2018/19

THE GUIDE TO

GRANTS FOR INDIVIDUALS IN NEED

16th edition

Judith Turner & Mairéad Bailie

Additional research by Denise Lillya,
Ian Pembridge, María Alejandra Puerta Reyes
& Jennifer Reynolds

dsc

directory of social change

Published by the Directory of Social Change (Registered Charity no. 800517 in England and Wales)

Head office: 352 Holloway Road, London N7 6PA

Northern office: Suite 103, 1 Old Hall Street, Liverpool L3 9HG

Visit www.dsc.org.uk to find out more about our books, subscription funding websites and training events. You can also sign up for e-newsletters so that you're always the first to hear about what's new.

The publisher welcomes suggestions and comments that will help to inform and improve future versions of this and all of our titles. Please give us your feedback by emailing publications@dsc.org.uk.

It should be understood that this publication is intended for guidance only and is not a substitute for professional or legal advice. No responsibility for loss occasioned as a result of any person acting or refraining from acting can be accepted by the authors or publisher.

First published 1987
Second edition 1990
Third edition 1992
Fourth edition 1994
Fifth edition 1996
Sixth edition 1998
Seventh edition 2000
Eighth edition 2002
Ninth edition 2004
Tenth edition 2006
Eleventh edition 2009
Twelfth edition 2011
Thirteenth edition 2013
Fourteenth edition 2014
Fifteenth edition 2016
Sixteenth edition 2018

ISBN 978 1 78482 043 5

British Library Cataloguing in Publication Data
A catalogue record for this book is available from the British Library

Cover and text design by Kate Griffith
Typeset by Marlinzo Services, Frome
Printed and bound by Page Bros, Norwich

Contents

Foreword

Our sector exists in order to provide support to those who need it – in the case of Age UK, to those who have reached later life. Every year, we offer information and advice to around 5.9 million people through online and written materials, as well as individual enquires by telephone, letter, email and local face-to-face sessions. In a similar way, directly through this guide, DSC gives so many charities and support agencies across the UK a tool to help support any individual in need.

Currently 1.9 million pensioners are living in poverty, yet we know many are missing out on vital benefits – some £3.8 billion worth of Pension Credit and Housing Benefit goes unclaimed by pensioners each year. This is why an important part of our work is helping older people claim their entitlements. We also hear from people who are well under pensionable age who are unable to work, perhaps due to caring responsibilities or living with a disability. They may have been affected by issues like the steep rise in the women's State Pension age and Pension Credit age. They may be finding it hard to manage on working age benefits alone, which have fallen in value over recent years as levels have been restricted or frozen. Watching every penny, going from shop to shop for the best deals, and sometimes having to cut back on essential items is debilitating. Whether old or young, living on a low income is hard work.

However, even when somebody has been managing to get by on a limited income, and are receiving any entitlements due, something can happen that throws everything off course. It could be an unexpected expenditure such as the cooker or washing machine breaking down, extra costs due to illness, or a major life change such as bereavement. At times like these, individuals, and those who advise and support them, can be at a loss to know how to find financial help. This is where *The Guide to Grants for Individuals in Need* is an essential resource, bringing together a wide range of sources of support and help to bring relief to people in financial hardship. Sadly, living in poverty is a reality for many people in the UK, but there are many charities that can help make life that bit easier – as long as you know how to find them.

Steph Harland, CEO, Age UK

Introduction

Welcome to the sixteenth edition of *The Guide to Grants for Individuals in Need*. The main focus of the book is to list sources of non-statutory help for people in financial need. This edition details more than 1,700 charities with over £308.5 million available in grant awards, compared with charities giving £66 million in this book's first edition in 1987.

Assistance given by charities in this guide ranges from food vouchers to grants for domestic items such as washing machines, wheelchairs and house adaptations, although few will cover the whole cost of these. This kind of help does not overcome long-term financial problems, but it can be extremely valuable in helping to meet immediate needs which the state does not currently cover.

This introduction looks at the charities included in this guide and how to locate them, before discussing what help is available and where alternative sources of help can be found. Helpful guidance explaining how to make a successful application to a relevant charity is also included; see page xiii.

Some grant-makers that have appeared in previous editions of this guide have not been included this time as they have ceased their grant-making activities, most notably The Fire Fighters Charity (Charity Commission no. 1093387) and Independent Age (Charity Commission no. 210729). Instead of providing financial assistance, these charities have narrowed their activities to providing emotional support and advice for their beneficiaries, which is part of a wider trend within the sector to address well-being and mental health issues. Many smaller charities have transferred their funds to local community foundations, for instance where the fund is too small to make a significant impact on its own or the trustees are not in a position, for a variety of reasons, to confidently make grants. Some local charities have also transferred the application process to their local community foundation to simplify the process for beneficiaries and ensure that the maximum number of people are helped.

About this guide

We aim to include publicly registered charities (including those in Scotland and Northern Ireland) which give at least £500 a year to individuals in need, although most give considerably more than this.

With a few exceptions, we do not include:

▷ Organisations which give grants solely for educational purposes
▷ Organisations which give grants to members only and not to dependants
▷ Individual employer or company welfare funds
▷ Friendly societies
▷ Local branches of national charities, although they may raise money locally for cases of need
▷ Organisations only providing services (such as home visiting) rather than cash (or in-kind) grants

Around 400 of the charities support individuals for educational causes as well. These are included in the sister guide to this book, *The Guide to Educational Grants*, which includes details of funding opportunities for all forms of education and training up to the end of a first degree – including apprenticeships, personal development and expeditions. Some charities support organisations such as community groups, and others have large financial commitments, such as providing housing. The entries in this guide concentrate solely on the charities' social welfare grants to individuals in need.

How charities are ordered in this guide

The charities are separated into seven sections. The first six sections contain most of the grant-makers, the majority of whom make grants to individuals across the UK. Indeed, most of the money in this book is given by the charities contained in these first six sections. The final, and largest, section of the guide contains grant-makers whose assistance is restricted to those residing in defined geographical areas. The flowchart on page xii shows how the guide works.

1. General charities (page 1)

This section is mostly made up of charities which operate with very wide objectives, such as the relief of 'people in need', rather than serving a distinct beneficiary group based on, for example, age, profession/trade or disability. General charities are among the best known and tend to be heavily oversubscribed.

In this part of the guide we have also included a subsection which lists charities whose purpose is to relieve individuals with utility debt and arrears. These charities are associated with utility providers (such as the British Gas Energy Trust), and while they are generally limited to helping only the customers of a certain provider, they can operate over broad geographical areas and assist with what is a specific but common need.

2. Charities by beneficiary (page 15)

This section features charities whose eligibility criteria is focused on individuals from defined beneficiary groups. The section contains alphabetically ordered subsections. Each subsection focuses on a specific group, including children and young people, older people, individuals belonging to a particular faith, and individuals whose needs are based on specific social circumstances, for example asylum seekers.

3. Illness and disability charities (page 41)

These charities give grants to people (and often their families/carers) who have an illness or disability and are in financial need as a result. Some have general eligibility criteria and support individuals with any kind of illness or disability; others assist only those affected by a particular condition. Many also give advisory and other support. For a detailed list of organisations providing these functions please see the 'Advice organisations' section, starting on page 427.

4. Armed forces charities (page 77)

This section contains exceptionally thorough charitable provision for people who have served in the forces, whether as a regular or during national service. These usually also provide for the widows, widowers and dependent children of the core beneficiaries. Many of these funds have local voluntary workers who provide advice and practical help and who, in turn, are backed up by professional staff and substantial resources. SSAFA, also known as The Soldiers, Sailors, Airmen and Families Association (Charity Commission no. 210760), is an influential member of this sector and a model of operation for other organisations. It is often the initial contact point, providing the application form for many of the regimental funds. This edition of the guide contains a useful flow chart on page xii of how to approach armed forced charities, following research undertaken by the Directory of Social Change funded by Forces in Mind Trust.

5. Occupational charities (page 93)

This section contains charities that benefit not only the people who worked in a particular trade but also, in many cases, their widows/widowers and dependent children. Membership or previous membership of the particular institute may be required, but many are open to non-members. Length of service can sometimes be taken into account. Some occupations are covered by a number of funds, while others do not have an established benevolent charity. Charities affiliated to trade unions can also be found in this section.

6. Livery companies, orders and membership organisations (page 181)

The charities in this section form a distinct and unique part of the grant-making sector. These are charities affiliated with membership organisations, from historic livery companies and orders to more recently established bodies. Some of the charities in this section only support members of their associated institution (and often their dependants) while others administer a range of funds with varying eligibility criteria.

7. Local charities (page 187)

Included in this section are those charities whose support is restricted to individuals in localised geographical areas within the UK. Northern Ireland, Scotland and Wales each have their own chapters; Scotland and Wales are divided further into regions and then into counties. Charities based in England are first organised by region, then subdivided into counties and then broken into districts/boroughs. Charities which could fall under two chapters have generally been given a full entry in one chapter and a cross reference in the other; charities relevant to three or more of the chapters have generally been included in the national section. Charitable help is unequally distributed across the UK, often with more money available in London and the south east of England than the rest of the UK. However, many of the largest cities contain at least one large charity that is able to give over £50,000 a year. This section starts with details on how to use and navigate the section.

Charities in Northern Ireland

Unfortunately, the section for Northern Ireland remains limited, as very little information is available at present on charities based there. It is estimated that there are between 7,000 and 12,000 charities operating in Northern Ireland.

The Charity Commission for Northern Ireland expects the completion of the registration process to take several years. In the meantime, up-to-date information on the progress of registration can be found on the Charity Commission for Northern Ireland's website: www.charitycommissionni.org.uk.

How grant-making charities can help

Some charities lament the fact that the people whom they wish to support might refuse to accept charity because of a desire to maintain their independence. A charity holds public money for the benefit of a specific group of people. As such, just as people are encouraged to access any statutory funds they can, they should also be encouraged to accept all charitable money which has been set aside for them.

However, it is not just people who are classified as 'poor' who are eligible for support from grant-making charities. Formerly known as the 'relief of sickness', this charitable purpose was re-defined under the provisions of the Charities Act 2006, and now comes under the purpose, 'the advancement of health or the saving of lives'.

The Charity Commission's guidance 'the advancement of health or the saving of lives' broadened the scope of the previous guidance, meaning a wider range of activities became charitable. Examples of help available concentrate on the alleviation of the physical aspect of 'relief' rather than on the financial position of people who are living with an illness or disability. This is not because grants for the advancement of health are not means-tested, but simply because these charities exist to relieve a physical need rather than a financial one. There are charitable organisations that exist to carry out either or both charitable purposes; they may either deal exclusively with the financial impact that an illness or disability can have on an individual's life or concentrate on the physical aspect of 'relief', or may address both.

Although these are the areas charities *may* support, it would be wrong to believe that any given grant-making organisation will support all of these needs. Each charity in this guide has a governing document, stating in which circumstances people can and cannot be supported. As noted earlier, to aid the reader in identifying those charities which are of relevance to them we have broken the charities listed into sections, and we would strongly advise that individuals do not approach a charity for which they are not eligible.

Many trustees have complained to us that they receive applications that are outside their charity's scope; meaning those which they would like to support but their governing document prevents them from doing so. These applicants have no chance of being supported and only serve to be a drain on the charity's valuable resources. With this in mind, please remember that it is not the number of charities you apply to which affects your chance of support but the relevance of them.

What types of help can be given?

Charity Commission guidance

The following guidance from the Charity Commission outlines the definition of the prevention or relief of poverty:

The prevention or relief of poverty

In the past, the courts have tended to define 'poverty' by reference to financial hardship or lack of material things but, in current social and economic circumstances, poverty includes many disadvantages and difficulties arising from, or which cause, the lack of financial or material resources.

There can be no absolute definition of what 'poverty' might mean since the problems giving rise to poverty are multidimensional and cumulative. It can affect individuals and whole communities. It might be experienced on a long or short-term basis.

Poverty can both create, and be created by, adverse social conditions, such as poor health and nutrition, and low achievement in education and other areas of human development.

The prevention or relief of poverty is not just about giving financial assistance to people who lack money; poverty is a more complex issue that is dependent upon the social and economic circumstances in which it arises. The commission recognises that many charities that are concerned with preventing or relieving poverty will do so by addressing both the causes (prevention) and the consequences (relief) of poverty.

Not everyone who is in financial hardship is necessarily poor, but it may still be charitable to relieve their financial hardship under the description of purposes relating to 'the relief of those in need by reason of youth, age, ill-health, disability, financial hardship or other disadvantage'.

In most cases, the commission will treat the relief of poverty and the relief of financial hardship the same. Generally speaking, it is likely to be charitable to relieve either the poverty or the financial hardship of anyone who does not have the resources to provide themselves, either on a short or long-term basis, with the normal things of life which most people take for granted.

Examples of ways in which charities might relieve poverty include:

- *grants of money*
- *the provision of items (either outright or on loan) such as furniture, bedding, clothing, food, fuel, heating appliances, washing machines and fridges*
- *payment for services such as essential house decorating, insulation and repairs, laundering, meals on wheels, outings and entertainment, child-minding, telephone line, rates and utilities*
- *the provision of facilities such as the supply of tools or books, payments of fees for instruction, examination or other expenses connected with vocational training, language, literacy, numerical or technical skills, travelling expenses to help the recipients to earn their*

living, equipment and funds for recreational pursuits or training intended to bring the quality of life of the beneficiaries to a reasonable standard

The provision of money management and debt counselling advice are examples of the ways in which charities might help prevent poverty.

See also the commission's guidance on the prevention or relief of poverty for the public benefit (www.gov.uk/ government/publications/charities-supplementary-public-benefit-guidance) and social inclusion (www.gov.uk/ government/collections/reviews-of-the-charity-register) and its decision on AITC Foundation (www.gov.uk/ government/publications/aitc-foundation).

Charity Commission, 2013

One-off grants

Some charities will only give one-off cash payments. This means that they will award a single lump sum which is paid by cheque or postal order either directly to the applicant, to the welfare agency applying on the person's behalf, or to another suitable third party or service provider. No more help will be considered until the applicant has submitted a new application, and charities are usually unwilling to give more than one such grant per person in any given year.

Recurrent grants

Other charities will only pay recurrent grants. Recurrent payments or grants in kind are disregarded when entitlement to Income Support and Pension Credit are calculated. Although this is a long-standing principle, be aware that the rules may change with the introduction of Universal Credit so it is wise to seek appropriate advice if you are in doubt.

Some charities will give either one-off or recurrent payments according to what is more appropriate for the applicant, although some charities which give small recurrent payments may also give one-off grants for irregular expenses.

Grants in kind

Occasionally grants are given in the form of vouchers or are paid directly to a shop or store in the form of credit to enable the applicant to obtain food, clothing or other pre-arranged items. Some charities still arrange for the delivery of coal. We have seen an increase in this edition of charities giving fuel vouchers that can be directly entered into a pre-payment meter. These are capped at £49 – the equivalent to approximately two weeks' dual fuel use.

More commonly, especially with disability aids or other technical equipment, the charity will either give the equipment itself to the applicant (rather than the money) or loan it free of charge or at a low rental price for as long as the applicant needs it. More common items, such as telephones and televisions, can also be given directly by the charity as equipment (the charity can get better trade terms than the individual).

Statutory funding

While there is a wide range of types of grants that can be given and a variety of reasons why they can be made, there is one area that charities cannot support. No charitable organisation is allowed to provide funds which replace statutory funding. The reason for this is that, for example, if a charity gives £100 to an individual that could have received those funds from statutory sources, then it is the state rather than the individual who is benefiting from the grant.

Advice for applicants

While there is still a large amount of money available to help applicants, the competition seems likely to remain strong. It is difficult to say how grant-makers will fare in the coming years, but it is unlikely that those who are dipping into reserves can continue to do so indefinitely, so charities will be looking to ensure that they are making the maximum possible impact with their grants.

For those individuals applying for funding the same basic principles apply – see page xiii for Ashley Wood's excellent step-by-step guide. However, in the current climate it is worth bearing a few extra things in mind.

- **Check the latest criteria**: Financial pressures and rising applications have led many charities to tighten up their eligibility criteria or limit the things for which they will give. Make sure that you have the latest guidelines and read them carefully to check that you are eligible to apply and the charity can help with your specific need. If in doubt, a quick phone call is usually welcomed and can save time for both parties in the long run.

- **Be open and honest when applying**: Take care to fill in any application form as fully as possible and try to be as clear and open as you can. The same applies if you need to write a letter of application. It will help grant-makers to assess your needs quickly and advise you on any other benefits or potential sources of funding for which you may be eligible.

- **Don't just apply to large, well-known charities**: These charities are likely to be the most oversubscribed, leaving you with less chance of success. Take the time to look for others you may also be eligible to apply for.

- **Apply to all appropriate charities**: Falling average amounts of grants may mean that one grant-maker cannot offer enough to cover the full cost of the item or service you need. You may have to consider applying to several charities and asking for a small contribution from each. If it has not been indicated already for any given charity in this guide whether calls are welcome or not, it is usually appropriate to make a quick phone call to establish how much they are likely to give for an individual grant.

- **Seek advice**: Some applications require a third-party endorsement. With advice services under increasing pressure, you may find an alternative organisation to contact in this guide; these organisations are listed on page 427. Also consider other impartial professionals who may be able to assist with an application form such as a school teacher if the application is on behalf of a child, or a medical practitioner such as a GP, consultant or therapist if the application is for a medical item or is related to a medical condition. Others who may be able to help include ministers of religion, social workers, local housing associations or probation officers. It is advisable to make a quick telephone call or send an email to the grant-maker to determine whether they can be flexible regarding who completes the application in exceptional circumstances.

Other sources of support

While there are many situations in which approaching a charity might be the best option, there is of course a limit to the support that they can provide, individually or collectively. There are a number of alternative sources of support that should be considered in conjunction with looking at grant-makers. These are beyond the scope of this publication, but the following sections offer signposts to where to find further information.

Statutory sources

There are some funding opportunities available to individuals from the state. The exact details of these sources vary in different countries in the UK, and in some instances among different local authorities. This area is likely to become ever more confusing in the light of further budget cuts and welfare reforms. Consequently, comprehensive details are beyond the scope of this guide.

However, full details should be available from government departments such as benefits agencies and social services, as well as many of the welfare agencies listed, starting on page 427. The government's website (www.gov.uk) and the Department for Work and Pensions (DWP) website (www.dwp.gov.uk) also have a wealth of information on what is available and how to apply.

There are a number of advice organisations that may be able to offer guidance and support to people who are unsure of their benefit entitlement or who are looking for extra support in the form of a grant. It may also prove useful to visit websites such as Turn2Us (www.turn2us.org.uk) which can offer advice on statutory and non-statutory sources of funding that are either given directly to individuals or available to individuals via the charities that are working on behalf of those individuals in need.

Citizens Advice provides an online advice guide (www.adviceguide.org.uk) and offers useful information on issues relating to statutory benefits and individual entitlement. Local branches of Citizens Advice can also offer people more assistance in this area.

Food banks

Food banks exist to support people who, due to a crisis or emergency, cannot afford to feed themselves. Food banks in the UK are diverse and how they operate varies, but they are generally run by volunteers who distribute food parcels via local churches and other community organisations. In the UK, the biggest provider of emergency food relief is The Trussell Trust, which has launched more than 420 food banks nationwide, and there are many more organisations and groups also working to support people who are facing food poverty.

The way to access assistance can vary depending on the food banks in your area; however, it is usually via referral from a care professional (such as a social worker, Citizens Advice or another welfare agency) who issues the individual who is in need of assistance with a voucher. This voucher can then be redeemed in exchange for a food parcel to last usually in the range of three to five days, depending on the food bank's policy. Some food banks can also provide other support through signposting to other welfare organisations and several charities included in this guide use them to reach potential applicants or liaise with existing beneficiaries. Information on food banks in your area can be found online or alternatively you can contact your local Citizens Advice.

Money advice

Many of the grant-makers in this guide specify that, before applying for a grant, individuals should seek professional financial or debt advice first. Your local Citizens Advice can provide free money advice, as can National Debtline (www.mymoneysteps.org and Debt Advice Foundation (www.debtadvicefoundation.org), which are both accredited by the Money Advice Service (www.moneyadviceservice.org.uk). Alternatively, the Money Advice Service provides an easy-to-use online search for local debt advice services, which lists Citizens Advice and other agencies that work to provide free financial advice in your area. You can also see the 'Advice organisations' on page 427 for contact details of free money advice providers.

Disaster appeals

In the event of a disaster or other humanitarian crisis the public's reaction is often to help the victims as quickly as possible, and one way to do so is by launching a disaster appeal. These are commonly set up as a public response to a well-publicised disaster, such as the Grenfell fire in 2017, where the public wish to show their support. They can also be established in response to a personal misfortune; The Mark Davies Injured Riders Fund, for instance, was established to support injured riders, by the parents of a talented rider killed during the Burghley Horse Trials. For comprehensive advice and guidance on whether to launch an appeal by an existing charity, assist an established charity in its efforts to help with the effects of the crisis, or set up a non-charitable appeal fund, please view the Charity Commission's online guidance, CC40 *Disaster Appeals*.

Companies

Many employers are concerned to see former members of staff or their dependants living in need or distress. Few have formal arrangements, but if you send a letter or make a telephone call to the personnel manager you should be able to establish whether the company will be able to assist.

Many large and some of the smaller companies give charitable grants, although most have a policy of only funding organisations. Those that will support individuals have their own charitable foundations or benevolent funds for ex-employees, and therefore are included in this guide.

There has been a growing trend for many prominent utility companies to establish charities which give to individuals who are struggling to pay their utility bills. These charities have continued to grow and have for a number of years provided much relief to the individuals involved, lessening the financial burden on them and ensuring that no legal action will be taken against them for non-payment of bills.

Community foundations

Over recent years, community foundations have established themselves as a key community resource. According to UK Community Foundations' website, there are 46 community foundations throughout the UK which distribute around £77 million grants a year and they hold, as of January 2018, £580 million in endowed funds.

Community foundations aim to be cause-neutral and manage funds donated to them by both individuals and organisations, which are then distributed to the local communities which they serve.

Whilst most community foundations only support organisations, some also have funds available for individuals and are therefore included in this guide. The UK Community Foundations' website has a complete list and a map of community foundations (see www.ukcommunityfoundations.org).

Please note, as is the case in most sources of financial support, funding for individuals is subject to frequent change. Even if your local community foundation is included in this guide, it is worth checking the availability on your local community foundation website.

Ministers of religion

There may be informal arrangements within a church, mosque and so on, to help people in need. Ministers of religion are often trustees of local charities which are too small to be included in the guide.

Hospitals

Most hospitals have patient welfare funds, but they are little-known, even within the hospitals, and so are not used as frequently as other sources of funds. It may take some time to locate an appropriate contact. Start with the trust fund administrator or the treasurer's department of the health authority.

Local organisations

Rotary Clubs, Lions Clubs, Round Tables and so on are active in welfare provision. Usually they support groups rather than individuals and policies vary in different towns, but some welfare agencies (such as Citizens Advice) have a working relationship with these organisations and keep up-to-date lists of contacts. All enquiries should be made by a recognised agency on behalf of the individual.

Orders

Historic organisations such as the Masonic and RAOB (known as Buffs) Lodges exist for the mutual benefit of their members and the wider community. Spouses and children of members (or deceased members) may also benefit, but people unconnected with these orders are unlikely to do so. Applications should be made to the Lodge where the parent or spouse is (or was) a member.

Hobbies and interests

People with a particular hobby or interest should find out whether this offers any opportunities for funding. Included in this guide are a number of sporting associations which exist to relieve people who are in need, but there may be many more which are not registered with the Charity Commission, or have less than £500 a year to give, but are of great value to the people they can help. It is likely that other sports and interests have similar governing bodies wishing to help their members either through making a donation or organising a fundraising event.

Educational support

This guide only deals with grants for the relief of those in need, ignoring grant-makers which can support individuals for educational purposes. However, many educational charities are prepared to give grants to schoolchildren, such as for uniforms for example. Receiving financial support for the cost of uniforms would obviously enable parents to spend the money budgeted for that purpose on other needs, so people with children of school age should check for any educational grants available to them. For information on statutory funds, contact your local educational authority or enquire for information at the office of the individual's school. For charitable funding, this guide's sister publication, *The Guide to Educational Grants*, provides information on over 1,100 grant-making charities that give throughout the UK.

Charity shops

Some charity shops will provide clothing if the applicant has a letter of referral from a recognised welfare agency.

Getting help

Unfortunately, these methods can only offer temporary relief. Applying for grants can be a daunting experience, especially if you are unfamiliar with the process; it is probably worth starting with the help of a sympathetic advisor. Most branches of Citizens Advice have money advice workers or volunteers who are trained in money advice work. If you find that you are in financial need, try going to the nearest Citizens Advice and talk to an advisor about your financial difficulties. They may be able to help you write an application to an appropriate charity, may know of a welfare benefit you could claim or be able to re-negotiate some of your debt repayments on your behalf. They will certainly be able to help you minimise your expenditure and budget effectively.

Acknowledgements

Throughout this introduction, we have commented on the guidelines and advice from the Charity Commission for England and Wales. While we are aware that the Charity Commission for England and Wales only has rule over those countries, readers in Northern Ireland and Scotland (as well as the Isle of Man and the Channel Islands) should note that, although the exact nature of charitable law differs in these countries, the spirit and guidance remains the same throughout the UK and the Charity Commission's advice should be considered to be just as relevant.

We would like to offer a special thank you to Steph Harland from Age UK for her contribution to this introduction.

We are extremely grateful to the many people, charity trustees, staff, volunteers, and others who have helped compile this guide. To name them all individually would be impossible.

How to give feedback to us

The research for this book was done as carefully as we were able, but there will be relevant charities that we have missed, some of the information may be incomplete or will become out of date. If any reader comes across omissions or mistakes in this guide, please let us know so we can rectify them. An email to the Research Department of the Directory of Social Change (research@dsc.org.uk) is all that is needed. We are also always looking for ways to improve our guides and would appreciate any comments, positive or negative, about this guide. We also welcome suggestions on what other information would be useful for inclusion when we research for the next edition.

References

Gov.uk, 'Charitable purposes: The advancement of health or the saving of lives' [web page], Charity Commission for England and Wales, 2013, www.gov.uk/government/publications/charitable-purposes/charitable-purposes#the-advancement-of-health-or-the-saving-of-lives, accessed February 2018.

Gov.uk, 'Charitable purposes: The prevention or relief of poverty' [web page], Charity Commission for England and Wales, 2013, www.gov.uk/government/publications/charitable-purposes/charitable-purposes#the-prevention-or-relief-of-poverty, accessed February 2018.

Gov.uk, 'Disaster appeals: Charity Commission guidance on starting, running and supporting charitable disaster appeals (CC40)' [web page], Charity Commission for England and Wales, 2012, www.gov.uk/government/publications/disaster-appeals-charity-commission-guidance-on-starting-running-and-supporting-charitable-disaster-appeals-cc40/disaster-appeals-charity-commission-guidance-on-starting-running-and-supporting-charitable-disaster-appeals, accessed February 2018.

How to use this guide

Below is a typical charity entry, showing the format we have used to present the information obtained from each of the charities.

Following on from this is a flowchart. We recommend that you follow the order indicated in the flowchart to look at each section of the guide and find charities that are relevant to you. You can also use the information in the sections 'About this guide' and 'How to make an application' to help inform your applications.

The Fictitious Charity

£24,000 (120 grants)

Correspondent: Ms I. M. Helpful, Charities Administrator, 7 Pleasant Road, London SN0 0ZZ (020 7123 4567; email: admin@fictitious.org.uk; website: www.fictitious.org.uk).

CC Number: 112234

Eligibility
People who live in London and are in need. Preference is given to older people and to single parent families.

Types of grants
Small one-off grants of up to £250 are given for a wide range of needs including white goods, beds and medical equipment.

Annual grant total
In 2017 the charity had assets of £132,000 and an income of £27,000. Grants to 120 individuals amounted to £24,000.

Exclusions
No grants are given for items already purchased.

Applications
Application forms are available from the charity's website. They can be submitted directly by the individual or, if necessary, by a third party such as a social worker or doctor. They are considered monthly.

Other information
The charity also makes grants to individuals for educational purposes.

Award and no. of grants

This shows the total (or estimated) amount given in grants during the financial year in question. Where further information was available, we have also included the total number of grants made.

Correspondent

This shows the name and contact details of the charity's correspondent. In many cases, this correspondent is the same contact listed on the charity's record at the Charity Commission; however, in cases where we could find a more appropriate correspondent on a charity's website, we have included their name here instead.

Charity Commission number

This is the number given to a charity upon registration with the Charity Commission. A small number of the grant-makers detailed in this guide are not registered charities and so do not have a Charity Commission number.

Eligibility

This states who is eligible to apply for a grant. Among other examples, criteria can be based on place of residence, age, health or occupation.

Types of grants

This section specifies whether the charity gives one-off or recurrent grants, the size of grants given and for which items or costs grants are actually given. This section will also indicate if the charity runs various schemes.

Annual grant total

This shows the total amount of money given in grants to individuals in the last financial year for which there were figures available. Other financial information may be given where relevant.

Exclusions

This field gives information, where available, on what the charity will not fund.

Applications

This section includes information on how to apply, who should make the application (meaning the individual or a third party) and when to submit an application.

Other information

This section contains other helpful or interesting information about the charity.

How to identify sources of help - a quick reference flowchart

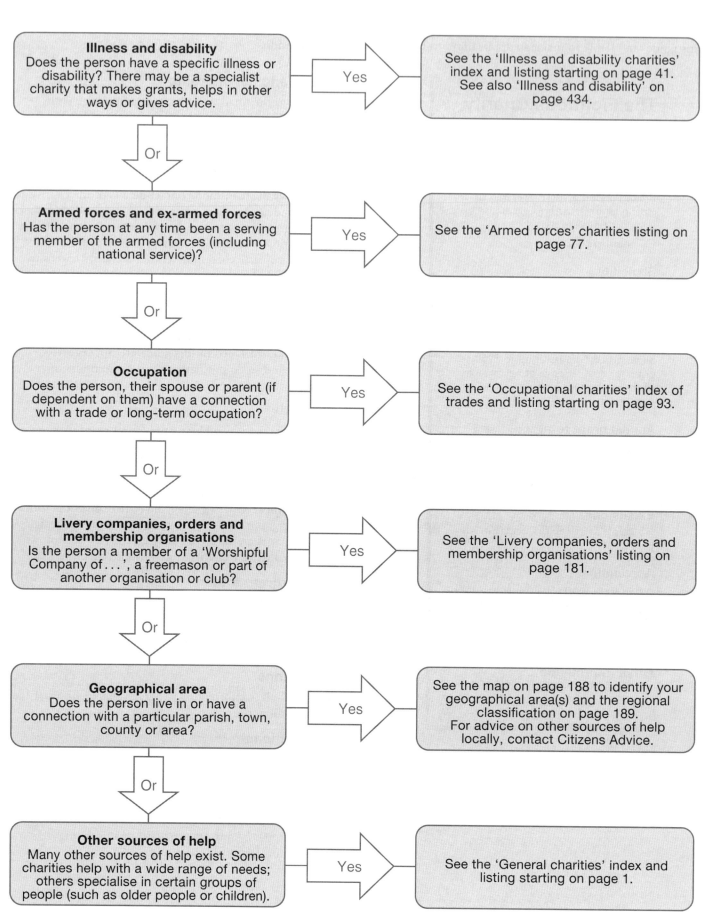

Illness and disability
Does the person have a specific illness or disability? There may be a specialist charity that makes grants, helps in other ways or gives advice.

Yes → See the 'Illness and disability charities' index and listing starting on page 41. See also 'Illness and disability' on page 434.

Or

Armed forces and ex-armed forces
Has the person at any time been a serving member of the armed forces (including national service)?

Yes → See the 'Armed forces' charities listing on page 77.

Or

Occupation
Does the person, their spouse or parent (if dependent on them) have a connection with a trade or long-term occupation?

Yes → See the 'Occupational charities' index of trades and listing starting on page 93.

Or

Livery companies, orders and membership organisations
Is the person a member of a 'Worshipful Company of . . .', a freemason or part of another organisation or club?

Yes → See the 'Livery companies, orders and membership organisations' listing on page 181.

Or

Geographical area
Does the person live in or have a connection with a particular parish, town, county or area?

Yes → See the map on page 188 to identify your geographical area(s) and the regional classification on page 189. For advice on other sources of help locally, contact Citizens Advice.

Or

Other sources of help
Many other sources of help exist. Some charities help with a wide range of needs; others specialise in certain groups of people (such as older people or children).

Yes → See the 'General charities' index and listing starting on page 1.

How to make an application

This section was kindly contributed by Ashley Wood, former Chief Executive of the Gaddum Centre, based in Manchester.

Once the appropriate charities have been identified, the next stage is the application itself. People often find making applications difficult and those who might benefit sometimes fail to do so because of the quality of the application submitted.

This article gives guidelines both to individuals applying directly and welfare agencies applying on behalf of individuals on how to make strong, clear and relevant applications.

The application form

The first stage in submitting an application is the question of application forms.

Applications on agency letter headings or personal letters directly from the applicant, no matter how well presented, are fairly pointless if the charity being approached has a specific application form which must be completed. This obvious point is often overlooked. It is frustrating when the application is returned with a blank form requesting largely the same information as has already been submitted. The resulting delay may mean missing a committee meeting where the application would have been considered and a significant wait until the next one.

Entries in this guide usually indicate when a particular application form is needed, but if there is any doubt the applicant should make a preliminary phone call to the charity.

Who submits the application?

Again, it is important that an appropriate person sends the application. The guide usually indicates whether an individual in need can apply on his/her own behalf, or whether a third party (professional or otherwise) must apply for them.

In recognition of 'empowerment' of service users, advisory bodies sometimes simply advise families of funds they can approach themselves. However, many charities require applications and forms (where appropriate) to be completed by a professional person who is sponsoring the application, for example. Therefore the individual in need may have to press the agency to make an application on his/her behalf.

The questions

When application forms are used, the questions asked can sometimes cause problems, often because they don't appear relevant. Applicants sometimes fail to realise all charities are governed by criteria laid down in their trust deeds and usually specific questions are designed to ensure these criteria are met.

For example, questions concerning date and place of birth are often answered very vaguely. 'Date of birth' is sometimes answered with 'late 50s' or, even worse, just 'elderly'. Such a reply reflects the appearance of the person

in question and not their age! If the charity can only consider applications for those below a pensionable age, and the request was on behalf of a woman, then the above answers would be too imprecise.

Equally 'Place of birth' is sometimes answered with 'Great Britain' which is again not precise enough for funds whose area of benefit is regional or local. It is always better to state the place of birth as well as town and county, even if they are different from the current home address.

Where application forms are not requested, it is essential to prepare clear, concise applications that provide the following information.

A description of the person or family and the need which exists

Although applications should be concise, they must provide sufficient detail, such as:

1 The applicant's name, address, place and date of birth

2 The applicant's family circumstances (such as married/ partners, separated/divorced/single parent, widow/ widower, the number and ages of dependent children)

3 The applicant's financial position (such as a breakdown of weekly income and expenditure, (where appropriate) DWP/housing benefit awarded/refused, savings, credit debts, rent/gas/electricity arrears, and so on)

4 Other relevant information, such as how the need arose (for example illness, loss of job, marital separation and so on) and why other sources (especially DWP/housing departments) have not helped. If applying to a disability charity, applicants should include details of the nature and effects of the disability (although see 'Medical Information'); if applying to a local charity, how long the applicant has lived in the locality.

The application, which says 'this is a poor family who need their gas reconnecting', is unlikely to receive proper consideration. It is also worth mentioning that applications are dealt with in the strictest of confidence, so applicants should aim to provide as much information as is relevant. The application form template on page xvi may serve as a useful checklist to ensure that all relevant information is included for the particular application.

How much money is requested and what it will be used for

This second point tends to cause the most difficulty. Applications are often received without any indication of the amount required or without sufficient explanation as to the desired use of the money.

For example, an applicant may have multiple debts totalling over £1,000. A grant of £100 would clear one of the debts and free much-needed weekly income. So the applicant approaches a suitable charity for a grant of £100. If the applicant explains the situation clearly, trustees can see that a £100 grant in this instance would be an effective use of their charity's resources. However, if it is not made clear, trustees can only guess at the possible benefits of the grant. Because they are unwilling to take undue risks with charitable money, trustees may either turn down an incomplete application or refer it for more information, which inevitably means delays.

Charity and the state

Charities are not supposed to give grants for items that are covered by statutory sources. However, the Big Lottery and increasing reforms to the welfare state have made it much more difficult to say where statutory provision ends and charitable provision begins.

Similarly, means testing under some state provision such as Disabled Facilities Grants regulations can create shortfalls between the amount that statutory sources can and will pay, and the full costs of equipment or adaptations to properties. Sometimes, because of what can and cannot be taken into account, assessments of what families can pay appear unrealistic. Where this is the case, it should be stated.

Changes arising from tightening of eligibility criteria and Community Care legislation are creating new areas of unmet need. If individuals are applying to a charity because statutory provision is clearly no longer adequate, they should make it clear in the application that they have exhausted all possible statutory sources of funding and are still left with a shortfall. A supporting reference from a knowledgeable agency may be helpful.

Where the identified need is not met, following any assessment process, applications for alternative or complementary finance should make the reasons clear.

The way that social and health care services are being provided is changing. Traditionally, the state assessed an individual's need and then provided, or arranged for those assessed services to be provided. The changes mean that money is now *given* to those assessed as eligible for services, in order to purchase the services themselves by way of an individual budget. The aim is to give more independence and a greater choice of services purchased. It is accepted that this is a radical change for many people. Applications to charities, particularly from those with social care needs, may well have to reflect the services already being purchased from an individual budget. These applications may also need a persuasive argument outlining the necessity of the thing you are applying for, and how it improves quality of life.

Realism

It helps to be realistic. Sometimes families have contributed to their own situation. An applicant who admits this and does not expect miracles, but rather seeks to hopefully plan afresh, will often be considered more positively than an applicant who philosophises about deprivation and the imperfections of the political regime of the day.

Likewise, avoid an application which tries to make the trustees feel guilty. Making them feel responsible for the impending doom which is predicted for the most vulnerable members of the family – unless money is given – is just as unlikely to impress experienced trustees, however sympathetic.

In general, be clear and factual, not moralising and emotional. In effect, a good application attempts to identify the need and promote possible resolutions.

Applications to more than one charity

Where large amounts are being sought, it can take months to send applications one at a time and wait for the outcome of each before applying to another. However, if a number of applications are being sent out together, a paragraph explaining that other charities are being approached should be included together with a commitment to return any surplus money raised. It is also worth mentioning if any other applications have been successful in contributing to the whole – nothing succeeds like success!

The same application should not be sent off indiscriminately. For example, if somebody is applying to a trade charity on behalf of a child whose deceased father had lengthy service in that particular trade, then a detailed description of the deceased father's service would be highly relevant. If an application for the same child was being made to a local charity, it would not.

Sometimes people who are trustees of more than one charity receive three or four identical letters, none tailored to that particular charity and none indicating that other grant-making organisations have been approached. The omission of such details and the neglect of explanations will raise questions in the minds of trustees, which in the end can result in delays or even refusal.

Timing

When applying to charities, remember the time factor – particularly in cases of urgent need. Committees often sit monthly, or even quarterly. A lucky break might mean that an application is received the day before the committees meeting. Although, if Murphy's Law is in operation, it will always arrive the day after! For the lack of a little homework, applications may not be considered in time.

From experience, few organisations object to a phone call being made to clarify criteria, dates of meetings or requests for application forms. Very often it seems that applicants leave the whole process to chance, which leads to disillusionment, frustration and wasted time for all concerned.

Savings

When awarding a grant, most trustees take the applicant's savings into account. Some applicants may think this is unnecessarily intrusive, but openness and honesty make for a better presented application and saves time. However, sometimes savings may not need to affect trustees' calculations.

For example, if a woman has a motor accident in which she was not at fault but which leaves her permanently disabled, she will receive compensation (often a one-off lump sum) through the guilty party's insurance company based on medical prognoses at the time. If her condition deteriorates faster and further than anticipated, requiring her to obtain an expensive item of equipment, it could well be argued that this should not be paid for out of the compensation awarded. The compensation was paid to cover factors such as loss of earnings potential, a reduced quality of life, reduced ability to easily fulfil basic household tasks and a general loss of future security, not to pay for unexpected and expensive pieces of equipment.

In such circumstances, the applicant should include a paragraph in the application to explain why their savings are not relevant to grant calculations.

In conclusion

Two final points should be borne in mind.

1. Be clear

Firstly, social and health care professionals often resort to the use of jargon when plain English would be more effective. There appear to be two extremes; one to present a report on the basis that the trustees are not very intelligent laypeople who need to be educated, or alternatively that they are all psychotherapists who need to be impressed. Usually, this only causes confusion.

2. Medical information

Secondly, medical information should not be presented without an accurate medical diagnosis to support it. Applicants' or social workers' presumptions on medical matters are not relevant. Often what is necessary is to explain why a financial need arises from a particular condition. This may be because of the rarity of the condition or the fluctuating nature of it.

The medical information should be presented by a professional in that field. The task of the applicant or the sponsor is to explain the implications of the condition.

Ashley Wood
Former Assistant Chief Exectuive
Gaddum Centre

Using the application form template for financial assistance

Over the page is a general-purpose application form. It has been compiled with the help of Gaddum Centre. It can be photocopied and used whenever convenient and should enable applicants (and agencies or people applying on behalf of individuals) to state clearly the basic information required by most grant-makers.

Alternatively, applicants can use it as a checklist of points to include in the letter. Applicants using this form should note the following things in particular:

1. It is worth sending a short, accompanying letter setting out the request in brief, even when using this application form.

2. Because this form is designed to be useful to a wide range of people in need, not all the information asked for in the form will be relevant to every application. For example, not all applicants are in receipt of state benefits, nor do all applicants have HP commitments. In such cases, applicants should write 'N/A' (not applicable) in the box or on the line in question.

3. If, similarly, you do not have answers for all the questions at the time of applying – for example, if you have applied to other charities and are still waiting for a reply – you should write 'Pending' under the question: 'Have you written to any other charities? What was the outcome of the application?'

4. The first page is relevant to all applications; the second page is only relevant to people applying for school or college fees. If you are applying for clothing or books for a schoolchild then it may be worth filling out only the first page of the form and then submitting a covering letter outlining the reasons for the application.

5. Filling out the weekly income and expenditure parts of the form can be worrying or even distressing. Expenditure, when itemised in this way, is usually far higher than people expect. It may be worth filling out this section with the help of a professional.

6. You should always keep a copy of the completed form in case the grant-maker has a specific query.

7. This form should not be used where the trust has its own form, which must be completed.

Application form template

Purpose for which grant is sought	Amount sought from this application	£

Applicant (name)	Occupation/School
Address Telephone no.	

Date of birth	Age	Place of birth
Nationality		Religion (if any)

☐ Single ☐ Married ☐ Divorced ☐ Partnered ☐ Separated ☐ Widow/er

Family details: Name	Age	Occupation/School
Parents/ Partner	. . . . . .	. . . .
Brothers/Sisters/ Children	. . . . . .	. . . .
. . . .	. . . . . .	. . . .
. . . .	. . . . . .	. . . .
Others (specify)	. . . . . .	. . . .

Income (weekly)	£	p	Expenditure (weekly)	£	p
Father's/husband's wage	. . . . . .		Rent/mortgage	. . . . . .	
Mother's/wife's wage	. . . . . .		Council tax	. . . . . .	
Partner's wage	. . . . . .		Water rate	. . . . . .	
Income Support	. . . . . .		Electricity	. . . . . .	
Jobseeker's Allowance	. . . . . .		Gas	. . . . . .	
Employment and Support Allowance	. . . . . .		Other fuel	. . . . . .	
Pension Credit	. . . . . .		Insurance	. . . . . .	
Working Tax Credit	. . . . . .		Fares/travel	. . . . . .	
Child Tax Credit	. . . . . .		Household expenses (food, laundry etc.).	. . . . . .	
Child Benefit	. . . . . .		Clothing	. . . . . .	
Housing Benefit	. . . . . .		School dinners	. . . . . .	
Attendance Allowance	. . . . . .		Childcare fees	. . . . . .	
Disability Living Allowance	. . . . . .		HP commitments	. . . . . .	
Universal Credit	. . . . . .		Telephone	. . . . . .	
Personal Independence Payments	. . . . . .		TV rental	. . . . . .	
Maintenance payments	. . . . . .		TV licence	. . . . . .	
Pensions	. . . . . .		Other expenditure (specify)	. . . . . .	
Other income (specify)	. . . . . .		. . . .	. . . . . .	
. . . .	. . . . . .		. . . .	. . . . . .	
. . . .	. . . . . .		. . . .	. . . . . .	
. . . .	. . . . . .		. . . .	. . . . . .	

Total weekly income £ _____   **Total weekly expenditure** £ _____

Savings £ _____

Debts/arrears Rent, fuels, loans, HP etc.		Has applicant received help from any other source? ☐ YES ☐ NO (If YES, please include details below)	
Specify in detail	Amount owed	Sources of grant obtained	Amount
. . . .	£	. . . .	£ . . . .
. . . .	£	. . . .	£ . . . .
. . . .	£	Other sources approached	
. . . .	£	. . . .	
. . . .	£	. . . .	
Total £ _____		**Total still required** £ _____	

Has applicant ever received previous financial help from this charity? ☐ YES ☐ NO   If so, when?

Reason for the application

Continue on a separate sheet if necessary

For applications being submitted through a welfare agency

Name of agency . . . .

Case worker . . . .

Address. . . . .

. . . .

Telephone. . . . .

How long has the applicant been known to your department/organisation?. . . . .

For all applications

Signature: **Date:**

About the Directory of Social Change

The Directory of Social Change (DSC) has a vision of an independent voluntary sector at the heart of social change. We believe that the activities of independent charities, voluntary organisations and community groups are fundamental to achieve social change. We exist to support these organisations in achieving their goals.

We do this by:

- Providing practical tools that organisations and activists need, including online and printed publications, training courses and conferences on a huge range of topics
- Acting as a 'concerned citizen' in public policy debates, often on behalf of smaller charities, voluntary organisations and community groups
- Leading campaigns and stimulating debate on key policy issues that affect those groups
- Carrying out research and providing information to influence policymakers, as well as offering bespoke research for the voluntary sector

DSC is the leading provider of information and training for the voluntary sector and publishes an extensive range of guides and handbooks covering subjects such as fundraising, management, communication, finance and law. Our subscription-based websites contain a wealth of information on funding from grant-making charities, companies and government sources. We run more than 300 training courses each year, including bespoke in-house training provided at the client's location. DSC conferences and fairs, which take place throughout the year, also provide training on a wide range of topics and offer a welcome opportunity for networking.

For details of all our activities, and to order publications and book courses, go to www.dsc.org.uk, call 020 7697 4200 or email cs@dsc.org.uk.

General charities

This chapter includes charities which could not be categorised to a specific occupation, disability, location or beneficiary group. Many have relatively broad criteria for their grant-making.

The charities listed under 'General' can give to a wide range of people, so if individuals are unable to find help from other sources in this guide then they should be able to approach one or more of these. However, note that most of these charities still have restrictions on who they can help. Applicants should not send indiscriminate applications to any charity under the 'General' heading; rather, they should first consider whether they are eligible.

The 'Utilities' section outlines charities, mainly set up by utility companies, with the specific purpose of providing assistance to those struggling to pay their utility bills or debts. Some of these are specific to those living in a particular geographical area, while others have a broader remit.

The charities in both sections are listed in alphabetical order.

The Acorn Foundation

£22,500 (24 grants)

Correspondent: Gill Snowdon, Secretary, 24 London Road West, Amersham, Buckinghamshire HP7 0EZ

CC number: 1068004

Eligibility
People in need who live in the UK.

Types of grants
Grants are given according to need.

Annual grant total
In 2015/16 the foundation held assets of £2.2 million and had an income of £108,500. Grants totalled £70,500 of which £22,500 was awarded to 24 individuals for welfare needs. One organisation also received funding.

Applications
Grants are made in partnership with a number of local authorities.

Other information
The foundation also works to promote the Christian faith through the ROPE organisation.

Al-Mizan Charitable Trust

£19,500 (90 grants)

Correspondent: The Grants Officer, PO Box 2488, Watford WD18 1YL (email: admin@almizantrust.org.uk; website: www.almizantrust.org.uk)

CC number: 1135752

Eligibility
The existing criteria for eligibility is: British citizens, those granted indefinite leave to remain in the UK and asylum seekers who are living in a condition of social or economic deprivation. Preference is given to the following groups:
▸ Orphans (a child who has lost either both parents or one parent who was the main bread-winner in the family)

- Children and young people under the age of 19 years (particularly those in care or who are carers themselves)
- Individuals who have disabilities, are incapacitated or terminally ill (particularly those who have severe mental health issues)
- Single parents (particularly divorcees and widows/widowers with children)
- Estranged or isolated senior citizens
- Individuals with severe medical conditions or their families
- Ex-offenders or reformed drug addicts or alcoholics
- Victims of domestic violence and/or physical or sexual abuse
- Victims of crime, anti-social behaviour and/or terrorism

Types of grants

At the time of writing (August 2017) the trust was reviewing its grant-making policy but previously, grants were mainly one-off, and have ranged from £34 to a maximum £500, with an average grant being £232. Grants have been awarded with the aims of: breaking the cycle of poverty, deprivation and/or disadvantage; improving the quality of life for individuals and/or families who 'are struggling to maintain a dignified existence and positively engage in society'; relieving suffering and helping individuals/families embark on a new start following a crisis or event. They are also given to assist with education and employability. Interest-free loans can also be given.

Annual grant total

In 2015/16 the trust had assets of £150,500 and an income of £102,000. Grants totalled £39,000 but we were unable to determine how much was given for social welfare and how much for education. We have estimated that £19,500 was awarded in social welfare grants.

Exclusions

The existing exclusions are: general appeals; applications from organisations or formal groups (except when assisting an individual or family); applicants who are not claiming all benefits for which they are eligible; applicants who have received funding from the trust in the last 12 months; applications for items or costs that have already been paid for; expenses relating to the practise or promotion of religion; debts, including rent and council tax arrears; fines or criminal penalties; university tuition fees; gap year projects; immigration costs; funeral expenses; gifts (including birthdays or festivals); holidays (however, the trust will consider funding trips for children and/or young people which 'enrich learning opportunities or very occasionally where a short vacation may serve a medical or social need');

international travel; applications for more than £500 (the trust will consider match-funding requests if the rest of the required amount is raised from other sources); products/services which contravene the ethos and values of the trust.

Applications

At the time of writing (August 2017) the website states: 'We are now closed for applications. This is while we review our Grants Policy and implement a new online grant application system.'

Note: in order to reduce administrative costs, the trust does not accept enquiries by telephone.

Other information

The 2015/16 annual report provides this useful account of the charity's grants policy:

> Our flexible Grants Policy meant that this support ranges from helping people access education and employment to escape the vicious cycle of poverty to simply putting food on the table for the families that cannot afford it. Our seasonal fundraising appeals, such as the Ramadan Food Parcels, Winter Warmer Packs, and Mother & Baby Kits, also provided items to poor families across the UK. These three appeals were run in partnership with grassroots organisations to ensure the packs reached those who genuinely needed them.

The trust has an informative website.

The Michael Barnard Charitable Trust

£6,200

Correspondent: Michael Barnard, Trustee, Brown Heath Park, Gregory Lane, Durley, Southampton SO32 2BS (07977 403 704)

CC number: 1157878

Eligibility

People who are in need due to their social or economic circumstances, natural disasters or because of crime, injustice or violence.

Types of grants

Grants are made for a wide range of goods and services that assist with the relief of poverty and need. In 2015/16 examples included bedroom furniture for a single-parent family and dental treatment for a young person who had been severely injured.

Annual grant total

In 2015/16 the trust had assets of £1.96 million and an income of £43,500. Grants were made totalling £28,000, of which £12,400 was awarded to individuals. We estimate that grants given to individuals for the relief of need totalled around £6,200.

Applications

Apply in writing to the correspondent.

Other information

The trust helps a small number of individuals each year.

The Biggart Trust

£12,000

Correspondent: The Trustees, c/o McClay Murray & Spens LLP, 1 George Square, Glasgow G2 1AL (0330 222 0050)

OSCR number: SC015806

Eligibility

People in need, with preference for people related to the founders and their descendants.

Types of grants

One-off and recurrent grants.

Annual grant total

In 2015/16 the trust had an income of £13,500 and a total expenditure of £16,400. We have estimated that grants to individuals totalled £12,000 during the year.

Applications

Apply in writing to the correspondent. The trustees meet on an annual basis to decide which individuals to support.

The Percy Bilton Charity

£142,000 (781 grants)

Correspondent: Tara Smith, Charity Administrator, Bilton House, 7 Culmington Road, Ealing, London W13 9NB (020 8579 2829; email: percybilton@aol.com; website: www. percy-bilton-charity.org)

CC number: 1094720

Eligibility

People who are aged over 65 and on a low income, children or adults with a physical, sensory or learning disability, or adults with a severe mental health problem which prevents them from working.

Types of grants

One-off grants of up to £200 for specific essential items only. For example, laundry equipment, cooking and heating appliances, basic furniture, beds and bedding, floor coverings, clothing and footwear, and other essential household items.

Annual grant total

In 2015/16 the charity held assets of £22.5 million and had an income of £839,000. A total of £142,000 was awarded in 781 grants to individuals broken down as follows:

White goods	358
Beds and other essential household items	162
Flooring	156
Clothing	105

The charity also distributed 2,007 Christmas food parcels worth £47,000. Organisations were awarded a further £475,000 in 171 grants.

Exclusions

No payments are made towards the following:

▶ Items costing over £200
▶ Travel expenses, sponsorship, holidays or respite care
▶ Educational grants, computer equipment or software
▶ House alterations and maintenance (including disabled facilities work or decorating)
▶ Debts
▶ Reimbursement of costs for articles already purchased
▶ Garden fencing or clearance
▶ Motor vehicle purchase or expenses
▶ Nursing and residential home fees
▶ Funeral expenses
▶ Removal expenses
▶ Medical treatment or therapy
▶ Course fees including driving or IT lessons

No repeat grants within a 12-month period.

Applications

Social workers or occupational therapists working within the local authority or NHS trust may apply on behalf of an individual who falls within the criteria of the charity. Applications must be made on a form available from the correspondent to be submitted by a social worker, community psychiatric nurse or occupational therapist, including a covering letter on local or health authority headed paper. Those applying should contact the charity by telephone to request an application form which will be sent by email. A full list of guidelines is available from the website. Applications are considered throughout the year.

Note: the charity is unable to respond to applications made by anyone other than a social worker or occupational therapist or to requests which fall outside the charity's funding criteria. Applicants should also ensure that they have applied to all statutory sources and any appropriate specialist charities (e.g. occupational funds and armed forces funds) before approaching the charity. Successful applicants should not reapply within 12 months of receiving a grant.

Catholic Clothing Guild

£6,000

Correspondent: Carmel Edwards, Trustee, 5 Dark Lane, Shrewsbury, Shropshire SY2 5LP (01743 243858; email: carmel.edwards17@gmail.com; website: www.catholicclothingguild.org. uk)

CC number: 277952

Eligibility

People in England who are in need of clothing, regardless of denomination.

Types of grants

The guild is a small charity which distributes new donated clothing (mainly to children). It may give small cash grants when this is not possible, however this only happens in exceptional circumstances as funding is limited.

Annual grant total

In 2015 the guild had an income of £6,300 and a total expenditure of £7,700. We have estimated that the total of grants awarded to individuals was approximately £6,000.

Applications

Clothing is distributed to organisations working with people in need and to individuals recommended by such organisations. There is a list of dioceses in which the guild operates on the website. Under no circumstances will applications be accepted from individuals directly. Telephone calls are not welcomed.

Other information

Note: The guild is only able to assist with up to six grants per month due to limited funding.

The Coats Foundation Trust

£70,000

Correspondent: Roslyn Cooper, Coats plc, 107 West Regent Street, Glasgow G2 2BA (0141 207 6835; email: andrea. mccutcheon@coats.com; website: www. coatspensions.co.uk/about-us/coats-foundation-trust)

CC number: 268735

Eligibility

People who are in need for whom there is no help available from statutory sources or from other charitable organisations.

Types of grants

One-off grants depending on need.

Annual grant total

In 2015/16 the trust had an income of £1,200 and a total expenditure of

£111,000. We estimate that the amount awarded in grants to individuals for the relief of poverty, and for the provision of social activities, totalled £70,000.

Exclusions

The trust does not have the funds to support regular payments or long-term needs such as food, rent or other day-to-day expenses.

The trust does not provide funding to other organisations.

Applications

Applications can be made using the application form, which is available to download from the website along with a financial statement, which must also be completed. Any other relevant information that may help the trustees when considering the applicant's case should be included.

Other information

The trust also provides grants for educational purposes.

The Cordwainers' Company Common Investment Fund Pooled Trusts

£19,700

Correspondent: John Miller, Secretary, The Cordwainers Company, Clothworkers Hall, Dunster Court, London EC3R 7AH (020 7929 1121; email: office@cordwainers.org; website: www.cordwainers.org)

CC number: 261891

Eligibility

The company administers a number of small trusts, the eligibility of which varies. Specific trusts exist for people who are blind, people who are deaf and dumb, widows of clergymen, ex-servicemen and widows of those who served in the armed forces, for example.

Types of grants

Small annual grants depending on the trust and the circumstances.

Annual grant total

In 2015/16 the charity had assets of £4.4 million and an income of £288,500. Grants to individuals totalled £19,700. The annual report states that around 70 individuals receive grants from the charity.

Applications

Apply in writing to the correspondent. If possible, applications should be made through referrals from welfare or other charitable bodies.

3

The Cross Trust

£108,000 (21 grants)

Correspondent: James Foskett, Cansdales, Bourbon Court, Nightingales Corner, Amersham HP7 9QS (01494 765428; email: mailto@cansdales.co.uk)

CC number: 1127046

Eligibility

Applicants' needs must be within the objects of the charity, which fall under the broad headings of: advancing any religious or other charitable object; work for the furtherance of religious or secular education; advancing the Christian faith in the UK or overseas; and the relief of the poor and needy and comfort of the sick and aged.

Annual grant total

In 2016/17 this charity had assets of £262,000 and an income of £338,500. Grants totalling £531,500 were awarded of which £108,000 was given to 21 individuals.

Applications

Apply in writing to the correspondent.

Family Action

£548,000

Correspondent: The Grants Service, 24 Angel Gate, City Road, London EC1V 2PT (020 7254 6251 (Wednesday and Thursday only between 2 pm and 4 pm); email: grants.enquiry@family-action.org.uk; website: www.family-action.org.uk)

CC number: 264713

Eligibility

The charity's website states:

In addition to living on a low income and having right of residency in the UK, welfare grant applicants must fall into one or more of the following priority areas listed below to be eligible to apply for a grant.

Grants available nationally

- Older People: Support to promote independence; improve the quality of life and isolation for those aged 60 and over
- Sickness/disability: Support to pay for disability aids that will benefit the applicant in their home. Funds are also available for medical treatment or to defray the expenses of convalescence and recuperation
- Mental Health: Support for adults (over the age of 18) with a clinical diagnosis of a mental health problem
- Domestic Abuse: Support for families or individuals who have recently experienced domestic abuse

Grants available for residents of Greater London only

- Holidays for Women living in Greater London: Support to provide recuperative holidays for women who are resident in greater London. Please note this fund is for women and their children of 16 years or less only
- Local Funds: Support for any welfare needs for those living in the following locations:
  St Pancras: support for single parents with children under four years of age resident in the following district postcode areas: WC1 and NW1
  Paddington: support for residents of the W2 W9 and NW8 (Westminster only) district postcode areas

Types of grants

Essential personal and household needs, such as clothing, fuel bills or household items (e.g. furniture or white goods). On average, grants are likely to be in the region of £200 to £300 (grants for holidays for women living in Greater London are likely to be in the region of £350 to a maximum of £600 per family).

Annual grant total

In 2015/16 the charity had assets of £12.2 million and an income of £21.5 million. A total of 1,770 grants were made to individuals totalling £740,000. Welfare grants to individuals totalled £548,000.

Exclusions

Grants are not available for:

- Day-to-day living expenses
- Council tax arrears or debts (including utility bills)
- Fines
- Rent deposits, arrears or payments
- Moving costs
- Funeral expenses (including associated expenses, such as headstones)
- Gifts (such as toys for birthdays, Christmas or other festivals)
- Repayment of Social Fund or other loans
- Bankruptcy or insolvency costs
- Items already purchased
- ICT equipment
- Citizenship applications
- Legal fees or passport applications
- Costs associated with employment or education
- Sponsorship or general appeals
- Funding for projects or groups
- Holidays (except for women living in Greater London)

Applications

All applications must be made online by a suitable referring agency. Suitable referring agencies include: statutory agencies or charities that provide health or social care; housing associations; probation services; and GPs.

Other information

Family Action provides a range of advice and support services across the country – see the 'Find us' facility on the website to find your local office. Support is given to help in the areas of some of the most complex issues, including financial hardship, mental health problems, social isolation, learning disabilities, domestic abuse, or substance misuse and alcohol problems. It is aimed to improve the lives of children and families, help through the early years of child development and ensure adult mental health and well-being.

The Farthing Trust

£6,400

Correspondent: Joy Martin, PO Box 277, Cambridge CB7 9DE

CC number: 268066

Eligibility

People in need, with priority given to those either personally known to the trustees or recommended by those personally known to the trustees.

Types of grants

One-off and recurrent grants are given to relieve poverty and hardship in the UK and overseas.

Annual grant total

In 2016/17 the trust had assets of £2.3 million and an income of £197,500. The trust awarded a total of £6,400 in grants to individuals in the UK.

Applications

Apply in writing to the correspondent. Applications can be submitted directly by the individual or through a social worker, Citizens Advice or other welfare agency.

Note: applicants will only be notified of a refusal if an sae is enclosed.

The trust has previously stated that it is only able to accept about one in every one hundred of the applications it receives; therefore, success is unlikely unless a personal contact with a trustee is established.

Other information

The majority of grants are made for the advancement of religion. The trust also awards grants to individuals and projects overseas, and to people in the UK for education.

The Fielding Charitable Trust

£1,000

Correspondent: Richard Fielding, West Hall, Longburton, Sherborne, Dorset DT9 5PF (01963 210234)

CC number: 1091521

Eligibility

People in need in the UK. Preference is given to older people and people who have disabilities.

Types of grants

One-off and recurrent grants are given according to need.

Annual grant total

In 2016/17 the trust had an income of £6,000 and a total expenditure of £4,000. We estimate that the trust awarded £1,000 to individuals in need during the year.

Applications

Applications should be made in writing to the correspondent.

Other information

The charity also makes awards for the furtherance of education and religion.

Elizabeth Finn Care

£3.1 million (3,278 grants)

Correspondent: Welfare Team, Hythe House, 200 Shepherds Bush Road, London W6 7NL (020 8834 9200; email: info@turn2us.org.uk; website: www.turn2us.org.uk)

CC number: 207812

Eligibility

There are three grant programmes with different eligibility criteria:

- **The Elizabeth Finn Fund** – People who are British or Irish and have a worked in a listed profession (available on the website), and their dependants. Applicants must have a low income or be claiming benefits and have less than £4,000 in savings. Applicants must also be living in Britain or Ireland for at least half of every year.
- **The Edinburgh Trust** – People who live in Edinburgh, have an annual household income that is below £16,000 and have less than £10,000 in accessible household savings.
- **The Turn2us Response Fund** – People who have experienced a life-changing event in the last 12 months. Grants are provided to meet specific needs to ensure the individual's/family's financial stability, well-being and independence. The website notes that at 'the current time applications

can only be made through intermediaries working for our partner organisations', a list of which can be found online.

Types of grants

Recurrent grants are made towards daily living expenses. One-off grants are also available towards needs such as car expenses, household items, funeral costs, house repairs and adaptations, specialist equipment and help with nursing/residential fees. All grants are means-tested.

Annual grant total

In 2016/17 the charity awarded 3,278 grants totalling £3.1 million to 4,401 beneficiaries (including family members).

Exclusions

Health-care costs; computer equipment; holidays; educational costs; debts, legal fees; funeral expenses.

Applications

Applicants should contact the charity to enquire about whether they are eligible via the online enquiry form on the website. A grants leaflet containing eligibility information is also available to download from the charity's website. If the charity thinks it may be able to help, an application form will be issued. This may be submitted either directly by the individual, through a third party such as a social worker or through an organisation such as Citizens Advice or other welfare agency.

Other information

If at any stage the charity cannot help, it will try to signpost applicants to other possible sources of funding.

The R. L. Glasspool Charity Trust

£1.6 million (5,598 grants)

Correspondent: Grants Team, Second Floor, Saxon House, 182 Hoe Street, Walthamstow, London E17 4QH (020 3141 3161 (9:30 to 12:30); email: grants@glasspool.org.uk; website: www.glasspool.org.uk)

CC number: 214648

Eligibility

People in need who are on a low income.

Types of grants

The trust's website states:

> We are able to consider requests for the following:
> - White goods
> - Beds and bedding
> - Essential household items and other household goods
> - Clothing, including school uniforms

- Baby needs
- Travel expenses for hospital visits, etc.
- Contributions towards equipment and adaptations for people with disabilities where there has been an occupational health therapist recommendation
- Vocational materials and training where there is clear evidence of an employment offer
- Driving lessons/tests where there is clear evidence of an employment offer
- Flooring where there is an exceptional circumstance for people with disabilities
- Educational computer equipment/television where there is a permanent or substantial disability/illness

Annual grant total

In 2016/17 the trust had assets of £42.5 and an income of £2 million. Grants to individuals totalled £1.6 million.

Exclusions

The trust's website states:

> We cannot consider requests for
> - Loans, debts e.g. catalogues/rent and council tax
> - Bursaries; project funding; research; educational grants
> - Bankruptcy and Debt Relief Order Fees
> - Holidays, outings and respite costs
> - Household repairs
> - Rent in advance/deposits
> - Funeral costs/headstones
> - Removal costs
> - Equipment and adaptations that should be funded by statutory services

Applications

The trust only accepts applications made through organisations. A list of criteria for organisations is available on the trust's website. Organisations should apply through the trust's www.grantsplus.org.uk website.

Other information

The trust is one of the few charities which operate nationally with no restrictions on its type of beneficiary.

Lady Hewley's Charity

£96,000

Correspondent: Neil Blake, Military House, 24 Castle Street, Chester CH1 2DS

CC number: 230043

Eligibility

Current or retired ministers of the United Reformed, Congregational and Baptist churches and their widows who are in need. This is a national trust, although preference is given to applicants whose ministry is in the northern counties of England.

Types of grants

Welfare grants to a maximum of about £1,000 (unless outside the scope of social security payments).

Annual grant total

In 2015/16 the charity held assets of £16.9 million and had an income of over £1 million. Grants to individuals totalled £146,000, of which £96,000 was for welfare needs. Grants made to specific groups of beneficiaries were broken down as follows:

Retired ministers	£50,000
Widows	£25,000
Ministers	£18,900
Daughters	£2,300

Grants to maintain almshouses totalled £58,500 and a further £41,500 was awarded to church institutions.

Exclusions

No grants will be given when local authority funds are available.

Applications

Applications are invited through contact with respective churches at local church, regional and provincial levels. Individual applications are considered twice a year and grants are made according to an individual's personal and financial circumstances.

The Houston Charitable Trust

£8,800

Correspondent: Geoffrey Houston, Trustee, Pednor Chase, Pednor, Chesham HP5 2SY

CC number: 1083552

Eligibility

People in need and those seeking funding for educational purposes, or for reasons relating to the advancement of the Christian faith. In practice, grants are available worldwide.

Types of grants

One-off and recurrent grants are given according to need.

Annual grant total

In 2016/17 the trust had assets of £206,000 and an income of £76,000. Grants to individuals totalled £9,000, of which welfare grants amounted to £8,800. A further £250 was awarded to individuals for purposes relating to the advancement of the Christian faith.

The majority of grants are given to organisations and during the year Christian institutions received £48,500 and welfare charities received further £75,000.

Applications

Apply in writing to the correspondent.

Hyde Charitable Trust

£27,000

Correspondent: Hyde Charitable Trust, Hyde Housing Association, 30 Park Street, London SE1 9EQ (020 3207 2762; email: hydeplus@hyde-housing.co.uk)

CC number: 289888

Eligibility

Residents of Hyde Housing Association who are in financial need.

Types of grants

Successful Tenancies Fund: Grants from this fund are intended to support the removal of tangible barriers that are preventing residents from maintaining their tenancies, or to pre-empt issues that may lead to greater risk of tenancy failure if not addressed.

Future Earnings Fund: Grants from this fund are intended to help residents on the path to maximising their household income and their ability to maintain current or future tenancies by assisting them to reach their employment goals.

Solutions for an Ageing Society Fund: Awards from £500 to £5,000 are available for individuals looking to set up social enterprises in the priority areas specified in the guidance notes.

Annual grant total

In 2016/17 the trust held assets of £9.1 million and had an income of £340,000. During the year, the trust gave around £27,000 in grants to individuals.

Applications

Applications can be made through the trust's online portal. Full guidelines on various schemes are available on the trust's website.

Grant funds are limited and awarded according to grant guidelines and on a first-come, first-served basis. Applicants are encouraged to submit applications as early as possible to avoid disappointment.

Other information

As part of an ongoing review the trust's grants programme may change, so check the website for current details before making an application.

The Johnston Family Trust

£28,000

Correspondent: B. J. S. Parsons-Smith, Aspen Cottage, Apse Manor Road, Shanklin PO37 7PN (0151 236 6666)

CC number: 207512

Eligibility

'Members of the upper and middle classes (and widows and daughters of such people) who, through no fault of their own, have fallen into impoverished circumstances.' Assistance is limited to men over 50 and women over 40.

Types of grants

Recurrent and one-off grants.

Annual grant total

In 2016 the trust had an income of £22,500 and a total expenditure of £31,000. We estimate that grants given to individuals totalled around £28,000.

Applications

Apply in writing to the correspondent. Applications are considered throughout the year.

The Heinz, Anna and Carol Kroch Foundation

£143,000 (867 grants)

Correspondent: Beena Astle, PO Box 327, Hampton TW12 9DD (020 8979 0609; email: hakf50@hotmail.com)

CC number: 207622

Eligibility

People who are in severe financial need who have ongoing medical problems. People who are homeless and people who have recently suffered domestic violence are also assisted.

Types of grants

One-off grants, typically ranging from £100 to £500, towards hospital travel costs, household bills, furniture, other hospital expenses, clothing, food, medical and disability equipment, living costs, home adaptations, help in the home, etc.

Annual grant total

In 2016/17 the foundation had assets of £7 million and an income of £248,000. During the year, 867 grants were made, totalling £143,000.

Exclusions

No grants are given for education or holidays.

Applications

Apply in writing to the correspondent. Most applications are submitted through other charities and local authorities. Applications should include full financial information including income and expenditure, what the grant will be used for and why it is needed. Applicants should also state if they have approached any other charities for financial assistance and how successful they have been to date. Applications are considered monthly.

Duchy of Lancaster Benevolent Fund

£3,500

Correspondent: Timothy Crow, Secretary, Duchy of Lancaster, 1 Lancaster Place, London WC2E 7ED (020 7269 1700; email: info@ duchyoflancaster.co.uk)

CC number: 1026752

Eligibility
The charity has a strong preference for applicants who reside in the county palatine of Lancaster or in the administrative counties of Lancashire, Greater Manchester and Merseyside.

Types of grants
Grants awarded to individuals tend to be one-off grants and are usually below £1,000.

Annual grant total
In 2016 the charity had a total income of £363,500 and a total expenditure of £428,000. During the year, the charity awarded 354 grants totalling £401,500. Grants awarded to individuals totalled £3,500 and grants awarded to organisations totalled £398,000.

The table below shows how the grants were distributed to individuals:

Community help	5	£2,300
Religious causes	1	£875
Youth and education	2	£350

Applications
Apply in writing to the correspondent.

The Elaine and Angus Lloyd Charitable Trust

£5,200

Correspondent: Ross Badger, Correspondent, 3rd Floor, North Side, Dukes Court, 32 Duke Street, St James's, London SW1Y 6DF (020 7930 7797; email: ross.badger@hhllp.co.uk)

CC number: 237250

Eligibility
People 'whose circumstances are such they come within the legal conception of poverty', particularly those who require assistance due to ill health or disability. Applications from south east England may be favoured.

Types of grants
One-off and recurrent grants are given according to need. Awards have ranged up to £2,000.

Annual grant total
In 2016/17 the trust had assets of £3.4 million and an income of £124,000. During the year, the trust awarded around £5,200 in grants to individuals for welfare purposes.

Applications
Apply in writing to the correspondent. The trustees meet regularly to consider grants.

Other information
The trust predominantly awards grants to organisations. Support may also be given for educational purposes.

The Douglas Martin Trust

£14,400

Correspondent: David Evans, Trustee, 45 Burnards Field Road, Colyton, Devon EX24 6PE (01297 553007; email: d.d. evans@btinternet.com)

CC number: 267876

Eligibility
People in need who live in southern England but only in cases personally known to the trustees. Unsolicited applications will not be responded to.

Types of grants
One-off grants typically up to £300 for items such as bedding, furniture, children's holidays, debt relief and educational grants.

Annual grant total
In 2016/17 the trust held assets of £622,000 and had an income of £31,500. During the year, the trust gave a total of £29,000 in grants. We estimate that around £14,400 of this amount was given to individuals.

The trust also gives grants to organisations.

Exclusions
The trust can only support cases known to the trustees.

Applications
Applications will not be accepted unless applicants are known by the trustees or referred by an organisation known to the trustees. Organisations which have recently made successful referrals include various Citizens Advice, SAFE and String of Pearls Project.

Morden College

£233,000 (112 grants)

Correspondent: Major-General David Rutherford-Jones, Clerk, Clerk's House, 19 St German's Place, Blackheath, London SE3 0PW (020 8463 8330; email: theclerk@mordencollege.org; website: www.mordencollege.org)

CC number: 215551

Eligibility
People in need who are aged over 50, from a professional or managerial background, who have retired from paid employment either on medical grounds or because they have reached the statutory retirement age.

Types of grants
One-off grants and quarterly allowances.

Annual grant total
In 2016/17 the charity held assets of £227.9 million and had an income of £11.1 million. The charity gave £233,000 in grants to 112 individuals.

Exclusions
The trust does not give for nursing home top-up fees or any services or products which should be funded by statutory authorities. Grants are generally not awarded to individuals who have received a grant within three years.

Applications
Apply on a form available from the correspondent, online or to download from the charity's website. Applications must include details of the applicant's income and expenditure as well as their employment history. Applicants are means-tested to ensure they are in need of assistance.

Other information
Morden College is the general title used for the administration of Sir John Morden's Charity and Dame Susan Morden's Charity. Sir John Morden's Charity provides grants and accommodation for older people. Dame Susan Morden's Charity is primarily concerned with the advancement of religion by assisting the Church of England with the upkeep of its churches and associated activities.

The charity runs a care home for beneficiaries no longer capable of living independently as well as accommodation for independent and supported living.

The National Benevolent Charity

£235,500

Correspondent: Dawn Swirczek, Peter Herve House, Eccles Court, Tetbury, Gloucestershire GL8 8EH (01666 505500; email: office@thenbc.org.uk; website: www.thenbc.org.uk)

CC number: 212450

Eligibility
The charity's website states:

In order to qualify for financial help from The National Benevolent Charity a person must:

 ▶ be in receipt of all available state benefits and have applied to any trade or professional charity or charities that support any medical condition to which they may suffer

- have been resident in the United Kingdom for not less than 24 months
- if under state retirement age, be in exceptional circumstances such as in receipt of long-term sickness benefits personal independence payments
- have no assets (excluding their home)
- have a disposable income after certain expenses have been disregarded (e.g. rent, council tax) of less that what is needed to provide a basic standard of living

Types of grants

The charity can make grants to meet essential needs, purchase and arrange delivery of household items and supply vouchers for goods and services. Occasionally, the charity can make a weekly payment to supplement a meagre income and help the beneficiary through a difficult period

Annual grant total

In 2016 the charity had assets of £14 million and an income of £796,500. Grants amounted to £235,500. Of this amount, £123,000 was given in regular payments to beneficiaries and £112,500 was awarded in one-off grants.

Applications

Applications can be made via the charity's website.

Other information

The charity also operates residential properties in Tetbury in Gloucestershire and Old Windsor in Berkshire, where it provides accommodation for people over 50 who are in financial need.

Newby Trust Ltd

£36,500 (272 grants)

Correspondent: Annabel Grout, Company Secretary, Newby Trust Ltd, PO Box 87, Petworth GU28 8BH (email: info@newby-trust.org.uk; website: www. newby-trust.org.uk)

CC number: 227151

Eligibility

People in the UK with welfare needs. The trust's website states that grants are usually given to individuals who are living in poverty which is 'exacerbated by additional misfortune including bereavement, divorce, abuse, homelessness, addiction, disability or ill health'. Applicants are expected to have claimed all statutory benefits available and to have applied for any available local authority funds. Grants are only given to those with substance misuse problems if they are in recovery. Applicants should have a household income of no more than £1,000 a month.

Types of grants

One-off grants of up to £250, for items such as household essentials, furnishings, clothing and school uniforms. Grants are occasionally made to support household adaptations and mobility equipment, travel costs, course fees or training equipment, rent deposits and respite breaks in the UK.

Annual grant total

In 2016/17 the trust held assets of £20 million and had an income of £483,500. Grants were made to 272 individuals for welfare purposes, totalling £36,500. Grants were also made to organisations for the purposes of welfare, health and education.

Exclusions

The trust does not provide grants for rent, council tax arrears, debts, bankruptcy or Debt Relief Order fees, or overseas respite breaks. Grants are not normally made for televisions and computers, tumble dryers and dishwashers, curtains, or carpets (except in the case of medical need or families with a young child).

Grants are generally not made to those without indefinite leave to remain in the UK; however, small grants of £50 may be made to those who are destitute.

Applications

Applications can be made online by statutory or voluntary agencies such as social or probation services, housing associations or registered charities, on behalf of individuals in need. Applications made directly by the individual are not accepted. Cheques are payable to the sponsoring organisation. Full guidelines are available on the website.

Open Wing Trust

£2,200

Correspondent: Jennifer Kavanagh, Clerk, Flat 2, 44 Langham Street, London W1W 7AU (020 7631 3551; email: clerk@openwing.org.uk; website: www.openwing.org.uk)

CC number: 1149773

Eligibility

Individuals over the age of 18 who are living in England and Wales at the beginning of their career and those contemplating a radical re-orientation of their life's work or the deepening of an existing vision. The trustees advise: 'We expect applicants to be in a process of inner change leading to a socially engaged commitment to working with those in need.'

Types of grants

One-off grants according to need. The guidelines note:

> [The] Trustees will consider funding specific living costs such as food and rent, training programmes, or offering support during voluntary work or an internship.

> The Trustees will expect clarity about what the applicant intends to do, what steps will be necessary to achieve it, and what they expect to be achieved during the period of the grant.

Annual grant total

In 2015 the charity had an income of £2,400 and a total expenditure of £2,400. We estimate that the charity gave around £2,200 in grants to individuals.

The website states: 'We expect to fund up to three small one-off grants a year, with an individual maximum of £2,000 (total available each year is £4,000).'

Exclusions

Grants are not given to individuals to pay off debt or repay loans.

No grants will be given to organisations or to fund specific work. Applications made on behalf of others will not be accepted.

Applications

Applicants must apply via an online form available on the website. Completed online forms must be submitted with a CV attached.

The trustees will expect clarity about what the applicant intends to do, what steps will be necessary to achieve it, and what they expect to be achieved during the period of the grant. Applicants will also need to demonstrate commitment to their purpose, and that they are in need of financial support to make it feasible.

The trustees expect to meet twice a year, but if necessary will consider applications between meetings.

Other information

At the time of writing (August 2017) the charity had no website or accounts available.

The Praebendo Charitable Foundation

Correspondent: Helen Leech, Trustee, The Redoubt, Second Drift, Wothorpe, Stamford PE9 3JH

CC number: 1137426

Eligibility

People in need in England, Scotland and Wales, with a possible preference for those living in Stamford, Lincolnshire.

Types of grants

Grants are made for items, services or facilities which will relieve poverty.

Annual grant total

In 2015/16 the foundation had assets of £288,000 and an income of £44,000. Charitable activities expenditure by the foundation amounted to £374,500, which we have taken to represent grants made. The annual report for the year explains that 13 grants were made, including 'direct financial assistance for relief of financial hardship' and support, totalling £45,000, to two local organisations. We were unable to determine the amount distributed to individuals, neither in total nor for social welfare purposes specifically.

Applications

Apply in writing to the correspondent.

Other information

The foundation makes a small number of grants to individuals and organisations each year.

Professionals Aid Council

£91,000 (117 grants)

Correspondent: Finola McNicholl, Chief Executive, 10 St Christopher's Place, London W1U 1HZ (020 7935 0641; email: admin@professionalsaid.org.uk; website: www.professionalsaid.org.uk)

CC number: 207292

Eligibility

Professionals with a strong educational background (degree level or equivalent, or working in a professional occupation requiring that level of education). Applicants must be resident in the UK and have less than £10,000 in savings.

Types of grants

Financial assistance is available in a number of forms, mainly: weekly grants, which in 2016 supported 77 beneficiaries; help with the costs of TV licences, household insurance, road tax and car insurance; one-off grants, which are given towards the purchase of clothing, cookers, beds, household items, travel and central heating.

Annual grant total

In 2016 the charity had assets of £5.3 million and an income of £118,000. Welfare grants totalled £91,000.

Exclusions

No grants are given for private medical fees, vet's bills or pet insurance, debts, mortgage repayments, utility bills or electronic equipment.

Applications

Initial enquiries can be made using the form on the website or, alternatively, by writing to the charity's Administration Department. Grants are means-tested.

Other information

The organisation also offers advice and assistance and can signpost individuals to specific occupational charities.

The J. C. Robinson Trust No. 3

£17,500

Correspondent: Christine Howe, Barnett Wood Bungalow, Blackboys, Uckfield, East Sussex TN22 5JL (email: jcrobinsontrust3@outlook.com)

CC number: 207294

Eligibility

Older people and people who are disadvantaged in England. Grants are also made to support the training and community spirit of young people.

Types of grants

Grants range from £50 to £1,000 according to need.

Annual grant total

In 2016/17 the trust had £773,500 in assets and an income of £40,000. During the year, the trust gave around £35,000 in grants. We estimate that around £17,500 was given to individuals.

Applications

Apply in writing to the correspondent, including supporting documents giving evidence of need, such as a letter from a doctor or social worker. Applications should usually be made through an organisation such as Citizens Advice or through a third party such as a social worker.

Skinners' Benevolent Trust

£32,500 (127 grants)

Correspondent: Grants Administrator, Skinners Hall, 8 Dowgate Hill, London EC4R 2SP (020 7213 5629; email: charitiesadmin@skinners.org.uk; website: www.skinners.org.uk/grants-and-trusts/skinners-benevolent-trust)

CC number: 1132640

Eligibility

Applicants must live in an area where the Skinners' Company has existing work or has historical links. These areas are: the City of London (the Square Mile only); Camden, Enfield, Hackney and Hounslow boroughs; West Kent (Tonbridge and Tunbridge Wells); and Romney Marsh (Kent).

The trust's main priority is to help:
- Those living with mental health issues
- Those in recovery from substance/ alcohol use
- Victims of domestic violence
- Those in receipt of a state retirement pension
- Those who have some kind of disability or chronic illness
- Families with dependent children (under 18) who are on a very low income

Types of grants

One-off grants of up to £250 towards essential household items such as white goods, furniture or children's clothing.

Annual grant total

In 2016/17 the trust held assets of £1.8 million and had an income of £60,500. During the year, a total of £32,500 was awarded in grants to 109 individuals and families in need and in pensions to 18 legacy residents of Hunt and Almshouse.

Exclusions

The trust cannot consider:
- Applications made directly by individuals
- Applications from organisations providing one-off support or advice
- Computers
- Mobility equipment
- Debts, payment of bills, or building modifications
- Items that have already been purchased

The trust cannot help individuals who have received a grant in the previous two years.

Applications

Application forms are available from the Grants Administrator who can be contacted by email, phone or post. Applications must made through referral from support agencies such as social and support services, housing associations, refuge and rehabilitation organisations, and local charities.

The trust has a very helpful website that provides further information for potential applicants. Applications are considered throughout the year.

The Henry Smith Charity (UK)

£1.27 million

Correspondent: Kindred Team, 6th Floor, 65–68 Leadenhall Street, London EC3A 2AD (020 7264 4970; website: www.henrysmithcharity.org.uk)

CC number: 230102

Eligibility

To register as kindred, individuals need to supply evidence showing they are a direct descendant of, or adopted by, one of the kindred previously registered with the charity.

Types of grants

One-off and recurrent grants for kindred who are in financial need. Grants have included: regular financial support to kindred of retirement age on low incomes, general financial assistance to those on low incomes, grants to students, training to equip young people for employment, and grants for white goods.

Annual grant total

In 2016 the charity had assets of £953 million and an income of £12.8 million. Grants to individuals totalled £1.27 million of which £776,000 was given to poor kindred.

Grants are also made to clergy and are administered by dioceses of the Church of England on behalf of the charity. These totalled £494,000 during the year.

Applications

To register, make an enquiry, or apply for assistance, contact the Kindred Team by email on kindred@henrysmithcharity. org.uk or by phone on 020 7264 4970 (option 4).

Other information

When Henry Smith died in 1628 he left funds to help his 'poor kindred', by which he meant descendants of his sister, who were in financial need. He did not have any children of his own. The Kindred Scheme is still in operation.

The Poor Clergy Fund now has two strands, the first of which is for individuals. The second strand is known as the Surplus of the Poor Clergy Fund and makes grants for projects which promote Christianity.

The charity also makes a large number of grants to organisations.

The Stanley Stein Deceased Charitable Trust

£100,000

Correspondent: Brian Berg, 14 Linden Lea, London N2 0RG (email: michael. lawson@williamsturges.co.uk)

CC number: 1048873

Eligibility

People over the age of 75 and people under the age of 21, who are in financial difficulty. There is a preference for assisting people who have a disability.

Types of grants

One-off and recurrent grants are given according to need. Previously, grants have been awarded for mobility and disability support, particularly for those who have sensory and physical disabilities. Grants have also been made for counselling support.

Annual grant total

In 2015/16 the trust had an income of £5,000 and a total expenditure of £204,000. We estimate that grants given to individuals totalled £100,000.

Applications

Application forms can be requested from the correspondent.

Other information

The trust also provides grants for individuals in education.

Mary Strand Charitable Trust

£52,000

Correspondent: Lynda Walker, Trustee, c/o Universe Media Group, Guardian Print Centre, Longbridge Road, Trafford Park, Manchester M17 1SN (0161 214 1200; email: lynda.walker@ catholicuniverse.com)

CC number: 800301

Eligibility

People who are in need due to poverty, sickness or old age.

Types of grants

One-off and recurrent grants, towards items like household goods, essential travel costs and clothing.

Annual grant total

In 2015 the charity had assets of around £303,000 and a total expenditure of £133,500. During the year, the charity awarded £52,000 in grants to individuals for welfare purposes. The charity also gave almost £65,500 in grants to organisations.

Applications

Apply in writing to the correspondent. Applications should be submitted through a local priest, charity or welfare agency.

Other information

The trustees publish a column in each edition of The Catholic Universe, a weekly Catholic newspaper. The column contains details of deserving causes with names changed to preserve anonymity, and appeals are made for specific requirements. Donations from readers are received in answer to these appeals and then distributed.

The charity's annual report (2015) states that:

> During the year a grant of £46,968 was paid to Caritas Salford for The Mary's Way Caritas Family Project. The aim of this project is to improve life chances and create new opportunities for people who live in the parishes within North Manchester by various ways including by reducing social disadvantages, increasing life skills and providing support.

The Talisman Charitable Trust

£156,500 (262 grants)

Correspondent: Philip Denman, Chief Executive, Basement Office, 354 Kennington Road, London SE11 4LD (020 7820 0254; website: www. talismancharity.org)

CC number: 207173

Eligibility

People in the UK who are living on a very low income.

Types of grants

One-off and recurrent grants are given according to need.

Annual grant total

In 2016/17 the trust held assets of £14.4 million and had an income of £218,500. The trust awarded 262 grants to individuals for welfare, totalling £156,500. The awards were broken down as follows:

Housing	156	£88,500
Disability	22	£21,500
'Small means'	46	£19,500
Child poverty	26	£18,000
Health	11	£9,400
Older people	1	£150

The trust also made grants to 29 individuals for educational purposes totalling £17,200 during the year.

Exclusions

The trust cannot accept applications made by recorded delivery or 'signed-for' services.

Applications

Applications should be made on behalf of an individual by a local authority, charitable organisation, or a social or professional worker and should be completed on letterheaded stationery. The trust's website provides a detailed list of all the information it needs to process the application. The applicant may need to provide further medical documentation, appropriate quotes for work or services and information on other assistance being received. The trust will only respond to successful applications and does not discuss applications before a decision has been made.

The Vardy Foundation

£69,000

Correspondent: Sir Peter Vardy, 4 Admiral Way, Doxford International Business Park, Sunderland SR3 3XW (0191 501 8555)

CC number: 328415

Eligibility

People in financial and circumstantial need. Preference is given to applicants in the North East and Scotland, but applications from across the UK are considered.

Types of grants

One-off grants according to need.

Annual grant total

In 2016/17 the foundation had assets of £36.3 million and an income of £1.8 million. During the year, £69,000 was distributed in grants.

Applications

Applications should be made in writing to the correspondent and should be supported by a professional or social agency such as a GP or Citizens Advice.

Other information

The foundation also makes grants to organisations with similar objectives, and is predominantly focused on funding early intervention programmes.

The Hon E. W. C. Weld-Forester Will Trust

£30,500 (nine grants)

Correspondent: Paul Rhodes, Padmore House, Hall Court, Hallpark Way, Town Centre, Telford TF3 4LX

CC number: 1105582

Eligibility

The annual report 2015/16 states:

> For the benefit of such one or more exclusively of the Hon. E W C Weld Forester's brothers, sisters, nephews and nieces and their respective issue and the surviving husband or wife of any such person who shall be poor and needy and in the opinion of the Trustees suitable recipients of charity as the Trustees shall think fit.

Types of grants

One-off grants.

Annual grant total

In 2015/16 the trust held assets of £917,000 and had an income of £35,500. During the year, the trust gave £30,500 in grants to individuals.

Applications

Apply in writing to the correspondent.

S. C. Witting Trust

£27,000

Correspondent: Christopher Gregory, S. C. Witting Trust, Friends House, 173 Euston Road, London NW1 2BJ (020 7663 1082; email: friendstrusts@quaker.org.uk)

CC number: 237698

Eligibility

Individuals in financial need, either under the age of 16, or over the age of 60.

Types of grants

One-off grants of up to £200 are available to assist with the provision of clothes, furniture, carpets, and white goods, etc.

Annual grant total

The correspondent has informed us there is a budget of £27,000 for relief-in-need grants.

Exclusions

Grants are not made towards debts, loans, or living expenses.

Applications

Applications must be made in writing by a social worker or other key professional. They must give a short case history, reasons for need and amount needed. Grants are only made to third party agencies, so include payee details. Requests are considered monthly and unsuccessful applications will not be acknowledged unless an sae is provided.

Other information

Grants are also made to students in university for educational items.

Utilities

Anglian Water Assistance Fund

£1.05 million

Correspondent: Charis Grants, Anglian Water Assistance Fund, PO Box 42, Peterborough PE3 8XH (01733 421060 (Charis Grants); website: www.anglianwater.co.uk/awaf)

Eligibility

The fund can consider helping if you are in debt with your water and/or sewerage charges to Anglian or Hartlepool Water and you are a current domestic account holder of Anglian or Hartlepool Water.

Types of grants

The fund may be able to help clear arrears of domestic water and sewerage charges by offering a number of solutions.

Annual grant total

In 2016/17 financial assistance to customers totalled £1.05 million.

Applications

Application forms are available to download from the fund's website. Alternatively you can call Charis Grants on 01733 421060 to request an application form. You will also need to send in proof with your completed application of the amount of income you have and where it comes from, e.g. wages, benefits.

British Gas Energy Trust

£8.2 million (16,675 grants)

Correspondent: Grants Officer, 3rd Floor, Trinity Court, Trinity Street, Peterborough PE1 1DA (01733 421021; email: bget@charisgrants.com; website: www.britishgasenergytrust.org.uk)

CC number: 1106218

Eligibility

Individuals and families who are in poverty, suffering or other distress who are struggling to pay their gas and/or electricity debts. Applications to the trust are welcomed from anyone living within England, Scotland or Wales.

Types of grants

Grants to clear gas and electricity debts and to clear other priority household debts or purchase essential household items such as:

- Boiler replacement
- Energy efficient white goods
- Funeral arrears
- Bankruptcy/Debt Relief Orders/LILA (Scotland) fees. These payments are known as Further Assistance Payments (FAPs)

Annual grant total

In 2015/16 the trust held assets of £2.4 million and had an income of £24.8 million. Grants to individuals in respect of energy debt totalled almost £2.4 million and grants to individuals in respect of further assistance payments totalled £5.8 million.

The average value of energy awards in 2015/16 was £630 and the average boiler award was £2,789

Exclusions

The trust cannot give loans or help with bills or items that have already been paid for. Nor can it help with the following: any household item that is not a white good; fines for criminal offences; overpayments of benefits; educational or training needs; business debts; debts to central government departments, for example, tax and national insurance; catalogues, credit cards, personal loans and other forms of non-secured lending; medical equipment, aids and adaptations; deposits to secure accommodation; or holidays.

Applications

The quickest way to apply is via the trust's online application form. Forms can also be downloaded from the website or requested by emailing or telephoning the correspondent. A local money advice centre such as Citizens Advice may be able to provide help in completing the form. Supporting documentation is required and the assessment of applications cannot begin without it. Evidence of income can be shown via bank statement, wage slips or benefit letters. Applicants are strongly advised to seek money advice before applying to the trust to increase the chance of a successful application. There are no deadlines for applications. Those in receipt of an award from the trust cannot reapply for two years. Applicants who do not receive an award can reapply if their circumstances change.

Other information

Grants are also made to voluntary organisations providing money advice, debt counselling or energy efficiency advice, in 2015/16 almost £4 million went to 28 advice organisations.

E.ON Energy Fund

£321,000

Correspondent: Fund Administrator, Freepost E.ON ENERGY FUND (03303 80 10 90; email: EONEnergyFund@ charisgrants.com; website: www. eonenergyfund.com)

Eligibility

Existing or previous customers of E.ON Energy who live in England, Scotland or Wales and need help paying current or final E.ON energy bills arrears. Applicants must be in receipt of Pension Credit or other means-tested benefits, credits or allowances. The fund also supports those who are seriously ill or have a terminal illness. Applicants must have a total household income of £16,190 or less.

Types of grants

Grants towards current or final E.ON energy bill arrears. The fund can also help applicants with replacement household items such as cookers, fridges, fridge-freezers and washing machines; and to replace and repair gas, calor gas and oil boilers.

Annual grant total

The website provides information on the top five areas that the fund has helped so far:

Birmingham	£90,000
Manchester	£77,000
Leeds	£60,000
Bradford	£48,000
Salford	£46,000

Exclusions

The fund cannot make grants for replacement radiators. The fund has different timescales for repeat applications, check the website for the most up-to-date information.

Applications

Application forms can be completed online or requested by telephoning 0330 080 1090. You will need to provide proof of income for the household and any medical confirmation to support your claim. If you are unsure what evidence you need to provide, contact Charis Grants.

Note: original copies of documents may not always be returned.

To apply to the E.ON Energy Fund for a boiler you must be the homeowner. Before applying, check if you are eligible for help under the Energy Company Obligation (ECO) Scheme before applying. You can find out whether you are eligible for help through the ECO Scheme by visiting eonenergy.com/heating or by calling 0330 400 1188.

Other information

The fund also offers applicants the option to apply for an e-learning voucher as part of its award package. These e-learning courses target core and specialist employability skills with the aim of helping people to find and retain employment.

If you are awarded an e-learning voucher, then you will have access to a range of training. You will be able to choose two core skills training courses from a range of seven options, including courses in using Microsoft Word and Excel. You will also be able to choose one specialist training course, from a range of over sixty options, including business, project management, and food health and hygiene courses. A full list of courses can be found on the fund's website.

Economy Energy Assistance Fund

Correspondent: (website: www. economyenergy.co.uk)

Eligibility

Economy Energy customers with debts over £100 or with household appliances (fridges, freezers and washing machines) over ten years old. Full eligibility guidelines are available from the fund's website.

Types of grants

Assistance with energy bills is available to Economy Energy customers with debt over £100. The fund can also replace household appliances which are over ten years old.

Annual grant total

We were unable to determine the fund's annual grant total.

Applications

Application forms are available to download from the fund's website.

EDF Energy Trust

£2.85 million (3,840 grants)

Correspondent: Grant Administrator, Freepost EDF Energy Trust (01733 421060; email: edfet@charisgrants.com; website: www.edfenergytrust.org.uk)

CC number: 1099446

Eligibility

Current domestic account holders of EDF energy (i.e. the person or people named on the bill) who are in need, hardship or other distress. The trust particularly looks to assist those who are struggling to pay for domestic electricity and/or gas services.

Types of grants

Grants are given to clear gas and electricity debts owed to EDF energy and other suppliers. Further Assistance Payments (FAPs) can also be given for: bankruptcy/Debt Relief Orders (DRO); sequestration and Minimal Asset Process fees; and the purchase of essential energy-efficient white goods and cookers.

Annual grant total

In 2016 the trust had assets of £2.9 million and an income of almost £1.46 million. During the year, 3,840 awards were made totalling £2.85 million. Of the awards made, 3,425, amounting to £2.7 million, were given to clear gas and electricity debts, and the remaining 415, given as Further Assistance Payments, totalled £108,500.

The trust's annual report informs that the average individual energy award was £797 and the average Further Assistance Payment value was £272.

Exclusions

The trust cannot assist with: loans, or bills or items already paid for; fines for criminal offences; educational or training needs; debts to central or local government departments; deposits to secure accommodation, or mortgage payments; medical equipment, aids or adaptations; overpayment of benefits; business debts; catalogues, credit cards, personal loans and other forms of non-secured lending; holidays; rent or council tax arrears; or beds or carpets.

Applications

Apply online or by downloading an application form from the website and returning it to: FREEPOST EDF Energy Trust. Application forms can also be requested from the trust directly by telephone, email or in writing.

All applicants are advised to seek appropriate money or debt advice from an organisation such as Citizens Advice before making an application in order to increase their chances of success. We would advise potential applicants to at first consider the guidelines available from the trust's website before beginning an application.

Those in receipt of an award from the trust cannot reapply for two years. Applicants who do not receive an award can apply again if their circumstances change. Payments for bills will be made directly to the supplier.

Other information

The trust also makes grants to organisations to support money and debt advice and fuel debt prevention services in communities.

The OVO Energy Fund

Correspondent: Citizens Advice Plymouth (01752 507703; website: www.ovoenergy.com/ovo-answers/topics/payments-and-statements/payments/what-is-the-ovo-energy-fund.html)

Eligibility

OVO Energy customers who've fallen behind with their payments, have fallen into debt and want to become more financially stable in the future. The fund's website states:

You can apply to the Fund if:

- You have an outstanding debt with OVO
- You've run up a debt on your gas or electricity account of at least £50
- Your annual household income is £16,190 or less
- You have a valid reason affecting your ability to pay

Types of grants

Payments directly into OVO accounts or gas or electricity meters.

Annual grant total

We were unable to determine the fund's annual grant total.

Applications

Applications can be made through the fund's website.

Scottish Hydro Electric Community Trust

£118,500

Correspondent: The Trust Secretary, Inveralmond House, 200 Dunkeld Road, Perth PH1 3AQ (01738 455113; website: shect.org)

OSCR number: SC027243

Eligibility

Members of the local community living in the Scottish Hydro Electric supply area. Grants can be given for domestic properties and properties used for not-for-profit community projects. Domestic properties must be the sole residence of the applicant.

Types of grants

Grants are awarded at the trustees' discretion and range from a few hundred pounds to a few thousand; however, the usual level is 50% of the connection cost. Connections or upgrades for renewable energy installations are also considered.

Annual grant total

In 2016/17 the trust held assets of £4.8 million and had an income of £137,500. Grants to individuals totalled £118,500 and a further £172,500 was awarded to organisations.

Exclusions

Applications for holiday homes or second homes will not be considered. Applications for retrospective connections may only be considered in exceptional circumstances.

Applications

Firstly, applicants should obtain a quotation for the electricity supply from the local Scottish Hydro Electric Power Distribution depot (or other authorised agent). Application forms can be completed online on the trust's website or downloaded and posted to the trust or to the quotation provider (who will then forward it to the trust on behalf of the individual). Applicants will also need to provide information of their financial circumstances and details of the need, including costs. Applications must be received three weeks before a trustees' meeting, dates for which are posted on the trust's helpful website.

The Severn Trent Water Charitable Trust Fund

£2.4 million (3,785 grants)

Correspondent: Grants Officer, 12–14 Mill Street, Sutton Coldfield, West Midlands B72 1TJ (0121 355 7766; email: office@sttf.org.uk; website: www.sttf.org.uk)

CC number: 1108278

Eligibility

People with water or sewage services by Severn Trent Water or by companies or organisations which operate on behalf of Severn Trent, who are in financial difficulty and unable to pay their water charges.

Types of grants

One-off grants are given to clear or reduce water and/or sewage debt. Further assistance can be given through the purchase of essential household items or by the payment of other priority bills and debts.

Annual grant total

In 2016/17 the fund held assets of £2.1 million and had an income of £5.3 million. Financial assistance to 3,785 individuals and families totalled over £2.4 million and was distributed as follows:

Water debts	£2.4 million
Other household needs	£62,000
Bankruptcy orders	£6,800
Rent	£1,300
Electricity	£500

Exclusions

No grants are made for court fines, catalogue debts, benefits/tax credit overpayments, personal loans or other forms of borrowing. No retrospective grants are given. Grants are usually one-off and applicants cannot reapply within two years of receipt.

Applications

Applications can be made through the fund's website or by using a form available to download from its website.

Other information

The fund also made grants totalling £182,500 to organisations which provide free debt advice and debt counselling services. Although this amount was paid to organisations, it was for services to individuals selected by the fund and has been included in the total amount of grants.

Severn Wye Energy Agency

£1.2 million

Correspondent: Severn Wye Energy Agency, Unit 15, Highnam Business Centre, Highnam, Gloucester GL2 8DN (01452 835060; email: info@severnwye.org.uk)

CC number: 1083812

Eligibility

Grants to private householders who suffer from cold and damp-related health conditions.

Types of grants

One-off grants according to need to improve the energy efficiency of properties.

Annual grant total

In 2015/16 the charity held assets of £1 million and had an income of £2.5 million. During the year, the charity gave almost £1.2 million in grants to individuals.

Grants were distributed as follows:

Warm and well	£1 million
Health grants	£162,500
Healthy people	£6,500

Applications

Contact the correspondent to request an application form.

Other information

Through its helpline, the charity also provides advice on how to reduce fuel bills and detailed bespoke advice on energy efficiency measures and renewable technologies.

Thames Water Trust Fund

£291,000

Correspondent: The Trustees, Thames Water Trust Fund, FREEPOST RSAJ-BXEA-LKLT, Sutton Coldfield B72 1TJ (0300 123 6001; email: office@twtf.org.uk; website: www.twtf.org.uk)

CC number: 1126714

Eligibility

Thames Water customers who are in need.

Types of grants

Grants are available to people struggling to pay their water bills. Grants are also available to help towards the cost of an essential household item or other needs.

Annual grant total

In 2016/17 the trust had assets of £972,500 and an income of £889,500. Grants to individuals totalled £291,000 and were broken down as follows:

Other household needs	£277,500
Bankruptcy	£12,100
Rent/mortgage	£1,000
Gas/electricity	£360

Applications

Application forms are available to download from the trust's website.

United Utilities Trust Fund

£4.4 million (4,971 grants)

Correspondent: The Secretary, Emmanuel Court, 12–14 Mill Street, Sutton Coldfield B72 1TJ (0845 179 1791; email: contact@uutf.org.uk; website: www.uutf.org.uk)

CC number: 1108296

Eligibility

People in need who live in the area supplied by United Utilities Water (predominantly the north west of England).

Types of grants

Payments for water and/or sewerage charges due to United Utilities Water. The charity can also help with water or sewerage charges which are collected by other companies or organisations on behalf of United Utilities Water. In certain cases, the charity can also consider giving some help to meet other essential bills, household needs or priority debts. Payments are made directly to the supplier.

Annual grant total

In 2016/17 the charity held assets of £337,000 and had an income of £5 million.

During the year, the charity awarded grants to 4,971 individuals, totalling £4.4 million.

Exclusions

No support is given for court fines, catalogue debts, credit cards, personal loans or other forms of borrowing, or statutory loans/benefit overpayments/tax credit overpayments now being reclaimed. The fund cannot make payments towards bills already paid or purchases already made.

The trust will not normally consider more than one application from the same person.

Applications

Application forms and full guidelines are available from the website. Money advisers and other referral agents may use the online application process. Applicants may receive a phone call or a home visit as part of the assessment process. All applications will be acknowledged and applicants will be issued with a reference number which they must use when making enquiries regarding the application. Successful applicants may not reapply for a period of two years. Unsuccessful applicants may apply again after six months.

For grants towards bankruptcy fees a separate application form is required; call 0845 179 1791 to request one.

Yorkshire Water Community Trust

£898,500 (2,185 grants)

Correspondent: Tasleem Salaq, Trust Officer, Freepost BD3074, Bradford BD3 7BR (0845124 24 26; fax: 01274 262265; email: info@ywct.org.uk; website: www.yorkshirewater.com/watersure)

CC number: 1047923

Eligibility

People who are in arrears with Yorkshire Water and have at least one other priority debt, such as gas or electricity, council tax, rent or mortgage repayments. Council and housing association tenants whose water charges are included with their rent may also apply.

Types of grants

No cash grants are given. One-off payments are made to Yorkshire Water and credited to the applicant's account.

Annual grant total

In 2016/17 the trust had both an income and a total expenditure of around £950,000. A total amount of £898,500 was awarded in 2,185 grants to individuals. There were 2,494 applicants during the year.

Exclusions

Successful applicants may not reapply within two years.

Applications

Application forms are available from the correspondent or to download from the trust's website. Helpful guidance notes are available on the trust's website and potential applicants are advised to read these carefully before making an application. Enquiries are welcomed.

Other information

The trust has a part-time Trust Manager with two part-time Assistant Trust Officers and a full-time Trust Officer. All resources are funded by Kelda Group Ltd and work within a Service Level Agreement for the trust. A Trust Secretary and a Treasurer provide their services on a voluntary basis.

Charities by beneficiary

This chapter includes all the charities that award grants to certain groups of beneficiary (for instance based on gender or age) or to individuals in specific circumstances (such as homeless people or refugees and asylum seekers).

The categories in this chapter are ordered alphabetically. 'Children and young people' includes charities that specifically award grants to people aged 25 or under, while 'Older people' includes grant-makers that give to people aged around 55 or older. Although this reflects the criteria of some of the grant-making charities in these chapters, the exact age restrictions specified by each individual charity do vary. The 'Miscellaneous' section includes charities with specific criteria that do not fall under any of the other categories in this guide. 'Religion' includes charities that support people of a particular religious group, while charities that specifically support those in religious occupations are listed in the 'Occupational charities' chapter in this guide (see page 93).

Please note that most of the charities within any given section still have further restrictions on who they can help. Individuals who fall into a particular category (such as 'older people') should not apply to all of the charities in the relevant section, but should first consider carefully whether they are eligible for each one.

The charities under any of the categories in this chapter are by no means the only charities in this guide that will give to that particular group of beneficiaries; they are simply the only charities that specify this group as their main criteria. For example, as well as the charities under 'Specific circumstances – Asylum seekers and refugees', there will also be charities in the 'General charities' chapter, or local sections, that will give grants to asylum seekers and refugees as part of a wider set of criteria.

Children and young people

Aberlour Child Care Trust

£15,200 (69 grants)

Correspondent: Correspondent, Aberlour Child Care Trust, 36 Park Terrace, Stirling, Stirlingshire FK8 2JR

OSCR number: SC007991

Eligibility

Families in Scotland, with children aged 16 and under, who are in urgent need of financial help.

Types of grants

Cash grants for basic items such as pram and cot bedding, single beds, microwaves, Moses baskets, children's clothing and shoes and sensory play equipment for children with disabilities. Grants are usually of around £100 per child.

Annual grant total

In 2015/16 the trust held assets of £9.3 million and had an income of £17.4 million. During the year, the charity gave around £15,200 in grants to 69 individuals.

Applications

Application forms can be found on the trust's website, along with full guidelines. The completed application form must be printed off and sent by post. Applications must be endorsed and submitted by a sponsor, acting in their professional capacity. The trust is unable to accept photocopied forms.

Other information

The trust awards grants to individuals through its Urgent Assistance Fund. Grant-making is only a small part of the trust's charitable activities.

The Avenel Trust

£4,500

Correspondent: The Trustees, 77 Comiston Drive, Edinburgh EH10 5QT

OSCR number: SC014080

Eligibility

Children in need under 18 and students of nursery nursing living in Scotland.

Types of grants

One-off grants, usually of £10 to £500, are given for safety items such as fireguards and safety gates, shoes, clothing, bedding, cots and pushchairs, money for bus passes, recreational activities for young carers and washing machines.

Annual grant total

In 2015/16 the charity had an income of £14,500 and a total expenditure of £12,800. We estimate that welfare grants to individuals totalled around £4,500.

Applications

Applications are considered every two months and should be submitted through a tutor or third party such as a social worker, health visitor or teacher. Applicants are encouraged to provide as much information about their family or individual circumstances and needs as possible. Applications can only be accepted from people currently residing in Scotland.

Bauer Radio's Cash for Kids Charities (England and Northern Ireland)

£13.5 million

Correspondent: Tracey Butler, Hampdon House, Unit 3, Falcon Court, Preston Farm, Stockton on Tees TS18 3TS (email: tracey.butler@ bauermedia.co.uk; website: www. cashforkids.uk.com)

CC number: 1122062

Eligibility

Children up to 18 years of age who are disadvantaged or have disabilities and live in one of the Bauer radio areas in England or Northern Ireland.

Types of grants

One-off grants for a range of needs including bedding, appliances, sensory equipment, wheelchairs, clothing and furniture.

Annual grant total

In 2016 the charity had assets of £2.4 million and an income of £15.7 million. Grants were made to a combination of individuals and institutions and totalled £13.8 million. Of this amount, individuals received £13.5 million, with the remainder awarded to organisations.

Applications

Applications can be made through local Bauer radio stations. A list of stations is available at www.cashforkids.uk.com. Individuals need a letter of support from a GP, health visitor, social worker, occupational therapist or some other professional involved with the child who can support the claim. Check your local station's website for application deadlines and grant criteria.

The Boparan Charitable Trust

See entry on page 51

Buttle UK – Small Grants Programme

£3 million

Correspondent: Alan Knowles, 15 Greycoat Place, London SW1P 1SB (020 7828 7311; email: info@buttleuk. org; website: www.buttleuk.org)

CC number: 313007

Eligibility

Children under 18 living with parents or carers and estranged, orphaned and vulnerable young people under 20 years of age and living independently. The trustees prioritise people facing exceptional difficulties or crisis, particularly living in severe poverty or facing domestic violence, drug and alcohol misuse, estrangement, illness, distress, abuse, neglect, behavioural or mental health issues.

Types of grants

One-off grants, for a range of essential household items or services which are critical to the well-being of a child. Grants are provided for cookers, fridges, washing machines and children's beds and bedding. Financial support is available for items of furniture, household equipment, baby necessities, and clothing. A full list of eligible and ineligible items can be found on the charity's website.

Annual grant total

In 2016/17 the charity held assets of £57.4 million and had an income of £4.5 million. The charity awarded over £3 million in grants to individuals through its small grants programme.

Exclusions

The charity cannot help:

- People over 21 years of age
- Families and young people not normally resident in the UK or who are non-EU residents on a student or work visa
- Parents who are not the main carer for the child
- Young people leaving care who can access funding under the provisions of The Children (Leaving Care) Act 2000

Applications

Applications can be made online on the charity's website and should be completed by a statutory or voluntary organisation that supports the family or the individual and is capable of assessing their needs and can also administer a grant on behalf of the charity.

Contact details for applicants resident in:

England: 15 Greycoat Place, London SW1P 1SB, info@buttleuk.org, 020 7828 7311

Scotland: PO Box 5075, Glasgow G78 4WA, scotland@buttleuk.org, 01505 850437

Wales: PO Box 2528, Cardiff CF23 0GX, wales@buttleuk.org, 029 2054 1996

Northern Ireland: PO Box 484, Belfast BT6 0YA, nireland@buttleuk.org, 028 9064 1164

Further information and guidelines are available on the charity's website.

Other information

Grants are also distributed through the BBC Children in Need Emergency Essentials Programme, which the trustees administer.

See the charity's website for other grant schemes.

Child Funeral Charity

£23,500

Correspondent: The Trustees, Unit 1, The Shield Office Centre, 186a Station Road, Burton Latimer, Kettering NN15 5NT (01480 276088; email: enquiries@childfuneralcharity.org.uk; website: www.childfuneralcharity.org.uk/ index.html)

CC number: 1156387

Eligibility

Families who are struggling to pay the costs of a funeral for a child aged 16 or under.

Types of grants

Financial support is available to help with funeral-related expenses.

Annual grant total

In 2016/17 the charity had assets of £28,500 and an income of £29,000. Grants to individuals totalled £23,500.

Applications

Application forms are available to download from the charity's website. Applications should be made by professionals who have knowledge of the bereaved family and their circumstances. This could include: funeral directors; celebrant or faith representatives; bereavement nurses or midwives; hospice managers; general practitioners; local authority registrars; hospital bereavement officers; and registrars.

Happy Days Children's Charity

See entry on page 55

Lifeline 4 Kids (Handicapped Children's Aid Committee)

£40,000

Correspondent: Roger Adelman, Correspondent, 215 West End Lane, West Hampstead, London NW6 1XJ (020 7794 1661; email: appeals@ lifeline4kids.org; website: www. lifeline4kids.org)

CC number: 200050

Eligibility

Children and young people under 18 who have disabilities.

Types of grants

Cash grants are never given. The charity will purchase specific requested items or equipment on behalf of the individual.

The charity's website explains:

> For the individual child we provide the full spectrum of specialised equipment such as electric wheelchairs, mobility aids and varying items including specialised computers and sensory toys. We are able to give emergency and welfare appeals immediate approval within the authorised limits of our welfare sub-committee. No appeal is too large or too small for us to consider.

Annual grant total

In 2015 the charity had assets of £358,500 and a total income of £161,500. We estimate that the amount given in grants to individuals during 2015 was around £40,000.

Exclusions

Funding is not normally provided for:

- Building or garden works
- Fridges or cookers/ovens
- Carpets or floor covering
- Washing machines
- Clothing
- Shoes (unless specialist)
- Childcare costs
- Transport expenses
- Tuition fees
- Driving lessons
- Recreational activities or holidays
- Therapy or treatment costs
- Cash grants

Applications

Firstly, applicants must email the charity. For an individual child, the email must outline: the specific requirement and the cost; brief factual information about the child including their name, date of birth, health condition and family name; and the applicant's postal address, email address and a contact telephone number.

Each request will be acknowledged and, provided it meets the trust's criteria, an application form will be sent by email or by post. The form contains questions relating to the child's medical condition and requires backup information from health professionals together with a financial statement of the applicant.

After a completed application form is received, it will be personally investigated by a member of the charity. The majority of appeals are discussed and decided upon at monthly meetings.

Emergency and welfare appeals, where possible, are dealt with immediately after receiving a completed application. The charity's decision to help can be made within days if vital.

Other information

The charity also supplies equipment and items for schools, children's hospices, respite care homes and clubs for children who have a disability or are underprivileged.

The charity notes that in the past it has often helped to equip hospital neonatal units with the latest incubators, infusion pumps and ultrasonic monitors among other life-saving equipment, although today its main activity is to help individual children.

The charity states on its website:

> We are inundated with applications for iPads and normally only consider funding a 16GB IPad for a child over the age of five on the following basis:
>
> 1) That your child's school recommends an iPad with one of the recognised communications apps such as Proloquo2go or MyTalkTools as your child's only means of communication.
>
> 2) The iPad must be for the exclusive use of your child.
>
> 3) The application must be in conjunction and collaboration with your child's school. If approved, the school must agree to purchase the iPad from our approved supplier and accept reimbursement from Lifeline 4 Kids.
>
> 4) Appropriate 'apps' should be specified and must be in use at school.
>
> 5) Your child should be able to use the iPad as a communications device without the need of adult supervision.
>
> 6) A suitable robust iPad case must be specified and may also be funded subject to our applications procedure.

Radio Bauer's Cash for Kids Charities (Scotland)

£2.5 million

OSCR number: SC041421

Eligibility

Children up to 18 years of age who are disadvantaged or have disabilities and live in one of the eight Bauer radio areas in Scotland.

Types of grants

One-off grants for a range of needs including bedding, appliances, sensory equipment, wheelchairs, clothing and furniture.

Annual grant total

In 2016 the charity had assets of £738,000 and an income of £3.4 million. Grants to individuals totalled £2.5 million, with a further £162,000 awarded to organisations.

Applications

Applications can be made through local Bauer radio stations. A list of stations is available at www.cashforkids.uk.com. Individuals need a letter of support from a GP, health visitor, social worker, occupational therapist or some other professional involved with the child who can support the claim. Check your local station's website for application deadlines and grant criteria.

Rees Foundation

£11,200

Correspondent: Jan Rees, County Court Buildings, 13 Church Road, Redditch B97 4AB (01527 839080; email: contactus@reesfoundation.org; website: www.reesfoundation.org)

CC number: 1154019

Eligibility

Young people and adults leaving foster or residential care.

Types of grants

The foundation has a limited crisis fund to provide immediate financial support for emergency situations 'to help care leavers keep body and soul together'.

Grants may cover expenses such as food, utility bills or transportation.

Annual grant total

In 2016 the foundation held assets of £56,000 and had an income of £255,500. Grants to individuals totalled £11,200.

Applications

In the first instance, applicants should get in touch with the foundation to discuss their needs. There is an online 'Request Support' facility on the website.

Other information

The foundation also offers practical advice and emotional guidance on a range of matters, as well as mentoring service and signposting.

The Rycroft Children's Fund

£20,000

Correspondent: Mark Stirzaker, Correspondent, Lower Dunisbooth House, Lane Head, Rochdale OL12 6BH (07778 671 012; email: rycroftchildrensfund@outlook.com; website: www.rycroftchildrensfund.co.uk)

CC number: 231771

Eligibility

Children in need who live in Cheshire, Derbyshire, Greater Manchester, Lancashire, Staffordshire, South and West Yorkshire. There is a preference for children living in the cities of Manchester and Salford and the borough of Trafford. Applicants should be aged 18 or under.

Types of grants

One-off grants according to need.

Annual grant total

In 2016/17 the charity had assets of £1.3 million and an income of £49,000. During the year, the charity awarded almost £40,000 in grants. We estimate that £20,000 was given to individuals for welfare purposes.

Exclusions

Grants are not given to individuals for education, overseas travel, individual holidays or computers.

Applications

Applications can be made through the charity's website.

Other information

The charity also gives grants to organisations.

Dr Meena Sharma Memorial Foundation
See entry on page 23

Eliza Shepherd Charitable Trust

£1,200

Correspondent: Carol Shepherd, Southview Cottage, Islington Road, Islington, Alton, Hampshire GU34 4PR (01420 520375)

CC number: 1064464

Eligibility

Children and young people who are in need.

Types of grants

Grants are awarded according to need, and can be used for clothing, household items, household adaptions (for example, for mobility aids) and general expenses.

Annual grant total

In 2015/16 the trust had an income of £2,500 and a total expenditure of £2,600. We estimate that the amount awarded to individuals totalled £1,200.

Applications

Applications should be made directly to the correspondent, detailing financial need. Applications are considered in May and November.

Other information

The trust also makes awards to young people for education fees.

Take a Break Scotland
See entry on page 194

Whizz-Kidz
See entry on page 58

Ethnic and national minorities in the UK

German Society of Benevolence

£13,000

Correspondent: David Leigh, Leigh Saxton Green, Mutual House, 70 Conduit Street, London W1S 2GF

CC number: 247379

Eligibility

Older people in need who are, or were, citizens of Germany, and their dependants. Applicants must live in Greater London, Essex, Hertfordshire, Kent or Surrey.

Types of grants

Small, one-off and recurrent grants for heating, clothing and other needs.

Annual grant total

In 2015/16 the society had an income of £9,100 and a total expenditure of £14,000. We estimate that grants given to individuals totalled £13,000.

Applications

Applications are considered from individuals or from agencies acting on their behalf.

The Netherlands' Benevolent Society

£10,700 (19 grants)

Correspondent: Social Work Co-ordinator, PO Box 858, Bognor Regis, West Sussex PO21 9HS (01932 355885; fax: 01932 355885; email: info@ koningwillemfonds.org.uk; website: www.koningwillemfonds.org.uk)

CC number: 213032

Eligibility

People in need who are Dutch nationals or of Dutch extraction and living in the UK. Assistance may also be given to widows, widowers and dependants of Dutch nationals.

Types of grants

One-off grants ranging between £100 to £1,000 and regular allowances of £80 per month. In the past, grants have included payments for: debts to allow someone to make a 'fresh start'; essential home repairs; clothing; basic living items; and the costs of a training course where it leads to employment. Loans may also be made.

Annual grant total

In 2016 the charity had assets of £951,500 and a total expenditure of £39,000. During the year, the charity gave around £10,700 in grants to individuals.

Exclusions

Beneficiaries must not have access to financial help from other sources.

Applications

Apply on a form available from the society administrator. Applications are usually made through churches, the Netherlands Embassy, the Netherlands Consulates, the Department of Work and Pensions regional offices or welfare charities. They are considered every month, except in August, at the trustees' monthly meetings, although emergency cases may be considered sooner. Information of the individual's financial situation, including details of any social security benefits, should be included. All enquiries are acknowledged.

Other information

The charity provides ongoing support, keeping in contact with applicants and beneficiaries.

Pusinelli Convalescent and Holiday Home

£3,000

Correspondent: David Leigh, Administrator, Leigh Saxton Green, 4–7 Manchester Street, London W1U 3AE (020 7486 5553; email: enquiries@lsg-ca.co.uk)

CC number: 239734

Eligibility

People who are or were German citizens and their dependants. Applicants must live in Greater London, Essex, Hertfordshire, Kent or Surrey.

Types of grants

Grants of up to £500 for families who would not otherwise be able to have a holiday.

Annual grant total

In 2015/16 the charity had an income of £4,300 and a total expenditure of £3,400. We estimate that grants given to individuals totalled around £3,000.

Applications

Applications should be made to the correspondent directly by the individual or by any welfare agency on their behalf.

Society of Friends of Foreigners in Distress

£20,000

Correspondent: Valerie Goodhart, 68 Burhill Road, Hersham, Walton-on-Thames KT12 4JF (01932 244916; email: vkgoodhart@gmail.com)

CC number: 212593

Eligibility

People living in London or its surrounding area who are from countries which are not in the Commonwealth, the USA or which were not once part of the British Empire.

Types of grants

Pensions and one-off grants can be awarded for electrical goods, clothing, living costs, household bills, food, travel expenses and repatriation, furniture and disability equipment.

Annual grant total

In 2015/16 the charity had an income of £13,000 and a total expenditure of

£22,000. We estimate that grants given to individuals totalled around £20,000.

Applications

Applications should be made in writing to the correspondent and can be submitted at any time.

Swiss Benevolent Society

£21,000

Correspondent: Suzanne Egloff, 79 Endell Street, London WC2H 9DY (020 7836 9119; email: info@swissbenevolent.org.uk; website: www.swissbenevolent.org.uk)

CC number: 1111348

Eligibility

Swiss citizens who are experiencing hardship and are temporarily or permanently resident in the UK.

Types of grants

Monthly pensions and one-off grants towards holidays, heating costs, travel to and from day centres, therapies, household equipment, telephone and TV licences, for example.

Annual grant total

In 2016 the charity had assets of £1.1 million and an income of £58,000. The charity awarded £21,000 in payments to individuals, £740 of which was awarded in pensions, and £20,300 was awarded in grants.

Applications

Apply in writing to the welfare officer including proof of nationality. Applications can be submitted directly by the individual, through an organisation such as Citizens Advice or another third party. They are considered at any time.

Other information

The charity has a welfare officer who also supports beneficiaries through: providing advice, counselling and support; offering advocacy with various agencies; co-ordinating overall care; and arranging visits from volunteers to homes, hospitals and nursing homes.

The Zimbabwe Rhodesia Relief Fund

£7,000

Correspondent: Hon. W. Walker, PO Box 5307, Bishop Stortford, Hertfordshire CM23 3DY (01279 466121)

CC number: 326922

Eligibility

Zimbabweans living worldwide who are distressed or sick.

Types of grants

One-off and small grants to relieve need in times of hardship.

Annual grant total

In 2015/16 the charity had an income of £32,500 and a total expenditure of £16,500. We estimate that the charity awarded £7,000 to individuals during the year.

Exclusions

Grants are not given for educational purposes or for travel.

Applications

Apply in writing to the correspondent. Applications should be made through somebody known to the charity and include proof of past or current Zimbabwean citizenship.

Other information

The charity also makes donations to charitable organisations with similar objectives.

Families

The Family Holiday Association

£711,500 (5,200 grants)

Correspondent: James Astley, Grants Officer, 3 Gainsford Street, London SE1 2NE (020 3117 0651; fax: 020 7323 7299; email: grantofficer@familyholidayassociation.org.uk; website: www.fhaonline.org.uk)

CC number: 800262

Eligibility

The Family Holiday Association was set up to help families, and considers a family to consist of dependent children and those who care for them. Carers can be parents, grandparents, guardians and others with caring responsibilities, such as an older child.

The family must:

▸ Be referred by someone who knows the family in a professional capacity and is aware of the family circumstances, for instance a social worker, health visitor, teacher or support worker, and who can support them until they go on the break
▸ Have at least one child in the family under 18 years old at the time of the holiday
▸ Be on a low income
▸ Not have had a holiday in the last four years

If the family is caring for a child who is ill or has disabilities, they should refer to The Family Fund at: www.familyfund.org.uk

The Family Fund is an independent charity funded by the four national governments of England, Northern Ireland, Scotland and Wales that gives grants to families living in the UK who are caring for such children aged 17 years or younger. Families in these circumstances should apply to the Family Fund before making an application to the Family Holiday Association. If the family is successful in their application to the Family Fund, they will no longer be eligible for support from the Family Holiday Association.

Types of grants

Day trips, short breaks, week-long holidays, group trips and group projects. Holidays are generally for holiday parks in the UK such as Haven or Butlins. Breaks include accommodation, linen rental (where available), entertainment passes and holiday insurance (subject to medical conditions). The charity may also make a contribution towards holiday expenses. Refer to the charity's excellent Q&A section on its website for further information.

Annual grant total

In 2015/16 the charity held assets of over £1 million and had an income of £1.5 million. Holidays for a record number of 5,200 families amounted to £711,500.

Exclusions

Note the following terms and conditions taken from the Q&A section of the website: 'The Family Holiday Association regrets that it is not in a position to help families with no recourse to public funds or those in receipt of foster care payments.'

If offered a break, families must abide strictly by the Family Holiday Association's terms and conditions. The family and referrer must agree that:

▹ The offer cannot be transferred to another family; it is only for the family and family members named on the application form
▹ The offer is valid for a limited time; offers not taken up in time will be withdrawn
▹ The offer has no cash value, if the family has to cancel their break they cannot claim a cash alternative
▹ If the family is unable to go on the holiday the Family Holiday Association must be notified immediately
▹ The family and referring agent must complete holiday feedback forms within four weeks of returning from the holiday

Failure to meet terms and conditions may jeopardise future applications.

Applications

Applications can be made on behalf of families by charities such as Barnardo's, social workers, health visitors or other caring agencies. Note the following from the association's website:

> The referrer acts as the point of contact throughout the process. As well as submitting the application, referrers should help the family book and prepare for their break, pass on our contribution towards expenses (if applicable) and ensure that feedback is sent in afterwards.

There is detailed information for both families and referrers on the association's helpful website.

Gender

Abortion Support Network

£58,500 (192 grants)

Correspondent: Jema Davis, Abortion Support Network, 2 Sheriffs Orchard, Coventry CV1 3PP

CC number: 1142120

Eligibility

Any woman from Ireland or Northern Ireland who would be unable to access an abortion without our financial assistance.

Types of grants

Grants ranging from £9 to £1,015 (2016) to help pay for treatment, travel and accommodation.

Annual grant total

In 2016 the charity held assets of £110,500 and had an income of £149,500. During the year, the charity gave grants totalling £58,500 to 192 individuals.

Applications

The charity asks applicants to call, text or email to get more information, or to discuss their circumstances. All contact information is available on the charity's website.

Other information

As of October 2017, those resident in Northern Ireland can access free abortions in England, and those facing financial hardship should be able to access financial assistance for travel direct from clinics in the UK. ASN is able to help those in NI who fall through any cracks in the government scheme, as well as those in the Republic of Ireland, the Isle of Man and the Channel Islands. ASN generally helps people travel to England but in some cases can help with clinics in Belgium or The Netherlands if necessary for reasons of cost or immigration status.

Frederick Andrew Convalescent Trust

£30,000

Correspondent: Karen Armitage, Clerk to the Trustees, PO Box 1291, Lincoln LN5 5RA (01522 705536; email: info@factonline.co.uk or frederick.andrew@icloud.com; website: www.factonline.co.uk)

CC number: 211029

Eligibility

Women who have been in paid employment at some time.

Types of grants

Grants of up to £1,000 for convalescence, domestic help or receiving therapy from Health and Care Professions Council-registered therapists. The trust also makes grants of up to £600 for therapy, including physiotherapy, occupational therapy, speech therapy, chiropody and podiatry and counselling.

Annual grant total

In 2015 the trust had assets of £1.8 million and had an income of £76,000. Grants to individuals totalled £30,000.

Exclusions

The grant must be used by the applicant, it cannot cover costs for convalescing partners or children. Retrospective costs are not covered. Grants cannot be awarded within two years of a previous grant, even if that grant was not taken for any reason within the six-month period the grant remains available.

Applications

An initial assessment form can be completed online and sent to the correspondent. The trust's website provides detailed guidance for the application process. The trust responds to every application and aims to notify applicants within four weeks. Grants are available for six months.

Other information

The trust also makes annual grants to the Pink Ribbon Breast Care Campaign.

Francis Butcher Gill's Charity

£16,000

Correspondent: The Trustees, c/o Freeths LLP Solicitors, Cumberland Court, 80 Mount Street, Nottingham NG1 6HH (0115 936 9369)

CC number: 230722

Eligibility

Unmarried widows or fatherless unmarried daughters of men who were 'clergymen, gentlemen, professional men or men engaged in trade or agriculture'. Beneficiaries must be members of the Church of England or of some other Protestant denomination, over the age of 50 and must reside in Nottinghamshire, Derbyshire or Lincolnshire.

Types of grants

Pensions are given to a fixed number of pensioners. One-off grants may also occasionally be available for items such as gas fires.

Annual grant total

In 2015/16 the charity had an income £16,700 and a total expenditure of £18,200. We estimate that grants given to individuals totalled around £16,000.

Applications

Application forms are available from the correspondent. Applications should be submitted either through a doctor or member of the clergy or directly by the individual supported by a reference from one of the aforementioned. Applications can be submitted at any time for consideration in March and October, or at other times in emergency situations. For pensions, applications will only be considered as a vacancy arises.

Baron Davenport's Charity

£466,000 (1,771 grants)

Correspondent: Kate Slater, Charity Administrator, Portman House, 5–7 Temple Row West, Birmingham B2 5NY (0121 236 8004; email: enquiries@barondavenportscharity.org; website: www.barondavenportscharity.org)

CC number: 217307

Eligibility

The charity's area of benefit is the city of Birmingham and West Midlands counties not extending 60 miles (or 96.56 kilometres) from Birmingham Town Hall.

The charity's website contains very detailed information about the application process and requirements.

The following extract is taken from there:

Twice-Yearly Grants to Older Ladies

- Ladies must live alone and be in receipt of State Pension and/or Pension Credit
- Ladies must have lived in a West Midlands county and no more than 60 miles from Birmingham Town Hall for at least 5 years
- Ladies' income must be less than £188 per week
- Ladies' savings must be less than £10,000
- Ladies must have a bank, building society or post office account in their own name which can accept BACs payments. Post office card accounts do not accept BACs payments and therefore cannot be accepted

At the moment ladies receive £260 twice yearly.

All the above are subject to review at each Trustees' Meeting.

Applications can be made by completing a simple form. Before applying, please read [the charity's] Guidelines for Twice-Yearly Grants to Older Ladies and Supplementary Guidance on Supporting Evidence.

The Charity prefers ladies to apply online through a referring body, for example Age Concern, Age UK, Citizens Advice or a Neighbourhood Office. Referring bodies will need to register before being able to submit online applications.

Individuals can request a paper application form by emailing enquiries@barondavenportscharity.org or telephoning the office on 0121 236 8004.

The following information regarding Emergency Grants is provided on the website:

Single ladies living alone or with their children and fatherless children living alone (children must be under 25 years old).

- Applicants must live in a West Midlands county and no more than 60 miles from Birmingham Town Hall
- Applicants must be in reduced financial circumstances
- Applicants must not have received an Emergency Grant from us in the last five years

Grants are given mainly to help purchase essential household items. Our maximum grant is £250.

PLEASE NOTE: We do not accept applications directly from individuals.

Online applications must be completed by a support worker who is part of an organisation that is supporting the lady or children and is capable of assessing their needs. The organisation must also be able to administer and supervise the grant on our behalf.

We can accept applications from a wide variety of organisations including charitable organisations, health care and advice services, tenancy support, education services, NHS and primary care trusts. Applications are not accepted from metropolitan districts, unitary authorities, county councils or district councils.

Organisations will need to register before being able to submit online applications.

Types of grants

There are two types of grant for individuals: twice-yearly grants to single women in their retirement and living alone, and emergency grants to single women and fatherless children.

Annual grant total

In 2016 the charity held assets of £34.28 million and had an income of £1.38 million. Grants totalled £1.17 million, of which £466,000 was distributed in 1,771 grants to individuals.

A further 481 grants, amounting to £601,000, were awarded to almshouses, hospices and children's charities in Birmingham and the West Midlands.

Exclusions

Contact the Charity Administrator for details of any current exclusions.

Applications

Except for emergency cases, applications should be made through local authority social services departments or recognised welfare agencies, although direct applications from individuals may also be considered. Application forms are available from the correspondent or to download from the website.

Applications for the spring distribution should be submitted by 15 March, and for the autumn distribution, 15 September. Grants are paid in May and November respectively. No more than one application should be submitted within twelve months.

Applications for one-off grants can be submitted at any time and are considered approximately every month. Enquiries are welcomed.

Other information

The charity and CVS regard as fatherless those whose fathers have died, and in some cases children abandoned by their fathers. For emergency needs, see the separate entries in: Shropshire, Staffordshire, Warwickshire, Worcestershire, and West Midlands.

Eaton Fund for Artists, Nurses and Gentlewomen

£262,500 (492 grants)

Correspondent: Anne Murray, Manager, PO Box 528, Fleet, Surrey GU51 9HH (020 3289 3209; email: admin@ eatonfund.org.uk; website: www. eatonfund.org.uk)

CC number: 236060

Eligibility

Artists, including painters, potters, sculptors and photographers but not performing artists; nurses, including SRN, SEN, medical carers and dental nurses who are in employment or retired; and women over 18, who are in need of financial assistance.

Full eligibility criteria is available from the fund's website.

Types of grants

One-off grants for artist's materials and equipment, picture framing for an exhibition, wheelchairs, and the setting up of a new home due to disability, family breakdown or homelessness.

Annual grant total

In 2015/16 the fund held assets of £9.2 million and had an income of £300,500. Grants were made to 492 individuals totalling £262,500. The 2015/16 accounts note that '23% of grants supported artists, 13% of grants supported nurses, and 64% of grants supported women in need.'

Exclusions

Grants are not given for educational fees, recurring expenses such as mortgage repayments, rent, fuel or phone bills, special diets, care home fees, private treatments or to clear debt.

Applications

Application forms are available to download from the website or can be requested from the correspondent. Forms can be submitted directly by the individual but the fund also asks that a supporting letter from an appropriate third party, such as a doctor or social worker be included as well as evidence of any benefits being received. Relevant documents such as invoices or quotations should also be sent with the form. Applications are considered six times a year and applicants will be notified of the decision within a month of the application deadline. For more information on specific application deadlines, see the 'calendar' section of the website.

Email applications are **not** accepted.

Mary MacArthur Holiday Trust

£39,000

Correspondent: Cheryl Andrews, Grants Administrator, Unite House, 1 Cathedral Road, Cardiff CF11 9SD (029 2035 9091; email: cheryl.andrews@mmht.org.uk; website: www.mmht.org.uk)

CC number: 209989

Eligibility

Women in need of a period of rest or holiday due to old age, poverty, illness, disablement or other socio-economic reasons. The website states that applicants must:

▷ Be 18 or over
▷ Not have had a holiday in recent years
▷ Not have received a grant from the trust for at least three years

Preference is given to women who are or have been normally in employment. Women in work are considered as well as those who are not. The trust recognises that a holiday may not be financially possible even for those in work

Types of grants

Grants of up to £350 for holidays, coach trips, family visits and stays in caravans, hotels and self-catering accommodation in the UK and abroad.

Annual grant total

In 2016/17 the trust held assets of £1.4 million and had an income of £67,500. Grants for holidays totalled £39,000. During the year, the management committee awarded 144 holidays and declined 62 applications that failed to meet the criteria.

Applications

Application forms can be downloaded from the trust's website, which also notes that a:

> Sponsoring body or person must support your application with a letter explaining why they feel you are eligible for a holiday grant. The sponsoring body or person must be supporting you on a professional basis regarding your personal circumstances, e.g. GP, social worker, support worker, trade union official, but not friends, family or work colleagues.

Grants are usually paid directly to the holiday provider, and it is up to the applicant to visit travel agents and other holiday providers.

The E. McLaren Fund

£70,500 (101 grants)

Correspondent: The Secretary of The E. McLaren Fund, Wright, Johnston & Mackenzie LLP, 302 St Vincent Street,

Glasgow G2 5RZ (0141 248 3434; fax: 0141 221 1226)

OSCR number: SC004558

Eligibility

Widows and unmarried women of a pensionable age who are in need, with preference for widows and daughters of officers of 'certain Scottish regiments'.

Types of grants

Annual pensions of £500 per individual, paid in May and November. One-off grants, holidays and Christmas gifts are also given according to need.

Annual grant total

In 2016 the fund had assets of £2.7 million and an income of £106,000. Grants totalled £70,500. There were 101 individuals in receipt of pensions by the year's end.

Applications

Application forms are available from the correspondent. Applications can be made throughout the year for consideration when the trustees meet at one of their three annual meetings. Beneficiaries' payments are reviewed annually at the discretion of the trustees and must be signed off by a person of responsibility who can verify the applicant's financial circumstances. Applicants are visited by the fund's female representatives before they are added to the pension roll and, where circumstances permit, after they are added to the roll.

Other information

The fund is registered with OSCR under the name E McLaren Fund for Indigent Ladies.

The Northern Ladies Annuity Society

£158,500

Correspondent: Jean Ferry, Secretary, MEA House, Ellison Place, Newcastle-upon-Tyne NE1 8XS (0191 232 1518; email: jean.ferry@nlas.org.uk)

CC number: 1097222

Eligibility

Single, unmarried and widowed ladies in need, who live or have lived for a number of years in Northumberland, Tyneside, Wearside, County Durham or Cumbria. At present only those over the state retirement age are considered.

Types of grants

Annuities paid quarterly. One-off grants are also available for those in receipt of an annuity for expenses such as holidays, domestic appliances, household items and other unexpected costs. Christmas hampers are also distributed to most annuitants. The society has also distributed fuel grants during recent spells of cold winter weather.

Note: individuals not already in receipt of an annuity are ineligible for any other form of help from the society.

Annual grant total

In 2016/17 the charity had assets of £5.8 million and an income of £388,000. During the year, the charity gave around £158,500 in grants to individuals.

Exclusions

The society does not give one-off grants to non-annuitants, nor will it support students. Any such requests for assistance will be ignored.

Applications

Applications to become an annuitant should be made on a form available from the correspondent. Completed forms can be submitted directly by the individual or through a third party such as Citizens Advice or a social worker. Applications are considered monthly.

The Pargeter and Wand Trust

£4,700

Correspondent: Marcus Fellows, Trustee, Broadening Choices for Older People, 1st Floor, 40B Imperial Court, Kings Norton Business Centre, Pershore Road South, Birmingham B30 3ES (0121 459 7670; email: marcus.fellows@bcop. org.uk)

CC number: 210725

Eligibility

Women who have never been married, are aged over 55 and live in their own homes. There is a preference for those living in the West Midlands area, but other areas of the country are considered.

Types of grants

Small annuities are paid quarterly and reviewed annually. Smaller, one-off grants, usually in the range of £50 to £150, are also available.

Annual grant total

In 2016/17 the charity had an income of £7,500 and a total expenditure of £4,900. We estimate that the charity gave around £4,700 in grants to individuals during the year.

Applications

Our previous research suggests that applications should be made via Age UK.

The Perry Fund

£29,000 (27 grants)

Correspondent: William Carter, Clerk to the Trustees, 7 Waterloo Road, Wolverhampton WV1 4DW (email: janeoliver@underhills.co.uk)

CC number: 218829

Eligibility

Annual top-up pensions to older women and one-off grants to women in need.

Types of grants

Annuities of around £2,000 to £3,000, as well as one-off grants.

Annual grant total

In 2015 the charity had assets of £652,500 and an income of £27,000. The charity paid regular annuities (of around £2,000 and £3,000) to five women throughout the year. Single grants were made to 22 women which totalled around £14,800. In total, the charity awarded around £29,000 in grants for welfare purposes in 2015.

Applications

Application forms are available from the correspondent. Applications can be submitted directly by the individual or through a third party such as a social worker, nursing home manager or welfare organisation. The trustees usually meet twice a year to consider applications.

Sawyer Trust

£65,000

Correspondent: Paul Denham, Trustee, PO Box 797, Worcester WR4 4BU (email: info@sawyertrust.org; website: www.sawyertrust.org)

CC number: 511276

Eligibility

Women over 50 who are in need through financial hardship, sickness or poor health. If there are surplus funds, men over 50 in similar circumstances may also receive assistance.

Types of grants

One-off grants of up to £500. Recent grants have been awarded for household items and fittings, removal costs, telephone bills, travel costs and rent arrears. The trust states that it will consider a wide range of assistance but does not pay cash directly to applicants.

Annual grant total

In 2015/16 the trust had assets of £2.2 million and an income of £74,500. During the year, the trust awarded around £65,000 in grants to individuals.

Exclusions

The trust will not give funding for: luxury goods or services; parties or outings; shortfall on insurance claims, except in certain circumstances; legal expenses; credit card debt; ongoing costs; or cash payments direct to individuals.

Applications

Apply on a form available from the correspondent or to download from the trust's website. Applications may be completed by the applicant or someone else on their behalf, and must be supported by an accredited third party; for example, Citizens Advice, a housing association, or a charitable organisation recognised by the trust. Refer to the website, or ask the correspondent for details of approved organisations. Written evidence such as a bank statement must be presented as evidence of applicant's circumstances. Applications must be posted or emailed. The trustees meet monthly to consider applications.

Dr Meena Sharma Memorial Foundation

£5,500

Correspondent: Dr B. K. Sharma, 14 Magdalene Road, Walsall, West Midlands WS1 3TA (01922 629842; email: gwalior@onetel.com)

CC number: 1108375

Eligibility

Children and women in the UK and India, especially those who have disabilities, are disadvantaged or underprivileged.

Types of grants

Small awards up to £500 (generally £100 to £250) are available to help children and women. Awards may include educational grants, travel expenses, financial help to further health and other needs.

Annual grant total

In 2015/16 the foundation had an income of £24,000 and a total expenditure of £23,000. We estimate that about £5,500 was given in welfare support to individuals.

Applications

Eligible candidates should apply in writing to the correspondent, providing an sae. Requests should give full contact details (including an email address) and reasons for seeking a grant. Applications can be made at any time. Only successful applicants are informed.

Other information

Grants are also made to organisations, especially in India, and individuals are supported for educational needs (teachers, other educational professionals and medical personnel or medical students may also be supported).

Smallwood Trust

£602,500

Correspondent: Paul Carbury, Lancaster House, 25 Hornyold Road, Malvern, Worcestershire WR14 1QQ (0300 365 1886; email: info@smallwoodtrust.org. uk; website: www.salrc.org.uk)

CC number: 205798

Eligibility

Women in need who: are living alone or with dependent children; have right of residency in the UK; are of working age; can provide evidence of savings of no more than £5,000; can provide evidence of debt of no more than £5,000; and have little income and/or are receiving all means-tested benefits to which they are entitled.

Types of grants

Regular monthly payments to support ongoing living expenses.

Annual grant total

In 2016 the trust had assets of £32.7 million and an income of £898,000. Grants to individuals totalled £602,500.

Exclusions

The trust is not able to offer: financial support for students; financial support to individuals who can access work-related or occupational charitable funds; or funding for one-off items such as white goods.

Applications

Applicants can either call the trust on 0300 365 1886 to make an application or complete the online grant enquiry form.

Ellen Rebe Spalding Memorial Fund

See entry on page 364

St Andrew's Society for Ladies in Need

£56,500

Correspondent: Maureen Pope, Secretary, 20 Denmark Gardens, Ipswich Road, Holbrook, Ipswich, Suffolk IP9 2BG (01473 327408; email: mpope1@btinternet.com; website: standrewssociety.btck.co.uk)

CC number: 208541

Eligibility

Single women from a well-educated, professional or semi-professional background who are now living alone in reduced circumstances, in receipt of all relevant state benefits and with very limited savings. Applicants must be retired or unable to work and of British nationality. Preference is given to women who are over 80 years of age.

Types of grants

Recurrent grants paid quarterly to help with daily living expenses. Priority is given to ladies who are trying to maintain their own homes but grants are also given to those struggling with nursing home fees. One-off special grants are also available for heating, the cost of moving house, domestic appliances, furniture, disability aids, holidays and convalescence.

Annual grant total

In 2016 the charity had assets of £1.8 million and an income of £65,000. During the year, a total of £56,500 was awarded in grants – £51,000 was given in regular grants, and £5,500 in special one-off grants.

Exclusions

No grants are given to younger women or non-retired ladies who are able to work. No assistance is given with the discharge of debts.

Applications

Application forms are available from the correspondent, and can be submitted directly by the individual or through a support agency such as Citizens Advice.

The Charles Wright Gowthorpe Fund and Clergy Augmentation Fund

£8,500

Correspondent: The Charles Wright Gowthorpe Fund & Clergy Augment, Lloyds TSB Private Banking Ltd, UK Trust Centre, 22–26 Ock Street, Abingdon, Oxfordshire OX14 5SW (01235 232758; email: pbuktccharityadmin@lloydsbanking. com)

CC number: 213852 and 213853

Eligibility

The Gowthorpe Fund supports widows and other women in need who live within a 12-mile radius of the Market Square, Nottingham.

The Clergy Augmentation Fund generally supports clergymen and their widows who live within a 10-mile radius of St Peter's Church, Nottingham.

Types of grants

Previous research indicates grants are typically of around £100, and paid annually in December.

Annual grant total

In 2016/17 the Gowthorpe Fund had an income of £4,700 and the Clergy Augmentation Fund had an income of £2,600. We estimate that combined grants from the funds totalled £8,500; around £6,500 from the Gowthorpe Fund, and £2,000 from the Clergy Augmentation Fund.

Applications

Apply on a form available from local Church of England vicars, to be returned by the end of October. Do not write to the correspondent initially; only send the application form once it has been completed.

Women In Prison Ltd

See entry on page 39

Miscellan-eous

The Andrew Anderson Trust

£35,500

Correspondent: Andrew Robertson Anderson, Trustee, 1 Cote House Lane, Bristol BS9 3UW (0117 962 1588)

CC number: 212170

Eligibility

People who are, or were, involved in charitable activities, and their dependants, who are in need.

Types of grants

One-off and recurrent grants are given according to need.

Annual grant total

In 2015/16 the trust had assets of £12 million and an income of £496,500. The vast majority of grants (£411,000) were awarded to organisations. Grants to individuals totalled £71,000 and we estimate that those for welfare purposes amounted to around £35,500.

Applications

The trust has previously stated that it rarely gives to people who are not known to the trustees or who have not been personally recommended by people known to the trustees. Unsolicited applications are therefore unlikely to be successful.

The Buchanan Society

£32,000

Correspondent: Ian Buchanan, 16 Ribblesdale, East Kilbride G74 4QN (01355 243437; email: Contact form on website; website: www.buchanansociety. com)

OSCR number: SC013679

Eligibility

Only people with the following surnames: Buchanan, McAuslan (any spelling), McWattie or Risk.

Types of grants

Pensions are available for older people in need. One-off hardship grants can also be given.

Annual grant total

In 2016 the society had assets of £1.6 million and an income of £54,000. Welfare grants to individuals totalled £32,000.

Applications

Application forms are available to download from the charity's website or can be requested from the correspondent.

Other information

The Buchanan Society is the oldest Clan Society in Scotland having been founded in 1725. Grant-making is its sole function. Grants are also made for educational purposes.

East Africa Women's League (United Kingdom)

£10,000

Correspondent: Sheila Heath, Nobles Farm, Gatehouse Road, Holton-le-Moor, Market Rasen LN7 6AG (01673 828393; email: eawlhq@gmail.com; website: www. eawl.org)

CC number: 294328

Eligibility

People of UK origin who have previously lived and worked in East Africa.

Types of grants

One-off and recurrent grants are given according to need. Grants range from around £100 to £800.

Annual grant total

In 2016 the charity had an income of £14,000 and a total expenditure of £21,000. We estimate that grants to individuals totalled £10,000.

Applications

Apply in writing to the Treasurer. Members of a fund sub-committee may visit applicants.

Friends of the Animals

£142,000

Correspondent: Martin Gomez, Trustee, 17A Riverway, Newport PO3 5UX (01983 522511; email: fotaiow@hotmail. com; website: www.friendsoftheanimals. co.uk)

CC number: 1000249

Eligibility

People who are in need and live on the Isle of Wight, in Portsmouth or the West Midlands.

Types of grants

Subsidised veterinary treatments such as spaying or neutering.

Annual grant total

In 2015/16 the charity held assets of £572,500 and had an income of £584,500. A total of £142,000 was spent on vet's bills for 3,385 treatments.

Applications

Requests for assistance can be made by calling the head office on 01983 522511 (Tuesday to Saturday, 10am to 4pm).

Other information

The charity's activities include the rehoming of animals and the provision of free advice and information on animal welfare, as well as loans of baskets, pens and other equipment to assist with animal care.

The Edmund Godson Charity

£3,000

Correspondent: Freya Villis, Trustee, 30 Hemingford Road, Cambridge CB1 3BZ (07866 267692; email: freya. villis@admin.cam.ac.uk)

CC number: 227463

Eligibility

People in need who wish to emigrate and who currently live in and around Woolwich, Charlton, Shooters Hill, Eltham, Abbey Wood and Plumstead in southeast London, Shinfield near Reading, Leominster in Herefordshire and Tenbury in Worcestershire.

Types of grants

One-off grants according to need.

Annual grant total

In 2016/17 the charity had an income of £14,000 and a total expenditure of £7,200. We have estimated that grants to individuals totalled £3,000.

Applications

Applications should be made directly by the individual on a form available from the correspondent. Details of the

proposed destination, occupation, emigration eligibility and financial circumstances should be given.

Eliza Haldane Wylie Fund

£12,500

Correspondent: The Trustees of Eliza Haldane Wylie Fund, Clyde & Co., Albany House, 58 Albany Street, Edinburgh EH1 3QR (0131 557 1545)

OSCR number: SC011882

Eligibility

People in need who are related to or associated with Eliza Haldane Wylie or her family, or are 'gentlefolk of the middle class'.

Types of grants

Small, one-off payments.

Annual grant total

In 2015/16 the charity had an income of £16,500 and a total expenditure of £12,900. We estimate that grants given to individuals totalled around £12,500.

Applications

Apply in writing to the correspondent.

The Agnes Macleod Memorial Fund

£5,000

Correspondent: Linda Orr, Secretary, Nurses Cottage, Hallin, Waternish, Isle of Skye IV55 8GJ (email: linda@m-orr. freeserve.co.uk; website: www.clan-macleod-scotland.org.uk)

OSCR number: SC014297

Eligibility

Women in need who are over 60, living in Scotland and were born with the name Macleod or whose mothers were born Macleod.

Types of grants

To provide monetary grants or donations of gift vouchers when benefits from the state are either not sufficient or not appropriate. Grants range from £100 to £250 and are one-off.

Annual grant total

In 2016/17 the fund had an income of £4,800 and a total expenditure of £5,200. We estimate that the fund gave around £5,000 in grants to individuals.

Applications

Apply in writing to the correspondent.

The Vegetarian Charity

£7,300

Correspondent: Susan Lenihan, 56 Parliament Street, Chippenham SN14 0DE (01249 443521; email: grantssecretary@vegetariancharity.org.uk; website: www.vegetariancharity.org.uk)

CC number: 294767

Eligibility

Vegetarians and vegans up to the age of 26 who are in need.

Types of grants

One-off and recurrent grants to relieve poverty and sickness, usually ranging up to £500. According to the website, the charity is 'keen to receive more applications from young people and parents experiencing financial hardship'.

Annual grant total

In 2015/16 the charity had assets of £1.1 million and an income of £53,000. The charity awarded a total of £29,000 in grants during the year to both organisations and individuals. We estimate that the charity gave around £7,300 in grants to individuals for welfare purposes, with funding also awarded for educational purposes.

Applications

Application forms are available to download, complete, and return to the correspondent. The charity prefers to receive applications by email.

The application forms ask for details of income, expenditure and debts in order to assess financial eligibility.

Older people

Age Sentinel Trust

£10,000

Correspondent: Francesca Colverson, Head of Fundraising, Longreach, Clay Lane, Chichester, West Sussex PO19 3PX (020 8144 4774 or 07823 880388; email: info@agesentinel.org.uk; website: agesentinel.org.uk)

CC number: 1133624

Eligibility

Older people who are in need. Priority is given to people with dementia, particularly Alzheimer's disease, and those with other debilitating illnesses.

Types of grants

One-off and recurrent grants to support independent living. Grants have been made to individuals with medical problems for purposes such as communication devices or home adaptations.

Annual grant total

In 2015/16 the trust had an income of £43,500 and a total expenditure of £43,500. The trust awarded £22,000 to both organisations and individuals and we estimate that £10,000 of that total was awarded directly to individuals.

Applications

Apply in writing to the correspondent.

Aid for the Aged in Distress (AFTAID)

£25,500

Correspondent: Major Brian Hudson, Trustee, 9 Bonhill Street, London EC2A 4PE (0870 803 1950; email: info@aftaid.org.uk; website: www.aftaid.org.uk)

CC number: 299276

Eligibility

UK citizens who are over 65, reside in the UK, are living on a low income and have minimal savings.

Types of grants

Emergency grants for essential items to facilitate the beneficiary to maintain their independence in the familiar surroundings of their home, e.g. heating appliances, bedding, cookers, washing machines or other white goods, essential furniture and carpets. Grants are also made towards more expensive items such as stairlifts, walk-in showers, motorised scooters, etc.

Grants are paid directly to the supplier of the goods or services.

Annual grant total

In 2015 the charity held assets of £361,000 and had an income of £124,500. Grants for older people totalled £25,500.

Exclusions

Grants cannot be made for any ongoing payments, retrospective funding, arrears or debts of any kind.

Applications

Apply on a form available through the charity's website. Applicants will initially need to fill in an online form which will automatically issue the application form by return email.

Applications can be made directly by the individual or through a welfare organisation and should include written support from a social worker, doctor or similar professional who is personally aware of the beneficiary's situation.

The charity's annual report states that, 'an increasing number of applications that are received are having to be declined as they fall outside the charity's remit and criteria. Unfortunately, this creates additional administration costs and a drain on resources.'

Barchester Health Care Foundation
See entry on page 58

Foundations Independent Living Trust
See entry on page 43

Friends of the Elderly

£157,000

Correspondent: The Trustees, 40–42 Ebury Street, London SW1W 0LZ (0330 332 1110; email: hello@fote.org.uk; website: www.fote.org.uk)

CC number: 226064

Eligibility

The charity's website states:

You can apply for a grant with us if you meet the following criteria:

- You are of state retirement age
- You live in England or Wales
- You are managing on a low income with savings of less than £4,000
- You are not living in a residential care home

Types of grants

The charity's website states that it has three types of grant:

- **Home essentials** – to cover the cost of replacing everyday items, small home repairs and mobility adaptations
- **Digital connection** – can be used towards the cost of equipment, such as tablets and smartphones, as well as broadband costs
- **Financial support** – to help with unexpected bills and large costs, such as utility bills, funeral costs or moving fees

The average amount awarded is £300.

Annual grant total

In 2015/16 the charity held assets of £32.7 million and had an income of almost £25.3 million. Grants to individuals totalled £157,000.

Applications

Applications should be made on a form available to download from the charity's website. Applications should be made through a third party organisation such as social services, Citizens Advice, Age UK or another welfare agency.

Other information

The charity offers a range of care and support options for its beneficiaries through residential homes, community nursing, befriending schemes and dementia support. A main aim of the charity is to reduce the level of isolation among older people, which is something its 'Phoning Friends' telephone service aspires to do.

The charity also helps older people to claim benefits for which they are eligible through its provision of welfare advice and assistance. Grants are also awarded to organisations to run events and activities for older people.

HWA (Home Warmth for the Aged)

£9,000

Correspondent: W. Berentemfel, Administrator, 19 Towers Wood, South Darenth, Dartford DA4 9BQ (01322 863836; email: w.berentemfel@btinternet.com)

CC number: 271735

Eligibility
People of pensionable age, who are at risk from the cold in winter and have no resources other than their state pension/income support and have savings of less than £4,000.

Types of grants
Provision of heating appliances, bedding, clothing and solid fuel. Grants are also available to pay fuel debts where the supply has been disconnected but these are one-off grants only.

Annual grant total
In 2016/17 the trust had an income of £8,900 and a total expenditure of £9,400. We estimate that grants given to individuals totalled £9,000.

Exclusions
No grants are made to people who have younger members of their family living with them.

Applications
Application forms are available from the correspondent. Applications should be submitted only through social workers, doctors, nurses, etc. to whom grants are returned for disbursement. If there is an armed forces connection, applications should be made through SSAFA (see the armed forces section of this guide). Applications made directly by individuals are not considered. Applications are considered monthly.

The William Johnston Trust Fund

£38,500 (22 grants)

Correspondent: B. J. S. Parsons-Smith, Administrator, Aspen Cottage, Apse Manor Road, Shanklin PO37 7PN (0151 236 6666)

CC number: 212495

Eligibility
Older people in need who live in the UK.

Types of grants
Recurrent grants paid twice annually, usually in June and December. One-off grants towards, for example, TV licences. Birthday gifts are also awarded.

Annual grant total
In 2016 the fund held assets of £1.16 million and had an income of £42,500. Grants to 22 individuals totalled £38,500.

Applications
Apply in writing to the correspondent. Applications can be submitted directly by the individual or family member and are considered throughout the year.

The John William Lamb Charity
See entry on page 233

Lady McCorquodale's Charity Trust

£7,600

Correspondent: Anina Cheng, Correspondent, Swan House, 17–19 Stratford Place, London W1C 1BQ (020 7907 2100; email: charity@mfs.co.uk)

CC number: 268786

Eligibility
People who are in need, with a preference for older people.

Types of grants
One-off and recurrent grants are given for day-to-day needs, such as clothing and food.

Annual grant total
In 2015/16 the trust had an income of £10,500 and a total expenditure of £15,300. We estimate that the trust gave around £7,600 in grants to individuals during the year.

Applications
Apply in writing to the correspondent. Applications can be submitted either directly by the individual or, where

applicable, via a social worker, Citizens Advice or other third party.

Other information
The trust also gives grants to organisations.

The Morris Beneficent Fund

£22,500 (eight grants)

Correspondent: Simon Jamison, No. 10 Evendons Centre, 171 Evendons Lane, Wokingham RG41 4EH (0118 979 8653)

CC number: 256473

Eligibility
The objective of the fund is to 'relieve financial hardship and social isolation among older people'.

Types of grants
Recurrent grants according to need.

Annual grant total
In 2016 the fund had assets of £1.1 million and an income of £41,000. Grants to eight individuals totalled £22,500.

Applications
The trustees put forward names to be included on the beneficiaries list. No unsolicited applications will be considered.

Other information
The trustees decide each year how many annuitants can be supported, although this number rarely exceeds 20 as the trustees prefer to raise the level of grants rather than awarding a larger number of smaller annuities.

The Muir Family Charitable Trust

£3,200

CC number: 255372

Eligibility
Older people who are in need.

Types of grants
One-off and recurrent grants.

Annual grant total
In 2015/16 the charity had an income of £7,200 and a total expenditure of £6,600. We estimate that grants given to individuals for welfare purposes totalled around £3,200.

Applications
Unsolicited applications are not accepted.

The Roger Pilkington Young Trust

£52,000 (89 grants)

Correspondent: Ben Dixon, Trustee, c/o Everys Solicitors, Magnolia House, Church Street, Exmouth, Devon EX8 1HQ (01395 264384; email: law@everys.co.uk)

CC number: 251148

Eligibility

People over 60 years of age whose income has been reduced through no fault of their own, through illness or accident.

Types of grants

Monthly pensions of about £60 for single people and £80 for married couples/civil partners.

Annual grant total

In 2016/17 the charity held assets of £1.5 million and had an income of £59,000. During the year, the charity gave around £52,000 in grants to 89 individuals.

Applications

Apply on a form available from the correspondent, after the pensions are advertised.

The Florence Reiss Trust for Old People

£5,000

Correspondent: Dr Stephen Reiss, Trustee, 94 Tinwell Road, Stamford, Lincolnshire PE9 2SD (01780 762710)

CC number: 236634

Eligibility

Women over 55 and men over 60 who are in need. Priority is given to those who live in the parishes of Streatley in Berkshire and Goring-on-Thames in Oxfordshire.

Types of grants

One-off and recurrent grants are given according to need.

Annual grant total

In 2015/16 the charity had an income of £10,800 and a total expenditure of £10,200. We estimate that the charity awarded around £5,000 in grants to individuals for welfare purposes. Grants are also awarded to organisations which support older people.

Applications

Apply in writing to the correspondent.

Other information

At the time of writing (August 2017) the charity had no website or accounts available.

Tancred's Charity for Pensioners
See entry on page 31

Religion

Christianity

The Alexis Trust

£4,300 (22 grants)

Correspondent: Prof. Duncan Vere, Trustee, 14 Broadfield Way, Buckhurst Hill, Essex IG9 5AG (020 8504 6872)

CC number: 262861

Eligibility

Members of the Christian faith.

Annual grant total

In 2015/16 the trust had assets of £531,000 and a total income of £45,000. Grants to 22 individuals totalled £4,300. A further £41,500 was awarded in grants to organisations.

Applications

Apply in writing to the correspondent.

The Appleton Trust (Canterbury)

£2,600 (two grants)

Correspondent: Mrs D. Parks, Clerk to the Trustees, Diocesan Board of Finance, Diocesan House, Lady Wootton's Green, Canterbury, Kent CT1 1NQ (01227 459401)

CC number: 250271

Eligibility

People in need connected with the Church of England in the diocese of Canterbury.

Types of grants

One-off grants normally ranging between £100 and £500. The trust also makes loans to members of the clergy, local parishioners and widows of clergymen for items such as cars, computer equipment and equity loans.

Annual grant total

In 2015 the trust had assets of £873,000 and an income of £31,000. Grants to two individuals totalled £2,600.

Exclusions

Our research suggests that grants are not given for further education.

Applications

Apply in writing to the correspondent. Applications should be submitted directly by the individual or a church organisation. They are considered every two months.

Other information

Organisations connected to the Church of England in Canterbury diocese are also supported.

Charity of Miss Ann Farrar Brideoake

£42,500

Correspondent: Alan Ware, Trustee, c/o Cowling Swift & Kitchin, 8 Blake Street, York YO1 8XJ (01904 625678)

CC number: 213848

Eligibility

Communicant members of the Church of England living within the dioceses of York, Liverpool and Manchester, who are in need. This includes parishioners, clergy and retired clergy.

Types of grants

Recurrent grants are given to help in 'making ends meet'. Support is given towards household outgoings, domestic equipment, holidays, and children's entertainment, etc. as well as special medical needs. One-off payments are made in special circumstances and debt relief can be supported in exceptional circumstances.

Annual grant total

In 2015/16 the charity held assets of nearly £2.2 million and had an income of £76,000. Grants to individuals totalled £42,500.

Applications

Apply on a form available from the correspondent, to be countersigned by the local vicar as confirmation of communicant status.

Charities of Susanna Cole and Others

£4,000

Correspondent: Tony Pegler, Central England Quakers Office, Frieds Meeting House, 40 Bull Street, Birmingham B4 6AF (0121 682 7575)

CC number: 204531

Eligibility

Quakers in need who live in the West Midlands (Birmingham, Coventry, Dudley, Solihull, Sandwell, Walsall, Warwickshire) with a preference for Worcester. Previously, the trust has preferred to support older people on low pensions.

Types of grants

One-off and recurrent grants are given according to need. Help may be given for a range of needs, including: domestic help or gardening for people with disabilities or older individuals; transport to and from meeting for worship or other Quaker gatherings; council tax; rent or accommodation fees; bills and fuel; furniture; white goods; food; clothing; convalescence or respite care; car expenses for those with limited mobility; complementary medicine; medical aids and equipment; media and communication needs, including TV licences; childcare; repairs; and counselling.

Annual grant total

In 2016 the charity had an income of £16,000 and a total expenditure of £8,500. We estimate that the charity awarded £4,000 in grants for welfare purposes.

Applications

Applications should be made in writing to the correspondent, detailing financial need and how the grant will be used.

Other information

Grants are made for both welfare and educational purposes, including training and starting work or a business.

The Deakin and Withers Fund

£27,500

Correspondent: Karen Alsop, Fund Administrator, South Yorkshire Community Foundation, Unit 9–12 Jessops Riverside, 800 Brightside Lane, Sheffield S9 2RX (0114 242 9003; email: grants@sycf.org.uk; website: www.sycf.org.uk)

CC number: 1140947–2

Eligibility

Single women in the UK, whether divorced, unmarried or widowed, who are in reduced circumstances and who are members of the Church of England or of a church with full membership of the Council of Churches for Britain and Ireland. Grants are given to women over the age of 40 across the UK.

Types of grants

One-off grants are available for help with the purchase of household items and the payment of utility bills.

Annual grant total

The fund is administered by South Yorkshire Community Foundation. In 2015/16 the fund had assets of £272,500 and an income of £53,000. A total of £27,500 was awarded in grants.

Exclusions

Holidays and retrospective payments cannot be funded.

Applications

Application forms are available from the correspondent or can be downloaded from the website. Applications must include details of personal income of expenditure.

William Gunn's Charity

£24,000

Correspondent: Jane Spiers, 3 Wesley Court, Duke Street, Broseley TF125LS (janespiers@gmail.com)

CC number: 210214

Eligibility

Members of the Society of Friends (Quakers) who are in conditions of need, hardship or distress.

Types of grants

One-off according to need.

Annual grant total

In 2016/17 the charity had assets of £1.2 million and an income of £33,500. Grants to individuals totalled £24,000.

Applications

Apply in writing to the correspondent.

Hoper-Dixon Trust

£17,200

Correspondent: The Provincial Bursar, The Dominican Council, Blackfriars Priory, St Giles, Oxford OX1 3LY (01865 288231; email: enquiries@hoperdixon.org.uk; website: www.hoperdixon.org.uk)

CC number: 231160

Eligibility

People in need connected with, or resident in or near, any house or pastoral centre under the direction of the Dominicans of the English Province Order of Preachers.

Types of grants

One-off and recurrent grants are given according to need. Recent grants have been given to assist with: medical expenses not covered by public funds; help for those unable to work due to sickness or injury; help with unexpected expenses; relocation expenses and basic household equipment for those setting up a new home; help for pilgrims going to Lourdes, both those who are sick and those caring for them; and the costs of attending a funeral for a close family member.

Annual grant total

In 2015/16 the trust had an income of £15,800 and a total expenditure of £22,500. We estimate that grants given to individuals totalled £17,200, with

funding also awarded for educational purposes.

Applications

Applications are normally made by a Dominican Friar for the benefit of someone connected with the order or living in the neighbourhood of a house of the order. A list of Dominican houses and contact details is available from the English Province of the Order of Preachers website.

Third-party welfare organisations applying on behalf of an individual should contact the trust in writing or by email to enquire about possible eligibility.

The Hounsfield Pension

£3,700

Correspondent: Godfrey Smallman, Administrator, Wrigleys Solicitors, Fountain Precinct, Balm Green, Sheffield S1 2JA (0114 267 5594; fax: 0114 276 3176)

CC number: 221436

Eligibility

Unmarried women, widows and widowers who are over 50 years old, live in England or Wales, are members of the Church of England and have never received parochial relief or public assistance. The charity tries to keep the numbers of male and female beneficiaries as equal as possible.

Types of grants

Grants are fixed annually and are paid in two instalments.

Annual grant total

In 2015/16 the charity had an income of £5,300 and a total expenditure of £3,900. We estimate that the charity gave around £3,700 in grants to individuals.

Exclusions

Applicants must reside in England or Wales.

Applications

Apply in writing to the correspondent. Only a limited number of pensions are available, and places become available at irregular intervals.

The Morval Foundation

£99,500

Correspondent: Tricia Cullimore, Secretary, Meadow Brook, Send Marsh Road, Ripley GU23 6JR

CC number: 207692

Eligibility

Older Christian Scientists living in the UK who are members of The Mother Church, The First Church of Christ, Scientist in Boston, USA.

Types of grants

Monthly grants to allow older Christian Scientists to continue living independently in their own homes and one-off grants according to need.

Annual grant total

In 2015/16 the foundation had assets of £4.7 million and an income of £280,000. During the year, the foundation gave around £99,500 in grants to individuals. Of this amount, £68,500 was given in monthly grants and £31,000 in one-off grants.

Applications

Application forms are available from the correspondent and can be submitted directly by the individual for consideration at any time.

Other information

The foundation administers three funds; the Morval Fund, the Ruston Bequest, the New Beechfield Fund and the New Chickering Fund.

North of Scotland Quaker Trust

£2,000

Correspondent: The Trustees, Quaker Meeting House, 98 Crown Street, Aberdeen AB11 6HJ

OSCR number: SC000784

Eligibility

People who are associated with the Religious Society of Friends in the North of Scotland Monthly Meeting area, namely Aberdeen City, Aberdeenshire, Moray, Highland, Orkney, Shetland, Western Isles and that part of Argyll and Bute from Oban northwards.

Types of grants

One-off and recurrent grants are given according to need.

Annual grant total

In 2016 the trust had an income of £17,900 and a total expenditure of £9,800. Grants are made to individuals and organisations. We estimate that grants given to individuals for welfare purposes totalled around £2,000.

Exclusions

No grants are given to people studying above first degree level.

Applications

Apply in writing to the correspondent.

Other information

Grants are also given for educational purposes.

The Ogle Christian Trust

£2,800

Correspondent: Fiona Putley, Secretary, 43 Woolstone Road, London SE23 2TR

CC number: 1061458

Eligibility

People who are experiencing financial hardship.

Types of grants

One-off grants.

Annual grant total

In 2016 the charity held assets of £2.2 million and had an income of £109,500. During the year, the charity gave around £2,800 in grants to individuals.

Applications

Apply in writing to the correspondent.

Mary Pittis for Widows

£800

Correspondent: Anthony Holmes, Correspondent, 62–66 Lugley Street, Newport, Isle of Wight PO30 5EU (01983 524431)

CC number: 262018

Eligibility

Widows who are aged 60 or over, live on the Isle of Wight and express Christian (in practice, Protestant) beliefs. Applicants must be known to the minister and have some connection with the church detailed on the application form. Preference is given to the candidates who were born on the Isle of Wight.

Types of grants

One-off grants for items such as essential kitchen equipment, semi-medical items such as remote control easy-lift armchairs.

Annual grant total

In 2015 the charity had an income of £11,600 and a total expenditure of £920. We estimate that the charity awarded around £800 in grants to individuals.

Applications

Application forms are available from the correspondent. Applicants should provide details of the church attended and the minister of that church. Submissions can be made directly by the individual, through a welfare agency or by a minister of religion on behalf of the candidate. Requests can be considered at any time.

Other information

At the time of writing (August 2017) the charity had no website or accounts available.

The Podde Trust

£5,500

Correspondent: Peter Godfrey, Trustee, 68 Green Lane, Hucclecote, Gloucester GL3 3QX (01452 613563; email: thepodde@gmail.com)

CC number: 1016322

Eligibility

Individuals involved in Christian work in the UK and overseas.

Types of grants

One-off and recurrent grants.

Annual grant total

In 2016/17 the trust had assets of £9,400 and an income of £49,000. There were 27 grants made to individuals totalling £11,200. The purposes for which awards were given were not specified. We estimate that grants for welfare purposes totalled around £5,500.

Applications

Applications may be made in writing to the correspondent.

Note: the trust has previously stated that it has very limited resources, and those it does have are mostly already committed. Requests from new applicants, therefore, have very little chance of success.

Other information

Organisations involved in Christian work in the UK and abroad are also supported (£30,000 was given to organisations in 2016/17). The trust awards grants for charitable purposes, including the advancement of religion, of education and the relief of poverty.

The Rehoboth Trust

£10,000

Correspondent: The Treasurer, 9 Arlington Close, Newport NP20 6QF (email: rehobothtrust@ntlworld.com; website: www.rehobothtrust.org.uk)

CC number: 1114454

Eligibility

Evangelical Christians working or living in Wales. Applicants are prioritised in the following order: those based in Newport, South Wales; those in the combined area of Monmouthshire, Torfaen, Blaenau Gwent and Caerphilly; those in the rest of Wales.

Types of grants

Grants given according to need.

Annual grant total

In 2016 the trust had an income of £23,500 and a total expenditure of £22,500. We estimate that grants given to individuals totalled around £10,000.

Applications

Apply in writing to the correspondent.

Other information

Grants are also made to organisations.

Tancred's Charity for Pensioners

£23,000

Correspondent: Andrew Penny, Forsters, 31 Hill Street, London W1J 5LS (020 7863 8522; email: andrew.penny@ forsters.co.uk)

CC number: 229936

Eligibility

Men and women aged 50 or over who are UK citizens and clergy of the Church of England or Church in Wales, or who have been commissioned officers in the armed forces.

Types of grants

Annual pensions of around £2,250 a year are paid quarterly to a limited number of beneficiaries.

Annual grant total

In 2016 the charity had an income of £33,000 and a total expenditure of £25,500. During the year, the charity awarded £23,000 to ten individuals.

The charity is administered by the Tancred's Charities which also administers the Tancred's Educational Foundation.

Applications

Apply in writing to the correspondent. Individuals may apply at any time, but applications can only be considered when a vacancy occurs, which is approximately once a year.

Other information

During the last financial year, all pensioners supported were retired clergy.

The Westward Trust

£5,000

Correspondent: Alison Ironside, 12 Green Meadow Road, Birmingham B29 4DD (0121 475 1179)

CC number: 260488

Eligibility

Quakers in who are in need and live in the UK.

Types of grants

One-off and recurrent grants can be given according to need.

Annual grant total

In 2015/16 the trust had an income of £12,000 and a total expenditure of £11,000. We estimate that the trust awarded £5,000 in grants to individuals during the year.

Applications

Apply in writing to the correspondent.

Other information

Grants are also made to organisations, particularly Quaker charities or projects in which members of the Religious Society of Friends are involved.

Islam

National Zakat Foundation

£1.3 million

Correspondent: Fund Administrator, NZF Zakat Centre, 41 Fieldgate Street, London E1 1JU (03333 123 123; email: info@nzf.org.uk; website: www.nzf.org. uk)

CC number: 1153719

Eligibility

The foundation's website states applicants must:

- Be Muslim
- Demonstrate that their circumstances mean that they cannot, or will soon not be able to finance basic needs (food, clothing and accommodation)
- Declare all income and expenses, assets and debts

Types of grants

Grants are available for a range of needs including: essentials (food, transport, utility bills, white goods, etc.); empowerment (education and business development); legal costs (asylum cases, residency, spouse visas, etc.); debt; emergency (voluntary permanent return to country of origin).

Full details of the grants available can be found on the eligibility page of the foundation's website.

Annual grant total

In 2016 the foundation held assets of £2 million and an income of £3.4 million. Grants to individuals totalled £1.3 million.

Exclusions

The foundation's website states:

Unfortunately, NZF cannot support the following applicants due to the nature of their circumstances:

- EU Nationals
- Non-Residents
- No Recourse to Public Funds
- Refused Asylum Seekers
- Overstayers/Illegal Immigrants

Applications

Applications can be made online or by using an application form which is available to download from the foundation's website. When completed, you can email your application to apply@nzf.org.uk, or post it to FREEPOST NZF.

Judaism

AJEX Charitable Foundation

See entry on page 79

Closehelm Ltd

£52,500

Correspondent: A. Van Praagh, 30 Armitage Road, London NW11 8RD (020 8201 8688)

CC number: 291296

Eligibility

People, particularly those of the Jewish faith, who are in need.

Types of grants

Grants and loans are given to those in need, depending on circumstance.

Annual grant total

In 2015/16 the charity had assets of £2.7 million and an income of £208,000. During the year, the charity awarded £52,500 in grants to individuals.

Applications

Applications should be made in writing to the correspondent.

The Engler Family Charitable Trust

£7,500

Correspondent: J. Engler, Trustee, Sunnydale, Bowdon Road, Altrincham WA14 2AJ (email: jengleruk@yahoo.co.uk)

CC number: 1108518

Eligibility

Members of the Jewish faith living in England or Wales, with a particular focus on young and older people.

Types of grants

Grants are given according to need.

Annual grant total

In 2015/16 the trust had an income of £15,500 and a total expenditure of £16,400. We estimate that grants given to individuals totalled around £7,500, with funding also awarded to organisations.

Applications

Apply in writing to the correspondent.

Isaac and Annie Fogelman Relief Trust

£9,000

Correspondent: Stephen Forman, 51 Barham Avenue, Elstree, Borehamwood, Hertfordshire WD6 3PW (email: stephenjforman1@gmail.com)

CC number: 202285

Eligibility

People of the Jewish faith aged 40 and over who live in Portsmouth and worship at the Portsmouth Jewish Synagogue.

Types of grants

One-off and recurrent grants are given according to need.

Annual grant total

In 2016/17 the trust had an income of £17,000 and a total expenditure of £10,000. We estimate that the amount awarded in grants to individuals was £9,000.

Applications

Apply in writing to the correspondent.

Friends of Boyan Trust

£185,500

Correspondent: Jacob Getter, Trustee, 23 Durley Road, London N16 5JW (020 8809 6051)

CC number: 1114498

Eligibility

People in need in the Orthodox Jewish community.

Types of grants

One-off grants according to need.

Annual grant total

In 2016 the trust had assets of £68,000 and an income of £675,500. Grants to individuals totalled £185,500, with a further £487,000 awarded to organisations.

Applications

Apply in writing to the correspondent.

Gur Trust

£5,500

Correspondent: The Trustees, 206 High Road, London N15 4NP (020 8801 6038)

CC number: 283423

Eligibility

People connected to the Jewish Orthodox faith in the UK.

Types of grants

One-off and recurrent grants may be offered according to need.

Note: that the trust primarily aims to support education in and the religion of the Orthodox Jewish faith.

Annual grant total

In 2015/16 he trust had assets of £1.4 million and an income of £44,000. We estimate that welfare grants to individuals totalled around £5,500.

Applications

Applications may be made in writing to the correspondent. Our previous research notes the trust stating that 'all calls for help are carefully considered and help is given according to circumstances and funds then available'.

Other information

The trust also makes grants to organisations, Talmudical colleges and to individuals for educational purposes.

The Jewish Aged Needy Pension Society

£17,500

Correspondent: Sheila Taylor, Secretary, 34 Dalkeith Grove, Stanmore, Middlesex HA7 4SG (020 8958 5390)

CC number: 206262

Eligibility

Members of the Jewish community aged 60 or over, who have lived in the UK for at least ten years or are of British nationality.

Types of grants

Regular pensions.

Annual grant total

In 2016 the society had an income of £12,900 and a total expenditure of £26,000. We estimate that pensions and grants totalled £17,500.

Applications

Apply in writing to the correspondent. Applications are considered quarterly.

Jewish Care Scotland

£11,700

Correspondent: The Trustees, The Walton Community Care Centre, May Terrace, Giffnock, Glasgow G46 6LD (0141 620 1800; fax: 0141 620 2409; email: admin@jcarescot.org.uk; website: www.jcarescot.org.uk)

OSCR number: SC005267

Eligibility

Jewish people who live in Scotland and are in need.

Types of grants

One-off grants are given towards clothing, food, household goods, rent, holidays, equipment, and travel. The charity also runs a food bank from Mark's Deli in Glasgow.

Annual grant total

In 2015 the charity held assets of £2.6 million and had an income of £1 million. During the year, the charity gave around £11,700 in grants to individuals through its hardship fund.

Applications

In the first instance, contact the correspondent.

Other information

The board also helps with educational costs and friendship clubs, housing requirements, clothing, meals-on-wheels and counselling, for example.

The Association of Jewish Refugees (AJR)

£1.3 million

Correspondent: Social Services Department, Jubilee House, Merrion Avenue, Stanmore, Middlesex HA7 4RL (020 8385 3070; fax: 020 8385 3080; email: enquiries@ajr.org.uk; website: www.ajr.org.uk)

CC number: 1149882

Eligibility

Jewish refugees from Nazi oppression, their dependants and descendants, who are settled in the UK. Potential applicants must be members of the

Association of Jewish Refugees (AJR) or be eligible to become members and be willing to join the association.

Specific conditions attached to each fund:

- Homecare: applicants must not have income exceeding £10,000 or assets (not including their home or vehicle) exceeding £50,000
- Emergency Fund and Hungarian Scheme: applicants must not have income exceeding £10,000, or £14,000 for a couple, with few or no assets, excluding a car
- Austrian Programme: Austrian survivors (or spouses of Austrian nationals) who live on low incomes, under £11,000 for one person or £15,000 for a couple, with limited assets (up to a maximum of £31,250)

Types of grants

The association administers emergency social, welfare and care funds on behalf of the Conference on Jewish Material Claims Against Germany, which can be used to pay for a number of services and essential items including dental treatment and specialist clothing as well as urgent house repairs, recuperative convalescence, respite breaks and homecare packages. Specifically these funds are:

- Homecare: the objective of the scheme is to assist clients to live in their homes for as long as possible. Homecare is assessed according to the client's functional capacity by a social worker. Homecare is funded by the German government and is only available to first-generation clients. In exceptional circumstances second-generation clients may be funded from the association's own funds
- Emergency Fund: grants of up to £2,000 (or £2,500 in exceptional cases) for essential items or services such as urgent house repairs, medical consultations, dental treatment or specialist clothing
- Austrian Holocaust Survivors Emergency Assistance Programme: financial assistance (up to a maximum of £10,000 in any 12-month period) for Austrian holocaust survivors on low incomes who require urgent medical attention or essential welfare services. Grants can be made for wheelchairs, disability aids, dental care, hearing aids, etc. Assistance to buy into the Austrian social security pension scheme can also be given
- Hungarian Government Scheme: grants for essential items or services for Hungarian survivors

Annual grant total

In 2015/16 the association held assets of £28.4 million and had an income of £3 million. During the year, the association gave around £1.3 million in grants to individuals for welfare purposes.

The association also gave £36,500 in grants to individuals for educational purposes.

Applications

Applications may be made by contacting the social work team by telephone.

Other information

The association provides support and advice on welfare benefits, foreign pension entitlements and reparations. It also has a day centre in Hampstead which runs entertainment programmes and serves Kosher lunches.

Kupath Gemach Chaim Bechesed Viznitz Trust

£289,000

Correspondent: Saul Weiss, Trustee, 171 Kyverdale Road, London N16 6PS (020 8442 9604 or 0781 125 3203)

CC number: 1110323

Eligibility

Members of the Jewish faith who are in need.

Types of grants

One-off and recurrent grants are given according to need.

Annual grant total

In 2015/16 the charity had an income of £404,500 and a total expenditure of £400,000. Grants to individuals totalled £289,000, with a further £109,500 awarded to organisations.

Applications

Apply in writing to the correspondent.

The Leeds Jewish Welfare Board

£4,000

Correspondent: Liz Bradbury, Chief Executive, 311 Stonegate Road, Leeds, West Yorkshire LS17 6AZ (0113 268 4211; fax: 0113 203 4915; email: theboard@ljwb.co.uk; website: www.ljwb.co.uk)

CC number: 1041257

Eligibility

Primarily people of the Jewish faith who live in Leeds or North and West Yorkshire.

Types of grants

Grants may be given as part of a 'support package'. They are rarely given on a one-off basis without a full assessment of the situation. Loans may also be given and depending on individual circumstances may be part

grant/part loan. A flexible approach together with budgeting advice is offered. The majority of grants are given to families with children. These may be for clothes, bedding requirements and so on. Grants are also given at Jewish festivals such as Passover. Counselling and meals-on-wheels services along with a comprehensive range of services and resources are also offered to children, families and older people primarily, but not exclusively, of the Jewish faith.

Annual grant total

In 2015/16 the charity had assets of £6.1 million and an income of £3.5 million. Each year a small amount is reserved for individual grant-making purposes. We estimate that grants given to individuals totalled around £4,000.

The charity also spent over £3.4 million on its various other charitable services, which include providing activities and support for older people, children and their families, people with physical and mental health problems from the Jewish community and the 'Survivors of the Holocaust' support group.

Applications

Applications for help can be made at any time by individuals, welfare agencies, friends or relatives. The board can respond quickly in urgent cases. The applicant will be seen by a case worker who will assess the application and gather the relevant information.

Other information

The organisation was established in 1878 as a voluntary Board of Guardians, with its main purpose being 'to hand out funds to the needy to prevent them from having to enter the workhouse'. Today, the Leeds Jewish Welfare Board employs more than 100 staff and hundreds of volunteers, who provide support in the community.

Mercaz Torah Vechesed Ltd

Correspondent: Joseph Ostreicher, Trustee, 28 Braydon Road, London N16 6QB (020 8880 5366; email: umarpeh@gmail.com)

CC number: 1109212

Eligibility

Members of the Orthodox Jewish community who are in need.

Types of grants

One-off grants.

Annual grant total

In 2016/17 the charity had an income of £2.1 million and a total expenditure of £2 million. During the last financial year, all of the charity's grant-making was to organisations. However, in previous years, it has awarded around £20,000 in grants to individuals.

Applications

Apply in writing to the correspondent.

Merseyside Jewish Community Care

£11,000

Correspondent: Lisa Dolan, Chief Executive, Shifrin House, 433 Smithdown Road, Liverpool L15 3JL (0151 733 2292; email: info@mjccshifrin. co.uk; website: www. merseysidejewishcommunitycare.co.uk)

CC number: 1122902

Eligibility

People of the Jewish faith who live in Merseyside and are in need due to poverty, illness, old age, social disadvantage, disability or mental health problems.

Types of grants

Small, one-off grants and loans to help towards medical equipment, respite breaks and basic essentials such as food and clothing. Grants are only paid on the provision of receipts for the goods/ services purchased or are simply made directly to the supplier.

Annual grant total

In 2015/16 the charity had assets of £1.9 million and an income of £413,000. During the year, the charity gave around £11,000 in grants to individuals.

Applications

Apply by letter or telephone to the correspondent, directly by the individual.

Other information

Merseyside Jewish Community Care provides a care and welfare service for Jewish people in Merseyside.

Vyoel Moshe Charitable Trust

£89,000

Correspondent: Sholem Cik, Trustee, 2–4 Chardmore Road, London N16 6HX

CC number: 327054

Eligibility

Grants are made to individuals who are in need to assist with the extra expenditure incurred during Jewish religious holidays.

Types of grants

One-off grants according to need.

Annual grant total

In 2016/17 the trust had assets of £40,500 and an income of £993,000. Grants to individuals totalled £89,000.

Applications

Apply in writing the correspondent.

The MYA Charitable Trust

£9,700 (six grants)

Correspondent: Myer Rothfeld, Trustee, Medcar House, 149A Stamford Hill, London N16 5LL (020 8800 3582)

CC number: 299642

Eligibility

Jewish people in need anywhere in the world.

Types of grants

One-off and recurrent grants to people in need of financial and medical aid. Short-term interest-free loans may also be made to help with to help with financial hardship or educational needs.

Annual grant total

In 2015/16 the trust had assets of £1.7 million and an income of £620,500. During the year, the trust gave around £9,700 in grants to individuals.

The trust gave around £233,500 in grants to organisations.

Applications

Applications may be made in writing to the correspondent.

Other information

The trust also gives grants for educational and religious institutions.

The Chevras Ezras Nitzrochim Trust

£215,500

Correspondent: Hertz Kahan, Trustee, 53 Heathland Road, London N16 5PQ

CC number: 275352

Eligibility

Jewish people who are in need due to sickness, disability, financial hardship or unemployment. The trust focuses on those living in the Greater London area, although help can also be given to individuals living further away.

Types of grants

One-off and recurrent grants are available according to need. Support is also given for the provision of food items, medical supplies and clothing.

Annual grant total

In 2016 the charity had assets of £10,200 and an income of £257,000. During the

year, the charity gave around £215,500 in grants to individuals.

Applications

Apply in writing to the correspondent. Applications can be made at any time.

NJD Charitable Trust

£3,400

Correspondent: Alan Dawson, Correspondent, St Brides' House, 10 Salisbury Square, London EC4Y 8EH (020 7842 7306; email: info@igpinvest. com)

CC number: 1109146

Eligibility

Members of the Jewish faith who are in need.

Types of grants

One-off and recurrent grants are given according to need. Our research indicates that grants awarded to individuals for welfare purposes are usually below £500.

Annual grant total

In 2015/16 the trust had assets of £188,000 and an income of £100,000. Grants to both organisations and individuals totalled almost £63,500. The majority of grants were awarded to organisations. A specific breakdown of the amount awarded to individuals was not provided in the accounts. We estimate that grants given to individuals totalled around £3,400.

Applications

Apply in writing to the correspondent. Applications are considered throughout the year.

Norwood

£55,000

Correspondent: Julian Anthony, Company Secretary, Broadway House, 80–82 The Broadway, Stanmore, Middlesex HA7 4HB (020 8809 8809; email: info@norwood.org.uk; website: www.norwood.org.uk)

CC number: 1059050

Eligibility

People with learning disabilities and children and families in need. Beneficiaries are mostly Jewish although one-quarter of their clients are of mixed faith. This is a national trust but concentrates on London and the south east of England.

Types of grants

According to need, but no regular allowances. Grants towards the celebration of Jewish religious festivals, social need and occasional holidays.

Annual grant total

In 2016/17 the charity held assets of £13.5 million and had an income of £31.5 million. We estimate that the charity gave around £55,000 in grants to individuals for welfare purposes during the year.

Applications

Grants are recommended by Norwood staff. Initial contact should be made by phone or by emailing info@norwood. org.uk.

Other information

Grants are made in conjunction with a comprehensive welfare service. Norwood provides a range of social services for Jewish children and families, including social work, day facilities, residential and foster care.

The Union of Orthodox Hebrew Congregations

£25,000

Correspondent: David Passey, c/o Landau Morley LLP, York House, Empire Way, Wembley, Middlesex HA9 0FQ (020 8782 1600; email: drp@ landaumorley.co.uk)

CC number: 1158987

Eligibility

Orthodox Jewish people who live in the UK and are in need.

Types of grants

One-off grants, awarded at times of Jewish Festivals, to assist with every day expenses.

Annual grant total

In 2016 the charity held assets of almost £2 million and an income of £1.6 million. Grants to individuals totalled £25,000. The majority of grants were awarded to Orthodox Jewish organisations and totalled £794,500 during the year.

Applications

Apply in writing to the correspondent.

The ZSV Trust

£643,000 (600 grants)

Correspondent: Z. V. I. Friedman, Trustee, 12 Grange Court Road, London N16 5EG (email: fllandzsv@gmail.com; website: www.foodlifeline.org.uk)

CC number: 1063860

Eligibility

Jewish people in need, particularly older people, refugees, orphans and families in distress.

Types of grants

One-off and recurrent grants are given according to need. Most of the trust's funds are spent on providing food parcels. Other recent grants have been given towards medical assistance, clothing, shoes and weddings.

Annual grant total

In 2015 the trust had assets of £91,000 and an income of £728,000. Grants to around 600 families totalled almost £643,000 and were broken down as follows:

Food parcels	£366,500
Endowments to poor brides	£129,000
Relief of poverty	£80,000
Families undergoing stress	£27,000
House repairs and utilities	£25,500
Clothing and shoes	£12,000
Assistance with health care	£2,700
Youth activities	£350

Applications

Apply in writing to the correspondent. Individuals need to apply through social services or are often recommended by Rabbis or other community leaders.

Specific circum- stances

Abortion Support Network
See entry on page 20

The Jack and Ada Beattie Foundation (Fund for the Forgotten)

Correspondent: Alexandra Taliadoros, Foundation Director, Soho Works, Unit 4.07, The Tea Building, 56 Shoreditch High Street, London E1 6JJ (020 3651 4706; email: info@beattiefoundation. com; website: www.beattiefoundation. com/fundfortheforgotten/index.htm)

CC number: 1142892

Eligibility

People who are facing social injustice or inequality 'against their dignity, freedom or sanctuary' in the Midlands and London.

Types of grants

According to the website, one-off grants between £500 and £1,000 are given to individuals who have 'no one fighting their corner'. Support is given to 'credible causes with measured and tangible outcomes'. There are case studies on the website providing details

of situations where the fund has been able to offer assistance, these include:

▶ A family who had escaped domestic violence and needed curtains and carpet for their new permanent accommodation

▶ Essential equipment and clothing to help a woman living with HIV on the arrival of her new baby

▶ Assistance with a rent increase for an individual living with Multiple Sclerosis while she waited to be rehoused

Annual grant total

In 2015/16 the foundation had an income of £20,500 and a total expenditure of £23,500. We were unable to determine how much was given to individuals through the Fund for the Forgotten.

Exclusions

The guidelines state that the foundation 'does not intend to engage in repeat funding of individuals'.

Applications

Initial applications can be made by sending a proposal, via email, summarising your situation. There are full guidelines for proposals on the website.

If your proposal is successful, you will be invited to submit an application form, which can be downloaded from the website. Applications must be accompanied by two references and identity documentation.

Pete's Dragons
See entry on page 390

The Prisoners of Conscience Appeal Fund

£165,000

Correspondent: Lynn Carter, PO Box 61044, London SE1 1UP (020 7407 6644; email: info@prisonersofconscience.org; website: www.prisonersofconscience.org)

CC number: 213766

Eligibility

The charity's website describes its eligibility criteria:

The recipients of our grants are people who have been persecuted for their conscientiously-held beliefs. These are people who have stood up for what they believe is right, usually in terrifying circumstances and often with the knowledge that their actions would bring themselves and their families into terrible danger. We cannot help anyone who has used or condoned violence.

Types of grants

Relief grants

One-off grants ranging up to £350 are awarded to cover or assist with life-sustaining items. Grants can be given towards, for example: basic essentials such as food, clothing, toiletries and travel costs; basic furniture; counselling/therapy sessions; or medical needs.

Family reunion grants

These grants pay for the related costs of bringing close dependants to join eligible individuals in the UK (see the website for eligibility criteria specific to these grants).

Bursaries Fund

Funds are allocated to help eligible individuals with larger educational grants specifically for postgraduate and professional conversion courses. To read more, visit the charity's website.

Annual grant total

In 2016 the charity had assets of £144,000 and an income of £336,500. The charity awarded £165,000 in grants to individuals.

Exclusions

No support is given to people who have used or advocated violence or supported a violent organisation or have willingly served in the armed forces.

Applications

Applications are not considered directly from individuals but rather from approved referral organisations that apply on behalf of individuals. The fund advises the following on its website:

> You can ask your solicitor to make an application or you can contact the many local Citizens Advice Bureaux who may apply to us on your behalf. If you are in touch with any other refugee organisations or official bodies, you could also ask them to make an application. If you do not know of any organisation who might be able to assist you, please contact us grantsofficer@ prisonersofconscience.org and we will try to help.

Referral agencies must register with the fund's online system in order to apply for a grant. See the website or contact the correspondent for more information.

Other information

The fund was initially established in 1962 as the relief arm of Amnesty International, but is now a charity in its own right. It is the only agency in the UK making grants specifically to prisoners of conscience – individuals who have been persecuted for their conscientiously-held beliefs, provided that they have not used or advocated violence. Grants recipients include political prisoners, human rights defenders, lawyers, environmental activists, teachers and academics who come from many different countries such as Burma, Zimbabwe, Sri Lanka, Tibet, Iran, Cameroon and Eritrea. The charity's aim is to raise and distribute money to help them and/or their families rehabilitate themselves during and after their ordeal. Financial grants cover general hardship relief, furniture, medicines, travel costs, family reunion costs, education, requalification and resettlement costs and medical treatment and counselling after torture.

The Spark Foundation

£11,800

Correspondent: Irene Hall, Trustee, c/o Highbank House, Stockers Hill, Rodmersham, Sittingbourne ME9 0PH (01795 476558; email: admin@ sparkfoundation.org.uk; website: www. sparkfoundation.org.uk)

CC number: 1097058

Eligibility

Young people under the age of 26 who either are, or have been, in care. Priority is given to those are homeless, in financial need or suffering from mental or physical disabilities.

Types of grants

Grants of up to £600 are available for household essentials, white goods, driving lessons, equipment and clothing for starting work or further education, activity holidays, sports kits, musical instruments, bikes and gym memberships.

Annual grant total

In 2015/16 the foundation held assets of £51,000 and an income of £25,000. Grants were awarded to 50 individuals and totalled £26,500 of which we have estimated that £11,800 was awarded to individuals for social welfare purposes. A further £3,100 was awarded to two organisations. Individual grants ranged from £84 to £620.

Exclusions

The foundation does not fund things which are the responsibility of the local authority, fostering agency or carer.

Applications

Application forms can be found on the foundation's website where you can find further guidance, examples of successful applications and deadlines.

WaveLength

£235,500

Correspondent: Anny Mills, Applications Officer, 159a High Street, Hornchurch, Essex RM11 3YB (freephone: 0800 018 2137; fax: 01708 620816; email: info@w4b.org.uk; website: www.wavelength.org.uk)

CC number: 207400

Eligibility

People who are isolated and lonely and who have limited ability to leave their homes.

Types of grants

The provision of radios and television. The charity does not provide television licences unless the applicant is in receipt of, or is applying for, equipment from the charity. The charity expects applicants to make provision for any subsequent licences.

Annual grant total

In 2015/16 the charity had an income of £308,500 and a total expenditure of £309,000. During the year, the charity spent around £235,500 directly on radios, TV sets, computer equipment and CD players for lonely people living in poverty.

Applications

Apply on a form available directly from the correspondent or to download from the website. Applications must be submitted through a third party such as a social worker, Citizens Advice, religious organisation or other welfare agency. Applicants must be UK residents and should provide evidence such as passport, birth certificate or citizenship document.

Other information

The charity was known as the Wireless for the Bedridden Society until 2010.

Asylum seekers and refugees

ASSIST Sheffield

£94,500

Correspondent: The Trustees, Victoria Hall Methodist Church, Norfolk Street, Sheffield S1 2JB (0114 275 4960; email: admin@assistsheffield.org.uk; website: www.assistsheffield.org.uk)

CC number: 1154862

Eligibility

Asylum seekers in Sheffield who are homeless.

Types of grants

Small weekly grants for food and basic living expenses. Bus passes, food vouchers, temporary accommodation and emergency support are also given.

Annual grant total

In 2015/16 the charity had assets of £203,000 and an income of £326,500. Grants were made totalling £94,500 for the following purposes:

Weekly payments	£65,000
Bus passes	£27,000
Emergency payments	£1,500
Other travel costs	£680

A further £12,200 was paid to host families providing temporary accommodation.

Applications

Preliminary contact should be made with the charity.

Other information

The charity provides advice, information, temporary accommodation and support with appointments, as well as running awareness-raising activities. In 2015/16 it opened a further three houses bringing the total of properties it runs to six. The charity also provides bus passes to allow clients to travel to medical, legal and Home Office appointments in Sheffield.

Fund for Human Need

£18,500 (235 grants)

Correspondent: Karen Drayton, Grants Officer, Trinity Cottage, 168 Watling Street, Brownhills WS8 7LU (email: kedrayton1@gmail.com; website: fundforhumanneed.org.uk)

CC number: 208866

Eligibility

Grants are made to refugees, asylum seekers, people who are homeless and other individuals in personal distress. The charity's website sates that 'priority is given to those who are destitute or have no income or benefits, to those who are particularly vulnerable, and to those where a small grant will make a major difference'.

Types of grants

Grants of up to £120 each. Grants can be made via another organisation but may also be made directly to individuals.

Annual grant total

In 2016/17 the fund held assets of £112,500 and had an income of £16,000. Grants were made to 235 individuals totalling £18,500. A further £23,000 was awarded to organisations working in disadvantaged communities.

Exclusions

Grants are not awarded for debt repayment, educational purposes, or to individuals outside the UK.

Applications

Applications may be made in writing to the correspondent or using the online application form. Applications should include details of the individual's financial situation, their reason for applying and the difference that receiving a grant would make. While applications can be made directly by an individual, it is preferred that applications are made by a recognised organisation, such as a local authority or voluntary organisation, on behalf of an individual. Grants are made on a monthly basis.

Domestic violence

The Heinz, Anna and Carol Kroch Foundation
See entry on page 6

Homelessness

Fund for Human Need
See entry on page 37

Housing the Homeless Central Fund

£50,500

Correspondent: Frankie Salton-Cox, Clerk to the Trustees, 2A Orchard Road, Sidcup DA14 6RD (email: hhcfund@gmail.com)

CC number: 233254

Eligibility

People who are either homeless or are at risk of homelessness. Priority may be given to expectant parents or those with children. Grants are given in three categories: those who are in danger of losing their home or essential services such as utilities; those caring for children in financial difficulties; those who have suffered a personal setback (such as mental illness, time in prison, addiction or domestic upheaval) and who are hoping to start a new home.

Types of grants

One-off grants, usually between £100 and £300, for household items and fuel bills. Recent grants have paid for cots and beds, basic kitchen equipment, clothing, and rent arrears.

Annual grant total

In 2016/17 the fund held assets of £382,000 and had an income of £64,000.

Grants to individuals are made via third party organisations and totalled £50,500 during the year.

Exclusions

No recurrent grants or grants for holidays, medical apparatus, funeral expenses, travel costs, vehicles, educational expenses, structural improvements to property, rent deposits, toys, computers or televisions.

Applications

Guidelines and application forms should be requested by and will be sent to a third party organisation, on headed paper and enclosing an sae. Decisions are usually made within a week, although no grants are made in March or December.

Note: telephone calls will not be accepted and applications must be made through by a representative of a recognised third party organisation for example Citizens Advice, social services or another welfare organisation.

The Heinz, Anna and Carol Kroch Foundation
See entry on page 6

The St Martin-in-the-Fields' Christmas Appeal Charity

£1.5 million

Correspondent: Tim Bisset, 5 St Martin's Place, London WC2N 4JH (020 7766 1134; email: vrf@stmartinscharity.org.uk; website: www.smitf.org/christmas)

CC number: 1156305

Eligibility

People who are at risk of, or currently experiencing homelessness or vulnerable housing.

Types of grants

Small crisis grants of up to £350. According to the charity's website it provides grants for:

Accessing accommodation – Rent deposits, rent in advance, admin fees, ID, or temporary accommodation costs.

Preventing eviction - Rent arrears, service charge arrears, Debt Relief Orders and bankruptcy fees or money to pay for a hoarding clean up.

Setting up home - Household goods or moving costs.

Annual grant total

In 2016/17 the charity had assets of £1.7 million and an income of £3 million. Grants to individuals totalled £1.5 million.

Exclusions

There are no grants for holidays, course fees, recurring costs, holidays, respite breaks, school trips, IT equipment, medical treatment, TVs and TV licences, childcare expenses, toys, books and play equipment, administrative charges, fines and professional fees, structural renovations or specialist equipment such as wheelchairs.

Applications

Applications can be made through the charity's online application portal. Applications are only accepted from applications from paid frontline workers providing support to people who are experiencing homelessness or vulnerable housing.

Offenders and ex-offenders

Michael and Shirley Hunt Charitable Trust

£7,500 (56 grants)

Correspondent: Deborah Jenkins, Trustee, Ansty House, Henfield Road, Small Dole, Henfield, West Sussex BN5 9XH (01903 817116)

CC number: 1063418

Eligibility

Prisoners and their relatives and dependants, such as their spouses and children.

Types of grants

One-off and recurrent grants for prisoners' families' welfare needs and for travel expenses for prisoners on care leave.

Annual grant total

In 2015/16 the trust held assets of almost £6.5 million and had an income of over £272,500. Grants were made to 56 individuals and totalled £7,500.

A further £62,500 was awarded to charitable organisations.

Applications

Apply in writing to the correspondent. Applications can be made directly by the individual or, where applicable, through a third party such as Citizens Advice, probation service or a social worker.

Sacro Trust

£5,000

Correspondent: The Trust Fund Administrator, 29 Albany Street, Edinburgh EH1 3QN (0131 624 7270; website: www.sacro.org.uk)

OSCR number: SC023031

Eligibility

People living in Scotland who are subject to a license/court order or who have been released from prison in the last two years, and their families.

Types of grants

Grants are usually to a maximum of £300, although applications for larger sums can be considered. Grants are given for household appliances and essentials, and for personal development.

Annual grant total

In 2016/17 the trust had an income of £33,500 and a total expenditure of £46,000. The trust awarded a total of £5,000 in grants for household items and personal well-being,

Exclusions

Grants are not made where financial help from other sources is available.

Applications

Applications can only be accepted if they are made through a local authority, voluntary sector worker, health visitor or so on. The forms may be obtained from the correspondent and are considered every two months. Payments cannot be made directly to an individual, rather to the organisation making the application. Other sources of funding should be sought before applying to the trust.

Other information

The trust also makes grants for educational purposes.

Lady Alice Shaw-Stewart Memorial Fund

£1,000

Correspondent: Bert Allison, Correspondent, Legal Services, Inverclyde Council, Municipal Buildings, Greenock, Inverclyde PA15 1JA (01475 712225; email: bert.allison@inverclyde.gov.uk)

OSCR number: SC019228

Eligibility

Female ex-prisoners recommended by the probation officer in the Inverclyde Council area.

Types of grants

On average one-off grants total about £200 each and are given for general welfare purposes, such as electrical goods, holidays and driving lessons.

Annual grant total

In 2015/16 the charity had an income of £220 and a total expenditure of £1,200. We estimate that grants given to individuals for welfare purposes totalled around £1,000.

Applications

Applications may be made in writing to the correspondent. They should be submitted by a probation officer on behalf of the individual.

Other information

Our research suggests that the council administers about 20 other small funds for people living in Greenock, Gourock, Inverkip and Kilmalcolm.

The Sheriffs' and Recorders' Fund

£176,000 (1,317 grants)

Correspondent: Fund Administrator, Central Criminal Court, Old Bailey, London EC4M 7EH (020 7192 2734 or 020 7248 3277; email: secretary@srfund.net; website: www.srfund.org.uk)

CC number: 221927

Eligibility

People on probation and the families of serving prisoners in the Greater Metropolitan Area of London. There is a preference for supporting drug or alcohol abusers.

Types of grants

One-off grants for people on probation to help them furnish a new home, buy clothes or contribute towards retraining and equipment they may need for work. Grants are also given to families of serving prisoners, primarily to allow their children to enjoy holidays and other recreational activities.

Annual grant total

In 2016/17 the fund held assets of £1.7 million and had an income of £309,000. Grants were made to 1,317 individuals and totalled £176,000. Grants were also made to 156 individuals for educational and training purposes and totalled £35,000. During the year, the average grant was £144.

Grants are also made to organisations working with prisoners and ex-offenders; these totalled £103,000.

Applications

All applications must be made through the probation service or through social workers. The fund immediately evaluates the applications and pays the grant to the recommending service.

Women In Prison Ltd

£12,300 (112 grants)

Correspondent: General Office, Women In Prison, 2nd Floor, Elmfield House, 5 Stockwell Mews, London SW9 9GX (020 7359 6674; email: info@ womeninprison.org.uk)

CC number: 1118727

Eligibility

Women with more than one year left to serve in prison

Types of grants

Small, one-off grants according to need.

Annual grant total

In 2016/17 the charity held assets of £303,500 and had an income of £1.9 million. During the year, the charity gave around £24,500 in grants to 218 individuals. We estimate that £12,300 of this amount was for welfare purposes, with the charity also giving educational grants.

Applications

Potential applicants can contact the charity by phone or email to discuss what help is available.

Illness and disability charities

There are many charities for people with illnesses or disabilities. The grant-makers detailed in this section are those that only give financial help. There are many others that provide non-financial support and advice and may be the starting point for getting financial help. For this reason we have a list of organisations which provide advice and support on page 427.

This section starts with an index of illness or disability. The entries are arranged alphabetically within each category, with charities supporting more than one illness or disability, or with broad criteria, listed at the start of the chapter. The 'Disability' section similarly lists charities which have a wide remit to support people with disabilities, rather than focusing on a specific condition. Individuals with any condition or disability, may therefore also look under these two general sections for support, as well as 'Specific conditions' or any other relevant section.

The sub-section 'Children' lists charities which give exclusively to children who have an illness or disability, with age as part of their key criteria – of course, many charities in other sections will also support children.

Similarly, the charities listed under 'Mental health' are by no means the only ones that will support those with mental health problems – rather, they are the only ones that specify this as their main criteria. Many charities with a broad remit to support those with an illness or disability will include people who have mental health problems; likewise with many of the grant-makers in the 'General charities' chapter.

Index of illness and disability funds

The ACT Foundation

£334,500 (345 grants)

Correspondent: The Grants Manager, 61 Thames Street, Windsor, Berkshire SL4 1QW (01753 753900; email: info@ theactfoundation.co.uk; website: www. theactfoundation.co.uk)

CC number: 1068617

Eligibility

The foundation has the aim of 'enhancing the quality of life for people in need', especially those who have physical or mental disabilities, are older or live in poverty. Applicants should be permanently resident in the UK.

Types of grants

Grants of up to £2,500 generally fall under three areas:

- Building: 'modifications to homes (where a Disabled Facilities Grant (DFG) has already been awarded)'
- Equipment: 'provision of specialist wheelchairs, other mobility aids and equipment including medical equipment and technology to assist independent living'
- Respite: 'help towards the cost of short-term respite breaks at registered respite centres'

Grants have been given towards: specialised seating and car seats; specialised beds and sleep systems; sensory toys and equipment, room padding; communication aids, specialised software; bathroom and vehicle adaptations; and stairlifts.

The current priorities are to help:

- People with physical and mental disabilities
- Older people and those in need
- Hospices and end of life care
- Support for young carers

Annual grant total

In 2015/16 the foundation held assets of £65.4 million and had an income of

£21 million. A total of £1.8 million was awarded in grants, consisting of around £334,500 to 345 individuals and about £1.5 million to 274 organisations.

Exclusions

Grants are not made for:

- Equipment or work for which there is statutory funding
- Building alterations where a Disabled Facilities Grant has not been applied for and has not been awarded
- Garden works
- Ordinary domestic items (e.g. flooring, white goods, furniture, clothing)
- Holidays
- Retrospective funding
- Deposits for vehicles

Applications

Application forms are available from the website or the correspondent. They must be submitted by post, as the foundation is unable to accept email applications. Requests can be made at any time and the trustees meet four times a year (approvals may be made between meeting dates if necessary). An acknowledgement letter is sent as soon as possible – if your application is in an unacceptable form, ineligible or of a low priority you will be advised of this in the letter. All acceptable applications are assessed, if appropriate you may be contacted for further information and/or paid a personal visit. The foundation notes: 'We aim to make decisions on 95% of grant applications within two months and on all applications within three months.'

Applications should be accompanied by supporting documentation (such as a letter from a qualified health professional) and financial evidence of need, if relevant. If the grant is intended for building modifications, a letter of permission from the owner of the property should be attached. Applicants are advised to read the terms and conditions on the website prior to applying.

Note the following stated on the website:

> We receive many more applications than we can fund and have to prioritise our grants towards those most in need. Where it is deemed that the beneficiary, the beneficiary's family or the applying charity/organisation are able to provide the equipment from their own resources we regret that the application will not be considered.

Other information

The foundation also supports organisations and has a number of strategic charity partnership; including one with Whizz-Kidz, which handles any applications the foundation receives for mobility aids for children up to the age of 18.

Barnwood House Trust

See entry on page 399

Clevedon Convalescent Fund

£56,000 (419 grants)

Correspondent: Joan Taffs, 4 Kenn Road, Clevedon BS21 6EL (01275 314777; email: joan@clevedonforbes.org; website: www.clevedonforbes.org)

CC number: 249313

Eligibility

People of limited means who are recovering from illness or who are in need of a break due to trauma or other distressing circumstances. Grants are also available for carers to have a break from caring for someone who is sick or who has disabilities.

Types of grants

One-off grants to provide convalescent breaks.

Annual grant total

In 2016/17 the charity had assets of £1.9 million and an income of £80,000. During the year, a total of £56,000 was awarded in 165 grants, benefitting 419 individuals.

Exclusions

Grants are not made for: debt relief; capital goods or the purchase of equipment; or breaks outside the UK. Individuals cannot apply for another grant until a three-year period has elapsed.

Applications

Applications need to be made through a professional in the statutory or voluntary sector, such as a social worker or welfare officer. Application forms are available on the charity's website or directly from the correspondent.

Other information

Grants recipients will also receive a booklet based on the gospels of Mark and Luke, unless otherwise requested. The charity also sends flowers to recipients upon their return from their break.

Harry Cureton Charitable Trust

See entry on page 259

Elifar Foundation Ltd

£109,500 (72 grants)

Correspondent: Adele Kimber, 6 Cambridge Road, Teddington TW11 8DR (020 8977 1770; email: enquiries@elifarfoundation.org.uk; website: www.elifarfoundation.org.uk)

CC number: 1152416

Eligibility

People of any age with any form of physical or learning disability. However, due to high application volumes, the charity is temporarily not accepting applications for the support of adults over the age of 28.

Types of grants

The maximum amount for a grant is £5,000. Grants can be made towards: the funding of manual or powered wheelchairs or other mobility aids; sensory toys and equipment; hoists; communication aids and specialised software; specialised seating, beds and sleep systems, trikes; and holidays.

Annual grant total

In 2015/16 the charity had an income of £157,300 and £100,000 in assets. There were 72 grants awarded to individuals, amounting to £109,500

Exclusions

Grants are not made for:

- Items or work for which there is statutory funding available
- Building works or garden works
- Ordinary computers/laptops/iPads
- Ordinary domestic items (e.g. furniture, flooring, white goods, clothing)
- Ordinary or family holidays
- Therapies
- Goods already purchased, for deposits paid, or goods already on order
- Where it is deemed that the beneficiary or the beneficiary's family are capable of providing the equipment from their own resources

Applications

Applications forms can be found on the charity's website, or they can be requested in writing or by email. They can be submitted by or on behalf of individuals, although a letter of support from a healthcare professional is required. All appeals are acknowledged.

If you are applying via post, submit your request to: c/o Shirley Baker, 21 Panmuir Road, London SW20 0PZ.

Other information

The name Elifar stands for Every Life Is For A Reason.

Foundations Independent Living Trust

£609,000 (406 grants)

Correspondent: The Trustees, The Old Co-op Building, 11 Railway Street, Glossop, Derbyshire SK13 7AG (0300 124 0316; email: info@filt.org.uk; website: www.filt.org.uk)

CC number: 1103784

Eligibility
People in need, particularly older people, people with disabilities and people who are unemployed.

Types of grants
Grants for repairs, minor adaptations, home improvements, heating and insulation measures.

Annual grant total
In 2016/17 the trust had assets of £171,000 and an income of £703,500. Grants to individuals totalled £609,000.

Applications
Apply through a local home improvement agency. Applications cannot be made directly to the trust but enquiries are welcome. Local home improvement agencies are listed on the trust's website.

Gardening for Disabled Trust

£20,000

Correspondent: The Secretary, PO Box 285, Tunbridge Wells, Kent TN2 9JD (email: info@gardeningfordisabledtrust.org.uk; website: www.gardeningfordisabledtrust.org.uk)

CC number: 255066

Eligibility
Members of the trust who wish to continue gardening despite disability or advancing illness.

Types of grants
One-off grants to adapt gardens to meet the needs of gardeners, for example by contributing to the costs of tools, raised beds, paving, or wheelchair access.

Annual grant total
In 2016 the trust had an income of £20,500 and a total expenditure of £34,500. Based on previous years' grants expenditure, we estimate that grants given to individuals totalled £20,000.

Exclusions
No grants are given to pay for a gardener for general maintenance or for clearing or fencing.

Applications
Apply in writing to the correspondent detailing the work you would like to be done and an estimate of the costs of tools, materials and labour (if necessary). Applications can be submitted through the online contact form on the website. If labour is required, the applicant should provide original copies of two quotes. Applicants should also include a note from their GP, social worker or occupational therapist describing their disability. Applications are considered monthly.

The Rob George Foundation

£52,000

Correspondent: Philip George, Chair, 1 Amphora Place, Sheepen Road, Colchester, Essex CO3 3WG (07831 504298; email: enquiries@therobgeorgefoundation.co.uk; website: www.therobgeorgefoundation.co.uk)

CC number: 1156026

Eligibility
Young people between the ages of 5 and 28 who have life-threatening or terminal illnesses and live in the UK.

Types of grants
Grants of up to £2,000.

Annual grant total
In 2016/17 the foundation had assets of £125,500 and an income of £114,500. Grants totalled £104,500. We estimate that around £52,000 was given to young people with life-threatening or terminal illnesses, with funding also awarded to young people for purposes relating to sports and the performing arts.

The annual report for 2016/17 stated that 'The number of applications for grants was 249...Approximately two-thirds of the applications were successful'.

Exclusions
The charity will not normally make grants for needs which are a statutory responsibility.

Applications
Individuals can apply directly using the online form or by downloading a form from the website and submitting a hard copy. Detailed guidance is available on the website. Applicants should be able to provide two referees, one of which can confirm their medical history and present condition/treatment. Supporting documentation (e.g. details of medical history, quotes, invoices) must be provided.

Hard copy applications/supporting documentation should be sent to: The Rob George Foundation, 4 Henry Villa Close, Colchester, Essex CO4 5XP.

Other information
The website states that financial support is also given to young people who 'demonstrate exceptional commitment and/or ability in the worlds of sport or the performing arts but may be held back by their financial situation from pursuing their goals'.

The Hospital Saturday Fund

£40,500 (91 grants)

Correspondent: Michelle Whittington, Company Secretary, 24 Upper Ground, London SE1 9PD (020 7202 1334; email: charity@hsf.eu.com; website: www.hospitalsaturdayfund.org)

CC number: 1123381

Eligibility
People in medical need in the UK and the Republic of Ireland.

Types of grants
Partial or full grants for the following: specialised mobility equipment, medical appliances and aids, specialised computer equipment, therapeutic equipment/treatment, home adaptations, and respite breaks at a therapeutic centre.

Annual grant total
In 2016 the fund held assets of £25.1 million and had an income of £28 million. During the year, 146 applications on behalf of individuals were assessed and 91 grants were awarded. Grants to individuals totalled £40,500, with a further £878,500 awarded to 280 medical charities, hospices and hospitals.

Exclusions
The fund does not make grants for the following:

- Financial assistance, such as repayment of loans or credit card debts, utility bills for household expenses (e.g. gas, water, telephone, etc.), rent or mortgage arrears
- Transport costs to hospitals/clinics
- In-home care or care home costs; or private treatment
- Experimental drugs/medication (those not recommended by The National Institute for Health and Care Excellence)
- Purchase of a car or driving lessons
- Building works neither inside nor outside the home, painting, decorating, or any gardening works
- New or replacement furniture/furnishings, or electrical household goods

- Installation or maintenance of any heating system
- Holidays/trips abroad/religious pilgrimages
- Clothing
- Education or tuition fees
- Funeral expenses
- Treatment outside the UK and Ireland

Applications

Application forms can be completed online by a third party 'supporter' such as a registered health professional, social worker, hospital consultant or specialist, nurse or occupational therapist, physiotherapist or Citizen Advice Bureau. Supporting evidence must be uploaded to confirm need. Full guidance can be found on the charity's website, and applications are considered quarterly.

Note: the charity does not accept paper or letter applications, or applications made directly by the individual. Cheques are made payable to the supplier of the goods/services or the organisation supporting the application, not the individual.

Hylton House and Specialist Support Fund

£2,500

Correspondent: County Durham Community Foundation, Victoria House, Whitfield Court, St John's Road, Meadowfield Industrial Estate, Durham DH7 8XL (0191 378 6340; fax: 0191 378 2409; email: info@cdcf.org.uk; website: www.cdcf.org.uk)

CC number: 1047625–2

Eligibility

People in the North East (County Durham, Darlington, Gateshead, South Shields, Sunderland and Cleveland) with cerebral palsy and related disabilities, and their families and carers. Applicants and/or their families must also be on a low income.

Types of grants

Grants of up to £1,000 can be applied for to cover costs of:

- Specialist equipment, e.g. communication, sensory, or mobility aids
- Respite care and holiday grants for families and carers
- Domestic equipment such as kitchen appliances
- Travel

(This list is not exhaustive).

Annual grant total

In 2016/17 we estimate that charity awarded grants of around £2,500.

Applications

Applications are available to complete online under the Hylton House funding page. Applications must be made by a social or professional worker on behalf of a client, and must include details of their home situation, medical condition and the impact it has on every day life, and how the funding will be used.

The charity states that it does not means-test applicants, however it does need to understand why the family may be unable to afford the resource applied for, e.g. because of low income.

Other information

The charity also makes awards to people with neurological conditions for education and training purposes that may have a significant impact on the applicant's well-being.

The fund is managed by the County Durham Community Foundation (Charity Commission no. 1047625).

Independence at Home

£378,500 (1,220 grants)

Correspondent: Liz Somerville, Applications Officer, UK Office, Independence at Home, 4th Floor Congress House, 14 Lyon Road, Harrow HA1 2EN (020 8427 7929; email: iah@ independenceathome.org.uk; website: www.independenceathome.org.uk)

CC number: 1141758

Eligibility

People who have substantial disabilities or are severely ill who live at home or who wish to do so.

Types of grants

Grants ranging between £100 and £750 towards specific additional costs associated with living at home with a disability, including equipment and adaptations. Grants can be made towards almost any expense which is not covered by statutory provision and which is related to a person with disabilities living at home.

Annual grant total

In 2016/17 the charity held assets of £6.4 million and had an income of £1.9 million. During the year, the charity gave around £378,500 in grants to individuals.

Exclusions

Grants cannot be made to people living in residential care or in hospital, groups of people or organisations. Grants are not made towards medical treatment or therapies, debt relief or arrears, funeral expenses, telephone rental or call charges, televisions or licences or motor vehicles (although car adaptations may be considered).

Applications

Applications should be made by a referrer. Any health or social care worker, or worker for a voluntary organisation, who is supporting the client, is capable of assessing their needs and willing to act on their client's behalf and take their application forward can apply. Application forms are available on the website and should be completed and returned by post along with a letter describing the individual's circumstances and medical diagnosis. For large pieces of equipment, an occupational therapist's report and a quote from a builder or supplier should be included. Applications are considered on an ongoing basis. The charity accepts informal contact to prior to applications being made.

The League of the Helping Hand (LHH)

£118,500

Correspondent: The Secretary, LHH, PO Box 342, Burgess Hill RH15 5AQ (01444 236099; email: secretary@lhh.org. uk; website: www.lhh.org.uk)

CC number: 208792

Eligibility

People who have a physical disability, learning difficulty or mental health problem and are in financial need. Those who care for somebody who has a disability or is older or ill may also be eligible.

Types of grants

One-off and recurrent payments. Grants of up to £250 are awarded towards essential household items, specialist equipment and carers' breaks. Quarterly gifts are available to help with daily living costs, the beneficiaries of which also receive newsletters, birthday and Christmas cards and, where possible, an annual personal visit from the Secretary.

Annual grant total

In 2015/16 the charity held assets of £2.4 million and had an income of £157,300. Grants to individuals totalled £118,500 and were distributed as follows:

Quarterly Gifts	£55,500
One-off Gifts	£53,500
Christmas gifts	£5,000
Visits	£2,700
Holidays	£2,200

Exclusions

No help is given for debts, business costs, holidays, tenancy deposits, building works, mobility scooters, wheelchairs, medical, dental or therapeutic treatments, or for education-related items.

Applications

Application forms are available to download from the charity's website. Applications must be submitted through a social worker, carers' support centre, Citizens Advice or other welfare body. If it is not possible to download the form, the correspondent should be contacted directly. An sae must be enclosed. The trustees meet every three weeks to consider applications, although emergency needs can be dealt with more quickly. Telephone enquiries are welcomed.

Note: applications submitted directly by individuals will not be considered.

Other information

A total of 720 applications were received during the financial year 2015/16 and 51% of requests were granted an award by LHH Trustees. Of the grants awarded, the average amount was £148 and the most frequently awarded amount was £100.

Newlife Foundation for Disabled Children

£2 million (1,283 grants)

Correspondent: Sheila Brown, Newlife Centre, Hemlock Way, Cannock, Staffordshire WS11 7GF (01543 462777; email: info@newlifecharity.co.uk; website: newlifecharity.co.uk/index.php)

CC number: 1001817

Eligibility

The foundation's guidelines state that the minimum eligibility requirements for an equipment grant are that the child/young person is:

- A UK resident
- Has a significant disability which affects their daily like, a life threatening/life limiting condition or has been diagnosed as terminally ill
- Under 19 years of age

Types of grants

The foundation's guidelines state: 'We fund a varied range of equipment, including specialist seating, wheelchairs, beds and communication aids. We will assess if we can help by considering the impact on the individual and their health, quality of life and safety.'

Annual grant total

In 2015/16 the foundation had assets of £4.35 million and an income of £11.4 million. Grants to individuals totalled £2 million and were broken down as follows:

Special cot/bed	161	£480,500
Wheelchairs/mobility/support	123	£480,500
Special car seat	355	£392,000
Special seating solution	175	£213,000
Special pushchair/buggy	228	£168,500
Play/sensory/development/ therapeutic	79	£119,500
Safety/behavioural/toileting	80	£103,000
Hoists/handling	26	£40,000
Other	18	£13,500
Bedding/clothing	26	£10,500
Shed/storage/exterior	12	£4,200

Applications

In the first instance, applicants should contact a Newlife nurse to check whether the foundation is able to provide the equipment needed. Newlife nurses can be contacted by phone on 0800 902 0095, by email at nurse@newlifecharity.co.uk or via live chat on the foundation's website.

The Florence Nightingale Aid-in-Sickness Trust (FNAIST)

£229,500 (332 grants)

Correspondent: Ann Griffiths, Grants and Funding Manager, Community House, Room 35, South Street, Bromley BR1 1RH (020 7998 8817; email: ann.griffiths@fnaist.org.uk; website: www.fnaist.org.uk)

CC number: 1157980

Eligibility

People of all ages who are in poor health, convalescent or who have disabilities. Preference will be given to people with professional, secretarial, or administrative qualifications or experience.

Types of grants

One-off grants are available for convalescence or respite care, medical equipment and other aids, sensory equipment, communications aids, telephone installation (or mobile phones in rare cases), computers and software, drug storage units, electric beds, household aids (for example, washing machines) and other needs to improve individuals' independent living. Partial funding may be provided where a large grant is requested.

Annual grant total

In 2016 the trust held assets of £10.7 million and an income of £391,500. During the year, the trust gave around £292,500 in grants to 315 individuals.

Exclusions

Grants are not usually given for:

- Car purchase or car adaptations
- Holidays, exchange visits or nursing home fees
- Debts or repayments
- General clothing
- General house furnishings
- House furnishings
- Stairlifts
- Clothing

Under normal circumstances, grants can only be given to any one household at intervals of three years.

Applications

Application forms are available to download from the trust's website or can be requested from the correspondent. They should be submitted by Citizens Advice, other charities, a social worker, an occupational therapist, doctor, health centre worker or a similar professional with a medical background. Candidates should provide a brief medical history of the applicant and proof of the need for assistance. Applications are considered monthly, although urgent requests can be dealt with between meetings.

The Rosslyn Park Injury Trust Fund

£19,600

Correspondent: Diane McIntier, Secretary, 102 Halfway Street, Sidcup, Kent DA15 8DB (020 8302 4082; email: bridihalfwayst@talktalk.net; website: www.rosslynpark.co.uk/information/injury-trust-fund)

CC number: 284089

Eligibility

Young people who have a disability or are in poor health as a result of an injury suffered while playing sports (amateur sports). Their dependants may also receive help.

Types of grants

One-off grants for computers, special care, medical equipment, computers and disability aids. The fund has a list of recent beneficiaries on its website.

Annual grant total

In 2016 the fund had an income of £19,200 and a total expenditure of £19,800. We estimate that grants given to individuals for welfare purposes totalled around £19,600.

Applications

Apply in writing to the correspondent. Applications can be submitted by either the individual or through social services and are considered as they are received.

Other information

The fund's website tells the story of how it was founded:

In 1981 the head boy of Llandovery College was playing as the captain of his team in the Rosslyn Park Schoolboy Sevens Competition. During the game he fell awkwardly in a tackle leaving him quadriplegic. At the time of this tragic injury there was very limited accident insurance available for schoolboys playing sport and that fact, coupled with the public sympathy felt for the player, led to the setting up on 2nd December 1981 of the registered charity now known as Rosslyn Park Injury Trust Fund.

Royalties from the book 'The Final Whistle: The Great War in Fifteen Players' support the fund.

The Stanley Stein Deceased Charitable Trust

See entry on page 10

See entry on page 10

AIDS and HIV

Eileen Trust

£57,500

Correspondent: Susan Daniels, Case Worker and Secretary, Alliance House, 12 Caxton Street, London SW1H 0QS (020 7808 1172; email: admin@ caxtonfoundation.org.uk)

CC number: 1028027

Eligibility

People who have contracted HIV through NHS treatment, for example, following transfusions or a needlestick injury. It provides financial support in the form of small regular payments or one-off payments to affected individuals and their dependants.

Types of grants

Financial help is given in three ways: regular monthly payments to contribute to meeting the additional costs of living with HIV, or assist those who have been bereaved; single payments in response to specific requests for help; and winter payments of £500 (supplementary to regular payments).

Annual grant total

In 2016/17 the trust held assets of £195,000 and had an income of £72,000. Grants and payments to individuals totalled £57,500 and were distributed as follows:

Regular payments	£38,000
Grants	£18,000
Winter payments	£1,500

Applications

Applications for assistance are received in the main via the trust's case worker and from time to time by direct approach.

The Terrence Higgins Trust – Hardship Fund

£68,000 (605 grants)

Correspondent: Grants Administrator, 314–320 Gray's Inn Road, London WC1X 8DP (020 7812 1600; email: hardshipfund@tht.org.uk; website: www. tht.org.uk)

CC number: 288527

Eligibility

People in the UK who have HIV and are in severe financial need.

Types of grants

One-off emergency grants for food, clothing, travel costs and other living expenses.

Annual grant total

In 2016/17 the trust held assets of £10 million and had an income of £15.6 million. Hardship grants totalled £68,000 and were awarded to 605 individuals.

Exclusions

No grants are given for council tax, rent, holiday expenses, air fares or funeral costs.

Applications

Apply in writing to the correspondent.

Other information

Terence Higgins Trust is the largest HIV and sexual health charity in Europe. Its Hardship Fund is supported by the Elton John AIDS Foundation, the Elizabeth Taylor AIDS Foundation and the MAC AIDS Fund.

The trust offers a range of services for people affected by HIV, such as: advice services, including benefits advice and counselling services.

THT also runs www.myhiv.org.uk, a website containing self-management tools, a community forum and information.

George House Trust

£57,000 (342 grants)

Correspondent: Lee Hardman, Services Adviser, 75–77 Ardwick Green North, Manchester M12 6FX (0161 274 4499; email: lee@ght.org.uk; website: www.ght. org.uk)

CC number: 1143138

Eligibility

People with HIV who live in the north west of England. The majority of services are provided in Greater Manchester.

Types of grants

Grants of £150 are available for beds and mattresses, white goods, clothing, bedding, utility bills and other items that will benefit your health or relieve need.

Annual grant total

In 2016/17 the trust held assets of £1.2 million and had an income of over £765,000. Welfare grants to 342 individuals totalled £57,000.

Applications

Applications are open to anyone known to George House Trust. The application form is available on the trust's website and must be completed in full and include as much relevant supporting information about the item(s) you are requesting. The trust asks that you book an appointment with an adviser before applying to the welfare fund. Full exclusions and eligibility criteria can be found on the trust's helpful website. The welfare team meets each month to review applications.

Other information

The trust's activities range from raising awareness through its information and community services, to providing advice, counselling and support for people affected by HIV and AIDS.

JAT

£5,000

Correspondent: Janine Clements, Director, JAT, 2A Dunstan Road, London NW11 8AA (07546 429885; email: j.clements@jat-uk.org; website: www.jat-uk.org)

CC number: 327936

Eligibility

Jewish people with HIV or AIDS.

Types of grants

One-off grants are available from the charity, which may share the costs of major items with other agencies. Past grants have been given towards the costs of Passover food, travel expenses for respite care, washing machines, cookers, moving costs and so on.

Annual grant total

In 2015/16 the charity had an income of £5,400 and a total expenditure of £9,600. Our previous research indicates that the charity usually gives around £5,000 in grants to individuals per year.

Exclusions

No grants are given towards rent, mortgage arrears, luxury items or repayments of loans, debts or credit cards.

Applications

Application forms are available from the correspondent. All referrals must be through a professional person such as a social worker, health visitor and so on. A referral must accompany every application and be on headed paper including: the client's name, date of birth and a breakdown of their weekly income; the details and nature of the request; the name, position and signature of the referrer; and details of whom the cheque should be made payable to. First applications require symptomatic proof of HIV diagnosis from the applicant's doctor.

Other information

The trust was established to provide support and advice for Jewish people affected by HIV. The trust provides 'confidential, non-judgemental' support services for its beneficiaries.

The Macfarlane Trust

£2.2 million

Correspondent: Keisha Hanchard, Support Services Officer, Alliance House, 12 Caxton Street, London SW1H 0QS (020 7808 1171 or 020 7233 0057 (main number); fax: 020 7808 1169; email: keisha@macfarlane.org.uk or admin@ macfarlane.org.uk; website: www. macfarlane.org.uk)

CC number: 298863

Eligibility

People with haemophilia who as a result of receiving contaminated blood products are living with HIV, and their dependants. No other people are eligible. The trust is in contact with those known to have haemophilia and to be HIV positive through infected blood products and therefore any further eligibility to register with the trust seems unlikely. Assistance is also given to the bereaved spouses or partners of beneficiaries.

Types of grants

One-off and recurrent grants are available towards the additional costs associated in living with HIV. Grants can be given towards health-related needs such as convalescence, respite, travel, clothes, medical care and specialist equipment. Grants are also given to primary beneficiaries towards winter fuel costs (payments of either £500 or £250) and towards supplementing the costs of children who are dependants. Payments to ensure that widows and dependants have a household income of at least £19,000 per year are also awarded.

Annual grant total

In 2016/17 the trust held assets of £2.1 million and had an income of £2 million. Grants to individuals totalled £2.2 million and were distributed as follows:

Widows payments and		
dependants	121	£1 million
Discretionary payments	261	£890,000
Dependants' supplementary		
payments	170	£243,000
Grants – current year	49	£97,500
Health and mobility-related		
grants	113	£12,700
Winter payments	–	£1,300

Applications

From 1 November 2017 the Macfarlane Trust no longer provides support to those with haemophilia who were infected with HIV as a result of contaminated blood, and their families. From 1 November 2017 support will be provided by a separate governmental organisation in each of the four UK countries, depending on where an individual was infected. For any other queries regarding support from 1 November, contact the relevant organisation in England, Wales, Northern Ireland or Scotland listed above.

Details on where to apply are available on the trust's website.

Other information

The trust offers benefits and financial advice and through its informative website, signposts to other helpful organisations. On its website, the trust also has online community resources to which its beneficiaries can login.

Positive East

£3,000

Correspondent: Alastair Thomson, Director of Finance, The Stepney Centre, 159 Mile End Road, London E1 4AQ (020 7791 2855; email: alastair. thomson@positiveeast.org.uk; website: www.positiveeast.org.uk)

CC number: 1001582

Eligibility

People affected by HIV who live and/or receive treatment in East London and are in need of short-term financial assistance to cover basic needs.

Types of grants

Grants of up to £25 each, up to a maximum of £50 in a year, with six months between each application. Each individual has a lifetime limit of £150, after which access to the fund will be closed to them. Grants are given for one-off, HIV-related expenses, child expenses such as school uniforms or medical treatment, utility bills, the cost of travel to an essential appointment and basic necessities such as food or clothing.

Annual grant total

Although grant-making is not the primary focus of the charity, around £3,000 is allocated each year for emergency hardship grants.

Exclusions

Grants are not given for: legal costs; non-essential travel or travel outside London; funeral costs; ongoing non-HIV-related treatment; household goods; and credit card or other debts.

Applications

Application forms are available from the correspondent. Applications can only be made through Positive East staff and are only available to registered members of the trust (new service users will need to fill in a registration form). Forms can be submitted at any time but applicants should note that the fund is a limited resource and will not be topped up again until the end of the financial year.

Before any grant is awarded, proof will be required that the individual is not eligible for any other financial assistance. Equally, if the person has been the victim of a crime, a crime reference number should be included in the application.

Other information

Positive East is a charity formed from the merger between the London East AIDS Network (LEAN) and the Globe Centre in 2005.

The charity provides a range of services for people affected by HIV including: counselling; support groups; employability services and training; and advice and information on HIV, living with the disease and health and well-being. A full list of services run by the charity, all of which are impartial and confidential, is available on its informative website.

Cancer

Ben's Heroes Trust

£154,000 (56 grants)

Correspondent: Kathrine Ross, Trustee, 10 Armada Close, Rownhams, Southampton SO16 8JY (email: info@ bensheroestrust.org; website: www. bensheroestrust.org)

CC number: 1146468

Eligibility

Children under the age of 18 in the UK who are being treated for cancer on an NHS paediatric oncology ward. The child must have a cancer which is registered by the child/young person's medical consultant onto the Teenager and Young Adult (TYA) or National Children's Cancer Registry.

Types of grants

Financial support of up to £2,000 but no less than £1,000 to access new treatments and/or drugs not available on the NHS but which are fully supported by the child's lead oncology consultant. The trust also makes weekly grants of £75 for a standard course of proton beam therapy – usually an 8 to 12-week period.

Grants may also be made to provide funding for projects which improve the quality of a child's life while they are on the ward or travelling to other locations for treatment.

Annual grant total

In 2016 the trust had an income of £133,000 and a total expenditure of £163,000. The trust received 66 applications and approved 56 of them. Grants totalled £154,000.

Exclusions

The trust does not consider grants for:

▶ Retrospective grants
▶ Non-medical interventions
▶ Non-UK residents
▶ International patients who are funded by their government/embassy/employer or themselves

Applications

Initial contact should be made by phone, email or in writing to see how the charity can help. Any applications for non-NHS treatments or therapies must be supported in writing and countersigned by the child's lead oncology consultant.

Other information

As well as offering grants the trust can offer support and advice on running fundraising events to help families with the costs of treatments. Grants may also be made to paediatric oncology units to improve the quality of life of the children being treated there.

Brad's Cancer Foundation

£8,200

Correspondent: Susan Bartlett, Trustee, 14 Crosslands Meadow, Riverview Park, Colwick, Nottingham NG4 2DJ (0115 940 0313; email: mick@brads.org.uk; website: www.brads.org.uk)

CC number: 1103797

Eligibility

Teenagers who have cancer and related illnesses who live in the East Midlands and are in need.

Types of grants

The provision of financial assistance to teenagers and their families, including grants towards equipment. Awards are usually of about £500.

Annual grant total

In 2015/16 the foundation had an income of £46,000 and a total expenditure of £45,500. Donations made during the year totalled £18,200, of which almost £8,200 was given to individuals.

Applications

Apply in writing to the correspondent.

Other information

Grants are also made to organisations, particularly the Teenage Cancer Trust,

which in 2015/16 received £10,000 from the foundation.

At the time of writing (January 2018) the foundation's website was undergoing maintenance and therefore was unavailable to view.

Children's Leukaemia Society

£32,000

Correspondent: Elaine Churchill, Trustee, The Library, Singleton Road, Splott, Cardiff CF24 2ET (029 2045 2483; email: childrensleukaemiasociety@hotmail.co.uk; website: www.childrensleukaemiasociety.co.uk)

CC number: 1008634

Eligibility

Children under 16 who are in need and have leukaemia. Grants are made to those living in South Wales and the West Country.

Types of grants

Gifts for children who are undergoing chemotherapy, usually in the form of an Argos voucher, and holidays for children and their families following treatment. The charity also gives 'special circumstance' gifts to children in hospital, usually those who are terminally ill.

Annual grant total

In 2016/17 the charity had an income of £15,400 and a total expenditure of £38,500. We estimate that grants totalled around £32,000.

Applications

Apply in writing to the correspondent.

Other information

The charity owns five holiday homes at Kiln Park in Tenby.

CLIC Sargent

£1.07 million (5,150 grants)

Correspondent: Kevin O'Brien, Horatio House, 77–85 Fulham Place, London W6 8JA (020 8752 2878; email: info@clicsargent.org.uk; website: www.clicsargent.org.uk)

CC number: 1107328

Eligibility

Children and young people aged 16 to 24 who are living in the UK and are receiving treatment for cancer.

Types of grants

One-off grants are available to young people and their families who have received a diagnosis within the previous 12 months. Grants are made to relieve the financial pressure faced following a

diagnosis. Funding can be used: to pay for various services including cancer treatment at home, or closer to home; to assist with household bills and general expenses; to provide palliative care; and to provide parents with free and specialist counselling following the death of a child.

Annual grant total

In 2016/17 the charity had assets of £17.1 million and an income of £24.8 million. According to the trustees' annual report, the charity awarded 5,150 grants to individuals, totalling £1.07 million.

Applications

Application forms can be found online and should be supported by the young person's clinician or nurse including their:

▶ Position/job title
▶ Contact details (telephone and NHS email address)
▶ Name and full address of the hospital where they work

Should you have any queries regarding the application process, call 020 8752 2895.

If you are a parent completing the form on behalf of your child, ensure you have permission to share their information and that you use their details when completing the application.

Other information

The annual report states: 'We provide our grants as quickly as possible to help reduce anxiety. 92% of grants were provided within the first five days of a diagnosis, and 86% within three days.'

Henry Dancer Days

£13,800 (55 grants)

Correspondent: The Trustees, Black Horse Inn, Cornsay, Durham DH7 9EL (07947 668993; email: henrydancerdays@aol.com; website: henrydancerdays.co.uk)

CC number: 1147982

Eligibility

Children under the age of 18 who have primary bone cancer, mainly osteosarcoma or Ewing sarcoma.

Types of grants

One-off grants of up to £250 to alleviate hardship. Grants are often used to help with winter fuel bills, transport costs, physiotherapy aids, home adaptations to make the home more accessible for the child or family trips. Grants can also contribute towards the cost of technology to enable patients to contact their friends when in hospital or when their immune system is compromised.

Annual grant total

In 2016/17 the charity held assets of £45,000 and had an income of £82,500. Grants were made to 55 families and totalled £13,800.

Applications

Applications for grants should be made through a healthcare professional who completes the application form on the family's behalf. This may be a CLIC Sargent social worker, a Macmillan nurse, a Marie Curie nurse, or an oncology consultant.

LATCH Welsh Children's Cancer Charity

£231,500

Correspondent: Ian Rogers, Trustee, LATCH Office, Children's Hospital for Wales, Heath Park, Cardiff CF14 4XW ((029) 2074 8858/9; fax: 029 2074 8868; email: info@latchwales.org; website: www.latchwales.org)

CC number: 1100949

Eligibility

Children who have cancer and leukaemia (including tumours) and have been referred to the Paediatric Oncology Unit at The Children's Hospital for Wales.

Types of grants

One-off and recurrent grants for children and their families who are in need of financial assistance towards, for example, travel costs to and from hospital, subsistence grants for daily expenses, utility bills, specialist equipment and other household needs (such as washing machines), childcare costs, car repairs, holidays and outings or other needs. After the emotional and disruptive time in hospital, LATCH gives all families a grant of £400 a year to put towards a well-deserved holiday.

Annual grant total

In 2016 the charity had a total income of £1,903,000 and a total expenditure of £1,525,000. A total of £231,500 was awarded in grants and comfort payments to individuals.

Applications

Applications should be made through one of the LATCH social workers, who can submit applications for consideration by the charity. More information on support given is available from other organisations, such as respite care.

Other information

The charity also supports the development of the specialist medical care at the oncology unit. Children and their families can also be provided on-site accommodation, advocacy and information services and emotional support.

In 2016 the charity spent a total of around £500,000 in services to patients and £98,500 in chemocare.

The Leukaemia Care Society

£1,400 (22 grants)

Correspondent: Monica Izmajlowicz, Chief Executive, One Birch Court, Blackpole East, Worcester WR3 8SG (01905 755977; email: info@leukaemiacare.org.uk; website: www.leukaemiacare.org.uk)

CC number: 259483

Eligibility

People with leukaemia and allied blood disorders. Financial support is open to all patients and carers who are no more than four years post-diagnosis or, if there has been bereavement, no more than two years after this.

Types of grants

Grants in the form of vouchers for a choice of three supermarkets.

Annual grant total

In 2015/16 the society held assets of £2 million and had an income of £1.2 million. The society awarded 22 grants to individuals for general living costs, totalling £1,400.

Exclusions

No repeat grants to individuals.

Applications

Applicants should at first call the care line on 0808 801 0444 to discuss their case and request the necessary forms. Applications usually take 14 to 30 days to complete. All applicants will be requested to complete an income and expenditure sheet and must provide proof of diagnosis such as a letter from their consultant.

Other information

The charity has a 24/7 care line which provides emotional support, information and signposting for patients. Throughout 2015/16 the charity responded to 3,885 requests from patients through its care line.

The charity runs a Nurse Advisor Service where people can contact a nurse by phone or email two evenings a week or arrange for a call back. Nationwide support groups are also available to patients, full details are available on the website.

Macmillan Cancer Support

£13.5 million (34,700 grants)

Correspondent: Macmillan Support Line, 89 Albert Embankment, London SE1 7UQ (0808 808 00 00 (free support line – Monday to Friday, 9am to 8pm); website: www.macmillan.org.uk)

CC number: 261017

Eligibility

People of any age who have cancer, or are still seriously affected by their illness or treatment.

Applicants must:
- Have less than £6,000 in savings if they are single, or less than £8,000 as a couple or family
- Have a low income (after paying rent/mortgage and council tax) that does not exceed (per week): £170 for a single person, £289 for a couple or household of two, £85 for each child, and £119 for each additional adult. Macmillan does not count Personal Independence Payment (PIP, Disability Living Allowance (DLA) or Attendance Allowance (AA) in its calculations for income

These are general conditions, but Macmillan does take into account individual circumstances. Macmillan can be contacted for more information.

Types of grants

Small, mostly one-off grants towards costs arising from or related to cancer or its treatment. As the website notes, a grant from Macmillan 'is an extra bit of help, not a replacement for other support'.

Assistance may be given with needs such as essential household items, extra clothing, help with heating bills, or a break in the UK, etc. The average grant is of around £380, but the amount given depends on the applicant's individual situation and needs.

Annual grant total

In 2016 the charity had assets of £64.3 million and an income of £247.4 million. Grants to 34,700 individuals totalled £13.5 million.

Exclusions

Grants are not made for daily expenses, private medical care or holidays outside the UK.

Applications

Applications should be made through a health or social care professional, such as a social worker, a district nurse, or a Macmillan benefits adviser or nurse, who will complete an application form and send it to the grants team at Macmillan. A short medical report from the applicant's specialist nurse, doctor or consultant should be included. Applications are usually processed on the day they are received and, if successful, payments are sent out within three working days.

Other information

Grants to patients are only one feature of the charity's work. Other work includes funding Macmillan Nurses (who are skilled in providing advice and support on symptom control and pain relief), Macmillan buildings for inpatient and day care, financing an education programme for professionals in palliative care, support and information sources for cancer patients and their families, and campaigning work.

The charity now offers support in the form of its financial guidance service, which can help you understand everything from mortgages to pensions and insurance to savings. There is a dedicated online financial support tool (finance.macmillan.org.uk), or individuals can speak to a financial guide by calling the support line or by emailing the team (financialguidance@macmillan.org.uk).

Sam Pilcher Trust

See entry on page 56

The Plymouth and Cornwall Cancer Fund

£9,400

Correspondent: P. W. Harker, Honorary Secretary, Curtis Whiteford Crocker Solicitors, 87–89 Mutley Plain, Plymouth PL4 6JJ (01752 220587; email: admin@pccf.org.uk)

CC number: 262587

Eligibility

People in need who have cancer, or who have a dependant or relative with cancer, and live in the county of Cornwall and within a 40-mile radius of Plymouth Civic Centre in Devon (a map is available on the charity's website) Also inpatients or outpatients of any hospital controlled by Plymouth Hospital NHS Trust.

Types of grants

One-off grants between £10 and £400 to relieve hardship which is caused by cancer, for example, towards the cost of travel to hospital for patients and visitors, additional clothing, bed linen, stairlifts and telephone installation and bills.

Annual grant total

In 2015/16 the fund held assets of £117,000 and had an income of £61,000. During the year, the fund gave around £9,400 in grants to individuals.

Applications

Apply in writing to the correspondent at any time. Applications should be submitted by a recognised health professional on behalf of a patient or carer. Applicants should have exhausted all other potential sources of help before approaching the fund. Further guidance is given on the charity's website.

Other information

The charity also supports improvements to local cancer facilities, research and education.

Mairi Semple Fund

£5,500

Correspondent: M. Sinclair, 4 Barrhill, Glenbarr, Tarbert, Argyll PA29 6UT

OSCR number: SC000390

Eligibility

People who live in Kintyre or the Island of Gigha and are suffering from cancer.

Types of grants

Provision of equipment and/or domestic nursing help, assistance with hospital travel costs for patients or relatives and the provision of measures to enable the 'greater privacy, quietness and dignity' of hospitalised patients with terminal cancer.

Annual grant total

In 2016/17 the fund had an income of £13,700 and a total expenditure of £23,000. We estimate that grants given to individuals totalled £5,500, with funding also awarded to organisations involved with cancer research.

Exclusions

No grants are given to students for research.

Applications

Apply in writing through the doctor, nurse or church minister of the patient, at the relevant address:

(i) Minister, Killean and Kilchenzie Church, Manse, Muasdale, Tarbert, Argyll.

(ii) Doctor, The Surgery, Muasdale, Tarbert, Argyll.

(iii) Nurse, The Surgery (same address as (ii)).

Carers

Carers Trust

£123,000

Correspondent: The Trustees, 32–36 Loman Street, London SE1 0EH (email: info@carers.org; website: www.carers.org)

CC number: 1145181

Eligibility

Individual adult carers aged 16 and over.

Types of grants

One-off grants. Carers can apply for grants, usually of up to £300, to purchase items or activities that will benefit them in their caring role, for example: breaks with or without the person they care for; items for the home; driving lessons and travel costs; home repairs; or short-term or time-limited replacement care.

Annual grant total

In 2016/17 the trust had assets of £2.3 million and an income of £4.3 million. Grants to individuals totalled £246,000. We estimate that social welfare grants to individuals totalled around £123,000, with funding also awarded for educational purposes.

Applications

Applications can be made through your local Carers Trust centre, a list of which is available on the website. Direct applications will not be considered.

Margaret Champney Rest and Holiday Fund

£12,000

Correspondent: Gillian Galvan, General Manager, The Gate House, 9 Burkitt Road, Woodbridge IP12 4JJ (01394 388746; email: ogilviecharities@btconnect.com; website: www.ogilviecharities.org.uk/grants/rest-and-holiday-fund/funding-for-holidays-for-carers.html)

CC number: 211646

Eligibility

Carers, particularly those caring for a relative with severe disabilities, who need a break away from the person they are caring for. The website explains:

> The primary aim is to give a complete break to a carer while the person cared for is receiving respite care. In exceptional circumstances we may assist where the carer and cared for wish to holiday together, provided they are husband and wife or partners, or an adult child caring for an aged parent or vice versa.

Types of grants

One-off grants, generally of between £200 and £300, towards respite breaks.

Annual grant total

In 2016 the charity had an income of £15,100 and a total expenditure of £13,500. We estimate that grants given to individuals totalled £12,000.

Exclusions

Applications are not accepted unless they have been made through a relevant third party. The website notes that the following groups are not supported

- 'Anyone living outside the United Kingdom'
- 'Refugees unless they have established legitimate status in the United Kingdom'
- 'Those individuals who have no recourse to public funds – whatever the circumstances leading to this position'
- 'Anyone in prison'
- 'Anyone in the UK unlawfully'

The fund cannot help with items already funded elsewhere, childcare costs or daily living expenses.

Applications

Applications must be made through a social worker, community nurse or similar professional agency. They are considered at any time and should include the professional's name, job title and the name and address of the organisation they represent as well as the name of the applicant and a brief summary of their circumstances. Candidates should also include full details of weekly income and expenditure, details of other agencies being approached for funding, details of who will care for the person while the break is being taken and the proposed holiday venue, date and likely costs. Income and expenditure forms can be downloaded from the website. Decisions are usually made within six to eight weeks of an application being received.

Holidays for Carers

£48,500

Correspondent: Lisa Dluska-Miziura, Administrator, 1 Marians Walk, Berry Hill, Coleford, Gloucestershire GL16 8QW (01594 834650; email: hols4carers@yahoo.com)

CC number: 1063523

Eligibility

Carers and the people they care for in England, Scotland, Northern Ireland and Wales.

Types of grants

One-off grants of up to £500 for holidays and respite breaks.

Annual grant total

In 2015 the charity had an income of £46,000 and a total expenditure of £48,500. Grants to individuals totalled £48,500.

Applications

Apply in writing to the correspondent.

Vitalise Holidays
See entry on page 60

Children

The Adamson Trust

£49,500 (134 grants)

Correspondent: Edward Elworthy, Administrator, The Adamson Trust, PO Box 7227, Pitlochry, Perthshire PH16 9AL (website: www. theadamsontrust.co.uk)

OSCR number: SC016517

Eligibility

Children aged 17 or under who have a physical, mental or emotional disability. Preference is given to those resident in Scotland.

Types of grants

Grants range from £150 to £5,000 and are given to help with the cost of a holiday or respite break. Grant recipients must take the trip before their eighteenth birthday.

Annual grant total

In 2015/16 the trust made 134 grants to individuals totalling £49,500, and a further 24 grants to organisations, amounting to £23,000.

Exclusions

No grants can be given for holidays that have already taken place or that will take place within a fortnight of a trustees' meeting. No grants can be given towards the costs of accompanying adults or for retrospective trips.

Applications

Apply on a form available from the correspondent, to be returned with: details of the planned holiday; booking confirmations (if possible); and information about the child beneficiary. Supporting evidence such as a letter from the child's GP, hospital or health professional should also be attached. **Note:** Disability Living Allowance letters are not accepted as evidence if a disability.

All applications are considered by the trustees four times a year in February, May, August and November with closing dates of 31 December, 31 March, 30 June and 30 September.

Other information

The trust also makes grants to schools and organisations.

Birkdale Trust for Hearing Impaired Ltd

£55,500

Correspondent: The Administrator, 21 Gleneagles Drive, Southport PR8 3PP (01704 225274; email: karen_fleetwood@ hotmail.com; website: www. grantsforthedeaf.co.uk)

CC number: 1103074

Eligibility

Children and young people up to the age of 25 with a hearing impairment.

Types of grants

Assistance with the purchase of specialist hearing equipment.

Annual grant total

In 2016/17 the charity had assets of £5.9 million and an income of £229,500. We estimate that around £55,500 was given in grants to individuals.

Applications

Application forms are available to download from the charity's website.

Other information

The charity also provides grants for education.

Blind Children UK
See entry on page 73

The Boparan Charitable Trust

£882,000

Correspondent: Lesley Williams, Colmore Court, 9 Colmore Row, Birmingham B3 2BJ (0121 214 9364; email: applications@boparan.com; website: www.theboparancharitabletrust. com)

CC number: 1129992

Eligibility

Children and young people up to the age of 18, throughout the UK, who are disadvantaged either through poverty, disability or life-limiting conditions.

Types of grants

One-off grants for household appliances and furniture, household goods, treatments, sensory items and disability aids.

Annual grant total

In 2016 the trust held assets of £2.6 million and had an income of £1.1 million. Grants to individuals totalled £882,000 and were broken down as follows:

Disability aids	£669,500
Treatments	£60,500
General household	£10,000
Household appliances	£5,000
Household furniture	£2,800
Other	£960

Exclusions

The trust's website states that it will not fund the following unless there are exceptional circumstances:

Donations to other charities; funeral services; ongoing appeals, treatments and therapies; holidays/short break programmes; help with legal costs; reimbursements of funds already paid out; repayment of loans; administration or salary costs; accommodation costs; travelling costs; lease or purchase of cars; faith healing; dolphin therapy; music therapy; alternative therapy; warrantees; room hire; service or autism dogs; trampolines/trampettes; home adaptations/renovations; family memberships; carpets and flooring; garden equipment/sheds; fencing; toys and computer consoles, e.g. Wii/Xbox/PlayStation/Nintendo; PCs, laptops or tablets under any circumstances; televisions/DVD players; portable DVD/TV players; hot tubs; private school fees; sofas/settees; non-medical body and face enhancements; ABA therapy.

Applications

Application forms are available to download from the trust's website and should be returned by post.

Note: official written confirmation by an independent professional body will be required stating the applicant's condition or circumstances. This letter must be on company letterhead paper, with contact details.

Brad's Cancer Foundation
See entry on page 48

The Campbell Burns Metabolic Trust

£26,000 (250 grants)

Correspondent: Mark Burns, Trustee, 3 Merganser Way, Coalville LE67 4QA (01530 482154; email: contact@ campbellstrust.co.uk; website: www. campbellstrust.co.uk)

CC number: 1148667

Eligibility

Families of children, aged 10 and under, who have been diagnosed with a metabolic disorder, so that they are assisted with the financial costs of day-to-day life following such a diagnosis.

Types of grants

The purpose of this scheme is to provide a small grant of up to £100 to assist families with the financial costs of day-to-day life following a metabolic disorder. Grants are awarded for various expenses including:

- Travel costs to and from hospital
- Parking costs at hospital
- Utility bills
- Some household bills
- Council tax

Annual grant total

In 2015/16 the trust had assets of £2,500 and an income of almost £33,000. Grants and donations awarded to 250 families totalled nearly £26,000.

Applications

Families can apply for four kinds of grants from the trust. Once your application forms have been completed, post to: The Campbell Burns Metabolic Trust, 3 Merganser Way, Coalville, Leicestershire LE67 4QA.

Other information

The trust was established in the name of Campbell Burns, born in January 2012 and diagnosed with Leigh's Disease in March 2012.

Caudwell Children

£2.4 million

Correspondent: Trudi Beswick, Minton Hollins Building, Shelton Old Road, Stoke-on-Trent, Staffordshire ST4 7RY (01782 600607; fax: 01782 600639; email: charity@caudwellchildren.com; website: www.caudwellchildren.com)

CC number: 1079770

Eligibility

People under 18 with a disability or serious illness who live in the UK. Household income/salary (not including benefits) should be less than £45,000 gross per annum.

Types of grants

One-off and recurrent donations for mobility, sensory and sports equipment; therapy, treatment and family holidays.

Annual grant total

In 2016 the charity held assets of £14.8 million and had an income of £13.8 million. During the year, the charity awarded around £2.4 million in grants to individuals.

Exclusions

No grants for: building works, fixtures and fittings; gardening and the making safe of gardens; respite care; dolphin therapy/faith healing; computers (unless specifically designed for people with special needs); iPads; motor vehicle purchase/adaptations; equipment repair

or maintenance; domestic appliances; non-specialist furniture, decoration, clothing or bedding; private education; speech or occupational therapy; or legal costs.

Applications

Application forms are available to download from the website or from the correspondent. The charity uses different application forms depending upon what is being applied for. Financial details must be included. The application process can, during busy periods, take up to six months and applicants may be visited by a trustee.

Other information

The charity provides family support services, equipment, treatment and therapies for disabled children and their families across the UK. It also runs the Enable Sport programme for talented athletes with disabilities and the Destination Dreams holiday for children fighting life threatening conditions. More details of all of the charity's activities are available from its informative website.

Cerebra for Brain Injured Children and Young People

£79,500

Correspondent: Christopher Jones, Chief Executive, 2nd Floor, Lyric Building, King Street, Carmarthen SA31 1BD (01267 244200; email: info@ cerebra.org.uk; website: www.cerebra. org.uk)

CC number: 1089812

Eligibility

Children and young people aged 16 or under who have a neurodevelopmental disorder or condition. The condition may be of a physical nature, a learning disability or both.

Examples of the types of conditions covered include, as further specified on the website: cerebral palsy; autistic spectrum disorders; developmental disorders; seizure disorders; ADHD; traumatic brain injuries; acquired brain injuries; Down's syndrome and other chromosomal/genetic conditions; brain abnormality or degenerative conditions; hydrocephalus; and conditions caused in utero.

This list is by no means exhaustive and applicants who are unsure as to whether they fit the criteria should contact Cerebra directly.

Types of grants

One-off grants of up to a maximum of 80% of the cost or £400, whichever is the lowest amount, of equipment or resources that would improve quality of life and which are not available from statutory agencies like social services or the NHS. Examples of grants made include those towards touch screen computers, specialist car seats, power wheelchairs, therapies, trampolines, sensory toys, and tricycles and quadricycles.

For anything where there is a medical need, the charity encourages potential applicants to check to see if it can help.

Annual grant total

In 2016 the charity held assets of £731,500 and had an income of £3.4 million. During the year, the charity awarded around £79,500 in grants to individuals for welfare purposes.

Exclusions

Grants are not given for: driving lessons; motorised vehicles such as quad bikes and motorbikes; anything that could be considered a home improvement, e.g. paint for decorating, conservatories, carpet or other flooring; garden landscaping; household items, e.g. vacuum cleaners, washing machines, wardrobes, standard beds (special beds may be considered); vehicle purchase or maintenance; assessments; general clothing; treatment centres outside the UK; lycra suits; holidays; and educational items such as home tutors, standard teaching materials or the Son-Rise programme.

Applications

Application forms and guidance notes can be downloaded from the Cerebra website.

Other information

The charity also provides other support services such as telephone counselling, parental advice and a wills and trust voucher scheme.

Children Today Charitable Trust

£226,500 (191 grants)

Correspondent: The Trustees, 17B Telford Court, Chester Gates Business Park, Dunkirk Estate, Chester CH1 6LT (01244 335622; fax: 01244 335473; email: info@children-today.org.uk; website: www.children-today.org.uk)

CC number: 1137436

Eligibility

Children and young people under 25 who have a disability.

Types of grants

Grants of up to £1,000 to provide vital, life-changing specialist equipment, such as wheelchairs, walking aids, trikes, educational toys, communication aids,

lifting and posturepaedic sleep equipment and specially designed sensory equipment like fibre optic sprays.

Annual grant total

In 2016/17 the charity held assets of £121,000 and had an income of £646,000. The annual report states that: 'During the year Children Today made 191 grants, totalling £226,472.' The average grant made was £1,185 with the largest single grant was about £10,700.

Exclusions

Grants are not made to organisations.

Applications

The following extract is taken from the charity's website:

> Call us on 01244 335622 to discuss your needs and request an application form. As part of our application process we ask that you please provide the following: Obtain a professional medical reference from someone who works with your child in a professional capacity saying how this piece of equipment will benefit your child (occupational therapist, doctor, hospital consultant etc.). Provide a valid quotation from the supplier of the equipment (please note we do not offer any retrospective funding and the quotation must still be in date). Provide some basic financial information on the application form.

Other information

Children Today was founded in 1994 to help children and young people up to the age of 25 with disabilities enjoy a better quality of life by providing them with the specialised equipment they need. The charity aims to build long-term relationships with children and their families, so encourages beneficiaries to reapply for funding as the child's needs change.

Children's Hope Foundation

£19,000

Correspondent: Tom Dora, 15 Palmer Place, London N7 8DH (020 7700 6855; fax: 020 7700 4432; email: info@childrenshopefoundation.org.uk; website: www.childrenshopefoundation.org.uk)

CC number: 1060409

Eligibility

Children and young people up to the age of 25 who are affected by illness, disability or poverty.

Types of grants

Grants for medical equipment or treatment which may help in the management of a condition or disability.

Annual grant total

In 2016/17 the foundation held assets of £116,500 and an income of £200,000. Grants to individuals totalled £19,000.

Applications

Application forms are available to download from the foundation's website.

Other information

Grants are also made to individuals for educational purposes.

Children's Leukaemia Society

See entry on page 48

Colchester Children's Charity Appeal

£14,200

Correspondent: Roy Kemp, Trustee, 11 Churchill Way, Colchester CO2 8ST (01206 860384; email: colchesterchildrenscharity@mail.com)

CC number: 800485

Eligibility

Children in the Colchester area who have disabilities or terminal illness.

Types of grants

One-off grants for unexpected hardship or financial difficulties caused by the child's illness.

Annual grant total

In 2016/17 the charity held assets of £285,500 and had an income of £90,000. Grants to individuals totalled £14,200, with a further £57,500 awarded to local organisations.

Applications

Apply in writing to the correspondent.

Roald Dahl's Marvellous Children's Charity

£70,000 (178 grants)

Correspondent: Jane Miles, Chief Executive, Montague House, 23 Woodside Road, Amersham, Buckinghamshire HP6 6AA (01494 890465; email: enquiries@roalddahlcharity.org; website: www.roalddahlcharity.org)

CC number: 1137409

Eligibility

Any families living in the UK that meet the following criteria, as set out on the charity's website:

> There is a child (or children) who has a serious illness that could be life-limiting, as described by the following:

Group 1 – Life-threatening conditions for which curative treatment may be feasible but can fail (e.g. epilepsy, irreversible organ failures of heart, liver, kidneys)

Group 2 – Conditions where premature death is inevitable (e.g. cystic fibrosis)

Group 3 – Progressive conditions without curative treatment options (e.g. Batten disease, mucopolysaccaridosis, muscular dystrophy)

Group 4 - Irreversible but non-progressive conditions causing severe disability leading to susceptibility to health complications and likelihood of premature death (e.g. sickle cell disease, cerebral palsy, multiple disabilities such as brain or spinal cord insult)

Group 5 – Syndromes without a name (SWAN) causing severe, chronic disability or illness

In addition:

- The child (or children) is eligible to receive Medium or High Rate DLA (the Care component) or the Enhanced Rate for 6 of the 12 activities in the PIP or has an equivalent level of need
- The child (or children) has yet to reach their 25th birthday
- The family are living in financial hardship
- The family has not received a grant for this child (or children) from the Marvellous Family Grants in the last 12 months
- The grant is for the benefit of the child directly

Types of grants

Grants of up to £1,000 are given to help families to access a wide range of support, including: play, art or music therapy sessions; peer group or counselling sessions; equipment or expenses so children can join in their friends' activities; access to social communications technology; expenses to attend a family support event or conference; payment of high heating bills because of the child's health condition; car seats, walkers, bicycles, pushchairs and mobility chairs; specialist furniture or household appliances required because of the child's health condition; beds, cots, bedding or clothing; travel expenses to and from hospital; and respite care.

Annual grant total

In 2016/17 the charity held assets of £1.5 million and had an income of £1.5 million. The charity supported 178 families with grants totalling £70,000.

Exclusions

The charity cannot support children who have any form of malignant cancer (due to levels of support available being far higher than for other conditions), or children who solely have learning or behavioural difficulties, including autism or ADHD.

Holidays, day trips or driving lessons cannot be funded. The charity is also unable to assist with requests where a statutory agency has a responsibility to provide the item required.

Applications cannot be submitted directly by parents or individuals, or by charitable organisations with a turnover exceeding £1 million and/or those which have been registered for less than two years. The charity is unable to offer funding where the applicant officer is from the organisation which will be providing the service (e.g. a charity that provides physiotherapy cannot apply on behalf of a child for funding for physiotherapy at their charity).

Applications

Applications can only be accepted through a healthcare professional, social services, a health visitor or a grant co-ordinator within a charitable organisation. This person (known as the 'Applicant Officer') should ideally be somebody who is familiar with the family's situation, their history and is happy to complete the application on their behalf. Applications are considered at monthly grant meetings and must be submitted by a set date in order to be considered at a specific meeting (these dates are listed on the website). Applications can take between four and eight weeks.

Other information

The charity also provides project grants, research grants and funding for specialised children's nurses.

The Family Fund

£32.6 million

Correspondent: Lora Timmins, Applications Officer, Unit 4, Alpha Court, Monks Cross Drive, Huntington, York YO32 9WN (01904 621115; email: info@familyfund.org.uk; website: www. familyfund.org.uk)

CC number: 1053866

Eligibility

Families who are caring at home for a child or young person aged 19 or under who has a severe disability or serious illness. Eligible families must show evidence of their entitlement to one of the following: Child Tax Credit; Working Tax Credit; income-based Jobseeker's Allowance (JSA); Incapacity Benefit; Employment and Support Allowance (ESA); Housing Benefit; or Pension Credit. If you do not receive any of the above, further information may be needed to complete your application. The charity also retains discretion to decline an application where a family has a significant level of capital or household income.

Types of grants

The help given must be related to the child's care needs. The top three types of grant in 2016/17 by total spend were holidays and outings (£13.7 million), computers (£6.9 million) and white goods (£3.8 million). Grants were also awarded towards: recreation/home entertainment, furniture, clothing and bedding, hospital visiting expenses and floor coverings. The charity is not always able to meet the full cost of every item requested due to limited funding.

Annual grant total

In 2016/17 the charity held assets of £2.2 million and had an income of £33.8 million. Grants totalling £32.6 million were made to over 71,100 families. A further 1,142 siblings were helped with a Siblings Matter Too grant. The annual report for 2016/17 notes that 90% of grants were for goods or services, rather than cash.

Exclusions

The charity cannot provide items which are the responsibility of statutory agencies, such as medical or educational equipment or small items for daily living, such as bath aids, which are the responsibility of social services. No funding is given for general household bills, utility bills, mortgage or rent payments or household repairs. No grants are given for families receiving National Asylum Support Service payments. The charity cannot help foster carers.

Applications

There are two separate application processes. If you are applying for the first time, you will need to download an application form from the website or request one from the charity. The website has detailed eligibility criteria and guidelines on what it can and cannot fund. Incomplete application forms cannot be processed and only one application per household can be made. If you are making an application on behalf of more than one child, there is an additional child form that must be completed.

If you have made a successful application in the past, you may be able to apply online by accessing your online account. If you need help accessing your account, you can contact the applications team by telephoning 01904 550055.

Families in Wales have to complete a slightly different application process following changes to the funding agreement with the Welsh government. There is a separate page on the charity's website that provides further details and clarifications.

Families can only receive a grant once every 12 months, your last award letter will include information about when you can next apply. The charity encourages applicants who have questions or need further help to contact them.

Other information

The charity is funded entirely by the government administrations of England, Northern Ireland, Scotland and Wales, and works within guidelines agreed by the trustees.

To meet the criteria for funding, the child or young person must have additional complex needs, or have a serious or life-threatening illness **and** there must be evidence that their additional needs impact on the family's choices and their opportunity to enjoy ordinary life. A full list of criteria is available on the charity's informative and comprehensive website.

The Rob George Foundation
See entry on page 43

Happy Days Children's Charity

£553,500 (22,944 grants)

Correspondent: Michelle McGillicuddy, Daytrip & Bookings Officer, Clody House, 90–100 Collingdon Street, Luton, Bedfordshire LU1 1RX (01582 755999; email: michelle@happydayscharity.org; website: www.happydayscharity.org)

CC number: 1010943

Eligibility

Children and young people aged 3 to 17 years (inclusive) who have special needs This includes children who: have disabilities, sickness or a terminal illness; have been abused or neglected and/or disadvantaged by poverty; have lost a parent; have been involved in a traumatic incident; or are young carers. Further information is given on the charity's website.

Types of grants

One-off two to four-night respite break holidays in the UK. All funding is paid directly to the providers. The charity offers funding for one suitable adult, which may be a parent, guardian or a trusted adult (e.g. a nurse or carer). In special circumstances, the charity may choose to make alternative arrangements.

Annual grant total

In 2016/17 the charity held assets of £244,000 and had an income of £945,500. In total, 22,944 children benefitted from holidays, trips and activities, with grants to individuals for these purposes totalling £553,500.

The annual report states that:

> 18,750 children were able to experience a performing arts production. 3,050 children went to either a theme park, zoo, animal park, seaside or place of interest. The Charity provided respite breaks for 209 children and their families to various destinations across the UK. We also enabled 935 children to benefit from a group activity holiday to various centres across the UK, and also a few abroad.

Exclusions

No extra adults are funded.

Applications

Apply on a form available to download from the website or from the correspondent. Applications may be submitted by a family member (a parent, guardian, grandparent or sibling) or by a GP, consultant, nurse or social worker.

There are separate applications for different holidays, see the website for further details. If you have any questions or need help completing the form, contact the correspondent. For family respite break queries contact Ann DaRocha on 01582 755804 or ann@happydayscharity.org.

Other information

Grants are also made to groups of children and young people who have special needs for day trips and holidays.

The Douglas Hay Trust

£29,000 (63+ grants)

Correspondent: John Ritchie, Secretary and Treasurer, Midlothian Innovation Centre, Pentlandfield, Roslin, Midlothian EH25 9RE (email: johndritchie@btinternet.com; website: www.douglashay.org.uk)

OSCR number: SC014450

Eligibility

Children aged under 18 who have physical disabilities and live in Scotland.

Types of grants

One-off grants towards shoes, clothes, bedding, home improvements, holidays, computers, equipment and education.

Annual grant total

In 2015/16 the trust held assets of £1.17 million and had an income of £43,500. Grants to 63 individuals totalled £27,000 during the year, with a further £2,100 distributed through the trust's shoe voucher scheme.

Applications

Apply using a form available from the website or by contacting the correspondent. The form should be submitted through a social worker, medical practitioner or other welfare agency. Applications are considered monthly.

Just Helping Children

£258,500

Correspondent: Jacqueline Tapp, Trustee, 85 Prince of Wales Road, Norwich, Norfolk NR1 1DG (0800 169 1601; email: office@just4children.org; website: just4children.org)

CC number: 1164473

Eligibility

Sick children living in the UK and Ireland. A full list of eligible conditions is available on the charity's website.

Types of grants

Grants for medical treatment, therapies, living environments, equipment and holidays.

Annual grant total

In 2015/16 the charity held assets of £622,500 and had an income of £676,500. Treatment costs totalled £258,500.

Applications

Contact the charity for further information.

Kayleigh's Wee Stars

£54,500 (37 grants)

Correspondent: Mr J. Cordiner, Kayleigh's Wee Stars, 4 Coutens Place, Oldmeldrum, Aberdeenshire AB51 0PU

OSCR number: SC043320

Eligibility

Families in Scotland who have a child with a terminal illness, and where life expectancy is likely to be less than two years.

Types of grants

One-off grants of approximately £1,500 for special holidays, travel expenses, memory keepsakes, financial pressures, specialised equipment or building modifications.

Annual grant total

In 2016/17 the charity held assets of £85,000 and had an income of £105,500. During the year, the charity gave £54,500 in grants to 37 individuals.

Applications

Application forms are available to download from the website. The form should be completed by a social worker who represents the family which will be receiving support. The form will also need to be signed by the parent/guardian to allow the charity to contact the child's medical consultant/doctor.

Completed applications must be sent by post.

Other information

The charity is now positioned in such a way that wherever there is a child who receives a terminal diagnosis in any Scottish Hospital, the paediatric social workers from CLIC Sargent, Children's Hospices Across Scotland (CHAS), Kindred and various others, can apply for support on behalf of the families.

Kidney Kids Scotland Charitable Trust

£84,500

Correspondent: Grants administrator, Merrow House, Church Street, Stenhousemuir, Stirlingshire FK5 4BU (01324 555843; email: office@kidneykids. org.uk; website: www.kidneykids.org.uk)

OSCR number: SC030284

Eligibility

Children in Scotland who have renal/ urological illnesses and their families who are in need.

Types of grants

Small grants to help families deal with the financial impact of having a sick child (e.g. to help with travel expenses to hospital or to support families who have taken time off from their job to be with their child).

Annual grant total

In 2015/16 the charity had assets of £72,500 and an income of £224,000. Grants to children and their families totalled £84,500.

Applications

In the first instance, contact the charity's office. Applications are usually made by a medical professional or social worker.

Other information

The charity supports The Royal Hospital for Children in Glasgow and bought the hospital all of the haemodialysis machines on its haemodialysis and transplantation unit.

Logans Fund

£8,100

Correspondent: The Trustees, 30 Dunbar Street, Lossiemouth IV31 6AL (07709 320879; email: info@ logansfund.org; website: logansfund.org)

OSCR number: SC040619

Eligibility

Children who have been affected by cancer, and their families.

The charity can support anyone diagnosed with cancer before their eighteenth birthday and can continue to offer support for up to five years after this age.

Types of grants

Grants are made to help with anything that will take the child's focus away from hospital and treatment. The website explains that its 'philosophy is to try and win back some of the childhood lost to time in hospital...to give your child's horizon a sprinkling of magic dust'. The charity has so far paid for a wide range of things, including driving courses, specialist dry suits, concert tickets, special days out and respite trips for children and their families. The website further notes: 'Just because we haven't done it just means no-one has asked yet.'

Annual grant total

In 2016/17 the charity had assets of £131,000 and an income of £43,000. We believe grants to individuals to have totalled around £8,100.

Applications

Applications can be made using the form on the charity's website and can be submitted either by the child's parent or guardian, or a third party outside the immediate family (e.g. a friend, charitable organisation, welfare professional or another family member, etc.).

Other information

Among its other activities, the charity works to raise awareness of childhood cancers and promotes research programmes and fundraising initiatives, and supports bereaved families in any possible way.

Families can also apply to spend some time together at the charity's 'Logan's Sunny Days' caravan at Lossiemouth Bay Caravan Park. Booking requests can be made on the website.

Nicola's Fund

£37,500

Correspondent: Stephen Riley, Chair, The Stables, Old Meadow Court, Gresford Road, Llay, Wrexham LL12 0NE (01978 856120; email: info@ nicolasfund.co.uk; website: www. nicolasfund.co.uk)

CC number: 1113095

Eligibility

Families of children with cancer or other long-term or terminal illnesses.

Types of grants

Grants to cover a weeks holiday in Centre Parcs or Black Rock Sands.

Annual grant total

In 2015/15 the charity held assets of £29,500 and had an income of £58,000.

Grants to families totalled £37,500. The Charity Commission record notes that Nicola's Fund has helped over 60 families go on holiday in the past two years.

Applications

Apply in writing to the correspondent.

The Joe Noakes Charitable Trust

See entry on page 69

Sam Pilcher Trust

£7,000

Correspondent: Colin Pilcher, Springhill Barn, Upper Slaughter, Cheltenham GL54 2JH (01451 824378; email: sam. pilchertrust@btinternet.com; website: www.sampilchertrust.org.uk)

CC number: 1151779

Eligibility

Families of children with cancer.

Types of grants

One-off grants are available to assist with the costs associated with having a child with cancer. Grants can be used for equipment at home, white goods, respite holidays, and to bridge a financial gap.

Annual grant total

In 2016 the trust had an income of £15,000 and a total expenditure of £18,000. We estimate that grants for welfare purposes totalled around £7,000.

Applications

Applications should be made in writing to the correspondent, detailing the situation and financial need.

Other information

The trust was established after the death of 11-year-old Sam Pilcher, who died from leukaemia. Before his death, Sam began fundraising to help other children suffering from cancer.

The trust mainly supports hospitals and other cancer care units, for example it helped to establish a dedicated Teenage Cancer Care Unit, and helped to refurbish the activity rooms in Bristol Royal Children's Hospital and Gloucester Royal Children's Hospital.

The trust also provides cuddly toys for new patients at Gloucester Royal Children's Hospital, and gives goody bags to inpatients at Bristol Royal Children's Hospital.

The trust also awards grants for educational equipment, such as computers and art supplies.

Power Pleas Trust

£18,000

Correspondent: Keith Berry, Trustee, 80 York Avenue, Wolverhampton WV3 9BU (01902 655962; email: admin@powerpleas.org; website: www. powerpleas.org)

CC number: 519654

Eligibility

Mainly young people, under 18 years, with muscular dystrophy and other mobility disorders living in the Wolverhampton area.

Types of grants

Grants are given primarily towards the purchase and provision of outdoor electric powered wheelchairs, trikes and other mobility aids.

Annual grant total

In 2016/17 the trust had an income of £940 and a total expenditure of £18,500. We estimate that grants given to individuals totalled £18,000.

Applications

Apply in writing to the correspondent directly by the individual or family member.

REACT (Rapid Effective Assistance for Children with Potentially Terminal Illnesses)

£347,000 (879 grants)

Correspondent: Grants Administrator, St Luke's House, 270 Sandycombe Road, Kew, Surrey TW9 3NP (020 8940 2575; email: react@reactcharity.org; website: www.reactcharity.org)

CC number: 802440

Eligibility

Families caring for a child with an illness which is life-threatening or has the potential to shorten their lifespan.

Types of grants

Grants are available for: specialist medical equipment (unavailable through your local health authority); educational or sensory equipment (to aid your child's development); and mobility equipment (to assist your child's physical development).

The charity also considers requests for basic, essential homecare items, travel and subsistence costs and end of life costs.

Annual grant total

In 2016/17 the charity held assets of £562,000 and had an income of

£871,500. Grants totalled £347,000 and were distributed as follows:

Safety and hygiene equipment	274	£108,000
Specialist equipment	190	£108,000
Mobile home holidays	242	£58,000
Funeral expenses	39	£34,000
Educational	55	£23,500
Travel and subsistence	50	£7,600
Respite holidays	29	£6,800

Applications

Application forms are available to download from the charity's website. They can also be requested by phone on 020 8940 2575 or by email at react@reactcharity.org.

Other information

The charity has eight mobile homes in six locations across the UK.

A Smile For A Child

£89,000 (41 grants)

Correspondent: Christopher Read, 17 Sugarhill Crescent, Newton Aycliffe, County Durham DL5 4FH (07904448296; email: asmileforachild@btinternet.com; website: www.asmileforachild.org)

CC number: 1123357

Eligibility

Disadvantaged children or those with disabilities in the UK.

Types of grants

Grants range from £25 to £8,000 for sports equipment, lessons and wheelchairs.

Annual grant total

In 2015/16 the charity held assets of £55,500 and had an income of £139,000. Grants to 41 individuals totalled £89,000, with a further £70,500 awarded to schools and organisations.

Applications

Application forms are available to download from the charity's website and should be returned to the correspondent.

The Smile of Arran Trust

£12,300 (84 grants)

Correspondent: Steve Tosh, Trustee, Honeysuckles, Bull Lane, Long Melford, Sudbury CO10 9EA (01787 371454; email: smileofarran@gmail.com; website: www.smileofarran.org)

CC number: 1161262

Eligibility

Children aged 0 to 19 who have been diagnosed with brain tumours.

Types of grants

Grants of up to £150 can be spent on anything needed by the child or young person.

Annual grant total

In 2015/16 the trust had an income of £55,000 and an total expenditure of £44,000. Grants to 84 individuals totalled £12,300.

Applications

Contact your CLIC Sarget social worker. Those without a CLIC Sargent social worker should contact the trust through its website.

Snowball Trust

£9,500

Correspondent: Pauline Blackham, Clerk to the Trustees, 11 Rotherham Road, Holbrooks, Coventry CV6 4FF (website: snowballtrust.wordpress.com)

CC number: 702860

Eligibility

Children and young people under 21 who are in poor health or who have a disability and live in Coventry and Warwickshire.

Types of grants

One-off grants mainly for medical equipment and disability aids. Grants may be made to agencies such as schools, medical bodies or other organisations, to purchase equipment which can then be loaned to the child. Further information is given on the charity's website.

Annual grant total

In 2016/17 the trust had an income of £22,000 and a total expenditure of £20,500. We estimate that grants given to individuals totalled around £9,500.

Applications

Apply on a form available from the correspondent or as a download from the charity's website. Forms can be submitted either by the individual or through a third party such as a special school, social worker or other welfare agency. Applications should include a firm quote for the equipment to be supplied, a letter of support from the individual's school and/or a medical professional, and confirmation of the parents'/guardians' financial need.

Other information

The trust also makes grants to organisations.

Tiny Tim Trust

£15,000

Correspondent: Jenny Anderson, 4 Gilbert Avenue, Chesterfield S40 3EU (01246 236890; email: tjanderson564@ gmail.com; website: tinytimtrust.org.uk)

CC number: 1038669

Eligibility

Children and young adults aged 0 to 19 with special health, educational and social needs living in Derbyshire. Applicants over 16 should be in full-time education.

Types of grants

One-off grants are available for: specialist therapeutic equipment; safety equipment; buggies and car seats; educational toys; sensory toys and equipment; early learning aids; IT equipment for children over eight years of age; and assistance with projects such as safe play outdoor projects and fencing.

Annual grant total

In 2016/17 the trust had an income of £43,500 and a total expenditure of £19,000. We estimate that grants given to individuals totalled around £15,000.

Exclusions

The trust cannot accept applications for: continuous or ongoing funding; clothing, except for specialist clothing; shoes; assistance with debt; or holidays.

Applications

Application forms are available to download from the trust's website. Check the website for application deadlines.

Variety, the Children's Charity

£521,000 (277 grants)

Correspondent: Stanley Salter, Trustee, The Variety Club Children's Charity, Variety Club House, 93 Bayham Street, London NW1 0AG (020 7428 8100; email: info@variety.org.uk; website: www.variety.org.uk)

CC number: 209259

Eligibility

Children (aged 18 and under) who have disabilities or are sick or disadvantaged. Applicants must be permanently resident in the UK.

Types of grants

Grants of between £100 and £6,000 can be made to both individuals and organisations for medical, basic care, mobility or sensory play equipment. This could include monitoring equipment, feeding tubes or hoists, or specially adapted car seats, for example.

Annual grant total

In 2016 the charity had assets of £2.8 million and had an income of £7.6 million. During the year, grants to individuals totalled £521,000. Of this amount, £321,000 was given for wheelchairs in 173 payments and £200,000 was awarded to 104 individuals.

Exclusions

The charity does not fund: standard household equipment or furnishings; repayment of loans; garden adaptations; garden sheds or summerhouses; the cost of a family/wheelchair adapted vehicle; laptops, iPads or computer hardware; maintenance or ongoing costs; travel costs; therapy sessions; reimbursement of funds already paid out; hire, rental costs or down payments; trikes, bikes or buggies; trips abroad or holiday costs; trampolines; medical treatment; or education or tuition fees.

Applications

Download the relevant application form from the website, where guidelines are also available. Note that there is a separate form for wheelchair applications. Applications can be made by parents, medical professionals, a school or organisation, hospitals and small registered charities, and must be supported by a letter from an appropriate medical professional. Two quotations for the equipment should accompany the application.

If you would like to request further information before making an application, Julie Thomas, the Grants Programme Manager can be contacted by telephone (020 7428 8120) or email (julie.thomas@variety.org.uk).

Whizz-Kidz

£1.5 million

Correspondent: Whizz-Kidz, 4th Floor, Portland House, Bressenden Place, London SW1E 5BH (0800 151 3350; email: kidzservices@whizz-kidz.org.uk; website: www.whizz-kidz.org.uk)

CC number: 802872

Eligibility

The charity's website states:

If you're a parent or carer of a child with a physical disability, you need to consider the following before applying:

- Is your child under 18 years old? Applications must be submitted before your child's 18th birthday
- Does your child have a physical disability that permanently affects their mobility and participation?
- Have you approached your local NHS wheelchair service and found that the mobility equipment that your child needs is not available/provided?

If you answered yes to the above questions then Whizz-Kidz may be able to help you.

If you've had mobility equipment from Whizz-Kidz in the past you can still make a new application as long as the young person still meets the above criteria and it's been two years since your last application.

Types of grants

Grants for a broad range of mobility equipment for children with a physical disability.

Annual grant total

In 2016 the charity had assets of £1.6 million and an income of £7.9 million. Grants to individuals totalled £1.5 million.

Applications

Application forms can be made through the charity's website where application forms can also be downloaded.

Disability

Barchester Health Care Foundation

£85,000 (100 grants)

Correspondent: Grants Management Team, 3rd Floor, The Aspect, 12 Finsbury Square, London EC2A 1AS (0800 328 3328; email: info@ bhcfoundation.org.uk; website: www. bhcfoundation.org.uk)

CC number: 1083272

Eligibility

Older people over the age of 65 and adults over the age of 18 with a physical or mental disability living in England, Scotland or Wales. In 2015 the main focus was on helping to combat loneliness and enable people to be active and engaged.

Types of grants

One-off grants of up to £5,000 can be given according to need. The foundation specifies that applications encouraging the person's mobility, independence and improved quality of life are favoured. Awards have previously been made for specialist equipment, electric and specialist sport wheelchairs, power packs, hoists, riser/recliner chairs, stairlifts, tricycles and mobility scooters, computers and other IT equipment and software, communication and visual aids, exercise, holidays and respite breaks, outings, transportation, home security, disability-related house and car adaptations or repairs, educational grants, white goods (where related to a disability/medical condition), home security, transportation, heating, storage for mobility scooters, house/garden/ ramp adaptations and so on.

Annual grant total

In 2015 the foundation held assets of £67,000 and had an income of £200,000. Grants to 100 individuals totalled £85,000.

Exclusions

Grants are not normally made:

▶ Retrospectively
▶ To candidates who have received a grant within the previous three years
▶ For services offered in a care home operated by Barchester Healthcare or by any other company
▶ Towards home repairs and alterations not related to a disability/medical condition
▶ For basic household items (white goods, furniture, carpets) not related to a disability/medical condition
▶ For daily living costs (rent, utility bills, clothing and so on)
▶ To repay debts
▶ For services for which the health and social care authorities have a statutory responsibility (e.g. medical and dental treatments)

Applications

Applications can be made online on the foundation's website or a form can be downloaded and submitted to the correspondent. All applications must be supported by a third party sponsor, for example, a health or social care professional, social worker or charity representative. The trustees meet quarterly, although applications can be dealt with between meetings.

Applicants can expect a response within ten weeks; however, the foundation is unable to acknowledge the receipt of postal applications.

Other information

Support is also given in grants to small community groups and local charities (£58,500 to 44 organisations in 2015).

Barchester Healthcare is the foundation's main benefactor and makes annual lump sum donations by matching pound for pound all fundraising by the company staff for the foundation, as well as providing in-kind donations of office space, equipment, accounting, marketing and IT support.

British Limbless Ex-Service Men's Association (BLESMA)
See entry on page 79

Challenger Children's Fund

£33,500

Correspondent: The Trustees, Suite 353, 44/46 Morningside Road, Edinburgh EH10 4BF (07531 580414; email: info@ ccfscotland.org; website: www. ccfscotland.org)

OSCR number: SC037375

Eligibility

The trust aims to help any child in Scotland under the age of 18 years living with a disability through a physical impairment of the musculoskeletal, neurological or cardiorespiratory system of the body

The following conditions on their own, however, are not accepted: psychiatric disorders, learning disabilities, behavioural disorders, development delay, Down's Syndrome, autism, visual or hearing impairment, cancer, diabetes, epilepsy, HIV, back pain and chronic fatigue syndrome. If they are associated with a physical disability, however, consideration will be given.

Types of grants

One-off grants of up to £500. More may be granted in some circumstances. Grants can be given towards anything which is not provided by statutory sources but is required to meet the special needs of the child. Items include clothing, apparatus, equipment, household appliances such as washing machines, furniture, travel and home or garden adaptations.

Annual grant total

In 2016/17 the trust had assets of £20,000 and an income of £30,500. Grants to individuals totalled £33,500.

Exclusions

Grants cannot be made retrospectively. Only one application per year.

Applications

Application forms can be obtained from the correspondent or on the website. Applications should be sponsored by a social worker, GP, health visitor, district nurse or therapist. Trainee workers and community care assistants may also apply, but a qualified person must countersign the application. Grants are given to the agency sponsoring the application or the company the purchase/s is/are being made from. They cannot be given directly to the child or child's family. Applications can be submitted once a year.

ECAS Ltd
See entry on page 202

Equipment for Independent Living

£19,700 (22 grants)

Correspondent: Alistair Stoker, Park Cottage, Donhead St Andrew, Shaftesbury SP7 9DZ (01747 828789)

CC number: 228438

Eligibility

People with disabilities in the UK.

Types of grants

One-off grants towards disability equipment enabling people to obtain 'mobility, independence and earning power'. Awards are usually in the range of £100 to £1,000.

Annual grant total

In 2016 the charity had assets of £42,500 and an income of £27,500. The charity awarded £19,700 in grants during the year.

Exclusions

Normally grants are not made towards: medical equipment; course fees and materials; welfare expenditure of a non-capital nature, e.g. holiday or moving expenses; equipment which is supplied by the NHS or social services; equipment running costs; building adaptations and decorating; household equipment (unless specially adapted for the person's disability); or private treatment, home care fees or computers (unless they are used as a speech aid or to enable the individual to earn their living).

Funds are not normally granted to cases submitted by other charities which have much larger resources than the charity.

Applications

Applicants must be referred in the first instance by a professional person involved with their welfare, for example, a social worker, occupational therapist or specialist nurse. The professional person should write to the Honorary Secretary describing the applicant's circumstances and saying what equipment is needed and why. If appropriate, a full application form will then be sent out.

Applications can be submitted at any time and are considered in January, April, July and October.

Get Kids Going

£14,000

Correspondent: Jane Emmerson, Chief Executive, 10 King Charles Terrace, Sovereign Close, London E1W 3HL (020 7481 8110; email: info@getkidsgoing. com; website: www.getkidsgoing.com)

CC number: 1063471

Eligibility

Children and young people up to the age of 26 who have a disability and wish to participate in sport.

Types of grants

One-off grants ranging from £500 to £15,000 for wheelchairs and sports equipment, repairs to sports equipment, travel to training and competitions, competition fees and sports physiotherapy.

Annual grant total

In 2015/16 the charity held assets of £10.5 million and had an income of almost £1.2 million. Grants to individuals totalled £14,000. During the year, the charity allocated most of its funding to the para-alpine ski team, other para-snowsports as well as other Paralympic sports. Grants to sports teams and organisations totalled £110,000.

Applications

Applications can be made directly to the charity.

The Gloucestershire Association for Disability

See entry on page 400

Mobility Trust II

£279,500

Correspondent: Denise Valentine, Chief Executive, 19 Reading Road, Pangbourne, Reading, Berkshire RG8 7LR (0118 984 2588; email: mobility@mobilitytrust.org.uk; website: www.mobilitytrust.org.uk)

CC number: 1070975

Eligibility

People who have severe physical disabilities.

Types of grants

The provision of powered wheelchairs or scooters for people who are unable to obtain such equipment through statutory sources or afford it themselves. If someone is unable to walk at all and requires a powered wheelchair, they should apply to their local NHS Wheelchair Service before making an application to the trust.

Note: the trust does not make direct cash grants but helps to obtain the required equipment.

Annual grant total

In 2016/17 the trust had assets of £295,500 and an income of £413,000. Expenditure on beneficiaries' equipment totalled £279,500.

Exclusions

Folding/portable scooters are not provided.

Applications

Individuals can complete the questionnaire on the trust's website. The trust uses the questionnaire to determine whether or not an individual is eligible to receive assistance.

Motability

£24 million (8,502 grants)

Correspondent: Customer Services, Warwick House, Roydon Road, Harlow, Essex CM19 5PX (0300 456 4566; email: communications@motability.co.uk; website: www.motability.co.uk)

CC number: 299745

Eligibility

People who receive one of the following benefits: Higher Rate Mobility Component of Disability Living Allowance (HRMC DLA); Enhanced Rate of the Mobility Component of Personal Independence Payment (ERMC PIP); War Pensioners' Mobility Supplement (WPMS); Armed Forces Independence Payment (AFIP); or a government vehicle, trike or mini.

Types of grants

Assistance can be given towards 'the best value suitable solution that meets basic mobility needs'. These could include: vehicle advance payments; supplying and fitting adaptations, for instance hand controls to enable somebody with a lower body disability to drive an automatic car or hoists to load electric wheelchairs into estate cars; driving lessons for people who have disabilities, or whose children or spouses have disabilities, especially people aged 16 to 24; or wheelchair accessible vehicles for customers who wish to get in a car while seated in their wheelchair.

Annual grant total

In 2016/17 the charity held assets of £68.7 million and had an income of £53.3 million. During the year, the charity gave around £24 million in grants to 8,502 individuals.

Applications

Potential applicants should contact the customer services team on 0300 456 4566. The trust usually requests that potential applicants have their national insurance number to hand.

Note the following from the website: 'financial help is only awarded towards the least expensive solution that meets your mobility needs and you should also expect to contribute as much as you can afford'.

At times there may be waiting lists for some of the schemes, check the website or contact the customer services team to check.

Other information

The group works in conjunction with the Department for Work and Pensions.

Vitalise Holidays

£620,000 (809 grants)

Correspondent: Bookings Team, 212 Business Design Centre, Upper Street, London N1 0QH (0303 3030145; fax: 020 7288 6899; email: bookings@ vitalise.org.uk; website: www.vitalise.org. uk)

CC number: 295072

Eligibility

Adults with physical disabilities and carers who might not otherwise be able to afford a break. Applicants must be aged 18 or over and must not have been on a break for over 12 months or have savings of more than £23,000. In exceptional circumstances, the charity may consider those who have been on a break in the previous 12 months. Applicants must not qualify for statutory funding.

Types of grants

Financial assistance towards the cost of a break at a Vitalise Centre.

Annual grant total

In 2016/17 the charity had assets of £7 million and had an income of £9.4 million. During the year, the charity gave grants to 809 individuals totalling £620,000.

Exclusions

Grants do not cover associated costs; for example, transport to and from the centre.

Applications

Both an online application form and a downloadable form are available on the website. Applications require a letter of support from a social worker or healthcare professional.

Provisional bookings must be made before completing the application form.

Other information

While the charity can only provide a limited number of grants, it also offers advice on other funding options for potential guests.

The charity mainly awarded 298 grants through the Joan Brander Memorial Fund. Revitalise has created its own support fund in 2016, which gave financial assistance to 298 people who were suffering from a demonstrable deterioration in their financial circumstances. A further 213 people were supported financially by a donation from Simplyhealth.

Bruce Wake Charity

£52,000 (37 grants)

Correspondent: Peter Hems, Trustee, c/o Grant Thornton UK LLP, Regent House, 80 Regent Road, Leicester LE1 7NH (0116 247 1234; email: wake@webleicester.co.uk; website: www.brucewaketrust.co.uk)

CC number: 1018190

Eligibility

People with disabilities (predominantly wheelchair users) in the UK.

Types of grants

The trustees will consider grant applications related to the provision of leisure activities for people with disabilities, but particularly favour applications where the potential beneficiaries meet one or all of the following criteria:

- The potential beneficiaries are wheelchair users with a physical disability
- Improved access for wheelchair users is proposed
- A sporting or leisure activity involving wheelchair users is proposed

Annual grant total

In 2016/17 the charity had assets of £9.2 million and an income of £213,500. Grants to individuals totalled £52,000.

Applications

Apply in writing through a charitable organisation or equivalent recognised body. Applications should include all appropriate financial information and are considered quarterly.

Other information

The charity has two narrowboats for hire which are both specially designed for wheelchair users. They are both berthed at Upton Marina on the River Severn.

Injuries

Mark Davies Injured Riders Fund

£14,500

Correspondent: Rosemary Lang, Lancrow, Par PL24 2SA (01726 813156; email: rosemary@mdirf.co.uk; website: www.mdirf.co.uk)

CC number: 1022281

Eligibility

People injured in horse-related accidents and their carers.

Types of grants

One-off cash grants and grants in kind according to need. Grants to beneficiaries vary from less than £100 to more than £40,000, depending on need. Assistance has recently been given in the form of travel expenses, physiotherapy, adapted motor cars, house adaptations and home and stable help.

Annual grant total

In 2016 the charity had assets of £391,000 and an income of £100,000. The charity awarded £14,500 in grants to individuals during the year.

Exclusions

Professional and amateur jockeys and those injured in the horse racing industry are not eligible to apply.

Applications

Apply in writing to the correspondent at any time. All applicants are visited by a local fund volunteer to discuss their medical and financial needs. A report is then made to the trustees, who will consider whether or not to award a grant.

The Matt Hampson Foundation

£137,500

Correspondent: Tommy Cawston, Chief Executive Officer, Office 14, Burrough Court, Burrough-on-the-Hill, Melton Mowbray, Leicestershire LE14 2QS (01664 454742; email: tommy@hambo.co.uk; website: matthampsonfoundation.org)

CC number: 1139823

Eligibility

The foundation's website states:

> The Foundation provides assistance to improve the quality of life and wellbeing for young individuals who have sustained catastrophic injury through sport or the pursuit of other physical recreational activities.

'Young' is defined by the Foundation as 'from school age to 30'. This definition does not however preclude anyone whose age falls outside of this definition from applying to the Foundation for assistance. A catastrophic injury can be defined as one that leaves a person suffering from permanent disability and has serious, long-term effects on the individual involved.

We mainly assist people who have received such injuries in the United Kingdom and the Republic of Ireland but that does not preclude us from helping those in other parts of the world who need urgent assistance.

Types of grants

Grants for items such as equipment, technology or everyday living expenses.

Annual grant total

In 2015/16 the foundation had assets of £639,000 and an income of £958,000. Grants to individuals totalled £137,500.

Applications

Contact the foundation for further information.

Other information

The foundation also provides information, mentoring and friendship.

The Injured Jockeys Fund

£630,000 (379 grants)

Correspondent: Lisa Hancock, Chief Executive, Millfarm Stud, Mill Lane, Cowlinge, Newmarket, Suffolk CB8 9HZ (01638 662246; fax: 01638 668988; email: kh@ijf.org.uk; website: www.injuredjockeys.co.uk)

CC number: 1107395

Eligibility

Jockeys who have suffered through injury, and their families. Applicants must hold (or have held) a licence to ride under the Rules of Racing, be in financial need and have obtained all state aid to which they are entitled.

Types of grants

One-off and recurrent grants to assist with medical care and to help alleviate financial problems and stress. Grants have included help with medical treatment and equipment, contributions to private medical insurance, wheelchairs, holidays, televisions and emergency cash. Assistance may also be given to help with the cost of education where children have special needs. Interest-free mortgage advances are available.

Annual grant total

In 2015/16 the fund held assets of £43.5 million and had an income of

£5.2 million. Grants to 379 injured jockeys totalled over £630,000.

Applications

Application forms are available from the correspondent. The fund has nine almoners who cover the whole of the UK and visit potential beneficiaries to assess their needs.

Other information

IJF also runs Oaksey House in Berkshire, 'a rehabilitation centre for jockeys past and present, the racing workforce, other sports men and women and those from the local community'. Jack Berry House in Malton, North Yorkshire is the fund's second rehabilitation centre.

RFU Injured Players Foundation

£1.08 million (141 grants)

Correspondent: Annabel Habart, Team Administrator, Rugby House, Twickenham Stadium, 200 Whitton Road, Middlesex TW2 7BA (0800 783 1518; email: ipfgrants@rfu.com; website: www.rfuipf.org.uk)

CC number: 1122139

Eligibility

People of any age who have suffered a catastrophic spinal cord or traumatic brain injury which has resulted in permanent disability while playing rugby in England at any level.

The foundation also has the Non-Catastrophic Injury (Non-CI) Grant Programme for individuals who have experienced injuries not classed as a catastrophic spinal cord or traumatic brain injury. The injury must have taken place during a rugby match or rugby training session with a school or club approved by the RFU. More information regarding eligibility is available from the foundation.

Types of grants

Grants, usually up to a maximum of £20,000, can be applied for to help with a wide range of essential needs. They are commonly given for home improvements to provide disability access, medical equipment and mobility aids, exercise and therapy equipment, communication aids, respite care and travel expenses.

Annual grant total

In 2015/16 the foundation held assets of £7.2 million and had an income of £1.7 million. More than £1 million was awarded to individuals: £470,000 through 117 applications for small and large grants from the grants programme, and £619,000 in case management (or benefits) framework grants to 24 individuals.

Exclusions

No grants are given for general household expenses such as food, clothing, utility bills or vehicle fuel costs.

Applications

Application forms for grants for essential needs may be downloaded from the website, along with guidance notes. Applications should include as much detail as possible, especially for amounts over £1,000. In most cases, applicants will be asked to provide at least one of the following pieces of information: a quote on business headed paper; a quote with a company signature included; a screenshot or web link to show the cost of the item required; or a receipt or invoice containing company details.

Grants should be applied for before any work is carried out or a purchase is made, although exceptions may be made in cases of emergency. The Team Administrator can be contacted for further clarification on this matter.

All applications will be acknowledged within five working days. Decisions on applications for amounts up to £20,000 will be made and the applicant informed within six to eight weeks. Applications for larger amounts (for over £20,000) can take around three months to process.

Contact by applicants to discuss any aspect of the application process is welcomed by the foundation. There is also a helpful FAQs section relating to the grants process on the website.

Applications for the Non-Catastrophic Injury (Non-CI) Grant Programme should be made via the individual's school or rugby club and are considered on a case-by-case basis. Individuals are advised to contact the IPF Team Administrator directly for more information.

Other information

The foundation supports injured rugby players and their families, as well as their clubs and team mates, with a range of immediate and long-term support. As part of its grants programme, the foundation also provides beneficiaries with the opportunity to experience match day hospitality in an adapted box at Twickenham.

The foundation also funds research into the causes and outcomes of serious injury, identifying the best ways to prevent and treat it and funds and informs the training of rugby coaches, players, referees and volunteers to protect players from serious injury.

The Welsh Rugby Charitable Trust

£185,500

Correspondent: Edward Jones, Hon. Secretary, 55 West Road, Bridgend CF31 4HQ (email: welshrugbycharitabletrust@gmail.com; website: www.wrct.org.uk)

CC number: 502079

Eligibility

People who have been severely injured while playing rugby union football in Wales, and their dependants.

Types of grants

One-off grants to help injured players regain their independence. Grants can be made towards cars, wheelchairs, hoists, domestic aids and gifts in summer (for a holiday break) and at Christmas.

Annual grant total

In 2015/16 the trust had assets of £3.78 million and an income of £414,000. Grants to individuals amounted to £185,500 and were distributed as follows:

Relief of injured players	£97,500
Summer grants	£63,000
Christmas gifts	£25,000

Applications

Apply in writing to the correspondent, including the circumstances of the injury and the effect it has had on the applicant's career. Information on the applicant's financial position before and after the accident should also be included. Applications are considered every two months (or sooner in emergency cases) and can be submitted either directly by the individual or by a club representative.

Players who have been seriously injured but do not have a permanent disability are usually visited by the trust to assess the degree of need before any grant is made.

Mental health

The Matthew Trust

£9,600

Correspondent: Annabel Thompson, Director, PO Box 604, London SW6 3AG (020 7736 5976; fax: 020 7731 6961; email: amt@matthewtrust.org; website: www.matthewtrust.org)

CC number: 294966

Eligibility

The trust is currently running four projects with the aims of: supporting children under 16 who have mental health problems; providing breaks for child carers; supporting young people aged 16 to 25 who have mental health problems; and enabling people with mental health problems who are over 60 through projects, with a view to promoting their inclusion in the wider community.

The priorities of the charity may change, so applicants are advised to consult the website before applying.

Types of grants

One-off grants of between £50 and £250 towards: counselling or medical bills; the provision of equipment and furniture to make a flat liveable; the provision of security equipment; and the provision of personal clothing items. The trust also helps with: second-chance learning and skills training; travel costs for prison visits; respite breaks; and debt support in special circumstances.

Annual grant total

In 2016/17 the trust had assets of £213,500 and an income of £35,000. During the year, the trust gave around £9,600 in grants to individuals.

Applications

Apply in writing to the correspondent through a professional agency such as a social worker, probation officer, community care worker or GP. The professional representative should also include their name and contact details in the application. Applications should include: the name, address, age and gender of the applicant; the health and age of other close family members; a summary of the mental health problem; the applicant's present circumstances; the type of support required, including costs where applicable; if the applicant has received support from the trust previously; and details of any other organisations that have been approached for support. Applications may be posted or emailed.

Note: The Matthew Trust is a 'last-stop' agency and will only consider applications when all other avenues of statutory and voluntary funding have been exhausted and then only where a care programme has been established.

The North Wales Psychiatric Fund

£7,100

Correspondent: Hilary Owen, Correspondent, Bryn Y Neuadd Hospital, Aber Road, Llanfairfechan, Gwynedd LL33 OHH (01248 682573)

CC number: 235783

Eligibility

People in North Wales who are mentally ill and are under the care of a social worker or health professional.

Types of grants

One-off grants for clothes, furniture, holidays and learning courses.

Annual grant total

In 2015 the charity had an income of £3,100 and a total expenditure of £7,300. We estimate that the charity gave around £7,100 in grants to individuals.

Exclusions

There are no grants available for the payment of debts.

Applications

Apply in writing to the correspondent through a social worker or health professional, including details of income and other possible grant sources. Applications are considered throughout the year.

Other specific conditions

The Nihal Armstrong Trust

£10,000

Correspondent: Rahil Gupta, Trustee, 111 Chatsworth Road, London NW2 4BH (020 8459 6527; email: info@nihalarmstrongtrust.org.uk; website: www.nihalarmstrongtrust.org.uk)

CC number: 1107567

Eligibility

Children living in the UK, up to and including the age of 18, with cerebral palsy. Applicants must be in receipt of means-tested benefits and be able to provide supporting evidence.

Types of grants

Grants of up to £1,000 towards equipment, communication aids or a particular service that will benefit children with cerebral palsy. Items/services must not be available from the local authority.

Annual grant total

In 2015/16 the trust had an income of £10,800 and a total expenditure of £11,000. We estimate that grants given to individuals for welfare purposes totalled around £10,000.

Exclusions

The trust does not fund holidays, refurbishment costs or household appliances. Grants are not available as part-funding for equipment or services that cost more than £1,000.

Applications

Applications can be made via the trust's website and must be supported by a doctor, school, social worker, health visitor, speech or occupational therapist or physiotherapist. The trustees meet three times a year, with application deadlines falling one week before each quarterly meeting. See the trust's website for specific dates.

The trustees prefer to receive applications via the website where possible. Individuals who are sending information on equipment/services or suppliers' estimates, can forward any documents to the address provided above. A short list of supporting documents required is available on the trust's website.

The trust's website also states that it will fund the basic model of the new iPad 2 and that the:

> Letter of evidence from a Speech and Language Therapist or Occupational Therapist or schoolteacher needs to state that the child has tried one and can use it. If you need a more advanced model, please ask the professional supporting your application to outline the reasons for it. Where possible parents applying for iPads should ask their child's school if they would order the iPad on their behalf. We will pay the school directly. This would help spread our money further as schools do not pay VAT.

ASPIRE (Association for Spinal Injury Research Rehabilitation and Reintegration)

£123,500

Correspondent: Kim Elliott, Grants Officer, ASPIRE National Training Centre, Wood Lane, Stanmore, Middlesex HA7 4AP (020 8420 6707; email: kim.elliott@aspire.org.uk; website: www.aspire.org.uk)

CC number: 1075317/SC037482

Eligibility

People in need who have a spinal cord injury. Applicants must be residing in the UK or Ireland, either as a UK or EU citizen, with definite leave to remain or with full refugee status. Priority is given to re-establishing independent mobility.

Types of grants

One-off grants to help towards the purchase of specialist equipment, such as wheelchairs, assistive technology, mobility aids and computers, to help them increase their level of independence. The charity states that it will rarely offer full funding, but will offer part funding and assistance with securing the remainder. Funding is given for essential items not upgrades or enhancement of existing property.

Annual grant total

In 2015/16 the charity held assets of £2.5 million and had an income of £3.6 million. Grants to individuals totalled £123,500.

Exclusions

Grants from the fund are solely for people with acquired non-progressive spinal cord injury. The charity states that it is unlikely to fund applications for:

- Holidays
- Vehicles
- House adaptations
- Passive exercise equipment
- Secondary functions on wheelchairs, including standing functions and cosmetic features, for reasons that could be met by other means

ASPIRE will not fund repairs, maintenance, insurance, replacement of parts or contracts for equipment, or equipment already purchased or ordered.

Second-hand equipment cannot be considered, except where it is sold through a reputable business and comes with a suitable warranty.

Only one application per applicant per five-year period is accepted, unless the previous provision is insufficient due to a change in medical circumstances.

The charity will not consider applications where statutory provision has not first been explored and exhausted.

Applications

Application forms are available from the charity's website. Each application requires a supporting statement: for medical equipment applications must be supported by an occupational therapist or medical consultant to explain why the specialist equipment is appropriate; for other equipment applications must be supported by a third party (check with the Human Needs Administrator as to the most appropriate individual to do this). The charity may request additional information or supporting evidence prior to considering an application. Completed applications will usually be considered within six weeks of receipt. Full guidelines are available on the website.

Other information

Aspire also provides a range of services for eligible individuals and has programmes in the areas of housing, independent living, sports development and assistive technology. It also established Aspire Law LLP which is the only law firm in the UK that deals exclusively with spinal cord injury claims. See the charity's informative website for a full list of its activities.

Bedford and District Cerebal Palsy Society

£3,500 (seven grants)

Correspondent: Jane Howard-White, CVS Mid and North Bedfordshire, 43 Bromham Road, Bedford MK40 2AA

CC number: 1156447

Eligibility

Individuals and families of those with cerebral palsy who are in need. Individuals must be resident within the Bedford district.

Types of grants

Grants for customised wheelchairs, second skins, splints, short residential breaks etc.

Annual grant total

In 2016/17 the society held assets of £418,500 and had an income of £225,500. During the year, the society gave grants of £500 each to seven individuals.

Applications

Applicants must contact the society by telephone or email in order to find out more about how to apply. The trustees meet quarterly to consider grants to individuals and families.

The Brittle Bone Society

£49,000

Correspondent: Patricia Osborne, Chief Executive, 30 Guthrie Street, Dundee DD1 5BS (01382 204446; email: bbs@brittlebone.org; website: www.brittlebone.org)

CC number: 272100

Eligibility

People with osteogenesis imperfecta (OI).

Types of grants

Grants are provided for manual and powered wheelchairs, trikes buggies and other types of equipment.

Annual grant total

In 2016/17 the society held assets of £395,500 and had an income of £240,000. Grants to individuals totalled £49,000, with £23,000 given for wheelchair purchases and repairs and £26,000 for welfare and equipment.

Exclusions

The society does not usually fund higher education, white goods or building works. Applications for retrospective funding are not accepted.

Applications

Application forms can be downloaded from the website or requested from the correspondent and should be completed and returned by post. Applications must be supported by a letter of support from a healthcare professional such as an occupational therapist or a physiotherapist.

Other information

The society also provides advice and support for people affected by osteogenesis imperfecta and works with children's medical institutions across the country.

Although the society does not offer advice on benefits rights directly, it can refer people seeking assistance to relevant organisations.

Chest Heart and Stroke Scotland

£286,500

Correspondent: Personal Grants Support Section, Third Floor, Roseberry House, 9 Haymarket Terrace, Edinburgh EH12 5EZ (0131 225 6963; email: webmaster@chss.org.uk; website: www.chss.org.uk)

OSCR number: SC018761

Eligibility

You could be eligible for a grant if:

- You are living in Scotland
- You are affected by an illness arising from a chest, heart or stroke condition
- You are struggling financially as a result of your illness
- You have someone who could act as a sponsor to support your application
- The item/service you wish to apply for would help with, or make a difference to your quality of life

Types of grants

Personal Support Grants to help with a variety of general and specific needs. Some examples of the type of items include, aids to daily living, adaptations, holidays, respite care, white goods, heating costs, telephone installation, driving lessons, clothing and travel costs. There are different grant limits for different grant purposes. For example, for standard grants the maximum amount that can be offered is £350, rising to £500 for travel costs or family holidays. There is a higher limit for aids to daily living of up to £750 and in exceptional circumstances, where a grant may enable a person to live independently rather than in care, funds of up to £2,000 can be considered.

Annual grant total

In 2016/17 the charity had assets of £7.6 million and an income of £11.58 billion. Grants to individuals for welfare purposes totalled £286,500.

Exclusions

The charity is unable to undertake ongoing costs or give retrospective grants. It also does not provide funding for nebulisers.

Applications

All applications are assessed by the Chest Heart and Stroke Welfare Committee on a regular basis. Applications must be made through a sponsor. This needs to be someone like a local authority social worker, a health professional employed by the NHS, or in some cases, a representative from a voluntary agency. Applications forms are only ever sent to the sponsor and successful grants can only be paid to the agency or organisation the sponsor represents. A section of the form also requires a short report from a GP or doctor to confirm relevant conditions. Applications for aids to daily living and adaptations must be sponsored by or include a report from an occupational therapist.

Crohn's and Colitis UK

£37,500

Correspondent: Julia Devereux, Support Grants Assistant, PO Box 334, St Albans AL1 2WA (0800 011 4701 or 0300 222 5700; email: support.grants@ crohnsandcolitis.org.uk; website: www. crohnsandcolitis.org.uk)

CC number: 1117148/SC038632

Eligibility

People in need who have Ulcerative Colitis, Crohn's Disease or related inflammatory bowel diseases (IBD). Candidates must have been resident in the UK for at least six months and be on a low income. Carers may also be supported.

Types of grants

One-off 'Personal Grants' of up to £500 are given to individuals for items or needs arising as a consequence of Crohn's or Colitis. Examples include: a washing machine or dryer; beds and bedding; a refrigerator; new clothing due to weight loss or gain; and a rehabilitation holiday in the UK.

Annual grant total

In 2016 the charity held assets of £3.6 million and had an income of almost £5 million. During the year, 236 grants were made for both educational and welfare purposes. We estimate that grants given to individuals for welfare purposes totalled around £37,500.

Exclusions

Recurring household bills or debts cannot be considered.

Applications

Application forms are available to download from the charity's website, along with guidance notes. The form has two extra sections, one of which should be completed by a doctor to confirm the individual's illness and one to be filled in by a social worker (or health visitor, district nurse, Citizens Advice advisor, or another 'professional person'). Full guidelines, application deadlines and eligibility criteria are available on the website.

Other information

Grants are also made for educational purposes and to institutions for research. Occasionally, local grants are made to hospitals. The main role of the association is to provide information and advice to people living with IBD. The information service can be contacted by calling 0300 222 5700 from 9am to 5pm on Monday, Tuesday, Wednesday and Friday, and 9am to 1pm on Thursday (except English bank holidays). Outside these hours, an answer phone service is available.

The Cystic Fibrosis Holiday Fund

£46,000 (132 grants)

Correspondent: Laurie Howard, Director, 1 Bell Street, London NW1 5BY (020 7616 1300; email: laurie@cfholidayfund.org.uk; website: www.cfholidayfund.org.uk)

CC number: 1088630

Eligibility

Children and young people up to the age of 25 who are diagnosed with cystic fibrosis, and their families.

Types of grants

Grants of around £350 towards enabling children with cystic fibrosis to go on holidays or short trips (this may also include the child's family).

Annual grant total

In 2016 the fund held assets of £62,500 and had an income of £104,000. Holiday grants totalled £46,000.

Exclusions

People who have received a grant within the previous two years cannot be assisted. The fund is usually unable to cover full costs and will not make retrospective grants (including where the trip takes place prior to the final grant approval).

Applications

Application forms can be downloaded from the fund's website, requested from the correspondent or completed online. A medical report form will be sent to applicants to be completed by their doctor/medical consultant. Applications are assessed by the fund's medical advisory panel which meets three times a year (see the website for the date of the next deadline or contact the correspondent).

Note: the approval procedure can take up to a few months so applicants should leave enough time before their proposed holiday when applying.

Cystic Fibrosis Trust

£186,000 (610 grants)

Correspondent: Welfare Team, 1 Aldgate, Second Floor, London EC3N 1RE (020 3795 2184; email: helpline@cysticfibrosis.org.uk; website: www.cysticfibrosis.org.uk)

CC number: 1079049

Eligibility

People in need who have cystic fibrosis.

Types of grants

The trust offers one-off emergency grants and health and well-being grants. According to the trust's website, emergency grants are given for the following purposes:

▶ Transplant grants: up to £250 to cover travel and related costs for people having a transplant or transplant assessment
▶ Small grants: up to £150 to cover emergency needs such as essential smaller cost items, emergency household repairs or unexpected travel costs
▶ Funeral grants of £750

Health and well-being grants, typically between £250 and £350, are awarded for the purchase of items which could improve health and quality of life, such as exercise equipment, white goods, furniture for a new home or gym fees.

The trust also makes holiday grants usually between £200 and £300 for people aged 18 and over who have cystic fibrosis – see the entry for the Cystic Fibrosis Holiday Fund for more information.

Annual grant total

In 2015/16 the trust held assets of £10.7 million and had an income of £11.3 million. A total of £186,000 was awarded in grants to 610 individuals. The annual report provides the following breakdown:

Funeral grants	85	£64,000
Health and well-being	248	£63,000
Emergency grants	139	£19,000
Transplant grants	24	£6,000

Through other programmes the trust awarded £44,000 in education grants, £28,000 through holiday grants and £7,000 in homecare grants.

Exclusions

Grants are not awarded for nebulisers, computers, cars, driving lessons, major home improvements, debts or to meet ongoing costs.

Applications

Application forms are available from the correspondent or can be downloaded from the website. Applications must be supported by a social worker or other professional and should state whether the applicant has applied to other charities and the outcome, and include details of the applicant's general financial circumstances, the cost of the services or goods required and the reason for the application. Individuals or their health professionals can contact the trust for assistance before submitting an application.

Further application guidelines are provided on the trust's website.

Other information

The trust also provides confidential advice, support and information on all aspects of cystic fibrosis in the form of factsheets and a dedicated helpline which can provide advice and support on a range of issues, including help with financial issues (020 3795 2184).

The Dystonia Society

£400

Correspondent: The Grants Administrator, The Dystonia Society, 1st Floor, 89 Albert Embankment, London SE1 7TP (02077933656; email: info@ dystonia.org.uk; website: www.dystonia. org.uk)

CC number: 1062595

Eligibility

People living with or affected by dystonia in the UK.

Types of grants

One-off and recurrent grants are given according to need. Grants do not usually exceed £300, except in special circumstances.

Annual grant total

In 2015/16 the charity had assets of £309,000 and an income of £465,000. The charity awarded just over £400 in grants to individuals.

Exclusions

Grants are not made for medical treatment or other therapies, or for items or services available from the NHS.

Applications

Our research suggests that applications can be made on a form available from the correspondent. They must be endorsed by a health or social care professional who has known the applicant for at least two years.

Other information

Note that the majority of the society's funds are spent on service provision. Grants are also made to organisations for research purposes.

The Haemophilia Society (The Tanner Fund)

£2,000

Correspondent: Liz Carroll, Chief Executive, Wilcox House, 140–148 Borough High Street, London SE1 1LB (020 7939 0784; email: info@ haemophilia.org.uk; website: www. haemophilia.org.uk)

CC number: 288260

Eligibility

People with haemophilia and related bleeding disorders, and their families.

Types of grants

One-off hardship grants of up to £200 for items relating to applicants' medical problems, such as bedding, fridges to store treatment, floor coverings and washing machines.

Annual grant total

In 2015/16 the society held assets of £860,500 and had an income of £645,500. Grants were made to individuals through the Tanner Fund and totalled £2,000.

Exclusions

No grants are given for debts, holidays, motor vehicles or ongoing bills such as gas or electricity.

Applications

Applications can be made on a form available from the correspondent. Applications must be completed in conjunction with a medical professional or a social worker. They are considered as received.

Note: each family may only make one application a year.

Other information

The society, founded in 1950, is the UK's 'only national independent charity for all people affected by bleeding disorders', with centres across the country. The organisation's central activities include the provision of information, advocacy with the government and the NHS, as well as providing support to sufferers of bleeding disorders in making informed decisions regarding treatment.

The Ben Hardwick Fund

£15,000

Correspondent: Anne Auber, 12 Nassau Road, Barnes, London SW13 9QE (020 8741 8499)

CC number: 1062554

Eligibility

Children with primary liver disease, and their families, who are in need.

Types of grants

One-off and recurrent grants to help with costs which are the direct result of the child's illness, such as hospital travel costs, in-hospital expenses, telephone bills and childminding for other children left at home.

Annual grant total

In 2016/17 the fund had an income of £2,400 and a total expenditure of £26,000. We estimate that grants given to individuals totalled £15,000, with funding also awarded to organisations.

Applications

Apply in writing to the correspondent, usually through a hospital social worker or other welfare professional. Applications are considered at any time.

Headway Emergency Fund

£50,500 (232 grants)

Correspondent: The Fund Administrator, Unit 1, College Fields Business Centre, 16 Prince George's Road, London SW19 2PT (020 8640 8413; email: emergencyfund@headway. org.uk; website: www.headway.org.uk/ supporting-you/headway-emergency-fund)

CC number: 1025852/SC039992

Eligibility

Families and individuals coping with the practical implications of a sudden and catastrophic brain injury. Applicants should have less than £1,000 in savings.

Types of grants

Grants of up to £500 are available to help people with the financial implications of sudden, acute brain injury. This may include the cost of travel to visit relatives in hospital or rehabilitation, emergency accommodation, additional costs in the immediate aftermath of the injury or breaks for carers (normally at a cottage in Yorkshire that Headway has access to).

Annual grant total

In 2016 the fund gave grants totalling £50,500 to 232 families.

Exclusions

Support cannot be given outside the UK.

The following are excluded:

- Taxi journeys
- Food
- Debts
- Rent deposits
- Utility bills
- Everyday household expenses

Applications

Application forms can be completed online or downloaded and returned to the correspondent once completed. Only one application per survivor of a brain injury can be considered.

Other information

Headway offers a range of services to people affected by a brain injury. There is a freephone helpline available (tel: 0808 800 2244; email: helpline@headway. org.uk).

The Family Emergency Fund is supported by the Stewarts Law Foundation.

Huntington's Disease Association

£11,000 (39 grants)

Correspondent: Specialist Huntington's Disease Advisory Service, Suite 24, Liverpool Science Park IC1, 131 Mount Pleasant, Liverpool L3 5TF (0151 331 5444; email: info@hda.org.uk; website: www.hda.org.uk)

CC number: 296453

Eligibility

People with Huntington's disease, their immediate families and those at risk, who live in England or Wales.

Types of grants

One-off grants to contribute towards the costs of specialist chairs, aromatherapy sessions, clothing, furniture, domestic equipment (e.g. washing machines and cookers) and so on.

Annual grant total

In 2016/17 the association held assets of £1 million and had an income of £1.5 million. Expenditure on welfare grants to individuals varies each year, and in 2016/17 totalled over £11,000.

Exclusions

No grants are given towards equipment or services that should be provided by statutory services. Support will not be given for the payment of debts, loans, bills, funeral expenses, holidays or travel.

Applications

Grants are made through the Specialist Huntington's Disease Advisory Service (SHDA), which can offer financial advice and co-ordinate support on your behalf. Contact details for local areas can be found on the website.

The British Kidney Patient Association

£783,500

Correspondent: Fiona Armitage, 3 The Windmills, St Mary's Close, Turk Street, Alton GU34 1EF (01420 541424; fax: 01420 89438; email: info@britishkidney-pa.co.uk; website: www.britishkidney-pa.co.uk)

CC number: 270288

Eligibility

Dialysis patients and their families who are on low incomes. Also, other patients, including transplant patients and those receiving conservative care, if their health and quality of life is being seriously affected by their renal condition.

Types of grants

Help can be given with the costs of domestic bills such as car insurance and tax, heating costs, telephone installations and TV licences, as well as with the purchase of domestic goods like washing machines and carpets.

If an individual cannot recover the costs of travel to their local hospital through their kidney unit, the association may be able to help if they have to visit regularly and have to travel a long way,

The association also gives grants to individuals and families towards the costs of a basic holiday in the UK or abroad. If the cost for a holiday is modest, a grant can be used to cover the entire amount, or for more considerable amounts, can be given as a contribution towards the total.

Annual grant total

In 2016 the association had assets of £33.9 million and an income of £1.8 million. Grants awarded through Patient Aid totalled £802,500. Of this amount, £783,500 was awarded to individuals for social welfare purposes.

The rest was awarded to individuals for educational purposes.

Exclusions

Grants are not made: to reimburse patients for bills already paid; for telephone bills, court fines, home improvements, the repayment of credit cards or loans, medical equipment, or council tax payments; or to help with the costs of getting ongoing dialysis. The guidelines also note: 'Whilst we don't pay for dialysis when on holiday either in the UK or abroad, it is free in European Community countries at centres which accept the European Health Insurance Card (EHIC).'

Applications

Application forms, along with guidelines, are available to download from the association's website. The form must be submitted by a renal social worker or a member of the patient's renal team, who must sign the form and attach a detailed social report on the hospital's headed paper.

Other information

The trust makes grants to hospitals and, as part of its work, supports the Ronald McDonald Houses at children's hospitals in Liverpool (Alder Hey), Birmingham, Bristol, London (Evelina Children's Hospital), Manchester and Glasgow (Royal Hospital for Sick Children, Yorkhill), which provide support for the families of young renal patients attending the units at these hospitals.

It also funds non-laboratory research and provides support services, information and advice to kidney patients, among other projects.

The Kingston Trust

£39,000 (94 grants)

Correspondent: Secretary, PO Box 6457, Basingstoke, Hampshire RG24 8LG (01256 352320; email: secretary@kingstontrust.org.uk)

CC number: 205591

Eligibility

Older ileostomists (over the age of 50) living in the UK and Ireland who are in need.

Types of grants

The trust can assist with a wide range of needs, including: beds and bedding; cookers; washing machines; bathroom modifications; home maintenance; mobility aids; and convalescent breaks.

Annual grant total

In 2016/17 the trust had assets of £2.5 million and an income of £78,500. Grants totalling £39,000 were paid to 94 individuals and included 28 Christmas box payments of £100 each.

Applications

Application forms are available to download from the website or from the correspondent. The form should be fully completed and include a financial summary page. If appropriate, two estimates should be supplied to support the amount requested. The doctor or stoma care nurse of first-time applicants will be required to verify details provided on the application form, particularly the applicant's date of birth and that they have had an ileostomy. The trustees aim to inform applicants of their decision as soon as possible.

Other information

The trust is registered as The Kingston Old Peoples Home Fund for Ileostomists.

Meningitis Now (formerly known as Meningitis Trust)

£71,500

Correspondent: Dr Tom Nutt, Chief Executive Officer, Fern House, Bath Road, Stroud GL5 3TJ (01453 768000; fax: 01453 768001; email: info@meningitisnow.org; website: www.meningitisnow.org)

CC number: 803016/SC037790

Eligibility

People in need who have meningitis or who have disabilities as a result of meningitis and reside in the UK.

Types of grants

Funding is given as part of the charity's service to help people to rebuild their lives following meningitis. Support can be given for counselling and creative and complementary therapy services, as well as for unexpected expenditure, such as home adaptations and equipment. Support can also be given with expenses relating to funerals.

Annual grant total

In 2016/17 the charity had assets of £939,500 and an income of £3.2 million. Grants to individuals totalled £143,000. We estimate that social welfare grants amounted to around £71,500.

Exclusions

Our previous research has found that support may not be given for: services or items which should normally be supplied by a statutory body, e.g. NHS or local authority; home adaptations on rented property; holidays; payment of domestic bills; arrears, e.g. mortgage payments; bedding, furniture or clothing; domestic appliances; or swimming pools.

Applications

Application forms for support with funeral expenses are available from the website. More information on eligibility criteria and how to apply for other support can be obtained by calling the Meningitis Helpline (0808 801 0388) or by emailing (helpline@meningitisnow.org).

Other information

Meningitis Now was formed following the merger of Meningitis Trust and Meningitis UK. The charity provides a wide range of information, advice and support for people affected by meningitis, as well as promoting meningitis awareness and education to the general public.

The Motor Neurone Disease Association

£940,000

Correspondent: Support Services, Support Services, MND Association, David Niven House, 10–15 Notre Dame Mews, Northampton NN1 2BG (01604 611802; email: support.services@mndassociation.org; website: www.mndassociation.org)

CC number: 294354

Eligibility

People with motor neurone disease, living in England, Wales and Northern Ireland.

Types of grants

The charity offers a range of grants including those for mobility aids, adaptations to buildings, holidays, advice and counselling. Potential applicants are advised to visit the charity's website and read through the MND Support Grant Guidance and Process information.

Annual grant total

In 2015/16 the charity had assets of over £10 million and an income of £16.6 million. During the year, the charity gave £940,000 in grants to individuals.

Grants and donations to institutions totalled around £11.9 million.

Exclusions

Retrospective funding in excess of three months and without prior agreement with the Support Services team; funeral and legal costs; emergency healthcare needs; equipment for assessment.

Applications

Application forms are available from the website. Applications must be submitted through a health or social care professional. In addition to stating what is requested, applications should include details of why the need is not met by statutory sources and where any payments should be made.

Other information

The charity has a network of association branches which can offer information about the grants available. Further information is available on its website.

Multiple Sclerosis Society

£1.48 million

Correspondent: The Grants Team, MS National Centre, 372 Edgware Road, Cricklewood, London NW2 6ND (020 8438 0700; fax: 020 8438 0701; email: grants@mssociety.org.uk; website: www.mssociety.org.uk)

CC number: 1139257

Eligibility

People with multiple sclerosis and their families and carers living in the UK. People living in Scotland or Northern Ireland may be subject to other conditions, contact MS Society Scotland (0131 335 4050) or MS Society Northern Ireland (028 9080 2802) for full details.

You can apply for a health and well-being grant if you have not had a grant from the MS Society in the last 12 months.

Types of grants

Health and well-being grants are available for items and activities that will have a significant positive impact on the individual's life, which includes everything from holidays and car adaptations to wheelchairs and exercise equipment.

Carers' grants can help fund activities that give unpaid carers a chance to relax or learn new skills.

Annual grant total

In 2016 the charity had assets of £17.3 million and an income of £1.4 million. During the year, the charity gave a total of almost £1.48 million in grants to individuals.

The charity also gave £4.67 million in grants to organisations.

Exclusions

Applicants with more than £16,000 in savings are not eligible for regular grants and those with more than £8,000 in savings are expected to contribute towards the cost of the item.

Grants cannot be made:

- Retrospectively, for purchases already made
- For any ongoing or long-term financial commitments (such as living costs and bills)
- For loans, debt assistance or legal fees (except for bankruptcy or Debt Relief Order fees)
- Towards paying for treatments
- To people who have received a grant from the individual support grant fund within the last two years
- To people who have received a grant from the short breaks and activities fund within the last one year

Statutory sources should be exhausted prior to applying to the society.

Further guidance on each of the grants programmes is given on the website.

Applications

Application forms are available to download from the website, or can be obtained from the correspondent or a local MS Society branch.

Applicants should send their completed forms by post or email to the correspondent. If there is a local branch in the applicant's area, their form will be sent on from the head office to the local branch. If the branch cannot give you a grant for the full amount, and the applicant is not able to make up the difference, it may send the application to the grants teams in London or Edinburgh to consider a top-up grant. The teams can also advise on other sources of funding that may be available.

Supporting information from a health and social care professional and evidence of financial circumstances will be required. The website notes that you should allow at least eight weeks for a decision to be made.

Other information

The society has a freephone helpline (tel: 0808 800 8000; email: helpline@

mssociety.org.uk), free information booklets on all aspects of living with MS for people with, and affected by, MS and a network of branches, manned by volunteers, across the UK offering local support to people with MS.

The Joe Noakes Charitable Trust

£1,500

Correspondent: Nina Noakes, Hampton House, The Street, Blo Norton, Diss IP22 2JB (01953 688127; email: nina@ joenoakestrust.org; website: www. thejoenoakestrust.org)

CC number: 1153550

Eligibility

Families applying for grants should have a combined household income of less than £45,000 per year and the child must be under the age of 5. Only people from the East Anglian region (Norfolk, Suffolk, Essex, and Cambridge) can apply.

Types of grants

Funding is available to cover the costs of applied behavioural analysis, a type of specialist therapy for children with autism.

Grant awards will only cover the cost of therapy for one year. During this time, parents are expected to use the data collected to apply for local authority funding. Applications to the trust may be repeated annually.

Annual grant total

In 2015/16 the trust had an income of £5,000 and a total expenditure of £2,000. We estimate that the trust awarded £1,500 in grants for health and welfare.

Applications

Potential applicants should email the trust, detailing their situation. If eligible, the trust will provide an application form. Completed application forms should be submitted together with the following:

- A covering letter
- A professional reference
- The child's diagnosis including all current statements, reports, etc.
- Bank statements including mortgage, overdrafts, credit card statements, etc.
- Proof of income, investments, social security benefits, maintenance payments, and child support maintenance
- Details of other commitments, e.g. council tax, water rates, utility bills, interest on loans, food, clothing, car payments, holiday costs, etc.

Applications can be repeated annually.

Other information

The charity was founded after the parents of Joe, a severely autistic child who could not walk or talk, discovered Applied Behavioural Analysis, which is a type of early intervention autism therapy. It is currently not funded by the NHS or local education authorities, so Joe's parents set up the charity to help other parents provide support for their children.

Parkinson's UK

£3,000

Correspondent: Sarah Day, Company Secretary, 215 Vauxhall Bridge Road, London SW1V 1EJ (020 7932 1327; email: hello@parkinsons.org.uk; website: www.parkinsons.org.uk)

CC number: 258197

Eligibility

People with Parkinson's disease who are in need. From May 2015, the scheme has been suspended for a review. The Parkinson's UK website states that:

> Our previous model of offering funding didn't reach out to everyone who needed help.
>
> We couldn't promote the fund as widely as we'd like as we didn't want to encourage levels of demand that couldn't be met within the funding available.
>
> We aim to do better and do more in providing financial help.
>
> We also want to consider how we can best harness the potential in our local networks. Any new arrangements need to be fair, transparent and support those people in the most need.
>
> We'll be developing new arrangements in 2016.

Types of grants

The charity previously gave one-off grants to people with Parkinson's through the Mali Jenkins Fund, for purposes such as equipment, home adaptations, respite breaks, professional fees, domestic appliances and other household goods.

Annual grant total

In 2016 Parkinson's UK held assets of £17.9 million and had an income of £32.86 million. During the year, the charity awarded grants totalling £3,000 to individuals.

Applications

Applicants should initially contact the charity to find out what support is available to them.

Other information

In previous years, eligible individuals could apply to The Parkinson's UK Mali Jenkins Fund; however, it has been suspended while the charity explores alternative options for financial assistance for people affected by Parkinson's and to put new arrangements in place.

Joseph Patrick Trust

£274,500 (231 grants)

Correspondent: Robert Meadowcroft, Correspondent, c/o Muscular Dystropy Group of Great Britain and Northern Ireland, 61A Southwark Street, London SE1 0BU (020 7803 4800; email: jptgrants@muscular-dystrophy.org; website: www.musculardystrophyuk.org/ get-the-right-care-and-support/ equipment-grants/jpt-grants)

CC number: 294475

Eligibility

People with muscular dystrophy or an allied neuromuscular condition.

Types of grants

On average about 150 one-off grants of between £200 and £1,250 are made each year to partially fund the purchase of wheelchairs (powered and manual), scooters, electric beds, trikes, computers, vehicle adaptations, riser chairs, mobile arm supports, portable aids, therapy equipment and so on. Discretionary payments can be made for funeral expenses and other emergencies.

Annual grant total

In 2016/17 the trust had assets of £237,000 and a total expenditure of £291,600. During the year, the trust awarded 231 grants totalling around £274,500. Of this amount, 161 grants were for adults and 70 awards for children. The breakdown of the grants was as shown:

Electric wheelchair	£93,300
Assistive technology	£27,500
Sports wheelchair	£27,500
Scooter	£24,700
Wheelchair adaptations	£22,000
Beds etc.	£11,000
Chairs etc.	£11,000
Portable aids	£11,000
Computer	£8,200
Discretionary grant	£8,200
Mobile arm supports	£8,200
Manual wheelchair	£5,500
Therapy equipment	£5,500
Trikes	£5,500
Vehicle adaptations	£5,500

Exclusions

Grants are not given for: holidays, household adaptations, building works or domestic appliances; equipment which has already been bought; recurring costs (e.g. wheelchair repairs); the purchase or lease of vehicles, vehicle deposits, maintenance or repair of vehicles. No grants outside the UK.

Applications

Application forms are available from the correspondent or to download from the website. Applications can also be completed online but supporting documentation should be sent to the trust by post.

Completed forms can be submitted directly by the individual or by a third party and should be supported by an assessment and quotation for the equipment requested, confirming the need and suitability of the equipment. The assessment must be carried out by an appropriately qualified professional, such as a physiotherapist, occupational therapist, social worker, etc. The assessment must be on headed paper. For guidance on what to include in the assessment check the trust's website.

Applications are considered six times a year. Grants are only be made payable to the supplier.

The British Polio Fellowship

£54,000

Correspondent: The Support Services Team, Unit 6, The Xchange, Wilmington Close, Watford WD18 0FQ (0800 043 1935; email: info@britishpolio.org.uk; website: www.britishpolio.org.uk)

CC number: 1108335/SC038863

Eligibility

People in need who have been affected by poliomyelitis (polio) and post-polio programme and live in the UK. Carers, families and healthcare professionals may also be assisted. Only members of the fellowship may apply for assistance.

Types of grants

Welfare grants – are given for disability-related equipment, such as scooters, electric or manual wheelchairs, riser/recliner chairs, specialised clothing and footwear and specialist beds and mattresses. Household aids and equipment to enable independence and home as well as car adaptations can also be supported. Assistance may occasionally be given for essential home improvement and crisis prevention.

Heating grants – are made annually to members on a low income who are too young to qualify for the Government' Winter Fuel Payment to help with heating costs.

Annual grant total

In 2015 the fellowship held assets of £2.8 million and had an income of £697,500. Grants to individuals totalled £54,000.

Exclusions

Grants are not given to non-members, or towards hospital expenses, household bills or home carers. Statutory sources must have been exhausted before an application is made to the fellowship, as financial support will not be made to substitute statutory help.

Applications

Welfare and heating grant forms are available from the correspondent or a local branch welfare officer. Applications should be submitted by the individual or by an appropriate third party on their behalf and include a medical certificate or doctor's note stating polio-disability. Welfare applications are considered throughout the year. Heating grants are awarded once a year in the autumn.

Holiday grant forms are available from the correspondent or by emailing Rosalind Evans at rosalindevans@ britishpolio.org.uk. They are assessed on a bi-monthly basis.

Other information

The fellowship has over 50 local branches and there is a range of information and support services offered to people affected by polio and post-polio syndrome (some, including grants, are only accessible to members).

Pulmonary Fibrosis Trust

£35,500

Correspondent: The Trustees, c/o E.B.S, Unit E1, City Wharf, Davidson Road, Lichfield, Staffordshire WS14 9DZ (01543 442191; email: info@ pulmonaryfibrosistrust.org; website: www.pulmonaryfibrosistrust.org)

CC number: 1149901

Eligibility

People living with pulmonary fibrosis or their carers.

Types of grants

One-off grants towards medical equipment such as portable oxygen concentrators, stairlifts, mobility scooters and travel expenses for transplant assessment.

Annual grant total

In 2016 the trust held assets of £193,000 and had an income of £76,500. We estimate that grants given to individuals totalled £35,500.

Applications

There is a short application form available to complete on the trust's website.

Other information

The trust also provides a dedicated phone line for those requiring counselling or emotional support and guidance (tel: 01543 442191).

The trust has recently partnered with Haven to help beneficiaries save up to 10% on holidays. To claim this discount or find out more, call Haven on 0333 202 5423 and quote CH_PFTRUST.

Spinal Muscular Atrophy Support UK

£10,000

Correspondent: Doug Henderson, The Jennifer Trust for Spinal Muscular Atrophy, 40 Timothy's Bridge Road, Stratford Enterprise Park, Stratford-upon-Avon CV37 9NW (01789 267520; fax: 01789 268371; email: office@smasupportuk.org.uk; website: www.smasupportuk.org.uk)

CC number: 1106815

Eligibility

Individuals diagnosed with any form of Spinal Muscular Atrophy.

Note: the charity cannot give grants to people with any other condition.

Types of grants

One-off grants for equipment to assist with every day life, such as home adaptions and mobility aids. The charity also provides multisensory toy boxes to children who have been diagnosed. Grants are typically £200 to £300.

Annual grant total

In 2016 the charity had assets of £123,500 and an income of £105,500. Welfare and equipment grants usually total around £10,000 per year.

Applications

Contact the charity for further information.

Other information

Individual financial grants are only one of the many ways in which the charity provides support. For more information, contact the charity or visit the website.

Stroke Association

£286,000 (1,107 grants)

Correspondent: Life After Stroke Services, Stroke Association House, 240 City Road, London EC1V 2PR (0303 3033 100; fax: 020 7490 2686; email: grants.external@stroke.org.uk; website: www.stroke.org.uk)

CC number: 211015

Eligibility

People who have had a stroke and are in need. Applicants must have less than £3,000 in savings and their income must not exceed their expenditure by more than £50.

Types of grants

One-off grants of up to £300 to help improve the individual's quality of life. Grants are available towards: specialised respite care or family holidays within the UK; white goods; cooking equipment; energy bills (but not arrears); installation of telephones or other telecommunications; beds and bedding; medical or disability aids; armchairs; driving assessments or lessons; and travel costs for, for example, hospital visits.

Annual grant total

In 2016/17 the charity held assets of £24.3 million and had an income of £37.3 million. According to the charity's impact report for 2016/17, grants totalling £286,000 were given to 1,107 individuals under the Life After Stroke programme.

Exclusions

The charity will not fund: private medical costs; labour costs (other than the installation of white goods) including item removal and structural alteration costs; nursing home fees (other than respite care); computer equipment or televisions; debts; or rent or bills arrears.

Applications

In the first instance, contact the charity by email (grants.external@stroke.org.uk) or call the helpline (0303 3033 100) to find out how to apply for a grant. Contact can be made directly by the individual or by a health, social care or other professional on their behalf. The individual's postcode and name should be provided.

Individuals who are receiving one of the charity's Life After Stroke Services can, alternatively, ask their co-ordinator for further information. All grants are means-tested.

Other information

The charity's website states:

> We were selected as Royal Mail's Charity of the Year in 2014, and we worked in partnership with the company for over two years. In March 2017 we were able to announce that £2 million had been raised to help stroke survivors.

> Every penny raised through the partnership is funding our Life After Stroke Grants, supporting up to 10,000 families as they build a life after stroke.

Strongbones Children's Charitable Trust

£100,500

Correspondent: The Trustees, Unit B9 Romford Seedbed Centre, Davidson Way, Romford RM7 0AZ (01708 750599; email: Trustees@strongbones.org.uk; website: www.strongbones.org.uk)

CC number: 1086173

Eligibility

Young people under the age of 21 with scoliosis, brittle bone disease, bone cancer, arthritis or any other condition of the bone.

Types of grants

Grants are available for disability equipment, manual wheelchairs, smart home technology, supportive seating and trikes. Up to a maximum of 70% of the cost of equipment will be provided.

Annual grant total

In 2016/17 the trust held assets of £24,000 and had an income of £257,000. Grants to individuals totalled £100,500.

Exclusions

Laptops/computers; spas/baths; driving lessons; debts/bills; Disabled Facilities Grant top-ups; household appliances and furniture; holidays; clothing; days out (except group trips); electric wheelchairs; iPads; game consoles; sensory equipment; garden and bedroom makeovers.

Applications

Applicants may apply using the trust's online application form. Applications should include details of the child's condition and why a grant is needed. The trust also requires that forms are signed and accompanied by a cover letter from the child's NHS consultant, physiotherapist, GP, school nurse or social worker. Applications for funding over £1,000 should be accompanied by a quote. Decisions can take up to three months. Families can only receive one grant in any 12-month period and unsuccessful applicants may reapply at a later date.

Other information

The trust also owns homes which it uses to provide respite holidays for children and their families. Information on these homes and the trust's activities is available on its website.

Tourettes Action

Correspondent: Tourettes Action Grants, The Meads Business Centre, 19 Kingsmead, Farnborough, Hampshire GU14 7SR (0300 777 8427 (helpdesk); email: (contact form on website); website: www.tourettes-action.org.uk)

CC number: 1003317

Eligibility

People with Tourette's Syndrome living in the UK.

All applications are considered, but the charity is unlikely to help applicants whose annual household income exceeds £40,000 or whose household savings exceed £8,000.

Types of grants

One-off grants of up to £500 are given for equipment that supports individuals with TS in day-to-day life. Past examples include: instruments for people whose tics reduce when playing music; electronic pens to help students take notes at school; and beds for people whose tics are so violent that normal beds break. The charity can be contacted to discuss the eligibility of particular items.

Annual grant total

A small amount is given in grants each year.

Exclusions

The charity cannot fund:

- Home improvements, e.g. paint, conservatories, carpets or other flooring (special items which are needed because of TS but not for a medical reason may be considered)
- Household items, e.g. vacuum cleaners, washing machines, wardrobes, or standard beds or chairs (special furniture needed because of TS but not for a medical reason may be considered)
- Therapies or alternative treatments
- Educational activities, e.g. home tutors or standard teaching materials
- Activities or holidays

The charity is unlikely to fund computer equipment but will consider specialist peripherals to assist individuals with TS to make the best use of existing computer equipment.

Successful applicants cannot apply within five years of receiving a grant.

Applications

Application forms are available to download from the website. Completed forms should be returned to the charity by post, along with supporting documentation. Applicants who would prefer a paper application form can request one by email (alison@tourettes-action.org.uk) or by calling the helpdesk (0300 777 8427). Larger print copies are also available.

The Tuberous Sclerosis Association

£9,100

Correspondent: TSA Support Fund, CAN Mezzanine, 32–36 Loman Street, London SE1 0EH (email: admin@ tuberous-sclerosis.org; website: www. tuberous-sclerosis.org)

CC number: 1039549

Eligibility

People in need who have tuberous sclerosis complex (TSC) and their parents and carers.

Types of grants

Grants of up to £250 are administered through the TSA Support Fund and can be given to help with: home adaptations; household essentials such as washing machines, carpets and flooring; short holidays with family, family visits or days out; or a holiday for a carer. The fund can also help with travel costs for those wishing to attend TSA events or for those needing to attend TSC clinics.

Four times a year, the charity awards the Janet Medcalf Award, which gives £300 to enrich the life of an individual with tuberous sclerosis complex.

Annual grant total

In 2015/16 grants from the benevolent fund totalled £9,100.

Exclusions

Support cannot be given for: items which are the responsibility of a statutory authority; items that have already been paid for, booked or ordered; any ongoing or long-term costs, including living costs and bills; or costs associated with debt.

Applications

Application forms and monitoring forms are available from the website. Applications should include evidence (photocopies) of any benefits you receive and quotes for the item(s) you wish to purchase.

Individuals living in England, Northern Ireland or Wales should return their forms to: TSA Support Fund, CAN Mezzanine, 32–36 Loman Street, London SE1 0EH. Applicants in Scotland should return theirs to: TSA Support Fund, PO Box 8728, Airdrie.

Applicants will be contacted within three weeks of receipt of their application and a reference from a health/social care or education professional may be requested. The charity aims to notify applicants of a decision within six weeks of receipt. Unsuccessful applicants will be informed of the reasons why and be able to submit another request.

Janet Medcalf Award – Applications can be made using the online form on the website. One successful application is chosen quarterly, in March, June, September and December.

Other information

As well as providing a range of support for people affected by tuberous sclerosis complex, the charity provides education and information about, and funds research into, the condition. More information is available from the charity's informative website.

Visual impairment

The Christina Aitchison Trust

£500

Correspondent: Revd Roger Massingberd-Mundy, Trustee, The Old Post Office, The Street, West Raynham, Fakenham NR21 7AD

CC number: 1041578

Eligibility

People who are blind or have any ophthalmic disease or disability, and people who have a terminal illness who are in need. Some preference may be given to individuals in the north east or south west of England.

Types of grants

One-off and recurrent grants to relieve blindness, ophthalmic disease or disability, and terminal illness.

Annual grant total

In 2016/17 the trust had an income of £1,800 and a total expenditure of £2,400. We estimate that welfare grants to individuals totalled around £500.

Applications

Application forms are available from the correspondent and should generally be submitted in March or September for consideration in April or November.

Other information

Grants are also given to individuals for educational needs and to organisations.

Blind Children UK

£204,000

Correspondent: Phillippa Caine, Association Secretary, Hillfields, Reading Road, Burghfield Common, Reading RG7 3YG (0800 781 1444; email: cypservices@guidedogs.org.uk or phillippa.caine@guidedogs.org.uk; website: www.blindchildrenuk.org)

CC number: 1051607

Eligibility

Children and young people aged up to 18 years in full-time education who are (or are eligible to be) registered blind or partially sighted and live in the UK.

Types of grants

One-off grants towards IT equipment or sensory/recreational equipment for use in the home or at school to aid with the individual's learning and development. This can include computer equipment and software, screen readers or magnifiers, braille devices, multisensory toys, resonance boards and so on. While there is no minimum or maximum amount available per application, only one item per applicant will be considered.

Annual grant total

In 2015 the charity had assets of £6.4 million and an income of £11.2 million. Grants were made through the Access Technology programme and totalled £204,000. The charity received 107 applications for equipment and software and 265 referrals for the programme during the year, but we were unable to determine how many grants were made.

Exclusions

The charity will not fund the following:

- Travel costs
- Respite care
- Activity/family holidays
- Childcare
- Mobile phones including iPhones
- Funds towards maintenance, insurance and extended warranties
- White goods
- TVs
- Items for which there is statutory funding

Applications

In the first instance, contact the charity to discuss the child's needs. The Access Technology advisors can carry out a technology assessment over the phone, to help children and young people and their families to choose the right technology for their needs. The charity requires a minimum 10% contribution towards the total cost of the items including VAT, should the application be successful. A qualified visual impairment professional must support all grant applications. Equipment and software must be for home use only. A detailed breakdown of the criteria and application process is available on The Guide Dogs for the Blind Association's website.

Other information

The charity offers a range of support, advice and services for children and young people with visual impairments and their families. In January 2017, the charity integrated with The Guide Dogs for the Blind Association but still carries out the same services and programmes.

Blind Veterans UK

£2.2 million

Correspondent: Membership Department, 12–14 Harcourt Street, London W1H 4HD (0800 389 7979; email: enquiries@blindveterans.org.uk; website: www.blindveterans.org.uk)

CC number: 216227

Eligibility

Eligibility for membership takes into account both military service and sight loss:

- All applicants must have served at any time in the regular or reserve UK Armed Forces (including National Service), or in the Merchant Navy during World War Two, or in the Polish/Indian Forces under British command
- The trust uses its own criteria for the level of sight loss required to receive help and the charity's doctors will assess this. The website advises that 'it doesn't matter how or when your sight loss was caused, or whether you were on active service at the time'

Types of grants

Grants are given to allow applicants to develop their independence through a combination of training, rehabilitation, holiday and respite care. The charity will also help with retraining and employability issues.

Annual grant total

In 2015/16 the charity held assets of over £150 million and had an income of £27.6 million. A total of about £27.5 million was spent in charitable activities, of which £2.2 million was spent on grants to individuals.

Grants were made for the following purposes:

Vision-impairment and computer equipment	£1.1 million
Domestic and personal care	£500,000
Well-being	£500,000
Employment and training	£100,000

Applications

Application forms are available on the charity's website or from the correspondent. There is also a form on the website which allows potential applicants to request a call back from the charity for further information. Applications must include details of the applicant's service (including service number and dates of service) and details of their ophthalmic consultant. On receipt, the charity will contact the respective service office and ophthalmic consultant for reports. The process can take about ten weeks.

All applicants are encouraged to get in touch with the charity to discuss their needs (free line 0800 389 7979).

Other information

The charity was previously known as St Dunstan's. Its activities cover four main areas: help and training for independent living; care centre activities; welfare services; and housing provision. Lifelong support and advice are offered to beneficiaries and their families. There are centres in Brighton, Sheffield and Llandudno which provide rehabilitation and training to individuals learning to cope with blindness. The Brighton and Llandudno centres also serve as nursing, residential and respite care centres.

This charity also administers the Diana Gubbay Trust which exists for the benefit of men and women in the emergency services (police, fire and ambulance) who have suffered severe loss of sight while on duty. The ophthalmic criteria are the same as for Blind Veterans UK.

BlindAid

£28,000 (96 grants)

Correspondent: Grant Co-ordinator, Lantern House, 102 Bermondsey Street, London SE1 3UB (020 7403 6184; fax: 020 7234 0708; email: referrals@blindaid.org.uk; website: www.blindaid.org.uk)

CC number: 262119

Eligibility

Blind and partially sighted people aged 18 and over who live on a permanent basis in one of the 12 central London boroughs or the City of London and who are in receipt of means-tested benefits, with a preference for those registered blind/partially sighted.

Types of grants

One-off grants typically up to £300 towards: computer equipment; equipment and gadgets, including talking clocks, big button phones, colour detectors, talking mobile phones and talking microwaves; and domestic items.

Annual grant total

In 2015 the charity had assets of £4.6 million and an income of £573,000. Grants for general purposes were made to 96 individuals and totalled £28,000. The charity also paid out £1,000 in smaller grants of less than £50 each. A further £11,800 was awarded in grants to organisations.

Exclusions

BlindAid does not make grants for the following purposes: payment of outstanding debts; non-essential furniture or home goods; payment of council tax or mortgage/rent arrears; legal fees for insolvency/bankruptcy; utility bills or other household bills (including internet connection); deposit payments for rented or leased accommodation; garden fencing or clearing; home modifications/adaptations; educational or occupational training; medical treatment/alternative therapies; funeral expenses; removal expenses; motor vehicle purchase or maintenance; fines or arrears; pest control; fixtures or fittings (including carpets, curtains and blinds); or holidays.

Applications

Applications can be made online or on a form available to download from the website or from the correspondent. Applications should be made through a third party such as social services, sensory teams, community health professionals, GPs or other charities. The trustees try to process applications within 28 days. A full list of guidelines is available to download from the website.

Only one application per person/household can be considered in any two year period.

Other information

BlindAid's core service is a home visiting service to provide company and conversation and lessen isolation in the community, on which it spends almost half its income; it also offers telephone support for those who choose not to have a visit, as well as advice, information and links to other appropriate organisations. The charity also supports small local organisations such as social clubs that help visually impaired people.

Colchester Blind Society

£8,000

Correspondent: Marilyn Theresa Peck, Trustee, Kestrels, Harwich Road, Beaumont, Clacton-on-Sea, Essex CO16 0AU (01255 862062; email: info@colchesterblindsociety.org.uk; website: www.colchesterblindsociety.org.uk/index.html)

CC number: 207361

Eligibility

People who are blind or sight impaired and live in the borough of Colchester.

Types of grants

One-off or recurrent grants according to need.

Annual grant total

In 2016/17 the society had an income of £2,700 and a total expenditure of £10,800. We estimate that grants given to individuals totalled around £8,000.

Applications

Apply in writing to the correspondent.

Gardner's Trust for the Blind

£32,000

Correspondent: Angela Stewart, 117 Charterhouse Street, London EC1M 6AA (020 7253 3757)

CC number: 207233

Eligibility

Registered blind or partially sighted people who live in the UK.

Types of grants

One-off grants for household items. The trust also gives grants in the form of pensions.

Annual grant total

In 2015/16 the trust had assets of £3.7 million and an income of £97,500. One-off welfare grants totalled £9,900 and regular quarterly grants totalled £22,000.

Applications

Apply in writing to the correspondent. Applications can be submitted either directly by the individual or by a third party, but they must also be supported by a third party who can confirm that the applicant has a disability and that the grant is needed.

Halifax Society for the Blind

£5,600

Correspondent: Victoria Le Feuvre, Trustee, 34 Clare Road, Halifax, West Yorkshire HX1 2HX (01422 352383; email: halifaxblindsociety@gmail.com)

CC number: 224258

Eligibility

People in need who are registered blind or partially sighted and live in Calderdale. Applicants should have savings of no more than £4,000 and a 'disposable' household weekly income of no more than £120 (after paying rent/mortgage, council tax and utilities bills).

Types of grants

One-off grants of cash up to £250 or equipment according to need. Grants have been given towards beds, school equipment, televisions and decorating costs.

Annual grant total

In 2016/17 the society held assets of £1.8 million and had an income of £70,000. Grants to individuals totalled £5,600.

Applications

Application forms are available from the correspondent and can be submitted when they are supported by a social worker or a rehabilitation officer. Members can also self-refer by discussing their needs with the HSB manager. Applications are considered on a regular basis.

Other information

The society runs five social centres and a resource centre, and operates a minibus service.

The Anne Herd Memorial Trust

£500

Correspondent: The Trustees of The Anne Herd Memorial Trust, 27 Bank Street, Dundee DD1 1RP

OSCR number: SC014198

Eligibility

People who are blind or partially sighted who live in Broughty Ferry. Applicants from the city of Dundee, region of Tayside or those who have connections with these areas and reside in Scotland will also be considered.

Types of grants

Grants, usually of at least £50.

Annual grant total

In 2015/16 the trust had an income of £112,500, of which £72,500 was derived from the sale of investments, and a total expenditure of £97,500, of which £68,500 was attributed to the purchase of investments. Grants totalled £2,000. We estimate that social welfare grants to individuals totalled £500.

Applications

Applications can be made in writing to the correspondent. They can be submitted directly by the individual in March/April for consideration in June.

The Kingston upon Thames Association for the Blind

£8,000

Correspondent: Jean Warwick, KAB Office, 2A Sussex Road, New Malden, Surrey KT3 3PY (020 8605 0060; email: kingstonassoc@btconnect.com; website: www.kingstonassociationforblind.org)

CC number: 249295

Eligibility

Blind and partially sighted people who live in the royal borough of Kingston upon Thames.

Types of grants

One-off grants of £50 to £2,000 towards the cost of subscriptions to RNIB Talking Books, computer equipment or software, holiday expenses, household items, and other aids like 'Easy Readers'.

Annual grant total

In 2015/16 the association held assets of £256,500 and had an income of £89,500. Grants to individuals totalled £8,000.

Applications

An application form is available to download from the website. If the applicant is not in receipt of income support, housing benefit, or family credit they will need to provide detailed financial circumstances. Applications are considered every other month from January onwards.

Other information

The association runs various initiatives specifically designed to improve the lives of blind and partially sighted people. This includes: the Eye Buddy home visiting scheme; exercise programmes such as the Tandem Scheme, Walking Buddies and Running Buddies; and a talking newspaper. It also supports other groups for visually impaired people in the local area.

Open Sight

£1,900

Correspondent: Stacey Allen, Administrator, 25 Church Road, Eastleigh, Hampshire SO50 6BL (023 8064 1244; email: info@opensight.org.uk; website: www.opensight.org.uk)

CC number: 1055498

Eligibility

People who are visually impaired, in need and live in Hampshire, excluding the cities of Portsmouth and Southampton.

Types of grants

One-off grants each to aid independent living for eligible people, e.g. towards special equipment, aids to daily living, holiday costs and costs incurred when moving into independent living.

Annual grant total

In 2016/17 the charity held assets of £367,000 and had an income of £434,000. During the year, the charity gave around £1,900 in grants to individuals.

Exclusions

No grants are given for educational purposes or to groups.

Applications

Applicants should at first contact the charity, to be put in touch with one of its Independent Living Advisors.

Other information

The charity's main activities are service delivery and community outreach. The charity's Independent Living Advisors offer support and advice on a wide range of issues.

The Surrey Association for Visual Impairment

£500

Correspondent: Bob Hughes, Chief Executive, Rentwood, School Lane, Fetcham, Leatherhead, Surrey KT22 9JX (01372 377701; fax: 01372 360767; email: info@sightforsurrey.org.uk; website: www.surreywebsight.org.uk)

CC number: 1121949

Eligibility

People who are blind or partially sighted and who live in the administrative county of Surrey.

Types of grants

Small, one-off grants are given when absolutely necessary. Grants are usually to help pay for equipment required to overcome a sight problem or a sudden domestic need. Applications from service users for small, interest-free loans are also occasionally considered.

Annual grant total

In 2015/16 the association had an income of £1.7 million and a total expenditure of £2 million. The charity awarded £500 to individuals for social welfare purposes and £1,200 to organisations in order to run clubs and classes.

Applications

Application forms are available from the correspondent. Applications can be submitted at any time by the individual or through a social worker, welfare agency, club or any recognised organisation for blind or partially sighted people.

Other information

The association's main focus is the provision of services, advice, IT training and information for visually impaired people. It runs a resource centre equipped with a wide range of aids and equipment as well as a home visiting scheme and outreach groups. The association has a successful children's services division and also provides support for those struggling to navigate the benefits system.

The Swansea and District Friends of the Blind

£8,600

Correspondent: John Allan, Secretary, 3 De La Beche Street, Swansea SA1 3EY (01792 655424; email: john_allan_10@hotmail.com)

CC number: 211343

Eligibility

People who are registered blind and live in Swansea and the surrounding area.

Types of grants

One-off grants which, in the past, have gone towards visual impairment aids such as talking watches, computers, etc. Gifts are also distributed at Christmas and Easter.

Annual grant total

In 2016/17 the charity had an income of £12,900 and a total expenditure of £46,500. In previous years, grants have totalled around £8,600.

Applications

Apply in writing to the correspondent. Applications are considered on a regular basis.

Other information

The majority of the organisation's funding goes towards the provision of information, advice and support services for registered blind people. It also arranges events and outings, particularly in summer and at Christmas.

Armed forces charities

Unlike other occupational associated charities, armed forces charities have been given their own section in this guide as they support a large beneficiary population which shares a specific background. This branch of the sector is committed to helping anyone who has done at least one day's paid service in any of the armed forces, including serving and ex-serving members of the UK armed forces, reserves and those who undertook National Service, and in most cases, their husbands, wives, children, widows, widowers and other dependants (collectively referred to as the armed forces community).

These charities are exceptionally well organised. Much of this is due to the work of the Soldiers, Sailors, Airmen and Families Association (SSAFA), which has an extensive network of trained caseworkers around the country who act on behalf of SSAFA and other Service charities. Many of the charities in this section use the same application procedures as SSAFA and assist members of the armed forces community. Other large charities (such as Royal British Legion) have their own procedures and ways of supporting the armed forces community, regardless of any specific eligibility criteria. Some charities cater for beneficiaries with specific needs (such as Blesma – supporting veterans with limb or sight loss), or provide support for those with particular affiliations to Service branches (such as The RAF Benevolent Fund) or individual regiments.

Many Service benevolent funds rely on trained SSAFA volunteer caseworkers to prepare applications, although some do have their own volunteers. Alternatively, some funds ask applicants to write to a central correspondent. In such cases, applicants may wish to follow the guidelines in the article 'How to make an application' earlier in this guide. Most entries in this section state whether the applicant should apply directly to the charity or through a caseworker. If in doubt, the applicant should ring up the charity concerned or the local SSAFA office.

Some people prefer to approach their own or their late spouse's regimental or corps association. Many of them have their own charitable funds and volunteers, especially in their own recruiting areas. In other cases, they will work through one of the volunteer networks mentioned previously on this page. Again, if in doubt or difficulty, the applicant should contact the regimental/corps association or local SSAFA office.

SSAFA is much more than just a provider of financial assistance. It also offers advice, support and training. It can assist members of the armed forces community on many issues, ranging from how to replace lost medals to advice on adoption. Its website (www.ssafa.org.uk) provides a wide range of information and useful links for members of the community.

DSC's armed forces research

Individuals connected to the armed forces should also refer to DSC's Armed Forces Charities website (www.armedforcescharities.org.uk). The website is an independent and comprehensive resource on armed forces charities created by DSC and funded by Forces in Mind Trust. The website contains information relevant to: past or present serving members of the UK armed forces; family members or dependants; or organisations working with the UK armed forces. This free-to-access online resource allows users to search for charities that support the armed forces community.

The website contains information on over 1,600 UK armed forces charities which provide a wide variety of support, either through their own activities or via grants. At least 200 of these charities make grants to individuals either directly or through another organisation. We have not included every armed forces charity in this book, but this chapter provides a sample of the types of help available for individuals and further information on some of the larger charities such as SSAFA, Royal British Legion and ABF The Soldier's Charity.

Armed forces charities use a process called almonisation to source and combine funds from several benevolent organisations in order to make one payment to a beneficiary. The flowchart on the following page is taken from DSC's *Sector Insight: UK Armed Forces Charities* report (2014) and shows the organisations which individuals should approach for support and how their application may be taken forward.

References
Pozo, A. and Walker, C., *Sector Insight: UK Armed Forces Charities,* London, Directory of Social Change, 2014.

Index of armed forces charities

How does the benevolent grant-making system work for the individual?

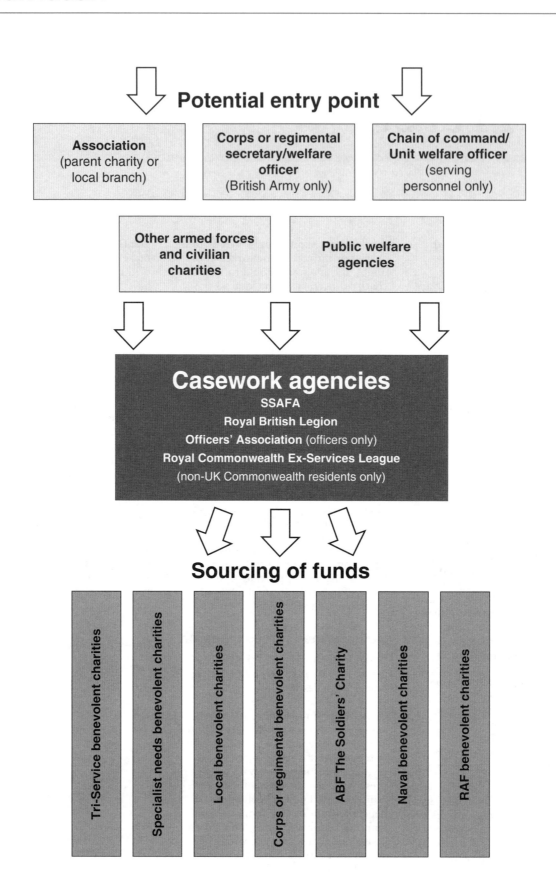

ABF The Soldiers' Charity

£2.5 million (3,375 grants)

Correspondent: The Welfare Team, Mountbarrow House, 6–20 Elizabeth Street, London SW1W 9RB (020 7901 8900; fax: 020 7901 8901; email: info@soldierscharity.org; website: www.soldierscharity.org)

CC number: 1146420

Eligibility

Members and ex-members of the British Regular Army and the Reserve Army (TA) and their dependants who are in need. Serving TA soldiers must have completed at least one year's satisfactory Service, and former TA soldiers should have completed at least three years' satisfactory Service.

Types of grants

Grants are awarded by the charity in seven broad areas: annuities; care home fees; bursaries (see this guide's sister publication, *The Guide to Educational Grants*); holiday schemes, for families under stress; special funds; general needs (grants for a wide variety of purposes which are not available from other sources e.g. mobility aids such as stairlifts); and the Current Operations Fund.

Annual grant total

In 2015/16 the charity had assets of £62.6 million and an income of £22.8 million. Grants totalled £6.6 million, of which £3.4 million was awarded to individuals. The charity's website states that it awards around 4,500 grants to individuals in each year. In this financial year, grants to individuals were given in the form of routine grants totalling £3.3 million, and from the Quick Reaction Fund (QRF) totalling £24,000. There were no grants made for specialist employment consultants (2015: £632,000). It has not been possible to determine how much of the total awarded in individual grants was for social welfare purposes. We have estimated a split of 75/25 in favour of social welfare, giving social welfare awards a total of £2.5 million.

Exclusions

Medical and legal fees, non-priority debt and memorials or headstones.

Applications

The charity does not deal directly with individual cases. Soldiers who are still serving should contact their regimental or corps association, which will then approach the fund on their behalf. Former soldiers should at first contact SSAFA Forces Help or The Royal British Legion. Applications are considered at any time, but all are reviewed annually in July.

Enquiries may be made directly to the charity to determine the appropriate corps or regimental association. See also, in particular, the entries for SSAFA Forces Help and The Royal British Legion.

Other information

As well as also making grants to individuals for educational purposes, ABF makes grants to other charities working to support service and ex-servicepeople. According to the annual report, in 2015/16 there was a focus on the following areas: care for older people, mental health and respite care, homelessness, supported housing, education and training for employment and welfare support to the army family.

AJEX Charitable Foundation

£59,000 (169 grants)

Correspondent: Ivan Phineas Sugarman, Trustee, Shield House, Harmony Way, Hendon, London NW4 2BZ (020 8202 2323; email: headoffice@ajex.org.uk; website: www.ajex.org.uk)

CC number: 1082148

Eligibility

Jewish ex-servicemen and women, and their dependants, who are in need.

Types of grants

One-off and recurrent grants are given according to need. Special grants are also made to cover emergencies and exceptional circumstances such as contributions towards the cost of stairlifts, electric motor scooters and so on.

Annual grant total

In 2015 the foundation held assets of £1.5 million and had an income of £158,500. Welfare grants and expenses totalled £59,000.

During the year, three regular grants were made to 44 single individuals and six couples, totalling £21,500 and 37 special grants were made totalling £18,000. Grants paid out of the AJEX Housing Fund during the year totalled £21,000.

Applications

Application forms are available from the correspondent, to be returned directly by the individual or through a third party. Evidence of Service in the British Army and of Jewish religious status is required.

Other information

The foundation works closely with SSAFA, The Royal British Legion and other regimental associations. Should there be leftover income towards the end of the year, the foundation will support older Jewish people suffering from financial hardship.

Blind Veterans UK
See entry on page 73

British Limbless Ex-Service Men's Association (BLESMA)

£760,000 (757 grants)

Correspondent: Grants Support Team, 185–187 High Road, Chadwell Heath, Romford, Essex RM6 6NA (020 8548 3516; email: membergrants@blesma.org; website: www.blesma.org)

CC number: 1084189

Eligibility

Serving and ex-serving members of HM or auxiliary forces who have lost a limb or eye or have a permanent loss of speech, hearing or sight, and their widows/widowers. Despite the association's name, it serves members of both sexes.

Types of grants

One-off and recurrent grants towards, for example, wheelchairs and scooters, stairlifts, car adaptations, gardening costs or home redecorating.

Annual grant total

In 2016 the association held assets of nearly £27 million and had an income of £6.6 million. During the year, 1,176 grants were made to 757 individuals and totalled £760,000.

Exclusions

The charity does not generally issue grants for prosthetic limbs, as this should be covered by NHS provision.

Applications

Application forms are available from the correspondent. Applications can be submitted at any time, either directly by the individual or through their local BLESMA representative, SSAFA Forces Help, Citizens Advice or similar welfare agency.

Other information

BLESMA also offers advice and support to members on a range of issues.

The Burma Star Association

£128,500 (161 grants)

Correspondent: Capt. (Retd) Mike Nelson, Benevolence Secretary, 34 Grosvenor Gardens, London SW1W 0DH (Monday and Wednesday: 01634 309681; Tuesday and Thursday: 020 7823 4283; email: mrnbsa@ btconnect.com; website: www.burmastar. org.uk)

CC number: 1043040

Eligibility

Burma Star holders and their spouses, widows and widowers. The association's website states:

In order for us to help the most needy and frail we ask that people requesting assistance meet the following criteria:

- You do not have more than £10,000 in savings – this includes investments, ISAs and premium bonds etc. (this does NOT however include the value of the home)
- You are prepared to allow a caseworker to visit you in your home to complete an application form. You may of course have a family member present during the meeting if that is your wish
- Where an application is for a home improvement grant (DFG) towards a bathroom conversion or a stair lift that has been refused by a local council, please keep all the correspondence as it will assist greatly in speeding up the process. If you are struggling with energy bills, please have the latest bill available

Types of grants

The association's website states that it can provide assistance with:

- Residential and care home fees and care home costs
- Respite placements to cover hospitalisation of the carer
- Contributions to the costs of wheelchairs and electronic scooters (EPVs)
- Contributions to the costs of mobility aids, riser/recliner chairs, profiling beds and stairlifts
- Communication aids like Care Call, life line pendant, help with travelling expenses for hospital visits, etc.
- Contributions to the cost of miscellaneous alterations and home repairs – bath-lifts or low-level showers, entrance alterations required because of mobility or disability, central heating/boiler repairs, etc., windows and doors repairs to or replacements
- Personal aids
- Household items (washing machine, refrigerator or furniture, etc.)
- Sundry debts (utility bills, etc.)

Annual grant total

In 2016 the association had assets of £747,500 and an income of £181,500. Grants to 161 individuals totalled around £128,500 and can be broken down as follows:

Nursing and residential homes	£96,000
Repairs	£13,500
Riser/recliner chairs and stairlifts	£7,100
Debts	£3,200
Wheelchairs and EPVs	£2,600
Communication aids	£920
Personal aids	£870

Applications

Applicants should contact the association's benevolence secretary for further information.

Other information

The association has 42 branches across the UK and four overseas, which offer support and advice to their local members and make small grants where possible. The contact details for local branch officers can be obtained from the correspondent.

W. J. and Mrs C. G. Dunnachie's Charitable Trust

£35,000 (100 grants)

Correspondent: The Trustees, c/o Low Beaton Richmond LLP, 20 Renfield Street, Glasgow G2 5AP (0141 221 8931; email: murdoch@lbr-law.co.uk)

OSCR number: SC015981

Eligibility

People who are in poor health or who have a disability as a result of their Service during the Second World War.

Types of grants

One-off and recurrent (quarterly) grants according to need. In 2016/17 grants ranged between £90 and £750.

Annual grant total

In 2016/17 the trust had assets of £2 million and an income of £86,500. Grants to 100 individuals totalled £35,000. A further £19,700 was awarded to organisations.

Applications

Most applications are submitted via SSAFA Forces Help or through a regimental association.

Help for Heroes

£756,500

Correspondent: Grants team, Unit 14 Parker's Close, Downton Business Park, Downton, Salisbury, Wiltshire SP5 3RB (01980 844354; email: grants@ helpforheroes.org.uk; website: www. helpforheroes.org.uk)

CC number: 1120920/SC044984

Eligibility

Current and former members of the armed forces who have suffered a life-changing injury or illness while serving, or as a result of their Service, and their dependants.

Types of grants

The website explains that 'swift' financial support is given through the Quick Reaction Fund (QRF) 'to alleviate the distress caused by injury or support you on your Road to Recovery'. Grants can be given for a wide range of needs, including: housing adaptations to accommodate injury; sports and therapeutic equipment and activities; white and brown goods; and support with priority debts. The QRF can be delivered directly by Help for Heroes or through the services' own charities and, in urgent cases, aims to provide support within 72 hours.

Annual grant total

In 2015/16 the charity had assets of £115.9 million and an income of £36.5 million. The annual report for the year provides the following information about the Quick Reaction Fund: 'Between 1 October 2015 and 30 September 2016 we have supported 1,182 cases totalling in excess of £1.44m and in September granted our 10,000th award to individuals.' We estimate that welfare grants to individuals totalled around £756,500.

Applications

Candidates are encouraged to contact the correspondent to discuss their needs and application procedure.

Other information

Help for Heroes provides a wide range of support and advice services for eligible individuals; the details of the support available can be found on the charity's informative website.

The charity works with the armed forces and other military charities. Funding is also given for training and educational needs and to organisations working for the benefit of members of the armed forces.

Individuals and their families or carers are also welcome to visit one of the 'Support Hubs' to receive further advice and support on a range of welfare issues. For more details and contact information of the recovery centres see the website.

Honourable Artillery Company

£16,000 (seven grants)

Correspondent: Andrew Elliott-Frey, Honourable Artillery Co., Finsbury Barracks, City Road, London EC1Y 2BQ (email: hac@hac.org.uk; website: www.hac.org.uk)

CC number: 208443

Eligibility

Individuals connected with the Honourable Artillery Company.

Types of grants

One-off grants according to need.

Annual grant total

In 2015/16 the charity held assets of £44.4 million and had an income of £5.7 million. During the year, the charity gave £16,000 in grants to seven individuals through its benevolent fund.

Applications

Apply in writing to the correspondent.

Other information

In some circumstances, grants are made to individuals to allow specific training to be undertaken or to support other military purposes.

Huddersfield and District Army Veterans' Association Benevolent Fund

£9,700

Correspondent: Cyril Ford, Secretary, 18 Grasscroft Avenue, Honley, Holmfirth HD9 6HY (01484 323107; email: cyril.ford@ntlworld.com; website: www.hdava.co.uk/index.html)

CC number: 222286

Eligibility

Veterans of the army, navy and air force who are in need, aged over 60 years, and who were discharged from the forces and live in Huddersfield and part of Brighouse.

Types of grants

One-off and recurrent grants are given according to need.

Annual grant total

In 2016 the fund had an income of £40,000 and a total expenditure of £35,000. Grants to individuals totalled £9,700.

Applications

Apply in writing to the correspondent, or on a form published in the fund's applications leaflet. The leaflet is available from doctors' surgeries, local libraries and so on.

Other information

The fund also provides social activities and trips to members of the forces in the Huddersfield area, spending £6,400 in 2016. It also has a welfare officer who can provide assistance with health and family problems and advice regarding funeral arrangements.

King Edward VII's Hospital Sister Agnes

£82,500 (19 grants)

Correspondent: PA to the Chief Executive, King Edward VII Hospital, Beaumont Street, London W1G 6AA (020 7486 4319; email: info@kingedwardvii.co.uk; website: www.kingedwardvii.co.uk)

CC number: 208944

Eligibility

People who have served in the armed forces, regardless of rank or length of service, who are uninsured and are either inpatients or outpatients at King Edward VII's Hospital Sister Agnes, and their spouses, ex-spouses, widows and widowers.

Types of grants

Means-tested grants for up to 100% of hospital fees, for both inpatient and outpatient services. In some cases, consultant fees, imaging and physiotherapy may also be covered.

Annual grant total

In 2015/16 the King Edward VII's Hospital had assets of £28 million and an income of £23 million. The Sister Agnes Benevolent Fund, which is administered by this charity, had an income of £65,000. Through the fund, the charity awarded 19 grants to individuals for welfare purposes totalling £82,500.

Applications

To apply, applicants must contact the charity via email or telephone, all contact details can be found on the website. All applications are considered in the strictest confidence by the trustees, and you will be informed of their decision before you are admitted.

Other information

The Sister Agnes Benevolent Fund is a restricted fund of King Edward VII's Hospital Sister Agnes. It was established in 1979 by an anonymous donation, to be held upon trust.

Lloyd's Patriotic Fund

£86,000

Correspondent: The Secretary, Lloyd's Patriotic Fund, Lloyd's, One Lime Street, London EC3M 7HA (020 7327 6144; email: communityaffairs@lloyds.com; website: www.lloyds.com/lpf)

CC number: 210173

Eligibility

Ex-servicemen and women of the Royal Navy, the Army, Royal Marines and Royal Air Force who are in need, and their dependants.

Types of grants

One-off grants, on average of about £300, can be given for essential domestic items, electric wheelchairs, home adaptations and 'exceptional' expenses. In deserving cases grants may also be given for debt relief and help with utility bills.

Annual grant total

In 2015/16 the fund had assets of £3 million and an income of £398,500. Welfare grants to individuals totalled £86,000.

Exclusions

Note: new annuity payments are no longer considered. Existing recipients will continue to be assisted.

Applications

Applications should be made through your local SSAFA Forces Help branch.

Other information

The fund works with SSAFA Forces Help and other partners through which funds are administered. Various military organisations are supported, with a particular focus on those helping people who have disabilities or individuals facing poverty, illness and hardship.

The Nash Charity

£15,000

Correspondent: Clare Brennan, Peachey & Co., 95 Aldwych, London WC2B 4JF (020 7316 5200; email: cmb@peachey.co.uk)

CC number: 229447

Eligibility

Ex-Service personnel who have been wounded or have suffered a disability during wartime.

Types of grants

Grants are usually paid through social services, Citizens Advice or other welfare agencies to purchase specific items.

Annual grant total

In 2015/16 the charity had an income of £14,900 and a total expenditure of £27,000. We estimate that the charity awarded around £12,500 to individuals for welfare purposes.

The charity also awards grants to organisations.

Applications

Apply in writing to the correspondent at any time. Applications can be submitted directly by the individual or through an appropriate third party.

Other information

At the time of writing (August 2017) the charity had no website or accounts available.

The Not Forgotten Association

£697,000 (10,000 grants)

Correspondent: Referral agencies, see 'Applications', 4th Floor, 2 Grosvenor Gardens, London SW1W 0DH (020 7730 2400; fax: 020 7730 0020; email: info@ nfassociation.org; website: www. nfassociation.org)

CC number: 1150541

Eligibility

This charity supports serving and ex-servicemen and women who have disabilities or who are suffering from some form of ill health. Applicants must have served in the Armed Forces of the Crown (or the Merchant Navy during hostilities).

Types of grants

The association does not give financial grants to applicants directly; rather it gives help in kind in the following areas: televisions and licences for those with restricted mobility or who are otherwise largely housebound, holidays for both groups and individuals (accompanied by carers if required), and day outings to events and places of interest. The association is now including more activity and adventure breaks and outings, in light of more recent military conflicts.

Annual grant total

In 2016/17 the association held assets of £2.3 million and had an income of £1 million. Assistance to nearly 10,000 individuals totalled £697,000 and was distributed as follows:

Holidays	£327,900
Outings	£216,000
Entertainment	£139,500
Televisions	£76,600

Exclusions

The association cannot help wives, widows or families (unless they are themselves ex-members of the forces or they are acting as carers).

Applications

Applications should be submitted through SSAFA Forces Help, The Royal British Legion, Combat Stress or the Welfare Service of the Service Personnel and Veterans' Agency. These agencies will complete the common application form on behalf of the applicant and then make the appropriate recommendation to the association, with the applicant's income and expenditure details and degree of disability. Applications are considered throughout the year. Successful applicants may reapply after three years.

Other information

The association organises two flagship events for war pensioners – its annual Garden Party at Buckingham Palace and a Christmas Party at St James's Palace. The association is now a charitable limited company (Charity Commission no. 1150541). The unincorporated association has now wound up and been removed from the Central Register of Charities.

The Officers' Association

£1.08 million (576 grants)

Correspondent: Kathy Wallis, Benevolence Department, 1st Floor, Mountbarrow House, 6–20 Elizabeth Street, London SW1W 9RB (02078084160; email: k.wallis@ officersassociation.org.uk; website: www. officersassociation.org.uk)

CC number: 201321

Eligibility

Officers who have held a commission in HM Forces, their widows and dependants. Officers on the active list will normally be helped only with resettlement and employment.

Types of grants

Grants fall into two main areas: regular allowances, predominantly for older beneficiaries on low incomes, and one-off grants towards specific items such as disability equipment. In addition, the OA provides grants to bridge the gap between the fees charged for residential care and the funds that the individual can provide from personal, family and/ or local authority sources.

Limited assistance may be given for educational or training needs in exceptional circumstances.

Annual grant total

In 2015/16 the association held assets of £17.6 million and had an income of £3.6 million. During the year, the charity gave around £1.08 million in grants to individuals for social welfare purposes.

Applications

Application forms are available from the Benevolence Secretary or can be downloaded from the website. Applications can be submitted either directly by the individual or via a third party. The association has a network of honorary representatives throughout the UK who will normally visit the applicant to discuss their problems and offer advice.

Other information

The association provides a series of advice leaflets on finding accommodation in residential care or nursing homes, how to get financial assistance and how to find short-term convalescence accommodation and sheltered accommodation for older people who have disabilities. It also has an employment department to help ex-officers up to the age of 60 find suitable employment. This service is open to officers just leaving the services and to those who have lost their civilian jobs.

The association has an informative website.

For applicants in Scotland: see entry for the Officers' Association Scotland.

Officers' Association Scotland

£90,000

Correspondent: Laura Darling, Welfare Services Administrator, New Haig House, Logie Green Road, Edinburgh EH7 4HR (0131 550 1575/1581; fax: 0131 557 5819; email: oasadmin@ oascotland.org.uk; website: www. oascotland.org.uk)

OSCR number: SC010665

Eligibility

Those 'who have held a Sovereign's Commission with embodied service in HM Naval, Military or Air Forces', and their dependants who are in need. Ex-officers who were commissioned into the Reserve, Auxiliary, or Territorial Forces are also eligible. Applicants must be resident in Scotland at the time of their initial application or have been members of a Scottish regiment or intend to settle in Scotland.

Types of grants

Recurrent grants and one-off grants, which in the past have been used to fund purposes such as home repairs, respite breaks, mobility aids, etc.

Annual grant total

In 2016/17 the association held assets of £7.5 million and had an income of £265,000. During the year, the charity gave around £90,000 in grants to individuals.

Applications

Potential beneficiaries can contact the correspondent to discuss eligibility. Alternatively, applications can be initiated by sending the individual's personal and Service details to the association via the online contact form on the association's website, by email or in writing. Applications are passed to the local SSAFA branch who will contact the individual to progress the application.

Other information

The association runs a 'friendship visits programme' to provide company for retired officers and their dependants who are feeling isolated.

It also offers support and advice to officers making the transition from Service to civilian employment and for the rest of their working lives.

Poppyscotland

£695,000 (1,336 grants)

Correspondent: Welfare Services, New Haig House, Logie Green Road, Edinburgh EH7 4HQ (0131 550 1557; email: GetHelp@poppyscotland.org.uk; website: www.poppyscotland.org.uk)

OSCR number: SC014096

Eligibility

People in Scotland who have served in the UK Armed Forces (regular or reserve) and their widows/widowers and dependants.

Types of grants

Grants are wide-ranging and can cover areas such as home repairs or adaptions, replacement household goods and clothing. Grant-giving criteria are kept deliberately so as to help as many people as possible.

Annual grant total

In 2015/16 the charity had an income of £4.7 million and assets of £9.9 million. Grants made to individuals totalled £695,000.

Applications

For more information call 0131 550 1557 or email gethelp@poppyscotland.org.uk.

Other information

Other services provided by Poppyscotland include respite breaks and programmes to support veterans into employment. The charity also collaborates with Citizens Advice Scotland to run the Armed Services Advice Project, offering advice to Armed Forces veterans on a wide range of issues such as finance, housing, employment, health and benefits.

The Royal British Legion

£10.1 million

Correspondent: Welfare Services, 199 Borough High Street, London SE1 1AA (Helpline: 0808 802 8080 (8am to 8pm, 7 days a week); email: info@britishlegion.org.uk; website: www.britishlegion.org.uk)

CC number: 219279

Eligibility

Serving and ex-serving members of the armed forces and their wives, partners, widows, children and other dependants in England, Wales, Ireland as well as any country overseas (for Scotland see the entry for the Earl Haig Fund Scotland in the Scotland section of the guide).

Types of grants

Following a standard assessment of the beneficiary's financial situation, the Legion makes grants to individuals, either financial or by the provision of goods or services. Grants can be given for any purpose within the scope of the Royal Charter, which governs the Legion. Financial assistance offered by the Legion includes an Immediate Needs Scheme, help for homelessness and a Property Repair Loan Scheme.

Annual grant total

In 2015/16 the charity held assets of £295.6 million and had an income of £151.2 million. Welfare grants to individuals totalled £10.1 million.

Exclusions

No assistance with business debts, legal expenses, loans or medical care.

Applications

Call the charity's helpline to be put in contact with your local welfare representative. An income and savings assessment may be required as part of the application process.

Note: most charities for ex-servicemen and women co-operate together in their work and The Royal British Legion may also be approached through other service organisations and vice versa.

Other information

The Royal British Legion is one of the largest providers of charitable help for individuals in the country and is financed mainly by gifts from individuals, especially through its annual Poppy Day collection.

It provides a comprehensive service for advising and helping ex-servicemen and women and their dependants. Direct financial assistance is but one aspect of this work. There are over 3,000 branches of The Royal British Legion, all of which can act as centres for organising

whatever help the circumstances may require. Support is available to all who served in the forces, whether in war or peacetime, as regulars or those who have done national service.

The Legion manages six cares homes in locations around the country and is dedicated to supporting the recovery of soldiers and ex-soldiers.

There are four break centres operated by the Legion, through which it facilitates holidays for serving and former service personnel and their families. It also provides adventure holidays for young people from service families.

Former members of the armed forces can seek support in their transition from military to civilian life through the Legion's website civvystreet.org, which 'gives beneficiaries and their partners information, advice and guidance on careers, skills and self-employment'.

More information on services provided can be found on the Legion's informative website or by calling the helpline.

Scottish War Blind

£906,000

Correspondent: Grants team, 50 Gillespie Cresent, Edinburgh EH10 4JB (0800 035640; email: enquiries@scottishwarblinded.org; website: www.royalblind.org/scottish-war-blinded)

OSCR number: SC047192

Eligibility

Applicants should be members of Scottish War Blinded.

Types of grants

Grants are provided to help members maintain and increase their independence and quality of life. Grants may be provided for household items, assistance with house moves, house adaptations, specialist equipment and mobility aids.

Annual grant total

In 2016/17 the charity held assets of £68 million and had an income of £3.1 million. Grants to individuals totalled £906,000.

Applications

Contact the charity for further information on membership and available support.

Other information

The charity provides rehabilitation, activities and education to veterans. It has 22 affordable houses on the Linburn estate which members can rent.

SSAFA (The Soldiers, Sailors, Airmen and Families Association) Forces Help

£13 million

Correspondent: The Welfare Team, Queen Elizabeth House, 4 St Dunstan's Hill, London EC3R 8AD (0845 241 7141 or 0800 731 4880 (UK freephone); email: via an online form or info@ssafa.org.uk; website: www.ssafa.org.uk)

CC number: 210760/SC038056

Eligibility

Service and ex-servicemen and women and their immediate dependants who are in need.

The charity's website provides an eligibility checklist and also states: 'If you have any connection with the Armed Forces, even if it isn't covered [in the list], then it's still worth getting in touch to see if we can help.'

Types of grants

One-off grants are available for a variety of needs, such as mobility aids, household goods and transition costs.

Annual grant total

In 2016 the charity had assets of £15.9 million and had an income of £51.8 million. Grants to individuals in need totalled £13 million.

Applications

Contact the charity by using the online enquiry form on its website.

Other information

SSAFA Forces Help operates throughout the UK and in garrisons and stations overseas. It is concerned with the welfare of Service and ex-servicemen and women and their families and provides a wide range of advice and support services. All SSAFA branches are empowered to give immediate help without reference to higher committees. Also, because of their extensive coverage of the UK, they act as agents for service and other associated funds. Indeed, SSAFA is much more of a case-working organisation than a benevolent fund.

A residential home is maintained on the Isle of Wight for older ex-Service personnel and their dependants. Eligible men and women can be accepted from any part of the UK. SSAFA also manages cottage homes for ex-servicemen and women and their spouses, some purpose-built for people with disabilities, for which residents pay no rent but make a modest maintenance payment.

Two SSAFA Norton Homes provide short-term accommodation so that families can stay nearby while visiting a loved one at Selly Oak Hospital in Birmingham or the Defence Medical Rehabilitation Centre at Headley Court, Surrey. The houses are designed as 'homes from home' and are both located in secure and peaceful environments.

Stepping Stone homes are provided for Service families facing relationship difficulties or marital breakdown who need somewhere to live while they consider their future.

Support services for serving and ex-Service prisoners, with the aim of reducing re-offending and helping prisoners resettle into society, are also available.

SSAFA provides a confidential telephone support line for serving personnel which is staffed all year round and is outside the chain of command (UK: 0800 731 4880; Germany: 0800 182 7395; Cyprus: 800 91065; Falkland Islands #6111; rest of the world: +44 (0)1980 630854). It also continues to grow and develop its health and social care services for serving personnel around the world with specialist health centres in Leicester and Nottingham. It also provides family support groups and adoption services.

For further information on all of the services listed here, and more, go to the charity's website or visit a local branch.

Todmorden War Memorial Fund (1914/1918)

£1,500

Correspondent: Stephen Ormerod, Trustee, 2 Maitland Close, Todmorden, West Yorkshire OL14 7TG (07941 195488)

CC number: 219673

Eligibility

Veterans of the First and Second World Wars who are sick or in need and live or have lived in the former borough of Todmorden, and their dependants. Other people in need in the area of benefit could also be assisted.

Types of grants

Our previous research indicates that grants are mostly one-off and recurrent grants are very occasionally given. TV licences are given to First and Second World War families. Food vouchers, medicine, medical comforts, bedding, fuel, domestic help and convalescence expenses are also given.

Annual grant total

In 2015 the charity had an income of £15,000 and a total expenditure of £3,200. We estimate that the charity gave around £1,500 to individuals for welfare purposes.

Applications

Apply in writing to the correspondent.

Other information

At the time of writing (September 2017) the charity had no website or accounts available.

The charity also gives grants to organisations.

The Victoria Cross and George Cross Association

£381,500

Correspondent: Rebecca Maciejewska, The Victoria Cross and George Cross Association, Horse Guards, Whitehall, London SW1A 2AX (020 7930 3506; email: secretary@vcandgc.org; website: vcgca.org)

CC number: 1162742

Eligibility

Recipients of the Victoria or George Cross and their dependants and partners.

To avoid confusion, the charity has defined 'dependant' as:

- Partners – referring to spouses and civil partners, of the same or different sex, with whom the medal holder lives as a partner in a family relationship
- Children, grandchildren, and great-grandchildren (whether illegitimate, adopted, step, or otherwise) and so forth through succeeding generations

Types of grants

One-off grants for welfare purposes and recurrent grants to supplement the pension annuity of members.

Annual grant total

In 2016 the charity held assets of £3.3 million and had an income of £3.5 million. During the year, the charity awarded around £381,500 in grants to individuals for welfare purposes. Grants are made in the form 'of welfare support and administering annuity payments to members'.

The charity's annual report (2016) states that 'supplementary payments were made to 23 members totalling approximately £362,000'. In 2016 total expenditure on welfare grants was approximately £20,000.

Applications

Applications should be made in writing to the correspondent, including proof of the Victoria or George Cross award, and income and expenditure details.

Other information

The charity organises reunions and ceremonies for medal holders. The charity also maintains the graves of medal holders.

Army

Airborne Forces Security (ABFS) Fund

£96,000 (112 grants)

Correspondent: Gwen Appleton, Secretary, Regimental Headquarters, The Parachute Regiment, Merville Barracks, Colchester, Essex CO2 7UT (01206 817079; email: syfund@parachute-regiment.com)

CC number: 206552

Eligibility

Serving and former members of the Parachute Regiment, the Glider Regiment and other units of airborne forces, and their dependants.

Types of grants

One-off grants are given according to need, including: clothing, bedding, furniture and household essentials; rent, living expenses, removals; education needs; monthly allowances; rehabilitation; etc.

Annual grant total

In 2016 the fund had assets of £7.2 million and an income of £429,000. Grants were made to 112 individuals totalling £96,000.

Additional grants of £40,000 and £35,000 were paid to the Army Benevolent Fund and the Parachute Regiment Charity respectively.

Exclusions

Grants are not normally given for repayment of private loans, legal proceedings or fines, or for purchase of private cars.

Applications

Apply in writing to the correspondent. Applications are usually made through the Army Benevolent Fund, SSAFA or The Royal British Legion.

The Army Dependants' Trust

£838,500 (74 grants)

Correspondent: Lt Col. Bill Graham, BSC Ceng Mimeche, The Army Dependants Trust, Trenchard Lines, Upavon, Wilts SN9 6BE (01980 615734; email: armydependantstrust@tiscali.co.uk; website: www.army.mod.uk/ADT)

CC number: 1064522

Eligibility

Dependants of servicemen and servicewomen who have died in Service, from whatever cause.

Types of grants

Cash grants according to need.

Annual grant total

In 2016 the charity held assets of £24.7 million and had an income of £1.8 million. During the year, the charity awarded 74 grants to individuals totalling £838,500.

Applications

The recipients of the awards need take no action themselves to claim as the charity completes the application process.

Other information

During the year the trustees awarded 65 (2015: 68) grants to the dependants of 60 (2015: 65) soldiers, officers and retired members who died during the year. Nine awards were made to members of the Army Reserve in 2016.

ATS and WRAC Association Benevolent Fund

£180,000 (344 grants)

Correspondent: Julia Doig, Finance Officer, Unit 39 Basepoint Business Centre, 1 Winnall Road, Winchester, Hampshire SO23 0LD (0300 400 1992; email: finance.officer@wracassociation.co.uk; website: www.wracassociation.co.uk)

CC number: 206184

Eligibility

Former members of the Auxiliary Territorial Service during the Second World War and members of the Women's Royal Army Corps who served up to April 1992, who are in need, and their dependants.

Types of grants

One-off grants generally up to £1,000, although requests for larger grants (up to £3,000) may be considered. The fund can also help with making up the shortfall for nursing home fees (up to £40 per week) and supports some annuitants who receive regular payments throughout the year – currently £34 per week with a £60 Christmas bonus.

Grants were awarded in over 20 categories, such as funeral expenses, carpets, house adaptations, disability aids, white goods and respite care.

Annual grant total

In 2015/16 the fund held assets of £6.2 million and had an income of £225,500. Grants to 344 individuals amounted to £180,000 and were distributed as follows:

Benevolent Fund	318	£146,000
Princess Royal's Memorial Fund	28	£34,000

Applications

All applications for financial assistance should go through the SSAFA, ABF The Soldiers Charity or The Royal British Legion caseworkers who will visit the applicants and submit whatever forms are necessary. Grants are distributed through these agencies.

Other information

If you feel that you might qualify for financial assistance, apply to your local The Royal British Legion or SSAFA office in the first instance.

The Black Watch Association

£16,000

Correspondent: The Trustees, Balhousie Castle, Hay Street, Perth PH1 5HR (01738 623214; email: bwassociation@btconnect.com; website: theblackwatch.co.uk/regimental-association)

OSCR number: SC016423

Eligibility

Serving and retired soldiers of the Black Watch, and their dependants, who are in need.

Types of grants

One-off grants are given towards rent arrears, clothing, household equipment, funeral expenses and mobility aids. There is also a holiday scheme for widows of Black Watch servicemen.

Annual grant total

In 2016 the charity had assets of £3 million and an income of £288,500. During the year, the charity awarded a total of £32,000 in grants to individuals. We estimate that the charity gave around £16,000 in grants to individuals for welfare purposes.

The charity also gave almost £25,000 in grants to organisations.

Exclusions

Our research suggests that no grants are made towards council tax arrears, loans or large debts.

Applications

The website states: 'Financial assistance is given when a report, prepared by SSAFA Forces Help, indicates a genuine need. Any grant given is authorised by an experienced Welfare Committee (who meet monthly) and is then paid to SSAFA Forces Help who administer the expenditure.' The contact details of local SSAFA branches can be found on the SSAFA website (www.ssafa.org.uk). Alternatively, SSAFA's Forcesline telephone service can be contacted from the UK by calling 0800 731 4880.

Churchill Lines Charitable Fund Ltd

£10,900

Correspondent: Robert Morgan, Hugh James, 114–116 St Mary Street, Cardiff CF10 1DY (029 2039 1038)

CC number: 1158677

Eligibility

Serving and former members of the Special Forces Support Group.

Types of grants

One-off grants according to need.

Annual grant total

In 2015/16 the charity had assets of £43,500 and an income of £49,000. Grants to individuals totalled £10,900.

Applications

Apply in writing to the correspondent.

The Commandos Benevolent Fund

£26,000

Correspondent: Michael Copland, Old Pinkneys, Lee Lane, Maidenhead SL6 6PE (01628 630375; email: mandlcopland@yahoo.co.uk; website: www.soldierscharity.org/need-our-help/individual-grants)

CC number: 229631

Eligibility

Members and ex-members of the British Regular Army who have completed basic adult training; preference is given to those who have been medically discharged as a direct result of an injury sustained during this period. Also, members and ex-members of the British Reserve Army who have completed one year's satisfactory service, ending in Phase 1 training. Dependants can also be supported.

Types of grants

One-off grants towards hospital transport, household bills, stairlifts, flooding costs, holidays, respite breaks, removal expenses, home adaptations, medical costs, funeral expenses, etc. The fund states that it will consider all applications on a case-by-case basis.

Annual grant total

In 2016 the charity had assets of £107,000 and an income of £305,500. The charity awarded £26,000 in grants to individuals during the year.

Exclusions

Medical fees, legal fees, non-priority debt, memorials and headstones cannot be funded.

Applications

Applications should be made in writing to the correspondent, accompanied by a written report from a partner organisation (usually SSAFA or The Royal British Legion), which details proof of Service, background to the case, financial position of the applicant, and what the grant will be used for.

Requests for grants for specialist equipment or home adaptations should also be supported by an occupational therapist and clinical recommendation.

The Hampshire and Isle of Wight Military Aid Fund (1903)

£19,100 (47 grants)

Correspondent: Lt Col. Colin Bulleid, Secretary, Serle's House, Southgate Street, Winchester, Hampshire SO23 9EG (01263 852933; email: secretary@hantsmaf.org; website: www.hantsmaf.org)

CC number: 202363

Eligibility

Members, or former members, of the British Army (whether regular, territorial, militia, yeomanry or volunteer), and their dependants, who are in need, and who are, or were:

a) Members or former members of any regiment or corps raised in Hampshire.

b) Members or former members of The Princess of Wales's Royal Regiment (Queen's and Royal Hampshire's) who were resident in Hampshire at the time of their enlistment.

Territorial Army soldiers must have had at least four years' Service with a TA unit in Hampshire or operational service.

The fund treats long-standing partnerships as marriages.

Types of grants

One-off grants for services or items such as: rent arrears; debts; household and boiler repairs; white goods and furnishings; nursing home fees; funeral costs; respite care; house moving costs; travel costs; and home adaptations such as stairlifts, riser chairs/beds, EPVs, wheelchairs, or showers.

Annual grant total

In 2016 the fund held assets of £498,500 and had an income of £31,000. During the year, 47 grants were made totalling £19,100.

Applications

The fund should not normally be approached directly. The following information is taken from the charity's website:

> Like all other military charities access to assistance is via a report from either SSAFA Forces Help or The Royal British Legion.
>
> A caseworker from your chosen organisation will visit you and complete a Form A with details about your connection to the Army, financial situation, your need, and a recommendation for appropriate assistance.

Consult the website for detailed information about the application process and how the money will be paid.

The Household Cavalry Foundation

£132,000

Correspondent: Col. Giles Stibbe, Household Cavalry Foundation, Horse Guards, Whitehall, Westminster, London SW1A 2AX (02078394858; email: admin@hcavfoundation.org)

CC number: 1151869

Eligibility

Household Cavalrymen who have been injured on operations or veterans and their dependants.

Types of grants

One-off grants.

Annual grant total

In 2015/16 the charity held assets of £3.3 million. During the year, the charity gave around £132,000 in grants to individuals.

Applications

The website states: 'To find out more information or to apply for support please email''admin@hcavfoundation.org.'

Other information

Formed in January 2013 The Household Cavalry Foundation was set up to raise funds to care for the Soldiers, Casualties, Veterans, Heritage and Horses of the Household Cavalry.

Its aim is to bring together regimental benevolent funds such as the Operational Casualties Funds (OCF), Household Cavalry Central Charitable Fund (HCCCF) and the Regimental Associations to operate as the Household Cavalry Foundation.

The Household Division Charity

£59,500

Correspondent: Maj. William Style, Treasurer, Household Division Funds, Horse Guards, Whitehall, London SW1A 2AX (020 7414 2270; email: hdftreasurer@gmail.com)

CC number: 1138248

Eligibility

Current and former members of the Household Division, and their dependants, who are in need.

Types of grants

One-off and recurring grants according to need.

Annual grant total

In 2015/16 the charity held assets of £6.9 million and had an income of £666,500. During the year, the charity spent a total of £237,000 in charitable activities. We estimate that around £59,500 was given in grants to individuals for welfare purposes.

The charity also awards grants to organisations and to individuals for educational purposes.

Applications

Apply in writing to the correspondent. Applications may be submitted by the individual or by a third party such as a representative from SSAFA, Citizens Advice or other welfare organisation.

Other information

The trustees' annual report for 2015/16 states:

> The trustees review financial commitments regularly. The Household Division is recognised by the nation as setting an international standard of excellence. With a legacy spanning 360 years, the Household Division Charity is driven primarily to generate even greater levels of military efficiency. Resources are allocated for the promotion of 'esprit de corps' based on optimal physical and mental fitness, breadth of knowledge, competence and experience to develop courage and professional effectiveness in the face of any danger. In support of this objective, funds are allocated to further education opportunities for individuals and groups, often abroad. Resources spent on welfare and memorialisation reinforce the sense of special unity that binds all members, serving and retired, able-bodied and injured, and their families including the bereaved.

Irish Guards Charitable Fund

£48,000 (72 grants)

Correspondent: Lt Col. Commanding, Regimental Headquarters, Irish Guards, Wellington Barracks, Birdcage Walk, London SW1A 6HQ (020 7414 3293; email: igwebmaster@btconnect.com; website: www.helpforirishguards.com)

CC number: 247477

Eligibility

Serving and retired officers of the Irish Guards and their dependants who are in need.

Types of grants

One-off grants according to need

Annual grant total

In 2016 the fund held assets of £2.7 million and had an income of £255,000. During the year, the fund gave around £48,000 to individuals.

Applications

Apply in writing to the correspondent.

K.O.S.B. Association Funds

£26,000 (70 grants)

Correspondent: The Trustees, Balcladach, Easter Ulston, Jedburgh, Roxburghshire TD8 6TF

OSCR number: SC033882

Eligibility

Members of the King's Own Scottish Borderers and their families and dependants.

Types of grants

One-off grants according to need.

Annual grant total

In 2016 the charity had assets of £686,000 and an income of £58,000. Grants to 70 individuals totalled £26,000.

Applications

Apply in writing to the correspondent.

The Military Provost Staff Corps Benevolent Fund

£2,100

Correspondent: Les Pearse, Secretary, MPSCA, Berechurch Hall Camp, Berechurch Hall Road, Colchester CO2 9NU (01206 783494; email: lespearse@mpsca.org.uk; website: www.mpsca.org.uk)

CC number: 1078437

Eligibility

Former members of the former Military Provost Staff Corps and of the Adjutant General's Corps (AGC), and their widows and dependants, who are in need.

Types of grants

Grants are given according to need.

Annual grant total

In 2016/17 the charity had assets of £299,000 and an income of £31,500. Welfare grants totalled almost £2,100, and included £800 given to widows.

Applications

Apply in writing to the correspondent.

Other information

Grants are also made to individuals for sports and adventure training, and to organisations.

At the time of writing (January 2018) the website was under construction.

Red Cypher

£36,500

Correspondent: Brian O'Neill, Unit 5, Blue Barns Business Park, Old Ipswich Road, Ardleigh, Colchester C07 7FX (01206 751999; email: enquiry@redcypher.com; website: www.redcypher.com)

CC number: 1161345

Eligibility

Past and present members of 3rd Regiment Royal Horse Artillery who are in need.

Types of grants

One-off grants according to need.

Annual grant total

In 2016/17 the charity had assets of £28,000 and an income of £61,000. Grants to individuals totalled £36,500.

Applications

Application forms are available to download from the charity's website and should be returned by email to enquiry@redcypher.com.

The REME Charity

£273,000 (370 grants)

Correspondent: Lt Col. Michael Tizard, Corps Sec. & CEO, RHQ REME, The Prince Philip Barracks, MOD Lyneham, Lyneham, Wiltshire SN15 4XX (01249 894507; email: corpssec@reme-rhq.org.uk; website: remecharity.org)

CC number: 1165868

Eligibility

Serving and retired members of the Corps of Royal Electrical and Mechanical

Engineers who are in need. Applicants should have served for at least one year in the regular army or at least three years as a reserve.

Types of grants

One-off grants are given for a wide range of welfare needs. In 2016 the average grant was £504.

Annual grant total

In 2016 the charity had assets of £14.06 million and an income of more than £2 million. The charity made 370 grants, totalling £273,000, from the benevolent fund. Of the grants made, 35 were to serving personnel and 335 to veterans.

Applications

Applications should be made through SSAFA or The Royal British Legion.

Other information

The charity's website explains:

> Charitable donations are collected through the days' pay scheme and spent on providing grants to regular, reserve and retired REME personnel and their families in line with the charitable objectives. Approximately a third is spent on benevolence, a third on developing our personnel through sport and adventurous training, and the remainder is spent on fostering espirit de corps though memorial, heritage and social events.

The Rifles Benevolent Trust

£156,000

Correspondent: Capt. I. I. Foster (Retired), The Rifles Benevolent Trust, Regimental Headquarters The Rifles, Peninsula Barracks, Romsey Road, Winchester, Hants SO23 8TS (01962 828530 OR 01962 828126; email: benevolence@the-rifles.co.uk)

CC number: 1119071

Eligibility

Serving and ex-serving members of The Rifles, their spouses, partners, widows or other dependants who find themselves in need of assistance.

The website states that 'In all cases there must be genuine hardship brought about through circumstances and not by the individuals own design.'

Types of grants

Grants in the form of weekly pensions. One-off grants for such things as disability adaptations, mobility equipment, rent, priority debts, clothing and household necessities.

Annual grant total

In 2016 the trust held assets of £18.9 million and had an income of £2.1 million. In 2016 the trust responded

to 534 applications, providing grants totalling £312,000. The trust also awards educational grants. We estimate that around £156,000 was given in grants to individuals for welfare purposes.

Applications

For weekly pensions, applications should be made to ABF The Soldiers Charity.

The Rifles Officers' Fund

£2,900

CC number: 1025591

Eligibility

Serving and former officers of the Rifles Regiment, its territorial units and its former regiments, and their dependants, who are in need.

Types of grants

Grants are given to individuals who are in conditions of need, hardship or distress. These can cover such things as disability adaptations (e.g. stairlifts, bath hoists), mobility equipment (e.g. wheelchairs, EPVs), rent, rates, bills, clothing or household necessities. Pensions are also available to people who are older or very sick.

Annual grant total

In 2016 the fund had assets of £1.8 million and an income of £45,000. Grants to individuals totalled £2,900.

Applications

Apply in writing to the correspondent. Applications are considered quarterly.

Royal Artillery Charitable Fund

£630,500 (1,243 grants)

Correspondent: Lt Col. I. A. Vere Nicoll, Regimental Secretary, Artillery House, Royal Artillery Barracks, Larkhill, Salisbury, Wiltshire SP4 8QT (01980 634309; email: rarhq-racf-welfaremailbox@mod.uk; website: www.theraa.co.uk/about/ra-charitable-fund)

CC number: 210202

Eligibility

All serving or retired officers and soldiers of the Royal Artillery and their dependants who are in need. Widowed or divorced partners are also supported.

Types of grants

The charity awards one-off and recurrent grants for a broad range of welfare purposes, including provisions for household items, paying bills, clothing, and transport.

Annual grant total

In 2016 the charity had assets of £30.7 million and an income of £1.57 million. During the year, the charity awarded 1,243 grants to individuals totalling £630,500. A further £253,500 was awarded to regiments and institutions.

The annual report states that the charity 'assisted 1,340 cases in 2016 of which 119 were serving. 25 other ineligible cases were declined, as they were not Gunners.' The average grant for welfare assistance was £488.

Exclusions

Grants are not given towards income tax, loans, credit card debts, telephone bills, legal fees or private medical treatment.

Applications

In the first instance, contact the correspondent for more information on how to apply.

Royal Commonwealth Ex-Services League

£2.6 million

CC number: 231322

Eligibility

Ex-servicemen and women of the crown, and their widows or dependants, who are living outside the UK.

Types of grants

All types of help can be considered. Grants are one-off and are generally for medical costs such as hearing aids, wheelchairs, artificial limbs, or for food or repairs to homes wrecked by floods or hurricanes, etc.

Annual grant total

In 2016 the charity held assets of £5.2 million and had an income of £1.6 million. The charity's total welfare expenditure amounted to £2.6 million during the year.

Applications

Requests are considered daily on receipt of applications from member organisations or British embassies/high commissions, but not directly from individuals. Applications should include proof of military service to the crown.

Other information

The league has members or representatives in most parts of the world through whom former servicemen or their dependants living abroad can seek help. The local British embassy or high commission can normally supply the relevant local contact. In a Commonwealth country, the local ex-Service association will probably be affiliated to the league. The league's annual report, available from the Charity Commission or from the league, gives an interesting breakdown and analysis of funds allocated according to location.

In 2016 the league assisted 9,835 ex-servicemen, women and widows.

Royal Engineers' Association

£338,000 (1,227 grants)

Correspondent: Lt Col. Neil Jordan, Deputy Controller, Brompton Barracks, Chatham, Kent ME4 4UG (01634 822982; email: benevolence@reahq.org.uk; website: www.reahq.org.uk)

CC number: 258322

Eligibility

Past or present members of the corps, and their dependants, who are in need.

Types of grants

One-off and recurrent grants. Grants are given for a wide range of purposes including mobility aids and walk-in showers. Regular weekly allowances are made to around 140 people. Christmas cards, and in some cases monetary gifts, are sent out in November to around 1,200 people who are resident in older people's homes, hospitals and care homes and to those in receipt of weekly pensions. Annuities for top-up fees for nursing homes are given in exceptional circumstances.

Annual grant total

In 2016 the association had assets of £12.3 million and an income of £1.2 million. Awards to 1,227 individuals totalled £338,000 and were distributed as follows:

Grants	£241,000
Weekly allowances	£78,500
Christmas Grants	£18,500

Exclusions

No grants are given for private education, private medical fees, court or legal fees or debts.

Applications

Application forms are available from the correspondent. Applications should be submitted through SSAFA or The Royal British Legion.

Further information about the provision of benevolence by the REA can be obtained by contacting HQ REA on 01634 847005.

Royal Military Police Central Benevolent Fund

£66,000 (83 grants)

Correspondent: Col. Jeremy Green, DVPG, Southwick, Fareham, Hampshire PO17 6EJ (02392284206; email: rhqrmp@btconnect.com)

CC number: 248713

Eligibility

People who are serving or have served in the Royal Military Police corps, or any of its predecessors, and their dependants.

Types of grants

One-off cash grants typically up to £1,000, although larger grants may be available. Grants have been made towards heating, funeral expenses, household furniture, debts, clothing and bedding, mobility aids, holidays, medical needs, special chairs, removals and other needs. Christmas grants are distributed to people who have received an individual benefit grant and are over 80 years of age.

Annual grant total

In 2016/17 the fund held assets of £4.4 million and had an income of £290,000. Grants to individuals totalled £66,000 and were distributed as follows:

Individual grants	£50,500
Annuities	£8,000
Christmas grants	£6,200
Nursing home fees	£1,000

Applications

Apply in writing to the correspondent.

The Royal Corps of Signals Benevolent Fund

£282,500 (565 grants)

Correspondent: Col. Terrance Canham, Secretary, RHQ Royal Signals, Griffin House, Blandford Camp, Blandford Forum, Dorset DT11 8RH (01258 482081; email: rsignalshq-regtsec@mod.uk; website: www.royalsignals.org/rsbf)

CC number: 284923

Eligibility

Members and former members of the Royal Signals, regular or territorial volunteer reserve, and their widows and other dependants.

Types of grants

One-off and recurrent grants are given according to need. Grants are given towards priority debts, such as rent and utilities, mobility aids, white goods, household repairs and Christmas allowances. Applications for amounts above £800 are approved only at Welfare Committee meetings.

Annual grant total

In 2016 the fund had assets of £11 million and an income of more than £1.4 million. During the year, 565 grants were made totalling £282,500.

In 2016 £43,000 was paid to other charities with similar objectives.

Exclusions

The fund does not distribute loans.

Applications

Applications should be made through SSAFA Forces Help or another charitable organisation and are considered as required.

Other information

The fund is an amalgamation of the Royal Signals Association Fund, the Royal Signals Officers Fund and the Royal Signals Corps Fund.

Welsh Guards Charity

£69,000

Correspondent: T.C.S Bonas, RHQ Welsh Guards, Wellington Barracks, Birdcage Walk, London SW1E 6HQ (020 7414 3288)

CC number: 1152766

Eligibility

Serving and ex-serving members of the Welsh Guards, and their dependants, who are in need.

Types of grants

One-off grants have been awarded in the past for medical equipment, therapy, essential items and short breaks.

Annual grant total

In 2016/17 the charity held assets of £6.7 million and had an income of £395,000. We estimate that around £69,000 was paid out to support the welfare of individuals during the year.

Applications

The charity's website states that applicants must contact the Regimental Veterans Officer (RV0), Jiffy Myers (tel: 07456 985727; email: welshguardsrvo@gmail.com).

Other information

The Welsh Guards Charity was established in 2013 as a result of amalgamating several different regimental charities and funds.

At the time of writing (January 2018) the Welsh Guards Charity's website was under construction. The charity's impact report (2017/18) states that it will:

Shortly be available at www. welshguardscharity.co.uk and will pull together all the various strands of the charity into one easily navigable place, giving examples of the work we do, details on fundraising, news on the Battalion, how to donate and much more besides.

Royal Air Force

The Royal Air Force Benevolent Fund

£7.08 million (7,713 grants)

Correspondent: Welfare Team, 67 Portland Place, London W1B 1AR (0800 169 2942; email: info@rafbf.org.uk; website: www.rafbf.org)

CC number: 1081009

Eligibility

Past and present members of the RAF, their partners, dependent children (under the age of 18), widows and widowers. Reservists and individuals who completed National Service are also assisted.

The charity notes on its website that in order to qualify for general support, you must have less than £16,000 in savings and less than £23,250 if you require home top-up assistance.

Types of grants

Grants or loans can be given for a wide range of welfare needs. Grants are given towards, for example: day-to-day living costs, such as utility bills or essential household items; mobility equipment; welfare breaks; sickness maintenance grants; funeral costs; and emergency needs. Assistance is also given with care home fees.

Annual grant total

In 2016 the charity had assets of £108.3 million and had an income of £23.3 million. We have estimated that grants made directly to individuals totalled over £7.08 million. This figure does not take into account a further £3 million spent on residential and respite care, £2.6 million spent on housing and £2.4 million spent on welfare programmes.

The annual report states that 7,713 individuals were directly supported by the fund with a further 4,310 individuals supported through programmes. An additional 53,070 individuals were awarded grants through RAF stations and other charities.

Exclusions

No grants are given for private medical costs or for legal fees.

Applications

Requests for assistance can be made by contacting the charity. There is an online contact form on the website. Alternatively, assistance can also be obtained through RAFA and SSAFA. The charity runs a free helpline which potential applicants are welcome to call for advice and support on the application process. Applications are considered on a continuous basis.

Other information

The charity provides advice and assistance on a range of issues including benefits, debt advice and relationships. It also can support its beneficiaries with residential and respite care and housing. See the website for more information on the services, support and financial assistance available.

The Royal Air Forces Association

£58,000

Correspondent: Welfare team, Atlas House, 41 Wembley Road, Leicester LE3 1UT (0800 018 2361; email: enquiries@rafa.org.uk; website: www.rafa.org.uk)

CC number: 226686

Eligibility

Serving and former members of the Royal Air Force (including National Service), and their dependants. The widows and widowers and dependants of those who have died in Service, or subsequently, are also eligible for assistance.

Types of grants

Small, one-off grants when all other sources of funding have been exhausted. Grants have been awarded for gas and electricity bills, clothing, bedding, electrical goods, furniture and hospital travel costs. Help can also be given for assistance in the home and respite breaks.

Annual grant total

In 2016 the association had assets of £30.3 million and an income of £12.85 million. Welfare grants were made totalling £58,000.

Exclusions

Grants are not made to help with credit card debts or medical fees.

Applications

Support can be accessed by contacting the relevant local area welfare office:

- **Head office** (contact details above)
- **Northern area:** 82–83 Fishergate, Preston PR1 2NJ (tel: 01772 426930)
- **Scotland and Northern Ireland area:** 20 Queen Street, Edinburgh EH2 1JX (tel: 0131 225 5221)
- **South East and Eastern area:** Atlas House, 41 Wembley Road, Leicester LE3 1UT (tel: 0116 268 8784)
- **Wales, Midland and South West area:** RAFA House, Chancel Lane, Pinhoe, Exeter EX4 8JU (tel: 01392 462088)

Other information

The association provides a range of welfare support and advice for its beneficiaries, including in relation to war pensions and the Armed Forces Compensation Scheme (AFCS). It also facilitates welfare breaks through its three Wing Breaks hotels, and manages three sheltered accommodation facilities. More information is available from the website or by contacting the relevant local area team.

The Royal Observer Corps Benevolent Fund

£49,000 (42 grants)

Correspondent: The Secretary, 120 Perry Hall Road, Orpington, Kent BR6 0EF (01572 768133; fax: 01689 839031; email: info@rocbf.org.uk; website: www.rocbf.org.uk)

CC number: 209640

Eligibility

All former members of the Royal Observer Corps who are in need, hardship or distress. Length of service is not a consideration, except that the person for whom the application has been made must have served long enough to have received their Royal Observer Corps official number. Eligibility also extends to their widows, widowers and dependants.

Types of grants

Almost all types of grants can be considered. Typically the fund can provide financial help for mobility aids, essential home repairs or modification, household goods and respite care.

Annual grant total

In 2016 the fund had assets of over £1 million and an income of £27,500. During the year, the fund gave almost £49,000 in grants to 42 individuals.

Exclusions

Grants are not given towards debts or arrears owed to government bodies.

Applications

Applicants can request help using a contact form on the charity's website. Individuals are also referred through SSAFA, The Royal British Legion, the Royal Air Forces Association or other organisation. Applications are considered on receipt and normally a decision is given within days.

Royal Navy and Marines

Help Our Wounded Royal Marines and Supporting Arms

£9,300

Correspondent: Julie Hutton, Secretary and Administrator, Bishop Fleming, 2nd Floor Stratus House, Emperor Way, Exeter Business Park, Exeter, Kent EX1 3QS (email: info@helpourwounded.co.uk; website: helpourwounded.co.uk)

CC number: 1150893

Eligibility

Serving Royal Marines and their Supporting Arms and former troops dating back to World War II. Dependants can also be supported.

Types of grants

One-off grants according to need. Grants are usually made for equipment and living costs.

Annual grant total

In 2016/17 the charity held assets of £83,000 and had an income of £52,500. Grants to individuals totalled £9,300 and a further £13,300 was awarded to armed forces charities.

Applications

Apply in writing to the correspondent.

Other information

The charity provides a wide range of services to support its beneficiaries to continue with their lives.

Hull Trinity House Charity

£401,500 (2,198 grants)

Correspondent: Richard East, Hull Trinity House Charity, Trinity House, Trinity House Lane, Hull HU1 2JG (01482 324956; email: secretary@ trinityhouse.karoo.co.uk)

CC number: 220331

Eligibility

Seafarers, their spouses and dependants, and spouses and dependants of deceased seafarers who are in need.

Types of grants

One-off grants according to need.

Annual grant total

In 2015/16 the charity held assets of £38 million and had an income of £1.7 million. During the year, the charity gave around £401,500 in grants to 2,198 individuals.

Applications

Apply in writing to the correspondent.

Other information

The charity provides 'rest homes' which provide accommodation for recipients of grants, or non-seafarers who are in need. The charity also supports the Trinity House Academy and Welton Waters Adventure Centre.

The Royal Naval Benevolent Trust

£2.2 million

Correspondent: The Grants Administrator, Castaway House, 311 Twyford Avenue, Portsmouth PO2 8RN (023 9269 0112; email: rnbt@ rnbt.org.uk; website: www.rnbt.org.uk)

CC number: 206243

Eligibility

Members of 'The RNBT Family'; serving and former Royal Navy ratings and Royal Marines other ranks, and their dependants, who are in need.

Types of grants

One-off and recurrent grants for a range of needs. The trust's website provides the following non-exhaustive list of categories of need: medical and dental; respite breaks; house repairs; food; funerals; clothing; furniture/furnishings; mortgage; household goods; education; rent; energy/fuel; removals; employment/ training; council tax and rates; telephone; care home top-up fees; domiciliary care; legal expenses; house adaptations (medical).

Annual grant total

In 2016/17 the trust had assets of £43.5 million an income of £5.6 million. Welfare grants to individuals totalled £2.2 million.

Applications

Contact your local Royal Marines or Royal Navy Welfare or local branch of SSAFA or The Royal British Legion. They will arrange a caseworker to visit you to complete an application form.

Other information

Among its activities, RNBT runs a residential and nursing home for older ex-naval men (not women) namely, Pembroke House in Gillingham.

The Royal Navy and Royal Marines Children's Fund

£443,500

Correspondent: Monique Bateman, Director, Castaway House, 311 Twyford Avenue, Stamshaw, Portsmouth PO2 8RN (023 9263 9534; email: caseworkers@rnrmchildrensfund.org.uk; website: www.rnrmchildrensfund.org)

CC number: 1160182

Eligibility

Dependants of serving and ex-serving members of the Royal Navy, the Royal Marines, the Queen Alexandra's Royal Naval Service or the former Women's Royal Naval Service, who are under the age of 25 and are in need.

Types of grants

One-off and recurrent grants are given for a range of welfare needs including food, clothing, hospital travel expenses, respite care, specialist equipment and childcare costs. Support is also available for children who have suffered bereavement or who have experienced a family breakdown or parental divorce.

Annual grant total

In 2016/17 the charity had assets of £10.5 million and an income of £1.2 million. Welfare grants totalled £443,500. Grants to individuals were broken down as follows:

School fees	£386,000
Clothing and equipment	£243,000
Childminding and respite	£161,500
Children's travel	£64,000
Extra tuition fees	£57,500
Other charitable expenditure	£270

Applications

Apply using a form available from the correspondent or for download from the website. Applications can be submitted directly by the individual or through the individual's school/college, SSAFA, social services or other third party. The fund can be contacted by telephone and can provide, where possible, assistance with the form's completion. Applications can be made at any time.

The Royal Navy Officers's Charity

£317,500

Correspondent: Commander Michael Goldthorpe, 70 Porchester Terrace, Bayswater, London W2 3TP (020 7402 5231; email: rnoc@arno.org.uk; website: www.arno.org.uk)

CC number: 207405

Eligibility

Officers, both in active Service and retired, of the Royal Navy, Royal Marines, QARNNS and WRNS and their reserves, and their spouses, former spouses, families and dependants, who are in need.

Types of grants

One-off grants and recurrent payments. Grants have been awarded towards nursing home fees, the provision of disability or mobility aids, the replacement of white goods, home repairs and to supplement inadequate incomes.

Annual grant total

In 2016 the charity had assets of £15 million and an income of £539,500 million. Grants to individuals for welfare purposes totalled £317,500.

Exclusions

Grants are not normally given for private medical care or education (other than from the RN Scholarship Fund), except in very exceptional circumstances.

Applications

Contact the Director for further details.

Other information

The society was founded on 16 May 1739 by a group of naval officers suffering from unreasonable treatment by the Admiralty. The benevolent function of the society emerged later and became its sole purpose in 1791.

In 2008, the Association of Royal Navy Officers Charitable Trust transferred its assets to the society and the charity changed its name from the Royal Naval Benevolent Society for Officers.

Special Boat Service Association

£520,500

Correspondent: The Association CEO, HQ SQN, RM Poole, Hamworthy, Poole, Dorset BH15 4NQ (01202 202692; email: ceo@association1664.com)

CC number: 1105052

Eligibility

Members and former members of the Special Boat Service, their families and dependants.

Types of grants

One-off grants for welfare purposes, memorials and funeral expenses.

Annual grant total

In 2016/17 the charity had assets of £11.5 million and had an income of £3.9 million. During the year, the charity gave around £520,500 in grants to individuals.

Applications

Apply in writing to the correspondent.

WRNS Benevolent Trust

£273,000 (236 grants)

Correspondent: Roger Collings, Grants Administrator, Castaway House, 311 Twyford Avenue, Portsmouth, Hampshire PO2 8RN (023 9265 5301; fax: 023 9267 9040; email: grantsadmin@wrnsbt.org.uk; website: www.wrnsbt.org.uk)

CC number: 206529

Eligibility

Ex-Wrens and female serving members of the Royal Navy (officers and ratings) who joined the Service between 3 September 1939 and 1 November 1993 who are in need.

Types of grants

One-off and recurrent grants. Recurrent grants are given in the following categories: general amenity; care enhancement; overseas (for beneficiaries who live overseas); weekly maintenance; and weekly support supplements. One-off grants are available towards a wide range of needs, for example: household goods and repairs; priority debts and arrears; medical aids; funeral expenses; removal and travel expenses; and rent and deposits.

Annual grant total

In 2016 the trust had assets of £4 million and had an income of £454,500. Grants to individuals totalled £276,000, with £3,100 of this awarded for educational purposes. Grants for social welfare purposes totalled £273,000.

Exclusions

People who deserted from the Service are not eligible.

Applications

Applications can be made directly to the correspondent; however, the trust states the following on its website:

> The WRNS Benevolent Trust is a small Charity. We have no caseworkers of our own and therefore work mainly with the Royal British Legion (RBL) and the Soldiers, Sailors, Airmen and Families Association (SSAFA), and their caseworkers call on any applicant on our behalf. They are discreet and knowledgeable, and can give friendly support and advice on a wide variety of matters. They complete a report, which is then put before our Grants Committee for consideration.

Applications can be made directly by the individual or, with their consent, by a relation or friend.

Other information

The trust states the following on its informative website:

> One of our biggest problems is raising awareness; it is surprising how many former Wrens do not even know of our existence. If you ever hear of a former Wren who you think may be having difficulties, do please tell her about us or approach us on her behalf. Many are too proud to ask for help, but we always stress that we are their special charity and one which they may have contributed to during their time in the Women's Royal Naval Service.

Occupational charities

This section begins with an index of categories of occupation, which are listed alphabetically.

First, the charities with wide occupational criteria, including trade unions, are listed. Whether members or not, individuals should check for any trade unions listed that cover their area of work, as they will sometimes have resources available for non-member workers in their sector, as well as benevolent funds and other support for members.

Following this section, the charities are arranged alphabetically within each occupational category. Grant-makers include both independent charities and benevolent funds associated with particular professional bodies.

Many of the grant-making charities listed here support not only members of a particular occupation, but also their dependants (such as parents, children and partners). This may present additional options to explore when identifying a relevant occupational category.

Being a member of a particular profession or trade is not necessarily enough to be eligible for support – charities may also specify further criteria, so do read the entries in each section carefully.

We have grouped together certain occupations to make relevant charities easier to identify. For example, 'Hospitality and retail' includes charities with general criteria supporting employees in these industries, as well as charities which support a very specific branch of occupation within this sector.

We have placed all 'Medical and health' workers in the same category, as again there are charities that support workers generally and some that will only support certain specific occupations. The 'Food and drink provision' section contains many different individual roles within the industry and similarly, the 'Skilled crafts and trades' section includes charities covering a wide range of occupations.

Some sectors have been further divided into sub-categories of occupation, such as 'Arts and Culture' or 'Public and government sector', which firstly lists charities with broad criteria within this sector, followed by sub-sections for 'Civil service', 'Emergency services', 'Prison services' and 'Social services'.

In some cases, paid employment is not necessary – for example, under 'Sports' there are some grant-making charities that support amateur sports people. In this edition, charities concerning clergy and missionaries have been listed under 'Religion' in this chapter; for charities that give based on religious group rather than religious occupation, refer to the chapter 'Charities by beneficiary'.

Please also note that charities which specify both occupation and location are still mainly listed under the appropriate occupational heading, but those with a very specific location (such as the 'Manx Marine Society', for example) may be listed in the relevant geographical chapter instead.

The National Association of Cooperative Officials (NACO) Benevolent Fund

£9,600

Correspondent: Lynne Higginbottom, Finance/Administration Manager, 6A Clarendon Place, Hyde, Cheshire SK14 2QZ (0161 351 7900; fax: 0161 366 6800; email: info@naco.coop; website: www.naco.coop)

CC number: 262269

Eligibility

Members and former members of the association, and their dependants, including widows and children of deceased members, who are in need.

Types of grants

One-off grants of up to a maximum of £1,000.

Additional grants of up to £2,500 are available to a spouse/civil partner (or other nominated person) upon the death of a member while in membership to help with bereavement costs and funeral expenses.

Annual grant total

In 2016 the fund had an income of £6,400 and a total expenditure of £9,800. We estimate that the fund gave around £9,600 in grants to individuals.

Applications

Application forms are available to download from the charity's website. They can be submitted directly by the individual including details of personal finance. Applications are considered at executive meetings, dates of which are available online.

Prospect Benevolent Fund and Death Benefit Scheme

£102,000 (92 grants)

Correspondent: Membership Team, New Prospect House, 8 Leake Street, London SE1 7NN (0300 600 1878; email: info@prospect.org.uk; website: www.prospect.org.uk/member-benefits/benevolentfund)

Eligibility

Members and retired members of the union (and the former Institution of Professional Civil Servants), and their dependants, who are experiencing financial problems.

Types of grants

Generally one-off grants with recurrent grants not exceeding £1,500. The trustees aim to relieve immediate problems and often point applicants to other channels and agencies for long-term solutions. Grants are usually sent to the applicant, but for speed and/or reliability, some awards are sent direct to the utility/body owed money. Occasionally this is processed through an agency or second party (such as a welfare officer, debt counsellor, branch officer or relative).

The union also makes death benefit grants to dependants of deceased members (except retired members) which are equal to five times the higher national rate annual subscription.

Annual grant total

In 2016 the fund held assets of £639,500 and had an income of £21,500. Grants for welfare support were made to seven individuals totalling £12,300. An additional £90,000 was given in 85 death grants, from a separate fund.

Exclusions

The fund does not make loans.

Applications

Application forms are available from the correspondent. They can be submitted directly by the individual or through the employer's welfare officers or branch representatives. Applications are considered throughout the year and generally are processed quickly.

Mr William Saunders Charity for the Relief of Indigent Gentry and Others

£8,000

Correspondent: St Andrew Trustees Ltd, c/o Charles Russell LLP, 5 Fleet Street, London EC4M 7Rd (020 7427 6500)

CC number: 212012

Eligibility

'Indigent gentry, tutors, governesses, merchants and others'; and their dependants, who are on low incomes and live throughout England and Wales.

Types of grants

Recurrent grants for people on low incomes.

Annual grant total

In 2015 the charity had an income of £9,300 and a total expenditure of £8,900. We estimate that pensions to individuals totalled £8,000.

Applications

Apply in writing to the correspondent.

There For You (UNISON Welfare)

£512,000

Correspondent: Tina Willis, Casework Team, UNISON Centre, 130 Euston Road, London NW1 2AY (08000857 857; email: thereforyou@unison.co.uk; website: www.unison.org.uk/welfare)

CC number: 1023552

Eligibility

Financial help is given to UNISON members and in certain circumstances former members of NALGO can apply. Partners/dependants of deceased members can apply in their own right.

Types of grants

One-off grants for individuals experiencing unforeseen difficulties such as redundancy, illness, bereavement or relationship breakdown. Recent awards have been given to help with household bills, travel costs, childcare, school uniforms, winter fuel costs, furniture, domestic appliances, funeral expenses, disability aids, etc. Emergency grants are available when there is a crisis and money is needed quickly.

Annual grant total

In 2016 the trust had assets of £6.8 million, an income of £1.3 million and a total charitable expenditure of £1.1 million. Grants were made totalling £512,000 and can be broken down as follows:

Household	£186,500
Income subsidy	£128,500
Other purposes	£65,500
Debt and bankruptcy	£61,500
Funeral expenses	£49,500
Well-being breaks	£11,000
Health	£8,500

Exclusions

Grants are generally not given for educational costs, private medical treatment, legal fees, car purchase or income lost due to industrial action.

Applications

Individuals should at first contact their branch welfare officer or secretary who will help them to fill in an application form. Applications are usually processed within two weeks, although urgent requests can be dealt with more quickly, sometimes within 48 hours. People who are having difficulty contacting their local branch may submit the form, available from the website, directly to the national office.

Note: there are separate application forms for welfare grants and well-being breaks.

Other information

The trust, previously known simply as UNISON Welfare, provides support and advice on a variety of issues including personal debt and state benefits.

UNITE the Union Benevolent Fund

£83,500

Correspondent: Steven Skinner, Trustee, Eastham Hall, 109 Eastham Village Road, Eastham, Wirral CH62 0AF (0844 880 1803; email: applications@unitebf. org; website: www.unitetheunion.org/ how-we-help/memberoffers/ benevolentfund)

CC number: 228567

Eligibility

Members, former members, employees or ex-employees of the union and their dependants.

Types of grants

One-off grants of between £100 and £1,000 to people who have fallen on hard times through being absent from work through prolonged sickness, retirement through ill health, family bereavements or a change in domestic circumstances. Grants have included payment towards a riser/recliner for person with back problems, help to somebody dismissed while on sick leave, heating grants for older people, Christmas bonuses for people who are older or have young children, and general assistance with bills.

Annual grant total

In 2016 the fund had assets of £1 million and an income of £157,000. Grants to individuals totalled £83,500.

Exclusions

Help with legal fees, educational grants and credit card bills is not usually available.

Applications

Application forms are available to download from the fund's website. The application form will ask you to give full details of your income, savings, capital, debts and housing expenditure, as well as information about your circumstances and Unite the Union membership or employment.

Architecture

Architects' Benevolent Society

£645,000 (264 grants)

Correspondent: Welfare Team, 43 Portland Place, London W1B 1QH (020 7580 2823; email: help@absnet.org. uk; website: www.absnet.org.uk)

CC number: 265139

Eligibility

People engaged or formerly engaged in the practice of architecture, and their dependants. This includes (but is not limited to) architects, assistants, technicians and technologists and landscape architects. Eligibility is based on work experience in the UK rather than being a member of one of the professional membership organisations.

Types of grants

Recurrent monthly grants, one-off grants and interest-free loans.

Annual grant total

In 2015/16 the society held assets of almost £33.4 million and had an income of £1.4 million. Grants and gifts to 264 individuals totalled £645,000. The annual report for 2015/16 provides the following breakdown: during the year, 482 separate cases were helped, of these 264 received direct financial assistance, the remainder received pastoral care and advice. Grants were made to 29 new cases.

Exclusions

No educational grants or grants to naval architects.

Applications

A short application form is available from the correspondent or to download from the website. Applications can be submitted directly by the individual or through a social worker, Citizens Advice or other welfare agency. Once received, the society will arrange a visit by one of their welfare officers. Applications are considered throughout the year.

Other information

The society also has a partnership with Anxiety UK through which applicants can receive helpline and email support, a well-being assessment which includes one year's membership to Anxiety UK and one-to-one therapy via a network of approved therapists.

Details of the grants available and the awards procedure are contained within the trustees' annual report for 2015/16. Grants are made to those who need help on a regular basis and gifts are provided for specific essential items that a person would otherwise be unable to afford. Interest-free loans are sometimes made where a beneficiary may be able to repay the society at some time in the future.

The committee works in close co-operation with two full-time welfare officers who visit most beneficiaries in person annually and as a result have first-hand knowledge of the circumstances of each case. Assessments and recommendations are prepared by the welfare team for consideration by the committee. Visiting people in their own homes is believed to be an essential part of the assistance given to people in need and visiting is written into the charity's constitution as one of the basic ways in which help is provided.

The welfare officers keep up to date with the latest information on state benefits in order to be able to give advice on subjects such as Universal Credit and with colleagues in other professional benevolent funds.

The society can provide financial assistance very rapidly in cases of pressing need and is able to do so within 24 hours when necessary. In this regard, the welfare team works closely with the chair of the case committee who is authorised to agree urgent applications for financial help between committee meetings. The society's trained welfare officers can offer support and information on various issues, including those relating to the state benefits system.

Arts and culture

Equity Charitable Trust

£102,000 (108 grants)

Correspondent: Kaethe Cherney, Plouviez House, 19–20 Hatton Place, London EC1N 8RU (020 7831 1926; email: kaethe@equitycharitabletrust.org.uk; website: www.equitycharitabletrust.org.uk)

CC number: 328103

Eligibility

Professionals in the field of entertainment, who are eligible for an Equity card. The trust typically assists those who are unable to work due to an illness or accident, although individuals who are experiencing financial hardship due to an emergency may also be eligible.

Types of grants

One-off grants to help with financial emergencies. Grants can assist with many needs – from utility bills and home

repairs, to convalescent care and health-care costs. Each case is considered on its merits and the trust tries to make grants in proportion to the individual's need.

Annual grant total

In 2015/16 the trust had assets of £10.8 million and an income of £419,500. Grants to 108 individuals for welfare purposes totalled £102,000. Education and training grants to 48 individuals totalled £100,500.

Exclusions

The trust cannot help amateur performers, musicians or drama students. Help cannot be given with credit card debt.

Applications

Applications can be made using a form, which is available to download from the website or on request by emailing rosalind@equitycharitabletrust.org.uk or by calling 020 7831 1926. They are considered at Welfare Committee meetings every six weeks.

Other information

As part of an application, beneficiaries are able to speak with an experienced money advisor who can help to find other sources of funding, including state benefits.

The Royal Literary Fund

£1.3 million (227 grants)

Correspondent: Eileen Gunn, Chief Executive, 3 Johnson's Court, Off Fleet Street, London EC4A 3EA (020 7353 7159; email: eileen.gunn@rlf.org.uk; website: www.rlf.org.uk)

CC number: 219952

Eligibility

Authors of published work of literary merit and their dependants. You are eligible to apply for help from the RLF if you have commercially published several works in the UK for a general readership and are suffering financial hardship. The work must be written in English. Books stemming from a parallel career as an academic or practitioner are not eligible.

Types of grants

One-off (outright) grants, instalment grants and pensions. Instalment grants and pensions are awarded over a three and five-year period respectively. Pensions are reviewed for renewal after the five-year period.

Recent examples of beneficiaries include:

- A writer suffering from ME. She had recently had a baby and lost some of her regular paid work. Her husband had also lost his job. The committee made her an annual grant

- A poet and his wife living on a tight budget. Their house needed urgent repairs and their savings had been depleted. The committee made him an annual pension
- An award-winning writer of science fiction taking time out from fiction to work on screenplays. This had not been a success and he had lost vital income. The committee made him a grant

Annual grant total

In 2016/17 the fund had assets of over £169.5 million and an income of £2.2 million. Grants and pensions totalled £1.3 million.

The total number of grants awarded to individuals in the year was 99.

Exclusions

No grants are given for projects or work in progress. The trust does not make loans. Books stemming from a previous academic or practitioner career do not count.

Applications

Application forms are available from the correspondent. Application forms request details of all income and expenditure, and a member of staff will subsequently arrange to meet with new applicants at their homes. Applicants are asked to supply copies of their published work which is then read by two members of the committee who decide on the question of literary merit. When requesting an application form applicants are asked to provide a list of their publications, including names of publishers, dates and whether they were the sole author. If this is approved, a grant/pension may be made based on an assessment of need.

Other information

One grant was paid to the Royal Society of Literature (£10,000).

The Guild of Motoring Writers Benevolent Fund

£11,500

Correspondent: Elizabeth Aves, Correspondent, 23 Stockwell Park Crescent, London SW9 0DQ (020 7737 2377; email: benfundadmin@gomw.co.uk; website: www.gomw.co.uk)

CC number: 259583

Eligibility

Motoring writers, journalists, photographers, broadcasters or web editors, who are in need and are, or have been, members of the guild. Their dependants may also be supported.

Types of grants

Mainly loans to help with short-term financial difficulties, for example following redundancy or injury. Loans may in some cases be converted to grants at the discretion of the trustees.

Annual grant total

In 2016 the fund had an income of £24,500 and a total expenditure of £11,700. We estimate that the charity gave around £11,500 in grants/loans to individuals.

Applications

Apply in writing to the correspondent at any time. Applications can be made either directly by the individual or through a third party.

Other information

See also the entry for Ben, the automotive industry charity, which supports anyone who has worked in the motor industry.

The Evelyn Norris Trust

£33,000 (43 grants)

Correspondent: Kaethe Cherney, Acting Secretary, Plouviez House, 19–20 Hatton Place, London EC1N 8RU (020 7831 1926; fax: 020 7242 7995; email: kaethe@ equitycharitabletrust.org.uk; website: www.equitycharitabletrust.org.uk/ evelynnorris.php)

CC number: 260078

Eligibility

Members or ex-members of the concert or theatrical profession who are older, sick, have a disability or are otherwise in need.

Types of grants

One-off grants of up to £700 towards convalescence or recuperative holidays following illness, injury or surgery.

Annual grant total

In 2016 the trust had assets of £917,500 and an income of £41,000. During the year, the trust gave around £33,000 in grants to individuals.

Exclusions

No grants are given for student/ education course fees.

Applications

Application forms are available to download from the website, although the trust advises potential applicants to at first call or email to discuss eligibility details and the application process. Applications are considered monthly and can be submitted directly by the individual or through a social worker, Citizens Advice, welfare agency or any third party. Applications should include any relevant financial or personal information.

Other information

Grants have also been made to residential homes.

The Miss M. O. Taylor and Alexander Nasmyth Funds

£10,000

Correspondent: Pauline Costigane, Royal Scottish Academy, The Mound, Edinburgh EH2 2EL (0131 624 6111; email: paulinecostigane@ royalscottishacademy.org; website: www. royalscottishacademy.org)

OSCR number: SC007352 and SC004198

Eligibility

Scottish artists of established reputation, mainly in painting, sculpture, architecture or engraving, who are in need. To be eligible you must have had some previous experience of success in the profession, namely, having exhibited and sold work with a recognised gallery or institution.

Types of grants

One-off grants according to need.

Annual grant total

The Nasmyth Fund is registered separately from the Taylor Fund which is held as fund within the Royal Scottish Academy (RSA). In 2016/17 the Nasmyth Fund had an income of £11,600 and a total expenditure of £9,000.

We estimate that grants given to individuals from both funds combined usually total £10,000 per year.

Applications

Application forms are available from the correspondent. Awards are made once a year and the deadline is usually early June, check the website for the exact date.

The Royal Theatrical Fund

£241,000

Correspondent: Sharon Lomas, Secretary, West Suite, 2nd Floor, 11 Garrick Street, London WC2E 9AR (020 7836 3322; fax: 020 7379 8273; email: admin@trtf.com; website: www. trtf.com)

CC number: 222080

Eligibility

People who have professionally practised or contributed to the theatrical arts (on stage, radio, film or television or any other medium) for a minimum of seven years, who are in need, and the dependants of such people.

Types of grants

Monthly allowances and one-off grants towards domestic bills, shortfalls in nursing and residential fees, car tax, stairlifts, computers, insurance, TV licences, etc. Winter fuel allowances and occasional gifts are also awarded.

Annual grant total

In 2016/17 the fund held assets of almost £12.3 million and had an income of £799,500. Grants to individuals totalled £241,000 and were distributed as follows:

One-off grants/gifts and birthday and Christmas gifts	£119,000
Monthly allowances	£76,500
Nursing home/residential/ convalescent/home care	£45,500

Exclusions

No grants are made to students or towards courses or projects.

Applications

Apply using the form on the fund's website. Alternatively apply in writing to the correspondent, making sure to include: a letter outlining your financial difficulties and how the fund may be able to help; any other relevant information; a letter of support from your GP or hospital, or a current medical certificate; and a full CV or details of your theatrical career. Applications can be submitted at any time. The Welfare Committee meet on a monthly basis to consider applications. Telephone enquiries are welcome.

Other information

In cases where the fund cannot assist, the Welfare Committee may choose to refer the applicant to another suitable fund or organisation.

The fund also works to provide advice relating to state benefits and emotional support for beneficiaries who are lonely or isolated.

Acting, theatre and film

The Actors' Benevolent Fund

£647,500 (210+ grants)

Correspondent: Jonathan Ellicott, General Secretary, 6 Adam Street, London WC2N 6AD (020 7836 6378; email: office@abf.org.uk; website: www. actorsbenevolentfund.co.uk)

CC number: 206524

Eligibility

Professional actors and theatrical stage managers who are unable to work because of an accident, sickness or old age.

If you are a dancer, a singer or a background artist or if you are a member of the theatrical profession and have children under 19, there are other charities which may be able to help. Telephone the office for advice.

Types of grants

Weekly allowances; grants paid monthly, in summer and at Christmas; hampers; and winter heating grants. The fund also provides assistance with general household expenses, the cost of replacing household equipment, mobility aids, physiotherapy, osteopathy, the shortfall of nursing home fees and holiday and funeral costs.

Annual grant total

In 2016 the fund had assets of £27.6 million and an income of £1.7 million. Grants to over 210 individuals totalled £647,500, with 170 receiving regular help.

Exclusions

No grants are available to students. Grants are unlikely to be made for credit card debts, loans or private dental or medical treatment which should be covered by the NHS.

Applications

Application forms are available from the correspondent, online or to download from the fund's website. Applications should be submitted directly by the individual and include a detailed CV and, if appropriate, the applicant's Spotlight link, Equity number or IMDB entry. If applying due to ill health or an accident, a recent doctor's letter giving details of the individual's condition should be included. It may also be helpful to include any Benefit Agency letters which confirm the level of benefits received. Applications are considered on the last Thursday of each month and forms should be submitted by the Friday before a meeting.

In cases of emergency, where potential beneficiaries need their application to be considered before the next scheduled meeting contact the fund's office on 020 7836 6378 for advice.

Other information

The Actors' Benevolent Fund also provides advice on welfare and debt and supports its beneficiaries through visits, telephone calls and birthday cards.

The fund occasionally approaches other theatrical charities on behalf of applicants, if given permission to do so. There is a list of charities with which the fund has links available on its helpful website.

The Actors' Children's Trust (TACT)

£199,000

Correspondent: Robert Ashby, General Secretary, 58 Bloomsbury Street, London WC1B 3QT (020 7636 7868; email: robert@tactactors.org; website: www. tactactors.org)

CC number: 206809

Eligibility

Children of professional actors. Eligible acting jobs include characters with speaking roles, whether on stage, TV or film, in role play, TIE, corporates or commercials. Grants are usually given to families where household income is less than £40,000.

Types of grants

Grants are available for a wide range of needs including childcare, clothing and small monthly payments towards household costs.

Annual grant total

In 2016/17 the trust had assets of £88,000 and an income of £356,000. Grants to individuals totalled £398,500. We estimate that welfare grants totalled around £199,000.

Exclusions

The trust is not able to fund presenters or people who have mainly played extra roles. Grants are not usually given for private school fees.

Applications

Details of how to apply for each type of grant can be found on the trust's website.

The Theatrical Guild

£58,000 (67 grants)

Correspondent: Adam Bambrough, Office Manager, The Theatrical Guild, 11 Garrick Street, London WC2E 9AR (020 7240 6062; email: admin@ttg.org. uk; website: www.ttg.org.uk)

CC number: 206669

Eligibility

People who work, or have retired from a role, either backstage or front-of-house in a professional theatre. Financial support may be given where accident, ill health or other circumstances have prevented the applicant from working. In special cases, support may be given to working members of the profession and to one-parent families who are prevented from accepting a job due to the cost of childcare.

Types of grants

One-off and recurrent grants are typically given for bills, equipment, special medical needs and retraining costs.

Annual grant total

In 2016 the guild had assets of £1.8 million and an income of £126,500. During the year, grants totalling £58,000 were awarded to 67 individuals.

Exclusions

No grants are given for the repayment of credit card debt. Help cannot be given to help drama students, amateur performers or anyone who has not worked or does not currently work in professional theatre.

Applications

Application forms can be downloaded from the website or can be requested by calling or emailing the office. Applications can be submitted either directly by the individual, through a third party such as a social worker or through an organisation such as Citizens Advice. They are considered monthly, with the exception of August and December. Those seeking emergency assistance should contact the office directly by email or phone.

Other information

The guild also offers access to counselling, welfare support, personal and financial advice, and educational sponsorship. It can also signpost individuals to other sources of support.

Artists

Artists' General Benevolent Institution

£389,000 (120 grants)

Correspondent: Brad Feltham, Secretary, Burlington House, Piccadilly, London W1J 0BB (020 7734 1193; email: info@ agbi.org.uk; website: www.agbi.org.uk)

CC number: 212667

Eligibility

Professional artists, i.e. painters, sculptors, illustrators, art teachers at A-level or above, who live in England, Wales and Northern Ireland who have earned their living (or a major part of it) from art and cannot work due to accident, illness or old age, and their dependants. Widows and orphaned children of artists are also eligible for assistance.

Types of grants

One-off and recurrent grants to artists who through old age, illness or accident are unable to work and earn. Grants cover a wide range of items and uses, such as domestic and utility bills, repair of equipment or replacement of worn-out items, help to cover costs of car replacements, visits to family and friends and respite care. Recent grants have been awarded towards the costs of assisted living to help an artist with dementia, as well as contributions towards household utility bills for an artist with a progressive illness. Applicants can submit a further application for support if their needs are ongoing.

Annual grant total

In 2015/16 the charity had an income of £631,000 and a total expenditure of £612,500. Grants to 120 professional artists in need amounted to £389,000.

Exclusions

The charity cannot help with career or legal difficulties, loss of earnings due to poor sales etc., expenses associated with exhibitions, or (except in exceptional circumstances) student fees.

Applications

Applications should initially be made in writing, including a full CV listing all training, qualifications, exhibitions in professional galleries and teaching experience (if any) at GCSE, A-level or above. They can be submitted directly by the individual, through a recognised referral agency such Citizens Advice, or by a doctor, social worker etc. The secretary visits most potential beneficiaries in order to carry out an assessment and to collect original works, as well as letters from two referees and a doctor or consultant (if applicable). The council meets to consider applications regularly throughout the year. Enquiries from potential applicants are welcomed.

Eaton Fund for Artists, Nurses and Gentlewomen
See entry on page 22

Scottish Artists Benevolent Association

£11,000

Correspondent: The Secretary, Scottish Artists Benevolent Association, c/o Robb Ferguson, Regent Court, 70 West Regent Street, Glasgow G2 2QZ (email: lesley@robbferguson.co.uk; website: scottishartistsbenevolentassociation.co.uk)

OSCR number: SC011823

Eligibility

Scottish artists in need and their dependants. While grants are mainly given to people who are older or in poor health, the association manages two

other funds – the Gertrude Annie Lauder Fund for female artists and their dependants, and the Tod Endowment Fund which provides holidays in Scotland for artists, resident in Scotland for at least two years, who are experiencing difficulties.

Types of grants

Regular or one-off grants according to need.

Annual grant total

In 2016/17 the charity held assets of £767,500 and had an income of £61,500. During the year, a total of £11,000 was awarded in grants, £2,000 of which came from the Tod Fund, which provides holidays in Scotland for artists.

Exclusions

Funds cannot be used to further education or to exhibit work.

Applications

Application forms can be requested from the correspondent. Applications are considered in March and November. Emergency applications are considered on an ongoing basis.

Other information

The charity also manages two separate funds: the Gertrude Annie Lauder Fund, and the Tod Endowment Fund.

Dance

The Royal Ballet Benevolent Fund

£95,000

Correspondent: Clementine Cowl, Charity Manager, Royal Opera House, Covent Garden, London WC2E 9DD (01273 234011; email: info@rbbf.org.uk; website: www.rbbf.org.uk)

CC number: 207477

Eligibility

People who have been employed in a ballet or contemporary dance company as a dancer, dance teacher, choreographer, choreologist or as an independent dance artist for at least five years. In certain circumstances, the fund may consider people who do not fit this criteria e.g. people who have had their careers prematurely ended by injury.

Types of grants

One-off grants and regular payments are available to relieve any form of hardship. This includes financial assistance to older people on a low income, aids for people with a disability, help with the transition from dance to another career, or specialist surgery/therapy for injured dancers. Typical grants cover items such as supplementary pensions, disability

equipment and adaptations, medical treatment and care.

Annual grant total

In 2016/17 the fund held assets of £7.3 million and had an income of £374,000. During the year, the fund gave around £95,000 in grants to individuals.

Exclusions

There are no grants available for students training to be dancers. The fund cannot help dancers whose careers have not been within ballet or contemporary dance companies, for example dancers whose main career has been in musical theatre.

The fund does not normally pay off credit card debts.

Applications

Application forms are available from the correspondent or to download from the website. Applications should be submitted directly by the individual along with a professional CV. The form may be completed by someone else on behalf of the applicant but the applicant must sign. An assessment of the applicant's income based on earnings from work or benefits and an assessment of the applicant's expenditure should be submitted as supporting evidence. Confirmation of the applicant's professional details must be provided by at least one referee. The trustees meet to consider applications four times a year.

The trustees welcome informal enquiries to discuss an application prior to the submission of a formal application.

Other information

The fund offers non-financial assistance in the form of advice services and home visits.

There is an informative website, with links to other agencies offering similar assistance.

The International Dance Teachers' Association Ltd Benevolent Fund

£30,000 (23 grants)

Correspondent: Keith Holmes, Secretary, International House, 76 Bennett Road, Brighton, East Sussex BN2 5JL (01273 685652; fax: 01273 674388; email: info@idta.co.uk; website: www.idta.co.uk)

CC number: 297561

Eligibility

Members and former members of the association, other dancers, former dancers, teachers or former teachers of dance, employees or former employees of the association, and their dependants who are affected by hardship. Support is mainly given in cases where individuals are unable to teach or work due to sickness, injury or disability.

Types of grants

One-off grants of up to £1,000 are available. Support is of benevolent nature for people in need during times of crisis or ill health rather than to develop career.

Annual grant total

In 2016 the fund had assets of £241,000 and an income of £229,000. Grants were made to 23 individuals totalling £30,000.

Applications

Applications are available from the correspondent.

Other information

The fund also organises various dancing events and may sponsor dance-related organisations.

Entertainment

The Concert Artistes Association Benevolent Fund

£20,000

Correspondent: Barbara Daniels, 3 Malm Close, Rickmansworth, Herts WD3 1NR (01923 771030; email: office@thecaa.org)

CC number: 211012

Eligibility

Members of the association, and their dependants, who are in need.

Types of grants

One-off and recurrent grants are given according to need. Grants have previously been given towards the payment of household bills, dentures, hearing aids, glasses, disability equipment and electrical goods. Monthly grants may also be distributed to pensioners.

Annual grant total

In 2015/16 the charity had an income of £20,500 and a total expenditure of £21,000. We estimate that grants to individuals totalled £20,000 during the year.

Applications

Application forms are available upon request from the correspondent, and are considered on an ongoing basis.

Royal Variety Charity

£89,000 (77 grants)

Correspondent: Giles Cooper, Chairman, Brinsworth House, 72 Staines Road, Twickenham, Middlesex TW2 5AL (020 8898 8164; email: enquiries@royalvarietycharity.org; website: www.eabf.org.uk)

CC number: 206451

Eligibility

Entertainment artistes, performers and other people who have been associated with the entertainment professions, and their dependants.

Types of grants

Regular top-up pensions and one-off grants for expenditure that eases financial hardship and improves quality of life, such as removals, medical treatment, travel costs, funeral costs and food vouchers.

Annual grant total

In 2016 the charity held assets of £8.6 million and had an income of £2.5 million. During the year, the charity awarded social grants and top-up pensions to some 28 families, totalling almost £40,000. In addition, one-off donations were awarded to 49 individuals to the sum of £49,000.

Applications

Applicants should contact the correspondent by email or telephone. Applications should include details of the applicant's difficulties, as well as evidence of their career in the entertainment industry. Requests for support are considered every couple of months.

Other information

Formerly known as The Entertainment Artistes' Benevolent Fund, the charity changed its name in June 2015. The charity's major fundraising event of the year is the Royal Variety Performance.

The fund also has its own residential and nursing care home for older entertainment professionals and supports its residents.

Scottish Showbusiness Benevolent Fund

£20,000

Correspondent: Grants Administrator, Caledonian Suite, 70 West Regent Street, Glasgow G2 2QZ (0141 255 0508; email: info@ssbf.co.uk; website: www.ssbf.co.uk)

OSCR number: SC009910

Eligibility

Members of The Showbusiness Association who are in need, and their dependants, including widows/widowers.

Types of grants

One-off and recurrent grants towards, for example, clothing, fuel, living expenses, funeral costs, and TV rental and licences.

Annual grant total

In 2016/17 the charity had an income of £24,000 and a total expenditure of £21,500. We estimate that grants awarded to individuals during the year totalled £20,000.

Applications

Applications should be made in writing to the correspondent.

Music

The English National Opera Benevolent Fund

£40,000

Correspondent: Welfare Team, Lilian Baylis House, 165 Broadhurst Gardens, London NW6 3AX (020 7845 9267; email: benfund@eno.org; website: www.eno.org/about/eno-benevolent-fund)

CC number: 211249

Eligibility

People who are or have been employed by the English National Opera and/or Sadlers Wells Companies and are in need.

Types of grants

One-off and recurrent grants are given according to need. Loans are also available. Previous research has suggested that medical/dental treatment is not normally supported, except where delay would affect a performing career. The fund will help with payments for treatment which is not generally available through the NHS.

Annual grant total

In 2015/16 the charity had an income of £12,000 and a total expenditure of £51,000. We estimate that grants given to individuals totalled around £40,000.

Applications

Applications should be submitted directly by the individual on a form available from the correspondent, to be considered quarterly.

ISM Members' Fund (The Benevolent Fund of The Incorporated Society of Musicians)

£89,500 (57 grants)

Correspondent: Deborah Annetts, Correspondent, 4–5 Inverness Mews, London W2 3JQ (020 7221 3499; email: membership@ism.org; website: www.ism.org)

CC number: 206801

Eligibility

Members and former members of the society and their dependants who are in need.

Types of grants

One-off and recurrent grants are given according to need.

Annual grant total

In 2015/16 the fund held assets of £3.8 million and had an income of £159,500. During the year, the charity gave around £89,500 in grants to 57 individuals.

Exclusions

No grants are given towards professional training.

Applications

Application forms are available from the correspondent and can be submitted directly by the individual at any time. An initial informal discussion with the primary contact would be beneficial. Applications are considered by a committee who assess the needs of each applicant and decide on the nature and amount of financial support given.

Other information

The fund provides an outsourced telephone counselling service which is available to all members and their families.

The Musicians Benevolent Fund

£1.7 million (1,063 grants)

Correspondent: Health and Welfare Team, 7–11 Britannia Street, London WC1X 9JS (020 7239 9101; email: help@helpmusicians.org.uk; website: www.helpmusicians.org.uk)

CC number: 228089

Eligibility

The fund can help if: you are a working professional musician; you are retired and your principal career was in music; you work in a related music profession; or (in some circumstances) if you are a dependant or partner of a musician. The fund defines a professional musician as:

> Someone who has earned their living substantially from music for a significant portion of their working life. We define 'working life' to be from the start of a career (i.e. the end of formal education, usually minimum age 18) to state pension age, or to the age at which a crisis occurs. This would normally be more than three years.

To qualify, you must be directly involved in the production of music, or in work for which the main qualification is a high level of music training.

Additionally, you must be able to show the fund that you are in financial need and be either resident in the UK, having spent the majority of your working life as a musician in the UK, or – if not currently living in the UK – have been resident in the UK for a minimum of three consecutive years having made an active contribution to British music.

Financial help is not normally given to individuals with savings of more than £16,000. For older and retired musicians, this limit is £20,000, however.

Types of grants

Support is given to professional musicians who are facing an unexpected crisis, a long-term illness or disability, or to help cope with retirement. The type of support given depends on the personal circumstances of the applicant. Contact the fund or see its informative website for more details.

Annual grant total

In 2016 the charity had assets of £71.6 million and an income of £5.5 million. During the year, financial assistance was given to 1,063 musicians to help with a crisis or continuing care, amounting to £1.7 million.

Exclusions

The fund is not able to assist amateur musicians or people whose paid musical work is clearly secondary to another career.

Applications

Contact the fund by calling the helpline or by email. If the fund feels it can help, you will be asked to complete a simple form, providing details of you, your career, your finances and the problem you are facing. You will be asked to provide details of a musical referee who can vouch for your career and status as a professional musician, as well as some evidence of finances, such as bank statements. Once the fund has received all the paperwork, it will aim to give a decision within ten working days and, if it is able to offer you support, will try to arrange a visit to your home within eight weeks of agreeing to help, in order to better assess your application and

personal needs. In a 'real emergency' a response may be made more quickly.

In the case of the fund being unable to help, it will try to signpost you in the direction of somebody who can.

Other information

The following information is taken from the fund's annual report:

> The charity supports musicians with a mix of advice, guidance and financial support...This support falls into 3 categories:
> - musicians at the point of entering the profession
> - musicians in their working lives who hit a serious crisis, illness or accident
> - musicians in retirement or later life

The fund's trained team can offer advice on a range of issues, including welfare advice, and can help put you in touch with other sources of support, such as debt advice services or medical specialists. Part of the way it offers support is through its successful home visiting scheme.

The Incorporated Association of Organists' Benevolent Fund

£7,000

Correspondent: Michael Whitehall, Secretary and Treasurer, 180 Lynn Road, Wisbech, Cambridgeshire PE13 3EB (01945 463826; email: michael@whitehalls.plus.com; website: www.iaobf.com)

CC number: 216533

Eligibility

Organists and/or choirmasters who are members/former members of any association or society affiliated to the Incorporated Association of Organists and their dependants who are in need.

Types of grants

Recurrent grants according to need. One-off grants are also available for young organists whose parents are unable to afford tuition fees.

Annual grant total

In 2016 the fund had an income of £18,700 and a total expenditure of £17,900. We have estimated that social welfare grants to individuals totalled around £7,000. Funding is also awarded to dependants of members or former members of the IAO to assist with pipe-organ course or examination fees.

Applications

An application form is available to download from the website or from the correspondent. Applications can be made by the individual but should be countersigned by the secretary of the applicant's local organists' association. They should be submitted by 31 March for consideration at the trustees' annual meeting in May. In urgent cases the Secretary may obtain approval at other times.

Organists' Charitable Trust

£5,000

Correspondent: The Trustees, 26 Fitzroy Square, London W1T 6BT (020 8318 1471; email: secretary@ organistscharitabletrust.org; website: www.organistscharitabletrust.org)

CC number: 225326

Eligibility

Organists, and their dependants, who are in financial difficulties.

Types of grants

One-off grants ranging between £500 and £1,000.

Annual grant total

In 2016 the trust had an income of £9,700 and a total expenditure of £11,000. We estimate that grants given to individuals for welfare purposes totalled £5,000, with a further £5,000 awarded to support organists through their education.

Applications

Application forms are available from the correspondent. Applications can be submitted directly by the individual or through a third party such as a social worker. They are considered at any time. Repeat applications are welcomed.

The Performing Rights Society Members' Benevolent Fund (PRS Members' Fund)

£351,500 (450+ grants)

Correspondent: John Logan, General Secretary, 2 Pancras Square, London N1C 4AG (020 3741 4067; email: fund@ prsformusic.com; website: www. prsformusicfund.com)

CC number: 208671

Eligibility

Songwriters and composers of music who have been a member of PRS for Music for seven years or more and their dependants (including dependants of deceased members), who are in need and/or unable to work because of old age, illness, accident or disability.

Types of grants

The fund offers a variety of grants and loans:

- One-off grants – towards unexpected costs, such as repair or replacement of furniture, specialist equipment, deposits for individuals moving home due to vulnerability
- Regular grants – up to £20 a week to help with general living expenses for those who are receiving benefits but still cannot maintain basic standards of living. Grants can also be given for expenses like gas or heating bills, telephone costs, TV rental and TV licences. Recipients of regular grants also receive Christmas gifts or bonuses
- Holidays for those in need of a break after a difficult period
- Short-term low-interest loans to those experiencing an unexpected financial crisis

Annual grant total

In 2016 over 450 grants totalling £351,500 were made to individuals for welfare purposes. This included: 33 grants totalling £14,100 towards unexpected costs (including repair or replacement of household items and rent or deposits for vulnerable people); 58 grants totalling £25,300 towards winter fuel bills; weekly grants to 451 people, as well as each receiving vouchers at Christmas; holidays or day trips for 32 people.

The charity received 954 applications during the year.

The charity also made 36 low-interest loans totalling almost £381,000 altogether.

Exclusions

The fund will not help:

- With the cost of buying a home
- To promote any commercial venture
- Composers who do not have any other employment
- Towards payments as an advance against future royalties

Applications

Application forms can be downloaded from the fund's website or requested from the correspondent. In cases of claims based on illness, a medical or GP's report is required. The committee generally meets on a monthly basis to consider applications.

All applications are means-tested in line with DWP income and savings criteria. Recipients of regular support are paid a visit by the fund at least once a year.

Other information

As well as offering financial assistance the fund can make referrals for specialist financial advice as well as provide specialist health assessments in

conjunction with their partners, the British Association for Performing Arts Medicine. The fund also provides sheltered accommodation and runs a career counselling service.

The Philharmonia Benevolent Fund

£15,000 (two grants)

Correspondent: Paul Townley, Philharmonia Ltd, 6 Chancel Street, London SE1 OUX

CC number: 280370

Eligibility

Present or former members of the Philharmonia Orchestra.

Types of grants

One-off grants according to need.

Annual grant total

In 2015/16 the fund held assets of £543,500 and had an income of £31,000. During the year, the fund awarded grants to individuals totalling £15,000.

Applications

Apply in writing to the correspondent.

Writing

The Society of Authors Pension Fund

£35,000 (17 grants)

Correspondent: Sarah Baxter, Contracts Advisor & Literary Estates, The Society of Authors, 84 Drayton Gardens, London SW10 9SB (020 7373 6642; email: sbaxter@societyofauthors.org; website: www.societyofauthors.org/ Grants/P-D-James-Memorial-Fund)

CC number: 212401

Eligibility

Members of the Society of Authors (SoA) who are either aged 60 or over or are medically unable to work. Applicants must have been a member of the SoA for at least ten years and be suffering financial hardship.

Types of grants

Annual grants of £2,000 per recipient which are given in the form of regular payments.

Annual grant total

In 2016 the charity had assets of £776,000 and an income of £83,000. During the year, almost £35,000 was awarded to 17 beneficiaries; £34,000 was given in awards and a further £850 in vouchers.

Applications

Applications are invited via the website and the society's journal when funds are available.

Other information

The charity is also known by its registered name, The P. D. James Memorial Fund.

The Authors' Contingency Fund

£24,000

Correspondent: Sarah Baxter, Contracts Advisor & Literary Estates, 84 Drayton Gardens, London SW10 9SB (020 7373 6642; email: sbaxter@societyofauthors. org; website: www.societyofauthors.org)

CC number: 212406

Eligibility

Professional authors in the UK and their dependants. The fund, in conjunction with the John Masefield Memorial Trust, makes grants to British poets and administers the Margaret Rhondda Awards to support women journalists.

Types of grants

One-off grants to relieve a temporary financial emergency.

Annual grant total

In 2015 the fund had an income of £23,500 and a total expenditure of £32,000. Welfare grants to individuals totalled £24,000.

Exclusions

The trust cannot help with the following:

- Grants to cover publication costs
- Grants to authors who are in financial difficulty through contributing towards publication costs
- Tuition fees

Applications

Application forms and guidelines are available from the fund's website. Applications should be submitted to the correspondent. The assessment process usually takes around three weeks.

Other information

The fund's website also provides information on how to apply for several different grant programmes for works in progress.

Francis Head Award

£18,500 (ten grants)

Correspondent: Sarah Baxter, Contracts Advisor & Literary Estates, 84 Drayton Gardens, London SW10 9SB (020 7373 6642; email: grants@societyofauthors.org or sbaxter@societyofauthors.org; website:

www.societyofauthors.org/Grants/ Grants-for-writers-in-need)

CC number: 277018

Eligibility

Professional writers (writing in the English language) who were born in the UK and are over the age of 35. The primary focus of the charity is those who are temporarily unable to support themselves or their dependants due to illness, accident or disability.

Types of grants

Emergency grants usually ranging from £1,000 to £2,000.

Annual grant total

In 2016 the charity held assets of £844,000 and had an income of £26,000. Grants were made to ten authors during the year and totalled £18,500.

Exclusions

No grants are given to cover publication costs, tuition fees or general maintenance while writing a book. Support is also unavailable to authors who are in financial difficulty because they have invested money in publication costs.

Applications

Apply on a form available from the correspondent or to download from the charity's website. Applications can be submitted directly by the individual and should include a covering letter explaining the circumstances prompting the application. A decision is usually made within three weeks.

Peggy Ramsay Foundation

£156,500

Correspondent: Neil Adleman, Trustee, Hanover House, 14 Hanover Square, London W15 1HP (020 7667 5000; email: prf@harbottle.com; website: www. peggyramsayfoundation.org)

CC number: 1015427

Eligibility

Playwrights who are resident in the British Isles. The charity also supports musical book writers and lyricists.

Types of grants

One-off grants. Individual grants never ordinarily exceed a standard commissioning fee. Grants are sometimes made for equipment, such as laptops, and for expenditure which makes writing possible.

Annual grant total

In 2015 the foundation had assets of £5.9 million and an income of £252,000. Welfare grants to individuals totalled £156,500.

Exclusions

Writers who write solely for media other than theatre; composers.

Applications

Apply by writing a short letter to the correspondent. Full details of what should be included can be found on the foundation's website.

Business, financial services and insurance

The AIA Educational and Benevolent Trust

£2,000

Correspondent: Tim Pinkey, Director of Professional Standards, Staithes 3, The Watermark, Metro Riverside, Tyne And Wear NE11 9SN (0191 493 0272; fax: 0191 493 0278; email: trust.fund@ aiaworldwide.com; website: www. aiaworldwide.com)

CC number: 1118333

Eligibility

Fellows and associates of the institute, and their close dependants, who are in need.

Types of grants

One-off grants according to need.

Annual grant total

In 2015 the trust had an income of £2,300 and a total expenditure of £5,000. The trust's annual report and accounts were not published on the Charity Commission's website due to its low income. We estimate that social welfare grants totalled around £2,000. Grants are also given to those wishing to undergo education and training in accountancy.

Applications

Apply using the form available from the trust's website which should be printed and posted to the correspondent. Applications are received on an ongoing basis.

The Baltic Exchange Charitable Society

£106,500 (31 grants)

Correspondent: Richard Butler, Secretary, The Baltic Exchange, 38 St Mary Axe, London EC3A 8BH (020 7283 6090; email: richard.butler@baltic-charities.co.uk)

CC number: 277093

Eligibility

Employees and ex-employees of member companies of the Baltic Exchange as well as companies in the oilseeds trade, and their dependants, who are in need. Assistance is available only to those who have joined as a member of the society.

Types of grants

Annual grants and emergency or one-off grants. One-off grants have recently been awarded towards physiotherapy, respite and care home fees, legal support, grave maintenance and gardening. Fuel payments were also made during exceptionally cold weather. Recurrent grants are paid quarterly to help with living expenses. In 2015 Christmas gifts were distributed to all beneficiaries. Loans may also be offered.

Annual grant total

In 2016 the society had an income of £164,000 and a total expenditure of £200,500. Grants to 31 individuals totalled £106,500; of which £73,500 was awarded in quarterly payments and £33,000 in special one-off grants.

Applications

Application forms are available from the correspondent. Applications on your behalf from a third party, such as care agencies or armed service organisations, are also welcomed. Applications can be submitted at any time, however if you are not a member then your application may take longer.

The Bankers Benevolent Fund (The Bank Workers Charity)

£564,000

Correspondent: The Client Advisor, Salisbury House, Finsbury Circus, London EC2M 5QQ (0800 023 4834 (helpline: 9am to 5pm, Monday to Friday); email: info@bwcharity.org.uk; website: www.bwcharity.org.uk)

CC number: 313080

Eligibility

Current and former employees of banks in the UK, and their families, who are in need.

Types of grants

One-off and recurrent grants for a wide range of needs.

Annual grant total

In 2015/16 the charity had assets of £46.7 million and an income of £1.9 million. Cash grants, all of which were paid to individuals, totalled £719,500. A breakdown of grants distributed according to purpose was not available; however, in previous years they have been awarded in three categories – child education, families and retirees. Based on allocations in the most recent year for which a breakdown was available (2013/14), we estimate that social welfare grants totalled around £564,000.

Exclusions

Non-priority debts; private medical fees; home improvements, except when essential repairs are needed to ensure independent living, safety and security. People who have worked in the insurance or stockbroking industries are generally not helped.

Applications

Contact the charity via its helpline or by using the contact form on the website to find out more about available support.

The charity notes in its annual report for 2015/16 that grants, and some services, 'are subject to an application process which takes into consideration various criteria, including length of banking service, income and savings as well as the individual circumstances and situation of the applicant'. All applications are considered on their individual merit and all grants are awarded on a discretionary basis. Regular grants are reviewed annually.

Other information

The annual report for 2015/16 explains that the charity 'aims to provide support for people in need based on early intervention, rather than picking up the pieces at crisis point'. It does, however, 'recognise that people in need do not always seek help at an early stage due to lack of awareness, pride and busy lifestyles as well as a variety of other reasons'.

A wide range of non-financial assistance is given, in the form of information, advice and expert assistance, in areas such as money, mental and physical health, relationships and employment.

The Chartered Accountants' Benevolent Association

£1.1 million (343 grants)

Correspondent: Donna Cooper, Grants Co-ordinator, 8 Mitchell Court, Castle Mound Way, Rugby CV23 0UY (0800 107 6163 (24-hour helpline); email: donna.cooper@caba.org.uk; website: www.caba.org.uk)

CC number: 1116973

Eligibility

Chartered Accountants' Benevolent Association (CABA) provides advice and practical support to current and former ICAEW chartered accountants and their dependants. Visit the website for full information.

Types of grants

One-off and recurrent grants towards daily living costs, respite care, household essentials and so on. The association also provides interest-free loans.

Annual grant total

In 2016 the charity held assets of £117.6 million and had an income of £2.7 million. Financial assistance to 343 individuals totalled £1.1 million, and loans of £18,000 were granted to three individuals.

Applications

Initial contact can be made by calling the 24-hour helpline or by using the live chat feature on the association's website.

The charity also has a 'grants search' tool where applicants can find various grants which are available to them.

Other information

The association offers a wide range of support and advice on issues such as accessing state benefits, debt and financial problems and stress management. Services are free and only direct financial support is means-tested.

The Chartered Certified Accountants' Benevolent Fund

£15,000

Correspondent: Hugh McCash, Hon. Secretary, c/o ACCA, 110 Queen Street, Glasgow G1 3BX (0141 534 4045; email: hugh.mccash@accaglobal.com; website: www.accaglobal.com/gb/en/member/membership/benevolent-fund/about.html)

CC number: 222595

Eligibility

Members of the ACCA, and their dependants, living worldwide.

Types of grants

One-off and regular grants are given for a wide range of needs. Secured loans can also be provided.

Annual grant total

In 2016/17 the charity had an unusually low income of £6,300 and a total expenditure of £37,000. Based on previous years' information, we estimate that grants given to individuals totalled around £15,000.

Exclusions

Students are not eligible for assistance.

Applications

Application forms are available to download from the website or can be requested from the correspondent in writing or by telephone.

The Chartered Institute of Management Accountants Benevolent Fund

£123,000 (46 grants)

Correspondent: Caroline Aldred, Secretary, CIMA Benevolent Fund, The Helicon, One South Place, London EC2M 2RB (020 8849 2221; email: benevolent.fund@cimaglobal.com; website: www.cimaglobal.com)

CC number: 261114

Eligibility

Past and present CIMA members and their dependants anywhere in the UK and the world.

Types of grants

One-off grants for specific needs such as television licence/rental, telephone rental, motor insurance/tax, disability aids, some repairs and necessary household items such as fridges, cookers, etc. Grants are also made for medical bills for members outside the UK. Regular grants are also made to help meet basic living costs. Interest-free loans may be provided in exceptional circumstances.

Annual grant total

In 2016 the fund had assets of £2.2 million and an income of £197,000. Grants to 46 individuals totalled £123,000, mostly for social welfare purposes.

Exclusions

No grants are given to enhance property, for investment in business ventures, or for private medical care: although assistance may be given to members

living outside the UK who do not have access to state-funded medical treatment or medical insurance and have large medical bills.

Applications

Apply in writing to the correspondent.

Other information

The charity can also signpost people to relevant services and provide support from a welfare officer.

Educational grants are also made for dependent children. CIMA has another charity, the General Charitable Trust Fund, which funds the advancement of education in accountancy and related topics.

The CTBI – The Salespeople's Charity

£624,500 (327 grants)

Correspondent: Mandi Leonard, Grants Secretary, Paramount House, Delta Way, Egham, Surrey TW20 8RX (01784 730875; email: info@salespeoplescharity. org.uk; website: www.salespeoplescharity. org.uk)

CC number: 216538

Eligibility

People in the UK who are in need and have worked as a sales representative/agent promoting or selling to the trade for at least five years, and their dependants. Sales must be business-to-business and involve the representative visiting client sites to sell or promote goods or services to the trade (rather than the public). Applicants must be in financial need and may be in work, retired, have been made redundant or be unable to work due to ill health or disability.

Types of grants

Recurrent grants and gifts in kind. One-off grants are also given towards respite breaks, disability aids, home adaptations and urgent maintenance work, Christmas and birthday payments and support with critical one-off payments. Gifts in kind have included vouchers for high street stores and food hampers.

Annual grant total

In 2016 the charity had assets of almost £6.4 million and an income of £646,500. Grants to 327 beneficiaries, comprising regular payments and new applicants totalled £624,500 which figure included gifts in kind but excluded support costs.

Exclusions

No help is given to those engaged in 'van sales', retail, telesales or general selling to the public.

Applications

Applications should be made on a form available from the correspondent or on the charity's website. Applications should include evidence of employment in commercial sales and be submitted either directly by the individual or through a third party. Applicants may be visited by a volunteer to discuss their application further. The trustees meet five times a year to consider applications, although emergency payments can be made quickly in cases of extreme hardship.

The Charles Dixon Pension Fund

£6,000

Correspondent: Caroline Duckworth, The Society of Merchant Venturers, Merchants' Hall, The Promenade, Clifton Down, Bristol BS8 3NH (0117 973 8058; email: enquiries@ merchantventurers.com)

CC number: 202153

Eligibility

Merchants who are in reduced circumstances who are over 60 years of age, and who live in Bristol, Liverpool or London.

Types of grants

Pensions, usually between £500 and £2,000 a year.

Annual grant total

In 2015/16 the fund had an income of £9,000 and a total expenditure of £6,700. We estimate that grants to individuals totalled £6,000.

Applications

Application forms are available from the correspondent. Applications can be submitted directly by the individual or, where applicable, through a social worker, Citizens Advice, other welfare agency or through an appropriate third party. They are dealt with as received.

The Institute of Financial Accountants and International Association of Book-Keepers Benevolent Fund

£12,000

Correspondent: The Secretariat, IFA & IAB Benevolent Fund, Brantwood, Sutton, Ipswich IP9 2TJ (email: secretary@ifaiabbenfund.org.uk; website: www.ifaiabbenfund.org.uk)

CC number: 234082

Eligibility

Past and present members of the institute or the association, their dependants, and all current IFA and IAB students.

Types of grants

The website explains that grants are 'usually in the form of one-off payments, where there is a critical situation that affects daily life'.

Annual grant total

In 2015/16 the fund had an income of £19,700 and a total expenditure of £27,500. We estimate that social welfare grants to individuals totalled £12,000, with funding also awarded to individuals for educational purposes.

Exclusions

No recurrent or ongoing payments are made where they could be considered to 'be in lieu of a steady income'.

Applications

Application forms are available from the correspondent or to download from the website. Applications can be submitted directly by the individual or on their behalf by a family member. Details of income and expenditure, as well as any relevant supporting evidence (for example, bank statements, payslips, tax return forms, proof of rent or mortgage payments) should be included. Every application is considered on its merits.

Other information

The trustees may choose to support the educational needs of those who are pursuing professional qualifications of the IFA or IAB when the fund has surplus income.

Alfred Foster Settlement

£12,000

Correspondent: Zedra Trust Company (UK) Ltd, Trustee, ZEDRA Trust Company (UK) Ltd, ZEDRA UK Trusts, Osborne Court, Gadbrook Park, Rudheath, Northwich CW9 7UE (01606 313118; email: charities@zedra.com)

CC number: 229576

Eligibility

Current and former employees of banks and their dependants who are in need.

Types of grants

One-off grants of £250 to £1,000 according to need.

Annual grant total

In 2015/16 the charity had assets of £866,500, an income of £37,000 and awarded over £23,500 in 11 grants. A further breakdown was not given. We

estimate that about £12,000 was given in social welfare grants.

Applications

Applications may be made in writing to the correspondent. They can be submitted directly by the individual or through the employee's bank or to their local regional office.

Other information

The charity also makes grants to individuals for educational purposes.

The Ruby and Will George Trust

£19,000

Correspondent: Damien Slattery, 125 Cloverfield, West Allotment, Newcastle upon Tyne NE27 0BE (0191 266 4527; email: admin@rwgt.co.uk; website: www.rwgt.co.uk)

CC number: 264042

Eligibility

People who are employed in commerce, and their dependants, who are in need.

Types of grants

One-off or recurrent grants for items which are needed but cannot be afforded.

Annual grant total

In 2015/16 the trust had assets of £3.5 million and an income of £136,500. A total of 47 grants were made to individuals during the year, amounting to £76.500. The annual report and accounts state that: 'The vast majority of the income generated by the trust's assets is paid out by means of either one-off or continuing grants, these being predominantly made to those in either secondary or further education.' With this in mind, we estimate that grants for social welfare purposes totalled around £19,000.

Applications

Applications can be made through the trust's website. Applicants will need to provide a brief explanation of their commerce connection and a recent payslip or a letter from their employer.

The Insurance Charities

£500,000

Correspondent: Annali-Joy Thornicroft, 20 Aldermanbury, London EC2V 7HY (020 7606 3763; fax: 020 7600 1170; email: info@theinsurancecharities.org.uk; website: www.theinsurancecharities.org.uk)

CC number: 206860

Eligibility

To be eligible, applicants must:

1) Be a current or past insurance employee:
- With at least five years' work in insurance within the last ten years
- With less than five years' insurance work, but where insurance has made up the majority of their career to date
- With at least five years' work in insurance immediately prior to retirement
- In receipt of a pension or deferred pension from an insurance employer in respect of at least five years' service

2) Be a dependant of a current or former insurance employee.

3) Be currently or previously employed by an insurance service in the UK or Irish insurance industries.

4) Must have restricted financial means in terms of income and capital.

5) Must have suffered an element of misfortune.

Types of grants

One-off grants for essential items (such as equipment to help someone with reduced mobility, an adaptation to a property which is not financed by local or central government, the replacement of an appliance or some essential property maintenance) and ongoing assistance are both considered.

Annual grant total

In 2015/16 the charity had assets of £33 million and an income of £3.8 million. We estimate that around £500,000 was awarded to individuals.

Other information

The charity also provides grants to insurance employees and their dependants for educational purposes, and it also runs a money and practical support service.

The Liverpool Merchants' Guild

£953,000

Correspondent: Trusts & Estates Team, Moore Stephens LLP, 110–114 Duke Street, Liverpool L1 5AG (0151 703 1080; fax: 0151 703 1085; email: info@ liverpoolmerchantsguild.org.uk; website: www.liverpoolmerchantsguild.org.uk)

CC number: 206454

Eligibility

People over 50 who have been employed in a professional, supervisory, or clerical capacity (or self-employed people) and their dependants who live on Merseyside (or who have lived there for a continuous period of at least 15 years) and are in need or distress.

Types of grants

Annual pensions of up to £6,000. One-off grants of up to £5,000 for items of exceptional expenditure e.g. equipment or adaptations to support independent living.

Annual grant total

In 2016 the guild had assets of almost £40 million, £30 million of which represents permanent endowment and is not available for grant-making. There is also a restricted legacies fund of around £1.3 million included in the assets figure. The guild's income was £1.4 million and grants were made totalling £953,000 which included £848,500 given in pensions and £104,500 given in grants.

Exclusions

Manual workers and their dependants.

Applications

Applicants can apply online through the website, or on a form available from the correspondent or to download from the website. Applications must be countersigned by two unrelated referees and include all relevant supporting documentation – refer to the website for details. They can be submitted at any time and are considered every three months.

Other information

The Liverpool Merchants' Guild was instituted in the year 1880 for the purpose of taking over and managing a fund bequeathed by the will of Catherine Wright, of Liverpool, who died in the month of September 1868.

Catherine Wright by her will bequeathed the sum of £10,000 to the trustees for the purpose of founding an institution to be called Wright's Institution, the object of which was to grant pensions to people who had been unable to make adequate provision for their declining years.

The name was changed in 1880 to Liverpool Merchants' Guild and in 2006 a Royal Charter was granted replacing the original of 1914.

The Lloyd's Benevolent Fund

£221,000 (25 grants)

Correspondent: Raymond Blaber, Secretary, Lloyd's Benevolent Fund, 1 Lime Street, London EC3M 7HA (020 7327 6453; email: raymond.blaber@lloyds.com)

CC number: 207231

Eligibility

People who work or have worked in the Lloyd's insurance market and their dependants, anywhere in the world.

Types of grants

One-off or recurrent grants can be given towards relieving general hardship.

Annual grant total

In 2015/16 the fund had assets of £11.4 million and an income of almost £330,500. During the year, the fund awarded almost £221,000 in grants to 25 individuals.

Exclusions

No assistance is given for underwriting members of Lloyd's. School fees and medical costs will not be covered.

Applications

Apply in writing to the correspondent.

Pawnbrokers' Charitable Institution

£63,500

Correspondent: Mrs K. Way, Correspondent, 184 Crofton Lane, Oprington BR6 0BW (01689 811978)

CC number: 209993

Eligibility

Pawnbrokers in need who have been in the business for at least five years, and their dependants. Help is primarily given to people over 60 but assistance may also be available to younger people if there is sufficient need.

Types of grants

Regular payments, Christmas gifts, equipment and one-off grants to meet emergency needs for those on a low income who cannot manage on a state pension.

Annual grant total

In 2015/16 the charity had assets of £3.4 million and an income of £115,000. During the year, the charity gave around £63,500 in grants to individuals.

Applications

Application forms are available from the correspondent.

The Prime Charitable Trust

£1,100

Correspondent: Pauline Weller, Correspondent, Federation of Small Businesses, Sir Frank Whittle Way, Blackpool FY4 2FE (01253 336000; email: admin@prime-charitable-trust.co.uk; website: www.prime-charitable-trust.co.uk)

CC number: 328441

Eligibility

Members or former members of the National Federation of Self-Employed and Small Businesses Ltd and their family and dependants, who due to illness or incapacity are unable to maintain themselves.

Types of grants

One-off and recurrent grants are given according to need.

Annual grant total

In 2015/16 the charity had an income of £800 and a total expenditure of £1,300. We estimate that the charity gave around £1,100 in grants to individuals.

Applications

Apply in writing to the correspondent.

Royal Bank of Scotland Group Pensioners' Association Benevolent Fund

£26,500 (22 grants)

Correspondent: David Walker, Trustee, Flat 4, Montagu Court, Montagu Road, Highcliffe, Christchurch BH23 5JT (01425 272703)

CC number: 277974

Eligibility

Support is open to all retired employees and their dependants irrespective of whether or not they have ever subscribed to the fund or belong to the Group Pensioners' Association. Assistance is mainly given to elderly people, but others in need, particularly those with a disability, are also considered. There are no fixed criteria to obtain assistance from the fund, each application is considered on its merits. However, it is unlikely that help would be approved by the trustees for those with significant savings/investments (excluding owner-occupied property) or income.

Types of grants

The fund helps towards the cost of providing one-off, specific items for individuals e.g. stairlifts; cookers; furniture; heating systems; dentures; wheel chairs; walk-in showers.

Annual grant total

In 2016/17 the fund had £1.15 million in assets and an income of £37,500. Grants to individuals totalled £26,500.

Applications

Apply in writing to the correspondent.

Scottish Chartered Accountants' Benevolent Association

£64,000

Correspondent: Caroline Christie, PO Box 28843, Edinburgh EH14 9BY (07722 932120; email: admin@scaba.org.uk; website: www.icas.com/our-charitable-work/scaba-scottish-chartered-accountants-benevolent-association)

OSCR number: SC008365

Eligibility

Members of the Institute of Chartered Accountants of Scotland who are in need, and their dependants.

Types of grants

One-off and recurrent grants and loans for a variety of needs. Previously grants have been given for hospital travel costs, house repairs, general living expenses, mobility aids, retraining and home help.

Annual grant total

In 2016 the association had assets of £2.1 million and an income of £139,000. Grants totalled £128,500. We estimate that around £64,000 was given in welfare grants to individuals.

Applications

An initial letter or telephone call should be made to the correspondent.

Other information

Grants are also given for educational purposes.

Scottish Stockbrokers' Benevolent Fund

£29,000

Correspondent: The Trustees, Flat 0/1, 23 Polwarth Street, Hyndland, Glasgow G12 9UD (email: Contact form on website; website: ssbf.org.uk)

OSCR number: SC013429

Eligibility

Former members of the Scottish stock exchange and their dependants.

Types of grants

The charity's website states:

> The fund carries out these objectives by providing grants to individuals in need, or to prevent or relieve poverty in the form of:
>
> ▶ Annuities on a discretionary basis
> ▶ Donations to those requiring temporary help
> ▶ Emergency grants for one-off payments
> ▶ Help to those that are sick or with disabilities, such as for medical equipment and carers

Annual grant total

In 2016/17 the fund had assets of £1.2 million and an income of £35,500. Grants to individuals totalled £29,000.

Applications

The fund's website suggests that potential applicants should at first make an informal enquiry to let the fund know their difficulties and circumstances.

Sears Group Trust

£120,000

Correspondent: Gary Branston, The Trust Partnership LLP, 6 Trull Farm Buildings, Trull, Tetbury GL8 8SQ (01285 841900; email: gary.branston@spearsgrouptrust.co.uk)

CC number: 1022586

Eligibility

Employees and former employees of any company that is, or has been, associated with Sears Ltd, who are in financial need, and their dependants.

Types of grants

One-off and recurrent grants are given according to need. Recurrent grants are made to top up low incomes. One-off grants have in the past been awarded towards respite care, decorating, beds, televisions and kitchen appliances.

Annual grant total

In 2016/17 the trust had an income of £349,000 and a total expenditure of £375,500. We estimate that grants given to individuals totalled around £120,000.

Exclusions

No grants are given for bankruptcy or funeral costs.

Applications

Apply in writing to the correspondent who will arrange for a visit from one of the trust's welfare visitors. The visitor will assess the applicant and make a recommendation to the trustees. The trustees meet to consider applications two to three times per year, however, applications can be processed between meetings.

The Stock Exchange Benevolent Fund

£629,000

Correspondent: The Secretary, 10 Paternoster Square, St Pauls, London EC4M 7DX (020 7797 1092/3120; email: admin@sebf.co.uk; website: www.sebf.co.uk)

CC number: 245430

Eligibility

Former members of the stock exchange and their dependants.

Types of grants

Annuities and one-off grants are given according to need. Grants have been made for medical equipment, motor repairs and household essentials.

Annual grant total

In 2016 the fund held assets of £24.4 million and had an income of £1.1 million. Grants were made totalling £629,000, of which £442,500 was given in pensions to 67 individuals and £110,000 in one-off grants.

Applications

Application forms can be downloaded from the fund's website.

Stock Exchange Clerks Fund

£78,500 (39 grants)

Correspondent: A. Barnard, Correspondent, 1–5 Earl Street, London EC2A 2AL (020 7797 4373 or 01245 322985; email: deanaball44@gmail.co.uk)

CC number: 286055

Eligibility

Former members of the fund and former employees of the London Stock Exchange or member firms of the London Stock Exchange, who are in need, and their dependants.

Types of grants

Monthly payments to help with living costs. One-off grants towards medical equipment, mobility costs, household goods and funeral expenses. Most beneficiaries also receive a Christmas food parcel.

Annual grant total

In 2016 the fund had an income of £117,000 and assets of £1.1 million. Grants were made to 39 individuals totalling £78,500.

Applications

Application forms are available from the correspondent. Applications can be submitted at any time by the individual or through a third party. New applicants are visited by the Funds Liaison Officer who will then make a report to the trustees.

Any information concerning individuals who were previously employed in the industry and who may be in need of assistance can be given in complete confidence to either the correspondent or any of the trustees.

The Vassar-Smith Fund

£9,500 (seven grants)

Correspondent: I. Partridge, Hon. Secretary, Vassar-Smith Fund, St John's Terrace, 3–7 Ampthill Street, Bedford MK42 9EY

CC number: 236381

Eligibility
Lloyds TSB staff and pensioners or their dependants in need.

Types of grants
One-off grants according to need.

Annual grant total
In 2015/16 the charity had assets of £1.1 million and had an income of £35,500. During the year, the charity awarded around £9,500 in grants to seven individuals.

Applications
Apply in writing to the correspondent.

Other information
The charity's annual report 2015/16 states that grant-making has been made more difficult by a slight decrease in investment income, although the seven grants have been issued during the year, equalling the previous year's issue.

Construction

Builders' Benevolent Institution

£58,500 (85 grants)

Correspondent: The Secretary, 12 Shepherds Walk, Chestfield, Whitstable, Kent CT5 3NB (01227 791623; email: bbi@fmb.org.uk; website: www.bbi1847.org.uk)

CC number: 212022

Eligibility
Those who are or who have been master builders (employers in the building industry), and their dependants. Applicants with less than ten years' experience are not eligible, nor are those who have been employees.

Types of grants
Mostly pensions and Christmas vouchers. Occasionally, the trust distributes one-off grants towards the cost of necessary items such as home alterations and urgent house repairs. The institution notes that the average length of time over which beneficiaries receive support is around 15 years.

Annual grant total
In 2016 the institution had assets of almost £1.3 million and an income of £106,000. Grants were made totalling £58,500 and were distributed as follows:

Pensions	£51,000
Christmas gift vouchers	£4,800
Temporary relief	£2,800

Applications
Apply on a form available from the correspondent, to be submitted directly by the individual, through a social worker, Citizens Advice, other welfare agency or third party. The trustees meet six times a year to decide on applications and review existing pensions.

Other information
The charity has a welfare advisor who visits beneficiaries regularly to offer support and to assist with applications for state benefits.

Chartered Institute of Building Benevolent Fund

£20,500

Correspondent: Franklin MacDonald, Secretary, 1 Arlington Square, Downshire Way, Bracknell, Berkshire RG12 1WA (01344 630780; email: fmacdonald@ciob.org.uk; website: www.ciobbenevolentfund.org.uk)

CC number: 1013292

Eligibility
Past and present members of the Chartered Institute of Building and their dependants who are in need. Financial support is usually given to individuals who are facing short-term financial difficulty (e.g. a period of unemployment or illness).

Types of grants
One-off and recurrent grants are given to assist with general household costs, essential travel to work, clothing and household items. Help is also given to members who have children living at home, and for short-term, skills-based training.

Annual grant total
In 2016 the fund had assets of £1.1 million and an income of £103,000. Welfare grants totalled £20,500.

Exclusions
The fund cannot normally assist with: membership fees; medical treatment; legal fees; business-related or educational costs; personal or business debts; the purchase of motor vehicles; or home improvements. Student members are not eligible to apply for assistance within their first year of CIOB membership.

Applications
Application forms are available to download from the website and can be returned to the correspondent by email.

Other information
The fund provides a range of support and advice for its beneficiaries, including on work, housing, money or other welfare issues. More information on how to access support is available on its informative website, or from the correspondent.

Lighthouse Construction Industry Charity (LCIC)

£456,000

Correspondent: Bill Hill, Chief Executive, 51 Church Road East, Crowthorne, Berkshire RG45 7NF (0161 429 0022; email: info@lighthouseclub.org; website: www.lighthouseclub.org)

CC number: 1149488

Eligibility
People, or dependants of people, who work or have recently worked in the construction industry, or in an industry associated with construction (e.g. civil engineering, demolition or design), in the UK or Republic of Ireland. Applicants must have worked in the construction industry for more than five years and be experiencing one of the following: be unable to work for more than six months due to an injury; be suffering from an illness which prevents them to work for six months; be in full-time primary care of a spouse or child; suffering from a long-term, life changing or life-threatening illness. The applicant must have applied to all government benefits available to him/her and have less than £6,000 in their savings account.

Types of grants
Recurrent grants to help towards living costs for those in need through accident, disability or ill health and for those in need because a member of their family (who was in the construction industry) has died or has a fatal illness. One-off grants are also available towards essential items or services, such as a new bed, a replacement washing machine, funeral costs and school uniforms.

Annual grant total
In 2016 the charity had assets of £810,500 and an income of £1.5 million. Grants were made totalling almost £456,000. Of this amount, £120,000 was awarded as one-off grants and £336,000 was awarded in monthly grants for social welfare purposes.

Applications

Contact the charity via the telephone or alternatively fill out the online application form. Details on how to apply are available on the website.

Other information

The charity also provides a Construction Industry Helpline which gives advice on a range of issues including:

- Occupational health and well-being issues as an employee or an employer
- Support and advice for sufferers of stress and addiction-related illness
- Advice on matters ranging from divorce to employment
- Advice on specific tax-related issues concerning employment within the construction sector
- Help to manage and reschedule debt
- Help to understand the benefits system and entitlement especially if caring for others
- Support on career changes, especially after accident or injury preventing return to your original job

Full details are available on the website.

Lionheart (The Royal Institution of Chartered Surveyors Benevolent Fund)

£478,000

Correspondent: Dawn Shirley, Office Administrator, Surveyor Court, Westwood Way, Coventry CV4 8BF (0845 603 9057; fax: 024 7647 4701; email: dshirley@lionheart.org.uk; website: www.lionheart.org.uk)

CC number: 261245

Eligibility

Members and former members of the Royal Institution of Chartered Surveyors (or organisations it has merged with) and their dependants. Applications are welcome from people in the UK and those living overseas. Applicants should visit the website for current eligibility criteria and are advised to contact one of the charity's support officers if in any doubt as to their suitability to apply for a grant. Support officers can also help with information and advice on the charity's other services.

Types of grants

One-off and recurrent grants are given towards: essential domestic appliances, furnishings, redecorating and property repairs; living expenses; care in the community, residential and nursing care; respite care and holidays; and medical aids, adaptations and equipment for children with disabilities and older people. Additional financial help is also available for those most in need at Christmas.

Annual grant total

In 2016/17 the charity held assets of £21.4 million and had an income of £2.5 million. During the year, the charity gave £478,000 in grants to individuals.

Applications

Application forms are available to download from the website. Evidence of RICS membership or details of the member of whom the applicant is a dependant should be provided. Applications are considered quarterly, although urgent cases can be considered between meetings.

Other information

The charity offers grants, confidential advice, counselling, befriending, information and help in kind to members of the profession and their dependants on a range of social welfare, financial, legal, employment and property-related matters. A helpline is operated on 0845 603 9057.

Scottish Building Federation Edinburgh and District Charitable Trust

£2,700

Correspondent: Jennifer Law, Charity Accounts Manager, Exchange Place 3, Semple Street, Edinburgh EH3 8BL (0131 473 3500; email: jennifer.law@scott-moncrief.com; website: www.scott-moncrieff.com/services/charities/charitable-trusts/scottish-building-federation-edinburgh)

OSCR number: SC029604

Eligibility

People in reduced circumstances who have been involved with the building trade in the city of Edinburgh or the Lothians, and their dependants. There is a particular emphasis on people who have been owners or senior employees of companies (supervisory grade, e.g. site agents, or above).

Types of grants

One-off grants according to need.

Annual grant total

In 2016 the trust had assets of £1.5 million and an income of £47,000. Welfare grants to individuals totalled £2,700 and were broken down as follows:

Scholarships and bursaries	£9,000
Academic prizes	£5,000
Charitable aid (welfare cases)	£2,700

Applications

Applications can be made using the appropriate form, which is available to download from the Scott-Moncrieff website.

Education and training

Church Schoolmasters and Schoolmistresses' Benevolent Institution

£16,900

Correspondent: Di Cara, Secretary, 3 Kings Court, Harwood Road, Horsham RH13 5UR (01403 250798; email: info@cssbi.org.uk; website: www.cssbi.org.uk)

CC number: 207236

Eligibility

Current or former teachers and lecturers, or their immediate families, who are members of the Church of England or another recognised Christian denomination and are suffering financial hardship. Applicants must be resident in England or Wales and be able to provide the details of two referees who can confirm their educational and church connections.

Types of grants

One-off grants are given to assist with, for example: general living expenses due to a change in circumstances such as illness, loss of employment or relationship breakdown; home repairs or adaptations; relocation costs; travel or childcare costs; and utility bill, council tax or rent arrears due to unavoidable circumstances. In exceptional circumstances, support over a longer period of time may be considered.

Annual grant total

In 2015/16 the institution had assets of £2.7 million and an income of £26,500. Grants totalled £33,500. We estimate that social welfare grants amounted to around £16,900, with funding also given to individuals for career development and retraining.

Applications

Application forms are available to download from the website. It is advised that applicants read the informative FAQ section of the website before submitting an application.

Education Support Partnership

£227,500

Correspondent: Charlotte Osborn, Education Sector Support Uk, 40A Drayton Park, London N5 1EW (020 7697 2752; email: enquiries@ teachersupport.info)

CC number: 1161436

Eligibility

Individuals who are working in or retired from the education sector and are suffering financial problems caused by unemployment, ill health, sudden life events, bereavement or a personal injury

Applicants must have worked for a minimum of one term in the educational sector.

The website states that:

1. You must have less than £4,000 in savings

2. You must be in receipt of all state benefits applicable to your circumstances

3. You may be referred to our debts advisory service prior to be assisted by the grants team. – Should the casework team need to refer you to a money advice service we will need to confirmation that you have discussed your financial circumstance with a money advice professional – e.g. a Common Financial Statement or Budget Pack.

4. If you are applying for disability aids/ adaptations you must have applied for a disability facilities grant from your local authority.

Types of grants

One-off grants awarded to help people with the burden of short-term debt, financial emergencies, pay for essential unaffordable items to improve health and well-being, and stay in or get back to work. All grants are paid to individuals.

Annual grant total

In 2015/16 the charity had assets of £6.9 million and had an income of £3.3 million. During the year, the charity gave around £227,500 in grants to individuals for welfare purposes.

Exclusions

Tutors who have worked solely in the private sector.

Applications

Applicants must submit their applications through the charity's online application form, available on the website.

Full guidelines are available on the website.

Educational Institute of Scotland Benevolent Fund

£130,000 (68 grants)

Correspondent: Local Benevolent Fund Correspondent, 46 Moray Place, Edinburgh EH3 6BH (0131 225 6244; email: enquiries@eis.org.uk; website: www.eis.org.uk)

OSCR number: SC007852

Eligibility

Members of the institute suffering from financial hardship due to unexpected illness, long-term health problems or a sudden change in financial circumstances, their widows/widowers and dependants. Applicants must have held a full membership for at least one year prior to application.

Types of grants

One-off and recurrent grants towards, for example, daily living costs, television licences, telephone rental and holidays. Emergency grants may also be available to members who have had an arrestment on their salary, who face eviction, or who have had their gas or electricity cut off.

Annual grant total

In 2015/16 the fund held assets of £3.1 million and had an income of £123,000. The fund awarded 68 grants to individuals in the year totalling £130,000. Grants ranged from £650 to £2,500.

Applications

Apply on a form available from a local Benevolent Fund Correspondent. Individual contact details are available from the EIS website. The correspondent may arrange a visit to discuss an application and can offer help to applicants completing the form.

IAPS Charitable Trust

£8,600 (three grants)

Correspondent: Richard Flower, Secretary, 11 Waterloo Place, Leamington Spa, Warwickshire CV32 5LA (01926 887833; email: rwf@ iaps.uk; website: iaps.uk/about/our-charities)

CC number: 1143241

Eligibility

Members, retired members and the dependants of current, retired or deceased members of the Independent Association of Prep Schools (IAPS). Support may also be given to association employees or, with the consent of the directors, anyone connected with education.

Types of grants

One-off grants are available according to need to relieve general hardship.

Annual grant total

In 2016/17 the trust had assets of £1.6 million and an income of £171,000. Grants totalled £61,000, of which £20,000 was distributed to organisations. Individuals were awarded grants amounting to £41,000.

The trustees' report states 'The restricted funds were used to make Bursary fund education grants of £8,500; Benevolent fund hardship grants of £8,584; Harrison Memorial fund music grants totalling £3,150; and School Access Scheme grants of £21,010.' Based on this information, we believe social welfare grants to individuals totalled almost £8,600.

Applications

Further information is available from the correspondent.

Other information

In 2012 the IAPS Benevolent Fund and the IAPS Bursary Trust, and in 2013 the IAPS Orchestra Trust merged with the trust allowing to extend its work.

The trust is also known as 'itrust'.

The Benevolent Fund of Her Majesty's Inspectors of Schools in England and Wales

£10,000

Correspondent: Clive Rowe, Trustee, Hassocks House, 58 Main Street, Newtown Linford, Leicester LE6 0AD (01530 243989; email: rowe.clive@sky.com)

CC number: 210181

Eligibility

Present and retired HM Inspectors of schools in England and Wales and their dependants who are in need or distress.

Types of grants

One-off grants of £500 to £5,000 and loans of up to £10,000.

Annual grant total

In 2016 the fund had an income of £14,300 and a total expenditure of £36,000. We estimate that grants given to individuals for welfare purposes amounted to around £10,000, with loans also given.

Applications

Apply in writing to the correspondent, either directly by the individual or through a third party such as a friend or colleague. Applications are considered as they arise and should include the applicant's financial situation and, for example, arrangements for repaying loans.

Other information

The fund also provides pastoral support, including advice, for its beneficiaries.

The Association of School and College Leaders Benevolent Fund

£20,000

Correspondent: Carole Baldam, 130 Regent Road, Leicester LE1 7PG (0116 299 1122; email: asclbf@ascl.org. uk; website: www.ascl.org.uk/help-and-advice/benevolent-fund)

CC number: 279628

Eligibility

Current or former members of the association and their dependants (including dependants of deceased members). Retired employees of the association are also supported.

Types of grants

Support for members during financial crisis or long-term problems resulting from events such as serious accidents, redundancy, chronic illnesses or disability.

Annual grant total

In 2016 the fund had an income of £189,500 and a total expenditure of £28,000. We estimate that grants given to individuals totalled around £20,000.

Applications

Apply in writing to the correspondent.

Other information

The association was previously known as The Secondary Heads Association Benevolent Fund.

The Society of Schoolmasters and Schoolmistresses

£3,800

Correspondent: Bill Puddicombe, Unit A2 Bybow Farm, Orchard Way, Dartford DA2 7ER (01322 293822; email: enquiries@sgbi.net; website: societyofss.org.uk)

CC number: 206693

Eligibility

Current or former members of the association and their dependants (including dependants of deceased

members). Retired employees of the association are also supported.

Types of grants

One-off and recurrent grants of up to a maximum of £600 per year. Grants are normally made to retired schoolmasters or schoolmistresses who have no adequate pension, but exceptions can sometimes be made for younger teachers. One-off grants have previously been given for purposes such as household items, nursing home fees and medical expenses.

Annual grant total

In 2016 the charity had an income of £7,200 and a total expenditure of £4,000. We estimate that grants given to individuals totalled around £3,800.

Applications

Application forms are available from the correspondent. Applications can be submitted directly by the individual. They are considered quarterly.

The National Association of Schoolmasters Union of Women Teachers (NASUWT) Benevolent Funds

£264,500 (647 grants)

Correspondent: Legal and Casework Team, NASUWT, Hillscourt Education Centre, Rose Hill, Rednal, Birmingham B45 8RS (0121 453 6150 (8.30am - 5.30pm); email: legalandcasework@mail. nasuwt.org.uk; website: www.nasuwt.org. uk)

CC number: 285793

Eligibility

The fund is available to members and former members of the NASUWT, their dependants and the dependants of deceased members, provided a subscription has been paid.

Types of grants

Short-term assistance to assist in times of financial hardship.

Annual grant total

In 2016 the fund had assets of £2.3 million and an income of £406,500. Grants to individuals totalled £264,500.

Applications

Applicants should contact their Local Association Secretary. Alternatively they can contact the Legal and Casework Team at NASUWT Headquarters, Hillscourt Education Centre, Rose Hill, Rednal, Birmingham B45 8RS.

Scottish Secondary Teachers' Association Benevolent Fund

£7,200

Correspondent: The General Secretary, West End House, 14 West End Place, Edinburgh EH11 2ED (0131 313 7300; email: info@ssta.org.uk; website: www. ssta.org.uk)

OSCR number: SC011074

Eligibility

Members and retired members of the association and, in certain circumstances, their dependants and families who are in need. Spouses and partners of deceased members are also supported.

Types of grants

One-off and recurrent grants (generally limited to a period of six months) to help members through a period of long-term illness or other difficulty. The SSTA website notes that support is most often given 'in cases of financial hardship but can also be used to meet for requests where the member is not actually experiencing financial difficulties but for whom additional funds would be useful'; one example includes a grant for a member to visit an ill friend at hospital.

Annual grant total

In 2016 the charity had an income of £11,300 and a total expenditure of £7,500. We estimate that grants given to individuals totalled £7,200.

Applications

Apply in writing to the correspondent. Applications can be submitted directly by the individual or through a third party. Applicants are asked to provide details of their financial circumstances.

The Teaching Staff Trust

Correspondent: Judith Smith, Unit 2 Bybow Farm, Orchard Way, Dartford DA2 7ER (01322 293822; email: enquiries@teachingstafftrust.org.uk; website: www.teachingstafftrust.org.uk)

CC number: 1168445

Eligibility

People who work in or have retired from working in a school, nursery or any other educational role for under 19s. People who have benefitted from the trust in the past include nursery workers, teaching assistants and learning support staff, teachers, lunchtime supervisors and school administrators.

Types of grants

One-off grants to help people stay independent and out of financial hardship. Examples of support include: debt relief or financial support; essential household repairs; maintaining people in their homes; helping people to take or keep jobs.

Annual grant total

The Teaching Staff Trust has taken over from the Schoolmistresses' and Governesses' Benevolent Institution. The charity was registered with the Charity Commission in July 2017 and therefore no financial information was available at the time of writing (January 2018).

Applications

Applications forms are available to download from the trust's website. Hard copies are available on request.

Other information

The trust has an advice service for those who have more complex financial problems and this service can also provide legal help and counselling.

The Woodard Schools (Southern Division) Benefit Fund

£1,600

Correspondent: Nigel Anthony Watts, 32 Springfield Park, North Parade, Horsham RH12 2BF

CC number: 306695

Eligibility

Members of the fund or their immediate dependants who are, for whatever reason, in severe financial difficulty.

Types of grants

One-off grants.

Annual grant total

In 2016 the fund had assets of £1.1 million and had an income of £36,000. During the year, the fund gave around £1,600 in grants to individuals for welfare purposes.

The fund also awarded £33,500 in educational grants.

Applications

The website states that applicants should; 'write in the first instance, to the Woodard School that you attended, who will pass your enquiry on to us'.

Other information

The fund was established by Canon Nathaniel Woodard, the founder of Woodard Schools. The fund is a registered charity administered by a committee of former students and the headmasters of the four schools in the Southern Division.

The website states: 'At a meeting of the General Committee which took place on 8th May 2015 it was decided to close the Fund to new members.'

Energy

BP Benevolent Fund

£8,500 (six grants)

Correspondent: Peter Darnell, Fund Administrator, BP Benevolent Fund Trustees Ltd, 4 Woodside Close, Shermanbury, Horsham RH13 8HH (email: peter.darnell@uk.bp.com)

CC number: 803778

Eligibility

Former employees of BP plc or subsidiary or associated companies and the dependants of such people.

Types of grants

One-off and recurrent according to need. Occasional hardship grants of up to a maximum of £750. In 2016 grants were paid for a variety of reasons including: mattresses, sofa beds, shoes and clothing, bathroom/bedroom extensions, installation of central heating, and car repairs.

Annual grant total

In 2016 the fund had assets of over £1.3 million and an income of £32,000. Awards were made to help six individuals and totalled £8,500.

The fund also provides interest-free loans. The trustees approved three new loans totalling £3,400 in 2016.

Applications

Apply in writing to the correspondent.

The Electrical Industries Charity (also known as EEIBA)

£438,000 (672 grants)

Correspondent: Welfare Team, Rotherwick House, 3 Thomas More Street, London E1W 1YZ (020 3696 1710; email: support@electricalcharity.org; website: www.electricalcharity.org)

CC number: 1012131

Eligibility

Employees and former employees of the UK electrical and electronic industries and allied sciences, including: electrical contracting and facilities management; electrical and electronic manufacturing; wholesaling, distribution and retail; electrical and mechanical engineering; lighting industry; and the generation, distribution and supply of electrical power, including nuclear and renewable energy.

Types of grants

Grants are available for a wide range of needs, including home repairs, disability adaptations, mobility equipment and everyday essentials such as heating and food. In certain cases, the charity may also be able to offer financial assistance for carers' respite breaks.

Annual grant total

In 2016/17 the charity held assets of £5.9 million and had an income of £1.8 million. Grants to 672 individuals totalled £438,000.

Exclusions

Grants are not normally given to cover the costs of private medical care, educational fees, bankruptcy fees, nursing/residential fees or for headstones or funeral plaques.

Applications

Application packs and a list of guidelines are available to download from the website or by calling the charity's helpline. Applicants must provide the latest letter/statement from the benefits or pensions office or their current payslip, copies of their latest bank statements from current and savings accounts and, if a specific item is required, two or three estimates. Medical equipment normally requires an occupational therapy assessment, which can be discussed at a later date. Enquiries are welcomed.

Other information

The Electrical Industries Charity was formerly known as the Electrical and Electronics Industries Benevolent Association (EEIBA). It also provides a confidential helpline (0800 652 1618), debt advice, respite for carers and careers advice and outplacement which supported 4,154 people in 2016/17.

Engineering

The Chemical Engineer's Benevolent Fund

£7,700

Correspondent: Jo Downham, Finance Manager, 165–189 Railway Terrace, Rugby, Warwickshire CV21 3HQ (01788 578214; email: info@benevolentface.org; website: www.benevolentface.org)

CC number: 221601

Eligibility

Chemical engineers and their dependants. This includes all chemical engineers worldwide, not simply members or former members of the Institution of Chemical Engineers.

Types of grants

The fund's website states:

We offer chemical engineers and their dependants a range of one-off gifts, grants and loans to help in the purchase of specialist equipment and to address financial difficulties arising through: ill-health, unemployment, bereavement or other changes of circumstance. We can also support with costs arising from the pursuit of postgraduate chemical engineering studies. However, we are unable to help with postgraduate living expenses or tuition fees and any costs arising from undergraduate study.

Annual grant total

In 2016 the fund had assets of £574,000 and an income of £55,000. Grants to individuals totalled £7,700.

Exclusions

Postgraduate living expenses or tuition fees and any costs arising from undergraduate study.

Applications

Applicants can register to make an application via the fund's website.

CIBSE (Chartered Institution of Building Services Engineers) Benevolent Fund Trust

£37,500 (50 grants)

Correspondent: Stuart Brown, Fund Administrator, CIBSE Benevolent Fund, 222 Balham High Road, London SW12 9BS (020 8673 0822; email: benfund@cibse.org; website: www.cibse.org/cibse-benevolent-fund)

CC number: 1115871

Eligibility

Members and former members of the institution and their dependants, who are in need.

Types of grants

Regular (quarterly) payments to supplement pensions and other income sources. One-off grants towards the cost of special equipment such as stairlifts or equipment which will enable the individual to work from home and major one-off bills such as essential repairs to the home. Help may also be given in the form of waived CIBSE subscriptions.

Annual grant total

In 2016 the trust held assets of £637,500 and had an income of £52,500. Grants to 50 individuals totalled £37,500.

Exclusions

Private health care or education.

Applications

Apply in writing or by contacting the helpline or a local almoner. Applications can be submitted at any time either directly by the individual or through a social worker, Citizens Advice or other welfare agency. An almoner will visit the applicant to obtain details. Applications are considered on receipt.

Other information

The fund's regional almoners visit applicants to assess circumstances, as well as providing advice.

The Institution of Engineering and Technology Benevolent Fund (IET Connect)

£751,500 (195 grants)

Correspondent: Christine Oxland, Chief Executive, Napier House, 24 High Holburn, London WC1V 6AZ (020 7344 5498; email: ietconnect@theiet.org; website: www.ietconnect.org)

CC number: 208925

Eligibility

Members and former members, including those of the Institution of Electrical Engineering and the Institution of Engineering and Technology, and their dependants.

Types of grants

The 2015/16 trustees' annual report details the support provided:

Assistance is offered in the form of grants of money where a financial need has been identified and may be either one-off for a specific purpose such as an adaptation of a house or a regular grant, perhaps on a monthly basis for a fixed period. Some of the items include routine expenses which are not met by State provision such as respite breaks, television licences, telephone charges, transport costs and essential replacement household items. Where possible regular grants are avoided as they can lead to a dependency rather than the individual trying to resolve their situation in the longer term. The preference is to give a larger initial sum, where appropriate, to help get the person or family back on their feet or to give them breathing space to resolve their difficulty and move forward independently.

Those struggling to pay their IET membership can contact the IET membership department directly on 01438 765 678

Annual grant total

In 2016/17 the fund held assets of £26.8 million and had an income of £1.2 million. During the year, the fund gave around £751,500 in grants to 195 individuals.

Exclusions

The fund is unable to fund items retrospectively.

Applications

Application forms are available from the correspondent.

Other information

The fund provides free advice on a wide range of welfare-related matters. Applicants are advised to visit the fund's very accessible, useful and informative website.

The Worshipful Company of Engineers Charitable Trust Fund
See entry on page 182

ICE Benevolent Fund

£577,000 (198 grants)

Correspondent: Lindsay Howell, Caseworker, 5 Mill Hill Close, Haywards Heath, West Sussex RH16 1NY (01444 417979 or 0800 587 3428 (free 24-hour helpline); email: info@icebenfund.com; website: www.icebenfund.com)

CC number: 1126595

Eligibility

Members of The Institution of Civil Engineers (ICE), and their dependants, who are in need.

Types of grants

One-off grants for: disability aids, adaptations and equipment; house repairs or maintenance; residential or nursing home fees; and carers' breaks and respite care. Regular, monthly payments are given to people who are not working and are on very limited incomes. Emergency grants can be given in times of crisis.

Annual grant total

In 2016 the charity had assets of £17 million and an income of £1.4 million. Grants to beneficiaries amounted to £579,000. A breakdown of grants distributed was not available in the annual report and accounts, however it is stated that the charity awarded funding to two individuals through its educational funding scheme for disadvantaged students. Based on this information, we estimate that grants for social welfare purposes totalled around £577,000.

Applications

Application forms are available to download from the website or from the correspondent. They can be submitted directly by the individual or through a third party, such as a social worker, Citizens Advice, welfare agency or a similar party. Supporting paperwork, which is detailed on the website, should be provided so that applications can be dealt with quickly, although the guidance notes state that 'you should not delay sending your application if you have not got everything to hand immediately'. If you are unsure about your eligibility or the support available, or are having difficulty with any of the questions on the application form, do not hesitate to get in touch with the charity.

Other information

The charity runs a 24-hour helpline (0800 587 3428) which offers support and advice on a wide range of issues, including counselling, stress management, relationship problems, financial troubles, parenting, illness and well-being and work life. Face-to-face support can also be arranged. There is the 'Back to Work' scheme operating providing advice and coaching for people who have been out of work for at least three months.

In 2016 the ICE supported 200 beneficiaries with financial help and advice, of which 164 were in the UK and 36 overseas. Many more individuals were supported through the helpline, online portal and workshop programme.

The Benevolent Fund of the Institution of Mechanical Engineers (IMechE) – known as Support Network

£146,500

Correspondent: Maureen Hayes, Casework & Welfare Officer, 1 Birdcage Walk, Westminster, London SW1H 9JJ (020 7304 6816; email: supportnetwork@ imeche.org; website: www.imeche.org/ support-network)

CC number: 209465

Eligibility

Current and former members of the Institution of Mechanical Engineers, and their dependants, who are in need. Former members must have paid subscription fees for at least five years.

Types of grants

Recurrent grants are given in the form of small, regular payments to help with living expenses. One-off grants are given for a wide range of needs, including: furniture; bedding; clothing; food; heating appliances; washing machines; fridges; fuel; telephone, broadband and online access (to promote inclusion); essential items for a new baby; and medical equipment.

Support is also given towards significant costs, such as medical equipment. IMechE members who own their own property may be able to apply for an interest-free loan to assist with the costs of house adaptations (e.g. stairlifts, bathroom conversions, ramps, grab rails, etc.) or repairs.

Annual grant total

In 2016 the charity had assets of £25.9 million and an income of £1.3 million. Grants for the relief of poverty totalled £293,500, which we have taken to also include amounts awarded for educational purposes. A breakdown of grants allocated was not included in the annual report and accounts. We estimate that social welfare grants to individuals totalled around £146,500.

Exclusions

Our research indicates that grants are not given for school fees, business ventures, private medical treatment or the payment of debts.

Applications

In the first instance, contact the charity directly by telephone or email. You will be asked a few questions about your situation and, if the fund is able to help, then an application form will be sent for you to complete.

Other information

Support Network provides information, advice and financial, emotional and practical support to eligible individuals who are in need. The charity has partnered with Law Express to provide its members with a telephone helpline to help with a broad range of everyday problems (helpline: 01275 376029 – 8am to 8pm, Monday to Friday; and 9am to 12pm, Saturday to Sunday). Full information on all of the support available can be found on its very informative website or from the charity itself by email or telephone.

The Matthew Hall Staff Trust Fund

£299,000 (175 grants)

Correspondent: Elaine Hanna, Secretary, AMEC, Booths Hall, Chelford Road, Knutsford WA16 8QZ (01565 683281)

CC number: 1019896

Eligibility

Former employees of Matthew Hall (1992) plc who are over the age of 65, suffering financial hardship and have completed at least two years of service, and their dependants. The spouses of deceased former employees who had completed between two and ten years of service are also eligible.

Types of grants

One-off and recurrent grants are given according to need.

Annual grant total

In 2016/17 the trust had assets of £1.47 million and an income of £35,500. During the year, the trust gave around £299,000 in grants through 175 payments.

Applications

Apply in writing to the correspondent. The trustees meet at least twice a year, normally in July and December, to consider applications.

Other information

The trust was founded using a gift from Bertram Baden, the then owner of the company.

The Institution of Plant Engineers Benevolent Fund

£14,000

Correspondent: Nicholas Humphrey, Trustee, 87 Overdale, Ashtead KT21 1PX (01372 277775; email: nick.jones87@ btopenworld.com)

CC number: 260934

Eligibility

Members/former members of the institution, and their dependants living in England, Scotland and Wales.

Types of grants

One-off grants according to need. Most grants are given to people who are financially stressed through serious illness, unemployment or bereavement.

Annual grant total

In 2016 the fund had an income of £13,500 and a total expenditure of £15,400. We estimate that grants awarded to individuals totalled approximately £14,000.

Applications

Apply in writing to the correspondent. Applications can be submitted directly by the individual or by a relative or close friend.

The Institution of Structural Engineers (ISTRUCTE) Benevolent Fund

£80,500 (19 grants)

Correspondent: Dr Susan Doran, Secretary, 47–58 Bastwick Street, London EC1V 3PS (020 7201 9110; email: benfund@istructe.org; website: www. istructe.org/about-us/funds-and-donations/benevolent-fund)

CC number: 1049171

Eligibility

Members of the institution and their dependants who are in financial difficulties due to circumstances such as: unemployment; illness, accident or disability; family problems; difficulties during retirement; or bereavement.

Types of grants

One-off and recurrent grants and loans up to a maximum of £13,000 per year towards, for example, home repairs, household equipment, property adaptations, disability equipment, carers' breaks and daily living costs for those on very modest incomes. Where appropriate, the fund will also pay the annual subscription fee of the beneficiary, as well as their fee to Engineering Council UK.

Annual grant total

In 2016 the fund had assets of £2.6 million and an income of £94,500. Grants were made to 19 individuals totalling £80,500.

Exclusions

No grants are given for private health care. If the fund settles debts for a beneficiary, it will not usually pay any subsequent debts. The fund will not normally help members' children over the age of 21 or any individuals legally separated or divorced from a member. Grants are assessed by the Benefits Consultant to ensure that the beneficiary's entitlement to statutory benefits will not be reduced.

Applications

Apply on a form available by emailing the correspondent which can be submitted by the individual or an appropriate third party. The trust likes to visit applicants before any grant is made.

Note: in cases of genuine emergency, the fund can pay up to £500, as a loan, normally within days.

Environment and animals

Agriculture

The Royal Agricultural Benevolent Institution

£1.3 million

Correspondent: Welfare team, Shaw House, 27 West Way, Oxford OX2 0QH (0808 281 9490 (freephone helpline); email: grants@rabi.org.uk; website: www. rabi.org.uk)

CC number: 208858

Eligibility

Farmers, farm managers, farm workers and their dependants who are in need. Applicants should have limited savings and be on a low income.

Types of grants

The institution can help with a wide range of short and long-term support. Assistance can be given with: essential white goods; TV licences, lifeline alarms and telephone rental costs; food vouchers and hampers; disability equipment and home adaptations; hospital travel costs; and heating costs. The institution may also be able to pay for relief workers to help around the farm if the individual has to go into hospital, or help with domestic bills for those who cannot work due to illness or injury. Emergency grants can also be given, as can help towards funeral costs.

Regular payments (usually paid quarterly) can be provided. Recipients are normally aged 65 or over and have worked in farming for at least ten years.

Annual grant total

In 2016 the institution had assets of £66.4 million and an income of £6 million. Direct grants awarded totalled more than £1.3 million.

Exclusions

No grants can be given towards business debts and expenses, medical expenses or the costs of private education.

Applications

Enquiries can be made by calling the freephone helpline (0808 281 9490). New applicants are usually visited by one of the institution's regional welfare officers. The grants committee meets every six to eight weeks to consider applications, although urgent cases can be fast-tracked.

Other information

The institution also operates two residential homes, one in Bury St Edmunds and one in Burnham-on-Sea and also associated sheltered flats for older members of the farming community.

The welfare team provides a wide range of support and advice, including assistance with statutory benefit claims, and access to debt advice and free business appraisals. There is a helpful leaflet detailing what the team can assist with on the website.

Barham Benevolent Foundation

£24,500 (19 grants)

Correspondent: Michael Cook, Trustee, 8 Stumps End, Bosham, Chichester, West Sussex PO18 8RB (01243 573993; email: mcook1158@googlemail.com)

CC number: 249922

Eligibility

People who have been employed in the dairy business, and their dependants, who are in need.

Types of grants

One-off grants according to need. In some circumstances the foundation will support the costs of holidays and provide assistance with accommodation expenses.

Annual grant total

In 2015/16 the foundation had assets of £5 million and an income of £183,000. Total expenditure amounted to £228,000.

Grants totalled £133,500, of which payments to 19 individuals amounted to £24,500. The foundation made grants to ten individuals directly totalling £9,500 and made a further nine payments totalling £12,000 through the National Dairymen's Benevolent Institution (NDBI).

Applications

Apply in writing to the correspondent.

Other information

Most funding given by the foundation goes towards supporting education relating to the dairy industry (£109,000 to five institutions in 2015/16).

The Bristol Corn Trade Guild

£3,500

Correspondent: Richard Cooksley, Secretary, Portbury House, Sheepway, Portbury, Bristol BS20 7TE (01275 373539; email: richard@bcfta.com; website: www.bcfta.org.uk/the-guild)

CC number: 202404

Eligibility

People who have a connection with the corn, grain, feed, flour and allied trades who are in need. Dependants of such people are also eligible. Current and former members of the Bristol Corn and Feed Trade Association may be favoured.

Types of grants

One-off grants can be given towards medical equipment or specialist treatment, repairs and household essentials. Recurrent grants can be made for utility bills.

Annual grant total

In 2016 the guild had an income of £12,700 and a total expenditure of £7,300. We have estimated that grants totalled around £3,500 during the year.

Applications

Apply in writing to the correspondent. Applications can be submitted directly by the individual or through a social worker, Citizens Advice or other welfare agency.

Other information

Members and former members of the Bristol Corn and Feed Trade Association are also invited to various activities organised by the guild, such as sporting events or Christmas lunch.

East Sussex Farmers' Union Benevolent Fund

£12,900

Correspondent: Desmond Lambert, Filsham Lodge, Horsted Lane, Isfield, Uckfield TN22 5TX (01825 751207)

CC number: 271188

Eligibility

Farmers, farmworkers and their dependants who are in need and live in East Sussex. When funds are available, eligible people living in the adjoining counties of West Sussex and Surrey may also be supported.

Types of grants

One-off and recurrent grants are given according to need. Hampers are also distributed.

Annual grant total

In 2016/17 the charity had assets of £1.9 million and an income of £44,500. Grants to individuals totalled £12,900.

A further £3,300 (which we have not included in the grant total) was spent on providing hampers for beneficiaries.

Applications

Apply in writing or by telephone to the correspondent.

The Sir Percival Griffiths' Tea-Planters Trust

£7,000

Correspondent: Stephen Buckland, Trustee, c/o Linton Park plc, Linton Park, Linton, Kent ME17 4AB

CC number: 253904

Eligibility

People who are or have been involved in tea planting in India, live in the UK and are in need. Dependants of such people are also eligible.

Types of grants

Our research suggests that one-off and recurrent grants are available to help with general living expenses.

Annual grant total

In 2016 the trust had an income of £580 and a total expenditure of £7,300. We estimate that grants given to individuals totalled around £7,000.

Applications

Application forms are available from the correspondent. They should include details of career in India (dates, tea garden and so on) and can be submitted at any time either directly by the individual or through a third party, such as a social worker, Citizens Advice, or another welfare agency.

RSABI (Royal Scottish Agricultural Benevolent Institution)

£535,500 (692 grants)

Correspondent: The Welfare Team, The Rural Centre, West Mains, Newbridge, Midlothian EH28 8LT (0300 111 4166; email: rsabi@rsabi.org.uk; website: www.rsabi.org.uk)

OSCR number: SC009828

Eligibility

People who have been engaged for at least ten years, full-time in a land-based occupation in Scotland, and their dependants. Applicants should be either retired or unable to work, on a low income (RSABI does not include non-means-tested disability benefits when calculating qualifying income) and have limited savings (£12,000 for a single applicant, £16,000 for couples) or be facing a crisis due to ill health, accident or bereavement

Qualifying occupations include: agriculture, aquaculture, crofting, forestry, fish farming, gamekeeping, horticulture, rural estate work and other jobs that depend on the provision of services directly to these industries.

Types of grants

The charity offers:

- Recurring payments made twice a year on a bi-annual basis to those on limited income with little or no savings. The charity can provide help with fuel and heating expenses, TV licences and seasonal bonuses, etc. to older people and those who are unable to work. RSABI welfare staff ensure that individuals receive their full entitlements to any other benefits due and will help and advise with other difficulties such as care services, housing or similar matters
- One-off grants for specific essential items, such as home repairs and modifications, disability aids, essential transport costs, car tax or insurance (where personal transport is essential) and respite breaks
- Awards to help individuals meet a particular crisis in their lives – by way of direct help, payments to suppliers (e.g. energy providers) and/or supermarket shopping vouchers
- Centenary Fund awards to help individuals in special circumstances 'where a significant improvement in their quality of life, or that of their carers, can be achieved'

There are 'Essential needs packages' available to assist with the costs of household appliances, furniture, floor covering and other home necessities.

Annual grant total

In 2016/17 the charity had assets of £11 million and an income of £867,000. The charity awarded £535,500 in grants to 692 individuals for welfare purposes, which can be broken down as follows:

Annual grants	559	£399,500
Single grants	-	£113,000
Orkney Crisis Fund	39	£23,000

Exclusions

Grants are not made to help with repayment of loans, the cost of bankruptcy, or business purposes (except towards the cost of professional and/or business advice and farm labour).

Applications

The charity has a very helpful website detailing all the support it offers and should be consulted before making an application.

All new applicants will be required to provide proof of identity, address confirmation, income and savings will be required. Applicants should be able to demonstrate that they meet the occupational criteria. Self-employed farmers and crofters will need to supply a Business Number/holding number or evidence of registration on the Register of Croft and recent business accounts. Any other self-employed worker or contractor will need to supply recent business accounts or proof of self-employment.

Other information

RSABI also offers advice on benefits and support from other organisations, provides guidance through key life events such as redundancy, and offers home visits by welfare officers to provide ongoing support and friendship. The charity also manage a confidential listening and support advice line for Scotland's land-based and farming community. The helpline is available from 7am to 11pm every day on 0300 111 4166.

In 2015 the charity established a Crisis Fund for Orkney, following a period of wet weather which meant that farmers could not let their cattle out to pasture. This scheme has now closed.

Animal care

Veterinary Benevolent Fund

£129,500 (36 grants)

Correspondent: Vanessa Kearns, Administration Manager, British Veterinary Association, 7 Mansfield Street, London W1G 9NQ (020 7908 6385; fax: 020 7980 4890; email: info@vetlife.org.uk; website: www.vetlife.org.uk)

CC number: 224776

Eligibility

Veterinary surgeons who are or have been on the register of the Royal College of Veterinary Surgeons (RCVS) and are ordinarily resident in the UK, and their dependants.

Types of grants

Regular monthly payments for people living on a low income and one-off grants of up to a maximum of £1,000 towards TV licences, telephone line rental, additional heating costs, car tax and insurance, holidays, medical equipment, disability aids and so on. The fund has previously noted an increasing trend towards providing more one-off support with less demand for recurrent grants. Short-term, interest-free loans may also be made to tide beneficiaries over in times of crisis.

Annual grant total

In 2016 the fund had assets of £7.6 million and an income of £552,500. Around £109,000 was paid out in the form of regular grants to 36 individuals and £20,000 was given as one-off special gifts, usually at Christmas time.

Exclusions

No grants are given towards:

- Grants to anyone before they have qualified and are on the RCVS register
- The costs of studying veterinary medicine as a second degree
- Business or partnership debt
- Mandatory training courses
- Indemnity insurance
- Private education
- Private medical care or care home fees
- Repaying loans to family and friends
- Improvements and repairs to rented property
- Support to individuals simply because they are unemployed

Applications

Application forms are available from the VBF office or can be downloaded from the Vetlife website and should be submitted with three months of recent bank statements and other supporting documentation (such as, a copy of a letter from the DWP with details of any state benefits received, recent mortgage/rent statement and copies of letters from creditors regarding arrears, if there are outstanding debts). Two references are required. A decision may be made immediately or VBF may request that one of their representatives make a home visit before a decision is reached. Applicants may be visited or asked to provide further information before a decision is made, although an immediate payment may be made for those in need of urgent help.

Other information

Alongside the benevolent fund the charity also runs a helpline, mental health support programme and the Vetlife website. It can also provide advice on a wide range of issues, including debt and welfare benefits. The fund owns four bungalows at Burton near Christchurch (Dorset) which are available 'for deserving veterinary surgeons and their families'.

Fishing

Fishermen's Mission

£975,000 (2,574 grants)

Correspondent: David Dickens, Secretary & Chief Executive, Fishermen's Mission Head Office, Mather House, 4400 Parkway, Fareham, Hampshire PO15 7FJ (01489 566910; email: enquiries@fishermensmission.org.uk; website: www.fishermensmission.org.uk)

CC number: 232822

Eligibility

Commercial fishermen, including retired fishermen, and their wives and widows who are experiencing unforeseen tragedy or hardship.

Types of grants

Immediate one-off payments to widows of fishermen lost at sea. There are also other individual grants to alleviate cases of hardship (e.g. provision of basic furniture for impoverished older fishermen). Grants are almost always one-off.

Annual grant total

In 2015/16 the mission held assets of £11.2 million and had an income of £2.7 million. Welfare support was given to 2,574 individuals and totalled £975,000.

Applications

Apply in writing to the correspondent or the local superintendent, either directly by the individual or through a social worker, Citizens Advice or other welfare agency. Record of sea service and names of fishing vessels and/or owners is required.

Other information

Grant-making is a small part/area of this mission's activities. It also has a team of welfare staff which provides advice and assistance to fishing communities throughout the UK. In addition it assists injured or ill fishermen and where appropriate arranges for them to receive enhanced medical attention, and can source emergency accommodation and catering facilities where there is no alternative provision.

Forestry

Forest Industries Education and Provident Fund

£600

Correspondent: Edward Mills, 5 Beech Court, Birkrigg Park, Ulverston, Cumbria LA12 0UH (07875 248115; email: info@edwardmills.co.uk; website: www.confor.org.uk/resources/education-provident-fund)

CC number: 1061322

Eligibility

Members of the Forestry and Timber Association (or Confor) and their dependants who are in need, hardship or distress (for example, due to illness, death or injury). Members must have been involved with the association for at least one year.

Types of grants

One-off grants are made towards expenses for those experiencing hardship.

Annual grant total

In 2015 the fund had an income of £6,900 and a total expenditure of £1,300. We estimate that welfare grants totalled around £600.

Exclusions

Retrospective funding is not given.

Applications

Application forms are available from the fund's website or can be requested from the correspondent.

Other information

Anyone can join Confor who has an interest in trees, woodlands or timber. Grants are also made for educational purposes.

The fund's website also directs beneficiaries to other potential sources of help: The Institute of Chartered Foresters' Educational and Scientific Trust and The Royal Forestry Society.

Gamekeepers Welfare Trust

£18,200

Correspondent: Helen Benson, Chief Executive and Charity Manager, Keepers Cottage, Tanfield Lodge, West Tanfield, Ripon, North Yorkshire HG4 5LE (0300 1233088 (helpline) or 01677 470180; email: enquiries@ thegamekeeperswelfaretrust.com or gamekeeperwtrust@btinternet.com; website: thegamekeeperswelfaretrust.com)

CC number: 1008924

Eligibility

Gamekeepers and those in similar occupations who are in need, and their dependants.

Types of grants

One-off and recurrent grants are given according to need. Some recent examples of support include housing assistance, home help, travel, medical equipment and aids, access to work vehicles, veterinarian assistance and small gifts and flowers.

Annual grant total

In 2016 the trust had assets of £139,500 and an income of £32,000. Welfare support totalled £18,200, with a further £1,300 awarded for educational needs.

Applications

Application forms are available from the correspondent or can be found on the website. They can be made at any time. The trust also invites applications for assistance by advertising through publications, on the website and by distributing its own brochure to associated organisations, to colleges and to gamekeepers and other members of the public at game fairs and similar countryside events.

Other information

In addition, the charity maintains a job register for gamekeepers, stalkers, ghillies and their families in difficult times to help them find gainful employment. The trustees have estimated that a further 600 people and their families were assisted in some way, either through signposting to other organisations, or through telephone support.

The New Forest Keepers Widows Fund

£22,500

Correspondent: Richard Mihalop, 17 Ferndale Road, Marchwood, Southampton SO40 4XR (023 8086 1136; email: newforestkwfund@gmail.com)

CC number: 1016362

Eligibility

Retired keepers of the New Forest and their dependants who are in need, or the dependants of deceased keepers who are in need.

Types of grants

One-off and recurrent grants ranging from £50 to £2,500.

Annual grant total

In 2015/16 the fund had an income of £15,200 and a total expenditure of £23,000. We estimate that the fund gave around £22,500 in grants to individuals.

Applications

Apply in writing to the correspondent directly by the individual or family member. Applications can be submitted at any time.

Horticulture

Gardeners' Royal Benevolent Society (Perennial)

£128,000

Correspondent: Sheila Thomson, Director of Services, 115 – 117 Kingston Road, Leatherhead, Surrey KT22 7SU (0800 093 8510; email: info@perennial. org.uk; website: www.perennial.org.uk)

CC number: 1155156/SC040180

Eligibility

People who are, or have been, employed or self-employed in the horticultural industry in the UK and their spouses/ partners, widows/widowers and other immediate dependants. This includes qualified and unqualified gardeners, nursery workers, landscapers, garden centre employees, arboriculturists, people running their own small businesses and others in the industry who are in necessitous circumstances, such as financial difficulties, illness, disability and so on.

Types of grants

The charity offers the following help:

- One-off grants towards a variety of needs, including: mobility aids; holidays; travel and transport costs; property adaptations and maintenance; domestic appliances; debt clearance; personal items; housing needs; housing benefit top-up; day-to-day living costs; energy bills; funeral expenses; community alarms; pet care; furniture and fittings
- Regular quarterly allowances payable on a long-term basis (in some cases for life), usually to those over retirement age
- Assistance and top-up for care home fees ranging from £10 to £100 per week
- Perennial also distributes grocery vouchers, makes winter fuel payments and provides referrals to food banks

Annual grant total

In 2015/16 the charity had assets of £53.9 million and an income of £4.5 million. Grants to individuals totalled £256,000. We estimate that welfare grants to individuals totalled around £128,000.

Applications

Applicants are advised to check the website for the application advice relating to separate schemes. Individuals are encouraged to get in touch with the charity to discuss their eligibility and support available.

Other information

The charity provides free and confidential advice, support and financial assistance to people of all ages working in, or retired from horticulture.

Food and drink provision

The Bakers' Benevolent Society

£8,500 (100+ grants)

Correspondent: Suzanne Pitts, Clerk to the Society, The Mill House, 23 Bakers Lane, Epping, Essex CM16 5DQ (01992 575951; fax: 01992 561163; email: bbs@bakersbenevolent.co.uk; website: bakersbenevolent.co.uk)

CC number: 211307

Eligibility

People in need who have worked in the baking industry and its allied trades and are now retired and their dependants and widows.

Types of grants

Quarterly pensions and one-off small grants to help people retain or increase their independence. Grants are available towards items such as mobility aids, lifelines and telephone rental, and household essentials.

Annual grant total

In 2015/16 the society held assets of £1.4 million and had an income of £570,000. Grants and pensions to individuals totalled £8,500.

Exclusions

The society cannot cover the costs of major home repairs, student loans or bursaries, respite breaks or holidays, funeral costs, or debt reduction. However, it can signpost to other services, organisations and benevolent funds.

Applications

Application forms are available from the correspondent. Applications should be submitted either directly by the individual or a family member or through an appropriate welfare agency. Applications should include details of

occupational history, age and financial circumstances. Applications are considered upon receipt.

Other information

The society was established in 1832 and provides sheltered accommodation for people who once worked in the baking industry and allied trades.

The Benevolent (The Wine and Spirits Trades' Benevolent Society)

£411,500 (563 grants)

Correspondent: Pam Jarrett, Office and Finance Manager, 39–45 Bermondsey Street, London SE1 3XF (020 7089 3888; email: support@thebenevolent.org.uk; website: www.thebenevolent.org.uk)

CC number: 1023376

Eligibility

People living in the UK who have worked for at least two years, or 20% of their working life, directly or indirectly, in the drinks industry – whether 'in a pub, brewery, bar, distillery, off licence, trade press publication, warehouse or in an office based role at a company producing, distributing, marketing or selling primarily alcohol'. Those applying for financial assistance are expected to have limited income and savings.

Types of grants

Regular beneficial grants towards general living expenses of up to £71.50 paid monthly and one-off discretionary grants for the purchase of large household items and unexpected expenses. Grants are given in exceptional cases for funeral costs. The society also makes Christmas gift donations (£71.50 each in 2015) and gives grants towards TV licence fees. Cases are assessed on an individual basis and larger grants can be made according to need.

Annual grant total

In 2015 the charity held assets of £5.2 million and had an income of over £1.1 million. Grants totalling £411,500 were made to 563 individuals during the year, the majority of which (£309,500) was paid in beneficial grants. A further £93,500 was given through the discretionary grants scheme and 59 people received grants (£8,500) through the TV licence scheme.

Exclusions

No grants are given towards business equipment.

Applications

Apply on a form available from the correspondent or to download from the charity's website, along with application

guidelines. Applications are considered throughout the year and should include history of employment within the drinks industry. All new beneficiaries are visited by one of the charity's welfare officers to assess the best form of support. Contact the trust with any queries or support needed with completing the application form.

E. F. Bulmer Benevolent Fund

£59,500 (174 grants)

Correspondent: James Greenfield, Administrator, The Fred Bulmer Centre, Wall Street, Hereford HR4 9HP (01432 271293; email: efbulmer@gmail.com; website: www.efbulmer.co.uk)

CC number: 214831

Eligibility

Former employees of H P Bulmer Holdings plc (before it was acquired by Scottish and Newcastle plc) or its subsidiary companies for a period of not less than one year, or their dependants, who are in need. Grants are occasionally made to other individuals in need in Herefordshire.

Types of grants

One-off grants, typically up to £500, are awarded according to need. Some top-up pensions are made from a historic list but the trust is not considering new pension applicants.

Annual grant total

In 2015/16 the trust held assets of £13.2 million and had an income of £456,000. Grants to 174 individuals totalled £59,500 and were distributed as follows:

Pension supplements	129	£37,000
One-off grants to other individuals	45	£22,500

A further £195,500 was awarded in grants to 65 organisations.

Applications

Initial enquiries should be made to the administrator, preferably by email. Applications should be made through a recognised organisation such as social services, Citizens Advice or other reputable organisations. Applicants are encouraged to consider the information noted on the trust's website before applying. The trust aims to inform eligible applicants of their outcome as soon as possible after a trustees' meeting. Ineligible applicants will not receive a reply.

Other information

The trust maintains the Fred Bulmer centre which provides facilities and accommodation for other charities.

Butchers' and Drovers' Charitable Institution (BDCI)

£187,000 (62 grants)

Correspondent: Tina Clayton, Vice Clerk to the Trustees, Butchers' and Drovers' Charitable Institution, 105 St Peter's Street, St Albans, Hertfordshire AL1 3EJ (01727 896094; email: info@bdci.org.uk; website: www.bdci.org.uk)

CC number: 1155703

Eligibility

People in the UK, who work or have worked in any aspect of the meat industry whether wholesale, retail or otherwise, and their widows, widowers, partners and dependent children. Applicants will normally have worked within the industry for at least ten years and will often be retired or medically certified unfit to work.

Types of grants

The charity gives assistance in two ways: one-off awards can be made towards heating bills, mobility aids, white goods, house repairs and clothing, for example; and small grants are given to top up nursing home fees. The charity also supports some beneficiaries with pensions.

Annual grant total

In 2016 the charity had assets of £13 million and an income of £647,000. Grants totalled £187,000 and were distributed as follows:

Pensions	£111,500
One-off grants	£75,500

During the year, 77 applications for assistance were considered by the Grants Committee, with 62 being approved.

Applications

Application forms can be requested from the correspondent or downloaded from the charity's website. They can be submitted directly by the individual or through a third party, such as a social worker, Citizens Advice or other welfare agency. Applications require the following information: the applicant's name, date of birth, address and phone number; details of other people living with the applicant; the presence of any children; the applicant's connection with the meat trade; financial details, including the income of the applicant and also, if applicable, their partner; details of the applicant's ownership of their own business, if applicable; the applicant's weekly expenditure; the type of assistance sought (i.e. financial, nursing or residential care). Applicants must provide proof of their connection with the meat trade as well as financial details. Applications are considered at bi-monthly meetings.

Other information

The charity also provides residential accommodation to those in need, see the charity's website for details.

The charity has initiated a new bursary scheme. Bursaries of up to £5,000 each per year will be awarded to students undertaking courses with relevance to the meat trade. The first awards were made with respect to the academic year 2015/16. Discussions with Harper Adams University to administer this scheme were successfully concluded during 2015. Harper Adams University has been appointed to administer the scheme for a trial period of three years.

Corn Exchange Benevolent Society

£38,500 (32 grants)

Correspondent: Richard Butler, Secretary, 38 St Mary Axe, London EC3A 8BH (020 7283 6090; fax: 020 7283 6133; email: richard.butler@baltic-charities.co.uk; website: www.baltic-charities.co.uk)

CC number: 207733

Eligibility

People who work/have worked in the UK grain trade (the corn, grain, seed, cereal, animal feeding-stuffs, pulses, malt, flour milling or granary-keeping trades) at any level (this includes the trading, processing, manufacturing, storage or transport parts of the trade), and their dependants.

Types of grants

Annual grants can be given to help with day-to-day living costs. Additional and special grants are available and in 2016 were given for needs including funeral costs, holidays, physiotherapy, rent, house cleaning, council tax, water rates, and the provision of a wheelchair and a new fridge. During the year, the charity also supported beneficiaries with heating grants in periods of exceptionally cold weather and distributed gifts and hampers at Christmas.

Annual grant total

In 2016 the charity had assets of £3.8 million and an income of £106,500. During the year, a total of £38,500 was awarded to 32 beneficiaries: £8,000 was awarded in quarterly grants, and £30,500 as one-off hardship grants.

Exclusions

Cereal growers, farmers, bakers and pastry cooks are not eligible.

Applications

Apply on a form available from the correspondent or to download from the website. Applications can be submitted directly by the individual or through a social worker, Citizens Advice or other welfare agency. Applicants are required to provide full details of income and expenditure. Initial approaches by phone, email or in writing are also welcomed.

The National Federation of Fish Friers Benevolent Fund

£1,900

Correspondent: The General Secretary, New Federation House, 4 Greenwood Mount, Meanwood, Leeds LS6 4LQ (0113 230 7044; fax: 0113 230 7010; email: mail@federationoffishfriers.co.uk; website: www.federationoffishfriers.co.uk)

CC number: 229168

Eligibility

Members or former members of the federation and their dependants (whether subscribers to the fund or not).

Types of grants

One-off grants in the range of £150 to £300 for necessities and convalescent holidays in the UK.

Annual grant total

In 2016 the fund had an income of £1,200 and a total expenditure of £2,100. We estimate that the fund gave around £1,900 in grants to individuals.

Exclusions

No grants are available for debts due to poor business practice or to organisations.

Applications

Application forms are available from the correspondent. Applications can be submitted by the individual, through a recognised referral agency (such as a social worker, Citizens Advice or AFF Associations/branches) or by the individual's family, and are considered throughout the year.

Other information

The fund maintains several convalescent homes.

The Fishmongers' and Poulterers' Institution

£15,200

Correspondent: Roy Sully, Secretary, The Fishmongers and Poulterers Institution, Top Floor, 14 Charterhouse Square, London EC1M 6AX (020 7600 4106; email: fpi@butchershall.com; website: www.butchershall.com/index.php)

CC number: 209013

Eligibility

People in need who are, or have been, involved in the processing, wholesale and retail fish and poultry trades for at least ten years, and their dependants.

Types of grants

Pensions and one-off grants. In the past, one-off grants were given for the purchase of white goods, replacement windows and assistance with care costs.

Annual grant total

In 2016 the institution held assets of £747,500 and had an income of £35,500. Grants to individuals totalled £15,200.

Applications

Application forms are available from the correspondent. Applications can be submitted directly by the individual or through a third party. The institution points out in its 2016 annual report that many applications are received through intermediary bodies such as The Royal British Legion or Care and Repair agencies. They are considered three times a year.

GroceryAid

£3.6 million

Correspondent: The Welfare Team, Unit 2, Lakeside Business Park, Swan Lane, Sandhurst, Berkshire GU47 9DN (01252 875925; email: welfare@groceryaid.org.uk; website: www.groceryaid.org.uk)

CC number: 1095897

Eligibility

Applicants should have at least three years' service in the grocery industry.

Types of grants

Crisis grants are available to people who experience an unexpected emergency, a change in circumstances or a sudden gap in income. Welfare grants which provide support over a longer period of time are available to people with at least ten years' service.

Annual grant total

In 2016/17 the charity held assets of £13.3 million and had an income of over £6.1 million. Grants to individuals totalled £3.6 million and were broken down as follows:

Quarterly payments	£2.5 million
Emergency assistance	£281,000
Christmas hampers	£200,000
Basic essentials	£194,000
Mobility	£135,000
Respite (carers)	£30,500
One-off payments	£25,000
Birthday vouchers and TV licences	£24,500
Beneficiary outings	£18,500

Applications

Application forms are available to download from the charity's website.

Other information

The charity runs a helpline to provide emotional support and advice to anyone who has worked in the industry regardless of length of service. The service is available 365 days a year on 0808 802 1122.

Licensed Trade Charity

£530,500 (596 grants)

Correspondent: Helpline Team, Heatherley, London Road, Ascot, Berkshire SL5 8DR (0808 801 0550; fax: 01344 884703; email: support@supportandcare.org; website: www.supportandcare.org)

CC number: 230011

Eligibility

People in need who are working, or have worked, in the licensed drinks industry, including their spouses/partners and dependent children. To qualify for assistance applicants should have worked in the trade for a minimum of five years continuously at some time in their working lives.

Types of grants

Recurrent grants are given to those on a very low income to help with utility bills, food costs, hospital travel expenses and other essential living expenses. One-off grants are also made towards: urgently needed equipment, such as household appliances and mobility aids; household improvements like door widening, stairlifts and ramps; convalescent care and nursing costs for those recovering from illness; winter fuel grants and funeral expenses.

Annual grant total

In 2016 the charity had assets of £64.4 million and an income of £26.3 million. Welfare grants to individuals totalled £530,500.

Exclusions

Support is not given for top-up fees for residential care or for private medical treatments.

Applications

In the first instance get in touch with the charity to discuss your needs. The charity can be contacted by email, live online chat, telephone or by writing. All contact details are available on the website.

Other information

The charity's annual report (2016) states, 'In terms of direct support, 596 individuals and their families benefitted from direct financial support, to help them out of difficult circumstances, including finding somewhere to live, support during severe or critical illness and financial hardship.'

The charity also operates an independent school in Ascot and SEN schools in Oxford and Hassocks, and offers bursaries to students whose parents have worked in the licensed drinks industry.

The charity's website offers advice and information on a range of issues, such as housing, money problems, education and health needs. Educational grants can also be made for families.

The Benevolent Society of the Licensed Trade of Scotland

£170,500

Correspondent: Chris Gardner, Chief Executive, 79 West Regent Street, Glasgow G2 2AW (0141 353 3596; fax: 0141 353 3597; email: chris@bensoc.org.uk; website: www.bensoc.org.uk)

OSCR number: SC005604

Eligibility

Members of the society and people who have been employed full-time in the licensed trade in Scotland for at least three years, the three years do not need to be consecutive.

Types of grants

Annual pensions usually of up to £640. Each pensioner also receives a substantial Christmas and holiday gift. One-off grants are also available for temporary emergencies.

Annual grant total

In 2016/17 the society had an income of £475,000 and a total expenditure of £491,500. Grants and donations to individuals totalled £170,500.

The table below shows how grants and donations were distributed during the year:

Pensions	£102,000
Christmas gifts	£27,000
Holiday gifts	£27,000
Grants	£14,300

Applications

A short online form is available on the website. Applicants must firstly submit the form online in order to find out if they are eligible for support. Alternatively, applicants can contact the correspondent by email or telephone (contact details are available on the website).

Other information

Pensioners are visited at least once a year.

The Liverpool Provision Trade Guild

£7,500

Correspondent: The Correspondent, KBH Accountants Ltd, 255 Poulton Road, Wallasey CH44 4BT (0151 638 8550)

CC number: 224918

Eligibility

Members of the guild and their dependants who are in need. If funds permit, benefits can be extended to other members of the provision trade on Merseyside who are in need, and their dependants.

Types of grants

Our previous research indicates that the charity awards recurrent grants.

Annual grant total

In 2015 the charity had an income of £3,200 and a total expenditure of £10,200. We estimate that the charity awarded around £7,500 in grants to individuals for welfare purposes.

Applications

Apply in writing to the correspondent directly. Meetings are held in May and December to discuss applications.

The Manchester Provision Trade Guild

£5,800

Correspondent: Laura McKeown, 2 The Granary, Sandlow Green Farm, Holmes Chapel Road, Holmes Chapel, Crewe CW4 8AS (01565 653388; email: admin@birchlittlemore.co.uk)

CC number: 244729

Eligibility

People in need in the provision trade, and their dependants. Applicants are normally retired and must have been employed in the trade for a number of years.

The provision trade covers the following: bacon, pork, canned meat/fish and dairy products.

Types of grants

One-off and recurrent grants are given according to need.

Annual grant total

In 2015/16 the charity had an income of £7,700 and a total expenditure £6,100. We estimate that grants given to individuals totalled £5,800.

Applications

Apply in writing to the correspondent.

The National Association of Master Bakers, Confectioners and Caterers Benevolent Fund

£6,000

Correspondent: The Secretary, 21 Baldock Street, Ware, Hertfordshire SG12 9DH (01920 468061; email: info@craftbakersassociation.co.uk; website: www.craftbakersassociation.co.uk)

CC number: 206691

Eligibility

Former master bakers and their families who are in need.

Types of grants

Quarterly grants to help towards living costs such as gas, electricity and telephone bills. One-off grants are also available for specific items such as wheelchairs and household adaptations.

Annual grant total

In 2016 the charity had assets of £888,000 and a total expenditure of £29,000. During the year, the charity gave a total of £12,000. We estimate that around £6,000 was given to individuals.

Exclusions

No grants are given for business debt or towards nursing home fees.

Applications

Application forms are available from the correspondent, to be submitted by the individual or through a recognised referral agency such as a social worker, Citizens Advice or doctor. Applications are usually considered on a monthly basis.

Other information

The charity also gives grants to organisations.

The Provision Trade Charity

£47,000

Correspondent: Mette Barwick, Secretary, 17 Clerkenwell Green, London EC1R 0DP (020 7253 2114; email: secretary@ptbi.org.uk; website: www.ptbi.org.uk)

CC number: 209173

Eligibility

People in need in the provision and allied trade, and their dependants. Applicants are normally retired and must have been employed in the trade for a number of years.

The provision trade covers the following: bacon, pork, canned meat/fish and dairy products.

Types of grants

Recurrent grants are issued quarterly. Summer and winter gifts and one-off grants can also be awarded where appropriate. One-off grants may also be issued to assist with special purchases or home improvements.

Annual grant total

In 2016 the charity held assets of £959,500 and had an income of £51,500. Grants to individuals totalled £47,000.

Exclusions

The charity does not provide loans and cannot support people employed in retail, catering or hospitality.

Applications

Application forms can be downloaded from the website. Applications may be returned by email or post. They can be submitted directly by the individual or through a social worker, Citizens Advice, other welfare agency or through a relation or friend. Prospective beneficiaries are visited by the charity's welfare visitor.

Other information

This charity was founded as the Cheesemonger's Benevolent Institution in 1835 'for pensionary relief of indigent or incapacitated members of the Provision Trade and their widows'. The charity is also referred to as 'PTBI'.

Scottish Association of Master Bakers Benevolent Fund

£15,000

Correspondent: Grants Administrator, Unit 2 Halbeath Interchange, Kingseat Road, Dunfermline, Fife KY11 8RY

OSCR number: SC010444

Eligibility

Members or ex-members of the Scottish Association of Master Bakers and their families who are in need. Other members of the Scottish baking industry may also be supported.

Types of grants

One-off grants, usually of up to £700, towards electrical goods, household repairs, repayment of small debts etc.

Annual grant total

In 2016/17 the association had an income of £23,500 and a total expenditure of £21,000. We estimate that grants given to individuals totalled around £15,000.

Applications

Application forms are available from the correspondent.

Scottish Grocers Federation Benevolent Fund

£9,000

Correspondent: The Grants Administrator, Federation House, 222–224 Queensferry Road, Edinburgh EH4 2BN (0131 343 3300; email: reception@scotgrocersfed.co.uk; website: www.scottishshop.org.uk/about/benevolent-fund)

OSCR number: SC047273

Eligibility

Past members or employees of the independent grocery trade in Scotland who have been employed in the trade for a minimum of six months, and are in need. Dependants, friends and family can also be supported.

Types of grants

One-off and recurrent grants to relieve hardship, depending on need. Grants are also made to friends and family of current and previous grocers for funeral costs relating to death in service.

Annual grant total

In 2016 the charity had an income of £17,000 and a total expenditure of £21,500. We estimate that grants given to individuals totalled £9,000.

Applications

Application forms are available to download from the website and should be returned to the correspondent via post.

Other information

Grants are also made to charitable organisations which provide support to those in need who work/have worked as an independent grocer in Scotland, and to give training to anyone who has worked as an independent grocer.

The charity is in the process of being wound up and will soon transfer its assets to Scottish Grocers Federation Benevolent Fund, charity number SC047273.

Hospitality and retail

ABTA LifeLine (The ABTA Benevolent Trust)

£35,000 (20 grants)

Correspondent: The Trustees, 30 Park Street, London SE1 9EQ (020 3117 0500; email: lifeline@abtalifeline.org.uk; website: www.abtalifeline.org.uk)

CC number: 295819

Eligibility

People in need who are or have been employed by ABTA members, ABTA itself or other organisations within the industry who are engaged in the sale of ABTA products, and their dependants.

Types of grants

One-off and recurrent grants unrestricted in size. Grants have been awarded for mobility equipment, disability and health needs, children's expenses, funeral costs, emergency home repairs, assistance with daily living costs and respite breaks for carers. The charity's lifeline stretches far and wide and nothing is too big or too small to be considered.

Guidance provided by the charity advises:

> Whilst we do not help with paying off debts, we may be able to help with priority debts (rent, mortgage, utility bills). The charity will request that you first seek guidance from the Citizens Advice Bureau. The CAB can help you plan and budget according to your needs, and provide advice on how to tackle the debts that you have.
>
> In exceptional circumstances, and where there is a clear need, we may be able to provide an immediate payment to help relieve the pressure.

We may, also in exceptional circumstances, be able to help the parent of someone working in travel. Both the parent and the person applying on behalf of the parent will need to be assessed.

Annual grant total

In 2015 the charity held assets of £546,000 and an income of £162,500. Grants were made to 20 individuals totalling £35,000. The charity also granted £2,900 in bursaries. During the year, the charity received a total of 28 applications.

Exclusions

The charity generally does not have any restrictions in relation to its grant criteria, except it cannot help with business costs including those arising from the failure of a company. Statutory help and assistance from other appropriate authorities or supportive agencies should be exhausted before applying for a grant from the charity.

Applications

Application forms are available from the correspondent or can be downloaded from the website. They should be submitted either directly by the individual, through a third party, such as a social worker, or through an organisation, such as Citizens Advice.

Other information

The charity also offers The ABTA Lifeline Bursary to assist 'an individual in [the] travel community who does not have the means to further their education and develop their career potential within the industry'. The bursary was established in partnership with Travel Weekly in memory of Colin Heal.

The Book Trade Charity

£148,000 (82 grants)

Correspondent: David Hicks, Chief Executive, The Foyle Centre, The Retreat, Abbots Road, Kings Langley, Hertfordshire WD4 8LT (01923 263128 or 01329848731; fax: 01923 270732; email: david@btbs.org or info@booktradecharity.org; website: www.booktradecharity.org)

CC number: 1128129

Eligibility

People in need who have worked in the book trade in the UK for at least one year (normally publishing/distribution/book-selling), and their dependants.

Types of grants

One-off grants and regular monthly grants of up to £2,000 a year. Grants are normally to supplement weekly/monthly income and for recuperative holidays. Other support is given in a variety of ways, for example, emergency payments for household repairs, disability aids or help moving house. Support is also available to help individuals and families through critical illnesses.

Annual grant total

In 2016 the charity had assets of £9.6 million and an income of £3.8 million. Welfare grants to individuals totalled £148,000.

Applications

Application forms are available to download from the charity's website.

British Office Supplies and Services Federation Benevolent Fund

£47,000 (158 grants)

Correspondent: Liz Whyte, Grants Adviser, 2 Villiers Court, Meriden Business Park, Copse Drive, Coventry CV5 9RN (0845 450 1565; email: liz@bossfederation.co.uk; website: www.bossfederation.co.uk)

CC number: 279029

Eligibility

Applications are welcomed from those who work or have worked in the stationery, office products and office machines sector, and their dependants, who are in need due to ill health, disability or loneliness, or are unable to work, are struggling to support a family or are otherwise in financial need.

Types of grants

One-off grants according to need are given towards, for example, wheelchairs, property repair, and school uniforms. Regular quarterly payments are also made.

Annual grant total

In 2015 the fund held assets of £960,500 and had an income of £59,500. During the year, 158 grants were made to individuals, totalling £47,000.

Applications

Applicants should contact the fund by telephone for an initial consultation, after which an appointment will be made for a member of the fund to visit the applicant at home for further information and to assess the situation.

Other information

This fund was previously known as The British Office Systems and Stationery Federation Benevolent Fund.

The British Guild of Tourist Guides Benevolent Fund

£10,000

Correspondent: Elizabeth Keatinge, The Guild House, 52D Borough High Street, London SE1 1XN (01980 623463)

CC number: 211562

Eligibility

Institute registered (blue badge) guides who are in need and have been qualified for at least one year and former and retired guides who have been qualified for five years or more. The dependants of guides qualified for at least five years may also be eligible for support.

Types of grants

One-off grants to relieve need and enable a guide to work.

Annual grant total

In 2016 the fund had an income of £7,800 and a total expenditure of £10,200. We estimate that grants given to individuals totalled £10,000.

Exclusions

Grants are not given for debts or private hospital care.

Applications

Apply in writing to the correspondent. Applications should include, the tourist board with which the applicant was registered, whether any statutory bodies have been approached and details of the specific need. Applications can be made directly by the individual or through a third party. They can be considered at any time. Each trustee has a portfolio of clients and is responsible for checking how the beneficiaries are getting on, sometimes through home visits.

Hospitality Action

£668,500 (745+ grants)

Correspondent: The Grants Team, 62 Britton Street, London EC1M 5UY (020 3004 5507; fax: 020 7253 2094; email: help@hospitalityaction.org.uk; website: www.hospitalityaction.org.uk)

CC number: 1101083

Eligibility

Former and current workers in the hospitality industry in the UK, and their dependants. Applicants must be either currently working, have worked for one continuous year in the past five years or have worked for seven years in their lifetime in the UK.

The individuals or the company they work for would need to have been involved in the direct provision of food, drink or accommodation away from home. Applicants must have limited savings. People who are suffering from a life altering illness, domestic violence, experience poverty, are in bereavement or older people who find themselves isolated are all assisted.

Types of grants

The charity offers support for:

- Essential Needs – 'towards the cost of an item or need considered essential for the well being or improving the quality of life of the applicant'
- Crisis Grants – usually for a maximum of one year 'to assist with the general living costs to applicants of working age who have suffered a sudden loss of income due to bereavement, illness or injury'
- Top-up Grants – 'to assist with their general living costs to ensure that an adequate standard of living is achieved'
- Winter Fuel Grants – to pay essential fuel bills

Loans are also available.

Annual grant total

In 2016/17 the charity held assets of £7.1 million and had an income of £1.5 million. During the year, the charity awarded a total of £668,500 in grants to individuals for welfare purposes.

Grants were distributed as follows:

Essential needs grants	540	£380,000
Crisis grants	136	£118,000
Top-up grants	69	£88,000
Other grants	-	£83,000

Exclusions

Funding is not available towards the following:

- Education-related costs, such as private school fees, fees for educational courses, student maintenance, and student loan repayment
- Most private medical treatments
- Residential care fee shortfalls
- Legal costs
- Property repairs/adaptations where equity release is a viable option

The charity cannot consider a grant for an item until all statutory sources of funding have been tried. Only one grant per applicant can be made in any twelve month period.

Applications

Application forms are available from the website and can be returned by post or email. Consideration normally takes about two weeks and all applicants are informed of the outcome in writing. The application must include the candidate's NI number, work history, reason for application, payee details and quotes (if applicable) and be signed. A supporting letter on headed paper must be provided. There are detailed and helpful application guidance notes on the charity's website.

The charity's annual report notes:

Applicants are required to complete a Hospitality Action application form unless a referring organisation has already supplied much of the relevant information. All applications need to be supported by an appropriate independent organisation such as Social Services, Citizens Advice Bureaux or charities such as British Legion, Help the Aged, etc. A copy of the grant rules is sent out on request by the Grants & Advisory Team.

The charity's website reminds:

If you have any questions about any part of this form or what we require please don't hesitate to get in touch on 020 3004 5500.

Other information

The charity was established and formerly known as the Hotel and Catering Benevolent Association (HCBA).

Hospitality Action runs The Ark Foundation Programme which offers seminars on drugs and alcohol misuse. The organisation has a Family Members scheme – a free scheme open to anyone who is of pensionable age and has worked within the hospitality industry in the UK for at least seven years. Christmas hampers and gift vouchers are offered to the members.

Johnson Charitable Trust

£26,500

Correspondent: Yvonne Monaghan, Trustee, Johnson Service Group, Unit 9, Monks Way, Preston Brook, Runcorn WA7 3GH (01928 704600; email: enquiries@jsg.com)

CC number: 216974

Eligibility

Employees and ex-employees of the Johnson Group plc and their dependants.

Types of grants

One-off and recurrent grants are given according to need.

Annual grant total

In 2015/16 the trust held assets of £1.7 million and had an income of £79,000. Allowances, grants and Christmas hampers to individuals totalled £26,500 and were distributed as follows:

Christmas hampers	£23,500
Widows/widowers allowance and	
gifts	£3,000
Lifeline	£100

Costs paid towards a pensioners' lunch amounted to a further £300.

Applications

Apply in writing to the correspondent.

The National Caravan Council (NCC) Benevolent Fund

£2,800

Correspondent: David Gale-Hasleham, Trustee, 6 Dee Banks, Great Broughton, Chester CH3 5UX (01244 328141; email: info@nccbf.org.uk; website: www.nccbf.org.uk)

CC number: 271625

Eligibility

People in need who are, or have been, employed in the caravan industry, and their dependants.

Types of grants

Normally one-off grants according to need. Smaller grants have been given to help with maintenance or unexpected bills, and larger ones have been made to help provide building adaptations or heating.

Annual grant total

In 2015/16 the fund had an income of £29,500 and a total expenditure of £13,900. Grants to individuals totalled £2,800.

Applications

Apply on a form available from the correspondent including details of employment within the caravan industry.

Other information

Through a partnership with Happy Days Children's Charity (1010943), the fund owns a touring caravan and a caravan holiday home which it uses to give disadvantaged children and their families the opportunity to enjoy a holiday experience.

Rainy Day Trust

£153,000

Correspondent: Diane Stevens, Federation House, 10 Vyse Street, Hockley, Birmingham B18 6LT (0121 237 1132; email: info@rainydaytrust.org.uk; website: www.rainydaytrust.org.uk)

CC number: 209170

Eligibility

People who have worked in the manufacture, wholesale, retail and distribution of builders' merchants, DIY, hardware, potteries and glass, housewares and garden centres. Applicants should have less than £10,000 in savings, be on a low income and have at least one year's service in the industry.

Types of grants

One-off grants towards, for example, household goods, home repairs, travel expenses and care home top-up fees. Monthly cash payments of up to £100 are also available.

Annual grant total

In 2016 the trust had assets of £1.9 million and an income of £281,000. Grants were made to individuals totalling £153,000. These were broken down as follows:

Quarterly pensions	£88,000
Other grants	£46,000
Holiday grants	£6,300
Telephone grants	£5,700
Christmas hampers/grants	£4,100
TV licence grants	£1,700
Funeral grants	£1,000

Applications

Application forms are available to download from the charity's website.

The National Federation of Retail Newsagents Convalescence Fund

£6,200

Correspondent: Michael Jenkins, Administrator, Yeoman House, Sekforde Street, Clerkenwell Green, London EC1R 0HF (020 7017 8855; email: michael@nfrn.org.uk; website: www.nfrn.org.uk)

CC number: 209280

Eligibility

Members of the federation and their spouses. Other people in the retail newsagency trade who are not members of the federation are not eligible.

Types of grants

One-off grants for convalescent holidays.

Annual grant total

In 2016 the charity held assets of £757,000 and had an income of £17,000. During the year, the charity gave around £6,200 in grants to individuals.

Applications

Apply in writing to the correspondent or by contacting the NFRN helpline on 0800 121 6376 (020 7017 8880 from a mobile phone) or emailing helpline@nfrn.org.uk. Applications can be submitted directly by the individual, through a third party such as a social worker or through a district office of the federation. They are considered at any time.

Retail Trust

£687,000

Correspondent: retailHUB team, Marshall Hall, Marshall Estate, Hammers Lane, London NW7 4DQ (0808 801 0808; email: helpline@retailtrust.org.uk; website: www.retailtrust.org.uk)

CC number: 1090136

Eligibility

People in need who have worked in retail or in manufacturing, wholesale or distribution for the supply of retail businesses, and their dependants.

To be eligible for support, applicants must have worked in retail for a particular amount of time, the length of which varies depending on the applicant's employment situation (e.g. if they are currently employed in retail, unemployed, or retired). See the website for more information.

Types of grants

The trust provides 'crisis grants' to help individuals facing a short-term financial crisis and 'welfare grants' towards longer-term needs.

Crisis grants can be given to help with emergency costs, including: rent, mortgage, council and utility arrears; deposits to secure accommodation; essential appliances; food; and emergency repairs (including boiler replacement).

Welfare grants are commonly given to assist with, for example: disability items; life-changing situations (health and capability); home repairs, adaptations and improvements; funeral expenses; and respite breaks.

The trust also makes educational and vocational grants to individuals.

Annual grant total

In 2015/16 the trust had assets of £30.4 million and an income of £9.6 million. Financial assistance grants totalled £687,000.

Exclusions

No grants are given for private medical treatment, legal fees, most personal debts or for items purchased prior to the application.

Applications

Applications can be made via the online grant portal. The application requirements are quite specific and potential applicants should read the information provided by the trust on its website before making an application.

Other information

Retail Trust provides free financial, legal, emotional, career and redundancy advice and support services for people who have been involved in retail through 'retailHUB'. More information on how to access these services is available from the website or through the trust's confidential helpline (0808 801 0808).

The trust also operates Cottage Homes, which has five retirement estates across the UK (in London, Derby, Glasgow, Liverpool and Salford), providing sheltered and extra-care accommodation for people who have retired from the retail sector. More information is available from the website.

Information and communication

BT Benevolent Fund

£700,000 (523 grants)

Correspondent: Dawn Bennett, Administrator, Room 323, Reading Central Telephone Exchange, 41 Minister Street, Reading RG1 2JB (020 8726 2145; email: benevolent@bt.com; website: www.benevolent.bt.com)

CC number: 212565

Eligibility

Present or past (whether pensionable or not) British Telecom Group employees and present or future BT Group pensioners, and their dependants. The fund's website specifies: 'Past BT employees may include workers from Telecoms side of former GPO.'

Types of grants

One-off grants are given towards: household appliances; disability aids; home adaptations; convalescence; carer's breaks; funeral costs; and debt arrears, especially when there is a risk of eviction and small children are involved. Weekly grants are available to older former employees, and their dependants, who are living on a low income. Recipients of weekly grants are also eligible to receive a £125 one-off Christmas grant.

The annual report for 2015 states the following: 'The normal maximum grant payment is £2,500, however during 2015 the trustees agreed to raise the maximum grant for home adaptations related to disability to £5,000.'

Annual grant total

In 2015 the fund held assets of £3.4 million and had an income of over £1 million. Grants totalled £700,000, of which £476,500 was given in one-off grants and £223,500 in weekly grants to 523 regular beneficiaries. Grants were made for the following purposes:

Weekly grants	£224,000
Disability aids and adaptations	£112,000
Debt	£97,000
Housing and heating repairs	£89,000
Funeral costs	£62,000
Other	£47,000
Furniture and appliances	£36,000
Re-housing	£33,000

Exclusions

The fund is unable to help contractors or staff employed through agencies.

Applications

Current and former BT and EE employees and BT pensioners should, in the first instance, contact the Employee Assistance Programme (EAP) by calling 0800 917 6767. The website notes that it is useful to have your BT pension number to hand when making an enquiry.

BT employees based outside the UK and Asia-Pacific should in their first email to the fund, enquire about their eligibility.

Other information

The fund also operates a 'contact scheme' to provide advice and support for BT pensioners who are over 75 years old and to ascertain whether they are eligible for support.

The Cinema and Television Benevolent Fund

£1.25 million (6,334 grants)

Correspondent: Welfare Department, 22 Golden Square, London W1F 9AD (0800 138 2522; email: welfare@ctbf.co.uk; website: www.ctbf.co.uk)

CC number: 1099660

Eligibility

People who have worked behind the scenes in the cinema, film and commercial television industries in the UK for two years in any capacity, i.e. the production, exhibition, distribution, administration or transmission of film or commercial television. Help is also available to dependants and for the National Care Plan, their parents. Refer to the charity's website for its application guidelines and full details of the set criteria.

Types of grants

Recurrent payments and one-off grants for a wide range of needs, for example, towards white goods, televisions, disability aids/special equipment, disability adaptations and home repairs.

Annual grant total

In 2016/17 the fund held assets of £34.6 million and had an income of nearly £3.2 million. Total expenditure was £5.8 million. Grants to individuals totalled £1.25 million (excluding administration costs associated with the various schemes). The following are the grant categories and amounts distributed:

Regular monthly grants	£506,000
JBA grants	£106,000
Other grants	£95,000
Financial arrears	£77,000
Support to Glebelands and Broccoli Cloisters residents	£50,000
Assistance with rent and mortgages	£49,000
Betty Box/Peter Rogers Awards	£40,000
Lord Attenborough Scholarships	£38,000
Christmas gifts and hampers	£30,000
Payments towards home telephones	£30,000
Household appliances	£25,000
Cold weather grants	£23,000
Birthday grants	£21,000
Medical	£17,000
Wheelchairs and mobility aids	£13,000
Utilities	£12,000
TV licences	£10,000
Grants from restricted reserves	£8,000

Exclusions

The fund is not able to assist individuals who have been employed solely by the BBC on a full-time basis. No grants are given for educational purposes (except in exceptional circumstances).

Applications

The CTBF's website states:

> We offer financial assistance (and can arrange a free consultation with a financial advisor), practical assistance, help with career matters and advice on government benefits you may qualify for. Call our free confidential helpline for support and information – 0800 138 2522.

Refer to the charity's website for full details of how to apply for its various means of support.

Other information

The fund owns and manages a home for older people at Glebelands, which gives priority to those who have worked in the world of film, cinema and television. For more information contact the fund or go to the Glebelands website (www.glebelands.org). The CTBF has also launched its National Care Plan, enabling those who have worked in the film or television industries for at least two years, and their parents, to receive a discount in any Anchor care home across England. According to the fund's website, 'the partnership with Anchor means that professionals and retirees from all parts of the country can now access care homes at preferential rates and receive help with finding retirement housing from a trusted and highly-regarded provider.'

The Grace Wyndham Goldie (BBC) Trust Fund

£2,500 (two grants)

Correspondent: Cheryl Miles, Secretary, BBC, Room M1017, Broadcasting House, Cardiff CF5 2YQ (029 2032 2000; website: www.bbc.co.uk/charityappeals/about/grants/grace-wyndham-goldie)

CC number: 212146

Eligibility

Individuals currently or previously engaged in broadcasting and their dependants.

Types of grants

One-off grants are given to help relieve short-term domestic hardship not covered by assistance from other sources.

Annual grant total

In 2016 the charity had assets of £1.5 million and an income of £60,000. The charity made two grants for welfare purposes, totalling £2,500. A further £25,500 was distributed in 13 grants for educational purposes.

Exclusions

The charity cannot provide continued support over a number of years.

Applications

Application forms are available to download from the fund's page on the BBC website. Applicants are asked to provide full information about the circumstances supporting their application. All applications are considered in confidence. Completed forms should be returned to: Trustees, Grace Wyndham Goldie (BBC) Trust Fund, BBC Pension and Benefits Centre, Broadcasting House, Cardiff CF5 2YQ.

iprovision

£4,000 (three grants)

Correspondent: Sharon Shortland, Grants Administrator, 52–53 Russell Square, London WC1B 4HP (020 8144 5536; email: administrator@iprovision.org.uk; website: www.cipr.co.uk/content/our-organisation/iprovision)

CC number: 1157465

Eligibility

Members of The Chartered Institute of Public Relations (CIPR) and dependants of members or deceased members.

In 2014 the charity re-registered as a CIO allowing it to widen the beneficiaries' categories to include past members and retired members with at least five years' IPR/CIPR membership.

Types of grants

One-off and recurrent grants and interest-free loans according to need. Grants can be given for respite care, medical equipment, and living expenses. Members receiving support may be entitled to abatement of membership fees for up to a year.

Annual grant total

In 2016 the fund held assets of £995,500 and had an income of £45,000. Grants were made to three individuals and totalled £4,000.

Applications

Initially contact the administrator in writing, by phone or by email outlining your situation and how you think the charity could help you. The administrator will then contact you personally, so make sure to include your contact details. The trustees meet to consider applications every three months, but if the need is urgent decisions may be made between meetings.

Note: If you are contacting the administrator by post, mark your envelope 'Private and Confidential'.

Other information

The charity can also provide support in other ways, for example, through: contact (by phone, emails and sometimes visits); information, including referral when appropriate to specialist statutory or voluntary organisations; and advice services and signposting members to employment, debt or money advice services. The helpline number is 020 8144 5536.

Journalists' Charity

£226,000 (187 grants)

Correspondent: Welfare Team, Dickens House, 35 Wathen Road, Dorking, Surrey RH4 1JY (01306 887511; email: enquiries@journalistscharity.org.uk; website: www.journalistscharity.org.uk)

CC number: 208215

Eligibility

Practising and former journalists and their dependants who are in need because of sickness, accident or other unforeseen circumstances. There are no age restrictions.

Types of grants

One-off grants normally in the range of £250 and £500 but all cases are decided on their merits. Regular payments may be provided on a weekly or monthly basis.

Annual grant total

In 2016 the charity held assets of £11.5 million and had an income of almost £2.2 million. Grants to individuals totalled £226,000.

Exclusions

The charity's website states that its 'aim is to give financial support in times of need however [they] cannot subsidise those who, in the long term, find it difficult to make a living from journalism unless through illness or other misfortune'. Grants are not offered to subsidise an existing lifestyle. Awards are not generally given towards holidays (although support may be given for convalescence or respite breaks) and it is unlikely that support will be given with care home fees. Only in exceptional circumstances will help be given with medical fees. Assistance is not given with the payment of credit card debts, bank loans, legal costs or fines, or with anything that is available through the state. Loans are not offered.

Applications

Application forms can be requested from the correspondent. They can be submitted directly by the individual or a family member. Applications should include details of the career in journalism and are considered monthly. Our research suggests that the consideration process may take between two and six weeks.

Chartered Institute of Library and Information Professionals (CILIP) Benevolent Fund

£8,900

Correspondent: Bridget Fisher, Chair of CILIP Benevolent Fund, 7 Ridgmount Street, London WC1E 7AE (email: benevolentfund@cilip.org.uk; website: www.cilip.org.uk)

CC number: 237352

Eligibility

Members and former members of CILIP and their dependants. This includes former members of the Library Association and the Institute of Information Scientists who may not have chosen to become members of CILIP.

Types of grants

According to the website, assistance can be given with 'any unusual or unexpected expenses that may be causing anxiety and hardship'. Examples listed on the website include: urgent house repairs; the replacement of essential household equipment; 'unexpectedly large heating bills which a member in difficulties might find it impossible to cope with'; or bank overdrafts or other debts that have 'accumulated unavoidably on account of illness'.

Annual grant total

In 2016 the fund had an income of £7,200 and a total expenditure of £9,300. We estimate that grants given to individuals totalled £8,900.

Exclusions

No grants are given to students. The fund is not able to offer recurrent grants or pension top-ups.

Applications

Applicants can contact the fund by submitting their details via the online form on the website or by downloading an initial contact form and returning it to the correspondent. With the applicant's agreement, a visit is arranged so that the applicant's difficulty can be discussed and it can be decided how the fund can best help to resolve it. The trustees usually meet three or four times a year to consider applications, although urgent requests can be dealt with more quickly.

Other information

While the fund can only offer short-term help, it has built up relationships with a number of charities and other bodies to which it may refer beneficiaries for further support.

The Market Research Benevolent Association

£21,500

Correspondent: Danielle Scott, Secretary and Treasurer, 11 Tremayne Walk, Camberley, Surrey GU15 1AH (0845 652 0303; email: info@mrba.org.uk; website: www.mrba.org.uk)

CC number: 274190

Eligibility

People who are or have been engaged in market research and their dependants.

Types of grants

Generally one-off grants for people in need. Funding has been given towards the costs of wheelchairs and other medical equipment, convalescence and other medical expenses, and emergency house and car repairs. Interest-free loans are also available.

Annual grant total

In 2016/17 the association held assets of £551,000 and had an income of almost £42,000. Grants totalling £21,500 were awarded to individuals during the year.

Loans totalling £1,700 were converted to grants.

Applications

Applicants should contact the correspondent by phone or by email to be assigned to an MRBA Regional Manager and sent an application form.

The regional manager will then contact the applicant and offer assistance throughout the application process. When completed, the application form will be the subject of a summary report which will then be reviewed by the MRBA Committee, which meets every six weeks. The regional manager will then inform the applicant on whether and how the association is able to assist. Urgent cases can be fast-tracked.

Other information

The association also provides advice, often in partnership with other organisations, as well as support for debt and bereavement.

The charity also offers loans to individuals.

NABS

£248,000

Correspondent: Support Team, 6th Floor, 388 Oxford Street, London W1C 1JT (0800 707 6607; email: support@nabs.org.uk; website: www. nabs.org.uk)

CC number: 1070556

Eligibility

People who work or have worked in advertising, marketing, marketing services and related industries, and their dependants.

Types of grants

One-off and ongoing assistance is given according to need. The annual report for 2014 provides the following information:

Grants for all beneficiaries are more targeted and focus on making a definitive difference as we continue to move away from providing long-term support. Grants for new applicants have largely been directed towards household utilities, rehoming and staving off homelessness....

Annual grant total

In 2016 NABS had assets of £5.8 million and an income of £4.9 million. During the year, the charity gave around £248,000 in grants to individuals.

Applications

In the first instance, contact the charity's Advice Line (0800 707 6607) or email support@nabs.org.uk.

The charity's website states that 'even if it's [we're] not able to offer you direct financial assistance, it's [we're] always available to give practical advice and support on the next step towards resolving financial issues'.

Other information

The society provides a wide range of advice, support, networking and career guidance for members of the advertising and media industry, including a telephone helpline, career coaching and workshops and a working parents programme. It also owns Peterhouse, a comprehensive retirement complex containing a registered care home.

NewstrAid Benevolent Society

£860,500

Correspondent: Alexandra Henry Van Straubenzee, Welfare Manager, Suites 1 and 2, Thremhall Estate, Start Hill, Bishop's Stortford CM22 7TD (01279 879569; fax: 01371 873816; email: oldben@newstraid.org.uk; website: www. newstraid.org.uk)

CC number: 1116824

Eligibility

People and their immediate dependants, who have been employed in newspaper and magazine distribution in the UK and who have fallen on hard times. Distribution means people who deal with newspapers and magazines from the time they leave the printing press until they reach the reader. All applications are assessed on their merits but the society states that applicants should have normally been connected with the trade for a minimum of ten years.

Types of grants

Annual payments and one-off grants for various items including household appliances, special chairs, mobility aids, small repairs and disability equipment. The charity offers interest-free loans to homeowners in respect of costly repairs, repayable on the sale of their property.

Annual grant total

In 2016 the charity had assets of £10.6 million and an income of £2.1 million. During the year, £860,500 was given in grants to individuals for welfare purposes.

Exclusions

No grants are given for private medicine or school or college fees.

Applications

Initial contact should be made by calling the welfare team or by submitting an enquiry form, available to download from the website. The application will then be followed up by a telephone call from the welfare team.

Other information

In 2012 there was a one-off payment of £200 to all beneficiaries to celebrate the 200th birthday of Charles Dickens.

NUJ Extra

£57,500

Correspondent: Lena Calvert, Fund Administrator, Headland House, 308–312 Gray's Inn Road, London WC1X 8DP (020 7843 3705; fax: 020 7837 8143; email: lenac@nuj.org.uk; website: www.nuj.org.uk/work/nuj-extra)

CC number: 1112489

Eligibility

Members and former members of the National Union of Journalists and the dependants of deceased members. Applicants must have paid at least one year's full subscription to the NUJ.

Note: Current members are only eligible for short-term assistance.

Types of grants

One-off grants are given for: urgent bills, mainly rent and utilities; wheelchairs; beds; domestic goods; medical equipment; and minor home adaptations. Bills or rent payments will generally be made directly to the supplier or landlord. Recurrent grants are available to top up the income of those living on a state pension and/or other benefits. Monthly payments are made to widows and orphans of former members of the NUJ, to provide a minimum monthly income, as determined by the committee annually. The value of recurrent grants is set at an annual meeting. Christmas bonus grants are also made.

Annual grant total

In 2016 the charity held assets of £2.4 million and had an income of £87,500. During the year, the charity gave around £57,500 in grants to individuals.

Exclusions

No grants are given for legal expenses, private medical treatment or private education. Help is unlikely to be available for consumer debts. Members who left owing the union contributions are not eligible for help. Applicants are expected to have claimed all available benefits before applying.

Applications

Application forms are available from the correspondent or to download from the website. Applications can be submitted by the individual or through an NUJ welfare officer or other third party. Applicants are required to provide details of their personal income and expenditure. Applications are considered throughout the year.

Other information

NUJ Extra is an amalgamation of charities previously known as National Union of Journalists Members in Need Fund and National Union of Journalists Provident Fund.

The Printing Charity

£690,500 (546 grants)

Correspondent: James Povey, Trustee, First Floor, Underwood House, 235 Three Bridges Road, Crawley, West Sussex RH10 1LS (01293 542820; email: support@theprintingcharity.org.uk; website: www.theprintingcharity.org.uk)

CC number: 208882

Eligibility

People who have worked for at least three years in the printing profession, graphic arts or allied trades, and their dependants, who are in need. A list of eligible trades can be found on the charity's website.

Types of grants

One-off grants of about up to £2,000 (depending on the type) and recurrent payments of up to £25 per week. The website gives exact details of types and amounts available and this includes: bereavement allowance; care home top-up fees; communications aids; home adaptation; independent living help; mobility aids; miscellaneous; nursing home top-up fees; respite breaks; residential care; day centre fees; care service at home. Home repairs and adaptations, household items, bankruptcy fees, travel costs to and from the hospital and also emergency relief for people affected by natural disasters are also supported.

During extremely cold winters, fuel allowances of £75 are sent to those who receive regular assistance from the charity.

Annual grant total

In 2016 the charity held assets of £37.7 million and had an income of £1.77 million. Grants were made to 546 individuals totalling £690,500.

Exclusions

Examples of what is not funded include:

- Grants for study or training overseas
- Grants for non-accredited or non-recognised training or education courses
- Grants above the charity's limits
- Holidays (with the exception of respite care breaks for the carer or person being cared for)
- To replace items or money that has been stolen unless the item is related to mobility or independent living
- Payments for parking fines or speeding tickets or any other fine imposed by the courts
- Legal fees or costs associated with solicitors' letters or interviews or any other kind of legal representation

- Applicants with high levels of savings that are over and above the set thresholds (for further information on this contact the correspondent)
- School fees unless there is a statemented educational need
- Pensions

Applications

Application forms and guidelines are available from the charity's website. Further information on the application process can also be obtained by contacting the correspondent. Assistance is means-tested so applicants should be prepared to make a full declaration of their finances, including state benefits and funding from other charitable sources. Applications can be made by individuals directly or through a welfare agency at any time.

The charity aims to acknowledge and assess all applications within 15 working days.

Other information

The charity also provides sheltered homes for older people at Basildon and Bletchley and gives education and training help to individuals.

The trustees are looking to ensure that at least 51% of their support is given to people outside London and the South-East.

Legal professions

Barristers Clerks Benevolent Fund

£16,000

Correspondent: Stephen Graham, 18 Woodcote Avenue, Wallington SM6 0QY (020 8647 0086; email: enquiries@westburypartnership.co.uk)

CC number: 1084609

Eligibility

Barristers' clerks, former barristers' clerks and their dependants.

Types of grants

One-off grants according to need.

Annual grant total

In 2015 the fund had an income of £9,700 and a total expenditure of £16,600. We estimate that grants given to individuals totalled around £16,000.

Applications

Apply in writing to the correspondent.

The Barristers' Benevolent Association

£78,000 (41 grants)

Correspondent: Susan Eldridge, 14 Gray's Inn Square, London WC1R 5JP (020 7242 4761; fax: 020 7831 5366; email: susan@the-bba.com; website: www.the-bba.com)

CC number: 1106768

Eligibility

Past or present practising members of the Bar in England and Wales, and their spouses, former spouses and dependants.

Types of grants

Assistance may be provided by way of grant or loan, or a combination of the two. Grants can be given for a range of causes for example; domestic end-of-life care, specialist medical treatments and equipment that fall outside the remit of the NHS, communication and mobility aids, school uniforms, and so on. Regular grants can be made to top up pensions or to help single-parent families.

Annual grant total

In 2015 the association had assets of £10.8 million and an income of £813,500. Grants totalled £156,000 and were awarded both for social welfare and educational purposes. We have estimated that welfare grants amounted to around £78,000 during the year.

Exclusions

Our research indicates that no grants were made to those who, when qualified, went straight into commerce.

Applications

Application forms are available to download from the website.

Other information

The association can also offer professional advice on IVA or bankruptcy as well as practical and moral support.

The Chartered Institute of Legal Executives Benevolent Fund

£1,000

Correspondent: Sharon Cooper, The Chartered Institute Of Legal Executives, Kempston Manor, Manor Drive, Kempston, Bedford MK42 7AB (01234 845713; email: benevolentfund@cilex. org.uk; website: www.cilex.org.uk/ membership/benevolent_fund)

CC number: 295527

Eligibility

Members and former members of the institute (including associates, fellows and student members), and their families or dependants. Help is particularly aimed at those who have become unemployed through old age, illness or other circumstances. Applicants must have been a member of CILEX for at least one year before applying. Applicants must be resident in England or Wales.

Types of grants

One-off grants are provided to meet unexpected costs such as utility bills, or for the provision of medical equipment. Grants will not be paid directly to the individual, rather they will be paid to the creditor.

Annual grant total

In 2016 the charity had an income of £3,000 and a total expenditure of £2,100. We estimate the amount awarded in grants to individuals for hardship relief to be £1,000.

Exclusions

Grants are not given for membership fees; student course fees; costs of joining CILEx; discharge of outstanding judgements; HMRC tax bills; IVA's; or bankruptcy. Assistance on an ongoing basis cannot be supported.

Applications

Application forms are available to download from the webpage listed. Full completion of the personal budget form is required, otherwise the application cannot be considered. Also include a supporting invoice or quote, including the cost and bank details of the creditor.

Other information

The fund also offers information, practical advice and advocacy services.

Faculty of Advocates 1985 Charitable Trust

£103,000 (11 grants)

Correspondent: Gaynor Adam, Secretariat Officer, Advocate's Library, Parliament House, Edinburgh EH1 1RF (0131 226 5071; website: www.advocates. org.uk)

OSCR number: SC012486

Eligibility

Widows, widowers, children or former dependants of deceased members of the Faculty of Advocates and members who are unable to practise by reason of permanent ill health.

Types of grants

Single grants, annuities or loans appropriate to the circumstances.

Annual grant total

In 2015/16 the trust held assets of £6.4 million and had an income of £198,500. Grants to eight annuitants totalled £85,500 and an additional £17,900 was awarded to three individuals.

Applications

The trust is regularly publicised among members and applications are often informal, by word of mouth via a trustee. Alternatively applications may be made in writing to the correspondent.

The Incorporated Benevolent Association of the Chartered Institute of Patent Attorneys

£19,500

Correspondent: Derek Chandler, c/o CIPA, 2nd Floor Halton House, 20–23 Holborn, London EC1N 2JD (020 8455 3822)

CC number: 219666

Eligibility

British members and former members of the Chartered Institute of Patent Attorneys, and their dependants.

Types of grants

One-off and recurrent grants or loans according to need for general relief-in-need purposes.

Annual grant total

In 2015/16 the charity had assets of £917,000 and an income of £58,000. We estimate that the charity awarded around £19,500 in grants.

Applications

Applications should be made in writing to the correspondent, detailing financial need and what the grant will be used for. Applications can be submitted at any time.

Other information

The charity also makes grants for educational purposes.

The Pritt Fund

£15,500

Correspondent: Liverpool Law Society, The Cotton Exchange Building, Second Floor, Edmund Street, Liverpool L3 9LQ (0151 236 6998; email: charities@ liverpoollawsociety.org.uk; website: www.liverpoollawsociety.org.uk)

CC number: 226421

Eligibility

Solicitors or clerks of solicitors, who are in need and have practised in the city of Liverpool or within the area of Liverpool Law Society, and their dependants.

Types of grants

One-off and recurrent grants are given according to need.

Annual grant total

In 2015/16 the charity had an income of £14,800 and a total expenditure of £16,000. We estimate that grants given to individuals for welfare purposes totalled around £15,500.

Applications

Application forms are available from the correspondent.

SBA The Solicitors' Charity

£761,000

Correspondent: Ricardo Premchand, CEO's Assistant, 1 Jaggard Way, London SW12 8SG (020 8675 6440; email: sec@ sba.org.uk; website: www.sba.org.uk)

CC number: 1124512

Eligibility

Solicitors who are or have been on the Roll for England and Wales and have practised, and their dependants, who are in need.

Types of grants

One-off and recurrent grants and interest-free loans (if sufficient equity is available). They can be used for a wide range of essential everyday needs, including food and heating.

Annual grant total

In 2016 the charity had assets of £22.6 million and an income of £1.9 million. During the year, grants and loans were made to 310 individuals. Grants totalled £761,000 and loans totalled £393,000.

Grants were broken down as follows:

Living allowances	£415,000
Supplementary, leisure, special and miscellaneous grants	£337,000
Nursing home fees	£9,000

Note: the charity no longer makes student grants.

Exclusions

Solicitors who are considered to have brought the profession into disrepute are not eligible but assistance may be available to their dependants.

Applications

Application forms are available from the website.

Scottish Solicitors Benevolent Fund

£20,000

Correspondent: The Secretary, Scottish Solicitors Benevolent Fund, 166 Buchanan Street, Glasgow G1 2LW (0141 352 4522; website: www.slas.co.uk)

OSCR number: SC000258

Eligibility

People in need who are or were members of the solicitors' profession in Scotland and their dependants.

Types of grants

One-off and recurrent grants are given according to need. A standard award is £500 for a period of six months.

Annual grant total

In 2015/16 the charity had an income of £17,500 and a total expenditure of £23,000. We estimate that grants totalled around £20,000.

Applications

Application forms are available to download from the website or can be requested from the correspondent. Applications should be completed in full, including financial details, and should be supported by another practising solicitor.

Manufacturing

The Spear Charitable Trust

£20,500 (nine grants)

Correspondent: Hazel Spear, Trustee, Roughground House, Beggarmans Lane, Old Hall Green, Ware SG11 1HB (01920 823071)

CC number: 1041568

Eligibility

Former employees of JW Spear and Sons plc, and their families and dependants.

Types of grants

One-off and recurrent grants to relieve financial hardship.

Annual grant total

In 2016 the charity had assets of £4.9 million and an income of £202,000. During the year, the charity awarded £20,500 in grants to nine individuals.

Applications

Applications should be made in writing to the correspondent, detailing financial need and what the grant will be used for.

Proof of employment with JW Spear and Sons plc should also be included.

Other information
The majority of the charity's grant-making is to organisations (£178,000 was awarded in 2016).

Marine occupations

The Coastguard Association Charity

£10,600 (nine grants)

Correspondent: Paul Davig, Almoner, 27 Church Lane, Skegness, Lincolnshire PE25 1ED (01754 768094; email: almoner@coastguardassociation.org.uk; website: www.coastguardassociation.org.uk)

CC number: 279359

Eligibility
Any serving or retired (by age or medically) coastguard personnel or volunteer coastguards and their dependants.

Types of grants
One-off grants to contribute towards medical expenses and equipment, funeral costs, holidays and respite breaks, living costs due to ill health. The charity also distributes Christmas gifts to retired coastguards.

Annual grant total
In 2016 the charity held assets of £278,000 and had an income of £27,000. Grants were made to nine beneficiaries and totalled £10,600.

Applications
For further information about this scheme contact the correspondent and they will offer further advice. The charity expects that applications should be made by a third party. The welfare committee may request information about the applicant's income, outgoings, and savings and a declaration of finances before any decision is made.

The Corporation of Trinity House, London

£25,500 (28+ grants)

Correspondent: Graham Hockley, Secretary, Trinity House, Tower Hill, London EC3N 4DH (020 7481 6914; email: graham.hockley@thls.org; website: www.trinityhouse.co.uk)

CC number: 211869

Eligibility
Mariners and their dependants.

Types of grants
The charity operates 18 almshouses at Walmer, Kent and makes provision for regular payments to up to 60 annuitants. Other direct support is made through occasional one-off grants to former seafarers and their dependants.

Annual grant total
The charity's significant assets are no reflection of the money available for grant-making which is a very small part of its activities.

In 2016/17 the charity had assets of £263 million and an income of more than £9 million. Grants were made to 28 retired seafarers in financial need at a rate of £728 per year. This totalled around £20,000. A further £11,700 was awarded in grants to individuals, some of which was distributed for educational purposes. We estimate that grants for social welfare purposes totalled around £25,500.

The vast majority of the charity's grants expenditure was distributed to organisations, with more than £1.5 million awarded during the year.

Applications
Enquiries regarding welfare grants can be made via email to the secretary.

Other information
The following information is taken from the corporation's website: 'The safety of shipping, and the well being of seafarers, have been our prime concerns ever since Trinity House was granted a Royal Charter by Henry VIII in 1514.'

Today there are three distinct functions:
- The General Lighthouse Authority (GLA) for England, Wales, the Channel Islands and Gibraltar. The remit is to provide Aids to Navigation to assist the safe passage of a huge variety of vessels through some of the busiest sea-lanes in the world
- A charitable organisation dedicated to the safety, welfare and training of mariners
- A Deep Sea Pilotage Authority providing expert navigators for ships trading in Northern European waters

Fawcett Johnston Charity

£2,000

Correspondent: Lisa Douglas, The Town Hall, Senhouse Street, Maryport CA15 6BH (01900 813205; email: maryport.council@talk21.com)

CC number: 208326

Eligibility
Grants for sailors and ships' carpenters, and their widows and children, who are in need.

Types of grants
One-off and recurrent according to need.

Annual grant total
In 2016 the charity had an income of £2,500 and a total expenditure of £2,500. We estimate that the charity awarded £2,000 in grants.

Applications
Apply in writing to the correspondent.

The Furness Seamen's Pension Fund

£10,000

Correspondent: Heather O'Driscoll, Waltons Clark Whitehill, Oakland House, 38–42 Victoria Road, Hartlepool, Cleveland TS26 8DD (01429 234414; email: heather.odriscoll@waltonscw.co.uk)

CC number: 226655

Eligibility
Seamen in need who are 50 or over and live in the borough of Hartlepool or the former county borough of West Hartlepool, or who had their permanent residence there during their sea service. All applicants must have served as seamen for at least 15 years and with some part of the sea service in vessels registered in Hartlepool, West Hartlepool or the Port of Hartlepool, or vessels trading to/from any of these ports.

Types of grants
Quarterly pensions.

Annual grant total
In 2015/16 the fund had an income of £9,900 and a total expenditure of £10,600. We estimate that pensions totalled £10,000.

Applications
Applications should be made on a form available from the correspondent. Advertisements have previously been placed in the Hartlepool Mail when vacancies are available.

Liverpool Marine Engineers' and Naval Architects' Guild

£22,000

Correspondent: Derek Gallagher, 4 Newton Hollows Cottages, Newton Hollows, Frodsham WA66JB (07477 535255)

CC number: 224856

Eligibility

Marine engineers, naval architects and families living in Merseyside.

Types of grants

One-off grants according to need.

Annual grant total

In 2016 the guild had assets of £652,500 and an income of £78,000. Grants to individuals totalled £22,000.

Applications

Apply in writing to the correspondent.

The Guild of Benevolence of The Institute of Marine Engineering Science and Technology

£79,000 (98 grants)

Correspondent: Mr A. D. Muncer, Chairman, 1 Birdcage Walk, London SW1H 9JJ (020 7382 2644; email: guild@ imarest.org; website: www.imarest.org/ guild)

CC number: 208727

Eligibility

Past and present members of The Institute of Marine Engineering, Science and Technology (IMarEST) or of The Guild of Benevolence; marine engineers who possess, or have possessed, Certificates of Competency or Certificates of Service issued by the relevant governmental department or agency, or equivalent qualifications; past and present employees of the IMarEST or the guild; the wives, husbands, widows, widowers, dependent children or other dependent relatives of any person qualifying under any of the previous categories.

Types of grants

The charity makes regular weekly grants to supplement low incomes as well as one-off grants for nursing home fees, home repairs, funeral expenses, respite care, debt relief and items that are essential for the recipient's well-being.

Annual grant total

In 2015/16 the charity had assets of £1.9 million and an income of £183,000. Grants to individuals totalled £79,000.

Applications

Application forms can be downloaded from the charity's website.

Other information

The charity's 2015/16 annual accounts state: 'The charity was originally set up by the Institute of Marine Engineers and the Daily Chronicle Newspaper for the widows and orphans of the Engineering Staff of the Titanic, all of whom perished when the ship sank on 15th April 1912.'

The Marine Society and Sea Cadets

Correspondent: Mark Hallam, Director of Finance, 202 Lambeth Road, London SE1 7JW (020 7654 7000; email: info@ ms-sc.org; website: www.marine-society. org/91-funding)

CC number: 313013/SC037808

Eligibility

Professional seafarers, active or retired, serving in the Royal Navy, the British Merchant Navy or fishing fleets or any other maritime career persons who are serving in the navies, merchant navies or fishing fleets, members of the Sea Cadet Corps.

Types of grants

It is the society's policy to help where financial hardship is evident. Assistance is aimed to improve the conditions of life of seafarers and their dependants in need by reason of their social and economic circumstances. Interest-free loans rather than grants are given where the need is short-term and the applicant expects to be earning again. Support is also given through bursaries, scholarships, one-off grants and loans towards educational and training needs.

Annual grant total

In 2015/16 the society had assets of £27.1 million and an income of £15.7 million. Grants were made totalling over £2 million, of which £922,000 was awarded to individuals and £1.1 million to organisations. We believe that the vast majority of grants to individuals were for educational and personal development purposes.

Exclusions

The society does not make recurrent grants.

Applications

Application forms are available from the correspondent and are considered as they arrive.

Other information

Grants are also made to sea cadet units and support can be given to 'nautical or other schools or training establishments which are charities or to other organisations established for charitable purposes'. In addition, grants are provided to volunteers to allow upkeep or purchase of uniforms on promotion or for wear and tear during the year.

The Honourable Company of Master Mariners and Howard Leopold Davis Charity

£22,500

Correspondent: Honourable Company of Master Mariners, HQS Wellington, Temple Stairs, Victoria Embankment, London WC2R 2PN (020 7836 8179; email: info@hcmm.org.uk; website: www. hcmm.org.uk/activities/charitable-giving)

CC number: 1127213

Eligibility

British master mariners, navigating officers of the merchant navy, and their wives, widows and dependants who are in need.

Types of grants

One-off and recurrent grants are given for general relief-in-need purposes.

Annual grant total

In 2016 the charity had assets of £4.1 million and an income of £103,000. We estimate that around £22,500 was given in grants to individuals.

Applications

In the first instance, members of the Honourable Company of Master Mariners should send their applications to the trust's address.

Non-member applications should be sent to: The Merchant Navy Welfare Board, 8 Cumberland Place, Southampton SO15 2BH

Contact can also be made by telephone (023 8033 7799) or by email (enquiries@mnwb.org.uk).

Other information

This charity is an amalgamation of four separate funds: the Education Fund, the Benevolent Fund, the London Maritime Institution and the Howard Leopold Davis Fund.

The charity also provides grants for education, and to seafaring organisations.

The Ann Molyneux Charity

£14,700

Correspondent: John Wilson, Trustee, Liverpool Seafarers Centre, 20 Crosby Road South, Liverpool L22 1RQ (0300 8008085; email: john.wilson@ liverpoolseafarers.org.uk)

CC number: 229408

Eligibility

Seafarers and their widows living in the city of Liverpool. Preference is given to individuals who sailed from the city for most of the last five years that they were at sea. Applicants must be in receipt of benefits.

Types of grants

Pensions of £200 a year (paid quarterly).

Annual grant total

In 2016/17 the charity had an income of £19,900 and a total expenditure of £14,900. We estimate that the charity awarded around £14,700 in grants to individuals.

Applications

Application forms are available from Liverpool Parish Church of Our Lady and St Nicholas. Applications should be accompanied by the seafarer's discharge books, details of income and a testimonial from a person of good standing in the community.

Nautilus Welfare Fund

£303,000

Correspondent: Amy Johnson, Case Manager, Trinity House Hub, Webster Avenue, Mariner's Park, Wallasey CH44 0AE (0151 639 8454; email: welfare@nautilusint.org; website: www. nautiluswelfarefund.org)

CC number: 218742

Eligibility

Former seafarers with significant careers at sea, and their dependants.

Types of grants

One-off grants towards household items, maintenance, independent living equipment and removal expenses.

Annual grant total

In 2016 the fund had assets of £23.6 million and an income of £3.6 million. Grants to individuals totalled £303,000.

Applications

Application forms are available from the fund's website.

Other information

The fund also manages the Mariners Park welfare complex in Wallasey, which accommodates independent older seafarers and their dependants in bungalows and flats, and older seafarers and their dependants assessed for residential or nursing care in the Mariners Park Care Home. The management and maintenance of this site takes up a large proportion of the fund's income.

Royal Institution of Naval Architects

£37,000 (1,720 grants)

Correspondent: Trevor Blakeley, Chief Executive, 8–9 Northumberland Street, London WC2N 5DA (020 7235 4622; email: hq@rina.org.uk; website: www. rina.org.uk)

CC number: 211161

Eligibility

Members and their dependants who are in need.

Types of grants

One-off grants for a variety of needs.

Annual grant total

In 2015/16 the charity had assets of £9.8 million and had an income of £2.2 million. During the year, the charity gave around £37,000 in grants to 1,720 members.

Grant-making is a small part of this charity's activities.

Applications

Apply in writing to the correspondent.

Other information

The Royal Institution of Naval Architects is an internationally renowned professional institution whose members are involved at all levels in the design, construction, maintenance and operation of marine vessels and structures. Members of RINA are widely represented in industry, universities and colleges, and maritime organisations in over ninety countries. The charity also runs training schemes and bursaries.

The Ropner Centenary Trust

£16,300 (24 grants)

Correspondent: Alan Theakston, Trustee, 15 The Green, High Coniscliffe, Darlington, County Durham DL2 2LJ (01325 374249; email: alantheakston@ btinternet.com)

CC number: 269109

Eligibility

Present and former maritime employees who are in need, and their dependants. Preference is generally given to people living in the north east of England and particularly those who have worked for Ropner Shipping Company Ltd.

Types of grants

One-off and recurrent grants are given according to need.

Annual grant total

In 2016/17 the trust had assets of £1.1 million and an income of £34,000. During the year, the trust gave around £16,300 in grants to 24 individuals.

The charity also gave £16,000 in grants to organisations with similar aims.

Applications

Apply in writing to the correspondent. Applications are considered annually, although urgent requests can be dealt with between meetings.

Sailors' Society

£16,000

Correspondent: Welfare Fund Manager, Sailors' Society, Seafarer House, 74 St Annes Road, Southampton, Hampshire SO19 9FF (023 8051 5950; email: enquiries@sailors-society.org; website: www.sailors-society.org)

CC number: 237778

Eligibility

Merchant seafarers and their dependants who are in need.

Types of grants

Emergency grants to ease financial hardship. Monthly payments are also made from the Leith Aged Mariners' Fund (OSCR no. SC003014).

Annual grant total

In 2016 the society had assets of £15.4 million and an income of £3.7 million. Welfare grants to individuals totalled £16,000.

Applications

In the first instance contact the correspondent via email.

Other information

The society maintains a network of chaplains at the various key ports around the world who carry out ship visiting routines and minister to seafarers. It also provides centres and clubs for seafarers and associated maritime workers at strategic seaports. International disaster relief is also given and organisations are supported.

Sailors' Children's Society

£457,500

Correspondent: Deanne Thomas, Chief Officer, Francis Reckitt House, Newland, Cottingham Road, Hull HU6 7RJ (01482 342331; email: info@sailorschildren.org. uk; website: www.sailorschildren.org.uk)

CC number: 224505

Eligibility

Seafarers' children under the age of 18 who are in full-time education and whose families are in severe financial difficulties. One of the child's parents must have served in the Royal or Merchant Navy or in the fishing fleets, including on ferries, tankers, cruise ships or cargo boats.

Applicants must be in receipt of Housing Benefit or Council Tax Reduction (other than single persons 25% discount or disablement reduction). The following information is given on the charity's website: 'All the families we help are on a means-tested benefit which ensures we only help those in most need.'

Types of grants

The charity provides financial assistance in a number of ways, including:

- Monthly child welfare grants – designed to boost income and enable families to provide basic essentials
- Clothing grants – payable per child twice a year to help children start off the new school year and, secondly, to buy a new winter coat and shoes
- Christmas grants – to help to buy a special Christmas present
- Emergency heating grants – in the event of extreme winter weather
- Special grants – one-off grants are given in extreme cases to provide, for example, furniture for a child's bedroom
- Caravan holidays – the charity owns eight caravans at seaside resorts across the UK. Travel grants are given to help with the costs of public transport or fuel expenses

Annual grant total

In 2015/16 the charity had assets of £2.1 million and an income of £601,500. Grants totalled £457,500, the majority of which was given for social welfare purposes.

Applications

Application forms are available from the correspondent and require details about children, income and expenditure. Copies of relevant certificates, for example birth certificates, and proof of seafaring service should also be provided. Applications can be submitted directly by the individual or through a social worker, Citizens Advice, other welfare agency, or through seafaring organisations. Applications are considered every other month, beginning in February.

Other information

The charity, which was previously known as Sailors' Families' Society, has an informative website where more details can be found.

Sailors' Orphan Society of Scotland

£54,500

Correspondent: Joyce Murdoch, Administrator, 18 Woodside Crescent, Glasgow G3 7UL (0141 353 2090; fax: 0141 353 2190; website: www. sailorsorphansociety.co.uk)

OSCR number: SC000242

Eligibility

Dependants of seafarers who are or may be in a position of need either through disadvantage or through the death or incapacity of one or both of their parents. Support is also given to disadvantaged young people within seafaring communities in Scotland.

Children must be under 16 or in full-time education if over 16.

Types of grants

Monthly grants of around £80 per child as well as two additional payments in July and December. One-off grants may also be paid at the trustees' discretion.

Annual grant total

In 2016/17 the charity had assets of £1.4 million and an income of £63,000. During the year, the charity gave around £54,500 in grants to individuals.

Applications

Apply on a form available to download from the charity's website. Applications should include a reference from a third party who can confirm the disadvantage suffered or the death or incapacity of a parent.

Grants are paid to the guardians of the beneficiaries, all of whom are individuals.

Scottish Nautical Welfare Society

£78,000

Correspondent: Gail Haldane, 937 Dumbarton Road, Glasgow G14 9UF (0141 337 2632; email: ghaldane@snws. org.uk; website: www.snws.org.uk)

OSCR number: SC032892

Eligibility

Former merchant seafarers or fishermen with ten years of sea service, although applicants with less than ten years of experience who have a specific need may be considered. Widows and widowers may also apply for financial support.

Types of grants

Recurrent quarterly grants provided with the help of Seafarers UK.

Annual grant total

In 2016/17 the charity had an income of £122,000 and assets of £394,000. Grants to individuals totalled £78,000.

Applications

Application forms can be retrieved from the charity's website. Some applicants may be visited by a caseworker who will provide a report and recommendations to the trustees as part of the individual's application.

Other information

This charity was established in April 2002 as an amalgamation of Glasgow Aged Seaman Relief Fund, Glasgow Seaman's Friend Society and Glasgow Veteran Seafarers' Association.

The charity also runs a range of social events for former seafarers: home/ hospital visits to those who are bedridden; social and lunch clubs on certain weekdays;, and periodic social outings.

Scottish Shipping Benevolent Association

£54,500 (19 grants)

Correspondent: Support Team, The Scottish Shipping Benevolent Association, c/o The Clyde Group, Seaforth House, Seaforth Road North, Hillington Park Glasgow G52 4JQ (0141 427 6655; email: info@ scottishshippingcharity.org; website: scottishshippingcharity.org)

OSCR number: SC004018

Eligibility

Any person who has worked or is currently working in a shore-based role within the Scottish maritime community, and their families. Applicants should be members of the association.

Types of grants

One-off grants for fuel bills and basic food supplies, etc.

Annual grant total

In 2016 the charity had assets of £1.1 million and an income of £85,000. Grants to individuals totalled £54,500.

Applications

Contact the support team using the online form on the website or by email.

The Shipwrecked Fishermen and Mariners' Royal Benevolent Society

£1.4 million (2,090 grants)

Correspondent: The Grants Team, 1 North Pallant, Chichester, West Sussex PO19 1TL (01243 789329; email: grants@shipwreckedmariners.org.uk; website: www.shipwreckedmariners.org.uk)

CC number: 212034

Eligibility

Fishermen, mariners and their widows and dependants, who are on a low income, especially those who are over 60 or in poor health. Priority is given to widows with young children. There is a minimum sea service of five years for one-off grants and ten years for regular payments, although this is reviewed periodically to reflect employment patterns.

Types of grants

According to the society's website there are five types of grant:

Biannual Grants are given twice each year to retired or permanently disabled fishermen, mariners, or their widows, whose situation means they require regular financial support. A minimum of 10 years of sea service is required.

Death Benefit Grants are a single grant paid to the widow of a Life Member of the Society under the former beneficial membership scheme.

Immediate Grants are given to widows and children left in need following the death of a serving fisherman or mariner.

One-off grants are given to fishermen, mariners, or their widows and children, who do not qualify for a Biannual Grant, but who have a specific need. A minimum of five years' sea service is required.

Funeral grants are awarded to the next-of-kin if they meet the qualifying criteria for a one-off grant subject to their having applied for and received a DWP funeral grant.

Assistance is also offered to shipwrecked survivors landed on the coasts of Great Britain and Ireland.

Annual grant total

In 2016/17 the society held assets of £27.2 million and had an income of £701,000. Grants to individuals totalled £1.4 million.

Exclusions

Applications for assistance are only accepted from eligible applicants residing in the UK and Ireland.

Applications

Application forms are available from the correspondent or to download from the website. Applications can be submitted by the individual or through a third party and are considered on a weekly basis.

Other information

This charity was founded in 1839 with the object of:

Giving relief and assistance to the widows and orphans of fishermen; and of mariners, members of the society, who lose their lives by storms and shipwreck on any part of the coasts of the United Kingdom, while engaged in their lawful occupations; and also to render necessary assistance to such mariners, soldiers, or other poor persons as suffer shipwreck upon the said coasts.

Shipwrecks still occur and the society is called upon to help but its main activity today is to provide financial assistance to retired or incapacitated fishermen and mariners and their dependants who are in need.

The society is one of the largest maritime charities in the UK and administers grants on behalf of some other funds such as the Royal Seamen's Pension Fund, the Hull Fishermen's Trust Fund and a subsidiary charity, the Fleetwood Fishing Industry Benevolent Fund. It manages the payment of grants from Trinity House, London, a fellow maritime charity.

The Tyne Mariners' Benevolent Institution

£90,500

Correspondent: Anthony Malia, Hadaway & Hadaway, 58 Howard Street, North Shields, Tyne and Wear NE30 1AL (0191 257 0382; email: tonym@hadaway.co.uk)

CC number: 229236

Eligibility

Former merchant seamen who live in Tyneside (about five miles either side of the River Tyne) and their widows. Applicants must be: (a) at least 55 years old and have served at least five years at sea; (b) under the age of 55, but unable to work owing to ill health; or (c) the widows of such people.

Types of grants

Pension payments.

Annual grant total

In 2016 the charity held assets of £1.33 million and had an income of £259,500. Pensions payments to individuals totalled £90,500.

Applications

Application forms are available from the correspondent. Applications should be submitted either directly by the individual or through a social worker, Citizens Advice or other welfare agency. Applications can be considered at any time.

Other information

The institution also administers and maintains the Master Mariners Homes in Tynemouth, providing 30 homes for beneficiaries.

Medicine and health

The 1930 Fund for District Nurses (No. 1)

£30,000

Correspondent: Mia Duddridge, The Trust Partnership, 6 Trull Farm Buildings, Tetbury, Gloucestershire GL8 8SQ (01285 841904; email: 1930fund@thetrustpartnership.com; website: www.1930fundfornurses.org)

CC number: 208312

Eligibility

Qualified nurses who have worked, are working or are unemployed in the community as a district nurse, community nurse, school nurse, health visitor, community midwife or community psychiatric nurse, and who are in need. Applicants must produce evidence of their employment as registered community nurses. Those applying for monthly or quarterly payments must hold a bank account solely in their own name.

Types of grants

One-off grants for a variety of needs, including home maintenance, to supplement income in cases of financial hardship or to purchase and install mobility aids. The fund also provides recurrent grants to help with living expenses, which are paid monthly or quarterly.

Annual grant total

In 2015/16 the fund held assets of £1.95 million and had an income of £57,000. Grants totalled £30,000, of which recurrent welfare grants totalled £15,500.

Exclusions

No grants are given for care home fees, educational fees, private healthcare, payment of debt, payment of rent/

137

council tax, or for expenditure incurred or committed prior to the date of the grant notification letter. Successful applicants for one-off grants can only apply once a year so it may be more appropriate to establish a short or long-term regular payment.

Applications

Apply on a form available from the correspondent or to download from the website. Applications can be submitted directly by the individual or through a family member, social worker, Citizens Advice or other welfare agency. They are considered at quarterly meetings. Applicants are required to supply evidence of having worked as a nurse, such as copies of any nursing certificates or qualifications and, if applicable, a recent payslip. A third party applying on behalf of a nurse should include a letter of endorsement from an approved authority. If the application is for home adaptations, repairs or the purchase of specific items, a copy of the invoice or quote must be supplied.

Enquiries are welcomed.

Other information

The charity, which was founded in 1930 by Ernest Cook, has an informative and helpful website.

The charity also runs a telephone befriending service for retired beneficiaries.

The Ambulance Staff Charity

£51,500

Correspondent: Tom Mitchell, Head Office, 12 Ensign Business Centre, Westwood Way, Coventry CV4 8JA (024 7798 7922; email: enquiries@theasc.org.uk; website: www.theasc.org.uk)

CC number: 1163538

Eligibility

Present and past ambulance staff, working within the NHS and independent sectors. Applicants should have less than £4,000 in savings and have worked in the UK ambulance service for a minimum of 12 months. The charity states that these are broad guidelines and where there are exceptional circumstances, the charity will consider all circumstances.

Types of grants

One-off grants for a wide range of needs.

Annual grant total

In 2015/16 the charity held assets of £2.4 million and an income of £2.1 million. Grants to individuals totalled £51,500.

Applications

Contact the charity using its support line on 0800 103 2999. Alternatively, complete the online enquiry form or email the charity at support@theasc.org.uk.

Other information

The charity also provides services such as counselling, debt advice, bereavement support and rehabilitation.

The Avenel Trust
See entry on page 16

The Barbers' Amalgamated Charity
See entry on page 169

The Birmingham and Three Counties Trust for Nurses

£10,800

Correspondent: David Airston, 16 Haddon Croft, Halesowen B63 1JQ (0121 602 0389; email: p.hyde@hotmail.co.uk)

CC number: 217991

Eligibility

Nurses on any statutory register, who have practiced or practice in the city of Birmingham and the counties of Staffordshire, Warwickshire and Worcestershire.

Types of grants

One-off or recurrent grants are awarded according to need. Grants are given to meet the costs of heating, telephone bills, cordless phones for the 'infirm', household equipment, household repairs, car repairs, electric scooters, wheelchairs, medical equipment and personal expenses such as spectacles and clothing. Grants are also made for convalescent care, recuperative holidays and to clear debt.

Annual grant total

In 2015/16 the trust had an income of £8,900 and a total expenditure of £14,900. Assistance in previous years has mostly been given for welfare purposes, although grants for educational needs are also made. We estimate that social welfare grants totalled around £10,800.

Applications

Applications can be made on a form available from the correspondent. Applications can be submitted either directly by the individual or through a friend, relative or a social worker, Citizens Advice or other welfare agency. Details of financial status including

income and expenditure, reasons for application, and health status where relevant should be included. Applications are considered throughout the year. Applicants are visited by a trustee (where distance allows) for assessment. Supportive visiting continues where considered necessary.

BMA Charities Trust Fund

£14,900

Correspondent: Marian Flint, Principal Officer, BMA House, Tavistock Square, London WC1H 9JP (020 7383 6142; email: info.bmacharities@bma.org.uk; website: www.bma.org.uk/about-us/who-we-are/bma-charities)

CC number: 219102

Eligibility

Employed and unemployed doctors, and medical students, who are in financial need. Applicants do not have to be a BMA member to apply.

Types of grants

One-off grants to ease financial hardship in times of crisis:

- Medical students in immediate and serious financial need
- Assistance with bills, travel, and equipment for unemployed doctors
- Working doctors in financial hardship for help with the GMC registration fee and professional indemnity insurance

Annual grant total

In 2016 the charity had assets of £5 million and an income of £309,000. The charity awarded £14,900 in welfare grants to individuals.

Exclusions

The fund does not help with general costs, legal fees, private medical treatment or career development projects.

Applications

Application forms are available from the correspondent and can be submitted at any time. Two personal references are required, one of which must be from a doctor. The trustees meet to consider applications four times a year.

Other information

The BMA Charities Trust Fund also provides grants to second degree medical students for educational purposes. The charity also administers the Dain Fund, for the education of the children of doctors.

British Dental Association (BDA) Benevolent Fund

£134,000

Correspondent: Laura Hannon, General Manager, 64 Wimpole Street, London W1G 8YS (020 7486 4994; email: administrator@dentistshelp.org; website: www.bdabenevolentfund.org.uk)

CC number: 208146

Eligibility

Dental students, dentists and their families in need, whether they are in training, in practice, have left the profession or are retired. Applicants must be living in the UK and do not need to be a member of the BDA to qualify for support but must have been registered at some time with the General Dental Council.

Types of grants

Regular monthly grants towards day-to-day living costs, back-to-work assistance following a period of illness; including help with retraining costs and professional fees, one-off grants towards specialist equipment, car or home adaptations. The fund can also make interest-free personal loans. In 2016 the fund made additional grants in December for fuel costs and to help meet the extra expenses of the festive season.

Annual grant total

In 2016 the fund had assets of £6.2 million and an income of almost £314,500. Grants were made totalling £134,000. In addition, a further £12,800 was paid in interest-free loans.

Exclusions

The fund cannot provide support towards:

- Private health care and medical insurance
- Private education
- Legal fees
- HMRC payments
- Repayment of loans from family or friends
- Business debts

Support will not be given to individuals with substantial savings, investments or capital.

Applications

The fund advises that potential applicants initially contact the fund by email or telephone to discuss whether they are eligible for support. Applications can then be made on a form available from the correspondent or to download from its website. Applicants will then be visited by the General Manager and their application will be considered at a bi-monthly executive committee meeting. Emergency grants can be made within a couple of days when the need is urgent. Further guidance notes are available on the website.

Other information

Every beneficiary receiving regular support from the fund is visited once a year to review their needs. The General Dental Council works closely with the fund and makes referrals for assistance for individuals who are in dispute with their commissioning bodies and are therefore unable to work.

The Cameron Fund

£113,000

Correspondent: David Harris, Company Secretary, BMA House, Tavistock Square, London WC1H 9HR (020 7388 0796; email: info@cameronfund.org.uk; website: www.cameronfund.org.uk)

CC number: 261993

Eligibility

Current and former registered general practitioners and their families and dependants. Doctors on postgraduate specialty training who have successfully completed the training or those who only completed it partially, due to unforeseen circumstances, are also considered.

Types of grants

One-off and recurrent grants towards essential living costs, rent, nursing home fees, help for pensioners and so on. Each application is considered on its own merits.

Annual grant total

In 2016 the fund had assets of £6.2 million and an income of £306,000. We estimate that welfare grants to individuals totalled £113,000.

Exclusions

Grants cannot be made towards items which should be provided through statutory sources.

Applications

Application forms can be found on the charity's website or requested from the correspondent.

The Care Workers Charity

£10,000

Correspondent: Alex Ramamurthy, The Care Workers Charity, Hill Place House, 55a High Street, Wimbledon Village SW19 5BA (email: info@ thecareworkerscharity.org.uk; website: www.thecareworkerscharity.org.uk)

CC number: 1132286

Eligibility

Current and former employees of the care profession who work/have worked in a registered domiciliary, residential care, or supported living service and have worked during one of the following time frames:

- One year's continuous service, if currently employed
- Three years' continuous service in the last five years, if no longer employed
- Six years' continuous service in the last ten years, if no longer employed
- Over ten years in their total working lifetime

Applicants can only be supported in the following circumstances.

1. Someone close to the applicant has died in the previous nine months
2. The applicant has experienced a sudden or unexpected illness or injury within the last six months
3. The applicant has experienced a sudden or unexpected loss of income within the last six months
4. The applicant has experienced a sudden or unexpected change in living circumstances or a loss of home in the last three months
5. There has been a recent relationship breakdown and/or domestic abuse within the last 12 months

Types of grants

One-off grants towards items necessary for health and well-being, for example household adaptions (up to £500); or support for essential living costs in an unforeseen circumstance, for example funeral costs (up to £250).

Annual grant total

In 2016 the charity had an income of £14,000 and a total expenditure of £13,700. We estimate that the amount awarded in grants to care workers was £10,000.

Exclusions

No grants are made towards debts.

Applications

Before applying, you will need:

- A completed and saved calculation report from the Turn2Us Benefits Checker
- A completed Turn2Us Grants Search Report
- A supporting statement from your adviser or supporter, confirming the support you need and how the need has arisen
- Proof of employment
- 3 full monthly bank statements for all accounts, including evidence of salary, benefits, and pensions

Applications can be completed online, or a paper version can be downloaded and returned to the correspondent.

Other information

Previously known as The Care Professionals Benevolent Fund; the charity also provides support and advice services.

Cavell Nurses' Trust

£439,500 (1,900 grants)

Correspondent: Welfare Team, Grosvenor House, Prospect Hill, Redditch, Worcestershire B97 4DL (01527 595999; email: admin@ cavellnursestrust.org; website: www. cavellnursestrust.org)

CC number: 1160148

Eligibility

Working and retired nurses, midwives and healthcare assistants, as well as student nurses suffering hardship, through illness, disability, accidents or family breakdowns. Applicants should hold no more than £4,000 in savings.

Types of grants

One-off and regular grants towards, for example, essential white goods, mobility aids and home adaptations, rent deposits, removal costs, bankruptcy and debt relief order fees. The trust can also help with travel expenses for medical treatment.

Annual grant total

In 2016 the trust held assets of £3.1 million and had an income of £500,500. Grants to 1,900 individuals totalled £439,500.

Exclusions

No grants are given for debt repayment, holidays, private medical fees, nursing home fees, educational costs, legal fees or car purchases.

Applications

An initial short eligibility form should be completed to see if your application is likely to be funded, which is available on the trust's website. A member of the welfare team will then contact you to discuss your circumstances and application. Applications may also be made by post or by telephone, and can be made either by the individual or by a referring agency.

Other information

The trust also provides advice and support on issues such as domestic violence, isolation and loneliness.

Chartered Physiotherapists' Benevolent Fund

£91,500 (54 grants)

Correspondent: The Administrator, Auriga Services Ltd, Emmanuel Court, 12 – 14 Mill Street, Sutton Coldfield B72 1TJ (0330 678 0655; email: info@ cspmbf.co.uk; website: www.csp.org.uk/ about-csp/what-we-do/members-benevolent-fund)

CC number: 219568

Eligibility

Members, past members, assistant members and student members of the society.

Types of grants

One-off grants and recurrent grants to help with living expenses, household repairs, heating bills and road tax (where car use is essential).

Annual grant total

In 2016 the charity held assets of £2.5 million and had an income of £139,000. During the year, the charity gave grants to 54 individuals totalling £91,500.

Exclusions

No grants are given towards payment of debts or when statutory help is available. Grants cannot be made to those who hold capital exceeding the maximum figure used by the Department of Work and Pensions to decide on benefit eligibility.

Applications

Application forms are available from the correspondent. Applications should be submitted directly by the individual or by a third party such as a carer or partner.

Cheltenham Aid-in-Sickness and Nurses Welfare Fund (Gooding Fund)

See entry on page 401

British Chiropody Association Benevolent Fund

£5,000

Correspondent: Sue Leech, Trustee, 9 Mill Road, Henham, Bishop's Storford CM22 6AD (email: sue@slahealthcare.co. uk)

CC number: 296490

Eligibility

People who are or have been fellows or full members of the British Chiropody Association for at least a year and are in need.

Types of grants

One-off grants according to need.

Annual grant total

In 2017 the fund had an income of £3,700 and a total expenditure of £5,600. We estimate that grants given to individuals totalled around £5,000.

Applications

Apply in writing to the correspondent.

The Benevolent Fund of the College of Optometrists and the Association of Optometrists

£63,500

Correspondent: Lynne Brown, 55 Colchester Road, White Colne, Colchester CO6 2PW (01787 223800; email: admin@opticalbenfund.com; website: www.opticalbenfund.com)

CC number: 1003699

Eligibility

Optometrists and their families who are in need.

Types of grants

Regular monthly grants and financial help with household expenditure. One-off grants are made towards more costly items in order to benefit an individual, or to help an applicant through a short-term crisis. The charity may also contribute towards the cost of counselling where an applicant is suffering from mental health issues. Assistance with professional fees is often available for younger practitioners unable to work.

The aim is to help beneficiaries remain independent in their own home, although help can be considered for those who need residential or nursing care.

Annual grant total

In 2015/16 the fund had assets of £1.4 and an income of £100,500. Grants to individuals totalled £63,500.

Applications

Applications can be made through the fund's website where application forms are also available to download. The fund's website states: 'If you are not sure about what to do, please make a preliminary telephone call to discuss your needs before filling in any forms.

We can then give you advice about the best way to proceed.'

Eaton Fund for Artists, Nurses and Gentlewomen

See entry on page 22

Environmental Health Officers Welfare Fund

£2,300

Correspondent: Anne Godfrey, Chief Executive, Chadwick Court, 15 Hatfields, London SE1 8DJ (020 7928 6006; email: membership@cieh.org; website: www.cieh.org/members/welfare-fund.html)

CC number: 224343

Eligibility

Past and present members of Chartered Institute of Environmental Health Officers, Association of Public Health Inspectors or The Guild of Public Health Inspection, and their dependants, who are in need.

Types of grants

Short-term support or one-off grants are given where needed due to a death, serious illness or catastrophe in the family.

Annual grant total

In 2016 the fund had an income of £340 and a total expenditure of £2,500. We estimate that grants totalled £2,300.

Exclusions

The fund cannot support long-term needs such as mortgage or rent. Students are generally not supported but can be assisted if they meet other criteria.

Applications

Initial enquiries should be made by telephone or using the contact form on the CIEH website.

The Ethel Mary Fletcher Fund For Nurses

£3,000

Correspondent: Henrietta Campbell, Vice-President, Cricket Green Medical Practice, 75–79 Miles Road, Mitcham, Greater London CR4 3DA (020 8685 1945; email: enquiries@rbna.org.uk; website: www.rbna.org.uk)

CC number: 209887

Eligibility

Retired state nurses who are sick or who have a disability and live in the UK. Applicants must have completed at least three years' postgraduate work.

Types of grants

Annuity payments are made twice yearly in July and December, with a bonus payment at Christmas.

Annual grant total

In 2016 the charity had an income of £4,500 and a total expenditure of £3,200. We estimate that grants given to individuals totalled £3,000.

Applications

Referrals are made by charitable organisations such as Age UK, Citizens Advice, other nursing organisations and SSAFA. Decisions are made by the executive committee at quarterly meetings.

Other information

The charity is administered by The Royal British Nurses' Association alongside three other charities: The Trained Nurses Annuity Fund; The Helena Benevolent Fund; and The Settlement Fund.

Forth Valley Medical Benevolent Trust

£5,000

Correspondent: The Correspondent, Meeks Road Surgery, 10 Meeks Road, Falkirk FK2 7ES (01324 619930)

OSCR number: SC000014

Eligibility

Medical practitioners and their families or relatives living in Forth Valley who are in need.

Types of grants

One-off grants according to need.

Annual grant total

In 2016/17 the trust had an income of £3,000 and a total expenditure of £10,500. The charity supports both educational and general welfare causes. We estimate that grants for welfare purposes totalled around £5,000.

Applications

Applications may be made in writing to the correspondent.

Other information

Educational needs are also supported.

The Royal Liverpool Seamen's Orphan Institution (RLSOI)

£119,500 (84 grants)

Correspondent: Linda Cotton, Treasurer, Suite 315, Cotton Exchange Building, Old Hall Street, Liverpool L3 9LQ (0151 227 3417 or 07747 607062 (mobile); email: enquiries@rlsoi-uk.org; website: www.rlsoi-uk.org)

CC number: 526379

Eligibility

Children of deceased British merchant seafarers, who are of pre-school age or in full-time education (including further and higher education). Help can also be given to seafarers who are at home caring for their family alone.

Types of grants

Discretionary awards for general living expenses and monthly maintenance grants. Support can be provided throughout the child's education.

Annual grant total

In 2016 the charity held assets of £2.7 million and had an income of £199,000. Grants to 84 individuals totalled £225,500 for both welfare and educational purposes. The breakdown between educational and welfare support was not specified; however, we estimate that about £119,500 was awarded for welfare needs.

Applications

Application forms are available from the correspondent and can be submitted at any time. Each application is considered on its own merits.

Other information

Support is given to both educational and welfare causes. While the proportions given for each cause were not specified, all grants are given to children and young people who are in attendance at school and further or higher education institutions. The charity's website also provides links to other organisations helping seafarers.

Medical Research Council Staff Benevolent Fund Association

£12,800

Correspondent: James Clerkin, Secretary to the Trustees, MRC Staff Benevolent Association, Medical Research Council, 14th Floor, 1 Kemble Street, London WC2B 4AN (020 7395 2289; email: james.clerkin@headoffice.mrc.ac.uk; website: sbfa.mrc.ac.uk)

CC number: 233839

Eligibility

Current and former Medical Research Council staff and their dependants.

Types of grants

Quarterly grants ranging between £150 to £250 and Christmas grants of £150. Interest-free or low-interest loans are also available.

Annual grant total

In 2015/16 the charity held assets of £758,000 and had an income of £35,500. Grants to individuals totalled £12,800.

Applications

The trustees meet six times a year on average.

The Royal College of Midwives Trust

£28,500 (40 grants)

Correspondent: Benevolent Fund Administrator, Royal College of Midwives, 15 Mansfield Street, London W1G 9NH (0300 303 0444; fax: 020 7312 3536; email: info@rcm.org.uk; website: www.rcm.org.uk)

CC number: 275261

Eligibility

Midwives, former midwives and student midwives who are in need. Preference is given to those who are members of the RCM or who have served as members of staff with the RCM or RCM Trust Ltd for at least five years.

Types of grants

Usually one-off grants for emergency or other unexpected needs (typically £50 to £200). Grants are given, for instance, towards the cost of a wheelchair, removal expenses, furniture, personal items and childcare costs.

Annual grant total

In 2016 the trust had assets of £2.3 million and an income of £416,500. During the year, the trust gave around £28,500 in grants to individuals.

Exclusions

The trust's website notes that 'unfortunately, the fund is not large enough to provide regular financial support, nor can it act as a top-up for low salaries or student midwives' bursaries, although it is able to advise on other sources of help'. However, Christmas grants are routinely paid to long-standing older members on low incomes.

Applications

Applicants must apply through the online portal which is available on the trust's website. A member of the trust's Welfare Services team will then be in contact within two working days.

Other information

The trust engages in a range of other activities such as providing information, advice and support to members as well as running educational programmes and conferences and undertaking campaigning work.

Junius S. Morgan Benevolent Fund

£239,000 (227 grants)

Correspondent: Shirley Baines, Grant Administrator, 8 Finsbury Circus, London EC2M 7AZ (020 7399 0110; email: grantadmin@juniusmorgan.org.uk; website: www.juniusmorgan.org.uk)

CC number: 1131892

Eligibility

Nurses and health care assistants who have practised for a minimum of five years post-registration.

Types of grants

Grants of up to £1,000 for essential decorating, furniture, and furnishings, e.g. walk-in baths, electric wheelchairs, and stairlifts. The charity will also consider providing grants for amenity bills.

Annual grant total

In 2016 the fund had assets of £3 million and an income of £204,500. Grants to 227 individuals totalled £239,000.

Exclusions

The fund will not consider educational and funeral costs, respite care, holidays or nursing home fees. The fund cannot help carers or student nurses.

Applications

Application forms can be downloaded from the fund's website. Applications should be accompanied by a letter of support from someone in a professional capacity such as a GP, health visitor, social worker, Citizens Advice worker or housing agency worker.

The NHS Pensioners' Trust

£58,000

Correspondent: Frank Jackson, Director, PO Box 456, Esher KT10 1DP (01372 805760; email: nhsptinfo@gmail.com; website: www.nhspt.org.uk)

CC number: 1002061

Eligibility

i) Any person who has retired from service in any capacity in the NHS in England, Wales or Scotland; ii) Any person who has retired from service in England, Wales or Scotland for any of the related health service organisations or caring professions prior to the creation of the NHS; and iii) Any person who is the wife, husband, widow, widower or other dependant of those specified above.

Types of grants

Grants of up to £350, for general upkeep to ease financial difficulty in cases of hardship, including the cost of living with a disability, aids and equipment, repairs to the home and fuel bills. Larger grants can be considered in particular circumstances. Grants are one-off, but individuals can reapply in the following year.

Annual grant total

In 2016/17 the trust had an income of £19,400 and a total expenditure of £78,000. We estimate that grants given to individuals totalled £58,000, based on previous years' accounts.

Exclusions

No grants are paid for top-up fees in nursing or residential accommodation.

Applications

Apply on a form available from the correspondent following receipt of an sae. Applications containing supporting information and/or the backing of social work agencies will be processed more quickly. Third party agencies may apply on behalf of individuals and may use their own application forms. A trust representative may follow up applications to verify information.

Other information

Advice services are also available from the trust.

The Benevolent Fund for Nurses in Scotland

£161,500 (972 grants)

Correspondent: Margaret Ramsay, Liaison Officer, 11 Avondhu Gardens, Grangemouth, Falkirk SK3 9BW (07584 322257; email: admin@bfns.org.uk)

OSCR number: SC006384

Eligibility

Current and former nurses, midwives or student nurses who trained or worked in Scotland and are experiencing financial difficulties.

Types of grants

Quarterly grants paid in March, June, September and December to applicants with limited income due to illness or disability, or those with minimal level of their pension. One-off grants towards general welfare needs, equipment or home adaptations are also given. During 2015, grants ranged from £50 to £700 and quarterly beneficiaries received a Christmas bonus of £200.

Annual grant total

In 2015 the fund held assets of £5.8 million and had an income of £244,000. During the year, 972 grants were made of which 738 were quarterly grants, the rest were single grants and Christmas gifts. Grants totalled £161,500.

Applications

Application forms are available from the correspondent and can be submitted by the individual directly or through a recognised referral agency (such as a social worker, Citizens Advice, doctor and so on). They are considered upon receipt. The trust may decide to visit potential beneficiaries.

The Nurses' Memorial to King Edward VII Edinburgh Scottish Committee

£101,000

Correspondent: Secretaries and Treasurers, Johnston Smillie Ltd, Chartered Accountants, 6 Redheughs Rigg, Edinburgh EH12 9DQ (0131 317 7377; email: info@nursesmemorial.org. uk; website: www.nursesmemorial.org. uk)

OSCR number: SC023963

Eligibility

Nurses or midwives with a strong connection to Scotland (including nurses who have worked in Scotland, or Scottish nurses working outside Scotland) who are retired, ill or otherwise in need.

Types of grants

One-off and monthly grants towards accommodation charges, domestic bills, equipment and to supplement inadequate income.

Annual grant total

In 2016 the charity held assets of £2.4 million and had an income of £93,500. During the year, the charity gave around £101,000 in grants to individuals.

Grants were distributed as follows:

Heating and Christmas payments	48	£54,900
Periodic support payments	24	£25,500
Single support payments	19	£15,000
Bursary awards	14	£5,500

Applications

Apply on a form available on the charity's website or from the correspondent. Details regarding the applicant's current financial circumstances and other information should be included. For further details, check the charity's website.

Pharmacist Support

£180,500

Correspondent: Diane Leicester-Hallam, Correspondent, 5th Floor, 196 Deansgate, Manchester M3 3WF (0808 168 2233; email: info@ pharmacistsupport.org; website: www. pharmacistsupport.org)

CC number: 1158974

Eligibility

You are eligible to apply for assistance if you are a pharmacist, a widow or widower of a pharmacist or a retired pharmacist and either you or your partner have been registered as a pharmacist with the General Pharmaceutical Council or RPSGB. Any member of a pharmacist's family who is dependent on you for financial support is eligible to apply. MPharm students at a university in Great Britain and pre-registration trainees are also eligible to apply for support.

Types of grants

The charity offers four types of grants:

- Health and well-being grants are given to support 'mental or physical quality of life'. Funding is typically given for respite care, counselling and therapies, convalescence, home help during convalescence, particular disability aids and for contributions towards residential and nursing home fees
- One-off grants are awarded for unexpected expenses such as essential car or home repairs, winter fuel bills or the purchase of a washing machine
- Recurrent grants act as 'top-ups' for those on very low incomes who 'are finding it difficult to make ends meet without getting into debt'. Recipients of these grants are often widows/widowers or retired pharmacists
- Student hardship grants are for pharmacy students who are facing extreme financial hardship due to unforeseen circumstances such as family issues, ill health or bereavement

Interest-free loans are also available.

Annual grant total

In 2016 the charity held assets of £15.1 million and had an income of £661,000. During the year, the charity gave around £180,500 in grants to individuals.

Exclusions

There are no grants available for pharmacy technicians or pharmacy assistants. Support is not available in Northern Ireland.

Applications

Apply on a form available for download from the charity's website, or by contacting the correspondent. Applications will be considered throughout the year and can be submitted either directly by the individual or through a social worker, Citizens Advice, other welfare agency, or other third party on behalf of an individual. The charity recommends that applicants make contact informally before applying in order to discuss eligibility and needs.

Other information

Pharmacist Support, formerly known as the Royal Pharmaceutical Society's Benevolent Fund, offers a range of services, information and specialist advice for pharmacists, former pharmacists and their families.

In partnership with Action on Addiction, the charity runs its Health Support Programme, which seeks to support pharmacists who are dealing with addiction and dependency issues through the provision of qualified addiction specialists. Those requiring more information on the Health Support Programme should call 0808 168 5132.

To talk to a trained volunteer about any work or home-related issues (including stress, bullying, ill health, financial worries, bereavement and anxiety about exams), call the 'Listening Friends' telephone helpline on 0808 168 5133.

General enquiries can be made by calling 0808 168 2233.

The Queen's Nursing Institute

£123,500 (159 grants)

Correspondent: Joanne Moorby, Welfare and Grants Officer, 1A Henrietta Place, London W1G 0LZ (020 7549 1405; email: joanne.moorby@qni.org.uk; website: www.qni.org.uk)

CC number: 213128

Eligibility

Queen's Nurses (district nurses who were trained by the QNI between 1887 and 1967) and community nurses who have worked in the community for a minimum of three years. The majority of beneficiaries are community nurses who are no longer able to work because of illness, age or disability.

Types of grants

One-off and recurrent grants ranging from help with household essentials, building repairs and adaptations to specialist aids and equipment.

The institute's website states:

> We will consider almost any request, but help is usually given, for example, with the provision of essential household items, building repairs or adaptations, respite care, specialist equipment such as walk-in baths, stair lifts, electric wheelchairs and amenity bills. In certain cases, the QNI may make regular quarterly payments to clients.

Annual grant total

In 2016 the institute held assets of £10.5 million and had an income of £949,000. Welfare support to 159 individuals was given in 447 grants and totalled £123,500.

Exclusions

Grants are not made for:

- Residential or nursing home fees
- Debts
- The costs of medical treatment
- Funeral expenses

Applications

Application forms are accessible on the institute's website. The applicant will need a copy of their latest bank statement and a utility bill. Applications are accepted from nurses, their friends, family or professionals and voluntary organisations supporting them. Initial contact may also be made to Joanne Moorby (020 7549 1405; joanne.moorby@qni.org.uk) to discuss the application. Requests can be made at any time.

Other information

Educational assistance is also given to nurses. The institute undertakes campaigning, lobbying and various projects. Organisations are also supported.

Debt and other advice services are available – see the website for more information.

The Society of Radiographers Benevolent Fund

£12,200

Correspondent: Benevolent Fund Trustees, 207 Providence Square, Mill Street, London SE1 2EW (020 8545 9944; email: help@sor.org; website: www.sor.org)

CC number: 326398

Eligibility

Past and present members of the society and their dependants in need.

Types of grants

One-off grants towards, for example, stairlifts, retraining, orthopaedic beds, house adaptations, car repairs, health-care travel costs, long-term residential

care, computer equipment and washing machines.

Annual grant total

In 2015/16 the charity had an income of £11,600 and a total expenditure of £12,400. We estimate that the charity awarded around £12,200 in grants to individuals for welfare purposes.

Exclusions

The charity does not award grants to repay debts or for further education.

Applications

Applicants must complete an application form and a financial circumstances form, both of which are available on request from the correspondent or to download directly from the fund's website. Applications can be submitted by the individual or through a third party such as a colleague or relative.

The RCN Foundation

£263,000

Correspondent: Grants Manager (Hardship or Educational), 20 Cavendish Square, London W1G 0RN (020 7647 3645; email: rcnfoundation@rcn.org.uk; website: www.rcnfoundation.org.uk)

CC number: 1134606

Eligibility

Registered or retired nurses, midwives, HCAs and health visitors in the UK, and their families in times of need, to help 'get their lives and careers back on track'. Student nurses may also be assisted in exceptional circumstances.

The fund is means-tested and an individual's circumstances would generally need to demonstrate the following:

- A shortfall between household income and essential expenditure (essential expenditure does not include consumer credit debt, such as credit cards or loans)
- Savings of under £2,000 (£5,000 for state retired nurses)
- Insufficient funds to meet the cost of essential items or services, such as disability adaptations or household appliances

Types of grants

Financial support can be provided to individuals who are experiencing financial difficulties or who have an essential cost that they cannot afford. Assistance is made with the full consideration of an individual's circumstances and support tailored to ensure the biggest impact. The type of assistance available is flexible to the needs of individuals.

Annual grant total

In 2016 the foundation had assets of £31.6 million and an income of £1.5 million. Benevolent grants to individuals totalled £263,000.

Exclusions

Postgraduate students are not eligible for support from the Lamplight Support Service.

There are certain costs the fund cannot directly assist with, these include:

- Funeral costs and costs associated with bereavement
- Educational or training costs, with the exception of support with living costs during a return to practice
- A shortfall between income and expenditure due to consumer credit debt, including credit cards and loans
- Private medical treatment where this treatment is available on the NHS
- Top-up fees for care homes
- Grants for dependants
- Costs associated with NMC hearings and legal fees
- Union membership fees

Applications

If you wish to apply for funding, contact the Lamplight Support Service on 0345 772 6200 between 8.30am and 8.30pm.

Royal Medical Benevolent Fund (RMBF)

£223,000

Correspondent: The Casework Department, 24 King's Road, Wimbledon, London SW19 8QN (020 8540 9194; email: help@rmbf.org; website: www.rmbf.org)

CC number: 207275

Eligibility

Doctors and their dependants, who are on a low income and unable to support themselves due to illness, disability, bereavement or being over state retirement age. Medical students experiencing unforeseen financial hardship, and their dependants.

Types of grants

Assistance is given to doctors, medical students and their dependants. Help ranges from financial assistance in the form of grants and interest-free loans to a telephone befriending scheme for those who may be isolated and in need of support. Assistance is tailored to the individual's needs. Support includes:

- One-off grants to help with costs such as home adaptations or specialist vehicles for those with disabilities

- Interest-free loans or grants to help where eligible applicants are in financial need
- Specialist money and debt management advice to renegotiate debts and secure all eligible state benefits
- Regular monthly grants towards day-to-day living costs
- Back-to-work awards for those returning to work following a period of illness (including retraining costs, professional fees and occasionally childcare costs)
- Top-up for residential care fees, extra care costs
- Support for medical students in exceptional financial hardship
- Support for refugee doctors retraining in the UK

For more detailed information on eligibility for financial help check the financial support section of the charity's helpful website or get in touch with the caseworkers.

Annual grant total

In 2016/17 the charity held assets of £32.9 million and had an income of £992,500. Grants to 234 individuals totalled £446,000. The breakdown between educational and welfare support was not given. We estimate that about £223,000 was given for welfare causes.

Exclusions

The following are excluded:

- Private health care and medical insurance/fees
- Legal fees
- HMRC payments
- Debts to relatives or friends
- Private education

Applications

For an application pack and further information, get in touch with the correspondent by email or phone. Applications can be submitted either directly by the individual or through a third party, for example a social worker, Citizens Advice, other welfare agency, medical colleague or other medical and general charities.

Two references are required (at least one of which should be from a medical practitioner). All applicants are visited before a report is submitted to the Case Committee, which meets on a bi-monthly basis (although emergency assistance may be given). The income/capital and expenditure are fully investigated, with similar rules applying as for those receiving Income Support.

Other information

Every year the RMBF helps hundreds of doctors, medical students and their dependants in a variety of ways. Voluntary visitors liaise between beneficiaries and the office. The fund has an informative website.

The Royal Medical Foundation

£71,000 (27 grants)

Correspondent: Helen Jones, Caseworker, RMF Office, Epsom College, College Road, Epsom, Surrey KT17 4JQ (01372 821010; email: rmf-caseworker@ epsomcollege.org.uk; website: www. royalmedicalfoundation.org)

CC number: 312046

Eligibility

Doctors (registered with the GMC) and their dependants who are in need. Doctors who have qualified outside the UK and are currently GMC registered may also apply, although they should have worked in the UK for at least three years prior to making an application.

Types of grants

One-off grants, monthly pensions and maintenance grants of £500 to £15,000. Previous applications have included support for doctors with debt problems, fall-out from divorce or suspension, retraining expenses, practical financial support during/after rehabilitation, help with essential domestic bills, respite breaks, home alterations for older people or people with disabilities and nursing home fees.

Annual grant total

In 2015/16 the foundation made 41 grants totalling £146,000. This included welfare grants amounting to £71,000 for 27 individuals. Grants were distributed as follows:

Short-term payments or one-off grants where urgent assistance is required	22	£55,000
Financial assistance with educational expenses at Epsom College	2	£37,500
Financial assistance with educational expenses	10	£36,500
Regular payments to medical practitioners and their widows/widowers	5	£16,200
Other grants	2	£650

Applications

There is an online financial assistance request form on the foundation's website. For more information contact the correspondent. Applicants must have applied for any state benefits to which they may be entitled before an application can be considered and will be visited by the caseworker as part of the application process. The foundation's board meets quarterly, in January, April, July and October and applications should be submitted well in advance (specific dates are listed on the website).

Other information

The Royal Medical Foundation is a charity founded by Dr John Propert in 1855 and administered by an Act of Parliament. Its original objects were to provide an asylum for qualified medical practitioners and their spouses and to found a school for their sons. Today, the foundation's aims and objectives are to assist registered doctors and their families who are in financial hardship.

The foundation is managed by a board of directors drawn from various professions and is located at Epsom College.

Society for Assistance of Medical Families

£34,500

Correspondent: Charlotte Farrar, Lettsom House, 11 Chandos Street, Cavendish Square, London W1G 9EB (01837 83022; email: info@ widowsandorphans.org.uk; website: www.widowsandorphans.org.uk)

CC number: 207473

Eligibility

Support is given in the following order of priority:

(i) necessitous dependants of deceased members of the society

(ii) necessitous members of the society

(iii) necessitous dependants of members of the society

(iv) necessitous medical practitioners not being members of the society and their dependants.

Types of grants

One-off and recurrent grants are available to assist with household and living expenses, expenses for those unable to work, moving expenses, and debts.

Annual grant total

In 2016 the charity held assets of £6.6 million and had an income of £221,000. Grants are made to individuals for educational and social welfare purposes and totalled £68,500 during the year. The figure given above is an estimate.

Exclusions

Grants are not normally made towards nursing home fees, loans, long-term assistance or second degrees.

Applications

Application forms and income questionnaires are available to download from the charity's website under the heading 'Media and Downloads'. The trustees meet four times per year, in February, May, August, and November.

Where possible, either the Secretary or a director prefers to meet with applicants.

Benevolent Fund of the Society of Chiropodists

£12,800

Correspondent: Grants Administrator, Society of Chiropodists Benevolent Fund, Second Floor, Quartz House, 207 Providence Square, Mill Street, London SE1 2EW (020 7234 8635; email: hbh@scpod.org; website: www.scpod. org)

CC number: 205684

Eligibility

Members/former members of the society or one of its constituent bodies and their dependants.

Types of grants

One-off grants according to need. The charity can also cover membership fees, make Christmas payments of £250, and provide interest-free loans where necessary.

Annual grant total

In 2016 the charity had assets of £1.2 million and an income of £29,000. During the year, charitable expenditure totalled £12,800, including Christmas grants and payment of membership fees to 12 individuals.

Applications

Application forms are available upon request from the correspondent, and where possible should be supported by a third party, such as a professional or social worker.

Somerset Local Medical Benevolent Fund

£27,500

Correspondent: Dr J. H. Yoxall, Somerset LMC, The Crown Medical Centre, Crown Industrial Estate, Venture Way, Taunton TA2 8QY (07796 267510 or 01823 331428; email: lmcoffice@ somersetlmc.nhs.uk; website: www. somersetlmc.co.uk)

CC number: 201777

Eligibility

General medical practitioners who are practising or have practised in Somerset and their dependants who are in need.

Types of grants

One-off or recurrent grants according to need. Recent grants have been given to contribute towards the locum costs of a young GP undergoing a cardiac procedure, to support a GP with a pre-

existing illness to get locum insurance, and to contribute to living expenses for a doctor unable to work due to a road accident. The fund also provides payments of £4,000 to dependants after the death in service of a practitioner.

Annual grant total

In 2016/17 the fund had assets of £592,500 and an income of £35,000. During the year, the fund awarded £27,500 in grants to doctors and their dependants.

Applications

Apply in writing to the correspondent. The charity's website states that the:

> Resources of the fund are there to be used by any GP facing extra costs, including locum expenses, due to unforeseen circumstances. Applications are not means-tested but the trustees may ask for some background information about PCT sickness payments and insurance income where appropriate. Please note that the Fund is not a substitute for adequate locum insurance arrangements.

Trained Nurses' Annuity Fund

£13,500

Correspondent: Angela Searle, Honourable Secretary, Cricket Green Medical Practice, 75–79 Miles Road, Mitcham, Surrey CR4 3DA (email: enquiries@rbna.org; website: www.rbna. org.uk)

CC number: 209883

Eligibility

Trained nurses with at least seven years' experience, who either have a disability or are aged 40 and over.

Types of grants

Annuities and occasionally one-off grants. Each year beneficiaries of annuities send a short report explaining whether their financial circumstances have changed and whether they are still in need of assistance. Annuities are paid twice-yearly in July and December.

Annual grant total

In 2016 the fund had an income of £18,200 and a total expenditure of £13,800. We estimate that grants given to individuals totalled £13,500.

Exclusions

No grants are given for education or house improvements.

Applications

Application forms are available from the correspondent. Previous research indicates applications are considered at quarterly meetings.

The West Sussex County Nursing Benevolent Fund

£3,000

Correspondent: Rod Shepherd, Trustee, Sheen Stickland LLP, 7 East Pallant, Chichester PO19 1TR (email: rod. shepherd@btinternet.com)

CC number: 234210

Eligibility

Nurses who are or have been engaged in community nursing in West Sussex and are in financial need. Beneficiaries must be in poor health, convalescing or have disabilities. The fund may also assist general or specialist nurses, both retired and serving, if such a need arises.

Types of grants

One-off and recurrent grants are given according to need. Gifts are also distributed at Christmas.

Annual grant total

In 2016 the charity had an income of almost £4,100 and a total expenditure of £3,200. We estimate that grants given to individuals totalled £3,000.

Applications

Application forms are available from the correspondent. They can be submitted directly by the individual or through a third party such as a social worker, Citizens Advice or other welfare agency.

Mining and quarrying

The Coal Industry Social Welfare Organisation

£549,000 (1,232 grants)

Correspondent: Vernon Jones, Secretary, The Old Rectory, Rectory Drive, Whiston, Rotherham, South Yorkshire S60 4JG (01709 728115; fax: 01709 839164; email: mail@ciswo.org.uk; website: www.ciswo.org.uk)

CC number: 1015581

Eligibility

Widows and families of miners who have died as a result of industrial accident or disease (mainly pneumoconiosis). Help is also available to mineworkers and their dependants who are experiencing financial difficulties.

Types of grants

- General hardship grants towards, for example, buying a motorised wheelchair, specialist equipment and home adaptations
- Grants to the dependants of miners who have died as a result of their work
- Grants to miners who are in hospital as a result of their work, up to a maximum amount per year
- Grants of up to a maximum amount for miners who have to travel to an outpatient centre as a result of an accident at work

Annual grant total

In 2016 the charity held assets of £31.3 million and had an income of £3.2 million. The total expenditure was £4.2 million, with relief-in-need grants totalling £549,000.

Applications

Apply in writing to the correspondent for consideration by the trustees. The charity usually sends one of its own social workers to visit the individual to assess their needs and assist with the application form.

Other information

The following information is taken from the charity's informative and helpful website:

CISWO provides a Personal Welfare Service to former miners and their families, including wives, partners, widows and any dependent children with a physical or learning disability. We aim to enhance the conditions of living, maintain independence and improve quality of life. Each led by a qualified Social Worker, our experienced regional teams offer:-

- **A Confidential Home Visiting Service** to provide advice and support across a range of issues
- **Advocacy –** to support and enable people to express their views and concerns, and defend and promote their rights and responsibilities, including access to information and services.
- **Emotional Support** at times of personal difficulty, including loss and bereavement, illness and caring responsibilities
- **Assistance to complete welfare benefit applications** and industry-related associated compensation schemes
- **Advice on Mining-Related Issues** including illness, disability, loneliness and social isolation
- **Support at times of exceptional hardship** where there is essential need to access available funds through CISWO (subject to eligibility) or to access external funding through working with like-minded agencies and charities

We will do our utmost to provide support, free of charge, to individuals in line with the policy of our National Trustees.

The Coal Trade Benevolent Association

£131,000

Correspondent: Nicholas Ross, Secretary, Unit 6 Bridge Wharf, 156 Caledonian Road, London N1 9UU (020 7278 3239; email: coalbenev@ btconnect.com; website: www. coaltradebenevolentassociation.org)

CC number: 212688

Eligibility

Non-manual workers of the coal industry in England and Wales who have worked in the production or distribution sectors and allied trades, and their dependants.

Types of grants

Weekly payments to supplement low income and help with telephone costs, televisions, respite holidays, birthday and Christmas cheques and shopping vouchers. One-off grants are also available towards capital items such as stairlifts, special bathrooms, washing machines, carpets and other items. Further special fuel payments have been distributed to regular beneficiaries during periods of exceptionally cold weather.

Annual grant total

In 2016 the association had an income of £269,500 and a total expenditure of £295,000. Grants to beneficiaries amounted to £131,000.

Applications

Apply on a form available from the correspondent for consideration throughout the year.

The Members Benevolent Trust of the Institute of Materials, Minerals and Mining

£29,000

Correspondent: Peter Waugh, Honorary Secretary, The Member's Benevolent Trust, 297 Euston Road, London NW1 3AD (07889 123373; email: mbt@ iom3.org; website: www.iom3.org)

CC number: 207184

Eligibility

Members of the institute and former members and their dependants who are in need.

Types of grants

One-off and recurrent grants in the range of £250 to £3,500. One-off grants in kind are also made. Grants are for general household needs, furniture, security installations, medical aids and adaptations, clothing, respite breaks and school uniforms. The trust is also keen to help unemployed and redundant members with travel costs, subscriptions, relocation costs and short course fees (where this will widen the scope for re-employment).

Annual grant total

In 2016 the trust held assets of over £1.8 million and had an income of £79,000. Grants to individuals totalled £29,000.

Applications

Requests for assistance are preferred in writing and application forms can be requested from the Honorary Secretary. Once returned, there is a preliminary review of the form. This is usually followed by a visit to the applicant by an established regional visitor or a trustee to talk through the application. Following the visit, the board assesses each application thoroughly and makes its decision.

Mining Institute of Scotland Trust

£1,500

Correspondent: Keith Donaldson, Hon. Secretary/Treasurer, 14/9 Burnbrae Drive, Edinburgh EH12 8AS (0131 629 7861; website: www.mining-scotland.org/ trust.htm)

OSCR number: SC024974

Eligibility

Former members of the Mining Institute of Scotland (MIS) and members or former members of IMM who live in Scotland or who worked in connection with Scottish mining matters for at least five consecutive years. The dependants of eligible people can also be supported.

Types of grants

One-off and ongoing hardship grants of up to £1,000 a year. Widows of members can receive Christmas and summer holiday grants.

Annual grant total

In 2016 the trust had assets of £873,000 and an income of £32,500. We estimate that welfare grants to individuals totalled around £1,500.

Applications

Applications for assistance can be made in writing to the correspondent.

North East Area Miners' Social Welfare Trust Fund

£2,800

Correspondent: Michael Lally, 4 Bilham Row, Brodsworth, Doncaster DN5 7DN (email: ian.lally@ciswo.org.uk; website: www.ciswo.org.uk)

CC number: 504178

Eligibility

People in need living in Durham, Northumberland and Tyne and Wear who are or have been employed by the coal industry, and their dependants.

Types of grants

One-off grants according to need. The fund aims to improve beneficiaries' health, social well-being and conditions of living.

Annual grant total

In 2015/16 the fund had assets of £3 million and an income of £110,000. We estimate that welfare grants to individuals totalled around £2,800.

Applications

Applications may be made in writing to the correspondent. They can be submitted directly by the individual or through a social worker, Citizens Advice or other welfare agency. Requests are usually considered four times a year.

Other information

The fund also makes grants to mining charities. It also provides group holidays for its beneficiaries and revenue/capital costs relating to the day-to-day running of the Sam Watson Rest Home. Educational and training support may also be given, although it would appear that most support is awarded for general social welfare needs.

The North Staffordshire Coalfield Miners Relief Fund

£3,500

Correspondent: Susan Jackson, Correspondent, c/o Coal Industry Social Welfare Organisation, 142 Queens Road, Penkhull, Stoke-on-Trent, Staffordshire ST4 7LH (01782 744996)

CC number: 209616

Eligibility

Mineworkers or retired mineworkers who worked in the North Staffordshire coalfield (including Cheadle), and their widows or dependants. The mineworker must have suffered an industrial accident or disease or died as a result of their duties.

Types of grants

One-off grants according to need.

Annual grant total

In 2015/16 the fund had an income of £2,600 and a total expenditure of £7,200. We estimate that the fund gave around £3,500 in grants to individuals.

Applications

Apply in writing to the correspondent or by telephone either directly by the individual or via a third party such as a social worker, Citizens Advice or other welfare agency. Applications are considered throughout the year.

Other information

Grants are also made to organisations.

The Nottinghamshire Miners' Welfare Trust Fund

£95,500

Correspondent: Donald Brookes, Secretary, CISWO, Welfare Offices, Berry Hill Lane, Mansfield, Nottinghamshire NG18 4JR (01623 625767; email: donald.brookes@ciswo.org.uk)

CC number: 1001272

Eligibility

Members of the mining community in Nottinghamshire who are in need, and their dependants.

Types of grants

One-off and recurrent grants are given to improve health and living conditions. Recent grants have been given for bathroom alterations, mortgage repayments, stairlifts, wheelchairs, scooters, beds and bedding, furniture and replacement boilers. Holiday grants of £100 to £250 are also available.

Annual grant total

In 2016 the fund had assets of £5 million and an income of £1.2 million. Grants were made totalling £95,500 and were distributed as follows:

| Personal welfare and hardship grants | £87,000 |
| Holiday grants | £5,500 |

Applications

Application forms are available from the correspondent. Applications should be submitted directly by the individual or through a third party such as the Coal Industry Social Welfare Organisation (CISWO), Citizens Advice, social worker or similar welfare organisation. Applications are considered regularly throughout the year. Some applicants may be visited by a CISWO social worker.

Other information

Grants are also made to organisations (£5,600 in 2016).

The Institute of Quarrying Benevolent Fund

£17,300 (six grants)

Correspondent: Lyn Bryden, Benevolent Fund Secretary, McPherson House, 8a Regan Way, Chetwynd Business Park, Chilwell, Nottingham NG9 6RZ (0115 972 9995; email: mail@quarrying.org; website: www.quarrying.org)

CC number: 213586

Eligibility

Members or former members of the Institute of Quarrying and/or their dependants.

Types of grants

One-off grants ranging from £100 to £2,500. No recurrent grants are made although most beneficiaries successfully reapply each year.

Annual grant total

In 2015/16 the fund held assets of almost £1.1 million and had an income of £27,000. Grants totalling £17,300 were made to six beneficiaries.

Exclusions

People who are involved in the quarrying industry but are not members of the institute cannot be considered.

Applications

Apply in writing to the correspondent. Each beneficiary is contacted on a regular basis by the welfare officer of the fund who is a carer by profession.

South Wales Area Miners' Benevolent Fund

£12,500

Correspondent: Wayne Thomas, General Secretary, NUM South Wales Area, Woodland Terrace, Maesycoed, Pontypridd, Mid Glamorgan CF37 1DZ (01443 404092; email: numsouthwales@fut.net)

CC number: 500118

Eligibility

Employees and former employees of the coal mining industry in South Wales.

Types of grants

Grants are given according to need.

Annual grant total

In 2016 the fund had an income of £5,200 and a total expenditure of

£30,000. We estimate that welfare grants to individuals totalled around £12,500, with funding also awarded for educational purposes.

Applications

Apply in writing to the correspondent.

South Wales Miners Welfare Trust Fund Scheme

£28,500

Correspondent: Andrew Morse, Regional Manager, CISWO, Unit 5 Maritime Offices, Woodland Terrace, Maesycoed, Pontypridd CF37 1DZ (01443 485233; email: andrew.morse@ciswo.org.uk)

CC number: 507439

Eligibility

Miners and their dependants in South Wales.

Types of grants

One-off grants towards the costs of home repairs, adaptations and other essential items.

Annual grant total

In 2016 the charity held assets of £8.6 million and had an income of £697,500. Grants to individuals totalled £28,500.

The charity also makes grants to organisations that support the welfare of miners. However, the majority of its expenditure is on the upkeep of its convalescent homes and organising day trips and other social activities.

Applications

Apply in writing to the correspondent. The trustees meet quarterly to discuss applications.

Other information

The trustees are also responsible for three convalescent homes that are open to all mineworkers, former mineworkers and their dependants, all of whom are eligible upon having worked a minimum of five years in the South Wales mining industry.

The charity also supports people employed by the Ocean Coal Company Ltd and their dependants to pursue full or part-time education. These scholarships are awarded through the David Davies Memorial Trusts. More details can be found on the charity's website.

Warwickshire Miners' Welfare Trust Fund Scheme

£6,900

Correspondent: Donald Brookes, CISWO, Welfare Offices, Berry Hill Lane, Mansfield NG18 4JR (01623 625767; email: donald.brookes@ciswo.org.uk)

CC number: 519724

Eligibility

People who work or have worked within the coal mining industry in Warwickshire, and their dependants. Widows, widowers and relatives of the deceased miners are eligible to apply.

Types of grants

Our research suggests that one-off grants from £50 to £1,500 can be given towards convalescent holidays, hospital visits, electrical appliances (such as, cookers and vacuum cleaners), carpets, beds and other furniture, wheelchairs, stairlifts, scooters and medical reports for industrial diseases.

Annual grant total

In 2016 the charity had an income of £13,200 and a total expenditure of £14,100. We estimate that grants given to individuals totalled £6,900, with funding also awarded to organisations in old coalfield areas.

Exclusions

According to our research, death grants are not provided and support is not given to people who have received redundancy pay within the last ten years. Awards will not be given for any purpose for which the DWP will pay.

Applications

Apply in writing to the correspondent. Applications can be submitted directly by the individual or through a third party, for example, a social worker, Citizens Advice or other welfare agency. Candidates should include weekly income and medical proof from a doctor (if applicable). Applications are accepted throughout the year.

Motor industry

Ben – Motor and Allied Trades Benevolent Fund

£183,000

Correspondent: Support Services Team, Lynwood Court, Lynwood Village, Rise Road, Ascot, Berkshire SL5 0FG (0808 131 1333; email: careservices@ben.org.uk; website: www.ben.org.uk)

CC number: 297877

Eligibility

People who are resident in the UK or the Republic of Ireland who are employed or formerly employed in the motor, agricultural engineering, cycle and allied trades and industries and their dependants.

Types of grants

Mostly one-off grants for essential household items, wheelchairs, adaptations and help towards costs such as essential school trips, clothing and specialist equipment for dependants.

Annual grant total

In 2015/16 the charity had assets of £28.7 million and an income of nearly £32.3 million. Grants to individuals totalled £183,000.

Exclusions

BEN cannot assist with top-up fees for people in care homes, property repairs or improvements (except heating and adaptations for people with disabilities), private education costs, private medical costs and medications, or costs associated with bankruptcy.

Applications

Individuals, or somebody referring an individual, can contact the charity directly via the helpline (0808 131 1333), email (supportservices@ben.org.uk), text (07764 411911), the online contact form, or by post. The charity requires a referral form to be completed, providing details of the individual's situation and the help they require. In order to confirm eligibility for assistance, the following documentation must be supplied: evidence of the connection with the motor industry (for example, a copy of a payslip, P45, contract or a letter from an employer); proof of address/residency status (such as a household bill or statement dated within the last three months); and a signed explicit consent form to store and/or share information. Referral forms can be downloaded from the website and returned to BEN by email (careservices@ben.org.uk) or by post.

The website notes the following helpful advice: 'If you are having difficulty providing proof of your eligibility then you can contact HMRC on 0300 200 3500 to request a record of your employment history (within the motor trade only) by asking for a Subject Access Request.'

Other information

BEN offers free support and advice on a broad range of issues through its support services team. Each of the following five regions has its own welfare officer assigned: Scotland and Northern Ireland; North of England; Midlands and Wales; East of England; South of England. The fund also runs care centres, more details of which are available from the fund's informative website.

Public and government sector

British Council Benevolent Fund

£41,500 (52+ grants)

Correspondent: Sarah Firth, Secretary, 10 Spring Gardens, London SW1A 2BN (020 3285 3828; email: benevolent.fund@ britishcouncil.org)

CC number: 1161805

Eligibility

Past and present staff of the British Council and their families or dependants. Staff include those who work as an employee or contractor of: the British Council; any wholly owned subsidiary of the British Council; a wholly or partly owned subsidiary of BC Trading Ltd; any organisation offering services to any of the previous entities.

Types of grants

One-off, quarterly and Christmas grants according to need.

Annual grant total

In 2016/17 the fund held assets of £749,500 and had an income of £31,000. Grants to individuals totalled £41,500.

One-off grants were paid to 31 individuals with three given in the UK and 28 overseas. Christmas grants were given to 21 individuals with four given in the UK and 17 overseas.

Loans were made to five individuals in the UK totalling £8,400.

Applications

Apply in writing to the correspondent.

Conservative and Unionist Agents' Benevolent Association

£220,000

Correspondent: Sally Smith, Conservative Campaign Headquarters, 4 Matthew Parker Street, Westminster, London SW1H 9HQ (020 7984 8172; email: sally.smith@conservatives.com; website: www.conservativeagentscharity. org.uk)

CC number: 216438

Eligibility

The charity's website states:

> Over the years CABA has supported those who have become seriously ill whilst still in employment, retired colleagues and their dependants, especially people who are very old whose salary will not have attracted a large pension, and the children and dependants of colleagues who have died in service.

Types of grants

The charity pays three types of grant, sometimes simultaneously. Firstly, some applicants receive regular monthly grants for day-to-day expenses.

Secondly, the charity provides additional grants for the following:

- Summer seasonal grant: £500 for a single person and £1,000 for a couple, paid in June.
- Heating grant: £900 paid in equal instalments in November and February.
- Winter seasonal grant: £700 for a single person and £970 for a couple, paid in November.
- TV license: full payment of the license for people under the age of 75.
- Telephone, broadband, and newspaper voucher bills: amounts vary according to the payment method by individuals. Call charges are not paid.

Thirdly, special requests for additional grants can be considered. The following items are considered 'urgent':

- Hearing aids: up to £3,000 for two ears.
- Glasses: particularly special prescriptions, up to £300 per pair. Designer frames are not included.
- Low vision aids: supported, subject to quotes.
- Mobility equipment: installation, rental, or outright purchase of stairlifts; mobility scooters; grab rails; and home conversions.
- Call alarms: running costs are covered if you choose to have one.

Annual grant total

In 2015/16 the charity had assets of almost £2.6 million and an income of £105,000. The amount awarded in grants was £220,000.

Exclusions

Grants cannot be made for nursing home fees, nor are loans given.

Applications

Initial enquiries can be made by post, email or telephone to the correspondent, who will then discuss the options available to the applicant. A member of the management committee or a local serving agent will then visit the applicant to discuss their application and their need for support, which is based on an assessment of household income and other circumstances. Every beneficiary is reassessed annually, either in winter or summer.

Other information

The majority of the association's grants are made for relief-in-need purposes but some help is given to the children of deceased members for the costs of education.

Corporation of London Benevolent Association

£2,100

Correspondent: Sacha Than, City of London Corporation, Town Clerk's Department, PO Box 270, Guildhall, London EC2P 2EJ (020 7606 3030; email: sacha.than@cityoflondon.gov.uk; website: www.cityoflondon.gov.uk)

CC number: 206643

Eligibility

People in need who are, or have been, members of the City of London's Court of Common Council, and their dependants.

Types of grants

One-off grants according to need.

Annual grant total

In 2015/16 the charity had an income of £10,000 and a total expenditure of £4,500. We estimate that welfare grants to individuals totalled around £2,100, with funding also awarded to individuals for educational purposes.

Applications

In the first instance, contact the correspondent.

Other information

Dependants of members of the Court of Common Council can be supported with grants for education and training.

Environmental Health Officers Welfare Fund

See entry on page 141

Public and Commercial Services Union Benevolent Fund

£74,000

Correspondent: Chris Baugh, Assistant General Secretary, PCS Member Benefits, Freepost BFH 1003, 160 Falcon Road, London SW11 2LN (020 7801 2810 or 020 7801 2601, option 3; email: benefits@pcs.org.uk)

Eligibility

Members and associate members of the union who are suffering severe financial hardship, through sickness, family troubles or other problems. Applications will be rejected if the individual is not a fully paid-up member, or associate member, of the union. Candidates must have been members for at least six months.

Types of grants

One-off grants to a maximum of £500 in any 12-month period.

Annual grant total

Benevolent services expenditure totalled £74,000 in 2016.

Exclusions

Grants are not given for:

▶ Private debts and credit card overdrafts
▶ Medical treatment
▶ Education costs
▶ Legal expenses
▶ Strike action

Loans are not provided.

Applications

Application forms are available from the correspondent or can be downloaded from the Public and Commercial Services Union website. Completed applications should be submitted either directly by the individual/family member, or through a third party (such as a union representative) and may be emailed or posted. They are reviewed weekly.

British Association of Former United Nations Civil Servants Benevolent Fund

£2,900

Correspondent: Geoffrey Ward, Clerk to the Trustees, Margalla, Higher Gunville, Milborne Port, Sherborne DT9 5AW (01963 250206; email: geoffreyward624@aol.com; website: www.bafuncs.org/benevolent.html)

CC number: 297524

Eligibility

Former employees of the United Nations or its specialised agencies, and their dependants who are in need.

Types of grants

One-off grants, grants in kind and loans of between £100 and £500. Grants can be made towards a wide range of needs, including remedial medical and surgical attention, respite care to release a family carer, aids for people with disabilities, household aids for older people, assistance towards transport costs for hospital outpatient visits; or visits by family or a BAFUNCS member to a hospitalised patient, convalescent visits to family and remedial holidays, loans or grants to meet short-term emergencies.

Annual grant total

In 2016 the fund held assets of £584,000 and had an income of £11,100. The latest application guidelines state that 'Since 1987 up to date (October 2016) a total of £85,899 has been used to make grants'. We estimate that grants in 2016 totalled approximately £2,900.

Applications

Application forms are available on the website and are normally referred to an appropriate BAFUNCS-registered welfare officer for immediate follow-up. Applications are considered throughout the year.

Other information

The fund is also known by its short title, 'BAFUNCS Benevolent Fund'.

Civil Service

Assist Fund

£102,000

Correspondent: Council of Management, Po Box 62849, London SE1P 5AE

CC number: 251419

Eligibility

Employees and ex-employees of the Government Communications Bureau and its associated organisations, and their dependants.

Types of grants

One-off or recurrent grants and loans towards telephone bills, house repairs and so on.

Annual grant total

In 2015/16 the fund held assets of £1.85 million and had an income of £410,500. Grants to individuals totalled £102,000.

Applications

Apply in writing to the correspondent, although applications are often made by word of mouth. Applications are generally considered throughout the year.

The Benevolent Fund of the Association of Her Majesty's Inspectors of Taxes

£3,000

Correspondent: Vicky Johnson, 58 High Street, Shirley, Solihull B90 1EY (0121 624 7216)

CC number: 207206

Eligibility

Current and former tax inspectors and other senior officers in the Inland Revenue who are members of the association, and their dependants, who are ill or in need.

Types of grants

One-off grants for people on sick leave to help towards the costs of medical equipment, hospital travel and medicines.

Annual grant total

In 2015/16 the fund had an income of £7,200 and a total expenditure of £3,500. We estimate that welfare grants to individuals totalled around £3,000.

Applications

Apply in writing to the correspondent at any time. Applications can be submitted directly by the individual.

The Charity for Civil Servants

£2.61 million (3,000 grants)

Correspondent: Help and Advisory Services, Fund House, 5 Anne Boleyn's Walk, Cheam, Sutton, Surrey SM3 8DY (0800 056 2424; email: help@foryoubyyou.org.uk; website: www.foryoubyyou.org.uk)

CC number: 1136870

Eligibility

Serving and former staff of the Civil Service, and their dependants, who are in need. Individuals who work for organisations directly funded by a government department may also be eligible to apply. If you are unsure of your eligibility, contact the help service.

Types of grants

Grants, loans and allowances according to need. Grants have previously been given for: essential household bills; utilities; appliances; childcare; daily living expenses; heating repairs; home adaptations; the relief of priority debts such as rent or council tax arrears; bereavement costs (funeral costs, cremation charges and solicitor's fees); hospital visiting costs; nursing home fees; mobility equipment (hoists, ramps, mobility scooters, walking aids and wheelchairs).

Annual grant total

In 2016 the charity had assets of £40.7 million and an income of £7 million. Grants to individuals totalled more than £2.6 million and were distributed as follows:

Reduced, low and insufficient income	£762,000
Ill health	£687,000
Relationship breakdown	£318,000
Disability	£268,000
Bereavement	£266,000
Unsafe and unstable living arrangements	£110,000
Poor well-being	£106,000
Domestic abuse	£67,000
Emergency situation	£34,000

Exclusions

The charity does not help employees of the NHS, the armed forces or local authorities.

Applications

By completing the online application form. The charity runs a freephone help service (0800 056 2424 or help@ foryoubyyou.org.uk, open every working day, 8.30am to 5pm) which provides advice and information as well as assistance with completing applications.

Other information

In addition to its grant-making, the charity runs services to give advice on, for example, money issues, stress and depression, carers' support, domestic abuse and mental well-being. Details regarding the full range of services provided are available on the website.

CSIS Charity Fund

£24,500

Correspondent: Helen Harris, Secretary, 7 Colman House, King Street, Maidstone, Kent ME14 1DD (01622 766963; fax: 01622 766963; email: helenharris@csis.co.uk; website: www. csischarityfund.org)

CC number: 1121671

Eligibility

Widows/widowers of policyholders of the Civil Service Insurance Society who are in need. Other dependants may also be supported.

Types of grants

Annual grants. One-off grants are also given to help with the costs of essential household bills, the replacement of white goods, and, occasionally, to help clear debts.

Annual grant total

In 2016 the charity had assets of £2.46 million and an income of £844,500. Grants to individuals totalled £24,500.

Applications

Application forms are available to download from the website. Completed forms can be returned to the correspondent by email or post. Applicants will have their financial circumstances assessed. Sometimes applicants are referred to other organisations with which the charity works.

Other information

CSIS's activities are focused mainly on providing grants and assistance to charities and organisations working to support civil and public servants, past and present, and their dependants who are in need. The website has a helpful list of organisations with similar aims that can provide advice and financial assistance to individuals.

The Overseas Service Pensioners' Benevolent Society

£116,000 (102 grants)

Correspondent: David Le Breton, Secretary, 138 High Street, Tonbridge, Kent TN9 1AX (01732 363836; email: bensoc@ospa.org.uk; website: www.ospa. org.uk)

CC number: 235989

Eligibility

Retired members of the Overseas Service Pensioners' Association, and their dependants, who are in need. In certain circumstances those with other relevant service in the Overseas Civil Service or in a former British dependent (colonial) territory can be supported as well as the dependants of such people.

Types of grants

Grants of up to £1,500 are usually paid quarterly to help with general living expenses. Occasionally, single grants are given for special needs and towards holidays. All cases are reviewed annually.

Annual grant total

In 2016 the charity held assets of £602,000 and had an income of £36,000. During the year, the charity awarded around £116,000 in grants to 102 individuals.

Exclusions

Grants are not normally made for residential care or nursing home fees.

Applications

Application forms can be requested from the correspondent. They can be submitted directly by the individual or by a third party, such as a close relative or legal representative.

Emergency services

Avon and Somerset Constabulary Benevolent Fund

£29,500

Correspondent: Caroline Peters, Company Secretary, PO Box 37, Valley Road, Portishead, Bristol BS20 8QJ (01275 816905; email: caroline.peters@ avonandsomerset.police.uk)

CC number: 1085497

Eligibility

Mainly serving and retired members of the Avon and Somerset Constabulary who are in need. Their dependants may also be supported.

Types of grants

One-off grants and interest-free loans are also available to cover debts or other urgent needs.

Annual grant total

In 2016 the fund held assets of £1.1 million and had an income of £48,000. Grants and donations to individuals totalled £29,500.

Applications

Applications must be submitted with a report and recommendation by a force welfare officer. They can be considered at any time.

Blackstock Trust
See entry on page 205

PC David Rathband's Blue Lamp Foundation

£2,000

Correspondent: Peter Sweeney, Trustee, Blue Lamp Foundation, PO Box 219, Newbiggin-by-the-Sea NE63 3FD (0871 234 5999; email: info@ bluelampfoundation.org; website: www. bluelamp-foundation.org)

CC number: 1138319

Eligibility
All operational personnel of the United Kingdom's police, fire and ambulance services who work on either a full-time, part-time or voluntary basis, who become injured while carrying out their duty.

Types of grants
The foundation makes four types of grants:

Re-enablement grants – suited to those who have been unable to work or are medically retired, this grant will help relieve financial burdens following a serious injury.

Specialist grant – help with adaptations or treatment for people who are seriously injured or incapacitated.

Immediacy grant – support to allow recipients to claim back the expenses that were incurred during the immediate aftermath of their injury.

Bereavement grant – assistance with funeral expenses.

Annual grant total
In 2015/16 the foundation had an income of £16,200 and a total expenditure of £153,500. We estimate that grants given to individuals totalled around £2,000.

Applications
Applications can be made through the foundation's website. Application forms are also available to download from the website.

Derbyshire Special Constabulary Benevolent Fund

£500

Correspondent: John Grubb, 23 Arbour Close, Chesterfield S41 0LG (01246 272460; email: thegrubbs@uwclub.net)

CC number: 213049

Eligibility
Any serving member of Derbyshire Special Constabulary or ex-member who resigned on the grounds of ill health, injury or reaching the age limit, and their dependants.

Types of grants
One-off grants according to need.

Annual grant total
In 2016/17 the fund had an income of £1,900 and a total expenditure of £530. We estimate that grants given to individuals totalled around £500.

Applications
Apply in writing to the correspondent.

Essex Police Force Benevolent Fund

£35,000 (33 grants)

Correspondent: Iain Logan, PO Box 2, Chelmsford CM2 6DA (email: loganiain@yahoo.co.uk)

CC number: 258273

Eligibility
Members and retired members of Essex Police and their dependants.

Types of grants
One-off according to need.

Annual grant total
In 2016/17 the fund held assets of £1.1 million and had an income of £52,500. Grants to individuals totalled £35,000.

Applications
Apply in writing to the correspondent.

Essex Police Support Staff Benevolent Fund

£4,100

Correspondent: Barry Faber, Trustee, Essex Police Headquarters, PO Box 2, Chelmsford CM2 6DA (01245 452597; email: jan.pyner@essex.pnn.police.uk)

CC number: 269890

Eligibility
People in need who work or worked full or part-time for Essex Police Authority, and their dependants.

Types of grants
One-off grants or loans for essential needs such as travel expenses for hospital visits and unforeseen bills such as car repairs.

Annual grant total
In 2016/17 the charity had an income of £5,100 and a total expenditure of £4,300. We estimate that grants given to individuals totalled £4,100.

Exclusions
Grants are not made for medical treatment.

Applications
Individuals should apply through the benevolent fund representative of their division or subdivision of Essex Police Authority. Applications are considered quarterly, but can be considered more quickly in emergencies.

The British Fire Services Association Members Welfare Fund

£11,500

Correspondent: George Halstead, Trustee, Copthorne, 9 Home Farm Close, Wray, Lancaster LA2 8RG (01524 221141; email: welfare.bfsa@btinternet. com; website: bfsa.org.uk/membership/ members-welfare-fund)

CC number: 216011

Eligibility
Firefighters and ex-firefighters who have held BFSA membership, and their dependants.

Types of grants
The Members Welfare Fund assists members, ex-members and their dependants. Assistance may be in the form of one-off grants to aid the purchase of mobility items, electrical appliances, furniture or repairs. Alternatively, the Management Committee of the fund may consider long-term maintenance grants, to those on a limited income.

Annual grant total
In 2015 the fund had an income of £59,000 and total expenditure of £23,000. Grants to individuals totalled £11,500.

Applications
Apply in writing to the correspondent, including details of income and expenditure and a record of fire service employment. Applicants are usually visited at home by a representative of the fund to assess their needs.

Other information
The fund has frozen its list of regular beneficiaries (currently 13) to enable more one-off grants to be made to a wider range of beneficiaries.

The Gurney Fund

£408,500

Correspondent: Christine McNicol, Director, 9 Bath Road, Worthing, West Sussex BN11 3NU (01903 237256; email: Contact form on website; website: www. gurneyfund.org)

CC number: 1156903

Eligibility

Children of police officers who have died or taken early retirement on ill health grounds within the 22 subscribing forces in England and Wales.

Types of grants

Weekly allowances paid quarterly. Additional assistance may also be available for educational trips (excluding skiing), musical instruments and tuition, books, school uniform and driving lessons.

Annual grant total

In 2016/17 the fund had assets of £9.1 million and an income of £500,000. Grants and allowances to children totalled £408,500.

Applications

Applications can be made via the fund's website.

Hampshire Constabulary Welfare Fund

£21,500 (32 grants)

Correspondent: Paul Robertson, Trustee, Federation House, 440 The Grange, Romsey Road, Romsey SO51 0AE (023 8067 4397; email: hampshire@polfed.org; website: www. hampshirepolfed.org.uk/services/welfare. htm)

CC number: 291061

Eligibility

Members, pensioners and civilian employees of the Hampshire Constabulary and their dependants. Assistance may also be available to special constables injured during police duty.

Types of grants

One-off and recurrent grants or loans to help support people experiencing a family crisis or recovering from injury or illness. Past grants have been given towards stairlifts, bath-lifts, car repairs, divorce fees, relationship breakdowns, unmanageable debt, wheelchairs, respite holidays and general living costs.

Annual grant total

In 2015/16 the fund held assets of £486,000 and had an income of £248,500. During the year, 32 grants were awarded totalling £21,500 and the average grant amount was about £2,000. A further eight loans were made totalling £21,000 and the average loan amount was about £1,750.

Applications

Application forms are available to download from the Hampshire Police Federation website. Applicants are requested to provide at least two quotes for amounts above £2,000 and one quote for amounts below £2,000. If a grant is for medical purposes, applicants should provide as much relevant information as possible, such as medical reports, occupational therapy reports and other supporting information. Details of any other agencies or charities that have been approached for funding must be provided. Applications are considered on a regular basis and eligible applicants may be contacted for further information. Urgent applications can be fast-tracked.

Other information

The trust also donates to other charitable trusts and organisations which support police officers.

Humberside Police Welfare and Benevolent Fund

£21,000

Correspondent: The Trustees, Humberside Police, Courtland Road, Hull HU6 8AW (08456060 222; email: webmail@humberside.pnn.police.uk)

CC number: 503762

Eligibility

Serving and retired officers of the Humberside Police and retired officers from other forces who live in Humberside, and their partners and dependants; and civilian employees of Humberside Police Authority, retired civilian employees and their partners and dependants.

Types of grants

One-off and recurrent grants. Loans are also available.

Annual grant total

In 2016 the fund had an income of £9,900 and a total expenditure of £22,600. We estimate that grants given to individuals totalled £21,000.

Applications

Apply in writing to the correspondent at any time, either through the branch/ divisional representative or the headquarters.

Metropolitan Police Benevolent Fund

(37 grants)

Correspondent: Natasha Raj, Secretary, Charities Section, 9th Floor, Metropolitan Police Services, Empress State Building, Lillie Road, London SW6 1TR (020 7161 1481; email: natasha.p.raj@met.police.uk; website: www.met.police.uk)

CC number: 1125409

Eligibility

Current and former officers of the Metropolitan Police and their dependants, who are in need.

Types of grants

Generally one-off grants according to need. Support can be given for bereavement expenses, building repairs and alterations, furniture and other household necessities, payment of debts and so on. Interest-free loans are also offered.

Annual grant total

In 2016 the charity had assets of £4.4 million and an income of £2.9 million. According to the annual report for 2016, the charity spent £164,000 on 'Officers and former officers (and their dependants) of the MPS'. We have taken this figure to include loans as well as grants; however, we were unable to determine the proportion attributed to each.

The annual report provided the following information:

In 2016 a total of 73 (2015: 79) applications were reviewed by the Relief Board. Of these 37 (2015: 44) were awarded a grant, 17 (2015: 30) were awarded a loan and 19 (2015: 5) were declined. There were 48 new applicants to the Charity and of the 25 return applicants, the majority were making a second application.

Applications

The individual should apply directly to the correspondent in writing. Applications are considered throughout the year.

Other information

The charity was created in 2008 following the amalgamation of four former charities (Metropolitan Police Convalescent Home Fund, Metropolitan Police Widows' and Widowers' Fund, Metropolitan Police Relief Fund and Metropolitan Police Combined Fund).

Grants are also made to other organisations supporting police officers and their families. Officers are also allowed free access to Flint House, the police rehabilitation centre in Goring.

Metropolitan Police Staff Welfare Fund

£15,400

Correspondent: William Tarrant, Charities Officer, Charities Section, Metropolitan Police Service, 10th Floor (East), Empress State Building, Lillie Road, London SW6 1TR (020 7161 1667; email: william.tarrant@met.police.uk)

CC number: 282375

Eligibility

Members and past members of the Metropolitan Police Staff and the Metropolitan Police Authority and their families and dependants who are in need.

Types of grants

One-off grants ranging from £100 to £2,000.

Annual grant total

In 2016/17 the fund held assets of £252,500 and had an income of £28,500. During the year, the fund gave around £15,400 in grants to individuals and £9,900 in welfare loans.

Exclusions

Grants are unlikely to be made towards private healthcare, private education fees, legal costs, business debts or bills that have already been paid.

Applications

Application forms are available from the correspondent. Applications should be submitted directly by the individual or, where applicable, through a social worker, Citizens Advice or other welfare agency.

Norfolk Constabulary Benevolent Fund

£11,800 (12 grants)

Correspondent: James Brown, Jubilee House, Falconers House, Wymondham NR18 0WW (0845 456 4567; email: benevolentfund@norfolk.pnn.police.uk)

CC number: 257462

Eligibility

Members and former members of the fund and their orphans, widows and dependants.

Types of grants

One-off grants according to need.

Annual grant total

In 2016/17 the fund held assets of £119,500 and had an income of £41,500. Grants to 12 individuals totalled £11,800.

Applications

Apply in writing to the correspondent.

North East Scotland Police Welfare Fund (NESPWF)

£4,700

Correspondent: Ron Findlay, Secretary, 21 Lochside Drive, Bridge of Don, Aberdeen AB23 8EH (email: secretary@nespwf.org.uk; website: www.nespwf.org.uk)

OSCR number: SC044963

Eligibility

Members of the NESPWF, former officers and support staff of Grampian Police or its constituent forces, or any future police divisions covering north east Scotland. Widows or widowers, and/or the dependants, of former officers or members are also eligible for support.

Types of grants

Supermarket vouchers and one-off grants according to need. Loans are also available.

Annual grant total

In 2015/16 the fund had an income of £29,500 and a total expenditure of £4,700. During the year, the fund supported a child that needed overseas treatment and provided over 100 supermarket vouchers to widows over the festive period.

Applications

Requests for help can be made by contacting the correspondent or completing a form on the fund's website. Applications can be made by members of the NESPWF or by family members or dependants. A welfare adviser or trustee will then visit the applicant to assess how the fund may help. The website notes that persons 'who are not yet members may apply to join immediately'.

The North Wales Police Benevolent Fund

£21,000

Correspondent: Mel Jones, North Wales Police Federation, 311 Abergele Road, Old Colwyn, Colwyn Bay LL29 9YF (01492 805404; email: mel.jones@nthwales.pnn.police.uk)

CC number: 505321

Eligibility

Members and former members of the North Wales Police Force, former members of previous forces amalgamated to form the North Wales Police, and their families and immediate dependants who are in need.

Types of grants

One-off and recurrent grants are given according to need. Grants are also made at Christmas.

Annual grant total

In 2016/17 the fund had an income of £11,800 and a total expenditure of £21,500. We estimate that grants given to individuals totalled around £21,000.

Applications

Apply in writing to the correspondent. Applications are considered quarterly, although urgent appeals can be considered as they arrive.

The North West Police Benevolent Fund

£107,500

Correspondent: Jackie Smithies, Trustee, St Michael's Lodge, Northcote Road, Langho BB6 8BG (01254 244980; email: jsmithies@nwpbf.org; website: www.nwpbf.org)

CC number: 503045

Eligibility

Serving and retired officers of Cheshire Constabulary, Greater Manchester Police, Lancashire Constabulary, Cumbria Constabulary, Merseyside Police, NCA and previous police forces amalgamated within the constituent forces, together with their dependants, who are in a condition of need and hardship. Former officers of the above forces may be considered at the trustees' discretion.

Types of grants

One-off or recurrent grants and interest-free loans are given for convalescence, medical and disability equipment (but not for private health care) or to help in other cases of need arising from unforeseen circumstances. Outpatient physiotherapy is also available at five locations.

In the event of the death of a serving police officer a grant of £5,000 is paid to the dependant family.

Annual grant total

In 2016 the fund had assets of £6.7 million and an income of £1.2 million. Welfare grants were made totalling £107,500. Support was given in the following categories:

Serving officers	£55,000
Death benefits	£30,000
Retirees	£19,500
Attendance at convalescent homes	£3,100
Christmas grants to pensioners and widows	£250

Exclusions

No grants are available for private health, education or legal fees.

Applications

Application forms are available from the correspondent. They are usually made through a force welfare officer or a member of the management committee.

Other information

The fund does not give grants to organisations but does contribute to other police funds and convalescent homes. Members are also able to use the police treatment centres or holiday lodges. See the website for further details.

Northern Ireland Police Fund

£1.7 million

Correspondent: The Secretary, Maryfield Complex, 100 Belfast Road, Holywood BT18 9QY (028 9039 3556; email: admin@nipolicefund.org; website: www. nipolicefund.org)

Eligibility

Serving and retired police officers in Northern Ireland, and their dependants, who have been directly affected by terrorist violence whether on or off-duty. This includes those with serious physical and/or psychological injuries which would be considered sufficiently serious to warrant the award of an IOD Band 2 medical discharge, as determined by an occupational physician. The applicant must also be able to demonstrate that the IOD was a result of the individual being the directly intended target of a terrorist attack. Applications are also considered from the families of officers who have committed suicide if a causal link can be established between a direct attack on the officer and their subsequent death.

Types of grants

Our research indicates that regular grants are given to those on a very low income and one-off grants are administered through a number of separate schemes. Contact the correspondent for more information.

Annual grant total

In previous years, grants have totalled around £1.7 million.

Exclusions

Once an application has been approved the applicant must wait 12 months before reapplying. Applicants cannot reapply for the same item if their first request has been declined nor can applications be split into separate parts to avoid the capping of awards.

Applications

Contact the correspondent for more information.

Other information

The fund was established in 2001 following the Patten Report into policing in Northern Ireland

In addition, the fund has a team of four occupational therapists who support clients.

Nottinghamshire Constabulary Benevolent Fund

£26,000

Correspondent: Andrew Roberts, West Bridgford Police Station, Rectory Road, West Bridgford, Nottingham NG2 6BN (07966 784118; email: andy.roberts@ nottinghamshire.pnn.police.uk)

CC number: 256806

Eligibility

Members of the fund and their widows, children and dependants.

Types of grants

One-off grants according to need.

Annual grant total

In 2016/17 the fund had assets of £294,000 and an income of £32,000. Grants to individuals totalled £26,000.

Applications

Apply in writing to the correspondent.

The Police Dependants' Trust Ltd

£254,500 (117 grants)

Correspondent: Welfare Team, 3 Mount Mews, High Street, Hampton, Middlesex TW12 2SH (020 8941 6907; email: office@pdtrust.org; website: www. pdtrust.org)

CC number: 1151322

Eligibility

Dependants of current or former police officers who have died or been incapacitated as a result of injuries received in the execution of their duties, or their dependants. Eligible officers include:

- Members of the British Transport Police
- Members of the Civil Nuclear Constabulary
- People performing temporary overseas or central police force duties who enjoy a statutory right of reversion to such a police force
- Special Constables appointed for any such police area
- Police cadets appointed to undergo training with a view to becoming members of such police forces

Grants are not restricted to those individuals who are living in the UK – if applicants have moved but would otherwise be eligible, they can still apply.

Types of grants

One-off grants for the following:

- Assistance Grants – to enable police officers and their families to maintain independence and improve their well-being. Grants can cover the following: specialist equipment, mobility aids, home adaptations, retraining and vocational training, extracurricular activities for children, or help towards the incidental costs of social activities and trips
- Maintenance Grants – regular annual benefits to those on low incomes. **Note:** This is a historic programme, new applicants must apply through the Assistance Grant programme
- Bereavement Grants – to assist families or next of kin following a police officer's death as a result of their duty

Support can include awards towards furniture and household appliances, essentials, for example, food and clothing, set-up costs to help with rented accommodation or to participate in sports and hobbies.

Annual grant total

In 2015/16 the trust held assets of £26.7 million and had an income of £982,000. There were 117 grants made totalling £254,500. Support was allocated as follows:

Maintenance Grants	48	£155,500
Assistance Grants	35	£94,500
Bereavement Grants	1	£4,000
Elderly Grants	-	£650

During the year, 35 Christmas grants were made totalling £4,800. Grants ranged from £100 to £12,500.

Exclusions

Grants are not normally awarded to individuals to:

- Help where state assistance or statutory services are available
- Repay debts
- Cover legal expenses such as county court costs and solicitor's fees
- Help in the form of a loan
- Assist with medical care
- Help where the impact of an injury was temporary (unless exceptional circumstances apply)

Applications

Application forms are available on the trust's website or from the correspondent. They can be submitted at any time but all applicants must first register with the trust. Supporting materials may be required. Applications are generally considered every month although urgent cases can be addressed between meetings. Generally applications are received, processed and concluded within 28 days. Accompanying guidance notes are also available on the website.

Other information

The trust offers support for both welfare and educational needs. The website notes that the trust 'also administers the National Police Fund, which shares broadly the same eligibility criteria i.e. financial support is provided to the families/dependants of police officers who have been killed or injured on duty, and this support is provided on the basis of need'. The National Police Fund provides grants to:

- Police dependants who are in further education (university degree or vocational qualification)
- Widows and orphans of police officers who were below inspector level at the time of their death or medical retirement (through the Mary Holt Fund)
- Police benevolent funds or sports/social clubs
- Police charities and other bodies which assist the police services

Port of London Authority Police Charity Fund

£4,300

Correspondent: Chair to the Board of Trustees, 14 Bedford Close, Rayleigh, Essex SS6 7QR (01268 777061; email: barry.smith@potll.com)

CC number: 265569

Eligibility

Former officers who have served in the port authority's police force, and their dependants.

Types of grants

One-off grants are given to help those in financial need.

Annual grant total

In 2016/17 the fund had an income of £700 and a total expenditure of £4,500. We estimate that the fund awarded around £4,300 in grants to individuals.

Applications

Apply in writing to the correspondent.

South Central Ambulance Service (Incorporating Hampshire Ambulance Service) Benevolent Fund

£5,800

Correspondent: Philip Pimlott, Trustee, 29 Beech Avenue, Lane End, High Wycombe HP14 3EQ (01494 881986)

CC number: 1041811

Eligibility

Serving and retired members of Hampshire Ambulance Service/South Central Ambulance Service NHS Trust and their dependants.

Types of grants

One-off grants according to need.

Annual grant total

In 2016/17 the fund had an income of £8,200 and a total expenditure of £6,200. We estimate that welfare grants to individuals totalled £5,800.

Applications

Apply in writing to the correspondent.

The South Wales Police Benevolent Fund

£40,000 (44 grants)

Correspondent: Head of Performance Management, Police HQ, Cowbridge Road, Bridgend CF31 3SU (01656 869342; website: www.south-wales.police.uk)

CC number: 501454

Eligibility

Serving and former members of the South Wales police force and their widows/widowers, civil partners and dependants who are in need.

Types of grants

One-off grants according to need. The annual report for 2016/17 notes that the 'majority of benevolent payments are still made to support some serving members who have been placed in considerable financial difficulty during periods of protracted sickness'.

Annual grant total

In 2016/17 the fund had assets of £728,500 and an income of £44,500. Grants to individuals totalled £40,000; benevolence assistance payments to 13 individuals totalled almost £31,000, and 31 death benefits amounted to £9,300.

Applications

Apply on a form available from the fund's in-house website or from the correspondent.

St George's Police Children Trust

£426,000

Correspondent: Peter Moore, Northern Police Convalescent Home, St Andrews, Harlow Moor Road, Harrogate HG2 0AD (01423 504448; email: enquiries@thepolicetreatmentcentres.org; website: www.stgeorgespolicechildrentrust.org)

CC number: 1147445/SC043652

Eligibility

Young people who are in full-time education and are the children of serving or retired officers who were members of a police force covered by the trust (see 'Other Information'), and who are now deceased or have been incapacitated while on duty and can no longer work. Young people not in full-time education who have lost a police officer parent but who are unable to earn their own living as a result of having special needs, may also be eligible.

Note: usually, to be eligible, the police officer parent must have donated to the trust while serving.

Types of grants

One-off and recurrent grants. The amount awarded is dependent upon household income and the potential need or hardship. Registration grants of £100 are given to all eligible applicants before full consideration at the trustees' meeting.

The trust offers:

- **St George's Police Children Trust Grants** – available to eligible beneficiaries in full-time education to statutory school leaving age, or up to the end of the school year in which they turn 19 years of age
- **Child Counselling Grants** – financial support to all beneficiaries who wish to access counselling to support a young person up to the age of 25, through a bereavement or difficult time
- **Driving Lesson Grants** – young people from the age of 17 up to the age of 25 to help with the cost of learning to drive
- **Special Needs Grants** – to children who are deemed as having a special need, i.e. are in receipt of the 'children's award' as defined in the police pensions regulations (poof of receipt will be required)

Annual grant total

In 2016 the charity held assets of £12.8 million and had an income of £966,500. During the year, the charity gave almost £852,500 in grants to individuals. We estimate that the trust gave around £426,000 in grants to individuals for welfare purposes, with educational grants also awarded.

Exclusions

People in education beyond first degree level cannot be assisted. Grants are not made for gap year activities. If applicants are applying for a Further Education Grant after a gap year, note that their applications can only be considered after a single gap period from education of not more than one year. The trust does not pay allowances or grants where the beneficiary is in work and earning money.

Applications

Application forms are available to download from the website or can be requested from Police Federation representatives or Police Force Benevolent Funds. They have to be submitted via the police force in which the parent served and **not** directly to the trust. This is usually done through the police federation office, the occupational health and welfare department or occasionally the force benevolent fund. Requests should be accompanied by relevant documentation.

Other information

The website notes that the foundation for The St George's Police Children Trust was laid by Catherine Gurney who opened Northern Police Orphanage in 1898 'for the care and welfare of Northern Police Force children who had lost one or both parents'. In the second half of the twentieth century, the orphanage was closed and St George's Fund and the Northern Police Orphans Trust, both providing grants to police officers children, were formed. The two charities merged in 2006 to form St George's Police Trust.

The trust covers the following police forces: Cheshire; Cleveland; Cumbria; Derbyshire; Durham; Greater Manchester Police; Humberside; Lancashire; Lincolnshire; Merseyside; Northumbria; North Wales; North Yorkshire; Nottinghamshire; Police Service of Scotland; South Yorkshire; Staffordshire; West Mercia; West Yorkshire. The accounts state that 'the number of serving police officers in this catchment area is now approximately 63,000 and the number of police offices making the voluntary donation is around 37,000 (the number of retired police officers is likely to be similar)'.

Suffolk Constabulary Benevolent Fund

£18,200

Correspondent: Trevor Barnes, Trustee, Suffolk Constabulary Headquarters, Potal Avenue, Martlesham Heath, Ipswich IP5 3QS (01473 613641; email: trevor.barnes@suffolk.pnn.police.uk)

CC number: 253149

Eligibility

Members of the fund and their dependants who are in need.

Types of grants

One-off grants according to need and pensions.

Annual grant total

In 2015/16 the fund had an income of £29,500 and a total expenditure of £32,000. Grants to individuals totalled £18,200.

Applications

Apply in writing to the correspondent.

Sussex Police Charitable Trust

£56,000

Correspondent: Lorna Stagg, Malling House, Church Lane, Lewes, East Sussex BN7 2DZ (101 ext. 544133; email: spct@sussex.pnn.police.uk; website: www.sussex.police.uk/SPCT)

CC number: 257564

Eligibility

Members of the Sussex Police Welfare Fund who are in need, and their dependants.

Types of grants

One-off grants towards, for example, hospital travel and parking costs, emergency accommodation, essential household items, mobility problems and emergency childcare. Assistance is also given to facilitate mediation and initial legal advice.

Annual grant total

In 2016 the fund held assets of £1.7 million and had an income of £180,000. Grants were paid totalling £56,000. Although the fund's Charity Commission record states that it also makes grants to organisations, we estimate that all grants expenditure went to individuals.

Applications

Apply by calling, emailing or writing to the fund. Cases will be dealt with by a trust adviser who will work with applicants to address their problems.

Other information

The trust owns a bungalow in Dorset which is available to members in need of a recuperative break.

The Thames Valley Police Benevolent Fund

£92,000

Correspondent: Simon Townsend, Thames Valley Police Finance Accounting, PO Box 238, Kidlington OX5 1XS (01865 855458; email: simon.townsend2@thamesvalley.pnn.police.uk)

CC number: 256865

Eligibility

Police officers who are serving or retired members of the fund and their widows, widowers and dependants.

Types of grants

One-off grants according to need.

Annual grant total

In 2016/17 the fund had assets of £990,500 and an income of £124,000. Grants to individuals totalled £92,000.

Applications

Apply in writing to the correspondent.

The Royal Ulster Constabulary GC – Police Service of Northern Ireland Benevolent Fund
See entry on page 192

West Yorkshire Police (Employees) Benevolent Fund

£2,000

Correspondent: Pat Maknia, Finance Department, PO Box 9, Wakefield, West Yorkshire WF1 3QP (01924 292841; email: diane.nelson@westyorkshire.pnn.police.uk)

CC number: 701817

Eligibility

Employees and ex-employees of the West Yorkshire Police Force or the West Yorkshire Metropolitan County Council under the direct control of the chief constable who are in need, and their widows, orphans and other dependants.

Types of grants

One-off and ongoing grants are given according to need.

Annual grant total

In 2016/17 the fund had an income of £4,300 and a total expenditure of £2,100. We estimate that grants given to individuals totalled around £2,000.

Applications

Apply in writing to the correspondent.

The West Yorkshire Police Benevolent and Loans Fund

£17,600

Correspondent: Catherine Laverick, Finance Department, Laburnum Road, Wakefield WF1 3QP (email: catherine. laverick@westyorkshire.pnn.police.uk)

CC number: 505514

Eligibility

Serving or former members of the force and their dependants.

Types of grants

One-off grants according to need.

Annual grant total

In 2016/17 the fund held assets of £705,500 and had an income of £36,000. Grants to individuals totalled £17,600.

Applications

Apply in writing to the correspondent.

Wiltshire Ambulance Service Benevolent Fund

£5,000

Correspondent: Andrew Newman, Treasurer, 82 Dunch Lane, Melksham, Wiltshire SN12 8DX (07966 534713; email: charliecopter@msn.com)

CC number: 280364

Eligibility

Serving and retired members of the Wiltshire Ambulance Service and their dependants.

Types of grants

One-off and recurrent grants are given according to need.

Annual grant total

In 2015/16 the fund had an income of £22,000 and a total expenditure of £23,000. We estimate that grants given to individuals totalled around £5,000.

Applications

Our previous research indicates that applicants should contact their station's benevolent fund representative, which will then contact the chair on their behalf.

Other information

The fund also owns and supports three properties that provide convalescence.

Wiltshire Police Benevolent Trust

£5,800

Correspondent: Mr G. S. Williams, Trustee, 3 Brookside, Hullavington, Chippenham SN14 6HD (email:federation@wiltshire.pnn.police.uk)

CC number: 1117765

Eligibility

Serving and retired Wiltshire Police staff, special constables and their dependants.

Types of grants

One-off grants according to need.

Annual grant total

In 2016/17 the trust had assets of £324,000 and an income of £13,300. Grants to individuals totalled £5,800.

Applications

Apply in writing to the correspondent.

Prison services

The Edridge Fund

£33,000 (85 grants)

Correspondent: Karen Monaghan, 160 Falcon Road, Battersea, London SW11 2NY (020 7223 4887; email: edridge.secretary@edridgefund.org; website: www.edridgefund.org)

CC number: 803493

Eligibility

Members and ex-members of the probation service and family court services who are (or were) eligible to be members of Napo, and their dependants.

Types of grants

Financial and welfare support, generally one-off grants, to alleviate cases of distress and hardship. Applications are assessed individually and grants are designed to help towards the applicant's specific requirements.

Annual grant total

In 2016 the charity had assets of £206,500 and an income of £43,000. During the year, the charity awarded £33,000 in grants to 85 individuals.

Applications

Application forms are available online, and can be completed on the website or downloaded and returned by email or post.

Other information

The charity also makes donations to organisations.

Scottish Prison Service Benevolent Fund

£20,000

Correspondent: The Trustees, HMP Glenochil, King O. Muirs Road, Glenochil FK10 3AD

OSCR number: SC021603

Eligibility

Scottish prison officers, both serving and retired, and their families who are in need.

Types of grants

One-off and recurrent grants are given according to need.

Annual grant total

In 2016/17 the fund had an income of £23,500 and a total expenditure of £25,000. We estimate that grants given to individuals totalled around £20,000.

Applications

Apply in writing to the correspondent.

Social services

Social Workers Benevolent Trust

£42,500 (92 grants)

Correspondent: Carol Dutton, Hon. Applications Secretary, Wellesley House, 37 Waterloo Street, Birmingham B2 5PP (0121 622 3911; email: swbt@basw.co.uk; website: www.swbt.org)

CC number: 262889

Eligibility

Social workers who hold a professional social work qualification and are experiencing financial difficulties, and their dependants. Unqualified social workers may also be considered depending upon the nature and length of their employment.

Types of grants

One-off grants are given for specific small debts and purchases.

Annual grant total

In 2015/16 the trust had assets of £234,500 and an income of £55,000. During the year, the trust awarded £42,500 in grants to 92 individuals.

Exclusions

Grants are not normally made for training or private education costs, health or social care, or supplementing income to cover daily living expenses.

Applications

Apply on a form available from the correspondent or to download from the website. Applications should be submitted directly by the individual and are considered bi-monthly.

Religion

Frances Ashton's Charity

£50,000 (60 grants)

Correspondent: Georgina Fowle, Grants Administrator, Beech House, Woolston, North Cadbury, Somerset BA22 7BJ (07775 717606; email: francesashton@ hotmail.co.uk; website: www. francesashton.co.uk)

CC number: 200162

Eligibility

Serving and retired Church of England clergy, or their widows/widowers, who are in need.

Types of grants

One-off grants. The trust has a number of areas of priority including emergency, medical or care needs.

Annual grant total

In 2015 the charity had assets of nearly £1.8 million and an income of £69,500. Grants were made to 60 individuals totalling £50,000.

Exclusions

Grants are not given towards: property purchase; school fees, private education or higher education costs (unless the child has a disability); sabbatical expenses; credit card debts and loans; general living expenses; parochial expenses.

Applications

Application forms are available from the correspondent. Applications should be submitted directly by the individual, usually by the beginning of June each year. Applications are considered at the autumn meeting of the trustees but urgent cases may be dealt with when they arise.

Other information

The charity also awards an annual grant to the charity Royal London Society (now merged with St Giles Trust) for £95 to support ex-offenders and their families in need.

Archdeaconry of Bath Clerical Families Fund

£2,200

Correspondent: The Trustees, The Bath and Wells Diocesan Board of Finance, The Old Deanery, Wells, Somerset BA5 2UG (01749 670777)

CC number: 230676

Eligibility

Widows and children of clergymen who have died and who last served in the deaneries of Bath, Chew Magna and Portishead.

Types of grants

One-off and recurrent grants are given according to need.

Annual grant total

In 2015/16 the fund had an income of £4,200 and a total expenditure of £2,200. We have estimated that around £2,200 was given in grants to individuals for social welfare purposes.

Applications

Apply in writing to the correspondent.

The Bible Preaching Trust

£5,500

Correspondent: Richard Mayers, Trustee, 34 Barleyfields, Didcot OX11 0BJ (01235 799219; email: richard. mayers@tesco.net)

CC number: 262160

Eligibility

Ministers of the Evangelical Christian faith who are in need. Theological students may occasionally benefit.

Types of grants

One-off grants.

Annual grant total

In 2015/16 the trust had an income of £9,000 and a total expenditure of £6,500. We have estimated the grant total to be £5,500.

Applications

Apply in writing to the correspondent.

Bishop of Lincoln's Discretionary Fund

£16,100

Correspondent: Revd Sally-Anne McDougall, Trustee, The Bishop's Office, The Old Palace, Minster Yard, Lincoln LN2 1PU

CC number: 1022582

Eligibility

Ministers of the Church of England who live and work in the Diocese of Lincoln, and their dependants.

Types of grants

One-off grants to assist sick clergy and their families.

Annual grant total

In 2015 the fund held assets of £61,500 and had an income of £30,500. Grants to individuals totalled £16,100 and grants awarded to organisations totalled £3,000.

Applications

Applications can be made in writing by the individual or one of the other local bishops to the Bishop of Lincoln. Applications are considered throughout the year.

Children of the Clergy Trust

£1,500

Correspondent: Revd I. Thomson, 4 Keirhill Gardens, Westhill, Aberdeenshire AB32 6AZ

OSCR number: SC001845

Eligibility

Children of deceased ministers of the Church of Scotland.

Types of grants

Grants are given according to need.

Annual grant total

In 2016 the trust had an income of £2,300 and a total expenditure of £3,300. We estimate that welfare grants totalled around £1,500, with funding also awarded for educational purposes.

Applications

Apply in writing to the correspondent. Applications should be submitted directly by the individual and should include information about the applicant's ministerial parent, general family circumstances and other relevant information.

Other information

The trust is known as the Synod of Grampian Children of the Clergy Trust.

Christadelphian Benevolent Fund

£277,000

Correspondent: David Ensell, Westhaven House, Arleston Way, Shirley, Solihull, West Midlands B90 4LH (0121 713 7100; website: christadelphianbf.com)

CC number: 222416

Eligibility

Members of the Christadelphian body who are experiencing difficult times and their families regardless of age.

Types of grants

One-off and recurrent grants are given according to need (listed below). Interest-free loans are also available in case unexpected problems arise. Irregular compassionate grants are given to individuals on the basis of representations made by the ecclesia of which those individuals are members.

- Help with fuel and water bills: grants of up to £300 towards fuel bills and up to £200 towards water bill
- Help with holidays and respite care: grants of up to £300 per person per week for a maximum of two weeks, and up to £200 per person towards the cost of travel
- Help with nursing and residential care in Christadelphian Care Homes: help through quarterly grants directly to CCH

Annual grant total

In 2016 the trust held assets of almost £3 million and had an income of £158,000. Grants to individuals totalled £277,000 and were distributed as follows:

Residential care costs	£155,000
Compassionate grants	£48,300
Regular grants	£21,000
Annual holiday scheme	£20,000
Fuel aid	£18,600
WaterAid	£10,800
Christmas grants	£3,500

Applications

Applicants should contact the Recording Brother or Secretary at their home ecclesia. They can offer local help, and will contact the charity for additional support if necessary.

The Church of England Pensions Board

£123,000

Correspondent: Lee Marshall, 29 Great Smith Street, London SW1P 3PS (020 7898 1000; email: housing@churchofengland.org; website: www.cofe.anglican.org/about/cepb)

CC number: 236627

Eligibility

Retired clergy and licensed lay workers of the Church of England, their widows, widowers and dependants.

Types of grants

Allowances for those participating in the retirement housing scheme and to clergy widows and widowers to supplement their low income. The standard of 'low income' is reviewed annually. Our research suggests that no new grants are made for assistance with private nursing or retirement care.

Annual grant total

In 2016 the board had assets of almost £118.7 million and an income of almost £28.4 million. A total of £123,000 was awarded in grants.

Applications

Application forms can be requested from the correspondent.

Other information

The trust's main concern is the administration of the pension scheme and the provision of supported housing and nursing care. It operates seven such complexes across the country. The trust also runs a retirement housing scheme which offers mortgages and loans to assist those vacating 'tied' housing.

The Clergy Rest Fund

£15,000 (15 grants)

Correspondent: R. H. A. MacDonald, Wickworth Sherwood LLP, Minerva House, 3–5 Montague Close, London SE1 9BB (020 7593 5000)

CC number: 233436

Eligibility

Church of England clergy who are in need.

Types of grants

One-off grants ranging from £500 to £1,500 for a variety of needs. In 2016 all grants paid were £1,000.

Annual grant total

In 2016 the fund had assets of £1 million and an income of £56,000. During the year, £15,000 was awarded to 15 members of the clergy.

Applications

Applications should be made in writing to the correspondent, detailing why the grant is needed.

Other information

The fund also makes grants to institutions connected with the Church of England.

The Collier Charitable Trust

£6,000

Correspondent: Michael Blagden, Cherry Tree Cottage, Old Kiln Lane, Churt, Farnham, Surrey GU10 2HX (01428 717534)

CC number: 251333

Eligibility

Retired Christian missionaries and teachers in the UK and overseas.

Types of grants

One-off and recurrent grants of around £300 each. The trust also provides accommodation.

Annual grant total

In 2016 the trust had an income of £6,000 and a total expenditure of £61,000. Previous research indicates around 10% of the total expenditure is spent on grants for individuals, therefore we estimate that £6,000 was awarded.

Applications

Apply in writing to the correspondent.

Other information

The trust can also make grants to organisations, although the trustees prefer to support charities that they already know.

The Cornwall Retired Clergy, Widows of the Clergy and their Dependants Fund

£6,400

Correspondent: Sophie Eddy, Director of Finance, Truro Diocesan Board of Finance Ltd, Church House, Woodland Court, Truro Business Park, Threemilestone TR4 9NH (01872 274351; email: finance@truro.anglican.org)

CC number: 289675

Eligibility

Widows, widowers and dependants of deceased members of the clergy who live in, or have worked in, the diocese of Truro. Retired Anglican clergy who are in need and have links with Truro are also eligible for support.

Types of grants

Grants are one-off and occasionally recurrent according to need. Grants have previously ranged from £50 to £500 and included funding for dental fees, spectacles, travel to hospital and assistance with equipment for people with disabilities.

Annual grant total

In 2016 the charity had an income of £11,900 and a total expenditure of £6,700. We estimate that grants given to individuals totalled £6,400.

Exclusions

No grants are given for assistance with school fees or university fees.

Applications

Apply in writing to the correspondent. Applications can be submitted directly by the individual or through a relative or a carer and are usually considered monthly.

Lord Crewe's Charity

£27,000 (23 grants)

Correspondent: Clive Smithers, The Miners' Hall, Durham DH1 4BD (0191 384 7736; email: enquiries@ lordcrewescharity.co.uk; website: www. lordcrewescharity.org.uk)

CC number: 1155101

Eligibility

Church of England clergy and their dependants who are in need in the dioceses of Durham and Newcastle. Grants may be given more generally to people in need who live in the area of benefit, with preference to people resident in parishes where the charity owns land or has the right of presentation to the benefice.

Types of grants

One-off and recurrent grants are given according to need in specific instances of hardship. Assistance is also given to clergy moving out of church housing on retirement.

Annual grant total

In 2016 the charity had assets of £42.5 million and an income of £1.4 million. During the year, the charity awarded £18,000 to 13 beneficiaries to assist with moving out of church accommodation upon retirement, and a further £9,000 to ten beneficiaries to relieve financial hardship.

Exclusions

Applicants who are not members of clergy are not supported and the trustees ask not to be contacted by people who do not fit the criteria.

Applications for church buildings and church projects are not assisted (except in the very small number of parishes in which the charity holds property or has rights of presentation).

Applications

Individuals wishing to apply for hardship assistance can make an initial enquiry to the charity via the contact form available on the website, or by telephone or email.

Other information

The majority of grant-making to individuals by the charity is to support the education of clergy dependants. During the year, the charity also made a large donation to Lincoln College Oxford, to provide bursaries, scholarships, and fellowships to students. Occasionally the charity makes grants to other organisations for general charitable purposes. Crewe's Library and Archives Trust (Charity Commission no. 1155101–2) has been established to own the libraries and archives collections currently held at Durham Cathedral, Durham University, the North East Religious Learning Resource Centre, and the Northumberland Records Office.

The Four Winds Trust

£1,500

Correspondent: Simon Charters, Trustee, 64 Station Road, Drayton, Portsmouth PO6 1PJ (email: fourwindstrust1971@gmail.com)

CC number: 262524

Eligibility

Evangelists, missionaries and ministers, including those who have retired, and their widows, widowers and other dependants who are in need.

Types of grants

One-off and recurrent grants are given according to need.

Annual grant total

In 2016/17 the trust had assets of £1.2 million and an income of £198,000. Grants to individuals totalled £1,500.

Applications

Apply in writing to the correspondent. The trust has previously stated that it does not consider unsolicited applications.

Anne French Memorial Trust

£51,000

Correspondent: Christopher Dicker, Hill House, Ranworth, Norwich NR13 6AB (01603 270356; email: cdicker@hotmail. co.uk)

CC number: 254567

Eligibility

Members of the Anglican clergy in the diocese of Norwich.

Types of grants

Holiday and other relief-in-need grants.

Annual grant total

In 2016/17 the trust had assets of £7.3 million and an income of £268,000. Grants to individuals totalled £51,000.

Applications

Apply in writing to the correspondent.

Other information

The trust has a close association with the Bishop of Norwich Fabric Fund Trust and the Norwich Diocesan Board of Finance Ltd.

Gibbons Charity

£16,000

Correspondent: Noel Fryer, 12 Shrewsbury Street, Hodnet, Market Drayton, Shropshire TF9 3NP (01630 684007; email: noelfryer@the-fryers.com)

CC number: 215171

Eligibility

Shropshire Church of England clergy, retired clergy and their widows, widowers, spouses, divorced partners or children.

Types of grants

One-off and recurrent grants are given according to need.

Annual grant total

In 2016 the charity had an income of £4,300 and a total expenditure of £18,300. We have estimated that grants to individuals totalled £16,000.

Applications

Apply in writing to the correspondent.

The Glasgow Society of the Sons and Daughters of Ministers of the Church of Scotland – also known as Manse Bairns Network

£28,000 (17 grants)

Correspondent: Jennifer Law, Secretary & Treasurer, Scott-Monicrieff, Exchange Place 3, Semple Street, Edinburgh EH3 9BL (0131 473 3500; email: jennifer. law@scott-moncrieff.com; website: mansebairnsnetwork.org)

OSCR number: SC010281

Eligibility

Children of deceased ministers of the Church of Scotland who are in need.

Types of grants

One-off and recurrent grants, which in 2015/16 ranged between £100 and £2,200, are given according to need.

Annual grants are made with an extra payment prior to Christmas.

Annual grant total

In 2015/16 the charity had assets of £1.57 million and an income of £60,500. Grants were made to 17 individuals and totalled £28,000. Educational support totalling £12,000 was given to 11 individuals.

Applications

Application forms are available to download from the charity's associated websites. Applications should be submitted to the correspondent no later than 31 May each year and grants are distributed by early September.

Other information

Further information on the charity is available from its website or from the charities page of Scott Moncrieff, the charity's administrator (www.scott-moncrieff.com/services/charities/charitable-trusts).

The I. W. Griffiths Trust

£20,000

Correspondent: Lord Brian Griffiths of Fforestfach, Trustee, 18 Royal Avenue, London SW3 4QF (020 7774 4015)

CC number: 1090379

Eligibility

People who are, or have been, engaged in Christian mission and are in need.

Types of grants

One-off and recurrent grants are given according to need.

Annual grant total

In 2016 the trust had an income of £25,000 and a total expenditure of £41,000. We estimate that grants given to individuals totalled around £20,000.

Applications

Apply in writing to the correspondent.

The Groveland Charitable Trust

£10,000 (22 grants)

Correspondent: Henry Mercer, Trustee, 8 Fairleigh Rise, Kington Langley, Chippenham SN15 5QF (01249 758877)

CC number: 289279

Eligibility

Gospel Standard Baptist ministers and their dependants.

Types of grants

One-off grants according to need.

Annual grant total

In 2017 the trust had assets of £1.8 million and an income of £74,000. Grants to 22 individuals totalled £10,000.

Applications

Apply in writing to the correspondent.

The John Henry King Fund

£44,500 (32 grants)

Correspondent: Canon Gerard Hetherington, Trustee, Le Platon Home, Clifton, St Peter Port, Guernsey GY1 2PW (01481 720755; email: anne@adh-consulting.co.uk; website: www.portsmouthdiocese.org.uk/directory/organisation/483.htm)

CC number: 224437

Eligibility

Sick or retired members of Catholic clergy of the Portsmouth Diocese.

Types of grants

One-off and recurrent grants are given according to need.

Annual grant total

In 2016 the charity held assets of £1.9 million and had an income of £68,000. Grants were paid to 32 beneficiaries and totalled £44,500.

Applications

Apply in writing to the correspondent.

The Lancashire Infirm Secular Clergy Fund

£106,000 (95 grants)

Correspondent: Revd Simon David, Correspondent, Hawksworth, High Wray Bank, High Wray, Ambleside, Cumbria LA22 0JD (01539 433160; email: simon.hawksworth@hotmail.co.uk)

CC number: 222796

Eligibility

Catholic secular clergy of the dioceses of Liverpool, Salford and Lancaster who are unable, through age or illness, to attend to their duties of office and are in need.

Types of grants

Grants usually range from £650 to £1,350.

Annual grant total

In 2015/16 the charity had a total income of £141,000 and a total expenditure of £136,000. The charity awarded a total of 95 grants, which totalled £106,000.

The table shows how the grants were distributed in 2016:

Salford	37	£42,000
Liverpool	35	£36,500
Lancashire	23	£27,500

Applications

Apply using a form available from the correspondent.

The Leaders of Worship and Preachers Trust

£27,000

Correspondent: Amelia Gosal, 77 Mortlake Road, Richmond TW9 4AA (020 8878 0701; fax: 01923 296899; email: lwptoffice@lwpt.org.uk; website: www.lwpt.org.uk)

CC number: 1107967

Eligibility

Preachers and leaders of worship, and their dependants, who are in need.

Types of grants

One-off and weekly grants for a broad range of needs.

Annual grant total

In 2015/16 the charity had assets of £273,000 and an income of £486,000. The charity awarded £1,200 in grants for financial hardship. Also listed in the accounts are two amounts for 'residents' subsidy' for housing and we have added these amounts to the social welfare grant total.

Applications

Application forms are available to download from the website. There are three parts: G1 – personal information form; G2 – application for a weekly allowance; and G3 – application for a one-off grant. G1 should be completed along with either G2 or G3, according to the applicant's need.

Other information

The charity also makes vocational grants to those wishing to train in the ministry. The 2015/16 annual report states:

> A distinct vocational grant programme has been established with clear guidelines and procedures. The emphasis will now to be to review and relaunch the hardship grants programme to ensure that grants are awarded to those involved in preaching and ministry in areas that are usually underfunded and to respond to need in crisis.

The charity's website provides information on how to apply for care at one of the Westerley Christian Care Homes managed by LWP Homes, which provide accommodation for people looking for actively Christian residential care in retirement.

Sylvanus Lyson's Charity

£31,000 (72 grants)

Correspondent: A. Holloway, Morroway House, Station Road, Gloucester GL1 1DW (01452 301903)

CC number: 202939

Eligibility

Widows and dependants of the clergy of the Church of England or retired ministers in the diocese of Gloucester who are in need.

Applications are also considered from individuals in need falling within the scope of the charity's objects, including support for education, training and welfare of members of the clergy.

Types of grants

One-off grants according to need.

Annual grant total

In 2015/16 the charity had assets of £11.36 million and an income of £353,500. During the year, the charity gave grants totalling almost £31,000 to 72 individuals.

The charity also gives grants to organisations.

Applications

Apply in writing to the correspondent.

The Methodist Church in Great Britain

£1.2 million

Correspondent: Revd Gareth Powell, Methodist Church House, 25 Marylebone House, London NW1 5JR (020 7486 5502; email: stipends@methodistchurch.org.uk; website: www.methodist.org.uk/for-ministers-and-office-holders/finance/stipends-and-payroll/ministerial-grants)

CC number: 1132208

Eligibility

Methodist presbyters, deacons, lay employees and local preachers and their families.

Types of grants

The charity's 2015/16 annual report states:

> Small grants are made to Methodist presbyters, deacons, lay employees and local preachers and their families towards the education of their children during times of ill health and for one-off financial support. Giving for this purpose draws on a variety of funds including the Fund for the Support of Presbyters and Deacons, Trinity Hall Trust and several benevolent funds.

Annual grant total

In 2015/16 the charity had assets of £222.3 million and an income of £43.3 million. Grants to individuals totalled £1.2 million.

Applications

Application forms are available to download from the charity's website.

Ministers' Relief Society

£22,500

Correspondent: Alan Lathey, Trustee, 2 Queensberry Road, Penylan, Cardiff CV23 9JJ

CC number: 270314

Eligibility

Protestant ministers, their widows and dependants who are in need, especially due to old age or disability. Children of deceased ministers generally must be under the age of 21 and of 'genuine evangelical and protestant convictions' to be eligible.

Types of grants

One-off and recurrent grants can be given according to need. In the past grants have been given to: ministers who are retired or have disabilities, and their widows, with inadequate income or savings; specific emergencies, such as serious illness, removal costs, enforced resignation or dismissal by congregation; candidates and students seeking vocational training in the ministry.

Annual grant total

In 2016 the charity had an income of £16,700 and a total expenditure of £22,500. We estimate that the charity gave around £22,500 in grants to individuals.

Applications

Application forms are available from the correspondent and can be submitted directly by the individual.

Other information

The charity is also known as the Society for the Relief of Necessitous Protestant Ministers, their Widows and Orphans.

Mitchell Bequest

£20,500 (54 grants)

Correspondent: The Trustees, Archdiocese of Glasgow, 196 Clyde Street, Glasgow G1 4JY

OSCR number: SC013478

Eligibility

Clergymen of Roman Catholic religion living in Scotland who are in need due to age or illness.

Types of grants

Annual allowances.

Annual grant total

In 2015/16 the charity had assets of £872,500 and an income of £29,500. Grants to individuals totalled £20,500.

Applications

Apply in writing to the correspondent.

The Monmouth Diocesan Clergy Widows and Dependants Society

£28,000 (seven grants)

Correspondent: Peter Lea, Secretary/Treasurer, Llwyn-Gwyn House, Old Hereford Road, Abergavenny NP7 7LE (01873 890265)

CC number: 1073775

Eligibility

Widows and dependants of deceased clerics of the Church in Wales who, at the time of their death, were in receipt of a stipend or pension from the Church in Wales arising from an appointment in the Diocese of Monmouth.

Types of grants

Financial support, including bereavement grants and birthday and Christmas gifts.

Annual grant total

In 2016 the charity had assets of £767,500 and an income of £27,500. Grants to individuals totalled £28,000.

The annual report for 2016 states that six widows and one dependant were supported with grants during the year. Grants made included four bereavement grants.

Applications

Apply in writing to the correspondent.

Other information

The charity supports beneficiaries with advocacy, financial advice and information. It also provides a lunch at a restaurant in Newport for widows.

The Mylne Trust

£44,000

Correspondent: Robin Twining, Secretary, PO Box 530, Farnham GU9 1BP (email: admin@mylnetrust.org.uk; website: www.mylnetrust.org.uk)

CC number: 208074

Eligibility

Members of the Protestant faith who have been engaged in evangelistic work, including missionaries and retired missionaries, and Christian workers whose finances are inadequate. Married ordinands with children are also supported when all other sources of funding have failed to cover their needs.

Types of grants
Annual and one-off grants for living costs and training expenses.

Annual grant total
In 2016/17 the trust had assets of £2.1 million and an income of £55,500. Grants to individuals totalled £87,500. We estimate that grants for welfare purposes totalled around £44,000.

Exclusions
The trust cannot support individuals who are not of a Protestant denomination.

Applications
The trust notes the following helpful information on its website:

> The trust has reviewed and, in 2013, changed its policy and procedure for making grants. Most grants are now being handled with partners already in Christian mission work. (Applications based on earlier procedures, using the old application forms, will no longer be considered by the trust.)

> *Worldwide except Africa*
> In principle, the only grant applications that will be considered by direct application to the trust are those from candidates for mission work who are studying or planning to study within the UK. Such applicants are invited to contact the Clerk to the Mylne Trust at admin@ mylnetrust.org.uk requesting a current application form.

> *Africa*
> There are special arrangements for applicants who are based in Africa.

We would advise potential applicants to at first visit the website for more information.

The Nazareth Trust Fund

£3,300

Correspondent: Revd David Hunt, 16 Wollaton Road, Ferndown BH22 8QR

CC number: 210503

Eligibility
The fund gives support to individuals known to the trustees who promote the Christian faith and/or are Christian missionaries.

Types of grants
One-off grants according to need.

Annual grant total
In 2016/17 the fund had assets of £41,000 and an income of £40,500. We

estimate that around £3,300 was given in grants to individuals.

Exclusions
No support is given for individuals not known to the trustees.

Applications
Apply in writing to the correspondent, although the trust tends to only support individuals and organisations personally known to the trustees.

Lady Peel Legacy Trust

£2,900

Correspondent: Christine Ruge-Cope, Trust Secretary, 21 Chace Avenue, Potters Bar, Hertfordshire EN6 5LX

CC number: 204815

Eligibility
Priests in the Anglo-Catholic tradition who, due to ill health or age, have had to resign their work or livings.

Types of grants
One-off or recurrent grants according to need.

Annual grant total
In 2015/16 the trust had an income of £5,500 and a total expenditure of £6,000. We estimate that the trust gave around £2,900 in grants to individuals.

Applications
Applicants can apply in writing to the correspondent.

The Harry and Katie Pollard Trust

£7,800 (six grants)

Correspondent: David Morgan, Trustee, 25 Newbiggen Street, Thaxted, Dunmow CM6 2QS (01371 830132)

CC number: 255080

Eligibility
Widows or unmarried daughters of the clergy. Applicants must be under the age of 50.

Types of grants
One-off grants according to need.

Annual grant total
In 2016 the trust held assets of £783,500 and had an income of £88,000. Grants were paid to six individuals and totalled £7,800.

Applications
Apply in writing to the correspondent.

The Pyncombe Charity

£19,000

Correspondent: Rita Butterworth, Wingletye, Lawford, Crowcombe, Taunton TA4 4AQ (email: joeandrita@ waitrose.com)

CC number: 202255

Eligibility
Serving Anglican clergy under 70 years of age and their immediate families who are resident with them, who are in financial need resulting from a serious illness, an injury or special circumstances.

Types of grants
Small, one-off grants.

Annual grant total
In 2016/17 the charity had an income of £19,100 and a total expenditure of £20,000. We estimate that grants given to individuals totalled around £19,000.

Exclusions
No grants are given towards educational expenses.

Applications
Applications must be made through the diocesan bishop on a form available from the correspondent. Applications should be submitted by April. No direct applications can be considered and the charity has told us the majority of the direct applications received are ineligible.

Note: It is important that the financial impact of the applicant's circumstances is clearly stated and quantified in the application.

The Retired Ministers' and Widows' Fund

£32,000 (32 grants)

Correspondent: Bill Allen, Secretary, 7 Wendover Lodge, Church Street, Welwyn AL6 9LR (01438 489171; email: billallen1960@gmail.com; website: www. retiredministers.org.uk)

CC number: 233835

Eligibility
Retired ministers, and ministers' widows of Presbyterian, Independent (including Unitarian, Free Christian, Congregational and the United Reformed) and Baptist churches, who live in England and Wales and are on a low income.

In 2016/17 this was defined as those with an income (not including state benefits) of less than £5,200 (£7,800 for married couples) and savings not exceeding £40,000. The savings limit for one-off grants is £10,000, although any of these limits may be disregarded in exceptional circumstances, such as when an application is made by a resident of a nursing home.

Types of grants

Half-yearly payments, which in 2016/17 totalled £850 a year for widows/widowers and £1,175 a year for married ministers. Christmas gifts are also awarded. One-off assistance may be provided to help in an emergency. Priority is given to those already registered with the charity.

A maximum of two grants will be paid to any individual in a four-year period.

Annual grant total

In 2016/17 the fund had assets of £827,000 and an income of £39,500. Distributions to beneficiaries totalled £32,000.

Applications

Application forms are available from the correspondent. Applications can be submitted by the individual but should be signed by a local minister.

Retired Missionary Aid Fund

£570,000

Correspondent: Roger Herbert, Secretary, 64 Callow Hill Road, Alvechurch, Birmingham B48 7LR (0121 445 2378; website: www.rmaf.co.uk)

CC number: 211454

Eligibility

Retired missionaries from the Christian Brethren Assemblies who are in need. Help may also be given to their dependants. According to the trustees' annual report for 2016/17, the trustees have established eligibility criteria for recipients of grants, relating to such matters as their length of missionary service, ill health, and age.

Types of grants

Quarterly grants, birthday gifts, Christmas hampers and funeral grants.

Annual grant total

In 2016/17 the fund held assets of £1.3 million and had an income of £427,000. Grants to individuals totalled £570,000 and were distributed as follows:

Gifts to retired missionaries	£536,000
Earmarked gifts for retired missionaries	£17,000
Gift vouchers and Christmas hampers	£9,200
Funeral grants	£8,000

Applications

The fund only gives support to its members, who should make their circumstances known to the correspondent.

Other information

The objects of the fund are to assist retired missionaries from Christian Brethren Assemblies who are in necessitous circumstances. Such missionaries have usually spent all or large proportions of their working lives in missionary work overseas without any salary or other fixed means of support.

George Richards' Charity

£20,000

Correspondent: Dr Paul Simmons, Flat 96, Thomas More House, Barbican, London EC2Y 8BU (020 7588 5583)

CC number: 246965

Eligibility

Church of England clergy who are in need and their widows and dependants. Preference is given to older people and those in poor health.

Types of grants

Our previous research indicates that the charity awards one-off and recurrent grants for heating expenses, household costs, travel, education, clothing, Christmas gifts and medical care. Pensions are available for those who have been forced to retire early from active ministry and are on a low income.

Annual grant total

In 2016 the charity had an income of £22,500 and a total expenditure of £22,500. We estimate that the charity awarded around £20,000 in grants to individuals for welfare purposes.

Exclusions

No grants are given for repaying debt.

Applications

Apply in writing to the correspondent.

Other information

At the time of writing (August 2017) the charity had no website or accounts available.

Samuel Robinson's Charities

£77,000 (34 grants)

Correspondent: Elizabeth Lawson, Grants Secretary, 113 Vesage Court, 8A Leather Lane, London EC1N 7RF

CC number: 222700

Eligibility

Pastors or ministers of Independent and Baptist Churches in England and Wales. Support is also given to their widows or widowers.

Types of grants

One-off grants according to need.

Annual grant total

In 2015/16 the charity held assets of £2.8 million and had an income of £78,000. Grants were made to 34 individuals totalling £77,000 and ranged between £1,000 and £4,000.

Applications

Apply in writing to the correspondent.

The Sheffield West Riding Charitable Society Trust

£4,000

Correspondent: Heidi Adcock, Diocese of Sheffield, Diocesan Church House, 95–99 Effingham Street, Rotherham, South Yorkshire S65 1BL (01709 309100; email: reception@sheffield.anglican.org; website: www.sheffield.anglican.org)

CC number: 1002026

Eligibility

Clergymen, deaconesses, and licensed lay people, and their dependants, in Sheffield. Also, housekeepers who have worked for any member of the clergy.

Types of grants

One-off, small grants to provide relief for those in need.

Annual grant total

In 2016 the trust had an income of £12,000 and a total expenditure of £8,000. We estimate that the trust awarded around £4,000 to individuals for relief-in-need purposes.

Applications

Application forms are available from the correspondent.

Other information

Grants are also made to individuals for education, and to local organisations.

The Society for the Relief of Poor Clergymen

£20,000

Correspondent: The Secretary, SRPC, c/o CPAS, Unit 3, Sovereign Court One, Sir William Lyons Road, University of Warwick Science Park, Coventry CV4 7EZ (email: secretary@sprc-aid.com)

CC number: 232634

Eligibility

Evangelical ordained ministers and accredited lay workers and their dependants or widows/widowers in the

Church of England, the Church in Wales, the Church of Ireland and the Scottish Episcopal Church.

Types of grants
Grants can be made to cover costs of bereavement, illness, and furniture/item removal. Hardship grants can also be made to families in debt.

Annual grant total
In 2016 the charity had an income of £20,500 and a total expenditure of £22,000. We estimate that grants to individuals during the year totalled £20,000.

Exclusions
Grants are not given towards school fees or normal travel expenses.

Applications
Application forms are available to download from the website or can be requested from the correspondent. Completed applications should be returned by email to secretary@sprc-aid.com or by post to:

The Secretary, SRPC, c/o CPAS, Unit 3, Sovereign Court One, Sir William Lyons Road, University of Warwick Science Park, Coventry CV4 7EZ.

Sons and Friends of the Clergy

£1.95 million

Correspondent: Jeremy Moodey, 1 Dean Trench Street, Westminster, London SW1P 3HB (020 7799 3696; email: enquiries@clergycharities.org.uk; website: www.clergycharities.org.uk)

CC number: 207736

Eligibility
The charity supports: serving and retired Anglican clergy and their dependants; divorced and separated spouses and civil partners of eligible clergy; widows, widowers and surviving civil partners of eligible clergy; Anglican ordinands training for ministry in the UK.

The relevant clergy must be working in or have been working in: the United Kingdom; the Republic of Ireland; the Diocese of Sodor and Man; the Channel Islands.

Types of grants
Grants are available for a wide range of needs such as accessibility modifications, bereavement, debt relief, legal fees on buying first property, medical expenses, nursing home fees, relationship counselling and resettlement.

Annual grant total
In 2016 the charity had assets of £104.2 million and an income of £4.17 million. During the year,

905 grants were awarded to individuals and three to organisations totalling £2.4 million. Grants for welfare purposes amounted to £1.95 million and were distributed as follows:

General welfare	£1.9 million
University maintenance	£196,500
School fees	£146,500
Ordinand grants	£129,000
Resettlement	£16,500
Bereavement	£6,800
Holidays	£4,200
Other education expenses	£2,100
School clothing	£1,300
Debt	£1,200

Exclusions
Exclusions are usually described on the charity's website. Contact the correspondent for more information.

Applications
Application forms are available to download from the charity's website.

Other information
According to the charity's website:

The charity was founded in 1655 by a group of merchants in the City of London and clergymen who were all sons of the cloth. During the Commonwealth, persecution of clergy who had remained loyal to the Crown was widespread and many who had been deprived of their livings by Cromwell were destitute. The charity's foundation dates from a recognition by a body of sons of clergymen that action was required to meet a pressing need among clergy families for charitable help. The charity's present name is often felt to be a misleading one, but it is in fact an accurate description of its founding fathers.

The Foundation of Edward Storey

£258,500 (278 grants)

Correspondent: Timothy Burgess, Clerk to the Trustees, Storey's House, Mount Pleasant, Cambridge CB3 0BZ (01223 364405; email: info@edwardstorey.org.uk; website: www.edwardstorey.org.uk)

CC number: 203653

Eligibility
'Financially unsupported' (i.e. single, separated, divorced or widowed) women who fall into either of two qualifying categories:

- Women over 40 living within the county of Cambridgeshire
- Widows, ex-wives or dependants of Church of England clergy; women priests, deacons or deaconesses of the Church of England; clergywomen, missionaries, or other women with a close professional connection with the Church of England

Types of grants
One-off grants or recurrent grants and pensions (which are annually reviewable and renewable). Pensions are occasionally available (only to those over 60). Some grants are issued with contractual terms of repayment. Christmas gifts may also be issued to residents or individuals in the local community.

Annual grant total
In 2016/17 the foundation held assets of £16.7 million and had an income of £2.4 million. Grants to individuals totalled £258,500 and were distributed as follows:

Parish grants	£164,000
Parish pensions	£35,000
Clergy pensions	£32,000
Clergy widow grants	£27,500

Applications
Application forms are available from the correspondent.

Other information
The charity also manages sheltered accommodation and a residential home based across four different sites.

Thornton Fund

£7,500

Correspondent: Dr Jane Williams, 93 Fitzjohn Avenue, Barnet EN5 2HR (020 8440 2211; email: djanewilliams@dsl.pipex.com)

CC number: 226803

Eligibility
Ministers of the Unitarian Church.

Types of grants
One-off grants. In the past, grants have been given towards convalescence, counselling, the replacement of equipment not covered by insurance and taxis for somebody unable to drive for medical reasons.

Annual grant total
In 2016 the fund had an income of £21,000 and a total expenditure of £18,500. We estimate that welfare grants to ministers totalled around £7,500.

Applications
Applications can be made in writing to the correspondent detailing your circumstances for consideration.

Other information
The fund also makes awards to students of Unitarian ministry and occasionally for project grants to the general assembly of Unitarian and Free Christian Churches.

The Wells Clerical Charity

£5,000

Correspondent: Ven. Nicola Sullivan, Trustee, 6 The Liberty, Wells, Somerset BA5 2SU (01749 670777; email: general@bathwells.anglican.org)

CC number: 248436

Eligibility

Clergy of the Church of England who have served in the historic archdeaconry of Wells, and their dependants, who are in need.

Types of grants

One-off grants according to need.

Annual grant total

In 2016 the charity had an income of £8,300 and a total expenditure of £10,500. Grants are made to individuals for both social welfare and educational purposes. We estimate that social welfare grants totalled £5,000.

Applications

Apply in writing to the correspondent.

WODS (The Widows, Orphans and Dependants Society of the Church in Wales)

£86,000 (56 grants)

Correspondent: Louise Davies, Hon. Secretary, 2 Callaghan Square, Cardiff CF10 5BT (029 2034 8228; email: ledavies@churchinwales.org.uk; website: www.churchinwales.org.uk)

CC number: 503271

Eligibility

Widows, orphans and dependants of deceased clergy of the Church in Wales who are on a low income.

The annual report for 2016 states: 'Each year the society sets minimum income levels for widows, dependants and orphans for which each diocesan committee should aim to achieve.' In 2016 these levels were set at £14,430 for widows, £13,800 for dependants and £2,620 for orphans.

Types of grants

One-off grants.

Annual grant total

In 2016 the society held assets of £862,500 and had an income of £86,000. Grants were made to 56 beneficiaries and totalled £86,000.

Applications

Apply in writing to the correspondent. Applications should be made through one of the six diocesan committees of the Church in Wales. Details of the applicant's financial situation should be included.

The Charles Wright Gowthorpe Fund and Clergy Augmentation Fund
See entry on page 24

Sciences and technology

The Royal Society of Chemistry Chemists' Community Fund

£34,000

Correspondent: Chemists' Community Fund Team, Thomas Graham House, Science Park, Milton Road, Cambridge CB4 0WF (01223 432227; email: Contact form on website; website: www.rsc.org/membership-and-community/chemists-community-fund)

CC number: 207890

Eligibility

People who have been members of the society for the last three years, or ex-members who were in the society for at least ten years, and their dependants, who are in need.

Types of grants

The fund can provide a range of support depending on an individual's circumstances. Forms of support include: regular monthly grants to assist with essential living costs and medical expenses; one-off grants for unexpected expenses such as a fridge or car repair; one-off grants towards redecoration and home adaptations; and support with respite breaks for carers.

Annual grant total

In 2016 the charity had assets of £60.7 million and an income of £55.7 million. Welfare grants to individuals totalled £34,000.

Applications

Individuals should, in the first instance, contact the correspondent to discuss their situation. An application form will then be sent.

Other information

The fund also provides advice and guidance services.

John Murdoch's Trust

£38,500 (17 grants)

Correspondent: The Trust Administrator, c/o The Royal Bank of Scotland plc, Trust Administrator, Eastwood House, Glebe Road, Chelmsford, Essex CM1 1RS

OSCR number: SC004031

Eligibility

People in need who are over the age of 50 and have pursued science, in any of its branches, either as amateurs or professionals.

Types of grants

Our research suggests that yearly allowances and one-off grants, on average of about £200 to £1,000, are offered. Awards are given for general relief-in-need purposes not for scientific needs.

Annual grant total

In 2016/17 the trust held assets of £1.6 million and had an income of £53,500. The trust awarded grants to 17 individuals totalling £38,500.

Applications

Application forms are available from the correspondent. Grants are normally considered twice a year.

The Nuclear Industry Benevolent Fund

£53,500

Correspondent: Elaine Price, Funding Secretary, Unit CU1, Warrington Business Park, Long Lane, Warrington WA2 8TX (01925 633005; email: info@tnibf.org; website: www.tnibf.org)

CC number: 208729

Eligibility

Past and present employees (direct or agency) of the UK nuclear industry.

Types of grants

Grants are awarded according to need. Previously, grants have been used for white goods, home repairs, clothing, and funeral expenses.

Annual grant total

In 2015/16 the charity had assets of £3 million and an income of £60,500. During the year, the charity awarded £53,500 in grants to individuals, and a further £12,000 in interest-free loans.

Exclusions

Grants are not given for private healthcare, legal, or business-related expenses.

Applications

To apply for funding: call the confidential helpline – 0800 587 6040; call the general enquiries number – 01925 633005; or email: info@tnibf.org.

The Benevolent Fund administered by the Institute of Physics

£16,600 (14 grants)

Correspondent: The Secretary of the Benevolent Fund, Institute of Physics, 76 Portland Place, London W1B 1NT (020 7470 4800; email: benfund@iop.org; website: www.iop.org)

CC number: 209746

Eligibility

Physicists and members of their family in need, whether members of the institute or not.

Types of grants

One-off and recurrent grants are given according to need. Interest-free loans are also available.

Annual grant total

In 2015 the fund held assets of £1.5 million and had an income of £51,500. Grants to 14 individuals totalled £16,600.

Applications

Apply in writing to the correspondent, marked 'Private and confidential'. The committee meets periodically through the year although emergency cases can be considered more urgently.

Other information

The benevolent fund also provides free access to legal advice; see the Institute of Physics website for details.

Secretarial and administration

The Chartered Secretaries' Charitable Trust

£43,500 (108 grants)

Correspondent: Elizabeth Howarth, Saffron House, 6–10 Kirby Street, London EC1N 8TS (020 7612 7048; email: icsacharities@icsa.org.uk; website: www.icsa.org.uk/about-us/charitable-trust)

CC number: 1152784

Eligibility

Members and former members, graduates, students, employees or former employees of the institute, and their dependants, who are in need and live in the UK, Eire and associated territories.

Note: there are more detailed conditions on the range and extent which govern eligibility.

Types of grants

Weekly allowances and regular support according to need, for example towards telephone line or mobile rental, broadband, white goods, house repairs, emergency alarm systems and TV rental and licences. One-off grants are given for specific items and services, often paid directly to the supplier, including those for clothing, dental work, medical aids, clearance of debts, decorating or property repairs. Interest-free loans are also considered.

Annual grant total

In 2015/16 the charity had assets of £6.3 million and an income of £360,000. During the year, the charity awarded £43,500 to those in need, distributed as follows:

General grants	£23,500
Christmas grants	£4,600
Rentals and licenses	£4,400
Irregular grants	£4,300
Winter grants	£3,500
ICSA membership	£2,100
Alarms	£1,000

During the year the charity also gave £1,900 in interest-free loans to individuals.

Applications

Application forms are available from the correspondent. Requests can be made throughout the year. Institute members (volunteers) visit beneficiaries, where necessary. Contact the correspondent if assistance in making the application is required.

Skilled crafts and trades

The British Antique Dealers' Association Benevolent Fund

£4,000

Correspondent: Mark Dodgson, Secretary General, 14 Dufferin Street, London EC1Y 8PD (020 7589 4128; website: www.bada.org)

CC number: 238363

Eligibility

Members and former members of the association who are in need, and their dependants.

Types of grants

One-off or recurrent grants.

Annual grant total

In 2015 the fund had an income of £8,500 and a total expenditure of £4,400. We have estimated that grants to individuals for welfare purposes totalled £4,000 during the year.

Applications

Application forms are available from the correspondent. Applicants should provide two references from members or former members of the association. Applications are considered on a regular basis.

The Barbers' Amalgamated Charity

£6,800 (five grants)

Correspondent: Col. P. J. Durrant, Clerk, The Worshipful Company of Barbers, Barber-Surgeons' Hall, 1A Monkwell Square, Wood Street, London EC2Y 5BL (020 7606 0741; email: clerk@barberscompany.org; website: www.barberscompany.org)

CC number: 213085

Eligibility

Poor, generally older, members of the medical professions or barbers' trade and their families.

Types of grants

Quarterly grants (called pensions) and one-off financial assistance.

Annual grant total

In 2015/16 the charity held assets of £521,500 and had an income of £164,500, the majority of which came from a transfer of funds from the John Bancks Charity. The charity made grants to five beneficiaries totalling £5,800 and made an additional one-off donation of £1,000 to one of those beneficiaries.

Applications

Only members of the Barbers' Company are eligible to apply. Apply in writing to the correspondent directly or via a family member, or through an organisation such as Citizens Advice or other welfare agency. Applications are considered throughout the year. The charity's annual report states the following:

New beneficiaries are accepted after their personal circumstances have been investigated by the Company's Honorary Almoner, a member of the Barbers' Company and the Charity Committee, who often seeks an independent report from organisations such as the Soldiers, Sailors, Airmen and Families Association (SSAFA).

The Bespoke Tailors' Benevolent Association

£83,500 (40 grants)

Correspondent: Elizabeth Fox, Secretary, 65 Tierney Road, London SW2 4QH (07831 520801; email: elizabeth.fox@ukgateway.net)

CC number: 212954

Eligibility

'Journeyman tailors and tailoresses' and their near relatives who were employed in the bespoke tailoring trade. Preference is given to past and present members of the institute but help can be given to other eligible applicants.

Types of grants

Small, one-off grants and regular allowances.

Annual grant total

In 2015/16 the charity had an income of £149,000 and held assets of almost £3.2 million. During the year, the charity provided grants of £83,500 to 40 beneficiaries.

Applications

Application forms are available from the correspondent. Applications should preferably be submitted through a social worker. However, those submitted directly by the individual or through another third party will be considered.

Other information

In late 2012 the Tailors Benevolent Institute and the Master Tailors Benevolent Association merged to form the Bespoke Tailors Benevolent Association.

The Ceramic Industry Welfare Society

£5,400

Correspondent: The Trustees, Unity Trades Union, Hillcrest House, Garth Street, Stoke-on-Trent ST1 2AB (01782 272755)

CC number: 261248

Eligibility

People in need who are or have been employed in the ceramics industry, or widows of former employees.

Types of grants

Recurrent grants are fixed at £45 per six week period, depending on the circumstances of the applicant (these are confirmed through a visit by a society representative).

Annual grant total

In 2016 the charity had an income of £830 and a total expenditure of £5,700. We estimate that grants given to individuals totalled £5,400.

Exclusions

No grants are payable beyond 12 months of the date of retirement.

Applications

Apply in writing to the correspondent.

Institute of Clayworkers Benevolent Fund

£5,100

Correspondent: Francis Morrall, Trustee, British Ceramic Confederation, Federation House, Station Road, Stoke-on-Trent, Staffordshire ST4 2SA (01782 571846; email: francism@ceramfed.co.uk)

CC number: 212300

Eligibility

People in the clay-working industry, namely current and former employees of the British Ceramic Confederation member companies and members and ex-members of the institute, and their dependants. Applicants will normally be unable to work due to ill health or an accident.

Types of grants

Recurrent pensions and one-off grants, usually of £250. Our previous research indicates that in exceptional cases where applicants have been identified by other charitable bodies as being in extreme need, larger grants may be given.

Annual grant total

In 2016 the charity had an income of £3,900 and a total expenditure of £5,300. We estimate that the charity gave around £5,100 in grants to individuals.

Applications

Apply in writing to the correspondent. Applications should include age, length of service, date of termination of employment (if applicable), brief description (two or three sentences) of circumstances leading to application, and brief testimonial (a sentence or two) from a supervisor/manager, if appropriate. Our research suggests that the fund only accepts applications made through a former employer and not usually those made directly by the individual. Requests may be made at any time.

The Cotton Industry War Memorial Trust

£66,500 (121 grants)

Correspondent: Peter Booth, Trust Secretary, Stables Barn, Coldstones Farm, Bewerley, Harrogate HG3 5BJ (01423 711205)

CC number: 242721

Eligibility

People in need who have worked in the cotton textile industry in the north west of England. This includes weaving, spinning and dyeing. Cotton industry workers who were badly injured while fighting for HM Forces in wartime may also be eligible.

Types of grants

Convalescence arrangements are made for people who are in poor health or who have suffered injury due to their work in the cotton textiles industry. The trust makes arrangements for beneficiaries' convalescence at commercial hotels in Blackpool. One-off grants may also be awarded for specific needs.

Annual grant total

In 2016 the trust had assets of £7.1 million and an income of £332,500. The trust arranged convalescence for 121 individuals through its Convalescent Scheme at a cost of £66,500.

Exclusions

People who have worked with clothing, footwear, hosiery and other man-made fabrics are not eligible.

Applications

Application forms are available from the correspondent. Note that the correspondent cannot send forms directly to applicants, only to employers, trade unions, SSAFA or similar welfare agencies for them to pass on to potential beneficiaries. Applicants must show that they have worked in the textile industry and provide medical evidence if claiming assistance due to employment injury or disability.

The Fashion and Textile Children's Trust

£55,500

Correspondent: Anna Pangbourne, Director, Victoria Charity Centre, 11 Belgrave Road, London SW1V 1RB (0300 123 9002; email: grants@ftct.org.uk; website: www.ftct.org.uk)

CC number: 257136

Eligibility

Children and young people under 18 whose parents or full-time carer work or have worked in the UK fashion and textile retailing and manufacturing industry for at least one year (within the last nine years).

Types of grants

The trust makes grants for essential items; these include day-to-day items such as winter clothing and shoes, and additional support such as mobility equipment, sensory toys, speech therapy and respite activities. Essential household items such as washing machines, fridges and children's bedding can also be considered.

Annual grant total

In 2015/16 the trust had assets of £8.25 million and an income of £380,500. Grants were made totalling £174,000, of which £55,500 was awarded for well-being. A small proportion of this (£8,000) was paid to organisations on behalf of individuals, with the remainder being awarded to individuals directly.

Exclusions

Funding cannot be given for childcare or home repairs.

Applications

In the first instance, contact the trust by telephone or by using the online enquiry form to discuss your child's needs. If the trust feels that it may be able to assist, an application form will be sent to you by post or email. Completed forms must be returned to the trust along with photocopies of three more documents: 1. a copy of your P45 or recent payslip; 2. a copy of your P60 or a letter from your employer confirming the length of your employment; 3. photocopies of a Child Benefit letter or a recent bank statement showing payment into your account. The trust cannot process applications without all of this supporting documentation. Applications for amounts over £750 require additional evidence, detailed on the website.

The Feltmakers Charitable Foundation

£12,800

Correspondent: Maj. J. Coombs, Clerk to the Trustees, Post Cottage, The Street, Greywell, Hook, Hampshire RG29 1DA (01256 703174; email: jcpartnership@ btopenworld.com; website: www. feltmakers.co.uk)

CC number: 259906

Eligibility

Hatting trade pensioners who are in need.

Types of grants

One-off grants according to need.

Annual grant total

In 2016/17 the foundation had assets of £698,500 and an income of £52,000. Grants individuals totalled £12,800. A further £27,500 was awarded to 12 charitable organisations.

Applications

Applicants must be nominated in the first place by their employer or former employer, or in exceptional circumstances, by a welfare organisation.

Footwear Friends

£63,000 (172 grants)

Correspondent: Gabi O'Sullivan, Secretary, Footwear Friends, Unit 116 Southbank House, 28 Black Prince Road, London SE1 7SJ (020 3735 8748; email: info@footwearfriends.org.uk; website: www.footwearfriends.org.uk)

CC number: 222117

Eligibility

People who are working or have worked in the boot trade and footwear industry, usually for a minimum of five years, and their dependants.

Types of grants

One-off grants and recurrent payments. Funding is also available towards convalescent holidays. Recurrent grants may be paid once every six months, or seasonally at Christmas and mid-year.

Annual grant total

In 2016/17 the charity held assets of £1.3 million and had an income of £145,000. Financial assistance to 172 individuals totalled £63,000.

Christmas grants	£16,200
Mid-year grants	£15,000
One-off grants	£11,700
Half-yearly allowances	£11,300
December bonus grants	£5,800
Cordwainers Christmas grants	£2,500
Holiday grants	£400

Applications

Apply on a form available from the correspondent or to download from the society's website. Applications can be completed by the individual or a third party. If completed by the individual, it must be verified by someone who has known the applicant for some time, who works in a professional capacity and is not related to the applicant; or a third party acting on behalf of the applicant, for example a welfare adviser.

Other information

The charity is also known as the Footwear Benevolent Society and formerly as The Boot Trade Benevolent Society.

The Hugh Fraser Foundation

£16,000 (four grants)

Correspondent: The Trustees, c/o Turcan Connell, Sutherland House, 149 St Vincent Street, Glasgow G2 5NW (0141 441 2111; email: enquiries@ turcanconnell.com)

OSCR number: SC009303

Eligibility

People in need who work or worked in the drapery, printing, publishing, bookselling, stationery and newspaper and allied trades and their dependants. The trustees consider applications particularly from individuals who are or were in the employment of House of Fraser Ltd, Scottish Universal Investments Ltd and Paisleys.

Types of grants

One-off grants according to need.

Annual grant total

In 2016/17 the foundation held assets of £82.3 million and had an income of £2.5 million. Grants were awarded to four individuals and totalled £16,000. Organisations received a further £1.3 million.

Applications

Apply in writing to the correspondent. The trustees meet on a quarterly basis and applications should be received three months before funding is required.

Note: the foundation's focus is on making grants to charitable organisations and only rarely, and in exceptional circumstances, will the trustees consider applications from individuals and their dependants.

The Furniture Makers' Company

£118,000 (145 grants)

Correspondent: The Welfare Officer, 12 Austin Friars, London EC2N 2HE (020 7562 8523; email: welfareofficer@ furnituremakers.org.uk; website: www. furnituremakers.org.uk)

CC number: 1015519

Eligibility

Current and former employees of the furnishing industry and their dependants who are in financial need. Applicants must normally have worked in the industry for a minimum of two years.

Types of grants

The charity's 2017 application guidelines state that grants can be awarded for:

- Essential household items
- Essential household bills
- Funeral expenses
- Disabled adaptations
- Property repairs considered essential due to age, security or access
- Disabled/medical equipment
- Respite/convalescent breaks
- General financial hardship
- Pre-tenancy costs and removal costs

The charity also provided annuities.

Annual grant total

In 2015/16 the charity had assets of £7.9 million and an income of £827,500. Grants to individuals totalled £118,000.

During the year the charity supported just under 100 people through quarterly grants and 45 people through one-off grants.

Exclusions

The charity's 2017 application guidelines state its current exclusions are:

- Assistance towards the clearance of consumer credit debt
- Bankruptcy fees and Debt Relief Orders
- Legal costs
- Private education fees
- Replacement of statutory funding
- Non-essential home improvements
- Ongoing financial assistance
- Loans of any kind
- Memorial stones
- Holidays

Applications

Application forms are available to download from the charity's website.

Other information

Bursaries are given to university students in order to complete their MA qualifications in Furniture Making and Design.

The charity states that the majority of people helped with welfare grants are over the age of 70.

The GPM Charitable Trust

£6,000

Correspondent: Keith Keys, 43 Spriggs Close, Clapham, Bedford MK41 6GD (07733 262991; email: gpmcharitabletrust@tiscali.co.uk; website: www.gpmtrust.org)

CC number: 227177

Eligibility

Workers, former workers and their dependants in the printing, graphical, papermaking and media industries.

Types of grants

Grants have been made: to help with the purchase of mobility aids; to finance home improvements to enable applicants to remain in their own homes; and towards the cost of a respite or convalescent break.

Annual grant total

In 2016/17 the trust had an income of £23,500 and a total expenditure of £12,500. We estimate that welfare grants to individuals totalled around £6,000.

Applications

An application form can be downloaded from the trust's website or requested from the correspondent. It must be printed and completed in black ink before being returned to the trust. The dates of application deadlines for subsequent trustees' meetings are listed on the website.

The Hairdressers' Charity

Correspondent: Jean Kelly, Secretary, 1st Floor, 1 Abbey Court, Fraser Road, Priory Business Park, Bedford MK44 3WH (01234 831888; email: info@thehairdresserscharity.org)

CC number: 1166298

Eligibility

Hairdressers with a minimum of three years experience or people who worked as a hairdresser for a minimum of five years. Help is available for the individual or for their immediate family or other dependants.

Types of grants

Regular quarterly payments and one-off grants to meet short-term needs. Clothing allowances for school uniforms as well as Christmas and birthday presents are available for children under the age of 16.

Annual grant total

The charity registered with the Charity Commission in 2016 but due to its low income its accounts were not available to view. According to the charity's website, it 'receives more than 300 applications for help each year and currently has more than 100 long-term beneficiaries'.

Exclusions

The charity does not help with debt, loan payments or bankruptcy fees except for in exceptional circumstances. Home improvements will only be considered if they are adaptations related to disability or other health conditions.

Applications

Application forms are available to download from the charity's website or can be requested from the

correspondent. In order to process the application the fund will need to know: what help is needed, why the help is needed, the applicant's length of involvement in the industry and when they last worked in the industry. The form should be completed and returned with copies of bank statements and proof of your involvement in the hairdressing industry.

Applications are reviewed on a monthly basis and the charity notifies all applicants of their decision.

The British Jewellery, Giftware and Finishing Federation Benevolent Society

£49,500 (51 grants)

Correspondent: Laura Banner, Board Liaison and Office Manager, Federation House, 10 Vyse Street, Hockley, Birmingham B18 6LT (0121 236 2657; email: laura.b.banner@gmail.com; website: www.thebenevolentsociety.co.uk)

CC number: 208722

Eligibility

People who are studying to begin their career in the industry sectors covered by the National Association of Jewellers, British Travelgoods and Accessories Association, The Giftware Association, the Jewellery Distributors' Association and the Surface Engineering Association, or those who used to work in these industry sectors. Applicants or their employer do not have to have been a member of any of the above-mentioned trade associations.

Types of grants

One-off grants are given towards the provision of essential items such as cookers, washing machines, fridges, freezers, bedding, winter clothing, telephone rental, television licence fees and household repairs. Recurrent grants are also paid to those on a low income. Interest-free loans and educational bursaries may also be awarded.

Annual grant total

In 2016 the society held assets of £954,500 and had an income of £105,000. Grants were made to 51 individuals totalling £49,500 and bursaries totalling £15,000 were awarded to two students so they could begin their careers.

Applications

Apply on a form on the charity's website. The charity can offer assistance with completing the form if needed. Applications can be submitted either directly by the individual or through a social worker, Citizens Advice, welfare agency or other third party. Applications are considered at quarterly trustees' meetings, but urgent requests may be dealt outside meetings. The charity visits applicants where possible.

Other information

In 2016 the charity changed its name to 'The Benevolent Society' to encompass all of the industries covered by the British Allied Trades Federation and assisted by the society and to allow the charity to help individuals beginning their career by providing support for education costs. To avoid confusion with similarly named charities we have kept its former name.

Leather and Hides Trades' Benevolent Institution

£60,500 (57 grants)

Correspondent: Karen Harriman, Secretary, 143 Barkby Road, Leicester LE4 9LG (0116 274 1500; email: karenharriman@btconnect.com; website: www.lhtbi.org.uk)

CC number: 206133

Eligibility

People who work or have worked in the leather trade (i.e. in the production of leather or in the handling of hide and skin) for ten years or more. Applicants are usually over 60, although people under 60 may also be considered. Bereaved spouses are also eligible to apply.

Types of grants

Currently, annuities of between £260 and £1,340 a year (paid quarterly). Applications for grants in cases of personal hardship are considered from persons who have at least ten years' service in the leather industry. Grants may be in the form of an annuity or one-off grant for a special need.

Annual grant total

In 2015 the charity had assets of £794,500 and an income of £61,000. Annuities and grants were made to around 57 individuals totalling £60,500.

Applications

Apply on a form available from the correspondent or through the charity's website. Applications can be submitted directly by the individual or through a social worker, Citizens Advice or other welfare agency. Applications can be considered at any time.

Note: Recurrent grants are subject to annual review.

The Society of Motor Manufacturers and Traders Charitable Trust Fund

£3,000

Correspondent: Simona Testa, Assistant Company Secretary, SMMT, 71 Great Peter Street, London SW1P 2BN (020 7344 9267; email: charitabletrust@smmt.co.uk; website: www.smmt.co.uk)

CC number: 209852

Eligibility

People in need who are associated with the motor industry, and their dependants.

Types of grants

One-off and recurrent grants are given according to need.

Annual grant total

In 2016 the charity had assets of £1.4 million and an income of £41,500. Grants totalled £39,500, the vast majority of which (£36,500) was awarded to the Foyer Federation. Grants made through BEN for the benefit of individuals totalled £3,000.

Applications

The annual report for 2016 explains that:

> Since 1990 under an informal arrangement, BEN [Motor & Allied Trades Benevolent Fund] have assisted in the administration of Trust beneficiaries' income payments. This relationship arose as BEN was able to provide an existing structure within which the suitability for payment of prospective SMMT Charitable Trust Fund beneficiaries could be assessed.

See the entry for BEN for details on how to apply for support.

Scottish Hide and Leather Trades' Provident and Benevolent Society

£10,000

Correspondent: Trust Administrator, c/o Mitchells Roberton Solicitors, George House, 36 North Hanover Street, Glasgow G1 2AD

OSCR number: SC004504

Eligibility

Retired members of the hide and leather trades in Scotland, their widows, and children of deceased members.

Types of grants

One-off and recurrent payments in the forms of grants, loans, pensions, donations, and gifts.

Annual grant total

In 2016 the charity had an income of £10,000 and a total expenditure of £10,500. We estimate that grants to individuals totalled £10,000.

Applications

Applications can be made in writing to the correspondent.

The Silversmiths and Jewellers Charity

£73,000

Correspondent: Julie Griffin, PO Box 61660, London SE9 9AN (020 8265 9288; email: info@thesjcharity.co.uk; website: www.tsjc.org.uk)

CC number: 205785

Eligibility

Any current or previous professionals in silversmithing and jewellery trade. No age restriction.

Types of grants

Quarterly payments together with summer gifts (£100 in 2016), Christmas gifts (£250 in 2016) and Christmas hampers are given to regular grantees. One-off grants are also made for special needs such as domestic goods, furniture, bedding and hospital travel costs.

Annual grant total

In 2016 the charity had an income of £186,000, and assets of £2.2 million. During the year, the charity paid £73,000 in grants to individuals.

Applications

Apply on a form on the charity's website or in writing to the correspondent, including the details of the applicant, a summary of why the grant is needed and the amount required. Applications can be submitted directly by the individual or through a social worker, Citizens Advice or other welfare agency.

Other information

This charity was previously known as The Goldsmiths', Silversmiths' and Jewellers' Benevolent Society.

The Timber Trades Benevolent Society

£147,500

Correspondent: Ivan Savage, 19 Church Lane, Oulton, Stone ST15 8UL (084489222 05; email: info@ttbs.org.uk; website: www.ttbs.org.uk)

CC number: 207734

Eligibility

People who have worked for a minimum of 10 (or five in exceptional circumstances) years for a firm selling timber commercially, such as timber merchants, importers or exporters or agents and their dependants. Note the society does not cover carpenters or joiners. Applications are also considered from employees of trussed rafter manufacturing companies, who are accredited members of the Trussed Rafter Association (TRA) subject to existing criteria and employees of accredited timber preservative processing companies.

Types of grants

Grants have been awarded towards heating installation, adaptation of cars for the use of people with disabilities, domestic appliances, phone rentals, TV rental or licences, hampers, funeral costs house repairs or essential car maintenance. Winter fuel grants are also made. Regular allowances are paid quarterly.

Annual grant total

In 2016 the society had assets of £3.3 million and an income of £278,500. Grants to individuals totalled £147,500 and were broken down as follows:

Quarterly allowances	£58,000
Winter fuel payments	£29,500
Christmas gifts	£23,500
Telephone rental	£14,100
Occasional and funeral grants	£13,000
Spring grants	£5,000
TV licences	£3,700
Respite grants	£200

Applications

Application forms are available from the correspondent. Applications can be submitted directly by the individual or through a social worker, Citizens Advice, welfare agency or other third party; they are considered on a regular basis.

The Tobacco Pipe Makers and Tobacco Trade Benevolent Fund

£190,000 (200+ grants)

Correspondent: Ralph Edmonson, Secretary, 2 Spa Close, Brill, Aylesbury, Buckinghamshire HP18 9RZ (01844 238655; fax: 020 8663 0949; email: info@ tobaccocharity.org.uk; website: www. tobaccocharity.org.uk)

CC number: 1135646

Eligibility

People who have been engaged for a substantial period of time in the manufacture, wholesale or retail sectors of the tobacco industry and their dependants, who are in need. Both full-time and part-time workers are eligible for assistance. Applicants should have no more than £12,000 in savings/capital (not including property).

Types of grants

Recurrent payments and one-off grants, mainly for household items, television licences and house repairs. Grants are also given to help with winter fuel costs and at birthdays and Christmas.

Annual grant total

In 2016/17 the fund held assets of £7.8 million and had an income of £373,500. Grants made to around 200 individuals totalled £190,000 and were distributed as follows:

Pensions and general relief	£61,500
Maintenance grants	£29,400
One-off grants	£25,500
Welfare assistance	£35,500
TV rentals and licences	£11,500
Christmas and birthday gifts	£21,000
House insurance	£1,000
Deprecation of buildings	£400

Applications

Application forms are available from the correspondent or to download from the website. They can be submitted directly by the individual or through a social worker, Citizens Advice, welfare agency or other third party. Applicants are asked to provide details of the length of their service in the tobacco trade, financial position and whether they own their own home. Applications are considered regularly throughout the year.

Other information

The fund was formed in April 2010 as a result of a merger between the Tobacco Trade Benevolent Association, the Worshipful Company of Tobacco Pipe Makers and Tobacco Blenders Benevolent Fund. The fund works alongside other charities such as GroceryAid, The Royal British Legion and SSAFA to help achieve its objectives.

Beneficiaries are visited regularly and are provided with a point of contact.

Grants are also awarded to charitable organisations.

The National Benevolent Society of Watch and Clock Makers

£192,000 (128 grants)

Correspondent: Anne Baker, Secretary, 19 Illet Way, Faygate, West Sussex RH12 0AJ (020 8288 9559; email: sec@ nbswcm.org; website: www.nbswcm.org)

CC number: 206750

Eligibility

Members of the UK watch and clock trade and their widows/widowers and dependants that are in need. Generally grants are given to those with an income

below £15,000 although the trustees have the discretion to act outside this criterion in certain circumstances.

Types of grants

Quarterly payments of £250 in December, March, June and September were made to each beneficiary during the year in review (an average of 130 grants per quarter), in addition a seasonal Christmas gift of £300 was made to each in December 2015 (131 gifts in total), a heating gift of £100 in March 2015 (128 gifts in total) and a summer gift of £100 in June 2016 (127 gifts in total).

Annual grant total

In 2015/16 the charity held assets of £2.7 million and had an income of £98,500. During the year, the charity gave around £192,000 in grants to individuals. Grants were distributed as follows:

Grants in aid	£127,500
Heating and seasonal gifts	£64,000
Television licence fees	£400

Exclusions

Grants are not usually awarded for individual items such as disability aids or home adaptations; however, the charity's website states that 'if an individual has a requirement for these and cannot find the funds, their income may be such that they qualify for a recurrent grant'.

Applications

Applications for grants should be made by contacting the secretary, providing the applicant's full name, address, telephone number and any relevant details. The secretary will then send an application form. Completed forms should be submitted by individuals or, if they require assistance, through a family member, social worker, welfare agency or Citizens Advice.

Sports

British Boxing Board of Control Charitable Trust

£18,100

Correspondent: Robert Smith, 14 North Road, Cardiff CF10 3DY (029 2036 7000, email: rsmith@bbbofc.com)

CC number: 1068585

Eligibility

People actively engaged or who have been actively engaged in the sport of professional boxing and their dependants.

Types of grants

One-off grants according to need.

Annual grant total

In 2016 the charity held assets of £177,500 and an income of £56,000. Grants to individuals totalled £18,100.

Applications

Apply in writing to the correspondent.

The Cardiff Blues Regional Benevolent Trust

£297,000

Correspondent: Martin Ryan, 36 Kew Green, Richmond TW9 3BH (020 8940 6616)

CC number: 1165480

Eligibility

Players or staff at a rugby club within the geographic area of the Cardiff Blues region who are in need.

Types of grants

One-off grants according to need.

Annual grant total

In 2016 the trust had assets of £14,500 and an income of £338,500. Grants to individuals totalled £297,000.

Applications

Apply in writing to the correspondent.

The Football Association Benevolent Fund

£27,000 (32 grants)

Correspondent: Richard McDermott, Secretary, Wembley Stadium, PO Box 1966, London SW1P 9EQ (0844 980 8200 ext. 6575; email: richard. mcdermott@thefa.com)

CC number: 299012

Eligibility

People who have been involved in Association Football in any capacity, such as players and referees, and their dependants, who are in need. The fund interprets people involved in football as broadly as possible, although it tends not to support professional footballers, passing their details on to the occupational benevolent funds which they can apply to.

Types of grants

One-off and recurrent grants are given to meet any need.

Annual grant total

In 2016 the fund held assets of £5.3 million and had an income of

£157,000. Grants were made to 32 individuals totalling £27,000.

Applications

Application forms are available from the correspondent. Applications should be made through the County Football Associations. They are considered on a regular basis.

Institute of Football Management and Administration Charity Trust

£1,400

Correspondent: Graham Mackrell, Trustee, The Camkin Suite, 1 Pegasus House, Tachbrook Park, Warwick CV34 6LW (01926 831556; fax: 01926 429781; email: ifma@lmasecure.com)

CC number: 277200

Eligibility

Members or former members of the institute (formerly the Football League Executive Staffs Association) who have worked for a Football League or Premier League Club and who are in need, and their widows/widowers.

Types of grants

One-off grants in particular cases of need, and Christmas vouchers.

Annual grant total

In 2015/16 the charity had no income for the year and had a total expenditure of £1,600. We estimate that grants given to individuals totalled around £1,400.

Applications

Apply in writing to the correspondent. Applications can be submitted directly by the individual or through a family member, friend or colleague.

Grand Prix Trust

£27,000

Correspondent: Sally Oliver, Case Advisor, Eighth Floor, 6 New Street Square, New Fetter Lane, London EC4A 3AQ (020 7842 2000; email: office@grandprixtrust.com; website: www.grandprixtrust.com)

CC number: 327454

Eligibility

Past and present Grand Prix mechanics and their dependants who are in need.

Types of grants

One-off and recurrent grants towards medical costs, bills, living expenses and so on.

Annual grant total

In 2016 the trust held assets of almost £2.6 million and had an income of £102,500. Grants were made to individuals and organisations and totalled £54,000. We have estimated that £27,000 was awarded to individuals for welfare purposes during the year.

Applications

Apply in writing to the correspondent or via the online contact form. The trustees consider donations at their Appeals and Awards Committee meetings and also bi-annual trustees' meetings. The trustees continue to monitor the requirements of potential beneficiaries and provides advice and guidance to beneficiaries, as well as providing financial support.

The Hornsby Professional Cricketers Fund

£51,500

Correspondent: The Revd Michael Vockins, Secretary, Birchwood Lodge, Birchwood, Storridge, Malvern, Worcestershire WR13 5EZ (01886 884366; email: mdvockins@btinternet. com)

CC number: 235561

Eligibility

Former professional cricketers and their dependants who are in need.

Types of grants

Monthly grants, special Christmas and mid-summer grants, and heating allowances. One-off payments may be given to help with a particular or urgent need. Assistance may also be given towards medical costs and special equipment such as electric wheelchairs and stairlifts.

Annual grant total

In 2015/16 the charity held assets of £388,000 and had an income of £35,500. Grants to individuals totalled £51,500 and were distributed as follows:

Monthly allowances	8	£28,500
Heating allowance	7	£7,400
Winter allowances	9	£6,800
Summer allowances	9	£6,300
Former WHMF recipients	5	£2,900

Applications

Apply in writing to the correspondent. Applications can be submitted either directly by the individual or by a county cricket club or similar association. Decisions are made at trustees' meetings three times each year.

In the Game

£33,000

Correspondent: The Trustees, In The Game, League Managers Association, National Football Centre, Newborough Road, Needwood, Burton upon Trent DE13 9PD (01283 576350; email: lma@lmasecure.com; website: www.leaguemanagers.com)

CC number: 1016248

Eligibility

Members of the League Managers Association who are in need and their wives, widows and children.

Types of grants

One-off and recurrent grants are given according to need.

Annual grant total

In 2015/16 the charity had a total income of £50,000 and a total expenditure of £56,500. The charity awarded a total of £33,000 in grants to individuals for welfare purposes.

The charity also gave £21,500 to organisations during the year.

Applications

Apply in writing to the correspondent. Applications are considered throughout the year.

Other information

The charity is otherwise known as The League Manager's Benevolent Trust.

PGA European Tour Benevolent Trust

£165,000 (15 grants)

Correspondent: Charlotte Duffain, PGA Building, Wentworth Drive, Virginia Water, Surrey GU25 4LX (01344 840400; email: cduffain@europeantour.com; website: www.europeantour.com/tourgroup/benevolenttrust/index.html)

CC number: 327207

Eligibility

'Members and former members of the PGA European Tour and other people whose main livelihood is, or has been, earned by providing services to professional golf', and their dependants.

Types of grants

One-off or recurrent grants according to need.

Annual grant total

In 2016 the charity held assets of £5.3 million and had an income of £37,500. During the year, the charity awarded around £165,000 in grants to individuals.

Applications

Apply in writing to the correspondent at any time. Applications can be submitted directly by the individual or through a social worker, Citizens Advice, other welfare agency or another third party.

The Professional Billiards and Snooker Players' Benevolent Fund

£10,000

Correspondent: Simon Brownell, Fund Secretary, World Snooker Ltd, 75 Whiteladies Road, Clifton, Bristol BS28 2NT (0117 317 8200; email: simon.brownell@worldsnooker.com; website: www.wpbsa.com/players/player-support/benevolent-fund)

CC number: 288352

Eligibility

Current or retired professional snooker or billiards players who are members of the World Professional Billiards and Snooker Association and their dependants, who are in need.

Types of grants

One-off grants and interest-free loans according to need. Trustees currently prioritise one-off payments on the death of players, payments to cover the private medical insurance policies of those who are ill or have suffered an injury related to the sport and the provision of loans for specific purposes to be repaid over a set period of time.

Annual grant total

In 2016/17 the fund had an income of £16 and a total expenditure of £15,200. We estimate that grants given to individuals totalled around £10,000.

Exclusions

The website notes the following:

> The Trustees have recently decided that they will no longer be able to provide financial assistance to tour players struggling with the cost of playing on the tour and that whilst they will consider all applications put to the board on a case by case basis, applications for such financial assistance are not likely to be approved.

Applications

Application forms are available to download from the website or from the correspondent. Personal and financial details and medical evidence should be included where appropriate. Applicants for loans will be asked to identify how the loan will be repaid.

Lower priority will also be given to members who suffer financial difficulty as a result of debt, alcohol, drugs, gambling or any other addiction. In the event that the trustees agree to support such an application the trustees reserve the right to pay any financial support to third party organisations to support the beneficiary.

Professional Footballers' Association Accident Insurance Fund

£2.5 million

Correspondent: Darren Wilson, Director of Finance, 20 Oxford Court, Bishopsgate, Manchester M2 3WQ (0161 236 0575; email: info@thepfa.co.uk; website: www.givemefootball.com)

Eligibility

Members or former members of the association in England and Wales who require medical treatment as a result of a specific injury or illness which results in their permanent total disability to play professional football.

Types of grants

Grants are to provide private medical treatment for all members and for members unable to claim under the terms of the PFA accident insurance policy due to the nature/circumstances of the injury. Grants are also given to meet operation costs which may not be covered by the insurance. Grants are also available to former members for treatment on injuries received as a result of their playing career.

Annual grant total

Direct expenditure (excluding support costs and legal and professional fees) totalled almost £2.5 million in 2016/17 and can be broken down as follows:

Insurance premiums	£901,500
Medical fees and grants	£899,000
Permanent total disability	£394,000
Spire costs	£221,500
Other costs	£63,000

Applications

Application forms are available from the correspondent. Completed applications should be returned directly by the individual or by a family member/social worker on their behalf. There are no deadlines and applications are considered as they are received.

Other information

The fund contributes to ensure that all Premier League and Football League contracted players are covered under the PFA's Accident and Sickness Insurance Scheme.

Racing Welfare

£186,000

Correspondent: The Welfare Team, 20B Park Lane, Newmarket, Suffolk CB8 8QD (0800 630 0443; email: info@racingwelfare.co.uk; website: www.racingwelfare.co.uk)

CC number: 1084042

Eligibility

People in need who are, or have been, employed in the thoroughbred horse-racing and breeding industry, and their dependants. Applicants must have worked in the industry for at least five years (with the exception of anyone who has had a work-related accident and/or is under the age of 25).

Types of grants

One-off grants according to need. Examples of where the charity may be able to help include: mobility equipment; counselling; utility bills; food; housing costs in emergency situations; physiotherapy; and white goods.

Annual grant total

In 2016 the charity had assets of £15.9 million and an income of £1.8 million. Grants to individuals in need were made totalling £186,000.

Applications

Contact the charity by calling its 24-hour helpline. A welfare officer will then assist with making an application.

Other information

The charity's main activity is the provision of support and guidance through its welfare officers based all over the country who offer information and advice, including on financial and personal issues, health and housing. There is a 24-hour helpline (0800 630 0443) offering advice. The charity also provides housing services, runs a holiday scheme for older beneficiaries and those with disabilities, continues to fund sporting events and sports centre memberships for those in need, and has a life skills programme at the Northern Racing College, British Racing School and National Stud, for young people between the ages of 16 and 19.

The Referees' Association Members' Benevolent Fund

£7,500

Correspondent: The Clerk to the Trustees, 63 Hazel Road, Rubery, Birmingham B45 9DY (0121 453 4622; email: ra@footballreferee.org; website: the-ra.org)

CC number: 800845

Eligibility

Members and former members of the association in England and their dependants who are in need.

Types of grants

One-off and recurrent grants to relieve an immediate financial need such as hospital expenses, convalescence, clothing, living costs, household bills, medical equipment and help in the home.

Annual grant total

In 2016/17 the fund had an income of £11,900 and a total expenditure of £7,700. We estimate that grants given to individuals totalled around £7,500.

Applications

Apply on a form available from the correspondent or to download from the fund's website. Applications should be submitted directly by the individual for consideration at any time.

The RFL Benevolent Fund (Try Assist)

£468,500 (195 grants)

Correspondent: Steve Ball, General Manager, Red Hall, Red Hall Lane, Leeds, West Yorkshire LS17 8NB (0844 477 7113; email: info@tryassist.co.uk; website: www.rflbenevolentfund.co.uk)

CC number: 1109858

Eligibility

People who play or assist, or who have played or assisted, in Rugby League in the UK or for a team affiliated to an association primarily based in the UK, and their dependants. Beneficiaries should be in hardship or distress, in particular, as a result of injury through playing or training, or when travelling to or from a game or training session.

Types of grants

Hardship grants, also donations towards special vehicles and repairs, home modifications, furniture, wheelchairs, gym equipment, funeral costs, computers, hotel accommodation, travel, physiotherapy, home appliances, educational courses and Christmas presents. Grants are also made for educational purposes.

Annual grant total

In 2016 the fund held assets of £565,000 and had an income of £452,500. Grants were made to 195 individuals and totalled £468,500.

Applications

In the first instance, contact the correspondent.

Welsh Rugby International Players Association

£1,400

Correspondent: John Williams, Trustee, 75 Village Farm Road, Village Farm Industrial Estate, Pyle, Bridgend, Mid Glamorgan CF33 6BN (01656 744311; email: enquiries@jjwilliamsltd.com (or use contact form on website); website: wrex.co.uk)

CC number: 1102484

Eligibility

Current and former Welsh international rugby players or their families and dependants who are in need. This specifically includes: those requiring medical treatment for physical or mental illnesses or injuries that may relate to their time playing rugby; and those whose earning capacity has been adversely impacted by injuries or illnesses relating to their time in the sport.

The charity's website notes: 'Whilst charities exist to help those seriously injured on the field, we wanted to provide support to those who have given so much for their country on the field of play but whose problems are very varied.'

Types of grants

One-off grants according to need.

Annual grant total

In 2015/16 the charity had an income of £13,200 and a total expenditure of £1,700. We estimate that grants given to individuals totalled around £1,400.

Note: The charity's income and expenditure tend to fluctuate each year.

Applications

Apply in writing to the correspondent.

Transport and storage

Railway Benefit Fund

£306,500

Correspondent: Jason Tetley, 1st Floor Millennium House, 40 Nantwich Road, Crewe CW2 6AD (0345 241 2885; email: support@railwaybenefitfund.org.uk; website: www.railwaybenefitfund.org.uk)

CC number: 206312

Eligibility

Current and former railway staff, and their dependants, who are in need.

Types of grants

One-off and recurrent grants of £100 to £1,500. The main types of grants are:

- Single benevolent grants – one-off grants provided to meet specific needs, for example, to assist with the costs of convalescence, disability equipment, funeral expenses, debts and arrears, minor house repairs and household equipment
- Annuities – paid quarterly to people on a low income
- Residential care grants – paid monthly to 'top up' care home fees
- Webb Fund grants – paid quarterly to assist the parents of underprivileged dependent children
- Childcare grants are one-off payments given towards clothing, footwear, school projects and the initial costs of entering higher education

Annual grant total

In 2016 the charity had assets of £4.1 million and an income of £943,500. Welfare grants to individuals totalled £306,500.

Applications

Applications are available to download from the website, or can be requested by telephone, via the Contact Us form on the website, or by emailing support@ railwaybenefitfund.org.uk.

Air

The Air Pilots Benevolent Fund

£12,000

Correspondent: Captain John Towell, Cobham House, 9 Warwich Court, Gray's Inn, London WC1 R5DJ (01276 47050; email: office@airpilots.org; website: www.airpilots.org)

CC number: 212952

Eligibility

Members of The Honourable Company of Air Pilots and those who have been engaged professionally as air pilots or air navigators in commercial aviation and their dependants.

Types of grants

One-off and recurrent grants ranging between £250 and £2,000. Grants and loans can be made to assist in the rehabilitation of people after accidents or to enable them to regain licences.

Annual grant total

In 2015/16 the fund had assets of £721,000 and an income of £71,000. Grants were made totalling £68,500 and consisted of:

PPL Scholarships via Air Pilots Trust	£27,000
Flying Instructor Development Bursary	£10,000
Regular grants	£9,500
Flying Scholarship for Disabled People	£9,000
Ray Jeffs Gliding Scholarships	£4,000
Inner London Schools Gliding	£3,600
City University Bursary via Air Safety Trust	£3,000
Occasional grants	£2,500

Exclusions

The fund cannot give grant or loan money for the repayment of debts or long-term expenses such as school fees, prolonged medical care or for obtaining professional pilots' licences and ratings.

Applications

Requests for support should be made on the 'Application for Financial Assistance' form. Appeals are reviewed at the quarterly meetings, although immediate grants may be made (the fund's office should be contacted directly if there is such an urgent need).

The fund works closely with the other aviation charities for individuals (both military and civilian). If an applicant has approached another such charity, they should say so in their application to this fund.

Other information

The fund was previously called The Guild of Air Pilots Benevolent Fund and provides both educational and welfare support.

The fund is administered by The Honourable Company of Air Pilots which is also managing Air Safety Trust and Air Pilots Trust.

People who want to become pilots or wish to gain further qualifications in the aviation industry are supported by The Honourable Company of Air Pilots.

The British Airline Pilots' Association Benevolent Fund (BALPA)

£12,900

Correspondent: Antionette Girdler, BALPA House, 5 Heathrow Boulevard, 278 Bath Road, West Drayton UB7 0DQ (020 8476 4029; email: tonigirdler@ balpa.org)

CC number: 229957

Eligibility

Current or retired British commercial airline pilots, flight engineers and winchmen, and their dependants.

Types of grants

One-off and recurrent grants and interest-free loans. The fund prefers to give grants for specific needs such as electricity bills, or school books for children.

Annual grant total

In 2015/16 the charity had assets of £1.6 million and an income of £34,500. Grants totalled £25,800 and interest-free loans were made to the sum of £89,000. We estimate that grants for welfare purposes totalled around £12,900.

Exclusions

Grants are not given for school fees.

Applications

Apply in writing to the correspondent to request an application form. Applications are considered quarterly.

British Airline Pilots Association Benevolent Fund

£36,000

Correspondent: Simon Collins-Dryer, 5 Heathrow Boulevard, 278 Bath Road, Sipson, West Drayton UB7 0DQ (020 8476 4029; email: scdaccountancy@ yahoo.co.uk)

CC number: 229957

Eligibility

Current and former commercial airline pilots and navigators, flight engineers and British Airline Pilots Association employees, and their families.

Types of grants

One-off grants and loans according to need.

Annual grant total

In 2015/16 the fund had assets of £1.7 million and an income of £34,500. Grants to individuals totalled £36,000.

Applications

Apply in writing to the correspondent.

British Airways Welfare and Benevolent Fund

£23,000

Correspondent: Roopal Radia, British Airways plc, PO Box 365, Harmondsworth, West Drayton UB7 0GB

CC number: 282480

Eligibility

Present and former employees of British Airways and their dependants.

Types of grants

One-off grants according to need.

Annual grant total

In 2016 the fund had assets of £2.4 million and an income of £59,500. Grants to individuals totalled £23,000.

Applications

Apply in writing to the correspondent.

Land

Associated Society of Locomotive Engineers and Firemen (ASLEF) Hardship Fund

£8,000

Correspondent: The General Secretary, ASLEF, 77 St John Street, Clerkenwell, London EC1M 4NN (020 7324 2400; fax: 020 7490 8697; email: info@aslef.org.uk; website: www.aslef.org.uk)

Eligibility

Members of ASLEF, and their dependants, who are in need.

Types of grants

One-off grants are given according to need.

Annual grant total

In 2016 the fund had assets of £1.5 million and an income of £89,500 from members' contributions. Grants to individuals totalled £8,000.

Applications

Apply in writing to the correspondent.

The Worshipful Company of Carmen Benevolent Trust

See entry on page 182

Removers Benevolent Association

£10,000

Correspondent: RBA administrator, The British Association of Removers, Tangent House, 62 Exchange Road, Watford, Hertfordshire WD18 0TG (01923 699480; fax: 01923 699481; email: rba@bar.co.uk; website: www.bar.co.uk/rba)

CC number: 284012

Eligibility

People in need who are, or have been, employed for a minimum of two years by a member of the British Association of Removers Ltd, and their dependants.

Types of grants

One-off grants to help those experiencing a temporary period of financial difficulty due to an illness or other difficulties. Occasionally, recurrent grants may be given.

Annual grant total

In 2016 the charity had an income of £19,300 and a total expenditure of £21,500. We estimate that grants given to individuals totalled around £10,000, with funding also awarded to organisations.

Applications

Application forms can be downloaded from the website. Applications should be made by the BAR member company the applicant has worked for on their behalf. They are considered upon submission.

RMT (National Union of Rail, Maritime and Transport Workers) Orphan Fund

£150,000

Correspondent: Collin Sharpe, Unity House, 39 Chalton Street, London NW1 1JD (020 7529 8291; email: info@rmt.org.uk; website: www.rmt.org.uk/member-benefits/orphan-benefit)

Eligibility

Children of deceased members of the RMT union who are under the age of 22.

Types of grants

Grants of £12 per week for each child under 16, and £12.75 per week for those between the ages of 16 and 22 who are in full-time education, payable on the member's death.

Annual grant total

Our research indicates that around £150,000 is distributed in grants each year.

Applications

Application forms are available from the local union branch or to download from the union's website. For children over the age of 16 in full-time education an education certificate should also be attached. Applications should be made through the local union branch and must be endorsed by the branch secretary. Grants are made quarterly, usually in March, June, September and December.

The Road Haulage Association Benevolent Fund

£15,000

Correspondent: Sheikh Ali, Correspondent, Road Haulage Association, Roadway House, The Rural

Centre, Newbridge EH28 8NZ (0131 333 4900; email: s.ali@rha.uk.net; website: www.rha.uk.net)

CC number: 1082820

Eligibility

Current and former members and employees/ex-employees, of the association, and their dependants.

Types of grants

One-off grants according to need.

Annual grant total

In 2016 the charity had assets of £874,500 and an income of £26,500. During the year, the charity gave around £15,000 in grants to individuals.

Exclusions

Grants are not usually awarded towards holidays (unless there are exceptional circumstances).

Applications

Application forms are available from the correspondent. Applications should be submitted directly by the individual or through a social worker, Citizens Advice or other third party. Applications are considered throughout the year.

Mail

Rowland Hill Memorial And Benevolent Fund

£446,500

Correspondent: Mary Jeffery, Manager, Rowland Hill Memorial and Benevolent Fund, Royal Mail, 185 Farringdon Road, London EC1A 1AA (0800 232 1762; email: rowland.hill.fund@royalmail.com; website: www.rowlandhillfund.org)

CC number: 207479

Eligibility

People in need who have been employed by the Royal Mail, Post Office, Parcelforce Worldwide, Romec or associated companies, for at least six months (full or part-time, not casual); retired employees in receipt of a Royal Mail pension; and people who no longer work for Royal Mail or Post Office and have not yet retired, but will receive a Royal Mail pension when they do. If none of the above apply, you must be able to prove that you were employed by Royal Mail or Post Office Ltd. The direct dependants of such people may also be eligible for assistance. Applicants must have less than £12,000 in savings.

Types of grants

One-off grants of up to £5,000 but usually less than £1,000 for dental work, rent and deposits, council tax, utility bills, mortgage arrears, household items, bankruptcy fees, boiler repairs and funeral expenses. The fund can meet part of the cost of expensive household adaptations. The fund notes that they are increasingly being asked to help pay for counselling, and can pledge to cover a set amount of sessions.

Occasionally the fund can make a regular grant of £100 per month for twelve months.

Annual grant total

In 2016/17 the fund held assets of £4.8 million and had an income of £576,000. Grants to individuals totalled £446,500.

Applications

Call the free 24-hour helpline operated by Royal Mail (0345 6004586). A trained adviser will conduct a telephone assessment (approximately 40 minutes in length) to discuss what you are applying for as well as requesting details of income, expenditure and any savings and documentary evidence that supports your application. This includes recent bank statements, details of Royal Mail service, medical evidence and cost estimates, if appropriate. They will then, with your agreement, prepare a report of the case for the trustees' consideration.

People applying through a third party such as a social worker or Citizens Advice may apply by telephone or in writing to the correspondent, including as much background information and supporting documentation as possible. The fund also accepts SSAFA Form A and will ask for bank statements.

The National Federation of Sub-Postmasters Benevolent Fund

£90,000

Correspondent: George Thomson, General Secretary, Evelyn House, 22 Windlesham Gardens, Shoreham-by-Sea, West Sussex BN43 5AZ (01273 452324; fax: 01273 465403; email: benfund@nfsp.org.uk; website: www.nfsp.org.uk)

CC number: 262704

Eligibility

Serving or retired sub-postmasters/sub-postmistresses, full-time employees of the NFSP, and the dependants of the above in the event of a breakdown in health, bereavement or domestic distress.

Types of grants

One-off and recurrent grants are given according to need. Support can be given in for a wide range of requirements, for example towards installing equipment in the post office to help the applicant work, holiday expenses for people with disability or those convalescing, for

home or car adaptations, specific items or equipment to aid medical conditions or disability.

Annual grant total

In 2016 the fund had assets of £1.1 million and an income of £48,500. Grants to individuals totalled £90,000.

Applications

Further information on the fund can be found in the Members Directory section of the website.

Other information

Fund also finances a Trauma Counselling Helpline to assist following a traumatic situation or incident in life, such as trauma reaction after an attack or raid.

Water

The London Shipowners' and Shipbrokers' Benevolent Society

£24,500

Correspondent: Richard Butler, Secretary, 20 St Dunstan's Hill, London EC3R 8HL (020 7283 6090; email: richard.butler@baltic-charities.co.uk)

CC number: 213348

Eligibility

Shipowners and shipbrokers and their dependants.

Types of grants

Annual cost of living grants, paid quarterly, as well as special grants at Christmas and during periods of cold weather. One-off and emergency grants are also available.

Annual grant total

In 2016 the society had an income of £23,500 and a total expenditure of £48,000. During the last financial year, the society was not required to submit its annual accounts. Based on previous years, we estimate that the society gave around £24,500 in grants to individuals through the form of quarterly and special grants.

Applications

Apply in writing to the correspondent.

Other information

The society can also provide advice and counselling.

Voluntary sector

WRVS Benevolent Trust

£30,000

Correspondent: Christopher Digby, 5 Rosemary Place, Maidstone Road, Paddock Wood, Tonbridge TN12 6DG (07894 060 517; email: enquiry@wrvsbt.org.uk; website: www.wrvsbt.org.uk)

CC number: 261931

Eligibility

Individuals who have volunteered or worked for the WVS, WRVS or Royal Voluntary Service and are on a low income.

Types of grants

One-off grants ranging from £50 to £6,000. Recent grants have been made for washing machines and other household items, personal alarms, contribution towards an electric wheelchair, household adaptations and dental treatment. Grants also cover the installation of electrical or white goods and the removal of old equipment.

Annual grant total

In 2016 the trust had an income of £12,500 and a total expenditure of £36,000. We estimate that grants given to individuals totalled around £30,000.

Applications

Applications should be made on a form available to download from the website, and are considered throughout the year. Applications can be made directly by the individual, or by a friend or family member on their behalf.

Livery companies, orders and membership organisations

This chapter includes the charities which award grants to members of a particular association or organisation. This chapter is divided into four sub-sections.

'Livery companies' are listed first. These are some of the oldest charities in the UK, originally set up as guilds by members of the same craft, trade or profession. With a historic connection to the City of London and in some aspects analogous to an early sort of trade union, the companies were originally responsible for training and regulation of their profession, with their halls providing a site for meetings and socialising. The existing Worshipful Companies all continue to practice charitable giving as an integral part of their work – often in the form of benevolence to members of their profession or trade, like those featured in this guide, but often more broadly to the wider community too.

'Orders' lists charities which generally support members of their particular order and their dependants.

'Sports clubs' includes charities which give grants to members of particular clubs, but please note that other sports charities are listed in the 'Occupational charities' chapter. The 'Other' section includes membership organisations that do not fit into any of the above categories.

All of the charities in each section are listed in alphabetical order.

Please note that trade unions are listed in the 'Occupational charities' chapter.

Index of livery companies, orders and membership organisations

Livery companies

The Worshipful Company of Carmen Benevolent Trust

£1,200 (one grant)

Correspondent: Chris Godbold, Hon. Secretary, Plaisterers' Hall, 1 London Wall, London EC2Y 5JU (020 7645 1405; email: carmenbentrust@hotmail.com; website: www.thecarmen.co.uk)

CC number: 1164687

Eligibility

Members (and former members) and employees of The Worshipful Company of Carmen and their dependants. People who have worked in the UK transport/ transport logistics industries can also be assisted.

Types of grants

One-off grants are given where the grant will make an exceptional difference to the individual. One example is a computer to assist an individual with disabilities.

Annual grant total

In 2016/17 the trust had assets of more than £2 million and an income of £159,000. One grant totalling £1,200 was awarded to an individual. All of the other grants made (£117,000) were to organisations.

Exclusions

The trust cannot help with holidays or bankruptcy fees.

Applications

Apply in writing to the correspondent, including as much information as possible about why the grant is needed, how much is required, and what it will be used for. Where appropriate, the trust will source additional evidence from social services or a doctor. The trustees meet at least four times a year – see the website for dates of specific meetings.

Note: grants are only rarely made to individuals.

The Worshipful Company of Engineers Charitable Trust Fund

£600

Correspondent: Anthony Willenbruch, Clerk, Wax Chandlers' Hall, 6 Gresham Street, London EC2V 7AD (020 7726 4830; fax: 020 7726 4820; email: clerk@ engineerscompany.org.uk; website: www. engineerstrust.org.uk)

CC number: 289819

Eligibility

Existing Engineers' Company members, retired members, or, the wives, husbands, widows, widowers, children, orphans and others depending on them can be considered for the relief of hardship; professional engineers who have been engaged in engineering at chartered engineer level in industry and commerce generally can be considered for the relief of hardship.

Types of grants

Grants are generally of up to £1,000 and can be given for various welfare purposes.

Annual grant total

In 2016 the trust had assets of £1.6 million and an income of £95,000. The annual report for the year stated: 'Monetary prizes to the value of £22,000 (2015 £22,362) were made to 7 (2015 7) individuals and grants to a total value of £50,459 (2015 £34,571) were made to individuals and organisations.' In previous years, welfare distributions to individuals have accounted for only a small amount of grants made, and have totalled around £600.

Applications

Applications should be made in writing to the clerk and should provide as much detail about the individual's circumstances as possible.

Other information

The trust also awards annual prizes for excellence in engineering and supports engineering research. Support can be given to organisations concerned with engineering or organisations in the City of London that further the interest of the history, traditions and customs of the city.

The Worshipful Company of Farriers Charitable Trust 1994

£3,800

Correspondent: Dr Ian Fifield, 92 Carshalton Road, Norwich NR1 3BB (07710 955276; email: theclerk@wcf.org. uk; website: www.wcf.org.uk/charity. php)

CC number: 1044726

Eligibility

Registered farriers, their widows and dependants who are in need.

Types of grants

One-off and recurrent grants are given according to need. Grants are usually given to people who are unable to work through injury or sickness.

Annual grant total

In 2015/16 the charity had assets of £1.7 million and an income of £64,000. The charity awarded £3,800 to individuals for welfare purposes.

Applications

Applications should be made in writing directly to the correspondent.

Other information

The charity also makes awards for education for farriers and prospective farriers. The trust also provides for the relief of suffering of horses.

The Anniversaries Fund of the Worshipful Company of Founders

£1,200

Correspondent: Andrew Bell, The Founders Co., Founders Hall, 1 Cloth Fair, London EC1A 7JQ (020 7796 4800; email: office@foundersco.org.uk; website: www.foundersco.org.uk)

CC number: 1006402

Eligibility

People who are in financial hardship, people with a disability, and older people.

Types of grants

Small grants for welfare purposes and poverty relief.

Annual grant total

In 2015/16 the charity had assets of £1.4 million and an income of £45,000. During the year, the charity gave a total of £2,400 in grants to individuals. We estimate that around £1,200 was given in grants to individuals for welfare purposes, with funding also awarded for education.

Applications

Applications can be made in writing to the correspondent. There is an online contact form if you wish to make any initial enquiries.

Other information

The charity's website states that 'the main focus is on young people, gifted or needy or quite often both'.

The Worshipful Company of Launderers Benevolent Trust Fund

£3,600

Correspondent: Margaret Campbell, Clerk, Launderers Hall, 9 Montague Close, London Bridge SE1 9DD (020 7378 1430; email: clerk@launderers.co.uk; website: www.launderers.co.uk)

CC number: 262750

Eligibility

Current and former members of the laundry industry and their dependants.

Types of grants

One-off grants according to need.

Annual grant total

In 2016/17 the charity had assets of £738,000 and an income of £42,000. Grants to individuals totalled £3,600.

Applications

Apply in writing to the correspondent.

Other information

Most of the charity's grant-making is to organisations, usually those working in within the City of London or Southwark.

The Worshipful Company of Scientific Instrument Makers

£2,300

Correspondent: The Clerk, Glaziers Hall, 9 Montague Close, London SE1 9DD (020 7407 4832; email: theclerk@wcsim.co.uk; website: www.wcsim.co.uk)

CC number: 221332

Eligibility

Members and past members of the company and their dependants.

Types of grants

One-off grants according to need. Grants have been used, for example, for bereavement and funeral costs.

Annual grant total

In 2015/16 the charity held assets of £2.9 million and had an income of £98,500. Grants to individuals for educational purposes totalled £51,000 and for social welfare purposes totalled £2,300.

Applications

Apply in writing to the correspondent.

Other information

The majority of the charity's charitable work is concerned with educational scholarships.

Orders

The Coventry Freemen's Charity

£558,500 (2,811 grants)

Correspondent: David Evans, Clerk to the Trustees, 3MC Middlemarch Business Park, Siskin Drive, Coventry CV3 4FJ (024 7625 8621; email: rob.anderson@baldwinandco.co.uk)

CC number: 229237

Eligibility

Freemen and their dependants, as well as the widows, widowers and other former dependants of deceased freemen, who are in need and live within the existing boundary of the city of Coventry or within seven miles of St Mary's Hall, Coventry.

Types of grants

One-off and recurrent grants.

Annual grant total

In 2016 the charity had assets of £14 million and an income of £880,000. Payments made totalled £558,500 and were distributed to 2,798 beneficiaries as follows:

Freemen and women	£437,500
Freemen's widows	£119,000
Special cases	£2,500

Grants for relief in need totalled £2,500.

Applications

Application forms are available from the correspondent and can be submitted directly by the individual.

Guild of Freemen of the City of London

£500

Correspondent: Christine Cook, The Guild of Freemen of the City of London, Rooms 78–79, 65 London Wall, London EC2M 5TU (020 7239 9016)

CC number: 227063

Eligibility

Past and present members of the Guild of Freemen of the City of London, their relatives and dependants.

Types of grants

One-off grants according to need.

Annual grant total

In 2016/17 the charity held assets of £838,500 and had an income of £49,500. Grants to individuals totalled £500.

Applications

Apply in writing to the correspondent.

Grand Lodge of Scotland Annuity Benevolent and Charity Funds

£71,500

Correspondent: The Trustees, c/o Freemasons Hall, 96 George Street, Edinburgh EH2 3DH (0131 225 5577; fax: 0131 225 3953; email: curator@grandlodgescotland.org; website: www.grandlodgescotland.com/about-masonry/charity)

OSCR number: SC001996

Eligibility

Members and their dependants, and the widows and dependants of deceased members.

Types of grants

One-off and recurrent grants which are given based on individual circumstances and are usually used to assist with the cost of day-to-day living expenses.

Annual grant total

In 2015/16 the charity had assets of £12.3 million and an income of £705,000. Grants were made totalling £118,000, of which £91,000 was awarded in 122 grants to individuals. Based on information available from the website, we have calculated that educational grants amounted to around £19,400, with the remaining £71,500 given to individuals for social welfare purposes.

Applications

Apply using a form available from the correspondent or by direct approach to your local lodge. The website explains that cases 'are managed and administered with the assistance of Lodges and Provincial Grand Lodges via [the Grand Lodge's] reporting system'.

Other information

The charity also makes grants to individuals for educational purposes, as well as to organisations, and runs care homes for older people.

The Leicester Freemen's Estate

£4,000 (six grants)

Correspondent: Jane Hammond, Estate Office, 32 Freemen's Holt, Old Church Street, Leicester LE2 8NH (0116 283 4017; email: office@leicesterfreemen. com; website: www.leicesterfreemen. com)

CC number: 244732

Eligibility

Leicester freemen and their widows who are in need due to age or sickness.

Types of grants

Monthly payments and Christmas hampers.

Annual grant total

In 2015 the estate held assets of £6 million and had an income of £240,500. Charitable payments totalling £4,000 was distributed to three freemen and three widows in 2015, by way of monthly payments and Christmas hampers.

Applications

Application forms are available from the correspondent and proof of status as a freeman/widow of a freeman should be included. Applications can be submitted directly by the individual and are considered monthly. Beneficiaries' eligibility is reviewed annually.

Other information

Dinner was provided for 23 people on Christmas day for people who may otherwise have spent the day on their own.

During 2015 sheltered accommodation was provided for 45 people and the provision of 36 bungalows for the charity's beneficiaries enables more council, social and private owned accommodation to be available for the public at large.

Masonic Charitable Foundation

£11.1 million (7,502 grants)

Correspondent: Enquiries Team, Freemasons Hall, 60 Great Queen Street, London WC2B 5AZ (0800 035 6090; email: help@mcf.org.uk)

CC number: 1164703

Eligibility

Freemasons and their families. Surviving partners, divorced or separated partners as well as children and grandchildren are also eligible although they must be able to prove they are/were financially dependent on a Freemason. The Freemason does not necessarily need to be a currently subscribing member, but must have joined before the need arose.

Support can only be given to Freemasons who are or were a member of a Lodge regulated by the United Grand Lodge of England. This includes England, Wales, the Channel Islands and the Isle of Man as well as members of overseas Lodges which follow the English Constitution.

The website notes the following, 'to demonstrate that any support required is beyond their financial means, those seeking our support must complete an assessment of household income, expenditure, savings and capital'.

Types of grants

Grants are available through the following three programmes:

- Financial Grants are available for household bills, food, living expenses, home adaptations for medical or mobility needs, essential home repairs, funeral costs, additional expenses following an accident, redundancy or any other life-changing event that has caused an unexpected loss of income
- Health Grants are available for private treatment or surgery, initial consultations or assessments, dental treatments and mobility equipment
- Family Grants are available for school uniforms, course materials, training and equipment for particular subjects and respite care

Annual grant total

In 2016/17 the foundation held assets of £416.7 million and had an income of £67 million. Grants were made to 7,502 individuals and totalled £11.1 million.

Applications

Before making an application you must contact either your Lodge Almoner or the foundation. If the enquiries team consider you eligible for a grant, a representative will visit you and help you complete the application form. Payments are made directly to the individual or to the supplier providing the equipment or service you require.

If your application is not approved the foundation can advise you on other organisations and services that may be able to help.

Other information

The foundation also runs a counselling careline and provides a range of nursing, residential and dementia care homes across England and Wales. Grants are also made to organisations and hospices.

Grand Charitable Trust of the Order of Women Freemasons

£2,700

Correspondent: The Trustees, 27 Pembridge Gardens, Notting Hill, London W2 4EF (020 7229 2368; email: enquiries@owf.org.uk; website: www.owf. org.uk)

CC number: 1059151

Eligibility

Women freemasons who are in need.

Types of grants

One-off and recurrent grants to help towards medical, household and living expenses.

Annual grant total

In 2015/16 the trust held assets of £862,500 and had an income of £180,500. Grants were made to individuals totalling £2,700.

The trust's grant-making activities mainly focused on funding for organisations, with The Adelaide Litten Charitable Trust, which owns sheltered housing properties, receiving £41,000, and outside charities a further £62,500.

Applications

Apply in writing to the correspondent, usually through the local lodge. The trustees meet regularly throughout the year to consider applications.

Other information

The trust is administered through The Order of Women Freemasons which was established as The Honourable Fraternity of Ancient Masonry in 1908.

Royal Antediluvian Order of Buffaloes, Grand Lodge of England War Memorial Annuities

£16,800

Correspondent: The Secretary, Grove House, Skipton Road, Harrogate, North Yorkshire HG1 4LA (01423 502438; email: hq@raobgle.org.uk; website: www. raobgle.org.uk)

CC number: 220476

Eligibility

Members of the order who are older or who have disabilities, and their dependants.

Types of grants

Annuities. The Grand Lodge may have other charitable funds available for one-off grants.

Annual grant total

In 2015/16 the charity had assets of £201,000 and an income of £30,000. Grants to individuals totalled £16,800.

Applications

Applications should be made through the member's lodge. All assistance originates at the local lodge level; if its resources are inadequate, the lodge may then seek assistance at provincial or ultimately national level. For dependants of deceased members, it is necessary to state the lodge to which the member belonged. If its name and number is known, the correspondent will probably be able to identify a current local telephone number or address. If only the place is known, this may still be possible, but not in all cases (particularly when the lodge concerned does not belong to this Grand Lodge group).

Other information

This charity was established by the Grand Lodge of England as a tribute to members of the order who died during the First World War.

The Grand Lodge also runs convalescent homes; one in Harrogate and the other in Paignton.

Other

Catenian Association Benevolent and Children's Fund

£116,500 (51 grants)

Correspondent: Phillip Roberts, Clerk, 39 Beechfield, Parbold, Wigan WN8 7AR (01257 462344; website: www. thecatenians.com)

CC number: 214244

Eligibility

Members of The Catenians and their dependants who are in need.

Types of grants

One-off and recurrent grants are given according to need. Loans are also available.

Annual grant total

In 2016/17 the charity had assets of £9.2 million and an income of £346,500. Grants totalling £116,500 were awarded to 51 beneficiaries during the year.

The annual report for 2016/17 also notes that 25 members were assisted with 'promissory note loans and second charge loans' amounting to £412,000.

Applications

Apply in writing to the correspondent. The trustees meet to consider applications at least four times a year, but urgent applications may be considered between the meetings.

Other information

The Catenians is an association of Catholic laymen.

There is a separate Catenian Association Bursary Fund Ltd (Charity Commission no. 1081143), which encourages Catholics between the ages of 16 and 25 to actively involve themselves with community projects in the UK and overseas.

The Moose International Welfare Service Fund

£7,200

Correspondent: Roger Williams, Trustee, 15 Higher Woodway Road, Teignmouth TQ14 8RG (01626 776683; email: admin@mooseintl.org.uk; website: www.mooseintluk.org)

CC number: 1153351

Eligibility

Members of the Grand Lodge of Great Britain Loyal Order of Moose or their families who are in need.

Types of grants

One-off grants according to need.

Annual grant total

In 2016 the fund held assets of £1.7 million and an income of £92,500. Grants to individuals totalled £7,200.

Applications

Apply in writing to the correspondent.

Soroptimist International of Great Britain and Ireland Benevolent Fund

£47,000

Correspondent: The Trustees, Beckwith House, Wellington Road North, Stockport SK4 1AF (0161 480 7686; email: hq@sigbi.org; website: sigbi.org/our-charities/benevolent-fund)

CC number: 211840

Eligibility

The relief of women in need who have been, for at least three consecutive years, members of a Soroptimist Club within the United Kingdom (including the Channel Islands and the Isle of Man) and the Republic of Ireland.

Types of grants

One-off grants to help with a particular need, or quarterly grants for general needs.

Annual grant total

In 2016/17 the charity had assets of £453,000 and an income of £44,500. Grants were awarded totalling £47,000.

Applications

Former soroptimists may apply to their Regional Representative (trustee) or they may apply directly to the Secretary. The annual report states that the business of the Benevolent Fund is strictly confidential.

Other information

Soroptimists are women who support projects, fundraising and advocacy to advance human rights and the status of women and girls. International and local initiatives are supported by raising awareness of issues and fundraising for specific charities.

Sports clubs

Auto Cycle Union Benevolent Fund

£68,000 (62 grants)

Correspondent: Regional Benevolent Fund Officers, ACU House, Wood Street, Rugby, Warwickshire CV21 2YX (01788 566400; email: dw@acu.org.uk; website: www.acu.org.uk)

CC number: 208567

Eligibility

Past and present members of the Auto Cycle Union, and their dependants, who are in need through accident, illness or hardship in England, Scotland or Wales.

Types of grants

One-off and recurrent grants. Loans may also be available.

Annual grant total

In 2016 the fund held assets of £2.8 million and had an income of £134,000. Grants were made to 62 individuals totalling £68,000.

Applications

Application forms are available from the local ACU officer or centre. Applications should be made directly by the individual and include details on current income and expenses. They are considered monthly. In very special circumstances the committee has the power to make emergency payments pending full information.

Other information

A full list of ACU clubs and centres is available on the website.

BRDC Benevolent Fund

£13,100 (nine grants)

Correspondent: BRDC Grants Administrator, Rawlinson and Hunter, Eighth Floor, 6 New Street Square, London EC4A 3AQ (020 7842 2000; email: brdcbenevolentfund@rawlinson-hunter.com; website: www.brdc.co.uk)

CC number: 1084173

Eligibility

Members of the BRDC and their families and dependants or persons involved with motor racing generally and their families and dependants.

Types of grants

One-off and recurrent grants are given according to need. For example, grants have previously been awarded for mobility aids, contributions to care costs and counselling.

Annual grant total

In 2016/17 the fund had assets of £695,000 and an income of £48,000. During the year, the fund gave £13,100 in grants to nine individuals.

Applications

Applications can be made using an initial enquiry form on the charity's website, or in writing to the correspondent, including details of income and expenditure, assets and liabilities. Applications can be submitted directly by the individual, by an organisation such as Citizens Advice or through a third party such as a social worker. There are no deadlines and applications are considered at trustees' meetings.

Other information

The charity's facilitator and social worker can offer advice about benefits and accessing further support.

British Motor Cycle Racing Club Benevolent Fund

£3,100

Correspondent: Mike Dommett, CEO, Unit D2, Seedbed Center, Davidson Way, Romford, Essex RM7 0AZ (01708 720305; email: mikedommett@hotmail.com; website: www.bemsee.net/ben-fund)

CC number: 213308

Eligibility

Members of the club and their dependants who are in need, with a particular focus on those who have been injured while riding.

Types of grants

One-off grants towards subsistence, travel and, as is the case most often, towards medical care and equipment costs.

Annual grant total

In 2016 the trust had an income of £9,700 and a total expenditure of £3,600. We estimate that grants given to individuals totalled around £3,100.

Applications

Apply in writing to the correspondent. Applications can be submitted at any time, either directly by the individual or through a third party such as a spouse or friend.

Sussex County Football Association Benevolent Fund

£6,500

Correspondent: Michael Brown, 10 Hillcrest, Brighton BN1 5FN (01273 708587)

CC number: 217496

Eligibility

Members of Sussex county FA clubs and their relatives or dependants.

Types of grants

One-off or recurrent grants to support players and officials affiliated to Sussex County FA who have suffered a football-related injury and, as a result, find themselves in financial hardship.

Annual grant total

In 2015/16 the charity had an income of £10,500 and a total expenditure of £28,000. We estimate that the charity awarded around £20,000 in grants to individuals during the year.

Exclusions

Claims for one week's incapacity should only be submitted in very exceptional circumstances as they are not considered necessitous.

Applications

Application forms are available from the correspondent. Requests for applications must be received by the secretary within 14 days of the injury and then completed and returned within a further 28 days.

Applications must include a full disclosure of financial and general circumstances alongside a medical certificate.

Local charities

This section lists local charities that award grants to individuals for welfare purposes. The information in the entries applies only to welfare grants and concentrates on what the charity actually does, rather than on what its governing document allows it to do.

Regional classification

We have divided the UK into 12 geographical areas, as numbered on the map on page 188. Scotland, Wales and England have been divided into unitary or local authorities, in some cases grouped in counties or regions. On page 189 you can find the list of unitary or local authorities within each county or area. Please note that not all of these unitary authorities have a grant-making charity included in this guide.

The Northern Ireland section has not been subdivided into smaller areas. Within the other sections, charities are ordered as follows.

Scotland

- First: Charities which apply to the whole of Scotland, or at least two areas in Scotland, are listed.
- Second: Scotland is further divided into electoral board areas, and then again into council areas.
- Should an entry apply for at least two council areas, it will appear in in the appropriate electoral board section.

Wales

- First: Charities which apply to the whole of Wales, or at least two areas of Wales, are listed.

- Second: Wales is subdivided into four regions. The entries which apply to the whole region, or to at least two local government areas within it, appear first.
- Third: Charities are listed under the relevant local government division.

England

- First: Charities which apply to the whole of England, or at least two regions within it, are listed.
- Second: England is divided into nine regions. The entries which apply to the whole region, or to at least two counties within it, appear first.
- Third: Regions are divided into counties.
- Fourth: The counties are subdivided into relevant local government areas.

London

- First: Charities which apply to the whole of Greater London, or to at least two boroughs are listed.
- Second: Charities serving London are further subdivided into the relevant boroughs.

Within each geographical category, the charities are listed alphabetically.

To be sure of identifying every relevant local charity, look at the charities in each relevant category in the following order:
1 Unitary or local authority (for England, Scotland and Wales) or borough (for Greater London)
2 County (for England)
3 Region (for England, Wales and in some cases, Scotland)
4 Country (for England, Northern Ireland, Scotland and Wales)

For example, if you live in Liverpool, first establish which region

Merseyside is in by looking at the map on page 188. Then, having established that Merseyside is in region 9, North West, look under the 'Geographical areas' list on page 189 to find the page where the entries for Merseyside begin. First, look under the heading for Liverpool to see if there are any relevant charities. Then work back through the charities under Merseyside generally, the charities under North West generally, and then charities listed under England generally.

Having found grant-makers covering your area, read any other eligibility requirements carefully. While some charities can and do give grants for any need for people in their area of benefit, most charities have other, more specific criteria which potential applicants must meet in order to be eligible.

Geographical areas

Northern Ireland

Church of Ireland Orphans and Children Society for Counties Antrim and Down

£49,000

Correspondent: The Secretary, Church of Ireland House, Diocesan Office, 61–67 Donegall Street, Belfast BT1 2QH (028 9082 8830; email: office@diocoff-belfast.org; website: connor.anglican.org)

CC number: NIC102840

Eligibility

Children in need, mainly orphans, who live in the counties of Antrim or Down, who are members of the Church of Ireland.

Types of grants

Grants to help orphans and other children in need, including bereavement grants on the death of a parent.

Annual grant total

In 2015/16 the society had assets of £6 million and an income of £212,500. During the year, grants to individuals totalled £49,000 and were distributed as follows:

Direct grant aid (to 47 children)	£42,000
Grants for special situations	£3,800
Bereavement grants (to three families	£3,300

A further £250,000 was awarded for 20 'special projects'.

Exclusions

No grants are made to applicants living outside the beneficial area.

Applications

Applications can be made at any time through the rector of the parish in which the individual lives. Direct applications cannot be considered.

Other information

The society also makes grants to support parochial and diocesan projects designed to help orphans and other children.

The Presbyterian Children's Society

£299,500

Correspondent: Dr Paul Gray, Executive Secretary, 5th Floor, Glengall Exchange, 3 Glengall Street, Belfast BT12 5AB (028 9032 3737; email: paulgray1866@gmail.com; website: www.presbyterianchildrenssociety.org)

CC number: NIC101444

Eligibility

Young people aged 23 or under who are in full or part-time education, living in Northern Ireland and Republic of Ireland, and are in need. Beneficiaries are usually from families where a parent is deceased or absent. One parent must be a Presbyterian.

Types of grants

Regular grants are paid each quarter. Exceptional grants are also given to help with, for example, basic clothing, repayment of debts, funeral expenses and general household expenditure. These are available to any family in need regardless of whether they are receiving help from the society and are usually of around £300, although in exceptional circumstances may be up to £600.

Annual grant total

In 2016 the charity held assets of £11.7 million and had an income of £784,500. Grants to 708 children and young people amounted to £599,500 and were given for both social welfare and educational purposes. We estimate that social welfare grants totalled around £299,500.

Grants are also made to small groups and clubs who provide childcare and family holidays (£8,500 in 2016).

Applications

Applications are to be made by Presbyterian clergy; forms are available from the correspondent or to download from the website. The Society's Board of Governors reviews all applications either in April or October of each year at

which point families are accepted formally for continued help.

The Presbyterian Old Age Fund, Women's Fund and Indigent Ladies Fund

£152,000 (98 grants)

Correspondent: The Secretary, Presbyterian Church in Ireland, Assembly Buildings, 2–10 Fisherwick Place, Belfast BT1 6DW (028 9032 2284; email: info@presbyterianireland.org; website: www.presbyterianireland.org)

Eligibility

Older people (over 60 years of age), women in need or ill members of the Presbyterian Church in any part of Ireland. Applicants will normally be living at home, have an income of less than £12,000/€17,500 per year, be in receipt of some type of state benefit, have less than £16,000/€20,000 in savings, have no significant support from their family members and have medical needs requiring extra expenditure (some, albeit not all, of the above criteria need to be satisfied).

Types of grants

Annual grants of £1,440 paid in quarterly instalments. A special gift of £360 was sent to every beneficiary prior to Christmas. One-off grants are also made to help in cases of immediate financial need.

Support can be given for equipment, services or activities, including: travel allowances to visit relatives or attend a funeral; household equipment; clothing and beddings; specialist medical or disability aids; home security; heating appliances and boilers; home insulation; respite care and a wide range of other needs.

Annual grant total

In 2015 a total of 98 people were assisted (44 in Old Age Fund, 35 in Women's Fund and 19 in Indigent Ladies' Fund) totalling £152,000 (£67,000 from the Old

Age Fund, £58,000 from the Women's Fund and £27,000 from the Indigent Ladies' Fund).

Exclusions

Requests normally covered by statutory sources are not supported.

Applications

Apply in writing to the correspondent. Applications should be supported by a minister and are usually considered in January, April, June and October.

The Royal Ulster Constabulary GC – Police Service of Northern Ireland Benevolent Fund

£185,000

Correspondent: The Administrator, RUCGC-PSNI Benevolent Fund, 77–79 Garnerville Road, Belfast BT4 2NX (028 9076 4200; email: benevolentfund@policefedni.com; website: policebenevolentfund.com)

CC number: NIC48380

Eligibility

Members and former members of the Royal Ulster Constabulary, and their dependants. The main objectives of the charity are to look after serving PSNI officers, widows/widowers, other dependants, injured officers and those with disabilities, pensioners and former members who are not pensionable and parents of deceased officers, all experiencing financial hardship or difficulties. Eligibility relates to financial hardship but 'the bottom line is simply that a case of need must be identified'.

Types of grants

One-off and recurrent grants and interest-free loans according to need. The fund offers a wide range of assistance, including adventure holidays for children, short breaks for widows, convalescence for injured officers, purchase of medical aids, wheelchairs and stairlifts, household goods, medical equipment and other necessities, and other financial help as required.

Annual grant total

In 2016 the fund had assets of £16.4 million and an income of £1.2 million. Grants to individuals totalled £370,000. We estimate that welfare grants to individuals totalled around £185,000.

Applications

Initial contact should be made in writing to the charity. Eligible applicants will then be advised on further application process. Candidates are visited by the representatives of the fund who then present the case to the management committee, which meets on the first Wednesday of each month. Each Regional Board has an appointed Benevolent Fund Representative. Applicants will be required to provide full financial breakdown and quotes where possible.

Other information

Additional help is offered by a number of other organisations, details of which can be found on the Northern Ireland Police Family Assistance website (www.northernirelandpolicefamilyassistance.org.uk).

The Society for the Orphans and Children of Ministers and Missionaries of the Presbyterian Church in Ireland

£13,700

Correspondent: Paul Gray, Secretary & Treasurer, Glengall Exchange, 3 Glengall Street, Belfast BT12 5AB (028 9032 3737; email: paulgray1866@gmail.com)

CC number: NIC101833

Eligibility

Children and young people aged under 26 who are orphaned and whose parents were ministers, missionaries or deaconesses of the Presbyterian Church in Ireland.

Types of grants

One-off grants are given for general welfare purposes.

Annual grant total

In 2016 the charity had assets of £1.15 million and an income of £53,500. Grants totalled £38,000; £13,700 was awarded for the welfare of orphaned children and young people, and a further £24,500 for educational purposes.

Applications

Application forms are available from the correspondent. Applications should be submitted directly by the individual in March for consideration in April.

Other information

The charity also gives educational grants to the children of living ministers and missionaries.

Scotland

General

Aberlour Child Care Trust
See entry on page 15

The Aged Christian Friend Society of Scotland

£2,000

Correspondent: The Trustees, Colinton Cottage Homes, 4a Redford Road, Edinburgh EH13 0AA (0131 441 2286/2502; email: office@ colintoncottages.org)

OSCR number: SC016247

Eligibility
Christians in need living in Scotland who are over the age of 65.

Types of grants
Annual pensions, usually of about £250 a year.

Annual grant total
In 2016 eight individuals were being paid £250 per year in pensions.

Applications
Apply in writing to the correspondent providing full details of the individual's situation.

Other information
The society is now a company limited by guarantee. Its principal activity is the provision of housing for older people in Scotland.

Barony Charitable Trust

£1,700

Correspondent: The Trustees, 8 New Mart Road, Edinburgh EH14 1RL

OSCR number: SC021091

Eligibility
People in need through age, ill health, financial hardship or disability who live in Edinburgh and Central Scotland.

Types of grants
One-off grants according to need.

Annual grant total
In 2016/17 the trust had an income of £2,300 and a total expenditure of £1,900. We estimate that grants given to individuals totalled around £1,700.

Applications
Apply in writing to the correspondent.

Other information
Note, this trust is linked to the Barony Housing Association and applications from their area of activity receive priority.

Challenger Children's Fund
See entry on page 59

Craigcrook Mortification

£37,500 (37 grants)

Correspondent: Jennifer Law, Charity Accounts Manager, c/o Scott-Moncrieff, Exchange Place 3, Semple Street, Edinburgh EH3 8BL (0131 473 3500; fax: 0131 473 3535; email: jennifer.law@ scott-moncrieff.com; website: www.scott-moncrieff.com/charities/charitable-trusts/craigcrook-mortification)

OSCR number: SC001648

Eligibility
People in need who are over 60 and were born in Scotland or have lived there for more than ten years.

Types of grants
Pensions of between £1,030 and £1,545 per annum payable in half-yearly instalments.

Annual grant total
In 2016 the charity had assets of £1.2 million and an income of £35,000.

During the year, the charity awarded £37,500 in pensions to 37 beneficiaries.

Exclusions
One-off payments are not available. Assistance is not normally given to those living with relations or in nursing homes.

Applications
At the time of writing (January 2018), the charity's webpage states that the application process is currently suspended. Check the website or contact the correspondent for current information.

Kayleigh's Wee Stars
See entry on page 55

The George McLean Trust

£9,900

Correspondent: Grants Administrator, Blackadders Solicitors, 30–34 Reform Street, Dundee DD1 1RJ (01382 229222; fax: 01382 342220; email: enquiries@ blackadders.co.uk)

OSCR number: SC020963

Eligibility
People in need who are living with a mental or physical disability and reside in Fife and Tayside. Older people may also qualify for assistance.

Types of grants
Grants typically range between £100 to £1,000 and are made towards convalescence, hospital expenses, electrical goods, clothing, holidays, travel expenses, medical equipment, nursing fees, furniture, disability aids and help in the home.

Annual grant total
In 2016/17 the trust had assets of £1.2 million and an income of £35,000. We estimate that the charity gave around £9,900 in grants to individuals.

Exclusions
No grants are made towards debts.

Applications

Application forms are available from the correspondent. Applications can be submitted directly by the individual or through any third party. They are considered monthly.

Other information

Our previous research indicates that roughly 20% of the trust's expenditure goes to individuals, with much of the rest going to local charitable organisations. This is flexible, however, as the trustees consider where funding is needed most.

James Paterson's Trust and Nursing Fund

£9,100

Correspondent: The Fund Administrator, Mitchells Roberton Solicitors, George House, 36 North Hanover Street, Glasgow G1 2AD (0141 552 3422; fax: 0141 552 2935; email: info@mitchells-roberton.co.uk)

OSCR number: SC017645

Eligibility

Women who have worked in cotton factories or mills in the Glasgow area. Principally the city of Glasgow and the contiguous districts of Dumbarton, Clydebank, Bearsden and Milngavie, Bishopbriggs and Kirkintilloch, East Kilbride, Eastwood and Renfrew.

Types of grants

Our research suggests that grants are given to pay primarily for short-term convalescent accommodation and occasionally for medical expenses and private accommodation in any private hospital.

Annual grant total

In 2015/16 the fund had assets of £880,000 and an income of £33,000. During the year, the fund gave around £9,100 in grants to individuals.

Applications

Applications may be made in writing to the correspondent. They can be submitted directly by the individual or through a social worker, Citizens Advice or other welfare agency. Requests are considered throughout the year.

Annie Ramsay McLean Trust for the Elderly

£650

Correspondent: The Trustees, Blackadders Solicitors, 30–34 Reform Street, Dundee DD1 1RJ (0131 222 8000; email: toni.mcnicoll@blackadders.co.uk)

OSCR number: SC014238

Eligibility

People aged 60 or over, who live in Fife and Tayside.

Types of grants

One-off and recurrent grants of £100 to £1,000 towards needs such as convalescence, travel expenses, furniture, clothing, medical and disability equipment, electrical goods, holidays, nursing home fees, help in the home, household items, electrically operated chairs, motorised scooters.

Annual grant total

In 2015/16 the trust had assets of £2.2 million and an income of £227,000. During the year, the charity awarded a total of £24,000 in grants. Of this amount, around £650 went directly to individuals for welfare purposes.

Exclusions

No grants are given towards debts.

Applications

Application forms are available from the correspondent. Applications can be submitted directly by the individual or through any third party. They are considered monthly.

Scottish Shipping Benevolent Association
See entry on page 136

See entry on page 136

Take a Break Scotland

£611,000

Correspondent: Applications Team, Take a Break, Family Fund, Unit 4, Alpha Court, Monks Cross Drive, York YO32 9WN (01904 571093, email: info@ takeabreakscotland.org.uk; website: takeabreakscotland.org.uk)

OSCR number: SC040810

Eligibility

Parents or carers of children and young people aged between 0 and 20 who are seriously ill or who have a disability. Applicants should reside in Scotland and have lived there continuously for six months or longer. Young people can also apply in their own right.

Types of grants

Grants can be used for breaks away, towards leisure activities or outings and sports equipment. The charity has previously given grants for: camping equipment; theatre breaks; horse riding; football kit and goals; gym memberships; holiday camp breaks.

Annual grant total

In 2016/17 grants to individuals totalled £611,000.

Exclusions

The charity is not able to fund: the purchase of vehicles; funds for an organisation; replacing existing funding; retrospective grants; IT equipment including laptops.

Applications

Applications can be made online through the charity's website.

Other information

The charity is administered by The Family Fund on behalf of the Scottish Government.

Mrs S. H. Troughton Charitable Trust

£3,400

Correspondent: Anina Cheng, Swan House, 17–19 Stratford Place, London W1C 1BQ (020 7907 2100; email: charity@mfs.co.uk)

CC number: 265957

Eligibility

People in need who receive a pension and live on the estates of Ardchatten in Argyll, and Blair Atholl.

Types of grants

One-off or recurrent payments to pensioners.

Annual grant total

In 2015/16 the trust had an income of £13,400 and a total expenditure of £13,800. We estimate that the charity awarded around £3,400 in grants to individuals for welfare purposes.

Exclusions

Grants are not given to people whose income is £1,000 above their personal allowance for income tax.

Applications

Apply in writing to the correspondent at any time. Applications can be submitted by the individual or, where applicable, via a third party such as a social worker or organisations such as Citizens Advice or other welfare agency. Unsuccessful applications will not be acknowledged.

Ayrshire

East Ayrshire

Miss Annie Smith Mair Newmilns Trust Fund

£900

Correspondent: The Grants Administrator, East Ayrshire Council, Council Headquarters, London Road, Kilmarnock KA3 7BU (website: www.east-ayrshire.gov.uk/CouncilAndGovernment/About-the-Council/Grants-and-funding/TrustsandBequests.aspx)

OSCR number: SC021095

Eligibility

People in need who live, or were born in, Newmilns.

Types of grants

Small, one-off grants towards clothing, household essentials, minor house or garden maintenance work/adaptations, mobility and personal aids, short breaks and small donations for living expenses.

Annual grant total

In 2016/17 the charity had an income of £260 and a total expenditure of £900. We estimate that the charity awarded £900 in grants to individuals.

Applications

Apply on a form available from the correspondent or from the East Ayrshire Council website. Applications can be made directly by the individual or through a GP, social worker, Citizens Advice or other welfare agency.

Note: If an application is being made on health grounds alone, a GP's certification of need will also be required.

Other information

The trust is administered by East Ayrshire Council and in recent years, has aided more than 100 people through its grant-making activities.

Archibald Taylor Fund

£19,900 (28 grants)

Correspondent: Democratic Services Trusts, East Ayrshire Council, Council Headquarters, London Road, Kilmarnock KA3 7BU (01563 576093; email: admin@east-ayrshire.gov.uk; website: www.east-ayrshire.gov.uk/Home.aspx)

OSCR number: SC019308

Eligibility

People who are either living in Kilmarnock, or were born there, and are

in need of special nursing, convalescent treatment at the coast or in the country; or a holiday during convalescence. Applicants must be in financial need.

Types of grants

Grants are given for the provision of special nursing or convalescent treatment and convalescent holidays of up to three weeks. Previous awards have ranged from £250 to £1,000. Support can also be given for beneficiaries to be accompanied on holiday by a carer or companion.

Annual grant total

In 2016/17 the fund had an income of £2,300 and a total expenditure of £27,500. We estimate that grants given to individuals totalled around £25,000.

Exclusions

Funding is not given for holidays abroad, only in the UK and Ireland, unless there are exceptional circumstances to support doing so.

Applications

Applications should be made a form available from the correspondent or to download from the East Ayrshire website, for consideration throughout the year. Applicants should be recommended for this by a GP. The following should be submitted with the application: household income, employer's certificate of earnings and/or a benefit award letter and a declaration by the applicant's GP.

Completed forms should be returned to: Head of Democratic Services, East Ayrshire Council Headquarters, London Road, Kilmarnock KA3 7BU. The administrator can answer queries by telephone, and help can be given to complete the application form and make holiday arrangements.

Central Scotland

Falkirk

The Anderson Bequest

£7,800

Correspondent: The Trustees, c/o Johnston & Co., 13 Register Street, Bo'ness, West Lothian EH51 9AE (01506 822112)

OSCR number: SC011755

Eligibility

Pensions for people in need who live in Bo'ness.

Types of grants

Annual grants or pensions.

Annual grant total

In 2015/16 the charity had an income of £27,500 and a total expenditure of £25,500. Grants totalled £16,000 of which £7,800 was given to individuals. The rest of the grant total was given to the West Lothian Education Trust.

Applications

Apply in writing to the correspondent.

Stirling

George Hogg Trust

£28,000

Correspondent: C. McRae, Ardagie, Main Street, Killin, Stirling FK21 8UT

OSCR number: SC001890

Eligibility

People who live in Killin and are in need.

Types of grants

One-off and recurrent grants are given according to need.

Annual grant total

In 2015/16 the trust had an income of £18,500 and a total expenditure of £30,500. We estimate that grants given to individuals totalled £28,000.

Applications

Apply in writing to the correspondent via a third party such as a local doctor or minister. There are no deadlines and applications are normally considered at the Annual General Meeting.

Dumfries and Galloway

Hart Knowe Trust

£600 (two grants)

Correspondent: The Trustees, Hart Knowe, Eskdalemuir, Langholm, Dumfries and Galloway DG13 0QH

OSCR number: SC044303

Eligibility

People in need living in Dumfries and Galloway.

Types of grants

General welfare grants.

Annual grant total

In 2015/16 the trust had assets of £14,500 and an income of £112,000. Welfare grants were made to two individuals totalling £600.

Applications

Apply in writing to the correspondent.

The Holywood Trust

£46,500

Correspondent: The Trustees, Hestan House, Crichton Business Park, Bankend Road, Dumfries DG1 4TA (01387 269176; email: funds@holywood-trust. org.uk; website: www.holywood-trust. org.uk)

OSCR number: SC009942

Eligibility

Primarily young people aged 15 to 25 living in the Dumfries and Galloway region. However, the trust is flexible and will consider applications from people under 15 who can demonstrate serious need.

Types of grants

Grants of up to £500 are available for purchasing household items, particularly for a young person leaving care; clothing; travel expenses etc.

Annual grant total

In 2015/16 the trust had assets of £97 million and an income of £2.4 million. We estimate that around £46,500 was awarded in grants.

Exclusions

Grants are not given towards carpets or accommodation deposits. Retrospective (backdated) awards are not made.

Applications

Application forms are available to download from the trust's website and should be returned to the correspondent by post in a large envelope. The trust states it is beneficial to include a letter from a third party, such as a social or professional worker, who can confirm your situation.

Other information

The trust also provides awards to individuals for educational purposes, and makes grants for organisations.

Lockerbie Trust

£3,600

Correspondent: The Trustees, Farries Kirk & McVean, Dumfries Enterprise Park, Heathhall, Dumfries DG1 3SJ (01387 252127; fax: 01387 250501)

OSCR number: SC019796

Eligibility

People in need who live in Lockerbie.

Types of grants

Our previous research indicates that the trust awards one-off grants of up to £500. Annual payments may be considered but only in exceptional circumstances.

Annual grant total

In 2016/17 the trust had an income of £17,400 and a total expenditure of £7,300. We estimate that the trust awarded around £3,600 in grants to individuals.

Exclusions

Educational grants are not awarded where Scottish Office grants are available.

Applications

Application forms can be downloaded from the Dumfries and Galloway Council website, along with full guidelines.

The trust normally holds meetings in February, July, September and December of each year. Applications must be submitted six weeks before a quarterly meeting. Applicants will be informed of the decision in writing following the relevant quarterly trust meeting. Payments will be made to successful applicants by cheque.

Other information

Organisations and groups or societies are also supported.

John Primrose Trust

£3,800

Correspondent: The Trustees, 1 Newall Terrace, Dumfries DG1 1LN

OSCR number: SC009173

Eligibility

People in need who live in Dumfries and Maxwelltown or have are connection with these places by parentage.

Types of grants

Our previous research suggests that grants of £100 to £150 are given twice a year to 10 to 20 older people.

Annual grant total

In 2016/17 the trust had an income of £16,400 and a total expenditure of £15,900. We estimate that grants given to individuals for social welfare purposes totalled around £3,800.

Applications

Application forms are available from the correspondent. They are generally considered in June and December.

Other information

The trust awards grants to both individuals and organisations for educational and social welfare purposes.

Dunbartonshire and Argyll

Argyll and Bute

Glasgow Bute Benevolent Society

£20,000

Correspondent: The Trustees, 2 Hunter's View, 34A Ardbeg, Rothesay, Isle of Bute PA20 0NL

OSCR number: SC016182

Eligibility

People in need who live in Bute, particularly older people. The length of time a person has lived in Bute and how long they have been connected with the area is taken into consideration.

Types of grants

Previous research suggests that the society does not award grants as such – suitable applicants are admitted to the Society's Roll of Pensioners and receive a pension payable half-yearly and a Christmas bonus payment.

Annual grant total

In 2016 the society had an income of £21,000 and a total expenditure of £20,500. We estimate that support to individuals totalled around £20,000.

Exclusions

People in receipt of parochial help are not supported, unless in extraordinary circumstances.

Applications

Application forms are available from the correspondent. Candidates should provide a supporting recommendation by a minister of religion, doctor, solicitor or other responsible person.

Other information

Small grants for educational purposes may be made on rare occasions.

June and Douglas Hume Memorial Fund

£1,000

Correspondent: Jennifer McPhail, Grant Programmes Executive, Glasgow Office, Empire House, 131 West Nile Street, Glasgow G1 2RX (0141 341 4964; email: jennifer@foundationscotland.org.uk; website: www.foundationscotland.org.uk/ programmes/june-and-douglas-hume)

OSCR number: SC022910

Eligibility

Terminally ill patients who wish to spend their final days in their own home. Priority will be given to applicants from the West of Scotland and in particular the Helensburgh area.

Types of grants

One-off grants of up to £1,000 to assist patients with specialist equipment, as well as any house modifications necessary to accommodate such equipment. Grants may be used for bath and stairlifts, reclining beds and chairs, wheelchairs and zimmer frames, for example.

Annual grant total

In 2016/17 the fund had a total expenditure of £1,000. We estimate that grants to individuals totalled around £1,000.

Applications

Applicants should contact Jennifer McPhail on 0141 341 4964 in the first instance and an application form will be sent out to applicants where funds are available.

Other information

The fund is administered by Foundation Scotland.

East Dunbartonshire

Lenzie Benevolent Society

£18,300 (five grants)

Correspondent: The Trustees, c/o French Duncan LLP, 133 Finnieston Street, Glasgow G3 8HB

OSCR number: SC011877

Eligibility

People in need living in the Lenzie area.

Types of grants

Monthly grants and holiday grants.

Annual grant total

In 2016 the charity had assets of £904,000 and an income of £495,500. Grants to five individuals totalled £18,300.

Applications

Apply in writing to the correspondent.

West Dunbartonshire

Lennox Children's Trust

£16,000

Correspondent: The Correspondent, c/o Citizens Advice Bureau, Bridgend House,

179 High Street, Dumbarton G82 1NW (01389 744690)

OSCR number: SC023740

Eligibility

Children up to the age of 18 who are in need through poverty, neglect, behavioural or psychological disorders, physical or mental disability, and who live in the West Dunbartonshire area.

Types of grants

One-off and recurrent grants are given according to need. Grants have been given for disability aids, educational and medical equipment and toys.

Annual grant total

At the time of writing (February 2018) this was the latest financial information available. In 2014/15 the trust had an income of £17,000 and total expenditure of £18,500. We estimate that grants given to individuals totalled £16,000.

Applications

Application forms are available from the correspondent, to be submitted by a third party with a connection to the child.

Fife

Fleming Bequest

£34,000

Correspondent: Grants Administrator, Thorntons Law LLP, Whitehall House, 33 Yeaman Shore, Dundee, Scotland DD1 4BJ (01382 229111)

OSCR number: SC016126

Eligibility

People living in the parish of St Andrews and St Leonards in the town of St Andrews who are older, in poor health or in financial difficulty.

Types of grants

One-off grants awarded towards clothing, carpets, fridge/freezers, special chairs and other essential household needs.

Annual grant total

In 2016/17 the charity had an income of £21,000 and a total expenditure of £36,000. We estimate that the amount awarded in grants during the year totalled £34,000.

Applications

Apply in writing to the correspondent preferably through a social worker, Citizens Advice or similar welfare agency. Applications are considered at any time and should include details of the applicant's postal address, date of birth and reason for the request.

The St Andrews Welfare Trust

£14,000

Correspondent: The Trustees, Thorntons Solicitors, Whitehall House, 33 Yeaman Shore, Dundee DD1 4BJ

OSCR number: SC008660

Eligibility

People in need who live within a four-mile radius of St Andrews.

Types of grants

One-off grants of up to £600 according to need.

Annual grant total

In 2016 the trust had assets of £226,500 and an income of £28,000. Grants to individuals totalled £14,000.

Exclusions

No grants are given for educational purposes, such as gap year projects.

Applications

Apply in writing to the correspondent through a social worker, Citizens Advice or other welfare agency. Applications should include applicant's date of birth, postal address and reason for request and are considered throughout the year.

Glasgow

The Association for the Relief of Infirmity in the West of Scotland

£111,500 (280 grants)

Correspondent: Secretary to the Trustees, c/o Wright Johnston & Mackenzie LLP, 302 St Vincent Street, Glasgow G2 5RZ (0141 248 3434; email: enquiries@wjm.co.uk)

OSCR number: SC014424

Eligibility

People over 18 years of age in financial need with long-term illnesses who are living at home. Applicants must be living in Glasgow or the West of Scotland.

Types of grants

Six-monthly pensions. One-off grants of up to £500 for specific needs, such as telephone installation, washing machines and cookers.

Annual grant total

In 2016 the charity had an income of £322,000 and a total expenditure of £164,000. Welfare grants to 280 individuals totalled £111,500, of which £4,900 was given in exceptional grants to ten individuals.

Exclusions

The charity will only assist individuals whose 'incurable' condition is 'the result of a contracted/untreatable disease and not due to a congenital state or the result of an accident'. Further detail on specific conditions is given in the charity's guidance notes, available online or by request from the correspondent. Grants are not given to clear debts or towards holidays.

Applications

Applications must be made through a social worker, Citizens Advice or other welfare agency on a form available from the correspondent. The applicant's GP must confirm their medical condition. Applications are considered quarterly with deadlines 14 days prior to each meeting.

The Glasgow Care Foundation

£277,000

Correspondent: The Trustees, Orkney Street Enterprise Centre, 18–20 Orkney Street, Glasgow G51 2BX (0141 445 2736; email: hello@ glasgowcarefoundation.org; website: www.glasgowcarefoundation.org)

OSCR number: SC000906

Eligibility

Residents of Glasgow who have lived in the city for a minimum of five years and are in need by reason of age, ill health, disability, financial hardship or other disadvantage.

Types of grants

Grants are given for essential support to those in need where support is not available through local authorities or other agencies. Support is given for items such as essential white goods e.g. cookers, fridges, freezers, washing machines, beds and bedding, basic furniture, children's clothing and holidays mainly in the UK.

Annual grant total

In 2016/17 the foundation had an income of £350,000 and a total expenditure of £347,500. Grants to individuals totalled £277,000.

Exclusions

People who are living in care are not eligible.

Applications

Applications can be made online, only through a recognised agency working in the community such as social services. Applicants will first have to apply for an online accounts. The foundation's welfare officers visit and investigate all cases.

Other information

The foundation was formerly known as the City of Glasgow Society of Social Service.

The Andrew and Mary Elizabeth Little Charitable Trust

£48,000

Correspondent: Ronnie Munton, Low Beaton Richmond Solicitors, Sterling House, 20 Renfield Street, Glasgow G2 5AP (0141 221 8931; fax: 0141 248 4411; email: gabrielle@lbr-law.co.uk)

OSCR number: SC011185

Eligibility

People in need whose sole source of income is income support, disability benefit or pension, who live in the city of Glasgow.

Types of grants

One-off and recurrent grants are given according to need.

Annual grant total

In 2015/16 the trust had an income of £58,000 and a total expenditure of £64,000. Our research indicates that typically grants to individuals account for 80% of the trust's charitable expenditure and grants to organisations the remaining 20%. Therefore, we estimate that individuals received around £48,000 in grants from the trust.

Applications

Apply in writing to the correspondent, to be submitted through social services. Applications should include financial details and are considered monthly.

The Trades House of Glasgow

£183,000

Correspondent: Janet Olverman, Administration Assistant, Trades Hall, 85 Glassford Street, Glasgow G1 1HU (0141 553 1605; email: info@ tradeshouse.org.uk or janet.olverman@ tradeshouse.org.uk; website: www. tradeshouse.org.uk)

OSCR number: SC040548

Eligibility

People in need who live in Glasgow. Several funds have different eligibility criteria around age or need, consult the website before making an application.

Types of grants

One-off grants according to need.

Annual grant total

In 2015/16 the charity had assets of £23.8 million and an income of £1.24 million. Grants totalling £183,000 were awarded for welfare purposes and a further £27,500 was awarded in bursaries and educational grants.

Exclusions

Grants are unable to fund:

- Rent/rent arrears
- Council tax/council tax arrears
- Funeral costs (in the majority or circumstances)
- Holidays
- Items/support/personnel effects which councils are legally required to provide (including shelter and accommodation)
- Cosmetic repairs and improvements to homes
- Items provided by the state

The funds are also unable to support those who are drug or alcohol dependent.

Applications

Applications can be made online through the respective funding pages.

Other information

Guilds and Craft Incorporations are the Scottish equivalent of the craft guilds or livery companies which developed in the Middle Ages. The Trades House also operates the Drapers Fund which distributes around £80,000 annually to children in need under the age of 17. The fund has its own application form that is available to download on the charity's website.

The Ure Elder Trust

£5,500

Correspondent: The Trustees, Dentons UKMEA LLP, 1 George Square, Glasgow G2 1AL

OSCR number: SC003775

Eligibility

People in need who live in Glasgow, especially Govan. Previous research indicates there is some preference to provide grants to widows.

Types of grants

One-off and recurrent grants are given according to need.

Annual grant total

In 2016 the trust had an income of £10,000 and a total expenditure of £16,300. We estimate that the trust awarded £5,500 in grants to individuals.

Applications

Applications should be made in writing to the correspondent.

Other information

The trust also makes grants for education and towards conservation and heritage protection.

Grampian

CALICO – Cancer and Leukaemia In Children Orientated

£4,400

Correspondent: M. Harcus, 67 Forest Road, Aberdeen AB15 4BJ

OSCR number: SC005795

Eligibility

Families who have children suffering from cancer, leukaemia or cancer-related illness

Types of grants

Grants to alleviate, where possible stress caused by additional expenses i.e. hearing, telephone and travel.

Annual grant total

In 2016/17 the charity had an income of £7,300 and a total expenditure of £9,000. We estimate that the charity gave around £4,400 in grants to individuals, with funding also given to local organisations.

Applications

Apply in writing to the correspondent.

Other information

CALICO also have access to CLAN's eight-berth luxury caravan at the Silver Ladies Caravan Park and Banchory. Parents and children can make use of this facility when available. Travel expenses will be met where necessary.

North East Scotland Police Welfare Fund (NESPWF)

See entry on page 155

Aberdeen and Aberdeenshire

Aberdeen Cheyne and Donald Trust Fund

£75,000

Correspondent: Trust Administrator, c/o Raeburn Christie Clark Wallace, 12–16 Albyn Place, Aberdeen AB10 1PS (01224 332400; website: www.raeburns.co.uk)

OSCR number: SC045666

Eligibility

People living in, with a strong connection to, Aberdeen and Aberdeenshire who are facing financial hardship. Preference is given to applicants with low income due to disability, age, or illness.

Types of grants

One-off and recurrent (half-yearly) grants are available according to need.

Annual grant total

In 2016 the charity had assets of £2.8 million and an income of £2.6 million. During the year, the charity awarded £75,000 in grants. Of this amount, £70,000 was awarded in half-yearly payments to 58 individuals, and £5,000 in one-off grants.

Applications

Applications should be made in writing to the correspondent, detailing financial need and what the grant will be used for.

Other information

The trust gained charitable status in 2015 after the transfer of funds from, and the cessation of, the Gordon Cheyne Trust Fund, the Aberdeen Widows and Spinsters fund, and the Donald Trust.

Aberdeen Female Society

£11,000

Correspondent: The Secretary, Aberdeen Female Society, c/o Messrs Burnett and Reid LLP, 15 Golden Square, Aberdeen AB10 1WF (01224 644333)

OSCR number: SC016491

Eligibility

Women who have reached retirement age and are resident in Aberdeen.

Types of grants

One-off grants to assist with the purchase of essential household items that are in excess of £100. Regular payments of £200 are paid half-yearly in May and November.

Annual grant total

In 2015/16 the charity had an income of £10,000 and a total expenditure of £11,900. We estimate that grants given to individuals totalled £11,000.

Applications

Application forms are available on request from the secretary and must be countersigned by a third party such as a health professional, social worker or minister.

James Allan of Midbeltie's Fund for Widows

£18,800

Correspondent: Michael McMillan, Burnett & Reid, 15 Golden Square, Aberdeen AB10 1WF (01224 644333; email: MDMcMillan@burnett-reid.co.uk)

OSCR number: SC003865

Eligibility

Widows who live in Aberdeen and are in need.

Types of grants

Recurrent allowances of around £400 a year payable in two instalments in May and November. A Christmas bonus is available if there are available funds.

Annual grant total

In 2015/16 the trust had an income of £61,000 and a total expenditure of £62,000. Grants to widows totalled £18,800.

Applications

Application forms are available from the correspondent. Applications can be submitted either directly by the individual, through a third party such as a social worker or through an organisation such as Citizens Advice or another welfare agency. Applications are usually considered in April and October.

Dr John Calder Fund

£2,800

Correspondent: The Trustees, St Machar's Cathedral, 18 The Chanonry, Aberdeen AB24 1RQ

OSCR number: SC004299

Eligibility

People in need who live in the parish of Machar. Our research suggests that preference is given to widows left with young children, where sufficient support cannot be obtained from the parish council. People in need living in Aberdeen may also be assisted.

Types of grants

One-off grants according to need.

Annual grant total

In 2016/17 the fund had assets of £618,000 and had an income of £130,500. Eight grants were made during the year, totalling almost £5,600. We estimate that welfare grants totalled around £2,800.

Applications

Apply in writing to the correspondent.

Other information

The fund also makes grants for educational purposes and to organisations.

The George, James and Alexander Chalmers Trust

£31,500 (46 grants)

Correspondent: Trust Administrator, c/o Storie Cruden & Simpson Solicitors, 2 Bon Accord Crescent, Aberdeen AB11 6DH (01224 587261; fax: 01224 580850; email: info@storiecs.co.uk)

OSCR number: SC008818

Eligibility

Women living in Aberdeen who have fallen on hard times as a result of misfortune and not through any fault of their own.

Types of grants

Recurrent grants of about £700 a year, payable in half-yearly instalments.

Annual grant total

In 2015/16 the charity held assets of £777,500 and had an income of £144,900. During the year, the charity awarded £31,500 in grants to 46 individuals.

Applications

Application forms are available from the correspondent.

Other information

Regular grants are also made to organisations.

Garden Nicol Benevolent Fund

£2,000

Correspondent: The Trustees, 100 Union Street, Aberdeen AB10 1QR

OSCR number: SC007140

Eligibility

Women in need who 'having been in a position of affluence have, by circumstances beyond their control, been reduced to comparative poverty'. Applicants must both have been born and be living in the city or county of Aberdeen.

Types of grants

One-off and recurrent grants are given according to need.

Annual grant total

In 2016/17 the fund had an income of £10,900 and a total expenditure of £2,600. We estimate that grants given to individuals totalled £2,000.

Applications

Apply in writing to the correspondent.

The Jopp Thomson Fund

£13,700

Correspondent: Douglas Watson, Fund Administrator, c/o Ledingham Chalmers LLP, 52–54 Rose Street, Aberdeen AB10 1HA (01224 408408; email: douglas.watson@ledinghamchalmers.com)

OSCR number: SC009106

Eligibility

People in need through age, ill health or disability. Preference is given for widowed and single women living in Aberdeenshire and those whose name or maiden name is Thomson or Middleton.

Types of grants

Annuities of £525 paid in two instalments to each beneficiary to be used at their discretion.

Annual grant total

In 2015/16 the fund held assets of £584,000 and had an income of £51,500. Grants to individuals totalled £13,700.

Applications

Application forms are available from the correspondent. They can be submitted directly by the individual or through a third party and are considered in April each year.

Other information

This fund is an amalgamation of the Henry John Jopp Fund and the Jessie Ann Thomson Fund.

The Mary Morrison Cox Fund

£15,000

Correspondent: The Trustees, 18 Bon-Accord Crescent, Aberdeen AB11 6XY (01224 573321)

OSCR number: SC007881

Eligibility

People in need who live in the parish of Dyce, Aberdeen. Preference is given to older people and people living with disabilities.

Types of grants

One-off grants, ranging from £100 to £400, to help with general living expenses.

Annual grant total

In 2015/16 the fund had an income of £11,300 and a total expenditure of £15,300. We estimate that the charity gave around £15,000 in grants to individuals.

Applications

The fund has a list of potential beneficiaries to whom it sends application forms each year, usually in November. In order to be added to this list, applicants should contact the fund.

Mrs Catherine Brook's Fund

£15,000 (30 grants)

Correspondent: The Trustees, 379 North Deeside Road, Cults, Aberdeen AB15 9SX

OSCR number: SC000675

Eligibility

People in need living in Peterhead. There is a preference for people with disabilities.

Types of grants

One-off grants of up to £500 according to need.

Annual grant total

In 2015/16 the fund had assets of £67,500 and an income of £23,000. Grants to individuals totalled £15,000.

Applications

Apply in writing to the correspondent.

Miss Caroline Jane Spence's Fund

£3,400 (four grants)

Correspondent: Fund Secretary, c/o Mackinnons Solicitors, 379 North Deeside Road, Cults, Aberdeen AB15 1SX (01224 868687; email: cults@mackinnons.com; website: www.mackinnons.com)

OSCR number: SC006434

Eligibility

People who live in Aberdeen and the surrounding area and are in need.

Types of grants

One-off and recurrent grants are given according to need. In 2015/16 the minimum amount awarded was £600 and the maximum was £1,100.

Annual grant total

In 2015/16 the fund had assets of £3.5 million and an income of £163,500. During the year, £3,400 was awarded in grants to four individuals.

The majority of grants made by the charity are to other organisations (£50,000 in 2015/16).

Applications

Application forms are available from the correspondent. Applications can be submitted either directly by the individual, or through a social worker, Citizens Advice or other welfare agency or third party. Applications are considered in January, April, and November.

Highlands and Na h-Eileanan an Iar (Western Isles)

Ewen Cameron's Trust

£21,500

Correspondent: The Trustees, PO Box 1, Park Street, Dingwall IV15 9JJ

OSCR number: SC010442

Eligibility

Older people in need who live in the parish of Fodderty and the part of the parish of Urray known as Ussie/Lochussie.

Types of grants

One-off grants according to need.

Annual grant total

In 2016/17 the trust had assets of £688,500 and an income of £26,000. Grants to individuals totalled £21,500.

Applications

According to its objectives, the trust distributes its income to the Free Church ministers at Maryburgh and Strathpeffer. Applications should therefore be directed to these ministers.

Dr Forbes Inverness Trust

£4,000

Correspondent: The Trustees, Munro & Noble Solicitors, 26 Church Street, Inverness IV1 1HX (01463 221727; email: legal@munronoble.com)

OSCR number: SC005573

Eligibility

People with a medical or similar need who live in the former burgh of Inverness or immediately surrounding areas to the south of the Beauly/Inverness Firth.

Types of grants

Generally one-off grants to help with the cost of medical treatment and equipment, convalescence or a period of residence in a nursing home, food, clothing and travel expenses to visit sick relatives.

Annual grant total

In 2016/17 the trust had an income of £9,300 and a total expenditure of £4,900. We estimate that grants given to individuals totalled around £4,000.

Applications

Application forms are available from the correspondent and can be submitted by the individual or through a recognised referral agency (e.g. social worker, Citizens Advice or doctor) or other third party.

Highland Children's Trust Scheme 1983

£4,200

Correspondent: The Administrator, Saffrey Champness LLP, Kintail House, Beechwood Park, Inverness IV2 3BW (01463 243872; email: info@hctrust.co.uk; website: www.hctrust.co.uk)

OSCR number: SC006008

Eligibility

Children and young people in need who are under 25 and live in the Highlands. There is some preference for orphans.

Types of grants

Grants are available for:

- Suitable accommodation
- Holidays – priority is given if the holiday will benefit the applicant's health or medical condition

Annual grant total

In 2016/17 the trust had assets of £1.4 million and an income of £50,000. We estimate that around £4,200 was given in grants to individuals.

Exclusions

Grants are not given to pay off debts, nor to purchase clothing, footwear, food, furniture or cars, etc.

Applications

Applicants should complete the 'HCT Application Form' which can be requested in writing from the correspondent, via email, or downloaded from the website.

Other information

The trust mainly awards grants for the advancement of education. The trust does not make grants to organisations or local clubs.

The William MacKenzie Trust

£14,500

Correspondent: Trust Administrator, 26 Lewis Street, Stornoway, Isle of Lewis HS1 2JF (01851 702335)

OSCR number: SC001598

Eligibility

People who are older or in poor health and live in Stornoway.

Types of grants

One-off grants to enable individuals to continue living in their own homes. Grants have been given for house adaptations, reclining chairs and domestic equipment such as washing machines.

Annual grant total

In 2015/16 the trust had assets of £1.1 million and an income of £44,500. During the year, the trust gave around £14,500 in grants to individuals.

The trust also gave almost £26,000 in grants to organisations.

Applications

Apply in writing to the correspondent.

Strathnairn Community Benefit Fund

£80,500

Correspondent: Company Secretary, Farr Community Hall, Inverarnie Park, Inverarnie, Inverness IV2 6AX (email: cosec@strathnairncbf.com)

OSCR number: SC036807

Eligibility

Residents of the Strathnairn Community Council area who are in need.

Types of grants

A grant of £220 is available annually to each permanent resident household within the Strathnairn Community Council area towards energy costs. Grants are also available to individuals or families in need or facing a crisis requiring professional respite care.

Annual grant total

In 2016/17 grants to individuals totalled £80,500, with £79,500 given in energy grants and £1,000 given in hardship grants.

Applications

Application forms are available to download from the fund's website.

Other information

The fund also provides grants for the installation of renewable technology and household energy saving measures.

Charlotte Sutherlands Trust

£6,300

Correspondent: The Administrator, Murdoch Stewarts, Suite 4/2, Merchants House, 7 West George Street, Glasgow G2 1BA (0141 412 2234)

OSCR number: SC006694

Eligibility

People in need who live in the parishes of Olrig – Caithness, Kirkwall and St Ola in the Orkney Isles.

Types of grants

Our research suggests that typically grants of around £50 each are awarded to relieve poverty.

Annual grant total

In 2015/16 the trust had an income of £5,700 and a total expenditure of £6,500. We estimate that the trust gave around £6,300 in grants to individuals.

Applications

Unsolicited applications are not considered. The trust's administrators write to the relevant social work departments and ask for a list of eligible beneficiaries, who the administrators then contact.

Lothian

Capital Charitable Trust

£20,000

Correspondent: The Trustees of Capital Charitable Trust, c/o Aitken Nairn WS, 7 Abercromby Place, Edinburgh EH3 6LA (0131 556 6644)

OSCR number: SC004332

Eligibility

People in need who live in the Edinburgh and Lothians area.

Types of grants

Small, one-off grants of about £10 to £20 towards clothes, decorating, household goods and other general welfare needs.

Annual grant total

In 2016/17 the trust had both an income and a total expenditure of £24,000. We estimate that grants given to individuals totalled around £20,000.

Applications

Application forms can be obtained from local authority social work departments and other responsible bodies who will forward them to the correspondent. Applications are not accepted directly from individuals.

ECAS Ltd

£6,000

Correspondent: Janice Todd, Administrator, Norton Park, 57 Albion Road, Edinburgh EH7 5QY (0131 475 2344; email: info@ecas-edinburgh.org; website: www.ecas-edinburgh.org)

OSCR number: SC014929

Eligibility

People living in Edinburgh and the Lothians who have a physical disability.

Types of grants

Grants are given for items which will 'enhance the applicant's life'. In the past, they have been given for: washing machines; fridge-freezers; cookers; laptops; furniture; car adaptations; sheds; iPads; holidays; and carpets.

Standard grants are of up to £750. Higher grants of up to £1,500 can also be considered, and grants exceeding £1,500 can be considered on an exceptional basis.

Annual grant total

In 2016/17 the charity had assets of £5.1 million and an income of £185,000. During the year, a total of £6,000 was awarded in grants.

Exclusions

People with the following conditions are not eligible to apply for support: arthritis; back pain; cardio-respiratory conditions; obesity; psychiatric disorders; learning difficulties; behavioural disorders; developmental delay; Down's syndrome; autism; visual or hearing impairment; cancer; diabetes; HIV; epilepsy.

Funding cannot be given retrospectively or to pay bills or debts. Grants are not made for small pieces of domestic equipment or for the purchase of powerchairs, scooters or battery packs.

Applications

Application forms, along with full guidelines and eligibility criteria, are available to download from the website or can be requested from the correspondent. Depending on the applicant's circumstances, some applications need to be sponsored by a social worker, health visitor, district nurse, support worker, occupational therapist, physiotherapist or GP – the helpful FAQ section of the website provides criteria for when a sponsor will be required.

Wherever possible, goods and holidays are purchased directly from the supplier – full details should be included on the application form. Applications for the maintenance or repair of battery packs, scooters or powerchairs must be accompanied by evidence of third-party

insurance. Applications for holidays should be submitted at least eight weeks before the date of departure – late applications may not be considered.

The charity aims to make a decision within eight weeks of all paperwork being received. Individuals requesting computer equipment may be subject to an ECAS assessment. More information about grants and how to apply is available from the FAQ section of the website or by contacting the charity.

Note that the application guidelines state that 'regrettably, ECAS does not have the resources to approve all the applications received, or to wholly fund many applications.'

Other information

ECAS also runs activities – ranging from arts and crafts, to yoga, swimming and ICT – as well as a befriending scheme, all of which aim to improve the quality of life for people living with physical disabilities.

The Edinburgh and Lothian Trust Fund

£76,500

Correspondent: Janette Scappaticcio, Trust Administrator, 1st Floor, 14 Ashley Place, Edinburgh EH6 5PX (0131 555 9100; fax: 0131 555 9101; email: grants@eltf.org.uk; website: www.eltf.org.uk)

OSCR number: SC031561

Eligibility

Individuals in need who live in the city of Edinburgh and the Lothians. Priority is given where there is a serious illness of an individual or within their family.

As part of its General Fund, the trust administers the Ponton House Trust on behalf of Lindsays W.S. Solicitors. Grants are made to young people in need living in Edinburgh, particularly those who have disabilities.

Types of grants

One-off grants of up to £250 where they will be of real benefit to the family or individual in need, such as for clothing and household essentials.

Annual grant total

In 2016/17 the trust had assets of £6.6 million and an income of £183,000. Grants to individuals from ELTF amounted to £68,000 and those from the Ponton House Trust (part of the General Fund) a further £8,700.

Grants were also administered by the trust on behalf of other charities, however we have not included these amounts in our grant total.

Exclusions

No grants are made for electrical equipment, white goods, holidays (except in special circumstances), students' fees/equipment or the repayment of debt. Only one application will be considered in a year.

Applications

Grants for individuals from the General Fund can be applied for using the online form on the website. Applications will only be accepted from a professional at a local authority, social services, hospital or voluntary sector agency. They are considered monthly. Grants are made to the applicant agency.

Other information

The trust was formerly known as Edinburgh Voluntary Organisations' Trust. It also makes grants to organisations working in social welfare, and manages The Edinburgh Fire Fund and the Edinburgh Police Fund for Children (see the individual entries for these funds for more information).

The Merchant Company Endowments Trust

£122,000

Correspondent: Gregor Murray, Secretary & Chamberlain, The Merchant Hall, 22 Hanover Street, Edinburgh EH2 2EP (0131 220 9284; email: gregor. murray@mcoe.org.uk; website: www. mcoe.org.uk)

OSCR number: SC002002

Eligibility

'Decent, indigent men and women' who are at least 55 years old on 1 July in the year of their application and have lived or worked in the city of Edinburgh or in Midlothian.

Help may also be given to younger individuals who are certified on medical grounds as unable to earn their living.

Types of grants

Assistance can be given in the form of a cash grant, bi-annual pension, gift or appliance, or provision and care support.

Annual grant total

In 2015/16 the trust had assets of £17 million and an income of £984,000. Grants totalled £122,000.

Applications

Contact the correspondent for more information. The trust employs an almoner who assesses need and reports to the trust prior to any grant being made.

Other information

The trust also provides almshouse accommodation.

John Wilson Robert Christie Bequest Fund

£76,000 (74 grants)

Correspondent: The Trustees, c/o Geoghegans, 6 St Colme Street, Edinburgh EH3 6AD (0131 225 4681; email: mail@geoghegans.co.uk)

OSCR number: SC000465

Eligibility

People over 60 who are in need and live in Edinburgh, Midlothian, East Lothian or West Lothian. In addition, a proportion of the fund is allocated to people who are suffering from 'acute and painful diseases'.

Types of grants

Annual allowances are given according to need.

Annual grant total

In 2015/16 the fund had assets of £3.1 million and an income of £113,500. Grants were made to 74 beneficiaries during the year, totalling £76,000. A further £15,500 was awarded to organisations.

Applications

According to the 2015/16 annual report, the fund invites applications by advertising funding and contacting medical practices and other professionals in the area of benefit. People over 60 who receive an allowance are visited by the fund's female visitors who ensure they meet the criteria for allowances. The female visitors also visit new applicants.

Other information

The fund changed its name to the John Wilson Robert Christie Bequest Fund in December 2009 following the transfer of assets from the John Wilson Bequest Fund to the Robert Christie Bequest Fund.

Edinburgh

The Airth Benefaction Trust

£12,500

Correspondent: The Trustees, HBJ Gateley Wareing, Exchange Tower, 19 Canning Street, Edinburgh EH3 8EH (0131 228 2400; email: info@gateleyuk. com)

OSCR number: SC004441

Eligibility

People in need in Edinburgh.

Types of grants

Recurrent grants and pensions.

Annual grant total

In 2015/16 the trust had an income of £14,900 and a total expenditure of £14,300. We estimate that grants given to individuals totalled £12,500.

Applications

Application forms are available from the correspondent. Applications should be submitted either directly by the individual or through a third party such as a social worker. These should be returned no later than 30 September for consideration in December. Beneficiaries are invited to reapply each year.

The William Brown Nimmo Charitable Trust

£20,500 (112 grants)

Correspondent: Grants Administrator, MHD Law LLP, 45 Queen Charlotte Street, Leith, Edinburgh EH6 7HT (0131 555 0616; fax: 0131 553 1523; email: fiona.marshall@mhdlaw.co.uk)

OSCR number: SC001671

Eligibility

Older women living on a low income who were born, and permanently live, in Leith or Edinburgh.

Types of grants

Annual grants of around £185.

Annual grant total

In 2016/17 the charity had assets of £1.18 million and an income of £35,000. During the year, the charity gave around £20,500 in grants to individuals.

Applications

Apply on a form only available from 1 June from the correspondent. It should be returned by 31 July for consideration in September/October. Applicants are visited.

Alexander Darling Silk Mercer's Fund

£29,000 (47 grants)

Correspondent: Gregor Murray, Secretary & Chamberlain, The Merchant Hall, 22 Hanover Street, Edinburgh EH2 2EP (0131 220 9284; fax: 0131 220 4842; email: gregor.murray@mcoe.org. uk; website: www.mcoe.org.uk)

OSCR number: SC036724

Eligibility

Women over the age of 55, who are (preferably) unmarried or widowed, and who:

- Were born in Edinburgh; or have lived in Edinburgh for the majority of their lives; or who were married to a man who was resident in Edinburgh

▶ **OR**, were employed in Edinburgh in the manufacture of garments for ladies and children

Preference is given to women with the surnames Darling, Miller or Scott, and to women born in Lanark.

Types of grants

Recurrent grants of £250 every six months to support living costs.

Annual grant total

In 2015/16 the charity had assets of £1.7 million and an income of £48,500. The charity awarded pension payments of £500 per year to 47 individuals, totalling almost £24,500. 'Grants and allowances' to individuals totalled around £4,800.

Applications

Applications should be made in writing to the secretary of the Merchant Company, either directly by the individual or through a third party such as a social worker or Citizens Advice. Every written application is followed up by a visit by the almoner, during which a declaration regarding the applicant's financial circumstances is required.

The Edinburgh Fire Fund

£2,800

Correspondent: Janette Scappaticcio, Trust Administrator, Edinburgh and Lothian Trust Fund, 1st Floor, 14 Ashley Place, Edinburgh EH6 5PX (0131 555 9100; fax: 0131 555 9101; email: grants@ eltf.org.uk; website: www.eltf.org.uk/ funds/the-edinburgh-fire-fund)

OSCR number: SC031561

Eligibility

Individuals and families living in the Edinburgh local authority area who have been affected by fire, including physical or psychological trauma or through fire damage to their home.

Applicants must be on state benefits or earning no more than the living wage according to the Living Wage Foundation (at the time of writing [January 2018] this was £8.75 gross per hour).

Applicants must also be able to provide a report from Fire and Rescue Scotland. Where the fire is still under police investigation or consideration by the Crown Office and Procurator Fiscal Service (COPFS), the trustees will defer their consideration until the investigations have been satisfactorily concluded.

Types of grants

Grants are made for: household contents, essential personal items and clothing not covered by appropriate insurance; redecoration (and any prior cleaning to remove smoke damage); and counselling or therapy needed as a result of trauma resulting from the fire.

Annual grant total

In 2016/17 grants from the fund totalled £2,800.

Exclusions

Grants are not made for structural repairs or work which would usually be covered by a building insurance policy. Applications are only accepted for fires that have taken place within the six months prior.

Applications

The fund is administered by The Edinburgh and Lothian Trust Fund. Applications can be made using the online form on the trust's website. Applications must be made by the person directly affected by the fire. An appropriate third party e.g. a social worker, community nurse, support worker, is usually expected to verify the information provided by the applicant.

Other information

The fund, which was founded in 1824, used to be known as The Surplus Fire Fund. In March 2014, the management of the fund was transferred to The Edinburgh and Lothian Trust Fund (OSCR no. SC031561).

Edinburgh Police Fund for Children

£4,900

Correspondent: Janette Scappaticcio, Trust Administrator, Edinburgh and Lothian Trust Fund, 1st Floor, 14 Ashley Place, Edinburgh EH6 5PX (0131 555 9100; fax: 0131 555 9101; email: grants@ eltf.org.uk; website: www.eltf.org.uk/ funds/edinburgh-police-fund-for-children)

OSCR number: SC011164

Eligibility

School-age children who are in need and live in the city of Edinburgh.

Types of grants

Grants of up to £50 for clothing and footwear, principally school shoes and jackets. In cases of self-referrals, a voucher will be provided.

Annual grant total

In 2016/17 grants from the fund totalled £4,900.

Exclusions

The charity does not make cash grants and does not provide assistance towards school uniforms.

Applications

Grants from the fund are administered by The Edinburgh and Lothian Trust Fund. Applications are usually made through a third party (e.g. a social worker, community nurse, head-teacher, police officer, etc.) using the online form, available on the trust's website. Families can self-refer if they do not have a suitable third party to do so on their behalf – in these cases, the Trust Administrator can be contacted directly and the family will receive an assessment visit from a police officer.

Other information

The fund, which was founded in 1892, used to be known as the Police Aided Clothing Scheme. Since January 2016, The Edinburgh and Lothian Trust Fund (OSCR no. SC031561) has administered its grant-making.

Edinburgh Royal Infirmary Samaritan Society

£21,000

Correspondent: J. Sheddan, 7 Fountainhall Road, Edinburgh EH9 2NL

OSCR number: SC004519

Eligibility

Patients of NHS hospitals in Edinburgh who are in need.

Types of grants

Specific sums of money for clothing, bills, travel expenses or other help for the families and dependants of patients while in these hospitals or on leaving them. Grants range between £5 and £150.

Annual grant total

In 2015/16 the charity had an income of £19,000 and a total expenditure of £22,500. We estimate that grants given to individuals totalled £21,000 during the year.

Applications

Through a medical social worker based at Edinburgh Royal Infirmary Social Work Department. Applications are considered fortnightly.

The Edinburgh Society for Relief of Indigent Old Men

£34,000

Correspondent: Trust Secretary, c/o Lindsays, Caledonian Exchange, 19A Canning Street, Edinburgh EH3 8HE (0131 229 1212; fax: 0131 229 5611; email: edinburgh@lindsays.co.uk)

OSCR number: SC005284

Eligibility

Men who live in Edinburgh, who are beyond the national retirement age and 'adjudged as being in some way deserving'.

Types of grants

The majority of spending is on monthly pensions. The charity also awards Christmas bonuses.

Annual grant total

In 2015/16 the charity had assets of £916,000 and an income of £47,500. During the year, £34,000 was awarded in grants.

Applications

Applications should be made in writing to the correspondent, detailing financial circumstance, and income and expenditure.

EMMS International – Hawthornbrae

£11,700 (24 grants)

Correspondent: UK Grants Administrator, 7 Washington Lane, Edinburgh EH11 2HA (0131 313 3828; email: info@emms.org; website: www.emms.org)

OSCR number: SC032327

Eligibility

Applicants must be resident in the Edinburgh city boundaries, be recovering from an illness, be of limited financial means, and be of 'good character'.

Types of grants

Grants of up to £300 for adults and £150 for children (under 18) for recuperative holidays. Grants to one family will not exceed £900.

Annual grant total

In 2017 the charity had assets of £1.3 million and an income of £1.7 million. The charity awarded £11,700 in grants to individuals.

Exclusions

The charity cannot give grants towards spending money.

Applications

Application forms are available to download from the website. Applications must be sponsored by a professional, social, or health worker. To protect applicant confidentiality, there are two forms:

1   Application form 1 requires basic information about the applicant and should be returned to EMMS International at care@emms.org
2   Application form 2 requires medical information about the applicant and should be returned to the medical assessor, Dr William Campbell, at william.campbell36@btinternet.com.

Other information

The majority of EMMS International's work is centred on health care in India, Malawi, and Nepal.

Orkney and Shetland

Tackling Household Affordable Warmth Orkney (THAW Orkney)

£261,000

Correspondent: THAW Orkney, 15 Victoria Street, Kirkwall, Orkney

OSCR number: SC045272

Eligibility

People in need who live in Orkney.

Types of grants

Small, one-off grants to cover the costs of heating installations, repairs, and occasionally bills. The trustees award grants to relieve fuel poverty.

Annual grant total

In 2016/17 the charity had assets of £95,000 and an income of £161,000. The charity awarded £261,000 in grants for individuals.

Applications

Applications can be made in writing to the correspondent.

Other information

The charity also makes awards for the improvement of education in energy and fuel conservation, and its efficient uses.

Renfrewshire

Inverclyde

Gourock Coal and Benevolent Fund

£3,500

Correspondent: S. Baldwin, 38 Taymouth Drive, Gourock, Renfrewshire PA19 1HJ

OSCR number: SC009881

Eligibility

People in need who live in the former burgh of Gourock. There is a preference for older people, especially people who live on their own.

Types of grants

Gas and electricity vouchers are available and coal deliveries can also be made.

Annual grant total

In 2016/17 the fund had an income of £4,800 and a total expenditure of £3,900. We estimate that grants given to individuals totalled around £3,500.

Applications

Apply in writing to any minister or parish priest in the town, or the local branch of the WRVS (not to the correspondent). Applications are normally considered in December and can be submitted either directly by the individual or through a social worker, Citizens Advice or other welfare agency.

Scottish Borders

Blackstock Trust

£16,700 (59 grants)

Correspondent: Trust Secretary, c/o Pike & Chapman, 36 Bank Street, Galashiels TD1 1ER (01896 752379)

OSCR number: SC014309

Eligibility

People who are older or sick, or people who have disabilities and live in the counties of Roxburgh, Berwick and Selkirk.

Serving and retired British police officers who have been injured or incapacitated while serving as a police officer, and their dependants.

Types of grants

Financial assistance ranging between £60 and £500 for accommodation, maintenance or welfare, short holiday breaks, respite care and the provision of amenities.

Annual grant total
In 2015/16 the trust held assets of £658,000 and had an income of £25,500. Grants were made to 59 individuals totalling £16,700.

Applications
Apply in writing to the correspondent, including details of financial position (income and capital).

Tayside

The Mair Robertson Benevolent Fund

£4,300

Correspondent: The Trustees, 144 Nethergate, Dundee DD1 4EB

OSCR number: SC007435

Eligibility
Older women living in Dundee and Blairgowrie who are suffering from financial hardship.

Types of grants
One-off grants.

Annual grant total
In 2015/16 the fund had an income of £9,400 and a total expenditure of £8,800. We estimate that the fund awarded around £4,300 in grants to individuals.

The fund also makes grants to charities based locally in Blairgowrie and Dundee.

Applications
Apply in writing to the correspondent.

Other information
At the time of writing (August 2017) the charity had no website or accounts available.

Angus

Angus Council Charitable Trust

£2,000

Correspondent: Head of Legal & Democratic Services, Angus Council, Angus House, Orchardbank Business Park, Forfar, Angus DD8 1AN (03452 777 778; email: accesslawcommittee@ angus.gov.uk; website: www.angus.gov. uk)

OSCR number: SC044695

Eligibility
Residents of Angus who are in need, including the wards of: Kirriemuir and Dean; Brechin and Edzell; Forfar and District; Monifieth and Sidlaw; Carnoustie and District; Arbroath East and Lunan and West and Letham; Montrose and District; as well as Angus-wide.

Types of grants
The purposes of funds available in each ward may vary; applicants should check the charity's website or contact the correspondent for further information.

Residents of Forfar may also apply to Strangs Mortification, which gives heating grants as well as one-off grants. Applicants must have lived in Forfar for at least two years and be in receipt of housing benefit.

Annual grant total
The council administers over 100 charitable trusts – the largest of which is Strangs Mortification. In 2015/16 the trust had an income of £7,200 and a total expenditure of £4,200. Grants were awarded to both individuals and organisations and we have estimated that grants to individuals for welfare purposes totalled £2,000 during the year.

Applications
Apply on a form available to download from the charity's website or from ACCESS offices or libraries. Applications to Strangs Mortification from those who live in Forfar must be approved by a social worker, health professional or minister, from whom an application form can also be obtained.

Other information
The Angus Council Charitable Trust was formed on 1 August 2014, consolidating 97 registered charities and 42 non-registered trusts.

Grants are also awarded to organisations meeting the charity's objectives.

The Colvill Charity

£650 (13 grants)

Correspondent: Trusts Administrator, Thorntons Law LLP, Brothockbank House, Arbroath DD11 1NJ

OSCR number: SC003913

Eligibility
People who are in need and live in the town of Arbroath and the parish of St Vigeans and the surrounding area. Any surplus funds will be awarded to applicants in the District of Angus.

Types of grants
Grants of £50, for general financial relief.

Annual grant total
In 2016/17 the charity had an income of £40,500 and a total expenditure of £22,500. The Colvill Charity awarded £650 in grants to 13 individuals during the year.

Applications
Application forms are available upon request from the correspondent.

Other information
The Colvill Charity also manages and distributes the funds of various other local organisations. The charity also makes an annual payment of £10 to the incumbent of the St Mary's Episcopal Church, and an annual payment of £100 to the Angus Educational Trust.

Angus Walker Benevolent Bequest

£6,900

Correspondent: The Trustees of Angus Walker Benevolent Bequest, c/o T. Duncan & Co. Solicitors, 192 High Street, Montrose, Angus DD10 8NA (01674 672533)

OSCR number: SC008129

Eligibility
People in need who live in Montrose.

Types of grants
One-off grants.

Annual grant total
This was the latest financial information at the time of writing (February 2018). In 2014/15 the charity had an income of £9,500 and a total expenditure of £7,100. We estimate that grants given to individuals totalled £6,900.

Applications
By formal application via a trustee, local district councillor, the minister of Montrose Old Church or the rector of St Mary's and St Peter's Episcopal Church, Montrose.

Dundee

Blyth Benevolent Trust

£1,500

Correspondent: Trust Administrator, c/o Bowman Solicitors, 27 Bank Street, Dundee DD1 1RP (01382 322267)

OSCR number: SC017188

Eligibility
People with disabilities or health problems who live in Dundee.

Types of grants
One-off and regular grants.

Annual grant total
In 2015/16 the trust had an income of £3,400 and a total expenditure of £2,100. We estimate that grants given to individuals totalled £1,500.

Applications

Apply in writing to the correspondent. Applications should be submitted either directly by the individual or through a third party such as a social worker, or through an organisation e.g. a Citizens Advice or other welfare agency.

Broughty Ferry Benevolent Trust

£14,000

Correspondent: The Secretary, 12 Tircarra Gardens, Broughty Ferry, Dundee DD5 2QF (01382 477723; email: ctgws@talktalk.net)

OSCR number: SC010644

Eligibility

People in need living in Broughty Ferry, Dundee.

Types of grants

One-off and recurrent grants are given according to need.

Annual grant total

In 2015/16 the trust had an income of £21,000 and a total expenditure of £16,300. We estimate that grants given to individuals totalled £14,000.

There are approximately ten beneficiaries, but the trust is seeking to help more people and encourages applications.

Applications

Application forms are available from the correspondent. They can be submitted either directly by the individual or through a social worker, Citizens Advice or other welfare agency.

Perth and Kinross
Mrs Agnes W. Carmichael's Trust

£3,500

Correspondent: Mrs Agnes W. Carmichael's Trust, Watson Lyall Bowie, Union Bank Building, Coupar Angus, Perthshire PH13 9AJ

OSCR number: SC004415

Eligibility

People with disabilities or other health problems and older people who live in Coupar Angus.

Types of grants

Grants, donations, loans, and gifts are given for the prevention and relief of poverty. The amount awarded is based on need.

Annual grant total

In 2016/17 the trust had an income of £7,500 and a total expenditure of £7,300. We estimate that grants totalled around £3,500.

Applications

Applications should be made in writing to the correspondent, detailing financial circumstances and what the grant will be used for.

Other information

The trust also supports organisations through grants, donations, loans, and gifts.

Neil Gow Charitable Trust

£16,000

Correspondent: The Trustees, c/o Miller Hendry Solicitors, 10 Blackfriars Street, Perth PH1 5NS (01738 630222)

OSCR number: SC012915

Eligibility

People in need who live in the district of Perth and Kinross or the immediate neighbourhood.

Types of grants

Regular pensions according to need.

Annual grant total

In 2016/17 the trust had an income of £9,200 and a total expenditure of £18,900. We estimate that grants given to individuals totalled £16,000.

Applications

Apply in writing to the correspondent.

The Guildry Incorporation of Perth

£37,500

Correspondent: Lorna Peacock, Secretary, 42 George Street, Perth PH1 5JL (01738 623195; email: secretary@perthguildry.org.uk; website: www.perthguildry.org.uk)

OSCR number: SC008072

Eligibility

Members of the guildry, their widows and dependants, and other people living in Perth who are in need.

Types of grants

One-off grants, weekly pensions and fuel allowances.

Annual grant total

In 2016/17 the guildry had assets of £6.7 million and an income of £232,500. Grants totalled £107,500, of which £77,000 was given in 89 grants to individuals. We estimate that grants to individuals for social welfare purposes totalled around £37,500.

Applications

Application forms can be requested from the correspondent. They are considered at the trustees' meetings on the last Tuesday of every month.

Scones Lethendy Mortification

£27,000

Correspondent: The Treasurer, King James VI Hospital, Hospital Street, Perth PH2 8HP (01738 624660)

OSCR number: SC015545

Eligibility

People over the age of 60 who are in need, and boys near to the age of 14 who can prove they are a descendant of Charles Cairnie or one of his brothers. Only residents of Perth can apply.

Types of grants

Pensions paid quarterly to older residents, and bursaries (paid yearly over ten years) to young boys who can prove their relation to Charles Cairnie.

Annual grant total

In 2015/16 the charity had an income of £45,000 and a total expenditure of £35,000. During the year, the charity awarded £27,000 in grants and pensions.

Applications

Apply on a form available from the correspondent. New applications are added to a waiting list although successful applicants are judged on need rather than when they applied.

Arthur and Margaret Thompson's Charitable Trust

£14,500

Correspondent: The Trustees, c/o Miller Hendry, 10 Blackfriars Street, Perth PH1 5NS (01738 630222)

OSCR number: SC012103

Eligibility

Residents of Kinross and the Parish of Orwell who are in need.

Types of grants

Annuities and Christmas gifts.

Annual grant total

In 2016/17 the trust had assets of £7.1 million and an income of £200,000. Grants to individuals totalled £14,500.

Applications

Apply in writing to the correspondent.

Mrs A. Unwin Trust

£9,700

Correspondent: The Trustees,
10 Blackfriars Street, Perth PH1 5NS

OSCR number: SC015126

Eligibility

Residents of the city of Perth who are in need.

Types of grants

One-off and recurring grants according to need. Grants have previously been awarded for household goods, clothing, bedding and flooring.

Annual grant total

In 2016/17 the trust had assets of £1.1 million and an income of £31,000. Grants to individuals totalled £9,700.

Applications

Apply in writing to the correspondent.

Wales

Mid Wales

Powys

The Brecknock Welfare Trust

£1,000

Correspondent: Fiona Williams, Brecon Town Council, The Guildhall, High Street, Brecon, Powys LD3 7AL (01874 622884; email: brecon.guildhall@btinternet.com)

CC number: 240671

Eligibility
People in need who live in the town of Brecon.

Types of grants
One-off grants in kind according to need, such as electrical goods, clothing, medical and equipment and furniture for people with disabilities.

Annual grant total
In 2016 the trust had an income of £1,100 and a total expenditure of £1,400. We estimate that around £1,000 was given in grants to individuals for social welfare purposes.

Exclusions
Grants are in kind and no cash awards are made.

Applications
Apply in writing to the correspondent. Applications should be submitted through a recognised referral agency (such as a social worker, Citizens Advice or doctor).

Llanidloes Relief in Need Charity

£1,500

Correspondent: Elaine Lloyd, Woodcroft, Woodlands Road, Llanidloes, Powys SY18 6HX (01686 413045; email: elainellloyd@gmail.com)

CC number: 259955

Eligibility
People in need who live in the area of Llanidoes.

Types of grants
Generally one-off grants for people in need.

Annual grant total
In 2015/16 the charity had an income of £1,200 and a total expenditure of £1,800. We estimate that about £1,500 was given in welfare grants to individuals.

Exclusions
Our previous research indicates that support is not normally given to applicants not living within three miles of the town.

Applications
Apply in writing to the correspondent.

Other information
At the time of writing (August 2017) the charity did not have a website or accounts available.

The Montgomery Welfare Fund

£1,100

Correspondent: Edward Humphreys, 2 Rowes Terrace, Pool Road, Montgomery SY15 6QD (01686 668790; email: ejhumphreys1@gmail.com)

CC number: 214767

Eligibility
People in need who live permanently in the ecclesiastical parish of Montgomery (not the county).

Types of grants
One-off grants.

Annual grant total
In 2015/16 the fund had an income of £2,800 and a total expenditure of £2,300. We estimate that welfare grants to individuals totalled around £1,100.

Exclusions
No grants are given to pay rates, tax or other public funds.

Applications
Apply in writing to the correspondent.

Other information
Our previous research indicates that the charity also awards grants to individuals for educational purposes.

Visual Impairment Breconshire (Nam Gweledol Sir Brycheiniog)

£1,000

Correspondent: Michael Knee, Secretary, 3 Beacons View, Mount Street, Brecon, Powys LD3 7LY (01874 624949; email: vibrecon@gmail.com; website: www.visualimpairment.breconshire.powys.org.uk)

CC number: 217377

Eligibility
People who have permanent and uncorrectable eye conditions who live in Breconshire.

Types of grants
One-off grants are given for equipment or aids, services and experiences (such as holidays). The need for the grant must be related to the individual's visual impairment.

Annual grant total
The 2014/15 accounts were the latest available at the time of writing (November 2017). In 2014/15 the charity had an income of £2,600 and a total expenditure of £3,500. We estimate that social welfare grants to individuals totalled around £1,000.

Exclusions
In general, the charity will not pay for anything that should be funded by the NHS or a local authority. Nor will it contribute towards the rental of book reading equipment and corresponding library subscriptions, or any equipment for use in care homes and similar institutions where there exists a statutory obligation or requirement to provide for client use.

Applications

Application forms, along with guidelines, are available to download from the website. They can be submitted directly by the individual, or by their relatives or carers.

Other information

This charity also runs activities, provides resources and makes grants to organisations. It also provides an annual bursary to enable an individual to pursue an educational or sporting activity.

North Wales

Conwy

The Evan and Catherine Roberts Home

£3,400

Correspondent: Ken Owen, Trustee, Ael Y Garth, 81 Bryn Avenue, Old Colwyn, Colwyn Bay LL29 8AH (01492 515209; email: kenowen@uwclub.net)

CC number: 244965

Eligibility

People over the age of 60 who live within a 40-mile radius of the Bethesda Welsh Methodist Church in Old Colwyn, with preference for members of the Methodist Church. Those living in parts of Conwy, Denbighshire, Flintshire and Gwynedd are eligible.

Types of grants

One-off grants ranging from £50 to £150.

Annual grant total

In 2016/17 the charity had an income of £5,700 and a total expenditure of £3,600. We estimate that around £3,400 was given in grants to individuals.

Applications

Application forms are available from the correspondent.

Denbighshire

Freeman Evans St David's Day Denbigh Charity

£6,100

Correspondent: Medwyn Jones, Town Clerk, Denbigh Town Council, Town Hall, Crown Square, Denbigh LL16 3TB (01745 815984; email: townclerk@denbightowncouncil.gov.uk)

CC number: 518033

Eligibility

People in need who live in Denbigh and Henllan. Particularly those who are older, have disabilities or an illness.

Types of grants

One-off grants according to need, including towards disability aids, furniture, carpets, travel costs, home adaptations, funeral costs, debt repayments, Christmas gifts. The charity appears to pay to service/item providers rather than making direct cash payments to individuals.

Annual grant total

In 2015/16 the charity had assets of £1.4 million and an income of £102,000. Grants were made totalling £58,500, of which welfare grants totalled £6,100.

Applications

Applications may be made in writing to the correspondent, either directly by the individual or through a third party, such as a social worker, Citizens Advice or other welfare agency. The trustees meet regularly throughout the year to consider applications.

Other information

Organisations are also supported and assistance is given to individuals for educational purposes.

Llanelidan Consolidated Charities

£4,000

Correspondent: Mrs E. Shakesby, Tyn Yr Erw, Llaneldian, Ruthin LL15 2RR (01824 750475)

CC number: 258225

Eligibility

Individuals in need living in the parish of Llaneldian.

Types of grants

One-off grants according to need.

Annual grant total

In 2016 the charity had an income of £3,500 and a total expenditure of £4,100. We estimate that grants given to individuals totalled around £4,000.

Applications

Apply in writing to the correspondent.

The Charity of Elizabeth Williams

£2,500

Correspondent: Alison Alexander, 19 Roe Parc, St Asaph, Denbighshire LL17 0LD (01745 583798; email: alison.alexander@btinternet.com)

CC number: 216903

Eligibility

People in need who live in the communities of St Asaph, Bodelwyddan, Cefn and Waen in Clwyd.

Types of grants

One-off and recurrent grants are given according to need. Grants can be for something specific, such as new white goods, or can be awarded as a Christmas gift.

Annual grant total

In 2016/17 the charity had an income of £7,700 and a total expenditure of £5,500. We estimate that the charity awarded £2,500 in grants to individuals.

Exclusions

Grants are not given for aid that can be met specifically by public funds, for private education or if the grant would affect a claimant's benefit from the DWP.

Applications

Applications should be made in writing to the correspondent. Previous research indicates that applications from individuals seeking specific help are dealt with on an ongoing basis. Applications for Christmas grants should be received by November.

Other information

One half of the income of the charity is to be awarded to Elizabeth Williams' Educational Foundation.

Flintshire

The Corwen College Pension Charity

£2,000

Correspondent: Diane McCarthy, Diocesan Secretary, The Diocese of St Asaph, Diocesan Office, High Street, St Asaph, Denbighshire LL17 0RD (email: dianemccarthy@churchinwales.org.uk)

CC number: 248822

Eligibility

Widows or widowers of clergy of the Church in Wales who are in need and who have held office in the district of Merionydd in Gwynedd or the communities of Betws Gwerfil Goch, Corwen Gwyddelern, Llandrillo, Llangar and Llansantffraid Glyndyfrdwy (all in Clwyd).

Types of grants

Recurrent grants according to need.

Annual grant total

In 2016 the charity had an income of £3,200 and a total expenditure of £2,200.

We estimate that social welfare grants to individuals totalled £2,000.

Applications

Apply in writing to the correspondent.

Owen Jones Charity

£2,700

Correspondent: Dr Jack Wolstenholme, Secretary, 18 St Peter's Park, Northop, Mold, Clwyd CH7 6DP (01352 840739; email: drjwolstenholme@aol.com)

CC number: 525453

Eligibility

People in need who live in Northop, Northop Hall, Sychdyn, Connah's Quay and Flint (the historic parish of Northop).

Types of grants

One-off and recurrent grants are given according to need.

Annual grant total

In 2016/17 the charity had an income of £11,600 and a total expenditure of £8,200. We estimate that grants made to individuals totalled £2,700.

The charity also makes grants to local schools and to individuals for educational purposes.

Applications

Apply in writing to the correspondent.

Gwynedd

Freeman Evans St David's Day Ffestiniog Charity

£36,500

Correspondent: Maldwyn Evans, Natwest Bank plc, Merionnydd Business Centre, Bridge Street, Dolgellau, Gwynedd LL40 1AU (01341 421242; email: maldevans@aol.com)

CC number: 518034

Eligibility

People who are older, in poor health or who have disabilities and live in the districts of Blaenau Ffestiniog and Llan Ffestiniog as they were prior to the 1974 reorganisation.

Types of grants

One-off and recurrent grants are given according to need, for example medical aids or equipment, transport and home adaptions.

Annual grant total

In 2016/17 the charity had assets of £1.6 million and an income of £53,000. During the year, the charity awarded £36,500 in grants to individuals.

Applications

Applications can be submitted directly by an individual to the correspondent. Where possible, applications should be endorsed by a professional or social worker, or an appropriate agency such as Citizens Advice.

Isle of Anglesey

Anglesey Society for the Welfare of Handicapped People

£3,500

Correspondent: Robert Jones, Administrator, 8 Gorwel Deg, Rhostrehwfa, Llangefni, Anglesey LL77 7JR

CC number: 218810

Eligibility

People living in Anglesey who have tuberculosis or any other disease, illness or disability.

Types of grants

One-off or recurrent grants according to need.

Annual grant total

In 2015 the charity had an income £2,500 and a total expenditure of £7,500. We have estimated that grants to individuals for welfare purposes totalled £3,500 during the year.

Applications

Apply in writing to the correspondent.

Other information

The charity also makes grants to organisations.

Charity of William Bold

£2,500

Correspondent: Rees Roberts, Talfryn, Bodffordd, Llangefni LL77 7DJ (01248 750368; email: reestalfryn@yahoo.co.uk)

CC number: 218152

Eligibility

People living on the Isle of Anglesey who are in need.

Types of grants

One-off grants according to need.

Annual grant total

In 2016/17 the charity had an income of £16,500 and a total expenditure of £11,100. We estimate that welfare grants to individuals totalled around £2,500, with funding also awarded to organisations and to young people for educational purposes.

Applications

Apply in writing to the correspondent.

Llanrhuddlad Charities (William Lloyd)

£500

Correspondent: Maldwyn Roberts, Trustee, 17 Maes Cynfor, Cemaes Bay LL67 0HS (01407 710549; email: mnlroberts@gmail.com)

CC number: 238565

Eligibility

Widows and older people who live in Llanrhuddlad.

Types of grants

Annual donations.

Annual grant total

In 2016/17 the charity had an income of £3,100 and a total expenditure of £2,100. We estimate that grants given to individuals totalled around £500.

Applications

Apply in writing to the correspondent.

Other information

The charity also pays for the maintenance of two properties it owns and for the building upkeep of the parish church.

Wrexham

The Jones Trust

£25,000 (126 grants)

Correspondent: Patricia Williams, Secretary, 33 Deva Way, Wrexham LL13 9EU (01978 261684; email: patmwilliams@tiscali.co.uk)

CC number: 229956

Eligibility

People who are sick or convalescing, have disabilities or are infirm in the city of Wrexham.

Types of grants

Grants for respite care. Grants for appliances and surgical aids not readily available through the health service are also considered.

Annual grant total

In 2016 the trust held assets of £1 million and had an income of £36,500. Grants were made to 126 individuals totalling £25,000.

Applications

Apply in writing to the correspondent.

Overton United Charity

£1,900

Correspondent: Jennifer Bellis, 6 Springfield Park, Overton, Wrexham LL13 0EX (01978 710567)

CC number: 1059405

Eligibility

People living in Overton who are older, ill or convalescent or who have disabilities.

Types of grants

One-off grants according to need.

Annual grant total

In 2015/16 the charity had an income of £2,400 and a total expenditure of £2,100. We estimate that grants given to individuals totalled around £1,900.

Applications

Apply in writing to the correspondent.

Other information

The Consolidated Charities of Ellis Lloyd and Others (Charity Commission no. 259621) is registered separately from Overton United Charity but shares its trustees and works under the same name. It also makes grants to support people who are older, ill or convalescent or who have disabilities, but operates in the parish of Erbistock.

Ruabon and District Relief-in-Need Charity

£1,000

Correspondent: James Fenner, 65 Albert Grove, Ruabon, Wrexham LL14 6AF (01978 820102; email: jamesrfenner65@tiscali.co.uk)

CC number: 212817

Eligibility

All people who are considered to be in need who live in the county borough of Wrexham, which covers the community council districts of Cefn Mawr, Penycae, Rhosllanerchrugog and Ruabon.

Types of grants

One-off and recurrent grants. Previously, grants have been made towards telephone installation, heating costs, children's clothing, cookers, furniture, musical instruments, electric wheelchairs, clothing for adults in hospital, travel costs for hospital visits and books and travel for university students.

Annual grant total

In 2016 the charity had an income of £3,100 and a total expenditure of £4,300. We estimate that grants for welfare purposes totalled approximately £1,000.

Applications

Apply in writing to the correspondent either directly by the individual or a family member, through a third party such as a social worker or teacher, or through an organisation such as Citizens Advice or a school. Applications are considered on an ongoing basis.

Wrexham and District Relief in Need Charity

£15,000

Correspondent: Frieda Leech, Holly Chase, Pen Y Palmant Road, Minera, Wrexham LL11 3YW (01978 754152; email: clerk.wpef@gmail.com)

CC number: 236355

Eligibility

People in need who live in the former borough of Wrexham or the communities of Abenbury, Bersham, Bieston, Broughton, Brymbo, Esclusham Above, Esclusham Below, Gresford, Gwersyllt and Minera in Wrexham.

Types of grants

One-off and recurrent grants to relieve financial hardship. Previous grants have been used for household furnishings and clothing.

Annual grant total

In 2016 the charity had an income of £18,000 and a total expenditure of £15,500. We estimate that grants given to individuals totalled £15,000.

Applications

Applications can be made in writing to the correspondent, detailing financial need and what the grant will be used for. Where possible, applications should have support from a professional or social worker. Applications are considered throughout the year.

South East Wales

Merthyr Tydfil

Merthyr Mendicants

£3,900

Correspondent: Allen Lane, 4 Georgetown Villas, Georgetown, Merthyr Tydfil, Mid Glamorgan CF48 1BD (01685 373308)

CC number: 208105

Eligibility

People in need who live in the borough of Merthyr Tydfil.

Types of grants

One-off grants according to need. Grants have been given towards: medical equipment not available from the NHS (providing it is recommended by a medical authority); Christmas parcels; holidays for children; telephone helplines for incapacitated people; and help with domestic equipment such as cookers, refrigerators, washing machines, bedding and beds.

Annual grant total

In 2016 the charity had an income of £10,500 and a total expenditure of £8,100. We estimate that grants given to individuals for social welfare purposes totalled around £3,900, with funding also awarded to organisations.

Applications

Apply in writing to the correspondent, including information on any other sources of income. Applications can be submitted directly by the individual or through a social worker, Citizens Advice or other welfare agency.

Other information

At the time of writing (August 2017) the charity had no website or accounts available.

Monmouthshire

Llandenny Charities

£1,100

Correspondent: Dr Graham Russell, Trustee, Forge Cottage, Llandenny, Usk, Monmouthshire NP15 1DL (01633 432536; email: gsrussell@btinternet.com)

CC number: 223311

Eligibility

People in need who are over the age of 65, in receipt of a state pension and have been living in the parish of Llandenny for more than one year.

Types of grants

Payments to people receiving a state pension.

Annual grant total

In 2016 the charity had an income of £2,300 and a total expenditure of £2,400. We estimate that grants for welfare purposes totalled around £1,100.

Applications

Applications may be made in writing to the correspondent. They can be made directly by the individual and should be submitted by 15 January for consideration in February.

Other information

Grants are also awarded to higher education students for educational purposes.

Monmouth Charity

£2,200

Correspondent: Andrew Pirie, Trustee, 2 St John Street, Monmouth NP25 3EA (01600 716202)

CC number: 700759

Eligibility

People who are in need and live within a ten-mile radius of Monmouth town.

Types of grants

One-off grants usually up to a maximum of £500.

Annual grant total

In 2015/16 the charity had an income of £8,800 and a total expenditure of £9,000. Grants are made to individuals and organisations for a wide range of charitable purposes, including for the relief of poverty, disability and education. We estimate that welfare grants to individuals totalled £2,200.

Applications

The charity advertises in the local press each September/October and applications should be made in response to this advertisement for consideration in November. Emergency grants can be considered at any time. There is no application form. Applications can be submitted directly by the individual or through a social worker, Citizens Advice or other welfare agency.

The Monmouthshire County Council Welsh Church Act Fund

£6,600

Correspondent: Joy Robson, Head of Finance, Monmouthshire County Council, PO Box 106, Caldicot NP26 9AN (01633 644657; email: davejarrett@monmouthshire.gov.uk; website: www.monmouthshire.gov.uk/welsh-church-fund)

CC number: 507094

Eligibility

People living in the boundaries of Monmouthshire County Council who are in need. Grants are also given to discharged prisoners and their families.

Types of grants

Grants of money or payment for items, services or facilities. Accommodation can be provided to older people who need it because of infirmities or disabilities. People who are visually impaired may also be given access to charitable homes and holiday homes.

Annual grant total

In 2015/16 the charity had assets of £5.2 million and an income of £226,000. Welfare grants to individuals totalled £6,600.

Applications

Application forms can be downloaded from the council's website. Applications are considered seven times a year.

Other information

The charity also makes grants to organisations.

Torfaen

The Cwmbran Trust

£15,000

Correspondent: Kenneth Maddox, Secretary, c/o Meritor HVBS (UK) Ltd, Grange Road, Cwmbran, Gwent NP44 3XU (01633 834040; email: cwmbrantrust@meritor.com)

CC number: 505855

Eligibility

People in need living in the town of Cwmbran, Gwent.

Types of grants

One-off and recurrent grants are awarded for a wide variety of educational and welfare purposes, such as stairlifts, home study courses, equipment, repairs, computer equipment, wheelchairs, holidays, debt clearance, removal costs, building renovation, funeral costs, travel expenses and respite care. Grants usually range between £100 and £3,000.

Annual grant total

In 2016 the trust had assets of £2.5 million and an income of £93,500. Grants to individuals totalled £17,000. Grants are mainly made for welfare purposes. We estimate that grants to individuals totalled around £15,000.

Applications

Applications may be made in writing to the correspondent. They can be submitted directly by the individual or through a social worker, Citizens Advice, welfare agency or other third party. Applications are usually considered in March, May, July, October and December.

Vale of Glamorgan

The Cowbridge with Llanblethian United Charities

£19,800

Correspondent: Clerk to the Trustees, 66 Broadway, Llanblethian, Cowbridge CF71 7EW (01446 773287; email: h.phillips730@btinternet.com)

CC number: 1014580

Eligibility

People in need who live in the town of Cowbridge with Llanblethian.

Types of grants

The provision of items, services or facilities that will reduce the person's need.

Annual grant total

In 2015/16 the charity had assets of £709,500 and an income of £26,500. Welfare grants to individuals totalled £19,800.

Applications

Apply in writing to the correspondent. Applications can be submitted directly by the individual or through a welfare agency.

South West Wales

Pembrokeshire

Haverfordwest Freemen's Estate

£8,000

Correspondent: P. K. Lucas, Clerk to the Trustees, R. K. Lucas & Son, 9 Victoria Place, Haverfordwest, Pembrokeshire SA61 2JX (01437 762538)

CC number: 515111

Eligibility

Hereditary freemen of Haverfordwest aged 18 years and over.

Types of grants

One-off grants according to need.

Annual grant total

In 2015/16 the estate had an income of £19,000 and a total expenditure of £16,100. We estimate that grants given to individuals totalled £8,000.

Applications

Freemen must be enrolled by the chair of the local authority. The honour is hereditary being passed down through the male or female line.

William Sanders Charity

£5,200

Correspondent: Julia Phillips, 11 Freemans Walk, Pembroke SA71 4AS

CC number: 229182

Eligibility
Widows and unmarried women who are in need and live within a five-mile radius of the parish of St John's, Pembroke Dock.

Types of grants
Christmas grants, typically ranging from £25 to £40, are available from November to December each year.

Annual grant total
In 2015/16 the charity had an income of £9,400 and a total expenditure of £5,400. We estimate that grants given to individuals totalled £5,200.

Applications
Applications can be made in writing to the correspondent, directly by the individual or a family member.

The Tenby Relief-in-Need and Pensions Charity

£26,000

Correspondent: Clive Mathias, Clerk to the Trustees, Lewis Lewis & Co., County Chambers, Pentre Road, St Clears, Carmarthen SA33 4AA (01994 231044; email: clive@lewislewis.co.uk)

CC number: 231233

Eligibility
Older people in need who live in the community of Tenby.

Types of grants
Pensions of £17 a month to help relieve financial difficulties. Most beneficiaries will also receive a small Christmas bonus of £20. Usually, once a grant has been agreed it will be paid indefinitely.

Annual grant total
In 2016 the charity had assets of £807,000 and an income of £34,000. Grants totalled £26,000.

Applications
Application forms are available from the correspondent and can be submitted directly by the individual or a family member.

William Vawer

£3,000

Correspondent: R. K. Lucas, R. K. Lucas & Son, 9 Victoria Place, Haverfordwest, Pembrokeshire SA61 2JX (01437 762538)

CC number: 213880

Eligibility
People in need who live in the town of Haverfordwest. The charity has a strong preference for those who are freemen of the town of Haverfordwest.

Types of grants
Pensions and one-off grants.

Annual grant total
In 2015/16 the trust had an income of £6,800 and a total expenditure of £3,300. We estimate that welfare grants to individuals totalled around £3,000.

Applications
Apply in writing to the correspondent.

Other information
At the time of writing (August 2017) the charity had no annual report or website available.

East Midlands

General

The Jack and Ada Beattie Foundation (Fund for the Forgotten)
See entry on page 35

DTD Charity
See entry on page 235

The John Heggs Bates' Charity for Convalescents

£20,000

Correspondent: Barbara Amos, Clerk, Unit 5, Friars Mill, Bath Lane, Leicester LE3 5BE (0116 204 6620; email: barbara. amos@stwcharity.co.uk)

CC number: 218060

Eligibility
'Necessitous convalescents' and their carers who reside in Leicester, Leicestershire and Rutland.

Types of grants
One-off grants.

Annual grant total
In 2016 the charity had an income of £17,000 and a total expenditure of £21,500. We estimate that grants given to individuals totalled £20,000.

Applications
Application forms are available from: Leicester Charity Link, 20a Millstone Lane, Leicester LE1 5JN. Applications should be submitted through a social worker, Citizens Advice, GP or church and are considered on a quarterly basis. The charity also works with local hospices to make grants to people staying there.

Leicestershire Coal Industry Welfare Trust Fund

£4,400

Correspondent: Peter Smith, Trustee, Miners Offices Unit 12, The Springboard Centre, Mantle Lane, Coalville, Leicestershire LE67 3DW (01530 832085; email: leicesternum@ukinbox.com)

CC number: 1006985

Eligibility
Miners and their dependants connected with the British coal mining industry in the Leicestershire area.

Types of grants
Grants to individuals have been described in the annual report (2015) as those which assist them with things such as home improvements or holidays. Grants have also been made to various groups to assist with running costs or competition expenses.

Annual grant total
In 2015 the fund had an income of £278,200 and a total expenditure of £23,000. Note that both the income and the expenditure vary each year. The charity awarded a total of £4,400 in grants to individuals experiencing financial hardship.

Applications
Apply in writing to the correspondent. Applications should include details of mining connections, residence in Leicestershire and dependence on the mineworker (in the case of children). The trustees meet throughout the year to consider applications.

Other information
Grants are also given to organisations.

The Leicestershire County Nursing Association

£43,000

Correspondent: Edward Cufflin, Treasurer, Charles Stanley, Mercury Place, St George Street, Leicester LE1 1QG (0116 366 6200; email: ed. cufflin@charles-stanley.co.uk)

CC number: 216594

Eligibility
Retired district nurses and people who are sick and in need, who live in Leicestershire or Rutland (excluding the city of Leicester). Priority is given to retired district nurses.

Annual grant total
In 2015/16 the charity had assets of £1.4 million and a total income of £58,500. During the year a total of £43,000 was awarded in grants to individuals for welfare purposes.

Applications
Apply in writing to the correspondent, directly by the individual in the case of retired district nurses or through Leicester Charity Link in other cases.

Other information
The charity also makes grants to organisations.

Thomas Monke

£1,500

Correspondent: Christopher Kitto, Correspondent, 29 Blacksmiths Lane, Newton Solney, Burton-on-Trent, Staffordshire DE15 0SD (01283 702129; email: chriskitto@btinternet.com)

CC number: 214783

Eligibility
People in need who live in Austrey, Measham, Shenton and Whitwick, especially older people over the age of 75 who live alone.

Types of grants

One-off and recurrent grants (up to a maximum of the £200) according to need. Support is mainly given to older people who need a little financial help, for example, with fuel costs or hospital travel expenses.

Annual grant total

In 2016 the charity had an income of £4,000 and a total expenditure of £3,300. We estimate that grants given to individuals for welfare purposes totalled around £1,500.

Applications

Application forms are available from the correspondent and should be submitted directly by the individual before 31 March, in time for the trustees' yearly meeting held in April.

Other information

The charity also supports young individuals for educational and training needs. Organisations may also be assisted. Educational support for individuals is, however, the primary concern.

The Quorn Town Lands Charity

£3,900

Correspondent: Trish Jonczyk, Clerk to the Trustees, 14 Mansfield Avenue, Quorn, Loughborough LE12 8BD (01509 620701; email: quorn.townlands@gmail. com; website: quorndon.com/townlands/ index.php)

CC number: 216703

Eligibility

People in need who live in the parish of Quorn.

Types of grants

One-off grants and recurrent grants. Grants given have included those for hospital expenses, convalescence, living costs, household bills, food, travel expenses and help in the home.

Annual grant total

In 2016/17 the charity had an income of £9,500 and a total expenditure of £8,000. We estimate that the charity gave around £3,900 in grants to individuals.

The charity also gives grants to local organisations.

Applications

By completing the application form, which is available for both individuals and groups from the Quorn Village website. Applications should be submitted directly by the individual or through a relevant third party. They are considered quarterly.

Other information

This charity consists of three different funds – Quorn Town Lands Charity, Quorn Aid in Sickness Fund and Quorn Education Fund.

Richard Smedley's Charity

£1,000

Correspondent: Ian Warton-Woods, 9 Blacksmith Croft, Marehay, Ripley DE5 8JL (07805031549; email: ianwartonwoods@aol.com)

CC number: 221211

Eligibility

People in need who live in the parishes of Breaston, Dale Abbey, Draycott with Church Wilne, Heanor, Hopwell, Ilkerton, Ockbrook and Risley (all in Derbyshire) and of Awsworth, Bilborough, Brinsley, Greasley and Strelley (all in Nottinghamshire).

Types of grants

One-off grants generally in the range of £50 to £350 are given towards items such as furniture, washing machines, mobility aids, clothing and carpets.

Annual grant total

In 2016 the charity had an income of £5,800 and a total expenditure of £2,600. We estimate that the charity awarded £1,000 in grants during the year.

Applications

Application forms are available from the correspondent and should be submitted either directly by the individual or through a social worker, Citizens Advice or other welfare agency. Applications can be submitted at any time and are usually considered quarterly.

Other information

Grants are also made to organisations.

Derbyshire

Tiny Tim Trust
See entry on page 58

Amber Valley

Alfreton Welfare Trust

£800

Correspondent: Celia Johnson, 30 South Street, Swanwick, Alfreton DE55 1BZ (01773 609782)

CC number: 217114

Eligibility

People in need who live in the former urban district of Alfreton in Derbyshire, namely, the parishes of Alfreton, Ironville, Leabrooks, Somercotes and Swanwick.

Types of grants

One-off grants of up to £200. Grants have previously been given to help with: hospital travel expenses; the provision of necessary household items and installation costs; recuperative holidays; costs brought on by a sudden event, such as theft of a pension or purse, funeral costs, or marital difficulties; telephone installations; and outstanding bills. Support can also be given to people with disabilities (e.g. for wheelchairs).

Annual grant total

In 2015/16 the trust had an income of £2,300 and a total expenditure of £965. We estimate that grants given to individuals totalled £800.

Exclusions

Grants are not given to organisations or groups or for educational purposes.

Applications

Apply in writing to the correspondent. Applications can be made directly by the individual and are considered throughout the year.

Chesterfield

The Chesterfield General Charitable Fund

£5,000

Correspondent: Keith Pollard, 266 Old Road, Chesterfield, Derbyshire S40 3QN (01246 221872)

CC number: 511375

Eligibility

People in need who live in the parliamentary constituency of Chesterfield. There is some preference for applications from older people or people with a disability.

Types of grants

One-off and recurrent grants are given according to need. Grants can be used for medical aids, furniture, home adaptions, clothing, etc.

Annual grant total

In 2016/17 the fund had an income of £8,800 and a total expenditure of £17,500. We estimate that the fund awarded £5,000 in grants to individuals during the year.

Applications

Applications should be sent to the correspondent by post. Previous research indicates applications are considered quarterly.

Other information

The fund mainly makes awards to organisations in the area.

Arthur Townrow Pensions Fund

£115,500

Correspondent: P. King, Secretary, PO Box 48, Chesterfield, Derbyshire S40 1XT (01246 560560; email: p. king15@sky.com; website: www. townrowfund.org.uk)

CC number: 252256

Eligibility

Women in need who are unmarried or widows, are over 40 years of age and who live in the Chesterfield and North East Derbyshire areas. The fund specifies that the applicant should be 'of good character' and be a member of the Church of England or a Protestant dissenting church that acknowledges the doctrine of the Holy Trinity. Applicants should have an income of £8,000 or less.

Types of grants

Recurrent grants of £60 a month (£720 per annum). One-half of the pensions granted must be paid to unmarried women and widows living in Chesterfield, Bolsover and North East Derbyshire. The remaining grants may be paid anywhere in England but only to eligible unmarried women over the age of 40.

Annual grant total

In 2016/17 the fund held assets of £4.2 million and had an income of £149,500. Grants to individuals totalled £115,500.

Applications

Application forms are available from the correspondent. Applications should be submitted either directly by the individual or through a third party.

Other information

Arthur Townrow was a Chesterfield-based miller who left a bequest to be used to support widows and unmarried women on low incomes.

Derby
Aston Welfare Trust

£3,300

Correspondent: Christine Scott, 6 Lodge Estate, Aston-on-Trent, Derby DE72 2AH (01332 792683; email: christine.scotti@btinternet.com)

CC number: 219985

Eligibility

People in need living in Derby.

Types of grants

One-off grants to people in need for health and social activities.

Annual grant total

In 2015 the trust had an income of £10,000 and a total expenditure of £3,500. We estimate that the trust gave around £3,300 in grants to individuals.

Applications

Apply in writing to the correspondent.

The Liversage Trust

£83,500

Correspondent: Yvonne Taylor, General Manager, The Board Room, London Road, Derby DE1 2QW (01332 348199; fax: 01332 349674; email: info@ liversagetrust.org; website: www. liversagecourt.org/charitable-grant-giving)

CC number: 1155282

Eligibility

Grants are made to subsidise almshouse residents, subsidise Liversage Court residents, local people in need and organisations. Subsidies for almshouse residents include Christmas bonuses and winter fuel allowances.

Types of grants

Small grants for essential items; subsidies to almshouse residents including Christmas bonuses and fuel allowances; up to £100 grants for essential household items and clothing.

Annual grant total

In 2015/16 the trust had assets of £19.6 million and an income of £2.2 million. The trust made grants to individuals for welfare purposes totalling around £83,500 and awarded £3,000 to organisations.

Exclusions

Usually only one grant per applicant within a two-year period, although the trustees do have discretion in cases of crisis. The charity does not accept applications for unborn children.

Applications

Applications should be completed using the online application form available on the charity's website.

Other information

The charity incorporated and re-registered with the Charity Commission in January 2014.

The charity's main concern is the management of almshouses and the care home, Liversage Court. The charity has 160 almshouses, including historic buildings dating back to the 1800s.

Spondon Relief-in-Need Charity

£26,500

Correspondent: Stephen Williams, 15 Dob Holes Lane, Smalley, Ilkeston DE7 6EN (01332 544689; email: info@ spondonreliefinneedcharity.org; website: www.spondonreliefinneedcharity.org)

CC number: 211317

Eligibility

People who live in the ancient parish of Spondon within the city of Derby.

Types of grants

One-off grants for items such as beds, white goods (fridges, freezers, etc.), carpets, furniture and cookers. Gifts are also distributed at Christmas.

Annual grant total

In 2016 the charity had assets of £752,500 and an income of £27,500. The amount awarded to individuals for welfare needs was £26,500.

Exclusions

No grants are made for the relief of rates and taxes, or any expenses usually covered by statutory sources.

Applications

Official application forms are available upon request from the correspondent. All returned applications should be accompanied by a letter of support from a social or professional worker. The trustees meet to consider applications in February, May, September and November.

Other information

The charity also provides funding for individuals in education.

Derbyshire Dales

The Margaret Harrison Trust

£4,000

Correspondent: Alexandra Mastin, Trustee, 273 Chesterfield Road, Matlock, Derbyshire DE4 5LE

CC number: 234296

Eligibility

'Gentlewomen of good character' aged 50 or over who have lived within a 15-mile radius of St Giles Parish Church, Matlock for at least five years.

Types of grants

Small quarterly pensions.

Annual grant total

In 2016 the trust had an income of £4,900 and a total expenditure of £4,500. We have estimated that grants to individuals totalled £4,000.

Applications

Application forms are available from the correspondent.

Erewash

The Old Park Ward Old Age Pensioners Fund

£1,200

Correspondent: J. Dack, 3 Knole Road, Nottingham NG8 2DB (0115 913 2118)

CC number: 201037

Eligibility

People over 65 who are in need and live in the Old Park ward of the former borough of Ilkeston.

Types of grants

One-off cash grants, usually at Christmas time.

Annual grant total

In 2015/16 the fund had an income of £13,000 and total expenditure of £13,200. We estimate that welfare grants to individuals totalled around £1,200.

Applications

Apply in writing to the correspondent.

Other information

The majority of the fund's income is spent on providing recreational facilities and events such as dancing, bingo, a monthly Sunday lunch club and other outings.

The Sawley Charities

£500

Correspondent: Joy Thuram, Trustee, 59 Northfield Avenue, Long Eaton, Nottingham NG10 3FH (0115 973 3326)

CC number: 241273

Eligibility

Older people who are in need and have lived in Sawley for at least six years. Normally only people in receipt of a state pension are considered.

Types of grants

Usually, small, one-off cash grants are given towards heating costs.

Annual grant total

In 2016 the charity had an income of £2,900 and a total expenditure of £2,100. We estimate that welfare grants to individuals totalled around £500.

Applications

Application forms are available from the correspondent. Applications can be submitted directly by the individual or a family member and should be received by September for consideration in October/November.

Other information

Grants are also made to organisations and for educational purposes.

High Peak

Mary Ellen Allen

£2,000

Correspondent: Tony Lawton, 8 Spinney Close, Glossop SK13 7BR (01457 852434; email: tony@tlawton.co.uk)

CC number: 512661

Eligibility

People over 60 who are in need and live in the former borough of Glossop (as it was in 1947). There is a preference for those who have lived in the area for at least five years in total.

Annual grant total

In 2015/16 the charity had an income of £5,200 and a total expenditure of £5,200. We have estimated that grants to individuals for welfare purposes totalled £2,000 during the year.

Applications

Apply in writing to the correspondent through a social worker, Citizens Advice or other welfare agency where applicable, or directly by the individual.

The Bingham Trust

£10,300

Correspondent: Ms E. Marshall, Secretary, Unit 1, Tongue Lane Industrial Estate, Dew Pond Lane, Buxton SK17 7LN (07966 378 546; email: binghamtrust@aol.com; website: www.binghamtrust.org.uk)

CC number: 287636

Eligibility

People in need who live in and around Buxton, Derbyshire (the SK17 postcode area).

Types of grants

One-off grants ranging from £200 to £1,500. Grants are made to individuals for a wide variety of needs, including further education. Grants made to individuals are usually by cheque made out to the provider of the service or goods.

Annual grant total

In 2015/15 the trust had assets of £4.3 million and an income of £193,500. Grants totalled £160,500, of which £20,500 was awarded to individuals. We estimate that grants given to individuals for social welfare purposes totalled around £10,300.

Exclusions

The trustees cannot consider applications from individuals outside the SK17 postcode area. Grants are not made to repay existing debts or for higher educational purposes (university and college level). No more than one application can be made in any 12-month period.

Applications

Applications can be made using the form available from the website, but will also be considered if sent by letter (the website does note, however, that applications sent by letter can take longer to deal with as the trustees may need to request more information). Applications from individuals must always be supported by an agency familiar with the applicant's circumstances, such as social services or a charity or community organisation. Individuals can apply directly but those not applying through an organisation must send a supporting letter with their application.

Applications can be sent by post at the address above, or as an email attachment (with no additional attachments). All applications are acknowledged by post or email. They are usually considered in January, April, July and October/November each year; the date of the next meeting and the closing date for applications are noted on the website. In cases of more complicated applications, the trustees may find it beneficial to arrange a visit if they feel it would help.

Other information

The trust was established through the will of the late Robert Henry Bingham who lived in the Buxton area. Today it supports a broad range of charitable causes that benefit people in the area.

John Mackie Memorial Ladies' Home

£3,500

Correspondent: David Wellens, Trustee, Axholme, Woodbourne Road, New Mills, High Peak, Derbyshire SK22 3JX (01663 742246; email: dhw111@hotmail.com)

CC number: 215726

Eligibility

Widows, unmarried women and divorcees, who are members of the Church of England, are over 50 and are in need. Applicants must have a connection with the parish of New Mills.

Types of grants

Christmas gifts and grants.

Annual grant total

In 2016 the charity had an income of £3,100 and a total expenditure of £3,700. We estimate that grants given to individuals totalled around £3,500.

Applications

Apply in writing to the correspondent.

Other information

At the time of writing (August 2017) the charity had no website or accounts available.

North East Derbyshire

The Eliza Ann Cresswell Memorial

£3,000

Correspondent: Anne Crowther, Trustee, Brierley Farm, Mill Lane, Brockhurst, Ashover, Chesterfield S45 0HS (email: elizacresswelltrust@gmail.com)

CC number: 230282

Eligibility

People in any kind of need who live in the former urban district of Clay Cross (now the civil parish of Clay Cross), particularly families with young children.

Types of grants

Usually one-off grants in whole or part payment of a particular need, for example heating costs, housing, debts, replacement of bedding and damaged furniture, removal costs and holidays.

Annual grant total

In 2016 the charity had an income of £2,400 and a total expenditure of £6,100. We estimate that social welfare grants to individuals totalled £3,000, with funding also awarded to organisations.

Exclusions

The charity does not give cash directly to applicants nor does it usually pay the full amount of a debt unless any repayment is beyond the individual's means.

Applications

Apply in writing to the correspondent. A description of the person's financial position, the gaps in statutory provision, what contribution the applicant can make towards the need and what help can be given to prevent the need for future applications should be included. Applications are considered throughout the year. Grants are given on the recommendation of social workers, health visitors, probation officers, home nurses, doctors, clergy and welfare organisations (e.g. Citizens Advice), and are paid through these bodies.

Dronfield Relief in Need Charity

£900

Correspondent: Dr Anthony Bethell, Trustee, Ramshaw Lodge, Crow Lane, Unstone, Dronfield, Derbyshire S18 4AL (01246 413276)

CC number: 219888

Eligibility

People in need who live in the ecclesiastical parishes of Dronfield, Holmesfield, Unstone and West Handley.

Types of grants

One-off grants, up to a value of £100, towards household needs (such as washing machines), food, clothing, medical appliances (such as a nebuliser) and visitors' fares to and from hospital.

Annual grant total

In 2016 the charity had an income of £3,500 and a total expenditure of £4,000. We have estimated that £900 was given to individuals for social welfare purposes.

Applications

Applications may be made in writing to the correspondent through a social worker, doctor, member of the clergy of

any denomination, a local councillor, Citizens Advice or other welfare agency. The applicants should ensure they are receiving all practical/financial assistance they are entitled to from statutory sources.

Other information

Grants are also given to local organisations and for educational purposes.

Leicester-shire

The Leicester Charity Link

£814,500 (4,425 grants)

Correspondent: James Munton, Director of Operations, 20a Millstone Lane, Leicester, Leicestershire LE1 5JN (0116 222 2200; fax: 0116 222 2201; email: info@charity-link.org; website: www.charity-link.org)

CC number: 1078271

Eligibility

People in need who live in Leicestershire, Rutland, and Northamptonshire. Beneficiaries have included those on a low income or experiencing hardship, vulnerable families, people who are homeless and older people.

Types of grants

One-off grants and occasionally recurrent grants or pensions. The charity makes payments from its own funds, administers funds on behalf of other charities and puts potential beneficiaries into contact with funds and charities which may be able to help.

Grants are available for a wide range of needs, although the charity most commonly funds essential, everyday items such as beds, cookers and, in emergencies, food. Recent grants for larger items have included stairlifts and specialist wheelchairs.

Annual grant total

In 2015/16 the charity held assets of £636,500 and had an income of £1.3 million. A total of 4,425 grants were awarded to individuals, amounting to £814,500.

The charity also distributed 416 awards totalling £343,500 on behalf of individuals and institutions.

Exclusions

It is expected that all statutory funding sources are explored before applying.

Applications

Individuals are referred through other organisations, such as charities and health, social or educational agencies, using an application form available on the website. The charity's website notes:

> We use a network of local organisations that are in the community working with individuals and families in need. Using organisations already in place keeps our overheads to a minimum, increases the efficiency of our services and ensures that we get the help to those who need it when they need it most.

While the charity aims to provide support within 20 days, urgent help on the same day can also be given if the charity is contacted by telephone.

Other information

The charity also makes small grants to organisations (seven grants totalling £2,900 in 2015/16).

The charity supports a food bank in conjunction with Leicester City Council, St Martin's House, Tomorrow Together and FareShare. Those working with vulnerable individuals or families wishing to access the food bank should telephone (0116 222 2200) or download an application form from the website.

The Nicholson Memorial Fund (The Rosehill Trust)

£4,500

Correspondent: The Clerk to the Trustees, The Nicholson Memorial Fund (Rosehill Trust), 20a Millstone Lane, Leicester LE1 5JN (0116 222 2200; fax: 0116 222 2201; email: info@charity-link.org; website: www.charity-link.org/trust-administration/trusts-we-support/the-nicholson-memorial-fund)

CC number: 1000860

Eligibility

Young people and children 'who are delinquent, deprived, neglected or in need of care' in Leicestershire or Rutland.

Types of grants

One-off grants according to need.

Annual grant total

In 2016/17 the charity had an income of £12,400 and a total expenditure of £9,100. We estimate that the charity gave around £4,500 in grants to individuals.

Exclusions

One grant per two-year period, except in exceptional circumstances.

Applications

Apply on a form available from Leicester Charity Link website.

Other information

Leicester Charity Link, the administrator of this fund, provides a wide range of support and advice to people in need.

The charity also gives grants to organisations assisting children and young people.

Thomas Stanley Shipman Charitable Trust

£32,500

Correspondent: Andrew York, Secretary to the Trustees, 6 Magnolia Close, Leicester LE2 8PS (0116 283 5345; email: andrew_york@sky.com)

CC number: 200789

Eligibility

People in need who live in the city and county of Leicester.

Types of grants

One-off and recurrent grants for living expenses and gifts at Christmas.

Annual grant total

In 2015/16 the trust held assets of £1.37 million and had an income of £62,000. Financial assistance for individuals was distributed as follows:

Grants administered by Leicester Charity Link	£15,000
Christmas gifts	£9,500
Grants and assistance to older people	£8,000

A further £7,100 was awarded to local organisations.

Exclusions

The trust does not usually provide educational grants due to a lack of resources, and in light of its other objectives.

Applications

Apply in writing to the correspondent either directly by the individual or, where applicable, via a relevant third party such as a social worker, Citizens Advice or other welfare agency, or through Leicester Charity Link. The trustees meet twice-yearly, normally in November and June. Applications should be submitted in mid-October and mid-April for consideration.

Charnwood

Babington's Charity

£4,500

Correspondent: Helen McCague, Trustee, 14 Main Street, Cossington, Leicester, Leicestershire LE7 4UU (01509 812271)

CC number: 220069

Eligibility

People in need in the parish of Cossington, Leicestershire.

Types of grants

One-off and recurrent grants are given according to need. Support includes assistance to people with disabilities and older people towards adequate heating expenses, household equipment and travel costs to hospital; help is offered to families suffering from hardship and other parishioners who are in need.

Annual grant total

In 2015 the charity had an income of £47,200 and a total expenditure of £49,800, of which £9,000 was awarded to individuals and students for both educational and social welfare needs. We estimate that about £4,500 was given for social welfare purposes.

Applications

Applications may be made in writing to the correspondent. The trustees meet at least twice a year.

Other information

The charity gives to individuals and organisations for both education and social welfare purposes.

The Loughborough Welfare Trusts

£10,900

Correspondent: Lesley Cutler, Bird Wilford & Sale, Solicitors, 20 Churchgate, Loughborough LE11 1UD (07765 934117; email: loughweltrsts@fsmail.net)

CC number: 214654

Eligibility

People in need who live in Loughborough and Hathern.

Types of grants

One-off and recurrent grants are given to people on low incomes for decoration costs, holidays and cookers, etc. Grants are also made towards clothing for primary schoolchildren under the age of 11.

Annual grant total

In 2016 the trust had an income of £31,000 and a total expenditure of £31,000. Welfare grants to individuals totalled £10,900, of which £6,400 was distributed for relief-in-need purposes and £4,500 for relief in sickness.

Applications

Apply in writing to the correspondent for consideration in January, March, May, July, September or November.

Other information

The trust administers Edgar Corah Charity, John Storer Education Foundation, The Reg Burton Fund, Loughborough Adult Schools, Herrick Charities, and The Loughborough Community Chest.

Mountsorrel Relief in Need Charity

£137,000

Correspondent: Rachel White, Benefit Secretary, c/o KDB Accountants and Consultants Ltd, 21 Hollytree Close, Hoton, Loughborough LE12 5SE (07931 129360; email: mountsorrelunitedcharities@outlook.com; website: www.mountsorrelunitedcharities.com)

CC number: 217615

Eligibility

People in need who live in the parish of Mountsorrel (for at least six months).

Types of grants

One-off grants towards essential needs. Grants towards Charnwood Lifeline, an emergency response service, are available.

The charity's website states: 'We offer help in a variety of ways with electrical household products, garden maintenance, decorating, carpeting, mobility equipment (that is not supplied by Social Services), i.e. mobility scooters, hospital travel expenses and many of other areas of need.'

The charity also runs foot care services and provides one-off or ongoing grants for gardening needs (offered April to November).

Annual grant total

In 2016 the charity had assets of £13.8 million and an income of £144,500. During the year, the charity gave around £137,000 in grants to individuals.

Applications

To apply, contact the correspondent who will visit you in your home and help you to complete the application form. You will need to provide some financial details, which will be kept strictly confidential.

Other information

This is one of the two funds administered under the Mountsorrel United Charities (Charity Commission no. 1027652) name.

The H. A. Taylor Fund

£19,900

Correspondent: Alexander Munton, Clerk to the Trustees, Leicester Charity Link, 20a Millstone Lane, Leicester LE1 5JN (0116 222 2200; email: info@charity-link.org; website: www.charity-link.org)

CC number: 516428

Eligibility

People in need who have been in resident in the parish of Syston for at least one year.

Types of grants

One-off grants, usually ranging from £50 to £1,000, towards a range of purposes, such as travel costs, furniture, clothing, fuel, household repairs, medical treatment, books and course fees, mobility aids and telephone and television expenses.

Annual grant total

In 2015/16 the fund had an income of £28,000 and a total expenditure of £36,300. The fund awarded a total of £19,900 to 28 individuals for welfare purposes and around £6,400 to organisations.

Exclusions

Applicants should not reapply within two years of receiving a grant, except in exceptional circumstances.

Applications

Application forms are available from Syston and District Volunteer Centre, Syston Health Centre and Syston Library or can be downloaded from the website. They can be submitted at any time, either through a third party or directly by the individual and are considered every two months.

Wymeswold Parochial Charities

£1,700

Correspondent: Jo Collington, Correspondent, 94 Brook Street, Wymeswold, Loughborough, Leicestershire LE12 6TU (01509 880538; email: jocollington@sky.com)

CC number: 213241

Eligibility

People in need who have lived in Wymeswold for two years prior to application.

Types of grants

One-off grants are given for educational and relief-in-need purposes. Winter gifts are given to pensioners, widows and widowers. One-off awards are also given to people who are ill.

Annual grant total

In 2015/16 the charity had an income of £5,100 and a total expenditure of £3,800. We estimate that about £1,700 was given to individuals for welfare purposes.

Applications

Applications may be made in writing to the correspondent at any time.

Other information

Educational needs are also assisted.

Harborough

United Charities Bitteswell

£5,000

Correspondent: John Booth, Trustee, The Brambles, Ashby Lane, Bitteswell, Lutterworth LE17 4SQ (07836 231377; email: johnpatbooth1@gmail.com)

CC number: 218278

Eligibility

People in need who live in Bitteswell, Leicestershire.

Types of grants

One-off grants according to need.

Annual grant total

In 2016 the charity had an income of £13,000 and a total expenditure of £10,900. We estimate that grants given to individuals totalled around £5,000, with funding also awarded to organisations.

Applications

Apply in writing to the correspondent.

Other information

Grants are made to both individuals and organisations for charitable purposes benefitting people living in the parish.

Valentine Goodman (Estate Charity)

£7,300

Correspondent: John Stones, Trustee, Blaston Lodge, Blaston Road, Blaston, Market Harborough LE16 8DB (01858 555688)

CC number: 252108

Eligibility

People in need who live in the parishes of Blaston, Bringhurst, Drayton, East Magna, Hallaton and Medbourne.

Types of grants

One-off or recurrent grants according to need.

Annual grant total

In 2016 the charity had an income of £16,600 and a total expenditure of £7,700. We estimate that grants given to individuals totalled £7,300.

Applications

Apply in writing to the correspondent.

Great Glen Relief in Need Charity

£2,100

Correspondent: Yannette Rea, Trustee, Old Vicarage, Church Road, Great Glen, Leicester LE8 9FE (0116 259 2946)

CC number: 231977

Eligibility

People in need (especially older people) who live in the parish of Great Glen and have been living there for a number of years.

Types of grants

One-off grants according to need. Older people receive grants in the form of vouchers at Christmas.

Annual grant total

In 2016 the charity had an income of £2,100 and a total expenditure of £2,300. We estimate that grants given to individuals totalled £2,100.

Applications

Apply in writing to the correspondent. Applications are considered twice a year, usually in November and April.

Illston Town Land Charity

£7,000

Correspondent: John Tillotson, 5 Barnards Way, Kibworth Harcourt, Leicester LE8 0RS (0116 279 2524)

CC number: 246616

Eligibility

People in need who live in the town of Illston in Leicestershire.

Types of grants

Grants towards the costs of council tax charges.

Annual grant total

In 2015/16 the charity had an income of £6,400 and a total expenditure of £7,800. We estimate that welfare grants to individuals totalled £7,000.

Applications

Apply in writing to the correspondent.

Keyham Relief in Need Charity

£15,000

Correspondent: David Witcomb, Trustee, Tanglewood, Snows Lane, Keyham, Leicester LE7 9JS (0116 259 5663)

CC number: 215753

Eligibility

People who live in the parish of Keyham (Leicestershire) and are in need. Applications from people who do not live in the area but have strong connections to residents in Keyham have previously also been considered.

Types of grants

One-off grants according to need.

Annual grant total

In 2016 the charity had an income of £22,000 and a total expenditure of £25,000. We estimate that grants given to individuals totalled £15,000.

Applications

Applications should be made in writing to the correspondent and submitted directly by the individual. If the applicant does not live in Keyham, information about their connection with residents should be provided with the application.

Other information

The charity's primary source of funding is rental income from the four cottages it owns.

Hinckley and Bosworth

Poor's Platt

£9,000

Correspondent: Jim Munton, Clerk to the Trustees, 20A Millstone Lane, Leicester LE1 5JN (0116 222 2200; email: info@charity-link.org; website: www. charity-link.org/trust-administration/ trusts-we-support/the-poors-platt)

CC number: 503580

Eligibility

People in need in the ancient parish of Barwell, Leicestershire.

Types of grants

One-off grants are given according to need.

Annual grant total

In 2016 the charity had an income of £23,500 and a total expenditure of £18,200. We estimate that grants given to individuals totalled around £9,000.

Applications

Applications can be made through the Leicester Charity Link using its application form or in writing to the correspondent.

Other information

Grants are also available for various organisations, projects and schools in the area of benefit.

Thomas Herbert Smith's Trust Fund

£5,000

Correspondent: Andrew York, 6 Magnolia Close, Leicester LE2 8PS (0116 283 5345; email: andrew_york@ sky.com)

CC number: 701694

Eligibility

People who live in the parish of Groby in Leicestershire.

Types of grants

One-off and recurrent grants, usually ranging from £100 to £500.

Annual grant total

In 2015/16 the fund had an income of £19,500 and a total expenditure of £11,200. Grants are made to individuals and organisations for both social welfare and educational purposes. We estimate that grants given to individuals for welfare purposes totalled £5,000.

Applications

Applications can be made using a form available from the correspondent. They can be submitted either directly by the individual, or through a social worker, Citizens Advice or other third party, and are considered throughout the year.

Leicester

The Leicester Aid-in-Sickness Fund

£11,000

Correspondent: Mark Dunkley, Correspondent, Shakespeares, Two Colton Square, Leicester LE1 1QH (0116 254 5454; email: mark.dunkley@ shakespeares.co.uk)

CC number: 219785

Eligibility

People living in the city of Leicester, who are in poor health and financial need.

Types of grants

One-off grants.

Annual grant total

In 2015/16 the fund had an income of £14,000 and a total expenditure of

£13,800. We estimate that grants given to individuals for welfare purposes totalled around £11,000.

Applications

Apply in writing to the correspondent. Applications are usually considered quarterly.

Other information

There were no accounts or website available for this charity.

Leicester and County Convalescent Homes Society (Leicester ARC)

£3,000

Correspondent: Lenore Headey, Charity Manager, 22 St Georges Way, Leicester LE1 1SH (0116 262 0617; email: enquiries@arcleicester.org; website: www. arcleicester.org)

CC number: 1016951

Eligibility

People in need who are ill, who have a disability or are receiving medical care and live in Leicester, Leicestershire and Rutland, and their dependants.

Applicants must be on a very low income or in receipt of one or more of the following statutory benefits:
- Employment Support/Allowance
- Income Support/Carers Allowance
- Jobseeker's Allowance (income based)
- Disability Living Allowance/ Attendance Allowance
- Pension Tax Credit
- Working Tax Credit
- Personal Budget

Types of grants

The charity considers requests for financial assistance towards rehabilitation e.g. recovery periods, respite, therapies and for medical equipment.

Annual grant total

In 2016 the charity held assets of £2.3 million and had an income of £51,500. During the year, the charity gave almost £3,000 in grants to individuals for welfare purposes.

Applications

Applications must be made in writing and marked for the attention of the Grants Committee. The charity's website further states that 'applications must be related to a genuine medical need and ultimately could require certified support from your GP/therapist.'

Other information

The charity also offers complementary therapies at concessionary rates to individuals who are in receipt of one of the benefits described (see eligibility).

During the year, convalescence was taken by seven patients in Dawlish and three patients had a respite break at a place of their choice. A total of 21 therapy treatments were taken by three clients.

The Leicester Indigent Old Age Society

£3,000

Correspondent: Katie Scranage, Trust Administrator, 20a Millstone Lane, Leicester LE1 5JN (0116 222 2200; fax: 0116 222 2201; email: info@charity-link. org; website: charity-link.org/trust-administration)

CC number: 208476

Eligibility

People aged 65 or over who are in need and live in the city of Leicester.

Types of grants

Pensions in payments of £10 per month to approximately 90 recipients. Grants are also made for coach trips and outings for older people living in Leicester.

Annual grant total

In 2016/17 the society had an income of £5,300 and a total expenditure of £6,500. We estimate that welfare grants to individuals totalled around £3,000, with funding also awarded to organisations in Leicester that assist older people who are in need.

Applications

Applications should be made through Leicester Charity Link using an application form which can be found on its website.

Alex Neale Charity

£1,300

Correspondent: Maurice Kirk, Administrator, 6 Ervin Way, Queniborough, Leicester LE7 3TT (0116 260 6851; email: mrakirk@btinternet. com)

CC number: 260247

Eligibility

Older people in need who live in the parish of Queniborough.

Types of grants

Grants towards gas and electricity bills.

Annual grant total

In 2015 the charity had an income of £3,200 and a total expenditure of £1,500. We estimate that grants given to individuals for social welfare purposes totalled around £1,300.

Applications

Our previous research indicates that the trustees publicise the grants, usually every two years, in The Queniborough Gazette. An application form is then available from the correspondent. The trustees may ask for copies of fuel bills for the two years prior to application, and then a grant would be made towards the costs of these bills.

Other information

At the time of writing (August 2017) the charity had no website or accounts available.

The Parish Piece Charity

£4,400

Correspondent: Revd Canon Barry Naylor, Trustee, St Martins House, 7 Peacock Lane, Leicester LE1 5PZ (email: magwill26@ntlworld.com)

CC number: 215775

Eligibility

People in need who live in the parish of St Margaret in Leicester. Priority is usually given to older people and people with disabilities.

Types of grants

One-off grants and small pensions. Grants have been given for heating costs and electrical appliances.

Annual grant total

In 2015/16 the charity had an income of £10,200 and a total expenditure of £8,900. We estimate that the charity gave around £4,400 in grants to individuals, with funding also going to local organisations.

Applications

Apply in writing to the correspondent or via Leicester Charity Link using its standard application form.

St Margaret's Charity

£2,000

Correspondent: Katie Scranage, Charity Link, 20A Millstone Lane, Leicester LE1 5JN (0116 222 2200; email: info@ charity-link.org; website: charity-link.org/trust-administration/trusts-we-administer/st-margarets-charities)

CC number: 234626

Eligibility

People in need who live in the city of Leicester.

Types of grants

One-off grants with a maximum value of £250.

Annual grant total

In 2015/16 the charity had an income of £4,100 and a total expenditure of £4,400. We estimate that the charity awarded £2,000 in grants for hardship relief.

Applications

Applications must be made through a welfare organisation such as Leicester Charity Link.

The Edward Wood Bequest Fund

£35,000

Correspondent: James Norris, Trustee, 63 Carisbrooke Road, Leicester LE2 3PF (0116 270 4223; email: andrew.norris@ brewin.co.uk)

CC number: 220606

Eligibility

Women who are 55 years old or over, are either unmarried or widows, who have lived in the area administered by Leicester City Council for at least ten years, and who are members of a Protestant non-conformist church.

Types of grants

Pensions of £400 a year only, paid quarterly.

Annual grant total

In 2015/16 the fund had an income of just £750, which was unusually low, and a total expenditure of £42,000, which was unusually high. As we have no access to the charity's accounts or annual report and there is no website, we consider that most of the outgoings have been spent on the objects of the charity and have estimated a total grant figure of £35,000. We would suggest that this figure is unlikely to be maintained.

Applications

Apply in writing on a form available from the correspondent either directly by the individual or through a third party. A reference from a church minister is also needed. There are only a limited number of pensions available and applications can only be considered when a vacancy arises.

Melton

Melton Mowbray Building Society Charitable Foundation

£3,000

Correspondent: Martin Reason, Trustee, Melton Mowbray Building Society, Leicester Road, Melton Mowbray LE13 0D3 (01664 414141; fax: 01664

414040; email: m.reason@mmbs.co.uk; website: www.mmbs.co.uk)

CC number: 1067348

Eligibility

Individuals in need who live within a 30-mile radius of Melton Mowbray – particularly young people, vulnerable adults, older people, people with disabilities and people with mental illnesses.

Types of grants

One-off grants in the range of £100 and £250, to provide, for example: opportunities for children from disadvantaged backgrounds; means of preparing young people for adult life; and help for those who have disabilities.

Annual grant total

In 2016/17 the foundation had an income of £102,000 and a total expenditure of £12,000. We estimate that the foundation awarded around £3,000 in grants to individuals for welfare purposes.

Exclusions

Grants are not made for expeditions or overseas travel.

Applications

Apply in writing to the correspondent. Applications should be submitted either directly by the individual or a family member, through a third party such as a social worker or teacher, or, where applicable, through an organisation such as Citizens Advice or a school. Applications should include details of the cash value sought, the nature of the expense, the reason for application and the location of the applicant. Applications are considered at meetings held on a quarterly basis.

North West Leicestershire

Ashby-de-la-Zouch Relief in Sickness Fund

£1,200

Correspondent: Leanne Cooper, Trust & Probate Executive, Crane & Walton, 30 South Street, Ashby-de-la-Zouch LE65 1BT (01530 414111; email: leannecooper@craneandwalton.co.uk)

CC number: 508621

Eligibility

People living in Ashby-de-la-Zouch who are sick, convalescent, have a disability or are caring for ill people and require financial assistance.

Types of grants

One-off grants are given for a range of needs. Examples include hospital expenses, electrical goods, convalescence, clothing, holidays, travel expenses, medical equipment, furniture, equipment to help with disabilities and help at home.

Annual grant total

In 2016/17 the fund had an income of £965 and a total expenditure of £1,500. We estimate that grants given to individuals totalled around £1,200.

Applications

Apply in writing to the correspondent. Applications can be made at any time either directly by the individual or through a social worker, Citizens Advice or other welfare agency. Anybody who thinks they know someone who needs help is welcome to submit an application on their behalf. Candidates are asked to specify whether any other source of help has been approached.

Northamp-tonshire

The New Appeals Organisation for the City and County of Nottingham

£22,000

Correspondent: Phil Everett, Joint Chair, 4 Rise Court, Hamilton Road, Nottingham NG5 1EU (0115 960 9644 (answering service); email: enquiries@ newappeals.org.uk; website: www. newappeals.org)

CC number: 502196

Eligibility

People in need who live in the city and county of Nottingham.

Types of grants

One-off grants ranging from £50 to £2,000 to meet needs which cannot be met from any other source. For example, wheelchairs, white goods, flooring, beds and bedding, rise/recliner chairs, adapted vehicles, holidays, sensory stimulation equipment, computers and other electrical goods. Christmas gifts are also given to older people and homeless people. Much of the money is raised for specific projects.

Annual grant total

In 2016/17 the charity had an income of £35,800 and a total expenditure of £46,000. We estimate that the charity gave around £22,000 in grants to individuals.

Exclusions

The charity does not usually help with debt arrears, building works, wages, educational costs, foreign travel for students or requests from outside Nottingham.

Applications

Applicants can apply on a form through the website, or download the form from the website and submit by email. Full guidelines are available on the charity's website.

The Nottingham Annuity Charity

£12,300 (24 grants)

Correspondent: David Simmons, Correspondent, c/o Intermediate Housing Team, Nottingham Community Housing Association Ltd, 12–14 Pelham Road, Sherwood Rise, Nottingham NG5 1AP (0115 844 3404; email: david.simmons@ncha.org.uk; website: www.ncha.org.uk)

CC number: 510023

Eligibility

People in need who live in Nottinghamshire, with a preference for widows and unmarried women.

Types of grants

Regular yearly allowances of around £200 are paid in quarterly grants, as well as Christmas gifts.

Annual grant total

In 2016/17 the charity held assets of £440,000 and had an income of £69,500. During the year, the charity awarded around £12,300 in grants to individuals.

Applications

Applications should be made on a form available from the correspondent to be submitted either directly by the individual or through an appropriate third party such as a social worker, Citizens Advice or other welfare agency. Applications are usually considered quarterly.

Daventry
The Chauntry Estate

£2,500

Correspondent: Rita Tank, Walnut Tree Cottage, Main Street, Great Brington, Northampton NN7 4JA (01604 770809; email: ritatank40@yahoo.com)

CC number: 200795

Eligibility

Older people in need who live in the parish of Brington.

Types of grants

One-off grants to relieve sudden need or illness, for example, towards travel expenses for visits to hospital, food, fuel and heating appliances, and aids not provided by health authorities.

Annual grant total

In 2015/16 the charity had an income of £11,200 and a total expenditure of £10,000. We estimate that welfare grants to individuals totalled £2,500.

Applications

Apply in writing to the correspondent.

The Daventry Consolidated Charity

£8,000

Correspondent: Maggie Dowie, PO Box 7692, Daventry, Northamptonshire NN11 1DW (email: daventryconsolidatedcharity@gmail.com)

CC number: 200657

Eligibility

People in need who live in the borough of Daventry.

Types of grants

One-off grants to assist with specific costs.

Annual grant total

In 2016 the charity had an income of £10,000 and a total expenditure of £17,000. We estimate that the charity awarded £8,000 in grants to individuals during the year.

Exclusions

There are no grants available towards debts or ongoing expenses.

Applications

Applications should be made in writing to the correspondent. Include the reasons for requesting the grant and approximate costs.

Other information

The charity also makes grants to organisations.

The United Charities of East Farndon

£3,500

Correspondent: Nigel Haynes, Newhouse Farm, Harborough Road, East Farndon, Market Harborough LE16 9SG (email: haynestripley@msn.com)

CC number: 200778

Eligibility

Families in need who live in East Farndon.

Types of grants

One-off cash grants of up to £50 are provided for travel expenses to hospital, fuel grants towards electricity, disability equipment, living costs and household bills.

Annual grant total

In 2016 the charity had an income of £6,800 and a total expenditure of £7,700. We estimate that grants given to individuals totalled around £3,500.

Applications

Applications can be made in writing to the correspondent directly by the individual or a family member, for consideration as they are received.

Yelvertoft and District Relief-in-Sickness Fund

£4,700

Correspondent: Richard Atterbury, Trustee, Crick Lodge, Crick, Northampton NN6 7SN (01788 822247)

CC number: 285771

Eligibility

People in need who live in the parishes of Yelvertoft, West Haddon, Crick, Winwick, Clay Coton and Elkington, who are sick, convalescent, or who have disabilities.

Types of grants

Small, one-off grants are given for items which assist recovery and alleviate suffering (wheelchairs, walkers, etc.)

Annual grant total

In 2016 the fund had an income of £8,200 and a total expenditure of £4,900. We estimate that grants given to individuals totalled £4,700.

Applications

Apply in writing to the correspondent. Applications should be submitted directly by the individual, a relative or district nurse, and can be considered at any time.

Kettering

Church and Town Allotment Charities and Others

£4,500

Correspondent: Anne Ireson, Kettering Borough Council, Council Offices, Bowling Green Road, Kettering NN15 7QX (01536 534398; email: anneireson@kettering.gov.uk)

CC number: 207698

Eligibility

Widows, widowers and single people over the age of 60 who live alone in Kettering or Barton Seagrave and are in receipt of retirement pension.

Types of grants

Grants of £25 towards winter fuel bills.

Annual grant total

In 2015/16 the charity had an income of £15,000 and a total expenditure of £10,000. We estimate that welfare grants to individuals totalled £4,500 with funding also awarded to individuals for educational purposes.

Applications

The charity places advertisements in local newspapers in November each year, after which an application form can be requested from the correspondent. Applications are considered in November. Applicants must include details of income, status, age and address.

Other information

Educational grants are available for people over the age of 16 who live in Kettering and Barton Seagrave.

The Desborough Town Welfare Committee

£4,000

Correspondent: Jonathan Gardiner, 36 Leys Avenue, Desborough, Kettering NN14 2PY (01536 764571; email: jonathan.gardiner36@gmail.com)

CC number: 235505

Eligibility

People who are older, sick or in need and living in Desborough.

Types of grants

One-off and recurrent grants, according to need.

Annual grant total

In 2015/16 the charity had an income of £5,600 and a total expenditure of £8,500.

We estimate that the amount awarded in grants to individuals totalled £4,000.

Applications

Apply in writing to the correspondent, for consideration within two to three months.

Other information

The charity also makes awards to local organisations.

Stockburn Memorial Trust Fund

£11,000

Correspondent: Andy Sipple, 62 Pipers Hill Road, Kettering, Northamptonshire NN15 7NH (01536 412511; email: andy.sipple@btinternet.com)

CC number: 205120

Eligibility

People in need who live in the borough of Kettering.

Types of grants

One-off grants according to need.

Annual grant total

In 2016 the fund had an income of £8,800 and a total expenditure of £12,000. We estimate that the charity awarded £11,000 to individuals during the year.

Applications

Apply in writing to the correspondent through a social worker, Citizens Advice or other welfare agency. Applicants should include details of age, address, telephone number, financial situation and health circumstances.

Northampton

The Betty and Charles Stilwell Fund

£1,400

Correspondent: Marina Eaton, Clerk to the trustees, 4 Grange Park Court, Roman Way, Northampton NN4 5EA (01604 876697; email: meaton@wilsonbrowne.co.uk)

CC number: 1047576

Eligibility

People living in the borough of Northampton who suffer from diseases of the heart.

Types of grants

One-off grants to alleviate hardship associated with heart disease, for example to purchase specialist medical equipment or aids.

Annual grant total

In 2016/17 the fund had an income of £4,200 and a total expenditure of £2,900. We estimate that grants given to individuals totalled around £1,400, with funding also awarded to organisations.

Applications

Apply in writing to the correspondent.

Other information

Grants may also be made to organisations.

The John and Mildred Law Fund

£15,400 (43 grants)

Correspondent: Jane Forsyth, Clerk to the trustees, Wilson Browne, 4 Grange Park Court, Roman Way, Grange Park, Northampton NN4 5EA (01604 876697; email: jforsyth@qswblaw.com)

CC number: 1121230

Eligibility

People in need who live in the borough of Northampton.

Types of grants

One-off grants of up to £1,000 according to need.

Annual grant total

In 2015/16 the fund had an income of £40,000 and a total expenditure of £45,500. During the year, the fund awarded a total of £42,500 in grants. Of the amount given in grants, £15,400 was awarded to 43 individuals for welfare purposes and £27,000 was awarded to organisations.

Applications

Apply in writing to the correspondent. The trustees meet twice a year to consider applications in May and November.

The Henry and Elizabeth Lineham Charity

£31,500 (64 grants)

Correspondent: Angela Moon, Clerk to the Trustees, Hewitson's LLP, Elgin House, Billing Road, Northampton NN1 5AU (01604 233233; email: mail@hewitsons.com)

CC number: 205975

Eligibility

Women in need who are at least 55 and live in the borough of Northampton.

Types of grants

Annuities, currently £512 per annum, are paid half-yearly in June and December.

Annual grant total

In 2016 the charity held assets of £1.4 million and had an income of £52,000. During the year, a total of £31,500 was given in grants to 64 women for welfare purposes.

Applications

Apply in writing to the correspondent. Beneficiaries are usually nominated by one of the trustees, mostly councillors or ex-councillors.

The Northampton Municipal Church Charities

£26,000

Correspondent: Jane Forsyth, Wilson Browne Solicitors, 4 Grange Park Court, Roman Way, Grange Park, Northampton NN4 5EA (01604 876697; email: jforsyth@wilsonbrowne.co.uk)

CC number: 259593

Eligibility

People in need who live in the borough of Northampton.

Types of grants

People aged over 55 are eligible for quarterly payments and a Christmas voucher. People of any age can receive one-off grants.

Annual grant total

In 2016/17 the charity had assets of £4.2 million and had an income of £241,500. During the year, the charity gave around £26,000 in grants to individuals. Of this amount, £1,150 was given in Christmas gifts.

Exclusions

The charity is unable to assist with debt.

Applications

Apply on a form available from the correspondent, including details of age, residence, income, assets and expenditure. Applications can be submitted either directly by the individual or through a third party such as a social worker, Citizens Advice or other welfare agency. They are considered on a regular basis.

Other information

The charity runs a sheltered housing scheme at St Thomas House in St Giles Street, Northampton. It is warden controlled and has 17 small flats for people over 55. The charity's income must firstly be used for maintaining St Thomas House, secondly for the benefit of residents, and thirdly for the relief in need of people who live in Northampton.

The Page Fund

£1,000

Correspondent: Marina Eaton, Clerk to the Trustees, c/o Wilson Browne LLP, Grange Park Court, Roman Way, Grange Park, Northampton NN4 5EA (01604 876697; email: meaton@wilsonbrowne.co.uk)

CC number: 241274

Eligibility

People in need who live in the borough of Northampton or within five miles of the Guild Hall and have done so for more than five years. Preference is given to older people, and to those who have experienced a sudden and unforeseen drop in income, for example widows following the death of a husband.

Types of grants

Pensions for people who have experienced a reduction in income due to widowhood or old age.

Annual grant total

In 2016/17 the fund held assets of £866,000 and had an income of £32,500. Most of the fund's expenditure is awarded to organisations, however over £1,000 was awarded to older people.

Exclusions

Applicants must have lived in the Northampton area for at least five years.

Applications

Application forms are available from the correspondent. Applications can be submitted directly by the individual or through a social worker, Citizens Advice or other welfare agency. They are accepted at any time and are usually considered in May and November.

St Giles Charity Estates

£45,500 (six grants)

Correspondent: Anthony Lainsbury, 5 Barrock Close, Southwaite, Carlisle CA4 0LL (01697 473898; email: info@nicholasrothwell.co.uk; website: nicholasrothwell.co.uk)

CC number: 202540

Eligibility

People in need who live in St Giles, Northampton borough, and Northamptonshire (preference is given in this order).

Types of grants

St Giles Charity makes one-off grants for the benefit of people in need residing in Northamptonshire. Grants to individuals and families towards, for example, helping to fund individual household requirements such as carpets, washing machines and so on. Grants are always made for a specific purpose, not as a financial 'top up'.

The trustees state that the charity's funds are limited, and consequently the grants made are in the low to moderate category. Sometimes it may be necessary to offer a reserved contribution grant payable on condition that the balance needed can be raised from other sources.

Annual grant total

In 2016 the charity had assets of £3.5 million and an income of £687,000. During the year, grants to individuals totalled £45,500.

Exclusions

Grants cannot be made in certain circumstances, for instance:

- Applications from, or on behalf of, people residing outside Northampton
- For building projects, staffing costs, etc.
- For educational course fees, expenses, or materials
- For gap year projects, overseas expeditions, etc.
- For the repayment of debts, arrears of council tax or rent, or other payments to public bodies
- For funeral expenses

General funding grants are not made to other charities and organisations.

Applications

Application forms and guidance on how to complete it can be obtained from the correspondent.

Note: all applications must be supported by, and submitted through, a relevant professional or social agency such as Citizens Advice. Applications received directly from individuals will not be successful.

Other information

The charity's main activity is the provision of almshouses and the support of Nicholas Rothwell House, a specially designed and purpose-built complex dedicated to providing both short and long-term residential care for older people.

South Northamptonshire

Edmund Arnold's Charity (Poors Branch)

£2,300

Correspondent: Maria Eaton, Grange Park Court, Roman Way, Grange Park, Northampton NN4 5EA (01604 876697; email: meaton@wilsonbrowne.co.uk)

CC number: 260589

Eligibility

People in need who live in the parish of Nether Heyford in Northamptonshire, the ancient parish of St Giles in Northampton and the parish of Stony Stratford in Buckinghamshire.

Types of grants

One-off cash grants for 'extra comforts'.

Annual grant total

In 2016 the charity had assets of £64,700 and an income of £48,000. Grants to individuals totalled £2,300.

Applications

Application forms are available on written request from the correspondent. Applications can be submitted either directly by the individual or through a third party such as a social worker, Citizens Advice or another welfare agency. They are considered in March/April and September/October.

Other information

The charity also makes grants to individuals through its Apprenticing and Educational Branch and to organisations.

Blakesley Parochial Charities

£3,500

Correspondent: Dee Lucas, Bradworthy, Main Street, Woodend, Towcester, Northamptonshire NN12 8RX (01327 860517; email: deelucas@uwclub.net)

CC number: 202949

Eligibility

People in need who live in Blakesley.

Types of grants

One-off and recurrent grants are given according to need. The charity provides funds for widows and widowers in the parish, and to older people who are facing financial hardship.

Annual grant total

In 2016 the charity had an income of £8,000 and a total expenditure of £5,000. We estimate that welfare grants to individuals totalled around £3,500.

Applications

Applications may be made in writing to the correspondent at any time.

Other information

The charity also makes grants for educational purposes and to local organisations.

The Brackley United Feoffee Charity

£7,500

Correspondent: Irene Bennett, 24 Broad Lane, Evenley, Brackley NN13 5SF (01280 703904; email: caryl.billingham@tesco.net)

CC number: 238067

Eligibility

People in need who live in the ecclesiastical parish of Brackley (which consists of the town of Brackley and the village of Halse only).

Types of grants

The charity gives funding to a wide range of causes, including the distribution of Christmas donations to around 60 elderly residents of Brackley. Grants made during 2015/16 included: payment for carpets where a family was rehomed due to domestic violence; payments for beds and bed linen where a family was rehomed due to domestic violence; various very small grants to assist people, generally with mental health problems, who had suffered a gap in benefits payments and needed a small sum to maintain, for example, electricity supply to their home.

Annual grant total

In 2015/16 the charity had assets of £1 million and an income of £258,000. We estimate that welfare grants totalled around £7,500.

Applications

Applications can be made in writing to the correspondent preferably by the individual or through a social worker, Citizens Advice or other welfare agency. The trustees meet every three to four months.

Other information

The charity awards grants to individuals and organisations for both educational and social welfare purposes.

Chipping Warden Smarts Charity

£1,700

Correspondent: N. J. Galletly, Trustee, 3 Allens Orchard, Chipping Warden, Banbury, Oxfordshire OX17 1LX (01295 660365)

CC number: 239658

Eligibility

People in need who live in the parish of Chipping Warden, Northamptonshire.

Types of grants

One-off grants can be given according to need.

Annual grant total

In 2016 the charity had an income of £4,100 and a total expenditure of £3,800. We estimate that grants given to individuals totalled £1,700, with funding also awarded to local organisations.

Applications

Apply in writing to the correspondent. Applications can be made either directly by the individual or through a third party, such as a social worker. They are considered at any time.

Gayton Relief in Need Charity

£2,200

Correspondent: Barry Steer, Secretary, 12 St Marys Court, Gayton, Northampton NN7 3HP (01604 858886; email: barrywendysteer@yahoo.co.uk; website: www.gayton-northants.co.uk/organisations/charities/index.html)

CC number: 201685

Eligibility

People in need who live in the parish of Gayton. In exceptional circumstances, assistance may be given to individuals resident immediately outside the parish.

Types of grants

Small, one-off grants are given to help with, for example, the purchase of food or clothing, heating costs and funeral expenses.

Annual grant total

In 2016/17 the charity had an income of £3,600 and a total expenditure of £4,800. We estimate that welfare grants to individuals totalled around £2,200.

Applications

Application forms are available from the correspondent. The trustees meet twice a year. Our research also suggests that applications can be made through the vicar of Gayton Church.

Other information

According to its Charity Commission record, the charity carries out its work under two working names: Gayton Poors, and Gayton Relief and Educational Charities. It also makes grants to organisations working to relieve poverty in the area of benefit.

Litchborough Parochial Charities

£3,300

Correspondent: Maureen Pickford, Trustee, 18 Banbury Road, Litchborough, Towcester NN12 8JF (01327 830110; email: maureen@ mojo1904.plus.com)

CC number: 201062

Eligibility

People in need who live in Litchborough.

Types of grants

Pensions are given to widows and grants are made to assist pensioners with heating bills.

Annual grant total

In 2015/16 the charity had an income of £7,300 and a total expenditure of £6,800. Grants are made to individuals for both educational and social welfare purposes. We estimate that welfare grants to individuals totalled £3,300

Applications

Apply in writing to the correspondent.

The Pattishall Parochial Charities

£21,000

Correspondent: The Clerk to the Trustees, 59 Leys Road, Pattishall, Towcester NN12 8JY (01327 830583; website: www.pattishallparish.org.uk/ parish-council/pattishall-charities)

CC number: 204106

Eligibility

People in need who have lived in the parish of Pattishall for at least three years. Preference is given to people who are over 65.

Types of grants

The 19 oldest applicants for the widows' and widowers' pension receive monthly payments of £35. Others can apply separately to receive grants for fuel at Christmas (currently £70 per household).

Annual grant total

In 2016 the charity had an income of £19,900 and a total expenditure of £21,200. We estimate that the charity gave around £21,000 in grants to individuals.

Applications

Apply in writing to the correspondent, making sure to include details of age, marital status and the length of time the applicant has been resident in the parish. Applications are usually considered in

November for fuel grants, July for pensions, and throughout the year for other grants. Applications can be submitted either directly by the individual or by anybody who hears of a need. Receipts (copies are accepted) should be included for the costs of travel for hospital visits and estimates for the purchase of large equipment (e.g. wheelchairs).

Other information

The Pattishall parish website states: 'Each year the charity clerk will advertise around Pattishall and on the website for new applicants. In an effort to help identify those who would benefit from a grant, members of the parish are requested to bring forward names to the attention of the clerk.'

The Roade Feoffee and Chivall Charity

£12,700

Correspondent: Michael Dowden, Trustee, 67 High Street, Roade, Northampton NN7 2NW

CC number: 202132

Eligibility

People in need who live in the ancient parish of Roade.

Types of grants

One-off grants usually ranging from £15 to £100. Past grants have been given at Christmas time and for such things as travel expenses to visit relatives in hospital.

Annual grant total

In 2016 the charity had an income of £24,100 and a total expenditure of £25,500. We estimate that the charity gave around £12,700 in grants to individuals for welfare purposes.

Applications

Apply in writing to the correspondent, specifying the reason for the application.

The Sponne and Bickerstaffe Charity

£1,400

Correspondent: Mrs T. Richardson, Clerk to the Trustees, Moor Field, Buckingham Way, Towcester, Northamptonshire NN12 6PE (01327 351206; email: sponneandbickerstaffe@ btconnect.com)

CC number: 204117

Eligibility

People in need who live in the civil parish of Towcester.

Types of grants

One-off grants of £50 to £250 towards household essentials, such as furniture, clothing and electrical goods.

Annual grant total

In 2016 the charity held assets of £747,500 and had an income of £102,500. During the year, the charity gave £1,400 in grants to individuals for welfare purposes.

Applications

Apply in writing to the correspondent, through a social worker, Citizens Advice or other welfare agency. Applications are considered monthly.

Wappenham Poor's Land Charity

£2,300

Correspondent: Mrs J. E. McNeil, Primrose Cottage, Main Street, Abthorpe, Towcester, Northants NN12 8QN (01327 857744)

CC number: 205147

Eligibility

People in need who live in the ecclesiastical parish of Wappenham.

Types of grants

The charity gives a small standard grant to pensioners in need. Grants are also given to widows, widowers and people who are sick or who have disabilities and are in need of specific items.

Annual grant total

In 2016/17 the charity had an income of £3,900 and a total expenditure of £3,500. We estimate that the charity gave around £2,300 in grants to individuals throughout the year.

Applications

Apply in writing to the correspondent.

Nottingham-shire

Dickinson Massey Underwood Charity

£24,000

Correspondent: Nigel Cullen, Freeths LLP, Cumberland Court, 80 Mount Street, Nottingham NG1 6HH (0115 936 9369; email: anna.chandler@freeths.co. uk)

CC number: 213884

Eligibility

Older people in need who live in the city of Nottingham or county of

Nottinghamshire. Preference is given to Christians.

Types of grants

Pensions are given to a fixed number of older people. One-off grants may also be available for emergency items such as replacing gas fires and safety alarm and telephone systems.

Annual grant total

In 2016 the charity had assets of £1.4 million and an income of £53,000. The total amount awarded in grants during the year was £24,000.

Applications

Application forms are available upon request from the correspondent. Applications can be submitted all year round and are considered in March, June, September and December, although emergency cases can be considered at any time.

The Fifty Fund

£27,000

Correspondent: Craig Staten-Spencer, Nelsons Solicitors, Pennine House, 8 Stanford Street, Nottingham NG1 7BQ (0115 989 5251; email: craig.staten-spencer@nelsonslaw.co.uk)

CC number: 214422

Eligibility

People in need who live in Nottinghamshire.

Types of grants

Monthly payments and one-off grants to help with debts, household items and white goods.

Annual grant total

In 2016 the fund had assets of £8.8 million and an income of £317,500. Grants totalled £214,500, of which £27,000 was awarded to individuals.

Exclusions

No grants are given for education, sponsorship, holidays, house moving costs, bonds or rents in advance.

Applications

Applications can be made in writing to the correspondent, to be submitted either by the individual or through a recognised referral agency (such as a social worker, Citizens Advice or doctor) or other third party. Applications are considered at quarterly meetings through the year.

Other information

Grants are made to both individuals and to charities with similar aims to the fund.

Long Bennington Charities

£5,000

Correspondent: Nicola Brown, Trustee, 61 Main Road, Long Bennington, Newark, Nottinghamshire NG23 5DJ (01400 282458; email: secretarylbcharities@yahoo.co.uk)

CC number: 214893

Eligibility

People in need who live in the parish of Long Bennington.

Types of grants

One-off grants according to need. Grants have previously been given for garden maintenance and disability aids.

Annual grant total

In 2016 the charity had an income of £6,300 and a total expenditure of £5,500. We estimate that the charity gave around £5,000 to individuals for welfare purposes.

Applications

Apply in writing to the correspondent.

Other information

At the time of writing (September 2017) the charity had no website or accounts available.

Municipal General Charities for the Poor

£14,800

Correspondent: Michael Gamage, Clerk, Payne and Gamage Solicitors, 48 Lombard Street, Newark, Nottinghamshire NG24 IXP (01636 640649)

CC number: 217437

Eligibility

People who live in the parishes of Coddington, Collingham, Farndon, Hawton, Holme, Langford, Newark and Winthorpe and are in need by reason of youth, age, ill health, disability, financial hardship or other disadvantage.

Types of grants

One-off grants of £200 to £300 are mainly given towards household items such as cookers, washing machines, furniture and other household equipment. Christmas gifts of £80 each are also available.

Annual grant total

In 2016 the charity had assets of £1.7 million and an income of £108,000. During the year, the charity gave a total of £14,800 in grants to individuals. This amount included, 81 Christmas gifts of £100 and £6,700 worth of items, services

or facilities bought on behalf of individuals.

Applications

Application forms are available from the correspondent. They should be submitted through a social worker, Citizens Advice or other welfare agency and must include details of the particular need. Awards are normally considered at quarterly meetings.

Other information

The charity also makes grants to organisations and is responsible for the administration of a number of charitable funds.

The Nottingham General Dispensary

£22,100

Correspondent: Nigel Cullen, Clerk to the Trustees, Cumberland Court, 80 Mount Street, Nottingham NG1 6HH (0115 901 5558; fax: 0115 901 5500; email: anna.chandler@freeths.co.uk)

CC number: 228149

Eligibility

People who are in poor health, convalescent or who have disabilities and live in the county of Nottinghamshire.

Types of grants

One-off grants ranging from £20 to £1,000 are given for a variety of needs including, home adaptations, mobility equipment, medical aids, hospital travel costs, computer equipment, holidays and respite breaks.

Annual grant total

In 2015/16 the charity had assets of £1.3 million and an income of £47,500. During the year, the charity gave around £22,100 in grants to individuals.

Exclusions

No grants are given where funds are available from statutory sources. No recurrent grants are made.

Applications

Apply in writing to the correspondent through a social worker, Citizens Advice, other welfare agency or a professional, for example, a doctor or teacher. Individuals can apply directly via an application form available from the correspondent but must include supporting medical evidence and details of the costs of the items or facilities needed. Applications are considered throughout the year, although requests for grants exceeding £1,000 may take longer.

The Perry Trust Gift Fund

£16,400

Correspondent: Anna Chandler, Correspondent, c/o Freeth Cartwright LLP, Cumberland Court, 80 Mount Street, Nottingham NG1 6HH (0115 901 5562)

CC number: 247809

Eligibility

In order of preference: people in need who have lived in the city of Nottingham for at least five years; people in need who have lived in Nottinghamshire for at least five years. Grants are mainly given to older people with low incomes but some help is available to younger people in need.

Types of grants

One-off grants of up to £200 towards, for example, electric bills, clothing, living costs, household bills, food, furniture, disability equipment and help in the home.

Annual grant total

In 2015/16 the fund had an income of £13,800 and a total expenditure of £16,600. We estimate that the fund gave around £16,400 in grants to individuals.

Applications

Application forms are available from the correspondent.

West Gate Benevolent Trust

£59,500

Correspondent: Stephen Carey, Secretary, 17 Storcroft Road, Retford DN22 7EG (01777 707677)

CC number: 503506

Eligibility

People in need who live in Nottinghamshire.

Types of grants

One-off grants towards, for example, washing machines, holidays and travel to visit relatives in hospital.

Annual grant total

In 2016/17 the trust had assets of £2,400 and an income of £64,500, of which £59,000 was donated from the Williamson Benevolent Trust. Grants totalled £59,500.

Applications

Applications must be made through a third party, such as a social worker or Citizens Advice.

Ashfield

The Hucknall Relief-in-Need Charity

£2,200

Correspondent: Kenneth Creed, 67 Glendon Drive, Hucknall, Nottingham NG15 6DF (0115 963 5929)

CC number: 215974

Eligibility

People in need who live in Hucknall, with a preference for 'poor householders'.

Types of grants

One-off and recurrent grants are given according to need.

Annual grant total

In 2016/17 the charity had an income of £6,300 and a total expenditure of £4,600. We estimate that the charity gave around £2,200 in grants to individuals during the year.

Exclusions

No grants are given for the relief of rates, taxes or other public funds.

Applications

Apply in writing to the correspondent at any time. Individuals should apply through a social worker, minister of religion or similar third party.

Other information

The charity also makes grants to organisations.

Bassetlaw

The Sir Stuart and Lady Florence Goodwin Charity

£6,500

Correspondent: Linda Dore, Grants Administrator, c/o Bassetlaw District Council, Queen's Buildings, Potter Street, Worksop, Nottinghamshire S80 2AH (01909 533249; email: goodwin.charity@bassetlaw.gov.uk)

CC number: 216902

Eligibility

People over 60 who are on a limited income and live in the wider rural district of East Retford.

Types of grants

One-off grants to improve quality of life. Recent grants have been used to pay utility bills, and to buy carpets, stairlifts, and furniture.

Annual grant total

In 2016/17 the charity had an income of £9,300 and a total expenditure of £6,700. We estimate that grants to individuals totalled around £6,500.

Exclusions

Grants cannot be paid retrospectively.

Applications

Contact the correspondent for further information and an application form. Applications can be submitted directly by the individual or through a third party such as Age Concern or social services. Grants will only be made to the person raising the invoice, not the individual.

Broxtowe

Beeston Consolidated Charity

£3,700

Correspondent: The Trustees, PO Box 10425, Nottingham NG9 9GN (07854 310 327; email: info@ beestonconsolidatedcharity.org.uk; website: www. beestonconsolidatedcharity.org.uk)

CC number: 1164090

Eligibility

People in need who are residents of Beeston, Nottinghamshire.

Types of grants

One-off grants, for example, to cover the cost of appliances or furnishings.

Annual grant total

In 2016 the charity held assets of £3.7 million and had an income of £141,000. Grants to individuals totalled £3,700 and a further £112,500 was made in grants to organisations.

Applications

Apply in writing to the correspondent, who welcomes questions and can offer further advice on how to apply. The trustees meet monthly but can respond more quickly if there is an immediate need.

Other information

This charity is a newly registered CIO that is a merger of four parochial charities for Beeston namely: the charities of Mary and Elizabeth Charlton, Henry Hanley, Elizabeth Wakefield and Henry Kirk.

Mansfield

Brunts Charity

£13,900

Correspondent: The Trustees, Brunts Chambers, 2 Toothill Lane, Mansfield NG18 1NJ (01623 623055; website: www. bruntscharity.org.uk)

CC number: 213407

Eligibility

Older people who are in need and live within the Mansfield District Council area or the surrounding area.

Types of grants

One-off grants are made towards items which will aid everyday comfort or relieve any illness or disability.

Annual grant total

In 2016/17 grants totalled £13,900 and were distributed as follows:

Other grants	£12,900
Christmas gifts	£840
Pensions	£150

Exclusions

Grants are not paid on a recurring basis or for items or services which are the responsibility of a statutory agency.

Applications

Application forms are available from the website or the correspondent. Forms should be returned to the charity office together with the applicant's birth certificate and details of their financial circumstances.

Other information

The charity's main concern is the provision of almshouses for older people who are in financial difficulty. It also makes grants to local organisations.

Warsop United Charities

£2,500

Correspondent: Jean Simmons, Trustee, Newquay, Clumber Street, Warsop, Mansfield, Nottinghamshire NG20 0LX

CC number: 224821

Eligibility

People in need who live in the urban district of Warsop (Warsop, Church Warsop, Warsop Vale, Meden Vale, Spion Kop and Skoonholme).

Types of grants

Our research suggests that one-off grants for necessities and quarterly grants to about 60 individuals are made.

Annual grant total

In 2015 the charity had an income of £7,500 and a total expenditure of £10,700. We estimate that grants given to individuals for social welfare purposes totalled around £2,500.

Applications

Applications may be made in writing to the correspondent. The trustees meet three or four times a year.

Other information

Grants are also made for educational purposes. Both individuals and organisations can be supported.

Newark and Sherwood

The Balderton Parochial Charity

£3,000

Correspondent: Louise Tetlaw, Administrator, 16 Gardiner Avenue, Fernwood, New Balderton, Newark NG24 3RG (07818 081490; email: bpc@ jimandlou.com)

CC number: 217554

Eligibility

People in need who live in the parish of Balderton.

Types of grants

One-off grants according to need. Recent grants have been given for cookers, electric wheelchairs, cycle trailers and garden alterations.

Annual grant total

In 2015/16 the charity had an income of £2,800 and a total expenditure of £3,500. We estimate that around £3,000 was made in grants to individuals for social welfare purposes.

Exclusions

No donations for the relief of rates, taxes, fines or other public funds.

Applications

Apply in writing to the correspondent either directly by the individual or through a social worker, Citizens Advice or other welfare agency. Applications are considered at any time.

The John and Nellie Brown Farnsfield Trust

£15,000

Correspondent: David Slight, 3 Fernbeck Cottages, Tippings Lane, Farnsfield, Newark NG22 8EP (01623 882349; email: dgcslight@gmail.com)

CC number: 1078367

Eligibility

People in need who live in Farnsfield in Nottinghamshire and the surrounding area.

Types of grants

One-off and recurrent grants are given according to need, to relieve hardship and/or protect and preserve health.

Annual grant total

In 2016/17 the trust had an income of £32,000 and a total expenditure of £31,000. The trust awarded £15,000 in grants towards welfare.

Applications

Applications should be made in writing to the correspondent.

Other information

Grants are also awarded to individuals for education.

Coddington United Charity

£6,000

Correspondent: A. F. Morrison, 26 Kirkgate, Newark, Nottinghamshire NG24 1AB (01636 700888)

CC number: 1046378

Eligibility

People in need who live in the parish of Coddington. Some preference is made for elderly applicants.

Types of grants

One-off grants for individuals to relieve financial hardship.

Annual grant total

In 2016 the charity had an income of £19,500 and a total expenditure of £14,000. We estimate that the charity awarded £6,000 in grants to individuals.

Applications

Applications should be made in writing to the correspondent.

Other information

The charity also provides and maintains almshouses in the area.

The Mary Elizabeth Siebel Trust

£63,000 (56 grants)

Correspondent: Sarah Allen, Secretary of Trustees, 3 Middlegate, Newark, Nottinghamshire NG24 1AQ (01636 671881; fax: 01636 700148)

CC number: 1001255

Eligibility

People over 60 years of age who are in poor health and live within a 12-mile radius of Newark Town Hall.

Types of grants

One-off grants ranging from £50 to £2,500. The trust aims to enable individual applicants to live in their own homes, e.g. help with the cost of stairlifts, essential home repairs, aids for people with disabilities, care at home, relief for carers.

Annual grant total

In 2015/2016 the charity had assets of £3 million and an income of £116,000. During the year, the charity awarded grants to 56 individuals totalling £63,000.

Applications

Application forms are available from the charity offices. Completed applications should be sent to the Secretary to the Trustees. Individuals are usually visited by the charity's assessor who will then make a recommendation to the trustees. The trustees meet every two months to consider applications.

Other information

Grants are also made to organisations.

Nottingham

The John William Lamb Charity

£11,600

Correspondent: Nina Dauban, Chief Executive, Nottinghamshire Community Foundation, Pine House B, Southwell Road West, Rainworth, Mansfield NG21 0HJ (01623 620202; fax: 01623 620204; email: enquiries@nottscf.org.uk; website: www.nottscf.org.uk)

CC number: 221978

Eligibility

People in need who have been living for at least one year within the city of Nottingham, or within 20 miles of the Nottingham Exchange, with a preference for older people.

Types of grants

Annuities are paid quarterly. One-off grants are also available for individuals.

Annual grant total

In 2016 the charity awarded a total of £11,600 in grants. Of this total, £10,100 was awarded in 20 annuities and a further £1,500 was given as grants to individuals.

Applications

Apply in writing to the correspondent. Applicants will be visited by a member of the charity.

Other information

The charity is administered by Nottinghamshire Community Foundation.

Nottingham Gordon Memorial Trust for Boys and Girls

£3,800

Correspondent: Anna Chandler, Charity Administrator, Cumberland Court, 80 Mount Street, Nottingham NG1 6HH (0115 901 5562; email: anna.chandler@ freeths.co.uk)

CC number: 212536

Eligibility

Children and young people under the age of 25 who are in need and live in Nottingham or the area immediately around the city. Preference can be given to individuals who are of the former Nottingham Gordon Memorial Home for Destitute Working Boys.

Types of grants

One-off grants are made for baby essentials, clothing, bedding, electrical goods (mainly cookers and washing machines), basic equipment for people with disabilities, those fleeing domestic violence or rebuilding their lives after a relationship breakdown. The trust also provides family holidays and trips.

Annual grant total

In 2016 the trust had assets of £1.3 million and an income of £47,000. We estimate that grants given to individuals totalled £3,800.

Applications

Application forms are available from the correspondent. They can be submitted through the individual's school, college, educational welfare agency, a health visitor, social worker, probation officer or similar professional. Our research suggests that individuals, supported by a reference from their school/college, can also apply directly. The trustees meet twice a year, although applications can be considered all year round.

Other information

The trust also supports organisations in the Nottingham area (£22,500 in 2016) and provides educational support for individuals.

The Thorpe Trust

£15,000

Correspondent: Mandy Kelly, Administrator, Actons Solicitors, 20 Regent Street, Nottingham NG1 5BQ (email: mandy.kelly@actons.co.uk)

CC number: 214611

Eligibility

Widows and unmarried women in need who live within a mile radius of Nottingham city centre. The recipients must be the widows or fatherless daughters of clergymen, gentlemen or professional people or of people engaged (other than in a menial capacity) in trade or agriculture.

Types of grants

Recurrent grants according to need.

Annual grant total

In 2015/16 the charity had an income of £17,000 and a total expenditure of £15,300. We estimate that grants given to individuals for welfare purposes to be around £15,000.

Applications

Application forms are available from the correspondent. Applications can be submitted directly by the individual or, where applicable, through a social worker, Citizens Advice or other welfare agency. They are considered once during the summer and at Christmas.

Other information

At the time of writing (August 2017) the charity had no website or accounts available.

Rushcliffe

Bingham United Charities 2006 (formerly known as Bingham United Charities)

£9,000

Correspondent: Susan Lockwood, 23 Douglas Road, Bingham, Nottingham NG13 8EL (01949 875453; email: lockwoodsue79@gmail.com)

CC number: 213913

Eligibility

People in need who live in the parish of Bingham.

Types of grants

One-off and recurrent grants for a wide range of welfare purposes.

Annual grant total

In 2016/17 the charity had an income of £9,800 and a total expenditure of

£10,500. The amount awarded in grants to individuals was £9,000.

Applications

Application forms are available from the correspondent, and should be supported by a professional worker where possible.

Rutland

The Brooke Charity

£2,000

Correspondent: Barbara Clemence, Trustee, Old Rectory Farm, Main Street, Brooke, Oakham, Leicestershire LE15 8DE (01572 770558)

CC number: 221729

Eligibility

People in need who live in the parish of Brooke and the adjoining parishes of Oakham, Braunston, Ridlington and Morcott, with priority given to people who are sick, older people and children.

Types of grants

One-off grants to relieve financial difficulty for items and services which will improve a person's daily life.

Annual grant total

In 2015/16 the charity had an income of £9,800 and a total expenditure of £4,900. We have estimated that grants to individuals totalled £2,000, with funding also awarded to local organisations.

Applications

Apply in writing to the correspondent. Applications can be submitted directly by the individual or, where applicable, through a social worker, Citizens Advice or other welfare agency. They are considered at any time.

The Rutland Dispensary

£4,700

Correspondent: The Trustees, 31 Springfield Way, Oakham, Leicestershire LE15 6QA (01572756120; email: angelaandfrancis@talktalk.net)

CC number: 230188

Eligibility

People who are poor, old or sick and live in Rutland.

Types of grants

One-off and recurrent grants, usually in the range of £100 to £250. Support is mainly given to relieve medical needs not covered by the NHS.

Annual grant total

In 2016 the charity had an income of £4,300 and a total expenditure of £4,900.

We estimate that the charity gave around £4,700 in grants to individuals.

Applications

Apply in writing to the correspondent. Applicants should include details of any medical conditions and their general circumstances.

The Rutland Trust

£3,500

Correspondent: Richard Adams, Clerk, 35 Trent Road, Oakham, Rutland LE15 6HE (01572 756706; email: rjaadams@btinternet.com)

CC number: 517175

Eligibility

People who have disabilities who live in Rutland and are in need.

Types of grants

Our research indicates that one-off and ongoing grants, usually ranging between £50 and £400, are given to buy medical equipment.

Annual grant total

In 2016 the trust had an income of £18,000 and a total expenditure of £17,500. We estimate that grants awarded to individuals for welfare purposes totalled around £3,500.

Applications

A telephone call to the trust is recommended.

West Midlands

General

The Jack and Ada Beattie Foundation (Fund for the Forgotten)
See entry on page 35

DTD Charity

£9,400

Correspondent: Zoe Lander, Fund Manager, 4 Millenium Way West, Phoenix Centre, Nottingham NG8 6AS (email: zoe@dtdcharity.com; website: www.sfcharity.co.uk)

CC number: 1104927

Eligibility

People of all ages who have severe disabilities. This can include people with significant sensory, physical and intellectual impairments and those with complex and challenging behavioural needs. The charity's website states that it is only able to accept applications from applicants in the counties of Nottinghamshire, Leicestershire, Derbyshire, Warwickshire and the West Midlands (primarily areas covered by the postcodes starting NG, LE, DE, CV, B, WS, WV, DY and some starting with S). There is a postcode searcher on the website.

Payments for or towards specific items or services which will make a 'positive' difference to the quality of life of individuals or groups.

Types of grants

Applications are treated on their merit. The majority of grants given are around £1,000.

Previously, grants have been given for special clothing, footwear, mattresses and beds, indoor/outdoor wheelchairs, mobility scooters, kitchen equipment, a Meywalker and structural amendments to houses and living areas. Grants may be given for ordinary household items if it can be shown that they will help to alleviate the disability rather than improving general family circumstances. Grants for UK holidays may also be considered, but applications should be submitted 6 to 12 months in advance of proposed holiday dates.

Annual grant total

In 2016 the charity had assets of £312,000 and an income of £74,500. We estimate that grants given to individuals totalled around £9,400.

Exclusions

The charity is unlikely to consider grants for salaries, transport costs, iPads or laptops.

The following are not funded: educational grants and course fees; debts of any kind, including utilities and rent arrears; money direct to other charities; reimbursement of costs for items already purchased; motor vehicle purchase or expenses, e.g. repairs/road tax/insurance/licence; nursing and residential home fees; funeral expenses/removal expenses; driving lessons; major home improvements including top-up grants; therapies such as swimming with dolphins, hyperbaric therapy, etc.; deposits for housing, vehicles and loads; alternative therapies, e.g. reflexology, acupuncture, faith healing.

Applications

Applications can be made via the foundation's website. Applications are welcomed from individuals, professional workers and representatives of organisations. Where the request is from a private individual, a detailed letter of support from a professional (e.g. family doctor, hospital consultant, social worker, teacher or a worker from a community or disability organisation) is essential. If applying for specialist seating, manual or powered wheelchairs, the letter must be from an occupational therapist or physiotherapist.

Other information

The charity was formerly known as SF Charity.

The W. E. Dunn Trust

£53,000 (334 grants)

Correspondent: Alan Smith, Secretary to the Trustees, 30 Bentley Heath Cottages, Tilehouse Green Lane, Knowle, Solihull B93 9EL (01564 773407; email: wedunn@tiscali.co.uk)

CC number: 219418

Eligibility

People who are in need and live in the West Midlands, particularly Wolverhampton, Wednesbury, north Staffordshire and the surrounding area. Preference is given to people who are very old or very young, who the trustees recognise as possibly being the least able to fend for themselves.

Types of grants

One-off grants usually ranging from £50 to £200.

Annual grant total

In 2016/17 the trust held assets of almost £5.4 million and an income of £185,500. Individuals received a total £53,000 in 334 awards. They were distributed as follows:

Clothing and furniture	165	£25,000
Domestic equipment	76	£12,000
Radio, TV and licences	51	£8,000
Social and welfare	37	£7,200
Education	5	£1,000

A further £110,500 was given in 150 grants to organisations.

Exclusions

Grants are not made to settle or reduce debts already incurred.

Applications

Applications should be made in writing via a social worker, Citizens Advice or other welfare agency. The trustees meet on a regular basis to consider applications.

Friends of the Animals
See entry on page 25

Grantham Yorke Trust

£4,500

Correspondent: Christine Norgrove, Clerk to the Trustees, Shakespeare Martineau, 1 Colmore Square, Birmingham B4 6AA (0121 214 0487)

CC number: 228466

Eligibility

People who are under 25 and were born in the old West Midlands metropolitan county area (basically: Birmingham, Coventry, Dudley, Redditch, Sandwell, Solihull, Tamworth, Walsall or Wolverhampton).

Types of grants

One-off grants according to need.

Annual grant total

In 2015/16 the trust had assets of £6.2 million and an income of £245,000. During the year, 21 grants were awarded to individuals, for both social welfare and educational needs, amounting to £9,100. We estimate that welfare grants to individuals totalled £4,500.

Applications

Applications can be made on a form available from the correspondent. They can be submitted directly by the individual or via a relevant third party such as a social worker, Citizens Advice or other welfare agency, in February, May, August and November for consideration in the following month.

The Persehouse Pensions Fund

£5,800

Correspondent: Clive Wheatley, 12A Oakleigh Road, Stourbridge, West Midlands DY8 2JX (01384 379775; email: clive.wheatley@virginmedia.com)

CC number: 500660

Eligibility

Older or distressed people belonging to the upper or middle classes of society who were born in the counties of Staffordshire or Worcestershire, or people who have lived in either county for ten years or more, and have been 'reduced to poverty by misfortune'.

Types of grants

Mainly pensions, but occasional one-off grants are also given.

Annual grant total

In 2016/17 the charity had an income of £13,200 and a total expenditure of £6,000. We estimate that welfare grants to individuals totalled around £5,800.

Applications

Application forms are available from the correspondent and can be submitted directly by the individual.

The Anthony and Gwendoline Wylde Memorial Charity

£2,500

Correspondent: Kirsty McEwen, Clerk to the Trustees, c/o Higgs & Sons, 3 Waterfront Business Park, Dudley Road, Brierley Hill, West Midlands DY5 1LX (01384 327322; email: kirsty.mcewen@higgsandsons.co.uk; website: wyldecharity.weebly.com)

CC number: 700239

Eligibility

People in need living in Dudley and Staffordshire, particularly Kinver and Stourbridge. The beneficial area is defined as the DY7, DY8 and DY9 postcodes.

Types of grants

One-off grants, usually up to £750, are given for a wide range of charitable needs.

Annual grant total

In 2015/16 the charity had assets of £908,500 and an income of £50,000. Grants were made totalling £37,000 and consisted of awards to 11 organisations amounting to £31,500 and awards to 15 individuals totalling around £5,100. We estimate that grants given to individuals for social welfare purposes totalled around £2,500.

Exclusions

Applications from areas outside the beneficial area may only be considered in exceptional circumstances. Support is not given where costs can be met by statutory resources.

Applications

The method of application depends on the type of grant being applied for. Full details of the types of grants available can be found on the website. Applications for grants of up to £750 (small grants), if necessary, can be dealt with quickly by the Small Grants Committee. Applications for amounts greater than £750 (large grants) can only be considered at trustees' meetings, held twice a year.

Other information

The charity was created by a trust deed dated 6 April 1988, in memory of Anthony and Gwendoline Wylde.

Hereford-shire

All Saints Relief-in-Need Charity

£3,000

Correspondent: Douglas Harding, Trustee, 6 St Ethelbert Street, Hereford HR1 2NR (01432 267821)

CC number: 244527

Eligibility

Individuals in need who live in the city of Hereford, with a preference for those resident in the ancient parish of All Saints.

Types of grants

One-off grants. The charity typically prefers to give items rather than cash sums.

Annual grant total

In 2016/17 the charity had an income of £7,600 and a total expenditure of £6,400. We estimate that welfare grants to individuals totalled around £3,000, with funding also awarded for educational purposes.

Applications

Application forms are available from the correspondent.

E. F. Bulmer Benevolent Fund

See entry on page 120

Hereford Municipal Charities

£5,500

Correspondent: Clerk to the Trustees, 147 St Owen Street, Hereford HR1 2JR (01432 354002; email: herefordmunicipal@btconnect.com)

CC number: 218738

Eligibility

People in need who live in the city of Hereford.

Types of grants

One-off grants of up to £200. Grants are given to help with household equipment, clothes, educational equipment, emergencies and so on.

Annual grant total

In 2016 the charity had assets of £5 million and an income of £364,000. We estimate that welfare grants to individuals totalled around £5,500.

Exclusions

Debts or nursery fees.

Applications

Application forms are available from the correspondent and should be submitted directly by the individual or through a relevant third party. Applications are considered five times a year but can be authorised within meetings if they are very urgent. Applicants are normally interviewed.

Other information

The charity also offers almshouse accommodation. There are two separate funds (eleemosynary and educational) administered by the Grants Committee.

The Norton Canon Parochial Charities

£11,000

Correspondent: Mary Gittins, Ivy Cottage, Norton Canon, Hereford HR4 7BQ (01544 318984)

CC number: 218560

Eligibility

People in need who live in the parish of Norton Canon.

Types of grants

One-off and recurrent grants are given according to need.

Annual grant total

In 2016 the charity had an income of £23,000 and a total expenditure of £11,200. We estimate that grants given to individuals totalled around £11,000.

Applications

Apply in writing to the correspondent.

The Rathbone Moral Aid Charity

£7,000

Correspondent: Carol Thompson, PO Box 181, Hereford HR2 9YN (01981 250899)

CC number: 222697

Eligibility

People who live in Herefordshire who are under 25 and in need of rehabilitation, 'particularly as a result of crime, delinquency, prostitution, addiction to drugs or drink, maltreatment or neglect'.

Types of grants

One-off and recurrent grants are given according to need.

Annual grant total

In 2016 the charity had an income of £15,000 and a total expenditure of

£14,900. We estimate that grants given to individuals totalled approximately £7,000.

Exclusions

No grants are given for nursery fees.

Applications

Apply in writing to the correspondent. Individual applications are considered throughout the year. All individual applications must be supported by a welfare agency or doctor, social worker, teacher or other professional.

Other information

Grants are also made to organisations.

Shropshire

The Lady Forester Trust

£70,500 (138 grants)

Correspondent: Janet McGorman, Grants Administrator, The Estate Office, Willey Park, Broseley, Shropshire TF12 5JN (01952 884318; email: lft@willeyestates.co.uk)

CC number: 241187

Eligibility

People living in of the county of Shropshire who have disabilities or are sick, convalescent or infirm, with priority given to inhabitants of the ancient borough of Wenlock.

Types of grants

One-off grants for medical equipment, nursing care, travel to and from hospitals and other medical needs not otherwise available on the NHS.

Annual grant total

In 2016 the trust held assets of £5.6 million and had an income of £226,500. Grants to individuals totalled £70,500, with a further £136,500 awarded to organisations.

Exclusions

No retrospective grants are made, nor are grants given for building repairs/alterations, home/garden improvements or household bills.

Applications

Application forms are available from the correspondent. Applications can be made directly by the individual or through a social worker or a GP and are considered on a quarterly basis.

The Gorsuch, Langley and Prynce Charity

£25,000 (244 grants)

Correspondent: Pamela Moseley, 116 Underdale Road, Shrewsbury SY2 5EF

CC number: 247223

Eligibility

People in need who live in the parishes of Holy Cross (the Abbey) and St Giles in Shrewsbury.

Types of grants

One-off and recurrent grants. Grants have been given towards furniture, carpets, washing machines, cookers, fridges, baby clothes and cots. Christmas gifts are also given.

Annual grant total

In 2015 the charity had assets of £1 million and an income of £41,800. During the year, the charity gave grants to 244 individuals and families, as well as to four local primary schools. The total of grants given was £37,000, although a breakdown of distributions was not available from the accounts. We estimate that grants given to individuals and families totalled £25,000.

Applications

Apply in writing to the correspondent through a social worker, healthcare professional, Citizens Advice or other welfare agency such as Home-Start. Applications should include details of the full amount required and why it is needed. They are considered on a regular basis.

The Basil Houghton Memorial Trust

£5,400

Correspondent: Julia Baron, Trustee, c/o Community Council Building, The Creative Quarter, Shrewsbury Business Park, Shrewsbury SY2 6LG (01743 360641; email: houghton.trust@shropshire-rcc.org.uk; website: www.basilhoughtontrust.org.uk)

CC number: 1101947

Eligibility

People with learning disabilities who are in need and live in Shropshire.

Types of grants

One-off grants. Grants should be additional to any services provided by statutory bodies. Typically, grants have been made towards travel expenses, achieving individuals' goals, the provision of life-improving items and services, and as contributions towards holidays.

Annual grant total

In 2016/17 the charity had an income of £13,900 and a total expenditure of £10,900. We estimate that the charity gave around £5,400 in grants to individuals, also awarding grants to local organisations.

Exclusions

Applicants for individual grants must be resident in Shropshire or Telford and Wrekin.

Applications

Application forms are available from the correspondent. The trustees meet quarterly in March, June, September and December.

Thompson Pritchard Trust

£15,000

Correspondent: Dr Nigel O'Connor, Trustee, 82 The Mount, Shrewsbury SY3 8PN (01743 343068; website: www. shropshirewelfaretrust.co.uk)

CC number: 234601

Eligibility

Individuals who live in Shropshire who have a serious health problem or disability and have a low income and little capital.

Types of grants

Small grants to assist with, for example, travel to and from hospital, convalescence, respite care, medical appliances, mobility items and essential household appliances.

Annual grant total

In 2016 the trust had an income of £22,000 and a total expenditure of £16,500. We estimate that grants given to individuals totalled £15,000.

Exclusions

Grants cannot be made for debts, bills or expenses already incurred.

Applications

Application forms are available from the website. Applicants should include as much information as possible about health problems along with any supporting letters (e.g. from a health care or social worker). Decisions on most awards can be made within weeks. The trustees meet to consider applications for larger amounts in March and October.

Shropshire

Albrighton Relief-in-Need Charity

£1,500

Correspondent: David Beechey, Trustee, 34 Station Road, Albrighton, Wolverhampton WV7 3QG (01902 372779; email: dabeechey@googlemail. com)

CC number: 240494

Eligibility

People in need who live in the parishes of Albrighton, Boningale, Boscobel and Donington. The charity aims to relieve temporary hardship.

Types of grants

One-off grants according to need. Grants could be given for clothing, household necessities, food, furniture, special medical and disability equipment, towards bereavement and funeral costs, travel expenses to people attending interview and recuperative holiday costs.

Annual grant total

In 2016 the charity had an income of £3,800 and a total expenditure of £3,000. We estimate that grants given to individuals for welfare purposes totalled £1,500 during the year.

Exclusions

Help is not given where the need can be addressed by the statutory sources.

Applications

Apply in writing to the correspondent.

Other information

The charity is a merger of a number of ancient local charities.

Alveley Charity

£6,500

Correspondent: Rachel Summers, c/o MFG Solicitors LLP, Adam House, Birmingham Road, Kidderminster, Worcestershire DY10 2SH (01562 820181; email: rachel.summers@ mfgsolicitors.com)

CC number: 1026017

Eligibility

People in need who live in the parishes of Alveley and Romsley.

Types of grants

One-off grants according to need.

Annual grant total

In 2015/16 the charity had an income of £21,000 and a total expenditure of £14,500. Part of the charity's activities involves the 'maintenance of property owned by the charity'. We estimate that

grants given to individuals totalled around £6,500.

Applications

Applications may be made in writing to the correspondent, either directly by the individual or through a social worker, Citizens Advice or other welfare agency.

Other information

The charity also maintains properties.

Bridgnorth Lions Club Trust Fund

£1,500

Correspondent: Colin Thomas, Trustee, 13 Stretton Close, Bridgnorth WV16 5DB (01746 766174; website: www.bridgnorthlions.org.uk)

CC number: 517786

Eligibility

Residents of Bridgnorth, Shropshire.

Types of grants

Small, one-off grants according to need in order to alleviate financial hardship.

Annual grant total

In 2016/17 the charity had an income of £37,500 and a total expenditure of £38,000. Grants awarded to individuals were not recorded separately in the accounts and we have based our estimate of £1,500 on previous years' giving and the increase in expenditure.

Applications

Apply in writing to the correspondent.

The Bridgnorth Parish Charity

£1,500

Correspondent: Elizabeth Smallman, Trustee, 37 Stourbridge Road, Bridgnorth WV15 5AZ (01746 764149)

CC number: 243890

Eligibility

People in need who live in the parish of Bridgnorth, including Oldbury, Quatford and Eardington.

Types of grants

Our research suggests that one-off grants are given according to need, including, for example, towards funeral expenses and heating costs.

Annual grant total

In 2015 the charity had an income of £14,300 and a total expenditure of £6,500. Note that the expenditure varies each year and in the past has fluctuated from £0 to £9,400. We estimate that the total awarded to individuals for welfare purposes was around £1,500.

Applications

Applications may be made in writing to the correspondent either directly by the individual or through a doctor, nurse, member of the local clergy, social worker, Citizens Advice or other welfare agency.

Other information

The charity also awards grants for educational purposes and to organisations.

The Hodnet Consolidated Eleemosynary Charities

£900

Correspondent: Wendy France, 26 The Meadow, Hodnet, Market Drayton, Shropshire TF9 3QF (01630 685907; email: wendy547@sky.com)

CC number: 218213

Eligibility

People in need who live in Hodnet parish.

Types of grants

Grants include Christmas parcels for people of pensionable age.

Annual grant total

In 2015 the charity had an income of £4,200 and a total expenditure of £3,700. Grants are made to individuals and organisations for a range of purposes. We estimate that welfare grants to individuals amounted to around £900.

Applications

Applications can be made in writing to the correspondent and are considered throughout the year. They can be submitted directly by the individual or through a social worker, Citizens Advice or other welfare agency.

Other information

This is essentially a relief-in-need charity. It also gives money to students for books.

Telford and Wrekin
The Roddam Charity

£2,100

Correspondent: Stuart Barber, Administrator, Merewood, Springfields, Newport TF10 7EZ (01952 814628; email: bougheyroddamha@btinternet.com)

CC number: 213892

Eligibility

People in need who live in the TF10 postcode area who have disabilities

or are sick, convalescent or infirm. The beneficial area includes the parishes of Newport, Chetwynd, Church Aston, Chetwynd Aston, Woodcote, Moreton, Sambrook, Tibberton, Edgmond and Lilleshall in Shropshire and Forton in Staffordshire.

Types of grants

One-off grants. Grants are made to help with items, services or facilities that are not readily available from other sources and which will relieve the suffering or assist the recovery of individuals in poor health and/or people living with disabilities.

Annual grant total

In 2016/17 the charity had an income of £4,400 and had a total expenditure of £4,300. We estimate that the charity gave around £2,100 in grants to individuals.

The charity also gives grants to organisations.

Exclusions

No grants are given for rates, taxes or other public funds.

Applications

Application forms are available from the correspondent and can be submitted directly by the individual. Applications are usually considered quarterly.

Charity of Edith Emily Todd

£8,000

Correspondent: The Grants Administrator, Charity of Edith Emily Todd, 4 Willmoor Lane, Lilleshall, Newport, Shropshire TF10 9EE (01952 606053)

CC number: 215058

Eligibility

People over the age of 60 who are in need and who live in the ecclesiastical parish of Lilleshall.

Types of grants

Monthly pensions.

Annual grant total

In 2016/17 the charity had an income of £7,100 and a total expenditure of £8,500. We estimate that the charity awarded £8,000 in grants to individuals during the year.

Applications

Apply in writing directly by the individual to the correspondent. Applications are considered on receipt.

Staffordshire

The Community Foundation for Staffordshire

£30,000

Correspondent: Sally Grieve, Grants Manager, Communications House, University Court, Staffordshire Technology Park, Stafford ST18 0ES (01785 339540; email: office@staffsfoundation.org.uk; website: staffsfoundation.org.uk)

CC number: 1091628

Eligibility

People in need who live in Staffordshire. The community foundation operates a number of funds, each with its own eligibility criteria. See the website for more information.

Types of grants

The support available depends on the fund being applied to. Assistance available from current funds can be given for a range of things, including medical equipment, respite holidays, white goods and emergency heating repairs, for example.

Annual grant total

In 2016/17 the community foundation had assets of £6.3 million and an income of £1.4 million. Grants totalled almost £500,000, the vast majority of which (£470,000) was awarded to organisations. A total of £30,000 was given to individuals from ten different funds during the year.

Applications

See the website for full guidance on how to apply to each fund.

Other information

The foundation operates a large number of grant schemes for community groups and individuals, made up of its own funding and also donations from local donors, philanthropists, businesses and national and regional grant-makers.

The Strasser Foundation

£4,000

Correspondent: The Strasser Foundation, c/o Knights Solicitors, The Brampton, Newcastle-under-Lyme, Staffordshire ST5 0QW (01782 627089; email: alfbhjb@gmail.com)

CC number: 511703

Eligibility

Individuals in need in the local area of Stoke-on-Trent and Newcastle-under-Lyme, with a preference for North Staffordshire.

Types of grants

Usually one-off grants for a specific cause or need, to help relieve poverty.

Annual grant total

In 2016/17 the charity had an income of £7,000 and a total expenditure of £12,000. We estimate that grants given to individuals totalled around £4,000.

Applications

Applications should be made in writing to the correspondent. Applications cannot be acknowledged unless an sae is enclosed. The trustees usually meet four times a year.

Other information

The foundation also makes grants to organisations and individuals for educational purposes.

East Staffordshire

Burton-on-Trent Nursing Endowment Fund

£3,300

Correspondent: Marilyn Arnold, 141 Newton Road, Burton-on-Trent, Staffordshire DE15 0TR (01283 567900)

CC number: 239185

Eligibility

People in need who live in the former county borough of Burton-on-Trent.

Types of grants

One-off grants are given towards, for example, chiropody treatment, bedding, removal costs, electric scooter batteries, fridges, freezers and childcare provision.

Annual grant total

In 2016 the charity had an income of £5,400 and a total expenditure of £6,900. We estimate that grants given to individuals totalled £3,300, with funding also awarded to organisations.

Applications

Application forms can be obtained from the correspondent. They can be submitted directly by the individual or through a recognised referral agency (social worker, Citizens Advice, local GP, etc.).

Consolidated Charity of Burton upon Trent

£50,500 (111 grants)

Correspondent: J. P. Southwell, Dains LLP, 1st Floor, Gibraltar House, Crown Square, First Avenue, Burton-on-Trent DE14 2WE (01283 527067; fax: 01283 507969; email: clerk@ consolidatedcharityburton.org.uk; website: www.consolidatedcharityburton. org.uk)

CC number: 239072

Eligibility

People who live in Burton-on-Trent and the neighbouring parishes of Branston, Outwoods and Stretton and are in need.

Types of grants

One-off grants are awarded up to a maximum of £300 per year for essential items such as cookers, fridge freezers, washing machines, carpets, furniture, bedding, mobility aids and school uniforms.

Annual grant total

In 2016 the charity had assets of £13.5 million and an income of £562,000. The total amount awarded to 111 individuals for welfare was £50,500.

Exclusions

Grants are not awarded for the relief of debt.

Applications

Application forms can be downloaded from the website to be returned by post, or are available to complete online. Applications must be supported by a support worker or other suitable professional, detailing why the grant is necessary. Support letters should be on headed paper and signed. The application should state what items are needed.

Other information

The charity also runs 29 almshouses in the local area, and provides grants for education.

The Tutbury General Charities

£1,800

Correspondent: Jeanne Minchin, 66 Redhill Lane, Tutbury, Burton-on-Trent, Staffordshire DE13 9JW (01283 813310)

CC number: 215140

Eligibility

Only people who are in need and live in the parish of Tutbury.

Types of grants

One-off and ongoing grants are given according to need. All residents in the parish who are over 70 receive a birthday card. Vouchers for fuel or goods at a local store (usually under £20) are also given at Christmas to about 200 people in need who live within the parish, regardless of their age. Special cases are considered on their merits by the trustees but applicants must live in the parish of Tutbury.

Annual grant total

In 2015/16 the charity had an income of £9,300 and a total expenditure of £7,800. We estimate that grants given to individuals totalled around £1,800.

Applications

Application forms are available from the correspondent and should be submitted for consideration in November for Christmas vouchers. Inclusion in the birthday voucher scheme can be made at any time (all that is needed is the name, address and date of birth of the person).

Other information

The Clerk has stated that details of the trust are well publicised within the village.

Lichfield

The Lichfield Municipal Charities

£9,100 (26 grants)

Correspondent: Simon James, Correspondent, Ansons Solicitors, St Mary's Chambers, 5 Breadmarket Street, Lichfield, Staffordshire WS13 6LQ (01543 267980; email: sjames@ansonsllp. com)

CC number: 254299

Eligibility

Individuals in need who live in the city of Lichfield (as it was pre-1974).

Types of grants

One-off grants according to need.

Annual grant total

In 2016 the charity had assets of £2.4 million and an income of £114,000. Grants were made to 26 individuals totalling £9,100 and to organisations totalling £2,500.

Applications

Grant application forms are available from the Clerk. The trustees meet four times a year in March, June, September and December.

Other information

Lichfield Municipal Charities comprises of thirteen almshouses known as William

Lunn Homes which are situated in Lichfield. Four are suitable for single people and the remaining nine are suitable for married couples. The almshouses are available for occupation for those who are experiencing financial hardship in the city of Lichfield.

Michael Lowe's and Associated Charities

£30,500 (239 grants)

Correspondent: Simon James, Clerk to the Trustees, Ansons LLP, 5–7 Breadmarket Street, Lichfield, Staffordshire WS13 6LQ (01543 267995; email: sjames@ansonsllp.com)

CC number: 214785

Eligibility
People in need who live in the city of Lichfield, particularly older people and those requiring help in an emergency.

Types of grants
One-off grants of up to £600 for domestic items, special chairs, school uniforms, wheelchairs and so on. People who are over 70 and living on a low income can also apply for fuel grants. The trustees may require the recipient to make a contribution of 10% to the cost of any item provided. Gifts in the form of second hand furniture are also distributed.

Annual grant total
In 2016/17 the charity had assets of £1.8 million and an income of £102,000. During the year, the charity gave around £30,500 in grants to individuals. Grants were distributed as follows:

Other grants	48	£16,300
Fuel grants	191	£14,300

The charity's Furniture Transfer Scheme distributed a total of 156 items of furniture to 25 families during the year, costing a total of £6,900. Grants to organisations amounted to a further £26,500.

Applications
Application forms are available from the correspondent. Applications are considered on their own merits and individuals are usually interviewed before any grant is awarded. Beneficiaries of the Furniture Transfer Scheme are usually recommended to trustees through a local welfare organisation. The trustees meet on average five times a year to consider grant applications, although special meetings may be called to deal with urgent requests.

Other information
Applicants are visited and may also be directed to other relevant organisations or services for welfare support.

Newcastle-under-Lyme

The Newcastle-under-Lyme United Charities

£2,700

Correspondent: Caroline Horne, Civic Offices, Merrial Street, Newcastle-Under-Lyme, Staffordshire ST5 2AG (01782 742232; email: caroline.horne@ newcastle-staffs.gov.uk)

CC number: 217916

Eligibility
People in need who live in the borough of Newcastle-under-Lyme (as it was before 1974).

Types of grants
Small donations are given at Christmas.

Annual grant total
In 2015/16 the charity had an income of £3,900 and a total expenditure of £2,900. We estimate that grants given to individuals for social welfare purposes totalled around £2,700.

Exclusions
No grants are given to older people living in sheltered housing.

Applications
Our previous research indicates that applicants must apply in writing to the correspondent. Applications should be submitted either directly by the individual or through a friend or family member. They are considered in October each year. The circumstances of beneficiaries are assessed on an annual basis by trustees.

Other information
At the time of writing (August 2017), a website did not exist and no accounts were available.

South Staffordshire

Enville Village Trust

£2,400

Correspondent: Richard Jones, Batfield House, Batfield Lane, Enville, Stourbridge, West Midlands DY7 5LF (01746 780350; email: enville.trusts@ btinternet.com)

CC number: 231563

Eligibility
People in need who live in the parish of Enville, with a preference for older people and children.

Types of grants
One-off and recurrent grants are given according to need. Grants may not always be paid to the individual, rather they may directly be paid to the creditor.

Annual grant total
In 2015/16 the trust had an income of £2,800 and a total expenditure of £2,800. The amount awarded in grants is estimated to be £2,400.

Applications
Applications should be made in writing to the correspondent. Previous research indicates applications are considered at any time.

Other information
The trust is made up of a combination of seven much smaller charities, all connected with the village of Enville.

Stafford

Church Eaton Charities

£7,000

Correspondent: Stephen Rutherford, 5 Ashley Croft, Church Eaton, Stafford ST20 0BJ (01785 823958)

CC number: 216179

Eligibility
People in need who have lived in the parish of Church Eaton for at least two years. In exceptional circumstances grants may be available to those living immediately outside the parish.

Types of grants
Previous research indicates support is generally given towards the heating costs or in provision of coal during the winter season. Grants are also available for other items, equipment or services, for example, TV licences, lifeline telephones and so on.

Annual grant total
In 2016 the charity had an income of £10,500 and a total expenditure of £7,300. We estimate that grants totalled £7,000.

Applications
Apply in writing to the correspondent. Applications are considered upon receipt.

Staffordshire Moorlands

Carr Trust

£44,000

Correspondent: Tina Mycock, Parish Administrator, St Luke's Church of England Church, Fountain Street, Leek, Staffordshire ST13 6JS (01538 373306; email: stlukesleek@hotmail.co.uk)

CC number: 216764

Eligibility

Residents of Leek, mainly older people, who are in need.

Types of grants

Mainly pensions, usually of around £20 a month towards items, services and facilities that will help to reduce need or hardship. One-off grants are also available and most beneficiaries receive a Christmas bonus.

Annual grant total

In 2016 the trust had an income of £14,000 and a total expenditure of £47,000. We estimate that grants totalled around £44,000.

Applications

Apply in writing to the correspondent. An advert about the grants appears in a local paper in March each year. The trustees require details of the applicant's age, marital status, income, savings and details of any property owned.

Tamworth

Beardsley's Relief in Need Charity

£5,000

Correspondent: Derek Tomkinson, Trustee, Barnfield, Comberford Lane, Wigginton, Tamworth, Staffordshire B79 9DT (01543 255612; email: enquiries@tomkinsonteal.co.uk)

CC number: 214461

Eligibility

People in need who live in the borough of Tamworth, especially older people, children and people with disabilities.

Types of grants

One-off grants and loans for health and welfare purposes.

Annual grant total

In 2015/16 the charity had an income of £12,900 and a total expenditure of £11,400. We estimate that grants given to individuals totalled £5,000, with funding also awarded to local organisations.

Applications

Apply in writing to the correspondent, either directly by the individual or, where applicable, through a social worker, Citizens Advice or other welfare agency.

The Rawlet Trust

£12,500

Correspondent: Christine Gilbert, 47 Hedging Lane, Wilnecote, Tamworth B77 5EX (01827 288614; email: christine.gilbert@mail.com)

CC number: 221732

Eligibility

People in need who live in the borough of Tamworth.

Types of grants

One-off and recurrent grants towards disability facilities, holidays, bibles for children and Home Link telephone expenses. Grants for educational purposes are also available for young people under the age of 25 who have parents resident in the area.

Annual grant total

In 2016/17 the trust had assets of £766,000 and an income of £25,500. Welfare grants to individuals totalled £12,500.

Applications

Apply using the application form available from the correspondent. Applications should be submitted either directly by the individual or through a third party such as a social worker or Citizens Advice. The clerk or one of the trustees will follow up applications if any further information is needed. The trustees meet in January, April, July and October to consider applications.

Tamworth Municipal Charity

£600

Correspondent: Anthony Goodwin, Trustee, Tamworth Borough Council, Marmion House, Lichfield Street, Tamworth, Staffordshire B79 7BZ (01827 709212)

CC number: 216875

Eligibility

People in need who live in the borough of Tamworth.

Types of grants

One-off grants towards, for example, equipment, household items and hospital travel costs.

Annual grant total

In 2016 the charity had a total income of £2,600 and a total expenditure of £1,400. We estimate that £600 was given to individuals for social welfare purposes, with funding also awarded to organisations.

Applications

Apply in writing to the correspondent.

Other information

At the time of writing (August 2017) the charity had no website or annual report available.

Warwickshire

North Warwickshire

Relief-in-Need Charity of Simon Lord Digby and Others

£2,500

Correspondent: Juliet Bakker, Administrator, The Vicarage, High Street, Coleshill, Birmingham B46 3BP (01675 462188)

CC number: 237526

Eligibility

People in extreme hardship who live in the parish of Coleshill.

Types of grants

One-off grants are given according to need.

Annual grant total

In 2016 the charity had an income of £12,000 and a total expenditure of £5,400. We estimate that around £2,500 was given in grants to individuals.

Applications

Apply in writing to the correspondent. The trustees meet four times a year to discuss applications. They can be submitted directly by the individual or through a social worker, Citizens Advice or other welfare agency. Candidates are requested to provide as much detail as possible including information about applications to other organisations/trusts.

Other information

Organisations may also be supported.

Nuneaton and Bedworth

Sir William Roberts Relief in Need Charity

£1,400

Correspondent: Leon Angrave, Trustee, Lower Ambion House, 1 Lower Ambion Farm, Ambion Lane, Sutton Cheney, Nuneaton CV13 0AD

CC number: 242296

Eligibility
People who live in the village of Sutton Cheney and are in need.

Types of grants
One-off grants, usually in the range of £150 to £200, for basic necessities only.

Annual grant total
In 2016 the charity had an income of £4,400 and had a total expenditure of £2,900. We estimate that grants given to individuals for welfare purposes totalled around £1,400.

Applications
Apply in writing to the correspondent or any of the trustees. Applications may be submitted directly by the individual at any time.

Other information
Grants are also made to organisations based in Sutton Cheney.

The Samuel Smith's and Spencer's Charities
See entry on page 252

Rugby

The Bilton Poors' Land and Other Charities

£1,500

Correspondent: Robin Walls, Trustee, 6 Scotts Close, Rugby CV22 7QY (email: biltoncharities@outlook.com)

CC number: 215833

Eligibility
People in need who live in the ancient parish of Bilton (now part of Rugby). Preference is given to older people and those referred by social services.

Types of grants
One-off grants, usually of between £15 and £250. Small cash grants are also made to older people at Christmas.

Annual grant total
In 2016/17 the charity had an income of £22,500 and a total expenditure of £22,000. At the time of writing (November 2017) the annual report and accounts for the year were not yet available to view at the Charity Commission. In the most recent year for which a grant figure was available (2015/16) awards totalled just over £6,000. Based on this figure, we estimate that grants given to individuals for social welfare totalled around £1,500, with funding also given to organisations and to individuals for educational purposes.

Applications
Applications can be made in writing to the correspondent, by the individual or through a third party such as a minister or welfare organisation. They are considered three times a year.

The Sir Edward Boughton Long Lawford Charity

£29,500 (91+ grants)

Correspondent: Debbie Groves, Clerk to the Trustees, 7 College Road, Willoughby, Rugby, Warwickshire CV23 8BN

CC number: 237841

Eligibility
People in need who live in the parish of Long Lawford or Rugby. Applicants for pensions must have lived in the parish for the last five years.

Types of grants
Pensions of £10 a month and Christmas bonuses of £40. One-off grants are awarded for various welfare purposes, including disability aids, hospital expenses and stairlifts.

Annual grant total
In 2016 the charity held assets of £1.7 million and an income of £134,500. Grants to individuals totalled £29,500, of which £14,500 was given to 91 individuals in pensions and 89 Christmas bonuses, and £15,200 was given to individuals in one-off grants. A further £38,500 was given in grants to organisations and local schools.

Applications
Apply on a form available from the correspondent, to be considered by the trustees every three months, usually February, May, August and November.

Rugby Relief in Need Charity

£3,200

Correspondent: Carol Davies, 14 School Street, Long Lawford, Rugby, Warwickshire CV23 9AU (01788 544630)

CC number: 217987

Eligibility
People in need who live in the ancient parish of Rugby, which includes the parishes of St Andrew's and St Matthew's.

Types of grants
Christmas vouchers to the older people of the parish. Some one-off grants may be made in cases of emergency.

Annual grant total
In 2015/16 the charity had an income of £3,400 and a total expenditure of £3,400. We estimate that the charity gave around £3,200 in grants to individuals.

Applications
Apply in writing to the correspondent. Applications are generally considered three or four times a year, although urgent cases can be considered at any time.

Stratford-upon-Avon

The South Warwickshire Welfare Trust

£11,000

Correspondent: Valerie Grimmer, Clerk, 62 Foxes Way, Warwick CV34 6AY (01926 492226; email: valerie.grimmer@sky.com)

CC number: 235967

Eligibility
People who are sick and in need and live in Warwick district and the former rural district of Southam.

Types of grants
One-off grants for items, services or facilities to alleviate suffering or assist recovery for people who have disabilities or are sick, convalescent or infirm. Grants are awarded towards holidays, cookers, carpets, white goods and home aids, for example.

Annual grant total
In 2016 the trust had an income of £11,300 and a total expenditure of £12,200. We estimate that grants given to individuals totalled around £11,000.

Exclusions
Grants are not repeated and are not given for relief of taxes or other public funds.

Applications

Apply on an application form available from the correspondent to be submitted through a social worker, Citizens Advice or other welfare agency, or through a doctor, church official or similar third party.

Stratford Town Trust

£12,900

Correspondent: The Trustees, 14 Rother Street, Stratford-upon-Avon, Warwickshire CV37 6LU (01789 207111; email: admin@stratfordtowntrust.co.uk; website: www.stratfordtowntrust.co.uk)

CC number: 1088521

Eligibility

Stratford town residents with less than £30 per month disposable income and be claiming all benefits to which they are entitled.

Types of grants

Small, one-off grants for items such as bedding, furniture, clothing, microwaves and fridges.

Annual grant total

In 2016 the trust held assets of £2.9 million and an income of £1.9 million. Grants to individuals totalled £12,900.

Applications

For more information on the grants available contact the Money Advice Caseworker, at Citizens Advice on 01789 298665.

Mayor's Fund Society of Stratford-upon-Avon

£1,800

Correspondent: Ros Dobson, Trustee, 155 Evesham Road, Stratford-upon-Avon, Warwickshire CV37 9BP (01789 293749; email: themayorsfund@yahoo.com; website: www.themayorsfund.webs.com)

CC number: 220136

Eligibility

Older people in need who live in the former borough of Stratford-upon-Avon.

Types of grants

One-off and recurrent grants are usually given in the form of grocery vouchers.

Annual grant total

In 2015/16 the fund had an income of £840 and a total expenditure of £2,100. We estimate that grants given to individuals in the form of grocery vouchers totalled around £1,800.

Applications

Apply in writing to the correspondent. Applications can be submitted directly by the individual or through a social worker, Citizens Advice, other welfare agency or other third party such as a member of the clergy. They should include a general summary of income, other relief received (such as housing benefits) and financial commitments.

Municipal Charities of Stratford-upon-Avon – Relief in Need

£10,000

Correspondent: Ros Dobson, Charities Administrator, c/o 6 Guild Cottages, Church Street, Stratford-upon-Avon, Warwickshire CV37 6HD (01789 293749; email: municharities@yahoo.co.uk or municharities@btinternet.com; website: www.municipal-charities-stratforduponavon.org.uk)

CC number: 214958

Eligibility

People in need, generally older people of state-pensionable age, who have been living within the town boundary of Stratford-upon-Avon for at least 18 months.

Types of grants

One-off grants, usually in the range of £100 to £500, are given for a variety of needs, including: essential items of furniture and household equipment, such as beds, support chairs and white goods; mobility aids not available through social services or occupational therapy services; and unexpected household bills.

Annual grant total

In 2016 the charity had assets of £116,000 and an income of £59,500. Grants totalled £52,500, of which grants for almshouses and other organisations accounted for at least £31,500 and educational grants a further £870. We estimate that social welfare grants to individuals totalled around £10,000.

Exclusions

Grants are not normally given for the repayment of debts, rent and council tax arrears or rental deposits. They are not generally considered unless the applicant is in receipt of all statutory benefits to which they are entitled.

Applications

Application forms are available from the correspondent. They should include details of the financial circumstances of the applicant (income and savings) and documentary supporting evidence will be requested. When applying for financial assistance in connection with a specific health condition, applicants are asked to include a letter from a GP, occupational therapist, social worker or similar professional in support of the application. Requests for help are considered throughout the year. Candidates are encouraged to contact the correspondent to clarify any questions or to discuss their case.

Other information

The Stratford-upon-Avon Municipal Charities is an amalgamation of seven different charities in the local area. A big part of the charity's activities is the provision of almshouse accommodation. Welfare support is given from the relief-in-need fund. Educational grants are also occasionally provided.

The charity's website explains how 'with an increasing number of applications being received, the Trustees have decided to award this year's grant for a specific need only'.

Warwick

The Barford Relief-in-Need Charity

£2,300

Correspondent: Terry Offiler, 14 Dugard Place, Barford, Warwick CV35 8DX (01926 624153)

CC number: 256836

Eligibility

People in need who live in the parish of Barford.

Types of grants

One-off cash grants and gifts in kind are given towards 'any reasonable need', including hospital expenses, electric goods, convalescence, living costs, household bills, holidays, travel expenses, medical equipment, nursing fees, furniture, equipment to help with a disability, and help in the home.

Annual grant total

In 2016 the charity had an income of £11,100 and a total expenditure of £9,500. Grants are made to individuals and organisations for both social welfare and educational purposes. We estimate that welfare grants to individuals totalled £2,300.

Applications

Applications can be made in writing to the correspondent, directly by the individual or a family member. One of the trustees will then visit the applicant to obtain all necessary information. Applications are usually considered in May and October.

Austin Edwards Charity

£2,300

Correspondent: Jackie Newton, 26 Mountford Close, Wellesbourne, Warwick CV35 9QQ (01789 840135; email: jackie.newton114@gmail.com; website: www.warwickcharities.org.uk)

CC number: 225859

Eligibility

People living in the old borough of Warwick (generally the CV34 postcode).

Types of grants

Grants, generally of no more than £300, are given for relief in need.

Annual grant total

In 2015/16 the charity had an income of £10,900 and a total expenditure of £9,300. Grants are made to individuals and organisations for both social welfare and educational purposes. We estimate that grants given to individuals for social welfare purposes totalled £2,300.

Applications

Apply in writing to the correspondent stating the purpose of the grant and the amount required, as well as details of any other charities approached with the same request. The individual's name and address must be supplied with the application. The trustees usually hold one meeting annually in July but will consider applications throughout the year.

Other information

The charity was named after Mr Austin Edwards who lived and worked in Warwick as a photographic manufacturer in the early years of the twentieth century. As a councillor of the borough of Warwick, he remained deeply interested in Warwickians and Warwick affairs generally. He gave generously to the Corporation of Warwick throughout his life.

Hatton Consolidated Fund (Hatton Charities)

£2,200

Correspondent: M. Sparks, Clerk, Weare Giffard, 32 Shrewley Common, Shrewley, Warwick CV35 7AP (01926 842533; email: bsparks1@talktalk.net)

CC number: 250572

Eligibility

People in need who live in the parishes of Hatton, Beausale and Shrewley. Applications from outside these areas will not be considered.

Types of grants

One-off grants, usually in the range of £50 to £500. Awards include those towards travel expenses to patients at convalescent homes, clothing and footwear, bedding, fuel costs, other household necessities and payments in a case of sudden distress, sickness or unexpected loss. Loans may also be available.

Annual grant total

In 2015/16 the fund had an income of £10,300 and a total expenditure of £8,900. We estimate that grants awarded to individuals for welfare totalled around £2,200.

Exclusions

Our research suggests that grants are not given to schoolchildren. Support is not made to cover council tax and other taxes or where public funds should be sought first.

Applications

Applications may be made in writing the correspondent, directly by the individual or a family member.

Other information

Grants are given to both organisations and individuals for educational and social welfare purposes.

Kenilworth United Charities

£5,000

Correspondent: Clerk to the Trustees, Damian J. Plant & Co., 29B Warwick Road, Kenilworth, Warwickshire CV8 1HN (01926 857741)

CC number: 215376

Eligibility

People in need who live in Kenilworth.

Types of grants

Support is usually given in the form of grocery vouchers to one-parent families. In the past, grants have also been made towards white goods.

Annual grant total

In 2016 the charity had an income of £23,000 and a total expenditure of £26,000. We estimate that grants given to individuals totalled around £5,000.

Applications

Application forms are available from the correspondent. Applications are considered quarterly, although urgent cases will receive special consideration.

Other information

The charity also funds almshouses and the Citizens Advice in Kenilworth.

The King Henry VIII Endowed Trust, Warwick

£2,500

Correspondent: Jonathan Wassall, Clerk and Receiver, 12 High Street, Warwick CV34 4AP (01926 495533; email: jwassall@kinghenryviii.org.uk; website: www.kinghenryviii.org.uk)

CC number: 232862

Eligibility

People who live in the former borough of Warwick. The area of benefit is roughly the CV34 postcode but exceptions apply so see the full list of eligible areas within the guidelines or contact the correspondent for clarification. The trust has a preference for providing relief in need to older people.

Types of grants

One-off grants can be given for general welfare purposes, according to need. Awards are usually made only if a previous application to The Warwick Relief in Need Charity has been unsuccessful.

Grants are intended to be supplementary and applicants are expected to raise additional funds themselves. Payments are normally made upon submission of receipts.

Annual grant total

In 2016 the trust had assets of £31.5 million and an income of £1.1 million. We estimate that around £2,500 was given in grants to individuals.

Exclusions

Grants are not made where support should be provided by the local or central government. Funding is not given retrospectively.

Applications

Application forms are available to download from the trust's website. Grants are usually considered on a quarterly basis in March, June, September and November. Check the trust's website for application deadlines.

Other information

The income is distributed to the historic Anglican churches in Warwick (50%), Warwick Independent Schools Foundation for allocation through scholarships and bursaries (30%), and to organisations and individuals in the town (20%).

Leamington Relief-in-Sickness Fund

£1,000

Correspondent: Hillary Holland, Trustee, 55 West Street, Warwick CV34 6AB (01926 401168; email: hilaryholland2@gmail.com)

CC number: 216781

Eligibility

People suffering from ill health and expectant mothers who live in the former borough of Leamington Spa and the neighbourhood, and are in need. People with disabilities or mental health problems are especially welcomed.

Types of grants

One-off grants including help with fuel debts, television licences, baby necessities, food for special diets, fares for visiting hospitals or sick relatives, replacing locks after a burglary, children's clothing and repairs to washing machines.

Annual grant total

In 2015/16 the fund had an income of £2,000 and a total expenditure of £2,500. We estimate that grants given to individuals totalled around £1,000.

Exclusions

Applicants can only receive one grant each year.

Applications

Our previous research indicates that applicants must apply in writing through a social worker, Citizens Advice, health visitor, doctor, probation service, Mind or other welfare agency. Applications submitted by individuals will not be acknowledged or considered. Applications are considered throughout the year.

Other information

At the time of writing (August 2017) there were no accounts or website available for this charity.

Warwick Relief in Need Charity (Warwick Combined Charity)

£21,000 (42 grants)

Correspondent: C. Houghton, 34 High Street, Warwick CV34 4BE (01926 491181; email: choughton@moore-tibbits.co.uk; website: www.warwickreliefinneed.org.uk)

CC number: 256447

Eligibility

People in need who live in the town of Warwick.

Types of grants

One-off grants of up to £1,000 towards, for example, washing machines, beds, mattresses, vacuum cleaners, carpets, holidays and home repairs.

Annual grant total

In 2016 the charity had assets of £3.8 million and an income of £171,000. During the year, the charity awarded £21,000 to individuals.

Applications

Apply on a form available from the correspondent or to download from the charity's website. Applications are normally submitted through social services or a similar welfare organisation and should be accompanied by a covering letter providing details of the applicant and the nature of the need. They are considered by the trustees at quarterly meetings.

Other information

The charity also awarded over £100,000 in grants to organisations during the year.

West Midlands

The Avon Trust

£1,500

Correspondent: Andrew Cashmore, Trustee, Trygva, Carthew Way, St Ives TR26 1RJ (01736 438347)

CC number: 219050

Eligibility

Retired Methodist ministers and their dependants with some preference for those living in the West Midlands, and people in residential homes who live in the West Midlands.

Types of grants

One-off and recurrent grants are given according to need.

Annual grant total

In 2015/16 the trust had an income of £7,300 and a total expenditure of £5,500. As the trustees predominantly focus on funding religious organisations, we estimate that grants given to individuals totalled around £1,500.

Applications

Apply in writing to the correspondent. The trustees meet once a year in July but can consider applications at other times.

The Harborne Parish Lands Charity

£46,000 (97 grants)

Correspondent: Sharon Sharratt, Grants Officer, 109 Court Oak Road, Harborne, Birmingham B17 9AA (0121 426 1600; email: sharon.sharratt@hplc.org.uk or info@hplc.org.uk; website: www.hplc.org.uk)

CC number: 219031

Eligibility

People in need who live in the ancient parish of Harborne, which includes parts of Harborne, Smethwick, Bearwood and Quinton. A map of the old parish is available to view on the website and individuals are advised to check that they reside in the area of benefit before making an application.

Types of grants

One-off grants of up to £800 are available for essential household items. Applications for carpets are only eligible if there is a health and safety issue and grants for washing machines are made only to families.

Annual grant total

In 2015/16 the charity held assets of £17.2 million and had an income of £1.4 million. Grants were made totalling £221,500, of which £46,000 was awarded to individuals.

Exclusions

Grants are not made in cash and cannot be used to pay debts such as utility bills or rent arrears.

Applications

Application forms are available from the Grants Officer by email or by telephone on 0121 426 1600. The trustees' report for 2015/16 notes that most applications are submitted through a third party such as a local charity, a health worker, or social services.

Other information

The charity also runs five almshouses with around 100 residents.

Jordison and Hossell Animal Welfare Charity

£1,300

Correspondent: Sally Reid, Trustee, Whitestones, Haselor, Alcester B49 6LU (01789 488942; email: sallyreid@me.com)

CC number: 515352

Eligibility

People in the Midlands who are on low incomes and are in need of financial assistance in meeting vets' bills for their pets.

Types of grants
One-off grants are made towards 'unpredictable' vets' bills.

Annual grant total
In 2015/16 the charity had an income of £2,000 and a total expenditure of £1,500. We have estimated that grants totalled around £1,300.

Exclusions
Support is not given with vets' bills for larger animals such as horses and farm animals. Grants are not made to support the continuing care of a pet.

Applications
Apply in writing to the correspondent. Applications must be made by a vet rather than from the client. Evidence that the beneficiary is on benefits is required.

The James Frederick and Ethel Anne Measures Charity

£8,500

Correspondent: Craig Sisson, The Measures Trust, 33 Great Charles Street, Queensway, Birmingham B3 3JN

CC number: 266054

Eligibility
Grants are awarded to people who live in Birmingham, Coventry, Dudley, Sandwell, Solihull, Walsall, and Wolverhampton who are in financial hardship or distress.

Types of grants
One-off and recurrent grants to relieve those in financial hardship.

Annual grant total
In 2015/16 the charity had assets of £1.1 million and an income of £36,500. We estimate that around £8,500 was awarded in grants to individuals.

Applications
Applications should be made in writing to the correspondent.

Other information
The charity also makes awards to individuals for educational purposes, and to local charities active in the community.

The Newfield Charitable Trust

£36,000 (135 grants)

Correspondent: Mary Allanson, Littleworth House, Littleworth, Warwick

CV35 8HD (024 7622 7331; email: m.allanson@rotherham-solicitors.co.uk)

CC number: 221440

Eligibility
Girls and women (under the age of 30) who are in need of care and assistance and live in Coventry or Leamington Spa.

Types of grants
The trust's objects are stated as: 'The relief of the physical, mental and moral needs of, and the promotion of the physical, social and educational training' of eligible people. Most grants are of under £500 and are given towards, for example: clothing, both school and general; beds and bedding; and essential household items.

Annual grant total
In 2016/17 the trust had assets of £1.7 million and an income of £64,000. Welfare grants to individuals totalled £36,000.

Exclusions
Grants are not made for arrears or utility bills.

Applications
Apply in writing to the correspondent to request an application form. Applications are accepted from individuals or third parties e.g. social services, Citizens Advice, school/college etc. A letter of support/reference from a professional third party (i.e. school, social services, etc.) is always required. Details of income/expenditure and personal circumstances should also be given. Applications are considered eight times a year.

The Norton Foundation

£12,700 (106 grants)

Correspondent: Richard Perkins, 50 Brookfield Close, Hunt End, Redditch B97 5LL (01527 544446; email: correspondent@nortonfoundation.org; website: www.nortonfoundation.org)

CC number: 702638

Eligibility
Young people aged under 25 who live in Birmingham, Solihull, Coventry and Warwickshire. Applicants must be 'in need through some aspect of disadvantage defined as: in care or in need of rehabilitation, lapsing into delinquency, suffering from maltreatment or neglect, or whose potential is not yet realised due to circumstances beyond their control'.

Types of grants
One-off grants are given towards clothing, household items and, occasionally, holidays. Grants of up to

£500 can be made, although they usually range between £50 and £250.

Annual grant total
In 2015/16 the foundation held assets of £4.5 million and had an income of £143,500. Grants totalled £88,500, of which £55,000 was awarded to organisations. A total of 106 grants were made directly to individuals totalling £12,700. They were distributed as follows:

Household	83	£9,600
Clothing	23	£3,100
Education and training	15	£2,200*

*The figure for educational grants was not included in the grants total.

In addition, £30,500 was paid in block discretionary grants to eight 'sponsors' for redistribution to individuals. Sponsors included South Birmingham Young Homeless Project (£13,900), St Basil's Centre (£12,300), Citizens Advice (£1,300) and Spurgeons (£1,000).

Applications
Applications should be made in writing and contain all the information described in the guidance notes, which are available from the website. Applications must be submitted through a social worker, Citizens Advice, probation service, school or other welfare agency, and should be typed or printed, if possible. They are considered on a monthly basis.

Other information
The foundation's website also lists helpful information on why applications fail:

- The trustees are not convinced by the case being presented
- Too many assumptions and unrealistic aspirations
- The amount requested is outside the range for the grant being applied for
- The bid was to fund long-term commitments
- Financial information was insufficient and inadequate
- The contact details were insufficient for the trustees to obtain further information

Pedmore Sporting Club Trust Fund

£4,600

Correspondent: The Secretary, Nicklin & Co. LLP, Church Court, Stourbridge Road, Halesowen, West Midlands B63 3TT (email: psclub@pedmorehouse.co.uk; website: www.pedmoresportingclub.co.uk)

CC number: 263907

Eligibility
People in need who live in the West Midlands.

Types of grants

One-off grants have included those for medical care equipment, travel to and from hospital, wheelchairs, other access aid and IT equipment. Money is normally paid directly to the service/ item provider, not the individual. Christmas and Easter parcels are given to senior citizens.

Annual grant total

In 2016 the charity had assets of £333,500 and an income of £52,500. During the year, the charity gave around £4,600 in grants to individuals.

Exclusions

The trust is unable to help with general living costs.

Applications

Our research indicates that candidates for the holiday food parcels should be recommended by a member of the sporting club. Other applications can be made in writing to the correspondent. The trustees meet quarterly and might interview the candidates.

Other information

Grants are mainly made to organisations, preferably local (£29,500 in 2014).

The Eric W. Vincent Trust Fund

£3,000 (24 grants)

Correspondent: Janet Stephen, Clerk, PO Box 6849, Stourbridge DY8 9EN (email: vttrust942@gmail.com)

CC number: 204843

Eligibility

People in need living in the West Midlands, within a 20-mile radius of Halesowen.

Types of grants

Grants ranging from £85 to £125.

Annual grant total

In 2015/16 the charity had assets of £1.5 million and an income of £52,500. The charity awarded a total of 24 grants to individuals which totalled almost £3,000.

Exclusions

The charity does not award grants to pay salaries, cover debts or to cover needs outside the local area.

Applications

Trustees normally meet bi-monthly. Applications should be in writing through a health professional, social worker, Citizens Advice or other welfare agency. Applications will not be considered if they are not made through a relevant third party. Details of financial circumstances must be included.

Other information

Small grants (generally under £1,000) are also made to organisations.

Birmingham

The Freda and Howard Ballance Trust

£4,500

Correspondent: The Trustees, Blackhams, Lancaster House, 67 Newhall Street, Birmingham B3 1NR (0121 233 0062; email: alankhawkins@gmail.com)

CC number: 513109

Eligibility

People who are in need and live in Birmingham.

Types of grants

One-off grants for social welfare. Grants are occasionally made for educational purposes.

Annual grant total

In 2015/16 the trust had an income of £3,000 and a total expenditure of £15,500. Grants are made to individuals and organisations and, occasionally, for educational purposes as well as for social welfare. We have estimated that grants made for welfare purposes to individuals totalled £4,500.

Applications

Apply using the form, which is available from the correspondent. A letter giving brief details of the application is required before an application form is sent out. Applications can be made either directly by the individual or via a third party such as a charity, social worker or Citizens Advice. They are usually considered quarterly.

Richard and Samuel Banner Trust

£4,000

Correspondent: Jaime Parkes, Charities and Education Associate, c/o Veale Wasbrough Vizards LLP, Second Floor, 3 Brindley Place, Birmingham B1 2JB (0121 227 3705; email: jparkes@vwv.co. uk)

CC number: 218649

Eligibility

People who are in need and live in the city of Birmingham.

Types of grants

One-off grants.

Annual grant total

In 2015/16 the trust had an income of £9,900 and a total expenditure of £8,100.

We have estimated that grants to individuals for welfare purposes totalled £4,000 during the year, with funding also awarded to individuals for educational purposes.

Applications

Applicants must be nominated by a trustee, doctor or the Council for Old People. Applications are considered on 1 November and grants are distributed immediately after this date.

Other information

The trust can also give apprenticeship grants to male students under 21, but this is done through certain colleges; applicants should not apply directly.

Thomas Bromwich Trust

£28,500 (84 grants)

Correspondent: Christine Norgrove, Clerk to the Trustees, c/o Shakespeare Martineau LLP, 1 Colmore Square, Birmingham B4 6AA (0121 214 0487)

CC number: 214966

Eligibility

People in need living in Handsworth. Great Barr and Perry Barr.

Types of grants

One-off grants of between £40 and £900 towards electric goods, clothing, household bills, food and help in the home.

Annual grant total

In 2015/16 the charity held assets of £902,000 and had an income of £121,500. Grants to 84 individuals totalled £28,500. Grants were also made to scout groups, schools and other local charitable organisations and these totalled £2,700.

Applications

Apply in writing to the correspondent either directly by the individual or through a social worker, Citizens Advice or other welfare agency. Applications are considered at any time.

Friends of Home Nursing in Birmingham

£3,500

Correspondent: Susan Bonner, 577 Walsall Road, Great Barr, Birmingham B42 1ND (0121 624 0021; email: fohnassociation@outlook.com)

CC number: 218182

Eligibility

Sick and older people who live in Birmingham city and who are patients nursed at home by the district nurse.

Types of grants

The trust provides goods, equipment and occasional monetary grants which are not available from other sources. In the past this has included digital thermometers, a dressing trolley, cameras and films for ulcer recordings, and part of the cost of holidays. No grants are made for double glazing or electrical work.

Annual grant total

In 2016 the trust had an income of £7,100 and a total expenditure of £7,300. We estimate that grants given to individuals totalled £3,500.

Applications

Apply in writing, via a district nurse, to the correspondent. Applications can be submitted at any time, for consideration in the spring and autumn. The trust has previously stated that if a real case of need occurs, it can be dealt with as soon as possible.

The Handsworth Charity

£8,000 (22 grants)

Correspondent: Dipali Chandra, Clerk to the Trustees, 109 Court Oak Road, Birmingham B17 9AA (email: info@handsworth-charity.com; website: www.handsworth-charity.com)

CC number: 216603

Eligibility

People in need who live in the parish of Handsworth (now in Birmingham). A map of the beneficial area is available on the website.

Types of grants

One-off grants of up to £500 according to need. Grants are given towards essential household items such as bedding, carpets, cookers, fridges and for small property repairs.

Annual grant total

In 2016 the charity held assets of £1 million and had an income of £28,000. Grants were made to 22 individuals and totalled £8,000, £280 of which was awarded to pensioners. Local schools and organisations received an additional £21,500.

Applications

Application forms are available to download from the website. Forms must be submitted through a recognised referral agency that is willing to act as a sponsor throughout the application process. The trustees meet three times a year, normally in mid-March, mid-July and mid-November. Applications should be received by the charity in the month before a meeting.

Note: successful applicants are expected to provide receipts of items purchased with the grant awarded. Sponsoring agencies are expected to accept some responsibility in making sure the grant is spent on its intended purposes.

A list of organisations that can act as a sponsor can be found on the charity's website.

The CB and AB Holinsworth Fund of Help

£1,300

Correspondent: Sanjeev Bhopal, Administrator, Birmingham City Council, Legal & Democratic Services, PO Box 15992, Birmingham B2 2UQ (0121 675 4673; email: sanjeev.bhopal@birmingham.gov.uk)

CC number: 217792

Eligibility

People in need who live in or near to the city of Birmingham and are sick or convalescing.

Types of grants

One-off grants can be given towards the cost of respite holidays, travelling expenses to and from hospital, clothing, beds and carpets.

Annual grant total

In 2015/16 the fund had an income of £5,600 and a total expenditure of £2,900. We estimate that grants given to individuals totalled £1,300.

Exclusions

Generally grants are not given for bills or debt.

Applications

Application forms are available from the correspondent. Applications are considered throughout the year and should be submitted through a social worker, Citizens Advice or other welfare agency. Confirmation of illness is needed, for example a letter from a doctor, consultant or nurse.

The King's Norton United Charities

£2,500

Correspondent: Revd Larry Wright, The Rectory, 273 Pershore Road, Kings Norton, Birmingham B30 8EX (0121 459 0560; email: parishoffice@kingsnorton.org.uk; website: www.knuc.org.uk)

CC number: 202225

Eligibility

The charity is able to assist only those who live within the boundary of the ancient parish of Kings Norton, formerly in Warwickshire and Worcestershire, now in Warwickshire and the West Midlands. This area includes the current Church of England parishes of Kings Norton, Cotteridge, Stirchley, parts of Bournville, Balsall Heath, Kings Heath, Moseley (St Anne's and St Mary's), Brandwood, Hazelwell, Highters Heath, Wythall, West Heath, Longbridge, Rubery and Rednal.

Types of grants

One-off, emergency grants of £50 to £350 are available to cover unforeseen expenses such as for new household items or repairs.

Annual grant total

In 2016 the charity had an income of £9,000 and a total expenditure of £5,500. We estimate that welfare grants to individuals totalled around £2,500.

Exclusions

Organisations are not supported.

Applications

The trustees prefer to receive referrals for help through a doctor or other agency, however there is a form available on the website if you wish to refer a friend or yourself. The trustees will then contact you to discuss the situation. Applications are considered on an ongoing basis.

Other information

The charity also makes awards for individuals in need of educational assistance.

Charity of Harriet Louisa Loxton

£22,000

Correspondent: Maureen Morris, Team Manager, Professional Support Services, 67 Sutton New Road, Erdington, Birmingham B23 6QT (0121 675 2501)

CC number: 702446

Eligibility

People in need who live in Birmingham, particularly older people, children and individuals with disabilities.

Types of grants

One-off grants. Grants have previously been given for needs such as essential household items, central heating and electric scooters.

Annual grant total

In 2015/16 the charity had assets of £1.6 million and an income of £28,000. Grants were made totalling £22,000.

Exclusions

According to our research, grants are not available to pay off debts, relieve public funds or towards the community charge.

Applications

Application forms are available from the correspondent. They must be made by a social worker (or an equivalent agency) The trustees normally meet four times a year to consider applications. Applications may take some considerable time to process; immediate decisions on applications cannot be given.

Other information

The charity was established from proceeds of the sale of Icknield, a property donated to the city by Harriet Louisa Loxton for use as a home for older people.

Organisations can also be supported at the approval by the advisory panel and general purposes committee.

The Newman Trust Homes

£7,900 (22 grants)

Correspondent: Judy Dyke, Trustee, Tyndallwoods Solicitors, 29 Woodbourne Road, Harborne, Birmingham B17 8BY (0121 693 2222; email: jdyke@tyndallwoods.co.uk)

CC number: 501567

Eligibility

People who are in need, hardship or distress who live, or have formerly lived, in the city of Birmingham. Grants are primarily paid to benefit people who are older, people with housing difficulties and people living within the area of Handsworth and its immediate vicinity.

Types of grants

One-off and recurrent grants are given according to need.

Annual grant total

In 2016/17 the charity had assets of £978,000 and an income of £43,500. During the year, the charity awarded around £7,900 in grants to individuals.

Exclusions

No funding is given for funerals.

Applications

Application forms are available from the charity. Applicants are encouraged to detail any additional information they believe may assist the trustees in their decision.

Sands Cox Relief in Sickness Charity

£5,100

Correspondent: Peter Combellack, Correspondent, 43 Shepherds Green Road, Erdington, Birmingham B24 8EU (0121 382 3295; email: pjcombellack@aol.com)

CC number: 217468

Eligibility

People who live in Birmingham and are in need due to illness, disability or other difficulties.

Types of grants

One-off grants.

Annual grant total

In 2015/16 the charity had an income of £7,500 and a total expenditure of £10,400. We estimate that the charity gave around £5,100 in grants to individuals.

The charity also gives to organisations.

Applications

Apply in writing to the correspondent.

Other information

At the time of writing (August 2017) the charity had no website or accounts available.

Sutton Coldfield Municipal Charities

£37,500 (30 grants)

Correspondent: The Almshouse Manager, Lingard House, Fox Hollies Road, Sutton Coldfield, West Midlands B76 2RJ (0121 351 2262 (Tuesday to Thursday, 9am to 4pm); fax: 0121 313 0651; email: info@suttoncharitabletrust.org; website: www.suttoncoldfieldcharitabletrust.com)

CC number: 218627

Eligibility

People who are in need and have lived in the four electoral wards of Sutton Coldfield (New Hall, Four Oaks, Trinity and almost all of Vesey) for at least five years.

Types of grants

Grants are made to help with the purchase of essential domestic equipment, to help people with disabilities, to help with education after normal schooling, to help people with long-term health problems and to meet other needs.

Annual grant total

In 2015/16 the trust had assets of £52.9 million and an income of £1.6 million. Welfare grants to individuals totalled £37,500.

Applications

Contact the Almshouse Manager for further details or to make an application.

Other information

The principal objective of the charity, which is also known as the Sutton Coldfield Charitable Trust, is the provision of almshouses, the distribution of funds and other measures for the alleviation of poverty and other needs for inhabitants and other organisations within the boundaries of the former borough of Sutton Coldfield.

Yardley Great Trust

£31,000

Correspondent: Karen Grice, 31 Old Brookside, Yardley Fields Road, Stechford, Birmingham B33 8QL (0121 784 7889; email: enquiries@ygtrust.org.uk; website: www.ygtrust.org.uk)

CC number: 216082

Eligibility

People living in south east Birmingham, with preference for applicants living in the ancient parish of Yardley in the city of Birmingham (this includes the wards of Yardley, Acocks Green, Fox Hollies, Billesley, Hall Green and part of the wards of Hodge Hill, Shard End, Sheldon, Small Heath, Sparkhill, Moseley, Sparkbrook and Brandwood).

Types of grants

One-off grants, up to £500, towards washing machines, fridges, cookers, clothing, beds and bedding and household furniture.

Annual grant total

In 2016 the trust had assets of £9.6 million and an income of £2.8 million. During the year, the trust awarded £31,000 in grants to individuals.

Exclusions

No grants are given towards the relief of rates, taxes or for items that should be met by local authorities, health authorities or social services. No grants are given for educational purposes, home improvements (redecoration excepted) or school uniforms.

Applications

Applications should be made through referral agents such as Neighbourhood Offices and Citizens Advice offices. A list of authorised referral agencies is available on the trust's website.

Other information

The trust also makes awards to local organisations, provides sheltered housing for independent older people, and residential care homes.

Coventry

The Children's Boot Fund

£4,000

Correspondent: Janet McConkey, 123A Birmingham Road, Coventry CV5 9GR (024 7640 2837; email: martin_harban@ btconnect.com)

CC number: 214524

Eligibility

Schoolchildren in the city of Coventry between the ages of 4 and 16.

Types of grants

Grants for school footwear for children in need. No other type of award is given. Grants are made directly to footwear suppliers in the form of vouchers. Normally one child per family can be supported within one year, but exceptions for families in difficult circumstances may be made. Twins are usually given an award each. People leaving school may receive a grant for shoes to attend interviews.

Annual grant total

In 2015/16 the fund had an income of £9,400 and a total expenditure of £15,000. We estimate that grants totalled around £4,000. Grants are only made for footwear.

Applications

Application forms are available from schools in the area. They should be made by the parents/guardians and supported by the headteacher of the child's school. Applications from social care services are also considered. Applicants are required to list their benefits and income. Requests are considered four times a year.

General Charity (Coventry)

£139,000 (453+ grants)

Correspondent: Susan Hanrahan, General Charities Office, Old Bablake, Hill Street, Coventry CV1 4AN (024 7622 2769; email: cov.genchar@outlook. com)

CC number: 216235

Eligibility

People in need living in the city of Coventry.

Types of grants

One-off grants in kind and recurrent grants, but not cash grants. Regular payments of around £45 a quarter can be given to a maximum of 650 pensioners over the age of 60.

Annual grant total

In 2016 the charity had assets of £10.4 million and an income of £1.5 million. Grants totalled £1.3 million and, of this amount, welfare grants to individuals totalled £49,000. A further £90,000 was given in pensions to 453 individuals.

Exclusions

Our research suggests that regular cash grants are not given.

Applications

Applications should normally be made through social workers, probation officers, Citizens Advice or other welfare agencies.

Other information

The charity consists of the charities formerly known as The Relief in Need Charity, Sir Thomas White's Pension Fund and Sir Thomas White's Educational Foundation. The trustees are also responsible for the administration of Lady Herbert's Homes and Eventide Homes Ltd providing accommodation for older people in the city of Coventry.

Most of the charity's assistance is given to organisations. Support is also given to individuals for educational purposes.

The Lant Charity

£62,500

Correspondent: Kirsty Hughes, c/o 27 Whitehead Grove, Balsall Common, Coventry CV7 7US (email: kah31@ hotmail.co.uk)

CC number: 234841

Eligibility

Individuals who reside in the area of Berkswell, Balsall Common or Temple Balsall experiencing hardship or distress. The charity also awards grants towards the stipends of ministers of the Church of England in the ecclesiastical parishes of St John the Baptist, Berkswell, St Mary Temple Balsall and St Peter, Balsall Common.

Types of grants

One-off and recurrent.

Annual grant total

In 2015/16 the charity had an income of £34,400 and a total expenditure of £62,700. We estimate that grants awarded to individuals totalled around £62,500.

Applications

Apply in writing to the correspondent.

Other information

At their quarterly meetings, the trustees approved grants to some residents in the area of benefit, undertook maintenance and upkeep of the sports ground and pavilion in Meeting House Lane, Balsall Common (either directly or through the Sports Association), undertook maintenance and upkeep of the Reading Room, Berkswell (either directly or through the Reading Room Committee).

Doctor William MacDonald of Johannesburg Trust

£2,200

Correspondent: Jane Barlow, Trustee, Lord Mayor's Office, Council House, Earl Street, Coventry CV1 5RR (024 7683 3047; email: jane.barlow@coventry. gov.uk)

CC number: 225876

Eligibility

People in need who live in the area of Coventry.

Types of grants

Our previous research indicates that the charity awards one-off grants.

Annual grant total

In 2015/16 the trust had an income of £3,300 and a total expenditure of £2,400. We estimate that grants given to individuals totalled £2,200.

Exclusions

No grants are made for the relief of debt.

Applications

Apply in writing to the correspondent. Applications can be submitted directly by the individual or through a third party such as a social worker.

John Moore's Bequest

£3,000

Correspondent: Ian Cox, Solicitor, c/o Sarginsons, 10 The Quadrant, Coventry CV1 2EL (024 7655 3181)

CC number: 218805

Eligibility

People in need, generally older people, living in the city of Coventry.

Types of grants

Grants are made according to need.

Annual grant total

In 2015/16 the charity had an income of £5,000 and a total expenditure of £3,000. We estimate that around £3,000 was given in grants to individuals for social welfare purposes.

Applications

Apply in writing to the correspondent. Previous research has suggested that grants are made through local churches.

The Samuel Smith's and Spencer's Charities

£34,500 (86+ grants)

Correspondent: The Trustees, Harrison Beale & Owen Ltd, 15 Queens Road, Coventry CV1 3DE (email: info@hboltd.co.uk)

CC number: 240936

Eligibility
People who live in Coventry and the ancient parish of Bedworth and are in need.

Types of grants
Pensions and one-off grants.

Annual grant total
In 2016 the charity had assets of £1.86 million and an income of £57,500. Grants totalled £34,500 and were distributed as follows:

Pensions	£27,500
Fuel (coal) payments	£3,600
May gifts	£2,200
Christmas gifts to pensioners	£1,100

A further £170 was expended on bibles.

During the year, 86 pensioners received recurrent grants.

Applications
Applications can be made directly in writing to the correspondent, but most beneficiaries are referred by the charity's almoner. The trustees meet three times a year to consider applications.

Other information
This charity was formed by the merger of the Samuel Smith, Coventry charity and Spencer's Charity (Charity Commission no. 212935).

The Tansley Charity Trust

£2,100

Correspondent: Lara Knight, Correspondent, Governance Services, Room 59, Council House, Earl Street, Coventry CV1 5RR (email: lara.knight@coventry.gov.uk)

CC number: 505364

Eligibility
Women over 50 years old who are in poor health and live in the city of Coventry.

Types of grants
Our research indicates that the trust awards one-off grants.

Annual grant total
In 2015/15 the trust had an income of £5,400 and a total expenditure of £2,300. We estimate that grants awarded to individuals for welfare purposes totalled around £2,100.

Exclusions
No grants are given for council tax or Inland Revenue payments.

Applications
Application forms are available from the correspondent. Applications can be submitted by the individual or through a recognised referral agency (e.g. a social worker, Citizens Advice or doctor). Grants are considered twice a year.

Other information
At the time of writing (August 2017) the trust had no website or accounts available.

Tile Hill and Westwood Charities

£5,000

Correspondent: Peter Tacon, 323 Cromwell Lane, Burton Green, Kenilworth CV8 1PG (024 7646 5633; email: ltacon@btinternet.com)

CC number: 220898

Eligibility
People who are both sick and in need and live in the parish of Westwood and Stoneleigh and elsewhere within a three and a half-mile radius of 93 Cromwell Lane, Coventry.

Types of grants
One-off grants according to need. The charity's main focus for giving is to relieve poverty and assist where there is medical need.

Annual grant total
In 2016 the charity had an income of £21,000 and a total expenditure of £12,000. We estimate that the charity awarded £5,000 in grants to individuals to relieve poverty during the year.

Applications
Apply in writing to the correspondent.

Other information
The charity also makes awards to organisations in the area.

Dudley

The Badley Memorial Trust

£38,500 (110 grants)

Correspondent: Christopher Williams, Clerk to the Trustees, 16 Manderville Gardens, Kingswinford DY6 9QW (01384 294019; email: badleymemorial@yahoo.com)

CC number: 222999

Eligibility
People in need who are in poor health, convalescent or who have disabilities and live in the former county borough of Dudley (as constituted in 1953). In certain cases the present metropolitan boroughs of Dudley and Sandwell may be included.

Types of grants
One-off grants have been made towards medical aids, clothing, beds/bedding, heating appliances, domestic appliances, televisions, radios, fuel, respite holidays and adaptations for people with disabilities. Recurrent grants are only given in exceptional cases.

Payments are made directly by cheque to the providers of goods or services, no cash payments are made to applicants.

The average grant in 2015/16 was £347.

Annual grant total
In 2015/16 the trust held assets of £1.6 million and had an income of £68,500. A total of £38,500 was distributed in 110 grants to individuals.

Exclusions
Grants are not given to pay off debts or for educational fees.

Applications
Application forms are available from the correspondent. Applications should be submitted directly by the individual or, where applicable, through a social worker, Citizens Advice, other welfare agency or a third party such as a relative, doctor or member of the clergy. Applications are considered quarterly. Those of an urgent nature may be dealt with more quickly by an authorised trustee.

Other information
Although none were awarded in 2015/16, the trust also makes grants to organisations.

The Dudley Charity

£3,200

Correspondent: David Hughes, Trustee, 53 The Broadway, Dudley, West Midlands DY1 4AP (01384 259277; email: dudleycharity@hotmail.co.uk; website: www.dudleyrotary.org.uk/dudleycharity.html)

CC number: 254928

Eligibility
People in need who live in the town of Dudley (as constituted prior to 1 April 1966) and its immediate surroundings, including Netherton.

Types of grants
One-off grants, usually in the range of £100 to £250. Examples of the types of

grants considered are: payments to relieve sudden distress; expenses for visiting people in hospitals or correctional facilities; assistance in meeting gas or electricity bills; the provision of furniture, bedding, clothing, food and other household appliances; the supply of tools, payment for training or equipment for recreational pursuits; respite care; contributions towards wheelchairs and scooters; and food for special diets, medical or other aids and nursing requisites or comforts. Weekly allowances may also be given for a limited period.

Annual grant total

In 2015/16 the charity had an income of £6,300 and a total expenditure of £6,700. We estimate that grants given to individuals totalled £3,200, with funding also awarded to organisations.

Applications

Application forms are available from the correspondent or from the charity's webpage. Applications can be submitted directly by the individual or through a third party such as a social worker. They are usually considered monthly.

Other information

The charity was formed in 1987 through the amalgamation of a number of small charities in Dudley. The charity's website notes that 'The earliest of these charities dates back to 1659 founded under the will of Jasper Cartwright that with two others became known as The Bread Charities.'

The Palmer and Seabright Charity

£9,400

Correspondent: Susannah Griffiths, Clerk to the Trustees, c/o Wall James Chappell, 15–23 Hagley Road, Stourbridge, West Midlands DY8 1QW (01384 371622; email: sgriffiths@wjclaw. co.uk)

CC number: 200692

Eligibility

People in need who live in the borough of Stourbridge.

Types of grants

One-off and weekly grants according to need.

Annual grant total

In 2016 the charity had assets of £313,500 and an income of £49,000. Grants were made totalling £16,400 (including £2,400 in Christmas grants). We estimate that welfare grants to individuals totalled £9,400.

Applications

Applications can be made on a form available from the correspondent. Applications can be submitted either directly by the individual or a family member, through a third party such as a social worker or teacher, or through an organisation such as Citizens Advice or a school.

The Edwin John Thompson Memorial Fund

£2,000

Correspondent: David Thompson, Long House Office, 56 High Street, Albrighton, Wolverhampton WV7 3JQ (01902 372036)

CC number: 213690

Eligibility

Older people, people who are sick or convalescing, and people with a disability who live in the county borough of Dudley or any other local district, area or administrative unit within a 15-mile radius of Dudley Town Hall.

Types of grants

One-off and recurrent grants are given according to need. Grants are used to purchase equipment for older people or people with disabilities, and to provide facilities and amenities for people who are sick or convalescing.

Annual grant total

In 2016/17 the fund had assets of £936,500 and an income of £33,000. The fund awarded a total of £2,000 in grants during the year.

Applications

Applications can be made in writing to the correspondent.

Other information

The fund also makes grants to young people to improve their education and employment skills (£4,600 was awarded in 2016/17). The fund mainly gives to organisations.

The Reginald Unwin Dudley Charity

£1,000

Correspondent: D. F. Hughes, 53 The Broadway, Dudley, West Midlands DY1 4AP (01384 259277; email: rududley@hotmail.com; website: www. dudleyrotary.org.uk/rududley.html)

CC number: 217516

Eligibility

People in need who live in Dudley.

Types of grants

One-off grants of up to around £200. Since the charity began grant-making in 1980, it has provided funding for items such as clothing, household appliances, respite holidays, funeral expenses, course fees, nebulisers, computers, software and wheelchairs.

Annual grant total

In 2015/16 the charity had an income of £3,100 and a total expenditure of £1,100. We estimate that the charity awarded £1,000 in grants to individuals.

Applications

Application forms are available from the correspondent or from the charity's page on the Dudley Rotary website. The application is more likely to succeed if accompanied with a supporting letter detailing the nature of the need for a grant.

Other information

The charity was originally established in 1904 by Reginald Unwin Dudley, who was a silk mercer in Dudley. Originally the charity was called The Reginald Unwin Dudley Highland Road Homes and consisted of four houses for older residents, which were sold in 1980 when the charity was organised into its current form.

The charity also makes awards to individuals for education, for example to assist with payment of course fees.

Chris Westwood Charity

£137,000 (102 grants)

Correspondent: Chris Westwood, PO Box 7131, Stourbridge DY8 9FP (07968 008098; email: chriswestwood@ waitrose.com; website: www. chriswestwoodcharity.co.uk)

CC number: 1101230

Eligibility

Children and young people under the age of 25 with physical disabilities, who live in Stourbridge and the surrounding areas (typically within a 50-mile radius).

Types of grants

Typical examples of support have included: special exercise equipment to assist in regaining and maintaining mobility; wheelchairs, special mobility chairs and lifting equipment; and contributions towards the costs of home modifications, to improve access, or provide specialised facilities that may be required.

Annual grant total

In 2017 the charity had an income of £113,7000 and assets of £29,100. During the year, 102 grants were awarded totalling £137,000

Applications

Apply in writing to the correspondent – there is no specific application form. Applications should detail: the name, age and address of the family and, where applicable, the school attended; background information and the reason for the request; a detailed quotation prepared after an assessment by the supplier; details of the financial position of the family; and details of any funds already raised. Applications should also be supported by a suitable professional person detailing the applicant's medical condition and any advantages the proposed equipment purchase would bring. The charity aims to respond to requests within 48 hours. Grants are made by cheque paid directly to the supplier.

Other information

The charity operates at zero administration cost, and aims to respond to requests within 24 hours.

Sandwell

The Chance Trust

£1,000

Correspondent: Revd Ian Shelton, Trustee, 192 Hanover Road, Rowley Regis B65 9EQ (0121 559 1251; email: ianshelton232@hotmail.co.uk; website: www.warleydeanery.co.uk)

CC number: 702647

Eligibility

People in need in the rural deaneries of Warley and West Bromwich (the area covered by the southern parts of Sandwell borough).

Types of grants

One-off grants, usually ranging from £50 to £400, can be given according to need.

Annual grant total

In 2016/17 the trust had an income of £2,600 and a total expenditure of £2,200. Grants are made to individuals for educational and social welfare purposes. We estimate that welfare grants to individuals totalled £1,000.

Exclusions

Grants are not normally provided where statutory funding is available.

Applications

Apply in writing to the correspondent. Applicants should specify the need and the amount required. Applications are usually considered in January and July.

The Fordath Foundation

£7,000

Correspondent: John Sutcliffe, Trustee, 33 Thornyfields Lane, Stafford ST17 9YS (01785 247035; email: fordath-foundation@ntlworld.com)

CC number: 501581

Eligibility

People who are in need and live in the metropolitan borough of Sandwell. Preference is given to older people and those in poor health.

Types of grants

One-off grants to meet a specific expense. Grants are also available for educational needs.

Annual grant total

In 2016 the foundation had an income of £7,100 and a total expenditure of £7,800. We estimate that grants given to individuals totalled £7,000.

Applications

Applications are usually only considered if they are made through Sandwell Social Services, Citizens Advice or a similar organisation. They should include brief details of the individual's circumstances. They are considered throughout the year, funds permitting.

George and Thomas Henry Salter Trust

£3,000

Correspondent: J. Styler, Lombard House, Cronehill Linkway, West Bromwich, West Midlands B70 7PL (0121 553 3286)

CC number: 216503

Eligibility

People who are in need and live in the borough of Sandwell.

Types of grants

One-off grants, usually in the range of £50 to £1,000, are given towards clothing and household equipment, for example.

Annual grant total

In 2016 the trust had assets of £1.7 million and an income of £42,500. Welfare grants to individuals totalled £3,000.

Applications

An application form is available from the correspondent.

Walsall

W. J. Croft for the Relief of the Poor (W. J. Croft Charity)

£3,500

Correspondent: Dr Paul Fantom, The Council House, Lichfield Street, Walsall WS1 1TW (01922 653484; email: paul.fantom@walsall.gov.uk; website: cms.walsall.gov.uk/charities)

CC number: 702795

Eligibility

Residents of the borough of Walsall.

Types of grants

Small, one-off grants to assist with the purchase of school uniforms and household items.

Annual grant total

In 2015/16 the charity had an income of £2,400 and a total expenditure of £4,000. We estimate that the charity awarded £3,500 in grants for the relief of hardship during the year.

Exclusions

Property deposits, taxes, rent arrears, mortgage payments and utility bills.

Applications

Application forms can be downloaded from the website or can be requested by telephone.

Walsall Wood (Former Allotment) Charity

£5,000

Correspondent: Craig Goodall, Democratic Services, Walsall Council, Council House, Lichfield Street, Walsall WS1 1TW (01922 654765; email: goodallc@walsall.gov.uk; website: www.walsall.gov.uk/charities)

CC number: 510627

Eligibility

Residents of the borough of Walsall.

Types of grants

The remit of the charity is wide, but awards are typically made for clothing and footwear, white goods and furniture.

Annual grant total

In 2015/16 the charity had an income of £23,500 and a total expenditure of £11,200. We estimate that grants for social welfare purposes totalled around £5,000.

Applications

A form is available to download from the council website and can also be requested from the correspondent by telephone. It is helpful, but not essential, to submit supporting evidence along with an application. This could include proof of income, such as a wage slip, benefit letter or bank statement, or a supporting letter from a professional familiar with the applicant's case. The trustees meet around six times a year.

Other information
The charity is administered by the Walsall Council Democratic Services team, which also administers a number of other funds.

Wolverhampton

Bushbury (Ancient Parish) United Charities

£4,500
Correspondent: Harold Hilton, Administrator, 23 Waterloo Road, Wolverhampton, West Midlands WV1 4TJ (01902 420208)
CC number: 242290

Eligibility
People in need living in the ancient parish of Bushbury.

Types of grants
One-off grants.

Annual grant total
In 2015 the charity had an income of £6,400 and a total expenditure of £5,000. We estimate that grants given to individuals totalled around £4,500.

Applications
Apply in writing to the correspondent.

Worcester-shire

The Astley and Areley Kings Sick Fund

£2,000
Correspondent: Alan Stanyer, Trustee, 56 Areley Common, Stourport-on-Severn, Worcestershire DY13 0NQ (01299 822700; email: alan.stanyer@ gmail.com)
CC number: 230709

Eligibility
People who suffer from ill health or have disabilities and who live in the parishes of St Peter Astley, St Bartholomew Areley Kings, St Michael and All Angels Stourport-on-Severn and All Saints Wilden.

Types of grants
One-off grants are made towards specialist equipment for home care, facilities for people with disabilities and additional home support.

Annual grant total
In 2016/17 the fund had an income of £1,500 and a total expenditure of £5,000. We estimate that around £2,000 was given in grants to individuals for social welfare purposes.

Applications
Apply in writing to the correspondent. Applications can be submitted either directly by the individual, or through a social worker, Citizens Advice or another third party. The trustees meet regularly throughout the year.

Other information
The charity also supports organisations.

Worcestershire Cancer Aid Committee

£12,000
Correspondent: Anthony Atkinson, Trustee, c/o Kennel Ground, Gilberts End, Hanley Castle, Worcestershire WR8 0AS (01684 310408)
CC number: 504647

Eligibility
People with cancer who live in the old county of Worcestershire.

Types of grants
One-off and recurrent grants and loans, including grants in kind to assist cancer patients in financial distress with home nursing, transport to hospital, specialist equipment and so on.

Annual grant total
In 2015/16 the charity had an income of £22,500 and a total expenditure of £24,000. We estimate that grants given to individuals totalled around £12,000.

Applications
Applicants must be referred by a medical professional, a hospice senior staff member or a social worker, etc. Applications are normally considered within one week.

Malvern Hills

Malvern Hils Nils

£6,000
Correspondent: Mary Walters, 5 The Howsells, Malvern WR14 1AD (01886 833683; email: malvernhillsnils@gmail. com)
CC number: 1163579

Eligibility
Residents of the district of Malvern Hills in Worcestershire.

Types of grants
One-off grants and loans according to need.

Annual grant total
In 2015/16 the charity had an income of £19,700 and a total expenditure of £6,000. We estimate that grants given to individuals totalled £6,000.

Applications
Apply in writing to the correspondent.

The Ancient Parish of Ripple Trust

£3,000
Correspondent: John Willis, 7 Court Lea, Holly Green, Upton-upon-Severn, Worcestershire WR8 0PE (01684 594570; email: willis.courtlea@btopenworld.com)
CC number: 1055986

Eligibility
People in need, hardship or distress living in the parishes of Ripple, Holdfast, Queenhill and Bushley.

Types of grants
Small, one-off cash grants are made. Christmas grants can also be made to older people.

Annual grant total
In 2015/16 the trust had an income of £13,700 and a total expenditure of £13,600. We estimate that grants given to individuals for welfare purposes totalled around £3,000.

Applications
Applications may be made in writing to the correspondent. Our research suggests that the trustees meet twice a year to consider appeals and the funds are advertised locally before these meetings.

Other information
The trust gives to both individuals and organisations and for educational and welfare purposes. The trust's record on the Charity Commission website notes that 50% of the net income is paid to the trustees of the Ripple Ecclesiastical Charity (Charity Commission no. 1059002) for the repair of the St Mary's Church, Ripple.

Worcester

The Armchair Trust CIO

(195 grants)

Correspondent: Richard Hines, Manager, Unit 6B, Checketts Lane Trading Estate, Checketts Lane, Worcester WR3 7JW (01905 456080; email: armchair@talktalkbusiness.net; website: armchairworcester.org.uk)

CC number: 1164966

Eligibility

People in need of furniture who have no savings and live in Worcester (generally, within a three-mile radius of the city centre).

Types of grants

The charity collects, recycles and provides good quality second-hand furniture at low cost (£31 per item in 2015/16) to families and individuals. Furniture provided includes beds, wardrobes, tables/chairs, desks and so on.

Annual grant total

In 2015/16 the charity had assets of £74,000, an income of £31,500 and a total expenditure of £25,000, all of which was spent on the overheads required for the distribution of second-hand furniture – the charity's main activity.

During the year, the charity received 195 referrals and delivered 803 items.

Exclusions

The charity cannot provide electrical goods, carpets, clothing, bedding, kitchen utensils and similar items. The website has links to other local organisations who can help source these things.

Applications

Applications should be submitted through local authorities, a social worker, Citizens Advice or other welfare agency. They are considered throughout the year. If the need is urgent, specify so in the application.

Other information

The trustees' annual report from 2015/16 notes that 'occasionally, gifts are collected from just outside the city but due to limited resources, the need to economise on fuel, and to achieve a low carbon footprint, all deliveries of household items are within the city boundary'.

The Mary Hill Trust

£5,000

Correspondent: Andrew Duncan, Clerk, 16 The Tything, Worcester WR1 1HD (01905 731731; email: a.duncan@wwf.co.uk)

CC number: 510978

Eligibility

People in need who live within the boundaries of the city of Worcester.

Types of grants

One-off grants according to need.

Annual grant total

In 2016 the trust had an income of £8,300 and a total expenditure of £12,200. We estimate that grants given to individuals totalled around £5,000, with funding also awarded to organisations.

Applications

Apply in writing to the correspondent either through a third party such as a social worker, Citizens Advice or other welfare agency, or directly by the individual. Applications from individuals are considered upon receipt. Applicants should include as many financial details as possible, for example income and weekly outgoings.

The United Charities of St Martin

£3,100

Correspondent: Michael Bunclark, 4 St Catherine's Hill, Worcester WR5 2EA (01905 355585)

CC number: 200733

Eligibility

People in need who live in the parish of St Martin, Worcester.

Types of grants

One-off grants and pensions are given according to need.

Annual grant total

In 2016 the charity had an income of £5,500 and a total expenditure of £6,700. We estimate that welfare grants to individuals totalled around £3,100.

Applications

Apply in writing to the correspondent.

Other information

The charity also supports the maintenance of the parish church of St Martin and St Peter on London Road, Worcester.

Henry and James Willis Trust

£4,500

Correspondent: John Wagstaff, 4 Norton Close, Worcester WR5 3EY (01905 355659; email: secretary@willistrust.org; website: www.willistrust.org)

CC number: 201941

Eligibility

People who are convalescing and live in the city of Worcester.

Types of grants

One-off grants of up to £700 per application, to allow people who have recently been treated in hospital, or who have an ongoing health condition, to rest and recuperate. The grants can also cover the costs for a partner or carer accompanying the individual, if it is necessary.

Annual grant total

In 2015/16 the trust had an income of £8,000 and a total expenditure of £5,000. We estimate that the trust awarded grants totalling £4,500 during the year.

Applications

Application forms can be requested from the correspondent or are available to download from the website.

Worcester City Parish Relief in Need Charity

£7,000

Correspondent: Tim Munslow, St Swithin's Institute, The Trinity, Worcester WR1 2PN (01905 25952; email: worcester.cityparish@btconnect.com)

CC number: 1077788

Eligibility

People in need who reside in Worcester.

Types of grants

One-off grants according to need.

Annual grant total

In 2016 the charity had an income of £7,800 and a total expenditure of £8,000. We estimate that grants totalled £7,000, with some awarded directly to the individual and some given through organisations to provide goods or services.

Applications

Apply in writing to the correspondent.

Worcester Municipal Charities (CIO)

£21,000

Correspondent: Maggie Inglis, Office Manager, Kateryn Heywood House, Berkeley Court, The Foregate, Worcester WR1 3QG (01905 317117; email: admin@wmcharities.org.uk)

CC number: 1166931

Eligibility

People in need living in the city of Worcester. People at risk of homelessness are also a priority.

Types of grants

One-off grants can be considered for essential items like cookers, fridges, fridge freezers, washing machines, clothes airers, food, clothes, fuel bills, carpeting, a television, a vacuum cleaner, other household items; in an exceptional circumstance, help may be considered for passports, holidays or holiday activities.

Annual grant total

In 2016 the charity held assets of £15.8 million and had an income of £16.2 million, which largely came from the consolidation of several charities assets. Grants to individuals totalled £21,000. Grants for white goods are available through the Discretionary Welfare Assistance Scheme and administered in part by the charity. DWAS grants totalled £74,500 during the year. A further £96,500 awarded to organisations and individuals for educational purposes.

Applications

Application forms can be downloaded from the charity's website and returned by email – handwritten forms are not accepted. Applications must be made through a support worker from a statutory or voluntary organisation. Guidance, other sources of support and deadlines are also available on the website.

Other information

This CIO consolidates Worcester's charitable trusts. All the assets and liabilities of the Worcester Municipal Exhibitions Foundation and the Worcester Consolidated Municipal Charity were transferred to this CIO on 30 June 2016. The charity provides accommodation for people in financial need and homeless people as well as making grants to individuals for educational purposes and to charitable organisations. The charity's website provides detailed guidelines on how to apply and other sources of support.

Wychavon

John Martin's Charity

£129,000

Correspondent: John Daniels, The Clerk to the Trustees, 16 Queen's Road, Evesham, Worcester WR11 4JN (01386 765440; email: enquiries@johnmartins. org.uk; website: www.johnmartins.org. uk)

CC number: 527473

Eligibility

People resident in Evesham, Worcestershire, who are in need.

Note: people who are suffering from chronic ill health living in designated parishes close to Evesham may also be able to apply for assistance with the costs of medical aids, equipment, etc. These parishes are listed on the charity's website.

Types of grants

Grants are available for the benefit of children, families, individuals, people who have disabilities and people who are on low incomes or who are in financial difficulty due to a variety of circumstances. Grants are considered for a range of purposes including essential household items, medical and mobility equipment, utility bills, gaps in income payments and school uniforms (for children aged 4 to 18 who live with a parent/guardian in the town).

Heating Award – Pensioners aged 63 and over may also apply for an award towards their heating costs. Criteria may be downloaded from the website and are also advertised throughout the town and in the Evesham Journal in November.

Annual grant total

In 2016/17 the charity had assets of £24 million and an income of £808,500. Grants were made to individuals totalling £396,000 and were distributed as follows:

Promotion of education	£267,500
Relief in need	£118,500
Health and other charitable purposes	£7,500
Religious support	£3,000

Exclusions

Payments are never considered for council tax or fines. The charity cannot replace statutory benefits or supply equipment that is normally available from statutory sources.

Applications

Application forms are available from the correspondent or as a download from the website, where criteria is also posted. Applications can be submitted directly by the individual or through a social worker, Citizens Advice or other welfare agency. All applications are subject to a financial assessment and evidence of income and housing costs must be provided. The charity's office can be contacted to discuss an individual's request and circumstances.

Other information

Grants are also made to organisations and to individuals for educational purposes. The charity has an informative website.

Randolph Meakins Patty's Farm and the Widows Lyes Charity

£2,000

Correspondent: Lesley Houghton, Hollyhocks, Main Street, Cropthorne, Pershore, Worcestershire WR10 3LT (01386 860217)

CC number: 500624

Eligibility

People in need who live in the village of Cropthorne, Worcestershire.

Types of grants

One-off grants based on financial need to cover unexpected costs or relieve hardship.

Annual grant total

In 2016/17 the charity had an income of £26,000 and a total expenditure of £5,000. We estimate that grants given to individuals totalled around £2,000.

Applications

Applications should be submitted directly to the correspondent.

Other information

The charity also makes awards for the advancement of education.

Pershore United Charity

£1,700

Correspondent: Cllr Christopher Parsons, Correspondent, Town Hall, 34 High Street, Pershore, Worcestershire WR10 1DS (01386 561561)

CC number: 200661

Eligibility

People in need who live in private or rented accommodation (not residential or nursing homes) in the parishes of Pershore and Pensham. Priority is given to older people and people in need who have lived in the town for several years.

Types of grants

Recurrent and occasionally one-off grants to help with heating costs at Christmas.

Annual grant total

In 2016/17 the charity had an income of £8,700 and a total expenditure of £3,600. We estimate that grants given to individuals totalled £1,700, with funding also awarded to local organisations.

Applications

Apply in writing to the correspondent. Applications are considered in October.

Wyre Forest

Kidderminster Aid In Sickness Fund

£26,500 (48 grants)

Correspondent: Rachel Summers, Clerk to the Trustees, c/o M. F. G. Solicitors LLP, Adam House, Birmingham Road, Kidderminster DY10 2SH (01562 820181; email: rachel.summers@ mfgsolicitors.com; website: kaisf.org.uk)

CC number: 210586

Eligibility

People who are sick, convalescent, or in need of rest or domestic help, are in financial need, and live in the borough of Kidderminster.

Types of grants

One-off grants typically ranging between £100 and £2,000 towards, for example, fuel expenses, equipment, furniture, beds and bedding.

Annual grant total

In 2016 the fund held assets of £508,500 and had an income of £64,000. Grants to individuals totalled £26,500. The trustees' report noted the following:

> 63 applications for assistance were considered during the year in question compared with 41 the previous year. Of those 63, 12 had to be rejected for various reasons; 4 never proceeded with their application; 48 grants, including 1 deferred from the previous year, were paid to individuals and averaged £556, the amounts varying between £69 and £2,550.

Exclusions

Applications from the wider Wyre Forest area cannot be considered. The fund cannot help with debt problems.

Applications

Application forms are available to download from the fund's website or hard copies can be obtained from the correspondent. Application forms must be accompanied by a covering letter and as much supporting information as possible and can be considered at any time.

East of England

General

Harry Cureton Charitable Trust

£14,700

Correspondent: Jane Darlington, Chief Executive Officer, c/o Cambridgeshire Community Foundation, Hangar One, The Airport, Newmarket Road, Cambridge CB5 8TG (01223 410535; email: hcct@cambscf.org.uk; website: www.cambscf.org.uk/the-harry-cureton-charitable-trust.html)

CC number: 1106206

Eligibility

People who have medical needs living in Peterborough and the areas of Cambridgeshire, Lincolnshire and Northamptonshire covered by Peterborough and Stamford hospitals.

Types of grants

Grants, generally of up to £20,000, are given towards pieces of medical equipment and small home adaptations. Examples of previous grants described on the website include: a comfort care chair for an individual with cerebral palsy; a specialist seating armchair for an individual with dementia; and a Theraplay tricycle for an individual with Down's syndrome. The trustees may consider applications for larger amounts providing the applicant can demonstrate a justifiable need.

Annual grant total

In 2015/16 the trust had assets of £3.8 million and an income of £91,000. Grants to individuals totalled £14,700, with a further £61,500 awarded to organisations carrying out healthcare activities.

Exclusions

Grants are not made: where the activity could be paid for by a surgery, the NHS or another source; where the grant will result in financial benefit of a person or group of people (e.g. improvements or alterations to a property); or to cover expenditure already incurred.

Applications

Application forms are available from the website. They should be submitted on behalf of the individual by an occupational therapist or other medical professional who has knowledge of the individual's overall health and financial situation. Applications are considered in October and March and should be received by the grants team by 1 September and 1 February respectively.

Other information

The trust is administered by Cambridgeshire Community Foundation.

The Hunstanton Convalescent Trust

£9,000

Correspondent: Fay Wilby, Trustee, 66 Collingwood Road, Hunstanton PE36 5DY (01485 533788; email: faywilby@msn.com)

CC number: 218979

Eligibility

People who are on a low income, physically or mentally unwell and in need of a convalescent or recuperative holiday, with a preference for those living in Norfolk, Cambridgeshire and Suffolk.

Types of grants

Grants are given to provide or assist towards the expenses of recuperative holidays, including for carers. The trust can sometimes provide other items, services or facilities which will help the individual's recovery.

Annual grant total

In 2015/16 the charity had an income of £1,100 and a total expenditure of £9,200. We estimate that the charity gave around £9,000 in grants to individuals.

Applications

Apply on a form available from the correspondent, through a social worker, GP or other welfare/medical professionals. Applications should be submitted at least one month before the proposed holiday. The full board of trustees usually meets in January, June and September.

Cambridge-shire

Cambridgeshire Community Foundation

£45,500

Correspondent: Jane Darlington, Hangar One, The Airport, Newmarket Road, Cambridge CB5 8TG (01223 410535; email: info@cambscf.org.uk; website: www.cambscf.org.uk)

CC number: 1103314

Eligibility

To be eligible for the Stay Well (Warm Homes) grant for heating costs, applicants must be in financial need, suffering from fuel poverty, and live in the Cambridgeshire area. For heating repairs/improvements, applicants must reside in Cambridgeshire, be aged 65 or over, or have a disability – referrals for this scheme must go through Age UK.

To be eligible for the Harry Curedon Charitable Trust fund, individuals must have a health condition or disability which requires additional medical aids or equipment, and must have an occupational therapist or other medical professional with knowledge of the medical and financial situation who can make the application on the individual's behalf.

Types of grants

The Stay Well (Warm Homes) fund provides grants of up to £300 to assist with heating costs and relieve fuel poverty. They also provide grants of up to £300 to cover small repairs or improvements to homes with a view to increase energy efficiency.

The Harry Curedon Charitable Trust provides grants to purchase specialist medical and disability equipment, for example care chairs for patients with cerebral palsy.

Annual grant total

In 2016/17 the foundation had assets of £6.8 million and an income of £2 million. During the year, a total of £45,500 was awarded in grants to individuals.

Exclusions

Grants cannot be made towards debts.

Applications

To apply for the Stay Well (Warm Homes) fund, download the application form from the website, to be completed by a professional or social agency such as Citizens Advice or Age UK. All applicants must be referred through a third party service.

To apply to the Harry Curedon Charitable Trust, download a form from the website. Applications must be made by an occupational therapist or other health/medical professional who has knowledge of the applicant's overall health and financial position.

Other information

The main focus of the foundation is to make grants to other organisations to ensure that they can continue to provide services to individuals in need in Cambridgeshire.

In 2016/17 the foundation awarded £1.7 million in grants to organisations.

Thomas Parson's Charity

£100 (one grant)

Correspondent: The Clerk, Hall Ennion & Young, 8 High Street, Ely, Cambridgeshire CB7 4JY (01353 662918; email: john@heysolicitors.co.uk; website: www.thomasparsonscharity.org.uk)

CC number: 202634

Eligibility

People over 50 years old, who are not in employment and live in Ely.

Types of grants

One-off and occasionally recurrent grants to relieve financial hardship and towards medical needs.

Annual grant total

In 2015/16 the charity had a total income of £299,500 and a total expenditure of £197,500. During the year, the charity awarded £100 to one individual.

Applications

Apply in writing to the correspondent. Applications can be submitted either directly by the individual, or through a social worker, Citizens Advice or other welfare agency. Applicants should

include as much detail about their financial situation and their need for the grant as is possible. Applications are considered monthly.

Other information

The charity's primary activity is the management of its 27 almshouses in Ely, more details of which are available on the website.

The Foundation of Edward Storey
See entry on page 167

City of Cambridge

Cambridge Community Nursing Trust

£4,000

Correspondent: Jan Croft, Trustee, 38 Station Road, Whittlesford, Cambridge CB22 4NL (01223 835412; email: enquiries@ cambridgecommunitynursingtrust.co.uk; website: www. cambridgecommunitynursingtrust.co.uk)

CC number: 204933

Eligibility

People in need who live in the boundaries of the city of Cambridge.

Types of grants

Grants are given to provide extra care, comforts and special aids which are not available from any other source.

Annual grant total

In 2016 the trust had an income of £16,900 and a total expenditure of £5,000. We have estimated that grants to individuals totalled £4,000 during the year.

Exclusions

Grants are not made retrospectively or to assist with debts.

Applications

Applications should be made by a professional on behalf of the individual, using the referral form on the trust's website. The receipt of applications will be acknowledged as soon as possible. The trustees meet regularly throughout the year and may consider applications between meetings to enable a swift response. The correspondent is happy to speak to potential applicants over the telephone before an application is submitted.

The Charities of Nicholas Swallow and Others

£1,200

Correspondent: Nicholas Tufton, Clerk, 11 High Street, Barkway, Royston SG8 8EA (01763 848888; email: nicholas@ntufton.co.uk)

CC number: 203222

Eligibility

People in need who live in the parish of Whittlesford (near Cambridge) and the adjacent area.

Types of grants

One-off cash grants at Christmas. Help can also be given towards hospital travel and educational costs.

Annual grant total

In 2016/17 the charity had assets of £846,000 and an income of £84,000. We estimate that welfare grants to individuals totalled around £1,200.

Applications

Individuals can apply in writing directly to the correspondent.

Other information

The principal activity of this charity is as a housing association managing bungalows and garages.

City of Peterborough

The Florence Saunders Relief-in-Sickness Charity

£2,200

Correspondent: Paula Lawson, 36 Tyndall Court, Commerce Road, Peterborough PE2 6LR (01733 343275; email: paula.lawson@stephensonsmart. com)

CC number: 239177

Eligibility

People in need who are in poor health, convalescent, or who have disabilities and live in the former city of Peterborough.

Types of grants

One-off grants typically range between £100 and £500, and have been awarded to assist with hospital expenses, convalescence, holidays, travel expenses, electrical goods, medical equipment, furniture, disability equipment and help in the home.

Annual grant total

In 2015/16 the charity had an income of £7,500 and a total expenditure of £5,600. We estimate that the charity awarded £2,200 in grants to individuals during the year.

Exclusions

No grants are given for the repayment of debts.

Applications

Applications should be made in writing directly to the correspondent, by the individual or a healthcare professional/social worker.

Other information

The charity also makes grants to organisations.

East Cambridgeshire

Swaffham Bulbeck Relief-in-Need Charity

£4,500

Correspondent: Cheryl Ling, 43 High Street, Swaffham Bulbeck, Cambridge CB25 0HP (01223 813885)

CC number: 238177

Eligibility

People in need who live in the parish of Swaffham Bulbeck.

Types of grants

One-off and annual grants.

Annual grant total

In 2015/16 the charity had an income of £9,700 and a total expenditure of £9,300. We estimate that the charity gave around £4,500 in grants to individuals.

The charity also awards grants to organisations.

Applications

Apply in writing to the correspondent.

Other information

At the time of writing (September 2017) the charity had no website or accounts available.

Fenland

Chatteris Feoffee Charity

£3,000

Correspondent: Brian Hawden, The Coach House, Beechwood Gardens, Chatteris, Cambridgeshire PE16 6PX (01354 692133; email: b.hawden@sky.com)

CC number: 202150

Eligibility

People in financial hardship who live in Chatteris.

Types of grants

One-off and recurrent grants are given according to need.

Annual grant total

In 2016/17 the charity had an income of £6,000 and a total expenditure of £6,000. We estimate the amount awarded in grants to be around £3,000.

Applications

Applications can be made in writing to the correspondent, or grant recipients may be identified by a trustee.

Other information

The charity also gives grants to local organisations.

The Leverington Town Lands Charity

£24,500

Correspondent: R. Gagen, Clerk to the Trustees, 78 High Road, Gorefield, Wisbech, Cambridgeshire PE13 4NB (01945 870454; email: levfeoffees@aol.com)

CC number: 232526

Eligibility

People in need who live in the parishes of Leverington, Gorefield and Newton.

Types of grants

One-off grants.

Annual grant total

In 2015/16 the charity had a total income of £46,000 and a total expenditure of £43,000. The charity awarded grants to individuals totalling £24,500. Of this amount, 220 grants were distributed through the charity's Charlton's Dole fund which supports older people in the area.

Applications

Application forms are available from the correspondent. Applications are considered in May and November.

Upwell (Cambridge) Consolidated Charities

£5,000

Correspondent: Nicholas Poolely, 19 Fridaybridge Road, Elm, Wisbech PE14 0AS (01945 860902; email: yeloopelm@hotmail.co.uk)

CC number: 203558

Eligibility

Older people who are in need and live in the parish of Upwell (on the Isle of Ely) and have done so for at least five years.

Types of grants

Grants, which in previous years have ranged between £10 to £40, are given at Christmas.

Annual grant total

In 2016 the charity had an income of £6,500 and a total expenditure of £5,200. We estimate that grants given to individuals totalled £5,000.

Applications

Apply in writing to the correspondent. Applications should be submitted directly by the individual and are considered in November.

Elizabeth Wright's Charity

£13,200

Correspondent: Dr Iain Mason, Trustee, 13 Tavistock Road, Wisbech, Cambridgeshire PE13 2DY (01945 588646; email: i.h.mason60@gmail.com)

CC number: 203896

Eligibility

People who live in the parish of Wisbech St Peter, Cambridgeshire.

Types of grants

One-off grants for essential items to offset hardship or cope with long-term illness.

Annual grant total

In 2015 the charity had assets of over £1.3 million and an income of £41,000. During the year, the charity awarded a total of £33,000 in grants; of this amount £13,200 was given to individuals for welfare purposes.

Applications

Applications can be made in writing to the correspondent. They can be submitted directly by the individual at any time. The trustees usually meet quarterly.

Other information

The charity also awards grants to organisations.

The charity tends to direct their funds towards young people and children from disadvantaged backgrounds.

Huntingdonshire

Huntingdon Freemen's Trust

£156,000

Correspondent: Karen Clark, Grants Officer, 37 High Street, Huntingdon, Cambridgeshire PE29 3AQ (01480 414909; email: info@huntingdonfreemen.org.uk; website: www.huntingdonfreemen.org.uk)

CC number: 1044573

Eligibility

People in need resident in Huntingdon (normally for at least one year but exceptions are sometimes made depending on circumstances).

Types of grants

The trust's website stated: 'We will consider grants for a variety of purposes including help with essential household items, medical and mobility equipment and adaptations.'

Annual grant total

In 2015/16 the trust had assets of £15.8 million and an income of £425,000. Welfare grants to individuals totalled £156,000.

Exclusions

The trust cannot substitute services that should be provided by the state but may supplement them. Relief-in-need support is not normally the payment of rent, council tax, debts, fines or funerals.

Applications

Apply in writing to the correspondent. Applicants should send their name, contact details and a brief description of the type of help required. Most applications will require the visit of an officer who will assess your needs and financial circumstances. Applications are assessed at monthly meetings.

Other information

The trust's website notes that applications are only considered 'from individuals, groups and organisations who live or are based within the area covered by Huntingdon Town Council, including Oxmoor, Hartford, Sapley, Stukeley Meadows and Hinchingbrooke Park'.

South Cambridgeshire

The Samuel Franklin Fund Elsworth

£20,000

Correspondent: Serena Wyer, 5 Cowdell End, Elsworth, Cambridge CB23 4GB (01954 267156; email: serena.wyersff@gmail.com; website: www.samuelfranklinfund.co.uk)

CC number: 228775

Eligibility

People who live in the parish of Elsworth and suffer from poverty, hardship or illness. Preference is given to older people and people with a disability.

Types of grants

Grants are made to individuals as: goodwill gestures on Trinity Sunday and at Christmas; for household needs, mobility equipment; and in appropriate cases, for funeral expenses.

Annual grant total

In 2016 the fund had assets of £112,500 and an income of £30,000. The amount awarded in grants to individuals in need was just over £20,000.

Applications

In the first instance, applicants should contact the charity by telephone or email.

Other information

Grants are also made to individuals entering work and to local organisations active in the parish. During this financial year, grants awarded to organisations totalled almost £23,000.

Thomas Galon's Charity

£3,500

Correspondent: Linda Miller, Clerk, 21 Thistle Green, Swavesey, Cambridge CB24 4RJ (01954 202982; email: thomasgaloncharity@swavesey.org.uk; website: www.swavesey.org.uk/thomas-galon-charity)

CC number: 202515

Eligibility

People in need who live in the parish of Swavesey. Preference is given to those who are over 70, single or widowed; married couples when one partner reaches 70; and widows and widowers with dependent children up to 18 years old.

Types of grants

One grant per household through the annual Energy Grant Scheme to provide a payment towards winter heating costs. Grants can also be made for educational or medical-related items or activities.

Annual grant total

In 2016 the charity had an income of £7,500 and a total expenditure of £7,900. We estimate that grants given to individuals totalled £3,500, with funding also awarded to local organisations.

Applications

Application forms can be downloaded from the website. Applications for the Energy Grant Scheme should reach the trustees before 30 September for consideration in November.

Girton Town Charity

£9,300

Correspondent: Dr Charles Hiley, 1 Fairway, Girton, Cambridge CB3 0QF (01223 277296; email: gtc@girtontowncharity.co.uk; website: www.girtontowncharity.co.uk)

CC number: 1130272

Eligibility

Individuals in need living in Girton.

Types of grants

One-off grants according to need. During the year, grants were made for nursery provision, walk-in showers and dismantling tasks such as sheds, clearance and removal.

Annual grant total

In 2015/16 the charity had assets of £30.7 million and an income of £962,000. Welfare grants to individuals totalled £9,300.

Applications

Apply in writing to the correspondent.

John Huntingdon's Charity

£8,400

Correspondent: Jill Hayden, Charity Manager, John Huntingdon House, Tannery Road, Sawston, Cambridge CB2 3UW (01223 830599; email: office@johnhuntingdon.org.uk; website: www.johnhuntingdon.org.uk)

CC number: 1118574

Eligibility

People in need who live in the parish of Sawston in Cambridgeshire.

Types of grants

Grants can be given for essential household items such as cookers, washing machines or beds. Assistance is also given towards school uniforms, school trips and, sometimes, nursery or playgroup fees.

Annual grant total

In 2016 the charity had assets of £16.4 million and an income of £394,000. We estimate that welfare grants to individuals totalled £8,400.

Applications

In the first instance, call the charity's office to arrange an appointment with one of its support workers.

Other information

The charity is proactive in supporting the community in Sawston and documents its activities in its informative annual report. Among its activities, the charity provides advice and housing services, sometimes in partnership with other local organisations. More details are available on the website or by contacting the charity's office.

Ickleton United Charities

£6,000

Correspondent: John Statham, Trustee, 35 Abbey Street, Ickleton, Saffron Walden CB10 1SS (01799 530258)

CC number: 202467

Eligibility

People in need who live in the parish of Ickleton, Cambridgeshire.

Types of grants

One-off grants towards fuel costs and necessities, and gift vouchers at Christmas. The charity often pays for Lifeline alarms for those who require them.

Annual grant total

In 2016 the charity had an income of £12,000 and a total expenditure of £6,300. We estimate that grants given to individuals totalled £6,000.

Applications

Apply in writing to the correspondent. Applications should be submitted directly by the individual.

Other information

Some of the charities in Ickleton date back to the Middle Ages; a fact given away by names such as Town House, Lettice Martin's Bequest and The Charity of Richard Swan. When they were amalgamated in 1970, the organisations were arranged into two separate funds: The Relief in Need charity, which makes grants; and The Gertrude Homes Charity, which runs three almshouses for people with close associations with the village.

Pampisford Relief-in-Need Charity

£3,000

Correspondent: Dennis Beaumont, 4 Hammond Close, Pampisford, Cambridge CB22 3EP (01223 833653)

CC number: 275661

Eligibility

People in need who live in the parish of Pampisford, particularly children and young people, older people and individuals who have a disability. In exceptional circumstances support may be given to otherwise eligible candidates who live immediately outside the parish.

Types of grants

Christmas gifts or small individual grants and services or other specific requirements. Contributions are also made for the improvement of village amenities, which can then be enjoyed by the parishioners, particularly older people, young people and people with disabilities.

Annual grant total

In 2016 the charity had an income of £15,600 and a total expenditure of £14,900. Our previous research indicates that around £3,000 is available for individuals each year.

The charity also supports organisations.

Applications

Apply in writing to the correspondent. Applications can be made directly by the individual at any time.

Lincolnshire

Committee for Kesteven Children in Need (KCIN)

£12,000

Correspondent: Alexandra Howard, Nocton Rise, Lincoln LN4 2AF (01522 791217; email: enquiries@kcin.org; website: www.kcin.org)

CC number: 700008

Eligibility

Children/young people up to the age of 16 who live in Kesteven (Lincolnshire) and are in need.

Types of grants

One-off and recurrent grants of up to £500. Examples of previous grants include clothing, educational holidays, days out, prams/pushchairs, beds/sheets, fireguards, second-hand washing machines, educational toys and playschool fees.

Annual grant total

In 2016 the charity had an income of £11,000 and a total expenditure of £23,500. We estimate that grants given to individuals totalled around £12,000.

Applications

The charity acts purely on referrals from professionals such as social workers, health visitors, teachers and education officers and similar. Applications should include the family situation, the age of the child and his/her special needs. Applications are considered throughout the year.

Other information

The charity also makes grants for children struggling to access education.

The Hesslewood Children's Trust (Hull Seamen's and General Orphanage)

See entry on page 411

Edward Hunstone

£5,400 (16 grants)

Correspondent: Tony Bradley, 58 Eastwood Road, Boston, Lincolnshire PE21 0PH (01205 364175)

CC number: 214570

Eligibility

Older gentlemen and those with disabilities who are in need and live in Lincolnshire.

There is a preference for descendants of: Edward Hunstone; the Gedneys of Bagarderly, Lincolnshire; Robert Smith of Saltfleetby, Lincolnshire; or the Woodliffes of Toft Grange, Lincolnshire.

The trustees also have a particular interest in helping retired clergymen, members of HM Forces, farmers and farm labourers.

Types of grants

Recipients receive £325 per year, paid in two instalments of £162.50 in April and October. The assistance will be given as long as the trustees consider necessary or until the death of the recipient.

Annual grant total

In 2016 the charity had an income of £30,500 and a total expenditure of £23,000. Grants to 16 beneficiaries totalled £5,400 during the year.

Exclusions

Grants are not given to women.

Applications

Application forms are available from the correspondent. They can be submitted directly by the individual or through a social worker, Citizens Advice or other welfare agency. Appeals are considered in May each year and should be received by 30 April; urgent applications can be considered at other times. Two references are required with each application.

The Lincoln General Dispensary Fund

£6,500

Correspondent: Michael Bonass, Administrator, Durrus, Scothern Lane, Dunholme, Lincoln LN2 3QP (01673 860660)

CC number: 220159

Eligibility

People who are in poor health, convalescent or who have disabilities and live within the 10-mile radius of the Stonebow (Lincoln).

Types of grants

One-off grants of up to around £250 to alleviate suffering or aid recovery. Our research tells us that past grants have been given for orthopaedic beds, alarm systems and recuperative holidays.

Annual grant total

In 2016 the fund had an income of £9,800 and a total expenditure of £12,200. We estimate that grants given to individuals totalled £6,500. Funding was also given to local organisations.

Exclusions

No grants are given for building adaptations, debts already incurred or anything that could be provided by public funds.

Applications

Our previous research indicates application forms are available from the correspondent and should be submitted through a recognised social or medical agency. Applications are considered throughout the year.

Lincolnshire Community Foundation

£9,400

Correspondent: Sue Fortune, Grants Director, 4 Mill House, Moneys Yard, Carre Street, Sleaford, Lincolnshire NG34 7TW (01529 305825; email: lincolnshirecf@btconnect.com; website: www.lincolnshirecf.co.uk)

CC number: 1092328

Eligibility

Generally, residents of Lincolnshire who are in need; however, different funds have different eligibility criteria attached. See types of grants section.

Types of grants

The type and amount of grant available depends on the fund being applied to. See the foundation's website for more information on open funds.

Annual grant total

In 2016/17 the foundation had assets of £5.64 million and an income of £945,000. Grants totalled £902,500 and we believe the vast majority were given to organisations. We estimate that grants given to individuals for social welfare purposes totalled around £9,400, awarded through The Colin Batts Family Trust.

Exclusions

Grants cannot be awarded retrospectively.

Applications

See the foundation's website for more information on the funds it operates and how to apply for assistance.

Lincolnshire Police Charitable Fund

£14,000

Correspondent: Amanda Watson, Correspondent, c/o Police Federation Office, Lincolnshire Police Headquarters, Nettleham, Lincoln LN2 2LT (01522 558303; email: charitable.fund@lincs.pnn.police.uk)

CC number: 500682

Eligibility

People in need who are present or former employees of Lincolnshire Police Authority, and their dependants. Former employees of other police authorities who have retired and now live in Lincolnshire may also qualify for assistance.

Types of grants

One-off grants according to need.

Annual grant total

In 2015/16 the fund held assets of £168,000 and had an income of £27,500. Grants to individuals totalled £14,000. A further £1,000 was awarded in grants to organisations.

Applications

Application forms are available from the Welfare Officer. Applications can be submitted directly by the individual or, where applicable, through a social worker, Citizens Advice or other welfare agency.

Other information

The charity awarded around £4,000 in loans to individuals who were experiencing hardship.

Boston

Charity of Thomas Cowley Exclusive of the Cowley Education

£5,500

Correspondent: Sue Hentley, Holmes House, Kyme Road, Heckington Fen, Sleaford NG34 9NA (email: sue.hentley@hotmail.co.uk)

CC number: 249415

Eligibility

People in need living in the parish of Swinehead.

Types of grants

One-off grants according to need.

Annual grant total

In 2016/17 the charity had an income of £10,800 and a total expenditure of £12,000. We estimate that grants given to individuals totalled around £5,500.

Applications

Apply in writing to the correspondent.

Frampton Charities

£4,500

Correspondent: Mark Hildred, Moore Thompson, Bank House, Broad Street, Spalding PE11 1TB (01775 711333)

CC number: 216849

Eligibility

People in need who have lived in the ancient parish of Frampton for at least five years. Preference is usually given to older people (aged over 65) and recently bereaved widows and their children.

Types of grants

One-off grants according to need.

Annual grant total

In 2015/16 the charity had an income of £9,400 and a total expenditure of £10,100. We have estimated that welfare grants to individuals totalled £4,500, with funding also awarded to local organisations.

Applications

Apply in writing to the correspondent. Applications are normally considered in October.

Sutterton Parochial Charity Trust

£5,500

Correspondent: Deirdre McCumiskey, 6 Hillside Gardens, Wittering, Peterborough PE8 6DX (01780 782668; email: deirdre.mccumiskey@tesco.net)

CC number: 234839

Eligibility

People in need who live in the parishes of Sutterton and Amber Hill. There is some preference to award grants that will help children or older people.

Types of grants

One-off grants to relieve financial need, for example to help with repair costs or to purchase new furniture.

Annual grant total

In 2016/17 the trust had an income of £14,000 and a total expenditure of £12,000. We estimate that the trust awarded £5,500 in grants to individuals during the year.

Applications

Applications should be made in writing to the correspondent and should include financial details and what the grant will be used for.

Other information

The trust also makes awards to organisations.

The Swineshead Poor Charities

£16,400

Correspondent: Lynne Richardson, Home Farm, Tumby Moorside, Boston PE22 7ST (01205 343627; email: lynne@hmtg.co.uk)

CC number: 216557

Eligibility

People in need who live in the parish of Swineshead.

Types of grants

One-off and recurrent grants are given according to need.

Annual grant total

In 2016/17 the charity had assets of £1.45 million and an income of £32,000. Monthly pension contributions were distributed to 15 individuals, totalling almost £8,000. Grants to other individuals amounted to £8,500.

A further £13,800 was awarded to organisations.

Applications

Apply in writing to the correspondent.

East Lindsey

Addlethorpe Parochial Charity (commonly known as Mottrams Charity)

£5,000

Correspondent: Maggie Boughton, Clerk, The Willows, Mill Lane, Addlethorpe, Skegness, Lincolnshire PE24 4TB (01754 760644; email: addlethorpeparishcouncil@gmail.com)

CC number: 251412

Eligibility

People who are sick, convalescent, infirm or who have a disability, and live in the parish of Addlethorpe, or who have previously lived in Addlethorpe and now live in an adjoining parish.

Types of grants

Support is given on an annual basis to assist with heating costs. One-off grants are given towards funeral expenses, household repairs and other necessities. Grants have also been given for hospital or doctor's visits.

Annual grant total

In 2015/16 the charity had an income of £4,800 and a total expenditure of £6,900. We estimate that grants given to individuals totalled £5,000.

Applications

Apply in writing to the correspondent. Applications can be submitted either directly by the individual or a family member, through a third party such as a social worker, or through an organisation such as Citizens Advice or other welfare agency.

Kitchings General Charity

£15,800

Correspondent: J. Smith, 42 Abbey Road, Bardney, Lincoln LN3 5XA (01526 398505)

CC number: 219957

Eligibility

People in need who live in the parish of Bardney, Southrey, Tupholme and Bucknall.

Types of grants

One-off grants are available to relieve hardship or distress and may include holidays/respite care for people with disabilities (mostly at a special home at Sandringham), specialised nursing equipment, including wheelchairs, funeral expenses and household essentials, such as carpets, flooring and bedding. Grants are usually in the range of £200 to £500 but can be of up to £2,000.

Pensions are available to eligible widows of Southrey (£10 per week).

Annual grant total

In 2016 the charity had assets of £6,700 and an income of £42,500. Widows pensions totalled £2,300 and we estimate that welfare grants totalled around £13,500.

Applications

Applications may be made in writing to the correspondent and should include some basic background details about the applicant and the nature of need. Our research indicates that applications are normally considered in May, October and January.

Other information

Grants are also given to local schools and organisations, and to individuals for educational purposes.

The Spilsby Poor Lands Charity

£1,250

Correspondent: J. Tong, Clerk, Rosedale Lodge, Ashby Road, Spilsby, Lincolnshire PE23 5DW (01790 752885)

CC number: 220613

Eligibility

People of retirement age in need who have lived in Spilsby for at least five years.

Types of grants

Our previous research indicates that one-off grants are made twice a year.

Annual grant total

In 2016 the charity had an income of £2,800 and a total expenditure of £2,700. We estimate that the charity awarded around £1,250 in grants to individuals for welfare purposes.

Applications

Our previous research indicates that applicants must apply on a form available from the correspondent. Applications must be submitted directly by the individual and are considered in June and December. Applicants must state how long they have lived in Spilsby.

Other information

At the time of writing (August 2017) the charity had no website or accounts available.

The Stickford Relief-in-Need Charity

£8,000

Correspondent: Katherine Bunting, 28 Wide Bargate, Boston, Lincolnshire PE21 6RT (01205 351114)

CC number: 247423

Eligibility
People in need who live in the parish of Stickford.

Types of grants
One-off and recurrent grants for relief-in-need purposes, towards school uniforms, and bonuses at Christmas.

Annual grant total
In 2015 the charity had an income of £17,100 and a total expenditure of £17,600. We estimate that welfare grants to individuals totalled around £8,000.

Applications
Applications can be made in writing to the correspondent. They should be submitted directly by the individual and are considered all year.

Lincoln

The Lincoln Municipal Relief-in-Need Charities

£37,500

Correspondent: M. Bonass, Clerk, Durrus, Scothern Lane, Dunholme, Lincoln LN2 3QP (01673 860660; email: m.bonass213@btinternet.com)

CC number: 213651

Eligibility
People in need who live in the city of Lincoln.

Types of grants
One-off grants of up to £500 each according to need.

Annual grant total
In 2015/16 the trust held assets of £803,000 and had an income of £43,000. Grants to individuals totalled around £37,500 and were distributed as follows:

Various individuals	£35,500
Quarterly payments	£2,100

Exclusions
No grants which will relieve public funds, contribute to the fabric of buildings or towards debts that have already been incurred. No recurrent grants.

Applications
Applications are generally only accepted through recognised social or medical agencies and are considered at any time. Requests for more than £500 must be approved at a quarterly trustees' meeting.

Other information
Grants are occasionally made to organisations.

North East Lincolnshire

Sir Alec Black's Charity

£5,900 (ten grants)

Correspondent: The Trustees, Wilson Sharpe & Co., 27 Osborne Street, Grimsby, North East Lincolnshire DN31 1NU (01472 348315; email: sabc@wilsonsharpe.co.uk)

CC number: 220295

Eligibility
Fishermen and dockworkers who are sick and poor, who live in the borough of Grimsby. Grants are also available to people employed by Sir Alec Black during his lifetime.

Types of grants
One-off and recurrent grants are given according to need.

Annual grant total
In 2015/16 the charity held assets of £1.8 million and had an income of £89,500. Grants to ten fishermen and dockworkers totalled £5,900 and grants to 25 charitable organisations totalled £43,000.

Applications
Apply in writing to the correspondent.

Other information
The charity also provides bed linen to hospices and other charitable organisations.

Grimsby Sailors and Fishing Charity

£20,500

Correspondent: Graham Johnston, Charities Administrator, 1st Floor, 23 Bargate, Grimsby DN34 4SS (01472 347914; email: grahamjohnston.gsfc@gmail.com)

CC number: 500816

Eligibility
Primarily the children of deceased Grimsby fishermen. However, help may also be available to other beneficiaries living in Grimsby and the surrounding area, at the trustees' discretion.

Types of grants
Weekly and quarterly grants to support children of deceased fishermen while they are still in full-time education.

Annual grant total
In 2016 the charity held assets of £5 million and had an income of £527,000. The majority of the charity's expenditure is spent on providing and maintaining almshouses. Individuals received £20,500 during the year.

Applications
Apply on a form available from the correspondent or from the Port Missioner. Applications should be submitted directly by the individual or through an appropriate welfare agency. They are considered when received.

North Kesteven

The Navenby Town's Farm Trust

£4,000

Correspondent: Leonard Coffey, 17 North Lane, Navenby, Lincoln LN5 0EH (01522 810273)

CC number: 245223

Eligibility
People in need who live in the village of Navenby.

Types of grants
One-off grants according to need.

Annual grant total
In 2016/17 the trust had an income of £19,900 and a total expenditure of £16,400. Grants are made to individuals and organisations for both social welfare and educational purposes. We estimate that welfare grants to individuals totalled £4,000.

Exclusions
No grants can be given to individuals resident outside the village.

Applications
Apply using a form available from the correspondent, the village post office, or the local newsagents. Applications are considered in September. Urgent applications may occasionally be considered at other times. Unsolicited applications are not responded to.

North Lincolnshire

Barton-upon-Humber Relief in Sickness Fund

£1,100

Correspondent: Harold Keith Ready, Market Place, Barton-upon-Humber, North Lincolnshire DN18 5DD (01652 632215; email: mail@keithready.co.uk)

CC number: 504255

Eligibility

People living in Barton-upon-Humber who are suffering from ill health or who have a disability. Where appropriate, their relatives/carers can also be assisted.

Types of grants

Grants can be awarded for a wide range of needs, but are usually given for medical aids and equipment.

Annual grant total

In 2015/16 the charity had an income of £3,200 and a total expenditure of £1,300. We estimate that grants given to individuals totalled around £1,100.

Applications

Apply in writing to the correspondent. Our research suggests that trustees discuss cases which are known personally to them, although written applications are equally welcomed and are considered when received.

Beeton, Barrick and Beck Relief-in-Need Charity

£5,000

Correspondent: A. Lawe, Barrow Wold Farm, Deepdale, Barton-upon-Humber, North Lincolnshire DN18 6ED (01469 531928)

CC number: 234571

Eligibility

People in need who are over 60 and live in the parish of Barrow-upon-Humber.

Types of grants

Christmas vouchers and one-off grants.

Annual grant total

In 2015/16 the charity had an income of £4,500 and a total expenditure of £5,600. We estimate that grants given to individuals totalled £5,000.

Applications

Application forms are available from the correspondent.

Blue Coat Charity

£28,500

Correspondent: The Trustees, c/o Keith Ready & Co., Market Place, Barton-upon-Humber, North Lincolnshire DN18 5DD (01652 632215)

CC number: 237891

Eligibility

People in need who live in Barton-upon-Humber.

Types of grants

One-off grants, usually in the form of vouchers which can be spent locally to contribute towards the purchase of footwear, clothing, school uniforms, bedding, food and other essential items.

Annual grant total

In 2015/16 the charity held assets of £789,000 and had an income of £30,000. Grants were made to individuals totalling £28,500.

Applications

Apply in writing to the correspondent.

Other information

The charity is also known as the Charity of John Tripp.

South Holland

The Moulton Poors' Lands Charity

£8,200

Correspondent: Richard Lewis, Maples & Son Solicitors, 23 New Road, Spalding, Lincolnshire PE11 1DH (01775 722261)

CC number: 216630

Eligibility

People in need, generally older people, who live in Moulton village and the surrounding areas (near Spalding in Lincolnshire).

Types of grants

Grants can be paid in cash or in kind. Relief-in-need grants are generally paid following a severe accident, unexpected loss or misfortune. The charity can provide bereavement grants and pension credits, among other needs.

Annual grant total

In 2016 the charity had assets of £935,000 and an income of £42,000. Welfare grants to individuals totalled £8,200.

Applications

Applications may be made in writing to the correspondent, usually through a trustee. Appeals are normally considered in April and December.

Other information

The charity also manages almshouses, the rent from which makes up a small part of its income.

Spalding Relief-in-Need Charity

£15,000

Correspondent: R. Knipe, Clerk and Solicitor, Dembleby House, 12 Broad Street, Spalding, Lincolnshire PE11 1ES (01775 768774; email: patrick.skells@chattertons.com)

CC number: 229268

Eligibility

People in need who live in the area covered by the district of South Holland. Preference is given to residents of the urban district of Spalding and the parishes of Cowbit, Deeping St Nicholas, Pinchbeck and Weston.

Types of grants

Support is given towards various items, services and facilities, including awards for furniture and domestic appliances, rent arrears and other debts, children's clothing and so on. Residents of the almshouses can be helped with the cost of TV licences.

Annual grant total

In 2016 the charity had an income of £51,000 and a total expenditure of £33,000. We estimate that grants given to individuals for welfare purposes totalled £15,000.

Exclusions

Grants are not intended to be made where support can be obtained from statutory sources.

Applications

Application forms can be requested from the charity. They can be submitted directly by the individual or assisted by a social worker, Citizens Advice or other welfare agency, if applicable. Grants are considered fortnightly. Payments are normally paid directly to suppliers.

Other information

This charity is connected with the Spalding Almshouse Charity (Charity Commission no. 220077) and shares the same body of administration, the Spalding Town Husbands.

The Surfleet United Charities

£2,800

Correspondent: Leanne Barlow, Clerk, Penryn, Northgate, Pinchbeck, Spalding PE11 3TB (email: leannebarlow100@ hotmail.co.uk)

CC number: 215260

Eligibility

Older people who are in need and have lived in the parish of Surfleet for over ten years (exceptions will be made on the age restriction in cases of extreme need).

Types of grants

Grants are normally given in the form of annual Christmas gifts of £15 (individuals) and £25 (couples). Other one-off grants are awarded according to need.

Annual grant total

In 2016 the charity had assets of £133,500 and an income of £70,500. Grants to individuals totalled almost £2,800.

Applications

Apply in writing to the correspondent. Applications can be submitted directly by the individual and are normally considered in November.

Other information

The United Charities consist of Samuel Elsdale, Joseph Burton, the Poor's Land and Salt Marsh Allotment charities. In 2017, a total of £12,000 was allocated to the Surfleet Parish Council.

Support is also given to the vicar and churchwardens of the ecclesiastical parish of Surfleet St Lawrence for the purchase of Old and New Testaments and other religious books to be distributed among the poor inhabitants of the parish.

The Sutton St James United Charities

£3,500

Correspondent: Keith Savage, 94 Wignals Gate, Holbeach, Spalding, Lincolnshire PE12 7HR (01406 490157)

CC number: 527757

Eligibility

People in need who have lived in the parish of Sutton St James and the surrounding area for at least three years.

Types of grants

One-off grants to relieve poverty and hardship. Previously, grants have been used to meet funeral expenses and find suitable living accommodation.

Annual grant total

In 2016/17 the foundation had an income of £25,000 and a total expenditure of £11,000. We estimate that welfare grants to individuals totalled around £3,500.

Applications

Application forms can be requested from the correspondent.

Other information

Organisations, including schools, can also be supported. Grants are made for both educational and welfare needs.

South Kesteven

Deeping St James United Charities

£14,200

Correspondent: Julie Banks, Clerk, The Institute, 38 Church Street, Deeping St James, Peterborough PE6 8HD (01778 344707; email: dsjunitedcharities@ btconnect.com; website: www. dsjunitedcharities.org.uk)

CC number: 248848

Eligibility

People in the parish of Deeping St James (including Frognall) who are in need, hardship or suffer from ill health, disability or are otherwise disadvantaged. There are no fixed income limits for applications.

Older residents of the parish who are in receipt of a state pension, have lived in the parish for at least two years, and are in need, can apply for a St Thomas' Day cash grant.

Types of grants

One-off grants are given to help with a wide range of welfare and medical needs. Small cash grants are made to older residents of the parish for St Thomas' Day each year.

Annual grant total

In 2016 the charity had assets of £3 million and an income of £118,500. Welfare grants to individuals totalled £14,200 and were distributed as follows:

Relief in need	£11,000
St Thomas' Day	£3,200
Relief in sickness	£24

Applications

Requests for assistance can be made through the charity's office, or by contacting the charity by telephone or email. Individual trustees can also be approached directly.

Application forms for St Thomas' Day grants are available to download online, from the charity's office (between 10am and 12pm on weekdays), or from the Deepings Advertiser when it prints the form in November. The awards are made on the nearest Thursday to 21 December. Grants are limited to one application per household.

Other information

The trust is an amalgamation of a number of small charities from the local area. This trust also gives grants to individuals for educational purposes (£5,400 in 2016), and to local projects which help the community (£16,800 in 2016).

The Farmers' Benevolent Institution

£3,500

Correspondent: Mark Foster, Duncan & Toplis, 3 Castlegate, Grantham NG31 6SF (01476 591200; email: duncan.andrew@duntop.co.uk)

CC number: 216042

Eligibility

People living within a 15-mile radius of Grantham who have been owners or occupiers of land, but who, from losses or other untoward circumstances, have become destitute. Applicants should be over 65 or, if they have been a subscriber to the fund for ten years or more, over 60.

Types of grants

Annual payments of around £150, with a supplementary payment at Christmas.

Annual grant total

In 2016/17 the charity had an income of £4,900 and a total expenditure of £3,800. We estimate that grants given to individuals totalled £3,500.

Applications

Apply in writing to the correspondent.

Haconby Parish Charity

£3,100

Correspondent: Sally Burton, Trustee, 36 Headland Way, Haconby, Bourne, Lincolnshire PE10 0UW (01778 571441)

CC number: 218589

Eligibility

People in need who live in the parish of Haconby and Stainfield.

Types of grants

One-off and recurrent grants are given according to need. Grants have been given as Christmas gifts to people aged over 60, help with home alterations for people with disabilities and towards funeral expenses and hospital travel costs.

Annual grant total

In 2016 the charity had an income of £4,600 and a total expenditure of £3,400. We estimate that grants given to individuals totalled £3,100.

Applications

Apply in writing to the correspondent. Applications can be submitted directly by the individual or through a third party such as a social worker, Citizens Advice or welfare agency.

West Lindsey

Gainsborough Dispensary Charity

£10,500

Correspondent: Jonathan Swatton, Trustee, 9 Priory Way, Lea, Gainsborough, Lincolnshire DN21 5HF (01427 615036)

CC number: 250376

Eligibility

People in need who live in Gainsborough and Morton.

Types of grants

One-off grants, usually up to about £300. Past grants have been given for furniture, domestic appliances, holidays (where there is a medical need) and clothing.

Annual grant total

In 2016 the charity had an income of £9,400 and a total expenditure of £11,100. We estimate that grants given to individuals totalled £10,500.

Applications

Apply in writing to the correspondent through a social worker, Citizens Advice or other welfare agency or through a third party such as a community nurse or a minister of religion.

Willingham and District Relief-in-Sickness Charity

£4,200

Correspondent: Lisa Brooks-Sleight, 13 The Close, Sturton by Stow, Lincoln LN1 2AG (01427 788440; email: willingham.sickness.charity@mail.com)

CC number: 512180

Eligibility

People in need who live in the parishes of Corringham, Heapham, Kexby, Springthorpe, Upton and Willingham in Lincolnshire.

Types of grants

Grants of money or providing or paying for items, services or facilities which help those in need.

Annual grant total

In 2016 the charity had an income of £6,000 and a total expenditure of £4,400. We estimate that grants given to individuals totalled £4,200.

Applications

Apply in writing to the correspondent. The trustees meet to consider applications in February, June and October.

Norfolk

Benevolent Association for the Relief of Decayed Tradesmen, their Widows and Orphans

£2,000

Correspondent: Nicholas Saffell, c/o Brown & Co., The Atrium, St George's Street, Norwich, Norfolk NR3 1AB (01603 629871; email: nick.saffell@brown-co.com)

CC number: 209861

Eligibility

People who are in need and live in Norwich or the parishes of Costessey, Earlham, Hellesdon, Catton, Sprowston, Thorpe St Andrew, Trowse with Newton and Cringleford. Preference is given to those who have carried on a trade in the area of benefit, as well as their dependants.

Types of grants

One-off and recurrent grants are given according to need.

Annual grant total

In 2015/16 the charity had an income of £5,900 and a total expenditure of £4,700. We have estimated that grants to individuals totalled £2,000, with funding also awarded to organisations.

Applications

Apply in writing to the correspondent.

Norfolk Community Foundation

£19,500

Correspondent: Grants Team, St James Mill, Whitefriars, Norwich, Norfolk NR3 1SH (01603 623958; email: grants@norfolkfoundation.com; website: www.norfolkfoundation.com)

CC number: 1110817

Eligibility

Unpaid carers living in Norfolk.

Types of grants

Grants for carers are available through the Norfolk Millennium Trust for Carers which is managed by the foundation. The trust aims to offer unpaid carers a better quality of life by giving grants for practical items like washing machines and laptops, power packs for wheelchairs and short breaks. Grants are typically up to a maximum of £250.

Annual grant total

In 2016 the foundation had assets of £21.9 million and an income of £5.2 million. Grants to individuals totalled £78,000. We estimate that around £19,500 was given to individuals for welfare purposes.

Applications

Contact the Grants Team for details of the application process. Applications must be supported by a referee who knows about your caring situation, and has the knowledge and skill to give a meaningful opinion on your request. A relative/member of your family, friend or neighbour is not acceptable.

Norwich Town Close Estate Charity

£109,000

Correspondent: David Walker, Clerk to the Trustees, 1 Woolgate Court, St Benedicts Street, Norwich NR2 4AP (01603 621023; email: info@norwichcharitabletrusts.org.uk; website: www.norwichcharitabletrusts.org.uk)

CC number: 235678

Eligibility

Freemen of Norwich and their families who are in need.

Types of grants

The charity provides annual pensions as well as one-off grants, generally for 'extraordinary and often unexpected items' as well as general relief in need. Examples may include decorating costs, house repairs, replacement of boiler, carpets, spectacles and dental work.

Annual grant total

In 2015/16 the charity had assets of £24 million and an income of £924,500. Welfare grants to individuals totalled £109,000.

Applications

Application forms are available from the correspondent. They are considered throughout the year. Applicants living locally will usually be required to attend an interview.

Other information

Awards are made for welfare as well as educational needs.

This is one of the three grant-making charities under the Norwich Charitable Trusts (others are Norwich Consolidated Charities and Anguish Educational Foundation).

The Shelroy Charitable Trust

£4,000

Correspondent: Norfolk Community Foundation, St James Mill, Whitefriars, Norwich NR3 1TN (01603 623958; fax: 01603 230036; email: jennybevan@ norfolkfoundation.com)

CC number: 327776

Eligibility

Residents of Norfolk who are in need.

Types of grants

One-off grants to assist with easing financial hardship. Previously, hampers have been distributed at Christmas to people who are isolated, older, bereaved, single parents or are otherwise in need.

Annual grant total

In 2015/16 the trust had an income of £3,000 and a total expenditure of £12,000. We estimate that grants given to individuals totalled around £4,000.

Exclusions

In previous years, the charity has not assisted with bankruptcy costs.

Applications

Application forms can be requested from the correspondent. Where possible, a social or professional worker should support the application.

Other information

The charity also awards grants to individuals for educational support, and to local organisations operating within the community.

The Watton Relief-in-Need Charity

£1,700

Correspondent: Derek Smith, Administrator, 39 Dereham Road, Watton, Norfolk IP25 6ER (01953 884044; email: derekismith@talktalk.net)

CC number: 239041

Eligibility

People in need who live in Watton.

Types of grants

One-off grants according to need. Recent grants have been given towards medical equipment, funeral expenses, clothing, carpets, kitchen and household expenses and to older people at Christmas time.

Annual grant total

In 2016/17 the charity had an income of £3,300 and had a total expenditure of £3,300. We estimate that the charity gave around £1,700 in grants to individuals, with funding also awarded to organisations.

Applications

Apply in writing to the correspondent, either directly by the individual or via a social worker, Citizens Advice, welfare agency or through a friend or neighbour. Applications are usually considered quarterly.

Other information

Grants are also made to organisations with similar objects.

Breckland

The Banham Parochial Charities

£5,000

Correspondent: Brian Harper, Trustee, 6 Pound Close, Banham, Norwich NR16 2SY (01953 887008)

CC number: 213891

Eligibility

People in need who live in the parish of Banham.

Types of grants

One-off grants according to need. Grants have been given towards such things as heating bills, fuel and 'illness needs'.

Annual grant total

In 2016 the charity had an income of £12,800 and a total expenditure of £10,500. We have estimated that grants to individuals for welfare purposes totalled £5,000, with grants also awarded to individuals for educational purposes.

Applications

Apply in writing to the correspondent. Applications can be considered at any time.

Charity of Thomas Barrett

£2,500

Correspondent: Nicholas Saffell, Administrator, Brown and Co., The Atrium, St George's Street, Norwich NR3 1AB (01603 629871)

CC number: 207494

Eligibility

Older people, children and young people in need who live in Swanton Morley.

Types of grants

One-off and recurrent grants are given according to need.

Annual grant total

In 2016/17 the charity had an income of £5,200 and a total expenditure of £5,200. We estimate that grants given to individuals totalled around £2,500.

Applications

The individual should apply directly to the correspondent in writing. Applications are considered in June and December.

Other information

The trust gives out a portion of its income towards the maintenance and repair of the parish church.

The East Dereham Relief-in-Need Charity

£4,000

Correspondent: Derek Edwards, Hon. Secretary, Lansdown House, 3 Breton Close, Dereham NR19 1JH (01362 695835)

CC number: 211142

Eligibility

People in need who live in East Dereham in Norfolk.

Types of grants

One-off and recurrent grants, usually ranging from £35 to £100, are given for electricity, coal and clothing.

Annual grant total

In 2015/16 the charity had an income of £9,400 and a total expenditure of £8,400. We estimate that grants given to individuals totalled around £4,000, with funding also awarded to organisations.

Applications

Application forms are available from the correspondent. Applications can be submitted either directly by the individual or through a social worker, Citizens Advice or other welfare agency.

Other information

In 2015/16 the charity made donations to Dereham Food Bank and to the Salvation Army for food hampers.

The Garboldisham Parish Charities

£4,000

Correspondent: Mr P. Girling, Treasurer, Sandale, Smallworth Common, Garboldisham, Diss IP22 2QW (01953 681646; email: pandw6@btinternet.com)

CC number: 210250

Eligibility

People in need who live in the parish of Garboldisham. Generally, this is covered by the Relief-in-Need Fund, although widows and those over 65 who have lived in the parish of Garboldisham for over two years may qualify for allowances given by the Fuel Allotment Charity.

Types of grants

One-off and ongoing grants usually in the range of £30 to £600. At Christmas, a cash grant is given from the Fuel Allotment to qualifying individuals.

Annual grant total

In 2016/17 the charity had an income of £8,900 and a total expenditure of £8,000. Grants are made to individuals and organisations for educational and social welfare purposes. We estimate that welfare grants to individuals totalled £4,000.

Applications

Applications can be submitted directly by the individual, including specific details of what the grant is required for. They are usually considered in July and December.

Old Buckenham Charities

£1,800

Correspondent: Jenny Sallnow, Arianne, Attleborough Road, Old Buckenham, Attleborough, Norfolk NR17 1RF (01953 860166)

CC number: 206795

Eligibility

People in need who live in Old Buckenham, Norfolk. Preference for pensioners (over 65) but other groups are also considered.

Types of grants

Normally recurrent grants in coal or cash in lieu for those without coal fires, although other needs may also be addressed. Grants are usually of £50 or equivalent and distributed yearly in early December. Cases considered to be of exceptional need may be given more. There is a reserve of money to help those in emergencies throughout the year.

Annual grant total

In 2016 the charity had an income of £2,500 and a total expenditure of £1,900. We estimate that grants given to individuals totalled £1,800.

Applications

Application forms are available from the correspondent, following posted notices around the parish each autumn. Requests are usually considered in early November and can be submitted either directly by the individual or through a third party, such as any of the trustees. Any relevant evidence of need is helpful, but not essential.

The Ella Roberts Memorial Charity for Saham Toney

£500

Correspondent: Rosemary Benton, Treasurer, 36 Richmond Road, Saham Toney, Thetford, Norfolk IP25 7ER (01953 881844)

CC number: 1025909

Eligibility

People in need who are older, sick or who have disabilities and live in Saham Toney.

Types of grants

One-off cash grants to cover half of the cost of dentures, glasses, physiotherapy or dental treatment, up to a maximum of £100 per application.

Annual grant total

In 2015/16 the charity had an income of £930 and a total expenditure of £530. We estimate that the charity gave around £500 in grants to individuals.

Applications

Application forms are available from the correspondent and should be submitted directly by the individual or a family member. Applications are considered on receipt.

Saham Toney Fuel Allotment and Perkins Charity

£2,600

Correspondent: Jill Glenn, 1 Cressingham Road, Ashill, Thetford IP25 7DG (01760 441738; email: jill@glenn8530.freeserve.co.uk)

CC number: 211852

Eligibility

People in need who have lived in Saham Toney for at least two years.

Types of grants

Small, recurrent grants to help with the cost of fuel.

Annual grant total

At the time of writing (February 2018) the charity's financial information for 2016 was overdue at the Charity Commission. The most recent year for which information was available was 2015, during which the charity had an income of £5,400 and a total expenditure of £2,900. We estimate that grants given to individuals totalled £2,600.

Applications

Application forms are available from the correspondent. Applications can be submitted directly by the individual. Applications should be submitted in May for consideration in June.

Shipdham Parochial and Fuel Allotment Charity

£11,000

Correspondent: Helen Crane, Trustee, Meadow Bank, Carbrooke Lane, Shipdham, Thetford, Norfolk IP25 7RP (01362 821440; email: hscmeadowbank@yahoo.co.uk)

CC number: 206339

Eligibility

People in need who live in Shipdham.

Types of grants

One-off grants according to need.

Annual grant total

In 2015/16 the charity had an income of £19,000 and a total expenditure of £24,500. We estimate that grants to individuals totalled £11,000, with funding also awarded to organisations.

Applications

Application forms are available from the correspondent. Applications are usually considered quarterly.

Swaffham Relief in Need Charity

£3,500

Correspondent: Richard Bishop, Town Clerk, The Town Hall, Swaffham, Norfolk PE37 7DQ (01760 722922; email: reliefinneed@swaffhamtowncouncil.gov.uk; website: swaffhamtowncouncil.gov.uk)

CC number: 1072912

Eligibility

People in need who have lived in Swaffham for at least 12 months. In exceptional circumstances, the trustees may decide to aid someone who is resident outside Swaffham or only temporary resident in the area.

Types of grants

Grants have been given for a number of reasons, for example to help with school uniforms, to provide disability access facilities or mobility scooters, towards central heating, to relieve long-term debt or to assist with basic home start-up facilities. Help is given where applicants are in need because of illness or disability, loss of work, emergencies and so on.

Annual grant total

In 2015/16 the charity had an income of £6,000 and a total expenditure of £7,300. We estimate that around £3,500 was given in grants to individuals for welfare purposes.

Applications

Application forms are available to download from the charity's website. The trustees meet six times a year to consider applications – in January, March, May, July, September and November.

Other information

Information on the charity is available via the Swaffham Town Council website. The charity supports both individuals and organisations for social welfare and educational needs.

Broadland

Horstead Poor's Land

£4,000

Correspondent: Barbara Gidney, Trustee, Mill Road, Horstead, Norwich, Norfolk NR12 7AT (01603 737900; email: barbaragdn@gmail.com)

CC number: 264730

Eligibility

People in need who live in Horstead with Stanninghall.

Types of grants

One-off and recurrent grants are given according to need.

Annual grant total

In 2016/17 the charity had an income of £7,500 and a total expenditure of £8,900. We estimate that grants given to individuals totalled £4,000, with funding also awarded to local organisations.

Applications

Applications, in writing to the correspondent, can be submitted directly by the individual, through a recognised referral agency (such as a social worker, doctor or Citizens Advice) or other third

party, and are considered throughout the year.

The Charity of Sir John Picto and Others

£750

Correspondent: Stephen Pipe, Correspondent, Beam End, Mill Street, Buxton, Norwich NR10 5JE (01603 279823; email: stephenpipe@live.co.uk)

CC number: 208896

Eligibility

People in need who live in the parish of Buxton Lamas, Little Hautbois, Brampton and Oxmead.

Types of grants

One-off and recurrent grants of £100 to £200 towards household bills, food, living expenses and other essential needs.

Annual grant total

In 2015/16 the charity had an income of £34,500 and a total expenditure of £10,000. We estimate that grants given to individuals totalled £750.

Applications

Applications may be made in writing to the correspondent directly by the individual or a family member, or through a third party, such as a social worker or teacher. Applications are considered at any time.

Other information

Educational help for families in need is also available. Grants are also made to organisations or groups within the parish boundary.

King's Lynn and West Norfolk

Edmund Atmere (Feltwell) Charity

£1,600

Correspondent: Edmund Lambert, Trustee, Hill Farm, Feltwell, Thetford, Norfolk IP26 4AB (01842 828156)

CC number: 270226

Eligibility

People, generally aged over 70 or who have a disability, or children with severe chronic illness, who have lived in Feltwell for at least ten years.

Types of grants

One-off grants.

Annual grant total

In 2015 the charity had an income of £3,000 and a total expenditure of £1,600. We estimate that grants given to

individuals totalled approximately £1,600.

Applications

Apply in writing to the correspondent.

Edmund Atmere (Northwold) Charity

£2,500

Correspondent: Helaine Wyett, Pangle Cottage, Church Road, Wretton, King's Lynn PE33 9QR (01366 500165; email: hwyett@tiscali.co.uk)

CC number: 270227

Eligibility

People in need who live in the parish of Northwold.

Types of grants

One-off grants according to need. Aids for people with disabilities are also loaned by the charity.

Annual grant total

In 2016 the charity had an income of £2,800 and a total expenditure of £2,800. We estimate that grants given to individuals for welfare purposes totalled £2,500.

Applications

Apply in writing to the correspondent.

The Beeston Fuel Charity (Fuel Allotment)

£1,500

Correspondent: Charles Brindley, Springfield, Beeston, King's Lynn PE32 2LZ (01328 701425; email: beestonbitteringpc@btinternet.com)

CC number: 213779

Eligibility

People over 65 years old who are in need and have lived in the parish of Beeston for at least five years.

Types of grants

Fuel grants of between £20 and £25 given at Christmas.

Annual grant total

In 2015/16 the charity had an income of £1,570 and a total expenditure of £1,360. We estimate that around £1,500 was given in grants to individuals for social welfare purposes.

Applications

Apply in writing to the correspondent for consideration in December. Application deadlines are in November.

Callibut's Estate Charity and Callibut's Charity (Hillington Share)

£5,100

Correspondent: William Tawn, Trustee, 2 Wheatfields, Hillington, King's Lynn, Norfolk PE31 6BH (01485 600641)

CC number: 243510/243511

Eligibility

People in need, usually over the age of 65, who live in Hillington or East Walton in Norfolk.

Types of grants

One-off and recurrent grants, usually ranging from £25 to £100.

Annual grant total

In 2016 the charities had a combined income of £5,600 and a total expenditure of £5,300. We estimate that grants given to individuals from the two charities totalled around £5,100.

Exclusions

Owner-occupiers are not eligible for support.

Applications

Applications can be made in writing to the correspondent and submitted directly by the individual. They are considered in November.

Other information

The charities are known by their working name, Hillington United Charities.

Jane Forby Charity

£1,200

Correspondent: Sarah Jane Scarrott, Warren House, Brandon Road, Methwold, Thetford IP26 4RL (01366 728238; email: janescarrott@btinternet.com)

CC number: 208899

Eligibility

People in need who live in the parish of Wretton.

Types of grants

One-off and recurrent grants are given according to need.

Annual grant total

In 2015/16 the charity had both an income and a total expenditure of £2,600. We estimate that grants given to individuals totalled around £1,200, with funding also awarded to organisations.

Applications

Apply in writing to the correspondent. Applications can be made directly by the individual or by a third party familiar with their circumstances. They are usually considered in November.

Gayton Fuel Allotment

£2,300

Correspondent: Tracey Haggas, Trustee, Well Hall Farm, Gayton, King's Lynn, Norfolk PE32 1QD (01553 636212; email: traceyhaggas@icloud.com)

CC number: 243082

Eligibility

People in need who live in the administrative parish of Gayton, which includes the village of Gayton Thorpe.

Types of grants

Small, one-off and recurrent grants are given according to need.

Annual grant total

In 2016/17 the charity had an income of £6,500 and a total expenditure of £2,600. We estimate that grants given to individuals totalled around £2,300.

Applications

Apply in writing to the correspondent. Applications can be submitted directly by the individual or a family member.

The Gaywood Poors' Fuel Allotment Trust

£3,500

Correspondent: The Trustees, 'Edelweiss', Station Road, Hillington, King's Lynn, Norfolk PE31 6DE (email: glno2ac@btinternet.com)

CC number: 209364

Eligibility

People in need and live in the parish of Gaywood in Norfolk.

Types of grants

Grants to help with fuel costs.

Annual grant total

In 2016/17 the charity had an income of £4,600 and a total expenditure of £3,800. We estimate that grants given to individuals totalled around £3,500.

Applications

Apply in writing to the correspondent through social services.

Hilgay United Charities (Non-Ecclesiastical Branch) (formerly known as The Hilgay Feoffee Charity)

£500

Correspondent: A. Hall, Windrush, Church Road, Ten Mile Bank, Downham Market, Norfolk PE38 0EJ (01366 377127; email: hilgay.feoffees@aol.com)

CC number: 208898

Eligibility

Older people who are in need and live in the parish of Hilgay.

Types of grants

Grants are given to help with fuels costs in winter.

Annual grant total

In 2015 the charity had an income of £23,000 and a total expenditure of £22,500. Our research has found that grants to individuals have, in the past, totalled around £2,000, with 75% for education, training and apprenticeships and the remainder for general grants.

Applications

Individuals can apply to the correspondent in writing.

Other information

The charity also supports the maintenance of two village halls.

Hundred Acre Common Charity

£5,500

Correspondent: Robin Pegg, Trustee, Willowbrook Cottage, Watermans Way, Salters Lode, Downham Market PE38 0BD (email: 100aclerk@gmail.com)

CC number: 208301

Eligibility

People in need who live in Downham Market, Downham West, Stow Bardolph and Wimbotsham. The charity prefers to support older people or people with disabilities.

Types of grants

Fuel and food vouchers.

Annual grant total

In 2016 the charity had an income of £11,000 and a total expenditure of £6,000. We estimate that grants given to individuals totalled £5,500.

Applications

Apply in writing to the correspondent, after local advertisements are placed in shops in the village. Applications can be submitted directly by the individual and are usually considered at the end of November.

The King's Lynn and West Norfolk Borough Charity

£11,300 (42 grants)

Correspondent: Andy Stephens, Secretary, 44 Gayton Road, King's Lynn PE30 4EL (01945 430599 or 07595 939769; email: andystephensobe@gmail.com)

CC number: 243864

Eligibility

People who live in the borough of King's Lynn and West Norfolk and are in need, hardship or suffer from illness or disability.

Types of grants

One-off grants. Recent assistance has included the purchase of cookers, washing machines, specialist clothing and help with relocation expenses within the borough.

Annual grant total

In 2016 the charity held assets of £252,000 and had an income of £29,500. Grants were made to 42 individuals and totalled £11,300.

Exclusions

Grants are not given to relieve public funds.

Applications

Application forms are available from the correspondent. They should be submitted through a social worker, Citizens Advice or other welfare agency. The trustees meet quarterly but can consider urgent applications between meetings.

The Marham Poor's Allotment

£22,000

Correspondent: Wendy Steeles, Trustee, Jungfrau, The Street, Marham, Kings Lynn, Norfolk PE33 9JQ (01760 337286; email: gary@tax.uk.com)

CC number: 236402

Eligibility

People of a pensionable age who are in need and live in Marham Village.

Types of grants

One-off vouchers usually of around £35 for food and fuel, to be spent in local shops.

Annual grant total

In 2016 the charity had an income of £40,500 and a total expenditure of £24,000. Welfare grants to individuals totalled almost £22,000 and were distributed as follows:

Food vouchers	£14,500
Fuel vouchers	£7,300

Applications

Apply in writing to the correspondent.

Marshall's Charity

£9,500

Correspondent: Lynda Clarke-Jones, Clerk to the Trustees, The Barn, Main Street, Littleport, Cambridgeshire CB6 1PH (01353 860449; email: marshallscharity1661@gmail.com)

CC number: 202211

Eligibility

Widows in need who live in the parish of Welney.

Types of grants

Grants of £125 paid quarterly.

Annual grant total

In 2016 the charity had assets of £577,500 and an income of £56,000. Quarterly payments to individuals totalled £9,500.

Applications

Apply in writing to the correspondent. The list of recipients is reviewed quarterly.

Other information

The charity also owns and maintains four alms bungalows and now supports many other village facilities including, among others, the parish hall and a playing field.

The village hall was completed during the year, with Marshall's charity giving a total donation of £127,000 to the project.

The Welney RUG (Residents Rec (and Green Spaces) Users Group) completed the children's play area this year, for which the charity donated £37,000.

A bingo machine for £220 was purchased for the village hall and £1,500 was donated to a local angling club for eight new fishing platforms.

The Harold Moorhouse Charity

£9,000

Correspondent: Christine Harrison, Trustee, 30 Winmer Avenue, Winterton-on-Sea, Great Yarmouth NR29 4BA (01493 393975; email: haroldmoorhousecharity@yahoo.co.uk)

CC number: 287278

Eligibility

Individuals in need who live in Burnham Market in Norfolk only.

Types of grants

One-off grants are made ranging from £50 to £200 for heating, medical care and equipment, travel to and from hospital, educational equipment and school educational trips.

Annual grant total

In 2015/16 the charity had an income of £21,500 and a total expenditure of £19,000. We estimate that grants given to individuals totalled around £9,000.

Applications

Applications can be made in writing to the correspondent. Applications should be submitted directly by the individual in any month.

Sir Edmund Moundeford Charity

£10,100

Correspondent: Barry Hawkins, The Estate Office, 15 Lynn Road, Downham Market, Norfolk PE38 9NL (01366 387180)

CC number: 1075097

Eligibility

Older individuals who live in Feltwell and are in need.

Types of grants

Grants are given at Christmas for heating. They can also be made to assist residents of the charity's almshouses.

Annual grant total

In 2015 the charity had assets of £5.7 million and an income of £128,00. Grants totalled £33,500. Individuals received grants totalling £13,800 for both social welfare and educational purposes. They were distributed as follows:

Fuel grants (Christmas)	£9,300
Student grants	£2,700
School leavers	£1,000
Almshouse tenants	£800

Applications

Applications can be made writing to the correspondent either directly by the individual or through an organisation such as Citizens Advice or a school. Applications are considered at meetings held quarterly.

Other information

The main purpose of this charity is the provision of almshouse accommodation.

EAST OF ENGLAND – NORFOLK

South Creake Charities

£3,500

Correspondent: Susan Hart, 26 Front Street, South Creake, Fakenham NR21 9PE (01328 823515; email: sccharities@hotmail.co.uk)

CC number: 210090

Eligibility
People in need who live in South Creake.

Types of grants
One-off grants according to need.

Annual grant total
In 2016/17 the charity had an income of £5,800 and a total expenditure of £7,000. We estimate that grants awarded to individuals for social welfare purposes totalled around £3,500.

Applications
Applications may be made in writing to the correspondent.

Walpole St Peter Poor's Estate

£1,800

Correspondent: Edward Otter, Correspondent, 1 Sutton Meadows, Leverington, Wisbech, Cambridgeshire PE13 5ED (01945 665018)

CC number: 233207

Eligibility
Older people over the age of 65 who are in need and live in the old parishes of Walpole St Peter, Walpole Highway and Walpole Marsh.

Types of grants
Annual Christmas grants for older people in the parish.

Annual grant total
In 2015 the charity had an income of £4,900 and a total expenditure of £3,800. We estimate that grants given to individuals for welfare purposes totalled around £1,800.

Applications
Applications may be made in writing to the correspondent. They can be submitted directly by the individual and are generally considered in November.

Other information
Grants are also made to college or university students for educational necessities.

The United Walsoken and Baxter Charities

£9,000

Correspondent: Derek Mews, 7 Pickards Way, Wisbech, Cambridgeshire PE13 1SD (01945 587982; email: derek. mews@hotmail.co.uk)

CC number: 205494

Eligibility
People over the age of 65 who have lived in the parish of Walsoken for at least five years. Applicants must also have been on the recipient list for at least one year prior to the next round of grant distributions.

Types of grants
Small, one-off grants and gifts in kind.

Annual grant total
In 2016 the charity had an income of £11,700 and a total expenditure of £9,500. We estimate that the charity awarded £9,000 in grants to individuals during the year.

Applications
Applications should be made by the individual and sent directly to the correspondent.

North Norfolk

The Blakeney Twelve

£10,000

Correspondent: Christopher Scargill, Trustee, 24 Kingsway, Blakeney, Holt NR25 7PL (01263 741020)

CC number: 276758

Eligibility
Individuals who are older, in ill health or who have disabilities and who live in the parish of Blakeney, Morston and surrounding district.

Types of grants
One-off and recurrent grants.

Annual grant total
In 2015/16 the trust had an income of £14,800 and a total expenditure of £13,700. We have estimated that grants to individuals totalled £10,000 during the year.

Applications
Apply in writing to the correspondent.

Other information
The charity also provides a Christmas meal for older people in Blakeney.

The Charities of Ralph Greenway

£1,000

Correspondent: Robert Harris, Administrator, East Barn, Hall Lane, Wiveton, Holt, Norfolk NR25 7TG (01263 740090; email: robertpharris@ btinternet.com)

CC number: 207605

Eligibility
People in need who are over 60 and have lived in the village of Wiveton for at least three years. Preference is given to widows. Consideration is also given to other villagers who are in need and have lived in the parish for three years.

Types of grants
Small weekly pensions and one-off fuel grants. Other needs can also be considered.

Annual grant total
In 2016/17 the charity had an income of almost £3,000 and a total expenditure of £2,800. We estimate that welfare grants totalled around £1,000.

Applications
Applications, on a form available from the correspondent, should be submitted directly by the individual and are considered twice a year. However, if a need arises, a special meeting can be convened.

Other information
Educational grants are also available from a subsidiary charity, for young people up to university age, including young people who are starting work.

The Pentney Charity

£5,200

Correspondent: Emma Greeno, Administrator, 19 Westfields, Narborough, King's Lynn, Norfolk PE32 1SX (email: emmagreeno@aol. com)

CC number: 212367

Eligibility
People over 65 who have lived in the parish of Pentney for the last two years are eligible for fuel grants. Other people in need may also apply for help.

Types of grants
One-off grants of £50 to £150 for fuel costs, travel to and from hospital, funeral expenses, medical expenses, disability equipment, clothing and household bills.

Annual grant total
In 2015/16 the charity had an income of £12,900 and a total expenditure of

£10,500. We estimate that the charity gave around £5,200 in grants to individuals, with funding also given to local organisations.

Exclusions

No grants are given where help is available from the social services.

Applications

Apply in writing to the correspondent either directly by the individual; through a social worker, Citizens Advice or other welfare agency; or by a third party on behalf of the individual, for example a neighbour or relative. Applications are usually considered twice a year.

Saxlingham United Charities

£5,000

Correspondent: Julie Queen, Correspondent, 22 Henry Preston Road, Tasburgh, Norwich NR15 1NU (01508 470759; email: saxlingham.uc@gmail.com)

CC number: 244713

Eligibility

People who live in the parish of Saxlingham and are in need. Our research suggests that applicants should generally be older people over the age of 70 and must have lived in the parish for at least five years.

Types of grants

Our research indicates that the charity offers recurrent grants for coal and electricity of £50 to £100 and one-off grants for widows and widowers.

Annual grant total

In 2015/16 the charity had an income of £7,300 and a total expenditure of £11,200. We estimate that grants for welfare purposes totalled around £5,000.

Applications

Applications may be made in writing to the correspondent. They can be submitted directly by the individual and are usually considered in October.

Other information

Grants are made for both welfare needs and educational purposes to people under the age of 21.

Norwich

Norwich Consolidated Charities

£164,500 (243 grants)

Correspondent: David Walker, Clerk to the Trustees, 1 Woolgate Court, St Benedicts Street, Norwich NR2 4AP

(01603 621023; email: info@ norwichcharitabletrusts.org.uk; website: www.norwichcharitabletrusts.org.uk)

CC number: 1094602

Eligibility

People in need who are permanent residents of the city of Norwich. Grants are generally only made to those with dependants, unless the application is supported by a social worker.

Types of grants

One-off grants, typically in the range of £50 to £500, are made for welfare purposes. They can be given to help with the purchase of essential household items (cookers, fridges, beds and carpets, for example), taking out a Debt Relief Order (DRO), or applying for a personal bankruptcy order.

Annual grant total

In 2016 the charity held assets of £34.3 million and had an income of £2 million. During the year, the charity gave grants of almost £164,500 to individuals.

The charity also gave grants of £429,000 to organisations.

Exclusions

Generally, the charity will only award an applicant a grant once in three years.

Applications

Applicants must contact the charity by email, telephone or post. If eligible, the charity will then arrange a meeting to discuss the application and will also visit the applicant's home to discuss specific needs.

Full details are available on the charity's website.

Other information

The main activity of the charity is the provision of almshouses, these are: Doughty's, which acts as residence for older people; and Bakery Court, which is managed by the charity Julian Support, for people who have mental health problems.

South Norfolk

Diss Parochial Charity

£4,300 (24 grants)

Correspondent: Sylvia Grace, Hon. Clerk, 2 The Causeway, Victoria Road, Diss IP22 4AW (01379 650630)

CC number: 210154

Eligibility

People in need who live in the town and parish of Diss.

Types of grants

The charity makes bereavement grants (of £150 each) and distributes hampers to bereaved individuals at Christmas. One-off grants are also made for a range of welfare purposes. Two one-off grants were made in 2016 – one for a hair removal pack and the other as a contribution towards a wheelchair powerpack.

Annual grant total

In 2016 the charity had assets of £827,000 and an income of £32,500. The charity awarded a total of £4,300 in 24 grants to individuals, for the following purposes:

Bereavements	22	£3,300
Individuals	2	£600
Bereavement Christmas gifts	*	£360

* made to follow up bereavement grants.

Applications

Apply in writing to the correspondent. They can be made directly by the individual or through a third party.

Other information

The charity also maintains four almshouses.

East Tuddenham Charities

£2,000

Correspondent: Janet Guy, Correspondent, 7 Mattishall Road, East Tuddenham, Dereham, Norfolk NR20 3LP (01603 880523)

CC number: 210333

Eligibility

People in need who live in East Tuddenham.

Types of grants

Christmas grants for fuel and occasional one-off grants.

Annual grant total

In 2016 the charity had an income of £27,500 and a total expenditure of £18,900. Grants to individuals totalled £2,000.

Applications

Applications may be made in writing to the correspondent.

Other information

The main activity of this charity is the provision of almshouse accommodation.

Woodton United Charities

£900

Correspondent: Daphne Littleboy, 34 The Ridings, Poringland, Norwich NR14 7GE (01508 494318)

CC number: 207531

Eligibility

People in need who live in the parish of Woodton. The charity is particularly interested in supporting pensioners and people with disabilities or their carers.

Types of grants

One-off and recurrent grants of £20 to £300 are given according to need. Annual grants are made to older people and people with disabilities. Contributions can also be made towards funeral expenses.

Annual grant total

In 2015 the charity had an income of £4,200 and a total expenditure of £3,900. We estimate that welfare support to individuals totalled around £900.

Applications

Applications may be made in writing to the correspondent. They can be submitted at any time directly by the individual, including full details and nature of the need.

Other information

Grants are also given for educational purposes.

Suffolk

The Martineau Trust

£20,000

Correspondent: Roger Lay, Clerk, 5 Princethorpe Road, Ipswich, Suffolk IP3 8NY (01473 724951; email: clerk@ martineautrust.org.uk; website: www. martineautrust.org.uk)

CC number: 206884

Eligibility

People living in Suffolk who have incurred expenses as a result of an illness or disability.

Types of grants

The trust makes approximately 100 one-off grants a year. These may cover the whole cost of an item or be a contribution to a larger sum. Grants have been made towards: new wheelchairs; transport costs for parents visiting children in hospital; clothing for a cancer patient; a bath-lift; a gas cooker for a family affected by a disability; and a new bed and mattress for a cancer patient. Further examples are available on the trust's website.

Annual grant total

In 2016/17 the trust had an income of £24,500 and a total expenditure of £26,500. We estimate that the trust gave around £20,000 in grants to individuals during the year.

Exclusions

Grants are not normally made for: holidays and 'breaks' for families, childcare costs, alternative treatment therapies, such as acupuncture, normal household running expenses, repayment of debts, retrospective grants, or for anything not relating to an illness or disability.

Applications

Apply on a form available from the correspondent or to download from the website. Applications must be completed by a suitable third party, such as a social worker, health visitor, nurse, doctor or charity welfare officer.

Mrs L. D. Rope's Third Charitable Settlement

£514,000 (2,141 grants)

Correspondent: Crispin Rope, Trustee, Crag Farm, Boyton, Woodbridge, Suffolk IP12 3LH (01473 333288; email: ropetrust@lucyhouse.org.uk)

CC number: 290533

Eligibility

People in need who live in east Suffolk, particularly in the parish of Kesgrave and the town of Ipswich. Some assistance is given in other parts of East Anglia.

Types of grants

One-off grants or vouchers according to need. Grants may be given to help with, for example, beds, furniture, white goods, food, child and baby care, the costs of obtaining a passport for ID purposes, problems with rent arrears, and funding for deposits for rented accommodation. The average size of grants in 2016/17 was £240.

Annual grant total

In 2016/17 the charity had assets of £65.9 million and an income of £1.6 million.

During the year, 2,141 grants were awarded to individuals totalling £514,000. The majority of these grants were distributed to people living in the charity's local area of east Suffolk (£411,500 in 1,746 grants), with the remainder received by individuals living in other parts of East Anglia.

The charity also awarded 187 grants to organisations to the sum of £647,000.

Exclusions

Grants are not given for individuals working overseas, debt relief, health/ palliative care or educational fees. Only in exceptional cases will more than one grant be awarded to the same individual or family in any one year.

Applications

Apply in writing to the correspondent, preferably through a social worker, Citizens Advice or another agency with which the charity works. Apply in a concise letter, saying what is needed and how charity may be able to help. It helps to include details of household income (including benefits), expenses, and a daytime telephone number.

Although the majority of applicants are referred by a local professional, unsolicited applicants are carefully reviewed.

Babergh

The Charity of Joseph Catt

£2,500

Correspondent: Keith Bales, Trustee, 34 Cattsfield, Stutton, Ipswich IP9 2SP (01473 328179)

CC number: 213013

Eligibility

People in need who live in the parish of Stutton only.

Types of grants

One-off grants and loans are given to help with fuel, hospital travel expenses, convalescent holidays, household goods and clothing.

Annual grant total

In 2016 the charity had an income of £10,900 and a total expenditure of £5,000. Grants are made to individuals for a range of purposes. We estimate that welfare grants totalled £2,500.

Applications

Applications can be submitted by the individual or through a recognised referral agency (e.g. social worker, Citizens Advice or doctor).

Sudbury Municipal Charities

£1,700

Correspondent: Adrian Walters, Clerk, Longstop Cottage, The Street, Lawshall, Bury St Edmunds IP29 4QA (01284 828219; email: a.walters@sclc.entadsl. com)

CC number: 213516

Eligibility

Older people (generally those over 70) who are in need and live in the borough of Sudbury.

Types of grants

Christmas and ascension day gifts in the form of food and clothes vouchers.

Annual grant total

In 2016 the charity had an income of £4,600 and a total expenditure of £3,700. We estimate that the charity awarded around £1,700 in grants to individuals. The charity also awards grants to organisations.

Applications

Grants are usually advertised in the local newspaper when they are available.

Other information

At the time of writing (August 2017) the charity had no website or accounts available.

Forest Heath

George Goward and John Evans

£9,400 (15 grants)

Correspondent: Laura Williams, 8 Woodcutters Way, Lakenheath, Brandon, Suffolk IP27 9JQ (07796 018816; email: laurawill@btinternet.com)

CC number: 253727

Eligibility

People who are in need living in the parish of Lakenheath, Suffolk.

Types of grants

One-off grants, usually in the range of £25 to £300, can be given according to need.

Annual grant total

In 2015 the charity had assets of £1.7 million and an income of £37,000. Welfare grants to 15 individuals and families totalled £9,400.

Applications

Applications can be made in writing to the correspondent. They can be submitted either directly by the individual or through a third party, such as a family member, social worker, teacher, or an organisation, such as Citizens Advice, for example. Applications should generally be submitted by February and August for consideration in March and September, respectively. Candidates should provide brief details of their financial situation and include receipts for the items purchased.

Other information

One-eighth of the charity's income is allocated to Soham United Charities. Grants are also made to other organisations, local primary, secondary, nursery and Sunday schools, and to individuals for educational purposes.

The Mildenhall Parish Charities

£15,000

Correspondent: Vincent Coomber, Clerk, 22 Lark Road, Mildenhall, Bury St Edmunds IP28 7LA (01638 718079)

CC number: 208196

Eligibility

Pensioners, widowers and widows in need who live in the parishes of Mildenhall and Beck Row.

Types of grants

The majority of the charity's giving is achieved through annual payments of £10 per person. One-off cash grants of up to £500 towards travelling expenses to hospital, assistance to persons preparing to enter into a trade or profession, and subscriptions to homes or hostels for infirm or homeless people are also available.

Annual grant total

In 2016 the charity had an income of £15,100 and a total expenditure of £15,100. During the year, the charity gave around £15,000 in grants to individuals.

Applications

Apply in writing to the correspondent.

Ipswich

John Dorkin's Charity

£11,000

Correspondent: J. Harvey, 20 Back Hamlet, Ipswich IP3 8AJ (email: mail@ johndorkincharityipswich.co.uk; website: www.johndorkincharityipswich.co.uk)

CC number: 209635

Eligibility

People in need who live in the ancient parish of St Clement's, St Helen, and Holy Trinity, Ipswich (a map of the area of benefit is provided on the charity's website). Preference for the widows and children of seamen.

Types of grants

One-off cash grants of about £200 towards electrical goods, essential household items and furniture, clothes, holidays, hospital travel costs and so on.

Annual grant total

In 2016 the charity had an income of £12,700 and a total expenditure of £22,000. We estimate that the amount awarded to individuals during the year totalled £11,000.

Exclusions

No grants are given to applicants resident outside the beneficial area.

Applications

Application forms can be downloaded from the charity's website and should be returned to the correspondent by post or email.

Other information

The charity also makes awards to organisations.

Mid Suffolk

Gislingham United Charity

£2,000

Correspondent: Sheila Eade, Woodberry, High Street, Gislingham, Suffolk IP23 8JD (01379 783541; email: gislinghamunitedcharity@gmail.com; website: gislingham.onesuffolk.net/ organisations/gislingham-united-charity)

CC number: 208340

Eligibility

People in need who live in Gislingham.

Types of grants

Usually one-off grants according to need. For example, the cost of hospital travel for older people, playgroup fees or specific items or equipment.

Annual grant total

In 2016 the charity had an income of £17,100 and a total expenditure of £24,500. In previous years around 10% of grants were given for welfare. We therefore estimate that around £2,000 was given in welfare grants.

Applications

Apply in writing to the correspondent.

Other information

The charity gives educational grants (education branch – the largest division), grants to individuals in need (non-ecclesiastical branch) and supports ecclesiastical causes (ecclesiastical branch – the smallest division). Village organisations are also assisted.

The non-ecclesiastical branch is divided into two 'moieties': 'for the relief of residents of Gislingham in need, hardship or distress' and 'for the provision and maintenance of facilities for recreation or other charitable purposes for the benefit of the inhabitants of the Parish of Gislingham'.

Earl Stonham Trust

£1,000

Correspondent: Sam Wilson, Trustee, College Farm, Forward Green, Stowmarket, Suffolk IP14 5EH (01449 711497)

CC number: 213006

Eligibility

People in need who live in the parish of Earl Stonham.

Types of grants

One-off grants are made up to a maximum of £200.

Annual grant total

In 2015/16 the trust had an income of £6,000 and a total expenditure of £5,000. We estimate that welfare grants to individuals totalled around £1,000.

Applications

Apply in writing to the correspondent. Applications should be submitted either by the individual or through a social worker, Citizens Advice or other third party. Applications are usually considered in March, June, September and December.

The Stowmarket Relief Trust

£28,000 (98 grants)

Correspondent: Philippa Richardson, Clerk, 9 Temple Road, Stowmarket IP14 1AX (07414 504513; email: clerk.relieftrust@gmail.com)

CC number: 802572

Eligibility

People in need who live in the town of Stowmarket. Depending on the amount of income available, the trust can also support people living in the adjoining parishes, and in the parish of Old Newton with Dagworth.

Applicants must have approached all sources of statutory benefit. People on Income Support will normally qualify for assistance.

Types of grants

Grants are given towards: the purchase and repair of white goods; the purchase and fitting of carpets and floor coverings; the purchase of beds, bedding and household furniture; the payment of living/household expenses; the purchase of clothing/footwear; the provision of specialist counselling; and the payment of court fees for individuals going into bankruptcy, including Debt Relief Orders.

Annual grant total

In 2015/16 the trust had assets of £1.6 million and an income of £68,000. Almost £28,000 was paid in 98 grants to individuals. A further two grants awarded to organisations totalled £250.

Exclusions

People with substantial capital funds are not eligible. People who are in full-time paid employment will not normally qualify for assistance, although there are cases in which exceptions may possibly be made.

Applications

Application forms are available from the correspondent. Applications should be submitted through a third party such as a social worker, probation officer, Citizens Advice or doctor. Applications are considered at trustees' meetings held three times a year, although urgent cases can be dealt with between meetings.

Town Estate Charity (Mendlesham)

£4,900

Correspondent: Shirley Furze, Clerk, Beggars Roost, Church Road, Mendlesham IP14 5SF (01449 767770; website: mendlesham.onesuffolk.net)

CC number: 207592

Eligibility

People who are in need and live in the parish of Mendlesham in Suffolk, particularly older people and those who are suffering from an illness.

Types of grants

One-off grants can be given towards, for example, heating, hospital visiting expenses and funeral expenses.

Annual grant total

In 2016 the charity had assets of £131,500 and an income of £26,500. Grants to organisations and 14 individuals totalled £9,800. We estimate that around £4,900 was awarded to individuals during the year.

Applications

Apply in writing to the correspondent. Applications can be submitted directly by the individual or through a third party, such as a social worker or Citizens Advice.

Other information

Grants are also made to the Church Estate Charity for the upkeep of St Mary's Church.

St Edmundsbury

The Pakenham Charities for the Poor

£2,300

Correspondent: Sally Smith, Clerk, 5 St Mary's View, Pakenham, Bury St Edmunds IP31 2ND (01359 232965; email: sally@sallysmithbooks.co.uk; website: www.pakenham-village.co.uk/main/pakenhamcharities.htm)

CC number: 213314

Eligibility

People in need who live in Pakenham.

Types of grants

Annual fuel grants and one-off payments for particular needs.

Annual grant total

In 2015 the charity had an income of £6,000 and a total expenditure of £4,700. We estimate that the charity gave around £2,300 in grants to individuals. Grants are also made to local organisations.

Applications

Apply in writing to the correspondent either directly by the individual, through a third party such as a social worker, or through an organisation such Citizens Advice or other welfare agency. Applications are considered in early December and should be received by 30 November.

The Risby Fuel Allotment

£3,500

Correspondent: Penelope Wallis, Trustee, 3 Woodland Close, Risby, Bury St Edmunds IP28 6QN (01284 81064)

CC number: 212260

Eligibility

People in need who live in the parish of Risby.

Types of grants

Annual grants, primarily to buy winter fuel but also for other needs.

Annual grant total

In 2015/16 the charity had an income of £7,300 and a total expenditure of £8,200. Grants are made predominantly for relief-in-need purposes. They are also made to organisations. We estimate that social welfare grants to individuals totalled £3,500.

Applications

Apply in writing to the correspondent.

The Stanton Poors' Estate Charity

£4,700

Correspondent: Michael Ronchetti, Trustee, 1 Grundle Close, Stanton, Bury St Edmunds, Suffolk IP31 2DX (01359 251535)

CC number: 235649

Eligibility

People in need who live in the parish of Stanton and are in receipt of means-tested benefits. Grants can be made in special cases of need or hardship outside these criteria at the trustees' discretion.

Types of grants

One-off or recurrent grants.

Annual grant total

In 2015/16 the charity had an income of £4,800 and a total expenditure of £4,900. We estimate that the charity gave around £4,700 in grants to individuals for welfare purposes.

Applications

Apply in writing to the correspondent.

Other information

At the time of writing (August 2017) the charity had no website or accounts available.

Suffolk Coastal

Aldeburgh United Charities

£1,000

Correspondent: Lindsay Lee, Moot Hall, Market Cross Place, Aldeburgh IP15 5DS (01728 452158; email: aldeburghtc@ moothall1.fsnet.co.uk)

CC number: 235840

Eligibility

People in need who live in the town of Aldeburgh. Its Charity Commission record describes its beneficiaries as 'senior citizens, people in specific sensitive situations, young and young minded people and people in the development stage of life's experience'.

Types of grants

One-off and recurrent grants are given according to need.

Annual grant total

In 2016 the charity had an income of £2,100 and a total expenditure of £1,700. We estimate that grants given to individuals for welfare purposes totalled around £1,000 during the year.

Applications

Apply in writing to the correspondent.

Other information

The charity is a combination of various charities in Aldeburgh, some hundreds of years old. Grants may also be given to organisations.

Chediston United Charities

£1,900

Correspondent: David Mantell, Clerk, Rosecroft Farm, Chediston Green, Chediston, Halesworth IP19 0BB (01986 785440; email: dpmantell@gmail.com; website: www.chediston.suffolk.gov.uk)

CC number: 206742

Eligibility

People in need who live in the civil parish of Chediston in Suffolk.

Types of grants

One-off and recurrent grants are given according to need. Christmas gifts are distributed to all pensioners and children in full-time education. Grants are also considered towards transport costs for essential hospital visits.

Annual grant total

In 2016/17 the charity had an income of £4,000 and a total expenditure of £3,900. We estimate that welfare grants to individuals totalled £1,900, with funding

also awarded to individuals for educational purposes.

Applications

Apply in writing to the correspondent. Applications are considered throughout the year, but mainly in November. The trust has no formal application procedure as requests are usually made in person to the trustees.

The Dennington Consolidated Charities

£3,300

Correspondent: Peter Lamb, 2 The Coach House, The Square, Dennington, Woodbridge IP13 8AB (01728 638897; email: peterlamb54@googlemail.com)

CC number: 207451

Eligibility

People in need who live in the village of Dennington.

Types of grants

One-off and ongoing grants according to need towards, for example, travel expenses for hospital visiting of relatives, telephone installation for emergency help calls for people who are older or unwell, and annual Christmas grants to older people. Grants usually range from £50 to £250.

Annual grant total

In 2016 the charity had an income of £17,000 and a total expenditure of £13,900. We estimate that welfare grants to individuals totalled around £3,300.

Applications

Apply in writing to the correspondent. Applications are considered throughout the year and a simple means-test questionnaire may be required by the applicant. Grants are only made to people resident in Dennington (a small village with 500 inhabitants). The charity does not respond to applications made outside this specific geographical area.

Dunwich Town Trust

£16,800

Correspondent: John Lavery, 24 Church View, Holton, Halesworth, Suffolk IP19 8PB (07779 585316; email: dttclerk@btinternet.com; website: www.dunwichtowntrust.org)

CC number: 206294

Eligibility

People in need who live in the parish of Dunwich.

Types of grants

Support with winter fuel costs, care alarms for older and vulnerable people, travelling costs, medical expenses (not covered by the NHS), home help, emergency needs and any other costs to help out in difficult circumstances. Awards can range from £600 to £3,500, depending on need.

Annual grant total

In 2016 the trust had assets of £1.8 million and an income of £99,000. Grants to individuals totalled £16,800 and were awarded as follows:

Winter Grants	£13,000
Contact care alarms	£1,900
General relief	£1,900

There were no grants for educational purposes in this financial year (2016) but they have been made in the past and we anticipate grants being made in the future.

Applications

Application forms can be requested from the correspondent or downloaded online. They should be returned two weeks prior to a meeting of the trustees – dates of meetings are published on the trust's website.

For Winter Grants 'the trust does not rely on individual applications, but on a list which is compiled each year using local information and candidates put forward by trustees'.

Other information

The trust makes grants to both organisations and individuals for social welfare and educational causes.

The Dunwich Town Trust was formed under a Charity Commission scheme in 1889 to administer the property of the dissolved Corporation of Dunwich and The Pension Charity was founded in 1899 under a separate Charity Commission Scheme to administer the endowments of a charity known as The Hospital of St James and The Maison Dieu. The two charities were amalgamated in 2010.

The Melton Trust

£6,500

Correspondent: Anthony Thompson, Trustee, Melton Rectory, Station Road, Melton, Woodbridge IP12 1PX (07952 992945; email: meltontrust.suffolk@ googlemail.com)

CC number: 212286

Eligibility

The present policy of The Melton Trust is to encourage applications from individuals who are residents of Melton, Suffolk (the Ecclesiastical Parish Boundary, not the present smaller Civil Parish), directly or through support organisations such as Suffolk CC Children's Centre, Citizens Advice,

SNAP, Social Services, and also applications from organisations that seek to alleviate or prevent hardship of the residents of Melton, Suffolk.

Types of grants

One-off and recurrent grants are given according to need.

Annual grant total

In 2016 the trust had an income of £10,700 and a total expenditure of £13,200. We estimate that the trust gave around £6,500 in grants to individuals.

The Mills Charity

£4,900

Correspondent: Deborah Stace, Correspondent, PO Box 1703, Framlingham, Suffolk IP13 9WW (01728 724370; email: info@themillscharity.co. uk)

CC number: 207259

Eligibility

Individuals in need who live in Framlingham or are very closely associated with the town.

Types of grants

One-off grants towards hospital expenses, electrical goods, living costs, household bills, travel expenses, medical equipment, furniture and disability equipment.

Annual grant total

In 2015/16 the charity had assets of £7.7 million and an income of £174,000. Payments for relief in need totalled £4,900.

A further £104,500 was given in grants to organisations.

Applications

The trustees hold their meetings every two months, they consider applications for assistance at these meetings. Cases for consideration should be made to: Chair of the Trustees, The Mills Charity, PO Box 1703, Framlingham, Suffolk IP13 9WW. The application should outline the need and also why the need has arisen. Provided the application falls within the remit of the charity all cases are considered. A supporting letter from a professional or other suitable referee to accompany the application is very useful.

Other information

The charity also provides and maintains almshouses.

Walberswick Common Lands

£3,700

Correspondent: Michelle Webb, Clerk, 7 Adams Lane, Walberswick, Southwold, Suffolk IP18 6UR (01502 725014; email: clerkwclc@gmail.com; website: walberswick.onesuffolk.net/walberswick-common-lands-charity)

CC number: 206095

Eligibility

People in need who live in Walberswick village.

Types of grants

Grants include quarterly payments to individuals, Christmas bonuses and one-off awards of £35 to £1,200 towards a range of needs, including gardening, veterinary expenses, domestic appliances, emergency repairs, hospital visiting, telephone rental and television licence payments, access adaptions and travel expenses. Personal loans are also available.

Annual grant total

In 2016 the charity had assets of £271,000 and an income of £96,500. Grants to individuals for welfare purposes totalled £3,700.

Applications

Applications should be made in writing to the correspondent. Requests can be made directly by individuals or on their behalf and must include details of the items required and a justification of the request. Consideration may take about two months. Applications are generally considered in February, April, June, August, October and December. Candidates are normally interviewed.

Other information

The charity no longer makes educational grants to individuals. Instead support is now given to schools on a per-capita basis, with the schools informing trustees of the specific projects on which the grants will be used.

Grants to groups, schools and projects totalled £32,500.

Waveney

Carlton Colville Fuel or Poors' Allotment

£13,000

Correspondent: Keith Vincent, Trustee, 23 Wannock Close, Carlton Colville, Lowestoft, Suffolk NR33 8DW (01493 852411)

CC number: 242083

Eligibility

People in need who live in the ancient parish of Carlton Colville. Preference is given for older people who only receive the basic state pension and have limited savings.

Types of grants

Recurrent grants for fuel and heating costs.

Annual grant total

In 2016 the charity had an income of £16,500 and a total expenditure of £14,400. We estimate that grants given to individuals totalled around £13,000.

Applications

Apply in writing to the correspondent.

Corton Poor's Land Trust

£4,800

Correspondent: Claire Boyne, 48 Fallowfields, Lowestoft NR32 4XN (01502 733978; email: claire.murray4@tesco.net)

CC number: 206067

Eligibility

People in need who live in the ancient parish of Corton in Suffolk.

Types of grants

Grants are given for various needs and in Christmas gifts for older people. Previously support has included funding for chiropody treatment, taxi fares to hospital, payment for home alarm installation and rent.

Annual grant total

In 2015/16 the trust had an income of £16,700 and a total expenditure of £9,800. We estimate that grants given to individuals totalled £4,800, with funding also awarded to organisations.

Applications

Apply in writing to the correspondent. Applications can be submitted at any time directly by the individual or by an appropriate third party.

Other information

The trust also maintains almshouses and makes grants to organisations which carry out the charity's aims within the area of benefit.

Gisleham Relief in Need Charity

£1,500

Correspondent: Elizabeth Rivett, Trustee, 2 Mill Villas, Black Street, Gisleham, Lowestoft NR33 8EJ (01502 743189; email: elizabethrivett@hotmail.co.uk)

CC number: 244853

Eligibility

People in need who live in the parish of Gisleham.

Types of grants

One-off and recurrent grants are given according to need. In the past grants have been given for household bills, travel expenses and disability aids.

Annual grant total

In 2016/17 the charity had an income of £2,200 and a total expenditure of £1,900. We estimate that grants given to individuals totalled £1,500.

Applications

Apply in writing to the correspondent. Applications should be submitted directly by the individual. Applications are considered at any time.

Kirkley Poor's Land Estate

£18,400 (762 grants)

Correspondent: Lucy Walker, Clerk to the Trustees, 4 Station Road, Lowestoft, Suffolk NR32 4QF (01502 514964; email: kirkleypoors@gmail.com; website: kirkleypoorslandestate.co.uk)

CC number: 210177

Eligibility

Individuals in need who live in the parish of Kirkley.

Types of grants

Vouchers of £25 are available to pensioners each winter to help towards the cost of groceries.

Annual grant total

In 2015/16 the charity had assets of £2.2 million and an income of £91,500. Grocery vouchers totalling £18,400 were distributed to 762 pensioners.

Applications

Applications can be made writing to the correspondent.

Other information

The boundaries of the parish are fully defined on the charity's website. The charity can support both individuals for welfare and educational purposes, and organisations.

Lowestoft Fishermen's and Seafarers' Benevolent Society

Correspondent: H. G. Sims, Secretary, 10 Waveney Road, Lowestoft, Suffolk NR32 1BN (01502 565161; fax: 01502 514382; email: lowestoftfpo@hotmail.com; website: infolink.suffolk.gov.uk)

Eligibility

Widows, children and dependants of fishermen and seamen lost at sea from Lowestoft vessels, who are in need.

Types of grants

One-off grants have previously been made for funeral costs, mobility aids and household adaptations. Monthly payments are also made.

Annual grant total

Our previous research suggests that grants generally total between £30,000 and £36,000 a year.

Applications

Apply in writing to the correspondent.

Other information

The charity is a constituent member of the Merchant Navy Welfare Board, more information about available help can be found on its website or through the Maritime Charities Welfare Guide where you can search for other charities that may be able to help.

Poors and Anguish's Charity

£3,600

Correspondent: David Cook, Trustee, Appletree Cottage, Somerleyton, Lowestoft, Suffolk NR32 5PY (01502 730265; email: djcookie54@googlemail.com)

CC number: 215061

Eligibility

Older people in Somerleyton.

Types of grants

Grants towards heating/fuel costs.

Annual grant total

In 2016/17 the charity had an income of £3,800 and a total expenditure of £3,900. We estimate that grants given to individuals totalled £3,600.

Applications

Apply in writing to the correspondent.

The Reydon Trust

£13,700

Correspondent: H. Freeman, Administrator, 22 Kingfisher Crescent, Reydon, Southwold, Suffolk IP18 6XL (01502 723746; email: h_freeman1@sky.com)

CC number: 206873

Eligibility
People in need who live in the parish of Reydon.

Types of grants
One-off grants towards hospital expenses, clothing, food, travel costs and disability equipment. Vouchers are also given as gifts at Christmas time.

Annual grant total
In 2015/16 the trust had an income of £27,500 and a total expenditure of £29,500. We estimate that the trust gave around £13,700 in grants to individuals.

The trust also gives grants to organisations.

Applications
Apply in writing to the correspondent. Applications can be submitted either directly by the individual, through a third party such as a social worker or via a doctor or health centre. They are considered upon receipt.

London

General

The Jack and Ada Beattie Foundation (Fund for the Forgotten)
See entry on page 35

BlindAid
See entry on page 73

Emanuel Hospital

£52,500 (34 grants)

Correspondent: Edward Gilbert, City of London Corporation, Aldermanbury, London EC2V 7HH (020 7332 1399; email: edward.gilbert@cityoflondon.gov. uk; website: www.cityoflondon.gov.uk)

CC number: 206952

Eligibility
People who are of 60 years of age or older, who are in need and who have lived in the London boroughs of Kensington and Chelsea, Hillingdon or Westminster for at least two years, and are in need by reason of poverty, old age, ill health, accident or infirmity.

Types of grants
Pensions of around £1,500 a year are paid in monthly instalments along with a Christmas bonus (£150 per person in 2015/16). One-off grants are also available for essential household items.

Annual grant total
In 2015/16 the charity had assets of £2.2 million and an income of £82,000. Grants were made totalling £52,500 to 34 pensioners.

Applications
Application forms can be requested over the phone. Application forms should be returned along with evidence of income such as benefit award notices, a copy of the applicant's birth certificate and two written testimonials confirming their eligibility and need for assistance, at least one of which must be from someone other than a friend or relative. Applications should be submitted directly by the individual.

The Hornsey Parochial Charities

£25,500

Correspondent: Lorraine Fincham, PO Box 22985, London N10 3XB (020 8352 1601; email: hornseypc@ blueyonder.co.uk; website: www. hornseycharities.com)

CC number: 229410

Eligibility
People in need who have lived in the ancient parish of Hornsey in Haringey and Hackney for at least 12 months. There are maps showing the area of benefit on the charity's website.

Types of grants
One-off grants to pay for items such as clothing, bedding, and other household equipment. Provisions can also be made for heating and lighting fees.

Annual grant total
In 2016 the charity had assets of £1.6 million and an income of £70,000. We estimate that around £25,500 was given in grants to individuals.

Applications
Application forms are available to download from the charity's website. There is also a postcode eligibility checker and a schedule of upcoming trustees' meetings available.

Other information
The charity also awards grants to individuals for education and starting work, and provides funds for organisations supporting education and welfare.

Mary Minet Trust

£19,700

Correspondent: The Correspondent, PO Box 53673, London SE24 4AF (07906 145 199; email: admin@maryminettrust. org.uk)

CC number: 212483

Eligibility
People who are living with a disability, sickness or infirmity and reside in the boroughs of Southwark or Lambeth.

Types of grants
One-off grants towards convalescence holidays, disability aids, medical equipment and household items such as washing machines, fridges, cookers, essential furniture, carpets, clothing, beds and bedding.

Annual grant total
In 2016/17 the trust had an income of £21,500 and a total expenditure of £19,900. We estimate that the trust gave around £19,700 in grants to individuals.

Applications
Applications for individuals are invited from sponsoring organisations, social workers, housing officers and other involved professionals. Applications should be made on the trust's application form, available by contacting the trust by email or telephone. Payments are made to the sponsoring organisation to ensure that the money is spent appropriately, and are paid by BACS transfer. Applications from families and friends, interested persons or the individual in need will be considered only in exceptional circumstances and supporting information will be required. Applications are considered quarterly.

North London Welfare and Educational Foundation

£152,500

Correspondent: Benedict Chayim Joseph, Trustee, 44 Warwick Avenue, Edgware HA8 8UJ (020 8905 4766)

CC number: 1155103

Eligibility

Primarily, people who live in North London and are in need.

Types of grants

Grants are made for items, services and facilities that relieve need.

Annual grant total

In 2015/16 the foundation had assets of £13,600 and an income of £437,500. Grants totalled £426,500, of which £305,000 was awarded to individuals. We estimate that social welfare grants to individuals totalled around £152,500.

Applications

Apply in writing to the correspondent.

The Pilion Trust Ltd

£2,500

Correspondent: Dolores Steadman, 39–41, North Road, Islington, London N7 9DP (020 7700 2498; email: dolores.mc@piliontrust.org.uk)

CC number: 1122628

Eligibility

Vulnerable people who live in Islington and struggle to maintain a home and a basic lifestyle or struggle to get to the next level of their life and seek to be independent.

Types of grants

One-off grants.

Annual grant total

In 2015/16 the trust held assets of £9,200 and had an income of £61,500. During the year, the trust gave around £2,500 in grants to individuals.

Applications

Apply in writing to the correspondent.

The Saint George Dragon Trust

£2,000

Correspondent: Di Emmerson, Trustee, 12 Lindsay Close, Epsom, Surrey KT19 8JJ (0777 963 6677; email: di.emmerson1@gmail.com)

CC number: 275674

Eligibility

People in need who live in Greater London and are moving, or have recently moved, from supported housing into independent accommodation.

Types of grants

One-off grants ranging from £100 to £400 for buying essential household equipment and furniture. Small grants of £50 to £100 are also available for the purchase of essential items following the move. Applicants should not be eligible for a Community Care grant or support from the Social Fund and have only minimal resources. (A rare exception may be where a very low Community Care grant has been awarded – see Applications section.)

Annual grant total

In 2016/17 the trust had an income of £1,700 and a total expenditure of £2,100. We estimate that the trust gave around £2,000 in grants to individuals.

Exclusions

Grants are not made to students or to 'able young people'.

Applications

Apply in writing, through a social, housing or welfare worker. Applications should be typed wherever possible and should be made on the headed notepaper of the organisation through which the application is being made. Guidance can be obtained by emailing sgdt@barraball.com.

Scotscare

£437,500

Correspondent: Shona Fleming, 22 City Road, London EC1Y 2AJ (020 7240 3718; email: info@scotscare.com; website: www.scotscare.com)

CC number: 207326

Eligibility

Scottish people, and their children and widows, who are in need, hardship or distress and live within a 35-mile radius of Charing Cross. Beneficiaries are usually in receipt of state benefits.

Types of grants

As well as giving weekly allowances (£87 per month) to people over the age of 60 who are on low incomes, Scotscare also gives support on a one-off basis to help with, for example: essential household items; family trips at Christmas and in summer; and children's items, such as clothing and school uniforms.

Annual grant total

In 2015/16 the charity had assets of £46 million and an income of £2.3 million. Grants to individuals amounted to £467,500. We estimate that around £437,500 was given in grants to individuals for welfare purposes.

Exclusions

No grants are made for debts or for items that have already been purchased.

Applications

There is an online Scotscare application request form on the website. Alternatively, call the freephone helpline on 0800 652 2989; the Scotscare team is there to give advice from Monday to Thursday 9am to 5pm and on Friday 9am to 4pm.

Other information

In addition to making grants, Scotscare also offers a range of services for beneficiaries in the areas of advocacy, employment and training, families, health, housing, money management, mental health, socialising and substance misuse.

The Sheriffs' and Recorders' Fund
See entry on page 38

Society for the Relief of Distress

£17,000

Correspondent: Caroline Armstrong, 21 Harstwood Road, London W12 9NE

CC number: 207585

Eligibility

People in need who live in one of the inner London boroughs.

Types of grants

One-off grants to relieve hardship and distress.

Annual grant total

In 2016 the charity had an income of £20,500 and a total expenditure of £18,000. We estimate that grants given to individuals totalled £17,000.

Exclusions

Grants are very rarely given towards general financial support, holidays, further education or debt repayment.

Applications

Applications can be sent in writing to the correspondent – applications must be made through a social or professional worker, a charity, GP, etc. Applications should include details of financial need and what the grant will be used for.

Miss Vaughan's Spitalfields Charity

£1,100

Correspondent: Philip Whitehead, Administrator, 45 Quilter Street, Bethnal Green, London E2 7BS (020 7729 2790)

CC number: 262480

Eligibility

People in need who live in the ecclesiastical parishes of Christchurch with All Saints in Spitalfields, St Matthew in Bethnal Green and St Leonard, Shoreditch.

Types of grants

Originally clothing and support was given to poor mechanics and weavers in Spitalfields who were unable to work. Now grants are given to individuals and families who are convalescing, unemployed or who have disabilities and also to large families on a low income.

Annual grant total

In 2016/17 the charity had an income of £1,300 and a total expenditure of £1,300. We estimate that the charity gave around £1,100 in grants to individuals.

Applications

Apply in writing to a member of the clergy from any of the eligible parishes.

The Victoria Convalescent Trust

£124,500 (386 grants)

Correspondent: A. J. Perkins, Grants Co-ordinator, 11 Cavendish Avenue, Woodford Green, Essex IG8 9 DA (020 8502 9339)

CC number: 1064585

Eligibility

People in medical need of convalescence, recuperative and respite care with a preference to people living in Surrey and Croydon. A small proportion of support is also given for general relief in need with a preference to women resident in the Greater London area.

Types of grants

Grants are available for services, items or equipment and awards up to £900 for recuperative holidays and respite care.

Annual grant total

In 2016 the trust had assets of £4.1 million and an income of £116,500. Grants to individuals totalled £124,500. Out of that sum, £108,500 was for convalescence and respite purposes and £15,900 was given in sundry grants.

Applications

Application forms are available from the correspondent. Applications must be submitted through a social worker, a health care worker or a welfare agency or another professional worker and will be considered every month. Medical and social reports supporting the need for a break must be provided.

Other information

Some support is given to women living in Greater London for vital equipment and services.

The trust incorporates Victoria Convalescent Trust Fund, King Edward VII Children's Convalescent Trust Fund and Princess Mary Memorial Trust Fund.

The Charity of Sir Richard Whittington

£237,000 (229 grants)

Correspondent: Mahvish Inayat, Grants Officer, Worshipful Company of Mercers, Becket House, 36 Old Jewry EC2V 8DD (020 7726 4991; email: mahvishi@mercers.co.uk; website: www.mercers.co.uk/grants-elderly-individuals)

CC number: 1087167

Eligibility

Older London residents who are on a low income. Applicants must be over the age of 60, although priority will be given to older and more frail applicants.

Types of grants

Regular grants of £1,140, paid quarterly, mainly for essential household goods and Christmas gifts of £100.

Annual grant total

In 2016/17 the charity held assets of £105.6 million and had an income of £3.2 million. During the year, the charity gave £237,000 in grants to 229 individuals.

Applications

Application forms may be requested by contacting the correspondent. The application must be submitted by an appropriate agency, such as social services, a registered charity, member of the clergy, etc., who must also provide a reference. This is followed by a home visit from a member of the Mercers' Company. The charity welcomes enquiries.

Note the following from the charity's website: 'our list of beneficiaries is currently full, so we are adding new applicants to a waiting list for future consideration'.

Other information

The Charity of Sir Richard Whittington is the amalgamation of both The Charity of Sir Richard Whittington and Lady Mico's Almshouse Charity.

The Charity of Sir Richard Whittington was founded in 1424 under the will of Richard Whittington (1354–1423) who was Mayor of London four times and Master of the Mercers' Company three times.

Lady Mico's Almshouses were founded under the bequest of Lady Jane Mico, widow of Sir Samuel Mico, Alderman and Mercer. In 1690 almshouses for eight older women were built opposite St Dunstan's Church, Stepney.

The charity still owns almshouses at Whittington College, Felbridge, Surrey and at Stepney, London.

Barnet

The Mayor of Barnet's Benevolent Fund

£8,000

Correspondent: Ken Argent, Grants Manager, The London Borough of Barnet, Building 4, North London Business Park, Oakleigh Road South, London N11 1NP (020 8359 2020; email: ken.argent@barnet.gov.uk; website: www.barnet.gov.uk/info/930094/grants_for_individuals/262/grants_for_individuals)

CC number: 1014273

Eligibility

People who are on an income-related statutory benefit (such as Income Support or Child Tax Credit), have lived in the London borough of Barnet for at least a year and are in need, hardship or distress. Children, young people, older people and individuals with disabilities are particularly supported.

Types of grants

Small, one-off grants of up to £200 are given towards essential household items, appliances (for example, cooker, refrigerator or washing machine), furnishing or equipping a new property, children and baby necessities, clothing items for adults where there is an exceptional need, small, one-off debts (such as telephone bills), the cost of school uniforms (up to £60) and for any other necessities arising from an unforeseen financial crisis. Up to two awards per applicant are provided.

Annual grant total

In 2015/16 the fund had an income of £21,500 and a total expenditure of £10,500. Most support is given in welfare grants. We estimate that welfare grants to individuals totalled around £8,000.

Applications

Applications have to be made in writing to the correspondent by post or email. Applications can be submitted directly by the individual or through a third party, such as a social worker, health visitor or an advice agency. Candidates should provide full details of their name, address, contact number, confirmation and length of residence in the borough, number and ages of the family members, family income, a proof of entitlement to a benefit, a summary of the applicant's circumstances, details of support requested, a quotation for any items required and information on other sources of funding approached.

Other information

Grants are also given for educational purposes such as for school uniforms.

The Finchley Charities

£9,900 (three grants)

Correspondent: Susan Faridi, Chief Executive, 41A Wilmot Close, East Finchley, London N2 8HP (020 8346 9464; email: info@thefinchleycharities. org; website: www.thefinchleycharities. org)

CC number: 206621

Eligibility

People in need who live in the former borough of Finchley.

Types of grants

One-off grants only.

Annual grant total

In 2016 the charity had assets of almost £14 million and an income of £1.4 million. During the year, three individual grants were made, totalling £9,900.

Note: Grant-making forms only a small part of the charity's work – see Other information for details.

Exclusions

Grants cannot be made for the relief of rates, taxes or other public funds. The trustees cannot commit to repeat grants.

Applications

Apply in writing to the correspondent, either directly by the individual or through a social worker, Citizens Advice or other welfare agency. Applications must include details of the amount being asked for and the reason for the application.

Other information

The trust's main concern is the provision of 156 flats for people in Finchley aged 55 and over who have insufficient funds to purchase their own property and have been resident in the London borough of Barnet for at least five years.

Awards are also made to local churches and organisations helping people in the area of benefit.

Jesus Hospital in Chipping Barnet

£4,900

Correspondent: Simon Smith, Ravenscroft Lodge, 37 Union Street, Barnet, Hertfordshire EN5 4HY (020 8440 4374; email: info@ jesushospitalcharity.org.uk; website: www.jesushospitalcharity.org.uk)

CC number: 1075889

Eligibility

People in need who live in Barnet.

Types of grants

One-off grants between £100 and £1,000 towards, for example, lifeline rentals, winter clothing, shoes, food vouchers, fridges/freezers, beds, gas cookers and utensils for single parent families and couples living on low incomes, as well as holidays for people with disabilities.

Annual grant total

In 2016 the charity held assets of £13.4 million and had an income of £679,000. Relief-in-need grants to individuals totalled £4,900. A further £51,000 was given in grants to organisations.

Applications

Apply on a form which can be downloaded from the charity's website. Applications are considered by trustees who meet every other month. Applicants may be visited by the clerk.

Other information

The charity maintains 54 almshouses in the Chipping Barnet and Monken Hadley area.

Eleanor Palmer Trust

£1,300

Correspondent: Fred Park, Clerk to the Trustees, 106b Wood Street, Barnet, Hertfordshire EN5 4BY (020 8441 3222; email: info@eleanorpalmertrust.org.uk; website: www.eleanorpalmertrust.org.uk)

CC number: 220857

Eligibility

People in need who live in the former urban districts of Chipping Barnet and East Barnet, This includes those living within the postal codes of EN4, EN5, N11 and N14. Applicants must have lived within the area for at least two years prior to submitting an application.

Types of grants

One-off grants towards, for example, carpets, furniture and clothing. Items or services are purchased directly from the supplier. No cash grants are made.

Annual grant total

In 2016/17 the trust held assets of £5.8 million and had an income of £1.6 million. During the year, the trust gave around £1,300 in grants to individuals.

The trust also gives grants to organisations.

Exclusions

No grants available towards educational purposes, bankruptcy fees, medical costs, taxes or debts.

Applications

Application forms are available from the correspondent. Applications are considered every two months. Applications should include details of the applicant's circumstances and income, the items or service required, and details of any other local charities to which the applicant has applied for assistance. The clerk visits applicants in order to assess need if this has not been done recently by a local charity.

Other information

The trust is named after Eleanor Palmer and was founded through the charitable bequest she made in 1558, just months before Queen Elizabeth I was crowned Queen of England.

The trust concentrates on running almshouses and a residential home for older people.

The Valentine Poole Charity

£36,000

Correspondent: Victor Russell, Ewen Hall, Wood Street, Barnet, Hertfordshire EN5 4BW (020 8441 6893; email: vpoole@btconnect.com; website: www. valentinepoole.org.uk)

CC number: 220856

Eligibility

People in need who live in Barnet, East Barnet, and Chipping Barnet.

Types of grants

One-off grants are given towards essential items such as household goods, children's clothing, travel and food costs. Pensions of £120 to £150 a month are made to older people. Christmas grants are also made to families at Christmas.

Annual grant total

In 2016 the charity had assets of £662,000 and an income of £68,000. Grants to individuals totalled £36,000 and were broken down as follows:

Monthly pensions	£25,000
Household equipment and travel	£9,200
Christmas grants	£1,700

Applications

Applications can be made in writing to the correspondent.

Other information

The charity also makes awards to individuals for education, and to organisations active in the local community.

Bexley

The Bexley Mayor's Benevolent Fund

£2,000

Correspondent: Ken Argent, Grants Manager, North London Business Park, Oakleigh Road, London N11 1NP (020 8359 2020; email: ken.argent@barnet. gov.uk; website: www.barnet.gov.uk/ citizen-home/council-tax-and-benefits/ grants-and-funding/grants-for-individuals.html)

Eligibility

People in need who live in the borough of Bexley.

Types of grants

Grants are available for household goods (up to £200), school uniforms (up to £60), clothing, relieving a financial crisis and essentials for families with new babies.

Annual grant total

An exact grant total figure was not available. Our research suggests that grants usually total around £2,000 per year.

Applications

Apply in writing to the correspondent. In practice, many applications are referred by the council's social services department who also vet all applications from individuals. Applications can be submitted at any time.

Bromley

Bromley Relief In Need Charity

£7,000

Correspondent: Revd Anne Jablonski, Trustee, Bromley Parish Church, Church Road, Bromley BR2 0EG (email: vicar@ bromleyparishchurch.org or

bromleyrelief@gmail.com; website: bromleyrelief.weebly.com)

CC number: 262591

Eligibility

People in need who live in both the ancient borough of Bromley and the wider area of the modern borough of Bromley.

Types of grants

One-off grants of up to £300. Examples of past grants include bedding, holidays, school trips, train tickets, carpets and furniture.

Annual grant total

In 2016 the charity had an income of £3,000 and a total expenditure of £7,900. We have estimated that grants to individuals totalled £7,000.

Applications

Applications should be made on a form available to download from the website or from the correspondent. All applications must be made through a professional third party, such as social worker, health worker, religious leader, other welfare organisation or charity. The trustees meet on alternate months to consider applications, but can respond quicker if necessary.

The Hayes (Kent) Trust

£11,900 (23 grants)

Correspondent: Andrew Naish, Trustee, 2 Warren Wood Close, Bromley BR2 7DU (020 8462 1915; email: hayes.kent.trust@gmail.com)

CC number: 221098

Eligibility

People in need who live in the parish of Hayes.

Types of grants

One-off grants, in the region of £75 to £1,500, are given according to need.

Annual grant total

In 2016/17 the trust had assets of £1.1 million and an income of £50,500. Grants to individuals totalled £18,200 and were broken down as follows:

Relief in need	45	£10,600
Advancement of education	10	£6,300
Relief in sickness	2	£1,300

Applications

Applications can be made in writing to the correspondent. They should include the full name of the applicant, postal address in Hayes (Kent), telephone number, email, date of birth, and details of why support is required. Applications may include any supporting information and can be made at any time either directly by the individual or through a

third party, such as a social worker, Citizens Advice or other welfare agency.

Other information

The trust is an amalgamation of the following charities: The Poors Land Cottage Charity; The Poors Land Eleemosynary Charity; The Hayes (Kent) Educational Foundation.

Camden

Hampstead Wells and Campden Trust

£183,000 (3,191 grants)

Correspondent: Sheila Taylor, 62 Rosslyn Hill, London NW3 1ND (020 7435 1570; email: grant@hwct.co.uk; website: www.hwct.org.uk)

CC number: 1094611

Eligibility

People who have a disability or are sick, convalescent, infirm, or in conditions of need, hardship or distress and who live in the former metropolitan borough of Hampstead. Grants to individuals, whether one-off payments or pensions, can only be made to residents of the former metropolitan borough of Hampstead (the area of benefit, a map of which is available on the website). A temporary stay in Hampstead, or in hospital in the area is not in itself a sufficient qualification.

Types of grants

In addition to pensions (£15 per week at the time of writing), one-off grants of up to £1,000 are given for a range of purposes including holidays, clothing, help with debts, removals and transport, furniture, gas, electric, fuel, TV and telephone bills and medical purposes. Kitchen starter packs and birthday and Christmas hampers are also given.

Annual grant total

In 2015/16 the trust had assets of £17 million and an income of £479,000. The trust made 3,191 grants for welfare purposes, totalling £183,000.

Exclusions

Grants are not made for: the payment of taxes, including council tax; the payment of fines; course or school fees.

Applications

Applications are accepted on behalf of individuals and families from any local constituted group, departments/units of Camden Council or the health service, a housing association, advice agency or other voluntary agency where the individual or family is known. The applying organisation must be willing to receive and account for any grant offered. The trust prefers to receive applications via the appropriate forms, which are available to download from the website; however, it also accepts applications in letter form. There is a list of essential information which must be included in any letter application on the website.

Other information

The trust's website lists additional eligibility criteria for individuals wishing to apply for a pension.

Lady Elizabeth Hatton's Charity

£7,000

Correspondent: Nicholas Hills, 5 St Andrew Street, London EC4A 3AF (email: info@standrewholborn.org.uk)

CC number: 213720

Eligibility

Residents of the ancient parish of St Andrew Holborn who are in need.

Types of grants

One-off grants according to need.

Annual grant total

In 2016 the charity had an income of £19,400 and a total expenditure of £10,700. We estimate that grants given to individuals totalled around £7,000.

Applications

Apply in writing to the correspondent.

St Andrew Holborn Charities

£97,000

Correspondent: Nicholas Hills, 5 St Andrew Street, London EC4A 3AB (020 7583 7394; email: charity@ standrewholborn.org.uk; website: www. standrewholborn.org.uk)

CC number: 1095045

Eligibility

People in need resident in a defined area of Holborn (applicants should call the charity or check the website for confirmation of the beneficial area).

Types of grants

One-off grants of up to £500 are given towards household items and clothing. Annual awards are also made to those with a long-term sickness or those with chronic illnesses.

Annual grant total

In 2016 the charity had assets of £11.8 million and an income of £347,500. We estimate that welfare grants to individuals totalled around £97,000.

Applications

Application forms can be downloaded from the website, where guidelines can also be found.

Other information

This charity is the result of an amalgamation of three trusts: The City Foundation; The Isaac Duckett's Charity; and The William Williams Charity. Grants are also given to organisations.

St Giles-in-the-Fields and Bloomsbury United Charity

£500 (one grant)

Correspondent: Hazel Capper, St Giles in the Fields Church, St Giles High Street, London WC2H 8LG (email: clerk@stgilescharities.org.uk; website: www.stgilescharities.org.uk)

CC number: 1111908

Eligibility

People in need who live in the ancient parishes of St Giles-in-the-Fields and St George's Bloomsbury. A map of the area of benefit is available on the website. In exceptional cases, the trustees may assist an individual outside the area of benefit. Applicants must have a low income (proof is required) and there is a preference to fund those with a physical and mental illness or disability.

Types of grants

One-off grants, usually of £500, towards the purchase of white goods, furniture, bedding, clothing and medical equipment.

Annual grant total

In 2016 the charity had assets of £2.85 million and an income of £135,000.

Grant-making makes up only a small part of the charity's work, however in October 2016 the charity launched a new individual grants programme, awarding up to £500 for household items where needed. By the end of the year, the charity had received one application for funding, and the trustees awarded up to £500 for a new dual fuel cooker.

Exclusions

Holidays are not funded except in extreme circumstances.

Applications

Grant application forms are available to download from the charity's website. Applicants need to provide proof of income and expenditure, and all new applicants will be visited by a Grants Officer.

Household items will be bought through a purchasing scheme.

Other information

The charity also provides almshouse accommodation, consisting of eight flats, for women over the age of 60 in the Covent Garden area. In addition, the charity also provides grants to organisations.

St Pancras Welfare Trust

£22,500 (274 grants)

Correspondent: Eleanor Sturdy, 124 Regents Park Road, London NW1 8XL (020 7483 2375; email: spwtrust@gmail.com; website: www.spwt. org.uk)

CC number: 261261

Eligibility

People in need or who are sick, convalescent, or have a disability and live in the old metropolitan borough of St Pancras (postal districts NW5, most of NW1, parts of N6, N19, NW3 and WC1). If you are unsure of whether you live in a qualifying area the trust website has a street directory on their website. Applicants must have the support of a sponsoring agency. The trust does not accept direct applications.

Types of grants

One-off grants, typically between £100 and £300, for a wide range of needs. Grants may be in the form of cash or vouchers.

Annual grant total

In 2016/17 the trust had assets of £865,000 and an income of £29,500. The trust awarded £22,500 in grants during the year – 134 grants were made for the relief of poverty, and 140 grants were issued as Christmas/winter vouchers.

Exclusions

No grants are made for educational purposes, computers, utility bills, statutory payments or rent arrears.

Applications

Applications can be submitted using an application form available from the trust's website or from the correspondent, with an accompanying cover letter. The trustees will only consider applications made through statutory bodies such as social services or community organisations like Citizens Advice. Applications are considered on a regular basis.

Stafford's Charity

£58,500

Correspondent: Nicholas Hills, 5 St Andrew Street, London EC4A 3AB (020 7583 7394; email: stafford@ standrewholborn.org.uk; website: www. standrewholborn.org.uk/charities)

CC number: 206770

Eligibility

People in need who have lived in the Holborn locality, centred on the ancient parish of St Andrew Holborn now comprising of the guild church of St Andrew Holborn and the parishes of St George the Martyr, Queen Square and St Alban the Martyr Holborn for at least three years (a map of the area of benefit is provided on the charity's website). Applicants must be living off a low disposable income (such as, those on jobseekers allowance, income support, Disability Living Allowance, etc.).

Preference may be given to older people or people with chronic disabilities or long-term sickness of any age (evidence of disability is required) and young widows or widowers with children.

Types of grants

Annual awards are given to those with a long-term sickness or those with chronic illness who are on a low weekly income (less than £75 a week for a single person, or less than £120 for a couple). One-off grants are also available to people on a low income for kitchen appliances, furnishings, carpets, medical equipment, clothing, redecoration costs and other household items or needs.

Annual grant total

In 2016 the charity had assets of £8 million and an income of £222,565. The charity awarded grants to individuals totalling £58,500, consisting of £58,000 in annual awards and £485 in individual grants.

Exclusions

No new application will be considered unless a year has elapsed since the last one and no grants are given for holidays (unless in exceptional circumstances).

The recipients of an annual award will lose the entitlement if they move into a residential home. Individuals will also lose their annual award if they move outside the area of benefit.

No grant will be given for holidays unless in exceptional circumstances.

Applications

Apply on a form available to download from the website or from the correspondent. Applications should be submitted to Anna Paterson (Grants Officer, 5 St Andrew Street, London EC4A 3AF). Applications can be submitted at any time. All new applicants are visited by the Grants Officer. Proof of income is required.

Other information

Note the following information from the charity's website: 'All grants for household items will be bought from Argos in Grays Inn Road or from IKEA, unless the applicant is known to other agencies i.e. Housing Support, a Housing Association etc. when a cheque can be made out to that organisation.'

City of London

The Aldgate Freedom Foundation

£18,800

Correspondent: Michael Sonn, Financial Officer, 140 Hall Lane, Upminster, London RM14 1AL (01708 222482)

CC number: 207046

Eligibility

Older people, generally aged over 65, who are in need and live in the parish of St Botolph's without Aldgate or the area to the boundary of the Portsoken ward.

Types of grants

Relief-in-need grants and Christmas bonuses.

Annual grant total

In 2015 the foundation had assets of £1.7 million and an income of £45,500. Grants to individuals, including Christmas bonuses, totalled £18,800.

Applications

Application forms are available from the correspondent. Requests for support can be considered at any time.

Other information

Grants are also given to organisations or hospitals within the city and towards the maintenance of St Botolph's church.

The Mitchell City of London Charity

£20,500

Correspondent: Lucy Jordan, Clerk to the Trustees, Ash View, High Street, Orston, Nottingham NG13 9NU (0845 600 1558; email: mitchellcityoflondon@ gmail.com)

CC number: 207342

Eligibility

Individuals of state pension age who are in need and who live or work, or have lived or worked, in the City of London for at least five years. Widows of men so qualified may also apply.

Types of grants

Pensions, which in 2016/17 were paid at £400 per annum, in quarterly sums of £100. Gifts are also given at Christmas (£150) and on the Queen's birthday (£125).

Annual grant total

In 2016/17 the charity held assets of £1 million and had an income of £81,500. During the year the charity gave around £20,500 in grants to individuals.

Applications

Apply on a form available from the correspondent including details of the applicant's income and expenditure. Applications can be submitted directly by the individual or through an organisation such as Citizens Advice. They are considered in March, June, September and November.

Other information

The charity is one half of the Mitchell City of London Charity and Educational Foundation. The Educational Foundation also makes grants.

City of Westminster

The Arthur Cross Charity

£3,000

Correspondent: Sylvia Kalisch, 83 Becklow Gardens, London W12 9ET (07970 860 685)

CC number: 210466

Eligibility

People who are sick, convalescing, or people with a disability. Individuals must live in the ecclesiastical parish of St Michael, Chester Square.

Types of grants

One-off grants of up to £150 for purposes including heating costs, clothing, holidays and furnishings.

Annual grant total

In 2016/17 the charity had an income of £7,000 and a total expenditure of £7,000. We estimate that the charity awarded £3,000 in grants to individuals during the year.

Exclusions

No grants are given towards arrears.

Applications

Individuals wishing to apply must do so through a professional or social worker, such as Citizens Advice. Applications received directly from an individual will not be considered.

Other information
The charity also makes awards to organisations.

Hyde Park Place Estate Charity

£7,200

Correspondent: Shirley Vaughan, St George's Hanover Square Church, The Vestry, 2A Mill Street, London W1S 1FX (020 7629 0874; website: www. stgeorgeshanoversquare.org)

CC number: 212439

Eligibility
People in need who are residents of the City of Westminster.

Types of grants
One-off and recurrent grants are available for individuals and families in need due to poverty, hardship or distress.

Annual grant total
In 2015/16 the charity had assets of £14 million and an income of £485,000. We estimate that around £7,200 was awarded in grants to individuals.

Applications
Applications should be sent directly to the correspondent. Applications are considered on an ongoing basis.

Other information
The charity also makes awards to organisations and individuals for education and welfare purposes. The charity also runs a grants programme for churches.

St John Southworth Caritas Fund

£18,000 (18 grants)

Correspondent: Marta Luiz, Diocese of Westminster, Vaughan House, 46 Francis Street, London SW1P 1QN (020 7798 9174; website: www.caritaswestminster. org.uk/grants.php)

CC number: 233699

Eligibility
Residents in the Diocese of Westminster.

Types of grants
Crisis grants can provide up to £1,500 per applicant, and can be used for: rent; fuel bills; children's expenses; white goods; furniture; school lunch money; and driving lessons. The charity also awards grants to assist with funeral expenses. Applicants applying for a

bereavement grant can receive up to £1,500.

Annual grant total
In 2016/17 the charity awarded £18,000 in grants to 18 individuals.

Applications
Application forms can be downloaded from the website and should be completed by the applicant's parish priest. Completed application forms should be returned by post, or by email to caritasgrants@rcdow.org.uk.

Other information
Funeral grants were introduced in September 2016 to help address funeral poverty. As a new grant, the charity has administered advertisements for these grants and hopes to see an increase in applications in the coming years.

The fund is managed and administered by the Westminster Roman Catholic Diocesan Trust.

The United Charities of St Paul's, Covent Garden

£2,400

Correspondent: Maggie Rae, Flat 9, 19 Henrietta Street, London WC2E 8QH (020 7379 6080; email: mrae@clintons. co.uk)

CC number: 209568

Eligibility
People in need who live in the city of Westminster.

Types of grants
One-off grants.

Annual grant total
In 2015/16 the charity had an income of £10,700 and a total expenditure of £5,000. We estimate that the charity gave around £2,400 in grants to individuals.

The charity also awards grants to organisations.

Exclusions
Tuition fees and holidays are not funded.

Applications
Apply in writing to the correspondent.

Other information
At the time of writing (September 2017) the charity had no website or accounts available.

Strand Parishes Trust

£25,500 (56 grants)

Correspondent: Roy Sully, 169 Strand, London WC2R 2LS (020 7836 3205; email: sptwestminster@aol.com; website: www.strandparishestrust.org.uk)

CC number: 1121754

Eligibility
Individuals who are disadvantaged through physical, or mental disability, or financial hardship and who live and/or work in the London borough of the City of Westminster, with preference for the parish of St Clement Danes and St Mary le Strand.

Types of grants
One-off grants of £50 to £500 to assist with the relief of poverty. The trust also provides pensions.

Annual grant total
In 2016 the trust had assets of £7.2 million and an income of £204,500. During the year, the trust made a total of 19 grants to individuals worth a total of £5,100. In addition, the trust also supported 37 older people with regular small payments totalling £20,500.

Exclusions
No grants are given for holidays abroad or the clearance of debt. Subsequent applications within a 12-month period are not usually considered unless in specific circumstances.

Applications
Application forms are available to download from the trust's website or can be requested from the correspondent. Applications must be supported by a sponsor, such as social services or Citizens Advice.

Other information
The Isaac Duckett's Charity, St Mary le Strand Charity and St Clement Danes Parochial Charities were amalgamated with other charities to form the Strand Parishes Trust.

Westminster Almshouses Foundation

£105,500 (243 grants)

Correspondent: Cristina O'Halloran, Clerk, 7 Allandale Place, Orpington, Kent BR6 7TH (020 7828 3131; email: cristina@westminsteralmshouses.com; website: www.westminsteralmshouses. com)

CC number: 226936

Eligibility
People in need who live in the London borough of Westminster.

Types of grants

One-off grants averaging around £400, as well as pensions. Grants are typically offered for help in obtaining cookers, washers, microwaves, as well as children's clothing and equipment.

Annual grant total

In 2016 the foundation had assets of £29.8 million and an income of £851,000. Pensions and grants to individuals for welfare purposes totalled £105,500.

Applications

Application forms are available from the correspondent. Forms must detail your request, current circumstances and how this award will help you towards self-sufficiency. Decisions are made quickly once all the necessary information is acquired.

Other information

The foundation's main activity is providing almshouse accommodation in central London for people over the age of 60 who are in need. The foundation also makes educational grants.

Westminster Amalgamated Charity

£33,000 (189 grants)

Correspondent: Keith Rea, School House, Drury Lane, London WC2B 5SU (020 7395 9460; fax: 020 7395 9479; email: wac@3chars.org.uk; website: www.w-a-c.org.uk)

CC number: 207964

Eligibility

People who live, work or study in the borough of Westminster; and people who have lived, worked or studied in Westminster for at least five years. Grants are awarded to those on low incomes or in receipt of benefits, those with disabilities, and those without a permanent residence and currently residing in a hospital. Note grants for holidays are only approved if the applicant is age 60 or over.

Types of grants

One-off grants between £100 and £400 to be used for: the purchase of clothing; household items (white goods, furniture etc.); decorating/carpeting/flooring; and holidays in the UK (for over 60s only). If the grant is for household repairs or items, the money will be paid directly to the supplier.

Annual grant total

In 2016 the charity had assets of £7.5 million and an income of £318,500. During the year, 189 grants were made to individuals totalling £38,000, broken down as follows:

Discretionary	68	£16,800
Household	52	£12,700
Holidays	11	£4,700
Clothing	58	£4,000

Exclusions

Grants will not be given for: TVs; CD/DVD players; mobile phones; computers/software; educational needs; holidays abroad; debt repayment or fees. No retrospective grants will be awarded.

Applications

Application forms are available to download from the charity's website and must be sponsored by a recognised agency, such as social services or Citizens Advice. Applicants must provide proof of their financial situation, for example payslips and bank statements, as well as details of what the grant will be used for.

Other information

The charity also makes grants to local organisations in the area.

Ealing

Acton (Middlesex) Charities – Relief in Need Fund

£2,500

Correspondent: Lorna Dodd, Clerk to the Trustees, c/o St Mary's Parish Office, 1 The Mount, Acton High Street, London W3 9NW (email: acton.charities@virgin.net; website: www.actoncharities.co.uk)

CC number: 211446

Eligibility

People in need who have lived in the former ancient parish of Acton for at least three years. (The John Perryn Relief in Need Charity fund considers awards from applicants who have lived in the parish for less than three years.)

Types of grants

One-off grants for the purchase furniture, white goods and other essential items of household equipment or other needs. Payments are made directly to suppliers.

Small awards are also available 'to encourage local talent', including help with mounting exhibitions if the group or artist involved is in the Acton area.

Annual grant total

In 2015 the charity had an income of £7,300 and a total expenditure of £3,400. The Acton (Middlesex) Charities' website notes that during the year a total of about £2,500 was given in relief-in-need grants (including the awards through the John Perry Relief in Need Fund). A further £2,500 was given to artists and arts organisations through the Athawes Art Gallery fund.

Exclusions

Anyone outside the area of benefit (there is a helpful map on the charity's website). Grants are not given for courses in private schools or institutions.

Applications

Application forms are available from the charity's website or the correspondent; however, referrals must be made by a professional third party, such as a doctor, district and health visitor or social services.

Note: any correspondence should be made by post or email only.

The charity advises that a quick response is not always possible. The trustees meet twice a year.

Further details of support for artists can be obtained from the correspondent.

Other information

This charity, together with Acton (Middlesex) Educational Charity (Charity Commission no. 312312) form part of the Acton (Middlesex) Charities, administered by the same body of trustees. The charities provide welfare, educational and arts grants and also support local schools and carnivals. The website states that 'in present times the charities try to help where other local services fail'.

During 2014 a total of £2,500 was paid to local organisations and artists (Athawes Art Gallery Fund).

The Ealing Aid-in-Sickness Trust

£3,300

Correspondent: Anita Sheehan, The William Hobbayne Community Centre, St Dunstan's Road, London W7 2HB (020 8810 0277; email: hobbaynecharity@btinternet.com; website: www.williamhobbaynecharity.co.uk)

CC number: 212826

Eligibility

People in need, who live in the old metropolitan borough of Ealing (this includes Hanwell, Ealing, Greenford, Perivale and Northolt but not Southall or Acton), who are incurring extra expense due to long- or short-term illness.

Types of grants

One-off grants according to need, to assist with the extra cost incurred through illness. Grants can be used for prescriptions, transport to medical appointments, home adaptions, mobility aids, etc.

Annual grant total

In 2015/16 the trust had an income of £4,100 and a total expenditure of £3,700. We estimate that the trust awarded £3,300 in grants to individuals during the year.

Applications

Application forms are available from the correspondent. The trust welcomes preliminary contact if there are any enquiries.

Other information

The trust has stated that funds are very limited.

The Eleemosynary Charity of William Hobbayne

£5,900 (29 grants)

Correspondent: Anita Sheehan, Administrator, The William Hobbayne Centre, St Dunstan's Road, London W7 2HB (020 8810 0277; email: hobbaynecharity@btinternet.com; website: www.williamhobbaynecharity. co.uk)

CC number: 211547

Eligibility

Primarily people in need who live in the civil parish of Hanwell. Very limited funds are also available for people with a medical condition who live in Hanwell, Perivale, Northolt, Greenford and Central Ealing.

Types of grants

One-off grants for clothing, furniture and domestic appliances. Grants are paid directly to the sponsors or suppliers.

Annual grant total

In 2015/16 the charity held assets of £2.4 million and had an income of £207,000. During the year, the charity gave almost £5,900 in grants to individuals.

The charity also gave around £35,500 in grants to organisations.

Applications

Application forms are available from the correspondent. Applications should be submitted through a sponsoring organisation such as a local health centre, church, outreach organisation or social services. Applications are considered on a monthly basis although urgent cases can be dealt with more quickly.

Other information

The charity owns the William Hobbayne Centre which runs activities and events for local people over the age of 50. It also has an outreach worker who, aside from encouraging grant applications, organises Christmas toy collections in more affluent parts of Hanwell for redistribution to families with difficult financial circumstances.

Enfield

Edmonton Aid-in-Sickness and Nursing Fund

£1,300

Correspondent: John Wells, Trustee, 54 Hyde Park Avenue, London N21 2PP (020 8292 5935; email: edmontonaidinsickness@gmail.com)

CC number: 210623

Eligibility

People in need who are in poor health and live in the old borough of Edmonton (mainly N9 and N18).

Types of grants

One-off grants, usually up to £300. In the past, grants have been awarded towards clothing, furniture, household necessities, convalescence, household bills and debts and medical equipment not covered by NHS provision.

Annual grant total

In 2016 the fund had an income of £6,100 and a total expenditure of £1,500. We estimate that grants given to individuals totalled £1,300.

Exclusions

The fund will not subsidise public funds, therefore applicants should have sought help from all public sources before approaching the fund.

Applications

Applications can be made in writing to the correspondent, either directly by the individual or through social services, Citizens Advice or other welfare agency. They can be received at any time.

The Old Enfield Charitable Trust

£115,000

Correspondent: Personal Grants Administrator, 22 The Town, Enfield, Middlesex EN2 6LT (020 8367 8941; email: enquiries@thetrustenfield.org.uk; website: www.toect.org.uk)

CC number: 207840

Eligibility

People in need, hardship or distress who live within the ancient parish of Enfield.

There is an eligibility checker on the charity's website.

Types of grants

One-off grants are given to help with unexpected expenses, including the replacement or provision of household goods and furniture, items associated with needs of individuals who have disabilities or chronic illnesses and, in exceptional circumstances, bills. Around 150 regular quarterly grants are made to people on a low income in financial need.

Annual grant total

In 2016/17 the trust had assets of £6.6 million and an income of £679,500. Grants to individuals totalled £231,500. We estimate that welfare grants totalled £115,000.

Exclusions

The trust will not provide support where local authority or central government should be assisting. Our research suggests that grants are not normally given to people who are homeless.

Applications

Application forms are available to download from the trust's website. There is also an eligibility checker on the website.

Other information

The charity makes 'community grants' to local organisations and individuals can also receive financial assistance to help with educational needs. The charity also administers Ann Crowe's and Wright's Almshouse Charity which owns almshouses that are let to people who are in need and already resident in the ancient parish of Enfield.

Greenwich

The Greenwich Charities

£6,000

Correspondent: The Trustees of The Greenwich Charities, c/o Grant Saw Solicitors LLP, Norman House, 110–114 Norman Road, London SE10 9EH (020 8858 6971; email: thegreenwichcharities@gmail.com; website: thegreenwichcharities.com)

Eligibility

Residents living within the postcodes SE10, SE3, SE7, SE13 and SE8 whose council tax is paid to the royal borough of Greenwich

Types of grants

One-off and recurrent grants are given according to need.

Annual grant total

In 2015/16 the three charities had a combined income of £10,600 and a total expenditure of £12,600. We estimate that grants given to individuals totalled around £6,000.

Applications

Applicants can download the application form on the charities' website or apply in writing to the correspondent. If applying in writing, applications should include: details of your circumstances; the amount of money you are requesting, what it is for and why it is needed; name, address and contact details; name and contact details of a supporting social worker if you have one. Friends, relatives or carers can apply on other people's behalf.

Other information

The Greenwich Charities is a group of three charities that share common objects and have one single application process. They consist of: the Charity of Charles Soames (Charity Commission no. 252262); Randall's Charity (Charity Commission no. 216731); The Greenwich Charity (Charity Commission no. 1074816).

The charities also make grants to organisations.

Greenwich Charities of William Hatcliffe and The Misses Smith

£18,200

Correspondent: Linda Clayton, Clerk to the Trustees, Greenwich Hatcliffe Charities, PO Box 70569, London SE9 9DT (email: clerk@greenwich-hatcliffe.org.uk)

CC number: 227721

Eligibility

People over the age of 55 who live within a five-mile radius of the almshouses operated by the charity.

Types of grants

One-off grants to help older people remain independent in their own homes and Christmas grants of £100 to almshouse residents.

Annual grant total

In 2015/16 the charity held assets of £1.7 million and had an income of £262,500. Grants made through the charity's Help at Home programme totalled £14,300 and an additional two grants totalling £3,900 were made to help with home adaptations. Christmas grants to individuals living in the charity's almshouses amounted to £1,400.

Applications

Apply in writing to the correspondent. The 2015/16 accounts note that applicants are normally referred through agencies such as Age UK.

Other information

The charity also provides almshouse accommodation for older residents in the ancient parish of East Greenwich.

The Woolwich and Plumstead Relief-in-Sickness Fund

£5,500

Correspondent: Dave Lucas, Royal Borough of Greenwich, The Woolwich Centre, 35 Wellington Street, Woolwich, London SE18 6HQ (020 8921 5261; email: dave.lucas@royalgreenwich.gov.uk)

CC number: 212482

Eligibility

People in need who have a physical illness or disability and live in the parishes of Woolwich and Plumstead. When funds allow, applications may be accepted from people living in the borough of Greenwich.

Types of grants

Small, one-off grants to relieve hardship and need. The grants can be used to cover the cost of items in part or in full, and can be used towards medical expenses, household items, travel, living expenses, etc.

Annual grant total

In 2016/17 the fund had an income of £11,500 and a total expenditure of £11,400. We estimate that grants given to individuals totalled £5,500.

Exclusions

No grants are given to help with debts, utility bills, recurrent expenditure, structural works or rent. Support for recurring items is not usually provided.

Applications

Applications should be made in writing to the correspondent, including details of the applicant's financial position and what the grant will be used for. A confirmation of diagnosis or supporting letter from a medical professional should also be included.

Other information

The fund also makes awards to organisations.

Hackney

Hackney Benevolent Pension Society

£4,500

Correspondent: The Trustees, 39 Sydner Road, London N16 7UF (020 7254 6145; email: fm.broadway@gmail.com)

CC number: 212731

Eligibility

People who are older and in need, and who have lived in Hackney for at least seven years.

Types of grants

Gifts of around £30 are given to pensioners at Christmas, on their birthday and at the society's annual general meeting in November. Payments are delivered in person through home visits.

Annual grant total

In 2016/17 the society had an income of £2,000 and a total expenditure of £4,800. We estimate that grants given to individuals totalled around £4,500.

Applications

Apply in writing to the correspondent.

The Hackney Parochial Charities

£10,000

Correspondent: Sarah Bennett, Correspondent, c/o Trust Partnership, 6 Trull Farm Buildings, Trull, Tetbury, Gloucestershire GL8 8SQ (020 3397 7805; email: hackney@ thetrustpartnership.com; website: www. hackneyparochialcharities.org.uk)

CC number: 219876

Eligibility

People in need who live in the former metropolitan borough of Hackney (as it was before 1970).

Types of grants

One-off grants for the purchase of clothing and essential household equipment, although grants can be given for many other welfare purposes, such as bedding, furniture and medical and travel expenses for hospital visits.

Annual grant total

In 2015/16 the charity had assets of £6 million and an income of £291,000. Grants were made totalling £223,500, most of which appears to be given to organisations. We estimate that around £20,000 was given to individuals for both social welfare and educational needs.

Applications

Applications can be made via a form available on the website.

The Lolev Charitable Trust

£8.39 million (2,800+ grants)

Correspondent: Abraham Tager, Chairman, 14a Gilda Crescent, London N16 6JP (020 8806 3457)

CC number: 326249

Eligibility

People who are sick or in need who live in Hackney and the surrounding area.

Types of grants

The trust's annual report stated: 'Assistance is given according to circumstances and available finance.'

Annual grant total

In 2016 the trust had assets of £35,000 and an income of £8.6 million. During the year, the trust gave around £8.39 million in grants to over 2,800 individuals.

Applications

Applications by individuals must be accompanied by a letter of recommendation by the applicant's minister or other known religious leader.

Other information

At the time of writing (November 2017) this was the only information available for the trust. We were unable to contact the correspondent for more details. Potential applicants are advised to write to the correspondent to confirm eligibility criteria and the types of grants available before submitting an application.

Hammer-smith and Fulham

Dr Edwards and Bishop King's Fulham Charity

£134,000 (211 grants)

Correspondent: Jonathan Martin, Clerk to the Trustees, Percy Barton House, 33–35 Dawes Road, London SW6 7DT (020 7385 9387; fax: 020 7610 2856; email: clerk@debk.org.uk; website: www.debk.org.uk)

CC number: 1113490

Eligibility

People in need who are on low incomes and live in the old metropolitan borough of Fulham. This constitutes all of the SW6 postal area and parts of W14 and W6.

Types of grants

One-off grants according to need are made towards essential items of daily living, including kitchen appliances, beds, furniture and clothing (including school uniforms), carpets, flooring, decorating materials, baby items, furnishings, cleaning or cleaning equipment, or essential medical equipment.

Annual grant total

In 2015/16 the charity had assets of £9.3 million and an income of £443,000. The charity made 211 welfare grants totalling £134,000.

Exclusions

According to the website, the charity does not:

- Normally help those who are homeowners
- Help those not in the area of benefit
- Give cash grants (unless they are to be administered by an agency)
- Give grants retrospectively or pay arrears on utility bills
- Provide funds for funerals
- Provide wheelchairs or electric scooters
- Provide computer equipment of any sort, unless you are housebound
- Provide dishwashers
- Provide laminate flooring
- Provide grants for equipment where government, or local government, or any other agency is required to provide that equipment by law

The charity prefers not to satisfy repeat requests and is extremely unlikely to help requests for which funding may be available from other places. Our research suggests that postgraduate courses are not funded.

Applications

Application forms are available to download from the charity's website or can be requested from the office. Applications can be submitted by an individual (or family) or on behalf of an individual (or family) by a supporting agency. There is a separate form for each type of application. Once the form has been submitted, the charity will be in touch to discuss what happens next. Further information on applications including dates of trustees' meetings are available on the charity's website.

Other information

The charity gives money to both individuals and organisations, with its main responsibility being towards the relief of poverty rather than assisting students.

There are also Summer Schemes whereby funding is given to help with 'organised activities and day trips for young local people from challenging backgrounds, over the July and August school holidays'. Assistance for longer trips – provided the destination venues are reputable, reasonably priced, and within the UK – may also be given under the scheme.

Fuelbanks and Families

See entry on page 306

Haringey

Tottenham District Charity

£96,500 (150+ grants)

Correspondent: Carolyn Banks, Secretary, 3rd Floor, River Park House, 225 High Road, London N22 8HQ (email: charities@virginmedia.com; website: www.tottenhamdistrictcharity.org.uk)

CC number: 207490

Eligibility

People in demonstrable financial need who have lived in Tottenham for a minimum of three consecutive years. Eligible individuals aged 65 and over can apply for a pension.

Types of grants

One-off grants and pensions. Grants of up to £400 are available towards, for example: basic household furniture or items, e.g. beds, bedding, wardrobes and carpets; white goods; clothing; hospital visit expenses; indirect educational expenses, such as transport costs; recuperative holidays; and home decoration or repairs.

Lifetime pensions totalling £260 each year (two payments of £130, at the end of April and October) are awarded to people over the age of 65.

Annual grant total

In 2016/17 the charity had assets of £2.8 million and an income of £87,000. A total of £96,500 was awarded to individuals; pensions/bonuses to more than 150 older people totalled £50,000, and £46,500 was given in one-off grants.

Exclusions

No grants are made to help with bills or debts.

Applications

Apply on a form available to download from the charity's website or from the correspondent. Completed forms should be returned to the correspondent by email or post. If possible, applications should be supported by a professional third party, such as a social worker, Citizens Advice or a welfare charity. Applications for grants should include information and costs of the specific items required (website, catalogue page, etc.).

The charity aims to make decisions on applications within a month. Organisations supporting successful applicants are required to find suitable shops that will accept the charity's cheque. Cheques are sent to the organisation/person that submitted the application. The charity does not normally make cheques out to individuals directly unless proof of purchase has been submitted.

Wood Green (Urban District) Charity

£12,000

Correspondent: Carolyn Banks, Clerk, 1st Floor, 48 Station Road, Wood Green, London N22 7TY (020 8489 5030)

CC number: 206736

Eligibility

People in need who have lived in the former urban district of Wood Green (roughly the present N22 postal area) for at least three years.

Types of grants

One-off grants according to need. Grants have previously been given for clothing and for household items such as beds and fridges. Pensions are given to eligible older people.

Annual grant total

In 2015/16 the charity had an income of £9,000 and a total expenditure of £12,800. We estimate that grants given to individuals totalled around £12,000.

Applications

Application forms are available from the correspondent. They can be submitted directly by the individual or through a social worker, Citizens Advice or other welfare agency or third party and are considered throughout the year.

Harrow

Mayor of Harrow's Charity Fund

£4,000

Correspondent: The Mayor's Office, London Borough of Harrow, Civic Centre, Harrow, Middlesex HA1 2UH (020 8424 1154; email: mayor@harrow. gov.uk)

CC number: 219034

Eligibility

People in need who live in the borough of Harrow.

Types of grants

One-off grants are given for basic items such as beds, food, heating appliances, cookers, clothing and so on. Grants are also given towards holidays/school trips for children.

Annual grant total

In 2015/16 the fund had an income of £4,300 and a total expenditure of £4,600. We estimate that grants given to individuals totalled approximately £4,000.

Applications

Application forms are available from the correspondent. Most applications come through a social worker, Citizens Advice or other welfare agency, although this does not preclude individuals from applying directly. Applications are considered at any time. Applicants must demonstrate that the individual/family is experiencing financial hardship and that the grant will alleviate ill health or poverty or improve essential living conditions. Grants are paid directly to the supplier or through a third party.

Hillingdon

Harefield Parochial Charities

£2,400

Correspondent: John Ross, Chair, 11 Burbery Close, Harefield, Uxbridge UB9 6QP (01895 823058; fax: 01895 823644; email: hpc@harefieldcharities.co. uk; website: www.harefieldcharities.co. uk)

CC number: 210145

Eligibility

People in need who live in the ancient parish of Harefield, especially those who are older or in poor health.

Types of grants

Cheques for £100 to older residents at Christmas with fuel costs. The trustees stress that grant-making is not the primary activity of the charity.

Annual grant total

In 2016 the charity held assets of £2.5 million and had an income of £132,000. Grants to individuals totalled £2,400.

Exclusions

Grants are not given towards relief of rates, taxes or other public funds.

Applications

Apply in writing to the correspondent. Applications can be made directly by the individual or through a social worker, Citizens Advice or other welfare agency.

Other information

The charity's main activity is the provision of alms accommodation for older people and families in need.

Uxbridge United Welfare Trusts

£71,000 (187 grants)

Correspondent: Mrs J. Duffy, Grants Officer, Woodbridge House, New Windsor Street, Uxbridge UB8 2TY (07912 270937; email: grants.officer@ uuwt.org; website: www.uuwt.org)

CC number: 217066

Eligibility

People in need due to financial circumstances, health problems, age and so on who live in or have a very strong connection with the Uxbridge area. The area of benefit covers Cowley, Harefield, Hillingdon, Ickenham and Uxbridge.

Types of grants

One-off grants can be given for services or specific goods, such as furniture, household equipment, clothing, baby equipment, and help with fuel bills.

Annual grant total

In 2016 the trust had assets of £14 million and an income of £660,500. Welfare grants to individuals totalled £71,000.

Applications

Application forms can be requested from the correspondent. They can be submitted directly by the individual or through a social worker, Citizens Advice or educational welfare agency, if applicable. Awards are considered each month. A trained member of staff will visit applicants for an interview to better assess their case.

Other information

Grants are also awarded for educational purposes and may be given to support organisations. The trust also runs almshouses.

Islington

Richard Cloudesley's Charity

£79,000

Correspondent: Melanie Griffiths, Director, Office 1.1, Resource for London, 356 Holloway Road, London N7 6PA (020 7697 4094; email: info@ cloudesley.org.uk; website: www. richardcloudesleyscharity.org.uk)

CC number: 205959

Eligibility

People in need who are sick or who have disabilities and live in the ancient parish of St Mary's Islington (roughly the modern borough, excluding the area south of the Pentonville and City Roads). A map of the area of benefit is available on the charity's website.

Types of grants

One-off grants, for a wide range of purposes, with the aim of relieving poverty and distress for those who are in need.

Annual grant total

In 2016/17 the charity held assets of almost £50.2 million and had an income of £1.38 million. Welfare grants made to individuals totalled £79,000.

Exclusions

No help for debts, education, computers, childcare, funeral expenses or for money that has been stolen.

Applications

Check the charity's website for up-to-date information. Under the interim welfare grants scheme, applications should be made to one of the charity's Welfare Grants Programme Trusted Partner organisations. The charity does not currently accept direct applications but can give further information and refer individuals to the appropriate partner agency.

Other information

The annual report of 2016/17 gives a short history of the charity which dates back to the 16th century:

> The charity was formed as the result of a gift of land (a 'Stoney Field' of 14 acres) from the will of Richard Cloudesley dated 1517. In his will it was stipulated that the proceeds from the rental of the land were to be used 'to bestow good deeds of charity and to fund masses at St Mary's

Church for his and his wife's souls'. During the Reformation, the proportion of the bequest allocated to fund masses was taken by the Crown and, in subsequent years, the charitable trusts have been amended several times. Today, Cloudesley is a significant grant-making charity in the borough of Islington. Half of the charity's grant-making focuses on its Health & Welfare programmes that support people with health and financial needs in the borough, while the other half supports the Church of England churches in the borough.

Cripplegate Foundation

£29,000

Correspondent: Kristina Glenn, Director, 13 Elliott's Place, Islington, London N1 8HX (020 7288 6940; email: grants@cripplegate.org.uk; website: www. cripplegate.org)

CC number: 207499

Eligibility

The foundation works to bring about change that will transform the lives of its most disadvantaged residents. Applicants must be in receipt of specified benefits. Full details of eligibility criteria are available from the Cripplegate Foundation website.

Types of grants

The foundation does not make cash payments and the form of payment varies depending on the type of assistance. The Resident Support Scheme (RSS) may be able to assist with, for example: payments for the purchase of essential household items; payments towards a shortfall in rent caused by the bedroom tax, for example; payments for removal expenses; help with living expenses for those affected by crisis or disaster; help managing a council tax bill. In the case of a crisis or disaster, assistance can be given in the form of grocery vouchers or help with help to connect or maintain access to gas or electricity supplies.

Annual grant total

In 2016 the foundation had assets of £38.7 million and a total income of £2.27 million. Grants made to individuals under the foundation's Islington Resident Support Scheme totalled £29,000 and from St Sepulchre's (which the foundation administers), totalled £34,000.

Exclusions

The foundation offers advice to new and returning applicants who are encouraged to contact the Programme Team for help by emailing grants@cripplegate.org.uk.

Applications

The foundation's website states that Cripplegate Foundation is a founding

partner of Islington's RSS which was launched in 2013 following the localisation of the discretionary elements of the old Social Fund. The foundation now contributes to this scheme rather than awarding individual grants. The RSS supports Islington residents who are experiencing financial hardship. Applications are usually made through statutory services or participating community organisations. To be considered, applicants must be resident in Islington, be considered vulnerable (such as being older, responsible for children, having a long-term sickness or having disabilities) and in receipt of a means-tested benefit. Full details of how to apply can be found on the foundation's website.

Other information

As well as administering grants to organisations, the foundation aligns its support to individuals with the London Borough of Islington's RSS and the St Sepulchre (Finsbury) United Charities. The St Sepulchre charity provides grants to individuals who are over the age of 45 and live in the old London borough of Finsbury. These grants are approved by St Sepulchre and the foundation receives a contribution towards administrative costs.

Lady Gould's Charity

£41,000 (80 grants)

Correspondent: Graeme Couch, Clerk, 50 Broadway, Westminster, London SW1H 0BL (020 7783 3769; email: andycouch@bdb-law.co.uk; website: www.ladygouldscharity.org)

CC number: 234978

Eligibility

People in need who live in Highgate (i.e. the N6 postal district and part of the N2, N8, N10 and N19 districts). A reference map and street index is available on the website. Most grantees are in receipt of income support and housing benefit, although the charity may also consider applications from people earning under £10,000 a year.

Types of grants

One-off grants generally ranging from £200 to £400, although more is available in exceptional circumstances. Grants are given for clothing, furniture, furnishings, baby necessities and white goods. Grants to help towards debts and holidays are available but will only be given in very needy cases. It is not usual for an individual or family to receive more than one grant in a year.

Annual grant total

In 2016 the charity made grants totalling £41,000 to 80 applicants.

During the year the average grant was £515 per person.

Exclusions

Grants are rarely made for educational or recreational purposes or for debt relief.

Applications

Application forms are available to download from the website. Applications should be accompanied by a supporting statement from a social worker, GP or other recognised body. If this is not possible attach evidence of your entitlement to benefits, such as a housing benefit letter. Applications can be submitted directly by the individual or through a third party such as a social worker, Citizens Advice or other welfare agency. They are considered at any time. Phillip Dann currently acts as Grants Adviser and will telephone applicants to discuss the application.

St Sepulchre (Finsbury) United Charities

£48,000

Correspondent: Elias Poli, Smithfield Accountants LLP, 117 Charterhouse Street, London EC1M 6AA (020 7253 3757; email: elias@smithfield-accountants.co.uk)

CC number: 213312

Eligibility

People aged at least 45 who are in need and live within the old metropolitan borough of Finsbury.

Types of grants

Quarterly pensions and one-off grants.

Annual grant total

In 2016/17 the charity held assets of £3.3 million and had an income of £124,000. Grants to individuals totalled £48,000, of which £17,700 was given in quarterly pensions and £30,500 in one-off grants. A further £16,500 was given to organisations operating within the charity's catchment area.

Applications

Grants from the charity are administered by the Cripplegate Foundation (see entry on page 298). Most beneficiaries are referred through the Islington Resident Support Scheme (RSS). Individuals who meet the eligibility criteria can also apply to the Cripplegate Foundation directly.

Other information

In April 2013 the charity joined the new Islington RSS, which is delivered through a partnership between Cripplegate Foundation and Islington Council. Applications to the scheme can only be made online through a designated access point. See the Cripplegate Foundation website (www.cripplegate.org) for a list of access points and further details of the scheme.

Kensington and Chelsea

The Campden Charities

£973,000

Correspondent: Christopher Stannard, Clerk, Studios 3&4, 27a Pembridge Villas, London W11 3EP (020 7243 0551 or 020 7313 3797; website: www.campdencharities.org.uk)

CC number: 1104616

Eligibility

Individuals applying for funding must: have been continuously living in Kensington for at least two years (there is a helpful area of benefit map on the website); be a British or European citizen or have indefinite leave to remain; live in rented accommodation and not be a homeowner; be in receipt of benefits, including housing benefits; or be in low-paid work.

Types of grants

Grants are given to relieve financial hardship. Examples include grants to assist older people with the replacement of household appliances and with bills.

Annual grant total

In 2016/17 the charity had assets of £152.3 million and an income of £3.6 million. During the year, the charity awarded a total of £973,000 in grants to individuals for welfare purposes.

The charity also gave £483,000 in grants to individuals for educational purposes and over £355,500 to organisations.

Exclusions

Previous research indicates that the charity will not give funding for: direct payment of council tax or rent; debt repayments; fines or court orders; foreign travel or holidays; career changes; personal development courses; postgraduate studies; computers; individuals whose immediate goal is self-employment; goods and services catered for by central government.

Applications

The charity's website advises that eligible applicants living in the area of benefit should call 020 7243 0551 to apply.

Other information

The charity provides debt advice for all of its beneficiaries through its partnership with Nucleus (nucleus.org.uk).

Kensington and Chelsea District Nursing Trust

£51,500 (126 grants)

Correspondent: Lady Margaret Rhodes, Clerk to the Trustees, 13b Hewer Street, London W10 6DU (020 8969 8117; email: kcdnt@tiscali.co.uk)

CC number: 210931

Eligibility

People who are in need who have lived for at least two years in the borough of Kensington and Chelsea. Beneficiaries have included people who are physically or mentally ill, people with disabilities, or people who have been rehoused after rehabilitation from substance abuse. Grants are given in exceptional circumstances to people who are in need outside the beneficiary area.

Types of grants

One-off grants for domestic appliances, medical and nursing aids and equipment, beds, bedding and other furniture and clothing. Heating allowances may also be made.

Annual grant total

In 2015/16 the trust held assets of £1.96 million and had an income of £94,500. Grants were made to 126 individuals and totalled £51,500. A further £11,000 was given to four organisations.

Exclusions

Grants are not given for payment of salaries, rents, court orders or fines.

Applications

Application forms are available from the correspondent. Applications must be submitted through a social worker, Citizens Advice or other welfare agency and are considered each month.

Kingston upon Thames

The Hampton Wick United Charity

£14,500

Correspondent: The Clerk, 258 Hanworth Road, Hounslow TW3 3TY (020 8737 0371; email: info@ hwuc.org.uk; website: hwuc.org.uk)

CC number: 1010147

Eligibility

People who are in need and live in the parishes of St John the Baptist in Hampton Wick, St Mark in Teddington, and St Mary with St Alban in Teddington. Beneficiaries are usually in receipt of a state benefit and proof of this may be required.

Types of grants

Relief-in-need grants have been given towards, for example: the purchase of a wheelchair; travelling expenses to enable the recipient to visit relatives in hospital; certain items of medical equipment not available on the NHS; heating repairs; the purchase of furniture; the purchase of a television set; school uniforms.

Annual grant total

In 2015/16 the charity had assets of £1 million and an income of £25,000. Welfare grants to individuals totalled £14,500.

Applications

In the first instance, contact the Clerk.

The Charities of Ann Savage

£1,000

Correspondent: Christopher Ault, Trustee, 18 Woodbines Avenue, Kingston upon Thames KT1 2AY (020 8546 8155)

CC number: 237108

Eligibility

People in need who live in the borough of Kingston upon Thames.

Types of grants

Mainly recurrent grants.

Annual grant total

Grants to individuals are generally around £1,000 a year. When funds allow, the charity donates half of its income to its local church.

Applications

The trustees usually support individuals known via their contacts at All Saints Parish Church in Kingston upon Thames. It is unlikely that grants would be available to support unsolicited applications.

Lambeth

The Clapham Relief Fund

£13,500

Correspondent: Clerk to the Trustees, PO Box 37978, London SW4 8WX (email: enquiries@claphamrelieffund.org; website: claphamrelieffund.org)

CC number: 1074562

Eligibility

People in need who live in Clapham. A map of the area of benefit is available on the website.

Types of grants

One-off grants, typically in the range of £100 to £300, are given for a wide range of needs.

Examples include: the purchase of furniture, white goods, heating, bedding, clothing and footwear, carpets and curtains; decorating, insulation and repair costs (especially where this will relieve pain, hardship or suffering); the costs of home adaptations for people who are ill or have disabilities (again, where this can relieve pain, hardship or suffering); travel, subsistence and accommodation expenses for attending or visiting relatives in hospitals, convalescent homes, children's homes or prisons; assistance with fuel bills; recuperative or respite holidays; and food for special diets, medical or other aids, nursing requisites or comforts. Weekly allowances can also be given over a limited period of time to meet a particular need.

Annual grant total

In 2016 the fund had an income of£26,000 and a total expenditure of £21,000. We estimate, based on information from previous years, that grants totalled around £13,500, with funding also awarded to organisations working locally.

Exclusions

No grants will be given where sufficient help is available from public sources. Support will only be given to permanent residents of Clapham. Grants are not given to meet the costs of any debts already incurred.

Applications

Application forms are available to download from the website, along with guidance notes. Applications should include details of monthly income and outgoings and verification by a sponsor. They can be submitted either directly by the individual, through a welfare agency or by a third party such as a district nurse, charitable agency worker, parish priest or doctor. Applications are considered at trustees' meetings held four times a year, usually in March, June, September and December. In exceptional circumstances they may be considered outside these meetings. Application forms should be submitted during the last week of the month before meetings.

Other information

The fund has an informative website.

Fuelbanks and Families
See entry on page 306

Waterloo Parish Charity

£800

Correspondent: Eileen Hamilton, Trustee, c/o The Vicarage, 2 Secker Street, London SE1 8UF (020 7633 9819; email: admin@stjohnswaterloo.org; website: www.stjohnswaterloo.org)

CC number: 251594

Eligibility

People in need who live in the parish of Waterloo, St John with St Andrew. Preference may be given to people resident in the area of the former ecclesiastical parish of St John the Evangelist, Lambeth.

Types of grants

Small grants are given to help with living expenses and domestic items.

Annual grant total

In 2015/16 the charity had an income of £1,300 and a total expenditure of £1,700. We estimate that grants given to individuals totalled around £800, with funding also awarded to organisations.

Applications

Application forms are available from the correspondent. They can be submitted either by the individual or through a social worker, Citizens Advice or similar third party and are considered quarterly.

Lewisham

The Deptford Pension Society

£6,500

Correspondent: Mike Baker, 144 Farnaby Road, Bromley BR1 4BW (020 8402 0775; email: mjpbaker@hotmail.co.uk)

CC number: 219232

Eligibility

People over the age of 60 who are in receipt of supplementary benefits and have lived in the former London borough of Deptford for at least seven years.

Types of grants

Pensions of £15 per month (with a bonus payment in December) to around 30 individuals.

Annual grant total

In 2016 the charity had an income of £5,300 and a total expenditure of £6,800. We estimate that grants given to individuals totalled £6,500.

Applications

Apply on a form available from the correspondent, for consideration bi-monthly. Applications can be submitted either directly by the individual or a family member, through a third party such as a social worker, or through an organisation such as Citizens Advice or other welfare agency. The application form must be signed by the individual.

Sir John Evelyn's Charity

£7,000

Correspondent: Colette Saunders, Clerk, Clerk's Office, Armada Court Hall, 21 McMillan Street, Deptford, London SE8 3EZ (020 8694 8953)

CC number: 225707

Eligibility

People in need who are in receipt of state benefits and live in the ancient parish of St Nicholas and St Luke (Deptford, South East London).

Types of grants

Grants for various needs, for example, household equipment or recuperative holidays. Pensioners are awarded regular payments.

Annual grant total

In 2016 the charity had assets of £3.46 million and an income of £76,000. Individuals received £7,000, of which £6,700 was distributed in payments to

pensioners and a further £300 in one-off grants.

Applications

Application forms are available from the correspondent. They are considered every two months.

Other information

During the year, the charity spent £4,600 on providing outings and meals for pensioners. Local organisations and community projects were also awarded grants.

The Lee Charity of William Hatcliffe

£18,500 (26 grants)

Correspondent: Anne Wilson, Clerk, PO Box 7041, Bridgnorth, Shropshire WV16 9EL (07517 527849; email: annewilsontc@hotmail.co.uk)

CC number: 208053

Eligibility

People in need in Lewisham, with preference to those living in the ancient parish of Lee, who are in need, hardship or distress.

Types of grants

Regular allowances.

Annual grant total

In 2016 the charity had a total income of £60,000 and a total expenditure of £33,500. The charity awarded 26 grants to individuals for welfare purposes totalling around £18,500. The charity awarded around £9,000 to charitable organisations.

Applications

Apply in writing to the correspondent. Many applications come via partner agencies in Lewisham.

Lewisham Relief in Need Charity

£2,500

Correspondent: The Finance and Administration Manager, Clerk's Office, Lloyd Court, Slagrove Place, London SE13 7LP (020 8690 8145; email: admin@lpcharities.co.uk; website: www.lpcharities.co.uk)

CC number: 1025779

Eligibility

People in need, including those who are who are older, disadvantaged or who have disabilities and who live in the ancient parish of Lewisham, which does not include Deptford or Lee.

Types of grants

Small, one-off grants of up to £500 for essential items such as kitchen equipment, beds or carpets. Small Christmas gifts are also awarded.

Annual grant total

In 2015/16 the charity had a total income of £116,500 and a total expenditure of £110,500. The charity awarded grants totalling £2,500 during the year. Included in this amount are Christmas gifts of £25 which were awarded to 15 individuals recommended by local churches.

Applications

Apply in writing to the Finance and Administration Manager clearly stating your requirements and enclosing quotes and examples of goods required, including as much information as you think will aid the trustees in their decision. Completed application forms for grants should be submitted by the following dates; 24 February, 2 June, 25 August and 24 November.

Other information

The charity is primarily engaged in providing sheltered accommodation for older people at its almshouse, Lloyd Court.

Funding is available for larger organisations working in the Ancient Parish of Lewisham requiring funding for projects. Grants are awarded up to £1,000.

Merton

Wimbledon Guild of Social Welfare (Incorporated)

£35,500 (217 grants)

Correspondent: Wendy Pridmore, Guild House, 30–32 Worple Road, Wimbledon, London SW19 4EF (020 8946 0735; email: info@wimbledonguild.co.uk; website: www.wimbledonguild.co.uk)

CC number: 200424

Eligibility

Individuals in need who live in the borough of Merton. The guild's activities focus on ageing well, supporting mental health and fighting poverty.

Types of grants

Small, one-off grants (averaging around £300) according to need towards kitchen equipment, children's clothing, household bills, emergency household repairs, exam entrance fees, mobility scooter batteries and so on. The guild also distributes food vouchers, emergency cash grants, and food collected through local harvest and Christmas festivals.

Annual grant total

In 2016/17 the charity had assets of £20.6 million and an income of £1.7 million. The charity awarded a total of £35,500 in grants to 217 individuals.

Exclusions

Continued funding, payment for debts or arrears, and improvements to council or privately rented property will not be considered. Applicants cannot apply more than once in a year.

Applications

Application forms are available to download from the website and must be completed by a professional or social worker with the individual's consent. Where possible, applications must be supported by the professional or social worker by a letter detailing their involvement. Applications can be returned by post or by email to welfare@ wimbledonguild.co.uk.

Applications are considered as they are received and a decision is usually made within two weeks.

Other information

The guild also donates to other charities and organisations with similar objectives, and runs an advice and advocacy service.

Redbridge

Ethel Baker Bequest

£3,700

Correspondent: Revd Charles Spencer, Trustee, 18 Chestnut Walk, Woodford Green IG8 0TE (020 8530 4916; email: neil@woodfordbaptist.org)

CC number: 270274

Eligibility

People in need who live in the parish of Woodford Baptist Church in the London borough of Redbridge. In the case of any excess income, applications from those living outside the area who have attended or are connected with the church will be considered.

Types of grants

One-off and recurrent grants are given according to need.

Annual grant total

In 2015/16 the charity had an income of £1,200 and a total expenditure of £4,000. We estimate that grants given to individuals totalled £3,700.

Applications

Apply in writing to the correspondent.

Richmond upon Thames

The Barnes Workhouse Fund

£17,200 (71 grants)

Correspondent: Miranda Ibbetson, Director, PO Box 665, Richmond, Surrey TW10 6YL (020 8241 3994; email: mibbetson@barnesworkhousefund.org. uk; website: www.barnesworkhousefund. org.uk)

CC number: 200103

Eligibility

People in need who live in the ancient parish of Barnes (this broadly corresponds with the SW13 postcode area).

Types of grants

It is the fund's policy to award a maximum of £350 to any one individual in one year; larger grants are made at the trustees' discretion. Grants are given for a wide range of essential items, including: fuel costs; food (in the form of supermarket vouchers); utilities bills; white goods; debt assistance; bankruptcy costs; bedding and beds; carpets; crisis/ emergency costs; furniture; removal costs; rubbish removal; and furniture.

Annual grant total

In 2016 the fund had assets of £11.3 million and an income of £721,000. Grants totalled £259,000, the majority of which (£223,000) was distributed to organisations. Of the £36,000 given to individuals, £17,200 was given for social welfare purposes.

Exclusions

Our research indicates that grants are not generally made to people who are homeless, as the scheme requires applicants to be resident in Barnes.

Applications

Applications must be made through a referral agency, such as Citizens Advice or a welfare organisation; applications cannot be accepted directly from individuals. Referral agencies wishing to submit an application on behalf of a client should contact the Director, who can then send a link to the fund's online application form. Subject to the form being completed correctly, applications are usually dealt with within two days of receipt. Applications for amounts exceeding £750 are considered at trustees' bi-monthly board meetings, unless the need is urgent. These meetings take place in January, March, May, July, September and November. For consideration at a specific meeting, applications must be submitted by the 6th of the preceding month. A home visit from two of the trustees may be suggested in order to determine the full extent of the applicant's need.

Other information

The Barnes Workhouse Fund provides 33 units of sheltered accommodation at Walsingham Lodge and Berkeley Road Bungalows.

The fund has an informative website and annual report, which both provide (in great detail) information on the fund's activities and its history.

Hampton Fuel Allotment Charity

£813,000 (1,671+ grants)

Correspondent: Carole Swinburne, Grants Manager, 15 High Street, Hampton, Middlesex TW12 2SA (020 8941 7866; fax: 020 8979 5555; website: www.hfac.co.uk)

CC number: 211756

Eligibility

People who are in poor health or financial need and live in Hampton, Hampton Hill, Hampton Wick, Teddington, Twickenham and Whitton. Applicants must either work part-time or be on a low wage; in receipt of state benefits; in receipt of help with rent or council tax; or have children who receive free school meals.

Types of grants

One-off grants are given for heating costs and other household essentials such as fridges, cookers, washing machines, wheelchairs and special medical equipment. Grants are made directly to the supplier and, in the case of fuel grants, credited to the applicant's account. School journey grants are available for children in their penultimate or final year at junior school.

Annual grant total

In 2015/16 the charity held assets of £54.5 million and had an income of £1.9 million. Grants to individuals in need totalled £813,000 and were distributed as follows:

Fuel grants	1,585	£764,000
Essential equipment and furniture	-	£44,500
Careline telephone equipment	62	£8,800
School journey grants	24	£4,900
Disability grants (for children with multiple and complex needs)	-	£1,000

Exclusions

The charity is unlikely to support: private and further education; building adaptations; holidays (except in cases of severe medical need); decorating costs, carpeting or central heating; anything which will replace statutory funds.

Applications

Application forms are available to download from the website, the charity's office or from the Greenwood Centre, Twickenham Citizens Advice or the White House. Applications should be submitted by post either directly by the individual or by a third party. Applications for fuel grants are considered every two months. Those for essential household items are reviewed weekly and should be verified through a letter of support from a welfare professional such as a social worker or housing officer. If this is not possible, the charity will visit the applicant at home.

Note: The charity does not accept applications by email.

To apply for a school journey grant, discuss the application with your school in the first instance.

The Richmond Aid-in-Sickness Fund

£4,500

Correspondent: Juliet Ames-Lewis, Director, 8 The Green, Richmond, Surrey TW9 1PL (020 8948 4188; email: info@richmondcharities.org.uk; website: www.richmondcharities.org.uk)

CC number: 200434

Eligibility

People in need who live in the borough of Richmond.

Types of grants

One-off grants ranging up to £250 towards, for example, fuel costs, extra bedding, nightwear and the costs of special equipment.

Annual grant total

In 2016 the fund had an income of £5,300 and a total expenditure of £4,700. We estimate that the fund gave around £4,500 in grants to individuals during the year.

Applications

Applications should be submitted through social services, Citizens Advice or other organisations such as Richmond Community Mental Health Resource Centre. Payments are received in February, May, August and November.

Richmond Parish Lands Charity (RPLC)

£84,500 (332 grants)

Correspondent: Jonathan Monckton, The Vestry House, 21 Paradise Road, Richmond, Surrey TW9 1SA (020 8948 5701; email: grants@rplc.org.uk; website: www.rplc.org.uk)

CC number: 200069

Eligibility

People who are in need or suffering from ill health or hardship in the TW9, TW10 or SW14 areas of Richmond, Ham, Sheen and Mortlake. Applicants must have lived in the area for at least six months prior to application and have no other possible sources of help.

Types of grants

Grants of up to £300 are made to individuals in extreme need. Grants can be made for items such as white goods, furniture, household items, utility bills, child-related expenditure, food and clothing.

Annual grant total

In 2016/17 the charity had assets of £98.8 million and an income of £2.1 million. Welfare grants to individuals totalled £84,500.

Applications

Crisis grants are made to individuals in extreme need following a referral from local agencies, such as Richmond Borough support teams or the Citizens Advice, Social Services, Age UK Richmond and the Community Mental Health Team. Applications are not accepted from individuals directly. The charity aims to respond to requests within 24 to 48 hours.

Other information

Grants are also made to organisations.

Richmond Philanthropic Society

£9,000

Correspondent: Juliet Ames-Lewis, Director, 8 The Green, Richmond, Surrey TW9 1PL (020 8948 4188; email: info@richmondcharities.org.uk; website: www.richmondcharities.org.uk)

CC number: 212941

Eligibility

People in need who live in the former borough of Richmond (Richmond, Kew, Petersham and Ham – the TW9 and TW10 postcodes).

Types of grants

One-off grants of up to £250 are given to help people who have run into short-term difficulties with basic amenities. Christmas hampers are distributed to older people who have been recommended by care workers and district nurses.

Annual grant total

In 2016 the charity had an income of £12,500 and a total expenditure of £10,500. We estimate that grants totalled around £9,000.

Exclusions

No grants are given for educational purposes or for the payment of council tax.

Applications

Applicants must be referred through Citizens Advice, social services, district nurses, health visitors or other established third parties. Individuals cannot apply directly.

Other information

Richmond Charities took over the administration of the charity in October 2010. It also administers three other welfare charities – Richmond Aid in Sickness Fund, Henry Smith's Charity (Richmond) and the Misses Thomson and Whipple Charity.

Henry Smith's Charity (Richmond)

£2,000

Correspondent: Juliet Ames-Lewis, Director, 8 The Green, Richmond, Surrey TW9 1PL (020 8948 4188; email: info@richmondcharities.org.uk; website: www.richmondcharities.org.uk)

CC number: 200431–4

Eligibility

People experiencing hardship or distress who live in the former borough of Richmond (Richmond, Kew, Petersham and Ham – the TW9 and TW10 postcodes).

Types of grants

One-off grants ranging up to £250 towards, for example, white goods, furniture, household items, assistance with utility costs, basic living expenses and special equipment.

Annual grant total

Previous research suggests that grants usually total around £2,000 per year.

Applications

There is an application form for the welfare charities administered by the Richmond Charities on the website. Applications are mostly received on behalf of individuals from Citizens Advice or social services.

Other information

The charity is administered by the Richmond Charities, along with the Richmond Aid in Sickness Fund, the Richmond Philanthropic Society (see separate entries), and the Misses Thompson and Whipple Charity. Its funds, however, are entirely separate and do not form part of the Richmond Charities' investments.

The Mayor of Southwark's Common Good Trust (The Mayor's Charity)

£5,000

Correspondent: Eric Bassett, 90 Sunnywood Drive, Haywards Heath RH16 4PB (01444 412812; email: eric.bassett@btinternet.com)

CC number: 280011

Eligibility

People in need who live in the borough of Southwark and the immediate surrounding area.

Types of grants

One-off grants, previously averaging around £160 each, for essential kitchen items, medical equipment, clothing, furniture and household items.

Annual grant total

In 2016/17 the trust had an income of £9,500 and a total expenditure of £11,500. We estimate that the amount awarded in grants to individuals was £5,000.

Applications

Applications should be made in writing to the correspondent, including a reference of support from a professional or social worker where possible. Applications should detail financial need and what the grant will be used for.

Other information

The trust also makes grants to organisations and provides an information and advice service.

Southwark

Camberwell Consolidated Charities

£54,500

Correspondent: Janet McDonald, c/o HFM Tax Accounts, 89 Worship Street, London EC2A 2BF (email: norahjanet@aol.com)

CC number: 208441

Eligibility

Primarily older people in need who have lived in the former parish of Camberwell for at least two years. Priority is given to those whose income is on or around the minimum state pension.

Types of grants

Annual pensions, paid at a rate of £360 per individual, and £540 per couple. The charity also provides £80 grants at Christmas to eight people.

Annual grant total

In 2016/17 the charity had assets of £1.4 million and an income of £56,000. During the year, a total of £54,500 was awarded in grants to individuals.

Applications

Application forms can be requested from the correspondent. Details of how to apply are usually distributed locally through leaflets. The trustees meet four times per year to consider applications.

Rotherhithe Consolidated Charities

£107,000

Correspondent: John Clarke, Administrator, Amwell House, 19 Amwell Street, Hoddeson, Hertfordshire EN11 8TS (01992 444466)

CC number: 211980

Eligibility

Recurrent grants are made primarily to widows who are in need and have lived in the ancient parish of Rotherhithe for at least ten years. Help is also given for the general benefit of those in need who live in the parish.

Types of grants

One-off grants for relief in need, Christmas donations and the provision of holidays. Annual pensions are also provided to widows in need.

Annual grant total

In 2016 the charity had assets of almost £5.2 million and an income of £175,500. Grants totalled £107,000 and were broken down as follows:

Holiday grants	£72,000
Stipend grants	£31,500
Other grants	£3,500

Applications

Apply in writing to the correspondent.

Other information

Grants are also made to organisations (£120,500 in 2016).

Southwark Charities

£114,000

Correspondent: Chris Wilson, Clerk to the Trustees, Charities Office, Edward Edwards House, Nicholson Street, London SE1 0XL (020 7593 2000; email: clerk@southwarkcharities.org.uk; website: www.southwarkcharities.co.uk)

CC number: 1137760

Eligibility

Older people in need who have lived in the former metropolitan borough of Southwark for at least five years.

Types of grants

Quarterly pensions, holiday costs, one-off grants and Christmas gifts.

Annual grant total

In 2015 the charity had assets of £25.3 million and an income of £735,000. The charity awarded around £114,000 in grants to individuals in the form of pensions, Christmas gifts, holiday benefits and grants for welfare purposes.

Applications

Apply in writing to the correspondent, either directly by the individual, via a third party or through a social worker, Citizens Advice or other welfare agency.

Other information

The charity's main objective is the maintenance of a number of almshouses for the benefit of older people who are in financial difficulties. The assets of the charity therefore bear no relation to the amount available for grant-giving.

The United Charities of St George the Martyr

£194,500

Correspondent: Paul Leverton, Clerk, Marshall House, 66 Newcomen Street, London SE1 IYT (020 7407 2994; email: stgeorge@marshalls.org.uk)

CC number: 208732

Eligibility

Older people in need in the parish of St George the Martyr (in north Southwark SE1). There is an area of benefit map on the charity's website.

Types of grants

Pensions and Christmas parcels. Pensions currently total £225 per annum. One-off grants according to need towards kitchen equipment, furnishing, flooring, mobility aids, accompanied transport to medical and dental treatments, easy-fitting slippers and shoes, and illuminated magnifying lenses. The charity also funds holidays and outings for its beneficiaries.

Annual grant total

In 2016 the charity held assets of £8.9 million and had an income of £352,500. Financial assistance for individuals totalled £194,500 and was distributed as follows:

Pensioner holidays	£91,500
Pensions	£46,000
Pensioner trips and outings	£25,00
Christmas hampers and parties	£21,500
Relief in need	£11,000

Applications

Apply in writing to the correspondent. The charity has previously stated that its grants and pensions are fully committed but that any new applications will be kept on file.

Other information

The charity also has a welfare visitor, who is able to visit beneficiaries and potential beneficiaries in their own homes.

St Olave's United Charity, incorporating the St Thomas and St John Charities

£200,000

Correspondent: Angela O'Shaughnessy, 6–8 Druid Street, London SE1 2EU (020 7407 2530; email: st.olavescharity@ btconnect.com)

CC number: 211763

Eligibility

People in need who live in Bermondsey (part SE1 and all SE16).

Types of grants

Individuals over the age of 70 can receive a birthday gift of £100 a year and a further grant towards holidays once every year or every two years. Depending on additional income, other one-off grants can be made for a wide variety of needs, including clothes, musical instruments and holidays.

Annual grant total

In 2016/17 the charity had assets of £16.5 million and an income of £520,500. Welfare grants to individuals totalled £200,000.

Applications

Applications should be made in writing to the correspondent and are considered four times a year.

Sutton

Cheam Consolidated Charities

£2,500

Correspondent: Nola Freeman, St Dunstan's Church, Church Road, Cheam, Surrey SM3 8QH (020 8641 1284)

CC number: 238392

Eligibility

People in need who live in Cheam. Some preference is given to older people.

Types of grants

One-off and recurrent grants are given according to need.

Annual grant total

In 2016 the charity had an income of £5,000 and a total expenditure of £5,000. We estimate that the charity awarded £2,500 in grants to individuals during the year.

Applications

Applications should be made in writing to the correspondent, and include a letter of reference from a support, social, or professional worker.

Other information

The charity also makes grants to organisations in the local area.

Sutton Nursing Association

£25,000

Correspondent: John Helps, 28 Southway, Carshalton SM5 4HW (020 8770 1095; email: admin@skingle.co.uk)

CC number: 203686

Eligibility

People who are in poor health, require financial assistance and live in the London borough of Sutton or the surrounding area.

Types of grants

One-off grants of up to £500 for domestic items, specialised equipment (such as, phones or buggies), furniture, beds, holiday expenses (including insurance), gym sessions, rent arrears, respite care, carpets, disability and other medical aids, computer equipment, clothing and school uniforms.

Annual grant total

In 2016 the association had an income of £24,000 and a total expenditure of £53,000. Grants are mainly made through various organisations. We estimate that support to individuals totalled around £25,000.

Applications

Applications are normally made through a social worker, Citizens Advice or other welfare agency. They are considered on a bi-monthly basis and should include as much information as possible, including estimated costs, funds available from other sources secured or applied to and the ability of the individual to contribute.

Other information

The association also makes grants to the community nursing services, hospitals and local organisations.

Tower Hamlets

The Bishopsgate Foundation

£100,500

Correspondent: Francesca Canty, Director of Programmes, Bishopsgate Institute, 230 Bishopsgate, London EC2M 4QH (020 7392 9251; email: enquiries@bishopsgate.org.uk; website: www.bishopsgate.org.uk)

CC number: 1090923

Eligibility

People who live and work, or have lived or worked, in the parishes of St Botolph's without Bishopsgate; Christchurch, Spitalfields; and St Leonard's, Shoreditch – all within the borough of Tower Hamlets.

Types of grants

Recurrent and one-off grants.

Annual grant total

In 2015/16 the foundation held assets of £33.8 million and had an income of almost £2.2 million. Grants to individuals totalled £100,500.

Applications

Application forms are available from the correspondent. Applications can be submitted either directly by the individual or, where applicable, through a social worker, Citizens Advice or other welfare agency.

Other information

The foundation's principal activity is the running of the Bishopsgate Institute and library.

The Henderson Charity

£15,000

Correspondent: Philip Hendry, Flat 8, Masters Lodge, Johnson Street, London E1 0BE (020 7790 1793; email: philipehendry@gmail.com)

CC number: 1012208

Eligibility

Older people who live in the parish of Ratcliff or the parish of St George-in-the-East in London.

Types of grants

Small pensions.

Annual grant total

In 2015/16 the charity had an income of £17,700 and a total expenditure of £15,600. We estimate that grants given to individuals totalled £15,000.

Applications

Previous research suggests that vacancies are normally advertised locally through social services and appropriate welfare agencies. When a pension is available, application forms can be obtained from social services or the correspondent.

Stepney Relief-in-Need Charity

£15,000

Correspondent: Jean Partleton, Clerk to the Trustees, Rectory Cottage, 5 White Horse Lane, Stepney, London E1 3NE (020 7790 3598; email: jeanpartleton194@btinternet.com)

CC number: 250130

Eligibility

People in need who live within the old metropolitan borough of Stepney.

Types of grants

One-off grants, usually of £100 to £500, are considered for a wide range of needs, including household items, clothing, holidays where individuals will benefit from a short break, convalescence costs following discharge from hospital, hospital travel expenses and mobility aids.

Annual grant total

In 2015/16 the charity had both an income and total expenditure of £17,500. We estimate that welfare grants totalled around £15,000.

Exclusions

No grants are made towards the repayment of loans, rent, council tax or utility bills.

Applications

An application form is available from the correspondent and may be submitted either directly by the individual or through a relative, social worker or other welfare agency. The trustees usually meet four times a year, but some applications can be considered between meetings at the chair's discretion.

Waltham Forest

Walthamstow and Chingford Almshouse Charity

£88,500

Correspondent: Liz Abbott, Monoux Hall, Church End, Walthamstow, London E17 9RL (020 8520 0295; email: office@wcac.org.uk; website: www.wcac.org.uk)

CC number: 1116355

Eligibility

Individuals and families in crisis who have limited income and live in Walthamstow or Chingford.

Types of grants

One-off grants are made for relief-in-need purposes.

Annual grant total

The correspondent has informed us that during the year 2016/17, the charity had assets of £21.5 million, and an income of £1.1 million. The total amount awarded in grants during the year was £88,500.

Applications

The majority of grants made are as a result of referrals from social or health services. Application forms are available online if an individual wishes to refer themselves. Most applicants will be visited at their home before a decision is made.

Other information

The charity is an almshouse charity, providing accommodation for older people in Walthamstow and Chingford.

Among its activities, the charity also makes grants to organisations working to prevent or relieve financial need in Walthamstow and Chingford, as well as occasionally to students and apprentices who live in the area and have limited family income for books, equipment or tools.

Wandsworth

Fuelbanks and Families

£33,500

Correspondent: Graham Slater, Chief Executive, 108 Battersea High Street, London SW11 3HP (020 3696 5335; email: admin@fuelbanksandfamilies.com; website: www.fuelbanksandfamilies.com)

CC number: 1161459

Eligibility

Families with children in need in Wandsworth, Lambeth, Hammersmith and Fulham.

Types of grants

Fuel vouchers of £49 that directly credit families' pre-payment meters. One-off grants for essential items such as school uniforms, shoes, winter coats and school trips.

Annual grant total

In 2016/17 the charity held assets of £164,500 and had an income of £277,000. We estimate that grants totalled £33,500.

Applications

Families are referred to the charity from third parties including food banks, teachers, social workers, hospitals and GPs. They will then be given a voucher which can be redeemed at a local food bank and the charity will assess whether the family has any other immediate or longer-term needs. Further help or support will then be offered if needed.

Other information

The charity has partnered with Centre 70 (www.centre70.org.uk) to offer specialist debt, benefits and housing support advice.

South London Relief-in-Sickness Fund

£7,000

Correspondent: Fiona Rae, Room 154, Wandsworth Town Hall, Wandsworth High Street, London SW18 2PU (020 8871 6010; email: fiona.rae@ richmondandwandsworth.gov.uk; website: www.wandsworth.gov.uk)

CC number: 210939

Eligibility

People who live in Wandsworth who are in need because of disability or ill health.

Types of grants

One-off grants of up to £300 are given towards, for example, furnishings, clothing and holidays. The average grant is £150.

Annual grant total

In 2016 the fund had an income of £13,800 and a total expenditure of £14,400. We estimate that grants given to individuals totalled £7,000, with funding also awarded to organisations.

Exclusions

Grants cannot be made to help with taxes or debts.

Applications

Applications can be made using a form available to download from the Wandsworth council website, and can be submitted through a social worker, Citizens Advice or other welfare agency. Applications are considered quarterly (usually in March, June, September and December). Full guidelines are available from the correspondent.

Wandsworth Combined Charity

£9,000

Correspondent: R. Cooles, 179 Upper Richmond Road West, London SW14 8DU (020 8876 4478)

CC number: 210269

Eligibility

Older people who have lived in Wandsworth for at least three years.

Types of grants

The charity provides regular pensions and also makes one-off grant payments to relieve hardship.

Annual grant total

In 2015/16 the charity had an income of £13,500 and a total expenditure of £9,500. We estimate the amount of grants to individuals totalled £9,000.

Exclusions

The grant cannot be used to fund work that is the responsibility of statutory agencies, statutory organisations, such as local authorities and schools, purely commercial ventures, political campaigns or concerns, religious organisations where the activities benefit only those of a particular faith, individuals, spending that has already taken place.

Applications

Applications should be made in writing to the correspondent.

North East

General

The Olive and Norman Field Charity

£21,000

Correspondent: Paddy Chapman, British Red Cross Society, Carrick House, Thurston Road, Northallerton DL6 2NA (01609 772186; email: olive&norman@redcross.org.uk; website: www.oliveandnormanfieldcharity.co.uk)

CC number: 208760

Eligibility

People who are in poor health, convalescent or who have disabilities and live in the following local government areas: Darlington; Hartlepool; Middlesbrough; Redcar and Cleveland; Stockton-on-Tees; County Durham; York; North Yorkshire; and the former North Riding of Yorkshire.

Types of grants

One-off grants to cover costs where the outcome will improve the quality of life. Awards have previously been made for:

- Wheelchairs and other mobility aids
- Specialised seating and car seats
- Sensory toys and equipment
- Technology to assist independent living
- Help towards short respite breaks or family holidays
- Home adaptions (after a Disabled Facilities Grant has already been awarded)

Annual grant total

In 2016 the charity had an income of £23,500 and a total expenditure of £22,000. We estimate the amount of grants to individuals totalled £21,000.

Exclusions

Grants cannot be given: for building work (unless a Disabled Facilities Grant has been secured); equipment or work where statutory funding is available; retrospective funding; or for debts.

Applications

Applications can be completed online, or the application form can be downloaded from the website to be completed and returned to the charity's address. Applications should be supported by a GP, professional/social worker, or the Citizens Advice. The trustees meet in March, June, September, and December, however applications are considered throughout the year.

The Greggs Foundation

£265,500 (918 grants)

Correspondent: Justine Massingham, Grants Manager, Greggs House, Quorum Business Park, Newcastle Upon Tyne NE12 8BU (0191 212 7626; email: greggsfoundation@greggs.co.uk; website: www.greggsfoundation.org.uk)

CC number: 296590

Eligibility

People in need who live in the north east of England (Northumberland, Tyne and Wear, Durham and Teesside). Priority is given to children and families.

Types of grants

Grants of up to £150 and are given for essential items such as white goods, furniture, baby equipment, flooring, clothing and school uniforms. The maximum grants for certain items are detailed on the website.

Annual grant total

In 2016 the foundation had assets of £17.7 million and an income of £3 million. Grants to individuals totalled £265,500.

Exclusions

Grants are not given to cover unspecified costs, loan repayments, bankruptcy fees, holidays, funeral expenses, medical equipment or computer equipment.

Applications

Applications can be made through the foundation's website. The foundation only accepts applications from recognised social organisations such as charities, housing associations and social services acting on behalf of a family or individual in need.

Other information

The foundation also has separate grants programmes for organisations.

Lady Elizabeth Hastings' Non-Educational Charity

£133,000 (119+ grants)

Correspondent: Andrew Fallows, Clerk, Carter Jonas, 82 Micklegate, York YO1 6LF (01904 558220; email: leh.clerk@carterjonas.co.uk; website: www.ladyelizabethhastingscharities.co.uk)

CC number: 224098

Eligibility

People who are in need and live in the ecclesiastical parishes of Collingham with Harewood, Ledsham with Fairburn or Thorp Arch. Clergy and former clergy who are working or have worked in the former counties of Yorkshire, Westmorland, Cumbria and Northumberland, and their dependants. Maps showing the boundaries of the areas of benefit are provided on the charity's website.

Types of grants

One-off grants for welfare purposes or payment of relevant items or services.

Annual grant total

In 2015/16 the charity held assets of £17.9 million and had an income of £544,500. A total of 119 clergy and their dependants, as well as other individuals in need, received a combined £133,000 in grants from the Non-Educational Charity. Grants were also given for the maintenance of churches in the beneficiary area.

A further 208 grants were made from the Educational Foundation, totalling £129,000.

Applications

Apply in writing to the correspondent.

Other information

The charity is managed by and derives its income from the Lady Elizabeth Hastings Estate Charity. Half of the charity's income goes is distributed to the Non-Educational Charity and the other half to the Education Foundation.

The John Routledge Hunter Memorial Fund

£12,000

Correspondent: Mary Waugh, Bond Dickinson LLP, One Trinity Gardens, Broad Chare, Newcastle upon Tyne NE1 2HF (0191 279 9000)

CC number: 225619

Eligibility

People who live in Northumberland and Tyne and Wear who have disabilities or are sick or convalescing. Previous research suggests that there may be a preference for people living in the area of the former county of Northumberland (pre-1974) who have, or have recently had, chest, lung or catarrhal complaints.

Types of grants

Grants of £200 to £500 towards a two or three-week recuperative holiday in a hotel in Lytham St Annes or Southport (including rail travel expenses, bed, breakfast, evening meal and £25 in cash). Holidays are taken between Easter and September.

Annual grant total

In 2015/16 the fund had an income of £16,600 and a total expenditure of £13,200. We estimate that grants totalled around £12,000.

Applications

Application forms are available from the correspondent. Applications should be supported by a certificate signed by a doctor. They are considered from January to April.

County Durham

County Durham Community Foundation

Correspondent: Grants & Donor Services, Victoria House, Whitfield Court, St John's Road, Meadowfield Industrial Estate, Durham DH7 8XL (0191 378 6340; email: info@cdcf.org.uk; website: www.cdcf.org.uk)

CC number: 1047625

Eligibility

People in need who live in County Durham and Darlington. The community foundation manages a number of different funds to which individuals can apply, each with its own eligibility criteria – see the website for details.

Types of grants

The type of grant available depends on the fund being applied to. At the time of writing (February 2018), there were funds making grants to help with, for example, essential domestic equipment, furniture, children's equipment and respite breaks.

Annual grant total

In 2016/17 the foundation had assets of £18.4 million and an income of £3.8 million. Grants to individuals totalled more than £1 million, the majority of which we believe was awarded for educational purposes. We were unable to determine the proportion of the grant total awarded for welfare purposes.

Applications

In the first instance, see the website for details of open funds, their eligibility criteria and guidelines.

Other information

The majority of the foundation's grant-making is to organisations (almost £2.5 million in 2016/17). The foundation also operates a number of funds from which grants are made to individuals for educational purposes.

Lord Crewe's Charity

See entry on page 162

The Sedgefield Charities

£2,100

Correspondent: John Hannon, East House, Mordon, Stockton-on-Tees, County Durham TS21 2EY (01740 622512; email: east.house@btinternet.com)

CC number: 230395

Eligibility

People in need who live in the parishes of Bishop Middleham, Bradbury, Cornforth, Fishburn, Mordon, Sedgefield and Trimdon, in County Durham.

Types of grants

One-off grants to relieve financial hardship, for example for furniture, disability or mobility aids, and for Christmas gifts.

Annual grant total

In 2016 the charity held assets of £941,500 and had an income of £31,000. The amount awarded to individuals who were in financial hardship was £2,100 (this figure includes a Christmas distribution of grants worth £300).

Applications

Application forms can be requested from the correspondent. Where possible, applications should be supported by a social or professional worker.

Other information

The charity also awards grants to local organisations, and to individuals in education.

Stockton-on-Tees

John T. Shuttleworth Ropner Memorial Fund

£16,000

Correspondent: Margaret Vaughan, County Durham Community Foundation, Victoria House, St Johns Road, Meadowfield Industrial Estate, Durham DH7 8XL (0191 378 6340; fax: 0191 378 2409; email: info@cdcf.org.uk; website: www.cdcf.org.uk)

CC number: 1047625–1

Eligibility

Individuals who are older, sick, or who have disabilities, and their carers in the Tees Valley area who are in need of respite care, or who need temporary support following hospitalisation, bereavement or because of dependency treatment. Applicants must live in Darlington, Hartlepool, Middlesbrough, Redcar and Cleveland or Stockton-on-Tees.

Types of grants

Grants of up to £1,000 for recuperative or respite care, home-help assistance, bereavement related costs, travel and accommodation for individuals (and for their families) undergoing dependency treatment at a clinic or centre away from their place of residence.

Annual grant total

In 2016/17 the charity made grants to individuals totalling £16,000.

Exclusions

Only one grant per family per financial year. Retrospective grants will not be made. No grants are given for medical equipment or treatment, or nursing care.

Applications

Application forms are available to download from the Durham Community Foundation website. A reference from a social or healthcare professional is required.

Northumber-land

Lord Crewe's Charity

See entry on page 162

The Eleemosynary Charity of Giles Heron

£4,000

Correspondent: George Benson, Trustee, Walwick Farmhouse, Humshaugh, Hexam NE46 4BJ (01434 681203; email: office@chestersestate.co.uk)

CC number: 224157

Eligibility

People in need who live in the parish of Wark and Simonburn.

Types of grants

One-off grants ranging from £100 to £500.

Annual grant total

In 2015/16 the charity had an income of £17,700 and a total expenditure of £17,400. We estimate that welfare grants to individuals totalled around £4,000.

Applications

The individual should apply directly to the correspondent in writing.

Morpeth Dispensary

£1,600

Correspondent: Michael Gaunt, Trustee, 15 Bridge Street, Morpeth, Northumberland NE61 1NX (01670 512336; email: alison@ brumellandsample.f2s.com)

CC number: 222352

Eligibility

People who are sick and poor and live in or around Morpeth.

Types of grants

Our research indicates that grants are usually one-off.

Annual grant total

In 2015 the charity had an income of £3,200 and a total expenditure of £3,500. We estimate that grants given to individuals for welfare purposes totalled around £1,600.

Applications

Apply in writing to the correspondent at any time through a third party such as a social worker, GP, Citizens Advice or other welfare agency. Applications must include detail of the applicant's age, whether a single parent, whether on benefits, their address and any details regarding health matters. Grants are made directly to the third party, not the applicant.

Other information

At the time of writing (August 2017) the charity had no website or accounts available.

Community Foundation Serving Tyne and Wear and Northumberland

See entry on page 311

Tyne and Wear

Community Foundation Serving Tyne and Wear and Northumberland

Correspondent: Jon Goodwin, Senior Philanthropy Advisor, Philanthropy House, Woodbine Bridge, Gosforth, Newcastle upon Tyne NE3 1DD (0191 222 0945; email: jg@communityfoundation.org.uk; website: www.communityfoundation.org.uk)

CC number: 700510

Eligibility

Girls/young women aged 16 to 25 in Sunderland and South Tyneside who are facing severe hardship.

Types of grants

The cost of clothes and provide small grants for furniture, carpets and any other important items required to set up a home or support someone in need.

Annual grant total

In 2015/16 the foundation had assets of £70.4 million and an income of £8.9 million. No grants were made during the year.

Applications

Apply through the foundation's website.

Gateshead

Gateshead Relief-in-Sickness Fund

£1,000

Correspondent: Rachel Ray, c/o Thomas Magnay & Co., 8 St Mary's Green, Whickham, Newcastle upon Tyne NE16 4DN (0191 488 7459; email: rachelray@thomasmagnay.co.uk)

CC number: 234970

Eligibility

People who are in poor health, convalescent or who have disabilities and live in the borough of Gateshead.

Types of grants

One-off grants towards providing or paying for items, services or facilities, which will alleviate need or assist with recovery, and are not readily available from other sources.

Annual grant total

In 2016 the fund had an income of £2,300 and a total expenditure of £1,900. We have estimated that grants to individuals totalled £1,000, as grants are also made to organisations.

Applications

Apply in writing to the correspondent. Applications can be submitted directly by the individual or through a social worker, Citizens Advice or other welfare agency.

Newcastle upon Tyne

The Non-Ecclesiastical Charity of William Moulton

£20,500

Correspondent: George Jackson, Clerk to the Trustees, 10 Sunlea Avenue, North Shields NE30 3DS (0191 251 0971; email: jgeorgelvis@blueyonder.co.uk)

CC number: 216255

Eligibility

People in need who have lived within the boundaries of the city of Newcastle upon Tyne for at least the past 12 months.

Types of grants

Grants typically range between £50 and £200 for general household/personal needs such as washing machines, cookers, furniture, clothing and so on.

Annual grant total

In 2016 the charity had assets of £1.3 million and an income of £36,500.

During the year, the charity gave a total of £41,500 in grants. We estimate that around £20,500 was given in grants to individuals, with the charity also making grants to local organisations.

Exclusions

Our previous research indicates that no grants are given for education, training or rent arrears.

Applications

Apply in writing to the correspondent.

Thomas Thompson's Poor Rate Gift

£1,400

Correspondent: Carol Farquhar-Johnston, Newcastle City Council, Civic Centre, Newcastle upon Tyne NE1 8QH (0191 211 6287)

CC number: 253846

Eligibility

People in need who live in Byker in Newcastle.

Types of grants

One-off grants for items such as washing machines, furniture and cookers. Grants have also been given to replace Christmas presents and children's bikes which have been stolen.

Annual grant total

In 2015/16 the charity had an income of £4,500 and a total expenditure of £1,600. We estimate that grants given to individuals totalled £1,400.

Applications

Apply in writing to the correspondent, for consideration throughout the year. Grants to replace stolen property are usually submitted through Victim Support.

The Town Moor Money Charity

£45,000

Correspondent: Richard Grey, Moor Bank Lodge, Claremont Road, Newcastle upon Tyne NE2 4NL (0191 261 5970; email: admin@freemenofnewcastle.org; website: www.freemenofnewcastle.org)

CC number: 248098

Eligibility

Freemen of Newcastle upon Tyne, Northumberland and Durham and their widows and children who are in need.

Types of grants

One-off and recurrent grants are given according to need. Grants are means-tested and paid in June and December.

Annual grant total

In 2015/16 the charity had an income of £16,500 and a total expenditure of £62,500. We estimate the amount of grants to individuals totalled around £45,000.

Applications

Application forms are available in April and October from the senior steward of the appropriate company. They are usually considered in May and November.

North Tyneside

Wallsend Charitable Trust

£10,400

Correspondent: The Secretary, North Tyneside Council, 16 The Silverlink North, Newcastle upon Tyne NE27 0BY (0191 643 7006)

CC number: 215476

Eligibility

People over 60 who are on or just above state benefit income levels and live in the former borough of Wallsend.

Types of grants

One-off grants.

Annual grant total

In 2016 the trust had an income of £47,000 and a total expenditure of £21,000. We estimate that grants given to individuals totalled around £10,400.

Exclusions

Our previous research indicates that the trust will not help with continuing costs such as residential care or telephone rentals and will not help a person whose income is significantly above state benefit levels. Applicants must have exhausted all statutory avenues such as DWP, social services department and so on.

Applications

Apply in writing to the correspondent.

Other information

Grants are given to organisations provided that the majority of members meet the same criteria as apply to individuals.

The trust is also known as the Victor Mann Trust Fund.

Sunderland

Houghton-Le-Spring Relief in Need Charity

£1,500

Correspondent: Brian Scott, 28 Finchale Close, Houghton Le Spring, Tyne & Wear DH4 5QU (0191 584 1608; email: rectorpinnington@gmail.com)

CC number: 810025

Eligibility

People in need living in the parishes of Bournmoor, South Biddick and West Rainton in County Durham, the parishes of Hetton and Warden Law in Tyne and Wear, and those parts of the borough of Sunderland and the parish of Framwellgate Moor, which formerly constituted part of the ancient parish of Houghton-Le-Spring.

Types of grants

One-off and recurrent according to need.

Annual grant total

In 2016/17 the charity had an income of £1,500 and a total expenditure of £1,600. We have estimated that grants to individuals totalled £1,500.

Applications

Apply in writing to the correspondent.

George Hudson's Charity

£26,000

Correspondent: Peter Taylor, Secretary, c/o McKenzie Bell, 19 John Street, Sunderland SR1 1JG (0191 567 4857; email: petertaylor@mckenzie-bell.co.uk)

CC number: 527204

Eligibility

People under the age of 18 whose father has died or is unable to work and are living in Sunderland, with first preference to children of seafarers or pilots belonging to the Port of Sunderland, and in second preference to those born and resident in the ancient township of Monkwearmouth.

Types of grants

The charity gives regular grants and clothing vouchers.

Annual grant total

In 2015/16 the charity held assets of £584,000 and an income of £40,000. Grants to individuals totalled £26,000, of which £10,200 was given in clothing and footwear grants. The charity spent an additional £125 on confectionary for children at Christmas and Easter.

Applications

Application forms are available from the correspondent. Applications are considered every other month.

Sunderland Guild of Help

£10,000

Correspondent: Norman Taylor, 4 Toward Road, Sunderland, Tyne and Wear SR1 2QG (0191 501 8690 (Wednesdays from 9.30am only); fax: 0191 567 2895; email: info@guildofhelp. co.uk; website: www.guildofhelp.co.uk)

CC number: 229656

Eligibility

People in need who live in Sunderland.

Types of grants

Support is given for the advancement of health and the relief of poverty. In special circumstances, refurbished goods have been given to those most in need in the form of beds, washing machines and fridges.

Annual grant total

In 2015/16 the guild had an income of £5,800 and a total expenditure of £11,300. We estimate that the guild awarded £10,000 in grants to individuals during the year.

Exclusions

New goods or goods made to order cannot be supplied. Applications requesting money or loans will be rejected.

Applications

Applications can only be considered if they are submitted through a social worker or professional familiar with the guild's system. They should include an income and expenditure statement and are considered throughout the year. The application form is available to download from the guild's website.

Other information

The guild administers funds including the Sunderland Queen Victoria Memorial Fund 1901 and the Sunderland Convalescent Fund.

In addition, the guild also acts as an enabling charity through its premises on Toward Road, Sunderland where other small charities are provided with accommodation at rents that reflect their charitable status.

The Sunderland Orphanage and Educational Foundation

£10,000

Correspondent: Peter Taylor, 19 John Street, Sunderland SR1 1JG (0191 567 4857; email: petertaylor@mckenzie-bell. co.uk)

CC number: 527202

Eligibility

Young people under the age of 25; who live in or around Sunderland and have one or two parents who are deceased, separated, divorced, or who have a disability; and attend a school, college or university approved by the trustees.

Types of grants

Provision is made for the following:

- Room and board
- Pocket money
- Clothing
- Instruments
- Recreation and leisure
- Holidays
- Medical treatment

Annual grant total

In 2015/16 the foundation had an income of £23,000 and a total expenditure of £25,500. We estimate that the foundation awarded a total of £10,000 in grants for welfare purposes.

Applications

Applications should be made in writing to the correspondent.

Other information

The foundation mainly makes awards for educational attainment.

North West

General

The Cotton Districts Convalescent Fund and the Barnes Samaritan Charity

£26,500 (52 grants)

Correspondent: Nicholas Stockton, c/o Cassons Chartered Accountants, Rational House, 64 Bridge Street, Manchester M3 3BN (0845 337 9409; fax: 0845 337 9408; email: manchester@cassons.co.uk; website: www.cotton-districts.co.uk)

CC number: 224727

Eligibility
People in need who have a severe/long-term illness, are convalescent or who have a disability and live: in the counties of Lancashire and Greater Manchester; the districts of Craven, North Yorkshire and High Peak, Derbyshire; the districts of Macclesfield and Warrington in Cheshire; and the district of Calderdale, West Yorkshire.

Types of grants
Monthly grants not exceeding £45 per month are available towards living costs for those who are in poor health, convalescent or who have a disability.

The charity makes grants to enable a subsidised convalescent holiday of one week to be taken at hotels in Blackpool and St Annes. Applicants are expected to pay an amount towards the cost of a week's half-board holiday with the fund paying the difference. Alternatively, the charity may instead make a contribution of £200 towards the costs of a holiday elsewhere in the UK. Consideration will be given to making a grant towards the costs of a special needs holiday proposed by the applicant (for example where nursing or other care is required).

Annual grant total
In 2016 the charity had assets of £1.1 million and an income of £45,500. During the year, the charity awarded £3,000 in holiday grants and £23,500 in monthly grants. There were a total of 52 beneficiaries.

Applications
Apply in writing to the secretary, providing details of your financial and medical circumstances. The application should be accompanied by a supporting letter from a sponsor, such as a doctor or social worker, confirming these medical and financial circumstances.

The Grant, Bagshaw, Rogers and Tidswell Fund

£10,500

Correspondent: Lawrence Downey, Ripley House, 56 Freshfield Road, Formby, Liverpool L37 3HW (01704 87933; email: lawrencedowney@btconnect.com)

CC number: 216948

Eligibility
Older people in need who live, or were born in, Liverpool, the Wirral, Ellesmere Port or Chester.

Types of grants
Small pensions are paid half-yearly. Occasional one-off grants may also be given.

Annual grant total
In 2015/16 the fund had an income of £15,900 and a total expenditure of £11,600. We estimate that grants given to individuals totalled £10,500.

Applications
Application forms are available from the correspondent.

Gregson Memorial Annuities

£2,700

Correspondent: Richard Hey, c/o Brabners Chaffe Street LLP, Horton House, Exchange Flags, Liverpool L2 3YL (0151 600 3000; email: richard.hey@brabners.com)

CC number: 218096

Eligibility
Female domestic servants and governesses who have been in service for at least ten years in Liverpool, Southport, Malpas and the surrounding area and who cannot work now for health reasons.

Types of grants
Annuities of about £300 a year, payable in two six-monthly instalments.

Annual grant total
In 2016/17 the charity had an income of £3,600 and a total expenditure of £3,000. We estimate that grants given to individuals totalled approximately £2,700.

Applications
Applications in writing to the correspondent are considered throughout the year.

Lancashire County Nursing Trust

£13,000

Correspondent: Hadyn Gigg, Trustee, Plumpton House, Great Plumpton, Preston PR4 2NJ (01772 673618; email: hadyngigg@yahoo.co.uk; website: www.lcnt.org.uk)

CC number: 224667

Eligibility
Members of the general public who are facing ill health or financial hardship living in Lancashire, Greater Manchester or South Cumbria; retired community nurses who have worked in Lancashire, Greater Manchester or South Cumbria.

Types of grants
One-off grants of up to £500. Grants awarded by the trust tend to go towards the replacement washing machines; part of a syndicate purchasing larger items/repairs to properties; food for special diets; assistance towards home adaptations; radio or TV for the housebound; purchase of a Kindle reader and funds to download books.

Annual grant total

In 2016 the trust had an income of £13,700 and a total expenditure of £15,600. We estimate that grants given to individuals for social welfare purposes totalled around £13,000.

Applications

Apply in writing to the correspondent. Applications can be submitted directly by the individual or through health and social work professionals, charities or other welfare organisations.

Cheshire

John Holford's Charity

£8,800

Correspondent: Kerris Owen, Clerk to the Trustees, Parish Office, St Peter's Church, The Cross, Chester CH1 2LA (07794 654212; email: jholfordcharity@ gmail.com; website: www. johnholfordcharity.org)

CC number: 223046

Eligibility

People in need who live in the parishes of Astbury, Clutton, Congleton and Middlewich.

Due to local authority changes the list of eligible parishes has been extended and now also includes: Alsager, Brereton, Church Lawton, Eaton, Goostrey, Holmes Chapel, Hulme Walfield, Mow Cop, North Rode, Odd Rode, Rode Heath, Sandbach, Smallwood, Swettenham and Wheelock.

Types of grants

One-off and recurrent grants for a variety of needs, ranging from £100 to £2,500.

Annual grant total

In 2016 the charity held assets of £1.8 million and had an income of £87,000. Grants can be made to individuals and organisations £17,600 and we have estimated that £8,800 was awarded to individuals.

Exclusions

According to our research, grants are not given for education or medical treatment.

Applications

Applications can be made online on the charity's website. Alternatively an application form can be downloaded from the website or requested from the correspondent. They can be submitted by the individual or through a social worker, carer, Citizens Advice, other welfare agency or also a relative. Two letters of support are required. Requests are considered on a regular basis.

The trustees prefer to award grants through third parties such as schools, school uniform suppliers or through social services.

Cheshire East

The Congleton Town Trust

£6,000

Correspondent: Jo Money, Clerk, Congleton Town Hall, High Street, Congleton, Cheshire CW12 1BN (01260 270908; email: info@congletontowntrust. co.uk; website: www.congletontowntrust. co.uk)

CC number: 1051122

Eligibility

People in need who live in the town of Congleton (this refers only to the area administered by Congleton Town Council).

Types of grants

Grants, usually in the range of £200 and £3,000, are given to individuals in need or to organisations that provide relief, services or facilities to those in need.

Annual grant total

In 2016 the trust had an income of £25,000 and a total expenditure of £26,500. We estimate that welfare grants to individuals totalled around £6,000.

Applications

We would advise potential applicants to, in the first instance, contact the correspondent for more information. This can be done using the online form on the website.

Lindow Workhouse Charity

£5,000

Correspondent: John Fallows, Correspondent, 1 Thornfield Hey, Wilmslow, Cheshire SK9 5JY (01625 533950; email: lwt@jfallows.org.uk)

CC number: 226023

Eligibility

People in need who live in the ancient parish of Wilmslow.

Types of grants

One-off grants to help with, for example, fuel bills, equipment repairs, property repairs. Any cases of real need are considered.

Annual grant total

In 2015/16 the charity had an income of £10,500 and a total expenditure of £10,700. We estimate that around £5,000

was awarded to individuals for welfare purposes.

Exclusions

Grants are not made towards relief of rates, taxes or other public funds.

Applications

Applications may be made in writing to the correspondent at any time. They can be submitted directly by the individual or a family member, through a third party (such as a social worker or teacher), or through an organisation (such as Citizens Advice or a school).

Other information

Our research suggests that children with special educational needs are also supported.

Macclesfield and District Relief-in-Sickness Charity

£2,100

Correspondent: Peter Womby, Trustee, Oak Crescent, Leek Old Road, Sutton, Macclesfield, Cheshire SK11 0JA (01260 252220)

CC number: 501631

Eligibility

People who are sick, convalescent or who have disabilities who live in Macclesfield, the rural district of Macclesfield and the urban district of Bollington.

Types of grants

One-off grants only for necessary items such as washing machines, telephone installation, removals or specialist wheelchairs and especially for health-related items that would improve the quality of the applicant's situation.

Annual grant total

In 2015/16 the charity had an income of £3,400 and a total expenditure of £2,300. We estimate that the charity awarded around £2,100 in grants to individuals for welfare purposes.

Applications

Our previous research suggests that applications must be made through a local social services office, doctor's surgery or other welfare agency, and they should verify the need of the applicant.

Other information

At the time of writing (August 2017) the charity had no website or accounts available.

The Wrenbury Consolidated Charities

£2,500

Correspondent: Helen Smith, Trustee, Eagle Hall Cottage, Smeatonwood, Wrenbury, North Nantwich CW5 8HD (01270 780262; email: helen@ peckfortonhouse.co.uk)

CC number: 241778

Eligibility

People in need who live in the parishes of Chorley, Sound, Broomhall, Newhall, Wrenbury and Dodcott-cum-Wilkesley.

Types of grants

One-off grants according to need.

Annual grant total

In 2016 the charity had an income of £10,000 and a total expenditure of £11,000. We estimate that welfare grants to individuals totalled around £2,500.

Applications

Apply in writing to the correspondent.

Other information

Grants are also given to churches, the village hall and for educational purposes.

Cheshire West and Chester

Chester Municipal Charities

£60,000

Correspondent: Peter Catherall, The Bluecoat, Upper Northgate Street, Chester CH1 4EE (01244 403277; email: administration@chestermc.org.uk; website: www.thebluecoat-chester.org.uk/about)

CC number: 1077806

Eligibility

Residents of Chester who are in need.

Types of grants

Mainly one-off grants for relief-in-need purposes.

Annual grant total

In 2016 the charity had an income of £554,000 and a total expenditure of £372,000. We estimate that grants given to individuals totalled around £60,000.

Applications

An application form is available from the correspondent.

Other information

The charity also manages almshouses.

Chester Parochial Charity

£13,700

Correspondent: Kerris Owen, Clerk, Parish Office, St Peter's Church, The Cross, Chester CH1 2LA (07794 654212; email: cprncharity@gmail.com)

CC number: 1001314

Eligibility

People in need who live in the city of Chester.

Types of grants

One-off grants, usually ranging from £50 to £1,000, are given for furniture, washing machines, cookers, electrical items, clothing, school uniforms, carpets, and so on. A supermarket voucher scheme is also available to help low-income families, mainly over the Christmas period.

Annual grant total

In 2015/16 the charity had an income of £30,500 and a total expenditure of £27,000 (this excludes amounts relating to the sale and purchase of assets). According to the year's receipts and payments accounts, grants were made totalling £13,700.

Applications

Application forms are available from the correspondent. Applications can be made directly by the individual, through a recognised referral agency, or through a third party such as a family member. All applicants will be visited by a trustee who will then report back to the subcommittee for a final decision. Applications are considered at any time.

Frodsham Nursing Fund

£2,500

Correspondent: Dr Andrew Faraday, Trustee, 22 Fluin Lane, Frodsham WA6 7QH (01928 731043; email: andrewfaraday@hotmail.com)

CC number: 503246

Eligibility

People in need who are sick, convalescent or living with disabilities and are resident in the town of Frodsham.

Types of grants

One-off grants according to need. Past grants have been given for items such as bedding, clothing, medical aids, heating and other domestic appliances. Temporary relief may also be provided to those caring for somebody who is sick or who has a disability.

Annual grant total

In 2016/17 the fund had an income of £3,000 and a total expenditure of £2,900. We estimate that social welfare assistance for individuals totalled around £2,500.

Applications

Apply in writing to the correspondent, either directly by the individual or on their behalf by a doctor, nurse or social worker. Applicants should briefly state their circumstances and what help is being sought.

The Ursula Keyes Trust

£9,000 (seven grants)

Correspondent: Dorothy Lawless, c/o RSM, One City Place, Queens Street, Chester CH1 3BQ (01244 505100; website: www.ursula-keyes-trust.org.uk)

CC number: 517200

Eligibility

People in need, especially those with a medical condition, who live in the area administered by Chester District Council and in particular those within the boundaries of the former City of Chester and the adjoining parishes of Great Boughton and Upton.

Types of grants

One-off grants according to need.

Annual grant total

In 2016 the trust held assets of £4.56 million and had an income of £276,000. Grants to seven individuals totalled £9,000. A further £99,000 was given in grants to organisations.

Exclusions

No grants are given to repay debts or loans or to reimburse expenditure already incurred.

Applications

Apply in writing to the correspondent. A summary form is available to download from the website and should be submitted along with your application. Applications must be supported by a social worker, a doctor (if relevant) or another professional or welfare agency.

Applications are considered by the trustees at their quarterly meetings, which take place on Fridays at the end of January, April, July and October. Applications should be received at least two weeks before these dates to be certain of consideration at any particular meeting. Dates of forthcoming meetings are posted on the trust's website.

Cumbria

Barrow Thornborrow Charity

£2,500

Correspondent: Fred Robinson, Trustee, The Parrock, Stankelt Road, Silverdale, Carnforth LA5 0TW

CC number: 222168

Eligibility

People who have a disability or are sick and live, or were born in, the former county of Westmorland, the former county borough of Barrow, the former rural districts of Sedbergh and North Lonsdale, or the former urban districts of Dalton-in-Furness, Grange and Ulverston.

Types of grants

One-off grants towards items, services or facilities which are calculated to alleviate suffering and assist recovery and are not available from other sources. In previous years grants have been awarded for household equipment, travel expenses in case of hospitalisation, clothing, computer aids and assistance with essential property repairs.

Annual grant total

In 2016 the charity had an income of £3,300 and a total expenditure of £2,900. We have estimated that grants to individuals for welfare purposes totalled £2,500 during the year.

Applications

Apply in writing to the correspondent including details of the applicant's circumstances. Applications can be submitted through a social worker, Citizens Advice or other welfare agency.

Cumbria Community Foundation

£3.55 million (1,521+ grants)

Correspondent: Grants & Donor Services, Cumbria Community Foundation, Dovenby Hall, Dovenby, Cockermouth, Cumbria CA13 0PN (01900 825760; email: enquiries@ cumbriafoundation.org; website: www. cumbriafoundation.org)

CC number: 1075120

Eligibility

People in need who live in Cumbria. Individual funds have their own specific eligibility criteria – see the community foundation's website for details.

Types of grants

The type of grant available depends on the fund being applied to. See the website for details of available grants.

Annual grant total

In 2016/17 the foundation had assets of £19.15 million and an income of £6.5 million (including almost £3.5 million from linked charities). Grants to 2,061 individuals for both welfare and education totalled £3.64 million. Of this amount, almost £3.55 million was distributed to 1,521 households from the Cumbrian Flood Recovery Fund 2015. It is likely that welfare grants were also made to individuals from other funds, although we were unable to determine an exact figure for this.

Applications

In the first instance, see the website for details of individual funds, their eligibility criteria and information on how to make an application.

Other information

The foundation makes grants to individuals for educational purposes, and also provides grants to local organisations working within the community (£3.07 million to 425 organisations in 2016/17).

Note: In recent years, the foundation has distributed an exceptionally large number of grants to individuals, owing to its response in helping people affected by the 2015 Cumbria floods. Before this time, grant-making to individuals made up only a small proportion of the foundation's activities.

Lakeland Disability Support

£32,000

Correspondent: Brenda Robinson, Trust Secretary, Boot Gate, Lily Lane, Windermere, Cumbria LA23 1NU (website: www.amblesideonline.co.uk/ useful-information/clubs/lakeland-disability-support)

CC number: 1102609

Eligibility

People with physical disabilities who live in South Lakeland, Cumbria.

Types of grants

One-off grants ranging from £200 to £5,000 towards, for example, the cost of respite care, garden access, special education, or equipment such as electric scooters, special chairs or computers.

Annual grant total

In 2016 the charity held assets of £1.9 million and had an income of £49,500. Grants to individuals totalled £32,000, with an additional £25,500 awarded to local organisations.

Exclusions

No grants are given for long-term care provision.

Applications

Application forms are available from the correspondent. Applications may be made by the individual or a third party and should be accompanied by a reference from a carer, doctor or social worker. Applications are considered quarterly in March, June, September and December. Successful applicants should wait for 12 months before reapplying.

Allerdale

The Bowness Trust

£2,700

Correspondent: Richard Atkinson, Trustee, Milburns Solicitors, Oxford House, 19 Oxford Street, Workington CA14 2AW (01900 67363)

CC number: 502323

Eligibility

People in need who live in Workington. Applicants must be living in their own home (i.e. not in a nursing home, hospital, etc.)

Annual grant total

At the time of writing (January 2018) the trust's financial information for the 2015/16 financial year was overdue at the Charity Commission.

In 2014/15 the trust had an income of £7,500 and a total expenditure of £3,000. We estimate that grants given to individuals totalled around £2,700.

Applications

Apply in writing to the correspondent.

Carlisle

Carlisle Sick Poor Fund

£8,300

Correspondent: Lynne Rowley, 15 Fisher Street, Carlisle, Cumbria CA3 8RW

CC number: 223124

Eligibility

People living in Carlisle and its neighbourhood who are in financial hardship due to ill health.

Types of grants

One-off grants of up to £200 are given towards bedding, food, fuel, medical aids and equipment, convalescence, holidays and home help.

Annual grant total

In 2016 the fund had an income of £8,600 and a total expenditure of £8,600. We estimate that grants given to individuals totalled £8,300.

Applications

Application forms are available from the correspondent.

Other information

Support can also be given to local organisations providing care and relief to people who are sick and in need.

Eden

Crosby Ravensworth Relief in Need Charities

£2,500

Correspondent: George Bowness, Ravenseat, Crosby Ravensworth, Penrith, Cumbria CA10 3JB (01931 715382; email: gordonbowness@aol.com)

CC number: 232598

Eligibility

People in need who have lived in the ancient parish of Crosby Ravensworth for at least 12 months. Preference is given to older people.

Types of grants

One-off and recurrent grants to relieve financial hardship. The charity also provides grants to assist people with disabilities, older people, and people suffering from ill health.

Annual grant total

In 2016 the charity had an income of £14,000 and a total expenditure of £4,000. We estimate that grants given to individuals totalled £2,500.

Applications

Applications may be made in writing to the correspondent, submitted directly by the individual. They should include details of the applicant's financial situation.

Other information

Grants are also awarded to individuals for educational and training purposes, and to organisations.

South Lakeland

Ambleside Welfare Charity

£39,000

Correspondent: Michael Johnson, 11 The Green, Bolton-le-Sands, Carnforth LA5 8FD (01539 431656; email: lakesparishclerk@yahoo.co.uk)

CC number: 214759

Eligibility

People in need who live in the parish of Ambleside, especially those who are ill.

Types of grants

One-off and recurrent grants are given according to need. Help is also given to local relatives for hospital visits.

Annual grant total

In 2015 the charity held assets of £977,000 and had an income of £51,500. Welfare grants amounted to £39,000.

Applications

Apply in writing to the correspondent.

Agnes Backhouse Annuity Fund

£3,500 (65 grants)

Correspondent: James Hamilton, Trustee, c/o Temple Heelis Solicitors, 1 Kent View, Kendal, Cumbria LA9 4DZ (01539 723757)

CC number: 224960

Eligibility

Unmarried or widowed women aged over 50 who live in the parish of Ambleside who are in need.

Types of grants

Annuities are paid out in December.

Annual grant total

In 2016 the fund had an income of £23,000 and a total expenditure of £29,500. Typically, annuities paid to individuals total around £3,500.

Applications

Apply in writing to the correspondent.

Other information

In the past, the fund has also made grants to a local branch of Age UK.

The Jane Fisher Trust

£2,100

Correspondent: S. Marsden, 9 Benson Street, Ulverston, Cumbria LA12 7AU (01229 585555; email: kathmarsden@hotmail.co.uk)

CC number: 225401

Eligibility

People in need over the age of 50 and people who have disabilities, who have lived in the townships of Ulverston and Osmotherly or the parish of Pennington for at least 20 years.

Types of grants

Small monthly payments.

Annual grant total

In 2015/16 the trust had an income of £2,400 and a total expenditure of £2,200. We estimate that grant to individuals totalled £2,100.

Applications

Application forms are available from the correspondent. Applications are considered when they are received. They must include details of income, capital, age, disabilities, marital status and how long the applicant has lived in the area.

Greater Manchester

J. T. Blair's Charity

£15,000

Correspondent: Kat Malin-August, Finance Manager, Gaddum Centre, Gaddum House, 6 Great Jackson Street, Manchester M15 4AX (0161 834 6069; email: info@gaddumcentre.co.uk; website: www.gaddumcentre.co.uk)

CC number: 221248

Eligibility

People over 65 who live in Manchester and Salford and are in need.

Types of grants

Pensions and grants towards specific expenses.

Annual grant total

In 2015/16 the charity had an income of £18,000 and a total expenditure of £35,000. We estimate that grants given to individuals totalled around £15,000.

Applications

Application forms are available from the correspondent. Applications should be submitted by a social worker or other professional person. The trustees meet three or four times a year. Applicants should contact the charity for specific deadlines. Those in receipt of a pension are visited at least once a year.

Other information

The charity funds a Befriending Service through the Gaddum Centre (which also administrates the charity). The service supports people in Manchester and Salford who are over the age of 60 and are socially isolated. The befriending coordinator matches older people up with a volunteer befriender who pays them regular visits. Further information is available by calling 0161 214 3934.

The Dr Garrett Memorial Trust

£3,000

Correspondent: Anne Hosker, Administrator, Gaddum Centre, Gaddum House, 6 Great Jackson Street, Manchester M15 4AX (0161 834 6069; email: info@gaddum.co.uk; website: www.gaddumcentre.co.uk)

CC number: 1010844

Eligibility

Families or groups in need who live in Manchester.

Types of grants

Grants are given towards the cost of convalescence or holidays for individual families and groups.

Annual grant total

In 2016/17 the trust had an income of £9,800 and a total expenditure of £6,900. We estimate that grants given to individuals totalled around £3,000.

Applications

Application forms are available from the correspondent and should be completed by a sponsor from a recognised social or health agency. Applications must be submitted by the end of April each year.

The Community Foundation for Greater Manchester (Forever Manchester)

£5,500

Correspondent: The Grants and Awards Officer, 2nd Floor, 8 Hewitt Street, Manchester M15 4GB (0161 214 0940; email: info@forevermanchester.com; website: forevermanchester.com)

CC number: 1017504

Eligibility

People in need who live in Greater Manchester.

Types of grants

Grants are usually one-off.

Annual grant total

In 2015/16 the foundation had assets of £9.5 million and an income of £3.2 million. During the year, the foundation awarded a total of £10,900 to individuals. There was no breakdown of the grants which were awarded. We estimate that around £5,500 went to individuals for welfare purposes.

Applications

Visit the foundation's website and contact the foundation for details of grant funds that are currently appropriate for individuals to apply for. The website states: 'Please contact our awards team on 0161 214 0940 to discuss deadline dates, eligibility and criteria and to receive guidelines and an application pack.'

Other information

The Community Foundation for Greater Manchester manages a portfolio of grants for a variety of purposes which are mostly for organisations, but there also are a select few aimed at individuals. Funds tend to open and close throughout the year as well as new ones being added – check the website for up-to-date information on currently operating schemes.

Manchester District Nursing Institution Fund

£6,600 (24 grants)

Correspondent: Katherine Malin-August, Correspondent, Gaddum Centre, Gaddum House, 6 Great Jackson Street, Manchester M15 4AX (0161 834 6069; email: info@gaddumcentre.co.uk; website: www.gaddumcentre.co.uk/trust-funds-more-info)

CC number: 235916

Eligibility

People on low income with health-related needs in the cities of Manchester and Salford and the borough of Trafford.

Types of grants

One-off grants. It is important that the request is directly related to the health issue of the applicant and is not related to a general condition of poverty.

Annual grant total

In 2016 the fund had assets of £960,500 and an income of £29,000. During the year, the fund awarded 24 grants to individuals totalling £6,600.

Financial figures include The Levenshulme Trust for the Relief of Sickness and Suffering (LTRSS).

Exclusions

Grants are not made for funeral expenses, rates, taxes or other public funds, bills, debts or fines.

Applications

Application forms and guidance can be obtained from the correspondent. All requests must be made by a sponsor from a recognised social and/or health agency or an appropriate third party professional.

Other information

The fund incorporates The LTRSS, the objective of which is to help people resident in the M19 postcode who have health-related problems.

Lord Mayor of Manchester's Charity Appeal Trust

£34,000

Correspondent: Correspondent, We Love MCR Charity, Lord Mayor's Office, Room 412, Level 4, Town Hall, Manchester M60 2LA (email: welovemcrcharity@manchester.gov.uk; website: www.welovemcrcharity.org)

CC number: 1066972

Eligibility

Families in need who reside in Manchester.

Types of grants

Holiday grants.

Annual grant total

In 2015/16 the trust had assets of £758,500 and an income of £114,000. During the year, the trust gave over £34,000 to individuals.

The trust also awarded around £27,000 to organisations.

Applications

The application form along with guidance notes are available to download from the website. Applications for individuals will be considered but must be nominated by a sponsor or third party. This can be an organisation or group on behalf of the individual, for example a school, social or support worker. Completed applications must be submitted by email.

Other information

Grants are awarded to individuals for short breaks which are taken locally in the UK and the families are nominated by a team of family support workers and social workers. In 2017, fifteen disadvantaged families from Manchester experienced a short break during the summer months. Since 2011, there have been 325 adults and 595 children who have benefitted from this programme.

Bolton

The Bolton and District Nursing Association

£800

Correspondent: T. Wallace, Bolton Guild of Help, Scott House, 27 Silverwell Street, Bolton BL1 1PP (01204 524858; email: guildofhelp@btconnect.com)

CC number: 250153

Eligibility
People who are sick or convalescing, or who have disabilities and live in the area of Bolton Metropolitan Borough Council.

Types of grants
One-off grants are made for items and services, such as the provision of medical equipment, disability equipment and convalescence.

Annual grant total
In 2016 the charity had an income of £3,400 and a total expenditure of £830. We estimate that grants given to individuals totalled around £800.

Applications
Apply in writing to the correspondent.

The Louisa Alice Kay Fund

£42,000 (183 grants)

Correspondent: Tracey Wallace, Secretary, Bolton Guild of Help (Inc.), Scott House, 27 Silverwell Street, Bolton BL1 1PP (email: guildofhelp@btconnect.com)

CC number: 224760–1

Eligibility
People in need who live in Bolton.

Types of grants
One-off grants for emergencies and relief in need, mostly for replacing household equipment and furniture.

Annual grant total
In 2016 grants were made to 183 individuals totalling £42,000 and were distributed in the following areas:

Washing machines	£17,500
Cookers	£8,300
Beds and furniture	£7,100
Fridges and fridge/freezers	£4,800
Other	£4,400

Applications
Application forms are available from the correspondent. Applications can be submitted either directly by the individual or a family member, through a third party such as a social worker, or through an organisation such as Citizens Advice or other welfare agency. Applicants will sometimes be interviewed before a grant is awarded.

Other information
The fund is administered by the Bolton Guild of Help Incorporated.

Bury

Bury Relief in Sickness Fund

£7,000

Correspondent: Gill Warburton, Trustee, c/o 2 Park Crescent, Haslingden, Rossendale, Lancashire BB4 6PS (01706 223578)

CC number: 256397

Eligibility
People living in the metropolitan borough of Bury who are in poor health, convalescent or who have disabilities.

Types of grants
One-off grants towards convalescence, medical equipment and necessities in the home which are not available from other sources.

Annual grant total
In 2016 the fund had an income of £1,600 and a total expenditure of £8,500. We have estimated that grants to individuals totalled £7,000.

Applications
Apply in writing to the correspondent.

The Mellor Fund

£2,700

Correspondent: Gillian Critchley, Trustee, 17 Marle Croft, Whitefield, Manchester M45 7NB

CC number: 230013

Eligibility
People who are sick or in need and live in Radcliffe, Whitefield and Unsworth.

Types of grants
One-off grants towards fuel, food and clothing, domestic necessities, medical needs, recuperative breaks and so on. Recurrent grants are generally not given.

Annual grant total
In 2015 the charity had an income of £5,500 and a total expenditure of £2,900. We estimate that grants given to individuals for welfare purposes totalled around £2,700.

Applications
Apply in writing to the correspondent. Applications can be submitted directly by the individual or through a social worker, Citizens Advice, other welfare agency or a relative, and should include brief details of need, resources, income and commitments. Applications are considered when received.

Manchester

The Dean of Manchester Crosland Fund

£10,000

Correspondent: John Atherden, Manchester Cathedral, Victoria Street, Manchester M3 1SX (0161 833 2220)

CC number: 242838

Eligibility
People affected by hardship who live in the city of Manchester.

Types of grants
One-off grants awarded quarterly, according to need.

Annual grant total
In 2015/16 the fund had an income of £7,200 and a total expenditure of £10,700. We estimate that grants given to individuals totalled £10,000.

Applications
Applications should be made by a recognised organisation such as Citizens Advice on behalf of the individual.

Manchester Relief-in-Need Fund and Manchester Children's Relief-in-Need Fund

£33,000

Correspondent: Grants Administrator, Gaddum Centre, Gaddum House, 6 Great Jackson Street, Manchester M15 4AX (0161 834 6069; email: info@gaddumcentre.co.uk; website: www.gaddumcentre.co.uk)

CC number: 224271 and 249657

Eligibility
People in need who live in the city of Manchester and are over 25 (Relief-in-Need) or under 25 (Children's Relief-in-Need).

Types of grants
One-off grants for domestic appliances, furniture, clothing, heating and fuel bills, and other general necessities. Cheques are made out to the supplier of the goods or services.

Annual grant total
In 2016/17 the fund had a combined income of £82,000. Welfare grants to individuals totalled around £33,000;

Manchester Relief-in-Need (awarded 1,114 grants amounting to £23,000) and the Manchester Children's Relief-in-Need (awarded an estimated £10,000).

Exclusions

Debts are very rarely paid and council tax and rent debts are never met. Normally an individual may only receive one grant in any 12-month period.

Applications

Apply on a form available from the correspondent which should be completed by a sponsor from a recognised social or health-related agency. The trustees meet during the last week of every month. Applications must be received by the 15th of the month.

Other information

Grants are also made to organisations.

Oldham

The Sarah Lees Relief Trust

£1,800

Correspondent: Catherine Sykes, Trustee, 10 Chew Brook Drive, Greenfield, Oldham OL3 7PD (01457 876606; email: cathiesykes@btinternet. com)

CC number: 514240

Eligibility

People living in Oldham who are sick or convalescent, or who have a disability.

Types of grants

One-off grants of up to £500 and gifts in kind.

Annual grant total

In 2015/16 the trust had an income of £3,400 and a total expenditure of £3,500. We estimate that grants given to individuals totalled £1,800.

Exclusions

No grants are given for items, services or facilities that are readily available from other sources.

Applications

Apply in writing to the correspondent through a social worker or other recognised welfare agency. The trustees meet three times a year, but urgent requests will be considered between meetings.

Oldham United Charity

£1,000

Correspondent: Phil Higgins, Administrator, 130 Denbydale Way, Royton, Oldham OL2 5TE (0161 624 2034; email: phil.higgins11@gmail.com)

CC number: 221095

Eligibility

People in need who live in the metropolitan borough of Oldham.

Types of grants

One-off grants according to need. Recent grants have been mainly for medical needs, e.g. wheelchairs and washing machines for people who are incontinent. Some grants are given to students towards educational expenses.

Annual grant total

In 2016/17 the charity had an income of £2,200 and a total expenditure of £2,400. We estimate that grants given to individuals totalled approximately £1,000, with funding also awarded to organisations.

Applications

Apply in writing to the correspondent. Grants are usually considered quarterly.

Rochdale

The Norman Barnes Fund

£3,500

Correspondent: S. Shahid, Clerk to the Fund, Governance and Committee Services, Floor 2, Number One Riverside, Smith Street, Rochdale OL16 1XU (01706 924713; email: committee. services@rochdale.gov.uk; website: www. rochdale.gov.uk/the_council/charitable_ trusts.aspx)

CC number: 511646

Eligibility

People over the age of 60 who live in Rochdale, Castleton, Norden or Bamford.

Types of grants

One-off grants of up to £250 can be made within any 12-month period. Grants can be made towards the purchase of white goods, carpets and furniture, essential house repairs, recuperative holidays, and travel expenses.

Annual grant total

In 2015/16 the fund had an income of £12,400 and a total expenditure of £8,100. We estimate that grants given to individuals for welfare purposes totalled £3,500, with funding also awarded to local organisations.

Exclusions

No payments for tax, council tax, or other statutory payments, except where relief or assistance is already provided out of public funds.

Applications

Application forms are available to download from the Rochdale Council website or by contacting the correspondent. It is recommended that applicants include a supporting comment from a doctor, social worker, Age UK representative or some other relevant professional. Standard items like fridges or cookers will be ordered directly by the trustees. For grants greater than £250, the support of an officer of Rochdale Council's Social Services Department is required.

Heywood Relief-in-Need Trust Fund

£8,500

Correspondent: Heywood Phoenix Trust, c/o 94 Whalley Road, Clayton-le-Moors, Accrington BB5 5DY (email: phoenixtrust@outlook.com)

CC number: 517114

Eligibility

People in need who live in the former municipal borough of Heywood are eligible. In exceptional cases, applications may be considered from those who are only temporarily located within the borough.

Types of grants

One-off grants have been given to help with fuel arrears, clothing and furniture.

Annual grant total

In 2016/17 the fund had an income of £6,000 and a total expenditure of £9,100. We estimate that grants given to individuals totalled £8,500.

Exclusions

No grants are awarded to pay for council tax or other statutory payments, or charges imposed or benefits reduced due to government policy, or payment of debts or fees for either bankruptcy or debt relief order processes. No repeat grants.

Applications

Apply in writing to the correspondent. Applications should be supported by a social worker, health visitor or similar professional.

The Rochdale Fund for Relief-in-Sickness

£8,900

Correspondent: Susan Stoney, Trust Administrator, The Old Parsonage, 2 St Mary's Gate, Rochdale OL16 1AP (01706 644187; email: law@jbhs.co.uk; website: www.rochdalefund.org.uk)

CC number: 222652

Eligibility

People living in the borough of Rochdale (including Wardle, Littleborough, Middleton, Heywood, Norden, Birtle, Milnrow and Newhey) who are in poor health, convalescent or who have disabilities. Help may also be given to those whose physical or mental health is likely to be impaired by poverty, deprivation or other adversity.

Types of grants

One-off grants according to need. The trustees will consider any requests for items which will make life more comfortable or productive for the individual. For example, recent grants have been given towards wheelchairs, hoists, IT equipment, house adaptations, special leisure equipment, medical aids, washing machines, cookers, clothing, beds, bedding and respite breaks.

Annual grant total

In 2016/17 the fund had assets of £1.7 million and an income of £59,000. During the year, the fund gave a total of £24,600 in grants. Of this amount, £15,700 was given to organisations and £8,900 to individuals.

Exclusions

Grants are not given for the payment of debts, including utility bills, council tax and Inland Revenue payments or to help with hardship not directly related to, or caused as a result of, sickness.

Applications

Apply on a form available from the correspondent or to download from the website. Applications can be made either directly by the individual (if no other route is available) or through a social worker, Citizens Advice, other welfare agency or other third party such as a doctor. Whether completed by the individual or a third party, all applications must be supported by a letter from a recognised body, such as social services, doctor, etc.

Other information

The fund's website states that it may also make grants to organisations, 'both statutory and voluntary, to assist them in providing equipment, services or facilities which may alleviate the suffering, or promote the recovery of, persons who qualify'.

Rochdale United Charity

£7,500

Correspondent: Saddleworth Parish Council, Saddleworth Parish Council, Civic Hall, Lee Street, Uppermill, Oldham OL3 6AE (01457 876665; website: parishcouncil.saddleworth.org/contact.html)

CC number: 224461

Eligibility

People in need who live in the ancient parish of Rochdale (the former county borough of Rochdale, Castleton, Wardle, Whitworth, Littleborough, Todmorden and Saddleworth).

Types of grants

One-off grants typically ranging from £50 to £250. Grants have been awarded for the provision of domestic appliances such as fridges and cookers, medical aids and equipment, telephones, televisions or radios for people who are lonely or housebound and towards the costs of arranging recuperative holidays.

Annual grant total

In 2016/17 the charity had an income of £10,600 and a total expenditure of £15,200. We estimate that the charity gave around £7,500 in grants to individuals, as well as awarding grants to local organisations.

Exclusions

No grants are given for the relief of rates, taxes or other public funds. No recurrent grants.

Applications

Application forms are available from the correspondent. Applications should be submitted through a social worker, GP, health visitor, Citizens Advice or other welfare agency. Applications are usually considered quarterly.

Salford

The Booth Charities

£1,000

Correspondent: Jonathan Aldersley, Clerk to the Trustees, c/o Butcher & Barlow LLP, 3 Royal Mews, Gadbrook Road, Rudheath, Northwich CW9 7UD (01606 334309; email: jaldersley@butcher-barlow.co.uk)

CC number: 221800

Eligibility

People who are retired, over 60, on a basic pension, live in the city of Salford and are in need.

Types of grants

Annual pensions and one-off grants. In 2015/16 the charity placed credit on electricity accounts of approved recipients of the Booth Benefit, and this was paid to the supplier.

Annual grant total

In 2015/16 the charity had an income of £1 million and a total expenditure of £1 million. The charity's main activity is making grants to organisations in Salford, and during the year, 48 organisations received £363,000. Grants to individuals totalled £1,000.

Applications

Application forms are available from the correspondent. Applications for one-off grants must be made by social services, ministers of religion or GPs. Distribution meetings are held regularly throughout the year.

Other information

The charity's main activity is supporting organisations working to alleviate poverty and ill health in Salford, and details of their activities can be found in the charity's thorough 2015/16 annual report. One of the charities in this group makes grants towards the upkeep of Sacred Trinity Church, where an annual commemoration service is held for beneficiaries.

Stockport

Sir Ralph Pendlebury's Charity for Orphans

£900

Correspondent: Stephen Tattersall, Correspondent, Lacy Watson & Co., Carlyle House, 107–109 Wellington Road South, Stockport SK1 3TL

CC number: 213927

Eligibility

Orphans who have lived, or whose parents have lived, in the borough of Stockport for at least two years and who are in need.

Types of grants

Recurring payments, usually of £5 or £6 a week, plus clothing allowances twice a year are available. Support can also be given for holidays. The main priority for the charity is relief in need.

Annual grant total

In 2015 the charity had an income of £13,500 and a total expenditure of £6,500. We estimate that around £900 was awarded in grants for welfare purposes.

Applications

Applications can be made in writing to the correspondent. They should be made by a parent/guardian.

Other information

Grants are also made for educational purposes.

Sir Ralph Pendlebury's Charity for the Aged

£2,800

Correspondent: Stephen Tattersall, Administrator, Lacy Watson & Co., Carlyle House, 107–109 Wellington Road South, Stockport, Cheshire SK1 3TL (0161 477 7400; email: help@lacywatson. co.uk)

CC number: 213928

Eligibility

People above pensionable age who have lived in the borough of Stockport for at least two years and are in necessitous circumstances.

Types of grants

Small grants to older people.

Annual grant total

In 2016 the charity had an income of £9,300 and a total expenditure of £6,000. We estimate the amount given to individuals to be around £2,800. The charity also awards grants to organisations.

Applications

Apply in writing to the correspondent.

Other information

At the time of writing (August 2017) the charity had no website or accounts available.

Wigan

The Golborne Charities – Charity of William Leadbetter

£4,500

Correspondent: Paul Gleave, 56 Nook Lane, Golborne, Warrington WA3 3JQ (01942 727627)

CC number: 221088

Eligibility

People in need who live in the parish of Golborne as it was in 1892.

Types of grants

One-off grants usually between £70 and £100, although larger sums may be given. Grants are usually cash payments,

but are occasionally in kind, for food, bedding, fireguards, clothing and shoes, for example. Help can also be given with hospital travel and necessary holidays.

Annual grant total

In 2016/17 the charity had an income of £6,600 and a total expenditure of £6,400. Grants are made to individuals for both social welfare and educational purposes. We estimate that social welfare grants to individuals totalled £4,500.

Applications

Apply in writing to the correspondent through a third party such as a social worker or a teacher, or via a trustee. Applications are considered at three-monthly intervals. Grant recipients tend to be known by at least one trustee.

The Lowton United Charity

£2,000

Correspondent: John Naughton, Secretary, 51 Kenilworth Road, Lowton, Warrington WA3 2AZ (01942 741583)

CC number: 226469

Eligibility

People in need who live in the parishes of St Luke's and St Mary's in Lowton.

Types of grants

One-off grants at Christmas and emergency one-off grants at any time.

Annual grant total

In 2015/16 the charity had an income of £7,400 and a total expenditure of £7,300. Our research suggests that grants for individuals total about £4,000 each year. About a half is given at Christmas for relief-in-need purposes and the rest are given throughout the year. We estimate that grants given to individuals for welfare purposes totalled about £2,000.

Applications

Applications are usually accepted through the rectors of the parishes or other trustees.

Other information

Some assistance may also be given to organisations. Educational support is also given to individuals.

Isle of Man

The Manx Marine Society

£5,000

Correspondent: Capt. R. Cringle, 10 Carrick Bay View, Ballagawne Road, Colby, Isle of Man IM9 4DD (01624 838233)

Eligibility

Seafarers and their widows, children and dependants, who live on the Isle of Man. Young Manx people under 18 who wish to attend sea school or become a cadet are also eligible.

Types of grants

One-off and recurrent grants of up to £400 are given according to need.

Annual grant total

Our research suggests that around £5,000 is awarded to individuals for social welfare purposes each year.

Applications

Application forms are available from the correspondent. Applications are considered at any time and can be submitted either by the individual, or through a social worker, Citizens Advice or other welfare agency.

Other information

The trustees also award grants for educational purposes.

Lancashire

Baines's Charity

£3,500

Correspondent: Duncan Waddilove, Correspondent, 2 The Chase, Normoss Road, Blackpool, Lancashire FY3 0BF (01253 893459; email: duncanwaddilove@hotmail.com)

CC number: 224135

Eligibility

People in need who live in the area of Blackpool and Fylde and Wyre.

Types of grants

One-off grants ranging from £100 to £250. Requests are considered on their merits.

Annual grant total

In 2016 the charity had an income of £19,000 and a total expenditure of £16,100. We estimate that the amount paid in grants to individuals for social welfare purposes was around £3,500.

Applications

Application forms are available from the correspondent. They can be submitted either directly by the individual or through a social worker, Citizens Advice or other welfare agency. Applications are considered upon receipt.

Other information

Grants can be made to individuals and organisations for both welfare and educational purposes, including support to schools. The charity works in conjunction with John Sykes Dewhurst Bequest (Charity Commission no. 224133).

The charity's area of benefit includes the ancient townships of Carleton, Hardhorn-with-Newton, Marton, Poulton and Thornton.

Daniel's and Houghton's Charity

£8,500

Correspondent: Helen Ryan, Brabners Chaffe Street LLP, 7–8 Chapel Street, Preston PR1 8AN (01772 823921; email: helen.ryan@brabners.com)

CC number: 1074762

Eligibility

People in need who live in Lancashire with preference given to those living in Preston, Grimsargh, Broughton, Woodplumpton, Eaves, Catforth, Bartle, Alston and Elston.

Types of grants

One-off and recurrent grants are given according to need.

Annual grant total

In 2015/16 the charity had a total income of £29,500 and a total expenditure of £33,500. We estimate that grants paid during the year totalled around £8,500.

Applications

Apply in writing to the correspondent.

Other information

Grants are also made to organisations.

The Harris Charity

£850

Correspondent: David Ingram, Secretary, c/o Moore and Smalley, Richard House, 9 Winckley Square, Preston PR1 3HP (01772 821021; email: harrischarity@mooreandsmalley.co.uk; website: theharrischarity.co.uk)

CC number: 526206

Eligibility

People in need under the age of 25 who live in Lancashire, with a preference for the Preston district.

Types of grants

One-off grants of £100 to £5,000 for electrical goods, travel expenses and disability equipment, for example.

Annual grant total

In 2015/16 the charity had an income of £127,000 and a total expenditure of £90,500. We estimate that grants given to individuals totalled around £850.

Applications

Application forms are available to download from the charity's website. Applications made by individuals must be accompanied by supporting references from responsible referees.

The half-yearly dates by which the applications must be submitted are 31 March and 30 September. Successful applicants are notified in July and January respectively.

Other information

The original charity known as the Harris Orphanage Charity dates back to 1883. A new charitable scheme was established in 1985 following the sale of the Harris Orphanage premises in Garstang Road, Preston. The charity also supports charitable organisations that benefit individuals, recreation and leisure and the training and education of individuals.

Swallowdale Children's Trust

£39,000 (232 grants)

Correspondent: Alexa Alderson, Swallowdale Children's Trust, PO Box 1301, Blackpool FY1 9HD (01253 767112; email: secswallowdale@hotmail.co.uk; website: www.swallowdaletrust.co.uk)

CC number: 526205

Eligibility

People who live in the Blackpool area who are under the age of 25.

Types of grants

The trust provides one-off grants for general welfare purposes and relief in need, such as for living expenses and recreational equipment. Payments are made to third parties or by issue of vouchers.

Annual grant total

In 2016/17 the trust had assets of £1.04 million and an income of £42,500. The amount awarded in grants to assist individuals in need was £39,000.

Applications

Application forms are available to download from the trust's website and should be countersigned by a social or professional worker. Completed applications should be returned to the correspondent's PO box.

The trustees meet on a bi-monthly basis to discuss and approve applications for grants.

Other information

The trust also makes awards to individuals for education.

Blackburn with Darwen

The W. M. and B. W. Lloyd Trust

£30,000

Correspondent: John Jacklin, Gorse Barn, Rock Lane, Tockholes, Darwen, Lancashire BB3 0LX (01254 771367; email: johnjacklin@homecall.co.uk)

CC number: 503384

Eligibility

People in need who live or have been educated in the borough of Blackburn with Darwen, Lancashire.

Types of grants

One-off and recurrent grants are given according to need to assist with the relief of poverty.

Annual grant total

In 2016/17 the charity had an income of £82,000 and a total expenditure of £93,000. We estimate that welfare grants to individuals totalled £30,000.

Applications

Applications should be made in writing to the correspondent. Previous research has shown applications are considered quarterly, in March, June, September and December.

Other information

Grants are made to both individuals and organisations for educational and social welfare purposes.

The trustees also administer the following funds:

- **The Peter Pan Fund** – for the benefit of people with mental disabilities
- **The Darwen War Memorial and Sick Poor Fund** – originally to help war widows and dependants after the First World War and the sick poor of Darwen
- **The Darwen Disabled Fund** – originally designed to assist with the social welfare of people with physical disabilities in Darwen

- **The Ernest Aspin Donation** – to support sporting activities and in particular training and educating young people in sports
- **The T. P. Davies Fund** – for the benefit of the residents of Darwen
- **Darwen Probation Volunteers Fund** – supporting people in Darwen who have come under the probation and aftercare service, and their families

Blackpool

The Blackpool Ladies' Sick Poor Association

£30,000

Correspondent: Patricia Dimuantes, Secretary, 22 James Avenue, Blackpool FY4 4LB (01253 694228; email: sand_grown@mac.com)

CC number: 220639

Eligibility
People in need who live in Blackpool.

Types of grants
Food vouchers are distributed monthly. Special relief grants can be made for immediate needs such as rent, second-hand white goods, furniture, clothes and other essential living costs.

Annual grant total
In 2015/16 the association held assets of £405,000 and had an income of £30,000. Grants to individuals totalled £30,000, with £21,000 given for general relief and £9,000 given for special relief.

Applications
Applications must include proof of extreme hardship and must be made in writing through health visitors, social workers, Citizens Advice or other welfare agencies. Health visitors and social workers can write to the association's treasurer directly, otherwise letters should be sent to the correspondent.

Other information
The association occasionally makes grants to organisations with similar objectives, for example in 2015/16 it made a grant to a local women's refuge to provide toiletries and clothes.

Chorley

The Shaw Charities

£2,500

Correspondent: Ms E. Woodrow, 99 Rawlinson Lane, Heath Charnock, Chorley, Lancashire PR7 4DE (01257 480515; email: woodrows@tinyworld.co.uk)

CC number: 214318

Eligibility
People in need who are over 60 and have lived in Rivington, Anglezarke, Heath Charnock or Anderton for at least five years.

Types of grants
Bi-annual grants.

Annual grant total
In 2016/17 the charity had an income of £5,000 and a total expenditure of £3,000. We estimate that grants given to individuals totalled around £2,500.

Applications
Application forms can be requested from the correspondent.

Hyndburn

The Accrington and District Helping Hands Fund

£15,000

Correspondent: The Trustees, 4 Grindleton Road, West Bradford, Clitheroe BB7 4TE (01200 422062; email: maryann.renton2@btinternet.com)

CC number: 222241

Eligibility
People living in the former borough of Accrington, Clayton-Le-Moors and Altham, who are in poor health and are either supported by benefits or are on a low income.

Types of grants
One-off grants towards the costs of: special foods and medicines, medical comforts, extra bedding, fuel and medical and surgical appliances; the provision of domestic help; convalescence; and the provision of mobile physiotherapy service. Grants are usually paid directly to the supplier.

Annual grant total
In 2016 the fund had an income of £14,700 and a total expenditure of £17,900. We estimate that grants given to individuals totalled £15,000.

Applications
Apply on a form available from the correspondent, to be submitted either directly by the individual or through a social worker, Citizens Advice or other welfare agency. Applications should include evidence of income and state of health, as well as estimates of what is required.

Lancaster

James Bond/Henry Welch Trust

£5,500

Correspondent: Jane Glenton, Secretary, Lancaster City Council, Lancaster Town Hall, Dalton Square, Lancaster LA1 1PJ (01524 582068; email: jglenton@lancaster.gov.uk)

CC number: 222791

Eligibility
People in need who live in the area covered by Lancaster City Council and have diseases of the chest/lungs. Children with disabilities and other special needs are also eligible.

Types of grants
One-off and recurrent grants.

Annual grant total
In 2015/16 the trust had an income of £10,200 and a total expenditure of £7,000. We have estimated that grants to individuals totalled around £5,500.

Applications
Apply in writing to the correspondent.

Brockbank's Annuities Trust

£4,000

Correspondent: Emma Edwards, Administrator, c/o Blackhurst Swainson Goodier LLP, 3 & 4 Allborg Square, Lancaster LA1 1GG (01524 386500; email: eje@bsglaw.co.uk)

CC number: 223595

Eligibility
Unmarried women or widows in need who are over 50 years old and have lived in Lancaster for the last three years. Applicants must not have an income of more than £1,000 from sources other than their state pension.

Types of grants
Quarterly grants.

Annual grant total
In 2016 the trust had an income of £7,000 and a total expenditure of £4,200. We estimate that grants given to individuals totalled £4,000.

Applications
Application forms are available from the correspondent. Applications should be submitted directly by the individual. Applications are usually considered every three months.

The Cottam Charities

£23,000

Correspondent: Emma Edwards, Blackhurst Swainson Goodier LLP, 3–4 Aalborg Place, Lancaster LA1 1BJ (01524 32471; email: eje@bsglaw.co.uk)

CC number: 223936 and 223925

Eligibility

People in need who are aged over 50 and have lived in Caton in Lancashire for at least five years.

Types of grants

One-off grants, usually ranging from about £100 to £140.

Annual grant total

In 2015/16 the charities had a combined income of £12,700 and a combined total expenditure of £24,000. We estimate that grants from the two charities totalled around £23,000.

Applications

Apply in writing to the correspondent directly by the individual or family member by mid-November for consideration in November/December each year. Applicants must reapply each year.

Other information

The Cottam Charities refers to Edward Cottam Charity (Charity Commission no. 223936) and Alice Cottam Charity (Charity Commission no. 223925).

Lancaster Charity

£2,300

Correspondent: Philip Oglethorpe, Clerk to the Trustees, William Penny's, Regent Street, Lancaster LA1 1SG (01524 842663; email: lancastercharity@ btconnect.com; website: www.lancaster-charity.org.uk)

CC number: 213461

Eligibility

People over 60 who are in need and have lived in the old city of Lancaster for at least three years. People under 60 may be considered if they are unable to work to support themselves due to age, accident or infirmity.

Types of grants

Top-up pensions according to need.

Annual grant total

In 2016 the charity had a total income of £231,500 and a total expenditure of £246,500. The majority of charitable expenditure was spent on maintenance of almshouses, and a total of £2,300 was awarded to older people over the age of 60 for welfare purposes.

Applications

Application forms are available from the correspondent. Applications are considered when vacancies occur.

Pendle

The Fort Foundation

£8,800

Correspondent: Edward Fort, Trustee, Fort Vale Engineering Ltd, Calder Vale Park, Simonstone Lane, Simonstone, Burnley BB12 7ND (01282 440000; email: info@fortvale.com)

CC number: 1028639

Eligibility

According to the trustees' annual report, the foundation operates throughout England and Wales and gives grants to individuals and organisations for general charitable purposes. Our research indicates that there may be a preference for people living in Pendle borough and district.

Types of grants

Our research indicates that one-off grants of £50 to £1,000 are available for purposes relating to social welfare and health.

Annual grant total

In 2016/17 the foundation had assets of £905,500 and an income of £338,000. Grants were made totalling £219,500, the vast majority (£201,000) of which was awarded to organisations. Of the £18,900 distributed to individuals, we have estimated that £8,800 was given for purposes relating to social welfare.

Exclusions

Our research indicates that awards are not made for fees.

Applications

Applications may be made in writing to the correspondent, directly by the individual. Appeals are considered at any time.

Nelson District Nursing Association Fund

£3,000

Correspondent: Joanne Eccles, Administrator, Democratic & Legal Services, Pendle Borough Council, Nelson Town Hall, Market Street, Nelson, Lancashire BB9 7LG (01282 661654; email: joanne.eccles@pendle. gov.uk)

CC number: 222530

Eligibility

Sick or poor people who live in Nelson, Lancashire.

Types of grants

One-off grants according to need, ranging from £50 to £500.

Annual grant total

In 2016/17 the fund had an income of £4,400 and a total expenditure of £3,200. We estimate that the fund gave around £3,000 in grants to individuals.

Applications

Apply in writing to the correspondent. Applications can be submitted directly by the individual or through a social worker, Citizens Advice or other welfare agency. All applicants will be visited by the fund's welfare officer as part of the assessment process.

Preston

The Goosnargh and Whittingham United Charity

£4,000

Correspondent: John Bretherton, Trustee, Lower Stanalea Farm, Stanalea Lane, Goosnargh, Preston PR3 2EQ (01995 640224)

CC number: 233744

Eligibility

Older people in need who live in the parishes of Goosnargh, Whittingham and Barton.

Types of grants

One-off and recurrent grants are given according to need.

Annual grant total

In 2016 the charity had an income of £6,500 and a total expenditure of £4,300. We estimate that grants given to individuals totalled £4,000.

Applications

Apply in writing to the correspondent. Applications should be submitted directly by the individual or family member.

West Lancashire

Peter Lathom's Charity

£1,900

Correspondent: Christine Aitken, 13 Mallard Close, Aughton, Ormskirk L39 5QJ (0151 520 2717; email: c.aitken@brighouse-wolff.co.uk)

CC number: 228828

Eligibility
People in need who live in West Lancashire.

Types of grants
One-off grants.

Annual grant total
In 2016 the charity had assets of £1.6 million and an income of £53,500. Welfare grants to individuals totalled £1,900.

Applications
Applications can be made using a form available from the correspondent. Grants are awarded in November/December of each year.

Merseyside

The James Greenop Foundation

£7,000

Correspondent: Russ Greenop, Trustee, 60 Hazel Avenue, Whiston, Prescot L35 2UZ (07799 620644; website: www. thejamesgreenopfoundation.org)

CC number: 1164640

Eligibility
Disadvantaged young adults and children living in Merseyside.

Types of grants
The foundation's website states:

> The purpose of our small grants scheme is to fund activities that promote inclusion, enhance wellbeing, improve prospects and raise aspirations. This may be through purchasing assistive technology and adaptations, equipment, training, educational resources, and activities that encourage personal and social development.
>
> Up to £500 can be awarded to individuals, their families or carers. Individual small grants may cover all or part of a purchase but must NOT be less than half the total cost. This therefore disqualifies applications for assistance purchasing any activities, services or products exceeding £1000.

Annual grant total
In 2016 the foundation held assets of £56,500 and had an income of £30,000.

Grants to organisations and individuals totalled £14,000. We estimate that grants given to individuals totalled around £7,000.

Applications
Application forms are available to download from the foundation's website.

Community Foundations for Lancashire and Merseyside

Correspondent: Sarah Mitchell, Community Foundation for Merseyside, 43 Hanover Street, Liverpool, Merseyside L1 3DN (0151 232 2420; email: info@ cfmerseyside.org.uk; website: www. cfmerseyside.org.uk)

CC number: 1068887

Eligibility
Refer to the foundation's website for eligibility details of the various current funds.

Types of grants
Refer to the foundation's website for details of current and open grants.

Annual grant total
In 2015/16 the foundation held assets of £12.4 million and had an income of £2.9 million. Grants paid were £2.2 million and the majority of this will have been awarded to organisations. We were unable to determine a figure for grants awarded to individuals.

Applications
All applications can be made online through the foundation's website. However, as the foundation administers funds from various grant-makers, check the application process of the fund to which you are applying by contacting the foundation staff directly.

Other information
The following is taken from the 2015/16 trustees annual report:

> In administering over 50 funds and foundations in 2015/16 we distributed £2.2 million to communities in Lancashire and/or Merseyside via 647 grant recipients, an increase of £400, 000 in grants compared to 2014/15. Our joint endowment fund stood at £11 million by March 2016, having begun endowment building in 2007 with around £130,000. This joint investment is a significant contributor to our sustainability as well as to ensure community philanthropy in Lancashire and Merseyside for future generations.

Liverpool Marine Engineers' and Naval Architects' Guild
See entry on page 134

Liverpool

Channel – Supporting Family Social Work in Liverpool

£6,000

Correspondent: Rebecca Black, 38 Brick Kiln Lane, Rufford, Ormskirk L40 1SZ (01704823408; email: beccavblack@ hotmail.com)

CC number: 257916

Eligibility
Families with young children, older people or people with disabilities, who live in Liverpool and are in need.

Types of grants
One-off grants of no more than £100 for childcare, clothing, food, furniture and kitchen equipment.

Annual grant total
In 2016/17 the charity had an income of £6,500 and a total expenditure of £6,500. We estimate that the charity awarded grants totalling £6,000 in the year.

Applications
Applications should be made in writing to the correspondent, detailing financial need and accompanied by a letter of support from a professional or social worker, where possible. Grant requests are considered on an ongoing basis.

The Liverpool Caledonian Association

£14,500

Correspondent: David Johnson, Correspondent, 46 Primrose Lane, Helsby, Frodsham WA6 0HH

CC number: 250791

Eligibility
People of Scottish descent, or their immediate family, who are in need and who live within a 15-mile radius of Liverpool Town Hall. The association states: 'generally speaking we do not welcome applications from people who have fewer than one grandparent who was Scots born'.

Types of grants

Previous research indicates that the charity awards regular monthly payment of annuities, heating grants and a limited number of Christmas food parcels.

Annual grant total

In 2015 the charity had an income of £13,100 and a total expenditure of £15,600. We estimate that grants given to individuals for welfare purposes totalled £14,500.

Exclusions

Holidays are generally excluded.

Applications

Apply in writing to the correspondent either directly by the individual, through a social worker, Citizens Advice, or other welfare agency or through any other third party. Applications are considered at any time and applicants will be visited.

Other information

At the time of writing (August 2017) the association had no website or annual report available.

Liverpool Corn Trade Guild

£6,000

Correspondent: Ian Bridge, Trustee, 1A St Johns Road, Southport PR8 4JP (01704 565596)

CC number: 232414

Eligibility

Members of the guild and their dependants who are in need. If funds permit, benefits can be extended to former members and their dependants. Membership is open to anyone employed by any firm engaged in the Liverpool Corn and Feed Trade.

Types of grants

One-off and recurrent grants are given according to need. Loans may also be provided.

Annual grant total

In 2015 the charity had an income of £8,400 and a total expenditure of £6,400. We estimate that the charity awarded around £6,000 in grants to individuals for welfare purposes.

Applications

Apply in writing to the correspondent. Applications can be made directly by the individual.

Other information

At the time of writing (August 2017) the charity did not have a website or accounts available.

The Liverpool Ladies' Institution

£5,000

Correspondent: David Anderton, Trustee, 15 Childwall Park Avenue, Childwall, Liverpool L16 0JE (0151 722 9823; email: d.anderton68@btinternet. com)

CC number: 209490

Eligibility

Single women in need who were either born in the city of Liverpool or live in Merseyside. Preference is given to women who are members of the Church of England, and to older women.

Types of grants

Recurrent grants.

Annual grant total

In 2016 the charity had an income of £3,600 and a total expenditure of £5,400. We estimate that the charity awarded around £5,000 to individuals for welfare purposes.

Applications

Application forms are available from the correspondent. Applications should be submitted, at any time, through a social worker, Citizens Advice or other welfare agency. The charity has previously stated that it receives a lot of inappropriate applications.

Other information

At the time of writing (August 2017) the charity had no website or accounts available.

Liverpool Wholesale Fresh Produce Benevolent Fund

£4,900

Correspondent: Thomas Dobbin, Correspondent, 207 Childwall Road, Liverpool L15 6UT (0151 722 0621; email: t.dobbin@virginmedia.com)

CC number: 1010236

Eligibility

People in need, who are or have been associated with the Liverpool fruit, vegetable or flower trade either as importers or wholesalers, and their families.

Types of grants

Small, one-off and recurrent grants.

Annual grant total

In 2016/17 the fund had an income of £181 and a total expenditure of £14,600. We estimate that the fund gave around £4,900 to individuals for welfare purposes.

The fund also gives grants to organisations.

Applications

Apply in writing to the correspondent.

Other information

The fund has previously stated that it predominantly makes grants to local charities in Merseyside due to a dwindling number of applications from individuals connected with the fresh produce trade.

West Derby Waste Lands Charity

£5,200

Correspondent: Lawrence Downey, Secretary, Ripley House, 56 Freshfield Road, Formby, Liverpool L37 3HW (01704 879330; email: lawrence@ westderbywastelands.co.uk; website: www.westderbywastelands.co.uk)

CC number: 223623

Eligibility

People who are in need who live within the boundaries of the ancient township of West Derby (this includes parts, but not all, of the L7, L11, L12, L13 and L14 postcodes; the Secretary holds a map of the defined area).

Types of grants

One-off grants are given according to need.

Annual grant total

In 2016 the charity had assets of £2 million and an income of £62,000. Grants to individuals totalled £5,200, with a further £47,500 awarded to local organisations.

Applications

Applications are available to download from the website or can be requested from the correspondent via the website's online contact form. Application forms must be completed and signed by the applicant before being submitted. They must be accompanied by an appropriate form of identification (e.g. a copy of a photo driving licence, passport, or a utility bill or bank statement in the name of the applicant). The trustees prefer applications to be supported by an independent organisation (e.g. social services or probation services). Applicants may be required to be interviewed before making a grant. Applications are considered quarterly.

Other information

The charity's website notes that it helps about 50 individuals and organisations each year.

Sefton

The Southport and Birkdale Provident Society

£21,500 (134 grants)

Correspondent: Charles O'Hara, 84 Lexton Drive, Southport PR9 8QW (01704 421403; email: sandbprov@mail.com)

CC number: 224460

Eligibility

People in need who live in the metropolitan borough of Sefton.

Types of grants

One-off grants in kind only after social services have confirmed that all other benefits have been fully explored. Grants have been awarded towards clothing, bedding, cookers, washing machines and other basic household needs.

Annual grant total

In 2016 the charity had assets of £450,500 and an income of £25,000. The charity awarded £21,500 in grants to 134 individuals during the year.

Exclusions

No cash payments. Grants are not given for education, training experience, rental deposits, personal debt relief or hire purchase. Medical services are not supported.

Applications

Apply in writing to the correspondent with as much information on family background and the reasons for the request as possible. Applications should be submitted through social services and are considered at any time.

Other information

The charity also makes grants to other organisations in the local area. In 2016 £7,100 was awarded to six charities.

Wirral

Birkenhead Relief in Sickness Charities

£4,800

Correspondent: Anna Barnish, Charity Trust Manager, North Birkenhead Development Trust, St James Centre, 344 Laird Street, Birkenhead CH41 7AL (0151 670 9974; email: anna@nbdt.org.uk)

CC number: 217686

Eligibility

People on a low income who have a long-term sickness and live in the old county borough of Birkenhead.

Types of grants

One-off grants usually up to a maximum of £250. Grants are given for essential items such as clothing, electrical appliances, furniture (e.g. beds), travel costs and household items (e.g. bedding, towels).

Annual grant total

In 2016/17 the charity had an income of £2,500 and a total expenditure of £5,100. We estimate that grants given to individuals totalled around £4,800.

Applications

Applicants must be referred by a recognised third party (e.g. social worker, health visitor, Citizens Advice, etc.) and are considered throughout the year. Evidence of the applicant's medical condition must be provided. Applicants are required to attend an interview to discuss their application.

Christ Church Fund for Children

£1,500

Correspondent: Robert Perry, Trustee, 28 Beresford Road, Prenton CH43 1XG (email: rperry4851@aol.com)

CC number: 218545

Eligibility

Children in need up to the age of 17 whose parents are members of the Church of England and who live in the county borough of Birkenhead. Preference is given to children living in the ecclesiastical parish of Christ Church, Birkenhead.

Types of grants

Grants for any kind of need, but typically for bedding, furniture, clothing and trips.

Annual grant total

In 2016/17 the fund had an income of £3,700 and a total expenditure of £1,700. We estimate that grants given to individuals totalled £1,500.

Applications

Apply in writing through a recognised referral agency (e.g. a social worker or Citizens Advice) or other third party. Applications are usually considered quarterly (January, April, September and December), but emergency applications can be considered at any time.

The Conroy Trust

£2,000

Correspondent: Barbara Pilkington, 2 Greenville Close, Wirral CH63 7SD (0151 645 2526)

CC number: 210797

Eligibility

People in need who live in the parish of Bebington. There is some preference for older people and young people.

Types of grants

One-off and recurrent grants. Grants usually range from £50 to £300.

Annual grant total

In 2016 the trust had an income of £5,500 and a total expenditure of £4,300. We estimate that the amount awarded in grants was £2,000.

Exclusions

No grants are made for educational purposes.

Applications

Apply in writing to the correspondent, detailing need and what the grant will be used for.

The Maud Beattie Murchie Charitable Trust

£11,100

Correspondent: Anthony Michael Bayliss, Duncan Sheard Glass, Castle Chambers, 43 Castle Street, Liverpool L2 9TL (0151 243 1209)

CC number: 265281

Eligibility

Retired members of Beattie stores who are in need and people in need who live on the Wirral.

Types of grants

One-off and recurrent grants are given according to need. Grants to organisations are mostly recurrent.

Annual grant total

In 2016 the trust had assets of £836,500 and an income of £30,500. During the year, the trust gave around £11,100 in grants to individuals.

The trust also gave grants to organisations totalling £15,200.

Exclusions

No grants are given for educational purposes.

Applications

Applications should be made through Wirral Social Services. Awards are made twice a year.

Other information

The trust also makes grants to charitable organisations.

West Kirby Charity

£17,000

Correspondent: Jane Boulton, 2 The Roscote, Wallrake, Heswall, Wirral CH60 8QW (07773 449123; email: ajaneboulton@btinternet.com)

CC number: 218546

Eligibility

People in need who have lived in the old urban district of Hoylake (Caldy, Frankby, Greasby, Hoylake, Meols and West Kirby) for at least three years. The charity supports older people with regular pensions, and preference is sometimes given to applicants with children or those who have a disability.

Types of grants

One-off and recurrent payments to people in financial need. Pensions are also provided for older people.

Annual grant total

In 2016 the charity had an income of £24,000 and a total expenditure of £18,000. We estimate that grants given to individuals totalled £17,000.

Applications

Applications should be made in writing to the correspondent.

South East

General

The Argus Appeal

£19,500

Correspondent: Elsa Gillio, Fundraising Co-ordinator, Argus House, Crowhurst Road, Hollingbury, Brighton BN1 8AR (01273 544465; email: elsa.gillio@ theargus.co.uk; website: www.theargus. co.uk/argusappeal)

CC number: 1013647

Eligibility

People in need, particularly older people and underprivileged children, who live in the Sussex area.

Types of grants

One-off and recurrent grants are given according to need and food parcels for older people. Past grants have been made to purchase purpose built communication aids and to contribute towards making a garden more accessible for wheelchair users. More than 500 Christmas hampers and food vouchers were given to pensioners and low-income families in 2015.

Annual grant total

In 2015 the charity held assets of £285,500 and had an income of £77,000. Grants to individuals totalled £19,500, of which £15,000 went towards the provision of food parcels for older people and people in need. The remaining £4,500 was given in eight one-off grants and donations to families.

A further £69,000 was awarded to local organisations.

Applications

Apply in writing to the correspondent including details of who you are, what you do, how much is needed, how it will be spent and what has been done so far to raise the necessary funds.

The B. V. MacAndrew Trust

£4,800

Correspondent: Roger Clow, Trustee, 4th floor, Park Gate, 161–163 Preston Road, Brighton, East Sussex BN1 6AF (01273 562563)

CC number: 206900

Eligibility

People in need who live in East and West Sussex.

Types of grants

One-off grants for a variety of needs including emergencies and household appliances.

Annual grant total

In 2016/17 the trust had an income of £990 and a total expenditure of £9,700. We estimate that the trust gave around £4,800 in grants to individuals.

Exclusions

The trustees are unable to assist with bankruptcy fees or debts.

Applications

Apply in writing to the correspondent. All applications must be made by welfare organisations or support groups on behalf of the individuals.

Other information

The trust also gives grants to organisations.

MidasPlus

£9,800

Correspondent: Michael Wylie, Trustee, 20 Island Close, Staines-upon-Thames TW18 4YZ (01784 440300 or 07803 706440; email: info@midasplus.org.uk; website: www.midasplus.org.uk)

CC number: 1110699

Eligibility

Individuals and community groups who have lived in Surrey and Middlesex and surrounding areas for at least six months. The charity usually supports those 'who demonstrate a need that cannot be fulfilled elsewhere'.

There is a particular emphasis on people from: Addlestone; Ashford (Middlesex); Camberley; Cobham; Feltham; Hampton; Heathrow; Hounslow; Isleworth; Richmond; Shepperton; Staines-upon-Thames; Stanwell; Sunbury-on-Thames; Teddington; Twickenham; West Drayton; and Wraysbury.

Types of grants

One-off grants, usually of less than £500, are given for medical and disability aids (e.g. wheelchairs and scooters), holidays, equipment, carpeting, communication aids, garden and home adaptations and any other needs to help those who are disadvantaged due to low income, ill health, disability or other reason.

Annual grant total

In 2016/17 the charity had an income of £22,500 and a total expenditure of £19,800. We estimate that the charity gave around £9,800 in grants to individuals.

Exclusions

Grants cannot be made to:

- People planning to move out of the area of benefit
- Those who have received three grants in the past
- Pay for general living costs
- Pay off debts
- Buy floor coverings of any type (unless there are very exceptional circumstances)
- Buy non-essential items

Applications

Application forms can be found on the charity's website. Candidates are required to have their application signed by a referring agency or person.

The website states that 'your application will be acknowledged as soon as it has been received and you should expect to hear the outcome of your application within four weeks'.

Other information

Organisations and community groups are also assisted.

Paradigm Foundation

£6,800

Correspondent: The Trustees, Paradigm Housing Group, Glory Park Avenue, Wooburn Green, High Wycombe, Buckinghamshire HP10 ODF (01628 811784; email: enquiries@ paradigmfoundation.org.uk; website: www.paradigmfoundation.org.uk)

CC number: 1156204

Eligibility

Paradigm Housing residents who are in need.

Types of grants

Grants of up to £1,500 to support individuals in times of crisis or to help people maximise their income, build their financial capacity and resilience and reduce and avoid debt

Annual grant total

In 2015/16 the foundation had assets of £111,500 and an income of £418,000. We estimate that welfare grants to individuals totalled around £6,800.

Applications

Application forms are available to download from the foundation's website.

Other information

The foundation also makes grants to organisations working with the community in the local areas where it operates.

South East Water's Helping Hand

£100,000

Correspondent: Customer Care Team, South East Water, Rocfort, Snodland, Kent ME6 5AH (0333 000 0001; email: contact form on website; website: www. southeastwater.co.uk/get-help/im-struggling-to-pay-my-bill)

Eligibility

South East Water customers who demonstrate that they are taking steps to achieve financial stability but need help clearing their water and sewerage debts.

Types of grants

Grants are made to South East Water customers who need help clearing their water and sewerage debts.

Annual grant total

Grants usually total around £100,000 per year.

Applications

Application forms are available to download from the South East Water website.

Other information

The fund was founded by South East Water upon the dissolution of the EOS Foundation in April 2010.

The Vokins Charitable Trust

£14,000

Correspondent: Trevor Vokins, Trustee, 56 Hove Park Road, Hove, East Sussex BN3 6LN (01273 556317)

CC number: 801487

Eligibility

People who live in Brighton and Hove and East and West Sussex, particularly people with disabilities or those suffering from ill health.

Types of grants

One-off and recurrent grants are given according to need. The trust also provides mobility scooters to individuals with disabilities.

Annual grant total

In 2015/16 the trust had an income of £58,800 and a total expenditure of £30,000. We estimate that the charity awarded around £14,000 in grants to individuals for welfare purposes. The trust also awards grants to organisations.

Applications

Apply in writing to the correspondent.

Bedfordshire

Bedfordshire and Luton Community Foundation

Correspondent: The Grants Managers, The Old School House, Southill Road, Cardington MK44 3SX (01234 834930; fax: 0700 600 6800; email: mail@blcf.org. uk; website: www.blcf.org.uk)

CC number: 1086516

Eligibility

Individuals in need living in Bedfordshire and Luton. The community foundation operates a number of funds, each with its own eligibility criteria. See the website for more information.

Types of grants

The type of grant available depends on the fund being applied to. See the website for details specific to each fund.

Annual grant total

In 2016/17 the community foundation had assets of £2.7 million and an income of £1.6 million. Grants totalled more than £1.1 million, the vast majority of which was awarded to organisations. We

were unable to determine the total of grants distributed to individuals.

Applications

See the website for full details of funds which are currently accepting applications.

Other information

The foundation operates a large number of grants schemes for community groups and individuals, made up of its own funding and donations from local donors, philanthropists and businesses, and national and regional grant-makers. The majority of these schemes benefit organisations working in the area of benefit.

Husborne Crawley Charity Estate

£3,600

Correspondent: Lyn Lyman, Trustee, Lodge Cottage, School Lane, Husborne Crawley, Bedfordshire MK43 0UY (01908 584159; email: lynlyman@yahoo. co.uk)

CC number: 248497

Eligibility

People in need who live in the ancient parish of Husborne Crawley.

Types of grants

One-off grants according to need for funeral expenses, fuel allowances and Christmas gifts.

Annual grant total

In 2016 the charity had an income of £5,100 and a total expenditure of £3,900. We have estimated that grants to individuals for welfare purposes totalled around £3,600.

Applications

Apply in writing to the correspondent either directly by the individual or via a third party. Applications are considered throughout the year.

Other information

Grants can also be made to the local church and to individuals for educational purposes.

Bedford

Bedford Municipal Charities

£22,000

Correspondent: Lynn McKenna, Administrator, Bedford Borough Council, Committee Services, Borough Hall, Cauldwell Street, Bedford MK42 9AP (01234 228193; email: lynn.mckenna@bedford.gov.uk)

CC number: 2005566

Eligibility

People in need who live in the borough of Bedford.

Types of grants

Pensions, grants towards fuel bills and other necessities, occasional one-off grants for special purposes and Christmas bonuses.

Annual grant total

In 2015/16 the charity held assets of over £1 million and had an income of £48,500. Grants to individuals totalled £22,000.

Applications

Apply in writing to the correspondent. Applications can be submitted directly by the individual or through an appropriate third party. Individual applicants may be visited to assess the degree of need.

The Norah Mavis Campbell Trust

£10,000

Correspondent: Lynn McKenna, Bedfordshire Borough Council, Borough Hall, Cauldwell Street, Bedford MK42 9AP (01234 228193)

CC number: 1073047

Eligibility

Older people in need who reside in the area of Bedford Borough Council.

Types of grants

Grants are given according to need.

Annual grant total

In 2015/16 the trust had an income of £1,200 and a total expenditure of £23,000. We estimate that the trust awarded £10,000 in grants to individuals during the year.

Applications

Applications should be made in writing to the correspondent, outlining the reasons for the request and any alternative funding that has been considered. Applications should be sent before 31 October.

Other information

The trust also provides additional benefits for residents at the Puttenhoe Home in Bedford. Grants are made to both individuals and organisations.

The Ravensden Town and Poor Estate

£1,500

Correspondent: Alison Baggott, Trustee, Westerlies, Church End, Ravensden, Bedford MK44 2RN (01234 771919; email: alisonbaggott@btinternet.com)

CC number: 200164

Eligibility

Older people who are in need and live in the parish of Ravensden.

Types of grants

Our previous research indicates that the estate awards one-off and recurrent grants according to need.

Annual grant total

In 2015 the charity had an income of £2,900 and a total expenditure of £1,800. We estimate that the charity awarded around £1,500 in grants to individuals for social welfare purposes.

Applications

Apply in writing to the correspondent.

Other information

The charity also gives grants to a local school.

Central Bedfordshire

Clophill United Charities

£2,500

Correspondent: Gillian Hill, 10 The Causeway, Clophill, Bedford MK45 4BA (01525 860539)

CC number: 200034

Eligibility

People who live in the parish of Clophill and are in need.

Types of grants

One-off and recurrent grants are given according to need, with the aim of relieving poverty.

Annual grant total

In 2016 the charity had an income of £10,000 and a total expenditure of £7,500. We estimate that grants given to individuals totalled around £2,500.

Exclusions

Grants are not given where statutory funds are available.

Applications

Application forms can be obtained from the correspondent.

Other information

Grants are also made to organisations and to individuals for educational purposes.

Dunstable Poor's Land Charity

£4,500

Correspondent: Yvonne Beaumont, Clerk, Grove House, 76 High Street North, Dunstable, Bedfordshire LU6 1NF (01582 660008; email: dunstablecharity@yahoo.com; website: www.associationofdunstablecharities.co.uk)

CC number: 236805

Eligibility

Older people who are on a limited income (i.e. in receipt of pension credit or housing benefit) and live within the old borough of Dunstable in Bedfordshire.

Types of grants

Small grants are made annually on Maundy Thursday, mostly to older people on a low income.

Annual grant total

In 2016 the charity had an income of £4,900 and a total expenditure of £4,700. We estimate that grants given to individuals totalled £4,500.

Exclusions

Only one grant per household is available.

Applications

Potential applicants should contact the correspondent by telephone for information on how to apply for assistance.

Flitwick Combined Charities

£5,000

Correspondent: David Empson, Trustee, 28 Orchard Way, Flitwick, Bedford MK45 1LF (01525 718145; email: deflitwick8145@aol.com; website: www.flitwickcombinedcharities.org.uk)

CC number: 233258

Eligibility

People in need who live in the parish of Flitwick.

Types of grants

Usually one-off grants for 'services or facilities to reduce hardship or distress'. The charity's website states: 'We also help the elderly in the community and are always looking for more people who genuinely require help, regardless of their situation.'

Annual grant total

In 2015/16 the charity had an income of £11,400 and a total expenditure of £10,350. We estimate that grants for social welfare purposes totalled around £5,000.

Applications

Application forms are available from the charity's website or the correspondent. The charity's website states:

> To apply for Relief In Need, applications must be made to the Trustees either directly, through the website or personally. Applications are periodically reviewed throughout the year. Anything not covered by these forms should be sent to us as a short paragraph outlining the reasons for the request and how any money will be spent, using the contact us form, following which we will then be in touch for extra information.

The trustees' meetings are held three times a year and the dates are publicised on the website. Applications need to be submitted at least two weeks in advance to the meeting.

Other information

There are three charities The Deacons Dole, The Poors Moor and The Town Lands Charity) collectively known as Flitwick Combined Charities. The objectives of the trustees are to provide both educational and relief-in-need help.

Mary Lockington Charity

£3,100

Correspondent: Yvonne Beaumont, Clerk, Grove House, 76 High Street North, Dunstable, Bedfordshire LU6 1NF (01582 660008; email: dunstablecharity@yahoo.com; website: www.associationofdunstablecharities.co.uk)

CC number: 204766

Eligibility

Individuals living in the parishes of Dunstable, Leighton Buzzard and Hockliffe who are in need due to hardship, disability or sickness.

Types of grants

One-off grants towards items, services or facilities.

Annual grant total

In 2016/17 the charity had an income of £11,700 and a total expenditure of £8,100. We estimate that grants given to individuals totalled around £3,100, with funding also awarded to organisations.

Applications

Apply in writing to the correspondent.

Other information

The charity also contributes to the upkeep of almshouses and makes grants to local organisations.

Potton Consolidated Charity

£700

Correspondent: Dean Howard, Clerk, 69 Stotfold Road, Arlesey, Bedfordshire SG15 6XR (01462 735220; email: clerk@potton-consolidated-charity.co.uk; website: www.potton-consolidated-charity.co.uk)

CC number: 201073

Eligibility

People who are in need and live in the parish of Potton.

Types of grants

Grants are given according to need.

Annual grant total

In 2015/16 the charity had assets of £4.1 million and an income of £152,500. Christmas grants to pensioners totalled £700.

Applications

The charity predominantly makes grants to individuals to assist with their education. We recommend that individuals seeking welfare assistance should, in the first instance, contact the Clerk for more information.

The Sandy Charities

£6,000

Correspondent: Charlotte Benjamin, 6 Bedford Road, Sandy, Bedfordshire SG19 1EN (01767 680251; email: cbenjamin@woodfines.co.uk)

CC number: 237145

Eligibility

People who live in Sandy and Beeston and are in need.

Types of grants

One-off grants are given for general welfare expenses, for example motorised wheelchairs, decorating costs and children's clothing.

Annual grant total

In 2015/16 the charity had an income of £9,500 and a total expenditure of £12,500. We estimate that grants given to individuals totalled around £6,000.

Applications

Applications should be made in writing to the correspondent.

Other information

The charity also makes educational grants to individuals.

Town Lands

£1,800

Correspondent: Julian Barrett, Trustee, South Cottage, 18 Broughton Road, Salford, Milton Keynes MK17 8BH (01908 583494)

CC number: 256465

Eligibility

People in need who live in the parish of Hulcote and Salford.

Types of grants

Grants can be made to relieve any social welfare need of people in hardship and distress. Grants are usually one-off and range from £60 to £200. Older people and children can also receive Christmas gifts.

Annual grant total

In 2015 the charity had an income of £7,900 and a total expenditure of £7,700. We estimate that welfare support to individuals totalled around £1,800.

Applications

Applications may be made in writing to the correspondent. They can be submitted directly by the individual or through any other parishioner.

Other information

Grants are also made to organisations supporting the local community. Educational support can also be given.

Berkshire

The Berkshire Nurses and Relief-in-Sickness Trust

£46,500 (128 grants)

Correspondent: Rosalind Pottinger, Honorary Secretary, 26 Montrose Walk, Calcot, Reading RG31 7YH (0118 901 0196; email: berksnursestrust@virginmedia.com)

CC number: 205274

Eligibility

People who live in the geographical area of the Royal County of Berkshire and parts of Oxfordshire which, prior to 1 April 1974, used to be part of the Royal County of Berkshire. Applicants must be under the care of the medical profession due to sickness or disability.

Types of grants

One-off grants according to need.

Annual grant total

In 2016/17 the trust held assets of £1.7 million and had an income of £68,000. A total of £46,500 was distributed in 128 grants to individuals. A further £2,600 was given in grants to organisations.

Applications

Application forms are available from the correspondent. Applications should be made through a social worker, Citizens Advice or other welfare agency known to the trustees and supported by a member of the statutory authorities. They are considered as received and are not accepted directly from members of the public.

The Slough and District Community Fund

£1,700

Correspondent: David Nicks, Trustee, 7 Sussex Place, Slough SL1 1NH (01753 577475; email: dave.nicks@btinternet. com)

CC number: 201598

Eligibility

People who are in need and live in Slough, New Windsor and Eton.

Types of grants

Our previous research suggests that the charity awards one-off grants according to need.

Annual grant total

In 2016 the fund had an income of £3,600 and a total expenditure of £1,900. We estimate that the fund awarded around £1,700 in grants to individuals for welfare purposes.

Applications

Application forms are available from the correspondent.

Other information

The fund was formed by the amalgamation of 'All Good Causes' and 'The Slough Nursing Fund'.

At the time of writing (August 2017) the fund had no website or accounts available.

Reading

Reading Dispensary Trust

£20,500 (80 grants)

Correspondent: Walter Gilbert, Clerk, 16 Wokingham Road, Reading RG6 1JQ (0118 926 5698; email: admin.rdt@ btconnect.com; website: www. readingdispensarytrust.org.uk)

CC number: 203943

Eligibility

People in need who are in poor health, convalescent or who have a physical or mental disability or illness and live in Reading and the surrounding area (within a seven-mile radius of the centre of Reading).

Types of grants

One-off grants from £70 to £1,000 for a wide range of needs. The trust makes grants for equipment and services not available through statutory sources to those suffering from physical, mental illness or disability. Examples in the 2016 annual report include clothing, powered wheelchairs, carpets, washing machines, holidays, beds and bedding, communication devices, cooking equipment, computer equipment, therapy and decoration.

Annual grant total

In 2016 the trust had assets of £1.4 million and an income of £51,000. During the year, 80 grants were made to individuals and totalled £20,500.

Exclusions

The trust cannot fund services or goods which are available from statutory sources.

Applications

Application forms can be downloaded from the website, along with guidelines. Applications are usually made through doctors, nurses, social workers or voluntary organisations. Grant applications are considered on the second Tuesday of each month. Further information can be obtained by contacting the Clerk.

St Laurence Relief In Need Trust

£2,700 (three grants)

Correspondent: Jason Pyke, Vale & West, Victoria House, 26 Queen Victoria Street, Reading RG1 1TG (0118 957 3238; email: mail@valewest.com)

CC number: 205043

Eligibility

Individuals in need or hardship who live in the ancient parish of St Laurence in Reading. Surplus funds may be provided to individuals living in the county borough of Reading.

Types of grants

One-off and annual grants are awarded according to need. Our research suggests that the minimum grant is £100.

Annual grant total

In 2016 the trust had assets of £125,500 and an income of £64,000. Grants to individuals totalled £2,700.

Exclusions

Grants are not made to students for training or research purposes or to people not resident in the area of benefit.

Applications

Applications should be made in writing directly to the correspondent.

Other information

The trust gives predominantly to organisations.

John Sykes Foundation

£1,500

Correspondent: Koichi Nicholas, 23/24 Market Place, Reading RG1 2DE (0118 903 5909; email: mail@ johnsykesfoundation.org; website: johnsykesfoundation.org)

CC number: 1156623

Eligibility

Individuals who live in and around Reading who are in need of help and support. A map showing the area of benefit can be found on the website.

Types of grants

Grants are given to individuals for purposes relating to arts and culture, education, science and sport (the details of which can be found in *The Guide to Educational Grants*), as well as for needs relating to health and disability. The website provides the following information:

▹ Health: 'The charity will support individuals who have a genuine need for medical support. It may be a piece of equipment to help everyday life or specialist treatment that may be out of reach'
▹ Disability: 'Life may have been changed by a disability or it may be a part of everyday life. The foundation wants to support individuals who may need help as a result of a disability or support when facing a newly diagnosed condition'

The foundation has four grant programmes and states on its website: 'Each grant is not currently time specific. The individual grants are structured with a grant total therefore it's important to apply to the correct grant programme.' The four grants programmes are: Minster – grants of £500 or less; Abbey – grants of £2,500 or less; Forbury – grants of £5,000 or less; and Maiwand – grants of £10,000 or less. It is important that applicants apply to the programme appropriate for the amount needed.

Annual grant total

In 2016 the foundation held assets of £14,700 and an income of £17,000. Grants to individuals totalled £1,500.

Applications

Application forms can be downloaded from the website and should be completed and returned to the foundation's office by post or email. When your application is submitted, you will be sent a notification to confirm it has been received. Your application will be assessed by the trustees and you will be informed whether it has been taken forward to the next stage. Applicants who are unsuccessful at this point will also be notified. If your initial application is successful, you will either be invited to the foundation's office or visited in your home to discuss your application, financial details, your reason for applying and what you hope to achieve. Following this meeting, you will be informed verbally of the foundation's decision and will receive confirmation in writing.

Note: As the foundation is a newly registered grant-maker and is in the early stages of its development, we would advise potential applicants to consider the information on the website thoroughly before beginning an application.

Other information

The foundation's informative website presents the following information:

> The foundation established by John Sykes in 2014 aims to help, support, and transform the lives of people living in and around the Reading area. John not only has a passion for business but his hometown of Reading too. It's from where over the last 15 years he has built his successful companies. He now wants to give something back for the people of Reading and his foundation is set to do just that.

Slough

The Datchet United Charities

£3,100

Correspondent: Anita Goddard, 25 High Street, Datchet, Slough SL3 9EQ (01759 541933)

CC number: 235891

Eligibility

People in need who live in the ancient parish of Datchet.

Types of grants

Grants of £15 to £1,500 are given for clothing, fuel bills, living costs, food, holidays, travel expenses and household

bills. Vouchers are distributed at Christmas.

Annual grant total

In 2015/16 the charity had assets of £913,000 and an income of £30,000. Grants to individuals totalled £3,100; Christmas vouchers amounted to £2,700, and £400 was given to assist five families.

A further £12,400 was given in grants to local organisations.

Applications

Applications can be made in writing to the correspondent, either directly by the individual or through a social worker, Citizens Advice or other welfare agency. All applicants will be visited by a social worker.

Other information

The charity owns a day centre which local groups are able to use free of charge. Loans of medical equipment are also available.

West Berkshire

The Newbury and Thatcham Welfare Trust

£2,500

Correspondent: Jacqui Letsome, Correspondent, Volunteer Centre West Berkshire, 1 Bolton Place, Northbrook Street, Newbury, Berkshire RG14 1AJ (07917 414376; email: ntwt@hotmail.com; website: www.newburyandthatchamwelfaretrust.org)

CC number: 235077

Eligibility

People in financial need who are sick, convalescent or who have a disability, and live in the former borough of Newbury as constituted on 31 March 1974 and the parishes of Greenham, Enborne, Hamstead Marshall, Shaw-cum-Donnington, Speen and Thatcham.

Types of grants

One-off grants of up to £250. Grants given include those for medical aids, food, holidays, respite care, travel, special equipment, TV licences, furniture and appliances.

Annual grant total

In 2016 the trust had an income of £4,900 and a total expenditure of £2,800. We estimate that grants given to individuals totalled around £2,500.

Exclusions

Grants are not given towards housing or rent costs and debts. The trust is unable to make payments to the individual; cheques can either be made payable to

the supplier, or to the referring organisation.

Applications

Apply on an application form available to download from the website, to be submitted either through a social worker, Citizens Advice or other welfare agency or through a third party on behalf of an individual such as a doctor, health visitor or other health professional.

The application must include details of the item, service or facility for which a grant is required and whether other sources of funding are being considered. In addition, the application must provide full disclosure of the individual's current financial status, such as a breakdown of all income received from employment and/or benefits, any savings and other relevant financial information.

Tilehurst Poor's Land Charity

£8,000

Correspondent: Clerk to the Trustees, PO Box 2802, Reading RG30 4GE (email: clerk@tilehurstplc.org.uk; website: www.tilehurstplc.org.uk)

CC number: 204048

Eligibility

People in need in the ancient parish of Tilehurst, which covers mainly, but not exclusively, postcodes RG30 and RG31.

Types of grants

One-off grants according to need.

Annual grant total

In 2016 the charity had an income of £18,100 and a total expenditure of £15,900. We estimate that grants given to individuals totalled £8,000, with funding also awarded to local organisations.

Applications

Application forms can be downloaded from the charity's website and should be printed out, completed and then posted to the contact address. Wherever possible, applications should include a supporting letter from a third party organisation, describing the applicant's personal circumstances. Copies of quotations/bills will be needed before the trustees make a decision.

Note: Grants are usually paid to the suppliers of goods and services.

Windsor and Maidenhead

Sunninghill Fuel Allotment Trust

£16,900

Correspondent: The Clerk, Sunninghill Trust, PO Box 4712, Ascot SL5 9AA (01344 206320; email: help@ thesunninghilltrust.org; website: thesunninghilltrust.org)

CC number: 240061

Eligibility

People in need who live in Sunninghill, Ascot and South Ascot.

Types of grants

One-off grants to relieve poverty and sickness. Grants have been used for utility bills, home appliances, and medical care.

Annual grant total

In 2015/16 the trust had assets of £3.8 million and an income of £281,500. Grants to individuals totalled £16,900 and were broken down as follows:

Other	£5,000
Physiotherapy	£4,200
Relief of poverty	£4,000
Day care	£3,700

Exclusions

Grants are not made for retrospective purposes.

Applications

Applications should be made in writing to the correspondent and should detail:

- Financial circumstances
- Why the grant is needed/how it will make a difference
- Whether there is a degree of urgency
- What process has been taken to gain assistance
- Why funding is unavailable elsewhere

The trustees meet four times per year to consider applications. Emergency applications are considered as they are received.

Other information

The majority of the trust's charitable giving is to organisations.

Wokingham

The Earley Charity

£5,900

Correspondent: Jane Wittig, Clerk to the Trustees, Liberty of Earley House, Strand Way, Earley, Reading RG6 4EA (0118 975 5663; fax: 0118 975 2263; email: enquiries@earleycharity.org.uk; website: www.earleycharity.org.uk)

CC number: 244823

Eligibility

People in need who have lived in Earley and the surrounding neighbourhood for at least six months. Applicants must be living in permanent accommodation and have UK citizenship or have been granted indefinite leave to remain in the UK.

In order to check whether you live within the area of benefit, see the map available on the website. If in doubt, get in touch with the correspondent to confirm.

Types of grants

One-off grants are given for the purchase of a specific item, equipment or service. Grants have been given for household goods, such as washing machines, cookers, fridges/freezers, beds and bedding, other furniture, kitchen appliances, and also mobility aids (wheelchairs, scooters, etc.) and sensory equipment.

Annual grant total

In 2016 the charity had and assets of £12.5 million and an income of £1.1 million. Grants to individuals totalled £6,400. We estimate that welfare grants to individuals totalled around £5,900.

Exclusions

Grants are not given to:

- Pay for general living costs
- Pay off debts
- Buy floor coverings of any type (unless there are very exceptional circumstances)
- Buy non-essential items

Applications

Application forms can be requested from the correspondent. They can be submitted either directly by the individual or through a social worker, Citizens Advice or other welfare agency. Applications for grants under £500 and applications for grants over £500 are considered at separate meetings around five times each year. The dates of these meetings, along with application submission deadlines, are published on the website.

Other information

Grants are also made to organisations and local voluntary and community groups.

The charity's website notes that currently the main focus is on various community initiatives and projects aimed at older people.

The Polehampton Charity

£4,700 (three grants)

Correspondent: Miss E. Treadwell, Assistant Clerk to the Charity, 65 The Hawthorns, Charvil, Reading RG10 9TS (0118 934 0852; email: polehampton. applications@gmail.com; website: www. thepolehamptoncharity.co.uk)

CC number: 1072631

Eligibility

People in need who live in the former ecclesiastical parishes of St Mary the Virgin – Twyford and St James the Great – Ruscombe.

Types of grants

The website notes: 'Charitable Grants are made for assistance in the case of personal hardship or special need where financial resources are not available.'

This may include items such as clothing, domestic appliances, holidays, medical equipment, furniture and equipment for people with disabilities.

Our research suggests that awards are generally are in the range of £100 to £250.

Educational grants are made to help with the costs of 'books and tools which are essential for the completion of courses of training at university, college, or other recognised educational establishments, including apprenticeships'.

Annual grant total

In 2016 the charity had assets of £3.4 million and an income of £106,500. Welfare grants to individuals totalled £4,700.

Applications

Applications should be made in writing to the correspondent, including full details of the applicant and their need and giving full costings.

The Wokingham United Charities

£8,000

Correspondent: Peter Robinson, Clerk, 66 Upper Broadmoor Road, Crowthorne, Berkshire RG45 7DF (01344 351207; email: peter.westende@btinternet.com; website: www.westende.org.uk)

CC number: 1107171

Eligibility

People in need who live in the civil parishes of Wokingham, Wokingham Without, St Nicholas, Hurst, Ruscombe and that part of Finchampstead known as Finchampstead North.

Types of grants

One-off grants towards household items, utility arrears and clothing.

Annual grant total

In 2015/16 the charity had assets of £1 million and an income of £171,500. Grants to individuals totalled £16,000. We estimate that welfare grants totalled around £8,000.

Exclusions

The charity is unable to fund items that are the obligation of the state or local authority.

Applications

Apply using a form available from the correspondent or website. Applications can be submitted directly by the individual although most often, grants are delivered through a social worker, school liaison officer or similar third party.

Other information

Wokingham United Charities 'is an amalgamation of some 21 Wokingham local charities – which date back to being some of the oldest charities in England'.

Buckingham-shire

The Archdeaconry of Buckingham Clergy Charity

£14,000

Correspondent: Brian Freshney, 16 Witchell, Wendover, Aylesbury HP22 6EG (01296 625629; email: archdbuc@oxford.anglican.org)

CC number: 1052475

Eligibility

Members of the clergy who are serving or who have served in Buckinghamshire Archdeaconry of the Oxfordshire Diocese and their dependants.

Types of grants

One-off according to need.

Annual grant total

In 2016 the charity had an income of £14,500 and a total expenditure of £15,000. We estimate that grants given to individuals totalled £14,000.

Applications

Apply in writing to the correspondent.

The Hitcham Poor Lands Charity

£2,500

Correspondent: Joy Brown, Trustee, 20 Weathered Drive, Burnham, Slough SL1 7NG (01628 664662; email: joybrown02@aol.com)

CC number: 203447

Eligibility

People in need who live in the parishes of Hitcham, Burnham and Cippenham.

Types of grants

Gifts in kind including furniture, white goods and school uniforms. Grants are available towards the costs of school trips and carer's holidays. Around 300 Christmas parcels are distributed each year.

Annual grant total

In 2016/17 the charity had an income of £7,400 and a total expenditure of £5,700. We estimate that grants given to individuals totalled £2,500, with funding also awarded to local organisations.

Applications

Apply in writing to the correspondent. Applications can be submitted directly by the individual or through a third party such as Citizens Advice or a social worker. There are no deadlines for applications and they are considered frequently.

Other information

The charity supports The Burnham Righthouse Project and Thames Hospice Care, which operate in the local area.

The Stoke Mandeville and Other Parishes Charity

£70,000

Correspondent: Caroline Dobson, Administrator, 17 Elham Way, Aylesbury HP21 9XN (01296 431859; email: smandopc@gmail.com; website: smandopc.org)

CC number: 296174

Eligibility

People in need who live in the parishes of Stoke Mandeville, Great Missenden and Great and Little Hampden. Applicants should have been resident in the area of benefit for at least two years.

Types of grants

The charity makes a range of grants to individuals. Examples include:

- **Lifeline alarms:** provided by Aylesbury Vale Housing Trust and available to older residents of Stoke Mandeville
- **Senior citizens railcards:** reimbursement for the cost of a senior railcard. Available to residents of Stoke Mandeville who are over 60 years old
- **Christmas grant:** an annual grant available to residents of Stoke Mandeville who are over 70 years old
- **Family day trip:** organised and paid for by the charity for families with children between 3 and 12 years old who live in Stoke Mandeville
- **Dementia screenings at The Waterside Theatre:** reimbursement for the cost of a ticket for a dementia screening at the Aylesbury Waterside Theatre, for people living in Stoke Mandeville or Great and Little Hampden

Annual grant total

In 2016 the charity had assets of £1.8 million and an income of £103,000. Grants are made for both welfare and educational purposes, however a breakdown was not included in the annual report and accounts for 2016. Based on the amounts distributed for education in previous years, we estimate that welfare grants totalled around £70,000.

Applications

Application forms are available to download from the charity's website.

Other information

Grants are also made to support residents of the parishes of Stoke Mandeville, Great Missenden and Great and Little Hampden who are studying at college or university, and to enable children resident in Stoke Mandeville to attend school trips.

Aylesbury Vale

John Bedford's Charity

£2,000

Correspondent: Richard Timothy, Friedlander, 14 Bourbon Street, Aylesbury, Buckinghamshire HP20 2RS (01296 318500)

CC number: 202972

Eligibility

People who are older and residing in the ancient parish of Aylesbury.

Types of grants

One-off grants.

Annual grant total

In 2016 the charity had an income of £2,600 and a total expenditure of £2,200. We estimate that the charity gave around £2,000 in grants to individuals.

Applications

Apply in writing to the correspondent.

Buckingham Almshouses and Welfare Charity

£1,900

Correspondent: Karen Phillips, Secretary, 78 London Road, Stony Stratford, Milton Keynes MK11 1JH (01908 563350; email: info@ buckinghamgeneralcharities.org.uk; website: www. buckinghamgeneralcharities.org.uk)

CC number: 1161308

Eligibility

People in need in the pre-1974 borough of Buckingham, which includes the modern day parishes of Buckingham, Bourton and Gawcott with Lenborough.

Types of grants

One-off grants.

Annual grant total

In 2015 the charity held assets of £517,500 and had an income of £63,500. Grants to individuals totalled £1,900. The charity also runs an almshouse and allotments in Buckingham.

Applications

Application forms are available to download from the charity's website. Applications should be made on behalf of an individual by a third party such as a social worker, Citizens Advice or a GP.

Other information

This charity used to be known as Buckingham General Charities until 2016. It is an amalgamation of 17 individual charities within the 1896 parish of Buckingham.

Cheddington Town Lands Charity

£3,300

Correspondent: Derek Berra, 9 Church Hill, Cheddington, Leighton Buzzard, Bedfordshire LU7 0SX (email: berraassociates@aol.com)

CC number: 235076

Eligibility

People in need who live in the parish of Cheddington.

Types of grants

One-off and recurrent grants are available according to need.

Annual grant total

In 2016/17 the charity had an income of £22,500 and a total expenditure of

£19,500. We estimate that the charity awarded around £3,300 in grants to individuals for welfare.

Applications

Applications can be made in writing to the correspondent, directly by the individual or a family member.

Other information

One-third of the charity's income goes to the maintenance of the parish church. The remainder is divided between village organisations, volunteer hospital drivers, students, and people in need.

Charity of Elizabeth Eman

£66,500 (126 grants)

Correspondent: John Reddington, Horwood & James Solicitors, 7 Temple Square, Aylesbury, Buckinghamshire HP20 2QB (01296 487361; email: enquiries@horwoodjames.co.uk; website: www.emans.co.uk)

CC number: 215511

Eligibility

Women and men who are resident in Aylesbury Vale and eligible to receive their pension.

Types of grants

Allowances of £111 per quarter, paid at the end of March, June, September and December. Grants are for life.

Annual grant total

In 2016 the charity had assets of £643,000 and an income of £60,500. During the year, the charity awarded £66,500 in 126 grants to individuals.

Applications

Application forms can be completed online, printed out from the website to be completed in writing, or over the telephone; call Sue Batchelor at Horwood and James on 01296 487361. Applications are considered as they arrive and a decision is usually made within a month.

Thomas Hickman's Charity

£45,000

Correspondent: John Leggett, Clerk to the Trustees, c/o Parrott & Coales LLP, 14–16 Bourbon Street, Aylesbury, Buckinghamshire HP20 2RS (01296 318501; email: john.leggett@ parrottandcoalesllp.co.uk)

CC number: 202973

Eligibility

People who live in Aylesbury town and are in need, hardship or distress.

Types of grants

One-off grants are given according to need.

Annual grant total

In 2016 the charity had an income of £696,000 and a total expenditure of £665,000. A total of 135 grants were made to individuals, amounting to £59,000. We estimate that welfare grants to individuals totalled around £45,000.

Applications

Application forms can be requested from the correspondent. They should be submitted either directly by the individual or through a third party, such as a family member, social worker, school or Citizens Advice. The trustees meet on a regular basis and applications are considered as they arise.

Other information

The charity also provides almshouses to older people, supports individuals with their education and makes grants to organisations.

Milton Keynes

The Ancell Trust

£2,500

Correspondent: Karen Phillips, Secretary, 78 London Road, Stony Stratford, Milton Keynes MK11 1JH (01908 563350; email: karen. phillips440@gmail.com)

CC number: 233824

Eligibility

People in need in the town of Stony Stratford.

Types of grants

Occasional grants to people in need, including those for health care or travel costs.

Annual grant total

In 2015/16 the trust had an income of £14,000 and a total expenditure of £10,200. We estimate that welfare grants to individuals totalled around £2,500.

Applications

Applications may be made in writing to the correspondent at any time.

Other information

The trust owns the sports ground in Stony Stratford, which provides cricket, football, bowls, croquet and tennis facilities.

Our research suggests that grants are given to students for books and may also be awarded for other training needs, including apprenticeships. Support is occasionally given to individuals for welfare purposes and to organisations or groups.

Emberton United Charity

£1,600

Correspondent: Warwick Clarke, Trustee, Old Pits, West Lane, Emberton, Olney, Bucks MK46 5DA (01234 713174)

CC number: 204221

Eligibility

Older people in need who live in the parish of Emberton.

Types of grants

One-off and recurrent grants, usually of up to £350. It would appear that grants are mainly distributed at Christmas.

Annual grant total

In 2016 the charity had an income of £42,000 and a total expenditure of £34,500. Welfare grants to individuals totalled £1,600, of which £1,400 was given as Christmas distributions.

Applications

Apply in writing to the correspondent, directly by the individual.

Other information

Grants are also given for educational purposes.

Catherine Featherstone

£5,500

Correspondent: Karen Phillips, Secretary, 78 London Road, Stony Stratford, Milton Keynes MK11 1JH (01908 563350; email: karen.phillips440@gmail.com)

CC number: 242620

Eligibility

People in need who live in the ancient parish of Wolverton. Preference is given to people who attend church regularly.

Types of grants

One-off and recurrent grants, usually ranging from £150 to £500. Grants have previously been given for household bills, food, medical and disability equipment, electrical goods, living costs and home help.

Annual grant total

In 2016 the charity had an income of £8,700 and a total expenditure of £11,300. We estimate that grants given to individuals totalled £5,500, with funding also awarded to organisations.

Applications

Application forms are available from the correspondent. Applications should be submitted either directly by the individual or through a social worker, Citizens Advice or other welfare agency.

Applications are considered in March, July and October.

South Buckinghamshire

Iver Heath Sick Poor Fund

£3,000

Correspondent: Tim L'Angellier, Trustee, 15 Warren Field, Iver SL0 0RU (01753 655799)

CC number: 231111

Eligibility

People with disabilities or who are sick, convalescing or infirm and who live in the Iver Heath ward of the parish of Iver and part of the parish of Wexham.

Types of grants

Usually one-off grants for clothing, medical needs, home help, fuel, lighting, chiropody and other necessities, although recurrent grants will be considered.

Annual grant total

In 2016 the fund had an income of £3,800 and a total expenditure of £6,500. We estimate that social welfare grants to individuals totalled £3,000. Grants can also be made to local organisations.

Applications

Apply in writing to the correspondent.

Stoke Poges Hastings Community Fund

£8,000

Correspondent: Mary Crocker, 129 Rogers Lane, Stoke Poges, Slough SL2 4LP (01753 646323; email: SPHCF11@outlook.com; website: www. stokepogescharities.com)

CC number: 206915

Eligibility

Individuals in need resident in the parish of Stoke Poges.

Types of grants

The fund's website states:

> The ways in which the Charity can help are wide and varied, providing there is a clear need in each case which is reasonable in the circumstances, taking into account any help available from other sources. For example, contributions (in full or in part) towards the cost of:
>
> - Grants to relieve sudden distress
> - Travelling expenses for visiting people in hospitals and the like
> - Items such as furniture, bedding, clothing, fuel, heating appliances, washing machines and other household equipment
> - Services such as essential house repairs
> - Facilities such as the supply of tools, equipment or books
> - Fees for instruction or examinations
> - Adaptations to the homes of disabled people
> - Items such as medical or other aids, nursing requisites, invalid chairs
> - Services in the home for disabled, handicapped or infirm people (including gardening)
> - Facilities for disabled, handicapped or infirm people such as arrangements for a recuperative holiday or respite care to provide temporary relief for carers

Annual grant total

In 2016 the fund had an income of £19,500 and a total expenditure of £12,500. We estimate that welfare grants totalled around £8,000.

Applications

Application forms can either be downloaded from the fund's website and returned by post or completed online.

Stoke Poges United Charity

£26,500

Correspondent: Mike Dier, 34 Hazell Way, Stoke Poges SL2 4DD (01753 642886; website: www. stokepogescharities.com)

CC number: 205289

Eligibility

People who are in need and live in the parish of Stoke Poges and the surrounding area. A map of the charity's area of benefit is available on its website.

Types of grants

Grants can be given for items such as: hospital travel expenses; tools, equipment and books; household items; home adaptations; medical aids; services in the home, e.g. gardening, respite care and recuperative holidays.

Annual grant total

In 2016 the charity had assets of £836,500 and an income of £40,000. Welfare grants totalled £26,500.

Applications

Application forms can either be downloaded from the charity's website and returned by post or completed online.

Other information

See the Stoke Poges Parish Council website for more information.

The Tracy Trust

£13,000

Correspondent: Jim Cannon, Trustee, 21 Ingleglen, Farnham Common, Slough, Bucks SL2 3QA (01753 643930; email: cannassoc@msn.com)

CC number: 803103

Eligibility

People of a pensionable age who are in need and live in the parish of Hedgerley.

Types of grants

Our previous research indicates that the trust awards one-off grants towards medical and welfare needs, such as spectacles, chiropody, hospital travel costs, aid alarms, TV licences, stairlifts and other related equipment or assistance.

Annual grant total

In 2015/16 the trust had an income of £18,600 and a total expenditure of £15,100. We estimate that grants given to individuals totalled around £13,000.

Applications

Apply in writing to the correspondent.

Wycombe

High Wycombe Central Aid Society

£300

Correspondent: Stuart Allen, Secretary, West Richardson Street, High Wycombe, Buckinghamshire HP11 2SB (01494 535890; email: office@central-aid.org.uk; website: www.central-aid.org.uk)

CC number: 201445

Eligibility

People in need, and those in receipt of benefits, who live in the old borough of High Wycombe. The society will also help ex-service personnel and their dependants.

Types of grants

Mainly one-off grants in kind and gift vouchers to a maximum of £100. Recent grants have been given for food, clothing and furniture.

Annual grant total

In 2016/17 the society held assets of £463,000 and had an income of £164,500. The annual report notes that:

> Sixty-one families and homes in crisis have been given free basic furniture, PAT tested appliances and carpet tiles to a value of £7,557 and a further 198 families in receipt of benefits have been assisted with similar items at very low prices (an increase over the last year).

The society can also make one-off grants to individuals in need but this is a small part of its charitable activities – these totalled £300 in 2016/17.

Exclusions

No grants are given towards council tax.

Applications

Apply in writing to the correspondent including details of income, savings, family situation and a quote for the goods needed along with any relevant supporting documents. Applications can be submitted through a social worker, Citizens Advice or other welfare agency and are considered on a monthly basis.

Other information

The society has a second-hand furniture warehouse and clothes and soft furnishings store (tel: 01494 443459; email: furniture@central-aid.org.uk).

Radnage Charity

£8,200

Correspondent: Ian Blaylock, Clerk to the Trustees, Hilltop, Green End Road, Radnage, High Wycombe, Buckinghamshire HP14 4BY (01494 483346)

CC number: 201762

Eligibility

People in need who live in the parish of Radnage.

Types of grants

One-off and recurrent grants.

Annual grant total

In 2016 the charity had an income of £17,000 and a total expenditure of £16,800. We estimate that grants given to individuals for welfare purposes totalled around £8,200.

Applications

Apply in writing to the correspondent either directly by the individual or, where applicable, through a social worker, Citizens Advice or other third party.

Other information

The charity also contributes to the upkeep of the village's twelfth-century parish church.

At the time of writing (August 2017) the charity had no website or accounts available.

Wooburn, Bourne End and District Relief-in-Sickness Charity

£20,000

Correspondent: Dorothea Heyes, 11 Telston Close, Bourne End SL8 5TY (01628 523498)

CC number: 210596

Eligibility

People who live in the parishes of Wooburn and Hedsor and the part of Bourne End which is in the parish of Little Marlow who are sick, convalescent or have physical or mental disabilities or illness.

Types of grants

One-off grants and gift vouchers, usually in the range of £50 to £400, are given for telephone installation, help with nursing costs, convalescence, holidays, home help and other necessities. All items for which a grant is requested must have a direct connection with the applicant's illness.

Annual grant total

In 2016 the charity had an income of £23,500 and a total expenditure of £21,500. We estimate that grants given to individuals totalled £20,000.

Exclusions

No recurrent grants are given.

Applications

Apply in writing to the correspondent through a doctor, health visitor, priest or other third party. Applications are considered throughout the year and should contain details of the nature of illness or disability.

East Sussex

The Mrs A. Lacy Tate Trust

£8,700

Correspondent: The Trustees, Heringtons Solicitors, 39 Gildredge Road, Eastbourne, East Sussex BN21 4RY (01323 411020)

CC number: 803596

Eligibility

People in need who live in East Sussex.

Types of grants

One-off and recurrent grants are given according to need.

Annual grant total

In 2015/16 the trust had assets of £697,500 and an income of £56,000.

There were 69 grants made to individuals totalling £17,400. We estimate that welfare grants totalled around £8,700.

Applications

Applications can be made in writing to the correspondent.

Other information

Grants are also made to individuals for educational purposes and to organisations.

The Doctor Merry Memorial Fund

£3,000

Correspondent: Ronald Pringle, Friston Corner, 3 Mill Close, East Dean, Eastbourne, East Sussex BN20 0EG (01323 423319; email: ronpringle@ hotmail.com)

CC number: 213449

Eligibility

People who are ill and who live in East Sussex.

Types of grants

One-off grants for nursing home care and medical equipment.

Annual grant total

In 2015/16 the fund had an income of £7,700 and a total expenditure of £5,900. We estimate that the fund gave around £3,000 to individuals during the year.

Applications

Our previous research indicates that individuals should apply via their doctor on a form available from the correspondent.

Other information

The fund was established in 1922 as a commemoration to a Dr Merry, who died of exhaustion while caring for the people of Eastbourne during a flu epidemic.

The fund also awards grants to local organisations.

Henry Smith (Rotherfield Share)

£3,200

Correspondent: Trevor Thorpe, Trustee, 82 Fermor Way, Crowborough TN6 3BJ (01892 664245; email: rotherfieldpc@ yahoo.co.uk; website: www. rotherfieldparishcouncil.co.uk)

CC number: 235516

Eligibility

People in need who live in the ancient parish of Rotherfield (Rotherfield and Crowborough civil parishes).

Types of grants

One-off and recurrent grants are given according to need. Grants have recently been awarded to help with the transport costs of regular hospital visits and the purchase of a mobility scooter.

Annual grant total

In 2016 the charity had an income of £2,600 and a total expenditure of £3,400. We estimate that the charity gave around £3,200 in grants to individuals.

Applications

Apply in writing to the correspondent. Applications can be submitted either directly by the individual, through a third party such as a social worker, or through an organisation such as Citizens Advice or other welfare agency. They are considered upon receipt.

City of Brighton and Hove

The Mayor of Brighton and Hove's Welfare Charity

£7,700

Correspondent: Michael Hill, Selborne Centre, 5 Selborne Place, Hove BH3 3ET (01273 779432)

CC number: 224012

Eligibility

Individuals in need who live in the old borough of Hove and Portslade.

Types of grants

One-off grants of up to a maximum of £250.

Annual grant total

In 2016/17 the charity had an income of £3,300 and a total expenditure of £8,100. We estimate that grants given to individuals totalled around £7,700.

Exclusions

No retrospective grants are made.

Applications

Apply on a form available from the correspondent along with full guidelines. Applications should be submitted directly by the individual or a relevant third party, for example, a friend, carer or professional (e.g. a social worker or health visitor). Grants are usually considered bi-monthly, in January, March, May, July, September and November. No money is given directly to the applicant, but rather directly to settle invoices. The committee will only consider one grant for each applicant and successful applicants should not reapply.

The Brighton Fund

£39,500

Correspondent: The Secretary, Brighton and Hove City Council, Democratic Services, Room 121, Kings House, Hove, East Sussex BN3 2LS (01273 291067 or 01273 291077; email: brightonfund@ brighton-hove.gov.uk; website: www. brighton-hove.gov.uk)

CC number: 1011724

Eligibility

Individuals in need (primarily people over the age of 60) who live within the administrative boundary of Brighton and Hove and are in need, hardship or distress.

Types of grants

One-off grants of up to £500 for white goods, flooring, carpets, etc.

Annual grant total

In 2015/16 the fund had assets of £1.3 million and an income of £49,000. Welfare grants to individuals totalled £39,500.

Applications

Application forms can be completed online or downloaded and completed by hand. All applications to the Brighton Fund must be made by support workers on behalf of clients who are residents of the city of Brighton and Hove. It can take up to a month for applications to be considered.

The Derek and Eileen Dodgson Foundation

£30,000

Correspondent: Gerry Wicks, Flat 5, 61 Wilbury Road, Hove BN3 3PB (01273 749576; email: gerald.wicks@btinternet. com)

CC number: 1018776

Eligibility

People in need who are over the age of 55, predominantly those living in the city of Brighton and Hove.

Types of grants

One-off grants, generally of up to £1,000. Most of the funds are given to local non-governmental organisations to pass on to individuals.

Annual grant total

In 2015/16 the foundation had assets of £2.3 million and an income of £108,500. Grants totalled £61,500 and were awarded to both individuals and organisations. The grant total above is an estimate for the amount received by individuals.

Applications
Application forms are available from the correspondent. Applications can be submitted either directly by the individual or through a social worker, Citizens Advice or other third party.

Hastings

The Isabel Blackman Foundation

£4,000 (four grants)

Correspondent: The Trustees, Stonehenge, 13 Laton Road, Hastings, East Sussex TN34 2ES (01424 431756; email: ibfoundation@uwclub.net)

CC number: 313577

Eligibility
People in need who live in Hastings and St Leonards district.

Types of grants
One-off grants based on disadvantage or need.

Annual grant total
In 2016/17 the foundation had assets of £6.3 million and an income of £303,000. The foundation awarded £4,000 to four individuals for welfare purposes.

Applications
Applications can be made in writing to the correspondent through a third party such as a social worker, Citizens Advice or other welfare agency.

Other information
The foundation mainly supports organisations and also makes grants to individuals for educational purposes.

The Catharine House Trust

£40,000 (146 grants)

Correspondent: Richard Palim, Ridge Cottage, New Cut, Westfield, Hastings, East Sussex TN35 4RL (email: catharinehousetrust@gmail.com)

CC number: 801656

Eligibility
Older individuals and people who have disabilities or are in poor health who live in the borough of Hastings.

Types of grants
One-off grants, which averaged just over £270 each in 2016/17. Funding is available for: medical equipment and treatment; household goods which are essential for maintaining health (this does not include general furniture); respite breaks for the client or carer; and relevant courses for instruction.

Annual grant total
In 2016/17 the trust had an income of £36,500 and a total expenditure of £41,000. The trust made 146 grants, totalling £40,000, during the year.

Exclusions
Usually only one application is accepted per person.

Applications
Apply in writing to the correspondent, supported by a written statement from a medical professional or social worker. Most applications are made through NHS trusts, local authority social services departments and other charities.

Other information
In 2016/17 about 14% of applications were received directly from individuals, with the remainder received through intermediaries such as social workers.

Hastings Area Community Trust

£32,500 (310 grants)

Correspondent: Anthony Bonds, Bolton Tomson House, 49 Cambridge Gardens, Hastings, East Sussex TN34 1EN (01424 718880; email: hact@btinternet.com; website: reliefhastings.weebly.com)

CC number: 1002470

Eligibility
People in need who are under 60 and live in the borough of Hastings or the district of Rother who are on a very low income and have children, or who have medical reasons for not working.

Types of grants
One-off grants mainly in the form of payments to suppliers for essential household needs, including white goods, beds, fuel costs, clothing and baby items.

Annual grant total
In 2015/16 the trust held assets of £944,000 and had an income of £88,500. Grants to 310 individuals totalled £32,500.

Exclusions
No grants are given for carpets, curtains or televisions.

Applications
Application forms are available from the correspondent. Applications can only be accepted from a recognised referral agency (e.g. social worker, Citizens Advice or recognised advice agency) and are considered throughout the year. The trust encourages applicants who wish to telephone to leave a message on the answer phone if there is no reply as messages are listened to daily.

Other information
The trust also provides accommodation and administration services to other local charities and organisations.

William Shadwell Charity

£7,600

Correspondent: C. R. Morris, Correspondent, 4 Barley Lane, Hastings TN35 5NX (01424 433586)

CC number: 207366

Eligibility
People who are sick or in need and live in the borough of Hastings.

Types of grants
One-off and recurrent grants.

Annual grant total
In 2016 the charity had both an income of £10,900 and a total expenditure of £15,400. We estimate that grants given to individuals totalled £7,600.

The charity also gives grants to local organisations.

Exclusions
No grants are given for the payment of debt, taxes, etc.

Applications
Apply in writing to the correspondent. Applications should be submitted in March and September for consideration in April and October, but urgent cases can be considered at any time. Applications can be submitted directly by the individual or through a third party.

Lewes

Elizabeth Ballard

£3,000

Correspondent: Revd Stephen Daughtery, The Refectory, Southover High Street, Lewes BN7 1HT (01273 472018)

CC number: 232587

Eligibility
Residents of Southover parish who are in need.

Types of grants
One-off according to need.

Annual grant total
In 2016 the charity had an income of £7,100 and a total expenditure of £6,900. We estimate that grants given to individuals totalled around £3,000.

Applications
Apply in writing to the correspondent.

The Newick Distress Trust

£3,500

Correspondent: Ian Reekie, Trustee, 3 High Hurst Close, Newick, Lewes, East Sussex BN8 4NJ (01825 722512; email: ianreekie24@gmail.com)

CC number: 291954

Eligibility

People in need who live in the village of Newick (East Sussex) and the surrounding area.

Types of grants

One-off or recurrent grants towards, for example, heating bills in very cold weather, school uniforms required due to a change of school and other basic living costs. The trust notes that most often requests for assistance come from people experiencing reduction in income due to bereavement, ill health, unemployment, marital breakdown or other unexpected circumstances.

Annual grant total

In 2016 the trust had an income of £5,700 and a total expenditure of £3,800. We estimate that grants given to individuals totalled around £3,500.

Applications

Apply in writing to the correspondent.

Rother
The Battle Charities

£3,000

Correspondent: Timothy Roberts, 1 Upper Lake, Battle, East Sussex TN33 0AN (01424 772401; email: troberts@heringtons.net)

CC number: 206591

Eligibility

People in need who live in Battle and Netherfield, East Sussex.

Types of grants

Grants are usually made towards fuel and children's clothing.

Annual grant total

In 2015 the charity had an income of £2,800 and a total expenditure of £3,500. We have estimated that grants to individuals for welfare purposes totalled £3,000.

Applications

Apply in writing to the correspondent. Applications can be sent directly by the individual or family member, through an organisation such as Citizens Advice or through a third party such as a social worker. Full details of the applicant's circumstances are required.

Crowhurst Relief-in-Need Charities

£900

Correspondent: Pauline Edwards, Trustee, 1 Lankester Square, Oxted, Surrey RH8 0LJ (01883 712874; email: crowhurstcharities@yahoo.com)

CC number: 200315

Eligibility

People in need who live in Crowhurst, Surrey.

Types of grants

One-off grants according to need.

Annual grant total

In 2015/16 the charity had an income of £2,500 and a total expenditure of £4,100. We estimate that social welfare grants to individuals totalled around £900. Grants are also given to organisations and for educational purposes.

Applications

Apply in writing to the correspondent.

Wealden
The Mayfield Charity

£2,200

Correspondent: Brenda Hopkin, Administrator, Appletrees, Alexandra Road, Mayfield, East Sussex TN20 6UD (01435 873279)

CC number: 212996

Eligibility

People in need who live in the ancient parish of Mayfield.

Types of grants

One-off grants according to need. Our previous research suggests that grants have been given towards hospital travel, clothing, equipment for people with disabilities, the purchase of aids and Christmas gifts for older people.

Annual grant total

In 2016 the charity had an income of £4,700 and a total expenditure of £9,000. We estimate that the charity gave around £2,200 in grants to individuals for welfare purposes.

The charity also gives grants to organisations and individuals for educational purposes.

Exclusions

Grants are not made for religious or political causes.

Applications

Apply in writing to the correspondent at any time either directly by the individual or a family member, through a third party such as a social worker or teacher, or through an organisation such as Citizens Advice or a school. Proof of need should be included where possible.

Essex
Colchester Catalyst Charity

£237,500

Correspondent: Peter Fitt, Secretary, 3 Dedham Vale Business Centre, Manningtree Road, Dedham, Colchester, Essex CO7 6BL (01206 323420; email: info@colchestercatalyst.co.uk; website: www.colchestercatalyst.co.uk)

CC number: 228352

Eligibility

People in north east Essex who are living with a disability or medical condition. The area of benefit is the entire CO postcode.

Types of grants

Special individual needs grants

Grants to purchase specialised equipment that is not provided by statutory organisations, with the aim of reducing the individual's medical condition. Items of equipment may include: wheelchairs; mobility scooters; special beds and mattresses; communication aids; computer software; and mobility aids.

Respite care grants

Grants are made towards respite care for people with medical needs or a disability. These grants are made through the charity's respite care partner organisations. Assistance may be given towards, for example: a residential or nursing home stay for the person being cared for; domiciliary help for a few hours each week, or as required; breaks for self-carers; or befriending, practical support or personal care.

Counselling grants

The charity works with partner organisations to provide therapeutic counselling support for people in the most urgent need of counselling who have identifiable clinical needs.

Annual grant total

In 2016 the charity had assets of £11.3 million and an income of £519,000. We believe grants to individuals totalled £237,500, and were distributed in the following categories:

Respite care	£145,500
Special individual needs	£89,000
Equipment pools	£3,600

A further £235,500 was awarded to other charities.

Exclusions

Funding will not be given for items already purchased or where there is an obligation for provision by a statutory authority. The charity does not take responsibility for the insurance, maintenance and repairs of any items funded. Grants towards replacement vehicles will only be considered where evidence of a replacement fund is available.

Applications

Application forms for 'special individual needs' grants are available to download from the website or from the correspondent. Supporting statements and professional assessments from medical practitioners must be attached, along with estimates.

Grants for respite care and counselling are administered by the charity's partner organisations. There is a full list of partner organisations on the website, or more information can be obtained from the correspondent.

Lenderhand

£54,000

Correspondent: Jennie Grant, PO Box 366, Loughton IG10 9E (020 8532 5066; email: contact@lenderhand.org; website: www.lenderhand.org)

CC number: 1161794

Eligibility

Families and individuals living in Essex who are in need. The charity's website states:

Circumstances that we will consider to be deemed suitable for grants will include but not be limited to:

- Family bereavement or tragedy
- Single parent families who are struggling and cannot work while looking after children
- Candidates who are unable to work due to disability or their partner's disability
- Unfortunate circumstances or incident i.e. house fire, accident, illness

Types of grants

One-off grants to help with essential goods and services.

Annual grant total

In 2016/17 the charity held assets of £14,500 and had an income of £59,000. Grants to individuals totalled £54,000.

Exclusions

Assistance cannot be provided for paying off debt, carpeting or vinyl.

Applications

Apply via the charity's website. Applications are processed within a six-week window.

David Randall Foundation

£13,300

Correspondent: Susan Randall, Secretary, 7 Browning Road, Maldon, Essex CM9 6BU (01621 858449; email: info@davidrandallfoundation.org; website: www.davidrandallfoundation.org)

CC number: 1151121

Eligibility

Individuals with life-limiting illnesses living in Essex.

Types of grants

Successful applicants will be offered vouchers/tickets for a range of outings and, as far as possible and if it is within its means, the foundation will try to provide vouchers for any outings in which the applicant would like to participate.

Annual grant total

In 2015/16 the foundation had assets of £77,500 and an income of £32,600. Grants to individuals totalled £13,300.

Applications

Application forms are available to download from the foundation's website.

Other information

The foundation's website states that:

David Randall died of bowel cancer aged 27 on 6th July 2012. He was diagnosed as being terminally ill on 14th February 2012. From that day his family and friends made sure he had regular enjoyable outings to look forward to and the David Randall Foundation aims to afford the same opportunity to people who are not in the position to provide these outings for themselves.

Braintree

Braintree United Charities

£2,000

Correspondent: The Administrator, 12 Medley Road, Rayne, Braintree, Essex CM77 6TQ (01376 321651; email: info@braintreeunitedcharities.co.uk; website: braintreeunitedcharities.co.uk)

CC number: 212131

Eligibility

People in need who live in the parishes of St Michael's and St Paul's, Braintree.

There is a map of the area covered by the charity on the website.

Types of grants

One-off and recurrent grants ranging from £50 to £100. Annual grants are given at Christmas to people in need who are registered with the charity.

Annual grant total

In 2016/17 the charity had an income of £3,000 and a total expenditure of £4,300. We estimate that grants given to individuals totalled around £2,000.

Exclusions

Loans are not normally made.

Applications

Application forms are available from the correspondent or can be completed online. They can be submitted either directly by the individual or through a third party, such as a social worker, Citizens Advice or other welfare agency. The trustees normally meet twice a year to consider applications, but urgent requests can be dealt with at other times.

Other information

Grants are also made to organisations working for the benefit of local people.

Helena Sant's Residuary Trust Fund

£3,200

Correspondent: Malcolm Willis, Trustee, Greenway, Church Street, Gestingthorpe, Halstead, Essex CO9 3AX (01787 469920; email: willis.malcolm@gmail.com)

CC number: 269570

Eligibility

People in need who live in the parish of St Andrew with Holy Trinity, Halstead who have at any time been a member of the Church of England.

Types of grants

One-off cash grants are given according to need.

Annual grant total

In 2016 the trust had an income of £5,100 and a total expenditure of £6,600. We estimate that the trust awarded around £3,200 to individuals.

The fund also gives grants to organisations.

Exclusions

Grants are not given to pay rates, taxes or public funds.

Applications

Applications can be submitted in writing to the correspondent directly by the individual, through an organisation such as Citizens Advice or through a third party such as a social worker. Applications are considered at any time.

Other information

At the time of writing (August 2017) the trust had no website or accounts available.

Brentwood

Ecclesiastical Charity of George White

£1,100

Correspondent: Revd Robert Wallace, Trustee, c/o St Peter's Parish Office, Claughton Way, Hutton, Brentwood, Essex CM13 1JS (01277 262864; email: dawn_shaxon@btconnect.com; website: www.huttonchurch.org.uk)

CC number: 208601

Eligibility

People in need who live in the parish of All Saints with St Peter, Hutton. Particular favour is given to children, young adults and older people. The usual length of residency is seven years.

Types of grants

Pensions and one-off grants.

Annual grant total

In 2015 the charity had an income of £6,000 and a total expenditure of £4,600. We estimate that grants given to individuals totalled around £1,100 for welfare purposes.

Applications

Apply in writing to the correspondent at any time. Applications can be submitted either directly by the individual, through a third party such as a social worker, or through an organisation such as Citizens Advice or other welfare agency. They are considered at any time.

Other information

The charity also makes grants towards the repair of the church fabric in the two local parish churches.

City of Chelmsford

Broomfield United Charities

£2,000

Correspondent: Brian Worboys, Trustee, 5 Butlers Close, Chelmsford CM1 7BE (01245 440540; email: brianbroomfield@ hotmail.co.uk)

CC number: 225563

Eligibility

People in need who live in the civil parish of Broomfield.

Types of grants

One-off grants according to need.

Annual grant total

In 2015/16 the charity had an income of £5,900 and a total expenditure of £5,400. We have estimated that grants to individuals totalled £2,000, with funding also awarded to local organisations.

Applications

Apply in writing to the correspondent directly by the individual for consideration at any time.

Springfield United Charities

£3,200

Correspondent: Nick Eveleigh, Civic Centre, Duke Street, Chelmsford, Essex CM1 2YJ (01245 606606)

CC number: 214530

Eligibility

Individuals in need living in the parish of Springfield.

Types of grants

One-off grants according to need.

Annual grant total

In 2016/17 the charity had an income of £7,700 and a total expenditure of £3,800. We estimate that the charity awarded £3,200 in grants to individuals during the year.

Applications

Applications should be made in writing to the correspondent.

Colchester

Colchester Children's Charity Appeal

See entry on page 53

Epping Forest

The George and Alfred Lewis (of Chigwell) Memorial Fund

£1,700

Correspondent: Elizabeth Smart, Trustee, 16 Forest Terrace, High Road, Chigwell, Essex IG7 5BW (020 8504 9408)

CC number: 297802

Eligibility

People in need and widows of those who served in HM Forces or the Merchant Service during the Second World War and were living in the parishes of

Chigwell and Chigwell Row at the time of their enlistment.

Types of grants

One-off grants to help people who are in need due to family illness, old age, domestic emergencies and so on.

Annual grant total

In 2016 the fund had an income of £2,600 and a total expenditure of £1,900. We estimate that grants given to individuals for welfare purposes totalled around £1,700.

Applications

Apply in writing to the correspondent. Applications can be made either directly by the individual or through a third party on behalf of the individual, such as a spouse or child, and should include as much detail of personal circumstances as is deemed appropriate. Applications are considered at any time.

Thurrock

East Tilbury Relief in Need Charity

£2,300

Correspondent: Robert Chaston, Trustee, 40 Queen Elizabeth Avenue, East Tilbury, Tilbury, Essex RM18 8SP (01375 851846)

CC number: 212335

Eligibility

People in need who live in the parish of East Tilbury.

Types of grants

One-off and recurrent grants have been given towards hospital visits and to children in need.

Annual grant total

In 2016 the charity had an income of £7,000 and a total expenditure of £4,800. We estimate that grants given to individuals totalled £2,300, with funding also awarded to organisations in the local area.

Applications

Applications can be made in writing to the correspondent and are considered in November.

Uttlesford

Hatfield Broad Oak Non-Ecclesiastical Charities

£3,000

Correspondent: Martin Gandy, Carters Barn, Cage End, Hatfield Broad Oak, Bishop's Stortford, Hertfordshire CM22 7HL (01279 718316)

CC number: 206467

Eligibility
People in need who live in Hatfield Broad Oak.

Types of grants
One-off and recurrent grants.

Annual grant total
In 2016 the charity had an income of £8,300 and a total expenditure of £3,300. We estimate that grants given to individuals totalled around £3,000.

Applications
Apply in writing to the correspondent directly by the individual or family member.

Other information
The charity's Charity Commission record states that it also assists with housing accommodation.

Lord Maynard's Charity

£2,900

Correspondent: Daniel Fox, Trustee, Moulton, Vicarage Lane, Thaxted, Dunmow CM6 2QP (01371 830470; email: thaxtedfox@gmail.com)

CC number: 278579

Eligibility
People who live in the parish of Thaxted and have more than three children in their family.

Types of grants
One-off grants according to need.

Annual grant total
In 2016/17 the charity had an income of £3,700 and had a total expenditure of £11,400. We estimate that the charity gave around £2,900 in grants to individuals for welfare purposes, with funding also given for educational purposes and to local organisations.

Applications
Apply in writing to the correspondent. Applicants traditionally queue in the local church on the first Saturday in August for the money to be handed out, but postal applications prior to this are accepted.

The Saffron Walden United Charities

£45,000

Correspondent: Jim Ketteridge, Clerk to the Trustees, c/o Community Hospital, Radwinter Road, Saffron Walden, Essex CB11 3HY (01799 526122; email: alfredjames.ketteridge@ntlworld.com)

CC number: 210662

Eligibility
People in need who live in the former borough council area of Saffron Walden, including the hamlets of Little Walden and Sewards End.

Types of grants
One-off grants in kind and gift vouchers. A range of help is considered including, for example, electrical goods, convalescence, clothing, household bills, food, holidays, travel expenses, furniture, disability equipment and nursery fees.

Annual grant total
In 2016 the charity had assets of £1.3 million and an income of £41,500. During the year, the charity gave around £45,000 in grants to individuals.

Exclusions
No grants are given for credit card debt.

Applications
Apply in writing to the correspondent either directly by the individual, through a third party such as a social worker, or through an organisation such as Citizens Advice or other welfare agency. Applications are considered as they arrive.

Thaxted Relief-in-Need Charities

£4,400

Correspondent: Michael Hughes, 3 Mill Row, Fishmarket Street, Thaxted, Dunmow CM6 2PD (01371 830642; email: michaelbhughes@hotmail.co.uk)

CC number: 243782

Eligibility
People in need who live in the parish of Thaxted.

Types of grants
One-off and recurrent grants are given according to need.

Annual grant total
In 2016 the charity had assets of £408,000 and an income of £29,000. During the year, the charity awarded £8,700 in grants to organisations and individuals. We estimate that the charity awarded £4,400 in grants to individuals for welfare purposes.

Applications
Applications should be made in writing to the correspondent.

Other information
The charity was established in at least 1549. The main priority of the charity is the provision and maintenance of almshouses, and it also gives grants to local organisations.

Hampshire

Hampshire Football Association Benevolent Fund

£2,600

Correspondent: Robin Osborne, Chair, Winklebury Football Complex, Winklebury Way, Basingstoke, Hampshire RG23 8BF (01256 853000)

CC number: 232359

Eligibility
People in need who have been injured while playing football, and others who have 'done service' to the game of football. Applicants must be playing for a team affiliated with Hampshire Football Association.

Types of grants
One-off and recurrent grants are given according to need.

Annual grant total
In 2016 the trust had an income of £3,300 and a total expenditure of £2,800. We estimate that grants given to individuals totalled £2,600.

Applications
The club secretary must apply to Hampshire Football Association or the Area Benevolent Officer for an application form on behalf of the applicant. The application should be completed by the applicant and endorsed by the secretary of the club.

A doctor's certificate clearly stating the nature of the injury and probable period of incapacitation must accompany each application. Completed application forms should be returned to the county office or the Area Benevolent Officer.

Hawley Almshouses

£33,500

Correspondent: The Secretary, Trustees' Office, Ratcliffe House, Hawley Road, Blackwater, Camberley GU17 9DD (01276 33515; email: hawleyalmshouses@ btconnect.com; website: www. hawleyalmshouses.org.uk/relief-in-need)

CC number: 204684

Eligibility
People in need who live in the area covered by Hart District Council and Rushmoor Borough Council.

Types of grants
Generally one-off grants for needs that cannot be met from any other source. Examples of grants made in recent years include: funding towards school trips for low-income families; one-off help with utility bills; rent deposits; the purchase of special equipment for people with disabilities; and contributions to specialist medical assessments.

Annual grant total
In 2016/17 the charity held assets of almost £1.8 million and had an income of £154,000. Grants to individuals totalled £33,500.

Applications
An initial contact form can be completed on the website by the individual or by an appropriate third party such as a social worker or close family member. It should include a brief summary of the problem and how a grant may be able to help. The charity will then make contact to discuss the applicant's situation and whether they may qualify.

Other information
The charity also provides warden-operated individual accommodation for older people in the area.

Hollis Charity
See entry on page 357

The Richard Kirkman Trust

£13,000

Correspondent: David Hoare, Trustee, Ashton House, 12 The Central Precinct, Winchester Road, Chandler's Ford, Eastleigh SO53 2GB (023 8027 4555)

CC number: 327972

Eligibility
People in need who live in Hampshire.

Types of grants
One-off grants according to need.

Annual grant total
In 2016/17 the trust held assets of £2.1 million and had an income of £73,500. Grants totalled £57,500 and were made to both organisations and individuals. We have estimated that grants to individuals totalled £13,000.

Applications
Apply in writing to the correspondent.

Portsmouth Victoria Nursing Association

£17,400

Correspondent: Susan Resouly, Secretary, Southlands, Prinsted Lane, Prinsted, Emsworth, Hampshire PO10 8HS (07717 718386; email: pvnacharity@gmail.com)

CC number: 203311

Eligibility
People in need who are sick and live in the areas covered by the Portsmouth City Primary Care Trust, the Fareham and Gosport Primary Care Trust and the East Hampshire Primary Care Trust.

Types of grants
One-off grants of up to £750 towards medical equipment, household essentials, special clothing and respite care.

Annual grant total
In 2016 the association held assets of £23,000 and had an income of £46,000. Grants to individuals totalled £17,400, with £17,000 given to patients and £400 given to nurses.

Exclusions
Items that should be provided by the NHS.

Applications
All applications must be made through the community nursing staff and help is confined to those for whom the nurses are in attendance. Referrals are made by the district nurses on a form which is considered by the committee at monthly meetings.

Basingstoke and Dean

Kingsclere Welfare Charities

£600

Correspondent: Roy Forth, PO Box 7721, Kingsclere RG20 5WQ (07796 423108; email: kclerecharities@aol.co.uk)

CC number: 237218

Eligibility
People in need who live in the parishes of Ashford Hill, Headley and Kingsclere.

Types of grants
The provision or payment for items, services or facilities, such as medical equipment, expenses for travel to hospital and grants to relieve hardship. Grants are mostly one-off, but recurrent grants can be considered.

Annual grant total
At the time of writing (January 2018) the most recent financial information available was from 2015.

In 2015 the charity had an income of £5,300 and a total expenditure £790. We estimate that grants given to individuals totalled £600.

Applications
Apply in writing to the correspondent. Applications are usually considered in February, April, June, September and November.

East Hampshire

Bordon Liphook Haselmere Charity CIO

£62,000 (425+ grants)

Correspondent: Sue Nicholson, Charity Administrator, Oaklands Farm, Smithfield Lane, Headley Down, Bordon GU35 8ST (01420 477787; email: grants@blhcharity.co.uk; website: www. blhcharity.co.uk)

CC number: 1153712

Eligibility
People in need who live in north east Hampshire and south west Surrey.

Types of grants
One-off grants and supermarket vouchers. The trustees consider a wide range of applications including furniture and furnishings, white goods, utility bills, debt relief and rent arrears, rent deposits, boiler repairs and bankruptcy. The charity also works with Furniture Helpline to provide families with starter packs of basic furniture and white goods worth around £420.

Annual grant total
In 2015/16 the charity held assets of £123,000 and had an income of £401,500. During the year, the charity made grants of £53,500 and gave away £8,000 in supermarket vouchers. The annual report for 2015/16 estimates that over 425 families and individuals benefitted. A further £12,600 was granted to four community projects.

Applications

Apply on a form available from the correspondent or to download from the website. Applications can be made either directly by the individual or through a social worker, Citizens Advice, other welfare agency, parent support advisor, health visitor or district nurse. Applications are considered monthly and the charity reserves the right to commission a case worker's report.

Other information

The charity raises money through its four charity shops in Bordon, Haslemere, Grayshott and Liphook and provides support to both individuals and organisations. It registered as a CIO in 2013.

Fareham

The Fareham Welfare Trust

£11,000

Correspondent: Anne Butcher, 44 Old Turnpike, Fareham, Hampshire PO16 7HA (01329 235186)

CC number: 236738

Eligibility

People in need who live in the ecclesiastical parishes of St Peter and Paul, St John and Holy Trinity, all in Fareham. Preference is given to widows.

Types of grants

One-off and recurrent grants are given according to need. Grants have been given for clothing, furniture, food, cookers, washing machines and other essential electrical items.

Annual grant total

In 2015/16 the trust had an income of £11,700 and a total expenditure of £11,700. We estimate that grants given to individuals totalled £11,000.

Applications

Applications should be submitted through a recognised referral agency (e.g. social worker, health visitor, Citizens Advice or doctor) or trustee. They are considered throughout the year. Details of the individual's income and circumstances must be included.

The Earl of Southampton Trust

£21,500

Correspondent: Sue Boden, 24 The Square, Titchfield PO14 4RU (01329 513294; email: earlstrust@yahoo.co.uk; website: eost.org.uk)

CC number: 238549

Eligibility

People in need who live in the ancient parish of Titchfield (now subdivided into the parishes of Titchfield, Sarisbury, Locks Heath, Warsash, Stubbington and Lee-on-Solent). Groups catering for people who are in need are sometimes considered.

Types of grants

One-off grants in the range of £25 and £1,000 are given for a wide range of purposes including, for example, furnishings, food, payment of household bills, household appliances, rent arrears, transport, holidays, respite care, and medical equipment.

Annual grant total

In 2015/16 the trust had assets of £1.65 million and an income of £94,000. Welfare grants to individuals totalled £21,500.

Applications

Application forms can be downloaded from the trust's website and must be submitted through a recognised agency (social services, a health visitor, etc.). Applications must include details of medical/financial status and are usually means-tested. They are normally considered on the last Tuesday of every month, although in the event of extreme urgency requests can be fast-tracked between meetings.

Other information

The trust runs almshouses and a day centre for older people.

Gosport

Thorngate Relief-in-Need and General Charity

£1,800

Correspondent: Kay Brent, 6 Hartspiece Road, Redhill RH1 6RS (01737 479729; email: kay.brent@btinternet.com)

CC number: 210946

Eligibility

People in need who live in Gosport.

Types of grants

One-off grants usually of between £100 and £500.

Annual grant total

In 2015/16 the charity had an income of £10,700 and a total expenditure of £7,500. Grants are made to individuals and organisations for a wide range of purposes. We estimate that welfare grants to individuals totalled £1,800.

Exclusions

No grants are made towards legal expenses.

Applications

Apply using a form available from the correspondent. Applications can be made either directly by the individual or through a social worker, Citizens Advice, probation service or other welfare agency.

New Forest

Dibden Allotments Fund

£162,500 (947 grants)

Correspondent: Valerie Stewart, Clerk, Dibden Allotments Charity, 7 Drummond Court, Prospect Place, Hythe, Southampton SO45 6HD (023 8084 1305; email: dibdenallotments@ btconnect.com; website: daf-hythe.org.uk)

CC number: 255778

Eligibility

People in need who live in the parishes of Hythe, Dibden, Marshwood and Fawley in Hampshire. Individuals should have lived in the Waterside area for at least 12 months.

Types of grants

One-off grants according to need are given for the relief of hardship or distress. Grants to individuals can take many forms, e.g. vouchers for food, clothes or household items, or the supply of white goods or furniture.

Shoe Vouchers Scheme: vouchers, mainly for children and older people, towards the costs of shoes at a number of participating local shoe retailers.

Garden Support Scheme: a scheme run in conjunction with a number of local gardeners to assist older people and people with disabilities with essential work in their gardens, such as grass cutting and hedge trimming, between March and November. **Note:** The majority of participants on the scheme are expected to make a small contribution towards its costs.

Annual grant total

In 2015/16 the fund had assets of £9.6 million and an income of £394,500. The charity awarded £91,000 to 180 individuals for general purposes; £55,500 to 229 individuals for garden maintenance; and £16,100 to 538 individuals through the shoe vouchers scheme.

Exclusions

The fund's website states: 'It would be unusual for an individual to receive more than a single grant in any one year or for goods already provided to an individual by the Fund to be replaced within what a manufacturer would consider to be a reasonable period of use.'

Applications

Apply for general assistance using the form available from the fund's website, where criteria, guidelines and the application process are also detailed. It is helpful to supply a supporting statement from a professional such as a health or social worker, midwife or teacher.

Shoe Vouchers Scheme: vouchers are distributed mainly through schools and organisations working with older people. People who don't have contact with either a school or participating organisation can apply using the same process as for a general grant (as described above).

Garden Support Scheme: applications can be made by letter or telephone at any time, although the fund encourages individuals wishing to join the scheme to make contact during January and February. When an application has been received, the charity will organise a meeting with the applicant to discuss their requirements and any contribution they will be expected to make.

Other information

Grants are also made to individuals for educational purposes (£2,300 in two grants in 2015/16), and to local organisations (£146,000 in 2015/16).

Groome Trust

£3,000

Correspondent: Patricia Dunkinson, Belmont, Burford Lane, Brockenhurst SO42 7TN (01590 622303)

CC number: 204829

Eligibility

People in need who live in the parish of Brockenhurst.

Types of grants

One-off grants towards lifelines for people living alone, gifts and food vouchers for older people at Christmas.

Annual grant total

In 2016 the trust had an income of £6,700 and a total expenditure of £7,500. We have estimated that grants to individuals totalled £3,000 during the year, with funding also awarded to local organisations.

Applications

Apply in writing to the correspondent.

The Sway Welfare Aid Group (SWAG)

£13,800

Correspondent: Jeremy Stevens, Trustee and Treasurer, Driftway, Mead End Road, Sway, Lymington SO41 6EH (01590 681500, select option 2; email: info@swaghants.org.uk; website: www. swaghants.org.uk)

CC number: 261220

Eligibility

Individuals and families in need who live in the parish of Sway (Hampshire) and its immediate neighbourhood. There is a map showing the area of benefit on the website.

Types of grants

One-off emergency grants can be given for a wide range of items. In the past, the charity has helped with council tax and rent arrears, replacement boilers, replacement carpets, car repairs, food bills, school trips and nursery places. Assistance is also available in the form of twice-yearly (in December and March) grants towards heating costs, up to a maximum annual total of £450.

Annual grant total

In 2016/17 the charity had assets of £245,500 and an income of £25,500. The charity awarded almost £13,800 in grants to individuals during the year: £6,100 in hardship grants; and £7,700 in heating grants.

Applications

Applicants should contact the charity directly (tel: 01590 681500, option 2) if they wish to make an application.

Other information

The charity also runs a transport service for people who need help to attend a hospital or other medical appointment, as well as a lunch club for people over the age of 65 who are living alone in the parish.

Portsmouth

Friends of the Animals
See entry on page 25

The Lord Mayor of Portsmouth's Charity

£22,000

Correspondent: Grants Team, Dame Mary Fagan House, Chineham Court, Lutyens Close, Basingstoke, Hampshire RG24 8AG (01256 776127; email: info@ hiwcf.org.uk; website: www.hiwcf.com)

CC number: 1100417–2

Eligibility

Contact the correspondent for current details. Formerly this charity funded individuals in need who lived in the city of Portsmouth, or former residents who lived in Havant, Waterlooville, Fareham or Droxford.

Types of grants

One-off grants.

Annual grant total

This is now a linked charity to the Hampshire and Isle of Wight Community Foundation, however, we could not find any information in the foundation's accounts for this particular fund's activities. The accounts did state that the Lord Mayor of Portsmouth's Charity had assets amounting to almost £536,000. In the past, we know that the charity awarded around £22,000 in grants annually.

Applications

Apply in writing to the correspondent.

Other information

Grants are also made to local organisations.

E. C. Roberts Charitable Trust

£10,900

Correspondent: Revd Wendy Kennedy, Administrator, First Floor, Peninsular House, Wharf Road, Portsmouth PO2 8HB (023 9289 9668; email: wendy. kennedy@portsmouth.anglican.org)

CC number: 1001055

Eligibility

Children in need who live in the city of Portsmouth, with a preference for those who are orphans, blind or have a disability.

Types of grants

One-off or recurrent grants according to need, including clothing and other essentials.

Annual grant total

In 2016 the charity had an income of £7,900 and a total expenditure of £22,000. We estimate that the charity awarded around £10,900 for welfare purposes, with grants also awarded to organisations.

Applications

Apply in writing to the correspondent. Applications can be submitted either directly by the individual or through a third party, for example, a social worker, Citizens Advice or other welfare agency. Requests for assistance are considered upon receipt.

Other information

At the time of writing (August 2017) the charity had no website or accounts available.

Rushmoor

The Farnborough (Hampshire) Welfare Trust

£2,400

Correspondent: M. Evans, Bowmarsh, 45 Church Avenue, Farnborough, Hampshire GU14 7AP (01252 542726; email: evans.bowmarsh@ntlworld.com)

CC number: 236889

Eligibility

People in need who live in the urban district of Farnborough, Hampshire.

Types of grants

Small, one-off and recurrent grants, mainly to older people at Christmas.

Annual grant total

In 2016 the trust had an income of £4,000 and a total expenditure of £2,500. We estimate that grants given to individuals totalled £2,400.

Applications

Apply in writing to the correspondent. Applications can be submitted either directly by the individual or by a third party and are usually considered in early December.

Southampton

The Southampton (City Centre) Relief-in-Need Charity

£7,700

Correspondent: Linda Page, Correspondent, 12 Westgate Street, Southampton SO14 2AY (023 8063 8968)

CC number: 255617

Eligibility

People in need who live in the ecclesiastical parish of Southampton (in practice, the city centre).

Types of grants

One-off grants usually ranging from £50 to £100. The charity supplies a leaflet detailing the types of grants it can give.

Annual grant total

In 2015 the charity had an income of £9,600 and a total expenditure of £7,900. We estimate that the charity gave around £7,700 in grants to individuals during the year.

Exclusions

No grants are given towards rent, debts or council tax.

Applications

Apply in writing to the correspondent through a social worker, Citizens Advice, health visitor or other welfare agency. Applications are considered quarterly, usually in March, June, September and December; those made directly by the individual will not be considered.

Southampton and District Sick Poor Fund and Humane Society (Southampton Charitable Trust)

£6,600

Correspondent: Matthew Pickett, BDO LLP, Arcadia House, Maritime Walk, Southampton SO14 3TL (023 8088 1915; email: matt.pickett@bdo.co.uk)

CC number: 201603

Eligibility

People who are sick and poor and live in Southampton and the immediate surrounding area. Grants and certificates are also awarded to people for saving or attempting to save someone from drowning or other dangers.

Types of grants

Our research suggests that one-off grants, usually ranging from £50 to £250, are available for bedding, food, fuel and specialist equipment to alleviate an existing condition or to assist with day-to-day living.

Annual grant total

In 2016 the charity had an income of £13,300 and a total expenditure of £13,600. We estimate that grants given to individuals totalled £6,600, with funding also awarded to organisations.

Applications

Apply in writing to the correspondent. Applications should preferably be submitted through a social worker, Citizens Advice or other welfare agency. The trustees usually meet twice a year, but applications can be dealt with outside these meetings. Candidates must clearly demonstrate that they are both sick and poor (such as evidence of Income Support or other state benefits).

Wincester

Twyford and District Nursing Association

£3,500

Correspondent: Giselle Letchworth, Sunnyside, High Street, Twyford, Winchester SO21 1RG (01962 712158; email: giselleletchworth@btinternet.com)

CC number: 800876

Eligibility

People who are in need and live in the parishes of Twyford, Compton and Shawford, Colden Common and Owslebury, in the county of Hampshire. Preference is made for applicants who are sick, have a disability, are convalescing, or otherwise suffering from ill health.

Types of grants

One-off, short-term grants for relief in need, including for medical care.

Annual grant total

In 2016 the charity had an income of £8,000 and a total expenditure of £4,000. We estimate that grants given to individuals totalled £3,500.

Exclusions

The charity cannot offer long-term care.

Applications

Applications should be made in writing to the correspondent and can be submitted at any time.

Hertfordshire

The Bowley Charity

£11,400 (52 grants)

Correspondent: Pam Hill, Clerk to the Trustees, c/o Hertfordshire County Council, Post Point 21, Apsley Two, Brindley Way, Apsley, Hemel Hempstead, Hertsfordshire HP3 9BF (email: pam.hill@hertfordshire.gov.uk; website: www.bowleycharity.btck.co.uk)

CC number: 212187

Eligibility

Disadvantaged children up to 16 years (or 18 if in full-time education) who live in Watford or Three Rivers. Applications for unborn babies can be made but items cannot be purchased until after the birth of the child.

Types of grants

Small, one-off grants for cookers, beds, bedding, prams, cots and other essential household items. Grants are also given for clothing and shoes for children. Grants should primarily benefit children, rather than adults, and usually come in the form of Argos vouchers.

Annual grant total

In 2015/16 the charity had an income of £9,800 and a total expenditure of £11,500. Grants to individuals totalled £11,400.

Exclusions

Trustees will not normally fund flooring, living room furniture, holidays, school uniform, outings or school trips.

Applications

Application forms are available to download from the charity's website or from the correspondent. Applications should be made through a social worker, health visitor or other support worker, who knows the applicant and has made a home visit. The trustees meet quarterly in March, June, September and December to consider grants. See the website for closing dates for applications.

The Hertfordshire Charity for Deprived Children

£3,500

Correspondent: David Williams, Clerk to the Trustees, 34 Cambridge Road, Langford, Biggleswade, Bedfordshire SG18 9PS (email: hertscfdc@gmail.com; website: mgtact0.wixsite.com/herts-charity-child)

CC number: 200327

Eligibility

Disadvantaged children up to the age of 17 living in Hertfordshire (excluding the Watford area). The charity's website states that it supports children who 'are facing difficulties that compromise their well-being and self-worth'.

Types of grants

One-off grants generally for clothing (such as school or cub uniforms or general clothing), bedding, furniture and other household items which would improve the quality of life for the child (such as beds, cookers or washing machines).

Annual grant total

In 2016/17 the charity had an income of £6,500 and a total expenditure of £3,800. We estimate that grants given to individuals totalled £3,500.

Exclusions

The charity is unable to help looked-after children in residential care or foster placements. Grants are not made towards loan repayments.

Applications

Apply on a form available to download from the charity's website or from the

correspondent. Applications should be made through a health visitor, social worker, housing officer or similar third party.

Hertfordshire Community Foundation

£27,000 (132 grants)

Correspondent: Grants Support Team, Foundation House, 2–4 Forum Place, Fiddlebridge Lane, Hatfield, Hertfordshire AL10 0RN (01707 251351; email: office@hertscf.org.uk; website: www.hertscf.org.uk)

CC number: 1156082

Eligibility

For the Hertfordshire Children's Fund: children below the age of 16 who are affected by disability or disadvantage and live in Hertfordshire. Applicants should check the foundation's website for details of eligibility criteria for other funds currently available.

Types of grants

For the Hertfordshire Children's Fund: one-off grants of up to £300 towards, for example, beds and bedding, baby equipment, white goods or specialised equipment for a child with a disability. Check the foundation's website for current guidelines, eligible items and amounts available.

The foundation manages a number of funds and applicants should check the website for other funds currently available.

Annual grant total

In 2016/17 the foundation held assets of almost £10.3 million and had an income of £1.1 million. During the year, 132 grants were made to individuals totalling £27,000, including:
- £14,200 through the Hertfordshire Children's Fund grants programme, supporting 68 families with an average grant of £209
- £11,300 through the Hertfordshire Healthy Homes grants programme, supporting 59 individuals with an average grant of £191

A further £390,000 was awarded to local organisations.

Exclusions

Grants are not given for: clothing or school uniform; holidays or school trips; carpeting or curtains; general furniture; gardening equipment; or debt repayment.

Applications

Apply to the Hertfordshire Children's Fund on a form available from the correspondent or to download from the website, where full guidelines are also provided. Applications can be made at

any time. They must be made through a recognised professional such as a social worker or health visitor.

Application details for other funds can be found on the website.

Other information

The foundation administers around 90 funds which provide grants to organisations and to individuals.

Hertfordshire Convalescent Trust

£19,800

Correspondent: Janet Bird, Grants Administrator, 140 North Road, Hertford SG14 2BZ (01992 505886)

CC number: 212423

Eligibility

People in need who are convalescing following an operation or period of ill health, chronically sick, terminally ill or children with special needs and their carers. Families suffering from domestic violence or relationship breakdown may also be eligible for assistance. Applicants must live in Hertfordshire.

Types of grants

One-off grants for respite breaks and holidays in hotels and caravans, or recuperative stays in a nursing home.

Annual grant total

In 2016 the trust held assets of £524,500 and had an income of £29,000. Grants totalled £19,800.

Exclusions

There are no grants available for equipment or transport costs.

Applications

Application forms are available from the correspondent. Applications should be sponsored by a health professional, social worker or member of the clergy. They are considered throughout the year.

Other information

The trustees' annual report for 2016 states that 'over 100 adults and children throughout the county of Hertfordshire were able to take a holiday due to receiving a grant from the Trust. Grants to each family or individual averaged between £450 and £500.'

Broxbourne

The Wormley Parochial Charity

£1,600

Correspondent: Carol Proctor, Trustee, 5 Lammasmead, Broxbourne, Hertfordshire EN10 6PF

CC number: 218463

Eligibility

People who are in need and live in the parish of Wormley as it was defined before 31 March 1935, particularly those who are older, sick or newly bereaved.

Types of grants

Support is given for/in the form of:

- Transport to or from hospital, either as a patient or visitor
- Food vouchers through local stores and utility bill donations
- Bereavement grants

Annual grant total

In 2016 the charity had an income of £13,300 and a total expenditure of £6,800. Grants are made to individuals and organisations for a range of purposes. We estimate that welfare grants to individuals totalled around £1,600.

Applications

Applications can be made in writing to the charity, either directly by the individual, or through a social worker, Citizens Advice, welfare agency or a third party such as a friend who is aware of the situation. Applications are considered in April and October.

Dacorum

The Dacorum Community Trust

£37,500

Correspondent: The Grants and Finance Officer, The Forum, Marlowes, Hemel Hempstead, Hertfordshire HP1 1DN (01442 253216; email: admin@dctrust.org.uk; website: www.dctrust.org.uk)

CC number: 272759

Eligibility

People in need who live in the borough of Dacorum.

Types of grants

The charity's website states:

> Dacorum Community Trust aims to help individuals, who through no fault of their own, are experiencing serious financial difficulties. We may be able to allocate small immediate grants (maximum £50) to help put the gas/electricity back on. We

may be able to supply you with a food voucher. We may be able to help you with household items and white goods. We may be able to help with baby clothing and nursery accessories. We are able to refer you to other agencies who may be able help you in your time of need.

Annual grant total

In 2016 the trust had assets of £122,500 and an income of £92,500. Grants to individuals totalled around £37,500.

Applications

Application forms are available to download from the trust's website.

Other information

This trust also gives to organisations.

East Hertfordshire

The Ware Charities

£12,500

Correspondent: Susan Newman, Correspondent, 3 Scotts Road, Ware, Hertfordshire SG12 9JG (01920 461629; email: suedogs@hotmail.com)

CC number: 225443

Eligibility

People in need who live in the area of Ware Town Council, the parish of Wareside and the parish of Thundridge.

Types of grants

Grants are made towards items or services not readily available from any other source. Awards are not paid to individuals directly, rather through a third party.

Annual grant total

In 2016/17 the charity had assets of £1.6 million and income of £72,000. Grants to individuals totalled £25,000 and we estimate that around £12,500 was given for welfare purposes.

Applications

Applications may be made in writing to the correspondent at any time. They should be submitted directly by the individual or a family member. Applications must include brief details of the applicant's income and savings and be supported and signed by a headteacher, GP, nurse, member of clergy or social worker.

Other information

Grants are also made to local organisations and individuals for educational needs.

North Hertfordshire

The Letchworth Civic Trust

£1,000

Correspondent: Sally Jenkins, Broadway Chambers, Letchworth Garden City, Hertfordshire SG6 3AD (01462 686919; email: letchworthct@gmail.com; website: letchworthct.org.uk)

CC number: 273336

Eligibility

People who have lived in Letchworth Garden City for two years or more.

Types of grants

Grants of up to £500 can be made for medical assistance, e.g. to provide mobility support, and for particular social needs such as rehabilitation.

Annual grant total

In 2015/16 the trust had assets of £820,000 and an income of £79,000. While we know that the trustees award grants other than for educational activities (there is a grant application form on the website for non-educational grants), it is not clear how much was awarded in the year for social welfare/other purposes. We have estimated that £1,000 was given in grants for social welfare needs.

Applications

Application forms are available to download from the trust's website. Be aware that there are separate forms for general financial needs and for medical assistance.

If applying for medical assistance or for a particular social need, the form must be completed by a relevant professional or social worker on behalf of the individual.

Applications should be returned by the beginning of January, March, June, September, October, and December, for consideration at the following trustees' meeting. Applications are not usually acknowledged before the trustees' meeting.

Other information

The charity's main object is to make grants to schoolchildren and higher education students to provide additional educational opportunities and equipment which would otherwise be unaffordable.

St Albans

The Harpenden Trust

£44,500 (609 grants)

Correspondent: Dennis Andrews, Secretary, The Trust Centre, 90 Southdown Road, Harpenden AL5 1PS (01582 460457; email: admin@ theharpendentrust.org.uk; website: www. theharpendentrust.org.uk)

CC number: 1118870

Eligibility

People in need who live in the AL5 postal district of Harpenden, with a preference for young and older people.

Types of grants

One-off grants are made to assist with household bills, as vouchers for food and clothing, and in the form of new and recycled furniture and white goods. Help can also be given to older people who have difficulty paying their winter utility bills (electricity, gas and water). Christmas parcels are delivered to older people who are housebound during the festive period.

Annual grant total

In 2016/17 the trust had assets of £5.1 million and had an income £626,000. Grants to individuals totalled £53,000, of which £8,500 was given in 59 grants to young people for what we consider to be educational purposes. They were distributed as follows:

General grants	402	£23,500
Utilities grants	82	£19,500
Youth grants	59	£8,500
Christmas parcels	125	£1,400

Exclusions

Grants are not given to individuals living outside Harpenden.

Applications

Apply in writing to the correspondent.

Other information

The Harpenden Trust was founded in 1948 by Dr Charles Hill. The trust organises outings, coffee morning, befriending and home visits for older people in the community.

Stevenage

The Stevenage Community Trust

£51,000

Correspondent: Caroline Haskins, Manager, Follett House, Primett Road, Stevenage SG1 3EE (01438 525390 or 07527 636469 (mobile); email: enquiries@stevenagecommunitytrust.org; website: stevenagecommunitytrust.org)

CC number: 1000762

Eligibility

People in need who live in Stevenage and the surrounding villages of Aston, Benington, Cromer, Datchworth, Graveley, Knebworth, Little Wymondley, Old Knebworth, Walkern, Watton-at-Stone, Weston, and Woolmer Green.

Types of grants

One-off grants according to need.

Annual grant total

In 2016/17 the trust had assets of £507,000 and an income of £132,000. We estimate that grants given to individuals totalled around £51,000.

Exclusions

Funding cannot be given retrospectively. The trust prefers not to fund medical treatment or the replacement of statutory funding.

Applications

Application forms and guidelines are available from the website and can be submitted at any time. All applications must be submitted by a relevant professional (e.g. a health professional, teacher, social worker or support worker) with knowledge of the beneficiary's situation.

Other information

The charity also makes grants to local organisations.

Watford

Watford Health Trust

£10,400 (18 grants)

Correspondent: D. I. Scleater, 23 Shepherds Road, Watford WD18 7HU (01923 222745; email: ian@ scleater.co.uk)

CC number: 214160

Eligibility

People in need who are in poor health, convalescent or who have a disability and live in the borough of Watford and the surrounding neighbourhood.

Types of grants

One-off and recurrent grants to assist recovery or improve quality of life.

Annual grant total

In 2015/16 the trust had assets of £1 million and an income of £28,000. During the year, the trust awarded £10,400 in 18 grant payments to individuals.

Applications

Applications should be made in writing to the correspondent.

Welwyn Hatfield

Wellfield Trust

£14,300

Correspondent: The Trust Manager, Birchwood Leisure Centre, Longmead, Hatfield, Hertfordshire AL10 0AN (01707 251018 (Monday to Friday, 9.30 am to 3 pm); email: wellfieldtrust@aol. com; website: www.wellfieldtrust.co.uk)

CC number: 296205

Eligibility

People in need who are on a low income and have lived in the parish of Hatfield for six months.

Types of grants

One-off grants, usually between £100 and £500, towards a range of welfare needs such as appliances, beds, clothing and carpets.

Annual grant total

In 2015/16 the trust had assets of £968,500 and an income of £66,100. Welfare grants to individuals totalled £14,300.

Exclusions

Applications are not normally considered from individuals who have received a grant from the trust within the last two years.

Applications

There is an application form available to download from the website, which must be completed by the individual or a member of the household in need and a sponsor. The sponsor should be somebody from an organisation who is familiar with the applicant's personal circumstances such as a social worker, health visitor, housing officer or warden. Applicants who cannot think of an appropriate sponsor should contact the trust for advice.

Unless the application is for household appliances or carpets, it needs to be accompanied by a shop-written estimate (a compliment slip with the details of the item will do). The trust also states this additional information on its website:

> If you are applying for a household appliance you just need to state the item you are in need of such a washing machine, fridge or cooker etc. and we will do the rest. If you are applying for carpet, the applicant needs to contact our supplier Colin Stuart of CCS Floorings Ltd (tel: 01727 822776) to arrange for any estimate. Only one type of carpet is considered and usually only for the main priority room.

The trust's committee meets on the second Tuesday of every month to consider applications which, to be considered at the next meeting, must be submitted by the first Monday of every month.

Other information

The trust also gives to organisations and has a room at a local leisure centre which can be hired free of charge to charitable organisations. It also runs the Scooter Loan Scheme, through which motorised scooters are loaned to residents of Hatfield, who would otherwise be virtually housebound, for as long as is required. The trust manager can be contacted for an initial discussion about the scheme.

Isle of Wight

The Broadlands Fund (Broadlands Home Trust)

£4,000

Correspondent: Mrs M. Groves, 2 Winchester Close, Newport, Isle of Wight PO30 1DR (01983 525630; email: broadlandstrust@btinternet.com)

CC number: 201433

Eligibility

Single women and widows who are over the age of 40, in need and live on the Isle of Wight.

Types of grants

Pensions of around £450 a year and Christmas boxes of between £50 and £100. General relief-in-need grants may occasionally be given.

Annual grant total

In 2015/16 the fund had an income of £11,100 and a total expenditure of £8,300. We estimate that welfare grants to individuals totalled around £4,000.

Exclusions

Grants are not made for married women or graduates.

Applications

Application forms are available from the correspondent and should be submitted either directly by the individual or a family member. Requests are considered quarterly in January, April, July and October. If you are applying by post, enclose an sae.

Other information

Educational support is also given to girls and young single women (under the age of 22) in need who are at school, starting work or are in further or higher education and are resident on the Isle of Wight.

Community Action Isle of Wight

£3,000

Correspondent: Helping Hands administrator, Riverside Centre, The Quay, Newport, Isle of Wight PO30 2QR (01983 524058; email: hello@actioniw.org.uk; website: www.communityactioniw.org.uk)

CC number: 1063737

Eligibility

People living on the Isle of Wight who are in need.

Types of grants

Small, one-off grants are made to assist people with a crisis or immediate need.

Annual grant total

In 2016/17 grants from the Helping Hands programme totalled around £3,000.

Applications

Applications must be made through a referring agent, such as a housing association or local charity.

Charity of Edgar Ralph Dore

£10,000

Correspondent: Anthony Bradshaw, Trustee, 62–66 Lugley Street, Newport, Isle of Wight PO30 5EU (01983 524431; email: ab@roachpittis.co.uk)

CC number: 255520

Eligibility

People in need on the Isle of Wight. Regular grants are available for people over the age of 60.

Types of grants

One-off and regular grants according to need.

Annual grant total

In 2016/17 the charity had an income of £16,500 and a total expenditure of £20,500. We estimate that grants given to individuals totalled £10,000. Grants are also awarded to animal welfare organisations.

Applications

Apply in writing to the correspondent.

Friends of the Animals
See entry on page 25

Greater Ryde Benevolent Trust

£8,900

Correspondent: Tricia Cotton, Correspondent, 40 Buckland Gardens, Ryde, Isle of Wight PO33 3AG (01983612913; email: cottontricia1956@gmail.com)

CC number: 249832

Eligibility

People who live in the former borough of Ryde (Isle of Wight) and are on low income and have health problems.

Types of grants

Small, one-off grants only.

Annual grant total

In 2016 the trust had an income of £7,800 and a total expenditure of £9,100. We estimate that the trust gave around £8,900 in grants to individuals.

Exclusions

Our research indicates that the trust is unable to provide recurrent grants.

Applications

Apply in writing to the correspondent.

Hollis Charity

£2,000

Correspondent: Mrs M. Groves, 2 Winchester Close, Newport PO30 1DR (01983 525630; email: cvhollistrust@btinternet.com)

CC number: 257875

Eligibility

Unmarried women and widows over the age of 40 who live on the Isle of Wight or in Hampshire.

Types of grants

One-off and recurrent grants are given according to need. Vocational grants are available for books, tools, fees and travelling expenses for young women.

Annual grant total

In 2016/17 the charity had an income of £5,800 and a total expenditure of £4,500. We estimate that grants for welfare purposes totalled £2,000, with a further £2,000 awarded to girls and young women undertaking vocational training.

Applications

Apply in writing to the correspondent.

Tom Woolgar

£1,300

Correspondent: Parish Clerk, Newport Parish Council, The Riverside Centre, The Quay, Newport PO30 2QR (01983 559119; email: clerk@newportwight.org.uk; website: www.newportwight.org.uk)

CC number: 204080

Eligibility

People in need aged 65 and over who live in the area of the former borough of Newport.

Types of grants

Winter fuel allowances.

Annual grant total

In 2016 the charity had an income of £1,400 and a total expenditure of £1,500. We estimate that grants given to individuals totalled around £1,300.

Applications

Apply in writing to the correspondent.

Kent

Headley-Pitt Charitable Trust

£22,000

Correspondent: Thelma Pitt, Old Mill Cottage, Ulley Road, Kennington, Ashford, Kent TN24 9HX (01233 626189; email: thelma.pitt@headley.co.uk)

CC number: 252023

Eligibility

Individuals in need who live in Kent, with a preference for those residing in Ashford. There is also a preference for older people.

Types of grants

One-off grants, usually in the range of £100 to £300.

Annual grant total

In 2015/16 the trust had assets of £2.4 million and an income of £76,000. A total of 122 grants were made to individuals, for both social welfare and educational purposes, totalling £43,500. We estimate that welfare grants to individuals amounted to £22,000.

An additional £35,000 was awarded in 165 grants to organisations.

Applications

Apply in writing to the correspondent, either directly by the individual or through a third party.

Other information

The trust also administers ten bungalows for the benefit of older people.

Kent Ambulance Service Benevolent Fund

£6,000

Correspondent: Stephen Bingham, Unit 1, Hall Avenue, Orbital Park, Sevington, Ashford, Kent TN24 0AA (01622 640401)

CC number: 1029472

Eligibility

Members of the Kent Ambulance Service who are in need.

Types of grants

One-off according to need.

Annual grant total

In 2015/16 the fund had an income of £3,600 and a total expenditure of £6,500. We estimate that grants given to individuals totalled around £6,000.

Applications

Apply in writing to the correspondent.

Kent Community Foundation

£44,000 (69 grants)

Correspondent: Grants Team, Evegate Park Barn, Evegate Business Park, Ashford, Kent TN25 6SX (01303 814500; email: admin@kentcf.org.uk; website: www.kentcf.org.uk)

CC number: 1084361

Eligibility

Individuals and families living in Kent or Medway who are financially disadvantaged. Each funding stream has its own specific eligibility criteria – see the foundation's website for more information.

Types of grants

The type of grant available depends on the fund being applied to. At the time of writing (January 2018) open funding streams provided for needs such as respite and short breaks for children with illnesses or disabilities, and holidays for adult carers, for example. See the website for details of funding streams currently accepting applications.

Annual grant total

In 2016/17 the foundation had assets of £22 million and an income of £7.66 million (of which £5.18 million was received from endowments). Grants were made totalling £1.52 million, of which individuals received £44,000.

The foundation's informative annual review, which can be found on the website, states that 69 individuals were helped during the year.

Exclusions

Support cannot be given for needs which are the responsibility of local or national statutory authorities.

Applications

In the first instance, see the website or contact the foundation for information on open funding streams, eligibility criteria and guidance on how to make an application. All applications must be made by a third party such as a charity employee, social worker, GP, occupational therapist or teacher.

Other information

The Kent Community Foundation administers a number of funding schemes for both organisations and individuals.

Kent Nursing Institution

£2,400

Correspondent: Canon Robert Stevenson, Trustee, Michaelmas Cottage, Stan Lane, West Peckham, Maidstone, Kent ME18 5JT (01622 817693)

CC number: 211227

Eligibility

People in need who are sick, convalescent or who have disabilities and live in west Kent.

Types of grants

One-off grants. Grants have been given to relieve hardship caused by family illness (for example, hospital visiting costs) and to assist with payments for specialist equipment to relieve discomfort (special beds, ultrasound matching, etc.).

Annual grant total

In 2016 the charity had an income of £4,800 and a total expenditure of £5,000. We have estimated that grants to individuals totalled £2,400, with local organisations also receiving funding.

Exclusions

The charity does not assist with debt or bankruptcy fees.

Applications

Apply in writing to the correspondent either directly by the individual or through a social worker, doctor, priest, Citizens Advice or other welfare agency. Applications are usually considered in March and October.

Littledown Trust

£5,500

Correspondent: Paul Brown, Trustee, Littledown Farmhouse, Lamberhurst Down, Lamberhurst, Tunbridge Wells TN3 8HD (01892 890867; email: paul.g.brown@btinternet.com)

CC number: 1064291

Eligibility

People in need, with a preference for older people and children and adults who are disadvantaged or who have disabilities who live in Kent or Devon.

Types of grants

Our previous research indicates that the trust awards one-off and recurrent grants according to need.

Annual grant total

In 2015/16 the trust had an income of £8,200 and a total expenditure of £8,200. We estimate that grants given to individuals totalled £4,000, with funding also awarded to organisations in Devon and Kent.

Applications

Apply in writing to the correspondent, or through Citizens Advice, a social worker or another relevant third party.

Other information

At the time of writing (August 2017) the trust did not have a website or accounts available.

Sir Thomas Smythe's Poor Fund (Skinners' Company)

£12,100

Correspondent: Grants Administrator, The Skinners' Company, Skinners' Hall, 8 Dowgate Hill, London EC4R 2SP (020 7213 0562; email: charitiesadmin@ skinners.org.uk; website: www. skinnershall.co.uk)

CC number: 210775

Eligibility

People in need who live within 26 parishes in Kent and London. Applicants must live in their own home, either as a tenant or an owner-occupier. Most beneficiaries are in receipt of a combination of benefits, disability allowances or state retirement pension, but each case will be examined individually.

A list of the eligible parishes can be found on the charity's website.

Types of grants

Pensions (£740 per annum in 2016/17) are distributed personally by a trustee and are reviewed every April. One-off

crisis grants (not exceeding £250) are typically made for items not covered by benefits, e.g. unexpected household repairs, the replacement of domestic appliances, or travel costs to and from hospital.

Annual grant total

In 2016/17 the charity had assets of £1.5 million and an income of £27,500. Grants to individuals totalled £12,100. Funding is also available to local social welfare organisations.

Applications

Applications must be made through agencies such as social and support services, housing associations, refuge and rehabilitation organisations, and local charities. Contact the Grants Administrator for an application form.

Ashford

Godmersham Relief in Need Charity

£1,500

Correspondent: David Swan, Fele Berge, Canterbury Road, Bilting, Ashford TN25 4HE (01233 812125)

CC number: 206278

Eligibility

People in need who live in the ancient parish of Godmersham in Kent.

Types of grants

One-off grants are given according to need.

Annual grant total

In 2015 the charity had an income of £7,000 and a total expenditure of £6,000 Grants are made to individuals and organisations for a wide range of purposes. We estimate that welfare grants to individuals totalled £1,500.

Applications

The individual or a third party can apply to the correspondent in writing.

The Thanet Charities

£5,000

Correspondent: Patricia Guy, Correspondent, Garden House, Bethersden Road, Hothfield, Ashford, Kent TN26 1EP (01233 612449)

CC number: 213093

Eligibility

People in need who live in the parish of Hothfield.

Types of grants

Small monthly payments to older residents of Hothfield village. There are

also a limited number of hardship grants available for individuals in need. These come in the form of one-off monetary payments or through the provision of services/facilities.

Annual grant total

In 2015/16 the charity had an income of £6,200 and a total expenditure of £5,600. We estimate that grants given to individuals for welfare purposes totalled around £5,000.

Applications

Apply in writing to the correspondent.

Other information

At the time of writing (August 2017) the charity had no website or accounts available.

City of Canterbury

The Canterbury United Municipal Charities

£4,500

Correspondent: Aaron Spencer, Furley Page, Solicitors, 39 St Margaret's Street, Canterbury, Kent CT1 2TX (01227 863140; email: aas@furleypage.co.uk)

CC number: 210992

Eligibility

People in need who have lived within the boundaries of what was the old city of Canterbury for at least two years.

Types of grants

One-off and ongoing grants and pensions are given. Food and clothing vouchers are also distributed at Christmas.

Annual grant total

In 2016 the charity had an income of £8,500 and a total expenditure of £9,900. We estimate that welfare grants to individuals totalled £4,500.

Applications

Applications can be made in writing to the correspondent through the individual's school/college/educational welfare agency or directly by the individual. Applications are considered on an ongoing basis and should include a brief statement of circumstances and proof of residence in the area.

The Lord Mayor of Canterbury's Christmas Gift Fund

£14,400

Correspondent: Jennifer Sherwood, Administrator, MHA MacIntyre Hudson, 31 St George's Place, Canterbury, Kent CT1 1XD (01227 464991; email: christmasgiftfund@gmail.com; website: www.christmasgiftfund.co.uk/about.php)

CC number: 278803

Eligibility
People in need who live in Canterbury and the surrounding area comprised in the former district of Bridge Blean. Preference is given to older people and to families with young children.

Types of grants
Food parcels and toy vouchers are distributed before Christmas.

Annual grant total
In 2015/16 the fund had an income of £17,200 and a total expenditure of £14,600. We estimate that the fund gave around £14,400 in grants to individuals, including 500 grocery parcels.

Applications
Direct applications should be made in writing to the correspondent. Gifts are delivered in person by volunteers.

Other information
The fund's website describes how it 'was set up 60 years ago by members of the business community, who approached the then Mayor, suggesting that they might launch an appeal to give parcels to the elderly and needy at Christmas time. In that first year the appeal raised between £200 and £300.'

Fordwich United Charities

£4,000

Correspondent: Dr Roger Green, Trustee, 15 Water Meadows, Fordwich, Canterbury, Kent CT2 0BF (01227 713661 or 07981 491654; email: rogergreen@fordwich.net)

CC number: 208258

Eligibility
People in need or with disabilities living in Fordwich.

Types of grants
One-off grants are mostly given towards household bills and 'coal grants'.

Annual grant total
In 2016 the charity had an income of £20,500 and a total expenditure of £19,400. We estimate that grants

awarded to individuals for welfare purposes totalled around £4,000.

Applications
Applications may be made in writing to correspondent. The deadline for applications is normally 1 September and a decision should be made within a month.

Other information
The charity gives to individuals and organisations for both educational and social welfare purposes. It also maintains its properties, particularly the Town Hall.

Streynsham's Charity

£26,500

Correspondent: The Clerk to the Trustees, PO Box 970, Canterbury, Kent CT1 9DJ (0845 094 4769)

CC number: 214436

Eligibility
People who live in the ancient parish of St Dunstan's in Canterbury.

Types of grants
One-off grants, up to a maximum of about £300.

Annual grant total
In 2015 the charity had assets of £94,000 and an income of £75,500. Welfare grants to individuals totalled £26,500.

Applications
Apply in writing to the correspondent. Applications should be made directly by the individual. They are usually considered in March and October but can be made at any time and should include an sae and telephone number if applicable.

Whitstable Non-Ecclesiastical Charities

£26,500

Correspondent: Garry Wootton, Furley Page LLP, 52–54 High Street, Whitstable CT5 1BG (01227 863179; email: gsw@furleypage.co.uk)

CC number: 248134

Eligibility
Residents of Whitstable who are in need.

Types of grants
One-off and recurring grants according to need.

Annual grant total
In 2016 the charity had assets of £3.3 million and an income of £130,000. Grants to individuals totalled £26,500.

Applications
Apply in writing to the correspondent.

Dartford

Wilmington Parochial Charity

£2,300

Correspondent: Regina Skinner, Correspondent, 101 Birchwood Road, Dartford DA2 7HQ (01322 662342)

CC number: 1011708

Eligibility
People in need who live in the parish of Wilmington.

Types of grants
In the past, grants have been made for groceries, heating and Christmas grants.

Annual grant total
In 2015/16 the charity had an income of £13,100 and a total expenditure of £9,600. The charity's record on the Charity Commission's website states that about 15% to 17% of its expenditure is given for educational purposes. We estimate that about £2,300 was given for welfare needs to individuals.

Applications
Applications should be submitted by the individual or through a social worker, Citizens Advice or other welfare agency. The trustees meet in February and November. Urgent applications can be considered between meetings in exceptional circumstances.

Other information
Grants are also given to local schools at Christmas and to individuals for educational purposes.

Dover

The Casselden Trust

£1,000

Correspondent: Leslie Alton, Administrator, 26 The Shrubbery, Walmer, Deal, Kent CT14 7PZ (01304 375499)

CC number: 281970

Eligibility
People in need who live in the Dover Town Council area.

Types of grants
One-off and recurrent grants, up to a maximum of £250.

Annual grant total

Grants usually total around £2,000 each year, split between educational and social welfare purposes.

Applications

Apply in writing to the correspondent.

The R. V. Coleman Trust

£58,000 (93 grants)

Correspondent: Glynis Farthing, 3 Church Farm Mews, East Langdon, Dover CT15 5FE (01304 851878; email: colemantrustclerk@btinternet.com)

CC number: 237708

Eligibility

People who live in Dover and the immediate neighbourhood and are sick, convalescing, or living with a mental or physical disability.

Types of grants

One-off grants according to need. In the past, grants have been given for periods in residential care and nursing homes, disability aids, telephone facilities and convalescent holiday breaks.

Annual grant total

In 2016 the trust had assets of £1.2 million and an income of £67,000. The total amount awarded in grants was £58,000.

Exclusions

No grants are given for furniture, home repairs or debts.

Applications

Applications should be made in writing by a professional or social worker, such as a GP or Citizens Advice, who has knowledge of the applicant's circumstances.

Gravesham

William Frank Pinn Charitable Trust

£144,500 (1,454 grants)

Correspondent: Trust Officer, HSBC Trust Company (UK) Ltd, 10th Floor Norwich House, Nelson Gate, Commercial Road, Southampton SO15 1GX (023 8072 2224)

CC number: 287772

Eligibility

People of pensionable age who live in the borough of Gravesham. Priority is given to those on lower incomes.

Types of grants

One-off grants averaging £100 are made for specific purposes only, mainly for household expenses and clothing.

Annual grant total

In 2015/16 the charity held assets of £7.8 million and had an income of £288,500. During the year, the charity gave around £144,500 in grants to 1,454 individuals.

Exclusions

No more than two grants may be made to any household per calendar year.

Applications

Application forms are available from the correspondent. Applications should be submitted directly by the individual and are considered as received.

Other information

This trust was formed from the estate of Mr William Frank Pinn who died on 18 June 1983.

Maidstone

Edmett and Fisher Charity

£10,500

Correspondent: Robin Rogers, 72 King Street, Maidstone, Kent ME14 1BL (01622 698000)

CC number: 241823

Eligibility

People in need who are aged over 60 and live in the former borough of Maidstone (as it was before April 1974).

Types of grants

One-off and recurrent grants are given according to need. Christmas gifts have also been distributed in previous years.

Annual grant total

In 2015/16 the charity had an income of £9,500 and a total expenditure of £11,000. We estimate that grants to individuals totalled £10,500.

Applications

Application forms can be requested from the correspondent.

Medway

Cliffe and Cliffe Woods Community Trust

£2,500

Correspondent: Paul Kingman, 52 Reed Street, Cliffe, Rochester ME3 7UL (01634 220422; email: paul.kingman@ btopenworld.com)

CC number: 220855

Eligibility

People in need who live in the ancient parish of Cliffe-at-Hoo.

Types of grants

One-off grants according to need; for example, grants towards household bills and nursing fees.

Annual grant total

In 2016/17 the trust had an income of £9,000 and a total expenditure of £5,000. We estimate that grants given to individuals totalled around £2,500.

Applications

Apply in writing to the correspondent. Applications can be submitted directly by the individual or a family member, or through a third party such as a social worker or Citizens Advice.

Other information

The charity also provides grants to individuals for educational purposes.

The Dobson Trust

£1,900

Correspondent: Margaret Taylor, Resources, Medway Council, Gun Wharf, Dock Road, Chatham, Kent ME4 4TR (01634 332144; email: margaret.taylor@ medway.gov.uk)

CC number: 283158

Eligibility

People in receipt of a state pension or over the age of 60 who are in financial need and live in the former borough of Gillingham.

Types of grants

One-off grants according to need.

Annual grant total

In 2016/17 the trust had an income of £1,600 and a total expenditure of £4,000. We estimate that the trust gave around £1,900 in grants to individuals for welfare purposes.

Applications

Application forms are available from the correspondent. Applications can be submitted at any time and the trustees meet about four times a year.

Richard Watts and The City of Rochester Almshouse Charities

£62,000

Correspondent: Jane Rose, Clerk and Chief Officer, Administrative Offices, Watts Almshouses, Maidstone Road, Rochester, Kent ME1 1SE (01634 842194; fax: 01634 409348; email: admin@richardwatts.org.uk; website: www.richardwatts.org.uk)

CC number: 212828

Eligibility

People in need who live in the city of Rochester and urban Strood.

Types of grants

The charity can fund essential items such as clothing, cookers and fridges for people of any age group living within the area of the charity who meet the charity's financial criteria. Grants may also be available for specialist equipment. Payments of £15 per week are available to retired applicants.

Annual grant total

In 2016 the charity had assets of £25.5 million and an income of £1.3 million. We estimate that one-off grants to individuals totalled around £9,200. During the year, pensions totalled £53,000.

Applications

Application forms are available to download from the charity's website.

Other information

This charity was founded in 1579 and, aside from making grants, also runs almshouses. There are four main sites: Maidstone Road; Reeves House in Watts Avenue; St Catherine's at the top of Star Hill; and Haywards House in Corporation Street.

The charity also offers a subsidised home help service for people who are in need of domestic help and a lawn cutting service.

Sevenoaks

Kate Drummond Trust

£1,500

Correspondent: Robin Lochhead, Trustee, 25 Bankside, Dunton Green, Sevenoaks, Kent TN13 2UA (07713 412333; email: kdtrustees@gmail.com)

CC number: 246830

Eligibility

People in need who live in Sevenoaks urban district and neighbourhood, with preference given older people and young girls.

Types of grants

The majority of grants are one-off and given according to need.

Annual grant total

In 2015/16 the trust had an income of £8,800 and a total expenditure of £6,500. We estimate that grants given to individuals for social welfare purposes totalled around £1,500.

Applications

Applications may be made in writing to the correspondent. Include an sae if a reply is required.

Other information

The trust owns and operates a residential house offering either rent-free or subsidised accommodation. Grant-making is available when there is surplus money. It can also give grants to organisations and for educational purposes.

Leigh United Charities

£31,000

Correspondent: Sally Bresnahan, Correspondent, 3 Oak Cottages, High Street, Leigh, Tonbridge TN11 8RW (01732 838544; email: sally@bresnahan.co.uk)

CC number: 233988

Eligibility

People in need who live in the parish of Leigh or Hildenborough.

Types of grants

Regular monthly grants towards the costs of heating and food, annual Christmas grants, and one-off grants for exceptional circumstances such as funeral expenses.

Annual grant total

In 2016/17 the charity held assets of £256,500 and had an income of £53,000. Grants to individuals in Leigh totalled £25,000 with a further £5,800 awarded to individuals in Hildenborough.

Monthly grants were made to 50 beneficiaries and annual Christmas grants to 56 beneficiaries. One-off grants were awarded to six beneficiaries.

Applications

The individual should apply directly to the correspondent in writing. Applications are considered throughout the year.

The Dorothy Parrott Trust Fund

£2,600

Correspondent: Gina Short, 10 The Landway, Kemsing, Sevenoaks TN15 6TG (01732 760263)

CC number: 278904

Eligibility

People in need who live in the area administered by Sevenoaks Town Council and the adjoining parishes (the TN13, TN14 and TN15 postcode areas). Preference is given to young children and older people.

Types of grants

Our previous research indicates that the trust usually awards one-off grants ranging from £25 to £100 according to need. Previous grants have been given towards a fridge, a school outing for the child of a single parent, house decoration, boots, ballet shoes, a mattress for twins and project trips such as Operation Raleigh.

Annual grant total

In 2015 the trust had an income of £18,000 and a total expenditure of £5,400. We estimate the amount awarded in grants to individuals for welfare purposes to be around £2,600, with funding also awarded to organisations.

Applications

Applications can be submitted either directly to the correspondent by the individual or through a social worker, Citizens Advice or similar third party, including a general history of the family. Applications are considered on the last Monday of January, April, July and October.

Other information

At the time of writing (August 2017) the trust had no website or accounts available.

Shepway

Folkestone Municipal Charity

£87,500

Correspondent: Michael Cox, Romney House, Cliff Road, Hythe CT21 5XA (01303 260144; email: gillyjc@btinternet.com)

CC number: 211528

Eligibility

People in need who live in the borough of Folkestone and have done so for at least five years. Preference is usually given to older people and single-parent families.

Types of grants
Pensions and one-off relief-in-need grants. Previous grants have been given for telephone installation, help after a burglary, loss of a purse/wallet, shoes for disadvantaged children, gas/electricity bills, beds/bedding, prams, clothing and household repairs. Relief-in-need payments, whenever possible, are made directly to the supplier.

Annual grant total
In 2016/17 the charity held assets of £3.56 million and had an income of £112,500. Grants and pensions totalled £87,500, with £63,500 given towards pensions and £24,000 for welfare.

Other charitable causes received a further £11,400 in grants and donations.

Applications
Application forms are available from the correspondent. Applications should be submitted through a third party such as a social worker, Citizens Advice or similar welfare agency. They are considered on a monthly basis, although urgent requests can be dealt with between meetings.

Anne Peirson Charitable Trust

£4,000

Correspondent: Ina Tomkinson, Trustee, Tyrol House, Cannongate Road, Hythe, Kent CT21 5PX (01303 260779; fax: 01303 238660)

CC number: 800093

Eligibility
People who live in the parish of Hythe and are in need due to, for example, hardship, disability or sickness. Our research suggests that support is primarily given for educational needs but grants for emergency needs will be made if financial hardship is demonstrated.

Types of grants
One-off grants ranging from £100 to £600. Grants have been made towards for example, nursery school fees, special needs for people with children who have disabilities, and household goods.

Annual grant total
In 2016 the trust had an income of £15,000 and a total expenditure of £17,300. We estimate that the amount given to individuals for social welfare purposes totalled around £4,000.

Exclusions
Grants are not made where statutory support is available.

Applications
Applications should be made in writing to the correspondent through Citizens Advice, a social worker, health visitor, school headteacher or other appropriate third party. Grants are considered at quarterly meetings of the trustees, but emergency applications can be considered in the interim.

Other information
Grants are awarded to individuals and organisations for both educational and social welfare purposes.

Swale
Almsland Charities and Others

£4,000

Correspondent: Mr Creed, 45C The Street, Boughton-Under-Blean, Faversham ME13 9BA (01227 750747; email: jeanburrows@jeanius.me.uk)

CC number: 213399

Eligibility
People in need living in the parish of Boughton under Blean.

Types of grants
One-off according to need.

Annual grant total
In 2016/17 the charity had an income of £6,900 and a total expenditure of £4,800. We estimate that grants given to individuals totalled around £4,000.

Applications
Apply in writing to the correspondent.

The William Barrow's Charity

£62,000

Correspondent: Stuart Mair, 43 Park Road, Sittingbourne, Kent ME10 1DY (01795 470556; email: stuart@ georgewebbfinn.com; website: www. thewilliambarrowscharity.org.uk)

CC number: 307574

Eligibility
People in need who live in the ancient ecclesiastical parish of Borden, Kent. Priority is given to people over the age of 60.

Types of grants
One-off grants and twice-yearly allowances may be given for pensions, disability and medical equipment, travel expenses and convalescence.

Annual grant total
In 2016 the charity had assets of £7.7 million and an income of £245,500. Grants to individuals totalled £62,000 and were broken down as follows:

Grants to pensioners	£32,000
Grants to students	£28,500
Other	£1,000

Applications
Applications can be made through the charity's website.

Thanet
Margate and Dr Peete's Charity

£6,200

Correspondent: Dorothy Collins, 31 Avenue Gardens, Cliftonville, Margate CT9 3AZ (01843 226173; email: dorothy_collins@talktalk.net)

CC number: 212503

Eligibility
People in need who live in the former borough of Margate (as constituted before 1974).

Types of grants
Small, one-off and recurrent grants.

Annual grant total
In 2015/16 the charity had an income of £8,400 and a total expenditure of £6,500. We estimate that grants given to individuals totalled around £6,200.

Applications
Application forms are available from the correspondent. Applications should be submitted either directly by the individual or, where applicable, through a social worker, Citizens Advice or other welfare agency.

Other information
The charity was established in 1907 following the death of Dr Thomas Peete, who left his entire estate – a total of £50,000 – to the Margate Philanthropic Institution. Since then, the charity has supported many of Margate's neediest residents.

Tonbridge and Malling

Leigh United Charities
See entry on page 362

Tunbridge Wells

Miss Ethel Mary Fletcher's Charitable Bequest

£6,000

Correspondent: Trust Administrator, Thomson, Snell & Passmore, Ref 1295, 3 Lonsdale Gardens, Tunbridge Wells TN1 1NU (01892 510000)

CC number: 219850

Eligibility
Older people in need who live in the Tunbridge Wells area.

Types of grants
The charity provides pensions and grants for clothing, fuel, medical treatment, food, and other items that provide comfort.

Annual grant total
In 2015/16 the charity had an income of £10,000 and a total expenditure of £18,500. We estimate that the charity awarded around £6,000 in grants to individuals during the year.

Applications
Applications should be made in writing to the correspondent.

Other information
The charity also makes grants towards improving access to education, and to other charitable organisations.

Oxfordshire

The Berkshire Nurses and Relief-in-Sickness Trust
See entry on page 336

The J. I. Colvile Charitable Trust
See entry on page 400

Ducklington and Hardwick with Yelford Charity

£750

Correspondent: Gillian Caton, 10 Lovell Close, Ducklington, Witney OX29 7YQ (01993 702261)

CC number: 237343

Eligibility
People in need or hardship who live in the villages of Ducklington and Hardwick with Yelford.

Types of grants
One-off grants of up to £200 can be given towards heating, transport costs, assistance with playgroup fees, furniture, funeral expenses, conversion of rooms for people who are older or have disabilities, provision of telephones, spectacles, school holiday assistance, help with rent arrears and other needs.

Annual grant total
In 2016 the charity had an income of £3,600 and a total expenditure of £3,100. We estimate that grants given to individuals for social welfare purposes totalled around £750.

Applications
Applications may be made in writing to the correspondent. The trustees normally meet in March and November but applications can be submitted at any time.

Other information
Grants are also made to organisations, clubs and schools. Support is also given for educational needs.

Ellen Rebe Spalding Memorial Fund

£2,000

Correspondent: Tessa Rodgers, Secretary, c/o The Spalding Trust, PO Box 85, Stowmarket IP14 3NY (website: www.spaldingtrust.org.uk)

CC number: 209066–1

Eligibility
Disadvantaged women, mothers, and children who live in Oxfordshire.

Types of grants
Small, one-off grants to help disadvantaged women and children. The majority of grants are used to pay for practical aids at home, and medical care and equipment.

Annual grant total
This fund is administered by The Spalding Trust. Previous research

indicates there is around £2,000 per year awarded in grants.

Applications
Applications should be made in writing to the Secretary.

Other information
The Ellen Rebe Spalding Memorial Fund is a linked charity to the larger Spalding Trusts. While a small amount is given in welfare grants through the Ellen Rebe fund, the majority of the Spalding Trusts' funds are spent on grants for the study of religion.

The Peter Ward Charitable Trust

£17,800

Correspondent: A. J. Carter & Co., 22B High Street, Witney, Oxfordshire OX28 6RB (01993 703414; email: ajc@ ajcarter.com)

CC number: 258403

Eligibility
People in need who live in Oxfordshire.

Types of grants
One-off and recurrent grants are given according to need.

Annual grant total
In 2015/16 the charity had an income of £6,700 and a total expenditure of £35,800. We estimate that the charity awarded around £17,800 in grants to individuals. The charity also awards grants to organisations.

Applications
Apply in writing to the correspondent although unsolicited applications are not encouraged.

Other information
At the time of writing (August 2017) the charity had no website or accounts available.

Whitton's Wishes (The Kathryn Turner Trust)

£10,000

Correspondent: Kathryn Turner, Founder and Trustee, Unit 3, Suffolk Way, Abingdon, Oxfordshire OX14 5JX (01235 527310; email: kathrynturnertrust@hotmail.co.uk)

CC number: 1111250

Eligibility
Children, young people, older people and people with disabilities/special needs in Oxfordshire. Grants can also be made for relieving the need, suffering and distress of members and former members of the services, their wives,

husbands, widows, widowers and dependants.

Types of grants

Grants towards the costs of equipment and other support.

Annual grant total

In 2015 the trust held assets of £7,500 and had an income of £178,500. Grants totalled £40,000 and we have estimated that £10,000 was awarded to individuals for welfare purposes.

Applications

Apply in writing to the correspondent.

Other information

The trust's registered name is The Kathryn Turner Trust and it also makes grants to organisations.

Cherwell

The Banbury Charities

£37,000

Correspondent: Nigel Yeadon, Clerk, 36 West Bar, Banbury OX16 9RU (01295 251234)

CC number: 201418

Eligibility

People in need who live within the former borough of Banbury.

Types of grants

One-off and recurrent grants towards living costs, household essentials and appliances, bedding, fuel and domestic help.

Annual grant total

In 2016 the charity had assets of £5.9 million and an income of £414,500. During the year, there were 236 grants made to individuals, totalling £74,000. We estimate that grants given to individuals for welfare purposes totalled around £37,000.

Applications

Apply in writing to the correspondent. Applicants are encouraged to obtain a letter of support from their social worker, carer or other person in authority to give credence to their application.

Other information

Banbury Charities is a group of eight registered charities. These are as follows: Bridge Estate Charity; Countess of Arran's Charity; Banbury Arts and Educational Charity; Banbury Almshouses Charity; Banbury Sick Poor Fund; Banbury Welfare Trust; Banbury Poor Trust; and Banbury Recreation Charity.

The Bletchington Charity

£1,000

Correspondent: Sue Green, Bletchingon Village Hall, Whitemarsh Way, Bletchington, Kidlington OX5 3FD (01869 350895; email: sue@sueg.co.uk)

CC number: 201584

Eligibility

People in need who live in the parish of Bletchington, in particular people who are older or infirm.

Types of grants

Grants to people who are older and infirm at Christmas and Easter towards fuel bills and other needs. Help is given for travel, chiropody and television licences. Also, one-off grants for social welfare, education and relief-in-sickness according to need.

Annual grant total

In 2016 the charity had an income of £11,000 and a total expenditure of £17,300. Grants are made to individuals and organisations for both educational and social welfare purposes. We estimate that welfare grants to individuals totalled £1,000.

Applications

Grants are generally made as the trustees see a need, but applications can be made in writing to the correspondent by the individual or by a social worker, doctor or welfare agency.

Other information

The charity seeks to support any educational, medical and social needs that will benefit the village community as a whole.

Fuel Allotment

£1,500

Correspondent: Mrs E. Cumberland, 9 Katrine Place, Bletchley, Milton Keynes MK2 3DW

CC number: 251127

Eligibility

Residents of Water Eaton who are in need.

Types of grants

One-off grants according to need.

Annual grant total

In 2015/16 the charity had an income of £2,500 and a total expenditure of £1,600. We estimate that grants given to individuals totalled around £1,500.

Applications

Apply in writing to the correspondent.

The Souldern United Charities

£1,500

Correspondent: Carolyn Couzens, Trustee, 2 Cotswold Court, Souldern, Bicester, Oxfordshire OX27 7LQ (01869 346694; email: caroldavidinsouldern@ btinternet.com)

CC number: 1002942

Eligibility

People in need who live in the parish of Souldern in Oxfordshire.

Types of grants

One-off and recurrent grants are given according to need.

Annual grant total

In 2015/16 the charity had an income of £11,000 and a total expenditure of £6,800. We estimate that welfare grants to individuals totalled around £1,500, with funding also awarded to organisations.

Applications

Apply in writing to the correspondent.

Other information

The charity also provides housing.

The Town Estate Charity

£11,500

Correspondent: Peter Morgan, Pond Cottage, Sibford Gower, Banbury OX15 5RT (01295 788207)

CC number: 253440

Eligibility

People who are in need and live in the civil parish of Sibford Gower.

Types of grants

One-off and ongoing grants.

Annual grant total

In 2016 the charity had an income of £34,000 and a total expenditure of £39,000. The charity awarded £4,500 in grants for relief in need, and £7,000 in grants for general benefit.

Applications

Applications should be made in writing to the correspondent, detailing financial need and what the grant will be used for.

Other information

The charity also makes an annual award of Sibford Gower Primary School.

City of Oxford

The City of Oxford Charity

£80,500 (243 grants)

Correspondent: David Wright, The Office, Stones Court, St Clements, Oxford OX14 1AP (01865 553043; email: enquiries@oxfordcitycharities.fsnet.co.uk; website: www.oxfordcitycharities.org)

CC number: 239151

Eligibility

People who have lived in the city of Oxford for at least three years who are in need and hardship. Our research indicates that priority is given to children and people who are older, have disabilities or a medical condition.

Types of grants

The charity can offer one-off relief in need grants, generally of up to £600, towards various welfare needs, such as furniture to people moving home, household appliances, washing machines, recuperation holidays for people with disabilities or medical problems and/or their carers, baby equipment, wheelchairs and mobility scooters and so on. Support is also available towards the payment of bankruptcy court fees.

Annual grant total

In 2016 the charity had assets of £6.2 million and an income of £418,000. Welfare grants to individuals totalled £80,500.

Applications

Application forms can be downloaded from the charity's website or requested from the correspondent. They can be submitted through welfare services/other organisations or by individuals directly. All applications have to be supported by a letter from a social worker/health visitor/similar professional commenting on the circumstances of the family and the need for a grant. The trustees meet every six weeks to consider applications. Candidates are required to specify exactly what the money is for and the costs involved, as applications without exact costings will be delayed.

Other information

The charity is an amalgamation of a number of charities working for the benefit of the people of Oxford city. It also gives grants to organisations, can support local schools, assists individuals for educational needs, and maintains almshouses in the local area.

South Oxfordshire

The John Hodges Charitable Trust

£2,900

Correspondent: Julie Griffin, 3 Berkshire Road, Henley-on-Thames RG9 1ND (01491 572621; email: juliegriffin2004@googlemail.com)

CC number: 304313

Eligibility

People in need living in the parish of St Mary the Virgin, Henley-on-Thames and the surrounding area.

Types of grants

One-off and recurrent grants towards, for example, white goods, carpets and flooring, clothing, mobility aids, bankruptcy fees and heating bills.

Annual grant total

In 2016/17 the trust had an income of £12,000 and a total expenditure of £6,000. We estimate that grants given to individuals totalled £2,900, with funding also awarded to organisations.

Applications

Apply in writing to the correspondent.

Tetsworth Cozens Bequest

£1,200

Correspondent: Dr John Stephen Lingard, Trustee, 12 The Mount, Tetsworth, Thame OX9 7AF (01844 281749; email: steve.lingard@vorticity-systems.com)

CC number: 204368

Eligibility

People need who live in the parishes of Tetsworth, Thame, Great Haseley, Stoke Talmage, Wheatfield, Adwell, South Weston, Lewknor and Aston Rowant.

Types of grants

One-off grants according to need.

Annual grant total

In 2015/16 the charity had an income of £5,900 and a total expenditure of £5,200. We estimate that grants given to individuals for welfare purposes totalled around £1,200.

Applications

Apply in writing to the correspondent.

Other information

The charity is registered under the name The Cozens Bequest and can make grants to individuals and organisations for a range of charitable purposes.

Thame Charities (The Thame Welfare Trust)

£10,000

Correspondent: John Gadd, 2 Cromwell Avenue, Thame, Oxfordshire OX9 3TD (01844 212564; email: johngadd4@gmail.com)

CC number: 241914

Eligibility

People in need who live in Thame and the immediately adjoining villages.

Types of grants

One-off grants of up to £1,000, where help cannot be received from statutory organisations. In the past, grants have been given towards a single parent's mortgage repayments and a wheelchair for a person who has disabilities.

Annual grant total

In 2016/17 the charity had an income of £15,000 and a total expenditure of £20,000. We estimate that grants given to individuals totalled around £10,000.

Applications

Apply in writing to the correspondent.

Other information

The charity also makes educational grants to residents of Thame.

Wallingford Relief in Need Charity

£2,500

Correspondent: Jamie Baskeyfield, Correspondent, Wallingford Town Council, 9 St Martin's Street, Wallingford, Oxfordshire OX10 0AL (01491 835373; email: queries@wallingfordtc.co.uk)

CC number: 292000

Eligibility

People in need who live in Wallingford and the neighbourhood (including the former parish of Clapcot).

Types of grants

One-off grants for necessities, including the payment of bills, clothing and shoes, cookers, fridges and so on. Payments are made to local suppliers; cash grants are not made directly to the individual.

Annual grant total

In 2015/16 the charity had an income of £8,700 and a total expenditure of £10,300. We estimate that grants for welfare purposes totalled around £2,500.

Applications

Application forms are form available from the correspondent. They should be submitted either directly by the individual or through a local organisation. The trustees meet about every three months, although emergency cases can be considered between the meetings. Urgent cases may require a visit by a trustee.

Other information

The charity also gives grants for educational purposes; however, the majority of grants are given for relief in need.

The Wheatley Charities

£3,500

Correspondent: R. F. Minty, Trustee, 24 Old London Road, Wheatley, Oxford OX33 1YW (01865 874676)

CC number: 203535

Eligibility

Residents of Wheatley, Oxford who are in need.

Types of grants

One-off and ongoing grants are given according to need.

Annual grant total

In 2016 the charity had an income of £4,300 and a total expenditure of £7,000. Grants are made to individuals and organisations for social welfare and educational purposes. We estimate that social welfare grants to individuals totalled £3,500.

Applications

Apply in writing to the correspondent.

Vale of White Horse

The Appleton Trust (Abingdon)

£2,200

Correspondent: David Dymock, 73 Eaton Road, Appleton, Abingdon, Oxfordshire OX13 5JJ (01865 863709; email: appleton.trust@yahoo.co.uk)

CC number: 201552

Eligibility

People who live in Appleton with Eaton and are in need or suffer from sickness, disability or other hardship.

Types of grants

One-off and recurrent grants.

Annual grant total

In 2015 the trust had an income of £5,000 and a total expenditure of £4,800. We have estimated that grants to individuals for welfare purposes totalled £2,200.

Applications

Apply in writing to the correspondent. Applications can be made either directly by the individual or through an appropriate third party.

Other information

Grants are also given to local organisations and for educational purposes to former pupils of Appleton Primary School.

The Faringdon United Charities

£2,500

Correspondent: Vivienne Checkley, Bunting & Co., Faringdon Business Centre, Brunel House, Volunteer Way, Faringdon, Oxfordshire SN7 7YR (01367 243789; email: vivienne.checkley@ buntingaccountants.co.uk)

CC number: 237040

Eligibility

People who are in need and live in the parishes of Great Faringdon, Littleworth or Little Coxwell, all in Oxfordshire.

Types of grants

One-off grants towards clergy expenses for visiting the sick, domestic appliances, holidays, travel expenses, medical and disability equipment, furniture and food, etc.

Annual grant total

In 2015/16 the charity had an income of £16,300 and a total expenditure of £10,000. We estimate that welfare grants to individuals totalled £2,500.

Exclusions

Grants cannot be given for nursing/ retirement home fees or the supply of equipment that the state is obliged to provide.

Applications

Applications can be made in writing to the correspondent throughout the year. They can be submitted either through Citizens Advice, a social worker or other third party, directly by the individual or by a third party, such as a neighbour, parent or child on their behalf.

The Lockinge and Ardington Relief-in-Need Charity

£4,200

Correspondent: Mrs A. Ackland, Correspondent, c/o Lockinge Estate Office, Ardington, Wantage, Oxfordshire OX12 8PP (01235 833200; email: aackland@lockinge-estate.co.uk)

CC number: 204770

Eligibility

People in need who live in the parish of Lockinge and Ardington. Help is given when statutory sources are not available or adequate.

Types of grants

One-off and recurrent grants.

Annual grant total

In 2016/17 the charity had an income of £5,200 and a total expenditure of £4,400. We estimate that the charity gave around £4,200 in grants to individuals.

Applications

Apply in writing to the correspondent.

Other information

The charity also provides support through advice and information.

The Steventon Allotments and Relief-in-Need Charity

£5,900

Correspondent: Patricia Effer, 19 Lime Grove, Southmoor, Abingdon, Oxfordshire OX13 5DN (01865 821055; email: info@sarinc.org.uk)

CC number: 203331

Eligibility

People who are in need and live in Steventon.

Types of grants

One-off grants for: the provision of food, fuel and personal items such as clothing; the repair and replacement of faulty domestic equipment or furniture; loans of electric wheelchairs; the provision of special equipment for people who are chronically ill; and help with unforeseen difficulties. Birthday grants of £50 are also given. Priority is given to assist young people in obtaining independent housing, to set up home within the community in which they were raised. Large loans will need to be secured as a percentage of a second mortgage.

Annual grant total

In 2016 the charity had assets of £3 million and an income of £127,000. Welfare grants to individuals totalled £5,900.

Applications

Apply in writing to the correspondent. The charity advertises regularly in the local parish magazine. Applications should include full details of income and expenditure, and will be treated in strictest confidence.

Other information

Grants are also made to individuals for educational purposes and to organisations.

The Wantage District Coronation Memorial and Nursing Amenities Fund

£3,000

Correspondent: Carol Clubb, 133 Stockham Park, Wantage, Oxfordshire OX12 9HJ (01235 767355)

CC number: 234384

Eligibility

People who are in poor health, convalescent or who have disabilities and live in the Wantage area of Oxfordshire.

Types of grants

One-off and recurrent grants typically ranging from around £20 to £100.

Annual grant total

In 2015/16 the charity had an income of £4,800 and a total expenditure of £6,100. We estimate that grants given to individuals totalled £3,000, with funding also awarded to organisations.

Exclusions

No grants are given towards the relief of taxes, rates or other public funds. Grants may, however, be applied to supplement relief or assistance provided out of public funds.

Applications

Apply in writing to the correspondent.

West Oxfordshire

The Bampton Welfare Trust

£5,000

Correspondent: David Pullman, Clerk to the Trustees, 1 Shrewsbury Place, Bampton, Oxfordshire OX18 2HF (01993 850589; email: david@dpullman. plus.com)

CC number: 202735

Eligibility

People in need who live in the parishes of Bampton, Aston and Lew.

Types of grants

One-off grants which can be repeated in subsequent years at the discretion of the trustees. Grants can be made for travelling expenses to hospitals, help with fuel and food costs, or to relieve immediate need.

Annual grant total

In 2016 the trust had an income of £8,500 and a total expenditure of £10,500. We estimate that grants given to individuals for welfare purposes totalled around £5,000, with organisations also receiving funding.

Applications

Applicants are advised to initially discuss their circumstances with the correspondent, who will advise the applicant on what steps to take. This initial contact can be made directly by the individual, or by any third party, at any time. The trustees meet twice a year.

Other information

The trust also makes grants to local primary schools playgroups and clubs for older people in the area.

The Bartlett Taylor Charitable Trust

£5,100 (13 grants)

Correspondent: Gareth Alty, Trustee, c/o John Welch and Stammers, 24 Church Green, Witney, Oxfordshire OX28 4AT (01993 703941; email: galty@ johnwelchandstammers.co.uk; website: www.btctrust.org.uk)

CC number: 285249

Eligibility

People in need who live in West Oxfordshire.

Types of grants

Relief-in-need grants range from £145 to £1,000 and medical support can be of around £500.

Annual grant total

In 2015/16 the trust had assets of almost £2.3 million and an income of over £88,000. Grants to 13 individuals totalled £5,100, of which one was a medical grant (£500) and 12 were relief-in-need grants (£4,600). A further £250 was awarded to one individual for educational purposes, however the trust states that it does not routinely make educational grants.

Applications

Apply on a form on the charity's website. The trustees meet bi-monthly.

Other information

Grants are also made to organisations, including national, international and local charities (£46,000 in 2015/16).

The Burford Relief-in-Need Charity

£25,000

Correspondent: Anne Burgess Youngson, Whitehill Farm, Burford, Oxfordshire OX18 4DT (01993 822894)

CC number: 1036378

Eligibility

People who are in need and live within seven miles of the Tolsey, Burford.

Types of grants

One-off grants towards hospital expenses, electrical goods, travel costs, convalescence, medical equipment and disability aids.

Annual grant total

In 2016 the charity had an income of £13,300 and a total expenditure of £55,000. We estimate that welfare grants to individuals totalled £25,000 with funding also awarded to individuals for educational purposes.

Applications

Apply in writing to the correspondent either directly by the individual or, where applicable, through a social worker, Citizens Advice or other welfare agency. Applications should include the individual's full name, address, age, and the number of years they have lived in Burford or their connection with Burford. Receipts are required for grants towards the costs of equipment. Applications are usually considered on a quarterly basis but urgent cases can be dealt with quickly.

Eynsham Consolidated Charity

£2,500 (18 grants)

Correspondent: Robin Mitchell, Clerk to the Trustees, 20 High Street, Eynsham, Witney, Oxfordshire OX29 4HB (01865 880665; website: eynsham-pc.gov.uk)

CC number: 200977

Eligibility

People in need who live in the ancient parish of Eynsham (which covers Eynsham and part of Freeland) in Oxfordshire. The website provides a map marking the area of benefit. In exceptional circumstances, grants can be made to people living immediately outside the parish; in practice, residents from most of Freeland may apply.

Types of grants

One-off grants, generally ranging from £50 to £200, can be given for specific items (glasses, furniture, washing machines, cookers, paint, school clothing or special equipment for people with disabilities), services (e.g. heating costs or insurance premiums) and for other unforeseen difficulties. The charity notes that where the cost of providing the necessary help will be high, help may be given in conjunction with other welfare organisations.

Annual grant total

In 2016 the charity had an income of £4,900 and a total expenditure of £3,100. Almost £2,500 was distributed in 18 grants to individuals.

Exclusions

Grants are not made to help with payment of rates, taxes or other public charges. Support is not given on a recurrent basis or in the form of personal loans.

Applications

Apply in writing to the correspondent by post or email via the form on the website. Applications can be made directly by the individual or on their behalf by a neighbour, friend or family member. Candidates should include details of what the grant is for, the costs involved and their personal circumstances. The trustees meet four times a year to consider applications, usually in February, May, September and November, although urgent requests can be dealt with between the meetings.

The Great Rollright Charities

£2,600

Correspondent: Paul Dingle, Correspondent, Tyte End Cottage, Tyte End, Great Rollright, Chipping Norton, Oxfordshire OX7 5RU (01608 737676; email: paul@pcdingle.plus.com)

CC number: 242146

Eligibility

People who are in need and live in the ancient parish of Great Rollright.

Types of grants

One-off grants towards, for example, fuel payments and to older people at Christmas.

Annual grant total

In 2015/16 the charity had an income of £9,900 and a total expenditure of £10,500. We estimate that the charity awarded around £2,600 in grants to individuals for welfare purposes.

Exclusions

No grants are given for the relief of rates, taxes or other public funds.

Applications

Apply in writing to the correspondent.

Over Norton Welfare Trust

£2,000

Correspondent: Christopher Sole, Trustee, Cotswold Edge, Choice Hill Road, Over Norton, Chipping Norton OX7 5PP (01608 644112; email: mail@soles.eclipse.co.uk)

CC number: 237881

Eligibility

People in need who live in the parish of Over Norton.

Types of grants

One-off grants for electricity stamps or coal vouchers.

Annual grant total

In 2015/16 the trust had an income of £3,000 and a total expenditure of £2,300. We estimate that grants given to individuals totalled around £2,000.

Applications

Apply in writing to the correspondent.

Surrey

The Bookhams, Fetcham and Effingham Nursing Association Trust

£4,000

Correspondent: Jenny Peers, Trustee, 1 Manor Cottages, Manor House Lane, Bookham, Leatherhead, Surrey KT23 4EW (01372 456752; email: j.peers@tiscali.co.uk)

CC number: 265962

Eligibility

People in need who are sick, convalescent or who have disabilities who live in Great Bookham, Little Bookham, Fetcham and Effingham.

Types of grants

Grants for medical items, services or facilities.

Annual grant total

In 2015/16 the trust had an income of £8,200 and a total expenditure of £8,100. We estimate that grants given to individuals totalled around £4,000, with funding also awarded to local organisations.

Applications

Applications should be referred through medical or social services, not directly from the public.

Elmbridge

Jemima Octavia Cooper for the Poor (Stoke D'Abernon Charities)

£2,500

Correspondent: Ron Stewart, Old Timbers, Manor Way, Oxshott, Leatherhead, Surrey KT22 0HU (07785 272590; email: ronandjackie@tecres.net)

CC number: 200187

Eligibility

People in need who live in the ancient parish of Stoke D'Abernon (which includes part of Oxshott).

Types of grants

One-off and recurrent grants are given according to need. Grants are made at Christmas and are of around £50 on average. Occasionally, smaller distributions are made in the summer.

Annual grant total

In 2016/17 the charity had an income of £2,800 and a total expenditure of £2,900. We estimate that the charity awarded £2,500 in grants to individuals.

Applications

Applications can be made formally in writing; however, in practice many applications are made informally by word of mouth given the small size and catchment area of the charity. If a formal application is to be made, the trustees prefer email, where possible.

Walton-on-Thames Charity

£82,000

Correspondent: Grants Team, Charities House, 2 Quintet, Churchfield Road, Walton-on-Thames KT12 2TZ (01932 220242; email: admin@waltoncharity.org.uk; website: www.waltoncharity.org.uk)

CC number: 230652

Eligibility

People in need who live in the borough of Elmbridge, with a preference for those living in Walton-on-Thames.

Types of grants

One-off grants are given to help with, for example: essential household goods (such as white goods) not funded by Surrey Local Assistance Scheme; contributions towards utility bills; essential health and care aids, and equipment not funded by statutory or other charitable sources; transport costs, if provision is not available; and support for young people and school-age children. Families on a low income can apply for assistance with school uniform, school shoes and winter coats.

Annual grant total

In 2016/17 the charity had assets of £31.1 million and an income of £3.2 million. Crisis grants to individuals totalled £78,000, with a further £4,100 distributed in the form of food vouchers.

Applications

Applicants must be referred to the charity by a recognised agency (however, applications for school uniform grants may be made by individuals directly). Applicants are required to complete an application form, including details of their personal and financial circumstances, and will also be asked to attend a meeting with a member of the Grants Team. More information can be obtained from either Amina Lawson (tel: 020 3328 0246; email: alawson@ waltoncharity.org.uk) or Nikki Howard (tel: 020 3195 8286; email: nhoward@ waltoncharity.org.uk).

Other information

The charity is involved with a wide range of activities in Walton-on-Thames, including through its partnership with Walton and Hersham food bank (part of the Trussell Trust's national network) and local churches. People must be referred to the food bank through a recognised agency, which will issue them with a food bank voucher. Those who are in urgent need of support but are unsure of which agencies can refer them can contact the charity for more information (tel: 01932 220242; email: admin@waltoncharity.org.uk).

Weybridge Poor's Land (Weybridge Land Charity)

£41,000 (333 grants)

Correspondent: Howard Turner, Little Knowle, Woodlands, Send, Woking GU23 7LD (01483 211728; email: treasurer@weybridgelandcharity.org.uk; website: weybridgecharity.org.uk)

CC number: 200270

Eligibility

People in need who live in Weybridge.

Types of grants

Emergency grants are provided for food, essential furniture, flooring, white goods, and children's expenses such as prams. The item is purchased directly by the charity.

Christmas grants are usually around £100 per applicant and cheques are awarded in December.

Annual grant total

In 2016 the charity held assets of £65,000 and had an income of £71,000. During the year, the charity awarded £41,000 in grants: £31,000 was awarded as Christmas grants to 310 applicants, and £10,000 was given in emergency aid to 23 applicants.

Exclusions

No funding towards credit card or debt relief.

Applications

Christmas grant application forms are available from the Weybridge Centre and Public Library in September and October. Individuals can apply directly during this time, with a maximum of one application per household.

Applicants for emergency grants must be referred to the charity through the local Citizens Advice, Weybridge Children's Centre, a health visitor, Home-Start Elmbridge, Paragon Community Housing Group, or a local church.

Other information

The charity also owns and operates allotments in Weybridge.

Epsom and Ewell

Chessington Charities

£2,000

Correspondent: Revd Scott Edwards, The Vicarage, Garrison Lane, Chessington KT9 2LB (020 8397 3016; email: stmaryschessington@hotmail.co.uk)

CC number: 209241

Eligibility

People in need who live in the parish of St Mary the Virgin, Chessington. Applicants must have lived in the parish for at least one year.

Types of grants

One-off grants available for short-term respite from financial hardship. Christmas gifts are also made to older people.

Annual grant total

In 2016 the charity had an income of £4,500 and a total expenditure of £4,000. We estimate that welfare grants totalled around £2,000.

Exclusions

Grants are not given to pay debts. The area of benefit is only the parish of St Mary the Virgin and excludes the rest of the Chessington postal area.

Applications

Application forms are available from the correspondent and can be submitted by

the individual or a social organisation such as Citizens Advice.

Other information

Educational grants are also available for individuals.

Epsom Parochial Charities (Epsom Almshouse Charity)

£10,400

Correspondent: John Steward, Trustee, 26 Woodcote Hurst, Epsom, Surrey KT18 7DT (email: vanstonewalker@ ntlworld.com)

CC number: 200571

Eligibility

People in need who live in the ancient parish of Epsom.

Types of grants

One-off grants ranging from £100 to £500 can be given according to need. Awards made include those for clothing, food, medical care and equipment and household appliances.

Annual grant total

In 2015 the charity had assets of £1.7 million and an income of £86,500. Grants to individuals for welfare purposes totalled £10,400.

Applications

Application forms are available from the correspondent.

Other information

Grants are also made for education. The charity also provides residential accommodation through its three almshouses.

Ewell Parochial Trusts

£25,000

Correspondent: Miriam Massey, Clerk & Treasurer, 19 Cheam Road, Epsom KT17 1ST (020 8394 0453; email: mirimas@globalnet.co.uk)

CC number: 201623

Eligibility

People in need who live, work or are being educated in the ancient ecclesiastical parish of Ewell and the domain of Kingswood.

Types of grants

One-off grants and pensions.

Annual grant total

In 2016 the charity had an income of £49,000 and a total expenditure of £39,000. We believe social welfare grants to individuals totalled around £25,000, with funding also given to individuals for educational purposes and to local organisations.

Applications

Apply in writing to the correspondent. Applicants are referred from Citizens Advice, charities, health services and other welfare agencies. Applications which do not meet the eligibility criteria will not be acknowledged.

Guildford

John Beane's Charity CIO

£85,000 (410 grants)

Correspondent: Brian France, Clerk to the Trustees, PO Box 607, Guildford, Surrey GU2 8WR (01483 572474; email: brian@accountingfacilities.co.uk)

CC number: 1161716

Eligibility

People in need who live in the administrative county of Surrey.

Types of grants

One-off or recurrent grants according to need.

Annual grant total

In 2015/16 the charity held assets of nearly £8 million and had an income of £321,000. Grants were made to 410 individuals and totalled £85,000.

Applications

Apply in writing to the correspondent.

Other information

The CIO is an amalgamation of three separate charities – the John Beane's Dorking and Guildford Eleemosynary Charities and John Beane's Charity – that have existed since the early 1700s.

Guildford Poyle Charities

£27,000 (171 grants)

Correspondent: Julia Bowman, Grants Administrator, 208 High Street, Guildford GU1 3JB (01483 303678; email: admin@guildfordpoylecharities.org; website: www.guildfordpoylecharities.org)

CC number: 1145202

Eligibility

People in need who live in the borough of Guildford as constituted prior to 1 April 1974 and part of the ancient parish of Merrow. A map showing the beneficial area can be viewed on the website.

Types of grants

Mainly one-off grants for kitchen items and appliances, furniture, baby equipment, travel and training costs. Grants are in the form of cheques or vouchers for suppliers with which the charity has arrangements or a cheque made out to the referral agency.

Annual grant total

In 2016 the charity held assets of almost £4.4 million and had an income of £167,000. A total of 171 grants were awarded to individuals, amounting to £27,000.

A further £110,000 was given to 26 local organisations.

Exclusions

Grants are usually not made to pay for basic items such as food, rent and utility bills. No help is given towards debts or arrears.

Applications

Application forms are available from the correspondent or to download from the website. Applications can be submitted at any time through a social worker, Citizens Advice or other welfare agency. Individuals may apply directly, although the charity has stated that an application has more chance of being successful if it is supported by a letter from a health or welfare professional who is familiar with the individual's circumstances.

The charity's office welcomes enquiries.

Other information

Applications for school uniforms are now handled through the Home School Link Worker (HSLW) attached to the child's school. Approach them for more details.

The Mayor of Guildford's Local Distress Fund

£10,000

Correspondent: Kate Foxton, Civic Secretary, Guildford Borough Council, Millmead House, Millmead, Guildford, Surrey GU2 4BB (01483 444031; email: kate.foxton@guildford.gov.uk.)

CC number: 258388

Eligibility

People in need who live in the borough of Guildford, with a preference for older people and people living with disabilities.

Types of grants

One-off grants. Grants have previously been given for purposes such as kitchen appliances, furniture and clothing. Grants are also made for Christmas events.

Annual grant total

In 2015/16 the trust had an income of £23,500 and a total expenditure of £11,500. We estimate that grants given to individuals totalled £10,000.

Exclusions

Grants are not given for ongoing expenses such as rent, utility bills or debt relief.

Applications

Apply on a form available for download from the Guildford Borough Council website, to be submitted through a social worker, Citizens Advice, local GP or other relevant third party. Applications are usually considered in January, April, July and October.

The Pirbright Relief-in-Need Charity

£1,700

Correspondent: Philip Lawson, Administrator, Stanemore, Rowe Lane, Pirbright, Woking GU24 0LX (01483 472842)

CC number: 238494

Eligibility

People in need, hardship or distress who live in the parish of Pirbright.

Types of grants

One-off grants for a variety of items, services or facilities that will reduce the need, hardship or distress of the individual, including buying or renting medical equipment to use at home.

Annual grant total

In 2015/16 the charity had an income of £2,800 and a total expenditure of £3,500. We estimate that £1,700 was awarded to individuals directly, with funding also awarded to organisations providing support for individuals in need.

Exclusions

Grants will not be given for taxes, rates or any other public funds. The trustees must not commit themselves to repeating or renewing any grant.

Applications

Apply in writing to the correspondent or any of the trustees.

The Henry Smith Charity (Ash and Normandy)

£2,500

Correspondent: Alan Coomer, 84 Queenhythe Road, Jacob's Well, Guildford, Surrey GU4 7NX (01483 300103; email: alancoomer@yahoo.co.uk)

CC number: 240485

Eligibility

People in need who live in Ash and Normandy.

Types of grants

One-off or recurrent grants according to need.

Annual grant total

In 2016/17 the charity had an income of £4,600 and a total expenditure of £5,700. We estimate that the charity awarded £2,500 in grants to individuals during the year.

Applications

Apply in writing to the correspondent, either directly by the individual or through a social worker, Citizens Advice or other welfare agency.

Other information

The charity also makes awards to organisations.

The Henry Smith Charity (Effingham)

£2,000

Correspondent: The Clerk, Effingham Parish Council, The Parish Room, 3 Home Barn Court, The Street, Effingham, Leatherhead KT24 5LG (01372 454911; email: clerk2009@ effinghamparishcouncil.gov.uk)

CC number: 237703

Eligibility

Older people and those with disabilities who live in Effingham.

Types of grants

One-off grants and gift vouchers according to need.

Annual grant total

Grants to individuals usually total £2,000.

Applications

Apply in writing to the correspondent.

The Henry Smith Charity (Send and Ripley)

£4,500

Correspondent: Geoffrey Richardson, Trustee, 2 Rose Lane, Ripley, Surrey GU23 6NE (01483 225322; email: shop@ richardsonsflorist.co.uk)

CC number: 200496

Eligibility

People in need who live in Send or Ripley, and have done so for five years.

Types of grants

One-off grants of around £30 at Christmas to 50 or 60 older people in Send and a similar number in Ripley.

Annual grant total

In 2016/17 the charity had an income of £4,900 and a total expenditure of £5,000. We estimate that grants given to individuals totalled around £4,500.

Applications

Apply in writing to the correspondent. Applications can be submitted directly by the individual or, where applicable, through a social worker, Citizens Advice or any other welfare agency or third party on behalf of the individual. Applications are considered as they arrive.

Smiths Charity (Shalford)

£2,500

Correspondent: Shalford Parish Council, Shalford Parish Council, Thursley House, 53 Station Road, Shalford, Guildford GU4 8HA (01483 459108; email: shalfordpc@gmail.com; website: shalfordpc.org.uk)

CC number: 240135

Eligibility

People in need who live in the parish of Shalford.

Types of grants

One-off and recurrent cash grants to relieve financial problems.

Annual grant total

In 2015/16 the charity had an income of £3,600 and a total expenditure of £2,700. We have estimate that grants totalled around £2,500.

Applications

Apply in writing to the correspondent. Applications can be submitted either directly by the individual or through a third party, such as a social worker, Citizens Advice or other welfare agency. Our research suggests that applications

are usually considered in March, after the grants are advertised locally.

Other information

The charity is registered as the Charity of Henry Smith (Warbleton Estate).

West Clandon Parochial Charities

£2,800

Correspondent: Stephen Meredith, Trustee, 11 Bennett Way, West Clandon, Guildford GU4 7TN

CC number: 200165

Eligibility

People in need, mainly older people, who have lived in the parish of West Clandon for at least five years.

Types of grants

One-off cash grants.

Annual grant total

In 2016 the charity had an income of £3,000 and a total expenditure of £2,900. We estimate that grants totalled around £2,800.

Applications

Apply in writing to the correspondent. The deadline for applications is 31 October. Grants are usually distributed during December.

Worplesdon United Charities

£2,200

Correspondent: Eric Morgan, Trustee, 21 St Michael's Avenue, Fairlands, Guildford GU3 3LY (01483 233344)

CC number: 200382

Eligibility

Individuals, mainly older people, who are in need and live in the parish of Worplesdon.

Types of grants

Our previous research indicates that grants are typically given to buy clothes, fuel or groceries at Christmas.

Annual grant total

In 2015/16 the charity had an income of £2,700 and a total expenditure of £2,500. We estimate that the charity awarded around £2,200 in grants to individuals.

Applications

Apply in writing to the correspondent.

Other information

At the time of writing (August 2017) the charity had no website or accounts available.

Mole Valley

The Abinger Consolidated Charities

£3,000

Correspondent: Mad Berry, The Rectory, Abinger Lane, Abinger Common, Dorking, Surrey RH5 6HZ (01306 737160)

CC number: 200124

Eligibility

People in need who live in the ancient parish of Abinger.

Types of grants

One-off grants according to need.

Annual grant total

In 2015/16 the charity had an income of £10,000 and a total expenditure of £9,800. We have estimated that grants to individuals for welfare totalled £3,000, with funding also awarded to organisations.

Applications

Apply in writing to the correspondent.

Betchworth United Charities

£7,500

Correspondent: Andrea Brown, Clerk, 15 Nutwood Avenue, Brockham, Betchworth, Surrey RH3 7LT (01737 843806; email: snowwhite15@btinternet.co)

CC number: 200299

Eligibility

People in need who live in the ancient parish of Betchworth.

Types of grants

Typically, one-off grants. The majority of funding is given for welfare purposes but a small amount is also available for educational needs from the Margaret Fenwick fund.

Annual grant total

In 2016 the charity had an income of £12,400 and a total expenditure of £16,300. We have estimated that welfare grants to individuals totalled £7,500. Grants are also awarded to organisations and to individuals for educational purposes.

Applications

Apply in writing to the correspondent. Applications should be submitted by a third party, such as a doctor, minister or social worker. Applications are considered at trustees' meetings.

John Bristow and Thomas Mason Trust

£11,500 (three grants)

Correspondent: Sam Longhurst, Trust Secretary, Beech Hay, Ifield Road, Charlwood, Surrey RH6 0DR (01293 862734; email: trust.secretary@jbtmt.org.uk; website: www.jbtmt.org.uk)

CC number: 1075971

Eligibility

People who are in need who live in the parish of Charlwood as constituted on 17 February 1926, including Hookwood and Lowfield Heath.

Types of grants

One-off and recurrent grants and loans are given according to need.

Annual grant total

In 2015/16 the trust had assets of £2.7 million representing mainly endowment funds with only £104,500 being unrestricted. The trust had an income of £102,000 and made grants totalling almost £56,000, of which £3,000 went to individuals for educational purposes and almost £11,500 to individuals for social welfare purposes. The remainder was awarded to organisations.

Applications

Application forms are available from the correspondent or to download from the website. Applications can be submitted directly by the individual or through a third party. They will normally be considered within two weeks but can be dealt with more quickly in urgent cases.

Leatherhead United Charities

£45,000

Correspondent: David Matanle, Clerk to the Trustees, Homefield, Forty Foot Road, Leatherhead, Surrey KT22 8RP (01372 370073; email: luchar@btinternet.com)

CC number: 200183

Eligibility

People in need who live in the area of the former Leatherhead urban district council (Ashtead, Bookhams, Fetcham and Leatherhead). Preference is given to residents of the parish of Leatherhead as constituted on 27 September 1912.

Types of grants

One-off grants, usually in the range of £100 and £750, are given for general relief in need. Pensions are also distributed.

Annual grant total

In 2016 the charity had assets of £6.4 million and an income of £313,500. During the year, 31 grants were made to individuals. Pensions totalled £41,000 and we estimate that welfare grants to individuals totalled £4,000.

Applications

Application forms can be requested from the correspondent. Our research suggests that they should be submitted through a recognised referral agency, such as a social worker, Citizens Advice or a doctor. Candidates should also provide details of their/their family income and include names of two referees. Awards are considered throughout the year.

Other information

The charity also provides residents of Mole Valley District Council with sheltered housing and associated services.

Ockley United Charities

£3,700

Correspondent: Tim Pryke, Trustee, Danesfield, Stane Street, Ockley, Dorking RH5 5SY (01306 711511)

CC number: 200556

Eligibility

People in need who live in Ockley (primarily older people living in sheltered accommodation provided by Ockley Housing Association or rented housing).

Types of grants

Recurrent annual cash gifts of £110. Assistance is also given to local families for nursery fees.

Annual grant total

In 2015/16 the charity had an income of £7,800 and a total expenditure of £7,600. We estimate that the charity gave around £3,700 in grants to individuals, with support also given to local organisations.

Applications

Apply in writing to the correspondent. Applications should include details of income, housing and need. They are considered on a regular basis.

Smith and Earles Charity

£3,200

Correspondent: Jeanette Gillespie, The Birches, Ifield Road, Charlwood, Horley, Surrey RH6 0DR (01293 862129; email: gillespie2@btinternet.com)

CC number: 200043

Eligibility

People with disabilities or those over 65 who are in need and have lived in the old parish of Charlwood for at least five years.

Types of grants

One-off and recurrent grants are made, usually of up to £80.

Annual grant total

In 2015/16 the charity had an income of £6,000 and a total expenditure of £6,700. We estimate that the charity awarded around £3,200 in grants to individuals for welfare purposes.

Applications

Apply using a form available from the correspondent. Applications for one-off (usually larger) grants should be submitted through a recognised referral agency (such as a social worker, Citizens Advice or other welfare agency). Applications for recurrent grants can be submitted directly by the individual. They are considered in November. Details of any disability or special need should be given.

Other information

Help is also given towards the hiring of halls for meetings for older people, hospices and school requirements.

Henry Smith (Worth Estate)

£3,600

Correspondent: Diana Salisbury, Trustee, Langholm, Village Street, Newdigate, Dorking RH5 5DH (01306 631435)

CC number: 200062

Eligibility

People in need who live in the parish of Newdigate.

Types of grants

One-off grants for a variety of needs. Grants are typically made to help residents with bereavement, health needs and special educational requirements.

Annual grant total

In 2015/16 the charity had an income of £5,000 and a total expenditure of £4,900.

We estimate that grants given to individuals totalled £3,600.

Applications

Apply in writing to the correspondent.

Other information

The trustees also hold an annual Christmas luncheon in the village hall for Newdigate's older residents.

The Henry Smith Charity (Capel)

£2,000

Correspondent: Jenny Richards, Old School House, Coldharbour, Dorking, Surrey RH5 6HF (01306 711885; email: jennyrichards1885@gmail.com)

CC number: 201507

Eligibility

People who live in Capel, Surrey.

Types of grants

Small, one-off and recurrent grants for bills, repairs, clothing, etc.

Annual grant total

In 2015/16 the charity had an income of £2,400 and a total expenditure of £2,300. We estimate that grants totalled around £2,000.

Applications

Apply directly in writing to the correspondent.

Other information

The charity is administered by the Warbleton Estate of the Henry Smith Charity.

The Henry Smith Charity (Headley)

£4,500

Correspondent: Anthony Vine-Lott, Trustee, Broom Cottage, Crabtree Lane, Headley, Epsom KT18 6PS (01372 374728; email: tony.vinelott@btinternet.com)

CC number: 237927

Eligibility

People in need who live in the parish of Headley.

Types of grants

One-off and recurrent grants are available to help with, for example, groceries and hospital travel.

Annual grant total

In 2015/16 the charity had an income of £5,100 and a total expenditure of £4,900. We estimate that grants given to individuals totalled around £4,500.

Applications

Apply in writing to the correspondent or any trustee, giving the reasons for the application.

The Henry Smith Charity (Leigh)

£4,500

Correspondent: Mrs J. Sturt, Littleton, Village Street, Newdigate, Surrey RH5 5AD (01306 632822)

CC number: 237335

Eligibility

People in need who live in Leigh, Surrey.

Types of grants

The trust has a list of all residents over 65; each receives support at Christmas in the form of food vouchers, or help with household bills. Gifts may also be given at Easter in the years when the trust receives more income. Help is also given to other residents of Leigh, who are in need.

Annual grant total

In 2015/16 the charity had an income of £5,100 and a total expenditure of £5,000. We estimate that grants given to individuals totalled around £4,500.

Applications

Apply in writing or by telephone to the correspondent, or through a third party.

The Henry Smith Charity (Wotton)

£4,500

Correspondent: Rosemary Wakeford, 2 Brickyard Cottages, Hollow Lane, Wotton, Dorking, Surrey RH5 6QE (01306 730856)

CC number: 240634

Eligibility

People in need who live in the ancient parish of Wotton.

Types of grants

One-off grants ranging from £100 to £500. Grants have previously been given to older people of the parish towards fuel and lighting bills and holidays, young people taking part in schemes such as The Duke of Edinburgh Award which will enhance their job prospects, and help towards the cost of independent projects or travel costs.

Annual grant total

In 2016 the charity had an income of £89 and a total expenditure of £4,800. We estimate that grants given to individuals totalled around £4,500.

Applications

Apply in writing to the correspondent. They can be submitted directly by the individual or through a third party.

Reigate and Banstead

Banstead United Charities

£2,000

Correspondent: Michael Taylor, Trustee, 6 Garratts Lane, Banstead SM7 2DZ (01737 355827)

CC number: 233339

Eligibility

People in need who live in the wards of Banstead village, Burgh Heath, Kingswood, Nork, Preston, Tadworth and Tattenhams (Surrey).

Types of grants

One-off grants, usually up to £500. Our research suggests that awards have been given towards funeral expenses, equipment for people with disabilities, travel for hospital treatment and rehabilitation, children's clothing, living expenses and towards minor educational needs.

Annual grant total

In 2016 the charity had an income of £3,500 and a total expenditure of £4,300. We estimate that grants given to individuals totalled £2,000, with funding also available for organisations.

Applications

Apply in writing to the correspondent. Applications can be submitted directly by the individual or through a social worker, Citizens Advice or other welfare agency. They are considered throughout the year.

Walton Parochial Charities

£2,000

Correspondent: The Trustees, St Peter's Church, Breech Lane, Walton-on-the-Hill, Surrey KT20 7SD (01737 668254)

CC number: 200568

Eligibility

People in need who live within the parish of Walton-on-the-Hill.

Types of grants

One-off or recurrent grants according to need.

Annual grant total

In 2016/17 the charity had an income of £3,100 and a total expenditure of £2,100. We estimate that grants given to individuals totalled £2,000.

Applications

Apply in writing to the correspondent.

Other information

This charity is the amalgamation of four older charities in the area, all of which were established to provide for people in need in the parish.

Runnymede

Chertsey Combined Charity

£3,000

Correspondent: Mike O'Sullivan, Secretary & Treasurer, PO Box 89, Weybridge, Surrey KT13 8HY (email: secretary@chertsey-combined-charity. org; website: chertsey-combined-charity.org)

CC number: 200186

Eligibility

People in need who live in the former urban district of Chertsey (this includes Addlestone, Chertsey, Lyne, Ottershaw, Rowtown and parts of Woodham).

Types of grants

One-off grants according to need.

Annual grant total

In 2016/17 the charity had assets of £132,500 and an income of £62,000. Grants to individuals totalled almost £6,000. We estimate that grants for welfare needs totalled around £3,000, with funding also given for educational purposes.

Applications

Application forms are available to download from the website, or from the correspondent. Applications are considered in February, May, August and November, and must be submitted before the first of that month for inclusion in the trustees' agenda.

Other information

Grants are also made to organisations.

The Egham United Charity

£8,500

Correspondent: Max Walker, 33 Runnemede Road, Egham, Surrey TW20 9BE (01784 472742; email: eghamunicharity@aol.com; website: www.eghamunitedcharity.org)

CC number: 205885

Eligibility

People in need who have lived in Egham, Englefield Green (West and East), Hythe or Virginia Water for at least five years.

Support is typically given to families, older people, people who have physical and mental disabilities, and people who are recuperating from mental illness.

Types of grants

One-off grants according to need. Grants are awarded towards, for example, fuel bills, household essentials, mobility aids and for school uniforms, trips and travel fares. Payments are made directly to the supplier/provider (in the case of settling bills) or to the sponsoring agency for distribution.

Annual grant total

In 2016 the charity had an income of £23,500 and a total expenditure of £17,400. We estimate that grants given to individuals totalled £8,500, with funding also awarded to individuals for educational purposes.

Exclusions

The website states that the charity cannot: fund necessities which are provided by local or central government (although it may top up partial provision); make up for income deficiencies or make recurring grants; pay for necessities which 'applicants, albeit with appropriate advice and befriending, could provide for themselves'; offer loans; or commit to any support outside a trustees' meeting.

Applications

Application forms are available to download from the website. The trustees prefer to receive applications through a referral agency, such as Citizens Advice or a social worker. Applications are only ever considered at trustees' meetings held every six weeks. On occasion, the trustees may arrange to visit an applicant.

Other information

The charity has trustees in common with other charities, including Egham Education Trust and Stewart's and Budgens's Almshouses.

The Henry Smith Charity (Chertsey)

£18,000

Correspondent: Bernard Fleckney, Runnymede Borough Council, Civic Offices, Station Road, Addlestone KT15 2AH (01932 425620)

CC number: 233531

Eligibility
People over 60 who are in need and live in Chertsey, Surrey.

Types of grants
Recurrent fuel vouchers which can be used as part payment of fuel bills.

Annual grant total
In 2015/16 the charity had an income of £21,000 and a total expenditure of £20,000. We estimate that grants given to individuals totalled around £18,000.

Applications
Apply in writing to the correspondent either through a social worker, Citizens Advice or other third party or directly by the individual. Applications can be considered at any time during the year.

The Thorpe Parochial Charities

£6,200

Correspondent: Dorothy Jones, Administrator, 9 Rosefield Gardens, Ottershaw, Chertsey, Surrey KT16 0JH (01932 872245)

CC number: 205888

Eligibility
People in need who live in the ancient parish of Thorpe, especially those over 60 years of age.

Types of grants
Our previous research suggests that grants are made for contributions to gas or electricity accounts and 'aids to the sick'.

Annual grant total
In 2016/17 the charity had an income of £1,100 and had a total expenditure of £6,400. We estimate that the charity gave around £6,200 in grants to individuals.

Applications
Apply in writing to the correspondent.

Spelthorne

Ashford Relief in Need Charities

£2,400

Correspondent: Peter Harding, Administrator, 8 Portland Road, Ashford TW15 3BT (01784 241257; email: pjlr_2000@yahoo.co.uk)

CC number: 231441

Eligibility
People in need who live in the ancient parishes of Ashford and Laleham.

Types of grants
One-off grants according to need.

Annual grant total
In 2016/17 the charity had an income of £15,000 and had a total expenditure of £4,900. We estimate that grants given to individuals totalled around £2,400, with funding also given to organisations.

Applications
Apply in writing to the correspondent. Applications can be made either directly by the individual, or through a third party such as a social worker, Citizens Advice or relative.

The Staines Parochial Charity

£4,500

Correspondent: Carol Davies, Honorary Clerk to the Trustees, 191 Feltham Hill Road, Ashford, Middlesex TW15 1HJ (01784 255432; email: candodavies@tiscali.co.uk)

CC number: 211653

Eligibility
Older people over the age of 60 who live in the parish of Staines, people who are unable to work, people caring for a person with disabilities, and occasionally other people in need who live in the area of the former urban district of Staines.

Types of grants
One-off grants according to need to alleviate hardship or distress, such as the payment of gas or electricity bills.

Annual grant total
In 2015/16 the charity had an income of £5,000 and a total expenditure of £4,800. We estimate that the charity gave around £4,500 to individuals for welfare purposes.

Exclusions
No grants are given to individuals living outside the beneficial area.

Applications
Apply on a form available from the correspondent including evidence of need, hardship or distress. Applications can be submitted either directly by the individual, through a social worker, Citizens Advice, welfare agency or other third party. The application must be submitted via a trustee who must countersign the application. Applications are normally considered in September.

Other information
At the time of writing (August 2017) the charity had no website or accounts available.

Surrey Heath

Frimley Fuel Allotments CIO

£64,500 (186 grants)

Correspondent: Frank Smithin, Trustee, 15 Winding Wood Drive, Camberley GU15 1ER (01276 28719; email: ffa.office1@gmail.com; website: www.frimleyfuelallotments.org.uk)

CC number: 1161717

Eligibility
People in need who live in the parish of Frimley. Priority is given to people who are older or who have a disability, and those who care for them.

Types of grants
One-off grants according to need.

Annual grant total
In 2016 the charity had assets of £1.7 million and an income of £141,500. Grants to individuals totalled £64,500.

Applications
Apply on a form available from the secretary or a local Citizens Advice, church or social services centre.

Henry Smith (Chobham)

£8,000

Correspondent: Elizabeth Thody, 46 Chertsey Road, Windlesham, Surrey GU20 6EP (email: cpa1831@aol.co.uk)

CC number: 200155

Eligibility
People in need who live in the ancient parish of Chobham (roughly the current civil parishes of Chobham and West End) in Surrey.

Types of grants
Small, one-off grants according to need.

Annual grant total
In 2016/17 the charity had an income of £1 and a total expenditure of £8,500.

Grants to individuals usually total around £8,000 each year.

Applications
Application forms are available from the correspondent.

Other information
This charity is a local branch of the wider Henry Smith Charity network.

The Henry Smith Charity (Bisley)

£2,300

Correspondent: Alexandra Gunn, Trustee, 213 Guildford Road, Bisley, Woking, Surrey GU24 9DL (email: sandy213@ntlworld.com)

CC number: 200157

Eligibility
People in need who live in Bisley in Surrey.

Types of grants
Grants to assist with food costs are distributed twice a year.

Annual grant total
In 2016 the charity had both an income and a total expenditure of £2,500. We estimate that grants given to individuals totalled £2,300.

Applications
Application forms are available from the correspondent and can be submitted directly by the individual.

The Henry Smith Charity (Frimley)

£2,000

Correspondent: Rachel Whillis, Democratic Services Officer, Surrey Heath Borough Council, Surrey Heath House, Knoll Road, Camberley, Surrey GU15 3HD (01276 707319; email: democratic.services@surreyheath.gov.uk)

CC number: 236367

Eligibility
People in need who live in the former parish of Frimley (Frimley, Frimley Green, Camberley and Mytchett).

Types of grants
One-off grants normally ranging from £100 to £200 towards clothing, bedding, furniture, disability equipment and electrical goods.

Annual grant total
In 2016/17 the charity had an income of £2,000 and a total expenditure of £2,300. We estimate that social welfare grants to individuals totalled £2,000.

Applications
Apply in writing to the correspondent through a social worker, Citizens Advice or other welfare agency.

Windlesham United Charities

£5,200

Correspondent: Carol Robson, 4 James Butler Almshouses, Guildford Road, Bagshot, Surrey GU19 5NH (01276 476158; email: jamesbutleroffice@btinternet.com)

CC number: 200224

Eligibility
Mainly older people and people with disabilities who are in need and have lived in the parishes of Bagshot, Lightwater and Windlesham (Surrey) for at least two years.

Types of grants
One-off grants, mainly in the form of small heating grants.

Annual grant total
In 2016 the charity had assets of £437,500 and an income of £66,000. Grants to individuals totalled £5,200.

Applications
Apply in writing to the correspondent at any time.

Other information
Windlesham United Charities consists of four separate funds: R. E. Cooper Educational Fund; The Duchess of Gloucester Educational Fund; Windlesham Poors Allotments; and Windlesham United Charities. The charity also maintains allotments.

Tandridge

Bletchingley United Charities

£5,000

Correspondent: Christine Bolshaw, Clerk to the Trustees, Cleves, Castle Street, Bletchingley, Surrey RH1 4QA (01883 743000; email: chrisbolshaw@hotmail.co.uk; website: www.bletchingley.org.uk)

CC number: 236747

Eligibility
People in need, hardship or distress who live in the parish of Bletchingley.

Types of grants
One-off and recurrent grants.

Annual grant total
In 2015/16 the charity had an income of £10,000 and a total expenditure of £10,500. We estimate that grants given to individuals totalled £5,000, with funding also awarded to local organisations.

Exclusions
Grants are not given for rates, taxes or other public funds.

Applications
Apply in writing to the correspondent. Applications can be submitted either directly by the individual, through a third party such as a social worker, or where applicable, through an organisation such as Citizens Advice or other welfare agency. They are considered throughout the year.

The Godstone United Charities

£5,000

Correspondent: Patricia Bamforth, Bassett Villa, Oxted Road, Godstone, Surrey RH9 8AD (01883 742625; email: clerk@godstonepc.org.uk; website: www.godstonepc.org.uk)

CC number: 200055

Eligibility
People in need who live in the old parish of Godstone (Blindley Heath, South Godstone and Godstone Village).

Types of grants
Food vouchers are usually given in December and March. One-off grants are also available.

Annual grant total
In 2016/17 the charity had an income of £6,800 and a total expenditure of £5,900. We estimate that grants given to individuals totalled around £5,000.

Applications
Apply in writing to the correspondent either directly by the individual or, where applicable, via a social worker, Citizens Advice or other welfare agency. Applications should include relevant details of income, outgoings, household composition and the reason for the request. All grants are paid directly to the supplier.

Other information
The charity may also assist with educational needs.

The Oxted United Charities

£5,200

Correspondent: Christopher Berry, Trustee, 9 Paddock Way, Oxted, Surrey RH8 0LF (01883 818549; email: cjboxted@aol.co.uk)

CC number: 200056

Eligibility

People in need who live in the parish of Oxted.

Types of grants

One-off grants. In the past, grants have been given for clothing, food, education, utility bills, television licences, furniture and floor covering.

Annual grant total

In 2016/17 the charity had an income of £5,500 and a total expenditure of £5,400. We estimate that the charity gave around £5,200 in grants to individuals.

Applications

Apply in writing to the correspondent. Applications are considered at any time and should be submitted directly by the individual or, where applicable, through a social worker, Citizens Advice or other welfare agency.

The Henry Smith Charity (Horne)

£3,500

Correspondent: Colin Buckley, Nutmeg Cottage, Domewood, Copthorne, Crawley RH10 3HD (01342 713822)

CC number: 201988

Eligibility

Older people and people in need who live in the ancient parish of Horne.

Types of grants

One-off grants are the norm, although recurrent grants can be considered.

Annual grant total

In 2016/17 the charity had no income and a total expenditure of £3,700. We estimate that grants given to individuals totalled around £3,500.

Applications

Application forms are available from the correspondent. Applications can be submitted either directly by the individual or through a social worker and should include details of the applicant's level of income.

Waverley

Miss Ada Oliver

£2,500

Correspondent: The Trustees c/o Marshalls Solicitors, 102 High Street, Godalming, Surrey GU7 1DS (01483 416101; email: lisa@marshalls.uk.net)

CC number: 234456

Eligibility

People who have cancer or rheumatism and are in financial need. Preference is given to people living in Surrey.

Types of grants

Grants are given for a variety of needs. Recent grants have been given for settling rent arrears, nursing home fees and necessities.

Annual grant total

In 2015/16 the charity had an income of £3,800 and a total expenditure of £7,000. We estimate that grants given to individuals for welfare purposes totalled £2,500, with funding also given to organisations.

Applications

Apply in writing to the correspondent, including details of income and circumstances. Applications can be submitted throughout the year by a social worker, Citizens Advice or other welfare agency on behalf of the individual.

The Churt Welfare Trust

£3,000

Correspondent: Eileen Kilpatrick, Hearn Lodge, Spats Lane, Headley Down, Bordon, Hampshire GU35 8SU (01428 712238; email: john@regalarch.f9.co.uk; website: churt.org/churtwelfaretrust.html)

CC number: 210076

Eligibility

People in need who live in the parish of Churt and its neighbourhood.

Types of grants

One-off and recurrent grants according to need. Previously, grants have been given for:

- Heating costs
- Home equipment and furnishings
- Specialist equipment, mobility aids and home nursing
- Travel and holidays
- Medical expenses
- Transport for long distance medical appointments
- Household repairs and maintenance

Annual grant total

In 2016/17 the trust had an income of £8,100 and a total expenditure of £8,600. We estimate that the trust awarded £3,000 in grants to individuals.

Exclusions

The trust cannot renew or commit to repeat grants.

Applications

Applications should be made directly to the correspondent, including details of financial need and what the grant will be used for.

Other information

The trust also makes grants to individuals for education, and to local organisations and charities in the area.

Dempster Trust

£5,000

Correspondent: Jon Curtis, Trustee, 21 Broomleaf Road, Farnham GU9 8DG (01252 721075; email: joncurtis@thedempstertrust.org.uk)

CC number: 200107

Eligibility

People in need, hardship or distress who live in Farnham and the general neighbourhood.

Types of grants

One-off grants or help for limited periods only. In the past, grants have been given towards nursing requisites, relieving sudden distress, travelling expenses, fuel, television and telephone bills, clothing, washing machines, televisions, radios, alarm systems and so on.

Annual grant total

In 2016/17 the trust had an income of £10,700 and a total expenditure of £10,100. We estimate that grants given to individuals totalled £5,000, with funding also awarded to local organisations.

Exclusions

Help is not given towards rent, rates or home improvements.

Applications

Apply on a form available from the correspondent or from the trust's website, to be submitted through a doctor, social worker, hospital, Citizens Advice or another welfare agency. Applications can be considered at any time.

Other information

Following the death of a long-standing trustee, the trust established The Jack Mayhew Education Grant to support students who may be in need of books, computers or other significant costs, to start their studies at university. Cash grants are not given but the trust will purchase the equipment on the student's behalf. Schools and colleges in Farnham should apply on behalf of the individual.

Margaret Jeannie Hindley Charitable Trust

£10,000

Correspondent: Lisa Rabinowitz, Trustee, c/o Marshalls Solicitors, 102 High Street, Godalming, Surrey GU7 1DS (01483 416101; email: lisa@marshalls.uk.net)

CC number: 272140

Eligibility
Relief of poverty among people in 'reduced or destitute circumstances'. Priority is given to people living in the Godalming area.

Types of grants
One-off and recurrent grants are given according to need.

Annual grant total
In 2016/17 the trust had an income of £21,500 and a total expenditure of £22,000. We estimate that grants given to individuals totalled £10,000, with funding also awarded to local organisations.

Applications
Apply in writing to the correspondent. The trustees meet regularly throughout the year to consider applications.

Shottermill United Charities

£1,000

Correspondent: Hilary Bicknell, Administrator, 7 Underwood Road, Haslemere, Surrey GU27 1JQ (01428 651276; email: hilary.bicknell@gmail.com)

CC number: 200394

Eligibility
People in need who live in the parish of Shottermill, Surrey.

Types of grants
Grants usually ranging from £40 to £50 according to need. The charity distributes grocery vouchers at Christmas.

Annual grant total
In 2016/17 the charity had an income of £2,100 and a total expenditure of £1,900. We estimate that around £1,000 was given in grants to individuals for social welfare purposes.

Applications
Apply in writing to the correspondent. Applications can be submitted directly by the individual or through a social worker, Citizens Advice or other welfare agency or third party. They are considered at any time, but particularly at Christmas.

Other information
The charity also gives grants to organisations.

Anthony Smith and Others

£1,200

Correspondent: Revd Peter Muir, Trustee, Yew Cottage, Dye House Lane, Thursley, Godalming GU8 6QA (01252 702360; email: peter.muir@thursleychurch.org.uk)

CC number: 239259

Eligibility
People in need, including those who have disabilities or are sick, older, single parents and bereaved young people, who live in the parish of Thursley in Surrey.

Types of grants
One-off and recurrent grants are given according to need.

Annual grant total
In 2015/16 the charity had an income of £2,400 and a total expenditure of £2,600. We estimate that the charity gave around £1,200 in grants to individuals.

Applications
Apply in writing to the correspondent. Applications can be submitted directly by the individual or through an organisation such as Citizens Advice, or through a third party such as a social worker. Applications are considered in November each year.

Other information
The charity is made up of the Charities of Anthony Smith and Henry Smith.

The Henry Smith Charity (Bramley)

£2,000

Correspondent: Kathy Victor, Administrator, Bramley Village Hall, Hall Road, Bramley, Guildford GU5 0AX (01483 894138; email: bramleyparish@gmail.com; website: www.bramleyparish.co.uk)

CC number: 200128

Eligibility
People in need who live in the parish of Bramley, Surrey.

Types of grants
One-off grants according to need.

Annual grant total
In 2015/16 the charity had an income of £3,600 and a total expenditure of £4,000. We estimate that grants given to individuals totalled £2,000, with funding also awarded to local organisations.

Applications
Apply in writing to the correspondent; there are no application forms. The letter should contain as much information as possible about why support is required.

Other information
This charity is also known as the Smiths Charity.

The Witley Charitable Trust

£900

Correspondent: Daphne O'Hanlon, Trustee, Triados, Waggoners Way, Grayshott, Hindhead, Surrey GU26 6DX (01428 604679)

CC number: 200338

Eligibility
Children and young people (normally under the age of 20) and older people (normally aged over 60) who are in need and who live in the parishes of Witley, Milford and small part of Brook.

Types of grants
One-off, modest grants ranging from £25 to £300. Support can be given towards telephone, electricity and gas debts (up to about £150, usually paid via social services), for medical appliances not available through the NHS, in Christmas gifts, food hampers or vouchers, and towards other needs.

Annual grant total
In 2016 the trust had an income of £3,700 and a total expenditure of £1,900. We estimate that grants for welfare purposes totalled around £900.

Applications
Applications can be made in writing to the correspondent. Applications should be submitted through nurses, doctors, social workers, clergy, Citizens Advice and other welfare agencies, but not directly by the individual. Awards are usually considered in early February and September, although emergency applications can be considered throughout the year.

Other information
Grants are also given for educational needs.

The Wonersh Charities

£3,300

Correspondent: Anna Pritchard, Correspondent, 8 Hullmead, Shamley Green, Guildford, Surrey GU5 0UG (01483 894191; email: wonershuc@gmail.com)

CC number: 200086

Eligibility

Older people and people with a disability who live in the parishes of Wonersh, Shamley Green and Blackheath.

Types of grants

Cash grants are given at Christmas. One-off grants are also available.

Annual grant total

In 2016/17 the charity had an income of £5,500 and had a total expenditure of £6,800. We estimate that the charity gave around £3,300 in grants to individuals. The charity is also responsible for maintaining a memorial tablet at Wonersh Church.

Applications

Apply in writing to the correspondent, preferably through a third party such as Citizens Advice, trustee of the charity, local clergy or welfare organisation. Applications are usually considered in early July and early December.

Woking

The Byfleet United Charity

£126,500

Correspondent: Director, 10 Stoop Court, Leisure Lane, West Byfleet, Surrey KT14 6HF (01932 340943; email: buc@byfleetunitedcharity.org.uk)

CC number: 200344

Eligibility

People in need who have lived in the ancient parish of Byfleet or West Byfleet area for at least a year (normally three years) immediately prior to their application.

Types of grants

Monthly pensions and one-off grants towards essential items, such as cookers, heaters, vacuum cleaners and nursery school fees.

Annual grant total

In 2015/16 the charity held assets of £10.7 million and had an income of £243,500. During the year, the charity awarded a total of £126,500 to individuals. Of this amount, £62,500 was given in pensions and £64,000 in grants.

Exclusions

People outside the area of benefit or resident there temporarily can only be assisted in exceptional circumstances.

Applications

Apply in writing to the correspondent. Applications can be made directly by the individual or through a third party, such as a social worker, Citizens Advice, local GP or church. Candidates are usually visited and assessed.

Other information

The charity gives money to local organisations. It also operates a sheltered housing complex of 24 flats available to people over the age of 55 who are in real need.

This charity is an amalgamation of smaller trusts, including the Byfleet Pensions Fund.

Chobham Poor Allotment Charity

£9,700

Correspondent: Elizabeth Thody, 46 Chertsey Road, Windlesham GU20 6EP

CC number: 200154

Eligibility

People in need who live in the ancient parish of Chobham, which includes the civil parishes of Chobham and West End.

Types of grants

The majority of grants are given in the form of vouchers, ranging between £30 and £50, as payment towards goods in local shops. Assistance is also given to provide stairlifts and electric scooters.

Annual grant total

In 2016/17 the charity had assets of £435,500 and an income of £49,500. Grants to individuals totalled £9,700.

Applications

Applications can be made on a form available from the correspondent. Applications should be submitted directly by the individual for consideration at any time.

Other information

The charity also manages almshouses and an area of allotment land. As well as making grants, the charity also supports local organisations through the provision of interest-free loans.

Henry Smith (Share Warbleton Estate)

£5,800

Correspondent: David Bittleston, Trustee, Pin Mill, Heathfield Road, Woking GU22 7JJ (01483 828621)

CC number: 232281

Eligibility

People in need who live in the ancient parish of Woking.

Types of grants

One-off grants only.

Annual grant total

In 2016/17 the charity had both an income and a total expenditure of £6,000. We estimate that grants given to individuals totalled £5,800.

Exclusions

Grants are not given for the relief of rates, taxes and other public funds.

Applications

Apply in writing to the vicar of the parish, either directly by the individual or, where applicable, through a social worker, Citizens Advice or other welfare agency. Successful grants are distributed by the vicars of each of the seven parishes in the area.

West Sussex

Midhurst Pensions Trust

£34,000

Correspondent: Anina Cheng, Administrator, 4th Floor, Swan House, 17–19 Stratford Place, London W1C 1BQ (020 7907 2100; email: charity@mfs.co.uk)

CC number: 245230

Eligibility

People in need who have been employed by the Third Viscount Cowdray, Lady Anne Cowdray, any family company or on the Cowdray Estate, and their dependants.

Types of grants

One-off grants typically in the range of £25 to £2,000.

Annual grant total

In 2015/16 the trust had an income of £90,000 and a total expenditure of £94,000. During the year, the trust gave around £34,000 in grants to individuals.

Applications

Apply in writing to the correspondent.

The Three Oaks Trust

£49,500 (241 grants)

Correspondent: The Trustees, The Three Oaks Family Trust Co. Ltd, 65 Worthing Road, Horsham, West Sussex RH12 1TD (email: contact@thethreeoakstrust.co.uk; website: www.thethreeoakstrust.co.uk)

CC number: 297079

Eligibility

People and families in need who live in West Sussex. There is a particular focus on people with a physical or mental disability (including learning difficulties), and on low-income families, single parents and the long-term sick.

Types of grants

One-off grants of up to £300 towards basic furnishings, clothing, washing machines, fridges, telephone connections and so on. For items over £300, the trust can make a contribution towards costs.

Annual grant total

In 2015/16 the trust had assets of £7.3 million and an income of £252,500. During the year, the trust made 241 grants to individuals totalling £49,500.

Exclusions

No funding for gap year work or similar activities.

Applications

Direct applications by individuals will not be considered. Applications can be made through Crawley and Horsham Social Services and Citizens Advice and other local, statutory and voluntary organisations. The trust has a helpful website where further details of how to apply on behalf of someone with multiple or complex needs are available.

Other information

The trust also supports a number of social welfare organisations in the UK and overseas through grants, and occasionally provides individuals with financial support for educational purposes.

Chichester
The Pest House Charity

£800

Correspondent: Tim Rudwick, Clerk, 31 Pretoria Avenue, Midhurst GU29 9PP (01730 812489; email: timrudwick@yahoo.co.uk)

CC number: 227479

Eligibility

People living in the parish of Midhurst who are in need and/or have ill health.

Types of grants

According to our research, one-off grants in the range of £60 to £500 are given towards various needs. In the past, support has been given towards transport and holiday costs.

Annual grant total

In 2016 the charity had an income of £12,400 and a total expenditure of £6,300. Our research suggests that the majority of the charity's expenditure is used to maintain the its properties. Previously, grants to individuals have totalled around £800 annually.

Exclusions

Requests from outside the parish will not be accepted.

Applications

Apply in writing to the correspondent. Applications can be made either directly by the individual or through a social worker, Citizens Advice or other welfare agency. They are usually considered in April and October and should be received in the preceding month.

Other information

Grants are also made to other organisations and occasionally to a local school.

Crawley
Crawley and Ifield Relief in Sickness Fund

£3,800

Correspondent: Roger Gibson, Trustee, 7 Priestcroft Close, Crawley RH11 8RL (01293 520752; email: roger.gibson7@talktalk.net)

CC number: 254779

Eligibility

People in need who are sick, convalescent or have disabilities and live within a three-mile radius of the church of St John Crawley.

Types of grants

One-off grants are given to alleviate suffering and assist recovery.

Annual grant total

In 2016 the charity had an income of £2,500 and a total expenditure of £4,000. We estimate that grants given to individuals totalled £3,800.

Applications

Apply in writing to the correspondent.

Horsham
The Ashington, Wiston, Warminghurst Sick Poor Fund

£5,500

Correspondent: Rod Shepherd, Trustee, c/o Sheen Stickland LLP, 7 East Pallant, Chichester, West Sussex PO19 1TR (email: rod.shepherd@btinternet.com)

CC number: 234625

Eligibility

People in need – typically those who are ill – who live, firstly in the villages of Ashington, Wiston and Warminghurst, and secondly, in West Sussex.

Types of grants

One-off grants according to need. Most grants are for equipment that will make an ill individual's life easier, although the trustees award grants towards anything that will improve their well-being. The average grant is £300.

Annual grant total

In 2016 the fund had an income of £520 and a total expenditure of £5,970 We estimate that grants given to individuals for welfare purposes totalled £5,500 during the year.

Applications

Application forms are available from the correspondent. Applications can be submitted directly by the individual or a relevant third party.

Mid Sussex
The Chownes Foundation

£17,000

Correspondent: Sylvia Spencer, Secretary, The Courtyard, Shoreham Road, Upper Beeding, Steyning, West Sussex BN44 3TN (01903 816699; email: sylvia@russellnew.com)

CC number: 327451

Eligibility

Former employees of Sound Diffusion plc who lost their pensions when the company went into receivership. Our research indicates that grants are also made to assist older people who live in mid-Sussex and are in need.

Types of grants

One-off and recurrent grants are given according to need.

Annual grant total

In 2016/17 the foundation had an income of £7,200 and a total expenditure of £68,000. Due to its low income, the foundation was not required to submit accounts. We estimate that around £17,000 was awarded to individuals for welfare purposes.

The foundation also awards grants to organisations and individuals for educational purposes.

Applications
Apply in writing to the correspondent.

Other information
The majority of the charity's funds are committed to long-term support for poor and vulnerable beneficiaries, so very few applications are successful.

South West

General

Viscount Amory's Charitable Trust

£750

Correspondent: Secretary to the Trustees, The Island, Lowman Green, Tiverton, Devon EX16 4LA (01884 254899; email: office@vact.org.uk; website: www.vact.org.uk)

CC number: 204958

Eligibility

People in need in the south west of England.

Types of grants

One-off and recurrent grants are given according to need. Short-term loans may also be awarded.

Annual grant total

In 2015/16 the trust had assets of £13 million and an income of £469,500. Grants to individuals for welfare purposes totalled £750.

Applications

Apply in writing to the correspondent, for consideration every month. Applications should be submitted by post, not email. Details of what should be included are outlined on the website.

Other information

The charity also gives grants to individuals for educational purposes and to organisations.

The Beckly Trust

£3,000

Correspondent: Stephen Trahair, Trustee, 10 South Hill, Stoke, Plymouth PL1 5RR (01752 675071; email: stephentrahair@blueyonder.co.uk)

CC number: 235763

Eligibility

Children under 18 who live in the city of Plymouth or district of Caradon, Cornwall and who have an illness or a disability and are in need.

Types of grants

One-off grants of around £100 to £300.

Annual grant total

In 2015/16 the trust had an income of £12,200 and a total expenditure of £3,600. We have estimate that grants to individuals totalled £3,000 during the year. Funding is occasionally also awarded to organisations.

Applications

Apply in writing to the correspondent giving brief details of income and outgoings of the applicant's parent/guardian and a description of the child's need. Applications should be made preferably through a social worker, Citizens Advice or other welfare agency but can also be made directly by the individual or through another third party. They are considered on an ongoing basis.

Grateful Society

£12,700 (18 grants)

Correspondent: FAO Robert Drewett, Hon. Secretary, c/o Womble Bond Dickinson (UK) LLP, 3 Temple Quay, Temple Back East, Bristol BS1 6DZ (email: robert.drewett@wbd-uk.com; website: gratefulsociety.org)

CC number: 202349

Eligibility

Women over 50 who have lived in Bristol and the surrounding areas (including the unitary authorities of North Somerset, South Gloucestershire or Bath and North East Somerset) for at least ten years and would benefit from financial assistance, typically to pursue an independent life in their own home.

Types of grants

Regular allowances, paid quarterly. One-off grants can be paid towards, for example, electrical goods, clothing, household bills, food, holidays, travel expenses, heating repairs, medical equipment, furniture and disability equipment.

Annual grant total

In 2016 the society had assets of £294,500 and an income of £160,000. During the year, annuities totalled £12,700. Other grants totalled a further £100,000, however we were unable to determine the proportion of this figure allocated to individuals.

Applications

Apply in writing to the correspondent. Applications may be submitted directly by the individual or through a third party.

Other information

The society also funds day centres and organisations with similar aims and a wide range of activities aimed at supporting and engaging older people.

The Pirate Trust

£1,400

Correspondent: Nicholas Lake, Correspondent, Pirate FM Ltd, Carn Brea Studios, Barncoose Industrial Estate, Redruth, Cornwall TR15 3XX (01209 314400; email: piratetrust@piratefm.co.uk; website: www.piratefm.co.uk/piratetrust)

CC number: 1032096

Eligibility

People in need living within the Pirate FM 102 broadcast area (Cornwall, Plymouth and west Devon). Preference is given to people with disabilities.

Types of grants

One-off and recurrent grants mainly towards disability equipment.

Annual grant total

In 2015/16 the trust had an income of £3,700 and a total expenditure of £3,100. We estimate that grants given to individuals for welfare purposes totalled around £1,400.

Applications

Application forms are available to download from the website.

South West Peninsula Football League Benevolent Fund

£4,500

Correspondent: Mark Hayman, Trustee, SCONICCA, 17 Nelson Place, Newton Abbot, Devon TQ12 2JH (01626 363376; email: phil@swpleague.co.uk; website: www.swpleague.co.uk)

CC number: 1079397

Eligibility
People in need who live in the counties of Devon and Cornwall who are or were involved with or connected to the South West Peninsula Football League, and referees in the league. Grants are given to people who have disabilities, a serious illness, or have experienced a personal misfortune.

Types of grants
One-off and recurrent grants. An example of support given in the past is an award made to a player with a depressed cheekbone fracture.

Annual grant total
In 2016/17 the fund had an income of £5,000 and a total expenditure of £4,800. We estimate that grants given to individuals totalled around £4,500.

Exclusions
Grants are not available to people with short-term injuries.

Applications
Applications can be made either directly by the individual or through a third party, such as a social worker, Citizens Advice or club secretary. Applications should include the individual's marital and employment status, number of children and length of incapacity. Supporting documentation may be required upon request. Our previous research indicates that the trustees meet to consider applications on the first Thursday of January, March, May, September and November, although emergency grants may be approved between meetings.

Other information
The charity is known as the Millennium Benevolent Fund.

St Monica Trust

£245,000 (468+ grants)

Correspondent: Community Fund Team, Cote Lane, Westbury-on-Trym, Bristol BS9 3UN (0117 949 4000; email: info@stmonicatrust.org.uk; website: www.stmonicatrust.org.uk)

CC number: 202151

Eligibility
People who have a physical disability or long-term physical health problem living in Bristol, South Gloucestershire, North Somerset or Bath and North East Somerset. Applicants must have a low income, limited savings and be over 40 years old.

Types of grants
Gifts: one-off grants averaging around £300 but never exceeding £500 to help towards mobility aids, home/car adaptations, domestic appliances, furniture and flooring, bedding, clothing, health costs, communication aids, bills and debts. This list is by no means exhaustive and gifts will be considered for anything that will make a positive difference to the applicant's everyday life.

Short-term grants: a period of monthly payments designed to help a person through a time of crisis. For example, help can be given for: debt relief; adjusting to a sudden loss of income; unexpected costs; and the extra costs involved when undergoing chemotherapy, interferon or similar treatments. Usually up to £25 each week for a period of time, ranging between a couple of months up to a maximum of three years. Help is usually given for around six months.

Annual grant total
In 2016 the trust had assets of £272.4 million and an income of £28.9 million. Grants were made to 530 individuals totalling £245,000 and were broken down as follows:

Gifts	332	£143,500
Short-term grants	187	£94,500
Annuities	1	£3,600

Applications
Apply on a form available to download from the trust's website or by contacting the trust directly. If possible, applications should be submitted via a social worker, advice worker or a similar professional, although individuals can apply themselves.

The trust expects applicants to have applied for available statutory funding (e.g. Community Care Grants or Disabled Facilities Grants) before applying. Applicants may be referred to a relevant trade or forces benevolent fund before their application is considered. The trust's website also advises: 'If you own your own home and are asking for help with repairs or improvements, we would expect you to investigate equity release schemes and charitable interest-free loans before you ask us for help.'

Other information
Grants are also made to organisations whose aim is to support a similar group of beneficiaries, with 15 organisations receiving a total of £163,000 in 2016. The trust also provides sheltered housing and retirement accommodation, support services, and nursing and residential care. The trust also works in partnership with Bristol City Council, the Clinical Commissioning Group and other local charities on a project called LinkAge, supporting older people.

Wessex Cancer Trust

£24,000

Correspondent: Cait Allen, 91–95 Winchester Road, Chandler's Ford, Eastleigh SO53 2GG (023 8067 2200; email: wct@wessexcancer.org; website: www.wessexcancer.org.uk)

CC number: 1110216

Eligibility
The applicant must be diagnosed with cancer, living in Dorset, Hampshire, the Isle of Wight, or Wiltshire, and in financial need. To qualify for transport to hospitals, the individual must live on the Isle of Wight or the Channel Islands.

Types of grants
Grants to relieve financial hardship that is brought on due to the costs associated with cancer. The trust also provides hospital transport and holiday homes for respite care.

Annual grant total
In 2016 the trust had assets of £543,000 and an income of £1.3 million. During the year, the trust awarded £24,000 in grants to individuals.

Applications
Individuals wishing to apply for hardship grants, hospital travel, or a respite holiday should contact the trust in the first instance.

Other information
The trust also makes grants to organisations with similar objectives.

City of Bristol

The Anchor Society

£47,500 (130 grants)

Correspondent: Catherine Watts, Administrator, 29 Alma Vale Road, Clifton, Bristol BS8 2HL (0117 973 4161; email: admin@anchorsociety.co.uk; website: www.anchorsociety.co.uk)

CC number: 208756

Eligibility

Isolated people over the age of 55 who are in genuine immediate need and live in the Bristol and former Avon postcode area (BS).

Types of grants

One-off and regular grants to help older people stay independent and in their own homes. Grants can be used for essential home repairs and adaptations, mobility aids and helping make homes more accessible and safe.

Annual grant total

In 2015/16 the society had assets of £3.9 million and an income of £119,500. Grants were made totalling £167,500, of which £47,500 was given to individuals and £120,000 to one organisation. During the year, the society paid £8,500 to its 14 regular annuitants and made 116 grants totalling £39,000 for specific purposes.

Exclusions

The society does not give grants for general living expenses, to pay off outstanding bills, to cover moving costs or travel expenses, holidays or respite breaks, insurance costs or funeral costs.

Applications

Applications should be made through the society's website and should be completed by a third party responsible for referring the individual for a grant.

Other information

The society operates a befriending service that is provided by volunteers and provides sheltered accommodation for older people on a long-leasehold tenure.

The society has also invested in the provision of a new form of day care for older people within the region through Link Age, which it supports with an annual grant (£120,000 in 2015/16) and has close links with other welfare charities in the area. It has invested in a number of housing projects as well as a robotics laboratory which allows researchers to trial new assisted living technology.

The Charity of Thomas Beames

£3,000

Correspondent: Anne Maddox, All Saints Centre, 1 All Saints Court, Bristol BS1 1JN (0117 929 2709)

CC number: 245822

Eligibility

People in need who live in the parishes of Christchurch with St George, St Stephen with St James or St John the Baptist with St Michael, Bristol. In exceptional cases, the charity may help people who live outside this area or those that live in the former parish of St George with St Augustine, who produce sufficient good reason why they should be treated as being resident within the parish.

Types of grants

One-off grants.

Annual grant total

In 2015 the charity had an income of £5,800 and a total expenditure of £3,500. We estimate that grants given to individuals totalled £3,000 during the year.

Applications

Apply in writing to the correspondent including details of why help is needed.

Elizabeth Blanchard's Charity

£1,800

Correspondent: Ruth Mico, 3 Springfield Grove, Bristol BS6 7X (email: gruthie_myo@hotmail.com)

CC number: 243122

Eligibility

Women who are in financial hardship; who are members of the congregation assembling for religious worship at the chapel known as Old King Street Baptist chapel in Cairns Road in the city of Bristol.

Types of grants

One-off, small grants.

Annual grant total

In 2016 the charity had an income of £2,100 and a total expenditure of £2,000. We estimate that the charity gave around £1,800 in grants to individuals.

Applications

Apply in writing to the correspondent.

The Bristol Benevolent Institution

£402,000 (235 grants)

Correspondent: Maureen Nicholls, Secretary, 45 High Street, Nailsea, Bristol BS48 1AW (01275 810365; mobile 07968 434274; email: secretarybbi@gmail.com; website: bristolbenevolent.org)

CC number: 204592

Eligibility

Older people with small fixed incomes and little or no capital. Applicants must be over 60 and have lived in Bristol for 15 years or more. People over the age of 55 who have chronic illness or severe disabilities are also eligible.

Types of grants

Mostly small recurrent grants paid quarterly, usually between £320 and £1,300 per annum. One-off grants may also be made for specific needs, such as household items, repairs or removal fees.

People over the age of 70 who own their own homes, free of mortgage, can apply for small interest-free loans to help supplement a low income or to help make essential repairs. Loans are repaid from the sale of the property upon the death of the beneficiary, or if the beneficiary sells their home. In the cases of couples, a loan can be transferred to the surviving spouse automatically.

Annual grant total

In 2016 the institution held assets of £14.5 million and had an income of £551,000. Grants to individuals totalled £402,000. An average of 229 grants were paid to individuals each quarter and 51 loans were also made during the year.

During the year, the trustees also awarded each beneficiary special grants of £225 to assist with heating costs in winter as well as a grant of £150 in summer. Beneficiaries also received a Christmas grant of £75.

A further £13,500 was awarded in grants to other charities to run local lunch clubs for older people and to Care and Repair to fund a large number of small repairs quickly.

Exclusions

The institution's website states that while it 'cannot give grants to people who own their own homes', it can offer interest-free loans to those homeowners over the age of 70.

Applications

Potential applicants should contact the Secretary by phone, email or in writing. A visitor from the institution will then call to complete an application. Applications can be submitted directly by the individuals or through a third party such as a family member, a friend, a social worker or GP, provided the individual concerned is notified and approves of the application. Applications are considered at quarterly trustees' meeting.

Other information

The institution notes that although it gives financial assistance, 'we believe that the most valued assistance we give is friendship and advice, ably provided by our visitors'. Newsletters, visits and telephone calls help the institution keep in touch with its beneficiaries.

Bristol Charities

£159,000

Correspondent: Grants Committee, 17 Augustines Parade, Bristol BS1 4UL (0117 930 0301; email: grants@ bristolcharities.org.uk; website: www. bristolcharities.org.uk)

CC number: 1109141

Eligibility

People in need who have lived in Bristol for more than two consecutive years.

Types of grants

Welfare grants are available for white goods (up to £250), small electrical equipment such as vacuum cleaners or microwaves, carpets and furniture, starter packs for the kitchen and the bedroom, medical equipment, respite breaks for carers, nursing and care services, support for carers after the death of the person being cared for.

The educational funds can make grants towards the cost of studying the arts, music, sport or religious instruction. It can also make grants for extracurricular activities such as school trips, instruments and tools, books or specialised clothing/sports kits. Note that these grants are typically given to organisations or suppliers, and not the individual.

Annual grant total

In 2015/16 the charity had a consolidated income of almost £1.7 million and a total expenditure of over £1.7 million. Welfare grants to individuals totalled £159,000 and grants for education totalled £2,800.

Exclusions

Welfare grants cannot be used for clothing, tumble dryers, TVs, PCs or audio equipment, baby equipment, fees for those in care, rent arrears or other debts. The educational grants programme cannot fund school uniforms or school fees.

Applications

Application forms are available from the Bristol Charities website; the charity is

no longer accepting paper applications. All applicants require the support of a sponsor who should be a healthcare professional. Applicants can apply for a number of grants of up to the value of £245 in a three-year period.

Other information

The charity owns four almshouses in Bristol and Monmouthshire which offer 73 flats for people over the age of 60 and who have entitlement to housing benefit or who have limited financial means. It also runs day centres in Bristol – see the website for more information.

The Lord Mayor of Bristol's Christmas Appeal for Children

£58,000 (1,650 grants)

Correspondent: Bruce Simmonds, Hon. Treasurer, 3 Park Crescent, Frenchay, Bristol BS16 1PD (07768 077864; website: www.lordmayorofbristolappeal. co.uk)

CC number: 288262

Eligibility

Children under 16 who are in need and who live in the city of Bristol.

Types of grants

One-off grants at Christmas in the form of vouchers. Each child receives two vouchers; one worth £20 to be spent on food, and another worth £20 to be spent on either clothing or toys.

Annual grant total

In 2015/16 the trust held assets of £69,000 and had an income of £74,500. The total value of food, clothing and toy vouchers, awarded to approximately 1,650 children, amounted to £58,000.

Applications

Through a social worker, Citizens Advice, welfare agency or other third party such as a parent or a person who can confirm the individual's needs.

Other information

The charity originated in the 1920s, when it was known as the Lord Mayor's Fund, and the money raised was used to provide Christmas dinners and boots for poor children.

Dolphin Society

£74,000

Correspondent: Sean Hollinswaite, Administrator, Bramford House, 23 Westfield Park, Bristol BS6 6LT (0117 929 9649; email: dolphinsociety@ btconnect.com; website: www.dolphin-society.org.uk)

CC number: 203142

Eligibility

Older people or people with disabilities who live in Bristol and its adjoining local authority areas, who have a low income and need help to maintain their independence and safety in their own homes.

Types of grants

Free pendant alarms are given to individuals who do not qualify for local authority assistance. The charity also channels funding through the charity WE Care and Repair to facilitate home adaptations (e.g. installing a walk-in shower or replacing steps with a ramp) and emergency repairs (e.g. for central heating).

Annual grant total

In 2015/16 the charity had assets of £179,500 and an income of £92,500. Direct charitable expenditure was broken down as follows:

Grants payable to WE Care and Repair	£37,500
Pendant alarms and telephone installation	£36,500
IT project	£1,000

We have taken the sum of grants to WE Care and Repair and expenditure on pendant alarms and telephone installation as our total.

Exclusions

No grants are made to applicants living outside the area of benefit.

Applications

For more information on pendant alarms, and how to apply for one, contact the correspondent.

Further information on assistance with home adaptations and heating repairs is available from WE Care and Repair (tel: 0117 954 2222; email: info@ bristolcareandrepair.org.uk).

The Peter Hervé Benevolent Institution

£61,000 (35 grants)

Correspondent: June Anderson, Grants Administrator, Suite F11B, Kestrel Court Business Centre, Harbour Road, Portishead, Bristol BS20 7AN (0117 929 1929)

CC number: 202443

Eligibility

People aged 60 and over who live within a 25-mile radius of Bristol city centre, own their own homes and have fallen on hard times.

Types of grants

Recurrent grants, averaging £200 a quarter, and one-off emergency grants of up to £500 towards, for example, the costs of a new boiler.

Annual grant total

In 2016 the charity held assets of almost £2.25 million and had an income of £99,500. Grants and annuities to individuals totalled £61,000 and were distributed as follows:

Emergency gifts	£38,000
Regular gifts	£21,000
Annuities	£1,900

Applications

The charity does not accept applications directly but rather invites organisations working with potential beneficiaries to apply for annuities and emergency gifts.

The Redcliffe Parish Charity

£1,500

Correspondent: Paul Tracey, Trustee, 18 Kingston Road, Nailsea, Bristol, North Somerset BS48 4RD (email: redcliffeparishclerk@mail.com)

CC number: 203916

Eligibility

People in need who live in the city of Bristol, with preference for those who live in the ecclesiastical parish of St Mary Redcliffe with Temple – Bristol, and St John the Baptist – Bedminster.

Types of grants

One-off grants usually of £25 to £50. The trustees generally limit grants to families or individuals who can usually manage, but who are overwhelmed by circumstances and are in particular financial stress rather than continuing need. Our research suggests that grants are typically given for electric goods, clothing, living costs, food, holidays, furniture and equipment for people with disabilities.

Annual grant total

In 2015/16 the charity had an income of £8,300 and a total expenditure of £6,200. We estimate that welfare grants to individuals totalled £1,500.

Applications

Awards are made through a third party, such as social services, housing associations, a doctor or health visitor, Citizens Advice or other appropriate body. Applications need to be made in writing on behalf of an individual for consideration each month. Ages of family members should be supplied in addition to financial circumstances and the reason for the request.

Other information

Grants to schoolchildren are also made as part of the charity's wider welfare work.

Cornwall

Blanchminster Trust

£31,000 (43 grants)

Correspondent: Jane Bunning, Blanchminster Building, 38 Lansdown Road, Bude, Cornwall EX23 8EE (01288 352851; email: office@blanchminster. plus.com; website: www.blanchminster. org.uk)

CC number: 202118

Eligibility

People who live in the parishes of Bude, Stratton and Poughill (the former urban district of Bude-Stratton), who are in need.

Types of grants

Assistance may be given in the form of a cash grant, disability equipment or travel costs for hospital visits, for example.

Annual grant total

In 2016 the trust had assets of £11.1 million and an income of £501,000. The trust awarded 43 grants to individuals for welfare purposes totalling £31,000.

Applications

Applications should be made in writing to the correspondent and outline exactly what assistance is needed and why. The trust does not have a standard application form, although it will send a financial enquiry form to individuals seeking assistance. Applications must include details of weekly income and expenditure, as well as information on any efforts that have been made to seek help from elsewhere.

Other information

Grants are also made to individuals for educational purposes and for community projects.

The Lizzie Brooke Charity

£33,000

Correspondent: Sheila Bates, Administrator, 13 Church Close, Lelant, St Ives TR26 3JX (01736 752383)

CC number: 254764

Eligibility

Older people, people who are sick and those in need who live in West Cornwall.

Types of grants

One-off grants.

Annual grant total

In 2016 the charity had an income of £2,200 and a total expenditure of £36,000. We estimate that grants given to individuals totalled £33,000.

Exclusions

Grants are not made to people living in other parts of Cornwall or for students for fees.

Applications

Apply on a form available from the correspondent, to be completed by a sponsor. Applications should be submitted through a social worker, Citizens Advice or other welfare agency. They are considered at any time.

Cornwall Community Foundation

£56,000

Correspondent: The Grants Team, Suite 1, Sheers Barton, Lawhitton, Launceston, Cornwall PL15 9NJ (01566 779865 or 01566 779333; email: office@ cornwallfoundation.com; website: www. cornwallfoundation.com)

CC number: 1099977

Eligibility

People in need living in Cornwall.

Types of grants

According to the foundation's website the following grants are available to individuals:

- **Duke of Cornwall's Benevolent Fund** - for young carers aged 18 or under where their duties go beyond what would be expected for a person of their age
- **Lord Lieutenant's Fund for Youth** - for young people who are exceptionally talented and gifted
- **The Emily Bolitho Trust** - for individuals faced with hardship through poor health and low income living in the old borough of Penzance including Gulval, Mousehole, Paul, Newlyn, Ludgvan, Marazion and Madron
- **Crisis Fund** - for people in crisis who are urgently in need of small, one-off amounts of money. Funds are made to charitable organisations throughout Cornwall for distribution to individuals
- **Crisis Fund, St Martin in the Fields Vicar's Relief Fund** - a grant can only be made by a sponsor or agency organisation, working to alleviate, and prevent homelessness, on behalf of the people they are supporting

Annual grant total

In 2016 the foundation had assets of £4.67 million and an income of £1.2 million. Grants to individuals totalled £56,000.

Applications

Application forms are available to download from the foundation's website.

Other information

Grants are mostly made to organisations, groups, clubs and community projects.

The Duke of Cornwall's Benevolent Fund

£2,000 (two grants)

Correspondent: Terry Cotter, Administrator, Duchy of Cornwall, 10 Buckingham Gate, London SW1E 6LA (020 7834 7346)

CC number: 269183

Eligibility

People who are in need because of sickness, poverty or age. In practice, funds are steered towards the South West and areas related to Duchy lands, which are principally in Cornwall.

Types of grants

One-off and recurrent grants are given according to need.

Annual grant total

In 2016/17 the fund held assets of £5.3 million and had an income of £526,500. During the year, the fund awarded grants of less than £1,000 each to individuals and organisations totalling over £16,000. There were two grants to individuals.

We estimate that grants given to individuals for welfare purposes totalled around £2,000.

Applications

Apply in writing to the correspondent. The trustees meet quarterly to consider grants.

Other information

The fund's main focus is on awarding grants to registered charities.

Charity of John Davey

£12,000

Correspondent: E. Pascoe, Tregenna Lodge, Crane, Camborne TR14 7QX (01209 718853; email: pbfhayle@hotmail.co.uk)

CC number: 232127

Eligibility

Ex-miners over 70 years of age and their widows who are in need and live in the ancient parish of Gwennap, near Redruth in Cornwall. Support is also given to miners of any age who are unable to work due to sickness or injury.

Types of grants

One-off and recurrent grants are given according to need.

Annual grant total

In 2015/16 the charity had an income of £12,000 and a total expenditure of £13,000. We estimate that the charity awarded £12,000 in grants to individuals.

Applications

Application forms are available to request from the correspondent.

The Heathcoat Trust

See entry on page 389

Charity of Thomas Henwood

£4,500

Correspondent: Jennifer Moyle, Trustee, Homeleigh, Gunwalloe, Helston TR12 7QG (01326 564806)

CC number: 206765

Eligibility

People who live in the parish of Gunwalloe who are unemployed, sick or retired and in need.

Types of grants

One-off or recurrent grants according to need, and grants for the provision of nurses and to assist people recovering from illness. Income is also used to care for graves in the churchyard if no relatives are still alive.

Annual grant total

In 2016 the charity had an income of £10,100 and a total expenditure of £4,700. We estimate that grants given to individuals totalled £4,500.

Applications

Apply in writing to the trustees. Applications are considered in March and December.

Pete's Dragons

See entry on page 390

Devon

Mrs E. L. Blakeley-Marillier Charitable Fund

£10,000

Correspondent: Lynn Young, Charitable Trust Administrator, Wollen Michelmore Solicitors, Carlton House, 30 The Terrace, Torquay, Devon TQ1 1BS (01803 213251; email: lynn.young@wollenmichelmore.co.uk; website: www.wollenmichelmore.co.uk)

CC number: 207138

Eligibility

Ladies over 55 who are in need and are not of the Roman Catholic faith or members of the Salvation Army. Preference is given to women from the counties of Yorkshire and Devon and in particular the towns of Scarborough and Torquay.

Types of grants

Annuities of a maximum £520 per year are paid in two instalments.

Annual grant total

In 2015/16 the fund had an income of £490 and a total expenditure of £10,700. We have estimated that annuities to individuals totalled £10,000.

Applications

Application forms are available from the correspondent. Applications should be submitted directly by the individual including a general financial overview.

Cranbrook Charity

£2,500

Correspondent: Stephen Purser, Venn Farm, Bridford, Exeter EX6 7LF (01647 252328; email: purseratvenn@hotmail.com)

CC number: 249074

Eligibility

People in need who live in the parishes of Dunsford, Doddiscombsleigh and 'that part of the parish of Holcombe Burnel as in 1982 constituted part of the parish of Dunsford'.

Types of grants

One-off and recurrent grants to those in need.

Annual grant total

In 2015/16 the charity had an income of £11,000 and a total expenditure of £5,000. We estimate that welfare grants totalled £2,500.

Applications

Applications may be made in writing to the correspondent.

Other information

Grants are made to individuals for educational purposes.

Devonian Fund

£7,200

Correspondent: Grants Administrator, The Factory, Leat Street, Tiverton EX16 5LL (01884 235887; email: grants@ devoncf.com; website: devoncf.com/ apply/apply-for-a-grant/individual-grants)

CC number: 1057923

Eligibility

People resident in Devon who are experiencing mobility or transport issues due to illness or disability.

Types of grants

Grants of £500 to £1,000 for items that relieve mobility problems, including specialised equipment or specialised transport such as accessible coaches or taxis.

Annual grant total

In 2016/17 the fund made grants to individuals for welfare and educational purposes totalling £14,400. We estimate that welfare grants to individuals, made through the Devonian Fund, totalled around £7,200.

Applications

Application forms are available to download from the Devon Community Foundation website. Applications must be made through a healthcare professional such as an occupational therapist, or a community group working with the individual. Applications can be made throughout the year.

Other information

This fund is administered by Devon Community Foundation.

The David Gibbons Foundation

£14,200 (31 grants)

Correspondent: Roger Dawe, Trustee, 14 Fore Street, Budleigh Salterton, Devon EX9 6NG (01395 445259; email: web.enquiry@gibbonstrusts.org; website: www.gibbonstrusts.org)

CC number: 1134727

Eligibility

People in need who live in Devon, with a preference for those from East Devon.

Types of grants

One-off grants according to need.

Annual grant total

In 2015/16 the foundation held assets of £2.8 million and had an income of £121,000. Grants to 31 individuals totalled £14,200.

Applications

Application forms can be downloaded from the website and posted to the foundation. Applications must be supported by at least one letter from a professional third party such as a social worker, teacher, doctor, etc. Applications without a letter of support will not be considered. It is also helpful, but not essential, to include a copy of personal identification. All applications will be acknowledged by letter or email. Trustees usually meet in January, April, July and October; therefore, it may be three months before the success of an application is confirmed. All grants are paid by cheque and successful applicants should acknowledge receipt of the grant through the foundation's office address, or risk ineligibility for any future applications.

The Heathcoat Trust

£141,500

Correspondent: Mrs C. Twose, Secretary, The Factory, Tiverton, Devon EX16 5LL (email: heathcoattrust@ heathcoat.co.uk)

CC number: 203367

Eligibility

People who are older, in poor health or financial need and live in Cornwall and Devon.

Types of grants

One-off and recurrent grants are given according to need. Grants are mostly to relieve poverty caused by ill health.

Annual grant total

In 2016/17 the trust had assets of £25.1 million and an income of £751,500. Grants totalling £141,500 were awarded to individuals and were broken down as follows:

Death grants	£43,000
Hospital visits	£30,500
Opticians' charges	£23,500
Chiropody	£23,000
Dental charges	£13,700
Employees in cases of sickness	£3,600
Cases of hardship	£3,500
Communication grant	£1,600
Telephone installation	£65

Applications

Applications should be made in writing to the correspondent.

Other information

The trust also awards grants for educational advancement, and provides grants to organisations.

Northcott Devon Foundation

£179,500

Correspondent: Emma O'Loughlin, Administrator, 1b Victoria Road, Exmouth, Devon EX8 1DL (01395 269204; fax: 01395 269204; email: emma.pat@live.co.uk; website: northcottdevonfoundation.com)

CC number: 201277

Eligibility

People living in Devon who are in need as the result of illness, injury, bereavement or exceptional disadvantage.

Types of grants

One-off and recurrent grants of up to £200 towards, for example, computers for children with physical disabilities, adaptations, repairs, holidays, clothing, furniture and wheelchairs.

Annual grant total

In 2015/16 the charity held assets of £5.6 million and had an income of £210,500. During the year, the charity gave around £179,500 in grants to individuals.

The charity also gave around £5,600 in grants to organisations.

Exclusions

No grants are given towards long-term educational needs, funeral expenses, energy bills or to relieve debts, council tax or other taxes.

Applications

Apply on a form available from the correspondent or to download from the foundation's website. Applicants must be sponsored by a doctor, social worker, Citizens Advice, health visitor, headteacher or a faith leader who is prepared to handle any grant on the applicant's behalf. The application must state the need for the grant, the applicant's income and expenditure, and must be accompanied by a supporting letter from the sponsor, complete with the sponsor's details. Any estimates should also be included. Grants are means-tested and cheques are made to the sponsor.

Note: Applicants must have explored all statutory funding options with no success. Successful applicants must wait at one year before reapplying.

Other information

The foundation was established in 1960 by George Northcott who relocated to Lympstone after World War ll.

Pete's Dragons

£15,000

Correspondent: Sasha Haithwaite, Trustee, 102 Exeter Rd, Exmouth, Devon EX8 1QA (01395 277780; email: hq@ petesdragons.org.uk; website: www. petesdragons.org.uk)

CC number: 1160644

Eligibility

Families living in Devon and Cornwall who are bereaved because of suicide. According to the website, the trustees 'particularly want to assist families in most need where they are unable to meet the costs themselves'.

Types of grants

Grants are given to purchase items such as white goods (washing machines, cookers, etc.) or brown goods (sofas, beds, furnishings, etc.). The website further explains that the trustees 'will also consider other goods which are not listed but where there is a recognisable and credible reason this would be beneficial to the family'. The trustees intend grant-making to be flexible so that money is directed to where it will have the biggest impact. Some examples of goods previously purchased by the charity include: mindfulness sessions; a memorial bench; vets bills; taxi expenses to an inquest; leisure activities which can be considered both therapeutic and beneficial to the family; and home fuel expenses.

The charity also provides 'life-affirming gifts' through its Hug in a Hamper scheme. The website states 'We hope that these gifts will bring a sense of shared understanding and support to those whose lives have been changed by the suicide of a loved one. They aim to break down the sense of shame and stigma that often surrounds loss through suicide.'

Annual grant total

In 2016/17 the charity had an income of £68,500 and total expenditure of £78,500. We estimate that grants given to individuals totalled around £15,000.

Applications

For referrals for financial support and for hampers contact admin@ petesdragons.org.uk.

Other information

Pete's Dragons has a colourful website containing, among other information, details of the support it can provide. In addition to financial assistance and the Hug in a Hamper scheme, the charity also provides suicide bereavement support services as well as suicide prevention training.

The Elizabeth Smith Trust for Widows

£4,000

Correspondent: Rod Harris, 6–9 Market Square, Ilfracombe, Devon EX34 9AX (01271 863495; email: robdharris@ btinternet.com)

CC number: 206557

Eligibility

Widows in Devon who are in need.

Types of grants

One-off according to need.

Annual grant total

In 2016/17 the trust had an income of £4,800 and a total expenditure of £4,400. We estimate that grants given to individuals totalled around £4,000.

Applications

Apply in writing to the correspondent.

City of Exeter

Central Exeter Relief-in-Need Charity

£4,400

Correspondent: Prof. Robert Snowden, Trustee, 50 Wonford Road, Exeter EX2 4LQ (01392 278425)

CC number: 1022288

Eligibility

People in need who live in the parish of Central Exeter.

Types of grants

One-off grants, usually of £50 to £150, for basic needs such as furniture, assistance with heating bills, children's clothing and mobility aids.

Annual grant total

In 2015/16 the charity had an income of £3,400 and a total expenditure £4,600. We estimate that grants given to individuals totalled £4,400.

Exclusions

Grants are not made for educational or training needs.

Applications

Applications are accepted through established care agencies such as social services or other welfare organisations. Applications are considered in June and December.

Exeter Dispensary and Aid-in-Sickness Fund

£29,500 (173 grants)

Correspondent: Carol Cathcart, Ridge Farm, Broadhembury, Honiton, Exeter EX14 3LU (01404 841401; email: carol.edfund@btconnect.com)

CC number: 205611

Eligibility

People living in Exeter who are in poor financial circumstances and who are sick or have disabilities.

Types of grants

One-off grants to be used for medical aids and equipment, chiropody, heating appliances, beds and bedding, clothing and shoes, flooring, and domestic appliances.

Annual grant total

In 2016 the fund had assets of £1.1 million and an income of £40,000. During the year, the fund awarded a total of £29,500 in grants to 173 individuals.

Exclusions

Grants are not given for items which are available from public funds or for structural alterations to property.

Applications

Applications should be made in writing to the correspondent, and supported by a professional or social worker, such as a GP or Citizens Advice. Applications should include details about current financial circumstances, disability or illness, and what the grant will be used for.

Other information

Grants are also given to other organisations with similar objectives (£7,000 in 2016).

The Exeter Nursing Association Trust

£1,500

Correspondent: John Charles Redwood, Lower Hawkerland, Sidmouth Road, Aylesbeare, Exeter EX5 2JJ (01395 232122; email: johncredwood@ btinternet.com)

CC number: 202314

Eligibility

People in need who are receiving, or in need of, medical/nursing care, or employees or ex-employees of the association and the nursing profession, who live in the city and county of Exeter.

Types of grants

Providing and supplementing nursing services of any kind. One-off grants are also made.

Annual grant total

In 2015/16 the trust had an income of £18,000 and a total expenditure of £7,700. We estimate that welfare grants totalled around £1,500.

Applications

Apply in writing to the correspondent. Patients should write via their attending health visitor or district nurse; nurses should write via a senior nurse at Community Nursing Services Exeter Localities.

The Exeter Relief-in-Need Charity

£8,500

Correspondent: Steven Sitch, The Exeter Municipal Charity, 6 Southernhay West, Exeter EX1 1JG (01392 421162; email: info@exetermunicipalcharity.org.uk)

CC number: 1002152

Eligibility

People in need who live within a 10-mile radius of Exeter centre.

Types of grants

One-off grants, usually of between £50 and £150. Grants can be made towards the purchase of clothing, children's shoes, school uniforms, bedding, soft furnishings and floor coverings. Assistance can also be given with the settlement of fuel, heating and lighting bills.

Annual grant total

In 2016 the charity had an income of £7,200 and a total expenditure of £8,800. We estimate that grants given to individuals totalled £8,500.

Exclusions

Grants cannot be made for debt repayment, interest on loans, rent, mortgage, or council tax arrears.

Applications

Application forms are available from the correspondent and are dispatched by post or email. Grants are means-tested and all applicants are interviewed by one of the directors.

Other information

This charity is part of Exeter Municipal Charities.

The Charity of John Shere and Others

£4,000

Correspondent: David Tucker, Trustee, 5 Elm Grove Gardens, Topsham, Exeter EX3 0EL (01392 873168; email: tucker-david@talktalk.net)

CC number: 220736

Eligibility

People in need who live in the parish of Topsham.

Types of grants

One-off and recurrent grants.

Annual grant total

In 2016 the charity had an income of £3,800 and a total expenditure of £4,700. We estimate that grants given to individuals totalled around £4,000.

Exclusions

Applicants must have lived in Topsham for at least three years.

Applications

Application forms are available from the correspondent. Applications can be submitted at any time either directly by the individual or through a third party such as a social worker.

Other information

At the time of writing (August 2017) the charity had no website or accounts available.

City of Plymouth

Joseph Jory's Charity

£10,500

Correspondent: Neal Mitchell, c/o Wolferstans Solicitors, 60–66 North Hill, Plymouth PL4 8EP (01752 292347)

CC number: 235138

Eligibility

Widows over 50 who are in need and have lived in the city of Plymouth for the last seven years.

Types of grants

Small pensions for utilities, paid quarterly. Amounts vary according to available income.

Annual grant total

In 2016 the charity had an income of £13,100 and a total expenditure of £10,600. We estimate that grants given to individuals totalled £10,500.

Applications

The charity advertises locally when funds are available; because ongoing grants are made, funds only become available to new applicants when someone leaves the

charity's list of beneficiaries. Any new applications are kept on file.

The Ladies Aid Society and the Eyre Charity

£9,000

Correspondent: Joyce Stephens, 14 Court Park, Thurlestone, Kingsbridge TQ7 3LX (01548 560891; email: joycestephens@onetel.com)

CC number: 202137

Eligibility

Unmarried women (including widows and divorcees) in need who live, or have lived, in Plymouth.

Types of grants

Grants are made according to need.

Annual grant total

In 2016 the charity had an income of £11,500 and a total expenditure of £10,000. We estimate that grants given to individuals totalled £9,000.

Applications

Application forms are available from the correspondent. Applications should be submitted through a social worker, Citizens Advice, member of the clergy, doctor, solicitor or similar third party.

Plymouth Public Dispensary

£33,000

Correspondent: Fiona Robertson, Clerk to the Trustees, 81D Higher Compton Road, Plymouth PL3 5JD (01752 782758; email: admin@ppdtrust.co.uk; website: www.ppdtrust.co.uk)

CC number: 267658

Eligibility

People in need due to low income, sickness, disability or general ill health and who are permanent residents of the city of Plymouth.

Types of grants

Grants are typically made on a one-off basis and can be between £20 and £2,000. Grants can be for medical equipment, home adaptations, convalescing and general relief in need.

Annual grant total

In 2016 the charity held assets of £981,000 and had an income of £49,500. Grants to individuals totalled £33,000.

Exclusions

The charity prefers not to support projects that 'encompass computer technology' or an 'exceedingly expensive project unless the charitable costs were shared elsewhere'.

Applications

Applications should only be made through a health professional, social worker, care agency or a charity. Application forms can be requested from the correspondent and returned by email or post. The trustees usually meet five times a year.

Other information

Local organisations can apply for funding but grants must benefit individual residents of Plymouth. Details of how individual beneficiaries have received support must be kept and reported back to the charity.

The annual report for 2016 states that 'in the case of the hospice, where household fittings or equipment are often required for a short loan period, the trustees require that [pieces of equipment] are returned to a 'pool' for subsequent further use'.

East Devon

The Non-Ecclesiastical Charity of Thomas Axe

£1,700

Correspondent: David Roberts, Administrator, 50 Claremont Field, Ottery St Mary EX11 1NP (01404 813961; email: david.coral683844@ btinternet.com)

CC number: 202725

Eligibility

Older people living in Ottery St Mary (the old Ottery St Mary Urban District Council area).

Types of grants

One-off grants ranging from £25 to £200 in 'marriage portions', and aids for older people and people with disabilities.

Annual grant total

In 2016 the charity had an income of £2,100 and had a total expenditure of £1,900. We estimate that the charity gave around £1,700 in grants to individuals.

Exclusions

Recurrent support cannot be given.

Applications

Apply in writing to the correspondent, directly by the individual. Applications are considered quarterly.

The Charity of Elizabeth Beaumont

£3,000

Correspondent: Richard Marker, c/o Carter Dawes IFA Solutions Ltd, 130 High Street, Honiton EX14 1JP (01404 46943; email: richardmarker@ combeestate.com)

CC number: 202065

Eligibility

People in need who live in the parish of Gittisham, Devon.

Types of grants

One-off and recurrent grants.

Annual grant total

In 2016 the charity had an income of £5,200 and a total expenditure of £3,600. We estimate that grants given to individuals for welfare purposes totalled £3,000 during the year.

Applications

Apply in writing to the correspondent.

Exmouth Welfare Trust

£12,000

Correspondent: Lynne Elson, 23 Hazeldene Gardens, Exmouth, Devon EX8 3JA (01395 264731)

CC number: 269382

Eligibility

People living in the former urban district of Exmouth, comprising the parishes of Withycombe Raleigh and Littleham-cum-Exmouth who are in need. A fund is available for modest awards for those setting up home on a minimal budget.

Types of grants

One-off grants according to need. In 2016 grants were awarded as follows:

Vouchers	£4,400
Miscellaneous	£2,500
Floor covering	£2,300
White goods	£1,500
Bedding	£670
Children's activities	£400
Clothing	£300
Transport	£150

Annual grant total

In 2016 the trust had an income of £38,500 and a total expenditure of £12,500. We estimate that trust awarded £12,000 in grants during the year.

Exclusions

No grants are given for rents, rates, debts or outstanding liabilities.

Applications

Applications can be made in writing to the correspondent and should be accompanied by a letter of support from a professional or social worker. Applications are considered as they are received.

Honiton United Charities

£4,800

Correspondent: Paula Land, Administrator, Ford Simey, 118 High Street, Honiton, Devon EX14 1JP (01404 540024; email: psl@fordsimey.co.uk)

CC number: 200900

Eligibility

People in need who live in the borough of Honiton.

Types of grants

One-off and recurrent grants. Pensions are paid quarterly.

Annual grant total

In 2016 the charity had an income of £11,000 and had a total expenditure of £9,800. We estimate that the charity gave around £4,800 in grants to individuals, with the charity also funding local organisations.

Exclusions

No grants are given to people living outside the beneficial area or for funding a gap year.

Applications

Apply in writing to the correspondent including details of income and savings. Applications can be submitted directly by the individual or through a social worker, Citizens Advice or other welfare agency, and are considered throughout the year.

Sidmouth Consolidated Charities

£13,200

Correspondent: Ruth Rose, 22 Alexandria Road, Sidmouth, Devon EX10 9HB (01395 513079; email: ruth. rose@eclipse.co.uk)

CC number: 207081

Eligibility

People in need who live in Sidmouth, Sidford, Sidbury or Salcombe Regis.

Types of grants

Our research suggests that one-off grants of up to £1,000 are available towards, for example, new cookers, washing machines and stairlifts, and to help with travel expenses to visit someone in hospital.

Annual grant total

In 2015 the charity had assets £1.4 million and an income of £39,000.

We estimate that welfare grants to individuals totalled around £13,200.

Applications

Applications may be made in writing to the correspondent, either directly by the individual or through a social worker, Citizens Advice or welfare agency. Applications are considered at monthly meetings.

Other information

The charity supports both organisations and individuals for social welfare and educational needs.

The charity's record on the Charity Commission's website notes that 'the objects of the John Arthur & William Slade branch are the relief of poverty, need or other hardship for beneficiaries over the age of 60 years who are resident in the area'.

Mid Devon

Charity of Edward Blagdon

£23,000

Correspondent: Adrian Richfield, 29 Lime Tree Mead, Tiverton, Devon EX16 4PX (01884 258595)

CC number: 244676

Eligibility

People in need who live in Tiverton and Washfield in Devon.

Types of grants

One-off grants only. Grants may be given in monetary form directly to the individual, or through payment for the provision of suitable services/facilities.

Annual grant total

In 2015/16 the trust had an income of £18,900 and a total expenditure of £24,000. We have estimated that grants to individuals totalled £23,000.

Applications

Apply in writing to the correspondent directly by the individual or through a social worker, Citizens Advice or other welfare agency.

Crediton United Charities

£3,000

Correspondent: Karen Limon, The Armstrong Room, 5 Parr House, Lennard Road, Crediton, Devon EX17 2AP (01363 776529)

CC number: 247038

Eligibility

People in need who have been resident in Crediton town and the parish of Crediton Hamlets for at least 12 months.

Types of grants

One-off grants of up to £300 towards, for example, nursery school costs, travel expenses, second-hand furniture, medical equipment, food, hospital expenses, electrical goods, household bills and disability equipment. 'General benefit tickets' of £5 each to buy food in local shops are also available from local health visitors.

The charity purchases goods and services from suppliers on behalf of beneficiaries whenever possible. Individuals generally do not receive payments directly.

Annual grant total

In 2015/16 the charity had an income of £36,000 and a total expenditure of £25,500. The amount awarded in grants to individuals totalled £3,000.

Exclusions

Grants are not given towards house improvements or to repay existing debts.

Applications

Applications should be made in writing to the correspondent, and where possible should be accompanied by a letter of support from a professional or social worker.

Other information

Crediton United Charities consists of the Crediton Relief in Need Charity, through which grants are made to individuals and organisations, and the Charity of Humphrey Spurway, which owns almshouses in the form of four flats and four bungalows.

Fuel Allotment Charity

£1,000

Correspondent: Rosalyn Channon, 24 The Brendons, Sampford Peverell, Tiverton EX16 7BQ (01884 820495)

CC number: 205327

Eligibility

People in need who live in the ancient parish of Culmstock.

Types of grants

Ongoing grants are given towards electricity and heating bills.

Annual grant total

In 2015/16 the charity had both and income and a total expenditure of £4,600. We estimate that grants for welfare purposes totalled around £1,000.

Applications

Individuals can apply directly to the correspondent in writing.

Sandford Relief-in-Need Charity

£4,600

Correspondent: H. Edworthy, 7 Snows Estate, Sandford, Crediton, Devon EX17 4NJ (01363 772550; email: chris@cctheedom.co.uk)

CC number: 235981

Eligibility

People in need who live in Sandford parish. Support is mostly given to pensioners.

Types of grants

One-off grants, usually of between £10 and £50, towards repair of household utility items, bereavement expenses, fuel bills, also recurrent grants of £12 a month (to around 30 households). Christmas vouchers of £25 are also available.

Annual grant total

In 2016 the charity had an income of £5,600 and a total expenditure of £4,800. We estimate that grants given to individuals totalled £4,600.

Applications

Application forms can be requested from the correspondent. They can be submitted either directly by the individual or through a social worker, Citizens Advice, or other welfare agency. The trustees usually meet in March, September and November. Applications may also be considered outside these times.

Silverton Parochial Charity

£2,500

Correspondent: The Revd Preb. Sue Sheppard, Secretary to the Trustees, Lamb Cottage, 49 Fore Street, Silverton, Devon EX5 4HZ (01392 860408; email: suesheppard59@gmail.com; website: www.silvertonparochialtrust.co.uk)

CC number: 201255

Eligibility

People in need who live in the parish of Silverton only.

Types of grants

One-off grants, with no minimum or maximum limit. Awards are given towards anything that will help relieve hardship or need, such as stairlifts, respite holidays and carpets.

Annual grant total

In 2016 the charity had an income of £24,000 and a total expenditure. We estimate that welfare grants totalled around £2,500.

Applications

Application forms are available to download from the website and should be returned to the correspondent or the trustees. The forms can also be obtained from the correspondent or Silverton Post Office. The trustees will need details of the applicant's financial situation (including the income and outgoings) as well as any additional information that may assist the application. The trustees meet eight times a year.

Other information

Grants are also made to organisations providing assistance for people in need who live in the parish and may be made for educational needs. The charity has an informative website.

North Devon

The Barnstaple and North Devon Dispensary Fund

£8,000

Correspondent: Christina Ford, Clerk to the Trustees, 17 Sloe Lane, Landkey, Barnstaple, Devon EX32 0UF (01271 831551; email: bandnddf@gmail.com)

CC number: 215805

Eligibility

People in need who live in the North Devon parishes.

Types of grants

One-off grants towards coal and heating bills, convalescence, medical equipment and other costs, bedding, clothing, travel expenses and food.

Annual grant total

In 2016 the fund had an income of £11,500 and a total expenditure of £8,700. We have estimated that grants to individuals for welfare purposes totalled £8,000.

Applications

Apply in writing to the correspondent, preferably through a doctor, health visitor, social worker or other third party.

Bridge Trust

£3,100

Correspondent: Peter Laurie, Chamberlain, The Bridge Trust, 7 Bridge Chambers, The Strand, Barnstaple EX31 1HB (01271 343995; email: chamberlain@barumbridgetrust.org; website: www.barumbridgetrust.org)

CC number: 201288

Eligibility

People who live in the borough of Barnstaple, Devon, with a preference for people who have disabilities and older and young people. The area of benefit extends within a five-mile radius of the Guild Hall at Barnstaple.

Types of grants

Individuals are eligible for Samaritan Grants (emergency grants of up to £400) towards furniture or domestic appliances and Support or Development Grants (for example, towards attendance of a competition, voluntary work, sports, special educational needs or skills development).

Annual grant total

In 2016 the trust had assets of £4.9 million and an income of £301,500. Most charitable expenditure is allocated to organisations. We estimate that around £3,100 a year is available for individuals through The Samaritan Fund and the Support and Development programme.

Exclusions

Recurrent grants are not given.

Applications

Apply in writing to the correspondent. Applications must be made via a third party, such as social worker, Citizens Advice or other welfare agency at any time. Applications should provide full contact information (including telephone and email), the amount required, the purpose for which it is to be used and any additional supporting information. Payments are normally made to organisations or the supplier of items/services, not the applicant.

All applications for Support or Development Grants must be supported in writing by the sponsor (such as a school/college or health professional).

Other information

The trust's main priority is the maintenance of properties in Barnstaple and making grants to local organisations.

South Hams

Brixton Feoffee Trust

£8,900

Correspondent: Sally Axell, Clerk, 15 Cherry Tree Drive, Brixton, Plymouth PL8 2DD (01752 880262; email: brixtonfeoffeetrust@googlemail.com; website: www.brixton-village.co.uk/feoffee.htm)

CC number: 203604

Eligibility

People in need who live in the parish of Brixton, near Plymouth.

Types of grants

One-off and recurrent grants are given according to need. Grants have been given for disability aids, essential household items, school travel costs, independent living alarms and assistance with rent payments.

Annual grant total

In 2016/17 the trust had assets of £1.36 million and an income of £40,500. Welfare grants to individuals totalled £8,900.

Exclusions

The charity cannot give grants where the funds can be obtained from statutory sources.

Applications

Application forms are available from the correspondent or to download from the charity's website. They can be submitted directly by the individual or through a social worker, Citizens Advice or other welfare agency or third party. They are considered throughout the year.

Other information

The trust's scheme states that its net income should be shared equally between people in need in the parish of Brixton and a local church, St Mary's in Brixton, for its upkeep and maintenance. If any of the allotted money is unspent at the end of the financial year it is transferred to a third fund which is distributed to charitable schemes that benefit Brixton parish as a whole. The charity also funds a car scheme which provides transport to those in need in the area.

The Dodbrooke Parish Charity (Dodbrooke Feoffees)

£9,300

Correspondent: Jane Balhatchet, Springfield House, Ashleigh Road, Kingsbridge TQ7 1HB (01548 854321)

CC number: 800214

Eligibility

People in need who live in the parish of Kingsbridge in South Devon.

Types of grants

One-off grants and pensions to older people.

Annual grant total

In 2016 the charity had an income of £21,500 and a total expenditure of £19,100. We estimate that grants given to individuals totalled £9,300, with funding also awarded to organisations.

Applications

Apply in writing to the correspondent. Applications are normally considered in January, March, June and September.

Other information

The charity also supports the parish church and rents property to local residents.

The Maudlyn Lands Charity

£2,000

Correspondent: Anthony Golding, Blue Haze, Down Road, Tavistock, Devon PL19 9AG (01822 612983; email: avda10@dsl.pipex.com)

CC number: 202577

Eligibility

People who live in the Plympton St Mary and Sparkwell areas and are in need.

Types of grants

One-off or recurrent grants, usually ranging between £250 and £500.

Annual grant total

In 2015/16 the charity had an income of £7,400 and a total expenditure of around £8,100. We estimate that about £2,000 was awarded to individuals for welfare purposes.

Applications

Applications may be made in writing to the correspondent and are considered in November.

Other information

This charity also gives grants to individuals for educational purposes, and to organisations.

Parish Lands (South Brent Feoffees)

£11,300

Correspondent: J. I. G. Blackler, Luscombe Maye, 6 Fore Street, South Brent TQ10 9BQ (01364 646180; website: www.sbrentfeoffees.btck.co.uk)

CC number: 255283

Eligibility

Individuals who live or have lived in the parish of South Brent.

Types of grants

One-off or recurrent grants and Christmas gifts. Awards are generally in the range of £50 to £300 and can be for a variety of needs, including hospital transport/travel costs and special treatment where the family is in desperate need of help.

Annual grant total

In 2015 the charity had assets of around £60,500 and an income of £53,500. A total of £35,500 was given in grants. We estimate that welfare support to individuals totalled around £11,300.

Applications

Application forms can be requested from the correspondent.

Other information

Grants are also given to organisations and for educational purposes. The trustees' annual report further specifies that one-third of the income of the charity is to be applied for upkeep of the parish church, one-third for the benefit of deserving people in need living in the parish and one-third to form the endowment of the Parish Lands Educational Foundation (to support the education and advancement in life of the parish children).

The Saint Petrox Trust Lands

£4,000

Correspondent: Hilary Bastone, Clerk/ Treasurer, 30 Rosemary Gardens, Paignton, Devon TQ3 3NP (01803 666322; fax: 01803 666322; email: hilarybastone@hotmail.co.uk)

CC number: 230593

Eligibility

People in need who live in the parish of Dartmouth and particularly within the ancient parish of St Petrox.

Types of grants

One-off grants of £100 to £500, to people affected by hardship through illness, homelessness, hospitalisation and so on, for items including electrical goods, hospital expenses, household bills, travel expenses, medical equipment and furniture.

Annual grant total

In 2016/17 the charity had assets of £788,000 and an income of £69,000. Our previous research indicates that grants for social welfare purposes are generally in the region of £4,000.

Exclusions

Recurring grants are not made.

Applications

Apply in writing to the correspondent either directly by the individual or through a social worker, Citizens Advice, other welfare agency, or other third party on behalf of the individual. Applications should include details of the purpose of grant, proof of need and estimates of costs. They are considered in January, April, July and October.

Other information

The trustees recently stated that they would like to support more individuals in need. They have therefore widened the charity's beneficial area to cover the whole of the parish of Dartmouth. Grants are also given towards the upkeep of ancient buildings within the ancient parish of St Petrox (Ancient Buildings Scheme).

Reverend Duke Yonge Charity

£3,800

Correspondent: Janet Milligan, 8 Chipple Park, Lutton, Nr Cornwood, Ivybridge PL21 9TA

CC number: 202835

Eligibility

People in need who live in the parish of Cornwood.

Types of grants

One-off and recurrent grants are given according to need. In the past, grants have been given to help with playgroup attendance fees, a sit-in shower facility, a support chair and winter heating costs.

Annual grant total

In 2016 the charity had an income of £14,500 and a total expenditure of £16,300. Grants are made to individuals and organisations for both educational and social welfare purposes. We estimate that welfare grants to individuals totalled £3,800.

Applications

Apply in writing to the correspondent via the trustees, who are expected to make themselves aware of any need. Applications are considered at trustees' meetings.

Teignbridge

Highweek Charities

£540

Correspondent: Lisa Hocking, Clerk & Collector, 4 Castlewood Avenue, Highweek, Newton Abbot, Devon TQ12 1NX (email: highweekcharities@ hotmail.co.uk)

CC number: 203004

Eligibility

People in need who live in the ancient parish of Highweek.

Types of grants

One-off Christmas grants and other grants usually of around £50 to £60.

Annual grant total

In 2016 the charity held assets of £97,500 and had an income of £40,000. Grants to individuals totalled £540.

Applications

Apply in writing to the correspondent, directly by the individual. Applications should be submitted in October, for consideration in November.

Other information

The charity's main priority is the management of almshouses in Highweek.

Torbay

Paignton Parish Charity

£5,500

Correspondent: Revd Roger Carlton The Revd Preb. Trustee, The Vicarage, Palace Place, Paignton, Devon TQ3 3AQ (01803 551866; email: roger.carlton@btinternet. com)

CC number: 240509

Eligibility

Individuals who are in need and are long-term residents of Paignton. In exceptional circumstances the trustees may decide to assist somebody who is resident outside Paignton.

Types of grants

Cash payments, usually of £50 to £60, are given twice a year for use as the recipient wishes.

Annual grant total

In 2016/17 the charity had an income of £10,600 and a total expenditure of £11,200. We estimate that the charity gave around £5,500 in grants to individuals, and also supported local organisations.

Exclusions

Payments are not made towards living expenses.

Applications

Application forms are available from the correspondent.

Torridge

The Bridge Trust (Bideford Bridge Trust)

£38,000

Correspondent: P. Sims, 24 Bridgeland Street, Bideford, Devon EX39 2QB (01237 473122)

CC number: 204536

Eligibility

People in need who live in Bideford and the immediate neighbourhood.

Types of grants

Grants of £150 to £500 are awarded for the relief of poverty and ill health. The trust also administers the Torridge Taxi Voucher Scheme, which provides transport for older people and those who are ill.

Annual grant total

In 2015/16 the trust had assets of £15.9 million and an income of £788,000. During the year, the trust awarded £17,700 under the Torridge Taxi Voucher Scheme, and £20,500 in grants for welfare purposes.

Exclusions

Applications from individuals in Barnstaple, Torrington and the areas beyond this are not accepted.

Applications

Application forms are available from the correspondent, to be submitted at any time during the year by the individual, although a sponsor is usually required. Applications are considered monthly.

Other information

The trust also makes grants to organisations and individuals for educational purposes.

Great Torrington Town and Lands Charity

£16,000

Correspondent: Ian Newman, Steward, 25 South Street, Great Torrington, Devon EX38 8AA (01805 623517; email: greattorringtoncharities@btconnect.com)

CC number: 202801

Eligibility

People in need who live in Great Torrington.

Types of grants

Usually one-off grants according to need. Individual grants are generally up to £200, although may reach up to £400 in extreme cases.

Christmas vouchers are made to residents of Great Torrington who qualify under certain criteria to be used only in local shops. The vouchers are of £15 to each resident.

Annual grant total

In 2015/16 the charity had assets £6.4 million and an income of £268,000. We estimate that welfare grants to individuals totalled £16,000.

Exclusions

Needs that should be addressed by statutory sources are not funded. The charity cannot make recurrent grants.

Applications

Applications should be made in writing to the correspondent, providing all relevant personal information.

Other information

The charity is concerned with the provision of almshouse accommodation and affordable rented housing. Grants are provided for organisations with various purposes, local churches, pensioners and other people in need.

Peter Speccott

£1,200

Correspondent: Claire Woolsey, 6–8 Fore Street, Holsworthy, Devon EX22 6ED (01409 253262; email: clairewoolsey@peterslaw.co.uk)

CC number: 203987

Eligibility

People in need who live in Holsworthy or Holsworthy Hamlets and also in the parish of Black Torrington, Devon.

Types of grants

One-off grants according to need.

Annual grant total

In 2016 the charity had an income of £2,600 and a total expenditure of £1,400. We estimate that grants given to individuals totalled £1,200.

Applications

Apply in writing to the correspondent. The charity also advertises in local colleges, careers offices, social services and so on.

West Devon

Nicholas Watts' Gift (Brownsdon and Tremayne Estate)

£10,500

Correspondent: Joan Stewart, 17 Chapel Street, Tavistock, Devon PL19 8DX

CC number: 203271

Eligibility

People who live in Tavistock who are in financial need.

Types of grants

One-off grants depending on need. Previous research indicates that, in addition to general relief in need, the trustees help towards the maintenance of homes owned by beneficiaries by providing, for example, new carpets, grants towards the costs of roof repairs and occasionally supplying computers to people with disabilities.

Annual grant total

In 2016/17 the charity had an income of £21,000 and a total expenditure of £11,000. We estimate that grants given to individuals totalled £10,500.

Applications

Applications should be made in writing to the correspondent.

Other information

The charity is known as Nicholas Watts' Gift and is made up of two different funds: the Brownsdon Fund; and the Tremayne Estate Charity.

Dorset

Dorchester Relief in Need Charity

£800

Correspondent: Robert Potter, 8 Mithras Close, Dorchester, Dorset DT1 2RF (01305 262041; email: robjoy1@talktalk.net)

CC number: 286570

Eligibility

People in need who live in the ecclesiastical parish of Dorchester.

Types of grants

One-off grants according to need, for general welfare purposes.

Annual grant total

In 2015/16 the charity had an income of £3,300 and a total expenditure of £1,500. We estimate that grants given to individuals totalled around £800.

Applications

Application forms are available from the correspondent and can be submitted by the individual or through a social worker, health visitor, etc.

Other information

Support is also given to individuals for educational purposes.

The MacDougall Trust

£10,000

Correspondent: Diana Ginever, Administrator, 96 Scarf Road, Poole, Dorset BH17 8QL (01202 676961; email: macdougalltrust@gmail.com; website: www.macdougalltrust.com)

CC number: 209743

Eligibility

People in need who live in Dorset.

Types of grants

One-off grants of up to £250 for all kinds of personal need. Only in exceptional circumstances will more than £250 be awarded, although the trust can contribute towards larger projects which will be jointly funded.

Annual grant total

In 2015/16 the trust had an income of around £14,700 and a total expenditure of £11,800. We estimate that the trust awarded around £10,000 in grants to individuals for welfare purposes.

Exclusions

No grants are made for education, sponsorship, childcare, debt, people living outside Dorset or to organisations. The trust cannot consider requests for ongoing funding.

Applications

Apply on a form available from the correspondent or to download from the trust's website. Applications should be supported by a recognised agency such as Citizens Advice, a local GP, social services or a similar organisation. Forms should be returned to the administrative secretary. Applications are considered quarterly – usually in March, June, September and late November/early December – although urgent requests may be considered between meetings. For consideration at a quarterly meeting, applications should be received the month before.

Note: If the application is being made on behalf of a minor, then details of the whole family will need to be included.

Other information

At the time of writing (August 2017) the charity had no website or accounts available.

St Martin's Trust

£3,200

Correspondent: Revd David Ayton, Trustee, 201 Kinson Road, Bournemouth BH10 5HB (01202 547054; email: davidj.ayton@ntlworld.com; website: www.stmartinsbooks.co.uk)

CC number: 1065584

Eligibility

People who are in need, people who have disabilities and older people who live in Dorset.

Types of grants

One-off and recurrent grants are given according to need.

Annual grant total

In 2015/16 the trust had an income of £6,100 and a total expenditure of £6,800. We estimate that grants given to individuals totalled around £3,200. The trust also awards grants to organisations.

Applications

Apply in writing to the correspondent.

Other information

The trust also maintains a bookshop. Funds raised by the sale of books are used to support local and other good causes.

> St Martin's Bookshop is a charity bookshop staffed by volunteers in Bournemouth, England. St Martin's Trust is an ecumenical charity, founded in 1997 by a group of Christians who wanted to work together for the good of the local community. The funds raised from book sales are used to support local and other good causes including Michael House (a Bournemouth charity for the homeless).

Bournemouth

Cole Anderson Charitable Foundation

£700

Correspondent: Martin Davies, Rawlins Davy, Rowlands House, Hinton Road, Bournemouth BH1 2EG (01202 558844)

CC number: 1107619

Eligibility

People in need who live in Bournemouth and Poole.

Types of grants

Grants are made to provide or pay for services or facilities which will help to relieve hardship.

Annual grant total

In 2015/16 the foundation had an income of £5,000 and a total expenditure of £2,000. We estimate that welfare grants to individuals totalled around £700.

Applications

Applications should be sent to the correspondent's address.

Other information

The foundation also provides grants for educational purposes.

Christchurch

Legate's Charity

£3,000

Correspondent: Sarah Culwick, Correspondent, 83 Brierley Road, Bournemouth BH10 6EG (01202 495273; email: sculwick@ christchurchandeastdorset.gov.uk)

CC number: 215712

Eligibility

People in need who live in the borough of Christchurch and the immediate surrounding area.

Types of grants

One-off grants for domestic items and clothes and small monthly allowances to help towards household bills.

Annual grant total

In 2015 the charity had an income of £9,000 and a total expenditure of £3,400. We estimate that social welfare grants to individuals totalled around £3,000.

Applications

Our previous research indicates that applicants must apply on a form available from the correspondent, to be submitted either directly by the individual or through a friend, relative, social worker, Citizens Advice or other welfare agency.

Other information

The charity did not have a website or annual reports available. The information provided is estimated based on previous accounts and research.

East Dorset

Boveridge Charity

£2,500

Correspondent: Rosemary Hunt, Brinscombe House, Lower Blandford Road, Cann, Shaftesbury, Dorset SP7 0BG (01747 852511; email: rosemary_hunt62@hotmail.com)

CC number: 231340

Eligibility

Poor people who are in need and have lived in the ancient parish of Cranborne (which includes the present parishes of Cranborne-cum-Boveridge, Wimborne St Giles, Alderholt, Verwood, Ferndown, West Parley and Edmondsham) for at least two years. People in need who live outside the beneficial area may also be supported in exceptional circumstances.

Types of grants

One-off grants.

Annual grant total

In 2015/16 the charity had an income of £6,600 and an overall expenditure of £6,700. We estimate that grants given to individuals totalled £2,500, with funding also awarded to local organisations.

Applications

Apply in writing to the correspondent, submitted directly by the individual, through a third party such as a social worker or through an organisation such as Citizens Advice or other welfare agency.

Brown Habgood Hall and Higden Charity

£14,000

Correspondent: Hilary Motson, White Oaks, Colehill Lane, Wimborne, Dorset BH21 7AN (01202 886303; email: bhhh.charity@btinternet.com)

CC number: 204101

Eligibility

Usually retired people on low incomes living in the ancient parish of Wimborne Minster in Dorset.

Types of grants

One-off grants and gifts in kind.

Annual grant total

In 2016 the charity had an income of £15,500 and total expenditure of £15,000. We estimate that grants given to individuals totalled £14,000.

Applications

Applications should be made in writing to the correspondent, either directly by the individual, through a social worker, Citizens Advice, other welfare agency or through another third party such as a doctor, health visitor or member of the clergy.

North Dorset

John Foyle's Charity

£2,500

Correspondent: Simon Rutter, Thomas House, Stour Row, Shaftesbury SP7 0QW (01747 851881; email: simonrutter@pwcr.co.uk)

CC number: 202959

Eligibility

People in need who live in the town of Shaftesbury.

Types of grants

One-off and recurrent grants and loans, including those for educational toys for people who have disabilities, moving expenses, fuel, equipment, carpets and decoration.

Annual grant total

In 2016 the charity had an income of £5,500 and a total expenditure of £5,700. We estimate that grants given to individuals totalled £2,500, with funding also awarded to organisations.

Exclusions

No grants are given for items/services which are the responsibility of the state.

Applications

Apply in writing to the correspondent. Applications can be submitted directly by the individual or through an appropriate third party and should show evidence of need and proof of address. They can be submitted at any time, for consideration at the discretion of the trustees.

The William Williams Charity

£49,500

Correspondent: Ian Winsor, Steward, Stafford House, 10 Prince of Wales Road, Dorchester, Dorset DT1 1PW (01305 264573; email: enquiries@ williamwilliams.org.uk; website: www. williamwilliams.org.uk)

CC number: 202188

Eligibility

People in need who live in the ancient parishes of Blandford Forum, Shaftesbury or Sturminster Newton.

Types of grants

Grants are usually made to help with the purchase of furnishings or white goods. The charity aims to provide goods or services directly to the applicant; it does not make cash grants.

Annual grant total

In 2016 the charity had assets of £9.1 million and an income of £460,500. Grants to individuals amounted to £160,000 with £49,500 of this awarded for social welfare purposes.

Exclusions

Grants cannot be made to relieve debt or towards rent/mortgage arrears.

Applications

In the first instance, applicants should write, either to the correspondent or to one of the local town administrative trustees, whose names and contact details are listed on the website. Letters from social services, GPs, Citizens Advice, healthcare workers, Lifestyle or similar organisations are accepted. They should include: the applicant's name, current address, telephone number or email (if preferred); the length of residence in the relevant town (or the previous place of residence if less than a year); some information on the applicant's personal background/situation; the reason for applying; and details of the applicant's financial circumstances, including income and main expenditure and whether or not they are in receipt of benefits. Following receipt of application, the town trustee will arrange to meet with the applicant to discuss their application.

Note: evidence of income will be required.

Purbeck

Corfe Castle Charity

£8,100 (40 grants)

Correspondent: Amanda Meaker, 2 Battlemead, Corfe Castle, Wareham BH20 5ER (01929 480873; email: cccharity1602@outlook.com)

CC number: 1055846

Eligibility

People in need who live in the parish of Corfe Castle.

Types of grants

One-off grants and loans according to personal need, generally for the relief of poverty and hardship.

Annual grant total

In 2015/16 the charity had assets of £3.2 million and an income of £206,500. The amount awarded in welfare grants to individuals was £8,100.

Applications

Application forms are available to request from the correspondent and should be returned by post. The charity accepts emergency applications.

Other information

Grants are also made to organisations in the local area, and to individuals for educational purposes.

West Dorset

Beaminster Relief in Need Charity

£4,500

Correspondent: John Groves, 24 Church Street, Beaminster, Dorset DT8 3BA (01308 862192; email: cnj@hand-n-head.uk)

CC number: 200685

Eligibility

Individuals in need who live in the parish of Beaminster. Preference is given to children.

Types of grants

One-off grants are given for a wide range of purposes, including for needs relating to illness and disability and the relief of poverty.

Annual grant total

In 2016 the charity had an income of £12,900 and a total expenditure of £20,000. We estimate that grants given to individuals totalled around £4,500, with funding also awarded to organisations and for educational purposes.

Applications

Applications can be submitted in writing to the correspondent directly by the individual or through a recognised referral agency, such as social worker, doctor or Citizens Advice. The trustees meet throughout the year.

Charmouth United Charities

£1,200

Correspondent: Anthea Gillings, Administrator, Swansmead, Riverway, Charmouth, Bridport, Dorset DT6 6LS (01297 560465; email: gilly@swansmead.co.uk)

CC number: 201885

Eligibility

People in need who, or whose immediate family, live in the parish of Charmouth.

Types of grants

One-off and recurrent grants. Grants have been given for hospital expenses, nursing fees, funeral expenses, special needs, health, sports and general living expenses. Grants can also be made towards the total or part payment of the costs of equipment, such as electric chairs and cars, arthritic supports, shopping trolleys, washing machines and nebulisers. Annual grocery vouchers are given to selected people.

Annual grant total

In 2016 the trust had an income of £3,200 and a total expenditure of £3,800. We estimate that grants given to individuals for welfare purposes totalled £1,200.

Applications

Apply in writing to the correspondent or other trustees. Applications can be submitted directly by the individual or through a third party such as a rector, doctor or trustee. They are usually considered at quarterly periods; emergencies can be considered at other times.

Other information

Grants are also given to individuals for further and higher education and overseas voluntary work, and to local organisations for specific purposes.

The Litton Cheney Relief in Need Trust

£900

Correspondent: Brian Prentice, Trustee, Steddings, Chalk Pit Lane, Litton Cheney, Dorchester DT2 9AN (01308 482535; email: fandspicer@gmail.com)

CC number: 231388

Eligibility

People in need who live in the parish of Litton Cheney.

Types of grants

Our research suggests that grants are distributed once a year at the beginning of December, although one-off emergency grants can be made at any time. One-off grants can be given to help where there is a serious illness in the family, or with bereavement costs or heating or utility bills, for example.

Older people on limited incomes can be assisted with the costs of heating and other needs.

Annual grant total

In 2016 the trust had an income of £6,200 and a total expenditure of £3,800. We estimate that grants given to individuals for welfare purposes amounted to £900.

Applications

Applications may be made in writing to the correspondent.

Other information

Organisations are also supported, including schools, churches and community associations.

Gloucestershire

Barnwood House Trust

£510,000 (1,160 grants)

Correspondent: Nicola Mosley, Chief Executive, Ullenwood Manor Farm, Ullenwood, Cheltenham, Gloucestershire GL53 9QT (01452 614429; fax: 01452 634011; email: info@barnwoodtrust.org; website: www.barnwoodtrust.org)

CC number: 1162855

Eligibility

People in need who live in Gloucestershire, have a long-term mental or physical disability that affects their quality of life, are on a low income and have little or no savings. Applicants are expected to seek statutory support first.

Types of grants

Wellbeing Fund: One-off grants are available, ranging from £50 to £1,000, to assist with everyday living. Previous funds have supported: the purchase of equipment for home use, such as riser-recliner chairs; the purchase of mobility aids and equipment, such as scooters; the purchase of domestic appliances and white goods; household expenses, including repairs and furniture; and some sundry expenses, e.g. computers.

Family Leisure Grant: A one-off grant of up to £50 per family member to pay for activities and day trips that the family can enjoy together, including wildlife park tickets or museum entry.

Annual grant total

In 2016 the trust had assets of £92.5 million and an income of £3.7 million. A total of £510,000 was awarded in grants to 1,160 individuals.

Exclusions

Grants are not usually made for:

- Funeral costs
- Medical equipment
- Private health care (for example, assessment, treatment or medication)
- Counselling or psychotherapy
- Top-up nursing home fees
- Private education or university tuition fees
- Council tax
- Court fines
- House purchase, rent deposits or rent in advance
- Regular payments to supplement income
- The needs of dependants or carers who do not have a disability
- Retrospective requests
- Appeals from people living outside Gloucestershire
- People with problems relating to drugs and alcohol – unless they also have physical disabilities or a diagnosed mental illness

Applications

The trust runs two types of grant for individuals. The application process is as follows:

Wellbeing Fund

Application forms are available to download from the website or can be requested from the correspondent. All applications must be made through, or endorsed by, a social or healthcare professional. Wherever possible, the grant-makers prefer to meet the applicants at their homes to discuss their needs in greater detail. Applicants are usually informed of the grant decision within ten working days of this home visit.

Family Leisure Grant

Application forms are available to download from the website or can be requested from the correspondent. The application form includes section which must be filled out by an appropriate professional who knows the applicant and their circumstances.

Other information

The trust also awards grants to individuals are organisations for educational purposes, and makes grants to communities to promote social inclusion.

The J. I. Colvile Charitable Trust

£2,700

Correspondent: Dennis Walker, 1 Weald Manor Cottages, Weald, Bampton OX18 2HH (01993 850736; email: jicolvilecharitabletrust@gmail.com)

CC number: 1067274

Eligibility

People in need, usually, but not necessarily, who are living in Gloucestershire or Oxfordshire. Our research has found that help is regularly given to ex-servicemen and their families via organisations such as SSAFA.

Types of grants

Small, one-off grants, usually ranging from £250 to £500.

Annual grant total

In 2016 the trust had an income of £2,900 and a total expenditure of £2,900. We estimate that grants given to individuals totalled £2,700.

Applications

Apply in writing to the correspondent. Applications can be submitted directly by the individual or family member, or by an organisation such as Citizens Advice. They are considered as necessary.

The Fluck Convalescent Fund

£38,500

Correspondent: Peter Sanigar, c/o Whitemans Solicitors, Second Floor, 65 London Road, Gloucester GL1 3HT (01452 411601; email: receptiongloucester@wspsolicitors.com)

CC number: 205315

Eligibility

Women of all ages and children under 16 who live in the city of Gloucester and its surrounding area and are in poor health or convalescing after illness or an operation.

Types of grants

Grants are available for clothing, bedding, furniture, food, fridges and freezers, vacuum cleaners, fuel, medical and other aids, holidays, respite care and nursery fees.

Annual grant total

In 2016/17 the fund held assets of £1.3 million and had an income of £47,000. Grants were made to individuals totalling £38,500.

Applications

Apply in writing to the correspondent through a professional person such as a social worker, medical professional or welfare organisation. Applications are considered throughout the year.

The Gloucester Charities Trust

£22,000

Correspondent: Kathryn Lewis, Century House, 100 London Road, Gloucester GL1 3PL (01452 500429; email: info@ gloschar.org.uk; website: www. gloucestercharitiestrust.co.uk)

CC number: 205177

Eligibility

People in need living in the county of Gloucestershire.

Types of grants

One-off grants according to need.

Annual grant total

In 2015/16 the trust had assets of £1.7 million and an income of £4.2 million. Grants to individuals totalled £22,000.

Applications

Apply in writing to the correspondent.

The Gloucestershire Association for Disability

£46,000

Correspondent: Christine Ellson, Secretary, c/o Centre for Deaf People, Colin Road, Barnwood, Gloucester GL4 3JL (01452 614890; email: info@ glosdisabilityfund.org.uk; website: www. glosdisabilityfund.org.uk)

CC number: 1048489

Eligibility

Gloucestershire residents of any age with a physical, sensory or learning disability who are in receipt of a disability benefit.

Types of grants

Grants of up to £750 for individuals needing help with one-off exceptional needs. Grants have been made for household goods, play equipment, holidays and disability-related equipment.

Annual grant total

In 2016/17 the charity held assets of £5.4 million and had an income of £175,500. We estimate that grants given to individuals totalled around £46,000.

Exclusions

The charity's website states:

Grants are not given for the following:

- Goods/services already ordered or purchased prior to making an application
- To help pay off outstanding debts
- For the client contribution element of Disabled Facilities Grants (DFGs)
- The cost of social or health care, medical procedures, rehabilitation or therapy courses
- Personal income payments, routine household expenses or for services that are normally available from statutory agencies
- Where the applicant's disability arises solely from a mental illness

Applications

Application forms can be downloaded from the charity's website.

Gloucestershire Football Association – Benevolent Fund

£4,500

Correspondent: Operations Manager, Gloucestershire FA Ltd, Oaklands Park, Gloucester Road, Almondsbury, Bristol BS32 4AG (01454 615888; email: info@ gloucestershirefa.com; website: www. gloucestershirefa.com/clubs-and-leagues/ benevolent-fund)

CC number: 249744

Eligibility

The fund supports individual players and referees who have contributed to the fund and suffered a loss of income following an injury incurred during an affiliated football match.

Types of grants

One-off and recurrent grants according to the nature of the accident and the applicant's personal circumstances.

Annual grant total

In 2016 the fund had an income of £5,300 and a total expenditure of £4,900. We estimate that grants given to individuals totalled around £4,500.

Applications

Application forms are available from the correspondent or can be downloaded from the website. Requests must be made within 28 days of the injury unless there are exceptional circumstances. All forms must be signed, include a report by and be countersigned by a member of the Gloucestershire FA Council and provide a medical certificate.

Cheltenham

Charlton Kings Relief in Need Charity

£1,100

Correspondent: Martin Fry, 7 Branch Hill Rise, Charlton Kings, Cheltenham GL53 9HN (01242 239903; email: reliefinneed@btinternet.com)

CC number: 204597

Eligibility

People in need living in the former urban district of Charlton Kings.

Types of grants

Small, one-off grants according to need. Grants have previously been given towards travel expenses and medical equipment and can be used to help people to make a fresh start.

Annual grant total

In 2016/17 the charity had an income of £7,600 and a total expenditure of £4,700. We estimate that social welfare grants to individuals totalled around £1,100.

Applications

Apply in writing to the correspondent.

Other information

Grants are also awarded to organisations and for educational purposes.

Cheltenham Aid-in-Sickness and Nurses Welfare Fund

£16,000

Correspondent: Emma Puschnik, 91 College Road, Cheltenham GL53 0JY (01242 522180; email: emma.cfwa@ btconnect.com; website: www. cheltenhamfamilywelfare.co.uk)

CC number: 205340

Eligibility

People in need who are engaged in domiciliary nursing in the Cheltenham area, or retired nurses who were so engaged.

Types of grants

One-off and recurrent grants to those in need.

Annual grant total

In 2016 the fund had an income of £13,500 and a total expenditure of £16,600. We estimate that grants given to individuals totalled around £16,000.

Applications

Applications should be made on a form available from the correspondent. Applications should be submitted through a third party such as a health visitor, social worker or Citizens Advice.

The Prestbury Charity (Prestbury United Charities)

£3,100

Correspondent: Brian Wood, Clerk, 2 Honeysuckle Close, Prestbury, Cheltenham, Gloucestershire GL52 5LN (01242 515941; email: puc.clerk@ prestbury.net; website: www.prestbury. net/puc)

CC number: 202655

Eligibility

People in need who live in the ecclesiastical parish of Prestbury and the adjoining parishes of Southam and Swindon village or immediately adjoining areas (most of north Cheltenham).

Types of grants

One-off grants according to need. Previously, support has been given towards: heating costs for a person with disabilities; security lights for an older person; repairs and decorating costs; and assistance for single-parent families.

Annual grant total

In 2016 the charity had an income of £14,200 and a total expenditure of £6,500. We estimate that the charity gave around £3,100 in grants to individuals for welfare purposes, with the charity also supporting local organisations.

Applications

Application forms are available to download from the charity's website and should be printed and returned directly to the clerk. Applications can be made directly by the individual or via a third party, such as a social worker, Citizens Advice or other welfare agency. Candidates should provide their home address, so that the charity can see that they live in the area of benefit.

Other information

Local organisations, groups and societies are also supported. The charity has an almshouse branch responsible for providing accommodation to those in need.

City of Gloucester
Gloucester Relief in Sickness Fund

£9,500

Correspondent: Tracey Bennett, 85 Sapperton Road, Gloucester GL4 6UN (07983 409501; email: traceyatgrisf@ hotmail.co.uk; website: gloucesterreliefinsickness.org.uk)

CC number: 243548

Eligibility

People experiencing both ill health and financial hardship who live in the city of Gloucester (under the 1969 boundary).

Types of grants

One-off and recurrent grants for a wide range of needs. Some examples of what the fund has previously assisted with include: fees for Debt Relief Orders and bankruptcy applications; rent arrears; white goods and furniture; food and clothing; hospital travel expenses; and retraining after major sickness.

Grants are not normally paid directly to individuals; they are usually awarded to the supporting organisation that will arrange purchase of the service or goods required or they are paid directly to the supplier.

Annual grant total

In 2015/16 the charity had an income of £9,700 and a total expenditure of £9,900. We estimate that grants given to individuals totalled around £9,500.

Exclusions

Grants are not made towards the payment of rates. The charity cannot commit to repeat funding.

Applications

Application forms are available to download from the website, although many of the organisations the charity works with will already have application forms.

Applications require supporting evidence relating to the applicant's medical and financial circumstances – the website states:

> Most people therefore find it easier to ask a representative of a recognised local support organisation such as a social worker, health visitor or occupational therapist, etc. to assist in the preparation of the claim. That person will usually be fully aware of the applicant's circumstances and therefore be able to better provide the necessary written evidence to support it.

The trustees also require evidence that either the applicant is not entitled to state benefits or that the benefits they receive do not fully meet their needs.

The trustees meet once a month (usually on the second Monday) and aim to consider all applications within one calendar month of the application being received.

United Charity of Palling Burgess and Others

£800

Correspondent: Jessica Gordon, Grants Administrator, Glasfryn, Cwmcarvan, Monmouth, Gwent NP25 4JP (email: nikkiarthy@btinternet.com)

CC number: 236440

Eligibility

People in need who live in the Gloucester City Council administrative area, including people with disabilities, children and young people, and older people.

Types of grants

One-off cash grants and grants in kind.

Annual grant total

In 2016 the charity had an income of £2,000 and a total expenditure of £1,800. We estimate that the charity gave around £800 in grants for welfare purposes, with funding also given for educational needs.

Applications

Apply in writing to the correspondent. Applications should be submitted through a social worker, nurse, health visitor, minister of religion or similar third party and are considered twice a year in March and October. Applications should be submitted by the end of February and September respectively.

Cotswold
Smith's Cirencester Poor Charity

£1,000

Correspondent: Maria Ann Bell, Administrator, 7 Dollar Street, Cirencester, Gloucestershire GL7 2AS (01285 650000)

CC number: 232383

Eligibility

People in need who have lived in the parish of Cirencester for the last three years.

Types of grants

One-off and recurrent grants towards disability aids, domestic appliances, furniture, heating bills and living expenses.

Annual grant total

In 2015/16 the charity had an income of £4,800 and a total expenditure of £2,200. We estimate that grants given to individuals totalled £1,000, with local organisations also receiving funding.

Applications

Applicants should be referred through local agencies such as a medical practice or hospital, social services, Citizens Advice, or another voluntary or charitable organisation. Applications are usually considered quarterly.

South Gloucestershire
Almondsbury Charity

£700 (two grants)

Correspondent: Peter Orford, Secretary, Shepperdine Road, Wayside, Oldbury Naite, Oldbury-on-Severn, Bristol BS35 1RJ (01454 415346; email: peter.orford@gmail.com; website: www. almondsburycharity.org.uk)

CC number: 202263

Eligibility

Individuals who are in need and have lived in Almondsbury, Bradley Stoke North, Easter Compton, Patchway or parts of Pilning for at least one year.

Types of grants

One-off grants according to need, for instance for household appliances.

Annual grant total

In 2015/16 the charity had assets of £2.5 million and an income of £72,000. Grants totalled £29,000 and were mainly awarded to organisations. Grants to four individuals from the Education and Relief Fund amounted to £1,400, although we were unable to determine how the grants were distributed between education and social welfare. We estimate that social welfare grants totalled around £700.

Exclusions

Grants are not given towards fuel bills.

Applications

Applications can be made using the appropriate form. Forms are available to download from the charity's website and should be completed and returned to the correspondent along with any other relevant information. The charity does not make cash awards.

The Chipping Sodbury Town Lands

£18,500 (137+ grants)

Correspondent: Nicola Gideon, Town Hall, 57–59 Broad Street, Chipping Sodbury, Bristol BS37 6AD (01454 852223; email: nicola.gideon@ chippingsodburytownhall.co.uk; website: www.chippingsodburytownhall.co.uk)

CC number: 236364

Eligibility
People in need who live in the parish of Sodbury.

Types of grants
One-off and recurrent grants are given according to need. Grants are given to help with winter heating bills, as well as for equipment for a variety of activities.

Annual grant total
In 2016 the charity had assets of £9.9 million and an income of £309,000. Welfare grants to individuals totalled £18,500.

Applications
Apply in writing to the correspondent.

Other information
Grants are also made to schools, clubs and other organisations in the area of benefit.

Thornbury Town Trust

£16,500 (72+ grants)

Correspondent: Amanda Powell, Cliff Farm, Passage Road, Aust, Bristol BS35 4BG (01454 631169; email: amandatowntrust1@talktalk.net)

CC number: 238273

Eligibility
People in need who live in the parish of Thornbury. Beneficiaries are often of pensionable age or have a disability, but anyone in the parish can apply.

Types of grants
One-off grants to help with the extra expense of Christmas, as well as one-off grants given at other times.

Annual grant total
In 2016 the trust had assets of £929,500 and an income of £50,500. Gifts to individuals totalled £16,500, with £3,200 given to individuals for general welfare purposes, £6,300 to residents in care homes and the rest given in Christmas grants.

Exclusions
Grants are not given where the need is covered by statutory authorities.

Applications
Apply in writing to the correspondent. Applications can be submitted directly by the individual or through a social worker, Citizens Advice or other welfare agency and should include details of income. They are considered in November for Christmas but applications for special needs can be made at any time.

Other information
The trust also owns almshouses.

Stroud

The Charity of the Ancient Parish of Bisley

£2,500

Correspondent: Jane Bentley, Secretary, The Old Post Office, High Street, Bisley, Stroud GL6 7AA (01452 770756; email: bisleycharity.capb@gmail.com; website: www.bisleycharity-capb.org)

CC number: 237229

Eligibility
Sick or older people in need who live in the ancient parish of Bisley. In the past, the charity has made grants for electrical and white goods and helped a family whose home had been flooded. The charity has also made grants towards funerals in cases where little or no other provision was available.

To be considered for a grant, whether financial or in kind, you need to be resident in the ancient parish of Bisley (see the map on the charity's website). The parish includes the Gloucestershire villages of Bisley, Eastcombe (east of the Toadsmoor Brook), Bussage, Oakridge, France Lynch, Chalford (north of the River Frome), Througham, Bournes Green and Waterlane.

Types of grants
One-off and in-kind grants according to need.

Annual grant total
In 2015/16 the charity had an income of £9,600 and a total expenditure of £5,800. We estimate that grants given to individuals totalled £2,500 during the year, with organisations also receiving funding.

Exclusions
No grants are given towards the relief of rates or taxes. No recurrent gifts.

Applications
The charity's website has an application form that can be submitted online, providing full details of the purpose for which the grant is required. Alternatively, apply in writing to the correspondent. Applications can be made by the individual or a third party.

Tewkesbury

The Gyles Geest Charity

£8,000

Correspondent: M. Simmonds, 10 Troughton Place, Tewkesbury GL20 8EA (01684 850697; email: simmondskandm@btinternet.com)

CC number: 239372

Eligibility
People in need who live in the borough of Tewkesbury.

Types of grants
One-off grants according to need.

Annual grant total
In 2016/17 the charity had an income of £8,200 and a total expenditure of £8,300. We estimate that grants given to individuals totalled £8,000.

Applications
Application forms are available from the correspondent and can submitted directly by the individual or through a third party.

Other information
The charity has been in existence since 1551, when Gyles Geest established a fund for the poor of Tewkesbury.

Somerset

J. A. F. Luttrell Memorial Charity

£1,500

Correspondent: Agnes Auld, Clerk to the Trustees, West Close, Church Road, Edington, Bridgwater, Somerset TA7 9JT (01278 722529)

CC number: 201495

Eligibility
People in need who live in Edington, Catcott, Chilton Polden, Burtle and Cossington.

Types of grants
One-off grants ranging from £25 to £500.

Annual grant total
In 2016/17 the charity had an income of £5,800 and a total expenditure of £6,200. We estimate that grants given to individuals totalled £1,500, with funding also awarded to local organisations and to individuals for educational needs.

Applications

Apply in writing to the correspondent, directly by the individual or a family member. Applications are considered in March and October and should be received by February and September respectively.

Other information

Grants are also awarded to organisations which have the objective of supporting older people, environmental needs and cardiac rehabilitation.

The Nuttall Trust

£6,700

Correspondent: Nicholas Redding, Trustee, Barrington & Sons, 60 High Street, Burnham-on-Sea, Somerset TA8 1AG (01278 782371; email: nredding@barrington-sons.co.uk)

CC number: 1085196

Eligibility

People in need who live in the parishes of Brent Knoll, East Brent, Mark and Lympsham in Somerset.

Types of grants

One-off grants according to need.

Annual grant total

In 2016/17 the trust had an income of £60,000 and a total expenditure of £20,500. During the year, the trust gave a total of £13,400 in grants. We estimate that £6,700 of this amount went to individuals, and the rest to organisations.

Applications

Apply in writing to the correspondent. Applications can be submitted directly by the individual or via a third party.

Somerset Local Medical Benevolent Fund

See entry on page 146

Bath and North East Somerset

Mayor of Bath's Relief Fund

£11,000

Correspondent: David Hobdey, Director of Finance, c/o St John's Hospital, 4–5 Chapel Court, Bath BA1 1SQ (01225 486400; email: david.hobdey@ stjohnsbath.org.uk; website: www. stjohnsbath.org.uk)

CC number: 204649

Eligibility

People in need who live in Bath.

Types of grants

One-off grants ranging from £50 to £350 for carpets, second-hand furniture and appliances, school uniforms and bills.

Annual grant total

In 2016 the fund had an income of £12,900 and a total expenditure of £11,900. We estimate that grants given to individuals for welfare purposes totalled around £11,000.

Exclusions

No grants are given for tuition fees or rent arrears.

Applications

The fund is administered by the St John's Foundation, and applications must be made through a third party and submitted through the foundation's website.

Note: Grants are only made as a last resort for those who have already exhausted all other funding channels such as social services and other local charities.

Combe Down Holiday Trust

£45,000

Correspondent: The Trustees, c/o Combe Down Surgery, The Avenue, Combe Down, Bath BA2 5EG (01225 837181; email: gr@cdht.org.uk; website: www.cdht.org.uk)

CC number: 1022275

Eligibility

People who have disabilities or illness (such as cancer), their families and carers, who live in the Bath and North East Somerset area.

Types of grants

One-off grants towards the cost of a holiday, short break or respite care.

Annual grant total

In 2016 the trust had assets of £1 million and an income of £57,000. During the year, a total of £45,000 was awarded in grants towards holidays and days out.

Applications

Application forms are available from the correspondent. Applications should be submitted directly by the individual or through a social worker, Citizens Advice or other welfare agency.

Other information

Note: specialised accommodation is usually booked months in advance, so applicants are advised to apply as early as possible to avoid disappointment.

The Henry Smith Charity (Longney Estate)

£1,800

Correspondent: Alistair Hardwick, Trustee, Church Farm, Stanton Prior, Bath BA2 9HT (01761 479625)

CC number: 240003

Eligibility

People in need who have lived in Stanton Prior for more than three years. Preference is usually given to those living in rented accommodation.

Types of grants

One-off cash grants and gift vouchers.

Annual grant total

In 2016 the charity had an income of £2,000 and a total expenditure of £2,000. We estimate that grants given to individuals totalled £1,800.

Applications

Apply in writing to the correspondent, directly by the individual, for consideration by the trustees in November and December.

The Henry Smith Charity (Longney)

£2,600

Correspondent: John Irons, Trustee, 48 Northend, Batheaston, Bath BA1 7ES (01225 852440; email: johnirons@dsl. pipex.com)

CC number: 204620

Eligibility

People in need who live in Batheaston, particularly widows.

Types of grants

One-off grants for fuel costs.

Annual grant total

In 2015/16 the charity had both an income and a total expenditure of £2,800. We estimate that grants given to individuals totalled around £2,600.

Applications

Apply in writing to the correspondent.

Ralph and Irma Sperring Charity

£19,000

Correspondent: E. W. L. Hallam, Company Secretary, Thatcher & Hallam Solicitors, Island House, Midsomer Norton, Bath BA3 2HJ (01761 414646; email: sperringcharity@gmail.com)

CC number: 1048101

Eligibility

People in need who live within a five-mile radius of the church of St John the Baptist in Midsomer Norton, Bath.

Types of grants

One-off and recurrent grants are given according to need.

Annual grant total

In 2015/16 the charity had assets of £6.1 million and an income of £220,000. We estimate that grants given to individuals for welfare purposes totalled £19,000.

Applications

Apply in writing to the correspondent. Applications are considered quarterly.

St John's Hospital (Bath)

£232,000 (500 grants)

Correspondent: Grants Officer, 4–5 Chapel Court, Bath BA1 1SQ (01225 486400; email: info@stjohnsbath.org.uk; website: www.stjohnsbath.org.uk)

CC number: 201476

Eligibility

People who live Bath and the surrounding area and are in need due to age, ill health, disability, financial hardship or other circumstances. There are no age restrictions.

Types of grants

Grants of up to £1,500 can be made towards a wide range of items and services.

Annual grant total

In 2016 the charity had assets of £130.8 million and an income of £5.5 million. Grants to individuals totalled £232,000.

Applications

Applications can only be made through recognised local welfare agencies, such as Citizens Advice, housing advice centre, health visitors, Developing Health and Independence (DHI), the Genesis Trust or others. There is an online system where applications can be made on behalf of the individual. Direct

applications from those in need are not accepted.

Mendip

Charity of John and Joseph Card (also known as Draycott Charity)

£4,500

Correspondent: Helen Dance, Leighurst, The Street, Draycott, Cheddar, Somerset BS27 3TH (01934 742811)

CC number: 203827

Eligibility

People in need who live in the hamlet of Draycott, near Cheddar, with a preference for those who receive a pension from the charity.

Types of grants

One-off and recurring grants according to need.

Annual grant total

In 2015/16 the charity had an income of £7,100 and a total expenditure of £9,500. We estimate that grants given to individuals totalled around £4,500.

Exclusions

No grants are given to pay normal household bills.

Applications

For pensions, apply on a form available from the correspondent and for hardship grants, apply in writing. Applications for pensions are considered in November and hardship grants are considered at any time. Applications can be submitted directly by the individual or by a family member.

Charity of George Cox

£2,500

Correspondent: Revd Sharon Walker, The Rectory, Vestry Close, Street BA16 0HZ (01458 442297)

CC number: 240491

Eligibility

People in need who live in the parish of Street.

Types of grants

One-off grants according to need. Grants have previously been given for: holidays; repair of domestic appliances such as washing machines and cookers; equipment for older people such as visual aids and Helping Hands; second-hand furniture and carpets; and hospital travel costs.

Annual grant total

In 2016 the charity had an income of £3,600 and a total expenditure of £5,300. We estimate that around £2,500 was awarded in grants to individuals.

Applications

Apply in writing to the correspondent. Applications are usually submitted through a social worker, Citizens Advice or other welfare agency, or through one of the trustees or someone known to the trustees.

Other information

Grants are made to both organisations and individuals.

North Somerset

Nailsea Community Trust Ltd

£2,500

Correspondent: Ann Tonkin, 1st Nailsea Scouts Training and Activity Centre, Clevedon Road, Nailsea, North Somerset BS48 1EH (email: info@ nailseacommunitytrust.co.uk; website: www.nailseacommunitytrust.co.uk)

CC number: 900031

Eligibility

People of any age or occupation who are in need due, for example, to hardship, disability or sickness, who live in Nailsea, Backwell, Chelvey, Tickenham or Wraxall.

Types of grants

One-off grants, usually up to £500, towards items, services or facilities.

Annual grant total

In 2015/16 the trust had an income of £3,000 and a total expenditure of £12,000. Grants are made to individuals and organisations for social welfare and educational purposes. We estimate that welfare grants to individuals totalled £2,500.

Exclusions

Applications from outside the area of benefit will not be considered.

Applications

The trust's website states that eligible individuals, or somebody who knows of an individual who may be eligible, should contact the trust by email or in writing. Applicants may be asked for a short interview with a couple of the trustees so a fuller understanding of their situation can be established. All applications are dealt with in confidence.

The Portishead Nautical Trust

£4,500

Correspondent: Liz Knight, Secretary, 108 High Street, Portishead, Bristol BS20 6AJ (01275 847463; email: portisheadnauticaltrust@gmail.com)

CC number: 228876

Eligibility

People who are disadvantaged, whose life chances are limited by difficult circumstances, such as ill health, poverty or parental neglect. Assistance is usually given to those under 25, who live in Portishead, North Somerset, Bristol and surrounding areas.

Types of grants

Small grants and bursaries, 'that will help young people to improve or alleviate their own situation'.

Annual grant total

In 2015/16 the trust had assets of £2 million and an income of £100,500. During the year, the trust gave a total of £69,000 in grants. Of this amount, £9,000 was given to individuals. We estimate that around £4,500 went to individuals for welfare purposes.

Applications

Application forms are available from the correspondent. The trustees meet four times a year to consider applications.

Charles Graham Stone's Relief-in-Need Charity

£900

Correspondent: Philip Baird, The Boardroom, Cottage Homes, Front Street, Churchill, Winscombe BS25 5NE (07861 802085; email: clerkhillarmshouses@gmx.co.uk)

CC number: 260044

Eligibility

People in need who live in North Somerset.

Types of grants

One-off grants of about £50 to £150 towards travel expenses to visit relatives in hospitals or nursing homes, help in the home, household bills or medical/disability equipment.

Annual grant total

In 2016 the charity had an income of £3,500 and a total expenditure of £1,100. We estimate that grants totalled £900.

Exclusions

Our research suggests that grants are not made for payment of national or local taxes or rates.

Applications

Applications may be made in writing to the correspondent providing a full explanation of the applicant's personal circumstances. Our research suggests that requests should be submitted by the end of February or August for consideration in the following month.

Note: the charity does not welcome initial telephone calls.

Wraxall Parochial Charities

£15,000

Correspondent: A. Sissons, Clerk and Treasurer, 2 Short Way, Failand, Bristol BS8 3UF (01275 392691)

CC number: 230410

Eligibility

Residents of the parish of Wraxall and Failand, Bristol who are in need due to hardship or disability.

Types of grants

One-off grants in the range of £50 to £100.

Annual grant total

In 2016 the charity had an income of £21,000 and a total expenditure £21,500. In previous years, welfare grants have totalled around £15,000.

Applications

Applications may be made in writing to the correspondent, directly by the individual. They are considered in February, June, September and November.

Other information

Grants made to individuals and organisations for educational and welfare purposes.

Sedgemoor

Cannington Combined Charity

£1,000

Correspondent: Betty Edney, Clerk to the Trustees, 1 Mill Close, Cannington, Bridgewater, Somerset TA5 2JA (01278 653026; email: betty@the-edneys.co.uk)

CC number: 290789

Eligibility

People in need who live in the parish of Cannington. According to a pamphlet distributed by the council 'You do not

need to be on benefits, perhaps you fall into the catch 22 category where you have a little savings, enough not to claim benefits but not enough to buy those essential items'.

Types of grants

Grants are made to meet regular or one-off bills where applicants cannot receive additional assistance from any other source.

Annual grant total

In 2015/16 the charity had an income of £3,500 and a total expenditure of £2,900. We estimate that grants given to individuals for welfare purposes totalled around £1,000.

Applications

Application forms are available from the correspondent. They can be submitted directly by the individual or through a social worker, family member, GP or similar third party. The trustees meet quarterly in January, April, August and November.

South Somerset

Charity of Elizabeth Blanford

£13,000

Correspondent: Andrew Stebbings, Goldsborough House, Sutton Montis, Yeovil BA22 7HE (01963 220232)

CC number: 235013

Eligibility

Residents of Sutton Montis who are in need.

Types of grants

Christmas grants towards the costs of food and clothing.

Annual grant total

In 2016 the charity had an income of £23,000 and a total expenditure of £14,000. We estimate that grants given to individuals totalled around £13,000

Applications

Apply in writing to the correspondent.

The Ilchester Relief in Need and Educational Charity (IRINEC)

£4,900

Correspondent: Kaye Elston, 15 Chilton Grove, Yeovil, Somerset BA21 4AN (01935 421208; website: www.ilchesterparishcouncil.gov.uk)

CC number: 235578

Eligibility

People in need who live in the parish of Ilchester only. Preference may be given to men over the age of 50.

Types of grants

One-off grants are given for goods and services to relieve need, hardship and distress.

Annual grant total

In 2016 the charity had assets of £457,500 and an income of £37,000. The charity awarded £4,900 in grants for welfare and relief in need.

Exclusions

Grants are not available where support should be received from statutory sources.

Applications

Application forms are available to request from the correspondent. The clerk welcomes initial telephone contact to discuss need and eligibility.

Other information

Grants are also awarded for educational support to college and university students.

Taunton Deane
The Pitminster Charity

£1,300

Correspondent: Bryan Thomas, Trustee, Greencrest, Sellicks Green, Taunton, Somerset TA3 7SD (01823 421616; email: bryn.thomas40@btinternet.com)

CC number: 281105

Eligibility

People who live or have recently lived in the parish of Pitminster and are in need.

Types of grants

Our previous research indicates one-off grants of at least £250 are given for items, services or facilities to reduce need. Funding has been given to assist with a hospital visit to a family member and to provide a personal alarm. Christmas gifts are given to those most in need.

Annual grant total

In 2015/16 the charity had an income of £6,100 and a total expenditure of £5,600. We estimate that welfare grants to individuals totalled around £1,300.

Applications

Apply in writing to the correspondent. Applications can be submitted at any time directly by the individual or family member. An sae should be enclosed.

Other information

When funds permit, the trustees may also make grants towards the upkeep of recreation grounds or for other charitable purposes which will benefit the residents of Pitminster.

At the time of writing (August 2017) the charity had no website or accounts available.

The Taunton Aid in Sickness Fund

£16,000

Correspondent: Ian Pinder, Lower Orchard, Spearcey Lane, Trull, Taunton TA3 7HW (01823 337689; website: www.tauntonaidinsicknessfund.co.uk)

CC number: 260716

Eligibility

People suffering from a medium to long-term illness who are in need and live within a four-mile radius of St Mary's Church, Taunton. Priority is given to those living in the former borough of Taunton and the parish of Trull.

Types of grants

One-off grants generally of up to £500. Recent grants have been given towards holidays, travel costs, outings and entertainment, laundry costs, furniture, food for special diets, help with childcare costs, and many other benefits for those in poor health.

Annual grant total

In 2016/17 the charity had an income of £32,000 and a total expenditure of £24,500. The charity awarded £16,000 to individuals during the year.

Exclusions

There can be no grant payments for council tax, other taxes, other public funds or payment of debts. Grants cannot be made on a recurring basis.

Applications

Applications should be made in writing to the correspondent. Applications need to be made through a professional, medical, or social worker. Citizens Advice can also make a claim on the applicant's behalf.

Other information

The charity also makes small donations to organisations.

Taunton Heritage Trust

£63,500 (174 grants)

Correspondent: Karen White, Huish Homes, Magdalene Street, Taunton, Somerset TA1 1SG (01823 335348 (Mon-Fri, 9am-12pm); email: clerk@ tauntonheritagetrust.org.uk; website: www.tauntonheritagetrust.org.uk)

CC number: 202120

Eligibility

People who live in the borough of Taunton Deane and are in conditions of need, hardship or distress. Applicants should not have had an application submitted on their behalf in the previous 12 months and should be eligible for/in receipt of housing benefit or another form of low-income support.

Types of grants

One-off grants for specific items, including furniture, white goods, equipment for babies/children, household repairs/decoration, flooring, holidays, clothing, disability aids, garden equipment, bedding, counselling, computers, etc.

Annual grant total

In 2016 the trust had assets of £7.3 million and an income of £700,000. Welfare grants to individuals totalled £63,500.

Exclusions

Grants are not given: to replace statutory support (supplementary grants may be available, however); for school trips, school bags or stationery; for retrospective applications; or for further/higher education course fees or books/materials.

Applications

Applications can be downloaded from the trust's website. They must be completed and typed (not handwritten) by a recognised referral agency such as social services or Citizens Advice. Applicants must not complete the forms themselves. Four copies of the completed form must be returned to the trust. The trust asks that, if possible, all information be included on one side of A4 (an accompanying letter should only be sent if absolutely necessary). The referral agency must check and provide details of the type and amount of benefits and/or other income that the applicant is receiving. The applicant's individual/family circumstances must also be described and the need for the grant fully explained. Specific items must be itemised and costed (more information on details to include is listed on the website).

The referral agency officer responsible for submitting the application, and for monitoring the use of any grant, must ensure that they have signed the form. Applications submitted by schools must be signed by the headteacher. If the applicant has moved home in the last 12 months, their previous address should be included. It is also essential (in order to arrange delivery of white goods) to include the applicant's correct telephone number.

Note: the trust cannot accept applications by email.

Other information

The primary role of the trust is to provide sheltered accommodation for people over the age of 60.

West Somerset

The Henry Rogers Charity (Porlock Branch)

£2,000

Correspondent: C. Corner, Administrator, Tyrol, Villes Lane, Porlock, Minehead, Somerset TA24 8NQ (01643 862645; email: dennis.corner@talktalk.net)

CC number: 290787

Eligibility

Older people who live in Porlock.

Types of grants

One-off grants and small monthly payments.

Annual grant total

In 2016 the charity had an income of £4,400 and a total expenditure of £2,200. We estimate that the charity awarded around £2,000 in grants to individuals.

Applications

Application forms are available from the correspondent and can be submitted directly by the individual.

Other information

At the time of writing (August 2017) the charity had no website or accounts available.

Wiltshire

Aldbourne Poors' Gorse Charity

£3,000

Correspondent: Terry Gilligan, 9 Cook Road, Aldbourne, Marlborough, Wiltshire SN8 2EG (01672 540205; email: terrygilliganaldbourne@gmail.com)

CC number: 202958

Eligibility

People in need who live in the parish of Aldbourne, with a preference for those over 65.

Types of grants

One-off grants towards fuel costs.

Annual grant total

In 2016 the charity had an income of £4,500 and a total expenditure of £3,400.

We estimate that welfare grants to individuals totalled £3,000.

Applications

Apply in writing to the correspondent, directly by the individual, usually on the charity's invitation.

Chippenham Borough Lands Charity

£33,500

Correspondent: Philip Tansley, 32 Market Place, Chippenham, Wiltshire SN15 3HP (01249 658180; fax: 01249 446048; email: sarah@cblc.org.uk; website: www.cblc.org.uk)

CC number: 270062

Eligibility

People in need who are living within the parish of Chippenham at the date of application, and have been for a minimum of two years immediately prior to applying.

Our research suggests that people applying for mobility equipment will be asked to attend the Independent Living Centre in order for them to assess which equipment would be most appropriate.

Types of grants

One-off, and occasionally recurrent, grants and loans are made according to need. Recent grants have included help with living costs, mobility aids, domestic appliances, debt relief, travel passes, food vouchers, furniture and childcare.

Annual grant total

In 2015/16 the charity had assets of £13.8 million and an income of £457,500. The charity awarded £33,500 in welfare grants to individuals.

Exclusions

The charity is unable to help towards:

▷ Funding of individual sports people
▷ Direct funding of the local authorities
▷ Religious organisations (except projects with an entire community benefit)
▷ First degrees
▷ Provision of carpets
▷ Council tax arrears

The charity will not consider an application if a grant has been received within the past two years (or one year for mobility aids) unless the circumstances are exceptional.

Applications

In the first instance, potential applicants should contact the charity by telephone or email to discuss their need and eligibility. Application forms will then be provided by the correspondent. Previous research has indicated that applications are considered on an ongoing basis.

Other information

The charity also supports individuals in Chippenham with educational grants. There are also funds provided to local organisations with similar objectives to the charity.

Note: after the changes to the parish boundary both the Cepen Park North and Cepen Park South estates are included.

Wiltshire

The Ashton Keynes Charity

£2,000

Correspondent: Richard Smith, Trustee, 4 Gosditch, Ashton Keynes, Swindon, Wiltshire SN6 6NZ (01285 861461; email: recsmith4@gmail.com)

CC number: 205302

Eligibility

People in need who live in Ashton Keynes.

Types of grants

Grants to pensioners. In previous years as many as 180 individuals have benefitted.

Annual grant total

In 2017 the charity had an income of £8,100 and a total expenditure of £5,300. We estimate that welfare grants to individuals totalled £2,000. Funding was also awarded to local organisations and to young people undertaking apprenticeships.

Applications

Apply in writing to the correspondent.

C. N. W. Blair Charity

£3,000

Correspondent: Robert Rogers, Clerk to the Trustees, 43 Clarendon Road, Trowbridge, Wiltshire BA14 7BR (01225 767228)

CC number: 202446

Eligibility

People in need who live in the civil parish of Trowbridge. Preference is given to those in receipt of Income Support, Jobseeker's Allowance or Pension Credit.

Types of grants

Small, one-off grants, mainly in the form of vouchers for food, fuel and clothing.

Annual grant total

In 2015/16 the charity had an income of £8,500 and a total expenditure of £7,300. We estimate that welfare grants to individuals totalled £3,000, with grants also being made to organisations.

Applications
The charity has previously advertised the date of distribution each year in the local press, with details of how to apply.

Charity of William Botley

£10,800 (seven grants)

Correspondent: Clerk to the Trustees, Trinity Hospital, Trinity Street, Salisbury, Wiltshire SP1 2BD (01722 325640; email: clerk@almshouses.demon.co.uk; website: www.salisburyalmshouses.co.uk)

CC number: 268418

Eligibility
Women in need who live in the city of Salisbury.

Types of grants
One-off grants to meet all kinds of welfare needs which cannot be met from public funds. Recent grants have been made for second-hand white goods, clothing for mothers and children, carpets and floor coverings and holiday costs.

Annual grant total
In 2015/16 the charity had an income of £9,200 and a total expenditure of £13,500. During the year, grants were made to seven individuals and totalled £10,800.

Exclusions
No grants are given for the payment of debts.

Applications
Application forms are available from the Salisbury City Almshouse and Welfare Charities' website. Applications are considered during the second week of every month and should be received at least two weeks prior to this. They should be submitted through a recognised professional such as a social worker.

Ernest and Marjorie Fudge Trust

£18,000

Correspondent: Fran Pearson, Trustee, 12 Rock Lane, Warminster, Wiltshire BA12 7HD (email: franpearson100@hotmail.com; website: www.fudgetrust.co.uk)

CC number: 298545

Eligibility
People in need who live in Warminster and surrounding areas, with a preference for people with learning difficulties.

Types of grants
One-off and recurrent grants are given according to need. Recent grants have been made for items such as mobility scooters, stairlifts and winter fuel payments.

Annual grant total
In 2015/16 the trust had assets of £1.36 million and an income of £61,500. A total of £45,000 was awarded to 15 individuals and 13 organisations. Grants are given for both educational and social welfare purposes. A breakdown of grants distributed was not available. We estimate that welfare grants to individuals totalled £18,000.

Applications
Applications should be made on a form available to download from the website, where deadlines for applications are also posted. Applications must be countersigned by a social worker, minister of religion, solicitor or some other professional person who is independent of the applicant. If you wish to discuss your application or eligibility before submitting a form, call the trust's chairperson, Fran Pearson, on 01985 213440 or fill out the contact form on the website.

Other information
The trust has an informative and helpful website.

Doctor C. S. Kingston Fund

£1,600

Correspondent: Nigel Godsiffe, Castle House, Castle Street, Trowbridge, Wiltshire BA14 8AX (01225 755621; email: rrogers2005@btinternet.com)

CC number: 265423

Eligibility
People in need who live in the urban district of Trowbridge.

Types of grants
One-off grants according to need. Grants have previously been given towards white goods, school uniforms and school trips for families not otherwise able to afford them.

Annual grant total
In 2015/16 the charity had an income of £4,500 and a total expenditure of £3,400. We estimate that grants given to individuals totalled £1,600, with funding also awarded to organisations.

Applications
Application forms are available from the correspondent. Applications can be submitted directly by the individual but are generally made through a social worker, doctor, Citizens Advice or other welfare agency.

Salisbury City Almshouse and Welfare Charities

£9,800

Correspondent: Clerk to the Trustees, Trinity Hospital, Trinity Street, Salisbury, Wiltshire SP1 2BD (01722 325640; email: clerk@almshouses.demon.co.uk; website: www.salisburyalmshouses.co.uk)

CC number: 202110

Eligibility
People in need who live in the district of Salisbury. Awards are aimed at relieving a temporary hardship.

Types of grants
One-off grants of between £100 and £300 are available to meet all kinds of emergency or other needs that cannot be met from public funds. Awards can be given towards, for example, essential items, such as electrical goods, heaters, (school) clothing, shoes, moving costs, beds/bedding, holidays and wheelchairs. Interest-free loans are also available.

Annual grant total
In 2016 the charity had assets of £16 million and an income of £2.1 million. Charitable activities totalled over £1.4 million, mainly consisting of almshouse operational costs. During the year, welfare grants were considered and approved totalling £19,000. This included grants to both individuals (£9,800) and local organisations helping people in need in Salisbury (£9,200).

Exclusions
Grants are not made to cover debts or where equivalent support is available from the state (although, the trustees may consider making a contribution towards statutory benefits in special circumstances). It is unusual for the charity to make more than one grant to an applicant in any one year. Only in exceptional circumstances will grants be made for holidays taken in consecutive years.

Applications
Application forms and full guidelines are given on the charity's website. Our research indicates that appeals are considered in the second week of each month and they should be submitted at least 15 days before. All applications

must be sponsored by a recognised professional who is fully aware of statutory entitlements and is capable of giving advice/supervision in budgeting and so on.

Note the following included in the guidelines: 'The demand on all charities is ever increasing and making any grant, which exceeds an applicant's minimum essential needs, can result in others in need receiving little or no help.'

Other information

The charity's main concern is the maintenance of almshouses – the charities own and manage 190 almshouses at 12 sites in and around Salisbury. This mainly includes housing for older people; however, accommodation is also offered to young families, especially single parents.

Educational support is given through Salisbury City Educational and Apprenticing Charity (Charity Commission no. 309523).

The Henry Smith Charity (Westbury)

£2,800

Correspondent: Bill White, Trustee, c/o Pinniger Finch & Co. Solicitors, 35 Church Street, Westbury, Wiltshire BA13 3BZ (01373 823791; email: info@ pinngerfinch.co.uk)

CC number: 243888

Eligibility

People in need who live in Westbury and are aged over 40 years.

Types of grants

Grants of around £40 are given towards, for example, fuel, food and clothing.

Annual grant total

In 2016 the charity had an income of £2,000 and a total expenditure of £3,000. We estimate that grants given to individuals totalled £2,800.

Applications

Apply in writing to the correspondent.

Yorkshire

East Riding of Yorkshire

The Joseph and Annie Cattle Trust

£163,000

Correspondent: Roger Waudby, PO Box 23, Patrington, Hull HU12 0WF (01964 671742; email: rogerwaudby@hotmail.co.uk; website: www.jacattletrust.co.uk)

CC number: 262011

Eligibility

Residents of Hull and East Riding of Yorkshire. Preference is given to people with disabilities, older people, and people who are financially disadvantaged.

Types of grants

One-off grants are available for relief-in-need purposes, and can be used for the purchase and installation of specialist equipment, medical expenses, travel, etc.

Annual grant total

In 2016/17 the trust had assets of £10.2 million and an income of £348,500. We estimate that around £163,000 was awarded in welfare grants to individuals.

Exclusions

Individuals cannot apply directly.

Applications

Applications cannot be made by individuals directly, instead they must be made on the behalf of an individual by a statutory organisation or charity. Application forms are available to download from the trust's website, and should be returned by post to the correspondent's address.

Other information

The trust also makes awards to children in education.

The Hesslewood Children's Trust (Hull Seamen's and General Orphanage)

£31,000

Correspondent: Lynne Bullock, 62 The Meadows, Cherry Burton, East Yorkshire HU17 7RQ (01964 550882; email: misslynneb@aol.com)

CC number: 529804

Eligibility

People who live in the county of Humberside, or in the districts of Gainsborough or Caistor in Lincolnshire.

Types of grants

One-off and recurrent personal grants according to need.

Annual grant total

In 2016/17 the trust had assets of £3.1 million and an income of £108,500. The trust awarded a total of £31,000 to individuals facing hardship.

Applications

Applications should be made in writing to the correspondent. Our previous research has indicated that applications should include family income and what the grant is for.

Other information

The grant also awards small funds to individuals in education, and to organisations active in the local communities.

The Sir James Reckitt Charity

£93,500 (368 grants)

Correspondent: The Administrator, 7 Derrymore Road, Willerby, Hull HU10 6ES (email: charity@ thesirjamesreckittcharity.org.uk; website: www.thesirjamesreckittcharity.org.uk)

CC number: 225356

Eligibility

Individuals and families in need who reside in Hull or East Yorkshire.

Types of grants

Aid is normally given in the form of household goods or equipment.

Annual grant total

In 2016 the charity had assets of £44.6 million and an income of £1.5 million. Grants to individuals totalled £93,500.

Applications

Applications for individuals are dealt with by the Consortium of Grant Giving Trusts (Hull and East Yorkshire) of which the Sir James Reckitt Charity is a member. Application forms are available to download from the charity's website. Applications should only be made by an agency such as social services or by a local charitable organisation.

East Riding of Yorkshire

The Garlthorpe Charity

£4,500

Correspondent: John Burman, c/o Heptonstalls Solicitors, 7–15 Gladstone Terrace, Goole, North Humberside DN14 5AH (01405 765661; email: clare.railton@heptonstalls.co.uk)

CC number: 224927

Eligibility

People in need who live in the parish of Barmby on the Marsh.

Types of grants

One-off grants according to need.

Annual grant total

In 2015/16 the charity had an income of £10,800 and a total expenditure of £4,800. We estimate that grants given to individuals totalled around £4,500.

Applications

Apply in writing to the correspondent.

Other information

The charity uses one-sixth of its income to fund the maintenance and repair of the church in the ecclesiastical parish of St Helen, Barmby on the Marsh.

Newton on Derwent Charity

£3,000

Correspondent: The Trustees, Grays Solicitors, Duncombe Place, York YO1 7DY (01904 634771)

CC number: 529830

Eligibility

People who are sick, older or in need who live in the parish of Newton on Derwent.

Types of grants

One-off grants according to need.

Annual grant total

In 2016 the charity had an income of £11,100 and a total expenditure of £13,000. Grants are made to individuals and organisations for both social welfare and educational purposes. We estimate that welfare grants to individuals totalled around £3,000.

Applications

Apply in writing to the correspondent.

The Ottringham Church Lands Charity

£1,000

Correspondent: Mary Fairweather, Trustee, South Field, Chapel Lane, Ottringham, Hull, East Yorkshire HU12 0AA (01964 626908; email: maryfairweather@hotmail.com)

CC number: 237183

Eligibility

People in hardship and/or distress who live in the parish of Ottringham.

Types of grants

Normally one-off grants, but recurrent grants may be considered.

Annual grant total

In 2016 the charity had an income of £10,900 and a total expenditure of £4,500. We estimate that welfare grants to individuals totalled £1,000.

Exclusions

No grants are given which would affect the applicant's state benefits.

Applications

Apply in writing to the correspondent at any time. Applications can be submitted either directly by the individual, through a third party such as a social worker or teacher, or through an organisation such as Citizens Advice or a school.

Robert Towrie's Charity

£1,000

Correspondent: Debbie Ulliot, Correspondent, The Cottage, Carlton Lane, Aldbrough, Hull HU11 4RA (01964 527255; email: roberttowerytrust@googlemail.com)

CC number: 222568

Eligibility

People in need who live in the parishes of Aldbrough and Burton Constable, especially older people and individuals with disabilities.

Types of grants

One-off and recurrent grants for food and fuel.

Annual grant total

In 2015/16 the charity had an income of £10,200 and a total expenditure of £4,400. We estimate that grants given to individuals for welfare purposes totalled around £1,000.

Applications

Applications may be made in writing to the correspondent, directly by the individual.

Other information

The charity makes grants to individuals and organisations for both educational and social welfare purposes.

Hull

The Charity of Miss Eliza Clubley Middleton

£15,800

Correspondent: Trust Administrator, Rollits LLP, Rowntree Wharf, Navigation Road, York YO1 9WE (01904 625790; email: andy.cook@rollits.com)

CC number: 229134

Eligibility

Poor women of the Catholic faith who have lived in the Hull area for over ten years.

Types of grants

Grants are distributed twice a year, at Christmas and in the summer. The typical average value of any individual grant is less than £75.

Annual grant total

In 2016/17 the charity had an income of £4,600 and a total expenditure of £16,000. We estimate that the charity gave around £15,800 in grants to individuals.

Applications

A list of current beneficiaries is circulated to all local priests each year. They then recommend any additions or note changes in circumstances.

The Hull Aid in Sickness Trust

£13,000

Correspondent: Daw Singleton, Clerk to the Trustees, 34 Thurstan Road, Beverley, Hull HU17 8LP (07835 472 512; email: info@hullaidinsickness.co.uk; website: www.hullaidinsickness.co.uk)

CC number: 224193

Eligibility

People who live in the city and county of Kingston upon Hull and are on a low income, in ill health or living with disabilities.

Types of grants

One-off grants to aid and improve quality of life. This can include grants for electrical goods, medical and disability equipment, food and living costs.

Annual grant total

In 2015/16 the trust had assets of £1.37 million and an income of £56,500. Grants were made totalling £41,500, of which £13,000 was given in grants to individuals.

Exclusions

No grants are given towards debts or where funds are available from public funds.

Applications

Application forms are available to download from the website and can to be submitted directly by the individual or through a social worker, Citizens Advice, other welfare agency or other third party. Applications must be supported by a doctor's certificate or similar. Applications should also include a quote for the requested items and details of who the grant cheque should be made out to. Grant requests are considered at the trustees' quarterly meetings.

Mother Humber Memorial Fund

£19,300

Correspondent: Malcolm Welford, Correspondent, The Hollies, Meadow View, Bainton, Driffield YO25 9NU (01377 219524)

CC number: 225082

Eligibility
People in need who live in the city of Kingston upon Hull.

Types of grants
One-off grants ranging from £50 to £500.

Annual grant total
In 2016/17 the fund had an income of £35,000 and a total expenditure of £38,500. We estimate that the fund gave around £19,300 in grants to individuals.

Exclusions
No grants are made for educational appeals and sponsorship (e.g. for Duke of Edinburgh Award students), the payment of debts, the payment of wages or administration expenses.

Applications
Application forms are available from the correspondent and can be submitted through a social worker, Citizens Advice or other welfare agency.

Other information
Organisations are also supported.

The Joseph Rank Benevolent Fund

£71,500

Correspondent: Debby Burman, Clerk to the Trustees, Artlink Centre, 87 Princes Avenue, Hull HU5 3QP (01482 225542; email: debby@be-think.co.uk; website: www.josephrankfund.org.uk)

CC number: 225318

Eligibility
Retired people on low incomes who have lived in Hull for at least ten years. Applicants should have no more than £10,000 in savings.

Types of grants
Recurrent grants of £30 per quarter to single people and £60 per quarter to married couples.

Annual grant total
In 2016 the fund held assets of £3.8 million and had an income of £117,000. Grants to individuals totalled £71,500.

Applications
Application forms are available from the correspondent. Applications are considered throughout the year.

Other information
The fund's website states: 'The Joseph Rank Benevolent Fund was founded in 1934 by Joseph Rank, of flour milling fame, to help those in need in the Hull area.'

Wilmington Trust

£3,000

Correspondent: Graham Wragg, Trustee, 16 Caledonia Park, Hull HU9 1TE (01482 223050; email: lindawickins@lindawickins.karoo.co.uk)

CC number: 250765

Eligibility
People in need who live in Kingston upon Hull (east of the river Hull).

Types of grants
Our research suggests that the charity awards one-off grants.

Annual grant total
In 2015 the charity had an income of £10,300 and a total expenditure of £6,200. We estimate that grants awarded to individuals for welfare purposes totalled around £3,000.

Applications
Application forms are available from the correspondent. Applications must be made through Citizens Advice, social workers or members of the clergy. The trustees usually meet twice a year to consider grants, although decisions can also be made between the meetings.

Other information
At the time of writing (August 2017) the charity had no website or accounts available.

North Yorkshire

The Carperby Poor's Land Charity

£1,500

Correspondent: David Brampton, Trustee, The Bastal House, Carperby, Leyburn, North Yorkshire DL8 4DD

CC number: 502524

Eligibility
People in need who live in the parish of Carperby-cum-Thoresby.

Types of grants
One-off and recurrent grants are given according to need.

Annual grant total
In 2016 the charity had both an income and a total expenditure of around £1,700. We estimate that social welfare grants to individuals totalled £1,500.

Applications
Apply in writing to the correspondent, with details of the financial need. Applications can be submitted directly by the individual or through a social worker, Citizens Advice or other welfare agency. They are usually considered quarterly.

The Olive and Norman Field Charity
See entry on page 309

The Gargrave Poor's Land Charity

£34,500

Correspondent: The Trustees, Kirk Syke, High Street, Gargrave, Skipton, North Yorkshire BD23 3RA

CC number: 225067

Eligibility
People who are in need and are permanently resident in Gargrave, Banknewton, Coniston Cold, Flasby, Eshton or Winterburn.

Types of grants
One-off and recurrent grants for debt relief, travel to hospital, household equipment, furniture, respite care, electrical goods and essential repairs. Christmas gifts are also made each year to permanent residents who are poor, older, disadvantaged or who have disabilities. Loans may also be given.

Annual grant total
In 2016/17 the charity had assets of £420,500 and an income of £29,000. Grants totalled £56,500 and were distributed as follows:

Hardship relief	£29,000
Educational assistance	£22,000
Christmas distributions	£5,300

Applications
Applications can be made on a form, which is available from the correspondent, and can be submitted at any time.

Goldsborough Poor's Charity

£1,200

Correspondent: Anthony Lovell, Trustee, 27 Princess Mead, Goldsborough, Knaresborough, North Yorkshire HG5 8NP (01423 863626; email: gtrotter@cooktrotterltd.co.uk)

CC number: 502912

Eligibility

Older people who live in Coneythorpe (or near Knaresborough), Flaxby or Goldsborough. Most recipients tend to be widows or widowers.

Types of grants

Recurrent grants are given to supplement pensions or low incomes.

Annual grant total

In 2016/17 the charity had an income of £1,400 and a total expenditure of £1,500. We have estimated the total of grants to individuals to be around £1,200.

Applications

Apply in writing to the correspondent. Applications can be submitted either directly by the individual or through a third party, for example, a social worker, Citizens Advice or other welfare agency. Grants are awarded twice a year.

Reverend Matthew Hutchinson Trust (Gilling and Richmond)

£6,000

Correspondent: Christine Bellas, Oak Tree View, Hutton Magna, Richmond DL11 7HQ (01833 627997; email: cbellas4516@gmail.com)

CC number: 220870 and 220779

Eligibility

People who are in need and live in the parishes of Gilling and Richmond in North Yorkshire.

Types of grants

One-off grants according to need. In the past, grants have been given towards medical care, clothing, nursery fees and home appliances.

Annual grant total

This charity has branches in both Gilling and Richmond, which are administered jointly, but have separate funding. In 2016 the combined income of the charities was £22,000 and their combined total expenditure was £12,000. We estimate that grants given to individuals for social welfare totalled £6,000.

Applications

Applications can be made in writing to the correspondent.

Other information

Grants are made to organisations and to individuals in the area of benefit for educational purposes.

The Rowlandson and Eggleston Relief-in-Need Charity

£3,000

Correspondent: Peter Vaux, Administrator, Clowbeck Farm, Barton, Richmond DL10 6HP (01325 377236; email: petervaux@brettanbymanor.co.uk)

CC number: 515647

Eligibility

People in the parishes of Barton and Newton Morrell who are in need.

Types of grants

One-off grants usually in the range of £100 to £500. Recent grants have been given towards funeral expenses, medical equipment, disability aids and lifeline telephone systems for older people.

Annual grant total

In 2016/17 the charity had an income of £5,200 and a total expenditure of £6,200. We estimate that the charity gave around £3,000 in grants to individuals.

Applications

Apply in writing to the correspondent including details of circumstances and the specific need(s). Applications may be submitted directly by the individual or through a social worker, Citizens Advice or other third party.

Other information

This charity also provides other facilities and make grants to individuals for educational purposes.

Craven

The Beamsley Trust

£3,600

Correspondent: Rowena Garton, Administrator, Central Hall, Alice Street, Keighley, West Yorkshire BD21 3JD (01535 665258; email: enquiries@ craventrust.org.uk; website: www. craventrust.org.uk)

CC number: 1045419

Eligibility

People resident within the Craven area who are in need, hardship or distress. The area of benefit includes Settle, Skipton and Bornoldswick and is

bordered by Sedbergh to the north, Keighley to the east, Denholme and Hurst Green to the South and Ingleton to the west. See the map on the website for the exact area.

Types of grants

One-off grants generally ranging from £100 to £1,500 for 'items, services or facilities which help to reduce their difficulties'.

Annual grant total

In 2016/17 the trust had an income of £15,300 and a total expenditure of £14,900. Grants to individuals totalled £3,600 and a further £11,300 was awarded to local organisations.

Exclusions

No grants are given for students, foreign travel or rates, taxes or other public funds. The trust cannot commit itself to repeat or renew a grant.

Applications

Application forms are available from the website, preferably to be submitted through a referral agency or a referee such as Citizens Advice, social services, a vicar or doctor. Supporting evidence such as copies of bank statements, correspondence or notices should be provided. After the application is submitted, and before the trustees meet, a telephone call or visit will be arranged. Applications are considered at trustees' meetings held twice a year. Applications are normally considered a month before the meeting. Exact deadlines can be found on the website.

Other information

The trust is a linked charity of The Craven Trust.

Raygill Trust

£2,500

Correspondent: John Brown, 6 The Fold, Lothersdale, Keighley BD20 8HD (01535 636682; email: stephen.z.brown@ btinternet.com)

CC number: 249199

Eligibility

Individuals who are in need and live in the ecclesiastical parish of Lothersdale. There is a preference for older people.

Types of grants

One-off grants are made to assist with living costs. Grants to assist with educational needs are also available.

Annual grant total

In 2015/16 the trust had an income of £11,600 and a total expenditure of £10,800. We estimate that grants given to individuals for welfare purposes totalled around £2,500.

Applications

Apply in writing to the correspondent. Applications can be submitted directly by the individual or through a third party or welfare agency.

Hambleton

Bedale Welfare Charity (The Rector and Four and Twenty of Bedale)

Correspondent: John Winkle, 25 Burrill Road, Bedale, North Yorkshire DL8 1ET (01677 424306; email: johnwinkle@awinkle.freeserve.co.uk)

CC number: 224035

Eligibility

People who are in need, hardship or distress and live in the parishes of Aiskew, Bedale, Burrill with Cowling, Crakehall, Firby, Langthorne and Rand Grange. Necessitous children and young people, older people suffering from illness or people with disabilities are particularly supported.

Types of grants

One-off grants can be given for various items and services according to need.

Annual grant total

In 2015/16 the charity had an income of £15,500 and a total expenditure of £2,200.

It has received a similar income for the last five years but its expenditure fluctuates between around £4,500 and £30,500 on average. It would appear that the charity distributes its income on a biennial basis. Therefore we have estimated that the charity makes grants to both individuals and organisations totalling £26,500 every two years, of which £13,000 is given to individuals.

Applications

Apply in writing to the correspondent.

Other information

There is a separately registered charity, Bedale Educational and Bedale 750 Charity (Charity Commission no. 529517) known under same working name – The Rector and Four and Twenty of Bedale – and sharing some of the trustees, which supports educational needs.

The Grace Gardner Trust

£1,300

Correspondent: The Secretary, c/o Town Hall, High Street, Northallerton, North Yorkshire DL7 8QR (01609 776718;

email: enquiries@northallertontowncouncil.gov.uk)

CC number: 511030

Eligibility

Older people, people with disabilities or those who are disadvantaged who live within the boundary of Northallerton parish.

Types of grants

One-off grants of up to £200 according to need including those for electric goods, home improvements, travel expenses, furniture and disability equipment.

Annual grant total

In 2016/17 the trust had an income of £4,800 and a total expenditure of £2,700. We estimate that the trust gave around £1,300 in grants to individuals, with funding also awarded to organisations.

Applications

Apply in writing to the correspondent including details of age and place of residence. Applications can be submitted directly by the individual or through a recognised referral agency (such as social worker, Citizens Advice or doctor) at any time.

Other information

The trust also makes grants to local organisations for day trips.

Harrogate

Knaresborough Relief In Need Charity

£8,700

Correspondent: Michael Dixon, Trustee, 9 Netheredge Drive, Knaresborough, North Yorkshire HG5 9DA (01423 863378; email: thedixongang@btinternet.com)

CC number: 226743

Eligibility

People in need who live in the parish of Knaresborough, with a preference for people who have lived there for at least five years.

Types of grants

Pensions of £30 a year and occasional one-off grants of up to £1,000.

Annual grant total

In 2016 the charity held assets of £423,000 and had an income of £27,500. Grants totalled £15,200, of which £6,500 was given to organisations. Around £4,300 was awarded to individuals in pensions, and a further £4,500 was given in one-off grants.

Applications

Apply in writing to the correspondent.

Richmondshire

The Smorthwaite Charity

£5,000

Correspondent: Geoff Clarke, Trustee, Pen Cottage, Main Street, West Witton, Leyburn, North Yorkshire DL8 4LX (01969 624393)

CC number: 247681

Eligibility

Older people in need who live in West Witton.

Types of grants

Annual grants usually ranging from £100 to £150.

Annual grant total

In 2015/16 the charity had an income of £11,100 and a total expenditure of £21,500. We estimate that grants given to individuals totalled around £5,000.

Applications

The charity usually advertises in the local post office. Most applications tend to be submitted by word of mouth and through conversations with the trustees, rather than through a formal application process.

Other information

Much of the charity's expenditure goes towards the upkeep of the rental properties it owns in the area.

Scarborough

Mrs E. L. Blakeley-Marillier Charitable Fund

See entry on page 388

The Scarborough Municipal Charity

£8,000

Correspondent: Fiona Mainprize Halmar, Pickering Road West, Snainton, Scarborough YO13 9PL (01723 859534; email: scar.municipalcharity@yahoo.co.uk)

CC number: 2177793

Eligibility

People who have lived in the borough of Scarborough for at least five years and are in need, hardship or distress.

Types of grants

Modest grants and the provision of goods, services and facilities to assist those who are in financial need or hardship.

Annual grant total

In 2016 the charity had assets of £2.5 million and an income of £191,000. The accounts show that the amount awarded to individuals was £8,000 and, as educational grants were not referred to in the trustees' annual report on activities, we have taken this figure to be the total for social welfare purposes alone.

Applications

Application forms can be requested from the correspondent.

Other information

The annual report for 2016 states:

> The principal activity of the charity is the management and administration of charities, for the benefit of almspeople, poor, aged and blind residents of the Borough of Scarborough. Benefits include the provision of accommodation and grants to assist in the purchase of essential items and those in need.

Selby

Elizabeth Fisher Charity

£2,500

Correspondent: Enid Roberts, 28 Broadacres, Carlton, Goole DN14 9NF (01405 947328)

CC number: 1071754

Eligibility

Residents of the parish of Carlton and Drax who are in need.

Types of grants

One-off grants according to need.

Annual grant total

In 2016 the charity had an income of £5,700 and a total expenditure of £5,800. We estimate that grants given to individuals totalled around £2,500.

Applications

Apply in writing to the correspondent.

York

Norman Collinson Charitable Trust

£12,100 (49 grants)

Correspondent: Dianne Hepworth, Clerk, Fairfield, The Mile, Pocklington, York YO42 1TW (01759 322102; email: info@ncct.org.uk; website: www.ncct.org.uk)

CC number: 277325

Eligibility

People in need living in the city of York, or the immediate surrounding area.

Types of grants

One-off grants for essential costs.

Annual grant total

In 2016 the trust had assets of £1 million and an income of £35,000. A total of 49 grants were made to individuals, totalling £12,100. A further £21,500 was awarded in 38 grants to organisations.

Exclusions

Grants are not usually made towards rent arrears or holidays.

Applications

All applications must be submitted through an appropriate third party (e.g. a health/mental health worker, child support services or educational services working on behalf of City of York Council, Leeds and York NHS PFT or North Yorkshire County Council). Application forms and guidance notes are available to download from the website. Signed applications must be returned to the clerk by post or email. In urgent cases where an immediate response is required, it is recommended that the clerk is contacted directly. Applications are usually considered within six weeks unless further information is required.

The Micklegate, York Charitable Trust

£6,700

Correspondent: John Whitehouse, 60 The Gallops, York YO24 3NF (01904 798478; email: jdfwhitehouse@hotmail.com)

CC number: 1094334

Eligibility

Residents of the city of York who are in need.

Types of grants

One-off according to need.

Annual grant total

In 2016 the trust had an income of £1,400 and a total expenditure of £6,700. We estimate that grants given to individuals totalled around £6,700.

Applications

Apply in writing to the correspondent.

The Purey Cust Trust CIO

£7,500

Correspondent: Kathryn Hodges, Secretary, 5 Grimston Park Mews, Grimston Park, Tadcaster, North Yorkshire LS24 9DB (01378 34730; email: pureycusttrust@btinternet.com; website: www.pureycusttrust.org)

CC number: 1159079

Eligibility

People with medical needs who live in York and the surrounding area.

Types of grants

One-off grants (to both individuals and organisations) for healthcare equipment, specialist medical equipment, respite care and domestic items. Grants given to organisations can be for services or equipment for individuals, for example a grant to Canine Partners for a support dog.

Annual grant total

In 2016/17 the trust had assets of £2.9 million and an income of £65,500. Grants to individuals totalled £7,500. Grants totalling £62,000 were awarded to local organisations. Some of these grants were given to organisations for equipment or opportunities for the benefit of an individual.

Exclusions

The trust tries to assist with one-off grants for specific purposes rather than ongoing routine costs, such as rent, rates and salaries.

Applications

Apply on a form which is available on the trust's website. Applications may be emailed or posted. Applications must show evidence of the medical need and can be submitted directly by the individual or through a social worker, Citizens Advice, other welfare agency or third party. Applications are considered throughout the year.

Other information

The annual report for 2016/17 notes that the trust received 36 applications for grants and approved 33.

Feoffee Estate of St Michael-le-Belfrey York

£4,700

Correspondent: Christopher Goodway, Clerk, c/o Grays Solicitors, Duncombe Place, York YO1 7DY (01904 634771)

CC number: 222051

Eligibility

People in need who live in the parish of St Michael-le-Belfrey, York.

Types of grants

One-off and recurrent grants ranging from £50 to £500. Quarterly pensions are available to older people as well as one-off payments to relieve special needs.

Annual grant total

In 2016 the charity had an income of £8,200 and a total expenditure of £9,700. We estimate that grants given to individuals totalled £4,700, with funding also awarded to organisations.

Exclusions

No grants are given for educational purposes.

Applications

Application forms are available from the correspondent. Evidence of financial circumstances will be required. Applications can be submitted directly by the individual or through a social worker, Citizens Advice, other welfare agency or other third party.

The Charity of Jane Wright

£2,800

Correspondent: Diane Grayson, Clerk, Harland & Co., 18 St Saviourgate, York YO1 8NS (01904 655555; email: cjw@harlandsolicitors.co.uk)

CC number: 228961

Eligibility

People in need who live in the city of York.

Types of grants

One-off grants and vouchers according to need.

Annual grant total

In 2015/16 the charity had an income of £94,000 and a total expenditure of £77,000. The charity gave around £2,800 in grants to individuals.

The charity also awards grants to organisations, our research suggests that the charity awards a recurrent grant to York College relief in need. In 2016 the charity gave £15,000 to York College relief in need.

Applications

Applications must be made directly or via recognised welfare agencies. They are considered at or between trustees' meetings.

Other information

The charity was founded on 21 December 1675 by Jane Wright who was born in York. Although she lived and died as a wealthy businesswoman in Whitechapel, London, she left her estate to benefit the poor in her hometown. In the present day, the charity also manages 11 almshouse flats.

York Children's Trust

£21,000

Correspondent: Margaret Brien, 29 Whinney Lane, Harrogate HG2 9LS (01423 504765; email: yorkchildrenstrust@hotmail.co.uk)

CC number: 222279

Eligibility

Young people under the age of 25 living within a 20-mile radius of the city of York.

Types of grants

One-off grants are given according to need where no statutory funding is available. Grants are awarded for social welfare, medical assistance, travel, and to support talent.

Annual grant total

In 2016 the trust had assets of £2.7 million and an income of £100,000. During the year, the trust awarded a total of £21,000 in grants to individuals.

Applications

Application forms are available upon request from the correspondent.

Other information

The trust was established through the amalgamation of five existing charities: St Stephen's Orphanage, Blue Coat Boys' and Grey Coat Girls' Schools, The William Richard Beckwith Fund, The Charity of Reverend A.A.R. Gill and The Matthew Rymer Girls Education Fund.

The charity also provides grants to individuals for education, and to organisations.

York Dispensary Sick Poor Fund

£10,000

Correspondent: Andrew Gowar, Secretary, c/o Langleys Solicitors, Queens House, Micklegate, York YO1 6WG (01904 683141; email: andrew.gowar@langleys.com)

CC number: 221277

Eligibility

People living in York and the surrounding districts who are suffering from both poverty and ill health.

Types of grants

Our research suggests that one-off grants are given for specific needs, such as clothing, domestic equipment or holidays.

Annual grant total

In 2016 the charity had an income of £19,700 and a total expenditure of £22,000. We estimate that grants given to individuals totalled £10,000.

Applications

Apply in writing to the correspondent. Applications should, preferably, be made through social services or a similar welfare agency, although direct application is possible. Requests are considered twice a year, normally in March and October.

Other information

The charity aims to meet those needs which fall outside the responsibilities of the NHS or other statutory sources. Most support is given to various organisations, some receiving annual payments.

York Moral Welfare Charity

£2,000

Correspondent: Sarah Birkett, c/o York CVS, 15 Priory Street, York YO1 6ET (01904 683825; email: forums@yorkcvs.org.uk)

CC number: 216900

Eligibility

Women and girls who live in York and who are in need.

Types of grants

Generally one-off grants, between £50 and £100, to help with accommodation, household items and furnishings, clothing, and leisure and recreational activities.

Annual grant total

In 2015/16 the charity had an income of £3,600 and a total expenditure of £5,600. We estimate that grants given to individuals totalled £2,000.

Exclusions

No grants are made for education or travel costs.

Applications

Application forms can be requested from the clerk.

Other information

Grants (usually up to £250) may also be made to local organisations which operate with similar aims.

South Yorkshire

Doncaster

Armthorpe Poors Estate Charity

£1,400

Correspondent: Tracey Ellis, 6 The Lings, Armthorpe, Doncaster, South Yorkshire DN3 3RH (01302 355180; email: apecharity@gmail.com)

CC number: 226123

Eligibility

People who are in need and live in Armthorpe.

Types of grants

One-off and recurrent grants, usually of £50 to £500, towards items such as mobility aids, aids for people with visual difficulties, hospital visits and the care of older people.

Annual grant total

In 2015/16 the charity had an income of almost £11,000 and a total expenditure of £5,900. Grants are made to individuals and organisations for a wide range of purposes. We estimate that grants given to individuals for social welfare purposes totalled £1,400.

Exclusions

Applications from individuals outside Armthorpe will be declined.

Applications

Contact the clerk by telephone who will advise if a letter of application is needed.

Other information

The annual report and accounts for 2015/16 were not available to view on the Charity Commission's website due to the charity's low income.

Cantley Poor's Land Trust

£13,000

Correspondent: Elizabeth Forbes, 27 Acacia Road, Doncaster DN4 6NR (01302 536106; email: artfelt@hotmail.co.uk)

CC number: 224787

Eligibility

People in need who live in the ancient parish of Cantley.

Types of grants

One-off grants ranging from £50 to £500 including those towards electric goods, clothing, medical equipment, furniture and equipment for people with disabilities.

Annual grant total

In 2015/16 the charity had an income of £130,000 and a total expenditure of £112,000. The charity awarded £13,000 in grants to individuals during the year.

Exclusions

Restrictions apply to the relief of rates, taxes and repeat grants.

Applications

Application forms are available from the correspondent. Applications should be submitted directly by the individual or through a welfare agency. Applications are considered on a monthly basis.

J. W. Chapman Trust

£44,500

Correspondent: Rosemarie Sharp, Trust Secretary, Jordans, 4 Priory Place, Doncaster DN1 1BP (01302 365374; email: info@chapmantrust.org; website: chapman-trust.org)

CC number: 223002

Eligibility

People in need who live in the metropolitan borough of Doncaster. Applicants are expected to have approached all available statutory sources of funding before applying to the trust.

Types of grants

One-off grants in kind, not cash, towards essential items such as cookers, fridges, beds and cots, bedding, mattresses, washing machines and tumble dryers, clothing and carpets.

Annual grant total

In 2015/16 the trust had assets of £3.6 million and an income of £190,000. Grants to and on behalf of individuals totalled £44,500. A further £23,000 was awarded to charities.

Exclusions

Grants are not made for non-essential items. Individuals cannot apply for more than one grant within a 12-month period, apart from in exceptional circumstances.

Applications

Applications can be submitted using the online form on the trust's website, where full guidance is available. Forms can also be submitted in person via the reception at the address above. Applicants must be able to provide a letter of support from a professional who is familiar with their circumstances, e.g. a health visitor, GP, probation officer or social worker. Documentary evidence to support an application must be submitted on paper.

Completed applications are passed on to the trust's visitor, who will then contact the applicant and arrange a visit to their home to assess their application. Following this, the application will be placed before the trustees at their next meeting.

Rotherham

Aston Charities

£4,000

Correspondent: Jim Nuttall, Trustee, 3 Rosegarth Avenue, Aston, Sheffield S26 2DB (0114 287 6047; email: jimnuttall@talktalk.net)

CC number: 225071

Eligibility

People in need who live in Aston-cum-Aughton, with a preference for older people.

Types of grants

One-off and recurrent grants are given according to need. Grants have previously been made towards the costs of holidays for a single-parent family and an unemployed couple and their three children. Help has also been given towards installing a telephone for an older couple. The charity does not normally give cash grants, paying the supplier of the services instead.

Annual grant total

In 2015 the charity had an income of £16,300 and a total expenditure of £9,200. We have estimated that grants to individuals for welfare purposes totalled £4,000, with funding also awarded to organisations.

Exclusions

The charity does not make loans or give to profit-making concerns.

Applications

Apply in writing to the correspondent or any trustee, directly by the individual or through a social worker, Citizens Advice or other welfare agency. Applications are considered quarterly.

The Brampton Bierlow Welfare Trust

£1,500

Correspondent: Jill Leece, Administrator, Newman & Bond, 35 Church Street, Barnsley S70 2AP (01226 213434; email: jill.leece@newmanandbond.co.uk)

CC number: 249838

Eligibility

People in need who live in Brampton Bierlow and West Melton, and those parts of Wentworth and Elsecar within the ancient parish of Brampton Bierlow.

Types of grants

One-off grants from £100 to £250 for necessities and comforts. Christmas grocery vouchers are also distributed.

Annual grant total

In 2016 the trust had an income of £11,500 and a total expenditure of £7,100. We estimate that social welfare grants to individuals totalled £1,500. Grants are also given to organisations and to individuals for educational purposes.

Applications

Applications in writing to the correspondent can be submitted by the individual and are considered at any time.

The Common Lands of Rotherham Charity

£1,500

Correspondent: Ann Ogley, 66 Moorgate Road, Rotherham, South Yorkshire S60 2AU (01709 365032; email: ann@maes-group.co.uk)

CC number: 223050

Eligibility

People in need who live in Rotherham. Preference is usually given to older people.

Types of grants

One-off grants are given according to need. Small monetary gifts are distributed at Christmas.

Annual grant total

In 2016 the charity had an unusually high income (£89,500) and total expenditure (£66,000), stemming from asset and investment sales and purchases. Welfare grants to individuals, in the form of Christmas gifts, totalled almost £1,500.

A further £2,000 was awarded in two scholarships for students attending university.

Applications

Apply in writing to the correspondent following advertisement in September.

Stoddart Samaritan Fund

£11,500

Correspondent: Peter Wright, 7 Melrose Grove, Rotherham S60 3NA (01709 376448; email: charlie0358-stoddartcfund@yahoo.co.uk)

CC number: 242853

Eligibility

People in need living in Rotherham and the surrounding area who have medical problems and would benefit from financial assistance to help their recovery.

Types of grants

One-off grants to assist people recovering from medical problems.

Annual grant total

In 2015/16 the fund had an income of £12,800 and a total expenditure of £11,900. We estimate that grants given to individuals totalled £11,500.

Applications

Application forms are available from the correspondent and can be submitted by the applicant's doctor. Applications are considered on a regular basis.

Sheffield

Beighton Relief-in-Need Charity

£4,000

Correspondent: Diane Rodgers, 41 Collingbourne Avenue, Sothall, Sheffield S20 2QR (email: beightonrelief@hotmail.co.uk)

CC number: 225416

Eligibility

People in need who live in the former parish of Beighton.

Types of grants

One-off grants according to need. In the past, grants have been given towards bath-lifts and childcare seats for people who have disabilities. Winter fuel grants of £15 per household were also given to older people.

Annual grant total

In 2016 the charity had an income of £16,000 and a total expenditure of £8,500. We estimate that welfare grants to individuals totalled around £4,000.

Applications

Apply in writing to the correspondent. Applications can be submitted directly by the individual or through a social worker, Citizens Advice, other welfare agency or a third party.

Other information

The charity also makes awards to individuals for educational purposes.

Sir George Franklin's Pension Charity

£7,000

Correspondent: Stephen Allen, West and Foster Ltd, 2 Broomgrove Road, Sheffield S10 2LR (0114 268 9950)

CC number: 224883

Eligibility

People in need aged 50 and over who live in the city of Sheffield.

Types of grants

Half-yearly grants according to need.

Annual grant total

In 2016/17 the charity had an income of £8,600 and a total expenditure of £7,400. We estimate that grants given to individuals totalled £7,000.

Applications

Application forms are available from the correspondent. Vacancies arise infrequently and are publicised locally. Applications should only be made in response to this publicity. Speculative applications will not be successful.

Other information

The charity is named after Sir George Franklin (1853–1916), who once served as Lord Mayor of Sheffield and Pro-Chancellor of the University of Sheffield.

Sir Samuel Osborn's Deed of Gift Relief Fund

£3,500

Correspondent: Grants Team, South Yorkshire Community Foundation, Unit 3 – G1 Building, 6 Leeds Road, Attercliffe, Sheffield S9 3TY (0114 242 4294; email: grants@sycf.org.uk; website: www.sycf.org.uk)

CC number: 1140947

Eligibility

Residents of Sheffield, with some preference for those with a connection to the Samuel Osborn Company.

Types of grants

One-off grants are made ranging between £250 and £1,000 for convalescent or recuperative holidays or care, medical comforts or equipment not available through the NHS. Other essential needs are considered on a case-by-case basis.

Annual grant total

In 2016 the fund had an investment income of £5,800 and awarded a total of £7,000 in grants. We estimate that around £3,500 was given to individuals for welfare purposes. The fund also awards grants to individuals for educational purposes.

Exclusions

Grants are not given for medical items available from the NHS or to individuals with large personal reserves of money. Individuals are limited to one grant per year.

Applications

Apply using the form, which is available to download along with guidelines, from South Yorkshire Community Foundation's website. The foundation welcomes informal approaches about applications prior to submitting. Applicants with a connection to the Osborn company should include written evidence. The foundation aims to assess cases within 12 weeks of receiving the completed application form with all enclosures.

Other information

The fund is now administered by South Yorkshire Community Foundation.

The Sheffield West Riding Charitable Society Trust

See entry on page 166

West Yorkshire

Bowcocks Trust Fund for Keighley

£2,000

Correspondent: Alistair Docherty, 17 Farndale Road, Wilsden, Bradford BD15 0LW (01535 272657; email: wendy.docherty4@btinternet.com)

CC number: 223290

Eligibility

People in need who live in the municipal borough of Keighley as constituted on 31 March 1974.

Types of grants

One-off grants of no more than £350 are given according to need.

Annual grant total

In 2015/16 the charity had an income of £9,600 and a total expenditure of £7,700. Grants are made to individuals and organisations for both social welfare and educational purposes. We estimate that social welfare grants to individuals totalled £2,000.

Applications

Initial telephone calls are welcomed. Applications should be made in writing to the correspondent by a third party.

Brook Charitable Trust

£2,100

Correspondent: Richard Mills, Trustee, 9 Camborne Drive, Fixby, Huddersfield HD2 2NF (01484 544749; email: richard.mills136@btinternet.com)

CC number: 1068335

Eligibility

People in need who live in Bradford, Calderdale, Wakefield, Kirkless or Leeds City.

Types of grants

One-off small grants.

Annual grant total

In 2016/17 the charity had an income of £12,000 and had a total expenditure of £4,300. We estimate that the charity gave around £2,100 in grants to individuals.

Applications

Apply in writing to the correspondent.

Charles Brook Convalescent Fund

£11,000

Correspondent: Carol Thompson, Mistal Barn, Almondbury, Huddersfield HD4 6TA (01484 532183)

CC number: 229445

Eligibility

People who are convalescing and live within the old Huddersfield Health Authority catchment area.

Types of grants

One-off grants for special foods, medicines or appliances, household goods such as washing machines and fridges, floor coverings, cleaning services, clothing, bedding and holidays for convalescence.

Annual grant total

In 2015/16 the fund had an income of £13,000 and a total expenditure of £12,000. We estimate that grants given to individuals totalled £11,000.

Applications

Apply on a form available from the social work department at Royal Infirmary, Huddersfield and St Luke's Hospital, Huddersfield. Applications must be submitted through a social worker and include details of weekly income/expenditure and family situation. Applications sent directly to the correspondent cannot be considered.

Bradford

John Ashton (including the Gift of Hannah Shaw)

£2,000

Correspondent: Ruth Richardson, Trustee, 262 Poplar Grove, Bradford, West Yorkshire BD7 4HU (01274 779455)

CC number: 233661

Eligibility

People in need who are over 65 and live alone in the Great Horton area of Bradford.

Types of grants

Small grants according to need.

Annual grant total

In 2016 the charity had an income of £2,300 and a total expenditure of £2,200. We estimate that grants given to individuals for welfare purposes totalled £2,000.

Applications

Application forms are available from the correspondent. Applications should be submitted directly by the individual or through a family member for consideration in June and December.

The Bradford and District Wool Association Benevolent Fund

£1,000

Correspondent: Sir James Hill, Trustee, Sir James Hill (Wool) Ltd, Unit 2 Baildon Mills, Northgate, Baildon, Shipley BD17 6JX (01274 532200; email: sirjameshill@btconnect.com)

CC number: 518439

Eligibility

Former workers in the wool trade in Bradford and district or their spouses, who are in need. Preference is given to older people and those with disabilities.

Types of grants

Normally recurrent grants are considered.

Annual grant total

In 2015/16 the fund had an income of £1,000 and a total expenditure of £1,400. We estimate that grants given to individuals totalled around £1,000.

Applications

Apply in writing to the correspondent.

Bradford Tradesmen's Homes

£5,700

Correspondent: Darren Broughton, Trust Administrator, 44 Lily Croft, Heaton Road, Bradford BD8 8QY (01274 543022; email: admin.bth@btconnect.com)

CC number: 224389

Eligibility

Individuals over the age of 60 who are in need, with preference for those who have held a position of responsibility in a profession in Bradford, and their dependants.

Types of grants

Pensions.

Annual grant total

In 2015/16 the charity had assets of over £1 million and an income of £223,000. Grants and annuities to individuals totalled £5,700.

Applications

Application forms are available from the correspondent. Applications can be submitted directly by the individual or, where applicable, through a social worker, Citizens Advice, other welfare agency, doctor, member of the clergy or other third party.

Other information

Bradford Tradesmen's Homes was first established in 1865, with the purpose of building and maintaining 30 homes for older tradesmen. Housing is still a priority for the charity and in 2015/16 £174,500 was spent on running its 45 almshouses for older men and women.

The charity's social committee organises events and activities for residents.

The Butterfield Trust

£1,000

Correspondent: Revd Sandra Benham, Trustee, The Vicarage, Church Hill, Baildon, Shipley BD17 6NE (01274 589005)

CC number: 216821

Eligibility

People in need who live in the parish of Baildon.

Types of grants

One-off grants for emergencies.

Annual grant total

In 2016 the trust had an income of £2,700 and a total expenditure of £1,200. We estimate that around £1,000 was given in grants to individuals for social welfare purposes.

Applications

Apply in writing to the correspondent. Decisions can be made immediately.

The William and Sarah Midgley Charity

£3,000

Correspondent: Eileen Proctor, 7 Lachman Road, Trawden, Colne, Lancashire BB8 8TA (01282 862757; email: eileenproctor@talktalk.net)

CC number: 500095

Eligibility

People who are in need, hardship or distress and live in Barcroft, Lees and Cross Roads in the former borough of Keighley, West Yorkshire.

Types of grants

Our research suggests that Christmas hampers are normally given to older people in the area. Occasional one-off cash grants and gifts in kind have also been made for electrical goods, clothing, food, travel expenses, medical and disability equipment and furniture.

Annual grant total

In 2016/17 the charity had an income of £6,200 and a total expenditure of £3,300. We estimate that the charity gave around £3,000 in grants to individuals.

Applications

Apply in writing to the correspondent.

The Moser Benevolent Trust Fund

£4,000

Correspondent: Donald Stokes, Correspondent, 33 Mossy Bank Close, Queensbury, Bradford, West Yorkshire BD13 1PX (01274 817414; email: moser@donaldstokes.co.uk)

CC number: 222868

Eligibility

People in need who are 60 or over and have lived or worked in the former county borough of Bradford for at least three years.

Types of grants

Our previous research indicates that an average of around ten recipients receive pensions of around £400 a year.

Annual grant total

In 2015/16 the charity had an income of £6,500 and a total expenditure of £4,300. We estimate that the charity awarded around £4,000 to individuals for welfare purposes.

Applications

Apply in writing to the correspondent.

Other information

The charity is named after Jacob Moser, Lord Mayor of Bradford from 1910 to 1911. In 1898, the mayor and his wife, Florence, donated £10,000, to establish a 'Benevolent Fund for the Aged and Infirm Workpeople of Bradford', and served the city as well-respected philanthropists throughout their lives.

Joseph Nutter's Foundation

£26,000

Correspondent: John Lambert, Administrator, 2 The Mews, Gilstead Lane, Bingley BD16 3NP (01274 688666; email: john@bradfordtextilesociety.org.uk)

CC number: 507491

Eligibility

People aged 16 or under who live in the metropolitan district of Bradford and have suffered the loss of a parent.

Types of grants

Our previous research indicates that the foundation awards one-off grants which are given towards clothing, bedding, beds and other household items that will specifically benefit the child. Other needs may occasionally be considered on an individual basis.

Annual grant total

In 2015/16 the foundation had an income of £19,100 and a total expenditure of £26,500. We estimate that the charity awarded around £26,000 to individuals for welfare purposes.

Applications

Apply in writing to the correspondent.

Other information

At the time of writing (August 2017) the charity had no website or accounts available.

Sir Titus Salt's Charity

£3,000

Correspondent: Norman Roper, Trustee, 6 Carlton Road, Shipley, West Yorkshire BD18 4NE (01274 599540)

CC number: 216357

Eligibility

People in need who are over the age of 75 and live in Shipley, Baildon, Saltaire, Nab Wood and Wrose of Bradford.

Types of grants

Food vouchers paid once a year, available from Shipley Information Centre.

Annual grant total

In 2016/17 the charity had an income of £5,400 and a total expenditure of £3,500. We estimate that social welfare grants to individuals totalled around £3,000.

Applications

Applications should be made through the Shipley Information Centre to be considered in November/December each year.

Paul and Nancy Speak's Charity

£10,000

Correspondent: Malcolm Dixon, 10 The Orchards, Bingley, West Yorkshire BD16 4AZ (01274 770878)

CC number: 231339

Eligibility

Women in need who are over the age of 50 and live in Bradford.

Types of grants

Regular allowances of £500 a year, paid quarterly.

Annual grant total

In 2016 the charity had an income of £24,000 and a total expenditure of £11,000. We estimate that the charity awarded £10,000 in grants to individuals during the year.

Applications

Apply in writing to the correspondent.

Samuel Sunderland Relief-in-Need Charity

£3,000

Correspondent: John Daykin, Weatherhead & Butcher Solicitors, 120 Main Street, Bingley BD16 2JJ (01274 562322; email: info@wandb.uk.com)

CC number: 225745

Eligibility

People who live in the former parish of Bingley and are in need. Some preference may be given to older people, and to children or young people.

Types of grants

One-off emergency payments to relieve hardship.

Annual grant total

In 2016 the charity had an income of £7,300 and a total expenditure of £6,100. We estimate that the charity awarded £3,000 in grants to individuals.

Exclusions

The charity stresses that it only accepts applications from individuals residing within the boundary of the former parish of Bingley. Applications from those living elsewhere will not be considered.

Applications

Applications should be made in writing to the correspondent. Include details of what the grant will be used for and quote costs.

Other information

The charity also makes grants to local organisations.

Calderdale

Bearder Charity

£108,500

Correspondent: Richard Smithies, Trustee and Secretary, 5 King Street, Brighouse, West Yorkshire HD6 1NX (01484 710571; email: bearders@ btinternet.com; website: www.bearder-charity.org.uk)

CC number: 1010529

Eligibility

Residents of Calderdale, West Yorkshire.

Types of grants

One-off grants according to need. Grants are made for welfare, education and the arts.

Annual grant total

In 2015/16 the charity held assets of £3.5 million and had an income of £130,000. Grants to individuals totalled £193,500, of which £108,500 was given for welfare purposes, £2,600 was given to artists and £26,500 was given in educational grants. The charity also made grants to 49 local organisations totalling £56,000 during the year.

Applications

All applicants are asked to apply in writing to the secretary. Applications may be made directly or through a local third party organisation. State what you need and how much it will cost. The trustees meet six times a year to assess grant applications.

Community Foundation for Calderdale

£576,000

Correspondent: Community Foundation for Calderdale, The 1855 Building (first floor), Discovery Road, Halifax, West Yorkshire HX1 2NG (01422 349700; fax: 01422 350017; email: grants@cffc.co.uk; website: www.cffc.co.uk)

CC number: 1002722

Eligibility

People in need who live in Calderdale.

Types of grants

Grants from the Individual Fund are awarded up to a maximum of £250 to help alleviate personal needs.

Annual grant total

In 2015/16 the foundation held assets of £11.4 million and had an income of £3.7 million. During the year, the foundation awarded 1,823 grants to individuals totalling £598,500. Of this amount, £576,000 was given to individuals for welfare purposes and £22,500 was given in educational grants.

Applications

Apply through a referring agency, the contact details of which are listed on the foundation's website.

Other information

The foundation also awards grants to organisations.

Mary Farrar's Benevolent Trust Fund

£6,000

Correspondent: Peter Haley, P. Haley & Co., Poverty Hall, Lower Ellistones, Saddleworth Road, Greetland, Halifax HX4 8NG (01422 376690)

CC number: 223806

Eligibility

Women of limited means over 55 years of age, who are native to the parish of Halifax, or have lived there for more than five consecutive years.

Types of grants

Pensions, paid quarterly.

Annual grant total

In 2015/16 the trust had an income of £5,000 and a total expenditure of £6,500. We estimate that the trust awarded a total of £6,000 in grants to individuals during the year.

Exclusions

A maximum of six grants are available each year for married women and widows.

Applications

Applications should be made in writing to the correspondent, detailing financial need.

The Goodall Trust

£3,300

Correspondent: Andrew Buck, 122 Skircoat Road, Halifax HX1 2RE (01422 255880; email: atbuck@tiscali.co.uk)

CC number: 221651

Eligibility

Widows and unmarried women who are in need and live in the present Calderdale ward of Skircoat or the parts of the parishes of St Jude and All Saints (Halifax) which are within the ancient township of Skircoat.

Types of grants

Recurrent grants are given according to need.

Annual grant total

In 2016 the trust had an income of £3,300 and a total expenditure of £3,500. We estimate that grants given to individuals totalled £3,300.

Applications

Application forms are available from the correspondent. Applications should be submitted either directly by the individual or by a relative, friend, neighbour or welfare agency on their behalf.

Halifax Tradesmen's Benevolent Institution

£16,500

Correspondent: Anthony Wannan, West House, Kings Cross Road, Halifax HX1 1EB (01422 352517; email: anthony.wannan@bm-howarth.co.uk)

CC number: 224056

Eligibility

People in need aged 60 or over who have been self-employed or a manager of a business for at least seven years and live in the parish of Halifax and the surrounding area, and their dependants. Applicants should have no other income than a pension and have only modest savings.

Types of grants

Pensions, which in recent years have amounted to around £550 per annum.

Annual grant total

In 2016/17 the charity had an income of £16,900 and a total expenditure of £27,900. We estimate that pensions paid to individuals totalled £16,500.

Applications

Apply in writing to the correspondent, applications are considered quarterly.

Charity of Ann Holt

£12,500

Correspondent: G. D. Jacobs, 9 Cross Street, Oakenshaw, Bradford, West Yorkshire BD12 7EA (01274 679835)

CC number: 502391

Eligibility

Single women over the age of 55, who have lived in Halifax for at least five years, and are in need.

Types of grants

Pensions of around £200 a year, paid in quarterly instalments until the recipient dies, moves out of the area or relocates to a residential home.

Annual grant total

In 2016/17 the charity had an income of £15,500 and a total expenditure of £12,800. We estimate that grants given to individuals totalled £12,500.

Applications

Applications should be made in writing to the correspondent, directly by the individual. Applicants will need to be prepared to provide two referees who are not relations, such as a vicar, ex-employer or someone else they have known for a number of years.

Kirklees

The Beaumont and Jessop Relief-in-Need Charity

£1,200

Correspondent: Leslie Chadwick, Trustee, 35 Westcroft, Honley, Holmfirth HD9 6JP (01484 662880; email: lesbuk@gmail.com)

CC number: 504141

Eligibility

People in need who are over 65 and live in the ancient township of Honley (near Huddersfield).

Types of grants

One-off grants ranging from £60 to £500 towards, for instance, Winged Fellowship holidays, heating grants (nominated by doctors), medical equipment, spectacles, or transport to luncheon clubs.

Annual grant total

In 2015/16 the charity had an income of £3,500 and a total expenditure of £2,600. We estimate that grants given to individuals totalled approximately £1,200, with funding also awarded to local organisations.

Applications

Apply in writing to the correspondent, indicating the purpose of the grant. Applications can be submitted directly by the individual or through a social worker, Citizens Advice, other welfare agency or other third party (nurses or doctors). Applications are considered throughout the year.

Dewsbury and District Sick Poor Fund

£11,000

Correspondent: John Winder, Correspondent, 130 Boothroyd Lane, Dewsbury, West Yorkshire WF13 2LW (01924 463308; email: alanwwayside@talktalk.net)

CC number: 234401

Eligibility

People who are sick and in need who live in the county borough of Dewsbury and the ecclesiastical parish of Hanging Heaton.

Types of grants

One-off grants according to need for household goods and holidays to aid recuperation after illness. Vouchers are also available for food, clothing and the purchase of medical aids.

Annual grant total

In 2016 the fund had an income of £2,800 and a total expenditure of £11,800. We estimate that grants given to individuals totalled around £11,000.

Applications

Apply in writing to the correspondent including details of illness and residential qualifications. Applications can be submitted either directly by the individual, through a third party such as a social worker or through an organisation such as Citizens Advice.

The H. P. Dugdale Foundation

£64,000 (76 grants)

Correspondent: Thomas Green, Bank Chambers, Market Street, Huddersfield, West Yorkshire HD1 2EW (0790 7294129; email: thomas.green37@btinternet.com)

CC number: 200538

Eligibility

People in need who live in the county borough of Huddersfield (comprising the urban districts of Colne Valley, Kirkburton, Meltham and Holmfirth). People who have previously lived in the area for a period of ten consecutive years are also eligible for assistance.

Types of grants

One-off and recurrent grants are given according to need.

Annual grant total

In 2016/17 the foundation had assets of £1.8 million and an income of £79,000. Grants were made to 76 individuals totalling £64,000. Of this, £48,500 was awarded in regular grants and £15,800 in one-off grants.

Applications

Application forms are given to local organisations such as social services and churches and may be submitted by or on behalf of the individual.

Leeds

The Bramley Poor's Allotment Trust

£1,200

Correspondent: Marian Houseman, 9 Horton Rise, Rodley, Leeds LS13 1PH (0113 236 0115)

CC number: 224522

Eligibility

People in need who live in the ancient township of Bramley, especially people who are older, poor and sick.

Types of grants

One-off grants between £40 and £120.

Annual grant total

In 2016 the trust had an income of £3,200 and a total expenditure of £2,400. We estimate that grants given to individuals for welfare purposes totalled around £1,200.

Applications

Apply in writing to the correspondent. The trust likes applications to be submitted through a recognised referral agency (social worker, Citizens Advice, doctor, headmaster or minister). They are considered monthly.

Chapel Allerton and Potter Newton Relief-in-Need Charity

£1,700

Correspondent: Christopher Johnson, Trustee, 6 Grosvenor Park, Leeds LS7 3QD (0113 268 0600; email: cacharities@btinternet.com)

CC number: 245504

Eligibility

People who live within the parishes of Chapel Allerton and Potter Newton, Leeds.

Types of grants

One-off grants are mainly available for household goods. Support can also be given to assist with fuel bills, rent and telephones.

Annual grant total

In 2016 the charity had an income of £2,300 and a total expenditure of £1,800. We estimate that grants given to individuals totalled around £1,700.

Applications

Applications must be made through the Leeds or Chapeltown Citizens Advice, a social services department, probation officer, health visitor or other referral agency. The trustees usually meet in March but applications can be dealt with at any time.

Kirke's Charity

£1,800

Correspondent: Bruce Buchan, Trustee, 8 St Helens Croft, Leeds LS16 8JY (01924 465860)

CC number: 246102

Eligibility

People in need who live in the ancient parishes of Adel, Arthington or Cookridge.

Types of grants

One-off grants, usually of around £100.

Annual grant total

In 2015/16 the charity had an income of £13,000 and a total expenditure of £7,300. Grants are made to individuals and organisations for both educational and social welfare purposes. We estimate that welfare grants to individuals totalled £1,800.

Applications

Applications can be submitted directly by the individual or through a social worker, Citizens Advice or other welfare agency.

Leeds Benevolent Society for Single Ladies

£31,000 (45 grants)

Correspondent: Anona Everett, Trustee, West Cottage, 12 Eastgate, Bramhope, Leeds LS16 9AB (0113 284 3815; email: anonaeverett@gmail.com)

CC number: 1155794

Eligibility

Single women who are living in the Leeds district.

Types of grants

One-off and recurrent. Individual grants for the previous year went towards supplements of state retirement pensions, television licences, telephone rentals, contributions towards holiday costs, outings and theatre visits, financial and general help.

Annual grant total

In 2016 the charity had an income of £150,000 and a total expenditure of £122,000. The charity awarded 45 welfare grants to older women in Leeds which totalled £31,000. Of this amount, £9,200 went towards holidays and outings. The charity also made donations to organisations throughout 2016 which totalled £33,500.

Applications

Apply in writing to the correspondent.

Other information

The charity also provides grants to organisations which fund social activities to alleviate loneliness and isolation of older single women. Additional grants totalling almost £33,500 were also made to the University of Leeds in respect of assistance with the Leeds Older Women Urinary Incontinence Self-Management (LOUISA) study.

In December 2016 the charity also agreed to support both OPAL and Caring Together in Woodhouse and Little London starting on 1 March 2017 with both organisations receiving £30,000 per year for a period of three years.

The Leeds Community Trust

£14,500

Correspondent: Lynn Higo, Administrator, McCarthy's Business Centre, Suite 23, Enterprise House, Leeds LS7 2AH (0113 237 9685; fax: 0113 278 3184; email: info@ leedscommunitytrust.org; website: www. leedscommunitytrust.org)

CC number: 701375

Eligibility

Families who are in need and live in the Leeds area. Families with children are usually given preference.

Types of grants

The trust provides assistance in a number of forms:

▶ One-off grants are given for emergency items such as beds, bedding, carpets, washing machines and removal costs, etc. The website states: 'Families with children are usually given priority, but we try to help all families in need who have problems such as physical or mental disabilities, child protection issues, homelessness or similar situations'

- Holiday grants are given to enable children and their families to go away on holiday; this could be to a caravan, a bed and breakfast, or even a guesthouse
- Christmas grants are given to disadvantaged families with children to cover food and gifts. Where funds permit, a grocery voucher is issued before Christmas
- The Millennium Project, whenever funds permit, helps to provide a bed for children who do not have a permanent bed
- Through the Kozy Kids Project the trust works with families who have experienced difficult circumstances in order to help the children furnish their bedroom/s
- Through the Keen Kids Project small, one-off grants are given to children to assist with educational, musical and sports costs

Annual grant total

In 2016 the trust had assets of £19,200 and a total expenditure of £14,500. During the year, the trust awarded a total of £14,500 to individuals for welfare purposes.

Applications

Applications can only be submitted by a social worker or care agency on behalf of the individual.

Other information

The trust runs two shops and distributes the profits to local charities, groups and individuals in need, particularly people who are in vulnerable situations.

Leeds Convalescent Society

£7,000

Correspondent: Peter Gallant, 21 Rose Croft, East Keswick, Leeds LS17 9HR (01937 573365; email: peter.gallant21@gmail.com)

CC number: 223831

Eligibility

Residents of Leeds who are in need, recovering from illness or require specialist equipment, e.g. wheelchairs.

Types of grants

One-off according to need.

Annual grant total

In 2016 the society had an income of £14,000 and a total expenditure of £14,500. We estimate that grants given to individuals totalled around £7,000.

Applications

Apply in writing to the correspondent.

The Leeds Tradesmen's Trust

£24,000

Correspondent: Grants Team, 1st Floor, 51A St Paul's Street, Leeds LS1 2TE (0113 242 2426; email: info@leedscf.org.uk)

CC number: 1096892

Eligibility

People over 50 who have carried on business, practised a profession or been a tradesperson for at least five years (either consecutively or in total) and who, during that time, lived in Leeds or whose business premises (rented or owned) were in the city of Leeds. Grants are also given to self-employed business/professional people who 'have fallen upon misfortune in business'; normally older people. Widows and unmarried daughters of the former are also eligible.

Types of grants

Quarterly pensions, normally of £10 to £500 a year, plus Christmas grants and spring fuel grants only to those already receiving a pension.

Annual grant total

In 2016/17 grants totalled £24,000.

Applications

Enquiries should be made to the Leeds Community Foundation's grants team by telephone or email.

Other information

Community Foundation for Leeds took over the administration of the trust in April 2013.

Metcalfe Smith Trust CIO

£11,200 (48 grants)

Correspondent: Geoff Hill, Secretary, c/o Voluntary Action Leeds, Stringer House, 34 Lupton Street, Hunslet, Leeds LS10 2QW (email: secretary@metcalfesmithtrust.org.uk; website: www.metcalfesmithtrust.org.uk)

CC number: 1164280

Eligibility

Adults or children who live in Leeds and have a physical disability, long-term illness or difficulties with their mental health.

Types of grants

One-off grants, usually ranging from £250 to £2,500, are given for items or services that will significantly improve the quality of life of the individual. Grants are given towards, for example, disability equipment, computers, respite breaks, heating costs, small items of furniture and course fees. Emergency grants of up to £100 are also available.

Annual grant total

In 2015/16 the trust had assets of £838,000 and an income of £21,500. Grants to individuals totalled £11,200, with £6,900 given to in 13 grants to individuals for relief in need and £4,300 distributed to 35 individuals through the emergency fund. A further £3,000 was awarded to organisations.

Exclusions

No support is given to individuals living outside the area of benefit. The trust will not commit to making recurrent grants.

Applications

Application forms are available on request by completing the application request form on the trust's website, where guidelines can also be found. Individual applications must be supported by a social worker or local welfare organisation. They are considered twice a year, normally in May and October/November. See the website for dates of application deadlines and trustees' meetings. Applications for emergency grants can be made at any time and applicants can use the online application form.

Wakefield

The Brotherton Charity Trust

£2,000

Correspondent: Christopher Brotherton-Ratcliffe, Trustee, PO Box 374, Harrogate HG1 4YW

CC number: 221006

Eligibility

People in need who are over 60 years old and live in Wakefield.

Types of grants

Annual pensions.

Annual grant total

In 2016 the trust had an income of £4,100 and a total expenditure of £2,400. We have estimated that pensions totalled around £2,000.

Applications

Application forms are available from the correspondent. When vacancies arise an advert is placed in the Wakefield Express and a waiting list is then drawn up. Applications can be made directly by the individual or family member.

Horbury Common Lands Trust

£6,600

Correspondent: Martin Milner, Clerk to the Trustees, Meadow View, Haigh Moor Road, Tingley, Wakefield WF3 1EJ (07550 085465; website: www. horburycommonlandstrust.org.uk)

CC number: 214613

Eligibility

Residents aged over 70 years, with a weekly income of less than £230, who have lived the urban district of Horbury for ten years or more are invited to apply for a Christmas grant from the trust.

Other grants are available for individuals in need.

Types of grants

One-off grants.

Annual grant total

In 2016 the trust held assets of £1.4 million and had an income of £66,500. Grants to individuals totalled £6,600, of which £5,000 was awarded to older people through the Christmas grant scheme. The trust also supports local organisations, schools and churches which received £44,500 during the year.

Applications

Forms can be downloaded from the charity's website. Applications can be submitted at any time of the year. Decisions are made in March, June, September and December. Applications need to be with the correspondent at the latest by the first day of the month of a meeting.

St Leonard's Hospital – Horbury

£1,200

Correspondent: Ian Whittell, Administrator, 31 New Road, Horbury, Wakefield, West Yorkshire WF4 5LS (01924 272762)

CC number: 243977

Eligibility

People in need, hardship or distress who live in the former urban district of Horbury.

Types of grants

One-off grants usually ranging from £20 to £200. Grants have been given towards adaptations, convalescence, nursing, renovation and repairs to homes for disability access and helping people who are homeless or experiencing marital problems.

Annual grant total

In 2016 the charity had an income of £3,400 and a total expenditure of £1,510. We estimate that grants given to individuals totalled approximately £1,200.

Exclusions

No grants are made towards maintenance of equipment already paid for. No loans are made, although recurrent grants are considered if necessary.

Applications

Apply in writing to the correspondent. Applications can be submitted directly by the individual, through a social worker, Citizens Advice or other welfare agency or through a church member. They are considered at any time and the trustees can act quickly in urgent cases.

Advice organisations

The following section lists the names and contact details of voluntary organisations that offer advice and support to individuals in need. The list is split into two sections – 'Welfare' and 'Illness and disability'. Each section begins with an index before listing the organisations by category.

The listings are a useful reference guide to organisations that individuals can contact to discuss their situation and receive advice and support. These organisations will have experience in tackling the sorts of problems that other individuals have faced, and will know the most effective and efficient ways of dealing with them. They may also be able to arrange for people to meet others in a similar situation. As well as providing advice and support, many of the organisations will be happy to help individuals submit applications to the trusts included in this guide. They may also know of other sources of funding available.

Some organisations included in this list have their own financial resources available to individuals. We have marked these with an asterisk (*). This list should not be used as a quick way of identifying potential funding – the organisations will have criteria and policies that may mean they are unable to support all the needs under that category and the guide will include many more potential sources of funding than there are organisations here.

Some organisations have local branches, which are better placed to have a personal contact with the individual and have a greater local knowledge of the need. We have only included the headquarters of such organisations, which will be happy to provide details for the relevant branches.

If you are requesting information from any of the organisations listed, it is helpful to include an sae.

This list is by no means comprehensive and should only be used as a starting point. It only contains organisations that have a national remit and does not include organisations that provide general advice and support solely to members of a particular religion, country or ethnic group. For further details of groups, look for charitable and voluntary organisations in your local phone book, or contact your local council for voluntary service (CVS) (sometimes called Voluntary Action) which should be listed in the phone book.

The following general welfare section includes 'Benefit and grants information' and 'Debt and financial advice', which may be of particular relevance during these difficult economic times.

Welfare

General

Advice NI, 1 Rushfield Avenue, Belfast BT7 3FP (tel: 028 9064 5919; email: info@adviceni.net; website: www.adviceni.net). For information on sources of advice and support in Northern Ireland.

Citizens Advice, 3rd Floor North, 200 Aldersgate Street, London EC1A 4HD (Adviceline: 03444 111 444 [England], 03444 77 20 20 [Wales], 03444 111 445 [TextRelay]; website: www.citizensadvice.org.uk). For details of your local Citizens Advice office please see the website.

The Salvation Army, Territorial Headquarters, 101 Newington Causeway, London SE1 6BN (tel: 020 7367 4500; email: info@salvation army.org.uk; website: www. salvationarmy.org.uk)

Samaritans, The Upper Mill, Kingston Road, Ewell, Surrey KT17 2AF (tel: 020 8394 8300; 24-hour helpline: 116 123; see the website for local numbers; email: admin@samaritans. org [general] or jo@samaritans.org [helpline]; website: www.samaritans. org)

Benefit and grants information

The Association of Charitable Organisations (ACO), 2nd Floor, Acorn House, 314–320 Grays Inn Road, London WC1X 8DP (tel: 020 7255 4480; email: info@aco.uk.net; website: www.aco.uk.net)

Child Benefit, PO Box 1, Newcastle upon Tyne NE88 1AA (helpline: 0300 200 3100 [Mon–Fri, 8am–8pm and Sat, 8am–4pm]; textphone: 0300 200 3103; email: use online form; website: www.hmrc.gov.uk/childbenefit)

Child Maintenance Options, (tel: 0800 988 0988 [Mon–Fri, 8am–8pm and Sat, 9am–4pm]; textphone: 0800 988 9888; website: www.cmoptions. org). Contact can also be made through an online live chat feature or use the online form.

Disability Service Centre, (Disability Living Allowance helpline: 0800 731 0122 [Mon–Fri, 8am–6pm]; Attendance Allowance helpline: 0800 731 0122; Personal Independence Payment (PIP) helpline: 0800 917 2222; website: www.gov.uk/pip)

Gov.uk, general information on money, tax and benefits (website: www.gov.uk)

Jobseeker's Allowance (JSA) (Universal Credit helpline: 0800 328 5644 [Mon–Fri, 8am–6pm]; textphone: 0800 023 4888; website: www.gov.uk/jobseekers-allowance/ further-information). You may also make a claim online.

Pension Credit Claim Line; (tel: 0800 991234 [Mon–Fri, 8am–6pm]; textphone: 0800 169 0133; website: www.gov.uk/pension-credit/overview) See the website for information on local offices.

Tax Credits helpline, Tax Credit Office, Preston PR1 4AT; (tel: 0345 300 3900 [Mon–Fri, 8am–8pm and Sat, 8am–4pm]; textphone 0345 300 3909; website: www.gov.uk/browse/ benefits/tax-credits)

Veterans UK, Ministry of Defence, Norcross, Thornton Cleveleys, Lancashire FY5 3WP; (helpline: 0808 191 4218 [Mon–Thurs, 7.30am–6.30pm and Fri, 7.30am–5pm]. Out of hours calls will be taken by Combat Stress or Samaritans, using the same number; email: veterans-uk@mod.uk; website: www.gov.uk/government/ organisations/veterans-uk)

Winter Fuel Payments, Winter Fuel Payment Centre, Mail Handling Site A, Wolverhampton WV98 1LR; (helpline: 0800 731 0160 [Mon–Fri, 8am–6pm]; textphone: 0800 731 0464; website: www.gov.uk/winter-fuel-payment)

Bereavement

Cruse Bereavement Care, Unit 0.1, One Victoria Villas, Richmond, Surrey TW9 2GW; (tel: 020 8939 9541; helpline: 0808 808 1677; email: info@cruse.org.uk or helpline@cruse.org.uk; website: www. cruse.org.uk)

Natural Death Centre, In The Hill House, Watley Lane, Twyford, Winchester SO21 1QX; (tel: 01962 712690; email: susan@naturaldeath. org.uk; website: www.naturaldeath. org.uk)

Stillbirth and Neonatal Death Society (SANDS), Victoria Charity Centre, Suite GF2 Ground Floor, 11 Belgrave Road, London SW1V 1RB (tel: 020

7436 7940; helpline: 0808 164 3332 [Mon–Fri, 9.30am–5.30pm and Tues and Thurs, 6pm–10pm]; email: accounts@sands.org.uk [general information] or helpline@sands.org.uk; website: www. sands.org.uk)

Survivors of Bereavement by Suicide (SOBS), The Flamsteed Centre, Albert Street, Ilkeston, Derbyshire DE7 5GU; (tel: 0115 944 1117; helpline: 0300 111 5065 [9am–9pm daily]; email: admin@uksobs.org; website: www. uksobs.org)

Children

Child Bereavement UK, Clare Charity Centre, Wycombe Road, Saunderton, Buckinghamshire HP14 4BF; (tel: 0800 028 8840; email: support@ childbereavement.org.uk; website: www.childbereavement.org.uk)

Winston's Wish, 17 Royal Crescent, Cheltenham GL50 3DA; (tel: 01242 515157; helpline: 0808 802 0021 [Mon–Fri, 9am–5pm and Wed, 7pm–9.30pm]; email: info@ winstonswish.org.uk; website: www. winstonswish.org.uk)

Parents

Child Death Helpline, Barclay House, 37 Queen Square, London WC1N 3BH; (tel: 020 7813 8416 [admin]; helpline: 0800 282986 or from mobiles 0808 800 6019 [Mon, Thurs and Fri, 10am–1pm; Tues and Wed, 10am–4pm; and every evening 7pm–10pm]; email: contact@ childdeathhelpline.org; website: www. childdeathhelpline.org.uk)

The Compassionate Friends, 14 New King Street, Deptford, London SE8 3HS; (tel: 0345 120 3785; helpline: 0845 123 2304 [10am–4pm and 7pm–10pm daily]; Northern Ireland helpline: 028 8778 8016 [10am–4pm and 7pm–9.30pm daily]; email: info@tcf.org.uk or helpline@tcf.org.uk; website: www.tcf. org.uk)

The Lullaby Trust, 11 Belgrave Road, London SW1V 1RB (tel: 020 7802 3201; helpline: 0808 802 6868 [Mon–Fri, 10am–5pm; weekends and public holidays 6pm–10pm]; email: office@lullabytrust.org.uk or support@lullabytrust.org.uk; website: www.lullabytrust.org.uk)

Carers

Carers UK, 20 Great Dover Street, London SE1 4LX; (tel: 020 7378 4945; Carers UK Adviceline: 0808 808 7777 [Mon–Fri, 10am–4pm]; email: advice@carersuk.org; website: www. carersuk.org)

Leonard Cheshire Disability, 66 South Lambeth Road, London SW8 1RL; (tel: 020 3242 0200; website: www. leonardcheshire.org). Contact can also be made by completing an online form.

Children and young people

Action for Children, 3 The Boulevard, Ascot Road, Watford WD18 8AG (tel: 01923 361500 [Mon–Fri, 9am–5pm]; email: ask.us@actionforchildren.org. uk; website: www.actionforchildren. org.uk)

Catch 22, 27 Pear Tree Street, London EC1V 3AG (tel: 020 7336 4800; email: use online form; website: www.catch-22.org.uk)

ChildLine, 42 Curtain Road, London EC2A 3NH (tel: 020 7825 2500; 24-hour advice helpline: 0800 1111; website: www.childline.org.uk). A personal inbox can be set up on the site which will allow you to send emails to ChildLine and save replies in similar way to a normal email service. Alternatively, send a message without signing in through the 'send Sam a message' function. You can also chat online with a ChildLine counsellor by going to www.childline. org.uk/get-support/1–2–1-counsellor-chat.

The Children's Society, Edward Rudolf House, Margery Street, London WC1X 0JL (tel: 0300 303 7000; email: supportercare@ childrenssociety.org.uk; website: www.childrenssociety.org.uk)

Coram Children's Legal Centre, Riverside Office Centre, Century House North, North Station Road, Colchester CO1 1RE (tel: 01206 714650 [general]; Civil Legal Advice Education Law Line: 0845 345 4345 [Mon–Fri, 9am–8pm and Sat, 9am–12.30pm]; Migrant Children's Project Advice Line: 020 7636 8505 [Tues–Thurs, 10am–4pm]) email: info@coramclc.org.uk; website: www. childrenslegalcentre.com)

National Youth Advocacy Service, Units 1–3, Tower House, 1 Tower Road, Birkenhead CH41 1FF (tel: 0151 649 8700; helpline: 0808 808 1001 [Mon–Fri, 9am–8pm and Sat, 10am–4pm]; email: main@nyas.net or help@nyas.net; website: www.nyas. net)

NSPCC, Weston House, 42 Curtain Road, London EC2A 3NH (tel: 020 7825 2500 [Mon–Fri, 9am–5pm]; helpline for adults concerned about a child: 0808 800 5000; ChildLine: 0800 1111; email: use online form; website: www.nspcc.org.uk)

Save the Children UK, 1 St John's Lane, London EC1M 4AR (tel: 020 7012 6400; email: supporter.care@ savethechildren.org.uk; website: www. savethechildren.org.uk)

Become 15–18 White Lion Street, London N1 9PG (tel: 020 7251 3117; care advice line: 0800 023 2033 [Mon–Fri, 10.30am–3pm]; email: advice@becomecharity.org.uk; website: www.becomecharity.org.uk)

Youth Access, 1–2 Taylors Yard, 67 Alderbrook Road, London SW12 8AD (tel: 020 8772 9900 [Mon–Fri, 9.30am–1pm and 2pm–5.30pm]; email: admin@ youthaccess.org.uk; website: www. youthaccess.org.uk [for an online directory of information, advice and support services for young people])

Bullying

The Anti-Bullying Alliance, National Children's Bureau, 8 Wakely Street, London EC1V 7QE (website: www. anti-bullyingalliance.org.uk; details of the regional offices are available on the website)

Kidscape, 2 Grosvenor Gardens, London SW1W 0DH (tel: 020 7730 3300; email: info@kidscape.org.uk; website: www.kidscape.org.uk)

Young People Leaving Care, Catch22, National Care Advisory Service (NCAS), 27 Pear Tree Street, London EC1V 3AG; (tel: 020 7336 4800; website: www.leavingcare.org)

Debt and financial advice

Age UK Money Matters, provides a range of advice on topics such as pensions, tax, financial management, consumer issues and benefits (website: www.ageuk.org.uk/money-matters; Age UK Advice: 0800 169 2081)

Business Debtline, (tel: 0800 197 6026 [Mon–Fri, 9am–5.30pm]; website: www.businessdebtline.org). The debtline does not provide advice by letter or email.

Gamblers Anonymous (GANON), (website: www.gamblersanonymous. org.uk).

GamCare, 2nd Floor, 1st Floor, CAN Mezzanine Old Street, London N1 6AH (tel: 020 7801 7000; helpline: 0808 802 0133 [8am–midnight daily]; email: info@gamcare.org.uk; website: www.gamcare.org.uk)

The Money Advice Service, Holborn Centre, 120 Holborn, London EC1N 2TD (tel: 0800 138 7777; typetalk: 18001 0300 500 5000 [Mon–Fri, 8am–8pm and Sat, 9am–1pm]; email: enquiries@ moneyadviceservice.org.uk; website: www.moneyadviceservice.org.uk; an online chat facility is also available.)

National Debtline, Tricorn House, 51–53 Hagley Road, Edgbaston, Birmingham B16 8TP (helpline: 0808 808 4000 [Mon–Fri, 9am–9pm and Sat, 9.30am–1pm]; website: www. nationaldebtline.org). Contact can also be made by completing the online form.

StepChange Debt Charity, Wade House, Merrion Centre, Leeds LS2 8NG (helpline: 0800 138 1111 [Mon–Fri, 8am–8pm and Sat, 8am–4pm]; email: use online form; website: www.stepchange.org)

TaxAid, Unit 2, 33 Stannary Street, London SE11 4AA (tel: 020 7803 4950 [advice agencies only]; helpline: 0345 120 3779; website: www.taxaid.org. uk). Contact can also be made by completing the online enquiry form.

TPAS (Pensions Advisory Service), 11 Belgrave Road, London SW1V 1RB (tel: 020 7630 2250; pensions advice: 0300 123 1047; helpline for women: 0345 600 0806; helpline for self-employed: 0345 602 7021; email: use online form; website: www. pensionsadvisoryservice.org.uk). An online chat facility for legal advice is also available from Mon–Fri, 9am–5pm and Tues, 7pm–9 pm.

Families

Home-Start UK, The Crescent, King Street, Leicester LE1 6RX (tel: 0116 464 5490; [Mon–Fri, 8am–8pm and Sat, 9am–12pm]; email: info@home-start.org.uk; website: www.home-start.org.uk)

Housing

Homes England, Fry Building, 2 Marsham Street, London SW1P 4DF (tel: 0300 1234 500; email: enquiries@homesengland.gov.uk; website: www.gov.uk/government/ organisations/homes-england/about)

Shelter, 88 Old Street, London EC1V 9HU (tel: 0300 330 1234; helpline: 0808 301 5978; email: info@ shelter.org.uk; website: www.shelter. org.uk)

Legal

Advice Services Alliance (ASA), Tavis House (Floor 7), 1–6 Tavistock Square, London WC1H 9NA (tel: 07904 377460; email: admin@asauk. org.uk or by using the online form; website: www.asauk.org.uk). Please note: ASA does not give advice to the general public.

Bar Pro Bono Unit, 48 Chancery Lane, London WC2A 1JF (tel: 020 7092 3960 [Mon–Fri, 10am–4pm]; email: enquiries@barprobono.org.uk or use the online form; website: www. barprobono.org.uk)

Civil Legal Advice, (helpline: 0345 345 4 345 [Mon–Fri, 9am–8pm and Sat, 9am–12.30pm]; email: use online form; website: www.gov.uk/civil-legal-advice). An online chat facility for legal advice is also available.

Law Centres Network, Tavis House (Floor 1), 1–6 Tavistock Square, London WC1H 9NA (tel: 020 3637 1330 [please note this is not an advice line but LCN's office line]; email: use online form; website: www.lawcentres. org.uk). See the website for information on your local law centre.

LGBT

Beaumont Society, 27 Old Gloucester Street, London WC1N 3XX (24-hour helpline: 01582 412220; website: www.beaumontsociety.org.uk). Contact can also be made by completing an online enquiry form.

LGBT Foundation, 5 Richmond Street, Manchester M1 3HF (helpline: 0345 330 30 30 [6pm–10pm daily]; email: info@lgbt.foundation; website: www.lgbt.foundation)

Stonewall, 192 St John Street, Clerkenwell, London EC1V 4JY (office [admin] tel: 020 7593 1850; information line: 0800 050 2020 [Mon–Fri, 9.30am–5.30pm]; email: info@stonewall.org.uk; website: www. stonewall.org.uk)

Missing people

Missing People, 284 Upper Richmond Road West, London SW14 7JE; (helpline: 116 000; text: 116 000; email: 116000@missingpeople.org.uk [if you are missing and want to talk about your situation] or use the online form [to report someone missing]; website: www. missingpeople.org.uk)

Offenders and ex-offenders

APEX Trust, 1st Floor, Century House, Hardshaw Street, St Helens, Merseyside WA10 1QU; (tel: 01744 612898; email: sthelens@apextrust. com; website: www.apextrust.com)

Hardman Trust, PO Box 108, Newport, IW PO30 1YN (tel: 01983 550355; email: info@hardmantrust. org.uk; website: www.hardmantrust. org.uk)

National Association for the Care and Rehabilitation of Offenders (NACRO), 46 Loman Street, London SE1 0EH (tel [Resettlement Advice Service]: 0300 123 1999; email: helpline@nacro.org.uk; website: www. nacro.org.uk)

Prisoners Abroad, 89–93 Fonthill Road, Finsbury Park, London N4 3JH (tel: 020 7561 6820; helpline: 0808 172 0098; email: info@ prisonersabroad.org.uk; website: www.prisonersabroad.org.uk)

Unlock, Maidstone Community Support Centre, 39–48 Marsham Street, Maidstone, Kent ME14 1HH (helpline: 01634 247350 [Mon–Fri, 10am–4pm]; text: 07824 113848; Skype: unlockhelpline; email: advice@ unlock.org.uk or use the online form; website: www.unlock.org.uk)

Families of offenders and ex-offenders

Offenders' families helpline, c/o Family Lives, 15–17 The Broadway, Hatfield, Hertfordshire AL9 5HZ (helpline: 0808 808 2003 [Mon–Fri, 9am–8pm and Sat–Sun, 10am–3pm]; email: info@offendersfamilieshelpline. org.uk). Information sheets are available on request by post or can be downloaded from the website: www. offendersfamilieshelpline.org.uk.

Partners of Prisoners and Families Support Group, POPS 1079 Rochdale Road, Blackley, Manchester M9 8AJ (tel: 0161 702 1000; helpline: 0808 808 2003 [Mon–Fri, 9am–8pm and Sat–Sun, 10am–3pm]; email: mail@ partnersofprisoners.co.uk or use the online form; website: www. partnersofprisoners.co.uk)

Prisoners' Families and Friends Service, 29 Peckham Road, London SE5 8UA (tel: 020 7735 9535; helpline: 0808 808 3444; email: info@ pffs.org.uk or use the online form; website: www.pffs.org.uk)

Female offenders and ex-offenders

Creative and Supportive Trust (CAST), Unit 1, Lysander Mews, Lysander Grove, Upper Holloway, London N19 3QP (tel: 020 7281 9928; mobile: 07435 967990; email: info@ castwomen.org.uk; website: www. castwomen.org.uk)

Older people

Age UK, 6th Floor, Tavis House, 1–6 Tavistock Square, London WC1H 9NA (helpline: 0800 169 2081 [Mon–Fri, 9am–4pm]; email: contact@ageuk.org.uk or by using the online form; website: www.ageuk.org. uk)

The Age and Employment Network, Headland House, 308–312 Gray's Inn Road, London WC1X 8DP (website: www.taen.org.uk; email: info@taen. org.uk)

Care & Repair, Unit 9, The Renewal Trust Business Centre, 3 Hawksworth Street, Nottingham NG3 2EG (tel: 0115 950 6500; email: info@ careandrepair-england.org.uk; website: careandrepair-england.org.uk)

Friends of the Elderly, 40–42 Ebury Street, London SW1W 0LZ (tel: 020 7730 8263; email: enquiries@fote.org. uk or use the online form; website: www.fote.org.uk)

Independent Age, 18 Avonmore Road, London W14 8RR, (tel: 020 7605 4200; advice line: 0800 319 6789; email: charity@independentage. org; website: www.independentage. org)

Parenting

Family Lives, 15–17 The Broadway, Hatfield, Hertfordshire AL9 5HZ (tel: 020 7553 3080; 24-hour helpline: 0808 800 2222; website: www. familylives.org.uk). Contact can also be made by using the online chat support service.

Home-Start UK, The Crescent, King Street, Leicester LE1 6RX (tel: 0116 464 5490; [Mon–Fri, 8am–8pm and Sat, 9am–12pm]; email: info@home-start.org.uk; website: www.home-start.org.uk)

Twins and Multiple Births Association (TAMBA), Manor House, Church Hill, Aldershot, Hampshire GU12 4JU (tel: 01252 332344; helpline: 0800 138 0509 [10am–1pm and 7pm–10pm daily]; email: asktwinline@tamba.org.uk; website: www.tamba.org.uk)

Abduction

Reunite (National Council for Abducted Children), PO Box 7124, Leicester LE1 7XX (tel: 0116 255 5345; advice line: 0116 255 6234; email: reunite@dircon.co.uk; website: www.reunite.org)

Adoption and fostering

Adoption UK, Units 11 and 12, Vantage Business Park, Bloxham Road, Banbury OX16 9UX (tel: 01295 752240; helpline: 07904 793974 and 07539 733079 [Mon–Thu, 10am–2.30pm]; website: www. adoptionuk.org.uk; email: aukhelpine@pac-uk.org or by using the online form)

After Adoption, Unit 5 Citygate, 5 Blantyre Street, Manchester M15 4JJ (tel: 0161 839 4932; Action Line: 0800 056 8578; email: information@ afteradoption.org.uk; website: www. afteradoption.org.uk)

CoramBAAF Adoption & Fostering Academy, Coram Campus, 41 Brunswick Square, London WC1N 1AZ (tel: 020 7520 0300; email: mail@corambaaf.org.uk; website: www.corambaaf.org.uk)

Fostering Network, 87 Blackfriars Road, London SE1 8HA (tel: 020 7620 6400; Fosterline: 020 7401 9582 [England], 0800 316 7664 [Wales], 0141 204 1400 [Scotland], 028 9070 5056 [Northern Ireland]; email: info@ fostering.net; website: www.fostering. net)

National Association of Child Contact Centres, Second Floor Offices, Friary Chambers, 26–34 Friar Lane, Nottingham NG1 6DQ (tel: 0845 450 0280 or from mobiles 0115 948 4557; email: contact@naccc. uk; website: www.naccc.org.uk)

Post-Adoption Centre, 5 Torriano Mews, Torriano Avenue, London NW5 2RZ (tel: 020 7284 0555; advice line: 020 7284 5879 [Mon, Tues and Fri, 10am–4pm, and Wed and Thurs, 2pm–7pm]; email: use online form; website: www.pac-uk.org)

Childcare

Family and Childcare Trust, The Bridge, 81 Southwark Bridge Road, London SE1 0NQ (tel: 020 7940 7510; email: info@familyandchildcaretrust. org.uk; website: www. familyandchildcaretrust.org)

Family Rights Group, Second Floor, The Print House, 18 Ashwin Street, London E8 3DL (tel: 020 7923 2628; advice line: 0808 801 0366 [Mon–Fri, 9.30am–3pm]; email: use online form; website: www.frg.org.uk)

Divorce

Both Parents Forever, 39 Cloonmore Avenue, Orpington, Kent BR6 9LE (helpline: 01689 854343 [8am–9pm daily])

CAFCASS (Children and Family Court Advisory and Support Service), 3rd Floor, 21 Bloomsbury Street, London WC1B 3HF (tel: 0300 456 4000; email: webenquiries@cafcass.gsi. gov.uk or telephoneenquiries@cafcass. gsi.gov.uk; website: www.cafcass.gov. uk)

Families Need Fathers, 134–146 Curtain Road, London EC2A 3AR (helpline: 0300 0300 363 [7am–midnight daily]; email: fnf@fnf. org.uk; website: www.fnf.org.uk)

National Family Mediation, Civic Centre, Paris Street, Exeter (tel: 0300 4000 636; email: use online form; website: www.nfm.org.uk)

NCDSW (National Council for the Divorced and Separated and Widowed), 68 Parkes Hall Road, Woodsetton, Dudley DY1 3SR (tel: 01902 679690; email: secretary@ phoenixclubs.org.uk; website: www. ncdsw.org.uk)

Grandparents

Grandparents Plus, 1 Addington Square, London SE5 OHF (helpline: 0300 123 7015 [Mon–Fri, 10am–3pm]; email: info@ grandparentsplus.org.uk; website: www.grandparentsplus.org.uk)

Mothers

Mothers Apart from their Children (MATCH), BM Box No. 6334, London WC1N 3XX (helpline: 0800 689 4140; email: enquiries@ matchmothers.org; website: www. matchmothers.org)

Mumsnet, (email: contactus@ mumsnet.com; website: www. mumsnet.com)

Pregnancy

ARC (Antenatal Results and Choices), 345 City Road, London EC1V 1LR (tel: 020 7713 7486; helpline: 0845 077 2290 [Mon–Fri, 10am–5.30pm]; email: info@arc-uk.org or by using the online form; website: www.arc-uk. org)

British Pregnancy Advisory Service (BPAS), 20 Timothy's Bridge Road, Stratford Enterprise Park, Stratford-upon-Avon, Warwickshire CV37 9BF (advice line: 03457 30 40 30; email: info@bpas.org; website: www.bpas. org)

Brook, 50 Featherstone Street, London EC1Y 8RT (tel: 020 7284 6040 [admin]; email: admin@brook. org.uk; website: www.brook.org.uk). You may also use the Ask Brook facility to ask questions via email or text 07537 402024.

Disability Pregnancy and Parenthood International (DPPI), 106 Muswell Hill Road, London N10 3JR (tel: 020 7263 3088; helpline: 0800 018 4730 [Tues–Thurs, 10.30am–2.30pm]; email: info@disabledparent.org.uk; website: www.disabledparent.org.uk)

National Childbirth Trust, 30 Euston Square, London NW1 2FB (helpline: 0300 330 0700; website: www.nct.org. uk; email: enquiries@nct.org.uk). Contact can also be made by completing an online enquiry form.

Single parents

Gingerbread, 520 Highgate Studios, 53–79 Highgate Road London NW5 1TL (tel: 020 7428 5420 [admin]; helpline: 0808 802 0925 [Mon, 10am–6pm, Tues, Thurs and Fri 10am–4pm and Wed 10am–1pm and 5pm–7pm]; website: www. gingerbread.org.uk). Contact can also be made by completing an online enquiry form.

Single Parents, The Silai Centre, 176–178 Easton Road, Bristol BS5 0ES (website: www.singleparents. org.uk)

Poverty

Care International, 9th Floor, 89 Albert Embankment, London SE1 7TP (tel: 020 7091 6000; website: www.careinternational.org.uk). Contact can also be made by completing an online enquiry form.

Counselling, 5 Pear Tree Walk, Wakefield, West Yorkshire WF2 0HW (website: www.counselling.ltd.uk)

*Family Action, 24 Angel Gate, City Road, London EC1V 2PT (tel: 020 7254 6251; email: info@family-action. org.uk; website: www.family-action. org.uk). Contact can also be made by completing an online enquiry form.

Law Centres Network, Tavis House (Floor 1), 1–6 Tavistock Square, London WC1H 9NA (tel: 020 3637 1330 [admin]; an online enquiry form is also available for non-legal advice; website: www.lawcentres.org.uk). See the website for information on your local law centre.

The Trussell Trust, Unit 9, Ashfield Trading Estate, Ashfield Road, Salisbury SP2 7HL (tel: 01722 580180; email: enquiries@trusselltrust.org; website: www.trusselltrust.org). You can also use the sites search facility to find your nearest food bank.

Refugees and asylum seekers

Asylum Aid, Club Union House, 253–254 Upper Street, London N1 1RY (tel: 020 7354 9631; advice line: 020 7354 9264 [Mon–Fri, 10am–12pm]; email: info@asylumaid. org.uk; website: www.asylumaid.org. uk)

Migrant Help, Charlton House, Dour Street, Dover, Kent CT16 1AT (tel: 01304 218700; email: info@ migranthelpline.org; website: www. migranthelp.org)

Refugee Action, Victoria Charity Centre, 11 Belgrave Road, London SW1V 1RB (tel: 020 7952 1511; asylum advice: 0808 800 0630; website: www.refugee-action.org.uk). See the website for a list of local offices.

Refugee Council, PO Box 68614, London E15 9DQ (tel: 020 7346 6700 [head office]; website: www. refugeecouncil.org.uk). Please visit the website for signposting to a specific service.

Refugee Support Centre, 47 South Lambeth Road, London SW8 1RH (tel: 020 7820 3606; email: rsctherapy47@hotmail.com)

Relationships

Albany Trust Counselling, 239A Balham High Road, London SW17 7BE (tel: 020 8767 1827; email: info@albanytrust.org; website: www. albanytrust.org.uk)

Family Planning Association, 23–28 Penn Street, London EC1Y 8QU (tel: 020 7608 5240; email: general@fpa.org.uk; website: www.fpa. org.uk)

Relate Premier House, Carolina Court, Lakeside, Doncaster DN4 5RA (tel: 0300 100 1234; email: use online form; website: www.relate.org.uk; there is also a live chat service available on the website)

Social isolation

The Farming Community Network, Manor Farm, West Haddon, Northampton NN6 7AQ (helpline: 0300 011 1999 email: chris@fcn.org. uk; website: www.fcn.org.uk)

Squatters

Advisory Service for Squatters (ASS), Angel Alley, 84B Whitechapel High Street, London E1 7QX (tel: 020 3216 0099; email: advice@squatter.org.uk; website: www.squatter.org.uk)

Victims of accidents and crimes

Abuse

Action on Elder Abuse (AEA), PO Box 60001, Streatham SW16 9BY (helpline: 0808 808 8141; email: enquiries@elderabuse.org.uk or use the online form; website: www. elderabuse.org.uk)

The Clinic for Boundaries, 49–51 East Road, London N1 6AH (tel: 020 3468 4194; email: info@ professionalboundaries.org.uk;

website: www.professionalboundaries. org.uk)

NSPCC, Weston House, 42 Curtain Road, London EC2A 3NH (tel: 020 7825 2500; helpline: 0808 800 5000; email: help@nspcc.org.uk; website: www.nspcc.org.uk)

Crime

Victim Support, Octavia House, 50 Banner Street, London EC1Y 8ST (tel: 020 7336 1730; Supportline: 0808 168 9111 [weekdays 8am–8pm and Sat–Sun, 9am–7pm]; email: supportline@victimsupport.org.uk; website: www.victimsupport.org.uk). For details on the regional offices please see the website.

Disasters

Disaster Action, No. 4, 71 Upper Berkeley Street, London W1H 7DB (email: admin@disasteraction.org.uk; website: www.disasteraction.org.uk)

Domestic violence

ManKind Initiative, Flook House, Belvedere Road, Taunton, Somerset TA1 1BT (helpline: 01823 334244 [weekdays 10am–4pm]; email: admin@mankind.org.uk; website: www.mankind.org.uk)

Men's Advice Line and Enquiries (MALE), (helpline: 0808 801 0327 [Mon–Fri, 9am–5pm]; email: info@ mensadviceline.org.uk or info@respectphoneline.org.uk; website: www.mensadviceline.org.uk)

National Centre for Domestic Violence, Edgeborough House, Upper Edgeborough Road, Guildford, Surrey GU1 2BJ (24-hour helpline: 0800 970 2070; text: 'NCDV' to 60777 for call back; email: office@ncdv.org.uk; website: www.ncdv.org.uk)

Refuge, 4th Floor, International House, 1 St Katherine's Way, London E1W 1UN (tel: 020 7395 7700; 24-hour helpline: 0808 200 0247; email: info@refuge.org.uk; website: www. refuge.org.uk)

Women's Aid Federation, PO Box 3245, Bristol BS2 2EH (tel: 0117 944 4411 [admin]; 24-hour helpline: 0808 200 0247; email: info@womensaid. org.uk or helpline@womensaid.org.uk; website: www.womensaid.org.uk). For details on the regional offices please see the website.

Medical accidents

Action for Victims of Medical Accidents (AVMA), 117 High Street, Croydon, London CR0 1QG (tel: 020 8688 9555 [admin]; helpline: 0845 123 2352 [Mon–Fri, 10am–5pm]; website: www.avma.org.uk)

Rape

Rape Crisis Centre, Suite E4, Joseph's Well, Hanover Walk, Leeds LS3 1AB (helpline: 0808 802 9999 [12pm–2.30pm and 7pm–9.30pm daily); email: rcewinfo@rapecrisis.org. uk; website: www.rapecrisis.org.uk). See website for contact information on local rape crisis centres.

Safeline, 6A New Street, Warwick, Warwickshire CV34 4RX (tel: 01926 402498; email: support@safeline.org. uk; website: www.safeline.org.uk)

The Survivors Trust, Unit 2, Eastlands Court Business Centre, St Peter's Road, Rugby, Warwickshire CV21 3QP (helpline: 0808 801 0818; email: info@thesurvivorstrust.org; website: www.thesurvivorstrust.org)

Women Against Rape (WAR) and Black Women's Rape Action Project, Crossroads Women's Centre, 25 Wolsey Mews NW5 2DX (tel: 020 7482 2496 [Mon–Fri, 1.30pm–4pm]; email: war@womenagainstrape.net or bwrap@dircon.co.uk; website: www. womenagainstrape.net)

Road accidents

Brake, PO Box 548, Huddersfield HD1 2XZ (tel: 01484 559909; helpline: 0808 800 0401; email: helpline@brake.org.uk; website: www. brake.org.uk)

RoadPeace, Shakespeare Business Centre, 245A Cold Harbour Lane, Brixton, London SW9 8RR (tel: 020 7733 1603; helpline: 0845 450 0355 [Mon–Fri, 9am–5pm]; email: info@ roadpeace.org; website: www. roadpeace.org)

Work issues

Acas, Euston Tower, 286 Euston Road, London NW1 3DP (helpline: 0300 123 1100; website: www.acas. org.uk)

Employment Tribunals Enquiry Line, (public enquiry line: 0300 123 1024; minicom: 01509 221564; website: www.gov.uk/employment-tribunals-enquiries). See website for the contact details of local employment tribunals.

Public Concern at Work, CAN Mezzanine, 7–14 Great Dover Street, London SE1 4YR (tel: 020 3117 2520; Whistleblowing Advice Line: 020 7404 6609; email: whistle@pcaw.org.uk; website: www.pcaw.org.uk)

Trades Union Congress, Congress House, Great Russell Street, London WC1B 3LS (tel: 020 7636 4030; email: info@tuc.org.uk)

Women

Refuge, Fourth Floor, International House, 1 St Katharine's Way, London E1W 1UN (tel: 020 7395 7700 [general]; 24-hour helpline: 0808 200 0247; email: info@refuge.org.uk; website: www.refuge.org.uk)

Women and Girls Network, PO Box 13095, London W14 0FE (tel: 020 7610 4678; advice line: 0808 801 0660 [Mon–Fri, 10am–4pm and Wed, 6pm–9pm]; Sexual Violence Helpline: 0808 801 0770 [please see website for opening times]; website: www.wgn. org.uk; an online contact facility is also available)

Women's Health Concern, Spracklen House, Dukes Place, Marlow, Buckinghamshire SL7 2QH (tel: 01628 890199 [telephone and email advice is available for a small fee, please check the website for more details]; website: www.womens-health-concern.org)

Illness and disability

Disability (general)

Action Medical Research, Vincent House, Horsham, West Sussex RH12 2DP (tel: 01403 210406; email: info@action.org.uk; website: www.action.org.uk)

Contact A Family, 209–211 City Road, London EC1V 1JN (tel: 020 7608 8700; helpline: 0808 808 3555; email: info@contact.org.uk or use the online form; website: www.cafamily.org.uk)

Disabled Living Foundation (DLF), Unit 1, 34 Chatfield Road, Wandsworth, London SW11 3SE (tel: 020 7289 6111; helpline: 0300 999 0004 [Mon–Fri, 10am–4pm]; email: helpline@dlf.org.uk; website: www.dlf.org.uk)

Disabled Parents' Network, Disability Resource Centre, 1A Humphrys Road, Woodside Estate, Dunstable LU5 4TP (tel: 07817 300103 email: information@disabledparentsnetwork.org.uk; website: www.voluntaryworks.org/organisation/disabled-parents-network)

Disabilities Trust, 32 Market Place, Burgess Hill, West Sussex RH15 9NP (tel: 01444 239123; email: info@thedtgroup.org; website: www.thedtgroup.org)

Disability Law Service (DLS), The Foundry, 17 Oval Way, London (tel: 020 7791 9800; email: advice@dls.org.uk; website: www.dls.org.uk)

Disability Pregnancy and Parenthood International (DPPI), 106 Muswell Hill Road, London N10 3JR (helpline: 0800 018 4730; website: www.disabledparent.org.uk)

Disability Rights, Plexal, 14 East Bay Lane, Here East, Queen Elizabeth Olympic Park, Stratford, London E20 3BS (tel: 0330 995 0400; email: enquiries@disabilityrightsuk.org; website: www.disabilityrightsuk.org)

I CAN's, Unit 31, Angel Gate (Gate 5), Goswell Road, London EC1V 2PT (tel: 020 7843 2510; email: info@ican.org.uk; website: www.ican.org.uk)

Jewish Care, Amélie House, Maurice and Vivienne Wohl Campus, 221 Golders Green Road, London NW11 9DQ (tel: 020 8922 2000; helpline: 020 8922 2222; email: helpline@jcare.org; website: www.jewishcare.org)

Kids, 7–9 Elliott's Place, London N1 8HX (tel: 020 7359 3635; email: use online form; website: www.kids.org.uk)

PHAB England, Summit House, 50 Wandle Road, Croydon CR0 1DF (tel: 020 8667 9443; email: info@phab.org.uk; website: www.phab.org.uk)

Queen Elizabeth's Foundation (QEF), Leatherhead Court, Woodlands Road, Leatherhead, Surrey KT22 0BN (tel: 01372 841100; email: use online form; website: www.qef.org.uk)

Respond, 3rd Floor, 24–32 Stephenson Way, London NW1 2HD (tel: 020 7383 0700; helpline: 0808 808 0700 [Thurs, 10am–4pm]; email: admin@respond.org.uk; website: www.respond.org.uk)

Addiction

Addaction, 67–69 Cowcross Street, London EC1M 6PU (tel: 020 7251 5860; email: use online form; website: www.addaction.org.uk)

Lions Lifeskills (formerly Tacade), 257 Alcester Road South, Kings Heath, Birmingham B14 6DT (tel: 0844 963 2427; email: mandy@lionslifeskills.co.uk or use the online form; website: www.lionlifeskills.co.uk)

Tasha Foundation, 89 Albert Embankment, London SE1 7TP (tel: 020 7582 6543; email: info@reachvolunteering.org.uk; website: reachvolunteering.org.uk/org/tasha-foundation)

Ageing

Age UK, Tavis House (6th Floor), 1–6 Tavistock Square, London WC1H 9NA (helpline: 0800 055 6112; email: use online form; website: www.ageuk.org.uk)

Independent Age, 18 Avonmore Road, London W14 8RR, (tel: 020 7605 4200; advice line: 0800 319 6789; email: charity@independentage.org; website: www.independentage.org)

AIDS/HIV

National Aids Trust, Aztec House, 397–405 Archway Road, London N6 4EY (tel: 020 7814 6767; email: info@nat.org.uk; website: www.nat.org.uk)

*Positive East, 159 Mile End Road, London E1 4AQ (tel: 020 7791 2855; email: talktome@positiveeast.org.uk; website: www.positiveeast.org.uk)

*Terrence Higgins Trust, 314–320 Grays Inn Road, London WC1X 8DP (tel: 020 7812 1600; advice and support line: 0808 802 1221 [Mon–Fri, 9.30am–5.30pm]; email: info@tht.org.uk; website: www.tht.org.uk)

Alcohol

Al-Anon Family Groups UK and Eire (AFG), 57B Great Suffolk Street, London SE1 0BB (helpline: 020 7403 0888 [10am–10pm daily]; email: enquiries@al-anonuk.org.uk; website: www.al-anonuk.org.uk)

Alcohol Concern, 27 Swinton Street, London WC1X 9NW (tel: 020 3907 8480; email: use online form; website: www.alcoholconcern.org.uk)

Alcoholics Anonymous (AA), General Service Office, PO Box 1, 10 Toft Green, York YO1 7NJ (tel: 01904 644026; helpline: 0800 917 7650; email: help@aamail.org; website: www.alcoholics-anonymous.org.uk)

Drinkaware, Finsbury Circus (Salisbury House), 3rd Floor (Room 519), London EC2M 5QQ (tel: 020 7766 9900; email: contact@drinkaware.co.uk; website: www.drinkaware.co.uk)

Drinkline (helpline: 0300 123 1110 [Mon–Fri, 9am–8pm and Sat–Sun, 11am–4pm])

Foundation 66, (now a subsidiary of Phoenix Futures Group) 68 Newington Causeway, London SE1 6DF (tel: 020 7234 9740; email: 020 7234 9740; website: www.phoenix-futures.org.uk/foundation-66)

Turning Point, Standon House, 21 Mansell Street, London E1 8AA (tel: 020 7481 7600; email: info@turning-point.co.uk; website: www.turning-point.co.uk)

Allergy

Action Against Allergy, PO Box 278, Twickenham TW1 4QQ (tel: 020 8892 4949; helpline: 020 8892 2711; email: actionagainstallergy@btconnect.com or use the online form; website: www.actionagainstallergy.co.uk)

Allergy UK, Planwell House, LEFA Business Park, Edgington Way Sidcup, Kent DA14 5BH (helpline: 01322 619898 [Mon–Fri, 9am–5pm]; email: info@allergyuk.org; website: www.allergyuk.org; a live chat facility is also available on the website)

Alopecia areata and alopecia androgenetica
Alopecia UK, PO Box 341, Baildon, Shipley BD18 9EH (tel: 07983 810490; email: info@alopecia.org.uk; website: www.alopeciaonline.org.uk)

Alzheimer's disease
Alzheimer's Society, 43–44 Crutched Friars, London EC3N 2AE (tel: 0330 333 0804; helpline: 0300 222 1122 [Mon–Fri, 9am–5pm and Sat–Sun, 10am–4pm]; email: enquiries@ alzheimers.org.uk; website: www. alzheimers.org.uk)

Arthritis/rheumatic diseases
Arthritis Care, Saffron House, 6–10 Kirby Street, London EC1N 8EQ (tel: 020 7380 6500; helpline: 0808 800 4050; email: info@arthritiscare. org.uk; website: www.arthritiscare. org.uk)

Arthritis Research UK, Copeman House, St Mary's Gate, Chesterfield S41 7TD (tel: 0300 790 0400; email: enquiries@arthritisresearchuk.org or use the online form; website: www. arthritisresearchuk.org)

Arthrogryposis
Arthrogryposis Group (TAG), Flat 22 Kirkland View, Kendal, Cumbria LA9 5EW (helpline: 07508 679351; email: help@arthrogryposis.co.uk or use the online form; website: www. arthrogryposis.co.uk)

Asthma
Asthma UK, 18 Mansell Street, London E1 8AA (tel: 0300 222 5800; Advice line: 0300 222 5800 [Mon–Fri, 9am–5pm]; email: info@asthma.org. uk; website: www.asthma.org.uk)

Ataxia
Ataxia UK, 12 Broadbent Close, London N6 5JW (tel: 020 7582 1444; helpline: 0845 644 0606 [Mon–Thurs, 10.30am–2.30pm]; email: helpline@ ataxia.org.uk; website: www.ataxia. org.uk)

Autism
National Autistic Society (NAS), 393 City Road, London EC1V 1NG (tel: 020 7833 2299; helpline: 0808 800 4104 [Mon–Fri, 10am–4pm]; email: supportercare@nas.org.uk; website: www.autism.org.uk)

Back pain
BackCare, 3rd Floor, Monkey Puzzle House, 69–71 Windmill Road, Sunbury-on-Thames TW16 7DT (tel: 020 8977 5474; helpline: 0845 130 2704; email: info@backcare.org.uk; website: www.backcare.org.uk)

Blind/partially sighted
CALIBRE (Cassette Library of Recorded Books), Aylesbury, Buckinghamshire HP22 5XQ (tel: 01296 432339; email: enquiries@ calibre.org.uk; website: www.calibre. org.uk)

International Glaucoma Association (IGA), Woodcote House, 15 Highpoint Business Village, Henwood, Ashford, Kent TN24 8DH (tel: 01233 648164; helpline: 01233 648170; email: info@iga.org.uk; website: www.iga.org.uk)

Listening Books, 12 Lant Street, London SE1 1QH (tel: 020 7407 9417; email: info@listening-books.org.uk; website: www.listening-books.org.uk)

National Federation of the Blind of the UK, Sir John Wilson House, 215 Kirkgate, Wakefield WF1 1JG (tel: 01924 291313; email: admin@ nfbuk.org or use the online form; website: www.nfbuk.org)

Partially Sighted Society, 1 Bennetthorpe, Doncaster DN2 6AA (tel: 01302 965195; email: reception@ partsight.org.uk; website: www. partsight.org.uk)

Royal National Institute for the Blind (RNIB), 105 Judd Street, London WC1H 9NE (helpline: 0303 123 9999 [Mon–Thurs, 8.45am–5.30pm]; email: helpline@rnib.org.uk; website: www. rnib.org.uk)

RP Fighting Blindness, PO Box 350, Buckingham MK18 5GZ (tel: 01280 821334; email: info@ rpfightingblindness.org.uk; website: www.rpfightingblindness.org.uk)

Voluntary Transcribers' Group, 8 Segbourne Road, Rubery, Birmingham B45 9SX (tel: 0121 453 4268; email: braillist@btinternet.com)

Bone marrow
Anthony Nolan Trust, Royal Free Hospital, Pond Street, Hampstead, London NW3 2QG (tel: 0303 303 0303; email: use online form; website: www.anthonynolan.org.uk)

Brain injury
British Institute for Brain-Injured Children (BIBIC), Old Kelways, Somerton Road, Langport, Somerset TA10 9SJ (tel: 01458 253344; email: info@bibic.org.uk; website: www. bibic.org.uk)

Brain tumours
The Brain Tumour Charity, Hartshead House, 61–65 Victoria Road, Farnborough GU14 7PA (tel: 01252 749990; information and support line: 0808 800 0004 [Mon–Fri, 9am–5pm]; email: support@ thebraintumourcharity.org; website: www.thebraintumourcharity.org)

Brittle bones
Brittle Bone Society, Grant Paterson House, 30 Guthrie Street, Dundee DD1 5BS (tel: 01382 204446; email: bbs@brittlebone.org or use the online form; website: www.brittlebone.org)

Burns
British Burn Association, Royal College of Surgeons of England, 35–43 Lincoln's Inn Fields, London WC2A 3PE (tel: 020 7869 6923; email: use the online form; website: www.britishburnassociation.org)

Children's Burns Trust, 2 Grosvenor Gardens, London SW1W 0DH (tel: 020 7881 0902; email: info@cbtrust. org.uk or use the online form; website: www.cbtrust.org.uk)

Cancer and leukaemia
Action Cancer, 1 Marlborough Park South, Belfast BT9 6XS (tel: 028 9080 3344; email: info@actioncancer.org; website: www.actioncancer.org)

Cancer Support Scotland, The Calman Centre, 75 Shelley Road, Glasgow G12 0ZE (tel: 0141 337 8199; email; info@cancersupportscotland.org; website: www.cancersupportscotland. org)

*CLIC Sargent Cancer Care for Children, No. 1 Farriers Yard, Assembly London, 77–85 Fulham Palace Road, London W6 8JA (tel: 0300 330 0803; email: use online form; website: www.clicsargent.org.uk)

*Leukaemia Care Society, One Birch Court, Blackpole East, Worcester WR3 8SG (tel: 01905 755977; 24-hour helpline: 0808 801 0444; email: care@leukaemiacare.org.uk; website: www.leukaemiacare.org.uk; online chat facility also available)

*Macmillan Cancer Support, 89 Albert Embankment, London SE1 7UQ (tel: 020 7840 7840; helpline: 0808 808 0000 [Mon–Fri, 9am–8pm]; email: use online form; website: www.macmillan.org.uk)

Marie Curie Foundation, 89 Albert Embankment, London SE1 7TP (helpline: 0800 090 2309; email: supporter.relations@mariecurie.org.uk; website: www.mariecurie.org.uk)

Tenovous Cancer Care, Gleider House, Ty Glas Road, Llanishen, Cardiff CF14 5BD (tel: 029 2076 8850; helpline: 0808 808 1010 [8am–8pm]; email: info@tenovuscancercare.org.uk or by using the 'ask the nurse' facility online; website: www.tenovuscancercare.org.uk)

Cerebral palsy

SCOPE, 6 Market Road, London N7 9PW (tel: 020 7619 7100; helpline: 0808 800 3333 [Mon–Fri, 9am–5pm]; email: helpline@scope.org.uk; website: www.scope.org.uk)

Chest/lungs

British Lung Foundation, 73–75 Goswell Road, London EC1V 7ER (tel: 020 7688 5555; helpline: 0300 003 0555; email: enquiries@blf.uk.org or by using the online form; website: www.blf.org.uk)

Child growth

Child Growth Foundation, 21 Malvern Drive, Sutton Coldfield B76 1PZ (helpline: 020 8995 0257 [Mon–Fri, 9.30am–4pm]; email: info@childgrowthfoundation.org; website: www.childgrowthfoundation.org)

Cleft lip/palate disorder

Cleft Lip and Palate Association (CLAPA), 1st Floor, Green Man Tower, 332B Goswell Road, London EC1V 7LQ (tel: 020 7833 4883; email: info@clapa.com or by using the online form; website: www.clapa.com)

Coeliac disease

Coeliac UK, 3rd Floor, Apollo Centre, Desborough Road, High Wycombe HP11 2QW (tel: 0118 939 1537; helpline: 0333 332 2033; email: use online form; website: www.coeliac.org.uk)

Colostomy

Colostomy Association (CA), Enterprise House, 95 London Street, Reading, Berkshire RG1 4QA (tel: 0118 939 1537; 24-hour helpline: 0800 328 4257; email: info@colostomyuk.org or use the online form; website: www.colostomyuk.org)

Cot death

Compassionate Friends, Kilburn Grange, Priory Park Road, London NW6 7UJ (helpline: 0345 123 2304 or 028 8778 8016 in Northern Ireland [Mon–Fri, 10am–4pm and 7pm–10pm]; email: info@tcf.org.uk; website: www.tcf.org.uk)

The Lullaby Trust (formerly Foundation for the Study of Infant Deaths), 11 Belgrave Road, London SW1V 1RB (tel: 020 7802 3200; helpline: 0808 802 6868; email: office@lullabytrust.org.uk or support@lullabytrust.org.uk; website: www.lullabytrust.org.uk)

Counselling

British Association for Counselling and Psychotherapy, 15 St John's Business Park, Lutterworth LE17 4HB, (tel: 01455 883300; email: bacp@bacp.co.uk; website: www.bacp.co.uk)

Samaritans, The Upper Mill, Kingston Road, Ewell, Surrey KT17 2AF (tel: 020 8394 8300; 24-hour helpline: 116 123; see website for local numbers; email: admin@samaritans.org [general] or jo@samaritans.org [helpline]; website: www.samaritans.org)

SupportLine, PO Box 2860, Romford, Essex RM7 1JA (tel: 01708 765222;

helpline: 01708 765200; email: info@supportline.org.uk; website: www.supportline.org.uk)

Crohn's disease and colitis

Children with Crohn's and Colitis (CICRA) Parkgate House, 356 West Barnes Lane, Motspur Park, Surrey KT3 6NB (tel: 020 8949 6209; email: support@cicra.org or use the online form; website: www.cicra.org)

National Association for Colitis and Crohn's Disease (NACC), 45 Grosvenor Road, St Albans AL1 3AW (tel: 0300 222 5700; helpline: 0121 737 9931 [Mon–Fri, 1pm–3.30pm and 6.30pm–9pm]; email: info@crohnsandcolitis.org.uk; website: www.crohnsandcolitis.org.uk)

Cystic fibrosis

Butterfly Trust, Swanston Steading, 109/3 Swanston Road, Edinburgh EH10 7DS (tel: 0131 445 5590; email: info@butterflytrust.org.uk; website: www.butterflytrust.org.uk)

*Cystic Fibrosis Trust, One Aldgate, Second Floor, London EC3N 1RE (helpline: 0300 373 1000; email: enquiries@cysticfibrosis.org.uk; website: www.cysticfibrosis.org.uk)

Deafblind

Deafblind UK, National Centre for Deafblindness, John and Lucille Van Geest Place, Cygnet Road, Hampton, Peterborough PE7 8FD (tel/textphone: 01733 358100; email: info@deafblind.org.uk or use the online form; website: www.deafblind.org.uk)

Sense, 101 Pentonville Road, London N1 9LG (tel: 0300 330 9250; textphone: 0300 330 9252; email: info@sense.org.uk; website: www.sense.org.uk)

Deafness/hearing difficulties

Action on Hearing Loss, 1–3 Highbury Station Road, London N1 1SE (tel: 020 7359 4442; text: 020 7296 8001; information line: 0808 808 0123 [voice] or 0808 808 9000 [text]; email: informationonline@hearingloss.org.uk; website: www.actionhearingloss.org.uk)

British Deaf Association (BDA), 3rd Floor, 356 Holloway Road, London N7 6PA (tel: 020 7697 4140 [office];

email: bda@bda.org.uk or use the online form; website: www.bda.org.uk)

The Guide Dogs for the Blind Association, Burghfield Common, Reading RG7 3YG (tel: 0118 983 5555; email: guidedogs@guidedogs.org.uk; website: www.guidedogs.org.uk)

Hearing Dogs for Deaf People, The Grange, Wycombe Road, Saunderton, Buckinghamshire HP27 9NS (tel and minicom: 01844 348100; email: info@hearingdogs.org.uk; website: www.hearingdogs.org.uk)

National Deaf Children's Society, Ground Floor South, Castle House, 37–45 Paul Street, London EC2A 4LS (tel: 020 7490 8656; minicom: 020 7490 8656; helpline: 0808 800 8880; email: ndcs@ndcs.org.uk or helpline@ndcs.org.uk; website: www.ndcs.org.uk)

Royal Association for Deaf People (RAD), Century House South, Riverside Office Centre, North Station Road, Colchester, Essex CO1 1RE (tel: 0845 688 2525; minicom: 0845 688 2527; email: info@royaldeaf.org.uk; website: www.royaldeaf.org.uk)

Depression

Mind, 15–19 Broadway, Stratford, London E15 4BQ (tel: 020 8519 2122; infoline: 0300 123 3393 [Mon–Fri, 9am–6pm, except for bank holidays]; text: 86463; email: info@mind.org.uk; website: www.mind.org.uk)

Depression UK, c/o Self Help Nottingham, Ormiston House, 32–36 Pelham Street, Nottingham NG1 2EG (email: info@depressionuk.org; website: www.depressionuk.org)

Samaritans, The Upper Mill, Kingston Road, Ewell, Surrey KT17 2AF (tel: 020 8394 8300; 24-hour helpline: 116 123; see website for local numbers; email: admin@samaritans.org [general] or jo@samaritans.org [helpline]; website: www.samaritans.org)

Diabetes

Diabetes UK, Wells Lawrence House, 126 Back Church Lane, London E1 1FH (tel: 0345 123 2399; [Mon–Fri, 9am–7pm]; email: helpline@diabetes.org.uk; website: www.diabetes.org.uk)

Disfigurement

Disfigurement Guidance Centre, PO Box 7, Cupar, Fife KY15 4PF (tel: 01337 870281)

Let's Face It, 1 Victoria Place, 90 Westgate Bay Avenue, Westgate on Sea, Kent CT8 8NG (tel: 01843 491291; email: chrisletsfaceit@aol.com; website: www.lets-face-it.org.uk)

Down's syndrome

Down's Syndrome Association, Langdon Down Centre, 2a Langdon Park, Teddington, Middlesex TW11 9PS (helpline: 0333 1212 300 [Mon–Fri, 10am–4pm]; email: info@downs-syndrome.org.uk; website: www.downs-syndrome.org.uk)

Drugs

ADFAM National, 2nd Floor, 120 Cromer Street, London WC1H 8BS (tel: 020 3817 9410; email: admin@adfam.org.uk; website: www.adfam.org.uk)

Cocaine Anonymous UK, PO Box 1337, Enfield EN1 9AS (helpline: 0800 612 0225 or 0300 11 2285 [10am–10pm daily]; email: info@cauk.org.uk; website: www.cauk.org.uk)

Early Break, Annara House, 7–11 Bury Road, Radcliffe M26 2UG (Bury: 0161 723 3880; Rochdale: 0161 723 3880; email: use online form; website: www.earlybreak.co.uk)

Families Anonymous, Doddington and Rollo Community Association, Charlotte Despard Avenue, Battersea, London SW11 5HD (helpline: 0845 120 0660 or 020 7498 4680; email: office@famanon.org.uk; website: www.famanon.org.uk)

FRANK (National Drugs Helpline), (24-hour helpline: 0300 123 6600; text: 82111; website: www.talktofrank.com; email: frank@talktofrank.com or by using the online form). Contact can also be made via an online chat facility from 2pm–6pm.

Narcotics Anonymous (NA), 202 City Road, London EC1V 2PH (tel: 020 7251 4007; helpline: 0300 999 1212 [10am–midnight]; website: www.ukna.org)

Turning Point, Standon House, 21 Mansell Street, London E1 8AA (tel: 020 7481 7600; email: info@turning-point.co.uk or use the online form; website: www.turning-point.co.uk)

Dyslexia

British Dyslexia Association, Unit 6a, Bracknell Beeches, Old Bracknell Lane, Bracknell RG12 7BW (tel: 0333 405 4555; helpline: 0333 405 4567 [Mon, Tues, Thurs and Fri, 10am–1pm and 1.30pm–4pm]; email: use online form; website: www.bdadyslexia.org.uk)

Dyslexia Action, Dyslexia Action House, 10 High Street, Egham, Surrey TW20 9EA (email: use online form; website: www.dyslexiaaction.org.uk)

Dyspraxia

Dyspraxia Foundation, 8 West Alley, Hitchin, Hertfordshire SG5 1EG (tel: 01462 455016; helpline: 01462 454986 [Mon–Fri, 9am–5pm]; email: info@dyspraxiafoundation.org.uk; website: www.dyspraxiafoundation.org.uk)

Dystonia

*Dystonia Society, Second Floor, 89 Albert Embankment, London SE1 7TP (tel: 020 7793 3651; helpline: 020 7793 3650; email: support@dystonia.org.uk; website: www.dystonia.org.uk)

Eating disorders

Eating Disorders Association (Beat), Unit 1 Chalk Hill House, 19 Rosary Road, Norwich, Norfolk NR1 1SZ (tel: 0300 123 3355; helpline: 0808 801 0677; youth helpline: 0808 801 0711; email: help@beateatingdisorders.org.uk or fyp@beateatingdisorders.org.uk [young people]; website: www.beateatingdisorders.org.uk)

Eczema

National Eczema Society, 11 Murray Street, London NW1 9RE (tel: 020 7281 3553; helpline: 0800 089 1122 [Mon–Fri, 8am–8pm]; email: helpline@eczema.org; website: www.eczema.org)

Endometriosis

Endometriosis UK, Suites 1 and 2, 46 Manchester Street, London W1U 7LS (tel: 020 7222 2781; crisis helpline: 0808 808 2227 [opening times vary depending on volunteer availability, see website for details]; email: support@endometriosis-uk.org or use the online form; website: www. endometriosis-uk.org)

Epilepsy

Epilepsy Action, New Anstey House, Gate Way Drive, Yeadon, Leeds LS19 7XY (tel: 0113 210 8800; helpline: 0808 800 5050 [Mon–Fri, 8.30am–5.30pm]; email: epilepsy@ epilepsy.org.uk; website: www. epilepsy.org.uk)

Epilepsy Society, Chesham Lane, Chalfont St Peter, Buckinghamshire SL9 0RJ (tel: 01494 601300; helpline: 01494 601400 [Mon–Fri, 9am–4pm and Wed, 9am–8pm]; website: www. epilepsysociety.org.uk; email: fromthehelpline@epilepsysociety.org. uk)

Growth problems

Child Growth Foundation, 21 Malvern Drive, Sutton Coldfield B76 1PZ (tel: 020 8912 0723; helpline: 020 8995 0257; email: info@ childgrowthfoundation.org; website: www.childgrowthfoundation.org)

Restricted Growth Association (RGA), PO Box 99, Lyndney GL15 9AW (helpline: 0300 111 1970; email: office@restrictedgrowth.co.uk; website: www.rgauk.org)

Haemophilia

*The Haemophilia Society, Wilcox House, 140–148 Borough High Street, London SE1 1LB (tel: 020 7939 0780; email: info@haemophilia.org.uk; website: www.haemophilia.org.uk)

Head injury

*Headway – National Head Injuries Association Ltd, Bradbury House, 190 Bagnall Road, Old Basford, Nottingham, Nottinghamshire NG6 8SF (tel: 0115 924 0800; helpline: 0808 800 2244; email: enquiries@headway.org.uk or helpline@headway.org.uk; website: www.headway.org.uk)

Heart attacks/heart disease

British Heart Foundation, Lyndon Place, 2096 Coventry Road, Sheldon, Birmingham B26 3YU (tel: 0300 330 3322; helpline: 0300 330 3311; website: www.bhf.org.uk). Contact can also be made by completing an online enquiry form.

Coronary Artery Disease Research Association (CORDA), Royal Brompton Hospital, Sydney Street, London SW3 6NP (website: www. corda.org.uk)

HeartLine, 9 Field Road, Watford WD19 4DR (email: intouch@ heartline.org.uk; website: www. heartline.org.uk)

Hemiplegia

Hemi-Help, 6 Market Road, London N7 9PW (tel: 0345 120 3713, helpline: 0345 123 2372 [Mon–Fri, 10am–1pm during term time]; email: support@ hemihelp.org.uk or helpline@hemihelp.org.uk; website: www.hemihelp.org.uk)

Hodgkin's disease

Lymphoma Association, 3 Cromwell Court, New Street, Aylesbury HP20 2PB (helpline: 0808 808 5555 [Mon–Fri, 9am–5pm]; email: information@lymphomas.org.uk; website: www.lymphomas.org.uk). Contact can also be made by completing an online enquiry form.

Huntington's disease

*Huntington's Disease Association, Suite 24, Liverpool Science Park IC1, 131 Mount Pleasant Liverpool L3 5TF (tel: 0151 331 5444; email: info@hda. org.uk; website: www.hda.org.uk)

Children with hyperactivity and ADHD

Hyperactive Children's Support Group, 71 Whyke Lane, Chichester, West Sussex PO19 7PD (tel: 01243 539966 [Mon–Fri, 2.30–4.30pm]; email: hacsg@hacsg.org.uk; website: www.hacsg.org.uk). If writing, the group requests that you enclose a large sae.

Incontinence

Association for Continence Advice (ACA), Fitwise Management Ltd, Blackburn House, Redhouse Road, Seafield, Bathgate, West Lothian EH47 7AQ (tel: 01506 811077; email: aca@fitwise.co.uk; website: www.aca. uk.com)

Industrial diseases

Mesothelioma UK, Unit 116, Greenacres, The Sidings, Station Road, Birstall, Leicester LE4 3BR (helpline: 0800 169 2409; email:

info@mesothelioma.uk.com; website: www.mesothelioma.uk.com)

RSI Action, 19 Station Road, Steeple Morden, Royston, Hertfordshire SG8 0NW (email: info@rsiaction.org. uk; website: www.rsiaction.org.uk)

Infertility

Fertility Network UK, 20 Egerton Drive, Greenwich SE10 8JS (tel: 01424 732361; email info@fertilitynetworkuk.org or support@fertilitynetworkuk.org website: www.fertilitynetworkuk.org)

Irritable bowel syndrome

The IBS Network, Unit 1.16 SOAR Works, 14 Knutton Road, Sheffield S5 9NU (tel: 0114 272 3253; email: info@theibsnetwork.org; website: www.theibsnetwork.org)

Kidney disease

*British Kidney Patient Association (BKPA), 3 The Windmills, St Mary's Close, Turk Street, Alton GU34 1EF (tel: 01420 541424; helpline: 01420 541424; email: info@britishkidney-pa. co.uk; website: www.britishkidney-pa. co.uk)

National Kidney Federation, The Point, Coach Road, Shireoaks, Worksop, Nottinghamshire S81 8BW (helpline: 0800 169 0936; email: use online form; website: www.kidney. org.uk)

Learning disabilities

Mencap, Mencap National Centre, 123 Golden Lane, London EC1Y 0RT (tel: 020 7454 0454; helpline: 0808 808 1111; email: help@mencap.org. uk; website: www.mencap.org.uk)

Limb conditions

*Blesma, 185–187 High Road, Chadwell Heath, Romford RM6 6NA (tel: 020 8590 1124; email: chadwellheath@blesma.org; website: www.blesma.org)

Limbless Association, Unit 10, Waterhouse Business Centre, 2 Cromar Way, Chelmsford CM1 2QE (tel: 0845 130 6225; helpline: 020 3478 0100; email: enquiries@limbless-association.org; website: www.limbless-association. org)

Reach (a charity for children affected by upper limb conditions), Pearl

Assurance House, Brook Street, Tavistock, Devon PL19 0BN (tel: 0845 130 6225; email: reach@reach. org.uk; website: www.reach.org.uk)

STEPS (a charity for people affected by childhood lower limb conditions), The Wright House, Wilderspool Business Park, Greenalls Avenue, Warrington WA4 6HL (helpline: 01925 750271; email: use online form; website: www.steps-charity.org.uk)

Literacy/learning difficulties

Learning and Work Institute, Chetwynd House, 21 De Montfort Street, Leicester LE1 7GE (tel: 0116 204 4200; email: enquiries@ learningandwork.org.uk; website: www.learningandwork.org.uk)

Liver disease

British Liver Trust, 6 Dean Park Crescent, Bournemouth BH1 1HL (tel: 01425 481320; information line: 0800 652 7330; email: info@ britishlivertrust.org.uk; website: www. britishlivertrust.org.uk)

Lowe Syndrome Trust (UK Contact Group) (LSA) 77 West Heath Road, London NW3 7TH (tel: 020 7794 8858; email: lowetrust@gmail.com; website: www.lowetrust.com)

Lupus

Lupus UK, St James House, Eastern Road, Romford RM1 3NH (tel: 01708 731251; email: headoffice@lupusuk. org.uk; website: www.lupusuk.org.uk)

Scleroderma & Raynaud's UK, 18–20 Bridge Lane, London EC4Y 8EE (tel: 020 7000 1925; email: info@sruk.co.uk; website: www.sruk. co.uk)

Mastectomy

Breast Cancer Care (BCC), Chester House, 1–3 Brixton Road, London SW9 6DE (tel: 0845 092 0800; helpline: 0808 800 6000 [Mon–Fri, 9am–5pm and Sat, 10am–2pm]; email: info@breastcancercare.org.uk; website: www.breastcancercare.org. uk)

Meningitis

*Meningitis Now, Fern House, Bath Road, Stroud, Gloucestershire GL5 3TJ (tel: 01453 768000; 24-hour helpline: 0808 801 0388; email: info@ meningitisnow.org or

helpline@meningitisnow.org; website: www.meningitisnow.org)

Menopause

The Daisy Network Premature Menopause Support Group, PO Box 71432, London SW6 9HJ (email: info@daisynetwork.org.uk; website: www.daisynetwork.org.uk)

Mental health

Anxiety UK, Zion Community Resource Centre, 339 Stretford Road, Hulme, Manchester M15 4ZY (tel: 0161 226 7727: infoline 0844 477 5774 [Mon–Fri, 9.30am–5.30pm]; text service: 07537 416905; email: support@anxietyuk.org.uk; website: www.anxietyuk.org.uk). Contact can also be made by completing an online enquiry form.

Bipolar UK, 11 Belgrave Road, London SW1V 1RB (tel: 0333 323 3880; email: info@bipolaruk.org.uk; website: www.bipolaruk.org.uk)

Mental Health Foundation, Colechurch House, 1 London Bridge Walk, London SE1 2SX (tel: 020 7803 1100; website: www.mentalhealth.org. uk). Note: the foundation does not offer a help or advice line and should not be contacted unless specific information on its work is required or you wish to collaborate with the foundation in a professional capacity. Its website advises that other organisations, such as Samaritans, can offer emotional support. Samaritans can be contacted by calling 116 123 or by emailing jo@samaritans.org.

Mind (National Association for Mental Health), 15–19 Broadway, Stratford, London E15 4BQ (tel: 020 8519 2122; infoline: 0300 123 3393 [Mon–Fri, 9am–6pm, except for bank holidays]; text: 86463; email: info@ mind.org.uk; website: www.mind.org. uk)

SANE (The Mental Health Charity), St. Mark's Studios, 14 Chillingworth Road, Islington, London N7 8QJ (tel: 020 3805 1790; helpline: 0300 304 7000 [4pm–10.30pm daily]; email: info@sane.org.uk; website: www.sane. org.uk). An online contact support service is also available.

Metabolic disorders

CLIMB (Children Living with Inherited Metabolic Disorders),

Climb Building, 176 Nantwich Road, Crewe CW2 6BG (tel: 0845 241 2173 or 0800 652 3181; email: contact@climb. org.uk; website: www.climb.org.uk)

Migraine

Migraine Action Association (formerly British Migraine Association), Fourth Floor, 27 East Street, Leicester LE1 6NB (tel: 0845 601 1033; email: info@migraine.org. uk; website: www.migraine.org.uk). Contact can also be made by completing an online enquiry form.

Migraine Trust, 52–53 Russell Square, London WC1B 4HP (tel: 020 7631 6970; email: info@migrainetrust.org; website: www.migrainetrust.org)

Miscarriage

The Miscarriage Association, 17 Wentworth Terrace, Wakefield, West Yorkshire WF1 3QW (tel: 01924 200795; helpline: 01924 200799 [Mon–Fri, 9am–4pm]; email: info@ miscarriageassociation.org.uk; website: www.miscarriageassociation. org.uk)

Tommy's, Nicholas House, 3 Laurence Pountney Hill, London EC4R 0BB (tel: 020 7398 3400; email: mailbox@tommys.org; website: www. tommys.org)

Motor neurone disease

*Motor Neurone Disease Association (MND), PO Box 246, Northampton NN1 2PR (tel: 01604 250505; helpline: 03457 626 262; email: enquiries@mndassociation.org or mndconnect@mndassociation.org; website: www.mndassociation.org)

Multiple sclerosis

*Multiple Sclerosis Society, MS National Centre, 372 Edgware Road, London NW2 6ND (tel: 020 8438 0700; helpline: 0808 800 8000 [Mon–Fri, 9am–9pm]; email: helpline@mssociety.org.uk; website: www.mssociety.org.uk). Contact can also be made by using the online form.

Muscular dystrophy

Muscular Dystrophy UK, 61A Great Suffolk Street, London SE1 0BU (tel: 020 7803 4800; helpline: 0800 652 6352; email: info@ musculardystrophyuk.org; website: www.musculardystrophyuk.org)

Myalgic Encephalopathy/ Chronic Fatigue Syndrome(ME/CFS)

Action for ME, 42 Temple Street, Keynsham BS31 1EH (tel: 0117 927 9551; helpline 0800 138 6544; email admin@actionforme.org.uk or welfare@actionforme.org.uk; website: www.actionforme.org.uk)

ME Association, 7 Apollo Office Court, Radclive Road, Gawcott, Buckinghamshire MK18 4DF (helpline: 0844 576 5326 [10am–12pm, 2–4pm and 7–9pm daily]; email: meconnect@ meassociation.org.uk; website: www.meassociation.org.uk)

Myotonic dystrophy

Myotonic Dystrophy Support Group, 19–21 Main Road, Gedling, Nottingham NG4 3HQ (tel: 0115 987 5869; helpline: 0115 987 0080; email: contact@mdsguk.org; website: www.mdsguk.org)

Narcolepsy

Narcolepsy UK, PO Box 26865, Kirkcaldy KY2 9BX (tel: 0345 450 0394; email: info@narcolepsy.org.uk; website: www.narcolepsy.org.uk)

Neurofibromatosis

The Neuro Foundation, 1st Floor, 44 Combe Lane, London SW20 0LA (tel: 020 8439 1234; email: info@nfauk.org; website: www.nfauk.org)

Osteoporosis

National Osteoporosis Society, Camerton, Bath BA2 0PJ (tel: 01761 471771; helpline: 0808 800 0035; email: info@nos.org.uk; website: www.nos.org.uk)

Paget's disease

The Paget's Association, Suite 5, Moorfield Road, Swinton, Manchester M27 0EW (tel: 0161 799 4646; nurse helpline: 07713 568197; email: use online form; website: www.paget.org.uk)

Parkinson's disease

*Parkinson's UK, 215 Vauxhall Bridge Road, London SW1V 1EJ (tel: 020 7931 8080; helpline: 0808 800 0303 [Mon–Fri, 9am–7pm and Sat, 10am–2pm]; email: hello@parkinsons.

org.uk; website: www.parkinsons.org.uk)

Pituitary disorders

Pituitary Foundation, 86 Colston Street, Bristol BS1 5BB (tel: 0117 370 1333; support line: 0117 370 1320 [Mon–Fri, 10am–4pm]; endocrine nurse helpline: 0117 370 1317 [Mon, 6pm–9pm and Thurs, 9am–1pm]; email: helpline@pituitary.org.uk; website: www.pituitary.org.uk)

Poliomyelitis

*British Polio Fellowship, Eagle Point, The Runway, South Ruislip, Middlesex HA4 6SE (tel: 0800 043 1935; email: info@britishpolio.org.uk; website: www.britishpolio.org.uk)

Post-natal

Association for Post-Natal Illness, 145 Dawes Road, Fulham, London SW6 7EB (tel: 020 7386 0868 [Mon–Fri, 10am–2pm]; website: www.apni.org)

Prader-Willi syndrome

Prader-Willi Syndrome Association, Craegmoor Suite 4.4, Litchurch Plaza, Litchurch Lane, Derby DE24 8AA (tel: 01332 365676; email: admin@ pwsa.co.uk; website: www.pwsa.co.uk)

Pre-eclampsia

Action on Pre-Eclampsia, The Stables, 80B High Street, Evesham, Worcestershire WR11 4EU (tel: 01386 761848; email: info@apec.org.uk; website: www.action-on-pre-eclampsia.org.uk)

Psoriasis

Psoriasis Association, Dick Coles House, 2 Queensbridge, Northampton NN4 7BF (tel: 01604 251620; helpline: 0845 676 0076; email: mail@psoriasis-association.org.uk; website: www.psoriasis-association.org.uk)

Scleroderma & Raynaud's UK, 18–20 Bridge Lane, London EC4Y 8EE (tel: 020 7000 1925; email: info@sruk.co.uk; website: www.sruk.co.uk)

Rett syndrome

Rett Syndrome Association UK, Victory House, Chobham Street, Luton LU1 3BS (tel: 01582 798910; helpline: 01582 798911; email: info@

rettuk.org or support@rettuk.org; website: www.rettuk.org)

Reye's syndrome

National Reye's Syndrome Foundation of the UK (NRSF), 15 Nicholas Gardens, Pyrford, Woking, Surrey GU22 8SD (tel: 01932 346843; website: www.reyessyndrome.co.uk). Contact can also be made using by completing the online contact form.

Sarcoidosis

SarcoidosisUK (Sarcoidosis and Interstitial Lung Association), Studio 1, 240 Portobello Road, London W11 1LL (tel: 020 3389 7221 or 0800 014 8821; website: www.sarcoidosisuk.org). The best way to contact the association is by completing the online contact form.

Schizophrenia

Rethink, 15th Floor, 89 Albert Embankment, London SE1 7TP (general enquiries tel: 0121 522 7007; advice service: 0300 5000 927; email: info@rethink.org or advice@rethink.org; website: www.rethink.org). The Advice Team can be contacted Mon–Fri, 10am–2pm, except on bank holidays. Note: Rethink cannot deal with emergency or crisis issues. See the website for a list of emergency contact details.

Scoliosis

Scoliosis Association (UK) (SAUK), 4 Ivebury Court, 325 Latimer Road, London W10 6RA (tel: 020 8964 5343; helpline: 020 8964 1166; email: info@sauk.org.uk; website: www.sauk.org.uk)

Sexually transmitted infections

FPA, 23–28 Penn Street, London N1 5DL (tel: 020 7608 5240 email: general@fpa.org.uk; website: www.fpa.org.uk)

Herpes Viruses Association (SPHERE), 41 North Road, London N7 9DP (helpline: 0845 123 2305; email: info@herpes.org.uk; website: www.herpes.org.uk)

Sickle cell disease

Sickle Cell Society (SCS), 54 Station Road, London NW10 4UA (tel: 020 8961 7795; email: info@

sicklecellsociety.org; website: www.
sicklecellsociety.org). Contact can also
be made by completing an online
enquiry form.

Smoking

QUIT (National Society of Non-
Smokers), 4 Sovereign Close, St
Katharine's and Wapping, London
E1W 3HW (tel: 020 7553 2132; email:
m.hussain@quit.org.uk or
m.akthar@quit.org.uk; website: www.
quit.org.uk)

Solvent abuse

Re-Solv, 30A High Street, Stone,
Staffordshire ST15 8AW (tel: 01785
817885; helpline: 01785 810762;
email: information@re-solv.org;
website: www.re-solv.org)

Speech and language difficulties

Association for All Speech-Impaired
Children (AFASIC), Lower ground
floor of 'Contact' offices,
209–211 City Road, London
EC1V 1JN (tel: 020 7490 9410;
helpline: 0300 666 9410; website:
www.afasic.org.uk). You can also
contact the helpline by completing an
online enquiry form.

British Stammering, 15 Old Ford
Road, London E2 9PJ (tel: 020 8983
1003; helpline: 0845 603 2001 or 020
8880 6590; email: mail@stammering.
org or info@stammering.org
[helpline]; website: www.stammering.
org). The helpline is open 2pm–5pm
and 7pm–9pm on Monday and
2pm–5pm on Thursday.

Royal Association for Deaf People
(RAD), Century House South,
Riverside Office Centre, North

Station Road, Colchester, Essex
CO1 1RE (tel: 0300 688 2525;
minicom: 0845 688 2527; email:
info@royaldeaf.org.uk; website: www.
royaldeaf.org.uk)

Spina bifida

SHINE, 42 Park Road, Peterborough
PE1 2UQ (tel: 01733 555988; website:
www.shinecharity.org.uk). Contact
can also be made by completing an
online enquiry form.

Spinal injuries

Spinal Injuries Association, SIA
House, 2 Trueman Place, Oldbrook,
Milton Keynes MK6 2HH (tel: 01908
604191; advice line: 0800 980 0501;
email: sia@spinal.co.uk; website:
www.spinal.co.uk)

Stroke

Stroke Information Service, Stroke
Association, Life After Stroke Centre,
Church Lane, Bromsgrove,
Worcestershire B61 8RA (helpline:
0303 303 3100; textphone: 18001 0303
3033 100; email: info@stroke.org.uk;
website: www.stroke.org.uk)

Suicide

Maytree, 72 Moray Road, Finsbury
Park, London N4 3LG (helpline: 020
7263 7070; email: maytree@maytree.
org.uk; website: www.maytree.org.uk)

Papyrus, Lineva House, 28–32 Milner
Street, Warrington, Cheshire
WA5 1AD (helpline: 0800 068 4141;
website: www.papyrus-uk.org)

Tinnitus

British Tinnitus Association (BTA),
Ground Floor, Unit 5, Acorn Business
Park, Woodseats Close, Sheffield

S8 0TB (tel: 0114 250 9933; helpline:
0800 018 0527; minicom: 0114 258
5694; email: helpline@tinnitus.org.uk;
website: www.tinnitus.org.uk)

Tourette's syndrome

*Tourettes Action, Kings Court, The
Meads Business Centre,
19 Kingsmead, Farnborough,
Hampshire GU14 7SR (helpline: 0300
777 8427; email: use online form;
website: www.tourettes-action.org.
uk).

Tracheo-oesophageal fistula

Tracheo-Oesophageal Fistula Support
Group (TOFS), St George's Centre,
91 Victoria Road, Netherfield,
Nottingham NG4 2NN (tel: 0115 961
3092; email: info@tofs.org.uk;
website: www.tofs.org.uk)

Tuberous sclerosis

The Tuberous Sclerosis Association,
CAN Mezzanine, 32–36 Loman Street,
London SE1 0EH (tel: 020 7922 7731;
email: admin@tuberous-sclerosis.org
or use the online form; website: www.
tuberous-sclerosis.org).

Urostomy

Urostomy Association, 4 Demontfort
Way, Uttoxeter ST14 8XY (tel: 01889
563191; email: secretary@
urostomyassociation.org.uk; website:
www.urostomyassociation.org.uk)

Williams syndrome

Williams Syndrome Foundation, (tel:
01732 365152; email: enquiries@
williams-syndrome.org.uk; website:
www.williams-syndrome.org.uk)

Index

What else can DSC do for you?

Let us help you to be the best you possibly can be. DSC equips individuals and organisations with expert skills and information to help them provide better services and outcomes for their beneficiaries. With the latest techniques, best practice and funding resources all brought to you by our team of experts, you will not only boost your income but also exceed your expectations.

Publications

We produce fundraising directories and research reports, as well as accessible 'how to' guides and best practice handbooks, all to help you help others.

Training

The voluntary sector's best-selling training, with courses covering every type of voluntary sector training.

In-house training

All DSC courses are available on your premises, delivered by expert trainers and facilitators. We also offer coaching, consultancy, mentoring and support.

Conferences and fairs

DSC conferences are a fantastic way to network with voluntary sector professionals while taking part in intensive, practical training workshops.

Funding websites

DSC's funding websites provide access to thousands of charities, grants, statutory funds and corporate donations. You won't get more funders, commentary and analysis anywhere else. Demo our sites free today.

www.dsc.org.uk/**fundingwebsites**

@DSC_Charity
For top tips and special offers

Visit our website today and see what we can do for you:

www.**dsc**.org.uk

Or contact us directly:
publications@dsc.org.uk